T0181739

Lecture Notes in Computer Science   **12423**

More information about this series at http://www.springer.com/series/7409

Constantine Stephanidis ·
Aaron Marcus · Elizabeth Rosenzweig ·
Pei-Luen Patrick Rau · Abbas Moallem ·
Matthias Rauterberg (Eds.)

HCI International 2020 - Late Breaking Papers

User Experience Design and Case Studies

22nd HCI International Conference, HCII 2020
Copenhagen, Denmark, July 19–24, 2020
Proceedings

 Springer

Editors
Constantine Stephanidis
University of Crete and Foundation
for Research and Technology –
Hellas (FORTH)
Heraklion, Crete, Greece

Elizabeth Rosenzweig
World Usability Day and Bentley User
Experience Center
Newton Center, MA, USA

Abbas Moallem
San Jose State University
San Jose, CA, USA

Aaron Marcus
Aaron Marcus and Associates
Berkeley, CA, USA

Pei-Luen Patrick Rau
Tsinghua University
Beijing, China

Matthias Rauterberg
Eindhoven Univesity of Technology
Eindhoven, Noord-Brabant, The Netherlands

ISSN 0302-9743 ISSN 1611-3349 (electronic)
Lecture Notes in Computer Science
ISBN 978-3-030-60113-3 ISBN 978-3-030-60114-0 (eBook)
https://doi.org/10.1007/978-3-030-60114-0

LNCS Sublibrary: SL3 – Information Systems and Applications, incl. Internet/Web, and HCI

This Springer imprint is published by the registered company Springer Nature Switzerland AG
The registered company address is: Gewerbestrasse 11, 6330 Cham, Switzerland

Foreword

The 22nd International Conference on Human-Computer Interaction, HCI International 2020 (HCII 2020), was planned to be held at the AC Bella Sky Hotel and Bella Center, Copenhagen, Denmark, during July 19–24, 2020. Due to the COVID-19 pandemic and the resolution of the Danish government not to allow events larger than 500 people to be hosted until September 1, 2020, HCII 2020 had to be held virtually. It incorporated the 21 thematic areas and affiliated conferences listed on the following page.

A total of 6,326 individuals from academia, research institutes, industry, and governmental agencies from 97 countries submitted contributions, and 1,439 papers and 238 posters were included in the volumes of the proceedings published before the conference. Additionally, 333 papers and 144 posters are included in the volumes of the proceedings published after the conference, as "Late Breaking Work" (papers and posters). These contributions address the latest research and development efforts in the field and highlight the human aspects of design and use of computing systems.

The volumes comprising the full set of the HCII 2020 conference proceedings are listed in the following pages and together they broadly cover the entire field of human-computer interaction, addressing major advances in knowledge and effective use of computers in a variety of application areas.

I would like to thank the Program Board Chairs and the members of the Program Boards of all Thematic Areas and Affiliated Conferences for their valuable contributions towards the highest scientific quality and the overall success of the HCI International 2020 conference.

This conference would not have been possible without the continuous and unwavering support and advice of the founder, conference general chair emeritus and conference scientific advisor, Prof. Gavriel Salvendy. For his outstanding efforts, I would like to express my appreciation to the communications chair and editor of HCI International News, Dr. Abbas Moallem.

July 2020   Constantine Stephanidis

HCI International 2020 Thematic Areas
and Affiliated Conferences

Thematic Areas:

- HCI 2020: Human-Computer Interaction
- HIMI 2020: Human Interface and the Management of Information

Affiliated Conferences:

- EPCE: 17th International Conference on Engineering Psychology and Cognitive Ergonomics
- UAHCI: 14th International Conference on Universal Access in Human-Computer Interaction
- VAMR: 12th International Conference on Virtual, Augmented and Mixed Reality
- CCD: 12th International Conference on Cross-Cultural Design
- SCSM: 12th International Conference on Social Computing and Social Media
- AC: 14th International Conference on Augmented Cognition
- DHM: 11th International Conference on Digital Human Modeling & Applications in Health, Safety, Ergonomics & Risk Management
- DUXU: 9th International Conference on Design, User Experience and Usability
- DAPI: 8th International Conference on Distributed, Ambient and Pervasive Interactions
- HCIBGO: 7th International Conference on HCI in Business, Government and Organizations
- LCT: 7th International Conference on Learning and Collaboration Technologies
- ITAP: 6th International Conference on Human Aspects of IT for the Aged Population
- HCI-CPT: Second International Conference on HCI for Cybersecurity, Privacy and Trust
- HCI-Games: Second International Conference on HCI in Games
- MobiTAS: Second International Conference on HCI in Mobility, Transport and Automotive Systems
- AIS: Second International Conference on Adaptive Instructional Systems
- C&C: 8th International Conference on Culture and Computing
- MOBILE: First International Conference on Design, Operation and Evaluation of Mobile Communications
- AI-HCI: First International Conference on Artificial Intelligence in HCI

Conference Proceedings – Full List of Volumes

http://2020.hci.international/proceedings

HCI International 2020 (HCII 2020)

The full list with the Program Board Chairs and the members of the Program Boards of all thematic areas and affiliated conferences is available online at:

http://www.hci.international/board-members-2020.php

HCI International 2021

The 23rd International Conference on Human-Computer Interaction, HCI International 2021 (HCII 2021), will be held jointly with the affiliated conferences in Washington DC, USA, at the Washington Hilton Hotel, July 24–29, 2021. It will cover a broad spectrum of themes related to human-computer interaction (HCI), including theoretical issues, methods, tools, processes, and case studies in HCI design, as well as novel interaction techniques, interfaces, and applications. The proceedings will be published by Springer. More information will be available on the conference website: http://2021.hci.international/

General Chair
Prof. Constantine Stephanidis
University of Crete and ICS-FORTH
Heraklion, Crete, Greece
Email: general_chair@hcii2021.org

http://2021.hci.international/

Contents

Design Case Studies

User Experience Case Studies

User Experience Design and Evaluation Methods and Tools

Detailed Usability Heuristics: A Breakdown of Usability Heuristics to Enhance Comprehension for Novice Evaluators

Anas Abulfaraj$^{(\boxtimes)}$ ⓘ and Adam Steele ⓘ

College of Computing and Digital Media, DePaul University, 243 South Wabash Avenue, Chicago, IL 60604, USA
Aabulfa2@mail.depaul.edu, Asteele@cs.depaul.edu

Abstract. Heuristic evaluation (HE) is one of the most commonly used usability evaluation methods. In HE, 3–5 evaluators evaluate a certain system guided by a list of usability heuristics with the goal of detecting usability issues. Although HE is popular in the usability field, it heavily depends on the expertise of the evaluator, meaning that there is a large gap in HE performance between expert evaluators and novice evaluators. One of the factors contributing to this gap is the difficulty of thoroughly understanding usability heuristics. Usability heuristics are abstract and require simplification to be better understood by novice evaluators. In this work, our goal was to simplify Nielsen's heuristics to make them easier to understand since they are one of the most popular sets of usability heuristics. We interviewed 15 usability experts with at least 4 years of experience in the field from both academia and industry and asked them to explain Nielsen's heuristics in detail. We analyzed their responses, and we produced a modified list that is more detailed than Nielsen's original list.

Keywords: Usability · Usability heuristics · Heuristic evaluation · Novice evaluators

1 Introduction

Usability is a central value in human-computer interaction (HCI) and user experience (UX). One of the main objectives of HCI/UX practitioners is to ensure that the system being evaluated is usable. One of the most well-known definitions of usability is that provided by Nielsen [1]. Nielsen's definition stated that usability is comprised of the following five components:

- Learnability: *"How easy is it for users to accomplish basic tasks the first time they encounter the design?"*
- Efficiency: *"Once users have learned the design, how quickly can they perform tasks?"*
- Memorability: *"When users return to the design after a period of not using it, how easily can they reestablish proficiency?"*

© Springer Nature Switzerland AG 2020
C. Stephanidis et al. (Eds.): HCII 2020, LNCS 12423, pp. 3–18, 2020.
https://doi.org/10.1007/978-3-030-60114-0_1

- Errors: "*How many errors do users make, how severe are these errors, and how easily can they recover from the errors?*"
- Satisfaction: "*How pleasant is it to use the design?*"

Based on this definition, for any system to be considered usable, it has to be learnable, memorable, be efficient, handle errors, and be satisfying. To measure the usability of a system, many methods have been developed and introduced. One of the most commonly used methods is heuristic evaluation (HE) [2, 3]. The idea behind HE is simple. In HE, a number of usability practitioners, ideally 3–5 [4], evaluate a system guided by usability heuristics. HE gained popularity because it is a discount method [5], meaning that it does not require much time, money, or resources. However, the level of expertise of the evaluator has an effect on the results of the evaluation. Originally, Nielsen stated that using HE, 3–5 usability experts can identify between 74% to 87% of the usability issues of a system, while the same number of novice evaluators can identify 51% of the usability issues [6]. However, a subsequent study showed that novices can detect only 23% of usability issues [7]. Therefore, the gap is even larger than what Nielsen expected. We investigated the reasons behind this discrepancy [8] and found that one of the main reasons is novices' lack of understanding of heuristics and the role that heuristics play in the detection of usability issues. This finding matches the results of other researchers. For example, [9] found that usability heuristics themselves are not usable due to their level of abstraction. Moreover, [10] reported that novice evaluators have difficulties understanding some usability heuristics, cannot differentiate between some heuristics, and think that some heuristics are the same. In [11], a questionnaire was designed to assess novice evaluators' perception of usability heuristics; the results showed that novice evaluators need more complete heuristics' specifications. Understanding anything is the first step to applying it. Therefore, without a proper understanding of usability heuristics, the gap between usability experts and novices will persist. Improving the performance of novice evaluators is important. Usability experts are not always available, either because it is difficult to find them or because they are expensive to hire them. Even in research studies, novices are recruited to perform HE [12, 13]. Small companies usually hire novices, as shown in a Brazilian study [14]. The 51% identification rate that Nielsen proposed can be achieved when 3–5 novices perform HE; however, some companies do not hire more than one usability practitioner, as shown by a Malaysian survey [15]. Therefore, it is important to start working to improve the performance of novices and provide them with more accessible and usable methods. In our work [8], we created a step-by-step protocol for HE. We stated that usability heuristics are too abstract and need to be further simplified to be easily understood by novices. In this study, we complemented that work by simplifying usability heuristics. We used a snowball sampling technique to recruit usability experts. We asked 15 usability experts with at least 4 years of experience from both academia and industry to thoroughly explain each of Nielsen's 10 usability heuristics, i.e., explain them; give examples; and describe their significance, their applicability and the consequences of ignoring them. After transcribing all the responses, we conducted thematic analysis to synthesize the responses and group all the concepts identified under each heuristic.

2   Related Work

HE as a method originally developed by Nielsen and Molish in the 1990s [16, 17], when they proposed a list of nine usability heuristics. This list was later revised by Nielsen to result in a list of ten usability heuristics [18]. This set of usability heuristics is considered to be one of the most famous in the field. The 10 heuristics are as follows:

- Visibility of system status: *"The system should always keep users informed about what is going on, through appropriate feedback within reasonable time."*
- Match between system and the real world: *"The system should speak the users' language, with words, phrases and concepts familiar to the user, rather than system-oriented terms. Follow real-world conventions, making information appear in a natural and logical order."*
- User control and freedom: *"Users often choose system functions by mistake and will need a clearly marked "emergency exit" to leave the unwanted state without having to go through an extended dialogue. Support undo and redo."*
- Consistency and standards: *"Users should not have to wonder whether different words, situations, or actions mean the same thing. Follow platform conventions."*
- Error prevention: *"Even better than good error messages is a careful design which prevents a problem from occurring in the first place. Either eliminate error-prone conditions or check for them and present users with a confirmation option before they commit to the action."*
- Recognition rather than recall: *"Minimize the user's memory load by making objects, actions, and options visible. The user should not have to remember information from one part of the dialogue to another. Instructions for use of the system should be visible or easily retrievable whenever appropriate."*
- Flexibility and efficiency of use: *"Accelerators — unseen by the novice user — may often speed up the interaction for the expert user such that the system can cater to both inexperienced and experienced users. Allow users to tailor frequent actions."*
- Aesthetic and minimalist design: *"Dialogues should not contain information which is irrelevant or rarely needed. Every extra unit of information in a dialogue competes with the relevant units of information and diminishes their relative visibility."*
- Help users recognize, diagnose, and recover from errors: *"Error messages should be expressed in plain language (no codes), precisely indicate the problem, and constructively suggest a solution."*
- Help and documentation: *"Even though it is better if the system can be used without documentation, it may be necessary to provide help and documentation. Any such information should be easy to search, focused on the user's task, list concrete steps to be carried out, and not be too large."*

Although Nilesen's heuristics are the most well-known heuristics in the field, there are other heuristics that preceded them and others that succeeded them. These heuristics include Shnideramn's 8 golden rules [19], which are 8 general principles for designing interfaces; Tognazzini's 19 interaction design principles [20]; Gerhardt-Powal's 10 cognitive principles [21], and Mandle's 3 golden rules [22]. These are just examples of the many other usability heuristics that have been produced over the years to aid usability practitioners in evaluating systems.

Since there are many usability heuristics that have been developed, some researchers prefer to combine some of the existing heuristics instead of creating new heuristics from scratch. In [23], the researchers devised a new list of 11 principles called the Multiple Heuristic Evaluation Table (MHET) based on multiple existing heuristics, such as Nielsen's heuristics and Shniderman's principles. In [24], the authors attempted a similar task; they created a new set of 15 heuristics based on Nielsen's heuristics and Tognazzini's principles.

Another approach to address the abundance of available usability heuristics is to compare them. In [25, 26], Nielsen's heuristics were compared with Gerhardt-Powals principles. Solh [25] showed that Gerhardt-Powal's principles are better than Nielsen's heuristics in detecting real problems, but Nielsen's heuristics were better in detecting severe problems, while Hvannberg et al. [26] reported no significant difference between the two.

All the previously mentioned heuristics are general heuristics, meaning they were not designed to target specific types of platforms, audiences or contexts. In contrast, some researchers have focused on producing domain-specific heuristics. The researchers in [27] developed a set of 43 heuristics to assess the playability of video games, which they called the Heuristics of Evaluating Playability (HEP). In [28], the researchers produced a list of 11 heuristics to evaluate the usability of touchscreen-based mobile devices. In [12, 29], the researchers developed heuristics targeted at specific audiences. The researchers in [29] focused on children and created a comprehensive list of heuristics to evaluate child e-learning applications, which they called the Heuristic Evaluation for Child E-learning Application (HECE), while in [12], the researchers focused on elderly people. These researchers produced a list of 13 heuristics to evaluate the usability of mobile launchers for elderly people.

This is by no means an exhaustive list of the domain-specific heuristics but rather some examples of what has been produced.

Some studies have aimed to facilitate the use of HE for novice evaluators. This trend was motivated by [7], which showed that novices' performance was far worse than that originally stated by Nielsen. Subsequently, many studies were conducted with the goal of enhancing the performance of novice evaluators. In [30], the researchers investigated the tactics that usability experts use when applying HE; they interviewed 4 usability experts and produced a list of 38 tactics that experts use. The goal was to help novices conduct HE by using the same tactics that experts use. In [31], the researchers decided to include real users in the HE process and examine whether the performance of nonexpert evaluators could be enhanced. They developed two methods, namely the user exploration session (UES-HE) and user review session (URS-HE), and both methods proved to be effective in enhancing the performance of novice evaluators. Other studies have tried to examine whether children are able to perform HE. In [32], they recruited 20 children between 12–13 years of age, explained the heuristics to them and asked them to evaluate a game; however, the results of their evaluation were not satisfactory. In a similar study [33], the researchers recruited 12 children aged between 10–11; however, they presented the children with heuristics written in a simplified manner appropriate for their age and asked them to evaluate a music game. The results of the evaluation showed that children faced some difficulties, however, that showed a potential for good HE performance.

As seen in the literature, there is a growing interest in facilitating the use of HE for novices. Although there are a large number of usability heuristics, both general and domain-specific, Nielsen's heuristics are still the most recognized and used heuristics. Therefore, instead of creating new usability heuristics, our goal in this study is to further enhance the understandability of Nielsen's heuristics by breaking down each heuristic.

3 Methodology

The goal of this study was to explain Nielsen's heuristics in detail. To do so, we decided to conduct interviews. Interviews give participants a chance to deeply explain their responses, which eventually helps the researchers obtain a better understanding of the matter at hand. We specifically chose to conduct semistructured interviews because, in contrast to structured interviews, they allow for some flexibility in asking additional questions when necessary, and in contrast to unstructured interviews, they still ensure that the specific points being investigated are addressed and prevent a loss of concentration.

Before conducting the interviews, we had to decide who we would interview. Obviously, the goal was to interview usability practitioners with some level of experience. However, defining who is an expert is difficult, not only in HCI but also in most fields to varying degrees. There is not much in the literature on defining who is an expert in HCI. To the best of our knowledge, the only work that has pursued this topic is [34]. In this work, the researchers defined an expert as someone with at least 10000 h of practice, as well as a Master's or PhD in the field. However, this definition is rather strict since the researchers based them on the idea of deliberate practice [35]. Such a criterion of deliberate practice suggests that for anyone to become an expert in a subject matter, he/she should have 10000 h/10 years of deliberate practice. However, this criterion has been widely criticized for not being accurate. In [36], the researchers showed that practice is not the only factor to determine who becomes an expert. There are other factors, such as when the person started to practice and the person's IQ. Therefore, one can become an expert with less than 10000 h of practice, and one might not become an expert even after 10000 h of practice. Since usability experts are difficult to find, and since this criterion is not necessarily appropriate, we decided to go with less strict criteria, such as those proposed in [30], in which an expert is defined as someone who has at least 4 years of experience in the field. In our study, along with this criterion, we stipulated that participants should be familiar with Nielsen's heuristics and have performed HE at least three times.

Our next step was to decide how many interviews should be performed. Interviews should be conducted until saturation is reached. For this study, the recommended number of interviews based on [37] was 12.

To recruit participants, we used a snowball sampling technique. We ultimately interviewed 15 usability experts with at least 4 years of experience who came from both academia and industry. We included 7 experts from academia and 8 experts from industry. Nine interviews were conducted online via conference calls, and 6 interviews were performed in person. The main questions in the interviews asked participants to explain each of the heuristics; give examples; and describe their significance, their applicability and the consequences of ignoring them.

After the interviews, we analyzed the responses of the participants by using thematic analysis [38].

4 Results

There are two main issues with the heuristics. First, some heuristics are too abstract, as they encompass multiple ideas that need to be listed; one overly abstract heuristic is the visibility of the system status. Second, some heuristics have interrelated ideas but are not the same. Therefore, they should be explained separately; otherwise, evaluators might focus on one of them and not the other. One example of a heuristic characterized by this issue is help and documentation.

The detailed heuristics are as follows:

1. Visibility of system status: The idea of this heuristic is to always keep the user informed. Under this heuristic, there are four subheuristics:

    1.1. State: Users should always know what the state of the system is and what they can do in the system at any given moment. For example, if there is a link in the page, it should appear in a different color and be underscored so that the user knows that he/she can click on it.

    1.2. Location: Users should always know where they are, including in which system they are, in which part of the system they are, and where they are in relation to other parts of the system. For example, the logo of the system on the top of the page lets users know in which system they are, the title of the page lets them know in which part of the system they are and the navigation bar lets them know where they are in relation to other parts of the system.

    1.3. Progress: Users should know how far they are from completing their task. This applies to both active and passive situations. Active situations occur when the user is completing a multistep task. For example, when a user is completing a multipage form, he/she should know how many pages have been completed and how many pages are left. Passive situations are when a user takes an action and waits for the system to complete it. For example, when the user downloads a file, the system shows him/her how long the file will take to download.

    1.4. Closure: Users should clearly know that their task is completed and whether it has been completed successfully. For example, when the user performs a financial transaction, he/she should know whether it went through.

2. Match between system and the real world: The idea of this heuristic is to provide users with content they understand and are familiar with. Under this heuristic, there are three subheuristics:

    2.1. Understandability: Users should be able to understand any content that is presented to them in the system. Content refers not only to text but generally anything presented in the system, such as pictures, icons, or metaphors. The understandability of the content depends heavily on the target audience;

therefore, the target audience should be kept in mind when examining the understandability of the content.

2.2. Natural and logical order: The content and the series of steps of an action in the system should follow a natural and logical order. A natural order refers to the order of steps that people usually follow when performing similar tasks in the real world. For example, in an e-shop, the steps to buy an item should be similar to the steps that users follow when they buy an item from a physical shop. However, not all tasks performed digitally have similar tasks in the real world; in such a case, the task should follow an intuitive and logical order as much as possible.

2.3. Appropriateness: The content should not only be understandable but also be appropriate and acceptable. For example, if the system is expected to be used by children, then certain words or phrases should not be used. Alternatively, if the system is expected to be used by users from a certain culture, then content that might be perceived as offensive should not be displayed. Therefore, the appropriateness also depends on the target audience of the system.

3. User control and freedom: The idea of this heuristic is to increase users' control over the system and their freedom. Under this heuristic, there are three subheuristics:

3.1. Reversibility: Anything users do should be reversible. Users should be able to undo or redo any action they make in the system. For example, if the user deletes a certain file, he/she should be able to retrieve the deleted file if desired.

3.2. Emergency exit: Users should be able to exit out of any undesirable situation in the system. If users are faced with a situation in which they do not know how to act or cannot find what they want, then there should be an easy way out of the situation. For example, on certain websites, there are continuous pop ups that the user does not know how to block, which is a violation of this heuristic.

3.3. Informing users: Users should be informed about any action they have taken in the system. This is specifically crucial when the actions that the user takes are important or critical. For example, when the system asks the user to enter personal information, the system should explain to the user why he/she is being asked to enter this information and how the system is going to handle this information.

4. Consistency and standards: This heuristic has two interrelated ideas. These two ideas are as follows:

4.1. Consistency: Once a certain element is used in one part of the system, it should be used in a similar way throughout the system. This consistency can take the following different forms: consistency in meaning, i.e., if one element has one meaning in one part of the system, it should have the same meaning in the whole system; consistency of function, i.e., if an element does one thing in one part of the system, it should do the same thing in the rest of the system; consistency of effort, i.e., if there is a multistep task, the effort should be divided equally between the steps so the user can know what to expect; consistency of organization, i.e., if one part is organized in a certain way, then the rest of the system should follow the same general organization; and consistency of feeling, i.e., there should be a consistent feeling throughout the system, and the system should be perceived as one unit.

4.2. Standards: The design of the system should incorporate the knowledge that users have from their previous experiences with similar systems. Therefore, common practices and conventions should be applied to the system to make the user's interaction with the system easier. For example, if most websites place the search bar at the top of the page and users are used to that placement, then the system should follow that and place the search bar at the top of the page.

5. Error prevention: The idea of this heuristic is that rather than waiting for users to make mistakes and then correct them, errors should be prevented in the first place. Under this heuristic, there are seven subheuristics:

5.1. Instructions: When a task has a specific way to be performed, the user should be provided with instructions on how to perform it. For example, when the system asks the user to enter a username and password, there should be instructions next this request to inform the user about what the username and the password should and should not contain. Otherwise, the user might have to enter the username and passwords multiple times until he/she determines what the requirements are.

5.2. Constraints: The system should not allow the user to enter certain inputs or use certain elements when the entry or use of those elements will inevitably produce erroneous/undesirable outcomes. For example, if the user is booking a flight, the user should not be allowed to enter a return flight date that precedes the date of the departure flight.

5.3. Confirmation: Users can sometimes take actions in the system that are unintended. Therefore, the system should ask users to confirm the actions they have taken to ensure that the actions that are about to be implemented are intended by the user. However, the confirmation should not be asked for every action the user takes in the system; it should be asked when the action is not easily undone or when it has serious consequences. For example, if the user is about to send a very large amount of money to someone, the system should ask the user to confirm the transfer to ensure that the correct amount is being sent and that the right person is going to receive it.

5.4. Notification: Changes and updates could occur in the system that could affect the outcomes and the performance of the user. Therefore, the user should be notified of any changes or updates to the system to avoid any undesirable outcomes. For example, if the user is using his/her phone, he/she might not notice that the battery is running low, so the system should notify him/her at a certain point that the battery is about to die to allow the user to take action. However, notifications should be used only when serious consequences are possible because continuous notifications could be annoying to users and could themselves have an adverse effect on the user's performance.

5.5. Autosaving: Various occurrences in the system can cause all the user inputs to be deleted or disappear. Therefore, the user's inputs should be autosaved so the user can retrieve them if anything happens to the system. Autosaving is most needed when the inputs are time-consuming or critical. For example, on e-learning websites, if the user is writing an essay on the site, the site should autosave the user's inputs so if anything happens, the effort put in by the user does not go to waste.

5.6. Flexible inputs: Sometimes, there is only one way for users to enter inputs; however, when there are multiple forms for the input, the system should allow users to enter the input in any form that they know/feel comfortable with, which will decrease the chance of them entering it incorrectly. For example, when entering a date, some users are comfortable entering the name of the month, while others are comfortable entering the month as a number; the system should accept both forms.

5.7. Defaults: In many systems, there are default states/modes that users start with. Defaults are critical because they determine the output and how the user interacts with the system. The user's lack of familiarity with or knowledge of the default state might lead to erroneous outcomes. Therefore, the defaults of a system should be used carefully and should be selected based on what the users are familiar with. Moreover, the user should clearly know what the default state is. For example, if the default of a phone is to not ring when someone calls, then the user would miss calls, as users do not expect that state to be the default when they use any new phone.

6. Recognition rather than recall: The idea of this heuristic is that users should not rely on their memory but rather should be provided with aids to remember. Under this heuristic, there are two subheuristics:

6.1. Availability: Anything users need to complete the task should be available in front of them. Therefore, the interface should clearly present everything that users need to accomplish their goal. Moreover, if users are completing a multistep task and there is a piece of information that they will need in more than one step, then this information should be presented not only at the first step but also at every step for which they need that information so they are not forced to remember it every time they need it. For example, when people go to a supermarket, there are signs on every aisle to tell them what every aisle contains so they do not need to remember what every aisle contains every time they go to the supermarket.

6.2. Suggestions: Users do not always know exactly what they want when using the system, and they might partially know what they want. Therefore, the system should provide users with suggestions to help them access what they want. For example, the suggestions that Google gives when one starts to type in the search bar help the user access what he/she wants. Additionally, in e-shops, when the user is browsing a certain item, the system gives suggestions of items that are frequently purchased with the item the user is browsing, which might remind the user to purchase an item he/she wanted. However, the suggestions provided should be as accurate as possible because inaccurate suggestions might be annoying to users.

7. Flexibility and efficiency of use: This heuristic has two interrelated ideas:

7.1. Flexibility: Most systems are used by multiple types of users and in different situations. Therefore, the system should be flexible enough to accommodate all different types of users and situations, which can be achieved through the provision of multiple ways to accomplish the same goal in the system, for example, providing a text reader to accommodate the user when he/she is driving or providing shortcuts for expert users.

7.2. Efficiency: Any task performed in the system should be in its simplest form. Therefore, there should not be any extraneous or unnecessary steps involved in completing the task. Any task performed in the system should be examined to ensure that every step can be performed in the required way; if it cannot be performed in this way, then it should be removed to simplify the task. For example, if the user is signing up for a website and is asked to enter his/her phone number, but the phone number will not serve any purpose, then the request for the phone number should be removed because it is just going to require additional unnecessary effort on the part of the user.

8. Aesthetic and minimalist design: The idea of this heuristic is that the design of the system should be appealing and easy to navigate. There are three subheuristics under this heuristic:

8.1. Aesthetic: The attractiveness and the beauty of the design is a crucial part of the system that might be overlooked. There is a principle called the esthetic-usability effect, which states that users perceive systems they find aesthetically pleasing to be more usable. Therefore, if the system is aesthetically pleasing, users will be more forgiving of any usability issues that the system has. However, users might be forgiving of minor usability issues but not major usability issues. Thus, the design of the system should also be examined in terms of how aesthetically pleasing it is.

8.2. Organization: The system should be clearly organized. The user should not spend a large amount of time trying to understand the organization of the system. The items that are related to each other should be organized in a way that shows their relation. The different sections should be separated to make the navigation easy.

8.3. Simplicity: The website should not present any extraneous information or elements. Only the elements that are necessary should be presented on the page. Extraneous content could make the system cluttered and crowded, which will affect the ability of the user to navigate it. Moreover, unnecessary content could divide users' attention, so instead of focusing on what they want to accomplish, they might become distracted by other things.

9. Help users recognize, diagnose and recover from errors: This heuristic has three interrelated ideas:

9.1. Recognizing errors: The first step in rectifying errors is knowing that an error has occurred in the first place. Therefore, the system should notify the user that something has gone wrong. The user should be able to clearly understand that an error has occurred. The notification could be a very clear error message, an alerting sound or a mixture of different formats. However, the end result should be that the user is able to recognize an error.

9.2.   Understanding errors: After learning that an error has occurred, users should be able to determine the exact error. They should be able to identify in which part of the system the error occurred and the nature of the error. By knowing all this information, users can more easily resolve the issue. For example, instead of showing a generic message that says there is an error when a user enters an existing user name, the system should tell the user that the error occurred in the user name field because the user entered an existing user name.

9.3.   Recovering from errors: In many cases, just telling users what the error is can make it easy for them to rectify it. However, in other cases, the notification might not be enough, and the user might need additional instruction on how to recover from the error. Therefore, specifically in cases in which the solution is not intuitive, instructions should be provided to the user on how to rectify the issue.

10.   Help and documentation: This heuristic has two interrelated ideas:

10.1.   Help: Providing help involves providing a direct interaction with the system support team to resolve any issues that the users face. Many people still prefer to interact with someone rather than reading a manual or documentation. Therefore, users should be provided with the former option. Moreover, regardless of how comprehensive the documentation is, it cannot cover all the issues that the users might face. Therefore, there should be ways that the users can contact the support team by chat, phone number, email, etc.

10.2.   Documentation: The documentation serves as the guide or manual of the system; it should explain the system and cover most of the issues that users might have while using the system. There should be contextual documentation that users can find in the places where difficulties are expected, such as documentation accessed with a question mark button. In addition, there should be general documentation that addresses the whole system, such as frequently asked questions (FAQs) and tutorials.

Table 1 shows a high level overview of the detailed version of Nielsen's heuristics.

Table 1. Nielsen's detailed heuristics.

Nielsen's Heuristics	Concepts
Visibility of system status	State: Users should know what the state of the system is. Users should know what they can do in the system at any given time
	Location: Users should know which part of the system they are in. They should know their location in relation to other parts of the system
	Progress: Users should know how far they are from accomplishing their goal
	Closure: Users should know that the task at hand is complete, regardless of whether it has been completed with desirable outcomes
Match between system and the real world	Understandability: The content presented in the system should be understandable by the target audience
	Natural and logical order: The content and actions presented in the system should follow a logical/natural order
	Appropriateness: The content presented in the system should be acceptable and appropriate for the target audience
User control and freedom	Reversibility: Users should be able to undo and redo any action they perform in the system
	Emergency exit: Users should be able to exit out of any undesirable situation in the system
	Informing users: Before asking users to enter any input or take any action, they should be presented with enough information so that they can make an informed decision
Consistency and standards	Consistency: Once a certain element of the system is used in one place of the system, it should be presented in the same way throughout the whole system
	Standards: The design of the system should follow the common practices and conventions of similar systems
Error prevention	Instructions: Users should be given enough guidance before they take any action to avoid making errors
	Constraints: Constraints should be placed on some types of inputs that are clearly invalid to save the time and effort of users
	Confirmation: Users should be asked to confirm their actions before they carry them out to ensure that they want the actions to occur
	Notification: Users should be notified of any changes in the system, especially if they have serious consequences
	Autosaving: Users' inputs should be saved in case something goes wrong. In such cases, users will not lose the effort they have put in
	Flexible inputs: Users should not be forced to enter inputs in a certain form; they should be able to enter inputs in any form they know
	Defaults: The default state of the system should be designed carefully to prevent users from making mistakes
Recognition rather than recall	Availability: Anything that users will need to accomplish a certain goal in the system should be presented to them. They should not have to rely on their memory as much as possible
	Suggestions: It is not possible to know what every user wants to accomplish in the system. Thus, users should be provided with suggestions to facilitate the process
Flexibility and efficiency of use	Flexibility: Every major goal or task in the system should be accessible and implemented in more than one way
	Efficiency: Any goal or task in the system should be performed in the simplest way possible
Aesthetic and minimalist design	Aesthetic: The design of the system should be esthetically pleasing to the target audience
	Organization: The content in the system should be presented in an organized and well-ordered manner
	Simplicity: The content presented in the system should be limited to the necessary content; extraneous content should be removed
Help users recognize, diagnose, and recover from errors	Recognizing errors: Users should notice that an error has occurred
	Understanding errors: Users should understand what the error is
	Recovering from errors: Users should know how to recover from that specific error
Help and documentation	Help: Users should be able to contact someone when they face some difficulties or have questions
	Documentation: The whole system or the most important aspects of it should be documented and presented to users in a written or visual material

5   Discussion

The main goal of this work was to better equip novice evaluators to conduct HE. One of the main advantages of HE is that it does not require many resources to be performed. The briefness of the usability heuristics is another advantage, as it makes the heuristics easy to recall so evaluators do not have to have the list with them every time they decide to conduct an evaluation. However, the briefness also introduces a problem, especially for novices, who might not fully grasp the different aspects of any given heuristic. Therefore, in this work, we aimed to balance the two extremes. Our goal was not to examine the completeness of Nielsen's heuristics and try to extend the list by adding new heuristics to the existing heuristics because in doing so, we might enhance the completeness of the list, but we might also make it difficult to digest. At the same time, we realized that the current version of the list of heuristics is not easy to understand and that keeping it that way will affect the quality of novices' HE results. Therefore, our objective was to focus only on the current heuristics and try to break them down and explain the different concepts and ideas that each heuristic contains. Although the detailed description of the heuristics requires more reading and effort on the part of evaluators, it will potentially enhance their understanding of the heuristics, which will potentially improve the quality of their evaluation. The main target audience of this work is novices, but experts can benefit from it as well. During the interviews, we noticed that not all experts have the same comprehensive understanding of the heuristics or are able to fully explain each heuristic. Therefore, this detailed list might help some experts enhance their understanding of heuristics. Finally, this list should be tested and compared to the original list to determine whether it actually enhances evaluators' understanding of them.

6   Conclusion

Usability is one of the main concerns of HCI. Therefore, usability experts evaluate systems to ensure their usability. One of the most popular methods to evaluate the usability of systems is HE. HE is a method in which 3–5 evaluators evaluate a system guided by a list of usability heuristics. Despite its popularity, HE is not as effective when used by novice evaluators as it is when used by expert evaluators. One of the reasons that makes HE less effective for novices is that usability heuristics are abstract to some degree, which makes fully understanding them challenging. Our goal was to simplify the usability heuristics by explaining each heuristic in detail to capture the different concepts that each heuristic encompasses. We chose Nielsen's usability heuristics since they are the most recognized usability heuristics. We interviewed 15 usability experts with at least 4 years of experience in the field from both academia and industry. We asked them to explain each of the heuristics; give examples; and describe their significance, their applicability and the consequences of ignoring them. Then, we analyzed their responses and produced a more detailed version of Nielsen's list of usability heuristics.

In future work, we would like to pursue two directions. First, we want to test whether, compared to Nilesen's original list, this detailed version enhances novices' understanding of the heuristics. Second, we want to examine whether a better understanding of usability heuristics leads to better evaluation performance.

References

1. Nielsen, J.: Usability 101: Introduction to usability. https://www.nngroup.com/articles/usabil ity-101-introduction-to-usability/
2. Rosenbaum, S., Rohn, J.A., Humburg, J.: A toolkit for strategic usability: results from workshops, panels, and surveys. In: Proceedings of the SIGCHI Conference on Human Factors in Computing Systems. ACM Press, The Hague, Netherlands, pp. 337–344 (2000). https://doi. org/10.1145/332040.332454
3. Fernandez, A., Insfran, E., Abrahão, S.: Usability evaluation methods for the web: a systematic mapping study. Inf. Softw. Technol. **53**, 789–817 (2011). https://doi.org/10.1016/j.infsof. 2011.02.007
4. Nielsen, J.: How to conduct a heuristic evaluation. Nielsen Norman Group **1**, 1–8 (1995)
5. Nielsen, J.: Guerrilla HCI: using discount usability engineering to penetrate the intimidation barrier. In: Bias, R.G., Mayhew, D.J. (eds.) Cost-Justifying Usability, pp. 245–272. Academic Press, Boston (1994)
6. Nielsen, J.: Finding usability problems through heuristic evaluation. In: Proceedings of the SIGCHI Conference on Human Factors in Computing Systems. ACM Press, Monterey, California, USA, pp. 373–380 (1992). https://doi.org/10.1145/142750.142834
7. Slavkovic, A., Cross, K.: Novice heuristic evaluations of a complex interface. CHI'99 Extended Abstracts on Human Factors in Computing Systems, pp. 304–305. Association for Computing Machinery, Pittsburgh (1999)
8. Abulfaraj, A., Steele, A.: Coherent heuristic evaluation (CoHE): toward increasing the effectiveness of heuristic evaluation for novice evaluators. In: Marcus, A., Rosenzweig, E. (eds.) HCII 2020. LNCS, vol. 12200, pp. 3–20. Springer, Cham (2020). https://doi.org/10.1007/ 978-3-030-49713-2_1
9. Cronholm, S.: The usability of usability guidelines: a proposal for meta-guidelines. In: Proceedings of the 21st Annual Conference of the Australian Computer-Human Interaction Special Interest Group: Design: Open 24/7. Association for Computing Machinery, Melbourne, Australia, pp. 233–240 (2009). https://doi.org/10.1145/1738826.1738864
10. de Lima Salgado, A., de Mattos Fortes, R.P.: Heuristic evaluation for novice evaluators. In: Marcus, A. (ed.) DUXU 2016. LNCS, vol. 9746, pp. 387–398. Springer, Cham (2016). https:// doi.org/10.1007/978-3-319-40409-7_37
11. Rusu, C., Botella, F., Rusu, V., Roncagliolo, S., Quiñones, D.: An online travel agency comparative study: heuristic evaluators perception. In: Meiselwitz, G. (ed.) SCSM 2018. LNCS, vol. 10913, pp. 112–120. Springer, Cham (2018). https://doi.org/10.1007/978-3-319-91521-0_9
12. Al-Razgan, M.S., Al-Khalifa, H.S., Al-Shahrani, M.D.: Heuristics for evaluating the usability of mobile launchers for elderly people. In: Marcus, A. (ed.) DUXU 2014. LNCS, vol. 8517, pp. 415–424. Springer, Cham (2014). https://doi.org/10.1007/978-3-319-07668-3_40
13. Paz, F., Paz, F.A., Pow-Sang, J.A.: Experimental case study of new usability heuristics. In: Marcus, A. (ed.) DUXU 2015. LNCS, vol. 9186, pp. 212–223. Springer, Cham (2015). https:// doi.org/10.1007/978-3-319-20886-2_21
14. de Salgado, AL., Amaral, LA., Freire, AP., Fortes, RPM.: Usability and UX practices in small enterprises: lessons from a survey of the Brazilian context. In: Proceedings of the 34th ACM International Conference on the Design of Communication. Association for Computing Machinery, Silver Spring, MD, USA, pp. 1–9 (2016). https://doi.org/10.1145/2987592.298 7616
15. Hussein, I., Mahmud, M., Tap, AOM.: A survey of user experience practice: a point of meet between academic and industry. In: 3rd International Conference on User Science and Engineering (i-USEr). IEEE, Shah Alam, Malaysia, pp. 62–67 (2014). https://doi.org/10. 1109/iuser.2014.7002678

16. Molich, R., Nielsen, J.: Improving a human-computer dialogue. Commun. ACM **33**, 338–348 (1990). https://doi.org/10.1145/77481.77486
17. Nielsen, J., Molich, R.: Heuristic evaluation of user interfaces. In: Proceedings of the SIGCHI Conference on Human Factors in Computing Systems. Association for Computing Machinery, Seattle, Washington, USA, pp. 249–256 (1990). https://doi.org/10.1145/97243.97281
18. Nielsen, J.: Usability heuristics for user interface design 10. https://www.nngroup.com/art icles/ten-usability-heuristics/
19. Shneiderman, B.: Designing the User Interface: Strategies for Effective Human-Computer Interaction. Addison-Wesley Publishing Co., Reading, MA (1987)
20. Tognazzini, B.: First principles of interaction design (revised & expanded). https://asktog. com/atc/principles-of-interaction-design/
21. Gerhardt-Powals, J.: Cognitive engineering principles for enhancing human-computer performance. Int. J. Hum. Comput. Interact. **8**, 189–211 (1996). https://doi.org/10.1080/104473 19609526147
22. Mandel, T.: The golden rules of user interface design. The Elements of User Interface Design, pp. 1–28. John Wiley & Sons Inc, Hoboken (1997)
23. Atkinson, B.F.W., Bennett, T.O., Bahr, G.S., Nelson, M.M.W.: Development of a multiple heuristics evaluation table (MHET) to support software development and usability analysis. International Conference on Universal Access in Human-Computer Interaction, pp. 563–572. Springer, Berlin (2007)
24. Granollers, T.: Usability evaluation with heuristics. New proposal from integrating two trusted sources. In: Marcus, A., Wang, W. (eds.) DUXU 2018. LNCS, vol. 10918, pp. 396–405. Springer, Cham (2018). https://doi.org/10.1007/978-3-319-91797-9_28
25. Sohl, M.: Comparing two heuristic evaluation methods and validating with usability test methods: applying usability evaluation on a simple website. Student thesis, Linköping University (2018)
26. Hvannberg, E.T., Law, E.L.C., Lárusdóttir, M.K.: Heuristic evaluation: comparing ways of finding and reporting usability problems. Interact. Comput. **19**, 225–240 (2007). https://doi. org/10.1016/j.intcom.2006.10.001
27. Desurvire, H., Caplan, M., Toth, J.A.: Using heuristics to evaluate the playability of games. CHI'04 Extended Abstracts on Human Factors in Computing Systems (Vienna, Austria, 24–29 April 2004), pp. 1509–1512. ACM, New York (2004)
28. Inostroza, R., Rusu, C., Roncagliolo, S., Rusu, V.: Usability heuristics for touchscreen-based mobile devices: update. In: Proceedings of the 2013 Chilean Conference on Human - Computer Interaction. Association for Computing Machinery, Temuco, Chile, pp. 24–29 (2013). https://doi.org/10.1145/2535597.2535602
29. Alsumait, A., Al-Osaimi, A.: Usability heuristics evaluation for child e-learning applications. In: Proceedings of the 11th International Conference on Information Integration and Web-Based Applications & Services. Association for Computing Machinery, Kuala Lumpur, Malaysia, pp. 425–430 (2009)
30. de Salgado, AL., de Lara, SM., Freire, AP., de Fortes, RPM.: What is hidden in a heuristic evaluation: tactics from the experts. In: 13th International Conference on Information Systems & Technology Management - Contecsi. Contecsi, São Paulo, SP, Brazil, pp. 2931–2946 (2016). https://doi.org/10.5748/9788599693124-13CONTECSI/PS-4068
31. Alqurni, J., Alroobaea, R., Alqahtani, M.: Effect of user sessions on the heuristic usability method. Int. J. Open Source Softw. Process. (IJOSSP) **9**, 62–81 (2018). https://doi.org/10. 4018/ijossp.2018010104
32. Wodike, OA., Sim, G., Horton, M.: Empowering teenagers to perform a heuristic evaluation of a game. In: Proceedings of the 28th International BCS Human Computer Interaction Conference (HCI 2014) 28, pp. 353–358 (Sep 2014)

33. Salian, K., Sim, G.: Simplifying heuristic evaluation for older children. In: Proceedings of the India HCI 2014 Conference on Human Computer Interaction. Association for Computing Machinery, New Delhi, India, pp. 26–34 (2014)

34. Botella, F., Alarcon, E., Peñalver, A.: How to classify to experts in usability evaluation. In: Proceedings of the XV International Conference on Human Computer Interaction. Association for Computing Machinery, Puerto de la Cruz, Tenerife, Spain, p. 25 (2014)

35. Ericsson, K.A., Prietula, M.J., Cokely, E.T.: The making of an expert. Harv. Bus. Rev. **85**(114–121), 193 (2007)

36. Hambrick, D.Z., Oswald, F.L., Altmann, E.M., Meinz, E.J., Gobet, F., Campitelli, G.: Deliberate practice: is that all it takes to become an expert? Intelligence **45**, 34–45 (2014). https://doi.org/10.1016/j.intell.2013.04.001

37. Guest, G., Bunce, A., Johnson, L.: How many interviews are enough?: An experiment with data saturation and variability. Field Methods **18**, 59–82 (2006). https://doi.org/10.1177/1525822X05279903

38. Blandford, A., Furniss, D., Makri, S.: Qualitative HCI research: going behind the scenes. Synth. Lect. Hum. Centered Inform. **9**, 1–115 (2016). https://doi.org/10.2200/S00706ED1V01Y201602HCI034

Investigating a Design Space for Developing Design Thinking in Electronic Healthcare Records

Ilyasse Belkacem[1]([⊠]), Isabelle Pecci[2], Anthony Faiola[3], and Benoît Martin[2]

[1] Luxembourg Institute of Science and Technology (LIST),
4362 Esch-sur-Alzette, Luxembourg
`ilyasse.belkacem@list.lu`
[2] Laboratoire de Conception, Optimisation et Modélisation des Systèmes (LCOMS),
Université de Lorraine, Metz, France
`{isabelle.pecci,benoit.martin}@univ-lorraine.fr`
[3] Department of Biomedical and Health Information Sciences, University of Illinois,
Chicago, USA
`faiola@uic.edu`

Abstract. In recent years, most hospitals have introduced an Electronic Health Record (EHR) systems to replace paper patient records. The satisfaction with these systems was lower than expected due to the poor organization of system data and the difficulty with obtaining actionable information. Data visualization and interface design are not as advanced in some parts of clinical medicine as it is in other scientific disciplines and commercial industries. In addition, the designers of electronic health record interfaces are confronted with a dizzying array of design choices. In this paper, we propose an 8-dimensional design space to provide a framework when designing interfaces for accessing a patient's record. We present our methodology to define this design space: first we used the 5W1H method to set the dimensions, then we studied existing systems and interviewed doctors to define main values or categories of each dimension, we present many illustrative examples of these categories. Finally, we showcase the utility of our work for designers of EHR systems through a scenario. Overall, our design space can help building systems which will improve health data visualization and interface design.

Keywords: Design space · Interface · Electronic health record

1 Introduction

The Electronic Health Record (EHR) focuses on the total health of the patient, going beyond standard clinical data collected and contained in the Electronic Medical Record (EMR) in the provider's office. EHRs are designed to share information with other health care providers and specialists. As such, they contain information from all the clinicians involved in the patient's care [15] thus allowing

C. Stephanidis et al. (Eds.): HCII 2020, LNCS 12423, pp. 19–41, 2020.
https://doi.org/10.1007/978-3-030-60114-0_2

different users (health professionals, patients, etc.) to access useful information that contributes to patient follow-up: history, problems, allergies, etc. Moreover, the EHR's format makes it more practical and accessible in different situations with different representations. The notion of time and context is much broader compared to a paper format, especially with mobile technology.

The EHR is also a communication tool between the different stakeholders facilitated by the user interface, which allows access to the health record. EHR adoption by hospital administrators is influenced (in part) by the quality and the effectiveness of the human-centered design of the EHR interface but many EHR systems lack usability when the user interacts with their interface [6].

The importance of designing suitable interfaces the meet the needs of end users is often overlooked. Users of the health record have different roles, so the information in the same health record can vary in importance depending on the user.

The presentation of information on the interface plays an important role in understanding the patient's record. Inappropriate visualization can involve many problems such as wasting time decision for health professionals or making errors when delivering care. Then the system will no longer be used. The interface and health data visualizations should help health professionals easily find the requested information at the right time. The task of designers is difficult. There are many challenges when designing an electronic health record interface to increase usability. This is why it is necessary for a designer to explore different possibilities before selecting the most appropriate option for its solution.

In this paper, we present a design space that explores different design possibilities organized into dimensions for electronic health record visualization. This structure can answer different questions to satisfy the needs of the end users. We first review what are EHR interfaces and design spaces (Sect. 2). Then, we present a study of EHR systems based on a comprehensive literature review of existing ones and on interviews of professionals' healthcare (Sect. 3). After presenting our design space to help the designer of EHR applications (Sect. 4), we introduce a novel design scenario based on our design space (Sect. 5). At the end, we discuss our space and its limitations (6) and we conclude by introducing our future work (Sect. 7).

Our contributions are threefold: (1) an eight-dimensional design space for helping design suitable electronic health record visualization, (2) a critical analysis of existing interfaces, and (3) new directions and future works for designing a new electronic health record visualization application.

2 Background and Related Work

An Electronic Health Record (EHR) is designed to contain information about a patient and to exchange it with all medical staff. An EHR is "the complete set of information that resides in electronic form and is related to the past, present and future health status or health care provided to a subject of care" [33]. EHR systems can support clinicians with improving quality of care, effectiveness, and coordination of work [3].

A frequent visualization in EHR systems is a flowsheet in the form of spreadsheets with graphs that contain different health variables for a patient over a period of time [4]. The US Institute for Medicine's 2011 Report noted that "The visualization of information is not as advanced in some parts of clinical medicine as in other scientific disciplines." [28]. Information visualization is a way to improve the understanding of complex data and, therefore, to increase the value of available medical data electronically [11].

Standards and guidelines such as Electronic Health Record Usability Evaluation and Use Case Framework [3] provide design principles and considerations that are well suited for health record visualization. However, they are limited in the range of possibilities that they offer to the designer. Previous surveys such as [22,23,35] analyze existing systems, but they only focus on what was already developed, and not on what should be important to develop. Our work is to support the designer to create an innovative EHR interface: we propose many alternative interfaces and guide them to the most suitable.

MacLean et al. [26] define a design space as a "space of possibilities" in order to outline and clarify thoughts and ideas. As it's difficult to design a suitable solution, designers need a tool to help them develop their ideas. A design space seems to be an interesting approach since it "limits design possibilities to certain dimensions, while leaving others open to creative exploration" [5]. Design spaces are not only used to study existing design options but also to propose innovative ones. This is why they differ from classifications and taxonomies [37].

Several design spaces have been developed in the different areas of Human-Computer Interaction to standardize and facilitate the role of the designer. Renate Haeuslschmid et al. [16] present a five-dimensional design space for an interactive windshield to help designers build different types of applications for cars. Schulz et al. [37] characterize the main aspects of interface tasks and Nancel et al. [30] structure menus and selecting items.

3   Electronic Health Record Application Analysis

3.1   Global Analysis: The 5W1H Method

At the outset of our research, we used the method of 5W1H which allows us to extract the dimensions of our design space by asking the right questions. 5W1H is an abbreviation of the questions: "Who? What? Where? When? Why?" and "How?". This method allows us to structure and identify the main dimensions of our design space. It is a formula for obtaining a complete history on a subject [31]. It is a widespread method in Journalism. But it is also used in other domains such as management [20], marketing [42] and even in interface visualization [49] or to build a design space [37]. The questions we asked to obtain the dimensions are as follows (see Fig. 1):

1. "**Who** needs to visualize or interact with the health record?" USER dimension.
2. "**What** the USER needs to visualize?" HEALTH RECORD dimension.

3. **"Where** should the visualization of patient record be hosted?" TECHNOLOGY dimension. **"Where** the USER interacts with the patient record?" LOCATION dimension.
4. **"When** does the user need to visualize the health record?" TIME dimension.
5. **"Why** the HEALTH RECORD interface is being used?". GOAL dimension.
6. **"How** does the USER view the HEALTH RECORD?" VISUALIZATION dimension. **"How** does the USER interact with the HEALTH RECORD?" INPUT INTERACTION dimension.

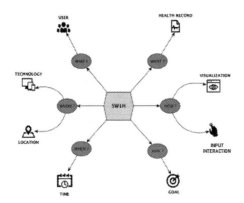

Fig. 1. The eight dimensions of our design space.

3.2   Detailed Analysis: Literature Review and Interviews

We have done extensive research in the literature: research papers, patents, and reports. To ensure the quality of our work, we carefully selected our keywords. We used first general terms to cover the field of study: "visualization of information" and "patient record". More than 150 references resulted from our initial research through electronic databases and search engines such as Google Scholar, ResearchGate, ACM Digital Library, IEEE Xplore and Web of Science. Furthermore, we searched for relevant articles cited in the bibliography of these articles. We excluded many articles because they didn't describe a specific visualization technique, or the visualization interface was not interactive. We identified a total of 54 papers that included the interface of EHR data. We report in this paper 12 works that include contemporary systems that provide design choices relevant to EHR visualization:

1. Plaisant et al., 2003 [32]: this system is considered a pioneer. It provides general visualization of health patient's record.
2. Ruchikachorn et al., 2014 [36]: it is an EHR system for preparing medical examinations.

3. Faiola et al., 2015 [13]: it's an EHR system for the Intensive Care Unit. It displays some medical data of the patient like life signs that come from monitors in the patient's room.
4. Jin et al., 2016 [19]: this system uses a 2D representation of a human's body to navigate in the various physiological data.
5. Thomas et al., 2017 [43]: this system uses wall-sized display to allow collaborative tasks between doctors and nurse in the Intensive Care Unit.
6. Dabek et al., 2017 [12]: this system uses a tree view and a timeline one to navigate more easily among data.
7. Zhang et al., 2018 [48]: it is an EHR system dedicated to patients who are suffering from cancer.
8. Vo et al., 2018 [44]: it is an EHR system dedicated to gastroenterologists.
9. Warner et al., 2015 [45]: this system allows exploring similar electronic health records.
10. Huang et al., 2015 [18]: this system allows following the development of chronic kidney illness over time.
11. Loorak et al., 2016 [25]: this system helps researchers to analyze data from patients' stroke.
12. Malver et al., 2017 [29]: this system helps medical staff during their daily medical round.

We completed our study by gathering the opinions of healthcare professionals who use health record interfaces of such systems. Nine volunteer doctors (eight males, one female) from the medical intensive care unit (MICU) at the University of Illinois Hospital, Chicago, participated in an interview. All spoke fluent English. All study procedures took place in the office of the doctors. The interview questions allowed the participants to express freely any concerns with any (positive/negative aspects).

3.3   Results

We collected different ideas and ordered them in our first level dimensions based on 5W1H questions. This led us to subdivide some dimensions into sub-dimensions. Table 1 provides a short description and illustrates each of them through examples of existing systems and suggestions from doctors' interviews.

LOCATION and TIME dimensions are not included in Table 1 since they did not appear clearly in literature reviews.

Table 1. Different design choice examples from literature and interviews

Subdimension	Description	Examples
Dimension		
User		
Target	The intended users of the application.	The system is designed to assist ICU clinicians [13,43], gastroenterologist doctors [44], patients with cancer [48], clinicians and researchers [45,18,25]] or all medical stuff [32,36,19,12,29].
Use	During the interaction, the number of users implicated.	The system was developed for large displays to facilitate teamwork [43].
Health record		
Cardinality	The number of records the system can display in the same view.	Some are developed to visualize single health record [32,36,13,19,12,48,44], multiple patients [45,18,25] or mixed where there is a unit-level view of all patients and a more detailed dashboard for each patient that opens when clicking a patient's name [43,29].
Dimension	The organization of the attributes of the medical data	One dimension like notes [36,13,43], temporal dimension is used in [32,36,13,19,12,48,25], tree dimension [12], network [45].
Data type	The two types of data covered by the application: quantitative and qualitative.	All systems use qualitative and quantitative data.
Variable number	The number of variables (e.g. Medications, vital signs) can support the application.	All variables [32,36,19,12,29], many variables [13,43,48,44], few variables [45,18,25]. The number of variables depends on the size of the screen (Interviews).
Level	The level of detail of data presented to the user.	All systems give a quick high-level overview and possibly necessary low-level data drill-down.
Technology		
	The device on which the user interacts with the health record	Desktop computers [32,19,12,18,25,29], laptop[13], tablets [36,13,44], Smartphone [48,45], wall-sized display [43]. Mobile device in mobility, desktop computer with large screen in office (interviews).
Goal		
Tasks	The task to be performed.	Decision making, exploratory analysis, care evaluation (interviews) [32,36,13,19,43,12,48,44,29], Statistical [45,18,25].
Use cases	The use cases that describe functionals scenarios.	Acute care [13,43], chronic disease [44.18].
Features	Features that exist in the interface to better assist users performing their tasks.	Medical imaging (interviews) [32,19] Diagnosis codes (ICD-9-CM) [45,18] Alerts and notifications (interviews) [32,36,19,43,29] Communication (voice message, texting, notes) (interviews). Recommendations for interventions (interviews). Statistics [45,18,25].
Input interaction		
Channels	The channels provided to interact with the system.	Touch screen [36,13,48,44,45] or a keyboard and a mouse for desktop computers [32,19,12,18,25,29]
Intent	A categorization that focuses on what the user wants to achieve.	Select: The clinician must select and drag-n-drop the needed vital sign into the timeline primary visualization display [13]."*I need to put on what I need*" (interviews). Explore: A clickable human body to interactively display health information [19], Expending and collapsing is possible to explore the tree [12]. Encode: The possibility of reordering the information with different reorderable attributes [25]. Abstract / elaborate: Touching a data-point brings the details of that point [44], a hover action can be used to show on demand the logged value for each graph-event [43]. Filter: A collapsing icon allows to hide some information and enlarge the rest [44], a filter button to reduce the data presented [12], Several tasks involve filtering patients according to a time period [25]. Connect: Search can highlight all parts of the record that match [32], machine learning used to analyze unstructured clinical notes to enables easy relation retrieval and show relevant information [36]. The visualization allows to show relationship [45].
Visualization		
Technique	The technique used to present different parts of information on the view.	Non-distortion techniques: Zooming in and out for images are available [32] or for graphs [13], A scrolling view that contains the entirety of the patient's history [12], new window [18], [43,44]. "Everything must be quickly accessible in one place" (interviews).
Representation	The way to represent information to the users	Table: by text and numeric [43]. Diagram: network [45], Sankey diagram [18], A tree representation [12], Kiviat diagram. [43] Graph: (interviews) [19,43,48,44,25]. Timeline: [32,36,13,12,48,44,25]. Map: a 2D human body representation [19]. Picture: like medical imaging [32,19]
Visual variables	The visual variables manipulated to encode information.	Size and position: size and position are used in systems that display data in a timeline [32,36,13,12,48,44,25]. Shape: circles and triangles for quantitative data, and square for qualitative data [44], symptoms are labeled with colored circles [19]. Color: is used to indicate severity or information category [32], to highlight related information [36], critical information such as allergies or alerts [13,29], abnormal test results [19], distinguish different combination of disease [18]. Transparency: transparency shows the different doses of a drug or the severity [32] or mapped to the morbidity score [43]. Texture: Some information is encoded by rectangles filled based on their data value. Crosses indicate missing data [25].
Adaptation and context awareness	An adaptive interface that can change according the clinical context	Highlighting values within the data in regard to the clinical context where you actually have models of the disease (interviews).

Table 2. Design space exploration (* exlusive selection)

Who? USER	Target	Doctors	Other medical staff	Patient	Patient family	Administrative staff	
	Use*	Individual			collaborative		

What? HEALTH RECORD	Cardinality*	Single patient		Multi patient		Mixed	
	Dimension	1 dimensional	n-dimensional	Temporal	Tree	Network	
	Data type	Qualitative			Quantitative		
	Variable number*	Few variables		Many variables		All variables	
	Level	Low			High		

Where? TECHNOLOGY	Screen size	Small			Large		
	Display number*	Single display			Multiple displays		
	Image quality	Resolution		Contrast		Luminance	
	Device type	Desktop	Exposed		Mobile	Wearable	

Where? LOCATION	Patient room	Care room	Doctor's office	Another place at the hospital	Home	Public building	Outdoor

When? TIME	Before the encounter		During the encounter		After the encounter	

Why? GOAL	Tasks	Exploratory analysis	Decision making	Care quality evaluation	Statistics		Non-medical task
	Use cases	Acute care		Chronic care	Preventive and health promotion		Undifferentiated symptoms
	Functionalities	Multimedia content	Diagnosis and treatment coding	Communication	Alerts and notifications	Care recommendation	Statistics	Educational tool

How? INPUT INTERACTION	Channel	Audio		Visual		Haptic	
	Intent	Select	Explore	Reconfigure	Encode	Abstract/Elaborate	Filter	Connect

How? VISUALIZATION	Technique	Distorsion		Non-distorsion			
	Representation	Table	Diagram	Graph	Timeline	Map	Picture
	Visual variables	Position	Size	Shape	Color	Transparency	Orientation	Texture
	Adaptation	Presentation		Navigation			
	Context awareness	User	Health record	Technology	Location	Time	Goal

4 Design Space Exploration

Based on the analysis of the existing systems and interviews with doctors, we have constituted different sub-dimensions and their values. Moreover, we added some values based on HCI papers. This section briefly describes each of the dimensions with the different sub-categories.

4.1 User

Target. Among the reviewed, the systems do not always target the same users. There are systems that they are addressed to all clinicians like [12,19,29,32,36], or a specific category of clinicians like ICU (Intensive Care Unit) clinicians [13, 43], gastroenterological doctors [44], patients with cancer [48]. Also, there are systems designed for researchers [18,25,45]. We notice that the EHR could even be used by medical secretaries, a legal service or even by the patient family and existing systems do not target all categories of end user.

The health record interface can be designed for only one type of users or intended for several user types. This will have an impact on the complexity task for the designer. Being able to identify the types of users will allow the system to consider a contextual adaptation as requested by the interviewees.

Use. During the interviews, doctors claimed EHR could be very useful as decision support and as a communication tool between colleagues. Only one system [43] among systems reviewed supports the collaboration. The use of visualization can be individual or collaborative. The doctor can visualize the health record with the nurse or different specialists involved in making a decision for a patient. A shared screen among different users can promote understanding of the visualized content [38] and also attention and participation. Individual use also promotes flexibility.

4.2   Health Record

Cardinality. This dimension refers to the number of health records the system can display on the same view. The relevant values we found in previous systems studied for this dimension are single health record at a timed [12,13,19,32,36, 44,48], multiple health records [18,25,45] or mixed (i.e. sometimes single health record or sometimes multiple health records) [29,43]. Including many records in the same interface should allow analysis of similar patients or study a phenomenon. If the system provides only a single health record, the visualization is mainly for healthcare delivery to display the different facets of the health record: allergies, problems, treatments, etc. This choice is therefore closely linked to the purpose of visualization. Cardinality is considered as an important dimension since it greatly influences the choices of other dimensions.

Dimension. We refer here to the dimension of data in the health record. For the values, we use the taxonomy of different types of data dimensions defined in [39]: one-dimension, multidimensional, temporal, tree, and network. The one-dimension is used when the data is linear (e.g. notes) [13,36,43]. But the data in the health record can sometimes have several attributes, and each attribute represents a dimension. Temporal data are widely used in the visualization of health records when the events produced are represented over time [12,13,19, 25,32,36,48]. The data can also be ordered as a tree like a family history [12]. However, data sometimes cannot be structured as a tree because relationships are much more complex like between problems, treatments, and drugs, so they take the structure of a network [45].

Data Type. When working on a health record, it is important to distinguish between the different types of data to be visualized. Depending on the type of data, the representation of information can vary. There are two types [50]: qualitative data and quantitative data. Qualitative data uses words to describe a health event like medical history (diabetes, asthma, hypertension) or allergies (penicillin, aspirin). The quantitative data represent data that can be counted such as heart rate. All systems reviewed use qualitative and quantitative data.

Variable Number. The electronic health record interface can represent few variables, many variables or all variables. For example, the doctor can focus on few variables in detail to analyze the patient's case for a problem in the Intensive Care Unit. In other cases, the doctor needs to have many variables or all variables of the health record according to the context. As a result, the designer must take care of the number of variables to be visualized to avoid cluttering the interface and adding information that has no value in accomplishing the necessary task. Most systems display many variables [13,43,44,48], but there are systems that display a very limited number of variables, especially systems that support multiple health records [18,25,45]. When the application is intended to all users it contains all variables [12,19,29,32,36].

Level. Data can be interpreted at different levels of abstraction. In our design space, we distinguish the low level that represents the data without interpretation (e.g. the temperature of the patient is 104 °F) and the high level that is an interpretation of the data (e.g. the patient has a fever since its temperature is 104 °F). A simple observation of the patient record or an in-depth analysis changes the level requested. Several characteristics of the other dimensions of our design space influence the data level such as "target" or "task". If there are multiple targets or tasks for the same view, a simple solution is to provide high level data and make low level data easily accessible on demand from the interface. All systems reviewed provide both a high-level overview and a low-level overview for more details.

4.3   Technology

Screen Size. Depending on the context, the screen size may vary. During the interviews, clinicians reported that they prefer a large screen when they are in their office and not time stressed, but in a mobile context (e.g. when visiting patient, when working in emergency services) they prefer a smaller screen if it is accessible more quickly.

On the one hand, a large screen can help when the task is complex, and the user must execute it quickly [21]. On the other hand, a small screen provides access to information at any time and any place. The designer must, therefore, find solutions to optimize the use of the screen depending on the context, choose the appropriate visualization technique and predict the appropriate interactions.

Display Number. Determining the number of displays is part of the designer's choices and he must be aware of the different possibilities. The sub-dimensions "adaptation", "context awareness", and "use" influence this choice. With multiple displays, we can facilitate collaborative use and display more information by sharing them on different displays.

This dimension is included in our design space to allow the user to have multiple displays depending on the context and switch between them. None of the studied systems offer different types of screens: big and small which reduces the possibilities of adaptation to the context.

Image Quality. During the interview, doctors claim they need images (in particular radiography) on EHR systems. Thus, we introduced a dimension about image quality, and we decomposed it in three factors as defined in [17] to maximize the quality of visualization for a radiologist: resolution, contrast, and luminance. The higher the resolution is, the better the visualization is. For medical imaging, for example, the doctor needs a high-resolution image [17]. As for contrast and luminance, they influence the user's interface, so these parameters must be adjusted so that the user can see more details easily.

Device Type. There are several available devices for health record visualization and the choice could be strategic toward the level of adaptivity required. The classic way is visualization on a desktop computer, which can be effective for some situations, but it's not suitable when the doctor has to visit patients in their rooms. In this case, for example, we can find a screen exposed in the room, but its use remains limited because display the patient's information in open areas is forbidden. Mobile devices are also available and can support the user while being on the move even outside the hospital. They can be in the pocket like phones or worn like a head-mounted display or smart glasses. These can even be used while allowing the hands to be free, which is useful during the examination of a patient or during surgery while keeping a private visualization of the health record. In aforementioned systems, a web-based interface was often developed for desktop computers [12,18,19,25,29,32]. We can find systems on laptop [13], tablets [13,36,44], smartphone [45,48], or wall-sized display [43].

4.4 Location

Ideally, the health record should be accessible anywhere, even outside the hospital: in the patient's room, in a care room, in the doctor's office, in another place at the hospital, at home, in a public building or outside. The location has a relationship with other dimensions. For example, if the user is outside, the system needs to balance luminance to allow reading. All systems using desktop computers [12,18,19,25,29,32] are located in the doctor's office. However, systems developed for laptops, tablets or smartphones [13,36,44,45,48] can be used anywhere at the hospital. All systems studied only run at the hospital.

4.5   Time

The time dimension shows when the system is used: before, during or after the encounter with the patient. This dimension is related to other dimensions like the task, the use, the location, the device type, the input interaction, and the visualization. Before the encounter, the doctor can prepare the visit by exploring the patient record (task dimension). The task could be collaborative (use dimension) if the doctor needs other points of view. He will have more comfort if he achieves this task in his office (location dimension). During the encounter, the doctor is with his patient, so the interface should not distract the doctor and interrupt his relationship with his patient. The designer should be aware of the interface proposed (input interaction and visualization dimensions). Moreover, the system should be mobile since the doctor visits patients in their room (device type dimension). After the encounter, the system can propose different tasks like making an evaluation of the care quality (task dimension). The systems examined do not all instantiate this temporal dimension with the same value were only 2 systems reporting on this category: before the encounter for [36], during the encounter for [29].

4.6   Goal

Tasks. Health record visualization has an important role in different types of task. The task is exploratory when the user does not know if he is looking for a problem or an existing treatment on the record and he is just trying to determine what will ensure a good action to be taken for the patient. Also, the user accesses the health record to make decisions: prescribing medications, ordering, analysis, or developing a treatment plan. The patient record allows for other medical tasks such as evaluation of care by comparing a patient's health status before and after cares. Moreover, health record visualization can have a completely different role depending on whether who uses it [2]. For example, a legal department may want to access the record to identify who is responsible for care issued or a statistical center may want to do a study such as identifying the cancer rate in the hospital. The purpose of visualizing data in a reviewed system is highly dependent on the "cardinality" sub-dimension. Systems that support a single health record [12, 13, 19, 32, 36, 44, 48] are designed for decision-making, exploratory analysis, and care evaluation. Others systems that support multiple health records [18, 25, 45] are designed for statistical tasks.

Use Cases. We introduced the use case dimension to better understand the usefulness of health record, and to design the user interactions. This dimension is based on the four scenarios from [43]: acute care, chronic care, preventive and health promotion, and undifferentiated symptoms. [43] used those scenarios to evaluate the patient record interface, and to define the conceptual requirements, and the major functionalities. In acute care, cases are severe, requires hospitalization and accurate follow-up during a short time. In chronic cares, the patient stays a long time, requires regular monitoring and evaluation of care to avoid complications. Prevention activities maintain the health of individuals through preventive testing or immunizations. As for undifferentiated symptoms scenarios, the doctor can use clinical decision support to evaluate symptoms from the health record and to make a good diagnostic. These use cases are a starting point for linking the healthcare professional's tasks with the interface content and the appropriate interaction. Some systems applied any use case like [19,32]. Some others feature a specific use case: chronic diseases for [44] and acute care for [13,18,43].

Functionalities. The designer must identify the functionalities that should exist on the interface to better assist users in performing their tasks. Based on interviews and the reviews of existing EHR systems, we propose six functionalities: multimedia content [19,32], diagnosis and treatment coding [18,45], alerts and notifications [19,29,32,36,43], statistics (in systems that support multiple health records [18,25,45]), communication, care recommendations (from the interviews). With the evolution of telemedicine, a health record should contain multimedia content. Multimedia content may include audio (e.g. audio recording of the fetal heartbeat during an echography of a pregnant woman) or other types of graphs or images that are relevant for some situations. During the interviews, doctors found pertinent to have other format data than text like an image (radio for example). It is also interesting that the interface contains information from the standards of medical coding (e.g. the International Classification of Diseases (ICD) standard). Standards facilitate public health research, sharing and statistical analysis. Doctors interviewed found really pertinent if the EHR system could help them to contact other colleagues. Messaging or video conferencing could promote collaborative work and improve diagnosis. However, no system provides diagnostic recommendations, additional information, or allows the user to communicate with another clinician via the interface. Moreover, alerts and notifications could avoid errors. The doctors were particularly interested in this functionality during the interview.

4.7 Input Interaction

Channel. We group the computer interface channel into three groups as in [14]: audio, visual and haptic. A channel is directly linked to some devices (e.g. audio channel with microphone). The system may use several channels to visualize the patient's record. For example, to navigate among data, the doctor could use voice commands (audio channel) or touch a tactile surface (haptic channel). All the systems studied only used the haptic channel.

Intent. This dimension aims to classify input interactions. We use the model proposed by [47] which contains seven general categories because it matches with all system studied:

1. Select: selecting information with a distinctive visual variable when there is a lot of information in a health record.

2. Explore: exploring the data space when the system doesn't show all data at a time.
3. Reconfigure: changing the location of the information or other adjustments.
4. Encode: changing the representation of the information.
5. Abstract/Elaborate: changing the level of details of information displayed.
6. Filter: changing the visualized content under certain conditions.
7. Connect: highlighting relevant information that is hidden and showing relationships between information.

We notice that few systems use the "Connect" intent [18, 32, 36, 45]. However, focusing on many implicit relationships could help the user in his task.

4.8   Visualization

Technique. When there is a lot of information in the health record, the content may be too large to be represented on the same view. Two techniques can overcome this problem [24]: the non-distortion technique and the distortion technique. The non-distortion technique allows the designer to display a part of the information, and to access to the rest with a scroll, pagination or a zoom. The best practice is to properly represent the information and divide it into parts to facilitate user navigation in the record. The distortion technique combines two views: a view of a local part with a high level of details and a view of the general context with fewer details. Several types of distortions exist. The role of the designer is to choose the best technique according to other dimensions such as device type, tasks, the complexity of the patient's health record, and the context. For example, on a mobile device, if the designer uses windows with pagination, the doctor will be lost within a health record that contains too much information.

All systems reviewed use the non-distortion technique. They proposed to scroll [12], to display a new window [18], to zoom [13, 32], or to hide some information [43, 44] for accessing to hidden data.

Representation. Spreadsheet forms or tables with graphics that contain graphical variables are the current representation in EHR systems [28]. The timeline metaphor is also used to order the events that occur to a patient in a time axis.

The representation depends on the information to be displayed: its complexity, its size, and other characteristics. But there are sometimes many possible representations for the same information. The challenge is to choose the best. Visualizing a patient's systolic pressure changes with a table or a graph are two possibilities, but it is necessary to find which one is more comprehensible according to context. The complexity of the representation increases learning time if it is not easy to explain the representation easily [46]. William Playfair [40] considers that a graphical representation of data will help the reader to understand and retain the information. During the interviews, doctors confirm this point of view. The timeline metaphor is the most common representation, as it is in almost all the reviewed systems. All systems use graphics to represent numerical variables and sometimes images are used for medical imagery. [19] uses a different representation: a patient's body as a map that can be zoomed in on for more details.

Visual Variables. The visual variables represent a critical dimension for the visualization of the health record. Jacques Bertin [7] identified seven visual variables to encode information: position (changes in location), size (changes in surface, length, width), shape (circles, squares, rectangles, symbols, etc), value (changes from light to dark), color (changes in hue), orientation (changes in alignment), texture (the pattern of filling the shape). In the design process, the appropriate use of these variables is a key component in interpreting, understanding and then using the visualized information [1]. For example, colors can encode the cholesterol values to show the degree of risk (e.g. green for low risk, orange for intermediate risk and red for high risk). In reviewed systems, color, size, shape, and position were used to encode information. The position was present in all systems that organize information in time. Size is used to compare quantitative data such as graphs. Color is widely used in systems to highlight: the category of information [32], related information [36], critical information such as allergies or alerts [13,29], abnormal test results [19] or a combination of disease [18]. Transparency is used to show the different doses of a drug or the severity [32] or to indicate the patient's state [43]. The form is used to differentiate between qualitative and quantitative data [44]. Regarding the texture, the filling of rectangles can code some values of information. Crosses indicate missing data [25].

Adaptation layout and elements to the needs of the user or the context [10]. Users of a health record system have different knowledge and the context of use is also different. The domain of health is an important field where adaptable user interfaces can be of great utility [34]. There are two main techniques for adaptation:

- the adaptive presentation, that adapts the content the user visualizes according to the situation and the context
- the adaptive navigation, that differentiates the way to interact with the visualization interface in different situations.

No reviewed system took into consideration this dimension of our design space. However, during the interviews, doctors report that well-done adaptation could help them for decision support.

Context Awareness. The adaptation of the user interface can be improved by selecting the contextual factors carefully. So, the challenge is to display the right health information with adequate representation according to the current contextual situation. Context awareness is a promising axis in the field of healthcare [9]. It can improve tasks performance for healthcare professionals and improve the quality of their care delivery [41]. We define a set of non-exhaustive factors of contexts that can be introduced for the health record visualization: user, health record, technology, location, time and goal. As the systems reviewed don't take into account the adaptation sub-dimension, they cannot handle context aware-ness.

5   Design Rationale

The design space that we have developed provides choices in the design of a health record interface. An explicit justification for the reasons behind each choice is required.

Design Space Analysis (DSA) is an approach to represent design justification and argumentation [27]. It helps to understand why certain possibilities were cho-sen during the design and to make the reasoning clearer [8]. It is based on the QOC notation which defines these three main concepts: Questions, Options, Cri-teria [26]. Questions are asked to draw the sub-categories of the various dimen-sions existing in our design space. The options are the possible choices for each sub-category and the criteria are the justifications, requirements, and consider-ations in making the choice. The criterion may be positive for one option and negative for another.

This approach will allow the designer to explain the different combinations of the possibilities selected during the design. The following figure shows a QOC notation that allows us to choose between individual or collaborative use. In this case, we have drawn two criteria: flexibility (which has a positive evaluation for individual use and a negative evaluation for collaborative use) and collaboration (which has a positive evaluation for collaborative use and a negative evaluation for individual use). If the designer feels that flexibility is more important than collaboration, then he chooses individual use.

From this decision, questions may arise for further decisions. The choice of a possibility in our design space is sometimes exclusive (noted by (*) in Table 2 of the design space) so the user is led to choose a single possibility like the example in Fig. 2. But in other cases, the user can choose several possibilities because the choice is not exclusive.

When the designer makes a decision and chooses a possibility, automati-cally other possibilities are eliminated which refines the solution. We also men-tioned that some sub-categories are strongly linked, so selecting a possibility in a sub-category eliminates even other possibilities in the other sub-categories and therefore facilitates the design choices.

6   Using the Design Space

In this section, we provide an example that elaborates how our design space can be utilized for health record interface design. Our example focused on the design of a health record system for display on smart glasses. Paul's wife is admitted to the MICU in acute respiratory distress with upper and lower GI bleeding. Her past medical history is significant for end-stage liver disease due to alcohol

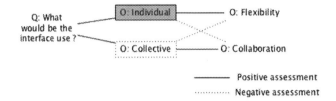

Fig. 2. QOC representation for the sub-category: use. The boxed option is the made decision.

abuse. The patient is intubated in response to worsening respiratory distress, aggressively resuscitated, and given a blood transfusion and vasopressor drugs.

Paul is very worried about his wife. Given the complex case of his wife, several doctors intervene: a pulmonologist, a gastroenterologist, a radiologist, an intensivist, etc. He notices that doctors sometimes check their desktop computers a few minutes before they come, and sometimes they do not even remember information that may be critically important.

Paul works as a "designer of new technology solutions" and wants to expose this problem to his work team to find a solution and launch a new product. He wants to use our design space to make his job easier.

Paul began with the analysis of an already existing system called MIVA [13]. (see Fig. 3) through our design space. However, he analyzed some limitations for the system and values to integrate to make the system more convenient. This is why he wrote a proposition based on the analysis of the MIVA system with integrating values of the sub-dimensions of the design space to overcome the various limitations. Table 3 shows the values that already exist on MIVA and the values that he integrated in the new prototype designed. He wrote his proposition based on the different dimensions with their categories.

We aim to create a patient record interface to help different doctors, nurses and medical secretaries (Target). This system will help them explore the patient record, evaluate the care provided, or for decision making (Tasks). The interface aims to help them with hospitalized patients in the ICU who need acute care (Use case). The period of hospitalization of a patient is a period that requires precision and speed in the delivery of services and care.

Usually, the clinician consults his desktop computer before making his rounds. This technology is inadequate in this use case for several reasons: the clinician does not have the right information in the right place at the right time. Relevant information is not exposed to him at the time of the consultation. He must have the patient's record at the consultation time (Time) in the patient room (Location). In addition, he cannot go back and forth to his office.

Mobile technology such as tablets and smartphones can solve this problem but with less efficiency. They do not respect the disruption of activity, and the clinician cannot keep his eye on the record and the patient at the same time. Technology such as smart glasses has a lot of potential in the work of the clinician

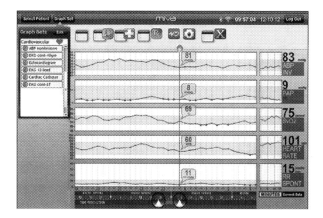

Fig. 3. MIVA main interface.

(Device type, Screen size). Each clinician can have individual glasses (Display number, Use) to access the patient file on which he will intervene (Cardinality).

With the small size of the screen, the non-distortion technique is less effective for viewing an entire patient record. Indeed, since it does not provide a global view of the context, the user can be lost during navigation. A distortion technique would simultaneously display a local part with details and the general context with less precision (Technique). The global view would display the high-level information in summary form and the user could access to low-level information on demand (Level).

In addition to tables with text, graphs will be included to facilitate the interpretation of some information and to make comparisons (Representation). The graphics will be chosen to fit the size and type of information. In a patient file, there will be many variables (Variable number) with different dimensions (One dimension, Several dimensions, and Temporal dimension): medical records, diagnostics, drugs, and vital signs (qualitative and quantitative). We can even consider the folder structure as a network and link the different information available. We identify these dimensions and types clearly to know which representation to avoid and select the most relevant ones (Dimension, Data type).

We take color into consideration to show the severity of a problem and place the information in the right place to display the information in a meaningful way (Visual variable).

To support the user accomplishing his tasks, we will include standards of different data (treatments, drugs, ...), and multimedia content (medical imaging) to maintain accurate understanding for all stakeholders and alerts to remind nurses of medicines and doses. In addition, the doctor can communicate with another care provider while using the design to better inform themselves (Functionalities). He must have a good resolution, contrast and luminance to view graphics and medical imaging (Image quality).

Users can interact with the interface using a stylus to point to patient record information, and a trackpad or gestures when they need their hands free. They can also use the camera to identify the patient or record a photo on his case (Channel).

In addition to the basic functions of selection, exploration, the user can reconfigure the interface: he can change the type of representation of the information if it is more meaningful to him. Also, he can connect different information by highlighting related information when he points to information (Intent).

To display the right information in the right place for the right person, the interface must be adaptive and take into account contextual information such as the user's profile. The information displayed for a neurologist is not the same for a nurse. Then, it will take into consideration his position in the hospital because the hospital patients are in different rooms. The content of the file changes the interface. For example, the placement medical tests are not the same for each patient's record (Context awareness and Adaptation).

Paul moves forward based on these values to design the next generation of MIVA using smart glasses called mCAREglass (Fig. 4). Table 3 shows the main interace of mCAREglass.

Table 3. The design space for Paul's scenario: values for each dimension. The red values are added to mCAREglass in addition to the values that exist in MIVA

USER-Target: Doctors, Other medical staff : nurse, Administrative stuff : medical secretaries
USER-Use: Individual, Collaborative
HEALTH RECORD-Cardinality: Single patient
HEALTH RECORD-Dimension:1 dimensional, n-dimensional, Temporal, Network
HEALTH RECORD-Data type: Qualitative, Quantitative
HEALTH RECORD-Variable number: Many variables
HEALTH RECORD-Level: Low, High
TECHNOLOGY-Screen size: Small
TECHNOLOGY-Display number: Single display, Multiple displays
TECHNOLOGY-Image quality-Resolution : good, Contrast : good, Luminance : good,
TECHNOLOGY-Device type: Mobile : Smart glasses
LOCATION:care room, doctor's office, Patient room, another place at the hospital
TIME: Before the encounter, during the encounter, after the encounter
GOAL-Tasks: Exploratory analysis, Decision making, Care quality evaluation
GOAL-Use cases: Acute care
GOAL-Functionalities: Multimedia content, Diagnosis and treatment coding,
        Communication, Alerts and notifications
INPUT INTERACTION-Channel: Audio, Visual, Haptic
INPUT INTERACTION-Intent: Select, Explore, Reconfigure, Filter, Connect
VISUALIZATION-Technique: Non-distorsion, Distorsion
VISUALIZATION-Representation: Table, Graph, timeline
VISUALIZATION-Visual variables: Position, Color
VISUALIZATION-Adaptation: Presentation, Navigation
VISUALIZATION-Context awareness:User, Health record, Location

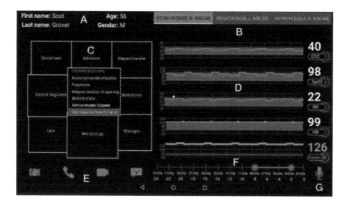

Fig. 4. MIVA main interface. (A) Basic patient information. (B) Tabs used for accessing multiple patients data (C) EHR data of selected patient in access through the Fisheye view, providing patient medical antecedents, and an expanded view of details. (D) Real time vital sign data from the bedside. (E) Communication tools. (F) 24-h time-line, showing trends across this period of time. (G) Voice recognition allows clinicians to be hands-free during clinical work

7   Discussion and Limitations

We provided an example that elaborates how our design space can help specify health record interfaces. It is interesting to note that many of the systems we analyzed did not meet the 8-dimensional criteria of our design space. The question is: are the current trends in electronic health record design the best ways to represent a health record or do designers need to innovate? Most health record interfaces use the timeline metaphor used by LifeLine [32].

Our design space allowed to show the shortcomings of existing systems. The systems we analyzed did not define dedicated techniques for devices in a mobile situation like smartphones or even wearables devices. In addition, adaptation and context awareness are missing. Providing information and interactions according to the user's situation using contextual factors can be a solution to improve the clinical user experience.

We believe our design scenario show a future of clinical health interface and interaction design where each dimension of our design space is addressed. A practitioner would have a more comprehensive user experience. The problem of health record interface design is far from being solved and requires a lot of focused attention. Our hope is for the designer to rely on our design space to find solutions to problems and gaps we have mentioned.

Our design space is coherent because it answers questions of health record visualization using the 5W1H method. We note that there are impossible combinations in the design space, e.g. choosing a wearable device (Device type) and large screen (Screen size).

We are aware that other aspects can be introduced with the evolution of research and technology by finding new ideas, but our design space can be extensible. For example, we focused on the visualization of the health record. Other output interactions could complete the design space. We highlight that we interviewed only ICU doctors even if we considered other target users in our design space.

8   Conclusion and Future Work

Electronic health record visualization is a complex issue that has interested many research groups. We analyzed existing EHR systems to extract important features and to identify weakness. We also interviewed doctors of the Intensive Care Unit to know their expectations when they use EHR systems. We concluded that EHR systems need improvements. We proposed a design space to help design process for future EHR systems. Our design space guides the designer to various alternatives to be compared and discussed. Our design space is flexible and allows the designer to explore novel aspects.

We showcased with a scenario how we could build a solid base and contribute to the implementation of new health record interface systems that can be very innovative if all dimensions are carefully explored and studied. We believe that the eight dimensions identified will be useful within their sub-categories.

The design space helps designers to choose between the different possibilities available. But as researchers, it is also useful as a tool to identify the gaps in existing health record interfaces and the potential for future work by observing combinations of new possibilities. To improve our design space, doing interviews with other target users is important (nurses, administrative staff, etc.).

Acknowledgement. This research was carried during the PhD studies of the first author and supported with funding from laboratoire LCOMS, Université de Lorraine. We thank Mary Bloodworth and Fintan Mc Gee for their careful reading of our paper and their many insightful comments and suggestions.

References

1. Alexander, R.: Interactive information visualization in patient care and clinical research: state of the art (2009)
2. Anaes, A.n.d.e.d.e.s.: dossier du patient : amélioration de la qualité de la tenue et du contenu réglementation et recommandations. https://has-sante. fr/upload/docs/application/pdf/2009-08/dossier_du_patient_amelioration_de_la_ qualite_de_la_tenue_et_du_contenu_-_reglementation_et_recommandations_-_2003. pdf. Accessed 01 Mar 2020
3. Armijo, D., McDonnell, C., Werner, K.: Electronic health record usability: evaluation and use case framework. AHRQ Publ. **9**(10), 1–57 (2009)
4. Bauer, D.T., Guerlain, S.A., Brown, P.J.: Evaluating the use of flowsheets in pediatric intensive care to inform design. In: Proceedings of the Human Factors and Ergonomics Society Annual Meeting, vol. 50, pp. 1054–1058. SAGE Publications, Los Angeles (2006). https://doi.org/10.1177/154193120605001011
5. Beaudouin-Lafon, M., Mackay, W.E.: Prototyping tools and techniques. In: Human-Computer Interaction, pp. 137–160. CRC Press (2009)

6. Belden, J.L., Grayson, R., Barnes, J.: Defining and testing EMR usability: principles and proposed methods of EMR usability evaluation and rating (2009). http://hdl.handle.net/10355/3719. Accessed 01 Mar 2020
7. Bertin, J.: Semiology of graphics: diagrams, networks, maps. Redlands (2010)
8. Biskjaer, M.M., Dalsgaard, P., Halskov, K.: A constraint-based understanding of design spaces. In: Proceedings of the 2014 Conference on Designing Interactive Systems, pp. 453–462 (2014). https://doi.org/10.1145/2598510.2598533
9. Bricon-Souf, N., Newman, C.R.: Context awareness in health care: a review. Int. J. Med. Inform. **76**(1), 2–12 (2007). https://doi.org/10.1016/j.ijmedinf.2006.01.003
10. Browne, D.: Adaptive user interfaces. Elsevier (2016)
11. Chittaro, L.: Information visualization and its application to medicine. Artif. Intell. Med. **22**(2), 81–88 (2001). https://doi.org/10.1016/S0933-3657(00)00101-9
12. Dabek, F., Jimenez, E., Caban, J.J.: A timeline-based framework for aggregating and summarizing electronic health records. In: 2017 IEEE Workshop on Visual Analytics in Healthcare (VAHC), pp. 55–61. IEEE (2017). https://doi.org/10.1109/VAHC.2017.8387501
13. Faiola, A., Srinivas, P., Duke, J.: Supporting clinical cognition: a human-centered approach to a novel ICU information visualization dashboard. In: AMIA Annual Symposium Proceedings, vol. 2015, p. 560. American Medical Informatics Association (2015)
14. Frohlich, D.M.: The design space of interfaces. In: Kjelldahl, L. (ed.) Multimedia, pp. 53–69. Springer, Heidelberg (1992). https://doi.org/10.1007/978-3-642-77331-0_5
15. Garrett, P., Seidman, J.: EMR vs EHR-what is the difference. HealthITBuzz, January (2011). Accessed 01 Mar 2020
16. Haeuslschmid, R., Pfleging, B., Alt, F.: A design space to support the development of windshield applications for the car. In: Proceedings of the 2016 CHI Conference on Human Factors in Computing Systems, pp. 5076–5091 (2016). https://doi.org/10.1145/2858036.2858336
17. Healthcare, B.: Optimizing image quality in the radiologist's field of vision (2017)
18. Huang, C.W., et al.: A novel tool for visualizing chronic kidney disease associated polymorbidity: a 13-year cohort study in Taiwan. J. Am. Med. Inform. Assoc. **22**(2), 290–298 (2015). https://doi.org/10.1093/jamia/ocu044
19. Jin, Y.: Interactive medical record visualization based on symptom location in a 2D human body. Ph.D. thesis, Université d'Ottawa/University of Ottawa (2016). https://doi.org/10.20381/ruor-5245
20. Kiron, B.: Project planning should start with the 5 w questions before getting to the how? https://kbondale.wordpress.com/2012/05/27/project-planning-starts-with-5-ws/. Accessed 01 Mar 2020
21. Klinke, H., Krieger, C., Pickl, S.: Analysis of the influence of screen size and resolution on work efficiency (2014). https://doi.org/10.18419/opus-3489
22. Kosara, R., Miksch, S.: Visualization methods for data analysis and planning in medical applications. Int. J. Med. Inform. **68**(1-3), 141–153 (2002). https://doi.org/10.1016/S1386-5056(02)00072-2
23. Lesselroth, B.J., Pieczkiewicz, D.S.: Data Visualization Strategies for the Electronic Health Record. Nova Science Publishers, Inc. (2011)
24. Leung, Y.K., Apperley, M.D.: A review and taxonomy of distortion-oriented presentation techniques. ACM Trans. Comput.-Hum. Interact. (TOCHI) **1**(2), 126–160 (1994). https://doi.org/10.1145/180171.180173

25. Loorak, M.H., Perin, C., Kamal, N., Hill, M., Carpendale, S.: Timespan: using visualization to explore temporal multi-dimensional data of stroke patients. IEEE Trans. Vis. Comput. Graph. **22**(1), 409–418 (2015). https://doi.org/10.1109/TVCG.2015.2467325
26. MacLean, A., Young, R.M., Bellotti, V.M., Moran, T.P.: Questions, options, and criteria: elements of design space analysis. Hum.–Comput. Interact. **6**(3-4), 201–250 (1991). https://doi.org/10.1207/s15327051hci0603%264_2
27. MacLean, A., Young, R.M., Moran, T.P.: Design rationale: the argument behind the artifact. ACM SIGCHI Bull. **20**(SI), 247–252 (1989). https://doi.org/10.1145/67450.67497
28. Institute of Medicine: Health IT and Patient Safety: Building Safer Systems for Better Care. The National Academies Press, Washington, DC (2012). https://doi.org/10.17226/13269
29. Mlaver, E., et al.: User-centered collaborative design and development of an inpatient safety dashboard. Joint Commission J. Qual. Patient Saf. **43**(12), 676–685 (2017). https://doi.org/10.1016/j.jcjq.2017.05.010
30. Nancel, M., Huot, S., Beaudouin-Lafon, M.: Un espace de conception fondé sur une analyse morphologique des techniques de menus. In: Proceedings of the 21st International Conference on Association Francophone d'Interaction Homme-Machine, pp. 13–22 (2009). https://doi.org/10.1145/1629826.1629829
31. Owen, S.T.: Press release: getting the facts straight. http://www.owenspencer-thomas.com/journalism/media-tips/writing-a-press-release/. Accessed 01 Mar 2020
32. Plaisant, C., Mushlin, R., Snyder, A., Li, J., Heller, D., Shneiderman, B.: Lifelines: using visualization to enhance navigation and analysis of patient records. In: The Craft of Information Visualization, pp. 308–312. Elsevier (2003). https://doi.org/10.1016/B978-155860915-0/50038-X
33. Potamias, G.: State of the art on systems for data analysis, information retrieval and decision support. INFOBIOMED project, Deliverable D **13**, 2006 (2006)
34. Ramachandran, K.: Adaptive user interfaces for health care applications. IBM developerWorks (2009). https://doi.org/10.1016/j.procs.2015.07.182
35. Rind, A., et al.: Interactive information visualization to explore and query electronic health records. Found. Trends® Hum.-Comput. Interact. **5**(3), 207–298 (2013). https://doi.org/10.1561/1100000039
36. Ruchikachorn, P., Liang, J.J., Devarakonda, M., Mueller, K.: Watson-aided nonlinear problem-oriented clinical visit preparation on tablet computer. In: The IEEE VIS 2014 Workshop on Visualization of Electronic Health Records, pp. 1–4 (2014)
37. Schulz, H.J., Nocke, T., Heitzler, M., Schumann, H.: A design space of visualization tasks. IEEE Trans. Vis. Comput. Graph. **19**(12), 2366–2375 (2013). https://doi.org/10.1109/TVCG.2013.120
38. Scott, S.D., Mandryk, R.L., Inkpen, K.M.: Understanding children's collaborative interactions in shared environments. J. Comput. Assist. Learn. **19**(2), 220–228 (2003). https://doi.org/10.1046/j.0266-4909.2003.00022.x
39. Shneiderman, B.: The eyes have it: a task by data type taxonomy for information visualizations. In: Proceedings 1996 IEEE Symposium on Visual Languages, pp. 336–343. IEEE (1996). https://doi.org/10.1109/VL.1996.545307
40. Spence, I.: William playfair and the psychology of graphs. In: 2006 JSM Proceedings, American Statistical Association, Alexandria, pp. 2426–2436 (2006)

41. Sridevi, S., Sayantani, B., Amutha, K.P., Mohan, C.M., Pitchiah, R.: Context aware health monitoring system. In: Zhang, D., Sonka, M. (eds.) ICMB 2010. LNCS, vol. 6165, pp. 249–257. Springer, Heidelberg (2010). https://doi.org/10. 1007/978-3-642-13923-9_27

42. Steve, B.: The 5 w's (and how) are even more important to business than to journalism. https://stevebuttry.wordpress.com/2011/04/27/the-5-w's-and-how-are-even-more-important-to-business-than-to-journalism/. Accessed 01 Mar 2020

43. Thomas, M.M., Kannampallil, T., Abraham, J., Marai, G.E.: Echo: a large display interactive visualization of ICU data for effective care handoffs. In: 2017 IEEE Workshop on Visual Analytics in Healthcare (VAHC), pp. 47–54. IEEE (2017). https://doi.org/10.1109/VAHC.2017.8387500

44. Vo, C., et al.: Electronic medical record visualization for patient progress tracking. In: International Symposium on Affective Science and Engineering ISASE2018, pp. 1–6. Japan Society of Kansei Engineering (2018). https://doi.org/10.5057/isase. 2018-C000018

45. Warner, J.L., Denny, J.C., Kreda, D.A., Alterovitz, G.: Seeing the forest through the trees: uncovering phenomic complexity through interactive network visualization. J. Am. Med. Inform. Assoc.: JAMIA **22**(2), 324 (2015). https://doi.org/10. 1136/amiajnl-2014-002965

46. West, V.L., Borland, D., Hammond, W.E.: Innovative information visualization of electronic health record data: a systematic review. J. Am. Med. Inform. Assoc. **22**(2), 330–339 (2015). https://doi.org/10.1136/amiajnl-2014-002955

47. Yi, J.S., ah Kang, Y., Stasko, J.: Toward a deeper understanding of the role of interaction in information visualization. IEEE Trans. Vis. Comput. Graph. **13**(6), 1224–1231 (2007). https://doi.org/10.1109/TVCG.2007.70515

48. Zhang, X., Deng, Z., Parvinzamir, F., Dong, F.: Myhealthavatar lifestyle management support for cancer patients. ecancermedicalscience 12 (2018). https://doi. org/10.3332/ecancer.2018.849

49. Zhang, Z., et al.: The five Ws for information visualization with application to healthcare informatics. IEEE Trans. Vis. Comput. Graph. **19**(11), 1895–1910 (2013). https://doi.org/10.1109/TVCG.2013.89

50. Éric, B.: Les variables. http://ebrunelle.profweb.ca/MQ/Chapitre2.pdf. Accessed 01 Mar 2020

The Effect of Device-Affordance Alignment with the User Goal on User Experience

Audrey Bond$^{(\boxtimes)}$ (ID), Pierre-Majorique Léger (ID), and Sylvain Sénécal (ID)

HEC Montreal, Montreal, QC H3T 2A7, Canada
audrey.bond@hec.ca

Abstract. Building upon the conceptualization of affordances, this article leverages the theoretical framework of task-technology fit in e-commerce to explore
the consequences of alignment and misalignment of technology's affordances and
user's intended goals. More specifically, the objective of this article is to investigate the effect of the alignment between the affordances of technological devices
and tasks performed on these devices on the user's shopping experience. A within-
subject controlled laboratory experiment was conducted. Twenty-five participants
were asked to complete six digital-grocery related tasks of equivalent nature on
both a computer and a smartphone. Study results highlight two primary findings.
First, the affordances of the device on which digital shopping tasks are performed
affect the user's cognitive and emotional states. Performing digital shopping tasks
on a smartphone generates a higher cognitive load (cognitive state), as well as a
more positive emotional valence and greater arousal (emotional state) for users.
Second, the results, however, do not provide enough evidence to conclude that the
type of task (user goal) moderates the previously found relationship. Limitations
and future research directions are discussed.

Keywords: Affordances · Task-technology fit · Smartphones · Computers · User
experience · Cognitive load · Emotional valence · Arousal · Human-computer
interaction

1 Introduction

One in ten dollars now flows through digital channels. In 2019, Canadians spent $64,56
billion on e-commerce and $20,34 billion on m-commerce, which represents 13,15% of
all retail sales [1]. With mobile sales anticipated to grow by 22,8% over the forthcoming
year and an all-time high smartphone penetration rate of 92% amongst Canadians [2],
the retail landscape has not seen its last disruption. The truly ubiquitous nature of digital
technologies, with different designs, different affordances, and different experiences,
therefore, implies a need for a deeper understanding of how these technologies impact
their users.

Over the past decade, many researchers have attempted to study the impact of these
technological devices on consumers. Indeed, research has shown that the interfaces of
technological devices such as smartphones and computers, can have a substantial effect

© Springer Nature Switzerland AG 2020
C. Stephanidis et al. (Eds.): HCII 2020, LNCS 12423, pp. 42–65, 2020.
https://doi.org/10.1007/978-3-030-60114-0_3

on how users explore, perceive, remember, and act upon online content [3]. This is a critical steppingstone because it highlights the importance of the device itself and what it affords, rather than only the content presented on this device. While there is a great number of studies that attempt to explain each technological device's characteristics and affordances [4–8], there are none, to our knowledge, that explores the effect of the device-affordance alignment with the user goal on the user experience.

The objective of this article is to explore the effect of the alignment between the affordances of technological devices and tasks performed on these devices on the user's shopping experience. More specifically, to what extent do the affordances of techno-logical devices influence the experience of a user? Also, to what extent does a user's goal moderate the effect of the affordances of technological devices on the user experi-ence? To answer these research questions, the article builds upon the conceptualization of affordances by Burlamaqui and Dong [9] and leverages the theoretical framework of task-technology fit in e-commerce by Klopping and McKinney [10].

To answer those questions, a within-subject controlled laboratory experiment was conducted. The twenty-five participants were asked to complete six digital-grocery related tasks of equivalent nature on both a computer and a smartphone. Data collection took place in a user experience laboratory specialized with psychophysiological mea-sures. Psychophysiological measures are physiological responses of the human body to psychological manipulations [11]. These responses are physical signals that make it possible to assess humans' mental processes by monitoring their bodily changes. Three psychophysiological metrics were used to measure the user's variation in the cognitive and emotional states: cognitive load, emotional valence, and arousal.

2 Literature Review

2.1 The Concept of Affordances

The Affordance Perspective. The term "affordance" was first coined by the ecological psychologist James J. Gibson [12] to conceptualize the action possibilities of animals in given environments [13]. In Gibson's [12] words, "the affordances of the environment are what it offers the animal, what it provides or furnishes, either for good or ill" (p.119). The goal of the original coinage of the term was to explain how species orient themselves to the objects in their environment in terms of possibilities of action [14]. It is essential to highlight that "affordance" refers to the relationship between the animal and the given environment, not the properties of either the animal or the environment. An affordance exists relative to the action capabilities of an actor and does not change if the actor's needs and goals change [14]. It represents the action possibility of a specific animal in a specific environment; the same environment can provide other affordances with a different animal. For example, a single object of the environment (i.e., a branch) offers different possibilities of actions for a dog (as a toy) and a beaver (as materials) [12, 15].

Donald Norman [15] appropriated the concept of affordances to the field of design and human-computer interaction. Norman adjusted the original meaning given by Gib-son [13], through his use of affordances to understand the relationship that binds agents and everyday objects. Norman [16] defines affordances as "a relationship between the properties of an object and the capabilities of the agent that determine just how the object could be used" (p.11). From Norman's perspective, affordances remain a relational concept, meaning that it represents the potential interactions between people and technologies, rather than properties of the agent or the technology [17]. Norman's conceptualization, however, varies from Gibson's on the notion of direct perception. While Gibson believes that animals (or agents) can pick up sensory information directly without internal processing and cognition, Normal argues that the brain must process the information arriving at the sense organs to interpret it coherently [16].

Human-computer interaction, information technology, communication scholars, among others, subsequently followed suit and leveraged affordances to study the relationship between various technologies and their users [9, 14, 17–23]. The affordance perspective provides a powerful lens to study technologies, because it provides a tool that focuses on the interaction between said technologies and its users [19, 21], while also providing theoretical grounding [24].

Given the ubiquity of the concept in a wide array of disciplines, affordances have been subject to extensive literature reviews and comparison analyses, which highlight the diverse uses of the term [9, 14, 23, 25–28].

Burlamaqui and Dong [9] reviewed the main articles covering the topic in different contexts (i.e., human-computer interaction, interaction design, and industrial design). They found five themes that emerge across all standpoints, which are artifact, agent, environment, perception, and potential use. Hence, it is possible to define the term in a manner that delineates the five foundational elements: "affordances are the cues of the potential uses of an artifact by an agent in a given environment" (p.13). Although differences of opinion still exist, this definition will serve as a reference point for this article.

Different Technologies have Different Affordances: Smartphones Versus Computers.
When looking at technology affordances more precisely, Hutchby [20] suggests that different technologies possess different affordances, and these affordances constrain the ways that the said technologies can be "written" or "read" by users [20].

Affordances represent the "cues of the potential uses of an artifact by an agent in a given environment" [9] (p.13). Consequently, there are endless potential affordances for each artifact (smartphone or computer), for each agent (user), and for each environment in which the interactions happen. Many scholars have studied both smartphones and computers as artifacts and have built many typologies of affordances in different contexts [17, 18, 21, 29–31]. To discuss the full published body of smartphone and computer affordances would take us beyond the concerns of the present article, given the sheer quantity. The key takeaway, however, is that different technologies have different affordances [20].

Smartphones are the main constituent of the mobile device category, which namely also includes tablets and smartwatches. Their distinctive features include an always-on network connection and "apps" to run the mobile software. In a review of the literature, Schrock [31] synthesizes a decade's worth of findings and formulates a typology of mobile affordances: portability, availability, "locatability" (based on the location-based GPS enabled features) and "multimediality" (based on the integrated photo and video capabilities) [31].

Other streams of research on the smartphone device provide other insights. Indeed, among other technologies, smartphones have high levels of both information capability (the ability of a device ecosystem to transmit, receive, and process information) and pervasivity (the extent to which the device is portable and operational) [32]. Relative to computers, mobile devices such as smartphones provide convenience across both temporal and spatial dimensions because of their ergonomic (i.e., size) and technological features (i.e., integrated telecommunication network [8]. However, smartphones usually have a smaller size than standard computers, which imposes constraints in terms of the screen size, and thus, the organization of the information [33].

Hence, it is possible to notice that based on smartphones' innate physical and design characteristics, this artifact provides cues of its potential uses that differ from the cues a computer provides, further reinforcing that different technological device have different affordances.

2.2 The Theory of Task-Technology Fit

The Task-Technology Fit Framework. The theory of task-technology fit was first introduced by Goodhue and Thompson [34] in the field of information systems. It refers to "the degree to which technology assists an individual in performing his or her tasks" (p.216). At its simplest expression, task-technology fit represents the match between a task and a technology that results in a positive outcome expressed in productivity or performance and technology use [35–37]. This framework can be applied to different settings, such as at the organizational-level, team-level, and individual-level. For example, at a team-level, Kerr and Murthy [38] compare the performance of computer-mediated and face-to-face teams on divergent and convergent brainstorm processes. Their results are consistent with the task-technology fit theoretical predictions, meaning that the alignment between the task (divergent or convergent brainstorm) and the technology (computer-mediated or face-to-face) used to perform the task, created a significant difference in the performance outcomes. Indeed, face-to-face teams performed better on the convergent aspect of the task, while computer-mediated teams performed better on the divergent aspects of the task [38].

The task-technology fit theory has been applied to several contexts to understand how specific tasks generate better outcomes when completing them on specific technologies [39, 40]. Authors in the field of information systems provide in-depth reviews of the literature and propose to refine and to extend the task-technology framework to a wide array of contexts [35, 37, 41–43].

Although the task-technology framework was developed to evaluate organizational technology interactions, it can be applied to the individual level in the field of e-commerce [10, 44]. In order to adapt it, authors have removed the "productivity" or "performance" outcome and instead included other outcomes, such as "actual use" [41], "perceived performance" [36], or "purchase intentions" [45].

In an e-commerce context, the technology component of the framework is often represented by the technological devices (namely smartphones, computers, and tablets) used by customers in carrying out their digital-shopping tasks. Thus, the task-technology fit theory considers the entanglement between the attributes of the technology and the specificities of given tasks and can begin to explain why some consumers gravitate towards specific devices to conduct specific tasks [46]. It represents a well-established framework that highlights that outcomes can significantly vary when using different technologies. For example, Lee and colleagues [45] propose a model that explores the adoption of mobile commerce in the insurance industry. They, more specifically, aim to understand which personal digital assistants' characteristics are best for which type of tasks of insurance agents.

The Task-Technology Affordance Fit Proposition. While the standard task-technology fit framework is a widely used tool to explain the positive outcomes that result from the alignment between tasks and technologies, this article proposes two variations.

First, this study suggests the use of the affordances of technological devices instead of the technology component only. Technologies can be used in a wide array of manners, given the context of the interaction and the user's characteristics. Hence, affordances, which are "the cues of the potential uses of an artifact by an agent in a given environment" [9] (p.13), could potentially provide an interesting lens to analyze the entanglement between human action and technological capability [14]. In the human-computer interaction literature, there are many research articles on affordances [18, 22], task-technology fit [37, 40, 44], and some that argue that it is the affordances themselves that embody the concept of fit [47, 48]. However, to our knowledge, no article leverages the affordance perspective within the task-technology fit theory to shed light on the relationship between users, technologies, and outcomes. The term "task-technology affordance alignment" is used in the following paragraphs to illustrate this proposition.

Second, this article suggests the use of the user experience as the outcome variable. Indeed, the performance outcome component of the original task-technology fit framework does not apply to all e-commerce contexts [36, 41, 45]. Thus, the user experience, which is the "user's perceptions and responses (i.e., emotions, preferences, and behaviors) that result from the use of a system, product or service" [49], would be an interesting outcome variable to consider as well. Considering the previous paragraphs, the concept of affordances provides vocabulary useful to analyze the entanglement between human action and technological capability [14]. Likewise, user experience focuses on the interaction between users and technologies. It is thus interesting to leverage the concept of affordances to better understand user experience, more specifically within the theoretical framework of task-technology fit. Leveraging the task-technology affordance alignment framework, better user experience should emerge from the alignment between a technological devices' affordances and the user's intended goal on the said device (the type of task performed). This is the case because the user should experience more positive responses when using a device that provides adequate affordances to complete a specific task.

3   Hypothesis Development

Figure 1 illustrates the conceptual model that guides the present article. In the following paragraphs, the hypotheses underlying this model are reported. We hypothesize that the affordances of technological devices, such as smartphones and computers, result in different user experiences, and that this relationship is moderated by the type of task performed on these technological devices. The direct effect section pertains to the effect of the affordances of technological devices on the resulting user experience, comprising both the cognitive and emotional state. The moderation effect section relates to the effect of the alignment between the affordances of technological devices and the tasks performed on these devices, on the resulting user experience comprising both the cognitive and emotional state.

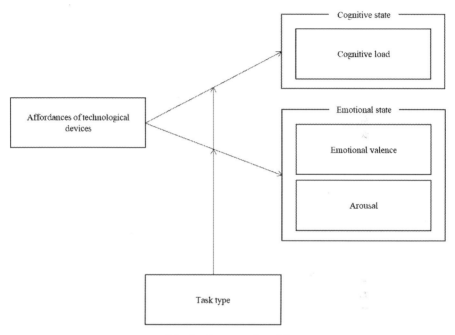

Fig. 1. Conceptual model

3.1 Direct Effect

Through the lens of affordances, it has been shown so far that different technologies possess different affordances. This article argues that the technologies (in this case, smartphones and computers) which possess different affordances, in turn, lead to different experiences when an agent is interacting with them. In the next paragraphs, the notion of experience is defined, as well as two of its essential components, cognitive and emotional states of users.

To compare the experience lived by a user with a smartphone and a computer (two technologies with different affordances), it is important to delineate what constitutes an experience. In simple words, user experience is a user's perceptions and responses (i.e., emotions, preferences, and behaviors) that result from the use of a system, product, or service [49]. In his conceptualization, Norman [16] emphasized the importance of human cognitive and emotional processing functions to give meaning to interactions with technologies or objects. In Norman's words, "cognition attempts to make sense of the world: emotions assign a value" [16] (p.47). Indeed, the user's internal and physical state resulting from the context of use is an essential component of user experience [50]. Zajonc's [51] research suggests that emotional and cognitive reactions are under the control of separate and partially independent systems that can influence each other in a variety of ways. With that in mind, the cognitive and emotional states of users represent essential components of the user experience.

First, regarding the cognitive state of users, cognition refers to the mental processes involved in gaining knowledge and comprehension, namely thinking, knowing, remembering, judging, and problem-solving. They represent higher-level functions of the brain and encompass language, imagination, perception, and planning [52]. The cognitive state refers to the level of an individual's cognitive processing [53] when making sense of the world. When studying the effect of affordances of technological devices (in this case, smartphones and computers) on a user's cognitive state, an excellent starting point lies the analysis of the level of effort required for the user to process the information [54] and, thus, gain knowledge and understand.

The literature provides some starting points to explore the cognitive impact of human-smartphone (vs. human-computer) interaction. On the one hand, research shows that the smartphone device itself, because of its prevalent and pervasive use, creates an increased cognitive effort that arises from the habit of multitasking on a smartphone [32]. Lurie and colleagues [32] also note the importance of the cognitive resources associated with mobile technologies. They argue that consumers on the mobile channel have fewer cognitive resources available to devote to information search and decision-making tasks. On the other hand, authors emphasize the cognitive impact of smartphone use because of the smartphone's natural device characteristics and specifications. Indeed, browsing on a smartphone induces a higher cognitive load because of the constraints in terms of the information structure and screen size, which significantly affect the navigation behavior and perceptions of users [33]. Compared to larger devices such as computers, the smaller keyboards and screens of smartphones increase the physical and cognitive effort required for using the device [55]. Hence, all things put into consideration; it might be the case that, for an equivalent task, more cognitive efforts are required when interacting with a smartphone (vs. computer). Thus, we posit our first hypothesis.

H1: For equivalent tasks, a user's interaction with a smartphone generates a greater cognitive load than a user's interaction with a computer.

Second, regarding the emotional state of users, Mehrabian and Russell [56] identify three primary factorially orthogonal emotional dimensions that are impacted by environmental stimuli (i.e., technological devices): pleasure (displeasure), arousal (nonarousal), and dominance (submissiveness). Given the argued cognitive nature of the dominance (submissiveness) dimension, many authors have followed not included the dominance dimension in their models [57–59]. Hence, in this research, the pleasure (displeasure) and the arousal (nonarousal) dimensions will serve as a basis to explore the emotional state of users.

For an equivalent task, we theorize that more positive emotions are experienced when using a smartphone (vs. computer). Thus, we posit our second hypothesis.

H2: For equivalent tasks, a user's interaction with a smartphone generates a greater emotional valence than a user's interaction with a computer.

Continuing with the arousal (nonarousal) dimension, it refers to the degree to which a person feels excited, stimulated, alert, or inactive in the situation [56, 60]. It can be defined as the state of reactivity of the body's nervous system to respond to a stimulus [61]. Although there are limited studies [62] that showcase the impact of smartphones and computers' affordances themselves on the arousal experienced by their users, it is possible to seek a potential explanation in connected fields. Namely, Warriner, Kuperman, and Brysbaert [63] explore the emotional meaning of 14 000 words in the English vocabulary and found that there is a U-shaped relationship between arousal and valence (which is the metric that represents the previously described "pleasure" dimension). More precisely, this means that words that are very positive or very negative generate more arousal that words that appear to be neutral [63]. The same type of relationship between valence (pleasure dimension) and arousal is supported by other authors [64–66]. Hence, all things put into consideration; it might be the case that the increase in positive emotions occurs in conjunction with a higher arousal level. More precisely, this means that, as per the previous hypothesis, for an equivalent task, a higher arousal level is experienced when using a smartphone (vs. computer). Thus, we posit our third hypothesis.

H3: For equivalent tasks, a user's interaction with a smartphone generates higher arousal than a user's interaction with a computer.

3.2 Moderation Effect

To explore the joint effect of affordances and user goals (tasks) [67], it is crucial to define more precisely the tasks that make up digital shopping.

According to Goodhue and Thompson [34], tasks are "actions carried out by individuals that turn inputs into outputs" (p.216). Shoppers undertake a variety of them while visiting a brick-and-mortar or digital store, for instance, searching for a product, comparing prices, and paying for the selected item.

A wide range of shopping-task taxonomies has been put forward to shed light on the phenomenon. Some authors agree that there are two significant categories of shopping tasks; searching tasks and browsing tasks [68, 69]. In searching tasks, consumers have specific predetermined goals that guide the shopping trip. In browsing tasks, however, consumers rather have a general objective for the shopping trip, which is often qualified as more experiential [70]. Building on this taxonomy, Moe [71] introduces a third category, comprising the purchase-related tasks.

The introduction of purchase-related [71] tasks echoes with other research that has shown there is a fundamental difference between hedonic and instrumental tasks, specifically in technology-mediated environments [72, 73]. One can argue that hedonic tasks pertain to shopping tasks (selecting and browsing), and instrumental tasks pertain to purchase-related tasks (administrative). Indeed, shopping-related tasks, whether searching or browsing, go beyond functional utility [74] and generate experiential implications. It is, therefore, essential to distinguish practical tasks from more hedonic ones [75].

Hence, if the affordances of the devices (smartphones and computers) on which digital-shopping tasks are performed do affect the users' cognitive and emotional states, it is possible to hypothesize that the type of task performed might modify this relationship. Leveraging the task-technology theory and analyzing a step further, it might be the case that utilitarian tasks provide a better user experience on a utilitarian technological device. In comparison, hedonic tasks provide a better user experience on a hedonic technological device. Indeed, the task-technology theory proposes that technologies positively impact user outcomes when they are utilized and match a task [34]. Given the hypotheses in the previous section, we hypothesize that the computer is the more utilitarian device, while the smartphone is the more hedonic one.

Therefore, regarding the cognitive state more precisely, it is hypothesized that, on a smartphone, shopping tasks require less cognitive efforts than administrative tasks, because the shopping task (task) and the smartphone (technology) fit together as they are both considered more hedonic. Conversely, on a computer, administrative tasks require less cognitive efforts than shopping tasks, because the administrative task (task) and the computer (technology) fit together as they are both considered more utilitarian. Thus, we posit our fourth hypothesis.

H4a: For equivalent shopping tasks, a user's interaction with a smartphone generates a lower cognitive load than a user's interaction with a computer.

H4b: For equivalent administrative tasks, a user's interaction with a smartphone generates a greater cognitive load than a user's interaction with a computer.

Regarding the emotional state, it is first hypothesized that, on a smartphone, shopping tasks generate a higher emotional valence than administrative tasks, because the shopping task (task) and the smartphone (technology) fit together as they are both considered more hedonic. Conversely, on a computer, administrative tasks generate a higher emotional valence than shopping tasks, because the administrative task (task) and the computer (technology) fit together as they are both considered more utilitarian. Thus, we posit our fifth hypothesis.

H5a: For equivalent shopping tasks, a user's interaction with a smartphone generates a greater emotional valence than a user's interaction with a computer.

H5b: For equivalent administrative tasks, a user's interaction with a smartphone generates a lower emotional valence than a user's interaction with a computer.

It is also hypothesized that, on a smartphone, shopping tasks generate more arousal than administrative tasks, because the shopping task (task) and the smartphone (technology) fit together as they are both considered more hedonic. Conversely, on a computer, administrative tasks generate more arousal than shopping tasks, because the administrative task (task) and the computer (technology) fit together as they are both considered more utilitarian. Thus, we posit our sixth hypothesis.

H6a: For equivalent shopping tasks, a user's interaction with a smartphone generates greater arousal than a user's interaction with a computer.

H6b: For equivalent administrative tasks, a user's interaction with a smartphone generates lower arousal than a user's interaction with a computer.

4   Method

A 2 (affordances of technological devices: smartphone or computer) X 2 (type of task: administrative or shopping) within-subject controlled experiment was conducted. Twenty-five participants ($\overline{x}_{Age}$ = 25,6 and P_{female} = 56%) completed six tasks of similar nature on both a smartphone (iPhone 6S Plus – IOS 12.1.4) and a desktop computer (Lenovo – Windows 10 Enterprise) for which they received a small monetary compensation. Participants were recruited from the University's research recruitment portal and an external marketing firm. Eligibility criteria required individuals to be older than 18, to understand oral and written English, and to be able to look at a computer or smartphone screen without wearing glasses. They also could not have any diagnosed neurological or psychiatric health problems, not suffer from epilepsy, not have astigmatism, and not have laser vision correction. The relatively small sample size is comparable to the average sample size used in NeuroIS research and is deemed adequate in research using neurophysiological tools [76, 77].

4.1   Study Context

A Quebec grocer's mobile application and website (using Chrome browser) were used for the experiment. Digital grocery serves as the context of this study for two main reasons. First, while online and mobile grocery shopping has been available for some time, both have had a low adoption rate since their inception. Canadian consumers' in-store grocery expenditures (91,58%) are much larger relative to their digital grocery expenditures on computers, tablets, and smartphones (8,42%) [78]. According to a 2019 study, only 15.72% of Canadians have shopped for groceries on a digital platform at least once [79], leaving 84,28% of Canadians having never interacted with such platforms. Hence, digital grocery allows the comparison of smartphones and computers on an even playing field and captures the variations caused by the devices' affordances themselves. Second, the current research follows previous work on online grocery, which analyses the user experience of shoppers through psychophysiological measures [80, 81]. These articles also serve as a guideline for the data collection protocol and procedure.

4.2   Procedure

Data collection took place in a laboratory that uses technological tools handled by trained research assistants. Upon arrival and following the guidelines of the University's Research Ethics Board, participants were indicated to read the study information to give informed consent to partake in the experiment. After proper permission from the participant and following protocol procedure, a research assistant proceeded to install and calibrate the psychophysiological measurement tools.

Participants took part in both conditions; they interacted with both devices studied (smartphone and computer) to minimize variations arising from individual differences [82]. The order in which the participants used the devices was randomized to reduce potential learning and transfer across conditions [83]. The six tasks performed (see Table 1) on both platforms are deemed equivalent, as per the careful evaluation of three experts during the pretest of the experiment [84]. The similar nature of each task on both devices allows for a higher comparison potential of the psychophysiological data, which ensures greater internal validity. Standardized instructions were provided to the participants. It is important to note that the smartphone was mounted on a stand to ensure consistency across interactions.

Table 1. Aggregation of digital-grocery tasks in two categories

Administrative tasks	Shopping tasks
(1) creating an account	(5) searching and selecting specific products
(2) selecting a favorite store	(6) browsing and selecting products of choice
(3) creating a grocery list	
(4) finding a promotion in the weekly flyer	

4.3 Measures and Materials

Psychophysiological measures are physiological responses of the human body to psychological manipulations [11, 85]. These responses are physical signals that make it possible to determine humans' mental processes by monitoring their bodily changes. Psychophysiological measures provide an objective [86], multidimensional [87], continuous [87], implicit [88], and unobtrusive technique to assess users' cognitive and affective states [89].

In comparison to self-reported data, physiological measures, which come from neuroscience methods and tools, enable the researchers to get a more objective view of a phenomenon [90]. It is noted that during a user's interaction with technology, some feelings do not reach the level of awareness, which grants the need for technology that allows researchers to investigate cognitive and emotional states implicitly in a human-computer interaction context [91]. NeuroIS research focuses on leveraging neuroscience methods and tools to complement traditional research approaches. Authors in the field provide in-depth overviews of psychophysiological measures, such as pupillometry, facial expression recognition, and electrodermal activity [76, 89, 91–93].

Three psychophysiological metrics are used to measure the variation in the cognitive and emotional states: cognitive load, emotional valence, and arousal.

Cognitive Load. The participants' pupil diameter (millimeters) is used as a proxy to measure their cognitive load [94], keeping the light level constant in a controlled laboratory environment [95]. Tobii Pro X3-120 eye tracker (Stockholm, Sweden) allows for tracking such data with its pupillometry feature. Tobii Pro X3-120 eye tracker is an unobtrusive stand-alone eye-tracker that can be used in various settings by attaching it to monitors, laptops, or other various supports [96]. Its wide-range head movement perimeter allows the participants to move naturally during the experiment to ensure data accuracy and ecological validity. Tobii Pro X3-120 eye-tracker has a sampling rate of 120 Hz (pupil measurement – 40 Hz), meaning that it captures 120 data samples per second [96]. Specifically, the Tobii Pro X3-120 eye tracker uses infrared diodes to generate reflection patterns on the corneas of the participant's eyes, which, combined with the visual stimulus and image processing algorithms, can identify various metrics related to the participant's gaze and pupil measurement [96]. Before each participant interacts with the smartphone and the computer, a calibration of the eye-tracker occurs to account for participant's features. Trained research assistants follow protocol procedures to do so. Tobii Pro eye trackers are cited in over 1400 peer-reviewed research articles (www.tob iipro.com), and they provide an accurate and precise measurement for adult participants [97].

Emotional Valence. Participants' facial expressions are tracked using facial recognition software to characterize their emotions. FaceReader Software (Noldus, Wageningen, Netherlands) classifies a user's facial expressions in one of the basic universal emotional categories: happy, sad, angry, surprised, scared, disgusted [98], and neutral. The software enables the observation of the extent and amount of positive and negative emotional reactions and generates the participant's emotional valence [99]. The users' emotional valence represents the extent of "happy" facial expressions from which the negative facial expressions are subtracted [100]. The result highlights whether the user's emotional state is positive or negative. During the experiment, a video of the participant's face is recorded with a webcam (Microsoft LifeCam HD-300; 30 frames per second) and afterward uploaded in FaceReader Software in the preprocessing phase to generate values of emotional valence. The FaceReader software has been frequently used and tested in the human-computer interaction [101], and it has been shown to provide an accurate depiction of human emotional reactions [102].

Arousal. Participant's electrodermal activity is used to measure their arousal level during the tasks on both interfaces [95]. Electrodermal activity is an involuntary response that measures the eccrine activity dependent on the sympathetic nervous system activity that arises from environmental stimuli [103]. Biopac System' (Biopac, Goleta, USA) tools and software with a 50 Hz sampling rate were used. The skin conductance is measured by placing two sensors on the participant's hands, which is in line with the sweat production glands found in human's extremities such as the palm [103]. A very low and constant voltage is subsequently applied (not felt by the participant), measured, and converted to the skin's conductance (microsiemens) following Ohm's law [103].

4.4   Data Analysis

Following the manipulations, three software were used to transform the data. First, eye-tracking data from Tobii Studio 3.4.6. [96] was coded to separate and discriminate each task performed and obtain the pupil size of users at various moments during the experiment. Second, the video data from users' interaction with each device was uploaded onto FaceReader 7.1. [104], which enables the computation of the emotional valence of the users at various moments during the experiment. Third, data from Biopac Systems [103] was transferred to the Acqknowledge 4.3. software to process the information for each participant and obtain the level of electrodermal activity of users. Data from these three sources were analyzed individually to ensure data quality and remove any outliers. It was subsequently exported into a compatible file format.

Each previously mentioned file was uploaded onto CubeHX's data triangulation platform (www.cubehx.com) to synchronize all psychophysiological data [105]. CubeHX's methodology allows triangulating data faster than manual triangulation while converting all measures on the same time scale to ensure their appropriate comparison potential [106].

Each participant that did not have a complete profile of psychophysiological measures (containing data for each task on each platform) was removed from analyses. A total of six participants were removed, which explains the sample size of twenty-five.

Before the statistical analyses, data were transformed in two ways. First, psychophysiological values for the pupil size and the arousal were adjusted to the users' initial states to account for individual differences in emotional and cognitive starting states [93]. The baseline value represents the average pupil size and electrodermal activity level of a participant before the start of the experiment. The change of measure that results from the experimental manipulation is the focus of the analysis [93]. Second, data obtained for each task were aggregated into two categories (see. Table 1) (administrative and shopping), following task-classification taxonomies as reviewed in the previous section [71, 74, 75].

5   Results

5.1   Descriptive Statistics

The distribution of data is relatively centered on the mean and has an acceptable level of skewness and kurtosis. It is, therefore, not submitted to normalization procedures. Table 2 provides greater details in the sample's descriptive statistics of the three metrics: pupil size, valence, and arousal. This data represents the descriptive statistics resulting from the smartphone and the computer interaction

Table 2. Descriptive statistics of the sample

	Smartphone			Computer			Total		
	pupil size	emotional valence	arousal	pupil size	emotional valence	arousal	pupil size	emotional valence	arousal
Mean	0,15	−0,05	0,71	−0,02	−0,16	0,23	0,06	−0,11	0,47
SD	0,16	0,23	1,12	0,19	0,23	1,31	0,19	0,24	1,24
Min	−0,20	−0,51	−2,33	−0,54	−0,69	−2,22	−0,62	0,13	−0,23
Max	0,61	0,52	3,20	0,33	0,36	2,43	4,81	2,71	2,45
Skewness	0,14	0,09	−0,07	−1,21	0,18	−0,20	−0,54	−0,69	−2,33
Kurtosis	1,38	−0,27	−0,07	1,74	−0,10	−0,98	0,61	0,52	3,20
n	50	50	50	50	50	50	100	100	100

5.2   Direct Effect

In this section, hypotheses H1, H2 and H3 are tested

The pupil size, the valence, and the arousal obtained during the participant's inter-action with each device studied (smartphone and computer) were compared to measure the direct effect of the affordances of technological devices on user experience.

Study results (see Fig. 2) highlight significant differences between the experience lived on a smartphone and a computer. Given the directionality of the hypotheses, one-tailed p-values are presented below.

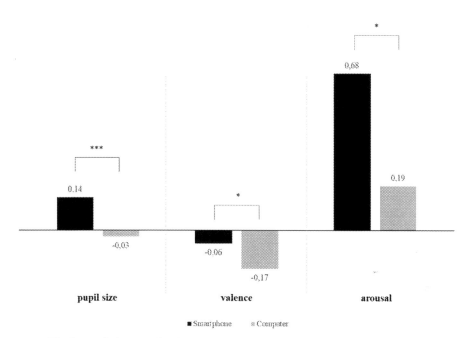

Fig. 2. Pupil size, emotional valence, and arousal for smartphones and computers

First, results of paired sample t-test with the device as the independent variable and pupil size as the dependent variable show that there is a significant difference in the average pupil size of participants when interacting with a smartphone (vs. computer) ($\overline{x}$ smartphone $= 0{,}14; \overline{x}$ computer $= -0{,}03;$ t $= -4{,}12;$p $= 0{,}00$). This result supports H1.

Second, results of paired sample t-test with the device as the independent variable and emotional valence as the dependent variable show that there is a significant difference in the average valence of the participants when interacting with a smartphone (vs. computer) ($\overline{x}$ smartphone $= -0{,}06; \overline{x}$ computer $= -0{,}17;$ t $= -1{,}68;$p $= 0{,}05$). This result supports H2.

Finally, results of paired sample t-test with the device as the independent variable and arousal as the dependent variable show that there is a significant difference in the average arousal of the participants when interacting with a smartphone (vs. computer) ($\overline{x}$ smartphone $= 0{,}68; (\overline{x}$ computer $= 0{,}19;$ t $= -1{,}97;$p $= 0{,}03$) This result supports H3.

5.3 Moderation Effect

In this section, hypotheses H4ab, H5ab and H6ab are tested

The results for the average measures in the four conditions are presented in the figure below (see Fig. 3). First, on average, pupil dilatation is the lowest when users perform administrative tasks on their computer ($\bar{x} = -0,03$), followed by shopping tasks on their computer ($\bar{x} = -0,01$), administrative tasks on their smartphone ($\bar{x} = 0,15$) and shopping tasks on their smartphone ($\bar{x} = 0,15$). Second, on average, emotional valence is the lowest when users perform administrative tasks on their computer ($\bar{x} = -0,18$), followed by shopping tasks on their computer ($\bar{x} = -0,15$), administrative tasks on their smartphone ($\bar{x} = -0,05$) and shopping tasks on their smartphone ($\bar{x} = -0,05$). Finally, on average, arousal is the lowest when users perform shopping tasks on their computer ($\bar{x} = 0,15$), followed by administrative tasks on their computer ($\bar{x} = 0,31$), shopping tasks on their smartphone ($\bar{x} = 0,67$) and administrative tasks on their smartphone ($\bar{x} = 0,74$).

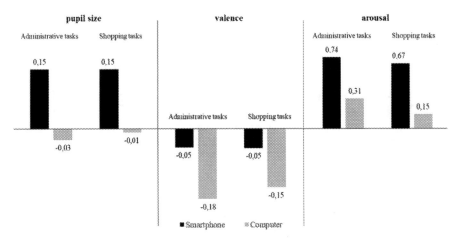

Fig. 3. Pupil size, emotional valence, and arousal for the four experimental conditions

First, a series of ordinary least squares (OLS) regressions [107, 108] were conducted to examine the overall effects of the device type (computer or smartphone) and the task type (administrative and shopping) on cognitive load (pupil size). Direct effect of device type ($\beta = 0,17$; $p = 0,0005$; R^2-ajd $= 0,1927$) is significant, while the direct effect of task type ($\beta = 0,01$; $p = 0,3563$; R^2-ajd $= 0,1849$) is not significant. Interaction of device type and task type was found and significant for both smartphone conditions: administrative tasks ($\beta = 0,16$; $p = 0,0008$; R^2-ajd $= 0,1768$) and shopping tasks ($\beta = 0,16$; $p = 0,0011$; R^2-ajd $= 0,1768$). This result does not support hypotheses H4a and H4b, which test the moderation effect of task type on the relationship between affordances of technological devices and the resulting cognitive load.

Second, a series of ordinary least squares (OLS) regressions [107, 108] were conducted to examine the overall effects of the device type (computer or smartphone) and the task type (administrative and shopping) on emotional valence. Direct effect of device type ($\beta = 0{,}11$; $p = 0{,}0869$; R^2-ajd $= 0{,}0493$) is significant (at $\alpha = 5\%$ for the one-tailed p-value), while the direct effect of task type ($\beta = 0{,}02$; $p = 0{,}2327$; R^2-ajd $= 0{,}0407$) is not significant. Interaction of device type and task type was not found nor significant. This result does not support hypotheses H5a and H5b, which test the moderation effect of task type on the relationship between the affordances of technological devices and the resulting emotional valence.

Third, a series of ordinary least squares (OLS) regressions [107, 108] were conducted to examine the overall effects of the device type (computer or smartphone) and the task type (administrative and shopping) on arousal. Direct effect of device type ($\beta = 0{,}48$; p $= 0{,}0933$; R^2-ajd $= 0{,}0281$) is significant (at $\alpha = 5\%$ for the one-tailed p-value), while the direct effect of task type ($\beta = -0{,}11$; $p = 0{,}3188$; R^2-ajd $= 0{,}0202$) is not significant. Interaction of device type and task type was found and significant for the administrative tasks on smartphone condition ($\beta = 0{,}59$; $0{,}0909$; R^2-ajd $= 0{,}0103$). This result does not support hypotheses H6a and H6b, which test the moderation effect of task type on the relationship between affordances of technological devices and the resulting arousal.

6   Discussion

The objective of this study is to explore the effect of the alignment between the affordances of technological devices and tasks performed on these devices on the user's shopping experience. The article builds upon the conceptualization of affordances by Burlamaqui and Dong [9] and leverages the theoretical framework of task-technology fit in e-commerce by Klopping and McKinney [10]. The following paragraphs discuss the results that stem from the first research question: to what extent do the affordances of technological devices influence the experience of a user?

Following the manipulations and analyses, it is possible to notice that the affordances of the technological devices have a significant impact on both the user's cognitive and emotional states.

Regarding the impact on the user's resulting cognitive state, results show that performing digital-shopping operations on a smartphone generates a higher cognitive load. As illustrated in Fig. 2 (see Fig. 2), the average pupil of the users was significantly more dilated when they interacted with the smartphone than when they interacted with the computer. This indicates that more considerable mental efforts resulted from the shopping session on the smartphone, which confirms the first hypothesis (H1: it might be the case that, for an equivalent task, more cognitive efforts are required when interacting with a smartphone in comparison to a computer).

There are many avenues to attempt to explain why smartphones require more considerable cognitive effort than computers. One approach lies in the design of smartphones, which provide different affordances than computers. Smartphones indeed have innate constraints in terms of screen size, and thus, the organization of information creates a need for additional mental resources to process the information efficiently [55].

Hence, the different affordances of the different technologies did generate a different experience, expressed in terms of the cognitive state.

Continuing with the impact of the device on the emotional state, more specifically, the pleasure (displeasure) dimension [56], results show that performing digital-shopping operations on a smartphone generates a higher emotional valence. As illustrated in Fig. 2 (see Fig. 2), the average valence of the users was significantly larger when they interacted with the smartphone than when they interacted with the computer. However, both the results of both devices average below zero. This indicates that more positive emotions resulted from the shopping session on the smartphone, which confirms the second hypothesis (H2: it might be the case that, for an equivalent task, more positive emotions are experienced when using a smartphone in comparison to a computer).

There are again many avenues to attempt to explain why smartphones generate higher emotional valence or pleasure. One direction pertains to the multisensory aspect of the experience, mainly driven by the touch-operated screen [3, 109–112]. Even if computers, like any other material object, afford touching because of their materiality, they do not react to on-screen touch-based commands (the computer did not have a touchscreen in the experiment). This "touchability-reactibility" affordance is an essential cornerstone for smartphones and can potentially explain why smartphones generate more positive emotions than computers.

Lastly, regarding the impact of the device on the emotional state, more specifically, the arousal (nonarousal) dimension [56]. Results show that performing digital-shopping operations on a smartphone generates higher arousal. As illustrated in Fig. 2 (see Fig. 2), the average electrodermal

Hence, the different affordances of the different technologies did generate a different experience, expressed in terms of the emotional state.

Now, what do these results mean for the overall experience of users with both technological devices? According to Norman [16], both positive and negative, cognitive and emotional states are valuable and powerful tools for human creativity and action. On the one hand, a positive emotional state is ideal for creative thought, but not very well suited for getting things done. On the other hand, a brain in a negative emotional state provides focus, which is what is needed to maintain attention on a task and finish it [16]. What is truly dangerous is the extremes of both the positive and negative states, whether cognitive or emotional. The second research question guiding this article attempts to delve deeper into the relationship between affordances of technological devices and the resulting user experience by exploring the impact of the type of task performed by the user while shopping. The following paragraphs discuss the results that stem from the second research question: to what extent does a user's goal moderate the effect of the affordances of technological devices on the user experience?

Following the manipulations and analyses, it is possible to notice that the task type does not significantly alter the relationship between the affordances of the technological device used to shop on a digital platform (smartphone or computer) and the resulting user experience (in terms of cognitive and emotional states).

Leveraging the task-technology fit theory, the rationale for the hypotheses was that it might be the case that utilitarian tasks provide a better experience on a utilitarian platform. In comparison, hedonic tasks provide a better experience on a hedonic platform.

However, results highlight that there is no significant interaction between the affordances of the technological devices (smartphone or computer) and the task type (administrative or shopping) on the resulting user experience (all metrics: cognitive load, emotional valence, and arousal). As illustrated in Fig. 3 (see Fig. 3), although the average pupil size, valence, and arousal of the users were significantly larger when they interacted with the smartphone than when they interacted with the computer, there is no overall significant difference when delving into the types of tasks. Given the lack of evidence, no conclusion can be made on the fourth, fifth, and sixth hypotheses.

This study contributes to the user experience and human-computer interaction literature. Indeed, there is a limited number of research articles that report the impact of technological devices themselves on user experience. By mobilizing the concept of affordances and the framework of task-technology fit, a novel approach, it has been possible to obtain psychophysiological data to improve our understanding of the shopping experience on a smartphone and a computer. Understanding the impact of the affordances of smartphones and computers on the user's cognitive and emotional states enriches current knowledge. It serves as a basis for future research related to the psychology of interface [113]. It is also a good starting point for practitioners, as they can understand the nature (more cognitive-laden or emotional-laden) of each device's experience, which can, in turn, help them create meaningful mobile and online experiences for their clients.

Limitations. There are many avenues to attempt to explain why the type of task performed (administrative or shopping) did not provide enough evidence to alter the relationship found between the affordances of technological devices used to shop on a digital platform (smartphone or computer) and the resulting user experience (in terms of cognitive and emotional states).

First, although the sample size is within the range of studies using psychophysiological measures [76], it is mostly comprising students. While it provides an opportunity to focus on the internal validity of the experiment, the sample would benefit from having a greater variety of participants and, of course, in higher numbers.

Second, the tasks comprised within the administrative and the shopping task categories could have affected the results. Indeed, four tasks were aggregated to the administrative category, while there were only two for the shopping category. Increasing the number of each task within each category and making sure that both categories contained an even amount could potentially provide a more significant picture.

Lastly, during the experiment, the smartphone was mounted on a stand and prevented participants from holding it naturally. It was necessary to have the smartphone mounted because there needed to be a reliable and stable base to position the eye-tracker and obtain useful eye-tracking data. The interaction with the smartphone was, therefore, not as natural as it could have been and has potentially affected the experience of the participants.

Those points could all be addressed in future research.

7 Conclusion

The objective of this research is to explore the effect of the alignment between the affordances of technological devices and tasks performed on these devices on the user's shopping experience. The results of the within-subject laboratory experiment show, on the one hand, that the affordances of the technological devices, in this case smartphones and computers, on which digital-shopping tasks are performed do affect resulting user experience, expressed in terms of the cognitive and emotional states. On the other hand, the results do not provide enough evidence to conclude that the type of task (administrative or shopping) alters the relationship found between the affordances of technological devices used to shop on a digital platform (smartphone or computer) and the resulting user experience, expressed in terms of the cognitive and emotional states.

References

1. Briggs, P.: Canada Ecommerce 2019. Emarketer (2019)
2. Statista: Consumer electronics usage in Canada 2019. Statista Inc. (2019)
3. Brasel, S.A., Gips, J.: Tablets, touchscreens, and touchpads: how varying touch interfaces trigger psychological ownership and endowment. J. Consum. Psychol. **24**, 226–233 (2014)
4. Ghose, A., Goldfarb, A., Han, S.P.: How is the mobile internet different? Search costs and local activities. Inf. Syst. Res. **24**, 613–631 (2013)
5. Lee, Y.-K., Chang, C.-T., Lin, Y., Cheng, Z.-H.: The dark side of smartphone usage: psychological traits, compulsive behavior and technostress. Comput. Hum. Behav. **31**, 373–383 (2014)
6. Melumad, S.: The Distinct Psychology of Smartphone Usage. Marketing, vol. Ph.D., pp. 226. Columbia University (2017)
7. Oulasvirta, A., Rattenbury, T., Ma, L., Raita, E.: Habits make smartphone use more pervasive. Pers. Ubiquit. Comput. **16**, 105–114 (2012)
8. Wang, R.J.-H., Malthouse, E.C., Krishnamurthi, L.: On the go: how mobile shopping affects customer purchase behavior. J. Retail. **91**, 217–234 (2015)
9. Burlamaqui, L., Dong, A.: The use and misuse of the concept of affordance. Design Computing and Cognition'14, pp. 295–311. Springer, Berlin (2015). https://doi.org/10.1007/978-3-319-14956-1_17
10. Klopping, I.M., McKinney, E.: Extending the technology acceptance model and the task-technology fit model to consumer e-commerce. Inf. Technol. Learn. Perform. J. **22**, 35 (2004)
11. Andreassi, J.L.: Psychophysiology: Human Behavior and Physiological Response. Psychology Press, United Kingdom (2010)
12. Gibson, J.J.: The Ecological Approach to Visual Perception: Classic Edition. Psychology Press, United Kingdom (1979)
13. McGrenere, J., Ho, W.: Affordances: clarifying and evolving a concept. In: Graphics Interface, pp. 179–186 (2000)
14. Faraj, S., Azad, B.: The materiality of technology: an affordance perspective. Materiality Organizing: Soc. Interact. Technol. world **237**, 258 (2012)
15. Norman, D.: The Psychology of Everyday Things. Basic Books, New York (1988)
16. Norman, D.: The Design of Everyday Things: Revised and Expanded Edition. Basic Books, New York (2013)
17. Majchrzak, A., Markus, M.L.: Technology affordances and constraints in management information systems (MIS). Encycl. Manage. Theory, (Ed: E. Kessler), Sage Publications, Forthcoming (2012)
18. Cochrane, T., Bateman, R.: Smartphones give you wings: pedagogical affordances of mobile Web 2.0. Australas. J. Educ. Technol. **26**(1) (2010)
19. Gaver, W.W.: Technology affordances. In: Proceedings of the SIGCHI Conference on Human Factors in Computing Systems, pp. 79–84 (1991)
20. Hutchby, I.: Technologies, texts and affordances. Sociology **35**, 441–456 (2001)

21. Leonardi, P.M.: When flexible routines meet flexible technologies: affordance, constraint, and the imbrication of human and material agencies. MIS Q. 147–167 (2011)
22. McEwan, B., Fox, J.: Why communication technologies matter: developing a scale to assess the perceived social affordances of communication channels. In: Paper presented the National Communication Association conference, Las Vegas, NV (2015)
23. Rietveld, E., Kiverstein, J.: A rich landscape of affordances. Ecol. Psychol. **26**, 325–352 (2014)
24. Rice, R.E., Evans, S.K., Pearce, K.E., Sivunen, A., Vitak, J., Treem, J.W.: Organizational media affordances: operationalization and associations with media use. J. Commun. **67**, 106–130 (2017)
25. Chemero, A.: An outline of a theory of affordances. Ecol. Psychol. **15**, 181–195 (2003)
26. Dohn, N.B.: Affordances revisited: articulating a Merleau-Pontian view. Int. J. Comput.-Support. Collaborative Learn. **4**, 151–170 (2009)
27. Evans, S.K., Pearce, K.E., Vitak, J., Treem, J.W.: Explicating affordances: a conceptual framework for understanding affordances in communication research. J. Comput.-Mediated Commun. **22**, 35–52 (2017)
28. Oliver, M.: The problem with affordance. E-Learning Digit. Media **2**, 402–413 (2005)
29. Cohen, M., Ranaweera, R., Ito, H., Endo, S., Holesch, S., Villegas, J.: Whirling interfaces: smartphones & tablets as spinnable affordances. In: ICAT: Proc. Int. Conf. on Artificial Reality and Telexistence, pp. 1345–1278 (2011)
30. Majchrzak, A., Faraj, S., Kane, G.C., Azad, B.: The contradictory influence of social media affordances on online communal knowledge sharing. J. Comput.-Mediated Commun. **19**, 38–55 (2013)
31. Schrock, A.R.: Communicative affordances of mobile media: portability, availability, locatability, and multimediality. Int. J. Commun. **9**, 18 (2015)
32. Lurie, N.H., et al.: Everywhere and at all times: mobility, consumer decision-making, and choice. Customer Needs Solutions **5**, 15–27 (2017). https://doi.org/10.1007/s40547-017-0076-9
33. Chae, M., Kim, J.: Do size and structure matter to mobile users? an empirical study of the effects of screen size, information structure, and task complexity on user activities with standard web phones. Behav. Inf. Technol. **23**, 165–181 (2004)
34. Goodhue, D.L., Thompson, R.L.: Task-technology fit and individual performance. MIS Q. **19**, 213–236 (1995)
35. Furneaux, B.: Task-technology fit theory: a survey and synopsis of the literature. Information Systems Theory, pp. 87–106. Springer, Berlin (2012). https://doi.org/10.1007/978-1-4419-6108-2_5
36. Zigurs, I., Buckland, B.K.: A theory of task/technology fit and group support systems effectiveness. MIS Q. **22**, 313–334 (1998)
37. Zigurs, I., Khazanchi, D.: From profiles to patterns: a new view of task-technology fit. Inf. Syst. Manage. **25**, 8–13 (2008)
38. Kerr, D.S., Murthy, U.S.: Divergent and convergent idea generation in teams: a comparison of computer-mediated and face-to-face communication. Group Decis. Negot. **13**, 381–399 (2004)
39. Chung, S., Lee, K.Y., Choi, J.: Exploring digital creativity in the workspace: the role of enterprise mobile applications on perceived job performance and creativity. Comput. Hum. Behav. **42**, 93–109 (2015)
40. Lu, H.-P., Yang, Y.-W.: Toward an understanding of the behavioral intention to use a social networking site: an extension of task-technology fit to social-technology fit. Comput. Hum. Behav. **34**, 323–332 (2014)
41. Dishaw, M.T., Strong, D.M.: Extending the technology acceptance model with task–technology fit constructs. Inf. Manage. **36**, 9–21 (1999)

42. Howard, M.C., Rose, J.C.: Refining and extending task–technology fit theory: creation of two task–technology fit scales and empirical clarification of the construct. Inf. Manage. **56**, 103134 (2019)
43. Mathieson, K., Keil, M.: Beyond the interface: ease of use and task/technology fit. Inf. Manage. **34**, 221–230 (1998)
44. Aljukhadar, M., Senecal, S., Nantel, J.: Is more always better? Investigating the task-technology fit theory in an online user context. Inf. Manage. **51**, 391–397 (2014)
45. Lee, C.-C., Cheng, H.K., Cheng, H.-H.: An empirical study of mobile commerce in insurance industry: task–technology fit and individual differences. Decis. Support Syst. **43**, 95–110 (2007)
46. D'Ambra, J., Wilson, C.S., Akter, S.: Application of the task-technology fit model to structure and evaluate the adoption of E-books by Academics. J. Am. Soc. Inf. Sci. Technol. **64**, 48–64 (2013)
47. Carte, T., Schwarzkopf, A., Wang, N.: How should technology affordances be measured? an initial comparison of two approaches (2015)
48. Davern, M.J.: Towards a unified theory of fit: task, technology and individual. Inf. Syst. Found.: Theory, Representation Reality, 49–69 (2007)
49. International Organization for Standardization
50. Hartson, R., Pyla, P.S.: The UX Book: Process and Guidelines for Ensuring a Quality User Experience. Elsevier, Netherlands (2012)
51. Zajonc, R.B.: Feeling and thinking: preferences need no inferences. Am. Psychol. **35**, 151–175 (1980)
52. American Psychological Association. https://dictionary.apa.org/cognition
53. Marshall, S.P.: Identifying cognitive state from eye metrics. Aviat. Space Environ. Med. **78**, B165–B175 (2007)
54. Kahneman, D.: Attention and effort. Citeseer (1973)
55. Raptis, D., Tselios, N., Kjeldskov, J., Skov, M.: Does size matter? Investigating the impact of mobile phone screen size on users' perceived usability, effectiveness and efficiency. In: Mobile HCI 2013, Munich (2013)
56. Mehrabian, A., Russell, J.A.: An Approach to Environmental Psychology. the MIT Press, Cambridge, Massachusetts (1974)
57. Russell, J.A.: A circumplex model of affect. J. Pers. Soc. Psychol. **39**, 1161 (1980)
58. Russell, J.A., Lanius, U.F.: Adaptation level and the affective appraisal of environments. J. Environ. Psychol. **4**, 119–135 (1984)
59. Russell, J.A., Weiss, A., Mendelsohn, G.A.: Affect grid: a single-item scale of pleasure and arousal. J. Pers. Soc. Psychol. **57**, 493 (1989)
60. Donovan, R.J., Rossiter, J.R.: Store atmosphere: an environmental psychology approach. J. Retail. **58**, 34–57 (1982)
61. Menon, S., Kahn, B.: Cross-category effects of induced arousal and pleasure on the internet shopping experience. J. Retail. **78**, 31–40 (2002)
62. vom Brocke, J., Hevner, A., Léger, P.M., Walla, P., Riedl, R.: Advancing a neurois research agenda with four areas of societal contributions. Eur. J. Inf. Syst. 1–16 (2020)
63. Warriner, A.B., Kuperman, V., Brysbaert, M.: Norms of valence, arousal, and dominance for 13,915 english lemmas. Behav. Res. Methods **45**(4), 1191–1207 (2013). https://doi.org/10.3758/s13428-012-0314-x
64. Bradley, M.M., Lang, P.J.: Affective norms for english words (ANEW): instruction manual and affective ratings. Technical report C-1, the center for research in psychophysiology (1999)
65. Redondo, J., Fraga, I., Padrón, I., Comesaña, M.: The Spanish adaptation of ANEW (affective norms for english words). Behav. Res. Methods **39**, 600–605 (2007)

66. Soares, A.P., Comesaña, M., Pinheiro, A.P., Simões, A., Frade, C.S.: The adaptation of the affective norms for english words (ANEW) for European Portuguese. Behav. Res. Methods **44**, 256–269 (2012)
67. Venkatraman, N.: The concept of fit in strategy research: toward verbal and statistical correspondence. Acad. Manage. Rev. **14**, 423–444 (1989)
68. Toms, E.G.: Understanding and facilitating the browsing of electronic text. Int. J. Hum.-Comput. Stud. **52**, 423–452 (2000)
69. Yüksel, A.: Tourist shopping habitat: effects on emotions, shopping value and behaviours. Tourism Manage. **28**, 58–69 (2007)
70. Hoffman, D.L., Novak, T.P.: Marketing in hypermedia computer-mediated environments: conceptual foundations. J. Mark. **60**, 50–68 (1996)
71. Moe, W.W.: Buying, searching, or browsing: differentiating between online shoppers using in-store navigational clickstream. J. Consum. Psychol. **13**, 29–39 (2003)
72. van der Hans, H.: User acceptance of hedonic information systems. MIS Q. **28**, 695–704 (2004)
73. O'Brien, H.L.: The influence of hedonic and utilitarian motivations on user engagement: the case of online shopping experiences. Interact. Comput. **22**, 344–352 (2010)
74. Bloch, P.H., Sherrell, D.L., Ridgway, N.M.: Consumer search: an extended framework. J. Consum. Res. **13**, 119–126 (1986)
75. Batra, R., Ahtola, O.T.: Measuring the hedonic and utilitarian sources of consumer attitudes. Mark. lett. **2**, 159–170 (1991)
76. Riedl, R., Fischer, T., Léger, P.-M.: A decade of NeuroIS research: status quo, challenges, and future directions. In: Thirty Eighth International Conference on Information Systems, South Korea (2017)
77. Riedl, R., Fischer, T., Léger, P.-M., Davis, F.D.: A decade of neuroIS research: progress, challenges, and future directions. Data Base Adv. Inf. Syst. In Press, ((Forthcoming)) (2020)
78. Statista: Do you typically spend more on groceries bought online or bought in-store? - Statistics & Facts (2018). https://proxy2.hec.ca:2554/statistics/822567/expenditure-on-onl ine-and-in-store-groceries/
79. Statista: Food Shopping Behavior in Canada - Statistics & Facts (2019)
80. Desrochers, C., Léger, P.-M., Fredette, M., Mirhoseini, S., Sénécal, S.: The arithmetic complexity of online grocery shopping: the moderating role of product pictures. Ind. Manage. Data Syst. (2019)
81. Giroux-Huppé, C., Sénécal, S., Fredette, M., Chen, S.L., Demolin, B., Léger, P.-M.: Identifying psychophysiological pain points in the online user journey: the case of online grocery. In: International Conference on Human-Computer Interaction, pp. 459–473. Springer (2019)
82. Charness, G., Gneezy, U., Kuhn, M.A.: Experimental methods: between-subject and within-subject design. J. Econ. Behav. Organ. **81**, 1–8 (2012)
83. Budescu, D.V., Weiss, W.: Reflection of transitive and intransitive preferences: a test of prospect theory. Organ. Behav. Hum. Decis. Process. **39**, 184–202 (1987)
84. Perdue, B.C., Summers, J.O.: Checking the success of manipulations in marketing experiments. J. Mark. Res. **23**, 317–326 (1986)
85. Riedl, R., Léger, P.-M.: Fundamentals of neuroIS. Stud. Neurosci. Psychol. Behav. Econ. Springer, Berlin, Heidelberg (2016)
86. Kivikangas, J.M., Chanel, G., Cowley, B., Ekman, I., Salminen, M., Järvelä, S., Ravaja, N.: A review of the use of psychophysiological methods in game research. J. Gaming Virtual Worlds **3**, 181–199 (2011)
87. Kramer, A.F.: Physiological metrics of mental workload: a review of recent progress. Multiple-task Perform. 279–328 (1991)
88. Ikehara, C.S., Crosby, M.E.: Physiological measures used for identification of cognitive states and continuous authentication (2010)

89. de Guinea, A.O., Titah, R., Leger, P.-M.: Explicit and implicit antecedents of users' behavioral beliefs in information systems: a neuropsychological investigation. J. Manage. Inf. Syst. **30**, 179–210 (2014)
90. Loos, P., et al.: NeuroIS: neuroscientific approaches in the investigation and development of information systems. Bus. Inf. Syst. Eng. **2**, 395–401 (2010)
91. Dimoka, A., et al.: On the use of neurophysiological tools in IS research: developing a research agenda for NeuroIS. MIS Q. 679–702 (2012)
92. Dimoka, A., Pavlou, P.A., Davis, F.D.: Research commentary—neuroIS: the potential of cognitive neuroscience for information systems research. Inf. Syst. Res. **22**, 687–702 (2011)
93. Riedl, R., Davis, F.D., Hevner, A.R.: Towards a neuroIS research methodology: intensifying the discussion on methods, tools, and measurement. J. Assoc. Inf. Syst. **15**, 4 (2014)
94. Zhang, Q., Gangwar, M., Seetharaman, P.B.: Polygamous store loyalties: an empirical investigation. J. Retail. **93**, 477–492 (2017)
95. Ganglbauer, E., Schrammel, J., Deutsch, S., Tscheligi, M.: Applying psychophysiological methods for measuring user experience: possibilities, challenges and feasibility. In: Workshop on User Experience Evaluation Methods in Product Development. Citeseer (2009)
96. Tobii AB: Tobii pro x3-120 eye tracker: Product description (2017). https://www.tobiipro.com/siteassets/tobii-pro/product-descriptions/tobii-pro-x3–120-product-description.pdf
97. Dalrymple, K.A., Manner, M.D., Harmelink, K.A., Teska, E.P., Elison, J.T.: An examination of recording accuracy and precision from eye tracking data from toddlerhood to adulthood. Front. Psychol. **9**, 803 (2018)
98. Ekman, P.: An argument for basic emotions. Cogn. Emot. **6**, 169–200 (1992)
99. Noldus Information Technology
100. Lewinski, P., den Uyl, T.M., Butler, C.: Automated facial coding: validation of basic emotions and FACS AUs in FaceReader. J. Neurosci. Psychol. Econ. **7**, 227–236 (2014)
101. Terzis, V., Moridis, C.N., Economides, A.A.: Measuring instant emotions based on facial expressions during computer-based assessment. Pers. Ubiquit. Comput. **17**, 43–52 (2013)
102. Dupré, D., Krumhuber, E.G., Küster, D., McKeown, G.J.: A performance comparison of eight commercially available automatic classifiers for facial affect recognition. PLoS ONE **15**, e0231968 (2020)
103. Biopac Systems Inc.: EDA introductory guide (2015). https://www.biopac.com/wp-content/uploads/EDA-Guide.pdf
104. Noldus: FaceReader reference manual 7 (2016). http://sslab.nwpu.edu.cn/uploads/150060 4789-5971697563f64.pdf
105. Courtemanche, F., Fredette, M., Senecal, S., Leger, P.-m., Dufresne, A., Georges, V., Labonte-lemoyne, E.: Method of and system for processing signals sensed from a user. Google Patents (2019)
106. Léger, P.-M., Courtemanche, F., Fredette, M., Sénécal, S.: A cloud-based lab management and analytics software for triangulated human-centered research. In: Davis, F.D., Riedl, R., vom Brocke, J., Léger, P.-M., Randolph, A.B. (eds.) Information Systems and Neuroscience. LNISO, vol. 29, pp. 93–99. Springer, Cham (2019). https://doi.org/10.1007/978-3-030-01087-4_11
107. Saunders, D.R.: Moderator variables in prediction. Educ. Psychol. Meas. **16**, 209–222 (1956)
108. Zedeck, S.: Problems with the use of "moderator" variables. Psychol. Bull. **76**, 295 (1971)
109. Hattula, J., Herzog, W., Ravi, D.: When touch interfaces boost consumer confidence: the role of instrumental need for touch. Adv. Consum. Res. **45**, 25 (2017)
110. Krishna, A.: An integrative review of sensory marketing: engaging the senses to affect perception, judgment and behavior. J. Consum. Psychol. **22**, 332–351 (2012)
111. Shen, H., Zhang, M., Krishna, A.: Computer interfaces and the "direct-touch" effect: can iPads increase the choice of hedonic food? J. Mark. Res. **53**, 745 (2016)

112. Xu, K., Chan, J., Ghose, A., Han, S.P.: Battle of the channels: the impact of tablets on digital commerce. Manage. Sci. **63**, 1469–1492 (2017)
113. Brasel, S.A., Gips, J.: Interface psychology: touchscreens change attribute importance, decision criteria, and behavior in online choice. Cyberpsychology, Behav. Soc. Networking **18**, 534–538 (2015)

Brainstorming for Sensemaking
in a Multimodal, Multiuser Cognitive
Environment

Shannon Briggs[1(✉)], Matthew Peveler[1], Jaimie Drozdal[1], Lilit Balagyozyan[1],
Jonas Braasch[1], and Hui Su[2]

[1] Rensselaer Polytechnic Institute, Troy, NY 12180, USA
{briggs3,pevelm,drozdj3,balagl,braasj}@rpi.edu
[2] IBM Thomas J. Watson Research Laboratory, Yorktown Heights, NY 10598, USA
huisuibmres@us.ibm.com

Abstract. This paper discusses a user study conducted on a brainstorming tool for brainstorming in intelligence analysis, situated in a cognitive and immersive system. The cognitive and immersive room is comprised of gesture technology, voice input, tablet input, and a 360 display to allow for group discussion and interaction. The brainstorming tool design is informed by sensemaking theory as defined by Pirolli and Card [1]. The basis for the digital brainstorming tool in our cognitive immersive environment is a structured analytic tool already in use by the intelligence analysis domain. We anticipate that this design will capitalize on cognitive familiarity to enable a more approachable design and facilitate a smoother and more useful tool. The user study (n = 26) is an A/B study conducted to compare the capabilities of the analog brainstorming tool with the digital brainstorming tool, and understand how the multimodal interaction system impacts brainstorming.

Keywords: HCI methods and theories · Multimodal interface · Evaluation methods and techniques · Qualitative and quantitative measurement and evaluation · User experience

1 Introduction

We have designed and implemented a digital brainstorming tool situated in the cognitive immersive room. This cognitive immersive room is comprised of a 360-degree screen ($14^0 h, 20^0 r$) [2], with five projectors displaying the system and five Microsoft Kinects interpreting gestural input for direct control of the system, as well as lapel microphones that allow verbal input [3]. The brainstorming tool in the cognitive immersive room is a digital tool based on a structured analytic technique that has been created by the intelligence analysis domain, which can be seen in Beebe and Pherson [4]. In general, the brainstorming method is a way for a group of analysts to identify new information or hypotheses, as well as broaden and diversify current ideas and hypotheses. The brainstorming tool is also informed by Pirolli and Card's sensemaking theory [1], which will

© Springer Nature Switzerland AG 2020
C. Stephanidis et al. (Eds.): HCII 2020, LNCS 12423, pp. 66–83, 2020.
https://doi.org/10.1007/978-3-030-60114-0_4

be discussed more in depth in the literature review. We have determined that the existing analog brainstorming structured analytic technique performs as an information foraging behavior for intelligence analysts as described by Pirolli and Card. In order to help support mindful software development for decision making in intelligence analysis, we have informed the design of our brainstorming tool by Pirolli and Card's model, that analysts need foraging tools, and from the design of the structured brainstorming technique.

The brainstorming tool is divided into two major views, the global view and the personal view. The global view is projected onto the 360-degree screen, allowing users to share information, make decisions, and work collaboratively [5, 6] (Fig. 1).

Fig. 1. Digital brainstorming tool global view

The brainstorming tool also allows for personal device input through the internet. Users can access a personal view of the brainstorming tool on any device that has access to a web browser. Users are able to create categories, and move notes from the global view (designated as "uncategorized" on the personal view) into categories.

We are interested in how our digital brainstorming tool compares against the capabilities of the analog pen and paper brainstorming technique. As such, we compare the words that participants used within sticky notes for both the analog and digital portions of the tool. We posit that the digital tool will help produce a more representative proportion of words than the analog tool. As each note is a piece of evidence from the case study, this metric displays how effectively each brainstorming method allows users to collect and transcribe evidence and information of interest, which is a primary function of the brainstorming tool. This also allows us to examine several points of the digital system that involve novel technology, particularly the gestures and voice system, and how these may help or hinder the brainstorming process. The results of our user study show that the digital brainstorming tool performs as well as the analog brainstorming tool in proportion to words created within sticky notes, when controlling for the proportion of information in each text segment compared to the number of pieces of information in the sticky notes (Fig. 2).

Fig. 2. Digital brainstorming tool personal view

2   Literature Review

2.1   Sensemaking Theory

Pirolli and Card's [1] sensemaking theory is the framework that informs our development of the brainstorming tool used for intelligence analysis, which is positioned within the cognitive immersive room. The authors created a notational sensemaking model to describe how intelligence analysts move though the sensemaking process, travelling through two major cognitive loops, the information foraging loop and the sensemaking loop. Sixteen smaller steps describe discrete cognitive phases that analysts move through during this sensemaking process. The two loops and the sixteen steps can be seen in Fig. 3. We posit that structured analytic tools that analysts have created are analog techniques to aid them in completing these sensemaking steps; therefore, designing a digital tool from these techniques will similarly aid analysts in completing this sensemaking process. We have designed the digital brainstorming tool from the structured analytic brainstorming technique; we believe this will aid users in steps 2 to 4 (see Fig. 3) in the information foraging process as described by Pirolli and Card [1].

The brainstorming tool, for example, is used by analysts during the information-foraging process, as it allows analysts to uncover and sort through new information. A digital brainstorming tool provides a more accessible record of decisions and insights; analysts can reach decisions about important evidence, collaborate with others, and finally store these for easy referral during other parts of the sensemaking process.

While analog brainstorming methods have been in wide use in intelligence analysis, the challenges of big data, increased communication potential through the internet, and increased data availability have presented analysts with new problems. Handling massive volumes of data, including organizing, sorting, and identifying relevant information are new challenges for the intelligence analysis domain [7]. Assembling, sharing, and presenting this data and insights generated from the data to other analysts and organizations are problems. Creating a digital version of tools that they are already familiar

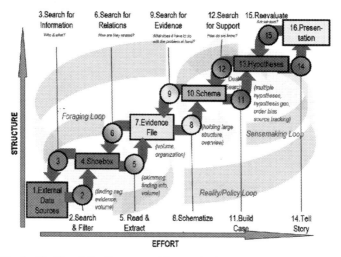

Fig. 3. Pirolli and Card's sensemaking model for intelligence analysis [1].

with, starting with the brainstorming tool, allows analysts to continue within the cognitive workflow as described by Pirolli and Card [1], without being disrupted or stymied by technological limitations. Similarly, the affordances provided by these digital tools, such as being able to ingest, filter, and display large amounts of data, allows analysts to leverage their training and insights in a more focused manner.

2.2 Electronic Brainstorming and Sticky Notes

Brainstorming, defined as generating, sharing, and combining ideas about a problem or task by more than one individual [8, 9] has long been supported by electronic media. The reported benefits of electronic brainstorming systems (EBS) include cognitive stimulation and synergy, reduced production blocking, and reduced evaluation apprehension in anonymous EBS [10–12].

Briggs et al. [9], for instance, report a 63% increase in the number of unique ideas generated during a brainstorming session when a highly salient social comparison mechanism was utilized in the brainstorming.

Grise and Gallupe [13] also conduct a review of electronic brainstorming capabilities, stating that they can generate a large number of ideas, while also supporting concurrent activities, such as entry and storage of ideas. The authors also posit that digital brainstorming enhances creativity, as users can access a larger group of ideas that had been created previously. Similarly, the authors also state that electronic brainstorming aids in better sensemaking, here defined as "the initial process of developing a set of ideas [13]." In brainstorming sessions using electronic means, participants produced more ideas that weren't in analog sessions, indicating that participants were able to produce a wider variety of ideas.

Electronic sticky notes have been proposed before in digital brainstorming literature, and varieties of such a tool have been implemented. Prior research has examined the application of sticky note tools in group and collaborative settings [14], in mediated group work accomplished remotely, and how sticky notes can be used to define affinity groups in collaborative work [15]. Jensen et al. conducted a study comparing the use of traditional analog sticky notes to a digital sticky-notes tool, and concluded that the digital sticky notes were superior in terms of increased note interaction, clustering, and labelling [16]. Existing digital sticky note tools can be found in examples such as Discusys [15], ECOPack [17], Padlet, and Quickies [18].

2.3 Structured Analytic Brainstorming

The brainstorming structured analytic technique is a cognitive tool used by intelligence analysts to generate new ideas and opinions about materials relevant to their job, and is one of the earliest techniques that can be carried out in the analysis process [4]. It is a multistep process that involves data collection, data analysis, and group discussion. The purpose of the exercise is to reduce cognitive bias, and to allow a diversity of perspectives to be taken into consideration in dealing with a problem. In Beebe and Pherson's description of structured brainstorming, it is a 12-step process with at least two analysts and a discussion facilitator, as portions of the brainstorming exercise are done independently before ideas are shared with the group [4].

Our digital sticky notes tool is informed by the brainstorming cognitive structured analytic technique. We have taken the pen-and-paper brainstorming exercise as described by Beebe and Pherson [4] and implemented it into an immersive, digital tool that can be used collaboratively in a multi-user context. The digital brainstorming tool is currently informed by documents from the training and educational literature that has been produced by the intelligence field concerning structured analytic techniques, specifically brainstorming.

Our digital brainstorming tool is designed to support analysts sensemaking by integrating educational and training materials that are already used by analysts in their own domain, such as those described by Beebe and Pherson [4] or Hall and Citrenbaum [19]. We believe that this will create a more accessible interface and will provide affordances that are already familiar to the user base. Providing analysts with a tool that provides a similar interface has proven to have some success with analysts as users, as has been discussed by Smallman [20]. We use the Pirolli and Card sensemaking notational model [1] to contextualize where the brainstorming process is positioned. This model depicts the cognitive tasks completed by intelligence analysts, and it includes a foraging phase and a sensemaking phase. The brainstorming tool is informed by the foraging phase from Pirolli and Card's model to allow analysts to search, discover, and filter information during the shoebox phase (see steps 1 through 4 in Fig. 3) [1].

3 User Study

3.1 Method

Our user study is an A/B study, designed to compare the analog brainstorming tool to the digital brainstorming tool. Comparing the analog and digital brainstorming method allows us to understand whether the intended users could find benefit from the digital tool; currently, the analog method is in wide use across many intelligence analysis applications; given its wide popularity in the domain, we have assumed that a digital tool using the same interactions and technique will be easily accessible. As the brainstorming technique is intended to include a range of ideas and opinions, our user study was conducted in small groups of 2-3 users per session. Participants were anonymized and given false names, which were also used as identifiers for our digital system. The digital system uses these names to distinguish verbal commands and sticky note ownership, so that a command will be carried out by the system as unique to the identity of the user issuing the command. Participants for the study were recruited from the student and faculty body at a local university, and were novices to the digital brainstorming tool. Inexperience to our tool was an important factor, as we anticipated that understanding how novices would interact with the tool would be helpful in understanding how the intended user would interact with the system. While several brainstorming tools and sticky-notes based systems are available, our gestural and verbal input system is a novel way for users to interact with a brainstorming tool.

The user study was divided into two 30-min segments, the analog portion and the digital portion. Participants first completed the analog portion of the study, allowing them to become acclimated to the brainstorming method. Participants in the digital portion were given an excerpt from the Jonathan Luna case study used in intelligence analysis classes and were then given five minutes to read this excerpt. Samples from this case study can be found in Beebe and Pherson's book [4]. Following this, participants were given five minutes to write pieces of evidence onto sticky notes, which were distributed at the beginning of the session. A piece of evidence would be constituted as a fact-based piece of information directly from the case study, rather than conjecture or hypothesis. For example, a piece of evidence could be, "He was a lawyer," but could not be, "I think he was traveling because he was a lawyer." Participants were then given five minutes to arrange their sticky notes on a shared wall, grouping their own sticky notes in categories based on topics in the evidence. Discussion for this portion of the brainstorming session was not allowed, as participants are supposed to rely on their own perspectives and ideas about what is important and salient, which is called the divergent thinking process [21]. Finally, participants were given five minutes to discuss sticky notes contents with other group members and rearrange sticky notes into shared categories. At the end of the session, a researcher running the user study asked the participants to give a verbal summary of their findings and major categories. Participants were encouraged to fill out a short survey on their experience with the analog brainstorming session.

The second portion of the user study was completed with the digital brainstorming tool. Participants either completed the digital brainstorming session in the lab-suite, where the system was projected onto a flat wall, or within the cognitive immersive room, where the system was projected onto the 360-degree screen. Participants were given tablets, in order to access the personal view to create sticky notes, and lapel microphones to allow them to issue verbal commands to the system. The lapel microphones were programmed with the identities given to them at the beginning of the study, which allowed them to issue separate commands to the global view. Participants were given a brief demonstration of the gestural and verbal input system, as well as a brief tutorial on how to create sticky notes on the tablet devices.

Participants were subsequently given five minutes to read a second excerpt from the same case intelligence analysis case study, which is available either on the projected global view, or with the same paper that was distributed during the analog portion. Participants were then given five minutes to use the tablets to create sticky notes; this feature was enabled in the digital brainstorming tool to resemble the analog method of separately writing on their sticky notes. Creating notes on the tablets within the personal view allows only the individual users to see their own notes. Participants then had five minutes to send their notes to the global view from the tablets, and group their own notes on the global screen using the gestural system. Again, this portion of the digital session was considered the divergent phase, and no discussion between participants was allowed. Finally, participants were allowed discussion during the last five minutes of the digital portion, where they discussed the notes created, and then agreed upon category names, and moved notes into categories. A researcher running the user study then asked the participants to give a verbal summary of their findings and encouraged the participants to voice any questions or concerns about the digital tool or anything from the study. Participants were then encouraged to fill out an optional survey about their experience with the digital tool. Participants were given a gift card for their participation in the user study.

3.2 Analysis

We are interested in how our digital brainstorming tool compares to the capabilities of the analog pen and paper brainstorming technique. This analysis examines how the participants were able to read, comprehend, absorb, and then reflect their understanding of the sample text segment in the notes themselves. Following an a-priori coding scheme, we created three major concept groups for analog tools from the text segment given to participants, and four major concept groups for the digital notes from another text segment given to participants. Our objective is to understand how the brainstorming format affects the range and diversity of words used in the sticky-notes, with the understanding that words in the sticky-notes that are the same or similar as words used in the text segment reflect a high understanding of the text. The sticky-notes content should also align well with the concept groups, which describe the major themes of the text.

Analog

For the analog sessions, there were 345 unique words across nine user study sessions, with a total frequency of all words of 1772. The words with the highest frequency can be seen in Fig. 4. When cleaned, the number of unique words is 320, with a total frequency of 1523. Using Catma.de [22], we performed a frequency search by the similarity of 80% to each word. For example, searching for "prosecute" also returned "suspect" because several of the characters are similar to "prosecute." We kept the similarity to 80% to capture the potential variability in representing specific words in the case. Finally, we hand-sorted the wordlist returned by Catma for similar words (Phil to Philadelphia, seek to seeking, etc.), to choose the words that were most important in a given text segment involving the three major themes.

Several interesting features of the data can be seen in the descriptive statistics, such as the resulting mode of 1, meaning that words that only appeared once in the analog

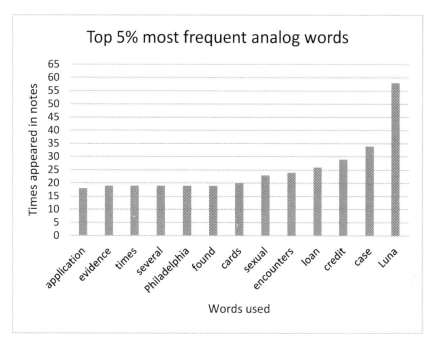

Fig. 4. Top 5% used words in analog sessions

sticky-notes data set were most frequent, indicating a high variance in words. The highest-occurring word was "Luna" with a frequency of 58 (80%). Most other words in the analog sticky-notes occurred only between 1 and 7 times, emphasizing the number of unique words in the sticky-notes, with nearly 60% of the words occurring only once or twice. There were 65 words that were most frequently used (between 7 and 58 times). Figure 4 shows the top 5% most frequent words in the analog notes, which include only 13 of the 345 words in total.

Figure 4 shows the frequency of the words in the three major concept groups, with additions of a mixed concept group. This last group included words that could be important to one or more categories, for example, Luna's name, mentions of his wife, and mention of his death. Overall, there were still 916 words otherwise non-categorizable to the four concept categories; these words were generally auxiliary verbs (is/was), articles (the/an), pronouns (he/that), and conjunctions (and/or), as well as punctuation that was also captured by Catma's software.

The percentage breakdown of the sticky-notes is a relatively straightforward reflection of the word frequencies in the three major concept groups in the analog text segment, which was distributed for participants to review for the analog portion of the user testing. Including all words in the text segment, there are 103 words related to Luna's work, 105 words related to Luna's debt, and 65 words related to Luna's sex life. Figure 5 displays the percentage of words per concept in text segment 1, which was used for the analog sticky-notes portion of the testing.

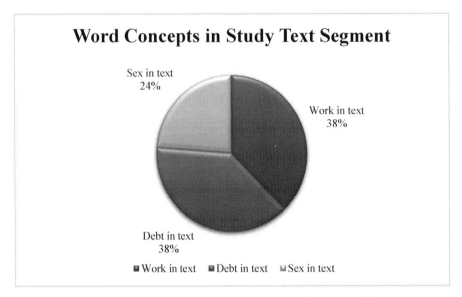

Fig. 5. Word Concepts in the analog text segment given to participants.

Figures 5 and 6 show that the concept percentages between the analog sticky-notes and the words in the text segment. The percentage breakdown of the note content has been cleaned for noise, where we removed articles, auxiliary verbs, and combined separately counted verb conjugations (i.e., sought was included with seek, cancel included with cancellation). Participants reinterpreted some of the information in the text segment in ways that could be attributed to several causes for Luna's death, which is represented in the Mixed Concepts category, which has taken up 23% of the total words across the 9 user sessions. Correspondingly, the other categories have shrunk. Table 1 shows a comparison of the word percentages between the text segment and the participants' sticky-notes text. In a direct comparison, participants were clearly able to absorb and reflect material through the brainstorming process, as the mixed category displays ways in which participants reinterpreted information in the text segment with their understanding of the cause of Luna's death. However, this also points to a possible weakness of the analog tool, where users do not thoughtfully examine ambiguous or unclear associations within the material they are working from. As we see in the brainstorming processes discussed by Beebe and Pherson (2014) and the CIA tradecraft manual [23], participants are encouraged to create clear categories with distinct themes.

Digital sticky notes
The digital notes brainstorming tool segment had roughly four content categories: work, body, knife, and death. As some words were used in multiple categories, we created a fifth category labeled "mixed" to demonstrate how some of the notes overlapped. We hand-sorted the words so each work that appeared in a concept chunk was sorted to a separate category. For example, the note containing the sentence, "Penknife believed to cause wounds on body" would be classified both under category "knife" as well as

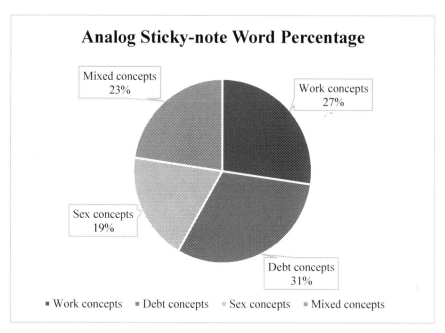

Fig. 6. Analog note word percentage

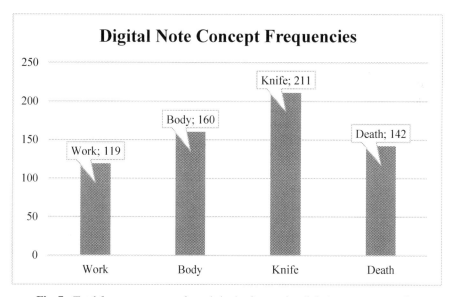

Fig. 7. Total frequency count of words in the four major digital concept categories

"body," as the note is referring to conceptually distinct points, both the knife and the wounds it caused.

Table 1. Percentages between analog notes and in-text words.

Work Concepts	Debt Concepts	Sex Concepts
In text: 38%	In-text: 38%	In-text: 24
Users: 27%	Users: 31%	Users: 19%
Difference: 11%	Difference: 7%	Difference: 5%

The sticky-notes content in the digital notes resulted in 372 unique words, and 1278 for a total word count. When cleaned to remove punctuation (such as periods, commas, and parentheses), the total unique words were 344, and the overall frequency fell to 982. Again, the overall word count is slightly lower than the analog sticky-notes (analog n = 1772, digital n = 1278), as sticky-note data was accidentally lost from CISL servers, amounting to roughly 38 words.

Figure 8 shows the number of notes participants created across eight sessions of user studies for the digital tool, grouped into the four major concept categories, as the words from Session 1 sticky-notes are not included in this analysis.

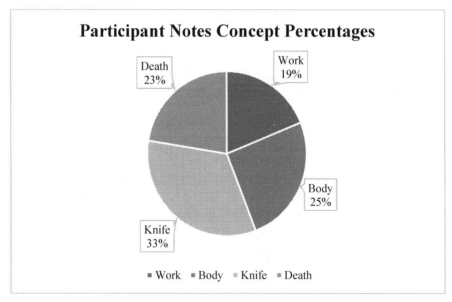

Fig. 8. Percentage of words in participants' sticky-notes related to the four major concepts

We found that the digital sticky-notes tool performed on par with the analog sticky-notes tool, and perhaps slightly better when looking at the statistical breakdown. Participants produced notes fitting the four major group concepts with the same frequency percentage found in the digital notes text segment that was provided to the participants. Figure 8 shows the percentage of notes created by participants, and Fig. 9 shows the percentage of text in concept categories in the digital text segment. Table 2 is a direct comparison of the frequency concept percentages proportionate to the text for the digital sessions (Fig. 7).

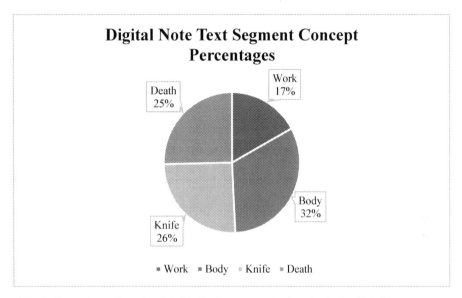

Fig. 9. Percentage of words related to the four concept categories in the digital text segment

Table 2. Concepts in digital notes between participants and text segment

Work Concepts	Body Concepts	Knife Concepts	Death Concepts
In text: 19%	In-text: 25%	In-text: 33	In text: 23
Users: 17%	Users: 32%	Users: 26%	Users: 25%
Difference: 2%	Difference: 7%	Difference: 7%	Difference: 2%

In terms of percentage difference, the digital sticky-notes created by participants differed from the in-text word totals between 2% (for "work" and "death" categories), and 7% (for "body" and "knife" categories). Therefore, the digital sticky-notes tool is better than the analog sticky-notes tool in allowing participants to create note content that accurately reflects the proportion of content in the given material, as Table 2 shows that the digital notes had a smaller percentage difference from the text. This is also shown for the comparison of unique word instances and total frequencies reported. The digital user study had roughly as many unique words as the analog tool, but contained fewer words overall, as can be seen in Fig. 10. This indicates the digital brainstorming tool resulted in more concise ideas within the brainstorming session, and the information content contained less noise and variability, and resulted in better sensemaking.

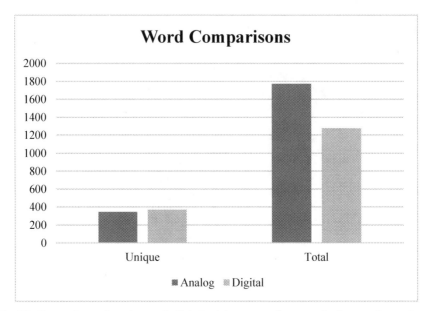

Fig. 10. Comparison of analog and digital sticky-note unique words frequencies and total frequencies

Comparisons between analog and digital

We also compared how the note content compared between the analog tool and the digital tool was categorizable into thematic units, and how many words were not categorizable. Figures 11 and 12 show the proportion of entirely relevant words (that is, all words directly categorizable and the mixed categories) between analog and digital is roughly proportionate, but the total percentage of unrelated words is 40% in the digital tool versus 49% in the analog tool. This indicates that the digital sticky-notes tool encourages a brainstorming session with more relevant sticky-notes overall, and therefore results in a better sensemaking session. Figure 10 shows a comparison of unique words in sticky notes, that is, words that were relevant only to the material in the text segment, per session compared to the total words produced per session. The graphic displays that participants produced a slightly higher amount of unique words with the digital brainstorming tool than the analog tool. Figure 10 also shows that participants produced fewer words total with the digital brainstorming tool, indicating a more concise and less noisy brainstorming session.

Finally, a Wilcoxon-Signed rank test between the analog note frequencies and the digital sticky-note frequencies indicated that the digital words displayed a lower frequency of words overall ($Z = -2.673$, $p = .008$). This result displayed that there were more of the same words used frequently, and more consistently, in words used in the digital sessions across nine sessions, compared to the analog digital brainstorming tool. When we compare this to the pie charts in Figs. 11 and 12, we can understand that the consistencies between the percentages of digital word frequencies and the in-text word frequencies indicate an efficient sensemaking process.

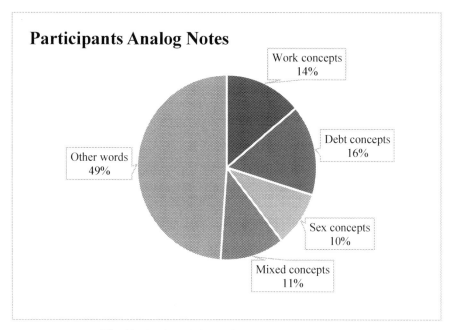

Fig. 11. Total breakdown of all words in analog notes

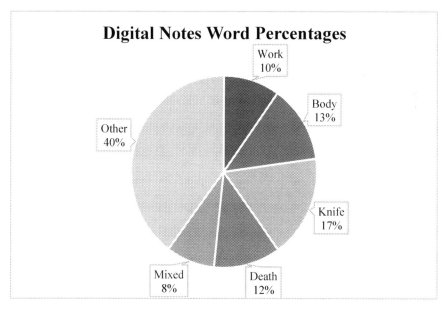

Fig. 12. Total breakdown of all words in digital notes

4 Discussion

We performed content analysis on participants' contents from the sticky-notes and categories across the nine user studies for both analog and digital brainstorming tools. We compared the proportion of relevant words in sticky-notes to their respective text segments from the testing. The following section discusses the implications of the findings in my analysis.

4.1 Sticky Notes

We posited that the digital brainstorming tool will have a more representative proportion of words related to the coded concept categories than the analog tool. We found that the analog sticky-notes tool had more words that only occurred once, indicating more variability in words used during the analog process. However, the brainstorming tool had a higher proportion of more consistent words, meaning that the participants across nine sessions used the same words to describe the same ideas. We found that the words within the overall concept frequencies were better represented in the digital notes sessions, with percentages of words used by participants matching more closely with the percentages of the words found in the text segment. Finally, using a Wilcoxon-Signed rank test, we determined that the digital portion of the user study had more of the same words used more frequently, meaning that users had a higher consensus concerning words, ideas, and concepts in the user study. The reason for more consistency in digital sticky-note words for participants using the digital tool may be due to the immersive environment affording users with an alternative route to process information compared to a purely physical environment, which I discuss further in the conclusions section. This information processing difference may have led to a different way of absorbing ideas from the text, resulting in higher word consistency in digital sticky-notes.

Our findings for comparing the words used in sticky-notes between the analog and digital brainstorming sessions showed that the digital tool displayed a more representative proportion of words to the text segment given to participants. This can be seen in the comparisons between the percentage of word proportions between participant sticky-notes and the text segments. This is also seen when comparing the number of unique words to the number of words overall in both brainstorming formats. As users had created their sticky-notes apart from each other during this phase, it appears that the digital tool's influence on word similarity is not simply due to collaboration. The reasons for the higher proportion of similar words across sessions may be due to their awareness of the immersive environment, and the nature of digital technology. This increased level of awareness may have led to increased caution for participants to represent their ideas more closely to the text segment given to them. The concept of presence in immersive environments may be tied to effects like the ones observed above, as different modes of information processing tend to be engaged when interacting with information in immersive environments [24]. Further research into participants' perception of how public their information is on the digital brainstorming format compared to the analog brainstorming format should be conducted to further understand this link.

4.2 System Interaction

Findings from our earlier sessions in this user study informed where the system was failing to support user actions and interactions. This also helped inform our user interface, as we were able to create a more intuitive interface that allowed users to fulfil specific actions, such as editing notes and deleting notes on the personal view. Part of the variability within digital sessions could be due to the change in system display. Users during the first five user study sessions were completed with the system display projected onto a flat wall, and as such it was slightly more difficult for users to interact with the far edges of the screen. This was solved in the second half of the session, which took place within the cognitive and immersive room.

We also found several points where the digital system addressed weaknesses of the analog system. Several participants reported the increased legibility of notes in the digital system, which increased both information understanding and helped group discussions. Participants also reported increased collaboration during the digital study, and increased unity in consensus for topic content.

Gestures

Users reported mixed feelings about the gestures system. Overall, users felt that the point, drag, and drop method of using the gestures system to move notes around the screen was intuitive and engaging. However, users tended to be frustrated if the system lagged, or if the system confused individuals' gestures. Similarly, as this is the first application within our system of multiple users using the gestures system within a single session, users were generally constrained to staying in place, as the system would confuse body frames. User perception of the gestures system improved dramatically throughout the user testing with the implementation of a more robust system, and we anticipate it will improve in future user responses with further improvements.

Verbal

Users reported mixed feelings about the verbal input system. While many users commented on survey responses about the utility of the transcript system in looking back over the history of a conversation, the verbal system frustrated users due to delayed registration of user commands. As the system records all speech, instead of just user commands, it would occasionally become slowed down as it tried to process large chunks of speech. However, in later user study sessions, with the implementation of more robust performance measures, users have reported more favorable interaction with the verbal system.

Tablet

Users reported largely positive feelings about tablet interactions. The tablets similarly allowed users a shortcut for interacting with the system, if the gestural and verbal systems were not reliably interpreting their commands. As a result, there were multiple user study sessions in which one user was interacting with the gesture systems by moving notes, another user would be categorizing notes via the tablet, and another user would use the verbal system. With a multi-input system, we found that users were generally able to work around each other as well as the pitfalls of the system, in order to complete their tasks. The tablet was the most useful tool in this regard, where participants were able to finish the digital brainstorming task by sharing and categorizing notes, while still using the global view for group discussions and an increased shared sensemaking process and perspective.

5   Conclusions and Future Work

We have presented a novel digital brainstorming system situated in a cognitive immersive environment. This system is comprised of a gestural system, a verbal input system, and enables sensemaking for intelligence analysis through the global view and the personal view. Through a user study (n = 26), we have found that the digital brainstorming tool performs as well as the traditional analog tool in capturing evidence into sticky notes, and enabling users to create more concise content with the digital brainstorming tool.

Future work for the brainstorming tool includes extraction of the sticky note content and category topic content through NLP, in order to further integrate the content from the tool into the Scenario Planning Advisor [25], which is another tool enabled in the cognitive immersive intelligence analysis room. We are also improving the smoothness of input systems in order to improve the overall perceived utility of the brainstorming system. The digital brainstorming system is novel among existing brainstorming and sticky note programs, in that it both integrates new technology via gestures, verbal input, and tablet input, as well as enabling these in a collaborative group setting. While these new technologies have the potential to hamper users due to their unfamiliar interface, we have discovered over the course of the user study that participants are able to complete tasks with the same success as they do in the similar analog setting. Future user studies will include experts in the intelligence analysis domain, and will also include testing new interaction methods with the digital brainstorming tool involving a smartphone based interaction tool.

References

1. Pirolli, P., Card, S.: Sensemaking processes of intelligence analysts and possible leverage points as identified through cognitive task analysis. In: Proceedings of the 2005 International Conference on Intelligence Analysis, McLean, Virginia (2005)
2. Allen, D., et al.: The rensselaer mandarin project—a cognitive and immersive language learning environment. Proc. AAAI Conf. Artif. Intell. **33**, 9845–9846 (2019). https://doi.org/10.1609/aaai.v33i01.33019845
3. Zhao, R., Wang, K., Divekar, R., Rouhani, R., Su, H., Ji, Q.: An immersive system with multi-modal human-computer interaction. In: 2018 13th IEEE International Conference on Automatic Face & Gesture Recognition (FG 2018). pp. 517–524. IEEE (2018). https://doi.org/10.1109/FG.2018.00083
4. Beebe, S.M., Pherson, R.H.: Cases in Intelligence Analysis: Structured Analytic Techniques in Action. CQ Press (2014)
5. Briggs, S., Drozdal, J., Peveler, M., Balagyozyan, L., Sun, C., Su, H.: Enabling sensemaking for intelligence analysis in a multi-user, multimodal cognitive and immersive environment. In: ACHI 2019 The Twelfth International Conference on Advances in Computer-Human Interactions, (2019)
6. Peveler, M., et al.: Translating the pen and paper brainstorming process into a cognitive and immersive system. In: Kurosu, M. (ed.) HCII 2019. LNCS, vol. 11567, pp. 366–376. Springer, Cham (2019). https://doi.org/10.1007/978-3-030-22643-5_28

7. Folker Jr, R.D.: Intelligence analysis in theater joint intelligence centers: an experiment in applying structured methods. Joint Military Intelligence College. Washington DC Center For Strategic (2000)
8. Reinig, B.A., Briggs, R.O., Nunamaker, J.F.: On the measurement of ideation quality. J. Manage. Inf. Syst. **23**, 143–161 (2007). https://doi.org/10.2753/MIS0742-1222230407
9. Briggs, R.O., Reinig, B.A., Shepherd, M.M., Yen, J., Nunameker, J.F.: Quality as a function of quantity in electronic brainstorming. Proc. Thirtieth Hawaii Int. Conf. Syst. Sci. **2**, 94–103 (1997). https://doi.org/10.1109/HICSS.1997.665465
10. Briggs, R.O., Kolfschoten, G., de Vreede, G.-J. Albrecht, C., Dean, D.R., Lukosch, S.: A seven-layer model of collaboration: separation of concerns for designers of collaboration systems. ICIS 2009 Proceedings, p. 26 (2009)
11. Fjermestad, J., Hiltz, S.R.: A descriptive evaluation of group support systems case and field studies. J. Manage. Inf. Syst. **17**, 115–159 (2001)
12. Pinsonneault, A., Barki, H., Gallupe, R.B., Hoppen, N.: Electronic brainstorming: the illusion of productivity. Inf. Syst. Res. **10**, 110–133 (1999)
13. Grisé, M.-L., Gallupe, R.B.: Information overload: addressing the productivity paradox in face-to-face electronic meetings. J. Manage. Inf. Syst. **16**, 157–185 (1999)
14. Dornburg, C.C., Stevens, S.M., Hendrickson, S.M.L., Davidson, G.S.: Improving extreme-scale problem solving: assessing electronic brainstorming effectiveness in an industrial setting. Hum. Factors **51**, 519–527 (2009). https://doi.org/10.1177/0018720809343587
15. Widjaja, W., Yoshii, K., Haga, K., Takahashi, M.: Discusys: multiple user real-time digital sticky-note affinity-diagram brainstorming system. Procedia Comput. Sci. **22**, 113–122 (2013). https://doi.org/10.1016/j.procs.2013.09.087
16. Jensen, M.M., Thiel, S.-K., Hoggan, E., Bødker, S.: Physical versus digital sticky notes in collaborative ideation. Comput. Support. Coop. Work (CSCW) **27**(3-6), 609–645 (2018). https://doi.org/10.1007/s10606-018-9325-1
17. Majd, S., Marie-Hélène, A., Véronique, M., Claude, M., David, V.: Integration of brainstorming platform in a system of information systems. In: Proceedings of the 8th International Conference on Management of Digital EcoSystems. pp. 166–173. ACM (2016)
18. Mistry, P., Maes, P.: Augmenting sticky notes as an I/O interface. In: Stephanidis, C. (ed.) UAHCI 2009. LNCS, vol. 5615, pp. 547–556. Springer, Heidelberg (2009). https://doi.org/10.1007/978-3-642-02710-9_61
19. Hall, W.M., Citrenbaum, G.: Intelligence analysis: how to think in complex environments: how to think in complex environments. ABC-CLIO (2009)
20. Smallman, H.S., St. John, M.: Macrocognition in Teams: Theories and Methodologies. CRC Press (2017)
21. Structured analytic techniques for improving intelligence analysis. (2009)
22. Meister, J.C., Horstmann, J., Petris, M., Jacke, J., Bruck, C., Schumacher, M., Flüh, M.: CATMA 6.0.0 (Version 6.0.0)
23. Primer, A.T.: Structured analytic techniques for improving intelligence analysis, (2009). http://doi.apa.org/get-pe-doi.cfm?doi=10.1037/e587102011-001https://doi.org/10.1037/e587102011-001
24. Riva, G., Davide, F., Ijsselsteijn, W.A., Grigorovici, D.: Persuasive effects of presence in immersive virtual environments. (2003)
25. Sohrabi, S., Riabov, A., Katz, M., Udrea, O.: An AI planning solution to scenario generation for enterprise risk management. In: AAAI (2018)

Open Source DMIs: Towards a Replication Certification for Online Shared Projects of Digital Musical Instruments

Filipe Calegario[1,2]([✉]), João Tragtenberg[2], Johnty Wang[3], Ivan Franco[3], Eduardo Meneses[3], and Marcelo M. Wanderley[3]

[1] MusTIC, Centro de Informática, Universidade Federal de Pernambuco, Recife, Brazil
fcac@cin.ufpe.br
[2] Batebit Artesania Digital, Recife, Brazil
[3] IDMIL, CIRMMT, McGill University, Montreal, Canada
http://mustic.cin.ufpe.br
http://batebit.cc
http://idmil.org

Abstract. The internet has allowed for the flourishing of several shared projects. Developers from different parts of the world can work asynchronously on the same project, formulating ideas, and implementing complex systems. For remote collaboration in software development projects, sharing information and code becomes more straightforward, given the textual and abstract nature of the source. However, for projects involving hardware and physical artifacts development, it is necessary to have a more detailed level of information, since many other characteristics of the project need to be covered in the documentation. In the case of digital musical instruments, which are physical artifacts aimed at musical interaction, we have several aspects such as mechanical structure, electronic, programming, mapping, and sound design. Currently, there are few initiatives in the literature that indicate possible ways to guide designers and developers in the process of documenting the replication of their projects. Given the importance of advancing the area of new interfaces for musical expression, the diffusion of ideas among innovators, and the popularization of innovative musical instruments, this paper discusses the challenges of sharing DMIs. Our main goal is to propose a checklist to help designers and developers to share their projects to increase the potential for replicability. As future steps, we hope to move towards a certificate that guarantees how replicable a given project is considering makers other than its developers. Besides, with better documentation and a more organized sharing process, we expect to encourage designers and developers to reproduce existing DMIs in different parts of the world so we could understand the adoption of these devices in different contexts and cultures. This paper presents a step towards making the projects more accessible to make the DMI community more connected.

C. Stephanidis et al. (Eds.): HCII 2020, LNCS 12423, pp. 84–97, 2020.
https://doi.org/10.1007/978-3-030-60114-0_5

Keywords: Open source share standard · Digital musical instrument · Development process

1 Introduction

In today's connected world, several projects are developed asynchronously and in distinct geographic parts. Open-source initiatives for sharing source code and documentation play a significant role in project development [7,18]. Package managers, repositories, virtual environments, and containers such as npm[1], $PyPI$[2], $GitHub$[3], and $Docker$[4] accelerate software development and allow developers from all around the world to run pieces of software seamlessly with few configuration requirements and, consequently, easily collaborate. Parametric design software empowers designers, developers, and end-users to adapt 3D models to their contexts and needs. Digital fabrication techniques such as laser cutting and 3D printing enable physical realization through digitally shared models. Additionally, there is an abundance of affordable and fast alternatives to produce printed circuit boards. This conjecture makes it possible to not only share pieces of code but also distribute complete instructions for replicating a particular physical artifact with a fine-grain level of detail.

All the mentioned collaborative tools can be used to aid in Digital Musical Instrument (DMI) design. DMI is a class of physical interactive objects that comprise a gestural control unit, mapping strategy, and sound synthesis module [11]. The development process of DMIs presents an exciting field of study as it covers different areas of skills that demand diverse approaches to share code, diagrams, schematics, 3D models, and document the replication process as a whole.

A number of aspects need to be considered for DMI design [3]:

- *Mechanical structure* (shape, color, appearance),
- *Electronics* (circuits, sensors, power unit, microcontrollers, actuators, communication modules, storage modules),
- *Programming* (firmware, software, communication protocol),
- *Mapping* (connections, data processing, data modification), and
- *Sound design* (synthesizers, DAWs, VSTs, samplers, drum machines).

A structural view of these aspects can be seen in Fig. 1. When the instrument design is a collaborative project, information regarding those aspects must be accessible to all participants, hence the necessity to adapt and use collaborative tools in DMI design.

---

[1] https://www.npmjs.com/.

[2] https://pypi.org/.

[3] https://github.com/.

[4] https://www.docker.com/.

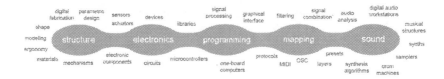

Fig. 1. Different Skills in DMI Development Process

2 Motivation

While there are many researchers, startups, and makers experimenting and developing novel musical instruments, there is often little communication between these innovators.

Although there are few examples, the reach of scientific publications on DMIs does not usually extrapolate academic audience. Additionally, startup companies are market-driven entities. In other words, they are limited to what sells well and interested in products that are compelling to a particular market. Considering the maker community, the driving force for individuals is based on what satisfies her or his needs. Thus their focus is specific. In sum, the paradigms are quite different from each community [10], but through an open innovation perspective, these communities can share knowledge and experience.

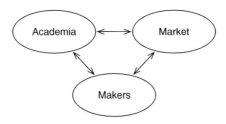

Fig. 2. Integration of DMI's innovators

We believe that, by sharing projects, these three innovators (Fig. 2) can collaborate, distribute technology, code, design files, and learn from each other.

3 Design Process and Replication

The DMI design process is reportedly idiosyncratic in literature [1]. Usually, the instrument is conceived and developed for one performer, or a person plays the roles of performer and designer. The process often varies from the user's context and intention, and, typically, there is little or no structured thinking about the process. We could speculate that can be the reason why many digital musical instruments are not adequately documented.

In an attempt to formalize the mindset, we borrow definitions from design theory for DMI context [5]. So we could formulate that the design process of a digital musical instrument is a set of steps that the design team, along with users, follow to achieve the desired result. The desired result is not an unchangeable monolith, but it evolves during the exploration and experimentation throughout the project. The process is, therefore, often cyclic and incremental. Features can always be improved from one cycle to another.

Inspired by processes from different areas such as engineering design, mechanical design, creative thinking, user-centered design, and innovation, we present a description of a general design process [2] is presented in Fig. 3. In the Definition phase, the team typically works on understanding the concepts behind the artifact, such as stakeholders, scenarios, shared knowledge of the area, the user's intention, and context of use. It defines the restrictions that comprise the project's design space. In Idea Exploration, the team explores possible paths in the design space, generating and selecting ideas that conform to the user's intentions and contexts of use. During Prototyping, the team realizes the abstract ideas into an artifact that can be utilized and tested, with which the user can interact. Finally, in the Evaluation, the team validates whether the artifact is adequate to the user's intention and context of use, rising corrections, enhancements, and modifications for the next cycles.

After finishing one or more cycles, the design team has a set of outcomes from the process typically. For instance, code, diagrams, schematics, 3D models, in sum, assets used to represent ideas. Working prototypes, general notes, and audiovisual records are also typical outputs from some cycles of the design process.

Although the process is cyclic and incremental, there is a moment that the implemented features partially fulfill the essential user's requirements. This is the moment in which the design team defines the release candidate that works as a project snapshot, i.e., the current status is satisfactory; therefore, one should save it. In Software Development, the semantic versioning[5] is commonly used to define major, minor, and fixing versions of the system.

Replication is the process of reproducing the project outside the environment in which it was developed. The replication documentation consolidates the project assets, working prototypes, general notes, and audiovisual records in a way to facilitate the comprehension of the project by an outside maker. After the development, the replication documentation is a reflection of the process and all the steps that were taken until the current version of the system. Besides, it is an empathy exercise, since the design team must put themselves into the maker's position, considering their possible lack of specific skills, mistakes, misinterpretations. It is a process of communication that can be arduous and more difficult than only implementing the system.

The design team should not only think about the maker and the replication process but also consider the operating instructions, which should also be explained. To raise the complexity, besides presenting a possible way of replicating a project,

---

[5] https://semver.org/.

the design of the project can allow for individual modifications. With the parametric design, the designer does not define the final object but a set of rules. The users, in their turn, manipulate parameters that, along with the rules, produce the final artifact.

In sum, the replication documentation is a deep dive into the abstract parts of the developed project and constitutes an essential step for making projects accessible to makers and users. In this paper, we intend to reflect on the documentation process for the replication of a digital musical instrument, discuss possible challenges and present a checklist to help designers and developers on the arduous process of documenting for replication.

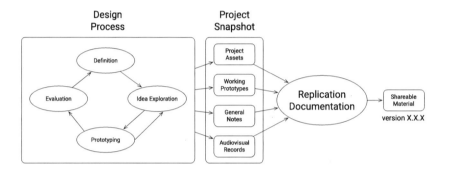

Fig. 3. Design process and replication documentation

4   Objective and Proposal

The main objective of this paper is to aid digital musical instrument designers to share their projects by providing ways that other people can reproduce them with the least effort in the shortest time possible.

This paper discusses approaches to the process of online sharing and documenting collaborative open-source projects of digital musical instruments. We examine the development process of DMIs and how can we expose the steps of this process into the structure of the source code repositories and how can we standardize the documentation to ease the comprehension and communication with collaborators.

We based our proposal on: 1) the previous experiences that our laboratories and research groups had during the development of different DMIs: the T-Stick [8,13], the Giromin [17], the Controllerzinho [3], the Pandivá [1], TumTá and Pisada [16]; and 2) DMI related toolkits (Probatio [2,4], Prynth [6]). The collaboration and attempted DMIs reproductions are the main motivation to develop this project.

As a contribution, we expect to offer initial guidelines and recommendations for DMI designers to share their projects, focusing on replication.

Inspired by the open-source hardware certification, we propose a checklist for sharing online projects in the form of questions. The checklist follows the different areas related to the musical instrument development process.

5 Inspirations

Although there are several examples in software development, the DMI development process presents a few structured attempts to organize how a project is shared and how the documentation covers the replication or reproduction of the artifact [6,12,14,15,19]. Due to the different sets of skills and their specific related tools, sharing and documentation is a challenge. The majority of the New Interfaces for Musical Expression (NIME) papers, for example, are concerned with a functional description, but only a few presents the means to reproduce the artifact. Consequently, this situation hinders communication between the project's collaborators or makers interested in replicating the instrument.

5.1 Open Source Hardware Certification

Regarding the lack of a standard definition of what an Open Source Hardware (OSHW) is, there have been many initiatives to create a certification program related to specific definitions. The Open Source Hardware Association (OSHWA)[6] holds a community ran a model of advocates for OSHW which helps the community to build a standard definition and stimulates designers to understand what they could and should do to release their projects as OSHW.

As stated in the association's website: "Open Source Hardware (OSHW) is a term for tangible artifacts – machines, devices, or other physical things – whose design has been released to the public in such a way that anyone can make, modify, distribute, and use those things. This definition is intended to help provide guidelines for the development and evaluation of licenses for Open Source Hardware."

The certification process is free and gives the product a unique ID for each OSHW. The benefit of the certification is that it helps the maker community to discern projects that are open from those that are only advertised as opened but have incomplete documentation. For instance, when the designer shares only a few low-resolution images of the PCB schematics instead of the actual CAD design files or the GERBER files.

Below, we present the guidelines organized by OSHWA to help the developers organize their projects to the certification process.

- **Documentation**
    - Have you made your original design files publicly available?
    - Have you made any auxiliary design files publicly available? (optional)
    - Have you made a bill of materials publicly available?

---

[6] https://www.oshwa.org/.

- Have you made photos of your product at various stages of assembly publicly available? (optional)
- Have you made any instructions or other explanations publicly available? (optional)
- Have you properly licensed your design files so that others may reproduce or build upon them?
- **Hardware**
  - Have you provided links to your original design files for your hardware on the product itself or its documentation?
  - Have you made it easy to find your original design files from the website for a product?
  - Have you clearly indicated which parts of a product are open-source (and which are not)?
  - Have you applied an open-source license to your hardware?
- **Software**
  - Have you made your project's software publicly available?
  - Have you applied an open-source license to your software?

They also suggest good practices after the certification process like labeling the hardware with a version number or release date, so people can match the physical object with the corresponding version of its design files and to use the OSHWA certification mark logo.

All the so far 395 licensed OSHW projects can be easily found in their website[7], helping makers to find projects they can make or modify as well as giving a big set of examples of ways to structure a new OSHW project for the community.

5.2   Other Initiatives

Maker Community: The Maker community is a substantial inspiration to our effort with motivating initiatives such as *Instructables'*[8], *Sparkfun's*[9], *Adafruit's*[10] tutorials; *Thingisverse's*[11] online 3D printing models sharing, and *Autodesk Fusion 360's*[12] online parametric design editor to name a few. Maker communities usually aim to provide images, videos, schematics, organized source code, and well-prepared content. There is also a focus on encapsulating technical details for beginners: Adafruit and Sparkfun have their libraries for Arduino, for example.

---

[7] https://certification.oshwa.org/list.html.
[8] https://www.instructables.com.
[9] https://www.sparkfun.com/.
[10] https://www.adafruit.com/.
[11] https://www.thingiverse.com/.
[12] https://www.autodesk.com/products/fusion-360/overview.

NIMEhub Initiative: The NIMEhub workshop [9] presented in 2016 during the International Conference on New Interfaces for Musical Expression reinforces the importance of the discussion about the replication process of Digital Musical Instruments in the context of the NIME community. Unfortunately, the results of the workshop discussion were not published. It was mentioned the use of standard approaches to share DMI designs, and we could see little advances towards the main subject of the workshop in the context of the NIME community.

6 Case Studies

In this section, we present projects developed by our research groups and laboratories, with which we could reflect upon the replication documentation process.

6.1 T-Stick

The T-Stick is a family of DMIs designed and developed since 2006 by Joseph Malloch and D. Andrew Stewart at the Input Devices and Music Interaction Laboratory (IDMIL) at McGill University. Expert performers and composers

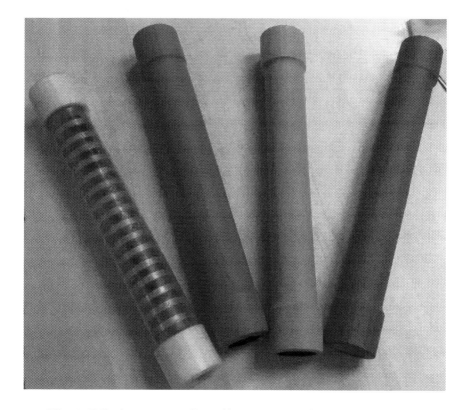

Fig. 4. T-Stick sopraninos (http://www.idmil.org/project/the-t-stick/).

have used the instrument as part of their musical practice, including D. Andrew Stewart and Fernando Rocha. It has been used in dozens of public appearances in countries such as Canada, the USA, Portugal, Brazil, Norway, and Italy.

From 2006 to 2018, there were no major hardware or software upgrades or modifications in the T-Stick. In 2018, Alex Nieva performed a significant upgrade [13], replacing hardware components for more modern versions, more noticeably the replacement of the accelerometer for a complete Inertial Measurement Unit (IMU), containing accelerometer, gyroscope, and magnetometer. The software was also revised to run on more recent microcontrollers, although the most significant modification was the ability to work wirelessly.

All documentation regarding the T-Stick development before Alex Nieva's research, as well as building and usage instructions, could only be found at academic publications and through IDMIL's archives. In October 2018, during the upgrading process, Nieva created a public repository[13] to organize documentation and make it publicly available. The documentation included the first version of the building instructions for the T-Stick Sopranino Wi-Fi, and it was used by McGill students in 2018 to build four instruments, as an assignment for a Music Technology course taught by Marcelo Wanderley in the same year.part o.

The building assignment was repeated in 2019 under the supervision of Eduardo Meneses. During this second iteration, Meneses used the students' feedback to improve the building instructions, tracking common mistakes that happened due to gaps in the documentation. The official T-Stick Github repository can be accessed at https://github.com/IDMIL/TStick.

6.2   Prynth

Prynth is a framework for the development of self-contained DMIs created by Ivan Franco at IDMIL and released to the public in September 2016. It started as a set of tools and procedures for embedded DMIs but soon evolved to become an open-source DMI development kit.

The framework is composed of hardware and software components that, once assembled, form a compact base system for sensor signal acquisition and audio synthesis. The sensor signal acquisition is made through a series of daughter-boards that sit on top of the Raspberry Pi, allowing for the direct connection of up to 80 analog sensors and 48 digital sensors. The audio engine is based on the programming language SuperCollider, and the user can interactively program new synthesis and interaction algorithms through a browser-based text editor.

Prynth is a tool for intermediate DMI developers. It assumes a considerable familiarity with electronics assembly and computer programming. The user is responsible for tasks such as PCB manufacturing, soldering components, installing custom Linux images, flashing micro-controller firmware, and programming the DMI interaction and audio synthesis in SuperCollider.

---

[13] The first T-Stick public repository can be accessed at https://github.com/alexnieva/TStick.

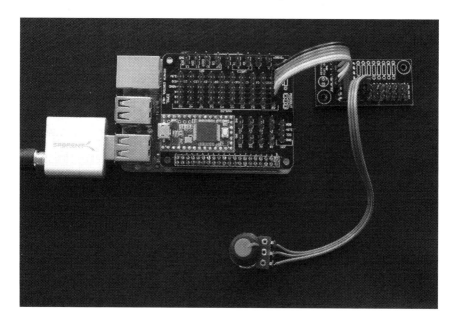

Fig. 5. Prynth board (https://prynth.github.io/).

The project's website contains a section titled *create*, divided into an overview of the framework, downloads, and documentation.

The downloads section contains links to the PCB board designs (distributed both in Eagle and Gerber file formats), the microcontroller software, and a ready-to-use Linux image file for the Raspberry Pi. Those that which to install Prynth on top of a previous Linux system can refer to the raw installation instructions on the project's Github repository.

The documentation is written in the form of a step-by-step *cookbook*, divided into chapters that include PC board assembly, flashing software/firmware, and the operation of Prynth's custom software to control the signal acquisition system and interact with SuperCollider. Finally, a set of "Hello World" examples show the path from connecting sensors to mapping them to SuperCollider audio examples. All of this information is relayed through text, screenshots, and high-resolution macro photography.

Prynth was covered in articles by specialized online publications such as Fact Magazine, Hackaday, and Synthopia, which triggered the quick growth of a user community. Some of those users reported having successfully built their first DMIs, much of it due to the quality of the documentation and support materials found on the project's website. Other users have also reported successfully modifying parts of Prynth to best suit their particular needs.

The Prynth webpage can be found at https://prynth.github.io/.

7   Open Source DMI

In this section, we discuss the concept of Open Source DMI and present the checklist that we hope can help to achieve a basic sharing structure for DMI projects.

7.1   Definition

An Open Source DMI is a digital musical instrument with a well-documented project, that is easy to reproduce or modify, accessible in terms of cost and components availability, and is obtainable publicly for any use. To this end, we have started developing a checklist that attempts to generate a comprehensive set of elements to support the process of replication.

7.2   Checklist

The checklist consists of a set of questions based on each step of the DMI development process and the previously discussed challenges, especially inspired by the OSHWA certification checklist:

General Aspects

- Is there a structured and organized website concentrating all the documentation and information about the project?
- Is there an open communication channel with the developers or makers to ask questions during the making process? (e.g., forum, e-mail)
- Is there a clear overview architecture diagram with the description of each part's details?
- Is there a description of the expected skills and resources required to realize the project?
- Does the documentation highlight critical, uncertain, difficult, or potentially confusing parts of the process of realization?

Hardware (Mechanical Structure and Electronics)

- Is the hardware made out of an accessible consumer product? (e.g., Bela, LEGO, Arduino, hardware synthesizers)
- Are the original design files for the instrument's structure and electronic circuits publicly available (e.g., CAD files, schematics, technical diagrams)?
- Is the bill of materials publicly available and accessible? (e.g., links, prices, detailed descriptions)
- Are there any instructions and explanations about the process of making the instrument's physical structure and electronic circuits publicly available? (e.g., wiki, Instructables, tutorials, images or videos about the process)
- Is there a source code version control publicly available for all the hardware and the mechanical structure? (e.g., git or SVN repositories)

- Are the design files licensed in a way that others may reproduce or build upon them? (e.g., Creative Commons)
- Is the construction and hardware design under an open-source license (e.g., CERN, TAPR, Solder Pad) so others may reproduce or build upon it?

Software

- Is the software/firmware publicly available and with an open-source license?
- Is there a source code version control publicly available for the software? (e.g., git or SVN repositories)
- Does the instrument rely on an easily accessible proprietary software? (e.g., Max/MSP, Ableton Live, VST Plugins)
- Are the support and configuration files publicly available? (e.g., mappings, software configuration diagrams, audio samples, presets, DAW project files)
- Are the presets, files, and projects licensed in a publicly available license (e.g., copyrighted audio samples)?
- Does the instrument use a standard communication protocol? (e.g., MIDI, OSC or Libmapper)

8   Future Works

By reflecting upon the digital musical instrument design and development process, we expect to improve the proposed checklist to achieve a certification level for DMI projects. Depending on the content and on how well the documentation is presented, the project would receive the title of Open Source DMI. We could also think on a scale that could classify the level of potential replication of the DMI. For example, if there were pieces of evidence that a different group apart from the initial design team replicated the DMI, that project would receive more points. The implementation of this system still an open question. However, we hope to have given an important step towards a more reliable way of sharing DMI projects to strengthen our community.

9   Conclusion

This paper is a step towards an actual standard to share DMI open-source project. The main contribution of this paper is to continue the discussion about sharing DMI designs around the world and how the process can be improved. We focused on discussing different challenges concerning the sharing of physical artifacts online. We presented an emerging checklist in the form of questions that serves as a starting point for designers interested in sharing their projects. Refining this list can lead to a more formal certification process that provides a universal set of standards. At the same time, since the nature of such projects are fundamentally creative in nature, care should be taken to tread the fine line between enforcing standards for the sake of reproducibility and hindering the creative process.

References

1. Barbosa, J., Calegario, F., Tragtenberg, J., Cabral, G., Ramalho, G., Wanderley, M.M.: Designing DMIs for popular music in the Brazilian northeast: lessons learned. In: Proceedings of the International Conference on New Interfaces for Musical Expression, pp. 277–280. Bâton Rouge, US (2015)
2. Calegario, F.: Designing Digital Musical Instruments Using Probatio: A Physical Prototyping Toolkit. Computational Synthesis and Creative Systems. Springer, Cham (2019). https://doi.org/10.1007/978-3-030-02892-3
3. Calegario, F., Tragtenberg, J., Cabral, G., Ramalho, G.: Batebit controller: popularizing digital musical instruments' development process. In: Proceedings of the 17th Brazilian Symposium on Computer Music. São João del-Rei, Brazil (2019)
4. Calegario, F., Wanderley, M.M., Huot, S., Cabral, G., Ramalho, G.: A method and toolkit for digital musical instruments: generating ideas and prototypes. IEEE MultiMedia **24**(1), 63–71 (2017). https://doi.org/10.1109/MMUL.2017.18
5. Cross, N.: Engineering Design Methods: Strategies for Product Design, 3rd edn. Wiley, Hoboken (2000). https://doi.org/10.1016/0261-3069(89)90020-4
6. Franco, I., Wanderley, M.M.: Prynth: a framework for self-contained digital music instruments. In: Aramaki, M., Kronland-Martinet, R., Ystad, S. (eds.) CMMR 2016. LNCS, vol. 10525, pp. 357–370. Springer, Cham (2017). https://doi.org/10.1007/978-3-319-67738-5_22
7. Kochhar, P.S., Kalliamvakou, E., Nagappan, N., Zimmermann, T., Bird, C.: Moving from closed to open source: observations from six transitioned projects to github. IEEE Trans. Softw. Eng. 1 (2019). https://doi.org/10.1109/TSE.2019.2937025
8. Malloch, J., Wanderley, M.M.: The T-stick : from musical interface to musical instrument. In: Proceedings of the 2007 Conference on New Interfaces for Musical Expression (NIME07), pp. 66–69 (2007). https://doi.org/10.1145/1279740.1279751
9. McPherson, A., Berdahl, E., Jensenius, A.R., Lyons, M.J., Bukvic, I.I., Knudsen, A.: NIMEhub: toward a repository for sharing and archiving instrument designs (workshop proposal). In: Proceedings of the International Conference on New Interfaces for Musical Expression. Queensland Conservatorium Griffith University (2016)
10. McPherson, A., Morreale, F., Harrison, J.: Musical instruments for novices: comparing NIME, HCI and crowdfunding approaches. In: Holland, S., Mudd, T., Wilkie-McKenna, K., McPherson, A., Wanderley, M.M. (eds.) New Directions in Music and Human-Computer Interaction. SSCC, pp. 179–212. Springer, Cham (2019). https://doi.org/10.1007/978-3-319-92069-6_12
11. Miranda, E.R., Wanderley, M.M.: New Digital Musical Instruments: Control and Interaction Beyond the Keyboard. A-R Editions, Middleton (2006)
12. Morreale, F., Moro, G., Chamberlain, A., Benford, S., McPherson, A.P.: Building a maker community around an open hardware platform. In: Proceedings of the 2017 CHI Conference on Human Factors in Computing Systems, CHI 2017, pp. 6948–6959. ACM, New York (2017). https://doi.org/10.1145/3025453.3026056
13. Nieva, A., Wang, J., Malloch, J.W., Wanderley, M.M.: The t-stick: maintaining a 12 year-old digital musical instrument. In: Proceedings of the International Conference on New Interfaces for Musical Expression (NIME), pp. 198–199. Blacksburg, USA (2018)
14. McPherson, A.P., Kim, Y.E.: The problem of the second performer: building a community around an augmented piano. Comput. Music J. **36**(4), 10–27 (2012). https://doi.org/10.1162/COMJ_a_00149

15. Tom, A.J., Venkatesan, H.J., Franco, I., Wanderley, M.: Rebuilding and reinterpreting a digital musical instrument - the sponge. In: Queiroz, M., Sedó, A.X. (eds.) Proceedings of the International Conference on New Interfaces for Musical Expression, pp. 37–42. UFRGS, Porto Alegre, Brazil, June 2019. http://www.nime.org/proceedings/2019/nime2019_paper008.pdf

16. Tragtenberg, J., Calegario, F., Cabral, G., Ramalho, G.: TumTá and pisada: two foot-controlled digital dance and music instruments inspired by popular Brazilian traditions. In: Proceedings of the 17th Brazilian Symposium on Computer Music. São João del-Rei, Brazil (2019)

17. Tragtenberg, J.N., Calegario, F., Cabral, G., Ramalho, G.L.: Towards the concept of digital dance and music instruments. In: Queiroz, M., Sedó, A.X. (eds.) Proceedings of the International Conference on New Interfaces for Musical Expression, pp. 89–94. UFRGS, Porto Alegre, Brazil, June 2019. http://www.nime.org/proceedings/2019/nime2019_paper018.pdf

18. Trimble, J., Henry, A.: Building a community of open source contributors the vision. In: Proceedings of the International Conference on Space Operations. Marseille, France (2018). https://ntrs.nasa.gov/search.jsp?R=20180003354

19. Vallis, O., Hochenbaum, J., Kapur, A.: A shift towards iterative and open-source design for musical interfaces. In: Proceedings of International Conference on New Interfaces for Musical Expression (NIME), June 2010. https://doi.org/10.5281/ZENODO.1177919

Great UI Can Promote the "Do Everything Ourselves" Economy

Christopher Fry[1] and Henry Lieberman[2]([⊠])

[1] Haddington Dynamics, Las Vegas, NV, USA
cfry@media.mit.edu
[2] MIT Computer Science and Artificial Intelligence Lab (CSAIL), Cambridge, MA 02138, USA
lieber@media.mit.edu

Abstract. As user experience designers know, great UI design isn't just a frill. It isn't just about aesthetics, and isn't just about efficiency or convenience. But what designers might not yet appreciate, is that great UI might actually hold the key to solving some of the major social problems of our time – like poverty, inequality, war, and climate change.

It might do so through an unusual route – enabling end-users to solve problems themselves that would otherwise require interactions with large industrial organizations. Great UI is now enabling "Do it Yourself" (DIY) culture, from home repair videos, to the Maker movement enabled by 3D printers. What if we could evolve these developments into a "Do Everything Ourselves" (DEO) economy? This could form the foundation of a more sustainable, more equitable economy for the new age of Artificial Intelligence and Personal Manufacturing.

Keywords: Artificial intelligence · 3D printing · User interface · User experience design · Maker movement

1 Introduction: Three Ways of Doing Things

Many human needs can be addressed in one of three different ways: First, you could try to address a problem yourself. If you need something, you could try to make it. If you need something done, you could try to do it yourself.

Another way is to have others help you. If you are blocked on some task, have a more competent friend offer advice. Families and friends routinely help each other out in this way.

The third way is to try to get "the marketplace" to take care of it. You could find a store that sells the thing you want. A professional you hire could offer a service you need. It just costs you money.

All three methods may work, and we all make use of each of them under different circumstances. But they each have their pros and cons.

Doing it yourself (DIY) has a bunch of advantages. You can customize the object or get the task done exactly the way you like it. You can work on it whenever or wherever you like. It can save you a lot of money, as your own labor is "free", and you may just

© Springer Nature Switzerland AG 2020
C. Stephanidis et al. (Eds.): HCII 2020, LNCS 12423, pp. 98–107, 2020.
https://doi.org/10.1007/978-3-030-60114-0_6

have to spend for materials. The downside is that you are limited to what you have the time, expertise, tools and raw materials to actually do yourself.

Enlisting family and friends to help you also has advantages. Now, you are not just limited to what you can do yourself, but the time and expertise of others. Both giving and receiving help can strengthen your relationship with people you care about. But the downside may be that their time and expertise (and perhaps willingness) is also limited.

The third option, the marketplace, results in a vastly expanded range of what you can do. People can specialize in making particular things or offering particular kinds of services. They can spend time improving their skills and become better at performing tasks. They can offer their expertise to anyone with the money to pay for it.

But there's the rub. Specialization of products and labor require money as a medium of exchange. Then, you need markets, stores, shopping, banks, factories, jobs, bosses, commuting, advertising, W2 forms, etc. etc. Welcome to 21st century Capitalism.

It's worked well for many people (but not everybody) for a long time. But Capitalism is already fraying around the edges, and there are serious questions about whether it is sustainable as an economic system in the long term.

One thing we'll observe is that the tradeoff between these ways of doing things depends on the state of technology at any given era. In the agricultural age, households had to be more or less self-sufficient. Growing your own food, building your own houses, and making your own clothes or other possessions, was the norm. There wasn't the option of the marketplace.

Now, most personal needs in first-world societies are taken care of by the marketplace. But in enabling the marketplace with industrial technology, somewhere along the way, we lost the DIY option. Products are now too complex for individual production; supply chains are too long; services too specialized. And individuals have to bargain to obtain them, earning money and spending wisely. They're competing with the very same marketplace that is supposed to be meeting their needs. And it's a competition that's far from fair.

But now we're entering a new era. Robots are automating production. AI is automating services. The network is facilitating sharing of expertise and building community. Individuals and small groups, armed with advanced technology, can now perform tasks that were once the province of professionals and big companies, through *disintermediation*. "Economies of scale" is not an iron clad business rule, it depends on tech. The new technologies may change the tradeoff between specialization of labor, and DIY.

Might it be possible to get the advantages of both? Can we get the customization, personalization and low cost of DIY, but be able to handle the range of products and services enabled by the collective wisdom of humanity? We think so.

But we're not quite there yet. The key to achieving this goal may well be in design of better user experience for tools and tutorials, including the tools and tutorials that help make tools and tutorials.

2 It's Now Amateur Hour

One effect of the popularization of digital technology is that it enables amateurs to perform tasks that were previously the domain of specialized experts. There are, for example, a wide range of home repair tasks that might lead many homeowners to hire a plumber or electrician. But a plethora of online videos and instructional materials now make it feasible for relatively unskilled homeowners (like your authors) to attempt the task themselves, even if they are not so-called "handymen" (amateur home improvement enthusiasts) (Fig. 1).

Fig. 1. Online tutorials from YouTube and WikiHow.

Graphic designers and user interface designers have experienced similar transformation to the handyman in their profession. It was once absolutely necessary to hire a professional graphic designer if one were preparing a publication-quality book, poster, or ad. Now, these (or their online versions) can be prepared by relatively unskilled authors using graphic editors and layout programs, if the task is not too complicated or demanding. In some professions, this caused a crisis, as professionals feared they would be put out of work. Indeed, there were many instances in which they lost business they otherwise might have gotten.

But plumbers and graphic designers have not disappeared. While routine tasks may now be handled by the customers themselves, professionals are still needed to handle more complicated tasks (or to clean up the disastrous mess left by an amateur who failed). Graphic designers can now focus on aesthetic decisions instead of the mechanics of printing processes.

Professionals seem to have made peace with the influx of amateurs. Now, many of the tutorials are authored and promoted by the professionals themselves. They educate potential customers about the subtleties of the task they are about to undertake, and build confidence in the DIY'ers competence. It can also be good for business of the pro. If you are indeed in need of a graphic designer, why not choose the one who helped you learn about the graphic program you're now using?

The process of better user interfaces replacing professionals has a long history. Telephone operators, gas station attendants and travel agents have all succumbed to do-it-yourself user interfaces. As the user interface to authoring tools and the how-to guides themselves improve, the breadth of activities they encompass can expand because domain experts who aren't programmers will be able to produce great UI experiences.

2.1 With a Little Help from My Friends

An intermediate scenario between doing this totally by yourself, or handing it off completely to a professional, is a *cooperative* approach. You can attempt a task by yourself, but then, if you run into trouble or need expertise beyond your current capability, you can reach out to others to collaborate with you on the solution.

This can take the form of a *panic button* on the DIY interface, that calls a helper. The helper can be a member of your friends or family circles, or a professional. Through *telepresence*, the helper can help as if he or she were in the room with you.

We need better interfaces for collaborative and remote problem solving. It's not just a matter of transmitting video and audio. The panic button could send the helper a history of the DIY'ers previous attempts to solve the problem and the current state of the work objects. It could bring up documentation, plans, schematics, costs, etc. in a just-in-time manner.

It's already starting to happen that professional services are marketed and/or delivered over the net. For some, it can replace onsite work, and its overhead, entirely. Our conventional plumber has to:

- Get and maintain a plumber's license.
- Drive to work and back.
- Drive to each work site and back
- Have a receptionist for scheduling jobs
- Have an accountant for billing, taxes, payroll and managing a bank account.
- Order, inventory and stock the truck daily with the right parts for a job.
- Find the customers (via advertising or other means) in addition to performing the actual work.

Many of these steps can be eliminated by online interfaces. The plumber doesn't have to hire an electrician, or a contractor, an accountant, etc., because all of those services have similar DIY interfaces.

3 Why Don't More People DIY?

To do a given task, you need:

- Know how
- Parts and/or raw materials
- Tools
- Time

and, most people, for numerous tasks they want to accomplish, are lacking in one or more of these needs. If we can supply these needs, more people could DIY for a much wider range of tasks. Internet resources, like the videos above and special-interest social media communities, can provide the know-how. What about the other requirements?

Parts and tools can be problematic. Many modern devices require specialized parts and tools that only professionals have. But help is on the way.

We'll need rather advanced "printers" that cannot just perform additive manufacturing, but subtractive, casting, origami, and pick and place. We call such tools *personal factories*. We'll need some specialized machines, such as contained aeroponic boxes for growing food efficiently without pesticides or weeds. Such specialized tools can be produced in a personal factory.

Once a 3D printer has enough capability to print out all the parts for another 3D printer, then they will be "reproducible" by DiY'ers and their effective cost will drop to the point where they will be accessible to all.

Going forward, we can try to rethink the design of products and services to put a priority on accessibility of parts and tools. We can prioritize using readily-available materials instead of special-purpose exotic substances. We can prioritize maintainability and repairability rather than planned obsolescence of products. We can end the so-called *connector conspiracy* that is constantly introducing new proprietary and incompatible interfaces, in order to trap the user into expensive additional purchases.

Finally, time. Right now, many middle-class professionals don't have the time to handle home repair, growing food or other tasks. But as the scope of DIY methodology increases, it will begin to encroach upon professional services. Perhaps to the extent that for increasing numbers of people, the value of DIY activities can increase to the extent that they will be competitive with earning a living in the marketplace. More on that shortly.

As we learn more about psychology, both cognitive and perceptual, we have new theoretical tools to enhance learning/know-how. As our communications and information presentation technologies improve, we will have new ways to deliver our advances in learning psychology. As our manufacturing technologies improve, we will have new ways to deliver hardware. If we are strategic, these techniques can save human labor, the greatest cost of pretty much anything.

4 Augmented Reality Brings Expertise to the Masses

Here's a future scenario (Fig. 2):

You're wearing corrective eyeglasses as usual, but these are fitted with a programmable transparent Augmented Reality (AR) display and a couple cameras to let a computer (or a remote person) see what you're seeing. We also have mics and earphones for audio I/O including speech synthesis and recognition. This is nothing that hasn't been imagined millions of times before now [1], and implemented to a weak degree.

The computer connected to this I/O has a model of your house. Every house design should be preserved for the actual occupants of the house to take advantage of, instead of disappearing in the architect's trash can.

A water pipe in your house springs a leak. You look at the water.

You: "Looks like a water leak." Your computer examines its 3D database of your house, sees "behind the wall" and notices a copper pipe with a straight connection fitting at that location.

Computer: "Shut off the water to the house in the basement." You go to the basement. A big green arrow in virtual space points at the valve, with a circular arrow telling you which direction to turn it in (clockwise).

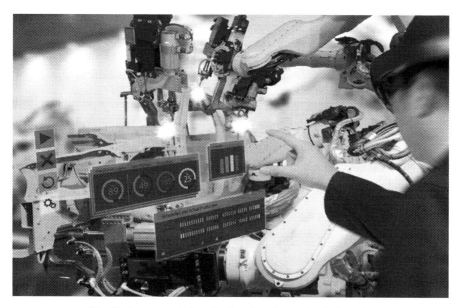

Fig. 2. An augmented reality interface for mechanical repair.

Computer: "You'll need a crowbar, a wrench and a new washer. You have the tools in your basement. You have the raw materials to print the washer. Printing will take 4 min. Shall I begin?"

You: "Yes". The computer knows about your 3D printer and what materials you have available.

A few minutes later. *Computer*: "The washer print is done." You go to your basement. The washer is outlined in green in your AR glasses. You pick the washer off of the printer. Looking at your tool shelf, the crowbar and adjustable wrench are outlined in green.

Computer: "Open up the wall with the crowbar. Example video *here*. You touch the virtual *here* with your real hand and watch the 2 min video. You open the wall and replace the washer. *Computer*: "Are you ready to patch the wall?"…

Our AR headset delivers the know-how. Our connected 3D printer makes parts for us, and can even make tools if we lack them. Even with such hi-tech we're not forecasting the manufacture of "time" (sorry). But if you had to find a plumber, schedule a time, wait for him to show up, be there while he's working and work for the money to pay him, perhaps the AR system we describe *does* save you time, even if you're several times slower on the actual task than a pro would be.

We need authoring tools to create the Augmented Reality how-to guides. These are similar to Software Development tools or authoring software. Difficult to make easy, but doable, especially with the collaboration of UI experts. They too will give away their expertise, if UI design is their passion and they have a personal factory to make what they themselves need.

First, one of the strongest motivations of people is to have an audience. Authoring a Great UI tutorial is a way to get an audience. Now for the real-time use of an expert for a specific situation, we'd have to have experts sign up for time slots and be "on call". An expert would do it just because most people actually like to help others. Those that don't, won't sign up to be on call. But we're guessing many will. We can give such helpful pros merit badges on top of the appreciation their "students" will show.

Medical pros now agree to the Hippocratic oath: "I will respect the hard-won scientific gains of those physicians in whose steps I walk, and gladly share such knowledge as is mine with those who are to follow". If a doctor doesn't have to go to the office, fill out insurance forms, or catch colds from their patients, we expect many will continue to fulfill their Hippocratic oath in a world of Great UI and sign up to be "on call" at least a few hours a week.

Finally, we need people to actually use the authoring tools to make great directions. As above, people love to give away their expertise. Make the tools easy to learn and they will be used for car repair, house building, food growing, health-care products, clothes making, augmented reality headset fabrication, computer maintenance, and whatever else people commonly need.

5   From "Do It Yourself" to "Do Everything Ourselves"

Imagine if *everyone* could become a DIYer. Would that make, overall, a more efficient economy? The conventional answer is: *No*. Specialization of labor means expertise can be concentrated and leveraged to great effect. You don't need to be an expert to get a job done, you just need to hire someone who is. However, new technologies can change that equation.

Does this mean you trade in your 40 h work week at a "job" for a 40 h work week at home fixing leaks and weeding your garden? Perhaps. But with advanced robotics, the repetitive tasks can be automated. Such capable robots are now expensive, but we've got this great UI to help us print the parts and the tools, plus deliver the know-how to put together our robot.

5.1   Makerism: The Antidote to Capitalism

We call this economy, where everyone is a do-it-yourselfer, *Makerism* [2]. Experts and remote factories aren't necessary for making and fixing most of the things you need done because you can follow excellent directions (not today's "some assembly required" nightmares.)

Compare our conventional economy to this new Makerism economy facilitated by great UI. Which one would take the least amount of labor to produce a comfortable lifestyle for all? First, its rather improbable that Capitalism could produce a comfortable lifestyle for all since it depends on inequality. But pretend some tweaks to Capitalism could, unlikely though that now appears

In Makerism, none of that is necessary. Yes our inexperienced home-owner will take longer than a pro to make a repair. But the overhead of our conventional economy is high. Just think of the lifecycle of a part in today's economy. Parts have to be redesigned for each competing company due to intellectual property laws and trade secrets. In Makerism, designers give away their design just like most of the rest of the content of the web. Design once, use by anyone. (Designers, like other Personal Factory owners, won't need a salary.) Thingiverse.com now contains more than a million designs for 3D printed parts, all freely downloadable. Facilitating the search for the best part is another opportunity for great UI!

Once our part is manufactured in a conventional factory, it has to be packaged, warehoused, transported to a store, retailed, marketed, money has to change hands (that alone is several percent!). Then it has to get from the store to your house. All of *that* is unnecessary under Makerism too. With great UI, we believe total labor for fulfilling humans' basic needs will decrease.

5.2   Can We Sustain the Status Quo?

No. Trends like climate change are accelerating, so one way or another, the status quo will change. Can we sustain Capitalism? Capitalism drives companies to maximize profit. The easiest way to do that is to cut costs (and perhaps ignore possible environmental consequences). The largest cost for production of physical objects, is labor. This is why automation is increasing. With smarter AI and more dexterous robots, it seems unlikely that humans can compete. We don't need AI and robots to be as good as humans, just good enough at the rather constrained tasks at most jobs to be cheaper than a human's salary to displace human workers. Without paychecks, people can't buy what the automated factories are making. Ergo, Capitalism itself is unsustainable.

Most economists disagree with this prediction. But most economists are not technologists. Yes, in the past, retraining for new jobs has allowed humans to compete with machines. The new jobs have come largely from replacing manual work with knowledge work. But when knowledge work starts getting automated, the generation of new jobs to replace technological unemployment, may come to a close. Sure, there will be esoteric services that only a human can provide. But once your basic needs are met with a personal factory, how many people will want to trade their time for such esoteric services?

Imagine we're wrong. Would most people rather work at a normal job, or stay home, fix leaks and tend a garden? With advanced tools, we believe the later will take less time than a normal job, and give a person more control over their remaining time. They may join organizations whose mission statements they revere (no salary required). They may join a band, write a book, teach (or attend) courses.

But it's not just a question of which economic strategy is more efficient, specialized labor economics vs DIY. Can we sustain today's specialized labor/"free" markets? A number of trends indicate that we might not be able to. Inequality is increasing, and Capitalism does not seem to have functioning mechanisms for relieving inequality. DIY becomes not just an alternative, but perhaps the only plausible means to accomplish the broadly shared goals of individuals.

6   Education

Having "Great UI" enabling a person to complete a task is a form of "Just in Time Education". There's no need to learn or remember the task prior to performing it. There's not much utility in remembering how you did it either, because you can reuse the just-in-time tutorial should you need it again. "Just in Time Education" is ideally suited to emergencies and rare tasks where repeats are unlikely. If its an often repeated task, you learn first from the "Great UI", then you can just do it on your own.

Useful though this may be for how-to scenarios, it doesn't foster the deep understanding of processes needed to adapt them to new situations or to invent whole new processes for novel circumstances. None-the-less, when a series of just-in-time tutorials is appropriately spaced, they can promote "learning by example". By making a second tutorial different enough from the first to contain new techniques, yet similar enough to demonstrate an analogy with the first tutorial, a student may gain some ability to generalize. By stringing together an orchestrated sequence of such well-spaced tutorials, deeper understanding of processes are possible, particularly if the sequence comes "full circle", tying together the first and last of the tutorials.

6.1 Programming by Example

A clever way of reducing the need for programming skills to create an application is called "programming by example" [3]. This involves the programmer showing the computer an example of what to do, The computer records the task and can repeat it later. With a more clever development environment, the programmer can show the computer a number of examples, and the computer can take note of both similarities and differences between the examples. These can be used to generalized the automatically generated algorithm for applicability to other contexts.

We can use this programming by example technique in reverse whereby the *computer* is showing the *human* examples, so that the human can learn and generalize from them. This is sometimes called *active learning.*

7 A Call to Arms: UX Design for Economic Independence and Peer Collaboration

Think about how User Experience design would change if it adopted the agenda we outline here. The constant, of course, would be that user interface designers are, as always, concerned with providing the best possible experience for the end user.

But most user experience design today is done primarily within the context of companies who are selling physical objects or software, promoting user engagement with web sites to attract attention to advertising, or in support of professional services delivered through the marketplace. These objectives may cause a conflict of interest with the primary goal of acting on behalf of the user. Social media, for example, has the positive purpose of connecting family and friends, but interfaces are also designed to deliver user attention to annoying advertising, and to encourage addiction. In the long run, the goal of serving two masters is not sustainable.

In the world we're envisioning, the purpose of user experience is to empower the end users to be more economically independent. It is to help the users solve problems and undertake positive activities in their life, by helping with them with the expertise they need. Rather than software which simply accrues "features", software should include step-by-step tutorials that teach users what they need to know; help them debug situations when things go wrong; and include general-purpose programming languages that allow users to customize or invent solutions to novel problems. It should be seamlessly integrated into their physical, social, and computational environments.

We also need better software for collaboration. Most software now is designed either to be operated by a single individual, or to deliver a commercial product or service that a user is paying for. We need software that better enables users, both amateur, enthusiast, and professional, to collaborate on problem solving. We need software that helps small groups of users collectively make informed decisions and embark on courses of action that satisfy their interests.

The "do it yourself"er takes joy and pride in their ability to meet their own needs and the needs of people they care about. Why not bring that joy and pride to everything?

References

1. Feiner, S., Blair, M., Dorée, S.: Knowledge based augmented reality. Commun. ACM (1993)
2. Fry, C., Lieberman, H.: Why Can't We All Just Get Along? Self-published book (2018). http://www.whycantwe.org/
3. Lieberman, H. (ed.) Your Wish is My Command. Morgan Kauffman (2001)

From UCD to HCD and Beyond. Conciliating the Human Aims Between Philosophy and Design Education

Romualdo Gondomar[1] and Enric Mor[2(✉)]

[1] Elisava, Barcelona School of Design and Engineering, Barcelona, Spain
rgondomar@elisava.net
[2] Universitat Oberta de Catalunya, Barcelona, Spain
emor@uoc.edu

Abstract. User-Centered Design (UCD) is defined as both design philosophy and process. Current education in UCD and Human-Centered Design (HCD) mainly focuses on teaching the process and set of specific UCD methods. Although HCD emphasizes on human factors, both forget the philosophical approach of the human being and how they interact with the environment. This paper presents the design, implementation and evaluation of a university-level course that broadens the traditional educational perspective of UCD and HCD. The course has been carried out during 5 semesters in a university-level Digital Design degree where 500 students have participated. During this period, the course design proposal has been evaluated and improvements were made, iteratively. The academic satisfaction surveys show significant results in relation to the course design. Learners find contents interesting and useful. One of the most interesting findings is that students explicitly highlight a change of mindset about design and its values.

Keywords: User-centered design · Human-centered design · Pragmatism · Design · Education

1 Introduction

User-centered design (UCD) can be understood as a design approach that places users at the center. UCD is defined as a design philosophy that has the premise that users must be involved in all phases of the design process. Additionally, UCD is defined as a design process, a way to plan projects and a set of methods and techniques to be used in each phase [1]. Human-Centered Design (HCD) is derived from UCD and includes in an explicit way a human approach in the design process. On a more formal level, the shift from "user" to "human" is used to provide a better understanding of the importance of this perspective [2].

Currently, there is a growing demand for UCD and HCI (Human-Computer Interaction) practitioners. Among other reasons, this is due to the increasing use of digital technologies in every human activity. Digital technologies require intuitive and easy-to-use software for a large and diverse number of people and these software products

© Springer Nature Switzerland AG 2020
C. Stephanidis et al. (Eds.): HCII 2020, LNCS 12423, pp. 108–122, 2020.
https://doi.org/10.1007/978-3-030-60114-0_7

need user-centered interfaces. Besides, the UCD perspective is also expanding to other areas beyond digital products and is being applied to the design of products, services and experiences.

Consequently, there is a higher UCD and HCD education and training demand. A wide range of user and human-centered courses can be found. Mainly, these courses focus on the aspects most demanded by the industry: design processes and methods. Furthermore, aspects related to process management such as Agile and Sprint have been gradually incorporated into UCD education [3]. Thus, the courses focus mainly on design process optimization, gathering user information fast and rapid production of design solutions [4]. As a result, design courses, where the human point of view should guide the design process, are not taking into account the philosophical perspective. The philosophical contribution of the human being and its modes of interaction can help restore the design process to its original purpose, serving individual and collective human needs. Under this perspective, UCD and HCD can provide value not only to the process of developing and selling products but can provide advantages to people and society. Regarding higher education courses, we believe that a holistic, open, deep and reflective approach to UCD and HCD is required. This approach will provide students not only with the necessary professional skills but also a human perspective and a way to develop critical thinking that can guide their design practice.

This paper presents the conceptualization, design and implementation of an HCD course that, in addition to the common contents related to design processes and methods, integrates the philosophical view. The paper is organized as follows: Sect. 2 presents a review of the UCD and HCI teaching and learning. Section 3 provides a philosophical framework for HCD. Section 4 presents a course design for HCD. Section 5 provides the experience of the course and, finally, Sect. 6 presents the conclusions of the work.

2 UCD and HCD Teaching and Learning

In this section, we review some of the literature on UCD and HCD in the context of HCI education, including approaches, design processes, methods and techniques. As mentioned above, there is a growing demand for UCD and HCD courses for practitioners, especially in the software development field. Human-Computer Interaction (HCI) is a multidisciplinary and broad field in the intersection of technology, human factors and design. HCI encompasess human and user-centered design processes, approaches and methods and "focuses on people and technology to drive human-centered technology innovation" [5]. The way to approach design education within HCI has been widely studied in the literature, identifying a diversity of voices, perspectives and educational practices.

ACM SIGCHI[1] is a professional and academic community that has been key to the development of HCI. From the beginning, SIGCHI had a strategic focus on HCI education, creating the Curriculum Development Group in 1998. The result of this group was the ACM SIGCHI Curricula for Human-Computer Interaction [6], published in 1992, which marked a turning point around the definition and design of educational courses

---

[1] www.sigchi.org.

and programs in HCI. The report was not intended to be prescriptive and provided a set of guidelines and content recommendations on the HCI field in order to promote the creation of courses. The report had a big impact and many of the courses that were developed at that time in several educational institutions were based on its recommendations. It had a great impact not only in the educational field but also in defining the HCI field itself as it provided one of the definitions of HCI most widely accepted and used over time.

The ACM SIGCHI report considers design and people-through human factors- as the first priority. However, it does not address specific issues about the educational practice of design. Content recommendations have a bias towards computing systems and do not include methodological aspects related to design and the human perspective of interaction. User-centered design is conceptually addressed but a methodological proposal on how to address UCD is missing. This was not an issue for the design HCI community as the curricula report was intended to be a starting point in HCI education. Over time, ACM SIGCHI has continued to promote initiatives focusing on education research, paying special attention not only to technological development but to people: "Students need to develop methods and skills to understand current users, to investigate non-use, and to imagine future users" [5].

Recent work highlights the need to create and work around communities of practice [7] and both educators and researchers have taken advantage of the CHI conference series. Design teaching and learning are in a continuous process of change due to the structural changes in the design field and HCI, both in education and in industry. The concept of living curriculum [8] is based on the idea that HCI education is an area of interdisciplinary knowledge that changes over time and must take into account the technological progress and social and cultural changes that may accompany it.

From an educational point of view, different educational approaches and practices can be distinguished in relation to design teaching and learning. In general, two approaches are identified: formal or creative [9]. The first is based on the formal design process, taking into account its iterative character and the evidence obtained through research. The second approach focuses on the creative side of working in a design or art studio: it focuses on ideation and the process is based on the designer's experience. It is important to note that these approaches are not mutually exclusive. Courses that include the UCD perspective do not have to choose between one or the other. The literature review carried out in this work did not find a significant difference between these two approaches in courses that include UCD or HCD. It is true that UCD and HCD typically have a formal approach at the process-level where evidence is researched and used to make design decisions. Depending on the design process to follow, the creative, ideation and solution generation aspects may be present at the same level of importance like, for example, the double diamond [10] design process. However, user-centered courses either with a formal, creative or mixed-focus approach, do not always include a holistic approach to aspects related with human experience of the world and often forget the philosophical aspects that configure the knowledge of the world around us.

Currently, industry demands user-centered practitioners trained in design and development of technological products in order to achieve better business competitiveness and market success. Furthermore, there is a need to follow the speed of technological change and the pace at which people and the market adopt technologies into daily life. These requirements have led to a significant growth in the demand for agile design and development methodologies.

Agile methodologies bring significant advantages in the process of designing and developing interactive digital products. The agile approach speeds up the software development process, provides flexibility to the workflow and the decision-making process, facilitates learning from errors, and significantly reduces the documentation required for the project. The UCD and HCD design processes are embracing the agile perspective [11] and, at the same time, creating challenges and opportunities. The design processes on which the UCD and HCD are based are compatible with an agile working perspective. However, the speed of projects tends to set aside the human aspects and minimize user involvement on all the process steps-research, ideation, prototyping, evaluation- either for financial reasons or in order to achieve fast results.

Current courses on HCI and UX are adapting to this situation and they include educational content and practices about the agile approach [4, 12]. As a consequence, courses increasingly focus on gathering user information fast, design process optimization and rapid production of design solutions. This is a way of understanding design education that leaves aside the philosophical and human perspective, prioritizing economic and market aspects. Considering this situation, we propose that philosophy, as a discipline that tries to explain human nature and its action, should identify and guide the necessary connections between human beings and technology. Basically, we understand that by incorporating the way human beings conceive reality, we will be able to design objects and products that will be properly embedded in the world around us. An approach that goes beyond the immediate and direct experience and that tries to incorporate into the discipline the common and general practices is needed. To understand human experiences, we must understand the value that people give to them and how this meaning can guide their individual and collective behavior. This is the broad and extensive philosophical vision of human experience that we want to integrate into the HCI's educational practice.

3   A Philosophical Framework for HCD

Digital advances require a general, human-centered perspective, which promotes a close connection between technological devices and people's real-life conditions. "Technology must be explicit" [13] to be adjusted to the practical activity of the users and their social and cultural referential frameworks.

Pragmatism, as a philosophical movement, emphasizes the practical perspective of human beings. It establishes a general framework that allows us to understand how the human being links up to his physical and socio-cultural environment. This philosophical approach places people in a world where interactions take place and it analyzes the relationships between human reasoning processes and how they connect with their experiences. According to Peirce [14], one of the founding fathers of pragmatism, the meaning of things arises from the complete conception of its possibilities of interaction. This meaning comes from the natural, coherent, and imaginable practical effects that derive from our cognitive processes. The pragmatic maxim, which supports and summarizes this philosophical perspective, says: "Consider what effects, that might conceivably have practical bearings, we conceive the object of our conception to have. Then, our conception of these effects is the whole of our conception of the object" [14].

The pragmatic vision of the human experience of the real world establishes meaningful relationships between the set of perceived information and our constant interaction with everyday things. Our way of knowing the world is based on the associative relationship that arises from these situations and, for this reason, the experience itself acquires epistemic value [15].

The act of thinking consists in conceiving and anticipating possible results, having an entire idea of a thing and knowing how to act constitute the fundamental premises of design. Therefore, we need a catalog of available action plans in order to drive our activities. The pragmatist notion of action habit connects our knowledge with the real world and establishes a constant and fluid cycle-based unit of analysis between action and perception: "Habits are formed when similar action is repeated in similar circumstances, and when one faces these circumstances again, one can anticipate similar future experiences" [15].

If we consider the design products and services directly involved in our relationships with the real world, we can examine them as elements of mediation. Designers must be aware of the relationships that structure our knowledge of the world, how things make sense to us and how we can formalize them so that people can use them properly [16]. Objects and services report and communicate to us how we can develop our activities and meet our expectations. Designers must acquire skills that notify the intentional communication of their products. The formalization of the designs should be planned in a way that their qualitative characteristics show the necessary and appropriate information in order to allow people to use them satisfactorily [17]. The usefulness of design must reach the set of human aspects that take part in the processes of interrelationships with the environment: emotions, meaning and technology.

Pragmatists reject the idea of a fixed and finished world and consider that our reality is changing. Our experiences are regularly built on our knowledge and thoughts. Therefore, this dynamic conception of reality is based on human sociocultural practices. This premise facilitated Dewey [18] to conceive his vision of education as a continuous reconstruction of experience. The author [19] developed some basic pedagogical principles that guide learning the real conditions of action. One of the main elements of this pedagogical approach is based on habit-forming from experience: "Habits give control over the environment, the power to utilize it for human purposes. Habits take the form both of habituation, or a general and persistent balance of organic activities with the surroundings, and active capacities to readjust activity to meet new conditions".

From this conception, Dewey considers that practice constitutes an experimental knowledge that, once acquired, encourages people's capabilities and their executive competences. The formation of cognitive and operational skills of the human being depends on his continuous and diverse interaction with the real world. This interaction facilitates the connection between thought, invention and initiative and constitutes the factor that guides the observation of reality and determines the decision-making. For Dewey this involves forecasting consequences and guiding the experience: "Thinking is the accurate and deliberate instituting of connections between what is done and its consequences. It notes not only that they are connected, but the details of the connection. It makes connecting links explicit in the form of relationships. The stimulus to thinking is found when we wish to determine the significance of some act, performed or to be performed... The projection of consequences means a proposed or tentative solution" [19].

From this pragmatic perspective, the generation of knowledge from reality includes: understanding the problem, observing its circumstances, inferring conclusions and experimentally verifying the state of affairs. This knowledge will transcend its direct meaning when it is shared with the group of people who constitutes the social environment. The relationships that emerge from experience connect doing with knowing and their analysis drives the development of solution proposals. What someone learns "in the way of knowledge and skill in one situation becomes an instrument of understanding and dealing effectively with the situations which follow" [18]. Thanks to this process of understanding reality, a context of meaningful relationships can be designed and planned that expands the conventional sense of things and the possibilities for common action. According to Dewey, continuity and interaction give value to the experience and give meaning to the educational process.

An educational program for HCD based on pragmatic principles must contemplate, at least, the survey of current status: constituent elements, instruments and resources involved, and general frameworks for understanding how to approach the interaction process. A methodological program that connects: the general processes of perception and analysis of reality, the cognitive processes that link personal and relational knowledge and, finally, the means used to represent, express and communicate that reality. In brief, identify and construct conditions of understanding [20] and therefore a human-centered design program must emphasize what things mean and how they are understood in a given community.

Krippendorff [21] states that an HCD should focus its attention on how people perceive, understand and experience the artifacts. Therefore, any act of communication and design should explore how people understand technology. The challenge is to establish elements of connection between the different ways of conceiving and constructing reality. That is, a way to promote effective dialogue between the technological world and the experiential world. In order to overcome the difficulties of mutual singular understanding and social scope of the facts, it is necessary to know the interests that rule the actions of each of the communities that shape reality.

We must understand that the comprehension of technological reality is linked to the behavior that individuals develop. In other words, the design of digitized devices depends on how people conceive and interpret them, their use and how they add them into their world of relationships [22]. In order to bridge the gaps in understanding, we must try to integrate the interests of the technological community, governed mainly by objective criteria with the expectations of people, directed by subjective interests. The transfer of knowledge between both worlds must be bidirectional, without prioritizing the conditions of one over the other, balancing the technological proposals with the design of experiences [23].

The analysis of the pragmatic experimentation of reality must be based on arranging the knowledge instruments that we use to understand how facts happen in a specific situation [24] and use them to plan means to generate understanding and collective participation. We can rely on the pragmatic components that structure the experiences of human beings. First, we should identify the elements that contribute to general conditions of understanding [20] and, later, we should define the frames of reference that humans use to organize meaning and participation in the real world [25]. These two pragmatic components must be screened with the system that humans use to collect information from reality: information based on perception [26].

It is important to differentiate and understand the levels of information from the perceived reality, the pragmatically structured reality and the formation of reference frames that connect these elements. This connection will drive the correct transmission of information to other members of a community. The understanding of interactive phenomena does not depend solely on the theoretical knowledge and observation of the structures that constitute reality. According to Habermas [20], it depends on the knowledge of our mechanisms of apprehension and on the reasoning processes that provide sense, meaning and regularity to interactive phenomena.

The basis of the design thinking, according to Papanek, a product must be conceived "as a meaningful link between man [read humans] and the environment. We must see man, his tools, environment, and ways of thinking and planning, as a nonlinear, simultaneous, integrated, comprehensive whole. This approach is integrated design. It deals with specialized extensions of man that make it possible for him to remain a generalist" [27].

Methodological processes are needed in order to adopt a holistic approach to HCD education. These processes should provide the necessary information to broaden the understanding of the problem to be solved. Henry Dreyfus in "Designing for People" shows how to deal with design problems: "We begin with men and women and we end with them. We consider potential users' habits, physical dimensions, and psychological impulses. We also measure their purse, which is what I meant by ending with them, for we must conceive not only a satisfactory design but also one that incorporates that indefinable appeal to assure purchase. The Greek philosopher Protagoras had a phrase for it, Man is the measure of all things" [28].

Additionally, Cross [29] establishes three fields of study that can promote and structure the knowledge necessary to develop design research: people, processes and products. We must address the interrelation between the set of factors that provide relevant data to plan the design of interaction artifacts. To balance the elements that compose HCD it is necessary to consider:

- factors that structure the human information capture system,
- cognitive processes that use the acquired knowledge and give meaning and sense to external stimuli,
- factors that guide behavior and determine contextual interaction capabilities and limitations, and
- information and communication processes that drive the formalization of creative design proposals so that they fit into the social and cultural context.

In short, to integrate intentionality into design, human needs and desires must be met, and the adaptation of technological means to this end must encompass both the private and collective levels [30]. Design intention, proposed forms, and consequent behavior must be based on the set of human capabilities. To link human abilities and practices together, it is important to connect the intention of design with the meaning that objects or services communicate to people. This meaning is what will give conceptual unity to design, will guide the interaction of individuals and will facilitate its evaluation. Nelson & Stolterman [30] define the conceptual unity of design through the attributes that evolve from the ideal towards the real and it takes shape through the creative arrangement of its elements.

This holistic approach is supported by one of the implicit characteristics of the design process itself: the reflective practice of the discipline [31]. We need to reflect on the diverse fields of experience in which design is involved to handle complex situations and share them with other people. It is needed to know the new communication resources and to make their relationships visible and convey them "through the senses, technology's potential within the categories of surface, body and space" [32]. In conclusion, this approach generates a dialectical process, of reciprocal and helpful relationships, between man and machine, which must be considered as the sociocultural element that underlies applied technology.

HCD research community recognizes the importance of embracing human, material, social, economic and technological domains [33]. Therefore, design education must transform its pedagogical practices to integrate the challenges derived from technological innovations. Saikaly [34] reviews the design research field and identifies three main areas. First, academic design research, related to methodologies of the sciences and humanities. Second, design research focused on professional praxis, where creative production is examined from the perspective of practice and production. Third, practice-based research that analyzes project development as an integral part of the design process. This one focuses its attention on the practice of design as an axis to understand the evolution of the research process. Specifically, it highlights the reflective, interpretive, dialectical and iterative research processes in the design process.

4   HCD Course Design

This section presents the design of an HCD course that, in addition to the contents related to the design process and methods, integrates a philosophical view. This course is part of the Design and Digital Creation degree at UOC, Universitat Oberta de Catalunya[2]. UOC is a completely online distance university based in Barcelona, Spain. UOC's educational model is based on breaking the barriers of time and space, making it possible to learn without the need to meet with teachers and other learners in time and place.

The degree in Digital Design and Creation is a three-year graduate program that trains students in design aspects connected to graphic design and interaction design, with a social change design perspective. The design of the educational program is based on the paradigm shift that the field of design has experienced in recent years. Industrial economy is transforming into a knowledge economy and this has led to a technological and social transformation of design practice. Design discipline increased its value thanks to its

---

[2] www.uoc.edu.

processes and methods, emphasizing the importance of its epistemological foundations. Consequently, design is expanding to new and different application areas including technological innovations. This is the context where the course "Human-Centered Design" is situated. It has a methodological approach and takes into account the design practices previously stated: design that goes beyond traditional application areas, being placed in hybrid spaces that transform people's activities and generating and exchanging new relation areas. Accordingly, the learning goals for future human-centered designers need to be expanded to meet interdisciplinary and increasingly complex challenges. Digital technologies changed design processes, and user-centered design is changing how technologies need to be designed, especially software applications. In addition to that, design must provide solutions to social, environmental and complex economic needs. Putting people at the center of design processes and practices is a key factor in understanding design today.

The driving force that shapes the learning path of the course is the way human beings interact with surrounding things, depending on the context they conduct their daily activities [15]. From a pragmatic point of view, the holistic understanding of human experience must be placed in our living environment. That is, in the same environment where experience occurs and, therefore, in the activity context where we give value and meaning to designed objects [35]. We classified social interaction environments based on the contexts of reference that humans use to understand and act. The dimensions that have guided this classification of experiences connect spatial conditions with human capabilities and limitations. We defined four major areas of study and analysis of people's interrelationship with the natural-artificial world: social urban space, shared human space, body space and hand space [36].

A group of design concepts provide the basis for the learning goals of the HCD course and allow to organize the methodological approach of the learning activities. Human interaction journey starts in an open environment, where people's activities are socially and culturally conditioned and ends in a close personal environment. Students begin their journey by facing a collective human perspective and they finish addressing personal experiences. The contents that provide support to the study and analysis of design processes are human diversity, people's dimensions, body measures and hand abilities. Universal design, anthropometry and ergonomics are connected to user-centered design processes, methods and techniques. This approach allows students to acquire the basics of HCD, learn how to structure a design process, apply the most appropriate UCD methods for each project, always keeping the meaning of human experience. The organization of the four learning activities of the course and how they include the main design concepts, processes and methods used are presented in Table 1.

The learning activities of the course and the conceptual and methodological elements that include are described below.

Activity 1: Universal Design. This learning activity addresses human interrelationship with public space. The design of the public urban space is perhaps the environment where human diversity becomes most clear and where it is more necessary to plan projects taking into account this variety of aspects [37]. In this first learning activity, design principles derived from the principles of universal design are studied and applied. The learning goal is to understand the importance of giving value to human diversity and

Table 1. Course organisation.

Human aspects	Activity	Concepts	Processes & Methods
Human diversity	1. Universal Design	Open & public space Universal design Human shared activity Context	Method: Observation
Human dimension	2. Design Process, Methods & Personal Space	Human size space Human measures Anthropometry Design process Design methods	Process: Iterative Method: Prototyping
Corporal measures	3. Body, Object & Space	Personal space Body interaction with objects and spaces Anthropometry Ergonomics	Process: J.C. Jones Process: Squiggle Process: User-centered design Process: Human-centered design Method: Storyboard Method: Scenarios
Manual abilities	4. Interaction & Object	Manipulation space Hand dimension Interaction design Ergonomics	Process: Iterative Method: Artefact analysis Method: Mapping Method: Observation Method: Prototyping

to learn how to apply the aforementioned principles to expand the benefits that design should provide to society.

Activity 2: Process, methods and personal space. This second learning activity reduces the contextual analysis and is focused on how human dimensions determine measures of non-public personal spaces. The concepts of design process and design method are introduced in this learning activity with the goal to facilitate understanding of how people plan and organize interior spaces. The activity focuses on the human innate tendency to adapt the experiential environment to human measures and proportions [38, 39]. Learners analyze spaces how they adapt to a specific human activity by means of physical models that allow them to test and iterate their project.

Activity 3: Body, object and space. This learning activity provides a hands-on perspective where learners are invited to experience the process of interaction with an object in order to identify activities and ergonomic relationships that are established between space, human being and object. The information collected on the interaction process with objects facilitates the understanding of physical and functional relationships between space, body and object. Design processes and methods proposed by Jones [40] and Newman [41] are studied.

Activity 4: Interaction and object. The last learning activity of the course is centered on the design of objects that expand human abilities. This activity connects all contents and abilities acquired on previous ones. Knowledge of how people interact with objects will provide guidelines to new design solutions and to define a sequence of actions that appropriately guide the user activities [42]. Learners are asked to design and prototype an interactive artifact by means of UCD process and methods.

The learning contents of the course are organized as follows. Specific and ad-hoc content has been developed to learn design processes and methods and the human approach. Contents related with the design process, methods and principles are delivered through the Design Toolkit [43], an educational content repository developed at UOC. Additionally, contents related with human activity, universal design, anthropometry, ergonomics and the theoretical concepts of design processes are available in a digital textbook that was created by faculty [44]. Course assessment is organized around the continuous assessment of the learning activities. Learners are expected to study the learning contents and complete each activity. The final mark of the course is based on the marks obtained in each learning activity.

5   Results

This section presents the results of this research based on data collected during the time the course has been running. The results are centered on academic performance and student satisfaction. The HCD course has been running 5 semesters since 2017-18 and is part of the Digital Design and Creation graduate program.

During this research 549 students were enrolled in the course. These students were distributed along 5 semesters: Semester 1: 74 students; semester 2: 56 students; semester 3: 116 students; semester 4: 100 students and semester 5 had 203 students. Participants were 60% female and 40% male. The age of the participants is distributed as follows: 28% are on the 19-24 age range; 24% on the 25-29 age group; 15% on the 30-34 age and the rest are in the age range between 35 and 55. Some participants had previous experience in higher education: 15% had a previous university degree and another 15% had higher education experience.

Regarding academic performance, two indicators have been used: performance rate and success rate. First, the academic performance rate is calculated taking into account the number of students who pass the course in relation to the number of students enrolled. Second, the academic success rate is calculated taking into account the number of students that pass the course and the number of students who followed the course. It is important to note here that in distance education, learners are more aware of their academic progress. At the point where a learner is aware that he will not pass the course (because he is not following the course or not doing the intended work), he will probably drop out of the course. In most of the cases, this dropout is a conscious student decision. As a summary, in distance education there is usually a higher dropout rate compared with traditional face to face education [45]. Therefore, the academic success rate tends to be higher than the academic performance rate. In this research, taking into account the 5 semesters period, the academic performance has ranged between 70% and 86%. In contrast, the academic success rate has ranged between 94% and 100%.

Two actions have been carried out in order to capture data on students' perceptions of the course. On the one hand, during the first two semesters students were asked to answer a short questionnaire right after they submitted each one of the four continuous assessment assignments. This questionnaire had 4 short and specific questions related with engagement [46]. On the other hand, at the end of the course students answer a more complete satisfaction survey. This survey included satisfaction questions around teaching, course methodology, learning resources, activities and assessment.

The short engagement questionnaire was carried out during the first two semesters of the course with the goal to collect agile and actionable feedback in order to iterate the course design. The questionnaire was designed with the goal to capture students' engagement in context, that is, not at the end of the course. Students were asked about cognitive, emotional and behavioral aspects. 91 students provided answers to this questionnaire. The results showed a neutral perception of the level of difficulty in completing the activities. Regarding the cognitive aspects of learning resources, students expressed high satisfaction on first activities that decreased slightly in the following activities. It is interesting to mention that this result is very different for the activities. In relation to students' own perception of the effort for solving each activity, more than 50% showed that they had worked "a lot" (3.5 on a scale of 5) on each activity. With reference to their level of happiness when completing an activity, more than 50% of students were happy and very happy (4,5 on a scale of 5). When asked about the time spent on activities, most of the students reported spending 20 or more hours to complete activities.

During the five semesters running the course that are analyzed in this work 190 students answered an academic survey satisfaction at the end of the term. As a general result, the satisfaction with the course improved over time. This could be the result of iterative improvements that have been made, mostly related to the design of the assessment activities and the learning resources. Satisfaction with learning resources increased from 49% to 66%. Satisfaction with the assessment grows from 50% to 70%. Satisfaction with the teacher increased from 48% to 77%. And finally, overall satisfaction with the course is set around 70%. The satisfaction survey also includes an open question. Through this option, students can express comments and concerns related to any course element. Three types of results can be identified from the analysis of open responses. First, a small group of students, about 10%, express some aspect that they did not like. The other responses can be divided into two large groups: neutral responses and comments and positive feedback. From the analysis of these answers, we highlight a change of student's mindset about the course contents. The results highlighted that the course helped the students to change their perspectives and provided a new point of view on human-centered design.

6   Discussion

HCI design perspective places the human being at the center of the design process and methods. This approach fosters the connection between technology and users and at the same time, it is one of the main aspects that boost innovation and research within the discipline.

Philosophy is the discipline that studies the meaning of human events and the way of knowing reality. Thus, the theoretical framework provided by philosophy is useful for connecting technology with interaction design, basically because the real-life of the human being constitutes the main objective of HCI. Over the years, the pragmatism tradition has developed a theoretical framework that facilitates the understanding of human activities in the physical environment and in the socio-cultural context. Two reasons motivated choosing this knowledge theory to design the curriculum of the HCD course. First, it facilitated planning the learning path, selecting the contents and the way they can be organized taking into account the spatial dimensions that human beings use to understand reality. Second, it allowed connecting environments and activities with human abilities and skills in a natural way thanks to the classification of the interaction contexts.

The natural way of human acts has contributed to the success of the HCI course. It is important to emphasize that students value very positively the change in their way of understanding and practicing the design that has involved following the HCD course. In all the scheduled activities of the course, the human experience has been the center of attention and this simple paradigm shift has been the main aspect that has facilitated the change of perspective of the students. This approach has been the key factor in the success of the course. It is important to emphasize that students valued very positively the change in their way of understanding and practicing design provided by the course. The human experience has been the focus of all learning activities. This simple paradigm shift facilitated students to change their perspective of design practice. The results obtained show that developing learning paths, contents and methodologies directly related to human abilities, the processes of perception and reasoning that guide human behavior, facilitated students to understand the importance of human experience for HCI.

References

1. Lowdermilk, T.: User-Centered Design: A Developer's Guide to Building User-Friendly Applications. O'Reilly, Beijing (2013)
2. Thomas, V., Remy, C., Bates, O.: The limits of HCD: reimagining the anthropocentricity of ISO 9241-210. In: Proceedings of the 2017 Workshop on Computing Within Limits (LIMITS'17), New York, USA pp. 85–92. ACM (2017)
3. Ormandjieva, O., Pitula, K., Mansura, C.: Integrating UCD within an agile software development process in an educational setting. In: Proceedings of the Canadian Engineering Education Association (2015)
4. Larusdottir, M., Roto, V., Stage, J., Lucero, A.: Get realistic!-UCD course design and evaluation. In: Bogdan, C., Kuusinen, K., Lárusdóttir, M.K., Palanque, P., Winckler, M. (eds.) HCSE 2018. LNCS, vol. 11262, pp. 15–30. Springer, Cham (2019). https://doi.org/10.1007/978-3-030-05909-5_2
5. Churchill, E.F., Bowser, A., Preece, J.: The future of HCI education: a flexible, global, living curriculum. Interact. **23**(2), 70–73 (2016)
6. Hewett, T.T., et al.: ACM SIGCHI Curricula for Human-Computer Interaction. Technical Report. Association for Computing Machinery, New York, USA (1992)

7. St-Cyr, O., MacDonald, C.M., Churchill, E.F., Preece, J.J., Bowser, A.: Developing a community of practice to support global HCI education. In: Extended Abstracts of the 2018 CHI Conference on Human Factors in Computing Systems, pp. 1–7 (2018)
8. Churchill, E., Preece, J., Bowser, A.: Developing a Living HCI Curriculum to Support a Global Community. In: CHI' 14 Extended Abstracts on Human Factors in Computing Systems (CHI EA' 14). ACM, New York, USA, pp. 135–138. ACM (2014). https://doi.org/10.1145/2559206.2559236
9. Wilcox, L., DiSalvo, B., Henneman, D., Wang, Q.: Design in the HCI classroom: setting a research agenda. In: Proceedings of the 2019 on Designing Interactive Systems Conference, pp. 871–883 (2019)
10. Council, D.: The design process: what is the double diamond. The Design Council (2015). https://www.designcouncil.org.uk/news-opinion/design-process-what-double-diamond
11. Beux, J., Bellei, E., Brock, L., Bertoletti, A.C., Hölbig, C.: Agile design process with user-centered design and user experience in web interfaces: a systematic literature review. Lat. Am. J. Comput. Fac. Syst. Eng. Escuela Politécnica Nac. Quito-Ecuador 5(2), 53–60 (2018)
12. Felker, C., Slamova, R., Davis, J.: Integrating UX with scrum in an undergraduate software development project. In: Proceedings of the 43rd ACM Technical Symposium on Computer Science Education (SIGCSE' 12). ACM, New York, USA, pp. 301–306. ACM (2012). https://doi.org/10.1145/2157136.2157226
13. McLuhan, M.: Understanding Media: The Extensions of Man. MIT Press, Cambridge (Mass.) (1994)
14. Peirce, C.S.: The Collected Papers of Charles Sanders Peirce, Electronic edn. InteLex Corporation, Charlottesville, VA (1994)
15. Määttänen, P.: Mind in Action. SAPERE, vol. 18. Springer, Cham (2015). https://doi.org/10.1007/978-3-319-17623-9
16. Määttänen, P.: Pragmatist semiotics as a framework for design research. In: S. Pizzorato, A. Arruda, & D. De Moraes (eds.), Design + Research: Proceedings of the Politechnico di Milano Conference, Politechnico di Milano, Milano, pp. 70–73 (2000)
17. Gondomar, R.: Pragmatic experience of digital media and environments. Hipertext.net: Revista Académica sobre Documentación Digital y Comunicación Interactiva, 17: The Digital Future of Facts. Universitat Pompeu Fabra, Barcelona (2018). https://doi.org/10.31009/hipertext.net.2018.i17.03
18. Dewey, J.: Experience and Education. Touchstone, New York (1997)
19. Dewey, J.: Democracy and education. Pennsylvania State University (2001)
20. Habermas, J.: Communication and The Evolution of Society. Beacon, Boston (1979)
21. Krippendorff, K.: Propositions of human-centeredness; a philosophy for design. In: D. Durling & K. Friedman (eds.), Doctoral education in design: Foundations for the future: Proceedings of the conference held 8–12 July 2000, La Clusaz, France, Staffordshire University Press, Staffordshire (UK) pp. 55–63 (2000)
22. Krippendorff, K.: Intrinsic motivation and human-centered design. Theor. Issues Ergon. Sci. 5(1), 43–72 (2004). https://doi.org/10.1080/1463922031000086717
23. Goodman, N.: Ways of Worldmaking. Hackett, Indianapolis [etc.] (1978)
24. Noveck, I.A., Sperber, D.: Experimental Pragmatics. Palgrave Macmillan, New York (2004)
25. Goffman, E.: Frame Analysis: An Essay on the Organization of Experience. Northeastern University Press, Boston (1974)
26. Gibson, J.J.: The Senses Considered as Perceptual Systems. George Allen & Unwin, London (1968)
27. Papanek, V.: Design for the Real World: Human Ecology and Social Change. Thames & Hudson, London (1984)
28. Dreyfuss, H.: Designing for People. Allworth Press, New York (2003)

29. Cross, N.: Designerly Ways of knowing. Springer-Verlag, London (2006)
30. Nelson, H.G., Stolterman, E.: The Design Way: Intentional Change in an Unpredictable World. The MIT Press, Cambridge [etc.] (2012)
31. Schön, D.A.: The Reflective Practitioner: How Professionals Think in Action. Routledge, New York (1994)
32. Buurman, G.M.: Total Interaction: Theory and Practice of a New Paradigm for the Design Disciplines. Birkhäuser, Basel [etc.] (2005)
33. Vaughan, L.: Practice Based Design Research. Bloomsbury Publishing Plc, London (2017)
34. Saikaly, F.: Approaches to design research: towards the designerly way. In: Proceedings of the 6th International Conference of the European Academy of Design, Design System Evolution. Hochschule fur kunste Bremen, Germany (2005)
35. Heft, H.: Ecological Psychology in Context: James Gibson, Roger Barker, and the Legacy of William James's Radical Empiricism. L. Erlbaum, Mahwah, N.J. (2001)
36. De Bonte, A., Fletcher, D.: Scenario-Focused Engineering: A Toolbox for Innovation and Customer-Centricity. Microsoft Press, Washington (2014)
37. Lahire, B.: L'homme Pluriel: Les Ressorts De L'action. Nathan, Paris (1998)
38. Hennessey, J., Papanek, V.: Nomadic Furniture 1. Pantheon, New York (1973)
39. Hennessey, J., Papanek, V.: Nomadic Furniture 2. Pantheon, New York (1974)
40. Jones, J.C.: Design Methods: Seeds of Human Futures. John Wiley & Sons, New York [etc.] (1970)
41. Newman, D.: The Process of Design Squiggle (2009). https://thedesignsquiggle.com/
42. Colborne, G.: Simple and Usable: Web, Mobile, and Interaction Design. New Riders, Berkeley, CA (2011)
43. Garcia-Lopez, C., Tesconi, S., Mor, E.: Designing design resources: from contents to tools. In: Kurosu, M. (ed.) HCII 2019. LNCS, vol. 11566, pp. 87–100. Springer, Cham (2019). https://doi.org/10.1007/978-3-030-22646-6_7
44. Gondomar, R., Mor, E.: Cuaderno de Diseño Centrado en las Personas. Universitat Oberta de Catalunya (UOC), Barcelona (2017)
45. Park, J.H., Choi, H.J.: Factors influencing adult learners' decision to drop out or persist in online learning. J. Educ. Technol. Soc. **12**(4), 207–217 (2009)
46. Balasooriya, Isuru., Mor, Enric, Rodríguez, M.Elena: Understanding user engagement in digital education. In: Zaphiris, Panayiotis, Ioannou, Andri (eds.) LCT 2018. LNCS, vol. 10925, pp. 3–15. Springer, Cham (2018). https://doi.org/10.1007/978-3-319-91152-6_1

Using Traditional Research Methods in Contemporary UX Surveying
Case Studies Applying Mental Model Research, Participant Observation, Projective Techniques

Csilla Herendy[1,2]([⊠]) [iD]

[1] Budapest University of Technology and Economic, Budapest, Hungary
herendycsilla@erg.bme.hu, herendy.csilla@uni-nke.hu
[2] National University of Public Service, Budapest, Hungary

Abstract. In my paper I write about three methods which are generally used and accepted in social sciences and market research, and can be effectively applied – not in a standard way, but innovatively – during the development of online interfaces, too. At the beginning of the paper I present how user interface research has become an indispensable component of web development, considering popular demand for ergonomic, user-friendly web pages and applications. The topic is also relevant from a business point of view, considering how web developments involving users prove to yield superior results.

There are several methods available for user surveys and researching. The appropriate choices and following through with the research (methodology, detail, depth) are subject to available funding and professional standards. There are many ways to do research, and even the most rudimentary research or survey always produces results.

In the following paper after a brief methodology overview (qualitative – quantitative, attitude – behavior, context and history, graphs and charts baser on C. Rohrer and McCrindle Research), I will go on to describe some of the common and lesser-used methods in UX research, even some which are not included in the chart but useful nonetheless. The latter account for innovative methods. It is these methodologies my study focuses on: participant observation, mental model research and various projective tests. For each method I describe its (standard) offline and its (innovative) online applications, and drawing on my own practice, I also describe their safe and reliable application to online surfaces. I present each method through case studies.

Keywords: User eXperience · Mental model research · Participant observation · Projective techniques

1 Introduction

1.1 General and Most Commonly Used UX Research Methods

User interface research has become an indispensable component of web development, considering popular demand for ergonomic, user-friendly web pages and applications.

© Springer Nature Switzerland AG 2020
C. Stephanidis et al. (Eds.): HCII 2020, LNCS 12423, pp. 123–132, 2020.
https://doi.org/10.1007/978-3-030-60114-0_8

The topic is also relevant from a business point of view, considering how web developments involving users prove to yield superior results.

There are several methods available for user surveys and researching. The appropriate choices and following through with the research (methodology, detail, depth) is subject to available funding and professional standards. There are many ways to do research, and even the most rudimentary research or survey always produces results.

The usual way to present available UX research is by saying they are surveying user attitudes or monitoring user behavior, and yield qualitative or quantitative results respectively. One of the best-known and most cited charts is the work of User Experience Design and Research Executive Christian Rohrer, from 2014 [1]. The chart arranges research methods by their behavioral and attitudinal focus (i.e. what the user does and says), and their quantitative or qualitative data yield (why or how often users do what they do). Another defining factor in method classification is the context of future use (Fig. 1).

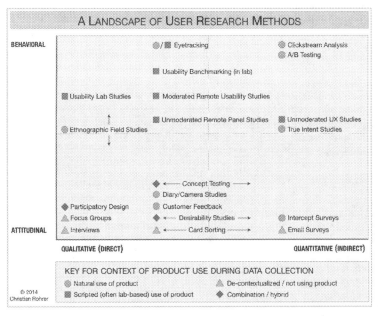

Fig. 1. A Landscape of User research Methods. Christian Rohrer, 2014.

Another cited chart is the one from McCrindle Research [2] that shows a range of methodologies broken down by generation. Of course, not all of these are used in examining User eXperience, they are more widely used in social science research, but many of these methods have been prominent in online interface testing as well (Fig. 2).

Certain methods developed for social science research are highly applicable to UX research, yet they are not featured on these charts. These are an increased sensitivity toward participant observation, mental modeling and cognitive schemas, as well as the application of projective testing.

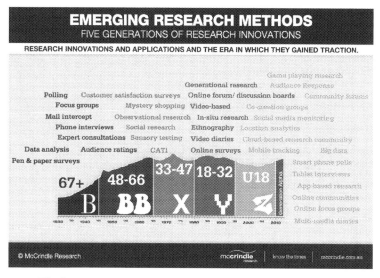

Fig. 2. Emerging Research Methods, McCrindle Research, 2013.

In the following Sect. 2 will describe three methods which I have used in my previous research, and introduce their potential innovative use for online interfaces.

2 Social Science Researching Methods in the Field of UX Research

2.1 Researching User's Mental Model in the Course of Mapping User Needs

One of the big, centuries-old questions facing not only psychology, but philosophy and linguistics as well is how we model the world inside our mind [3], how we conceptualize complex processes. For example, how we might imagine a shopping excursion, mailing a letter, or unwrapping a chocolate egg. These practical and accurate mental maps determine how we set about doing such a complex series of tasks: essentially, it is a mental model of our attitude object [4]. Mental models are shaped and molded by previous experience [5]. These models are relevant to both on- and offline environments, and pre-define our expectations toward how things should work. Some important shared features of mental models is their occasional instability, irrationality, rapid emergence and mutability, scientific unfeasibility and blurred demarcations [6].

In a sense, we would do well to start off all research and development with mapping the user's relevant models of attitude objects (including services, apps, issues etc.) [4].

Rohrer mentions the study of mental models, namely in connection to card sorting tests [1], and the same card sorting method was applied by Jakob Nielsen in redesigning SunWeb's intranet [7].

However, if we were to become acquainted with users' mental models relevant to an application undergoing development, we can start by conducting some individual in-depth interviews, followed up with group interviews. Analyzing the data, we can then

then classify and describe the views and models we found [8]. In case data visualization is more convenient, we may use Indi Young's methodology [9]. For this paper, I am describing a case study involving in-depth interviews, the contents of which was categorized and analyzed.

2.2 Case Study: Researching Mental Models During a Bank Development Project

As a case study for applying this method, I will present a study commissioned by a bank. Ergománia UX agency developed a new web interface for a Hungarian bank in 2016. The interface introduced an entirely new complex service to Hungarian banking, a digital innovation supporting small business financial administration. As per the bank's instructions, everything works online in a transparent and simple manner, including photographed invoice uploading for accountancy. The agency organized in-depth interviews for the novel service concept, attempting to explore participants' relevant attitudes and mental models. The service itself was novel to Hungarian banking, therefore all I had to work with was extrapolations of participants' previous experience, somewhat hazy ideas overall. My central focus was a question borrowed from partner therapy: "How would this solution improve your day?" My experience during these interviews was that participants were highly enthusiastic and vocal about possible online solutions, which they were not yet familiar with (i.e. which did not exist), but once developed, would make their business affairs more easily manageable, by simplifying accountancy correspondence and financial administration.

It was my experience that these participant interviews yielded multiple mental models, both parallel and subsequent. Finally, I ended up with far more mental models than the number of interviewees, in fact there were individual versions for several of these models. The reason behind this phenomenon is that mental models are elusive, mutable, and generally difficult to grasp. According to the bank, the research yielded some highly remarkable concepts, and the user needs it revealed provided plenty of inspiration for subsequent web design and development. Mental models were not encountered through thematic exploration (as per card sorting), through webpage assessment of existing or missing features, but in-depth mapping of user needs and ideas.

2.3 Participant Observation and Its Potential Application in Menu System Design and Development

About Participant Observation
Participant observation is one of the oldest and most widespread qualitative research methods. Its origins trace back to cultural anthropology, first proponents being Bronislaw Malinowski (1884–1942) and Clifford Geertz (1926–2006), but later adapted by social researchers to their examination of immigrant communities. This is the only method we can use to learn how subjects actually behave, rather than learn what they report on their own behavior. Field research offers direct and complete observation of subjects in their natural surroundings. It is suitable for exploring qualitative, unquantifiable details

and minutia, and is therefore highly suited for mapping the fine details of attitude and behavior [10].

As far as we are discussing online interfaces and menu structures, mental model exploration is conducted foremost (and in case of online content, longest) through the card sorting test method. This was the first method applied by Nielsen to the Sun intranet development project in 1994 [7]. However, even though we had used this same method in our presented research, we chose participant observation for instead of this method for menu development, and I will now present its innovative use. These methods were used in the successful restructuring of a webshop's menu system.

Case Study: Participant Observation and Card Sorting Test, as Support for Menu Tree Design and Development

Participant observation is a widely used method in market research as well as cultural anthropology. This fact, as well as researcher curiosity, encouraged me to apply this method in developing an interface for an online household appliance webshop called markabolt.hu. Research aimed to find solutions to resolve blocks in the shopping process as well as mapping the process in as much detail as possible. The research ws conducted by Hungarian UX agency Ergománia in 2017. We were interested in finding out about shoppers' product selection and shopping behavior in an offline shop's online environment. Also, we were focusing on comparing this behavior with the planned online selection and shopping process. To this end, a UX colleague and I spent a few mornings working alongside household appliance store employees, listening in on client inquiries. Sometimes we asked shoppers questions to pinpoint their product selection and shopping issues, including their priorities for finding the right oven or washing machine. What were their basic considerations for making a choice? Another of our priorities was specifying the exact parameters they used to select a product. Would shoppers arrive at the store looking for a specific appliance, possibly as far as its product code? Do they have a special function or feature in mind, like a freestanding or built-in set? How relevant are size dimensions? Our experience in this department proved fundamental in formulating the menu tree design.

To balance what we had seen and heard, we also kept up a conversation with the store employees in between sessions. We encouraged them to tell us their experience of typical shoppers and distinct shopping processes. We also asked employees to relate their previous pleasant or annoying experiences. This proved highly entertaining, as well as instructive for us.

Inbetween participant observations, and as follow-up, we asked employees as well as shoppers to participate in individual card-sorting tests. During the card sorting, researchers ask participants to arrange items destined for webpage display in a system they find intelligible. They can name and re-name their groups. Via this card-arrangement method, we can map users' concepts for webpage content and its respective arrangements, as well as how users would categorize information featured on the webpage, and their terms for groups of content. In this case, our questions pertained to how they would find it logical and navigable to arrange store goods on an online interface. They used little cards to provide us with answers. We included this input in the development of the webpage menu tree.

Our participant observation experience definitely benefited our redesigning of the webpage search bar, product filter and menu tree, down to the actual wording of interface sections. We thereby applied experience from offline behavior observations to planning an online interface.

2.4 Applying Projective and Enabling Methods to Collecting Interface-Relevant Feedback

About Projective Methods

Focus groups and projective methods used in group interviews provide invaluable assistance to gain insight to what lies under the surface of rationalized replies. These techniques are typically used in market research, and may enable a deeper exploration of subject attitudes toward situations, products and activities [11]. They are also helpful in accessing interviewees' inner perspectives, and give us a means of looking beneath the surface of rationalization i na way perfectly acceptable to the respondents.

Projective technique has five important methods: Associative, Complementary, Constructional, Self-expressive and Sorting-arrangement. Complementary procedures including sentence completion, and the picture sorting technique were applied in my research presented below. For the picture sorting exercise, it is crucial for participants to provide the explanation for their choices, rather than the researcher.

Case Study: Projective Tests for Deeper Examinations of Interface-Relevant Attitudes

In spring 2007, I applied an eye tracking study and a follow-up online focus group study to examine the webpage magyarorszag.hu, which was Hungary's central administrative portal at the time.

Both in terms of its composure and the issues explored, the online focus group activity was based on traditional, in-real-life focus group methodology. Research participants meet in a chatroom-like online virtual environment at a given time, and have individual nicknames for participation. The procedure and aims of the online focus group research are much like a traditional focus group's, the only difference being that the conversation takes place in a virtual, home-accessible chat room rather than a designated offline space. Online focus group participants are introduced to a variety of stimuli, and may even apply the projective methods familiar to traditional focus group studies [11]. Such projective methods include semantic differential, collage making, picture sorting and completing unfinished sentences (Fig. 3).

These were the studies I conducted in 2007 for the webpage as it was at the time; and this same study was repeated for the since revamped magyarorszag.hu webpage. National Infocommunications Service Company Ltd. informed me that the new webpage was developed using agile methodology, and several rounds of progressive internal testing. User testing was not applied to the new webpage, nor was it for the 2007 version.

Due to the circumstances of COVID-19 lockdown, there was no way to conduct an eye-tracking study for May 2020. Instead, participants were asked to solve projective tasks from the online focus group study. There were 11 participants in total, and the questions were relayed via Google Forms. Two participants were high school graduates,

Fig. 3. magyarorszag.hu (May 2007)

the rest held college degrees. Ages ranged from 30 to 66. 62% were women (8/5), 38% men (8/3), residents of Budapest (9/4), other towns (9/3) and villages (9/2).

In both instances, online focus group projective testing took place in the same manner. Lead-up questions focused first on their personal, then online experiences of administration management.

In this study, responses relevant to personal administration were 50% positive and 50% negative, such as connection, smile, complicated or time-consuming. Online administration was categorized as positive for the most part, with terms like "simple" or "no cue", but one participant stressed "simple, as far as the site is navigable". Participant memories relevant to the magyarorszag.hu website however were grouped around terms like "total waste", "annoyance", "searching", "illogical", "complicated", "tangled". Afterward, I showed participants the webpage starting screen for that day (see Fig. 4), and asked for their feedback. Most participants reported the webpage is simple, clear, and transparent, and only few thought it was complicated. In comparison, every single participant rated the webpage negatively during its 2007 testing, as "illogical", "gray", "dim", 'bleak", "cluttered", "austere".

My next step was to ask for feedback via a differential scale. The two end parameters were, with little exception, identical to those applied in the 2007 study. For the sake of brevity I will only highlight the most prominent and differing resposes, based on the

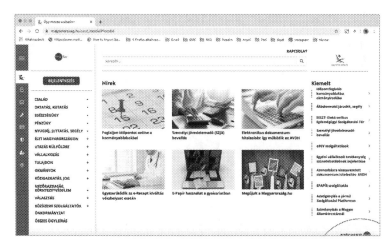

Fig. 4. magyarorszag.hu (May 2020)

response diagrams. Semantic differential scale responses for the 2007 webpage study favored overall the idea of "complicated" as opposed to "simple", "monotonous" rather than "colorful", and "boring" rather than "interesting". Prominent values for the 2020 study included characterizing the webpage as "slow" rather than "fast", more "in-depth" than "superficial", "reliable" rather than "unreliable", more "thorough" than "superficial", more "boring" than "interesting", more "official" than "casual", and the like/dislike categorization was in favor of the dislikes.

One of the most interesting parts of the study was picture sorting, which focused on opinions and attitudes which are more difficult to express and less readily translated to stereotypes. Software applied for the 2007 study [12] enabled the selected pictures' assembly into collages. For this present study, the software was no longer available for use, so we used a Google survey to pick images, and there was no option for collage-making, regrettably. Participants were asked to select their pictures from sets including various animals, landscapes, different price-range automobiles, reps of various ages and characteristics, various landscapes, differently styled HQ's (trendy office blocks to classicist halls), office interiors, cues (from single-person to snaking lines), picking the ones that they thought best reflected on the magyarorszag.hu main page. I also asked them to write down why they thought their choice appropriate.

The most frequently picked animals were the vizsla dog (10/4) and snail (10/3), and justifications included "vizsla are swift, curious and Hungarian", and for snails: "not pretty or quick, but ours al lthe same". For the "Administrative support at magyarorszag.hu webpage is…" section, there were images of different cues and administration service situations. Most participants picked personal support sessions (10/3), and the employee sitting next to a pile of paperwork (10/4). Most participants' automobile of choice was the used Honda Jazz (10/4), citing reasons like "Because Hungarian administration is so bureaucratic, I picked an older but reliable car", some even ventured as far as "Give me a round-headlight Zhiguli anyday!" The runner-up was a modern, mustard-colored Audi (10/3), with justifications like "it is up to the challenges of today", and "reliable quality". The other car choices were disparate. The most popular landscape (10/4) was the green hill familiar as a default Windows background. Interestingly, only one respondent took time to justify their choice, namely "this is as functional as a blank Windows screen". The winning building photo was a modern, all-glass block because "it is a well-thought-out piece of engineering", "stability", "block".

Another interesting part of the study was finishing the incomplete sentences. For brevity's sake, I will only give a few examples from three questions and the respective responses' summary evaluation. Regarding page navigability, the 2007 study had the incomplete sentence "Navigating the magyarorszag.hu webpage is…", which most respondents completed to the effect that page navigation is difficult and confusing. They specified two main reasons for this, one, that there was too much information crammed into one space, and two, that menu points and information was not found where one would expect to look. The visual experience was reported as "drab", "dreary", "too much gray", "needs improvement".

The sentence "Support personnel at magyarorszag.hu are…" elicited responses including: "unimaginative", "bureaucrats", "helpful and quick to react", "as confused by the webpage as I am", "not circumspect", "on a coffee break", "bored and unhurried", "dressed in gray and beige, with a seasonal red ribbon for Christmas".

In contrast, the interface tested in 2020 was more positively rated by participants. Reporting on their navigation experience, most participants reported "easy" and "simple", and only a small minority (11/3) said it was "very complicated" or "impossible". The website visuals were also less negatively received than in 2007, although one-third of respondents (9/3) were again quick to point out its drabness, while replies included terms like "official", "boring", "a bit tedious", "navigable, but complicated". As for the support staff, they were rated mostly positive or neutrally: "proper", "likeable", "competent". Yet here again we found responses probably rooted in stereotypes regarding public services, like "lost in the maze of bureaucracy", or "waiting to get off work at 5".

Apparently, these projective tests, while taking longer to evaluate due to their complexity, yield more subtle insight to user opinion exploration, revealing stereotypes and attitudes, as well as supporting the articulation of less straightforward opinions.

3 Summary

This paper was an attempt to present examples on how well-known methods used in less familiar settings can enable us to gain insights to user feedback regarding websites and online interfaces. These methods may prove highly useful in the field of UX research, giving access to user opinions, attitudes and stereotypes that lie beyond the issues of mere interface utility. These methods also help to learn how users think about issues, and user observation allows us to experience this as a reality [14]. Because the subject of observation is actually performing what we want to examine, we are in a position to ask direct questions about the reasons and motives behind their actions and choices. Projective testing is a familiar staple from market research, and can give very detailed and insightful feedback on users' non-reflected opinions.

References

1. Rohrer, C.: When to Use Which User-Experience Research Methods. Nielsen Norman Group (2014). xdstrategy.com, https://www.xdstrategy.com/wp-content/uploads/2018/08/When-to-Use-Which-User-Experience-Research-Methods-2014-10-12-Print.pdf. Accessed 13 May 2020
2. McCrindle, M.: Emerging research-methods-infographic mc-crindle-research. https://www.slideshare.net/markmccrindle/emerging-researchmethodsinfographic-mccrindleresearch. Accessed 13 May 2020
3. Eysenck, M.W., Keane, M.T.: Cognitive Psychology, 5th edn. Psychology Press, Taylor & Francis Group, East Sussex (2005)
4. Herendy, C.: "Mental images" mental and conceptual models. https://ergomania.eu/mental-images-mental-and-conceptual-models-1/. Accessed 13 May 2020
5. Weinschenk, S.: 100 Things Every Designer Needs to Know About People (Voices That Matter). New Riders, Berkeley (2012)
6. Don, N.: Some observations on Mental Models [Norman] – Mental Models Research (2009). https://phdproject01.wordpress.com/2009/05/06/some-observations-on-mental-models-norman-mental-models-research/. Accessed 13 May 2020
7. Nielsen, J.: Design of SunWeb: Sun Microsystems' Intranet. https://www.nngroup.com/articles/1994-design-sunweb-sun-microsystems-intranet/. Accessed 13 May 2020
8. Snyder, C.: Prototyping: The Fast and Easy Way to Design and Refine User Interfaces. Morgan Kaufmann Publishers, San Francisco (2003)
9. Young, I.: Mental Models: Aligning Design Strategy with Human Behavior. Rosenfeld Media, Brooklyn, New York (2008)
10. Babbie, E.: The Practice of Social Research. Wadsworth, Cengage Learning, Belmot, CA (2010)
11. Gordon, W., Langmaid, R.: Qualitative Market Research, 1st edn. Gower Publishing Company Limited, Brookfield (1988)
12. Herendy, C.: How to research people's first impressions of websites? Eye-tracking as a usability inspection method and online focus group research. In: Godart, C., Gronau, N., Sharma, S., Canals, G. (eds.) I3E 2009. IAICT, vol. 305, pp. 287–300. Springer, Heidelberg (2009). https://doi.org/10.1007/978-3-642-04280-5_23
13. Herendy, C.: Weboldal-fejlesztés: innovatív és hagyományos módszerek II. Médiakutató (2009). http://epa.oszk.hu/03000/03056/00034/EPA03056_mediakutato_2009_tavasz_04.html. Accessed 13 May 2020
14. Herendy, C.: 20. századi módszertanok a 21. századi UX kutatásban JEL-KÉP: Kommunikáció közvélemény media 2018, vo. 2, pp. 29–44 (2018)

Dynamic Generative Design System

Yinghsiu Huang[✉] and Huan-Nian Chen

National Kaohsiung Normal University, 82446 Kaohsiung, Taiwan
yinghsiu@nknu.edu.tw

Abstract. The form of a stool is based on its function which is hard to satisfy all user due to the differences of physical statures. Therefore, CAD can assist the final production and manufacturing process. By doing so, Designers can quickly explore the large number of possibilities under specific styling definitions and evaluate alternatives through the generative design system. Thus, Design results are achieved by continuously repeating the operating system, further analysis, and evaluation system and then modify the system. Therefore, the purpose of this study is to design some types of stools by conforming parameters from users' buttocks and adjusting the form according to the body weight which allows users to seat comfortably. This study constructed the structure, shape, and surface of stool design in a parametric modelling manner conducted with Grasshopper, which is a plug-in of Rhinoceroses, to deform a stool that meet the requirement for users. By using generative design to break through the traditional design thinking, the physical stature and weight of users are simulated and adjusted by appropriate parameters in the generative system to change forms of a stool which can generate a variety of stools in short time and provide different users suitable stools.

Keywords: Generative design · Parametric design · Stool design · Grasshopper · Arduino

1 Introduction

Designers often use the computer to build design models for visualizing ideas from their minds. However, it is difficult and complicated to construct the model with a large number of parameters, especially in complex models, for example, to adjust a part of the model needs to go back to lower layers which might affect or damage the entire model. In order to solve this problem, the designers start to utilize parametric design software which allows the designer to adjust the model by setting the corresponding variables or parameters. Thus, the advantage is that designers are allowed to changes parameters, and relative ones will make corresponding changes.

The derived and continuative changes are controlled by software, which formulated by designers based on relevant regulations. The logic of regulations are not only important descriptions of relevance and parametric forms, but also design proposals instead of fixed forms themselves. By doing so, this kind of generative designs can help designers to create a powerful interactive tool that allows designers to explore and optimize possibilities of the design ideas, and also to reduce the amount of time. It is necessary

© Springer Nature Switzerland AG 2020
C. Stephanidis et al. (Eds.): HCII 2020, LNCS 12423, pp. 133–141, 2020.
https://doi.org/10.1007/978-3-030-60114-0_9

to switch from operational product presentation to the coding design based on the logic program, engaged in this process of parameterization and calculation.

The calculating-based design thinking is the transformation from the original high realistic product models to parameterized ones. The advantage of calculating-based design thinking is to produce 3D models by structural, relevant, flexible, and intelligent structures. Moreover, some constructions through parametric and calculation formula can truly reflect the life of the model itself, not only changing the parameters of the model, but also the force field of the structure, material, temperature and humidity, the variation of light, and even the state of the content. These factors can accurately represent the logic of the internal structure, and the parametric models can easily convert into a form built by digital tools.

Therefore, the parametric form, a powerful digital process, is influenced by the purpose of the design, like the logic of appearance analysis and the digital manufacturing, can be used to define the characteristics of digital architecture. Contemporary architect Patrik Schumacher, partner of ZAHA, defined "Parametricism" as the new movement of architectural after "Modernism" [1]. Patrick addresses that we must pursue parametric design, and it will penetrate into any corner of the construction field. Systematic variables related to all architectural designs, including structural details from the city to all stages, which means all the scales are completely flowing (dynamic). He also pointed out the fundamentals of parametric design including the vision repetition, a large number of customizations and continuous changes.

Following the calculating-based design thinking, the problem of this research is how to assist designers to generate design concepts through the user's body dynamic and digital information. In order to solve the problem of this research, the main objective is to utilize the sensors built by Arduino, combined with the parametric software Grasshopper, which is a plug-in in Rhinoceros, conducted with the parameters of dynamic information to construct the stool deformation by structure, form, size of the stool, etc., and, finally, conformed the shape of hip from different users. By using generative design to break through the traditional design thinking, the generative system could not only change the form of the stool through dynamic sensing parameters, but also quickly generate multiple stools to provide suitable solutions for different uses.

Therefore, the first step of this study is to analyze forms and structures of some kinds of stools and to construct a stool generative modeling system by Grasshopper. The second step, then, is to integrate the pressure sensors in Arduino to obtain the pressure values of users, instantly. After obtaining the information from users, finally, the generative system could build stools based on dynamic values from different body types, and then the dynamic informs also could be applied to different models of stools or chairs.

2 Related Works

The parametric-oriented CAD (Computer-Aided Design) software, such as Pro-E and any Generative Component, has functions for parameter adjustment, construction history, and open-coded script to achieve divergent design or optimization effect in a more intuitive and non-linear way. For example, Grasshopper (https://www.grasshopper3d.com) with the logic components and object-oriented interface, which is fully integrating with the modeling instructions, had been developed as a well-known plug-in of

Rhinoceros. Grasshopper is programmed in series to make the parameter data flow, processing easier to grasp, and the history of model construction. Another application of Grasshopper, named Firefly (https://www.grasshopper3d.com/group/fireflyplugin), connected the entities of Arduino and robotics, which modeling purposes beyond the original derivative, but also successfully lead the trend for other object-oriented programming languages to emulate, such as Nudebox (https://machinebox.io/docs/nudebox) and so on.

Moreover, Grasshopper has rapidly developed and popularized in the field of digital architecture, and has widely used in recent years. Especially for free-form surfaces and digital construction has achieved by this parametric modeling tool. The advantage of being able to perform monotonous and large computations in a computer is helpful for processing in a large amount with small components in digital buildings. Also, its advantage of fast calculations to present the change in time allows designers to repeatedly seek for the best form and structural performance with dynamic non-linear design techniques. Therefore, a generative system can build a model based on some crucial parameters of functional requirements, such as size, input, cost, etc. Through generative system, the outputs are consistent with the designers' needs, such as CAD model files, design procedures, rules, feature limits, formulas, etc. For example, the Cell Cycle System (Fig. 1) could generative customized form based on users' inputs, such as size, shape and density of holes, materials…etc., and finally, the cost of design will be calculated.

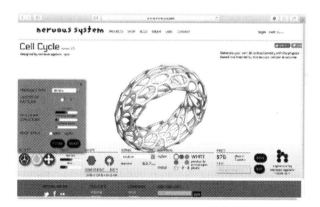

Fig. 1. The cell cycle system.

In the application of design computation, Oxman formally established the fundamental definition of generative design in terms of theory and practice [2]. By manipulating some parameters in the pre-compiled generative system, designers could obtain preliminary models from the generative system. Designers, furthermore, could limit parameters and determine the interaction judgments between the drawing instructions and the data transfer function in order to derive new modified results, which is closer to designers purposes. The dynamic design-concept generation is very different from the traditional design thinking and modeling. Based on a large number of information which is as design reference or design space, design ideas from generative system have better optimization or insight compared with the traditional design thinking, in which designers have limited and fixed brain recourses.

Another well-known system, SketchChair, allows the user to sketch the chair with his own body, shown as Fig. 2. Using the programmatic algorithm can automatically generate a 3D chair structure from a 2D sketch. At the same time, the user can improve the chair form by changing the sketches and exercises multiple times in this operation interface. This interface is more suitable for inexperienced users. Meanwhile, the software can draw a laser cutting pattern directly, which can be assembled into a chair directly after cutting [3].

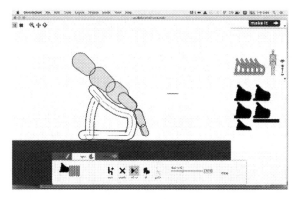

Fig. 2. SketchChair.

Please note that the first paragraph of a section or subsection is not indented. The first paragraphs that follows a table, figure, equation etc. does not have an indent, either.

In addition, Krish proposed a generative system based on parametric computer-aided design, Generative Design Method (GDM) [4]. The parameters in the system contain a certain range, and the range is the space for the program search from the maximum to the minimum value. The search range of each parameter can form the entire design space while limiting the range that the computer can search. The generative design system will randomly generate new design output based on the parameters, and the parameters are like the genes of design. Through the Genoform plug-in, the designer can quickly synthesize a large number of parameters and allows the system to generate dozens or even hundreds of design idea which can save lots of time. However, Krish also added the concept of filtering to Genoform. Performance Filters is based on the design requirements and condition to filter the conception which meet the design requirements. Another similarity filter, Proximity Filter, removes the high similarity idea to ensure a different vision. These data will be stored for further modification [4]. This filtering mechanism can be adjusted by the designer to improve the efficiency of dealing with a large number of unsuitable forms, and also find the best solution in the large solution space (Fig. 3).

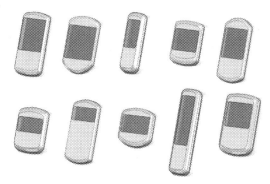

Fig. 3. Generative Design Method (GDM)

3 Process of Constructing Generative System

There are three steps to achieve the objective of this study, which including construction of generative models, interactive devices with Arduino, and applications for different types of chairs.

3.1 The Construction of Generative Models

Based on the shape of stool surface, there are a variety of types of stools, such as square stools, round stools, benches, T-stools, I-stools…etc., and the numbers and shapes of stool legs are also very diverse with no limitations. The purpose of this study is to investigate the form changed based on the users' body shape. Thus, to represent the users' inputs simply and clearly in generative system, the basic shape of a stool is a simple rectangle of surface with arc-shape legs. Moreover, the deformation control directions of the stool are setting to the left and right sides and upper and lower axial in order to observe the deformation clearly through the front view of the stool. Different thickness with same material in the same force, however, has different levels of deformations. To avoid the factor of thickness, therefore, this study is regardless of the thickness parameters by defining the same thickness.

According to the basic form analysis of the stool, described above, process of constructing generative system of stools by Grasshopper in Rhinoceros is followed.

Definitions of the Deformation Control Points. The basic structure of a stool is including two parts: stool surface line, and two legs perpendicular to the stool from the front view. Thus, in Grasshopper, there are some parameters to control the width of the stool surface and the length of the stool legs. Then, connection between the stool surface and legs is through the rounded curve tangent, and adjust the size of the fillet curve by changing the fillet radius setting. The deformation control points can be changed linkage with baseline and changed the curvature of the stool surface and legs to simulate the changes caused by the different weight of the people, shown as Fig. 4.

After reformatting the control points, the system could extrude the contours of stool into 3D models, and also modify the depth and size of stools in Fig. 5.

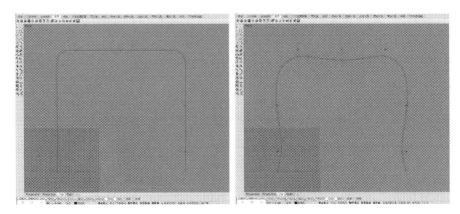

Fig. 4. The deformation control points

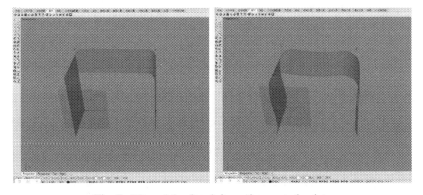

Fig. 5. 3D models after deformation control points

Construction of Concave-Seat Surface. The curve can be adjusted through the deformation control points and constructed into a concave surface by adjusting the width, depth, and degree of down-concave through parameters setting, shown as Fig. 6.

Construction of Fixed Thickness. Finally, fixed thickness, mentioned above, has been conducted by the combined blending surfaces into a solid model, which applied the offset curve function in Rhinoceros, shown as Fig. 7.

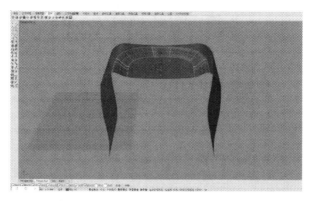

Fig. 6. Construction of concave-seat surface

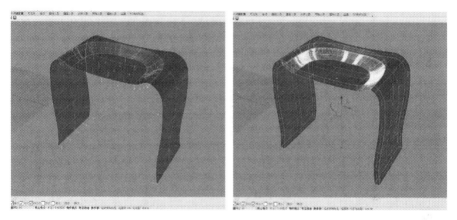

Fig. 7. Construction of fixed thickness

3.2 The Interactive Devices with Arduino

The interactive sensing device was built by placing several pressure sensors on the specific parts of the stool surface and detected the dynamic pressure data instantly through Arduino, shown as Fig. 8: left. Sitting on the interactive sensing device, the device can detect the pressure data of each part, and generate the form of stool in Grasshopper instantly based on the users' body shape of subjects, shown as Fig. 8: right.

The dynamic data measured by the interactive sensing device used as input parameters for Grasshopper is used to construct a generative system for stools, shown as Fig. 9.

3.3 Applications for Different Types of Chairs

Dynamic data information from users' bodies, finally, could be applied into different kinds of chair designs, shown as Fig. 10.

Fig. 8. left: Interactive sensors with Arduino; right: dynamic input for forming stools

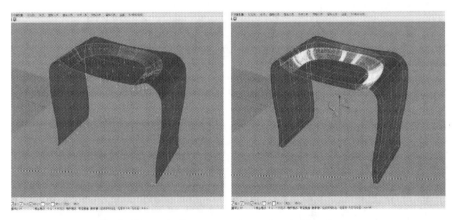

Fig. 9. Dynamic-form generative system in Grasshopper

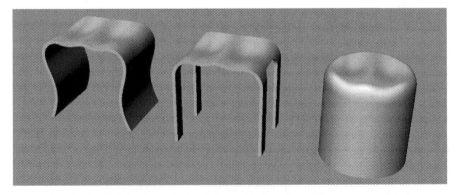

Fig. 10. Applied the dynamic data information into three different types of chairs

4 Conclusions

The objective of this study attempts to generate the dynamic design generative system by using information of users' body. Applying the sensors constructed by Arduino combined with the parametric software, Grasshopper in Rhinoceros, is to generate deformed stools, fitting hip of different users. In the generative design system for stools, forms of stools are reformed through dynamic sensing parameters and further applied to different types of chair. By doing so, this kind of generative design is also applied to break through the traditional design thinking.

The computer-aided design and parametric design not only can reform the width, height, and depth of the stool through adjusting the parameters, but also possible to control the bending degree deformation of the stool in response to the weight and size of the occupant. For a generation of strong customer demand era, it is a very convenient tool for the designer whether it is furniture or product designs.

References

1. Jabi, W.: Parametric Design for Architecture. Laurence King Publishing Ltd. (2013)
2. Oxman, R.: Theory and design in the first digital age. Des. Stud. **27**(3), 229–265 (2006)
3. Saul, G., Lau, M., Mitani, J., Igarashi, T.: SketchChair: an all-in-one chair design system for end users. In: Proceedings of the International Conference on Tangible, Embedded, and Embodied Interaction (TEI), pp. 73–80. ACM Press, New York (2011)
4. Krish, S.: A practical generative design method. Comput.-Aided Des. **43**, 88–100 (2011)

Detriments to Cultural Sensitivity in HCI Design Processes: Insights from Practitioners' Experiences in India

Jyoti Kumar and Surbhi Pratap(⊠)

Department of Design, Indian Institute of Technology Delhi, New Delhi, India
meetjyoti@gmail.com, surbhi.pratap@gmail.com

Abstract. Culture influences human preferences and behaviour. Many HCI products are being designed and developed in cross cultural contexts. Culture's influence needs to be accommodated in the HCI design process. There is a need to understand how the current design processes for HCI products are accommodating for culture's influence. Discussion with HCI designers is one possible method to do this. This paper reports findings of interviews with 30 HCI designers from India. The one on one semi structured qualitative interviews were conducted to understand whether the current design processes under practice are sensitive to culture's influence on design and what are the detriments to accommodate cultural influences in the design process. The key findings suggest that the inclusion of cultural concerns in the design process are directly influenced by the project leadership's awareness and the client's awareness of the impact of culture in acceptance of HCI products. In projects where the client had not specifically asked for cultural sensitivity of the HCI product, design processes did not include the cultural concerns in the development of the product.

Keywords: Culture · Interaction designers · UX design process

1 Introduction

Design of Human Computer Interaction (HCI) is the process of shaping up of digital artefacts (products, spaces, services) in social, cultural and business contexts while paying particular attention to the user experience [1]. Localisation of HCI products as a way to improve the user experience (UX) has been argued often [2]. One of the aspects of localisation is the cultural suitability of HCI products. Culturally suitable products would also need a culturally sensitive design process of HCI products. The need for cultural sensitivity of design processes has been argued in literature [3, 4] and also methods which can make the design processes culturally sensitive have been discussed [5]. However, the processes of HCI product design in Industry have yet not been reported to use these culturally sensitive design methods [6, 7].

India is one of the largest exporters of HCI products in the world [8, 9]. Often, HCI products which are targeted at users from different cultures are developed in India. This paper reports findings from one on one semi structured qualitative interviews with 30

© Springer Nature Switzerland AG 2020
C. Stephanidis et al. (Eds.): HCII 2020, LNCS 12423, pp. 142–155, 2020.
https://doi.org/10.1007/978-3-030-60114-0_10

design professionals working in different organisations in India. The findings suggest that in spite of the willingness of the design teams to conduct user centred design process of designing for culturally sensitive products, industry constraints are often forcing the design teams to deliver products otherwise.

1.1 Culture and HCI Design Process

Influence of culture on human preferences has been discussed in literature [10]. Also, study of the effects of cultural differences on organizational behaviour has been reported [11]. Some discussion on the influence of culture on design practice are also available in the literature [12]. However, most of the reported literature has centred its discussions on the difference between users' behaviours and their preferences due to cultural differences. There is very little literature reported where the practices of the design teams have been studied. Design teams and the processes that they follow are key factors in ensuring that HCI products are culturally suitable. The practices of the HCI design team thus become central to the whole cultural focus of the HCI products.

While, HCI products are often developed by multi-disciplinary teams, HCI design professionals are one of the key players. HCI designers are often responsible for bringing an intentional change in the way humans interact with computers by using both opportunistic (artistic/creative) and systematic processes (scientific) which makes their role more power laden [13]. The design teams have the potential to influence the entire socio-technical system [7]. It is thus required that the HCI designers are informed and invested in the socio technical concerns of the HCI products. Sensitivity to cultural needs is one such expectation from the HCI design professionals.

It has been argued that contemporary design should be a solution oriented design for which the defining characteristics are the 'tools and methods' it uses and not the artefacts it produces. However, limited focus on cultural dimension at the 'tools and methods' level in the design process has limited the impact of design practice at artefactual level [7].

2 Research Methodology

This paper reports findings from qualitative interviews. 'Conversation analysis' of the qualitative data from the interviews has been the methodology of this paper. The purpose of this paper is to report the HCI design processes being followed in industry and then to dig deeper into why the prevalent processes do not have cultural sensitivities. The qualitative research was conducted to identify the detriments to the cultural sensitivity of the HCI design process.

'Conversation Analysis' has been used in sociology, linguistics, psychology, anthropology, ethnography etc. [14] to understand the deep semantic connotations of an existing phenomena. Design researchers have also been using the 'conversational analysis' as a method to dig deeper into the interpretations of perspectives and arguments around the profession [15]. The benefits of this research methodology has been its ability to bring forth the underlying causes of a reported effect rather than count of instance of occurrence of an effect. Given the nature of human experiences and understanding, there are deeper beliefs and feelings beneath the reported phenomena. The open ended interviews, guided by deep probes into reported experiences, have the potential to identify causal structures in reported experiences which otherwise is difficult to study. One on one interviews over skype were conducted over a duration of 45–60 min (average) each with practising designers of the Indian UX design industry. The contacts were sourced through personal references as well as LinkedIn profiles. Designers were requested for a suitable time for a skype conversation after introducing to them the intent and the objective behind this interview. The interviews were recorded after seeking their consent. For most of the interviews, the time slot was after their office hours, where they would take their laptops at home or cafe. The interviews were semi structured, with the designers explaining the HCI design processes they have followed initially and then responding to probes on their specific experiences in the UX design industry. The probes were developed upon the conversations of the design practitioners.

The interviews started with an introduction of the interviewers and the purpose of the interview. An informed consent was obtained on the call itself and was recorded along with the rest of the interview. Permission for the recording was also obtained on the call and was also recorded. The interviewer then asked about the personal details and prior work experiences. The sequence of conversations initiated by the interviewer was planned as: Can you please narrate the design process followed by you in the last two design projects?

- How was the design brief generated?
- How was the design process selected?
- How were the users of the design identified?
- How were the user's needs understood?

If the discussion on cultural consideration did not emerge in the conversation automatically, then a specific question "did you consider for the user's culture in the design process?", "have you ever considered users' cultural differences in any of the earlier projects" was asked to the design professionals. The qualitative responses from interviews were recorded and then transcribed. Discussions on semantics of each uttered response and its intent were discussed between the two authors. Then thematic areas within the reasons for not following a culturally sensitive HCI design process were identified. Responses of the designers were clustered under the thematic areas [16, 17].

Participants
All the 30 participants were from 30 different organisations. Each of the participants had a good experience of handling different HCI design projects. There was a range of years that they had spent as a design professional. While the youngest professional had spent 3 years, the most senior participant had spent 17 years as a design professional. All the professionals had worked in India for most of the duration of their professional career. Out of the 30 professionals 12 had worked on HCI products which was aimed at users of a different culture at some point of time in their career. The average age of the design professionals interviewed was 33 years with Std. Dev. of 4.7 years. The average professional experience of participants was 8 years with Std. Dev. of 4.2 years. Out of the

30 participants 25 were males and 5 were females. An overview of participants profiles is displayed in Table 1.

Table 1. Design Professional profiles who participated in the interviews

Sl. no	Gender	Exp (yrs)	Age (yrs)	Current designation	Type of organization
1	M	8	32	UX Lead	e-commerce
2	M	3	29	UX Designer	Insurance product
3	M	6	30	Sr. Designer	Design consultancy
4	M	2	26	Designer	Design consultancy
5	M	4	27	Product Designer	Travel Product
6	M	3	25	Designer	Insurance product
7	M	12	36	Director of Design	Cloud product
8	M	2	26	UX Designer	e-commerce
9	M	16	42	Design Head	e-commerce
10	F	4	29	UX Designer	News & Marketing
11	F	8	32	Design Lead	Software product
12	M	3	28	UX Designer	Software product
13	M	12	36	Head of Design	Service Product
14	M	12	35	Senior Designer	Software product
15	M	15	38	UX Head	Software product
16	M	6	32	Designer	Software product
17	F	9	36	Design Lead	Travel Product
18	M	12	36	Head of Design	Service Product
19	M	6	30	UX Designer	Software product
20	M	8	32	Designer	Software product
21	F	17	45	Senior Designer	Design consultancy
22	M	15	35	Design Lead	Service Product
23	M	12	35	Design Head	Software product
24	F	5	30	UX designer	Software product
25	M	6	30	UX designer	Banking Product
26	M	5	29	Designer	News & Marketing
27	M	4	28	Designer	Design consultancy
28	M	6	38	Senior Designer	e-commerce
29	M	10	34	Senior Designer	Software product
30	M	5	29	Designer	e-commerce

3   Findings

The most striking finding from the interviews was that none of the 30 professional designers had used any consideration for user's culture in their design processes in the last two projects that they reported. Further, only 5 of the 30 professionals had used culture's consideration in their design process at least once in their professional career. However, almost all the design professionals interviewed expressed their interest to accommodate the users' culture given support by the organisation's processes. Also, almost all of them were aware that users' culture has an influence on the design outcomes.

The detriments to inclusion of users' culture in the design process were 1. Lack of clients' emphasis for inclusion of cultural concerns 2. Lack of awareness of the design leadership in companies who drive the projects 3. Lack of project resources for inclusion of culture in the design process 4. Extensive focus on delivering bare minimum products and 5. Fast sprints of agile methodology. Details of each of the five identified detriments to inclusion of users culture during the design process as reported by design professionals has been organised under five themes in the following subsections.

3.1   Client Briefs

Almost all the professionals mentioned that clients gave the design brief for the project. The design brief given by the client drove the project processes. As the client brief did not mention for consideration of the users' culture, therefore, the design team did not accommodate the users' culture in the design process. Table 2 shares some instances of the interview where design professionals had mentioned how client brief became detriment to inclusion of users' culture in the HCI design process. The sl nos. in Table 2 reflects the sl nos. in Table 1 so a reader can check against the company type and the professional's profile. The verbal reports on the right column have been paraphrased to make sense in this context of discussion, however it has been ensured that the meaning remains the same as narrated by the professionals.

Table 2. Instances of how client brief affects the design process

Serial no.	Verbal report
Sl no. 16	The client has a Customer Relationship Management (CRM) system which gathers the customers feedback. The client shared with us the design insights based on their CRM The design brief is generated by the client on the basis of the CRM and they did not trust the user research. The client does not expect deep insights to emerge from user research
Sl no. 17	Service companies present the academically advised processes for user centred design as they have to sell it to the clients, however the design team does not get to practice the process as the clients are not particular about it. Almost all design briefs by clients are data driven from their website analytics. There is very little scope of revising the brief
Sl no. 20	In the service based industry, we have clients from different domains. Thus for bidding, quick wireframes and visual design is done for bidding and the user centred design process is skipped. In cases where the client asks to do user research, a different team gets involved in the user research, design team is not involved in the research. At most, the design team does testing informally with internal colleagues. We do not work for consideration of user culture because we work on the user expectations as shared by the clients
Sl no. 21	When we worked for an Australian client who was creating a product for Indian users, I got exposed to their focus on user centred design. However, when we worked in Indian teams, we were given very little time to deliver and hence the focus shifts to delivery rather than the details of the process. We once did remote testing when the client asked
Sl no. 23	Service based companies don't own the product. So they are not so much invested in its success. And the clients are result oriented. They would not provide enough bandwidth to do user research, so a lot of user-research steps are skipped during the design process. Convincing the clients about the actual problem at hand also takes up a lot of time and effort. Development companies are engineering or cost driven and here design is not taken seriously
Sl no. 24	In my experience the clients give the design brief which consists of what the user requirements are. We have internal meetings to detail out the design brief. As a design team we are supposed to deliver as per the brief and not add any other considerations. Once with a South African client, the brief was not clear then the designer had to hold a stakeholder meeting to clarify the design brief. Another example where a US client did not document the design brief, so we had to spend longer to understand the needs. But almost always in my experience, it is the client who gives the design brief

3.2 Leadership Led Design Process

The next most recurrent reason iterated by the professionals for not having any cultural considerations in the design process was that the design team lead had a strong influence on the selected design process and often the leader of the design team did not have an

Table 3. Instances of how leadership has affected the design process

Serial no.	Verbal report
Sl no. 2	Our CEO does not believe in user centred design as in his eyes the credibility of the design team to do user research is low. Even usability testing in our company is done superficially. The design team wants to do more user centric practices including rigorous UTs but due to lack of leadership support we are not able to do it. Our design team's whole focus is to convince the CEO and the marketing team. If they approve a design then our job is done
Sl no. 3	We have a strong team hierarchy in the company. Our seniors in the company share their understanding of the users. Whatever our seniors in the company tell us, our design team aims to achieve it. There is no further consideration of users in the design process. In my experience users' culture has never been considered formally
Sl no. 5	Ours is a product company. We first develop a product and then sell it. The design brief is generated by the top management of the company. Often the sales team is involved in generating the design brief. The design team has to deliver the brief given. There is no involvement of users in the process. There is no research to validate the problem statement. Culture of the company reflects in the design more than the culture of the user
Sl no. 11	Our design brief comes from product managers who jots down the use cases based on their understanding of the market. In India, more development work comes rather than strategic design work, hence design team assists the development teams rather than lead them
Sl no. 13	Data science team gives inputs to the design head. People in my company do not realise the importance of design. In my company, design is understood as 'making things beautiful' therefore the design process is aimed at making the products 'pixel perfect' rather than to understand the user needs. Also, there is a time crunch in projects. Thus when we ask questions about the users, the marketing team sees us as slowing down the process
Sl no. 14	The design team in our company has a mentality to 'serve'. So they serve the clients but don't question them. And this also results in not making an effort into innovating anything. We get requirements from the senior business analysts who have a huge pressure of time. They force us to skip steps from the design process
Sl no. 16	Boss says don't go so deep. I love to do user research, competitor analysis and market trend analysis, but my boss suggests not doing that because of time pressure. The vision is to please the client and not the users. Hence understanding client has far more importance than understanding the user
Sl no. 18	Design team members are often seen as young by the leadership of the organization and therefore not expected to understand the complexities of the business of the product. The design team is not expected to do the user research to develop the user understanding, user needs are given to them by the leadership
Sl no. 26	Managers in my company think that they are the users. They share the user considerations as per their knowledge. We only focus on competitor analysis and no other user research

(continued)

Table 3. (*continued*)

Serial no.	Verbal report
Sl no. 30	Time constraints are high, hence we are asked to make things look 'nice' as there is no time for detailed user investigations. 'User data' is all that the product manager has and gives the design brief based on the data that he has. Design team is not expected to study the 'user data' that the product manager has

orientation in nuances of cultural influence on HCI products. Most of the design professionals reported that their design teams haven't followed user centred design process. Many of them did not get a chance to collect user data or to analyse any aspect of users' needs, be it cognitive, affective or cultural. The sheer lack of focus on user centric design process further made it impossible for design professionals to consider for users' culture in the design process. The entire design process was focussed on delivering the business goals because the head of the design team had that as the priority. Some of the instances of how design leadership affected the design process has been tabulated in Table 3.

3.3 Lack of Project Resources

All of the 30 professional designers who were interviewed, also reported that one of the major reasons for not considering the user's culture in the design process was that the resources required to do so were not available. These resources were design professionals with cultural understanding; time required to do the design iterations and funds available to facilitate the design teams. The user centric design process was found to be more resource expensive and hence the project focus was on implementing the design brief given by the client and stakeholders. Table 4 presents some of the instances of how lack of resources affected the design process.

Table 4. Instances of how lack of resources affect the design process

Serial no.	Verbal report
Sl no. 1	User centred design is a very time consuming process. As our projects have highly constrained on budget and time hence people in my company are not interested in user centred design
Sl no. 3	We have a very limited budget for projects, hence we can afford only one UT which is taken up only after the design team is confident of the design. We do not do any other user data collection for our projects apart from UT
Sl no. 7	In the design process, depth is missing because of time crunch. Most start-ups cannot afford usability testing. And even with bigger companies, it is not carried out seriously unless it's a broad feature of the product
Sl no. 8	Designer's appraisals depend on conversion rates. The final design is sought as soon as the research report is completed, so we actually don't use findings of the research properly in the design. Because there is a lack of bandwidth and resources things like culture cannot be discussed
Sl no. 14	Time crunch ensures that we cannot focus on the design process and thus the quality of the outcomes suffer. We don't get to hear words like user culture or empathy while designing because of this, even though implicitly sometimes it does get covered when we map out journey maps
Sl no. 16	There is a limited time for research, so it is limited to only competitor analysis, user requirements are received from the clients and designs are made according to those requirements
Sl no. 20	The main design process is given a skip, quickly wireframes and VD are done for RFP(Request for Proposal). Interviews are not easy to get because of logistics constraints especially in service industry
Sl no. 21	For most of the projects, I have to buy time for doing research from the limited available for the entire project. Time constraints drive the process. People don't really value user experience or the time taken for design. We have to convince the leadership or the development team about time needed to do even basic research
Sl no. 22	User research is done for namesake initially because of time constraints. We take feedback from the end-users but they are mostly on the user interface design and not on the user experience. The process is agile, so we plan subsequent research studies after the product is launched
Sl no. 27	Ours is a design consultancy and that can never compete with product companies because of lack of time. We do remote research sometimes, but mostly we try to get insights through role play, though we would love to do in-depth research
Sl no. 29	Usually there is not much time to do detailed research, so we work with a basic sequence of steps. To make up for this, we work with domain experts and they become our reference points. We also rely a lot on heuristics and best practices

3.4   Extensive Focus on Delivering a Bare Minimum Working Product

One constant complaint that was the focus of the entire design team and the design process followed was that the product at hand had to work. That the product had to reach the users and lead to conversions and profit. In order to deliver the product with the desired functionality as required by the top management, the design teams were conducting competitor analysis [18, 19] to identify the features that worked. The understanding was that if something was working in the market, it must be good and therefore there was no need to 'reinvent the wheel'.

Table 5 lists instances where participants reported how extensive focus on delivering the bare minimum product affected the design process.

Table 5. Instances of how focus on a minimum working product affects the design process

Serial no.	Verbal report
Sl no. 5	We make our own product and hence do not have too many stakeholders. We draft the design process on our own and it is orientated towards making a minimum viable product. So after conceptualization, we do a technical feasibility meeting and then directly go to the prototype stage. Not much user research is done
Sl no. 6	For us, the technical marketing team gives us the use cases and tasks are completed in order of priorities set by the company. We do competitor benchmarking and make a basic product based on that. So as designers, we don't do hands on research on the users ourselves. The conversation around user culture doesn't come up
Sl no. 7	For the product, the design team makes brief but it is mostly a version of the brief that has come up from the marketing team. In India, focus is on making basic digital products accessible to a large number of people rather than working on the experiential aspects
Sl no. 12	We start with fixed primary goals for the product and the minimum features required for it to be working. We then decide on indices to be focused on to define its success. Design is sometimes regarded as an afterthought
Sl No. 13	The start-up environment mostly works for the usefulness of the product, and not the experience. Customer is different from the user and the product is designed for customer satisfaction and not user satisfaction
Sl no. 17	We have phased rollouts of the product and the entire process is highly data driven. We are a risk averse company and data and analytics matter more than studying the users
Sl no. 20	Quick wireframes and visual designs are done for requests for proposal (RFP). The design process is given a skip. During this time only a user story is chalked out by the client or the business analyst. We design according to that user story. There is an overview of the project and then heuristic analysis is done to test the design
Sl no. 22	In the start-up environment, product development is required at a very fast pace. We however do not have enough resources for that. User research is a time consuming process. So we create a minimum working product and test it within the company team to get a basic start on the product
Sl no. 26	We get the requirements from the reporting manager who does his basic research and then clearly defines the features that are to be used for the new product. We get a list of 'must have' and 'nice to have' features and work on them to create the wireframes. We don't do user research ourselves

3.5 Fast Sprints of Agile Development Process

The development culture of the companies have shifted to fast sprints as reported by 5 of the 30 professionals. The fast sprints of the agile method give very little time to the design professionals to have a fresh strategic look at the user needs. This was observed as another reason why the cultural considerations of the users were not being addressed in the design process.

Table 6 lists instances where participants reported how shifting to fast sprints of agile development process limited designers' involvement with in-depth user research.

Table 6. Instances of how fast sprints of agile development has affected the design process

Serial no.	Verbal report
Sl no. 4	Since we cater to start-ups, who do not have established products, We follow an agile process strictly. We depend on client's research for user context and requirements and focus on creating a mind map document based on our understanding of the client's brief followed by the information architecture of the product. This does not involve any user research from our end
Sl no. 14	While working for the government, agile processes result in random steps and sometimes more wastage of time. After conceptualization, mock-ups were created and were shown for approval by the ministry. However the process was wrong, as approval should be sought after usability testing
Sl no. 22	Our design process is agile, so we plan subsequent research studies after the product is launched. In the first phase we focus on creating the product and launching it. Not much time goes into developing an experience
Sl no. 23	The design process followed here is agile. So the design process does not follow a linear route. Everything is done parallelly. It's iterative and though iterations should ideally happen earlier, it happens late in most of the cases and even during product testing, changes are required which could have been done earlier
Sl no. 29	We use heuristics and best practices approach to reduce the time taken for designing. In agile, we follow a 2 week sprint model. We create the design in one week and then it is available for coding. Agile is focussed on the technical development goal and not on the product experience

To summarise, the above thematic reports suggest that the client and the leadership in the design organisation are the most important influencing factors that lead to selection of tools and process that make the design culturally sensitive to users' needs. A lack of awareness of the impact of user centred design process and culturally suitable products amongst the clients and the leadership results in fast sprints of design process which focus on a minimum working product rather than the experiential aspects. This leads to a lack of understanding of users' context and users' culture in designers while designing products for them. Figure 1 visually represents the flow of influences on culturally sensitive processes in an organisation.

In the one on one interviews, designers also reported that they were aware of the impact of user research and in fact enjoyed that during the design process. But the industry

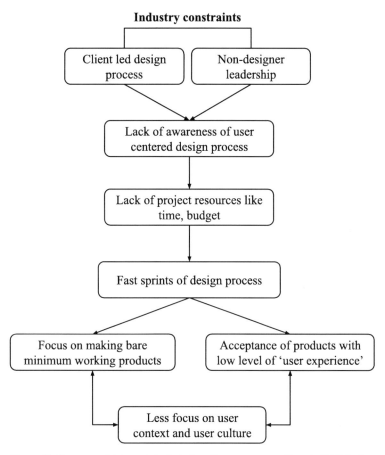

Fig. 1. Flow of influences which contribute to less focus on user culture in HCI design process

constraints of time and resources limited them while doing user centric research. They also reported that literature on culturally sensitive design methods like guidelines, skills and tools would be of help in following a user centred design process.

4 Discussion and Conclusion

In the light of the reporting of the professional designers who were interviewed in this research, it can be concluded that it is not the lack of interest of the HCI professionals to include user's cultural considerations but rather the organisational processes employed in designing HCI products that are detriments to the cultural sensitivity of the HCI design processes. The design processes are either driven by the client or the leadership of the organization. There is a need to influence the design ecosystem of the HCI products to include the cultural considerations of the users. For this, an awareness in both the client as well as the leadership is required for an understanding about the impact of including culture's consideration in user centred design.

Figure 2 summarizes the findings of this research in a schematic diagram. The right side of the figure represents the organizational factors that influence the designer of an HCI product. The culture of an organization determines if the leadership of the design team is aware and understands the return of investment for cultural considerations while designing an HCI product. If they are aware, they would facilitate the designer in following a user centred design process. The left side of the schematic represents the project specific factors that influence the designer. If the client is aware of and understands the return of investment of cultural considerations in the design of a product, resources like time, budget would be facilitated to the designer to follow a user centred design process. And if guidelines, skills and tools that help in following culturally sensitive design processes are made available to the designers, then it would help to include culture's consideration in user centred design.

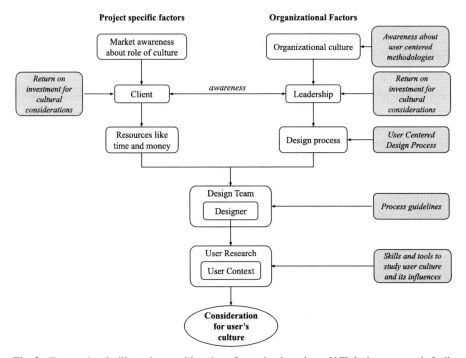

Fig. 2. Factors that facilitate the consideration of users' culture in an HCI design process in India

References

1. Fallman, D.: The interaction design research triangle of design practice, design studies, and design exploration. Des. Issues **24**, 4–18 (2008)
2. Rau, P.L.P. (ed.): CCD 2015. LNCS, vol. 9180. Springer, Cham (2015). https://doi.org/10.1007/978-3-319-20907-4
3. Gray, C.M., Boling, E.: Designers' Articulation and Activation of Instrumental Design Judgements in Cross-Cultural User Research. Analysing Design Thinking: Studies of Cross-Cultural Co-Creation, pp. 191–212 (2017)
4. Horn, M.S.: The role of cultural forms in tangible interaction design. In: Proceedings of the 7th International Conference on Tangible, Embedded and Embodied Interaction, TEI 2013 (2013). https://doi.org/10.1145/2460625.2460643
5. Hakken, D., Maté, P.: The culture question in participatory design. In: Proceedings of the 13th Participatory Design Conference on Short Papers, Industry Cases, Workshop Descriptions, Doctoral Consortium papers, and Keynote Abstracts, PDC 2014, vol. 2 (2014). https://doi.org/10.1145/2662155.2662197
6. Nielsen, J., Bødker, M., Vatrapu, R.: Culture and (i)literacy as challenges to scandinavian cooperative design. In: Proceedings of the 3rd International Conference on Intercultural Collaboration, ICIC 2010 (2010). https://doi.org/10.1145/1841853.1841905
7. Manzini, E.: Design culture and dialogic design. Des. Issues **32**, 52–59 (2016)
8. Thomas, P.N.: Digital India: Understanding Information, Communication and Social Change. SAGE Publications, India (2012)
9. McKinsey & Company, Inc.: Reimagining India: Unlocking the Potential of Asia's Next Superpower. Simon and Schuster (2013)
10. Fehr, E., Hoff, K.: Tastes, castes, and culture: the influence of society on preferences. PsycEXTRA Dataset (2011). https://doi.org/10.1037/e596062012-001
11. Sinha, J.: Culture and Organizational Behaviour (2008). https://doi.org/10.4135/9788132100997
12. Singh, N., Pereira, A.: The Culturally Customized Web Site. Routledge (2005)
13. Nelson, H.G., Stolterman, E.: The Design Way (2012). https://doi.org/10.7551/mitpress/9188.001.0001
14. Nielsen, M.F., Wagner, J.: Diversity and continuity in conversation analysis. J. Pragmatics **39**, 441–444 (2007)
15. Oak, A.: What can talk tell us about design?: analyzing conversation to understand practice. Des. Stud. **32**, 211–234 (2011)
16. Charles Romesburg, H.: Cluster Analysis for Researchers (2004)
17. Kaufman, L., Rousseeuw, P.J.: Finding Groups in Data: An Introduction to Cluster Analysis. Wiley, Hoboken (2009)
18. Competitor Analysis. Dictionary of Marketing Communications. https://doi.org/10.4135/9781452229669.n734
19. Youngman, I.: The need for competitor analysis. Competitor Analysis in Financial Services, pp. 1–21 (1998)

Human Factors Evaluation Principals for Civil Aircraft Flight Deck Controls Design and Integration

Fei Li[(✉)], Kaiwen Chen, Yuan Wang, and Pu Hong

Shanghai Aircraft Design and Research Institute, Shanghai 201210, China
lifei@comac.cc

Abstract. The Flight Deck Controls are the components of a flight deck interface that allow pilots to provide information to an aircraft system. Example control functions are to operate, configure, and manage systems. This document addresses controls on civil aircraft flight decks from primarily a human factors perspective. This paper introduced a practical evaluation principles, which including general evaluation principles, arrangement and accessibility evaluation principles and operational and usability evaluation principles, for Civil Aircraft Flight Deck Controls Design and Integration.

Keywords: Flight deck · Human factors · Control

1 Introduction

Controls are the primary means of interfacing with the system. The term "controls" is used here to refer to the hardware and software related to an input device, the label, and other components that address its intended function [1]. Conventional aircraft control devices consist of buttons, knobs, keyboards, and switches, but cursor control devices, such as a mouse, touchpad, trackball, or joystick are becoming more frequent. Each control device has unique characteristics that may affect the design of the functions being controlled. Consideration must be given to the appropriateness of a control to a particular application and/or system and its usability.

2 General Evaluation Principles

Flight deck controls must be installed to allow accomplishment of all the tasks required to safely perform the equipment's intended function, and information must be provided to the flightcrew that is necessary to accomplish the defined tasks [2].

Flight deck controls and information intended for the flightcrew's use must:

- Be provided in a clear and unambiguous manner, at a resolution and precision appropriate to the task.

C. Stephanidis et al. (Eds.): HCII 2020, LNCS 12423, pp. 156–165, 2020.
https://doi.org/10.1007/978-3-030-60114-0_11

- Be accessible and usable by the flightcrew in a manner consistent with the urgency, frequency, and duration of their tasks, and
- Enable flightcrew awareness, if awareness is required for safe operation, of the effects on the airplane or systems resulting from flightcrew actions.

For each of these requirements, the proposed means of compliance should include consideration of the following control characteristics for each control individually and in relation to other controls [3]:

- Physical location of the control.
- Physical characteristics of the control (e.g., shape, dimensions, surface texture, range of motion, colour).
- Equipment or system(s) that the control directly affects.
- How the control is labelled.
- Available control settings.
- Effect of each possible actuation or setting, as a function of initial control setting or other conditions.
- Whether there are other controls that can produce the same effect (or affect the same target parameter) and conditions under which this will happen.
- Location and nature of control actuation feedback.

Controls shall be designed so as to minimize the risk of erroneous or inadvertent operation. The following criteria should be met:

- Identification shall be facilitated by logical arrangement and coding of controls. (Differing shapes, sizes, colours, etc.)
- Control position shall be readily discernible in all lighting conditions.
- Differing types of control shall be limited to the minimum, sense of actuation standardized and related effect made as uniform as possible. Keyboards and rotary controls are preferred to thumb wheels and slew controls.
- Where appropriate, detents shall be provided f o r each unit or increment of the controlled parameter (e.g., degrees, KHz).
- Safety devices (gate, balk, and override) shall be designed to prevent incorrect or premature selection.
- Where damage to the aircraft can result from exceeding a placarded limitation, initial movement of a control (e.g., flap, landing gear) should excite the appropriate aural or visual alert.

Controls should be designed to maximize usability, minimize flight crew workload, and reduce pilot errors. The recommendations for manual control functions is shown in Table 1.

Table 1. Recommended manual controls

Control function	Control type for small actuation forces	Control type for large actuation forces
2 discrete positions	Keylock Legend switch Push button Slide switch Toggle switch	Detent lever Foot push button Hand push button
3 discrete positions	Push button Rotary selector switch Toggle switch	
3 to 24 discrete positions		Detent lever Rotary selector switch
4 to 24 discrete positions	Rotary selector switch	
Continuous setting (linear and less than 360°)	Continuous rotary knob Joystick or lever	Crank Handwheel Joystick or lever Two-axis grip handle
Continuous slewing and fine adjustment	Continuous rotary knob Crank Joystick or lever	Crank Handwheel Two-axis grip handle Valve

3   Arrangement and Accessibility Evaluation Principles

3.1   Environment and Use Conditions

Consider a variety of environments, use conditions, and other factors that can impact flightcrew interaction with controls during aircraft operations that can be reasonably expected in service, including:

- Appropriate representation of pilot population;
- Bright and dark lighting conditions;
- Use of gloves;
- Turbulence and other vibrations;
- Interruptions and delays in tasks;
- Objects that may physically interfere with the motion of a control;
- Incapacitation of one pilot (multi-crew aircraft);
- Use of the non-dominant hand; and
- Excessive ambient noise.

Since all possible environment and use conditions cannot be specifically addressed, develop a representative set that includes nominal and worst cases. These cases should cover the full environment in which the system is assumed to operate, given its intended function. This includes operating in normal, non-normal, and emergency conditions. The following paragraphs describe the above list of environment and use conditions in more detail.

Controls are designed with an assumption of a certain range of pilot attributes. These assumptions may include physical attributes, such as body size and proportion, and non-physical attributes, such as experience with a given type of controls.

Controls should be operable under foreseeable lighting conditions. Labels and other information related to a control's function and method of operation should be readable over a wide range of ambient illumination, including, but not limited to:

- Direct sunlight on the controls;
- Indirect sunlight through a front window illuminating white clothing (reflections);
- Sun above the forward horizon and above a cloud deck in a flightcrew member's eyes; and
- Night and/or dark environment.

3.2 Layout and Organization

Controls shall be located so that they are accessible to the crew member to whom they are assigned.

Controls for managing the information content of flight and navigation displays shall be located in a prime position for each pilot. It is desirable that both pilots be able to operate the controls of both pilots' displays.

The controls of individual equipment which are functionally and directly related shall be grouped together. Controls for equipment not clearly related by function can be separated.

Controls which are likely to be operated simultaneously by both pilots shall be located and arranged so as to minimize the risk of physical interference.

Normal operation of controls shall not obscure the associated display from the pilot's view.

For compliance with § 25.777, the flightcrew must be able to see, identify, and reach the means of controlling the HUD, including its configuration and display modes, from the normal seated position. To comply with §§ 25.777 and 25.1301, the position and movement of the HUD controls must not lead to inadvertent operation [6].

For compliance with § 25.777, the flightcrew must be able to see, identify, and reach the means of controlling the HUD, including its configuration and display modes, from the normal seated position. To comply with §§ 25.777 and 25.1301, the position and movement of the HUD controls must not lead to inadvertent operation.

The dimensions and location of the input device should be usable by the 5th through 95th percentile of the end user population, when appropriately clothed and equipped [7].

Pilots might wear gloves during operations, such as in cold weather. Design assumptions regarding skin contact (e.g., tactile feedback, system capacitive sensing), finger size (e.g., button spacing), and other finger characteristics alone might not adequately cover situations in which pilots wear gloves. Therefore, include gloved pilot operations in environment and use conditions. In cases where controls cannot be operated with gloves, clearly describe any limitations or methods for determining limitations, in the aircraft flight manual or flight manual supplement, as appropriate.

4 Operation and Usability Evaluation Principles

4.1 Movement of Controls

Control devices typically transform their movement and/or force to achieve a control's function. Ensure that the interaction between a control and its related elements (e.g., aircraft systems, displays, indications, labels) are readily apparent, understandable, logical, and consistent with applicable cultural conventions and with similar controls in the same flight deck. Table 2 provides examples of conventional relationships between the movement of a control and its function.

Table 2. Examples of Conventional Relationships between Control Functions and Movements.

Function	Direction of movement
Increase	Up, Right, Forward, Clockwise, Push
Decrease	Down, Left, Rearward, Counter-Clockwise, Pull
On	Up, Right, Forward, Pull, Depress, Rotate Clockwise
Off	Down, Left, Rearward, Push, Release, Rotate Counter-Clockwise
Right	Right, Clockwise
Left	Left, Counter-Clockwise
Up	Up, Forward
Down	Down, Rearward
Retract	Rearward, Pull, Counter-clockwise, Up
Extend	Forward, Push, Clockwise, Down

4.2 Sensitivity and Gain of Controls

Since many controls transform their movement and force to achieve a function, the gain or sensitivity is a key design parameter. In particular, it strongly affects the trade-off between task speed and error. High gain values tend to favour pilot comfort and rapid inputs, but can also contribute to errors (e.g., overshoot, inadvertent activation). Low gain values tend to favor tasks that require precision, but can also be too slow for the task. Gain and sensitivity of the control typically need to be traded off to support the intended function. Give special consideration to variable-gain controls. Accurately replicate the response lag and control gain characteristics that will be present in the actual airplane, and show that gain and sensitivity of the control are acceptable for the intended function.

4.3   Feedback of Controls

Design the controls to provide feedback to the pilot when operated. Feedback from controls provides pilots with awareness of the effects of their inputs, including the following effects, as applicable:

- Physical state of the control device (e.g., position, force);
- State of data construction (e.g., text string);
- State of activation or data entry (e.g., "enter");
- State of system processing;
- State of system acceptance (e.g., error detection); and
- State of system response (e.g., cursor position, display zoom, autopilot disconnect).

Feedback can be visual, aural, and/or tactile. If feedback/awareness is required for safe operation, it should be provided to inform the flightcrew of the following conditions:

- State of activation or data entry;
- State of system processing (for extended processing times); and
- State of system response, if different from the commanded state.

Provide clear, unambiguous, and positive feedback to indicate the successful or unsuccessful actuation of a control action. Feedback within the control device (such as the tactile snap of a switch) without any other system effect should not be the sole means of detecting the actuation of a control.

The type, response time, duration, and appropriateness of feedback will depend upon the pilots' task and the specific information required for successful operation.

The final display response to control input should be fast enough to prevent undue concentration being required when the flightcrew sets values or display parameters (§25.771(a)). The specific acceptable response times depend on the intended function.

Once a control device is activated, if processing time is extended it might be appropriate to display progress to provide the pilot with a sense of time remaining for completion.

If control device position is the primary means of indicating the status of a function (e.g., switch in the Up position indicates that the function is On), the control position should be obvious from any pilot seat.

When a control is used to move an actuator through its range of travel, the equipment should provide operationally significant feedback of the actuator's position within its range.

Show that feedback is adequate in performance of the tasks associated with the intended function of the equipment.

4.4   Identifiable and Predictable Controls

Pilots must be able to identify and select the current function of the control with speed and accuracy appropriate to the task, per § 25.777(a). Make the function and method of operation of a control readily apparent (i.e., predictable and obvious), so that little or no familiarization is needed. Show that the intended pilot population can rapidly, accurately and consistently identify and execute all control functions, assuming qualified and trained pilots.

The applicant should evaluate consequences of control activation to show that the consequences are predictable and obvious to each flight crewmember. Such an assessment would include evaluation of the control of multiple displays with a single device and evaluation of shared display areas that flightcrew members access with individual controls. The use of a single control should also be evaluated.

Controls can be made distinguishable or predictable by differences in attributes such as form, colour, location, and labeling. For example, buttons, which are pushed, should be readily discernable from knobs, which are rotated. Control shapes that are easily determined with tactile senses can improve ease of operation, particularly during periods when pilot tasks require significant visual attention.

Colour coding as a sole distinguishing feature is usually not sufficient. This applies to physical controls as well as to controls that are part of an interactive graphical user interface.

The labeling design should avoid hidden functions such as clicking on empty space on a display to make something happen.

4.5   Labeling of Controls

Control labels must be visible, legible, and understandable for the population of pilots that will use the controls, per § 25.1555(a).

Unless the control function and method of operation are obvious or indicated through other means (e.g., form, location), the control labeling scheme should clearly and unambiguously convey:

- The current function performed by each control,
- The method for actuating the control when performing the current function.

Size control labels to be easily legible from the pilot's normally seated position [8].

For controls using icons in lieu of text labeling, substantiate that pilots, with the minimum expected training program, can adequately perform their duties at an acceptable level of workload, as required by normal, non-normal, and emergency situations. If appropriate, consider incorporating icons in controls to complement rather than replace text labels (e.g., continuous text display, temporary "mouseover" display).

If multiple controls exist for the same function, clearly label all such controls. Exceptions can include alternate controls that provide flexibility to accommodate a wide range of pilots.

If multiple controls exist (multi-crew aircraft) for the same function, show that there is sufficient information or other means available to make each crewmember aware of which control is currently functioning.

Use only one abbreviation and/or one icon for labeling a function. This is to prevent confusion when a label appears in multiple locations.

Ensure that the labels resist scratching, hazing, erasure, disfigurement, and other legibility degradation that might result from normal use.

4.6   Controls Lighting

For controls with visual markings that are intended for use in low-light conditions, the markings must be lighted in some way that allows them to be easily read, for compliance with § 25.1555(a) and § 25.1381(a).

Ensure that lighting of controls is consistent with flightcrew alerting such as warning, caution, and advisory lights (§ 25.1322).

For low-light conditions, make lighted controls dimmable to brightness levels commensurate with other flight deck instrument lighting. This allows for the flightcrew's adaptation to the dark, so controls are legible, and outside vision is maintained.

Ensure that lighting of controls from an internal source is not dimmable to brightness levels so low that the controls appear inactive.

Ensure that lighting of controls from an internal source does not produce light leaks, bright spots, or reflections from the windshield that can interfere with pilot vision or performance.

Automatic adjustment of lighted controls may be employed. Consider preference differences in multi-crew operations.

Ensure that lighted controls intended for operation in a night vision imaging system (NVIS) lighting-modified cockpit meets AC 20-175, 2-9.a through 2-9.e, and are compatible with night vision goggles (NVG).

4.7   Prevention Inadvertent Operation of Controls

Protect controls against inadvertent operation. This type of error can occur for various reasons, such as when a pilot accidentally bumps a control, or accidentally actuates one control when intending to actuate a different control.

Provide mitigation for inadvertent operation as appropriate. Consider these questions when designing and installing the control:

- Are there any safety-critical consequences if the pilot is not aware of the inadvertent operation?
- What will the pilot need to do to correct an inadvertent operation?
- Is the control designed to support "eyes free" use (i.e., when the pilot is not looking at the control)?
- Are there aspects of the design that will decrease the likelihood of inadvertent operation?
- Are there aspects of the design that will increase the likelihood of the pilot detecting an inadvertent operation?

The following paragraphs provide multiple methods that reduce the likelihood of inadvertent operation of controls.

- **Location & Orientation.** Title § 25.777 requires controls to be located to prevent inadvertent operation. Locate, space, and orient controls so that the operator is not likely to strike or move them accidentally in the normal sequence of control movements. For example, switches located close to a frequently-used lever could be oriented so the axis of rotation for the switches is perpendicular to the axis of rotation for the lever.

- **Physical Protection.** Physical obstructions can be built into the design of a control to prevent accidental actuation of the control. Examples include: recessed controls, shielded controls, flip-covers, and guards. Make physical protections so they do not interfere with the visibility or operation of the protected device or adjacent controls. Physical protections should be appropriately durable to ensure continued airworthiness.
- **Slippage Resistance.** The physical design and materials used for controls can reduce the likelihood of finger and hand slippage (especially in the presence of vibration). For example, buttons can be designed with concave, textured, or tacky upper surfaces to prevent finger slippage.
- **Hand Stabilization.** Provide hand rests, armrests, or other physical structures as a stabilization point for the pilot's hands and fingers when they are operating a control. This can be particularly useful for controls used in the presence of turbulence and other vibration, helping the pilot make more precise inputs.
- **Logical Protection.** Software-based controls and software-related controls may be disabled at times when actuation of the control would be considered inappropriate, based on logic within the software. Make disabled (inactive) controls clearly discernable from active controls.
- **Complex Movements.** The method of operation for a control can be designed so that complex movement is required to actuate it. For example, a rotary knob can be designed so that it can only be turned when it is also being pulled out. Double-click or push-and-hold methods are not recommended methods of protection.
- **Tactile Cues.** The surfaces of different controls can have different shapes and textures, supporting the pilot in distinguishing different controls when operating in a dark or otherwise "eyes free" environment. For example, most keyboards have a small ridge on the "J" and "F" keys, cuing the user to the proper placement of their index fingers. Similarly, § 25.781 requires specific shapes for certain cockpit controls.
- **Locked/Interlocked Controls.** Locking mechanisms, interlocks, or the prior operation of a related control can prevent inadvertent operation. For example, a separate on/off control can activate/deactivate a critical control, or physically lock it in place.
- **Sequential Movements.** Controls can be designed with locks, detents, or other mechanisms to prevent the control from passing directly through a sequence of movements. This method is useful when strict sequential actuation is necessary.
- **Motion Resistance.** Controls can be designed with resistance (e.g., friction, spring, inertia) so that deliberate effort is required for actuation. When this method is employed, the level of resistance cannot exceed the minimum physical strength capabilities for the intended pilot population.

Any method of protecting a control from inadvertent operation should not preclude operation within the required pilot task time, or interfere with the normal operation of the system. If a control is inadvertently operated, multisensory information can assist pilots in detecting the error. Feedback can include one or more auditory cues, tactile cues, or visual cues. As a general rule, the greater the consequence of an unintended operation, the greater the prevention method needed, and the more salient the cues that should be provided for detection.

5 Summary and Conclusions

The evaluation of flight deck controls should include a thorough examination of the control location and mechanization. The physical arrangement of the controls on multi-engine should be consistent with the physical location of the engines on the airplane as far as left to right sequence. They should also be examined in conjunction with their associated displays and warning indications when failures occur. Every effort should be made to provide clear unmistakable indications to prevent these situations from occurring. Also, marking and lighting of the engine controls needs to be clear and distinct to prevent any confusion to the pilot. Compliance testing identified in the human factors certification plans should begin with analysis of initial engineering studies and continue through mock-up, simulator and aircraft ground/flight test evaluations.

Acknowledgments. The author gratefully acknowledges the helpful reviews by Ph.D. Dayong Dong and useful discussions with Dr. Wenjun Dong, Mr. Kaiwen Chen, Mr. Pu Hong, and Miss. Yuan Wang.

References

1. AC20-175: Controls for Flight Deck Systems
2. FAR25.1302 Installed Systems and Equipment for Use by the Flightcrew
3. MIL-STD-1472G Human Engineering, Table II
4. AC 25.1302-1: Installed Systems and Equipment for Use by the Flightcrew
5. AC 25-11B: ELECTRONIC FLIGHT DECK DISPLAYS
6. RTCA DO-257A Minimum Operational Performance Standards for the Depiction of Navigation Information on Electronic Maps
7. MIL-HDBK-759C: Human Engineering Design Guidelines
8. SAE 4102/7: Electronic Displays

Reviewing and Predicting Human-Machine Cooperation Based on Knowledge Graph Analysis

Yujia Liu[✉]

College of Design and Innovation, Tongji University, Shanghai, China
liuyujia@tongji.edu.cn

Abstract. Human-Machine Cooperation involves multiple fields and disciplines such as automated vehicles, robots, machine manufacturing, psychological cognition, and artificial intelligence. As research in these areas progresses rapidly, it is important to keep up with new trends and key turning points in the development of collective knowledge. Based on the visualization method, we can quickly sort out the ins and outs of this field in the vast literature and search for valuable and potential literature. First, we introduced the principles of scientific visualization of knowledge graphs. Then we extracted 3257 articles from Web of Science Core Collection and established a research field of bibliographic records of representative data sets. Next, we carried out a visual analysis of the discipline Dual-Map overlay, Co-words, Co-citation, and reviewed some key Highly-Cited documents. Finally, we summarize and analyze the literature with high betweenness centrality, citation bursts, and Sigma value. This review will help professionals to have a more systematic understanding of the entire field and find opportunities for future Human-Machine Cooperation development.

Keywords: Human-Machine Cooperation · Knowledge graph · Domain analysis · Systematic review

1 Introduction

Since the 1960s, research on Human-Machine Interface (HMI) or Human-Computer Interaction (HCI) has been extensively developed due to the rapid growth of information systems [1]. And now, it has been covered in various Human-Machine interfaces (such as robots, computers, mobile smart devices, etc.). However, the environment in which we live is constantly becoming more and more complex. While we rely too much on machines for convenience, it also causes many problems (such as friendliness, usability, trust, transparency, acceptance, etc.). Hence, using the Human-Machine Cooperation (HMC) method can effectively address the stakes caused by the uncoordinated interaction between humans and machines [2]. Research on HMC has attracted widespread attention in the community. Many scholars have tried to explain how machines (systems) and humans can cooperate safely and efficiently, and create models to define the nature and laws governing human and machine (system) interaction [3].

C. Stephanidis et al. (Eds.): HCII 2020, LNCS 12423, pp. 166–183, 2020.
https://doi.org/10.1007/978-3-030-60114-0_12

New scientific discoveries can expand and deepen existing knowledge, and can also eliminate the original or even once brilliant cognition. The HMC literature that appears in any time period may play a key role. Any perspective may bring new inspiration to the HMC research, and any details may become the beginning of the next breakthrough in this research. A systematic review can help us sort out the knowledge of an academic field, and we can extract exciting clues from the vast academic literature. However, in such a rapidly developing field of HMC research, any existing review may soon become outdated, and the limitations of the reviewer's personal cognition may miss some very critical issues. The knowledge graph drawn based on the quantitative data of the literature has unique advantages in clarifying the development context and trends of a certain research field or discipline. It can help researchers quickly understand the development history of this knowledge field, and find the key breakthroughs that trigger future research point.

We used CiteSpace[1], a visual analysis software for scientific research, to analyze 3257 documents in Web of Science Core Collection about the field of Human-Machine Cooperation. To understand the development status and future trends of human-machine cooperation, we analyze discipline Dual-map overlay, Co-words, Co-citation, etc., and reviewed some key High-Cited literature. Then, we summarize and analyze the literature with high betweenness centrality, citation bursts, and Sigma value, to clarify the opportunities for the future development of HMC.

2 Related Work

Thomas S. Kuhn proposed the structure of the scientific revolution in the 1960s [4]. He believes that the advancement of science is an endless process based on the scientific revolution. People accept new ideas through one scientific revolution after another. The importance of new ideas lies in whether they can make a more convincing explanation of the objects we observe. Kuhn's scientific revolution refers to the alternation of the rise and fall of old and new scientific paradigms. If the scientific process is just as Kuhn had observed, then we should be able to find the footsteps of the rise and fall of the paradigm in the scientific literature. The specific expression of Kuhn's paradigm shift in the graph of scientific knowledge is the clusters that appear in one time period after another. The dominant colors of the clusters reveal their prosperous years. For analyzing the current status of HMC research, we use visualization software (CiteSpace) according to Co-occurrence network relationships (such as literature Co-citations, Co-word analysis, etc.) to find classic documents in the field. The review of classic and Highly-Concerned literature will help understand the knowledge base in this field, to interpret the current research status and find valuable research points.

Ronald S. Burt proposed the theory of structural holes research on social networks and social values [5]. Burt found that people located around structural holes often have a more significant advantage, and this advantage can often be attributed to the fact that they have access to different types of information and thus have greater imagination space. The theory of structural holes in social networks can be extended to other types of

---

[1] http://cluster.ischool.drexel.edu/~cchen/citespace/download/.

networks, especially citation networks. Burt's structural holes connect different clusters, from which we can gain a deeper understanding of how one cluster is connected to another almost completely independent cluster, and which specific literature plays a key role in paradigm shifts. Therefore, the idea of structural holes is reflected in the visual knowledge graph as finding pivotal points with a high degree of betweenness centrality [6]. In this way, we are no longer confined to the local contributions of specific papers, but to focus on their role in the overall development of the academic field. This is precisely the leap pursued by systematic academic reviews. From this, we can peek into the future trend of HMC research by looking for pivotal points of betweenness centrality.

Besides, for predicting the future trend of research, we can also find the burst detection points with the frequency surge in the knowledge graph. Chen, the founder of Citespace, proposed the method of burst detection for detect terms [6]. If the frequency of citations for an article increases rapidly, the most appropriate explanation is that the work of the article has great potential or interest, and it acts as a very critical node in the citation network. Therefore, he used the algorithm Jon Kleinberg [7] which can be used to measure how fast a given type of events taking place. In the design of CiteSpace, the potential papers can be detected by monitoring the possible response of the knowledge system to new papers. Scientific knowledge itself is an adaptive and complex system. Its input and output are not linearly related. New discoveries and new ideas may change our beliefs and behaviours. If a new paper can be regarded as the signal received by an adaptive complex system, then whether the modularity of the measurement system changes will provide us with very valuable information to understand the potential.

3   Method

3.1   Data Collection

Based on the above theories and methods, this paper extracts 3,257 related documents from the Web of Science Core Collection with the search topic: Human-Machine Cooperation, Human-Computer Cooperation, Human-Machine Collaboration and Human-Computer Collaboration. The four subject keywords are connected by "or" to expand the search scope and ensure that relevant documents are included as much as possible. From a practical point of view, as opposed to refining and cleaning the original search results until all irrelevant research topics are excluded, an accessible and more effective method is to keep them, then in the Knowledge Graph, skip these irrelevant branches when interpreting [8]. The document time span is the full period in WOS from 1990 to now (May 2020). From Fig. 1, it illustrates that the number of relevant bibliographic records on Human-Machine Cooperation is showing an upward trend year by year, which indicates more and more scholars are participating in research in this field.

3.2   Visualization and Analysis

We visualize and analyze the dataset with the software of CiteSpace. We use the knowledge graph visualization analysis software to analyze the collected data through some

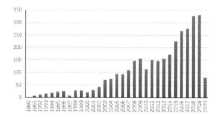

Fig. 1. The annual distribution of the bibliographic records.

methods such as Dual-Map overlay, Co-words, Co-citation, research hotspots, between-ness centrality, burst detection, etc. The document Co-citation analysis function in CiteS-pace constructs networks of cited references and connections between references represent Co-citation strengths [8]. CiteSpace can establish a citation network that changes with time according to the time slicing interval, and synthesizes these separate networks to form an integrated citation network for systematic analysis through quantitative methods.

Through the scientific analysis of visual analysis methods, researchers are freed from some Time-Consuming and Labour-Intensive burdens, focusing on more important and critical analysis problems, abstract and creative thinking. This article will help get a quick and iterative understanding of the development history, and has a systematic summary, review, and outlook on the overall HMC research status and look for future futures from new papers with potential research direction.

4   Results

To understand the current research status in Human-Machine Cooperation, it is feasible to analyze initially from the Macro-level (discipline level). A Dual-Map overlay represents the entire dataset in the context of a global map of science generated from over 10,000 journals indexed in the WoS [9]. In this Dual-Map overlay of the HMC literature (see Fig. 2), on the left is the distribution of journals where the Co-cited documents are located, representing the main disciplines where Human-Machine Cooperation belongs; on the right is the distribution of journals where the cited literature is located, representing which disciplines are mainly cited by Human-Machine Cooperation. This figure shows that HMC literature is published in many disciplines such as computer science, engineering, automation control system, education research, psychology, and so on. Literature in the disciplines of computer science and psychology (shown in the map as curves in red and cyan) are citing each other. This suggests that, in the field of HMC, it is necessary to study two levels from the machine and human, and the disciplines of computer science and psychology are directly related to those two.

Looking for topic keywords can intuitively understand the field research content from the Micro-level. The topics involved in HMC can be delineated in terms of the keywords assigned to each article in the dataset [8]. Figure 3 shows a minimum spanning tree of a Keywords-Network and adjacent keywords are often assigned to the same articles [9]. For instance, system, design, cooperation (collaboration) and Human-Computer interaction are near to each other in the middle of the diagram.

Fig. 2. A Dual-Map overlay of the HMC literature. (Color figure online)

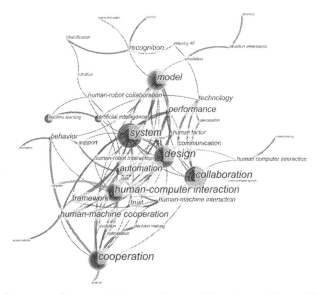

Fig. 3. A minimum spanning tree of a keyword network based on articles published between 1990 and 2020.

Taking Human-Computer Interaction as the center (see Fig. 4 left), it can be found that in addition to some large nodes such as cooperation and design, it is also closely connected with small nodes such as artificial intelligence, human factor, behaviour, and task. For another example, with cooperation as the center (see Fig. 4 right), small node keywords such as automation, decision making, communication, and trust are related.

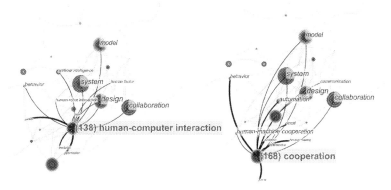

Fig. 4. Keyword network centered on Human-Computer Interaction and Cooperation respectively.

4.1 Landscape View

Figure 5 is generated based on publications from 1990 to 2020. Top 30% of most Co-cited or occurred publications in each period slicing (one year) are used to construct a references network. This synthesized network contains 90370 references, 11 main Co-citation clusters and 1,508 nodes. The modularity of network is 0.9545, which is considered as extremely high (more than 0.5 is considered significant clustering, and more than 0.8 is considered extremely significant [9]), suggesting that the effect of clustering is very significant. Some other literature cannot form clusters because the modularity value is too low. Therefore, the serial numbers of clusters are not continuous. The mean silhouette value of 0.299 is relatively low mainly because of the numerous small clusters. The mean silhouette score of the large clusters we are concerned with is extremely high, so it has good research value.

The areas of different colors indicate the time when Co-citation links in those areas appeared for the first time [8]. The top colours bar in Fig. 5 from left to right represents the period from 1990–2020. The youngest cluster in the picture is #11 artificial intelligence, and the oldest cluster is #27altrulism (the cluster colour is close to white). Among the several largest clusters, the largest cluster cluster#0 is earlier than other clusters. The naming of each cluster comes from headline terms, keywords, and abstract terms that refer to the articles of the cluster. For instance, the Yellow-Coloured area at the middle center is labelled as #0 shared control, indicating that Cluster #0 is cited by articles on shared control. The size of the node represents the frequency of citations of this article, the greater the number of times. And the big red node indicates that this is a burstiness citation.

4.2 Timeline View

The timeline view explains the arrangement of clusters along the horizontal timeline, with time increasing gradually from left to right, and clusters arranged from large to small from top to bottom (see Fig. 6). Coloured arcs indicate Co-citation links added

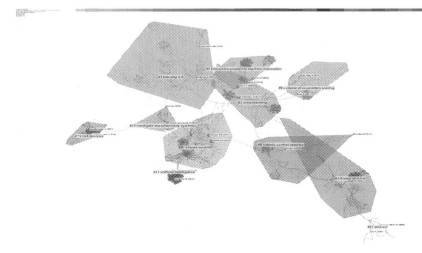

Fig. 5. A landscape view of the Co-citation network.

in the corresponding colour year. Like landscape view, the Co-citation and burstiness citation nodes behave in the same way. Below each node, at most the three references with the most citations are displayed.

Table 1. Temporal properties of major 11 clusters.

Cluster#	Size	Silhouette	From	To	Duration	Theme
0	87	0.936	2007	2019	13	Shared control
1	78	0.951	2008	2020	13	Industry 4.0
2	59	0.934	2008	2017	10	Crowdsensing; gesture recognition; Internet of things
4	56	0.957	2001	2015	15	Theory of mind
6	43	0.985	2008	2017	10	Holonic control solution; Multi-agent system
7	35	0.971	2009	2016	8	Interactive-Predictive machine translation
9	29	0.987	2010	2014	5	Collaborative problem solving;
11	27	0.998	2011	2018	8	Artificial intelligence; Social sustainability; Logistics performance
13	25	0.998	2005	2016	12	risk analysis
23	15	0.955	2011	2017	7	Intelligent manufacturing systems; Crisis management
27	13	0.996	1998	2008	11	Altruism

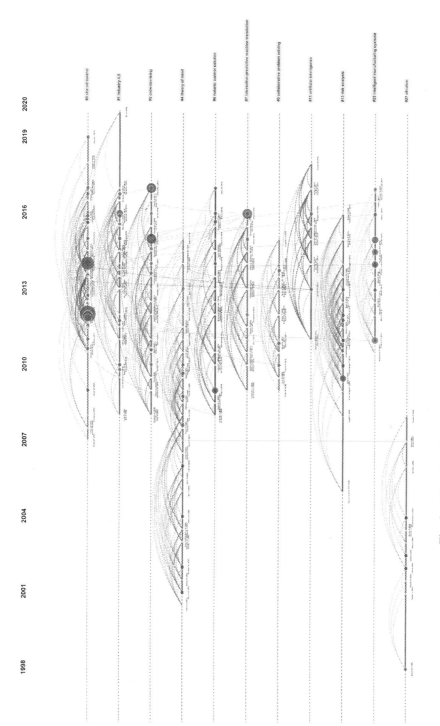

Fig. 6. A timeline view of the Co-citation network (Color figure online)

The timeline view very intuitively shows the timeliness of the cluster, each cluster has a different start time, end time, and duration. Table 1 lists the detailed information of 11 clusters. Some clusters have a long lifetime, such as clusters #0, #1, and #4. Some clusters have relatively short lifetimes, such as clusters #9 and #23. Until now, cluster #1#2 has remained active. Some clusters are already inactive, such as cluster #27. Cluster #6 on intelligent manufacturing systems ends by 2014, but some of its articles provide references for other clusters.

4.3 Main Specialties

In the following discussion, we will particularly focus on the three largest clusters. The research status and frontiers of a research field can be reflected through Co-cited references and cited articles. The Co-cited literature shows that this reference has become the basis of other people's knowledge to some extent, and the citing literature is a new reflection caused by referring to the views of others.

Cluster #0 – Shared Control. Cluster #0 is the largest group and contains 87 citations in the 13 years from 2007 to 2019. Timeline visualization can be discussed in three periods (See Fig. 7). The first period is from 2007 to 2011. During the period, there are few studies on this cluster and few high Co-cited articles. But there is an article about the classification, overview and future prospects of lateral control in car driving [10] as the end of this period, which has attracted the attention of others.

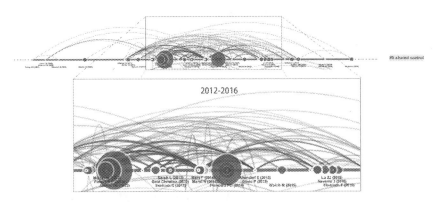

Fig. 7. High-Impact members of Cluster #0.

The second period is from 2012 to 2016. In the top ten citation articles of cluster #0, a total of 9 articles were born in this period (See Fig. 8). The types of High-Impact articles that emerged during this period can be divided into:

- Conceptual frameworks - [11, 12]
- Interaction approach - [13, 14]
- Concepts in System design - [15]
- Human behaviour - [16]
- Design and evaluation - [17, 18]

Freq	Burst	Degree	Centrality	Σ	Author	Year	Title	Source	Vol	Page	HalfLife	DOI	Cluster
25	12	0.92	1.00		Flemisch FO	2014		ERGONOMICS	57	343	4	10.1080/00140139.201...	0
20	9	0.93	1.00		Abbink DA	2012		COGN TECHNOL WORK	14	19	6	10.1007/s10111-011-0...	0
17	12	0.93	1.00		Flemisch F	2012		COGN TECHNOL WORK	14	3	6	10.1007/s10111-011-0...	0
15	23	0.93	1.00		Mulder M	2012		HUM FACTORS	54	786	5	10.1177/0018720812298...	0
6	7	0.96	1.00		Marti N	2014		TRANSPORT RES F-TRAF	27	274	5	10.1016/j.trf.2014.09.005	0
6	6	0.90	1.00		Tomosello M	2014		NATURAL HIST HUMAN T	0	0	5		0
6	6	0.90	1.00		Itoh M	2014		ERGONOMICS	57	361	3	10.1080/00140139.201...	0
6	12	0.95	1.00		Navarro J	2011		IET INTELL TRANSP SY	5	297	3	10.1049/iet-its.2016.0387	0
6	8	0.90	1.30		Flemisch F	2016		IFAC PAPERSONLINE	49	72	3	10.1016/j.ifacol.2016.10...	0
6	7	0.90	1.00		Mars F	2014		IEEE T HAPTICS	7	324	5	10.1109/TOH.2013.229	0

Fig. 8. Top 10 most Co-cited articles to the largest cluster (#0).

In cluster #0 (also in entire Co-citation network), the highest Co-cited article is published by Flemisch about collaborative guidance and control of human and automated vehicles [11] in 2002. Under different driving tasks, the driver engages in the guidance by means of "Conduct-by-Wire", and can delegate the operation to the automation system through a special operation interface. This article proposes the H (orse)-Metaphor framework, where human collaborate with automation through H-mode—that is, guidance and control are mainly through a tactile and effective interface. Flemisch believes that cooperation is a key factor for the future development of human and automation systems, especially for highly automated vehicles, cooperative guidance and control is a research direction.

The second highest Co-cited article is the interaction method published by Abbink that discusses haptic shared control between human and automation systems. Abbink believes that the problem of persistence of interaction between people and automation should be solved, and haptic shared control is a promising method when studying the problem of HCI. Through experimental evidence, the authors conclude that haptic shared control can bring Short-Term performance advantages—faster, more accurate vehicle control, lower control effort, and reduced need for visual attention. And Abbink's view of future research on tactile shared control should pay more attention to issues related to Long-Term use, such as trust, excessive dependence, dependence on the system, and skill retention.

The third period is from 2017 to the present. Although no highly Co-cited articles appeared during this period, the researchers still have a better understanding of the latest development of the cluster. Most cited publications in this period include a study of the human factors [19] and ergonomics science [20].

As mentioned before, the citing articles of the cluster help us understand the development of the cluster. According to the types of the top ten cited articles (See Fig. 9), they can be roughly divided into the following categories, namely framework and approach (3, 4, 7, 8), analysis and reviews (9), application of cooperation (1, 6, 8, 10) and design and evaluation (2, 5) (Table 3). This is basically similar to the type of Co-cited literature, indicating that the topic under discussion is still continuing.

1. Benloucif, M A (2017). Online adaptation of the Level of Haptic Authority in a lane keeping system considering the driver's state
2. Navarro, Jordan (2018). Does False and Missed Lane Departure Warnings Impact Driving Performances Differently?
3. Thanoon, Mohammed I (2018). A Multi-Modular Sensor Fusion and Decision-Making Approach for Human-Machine learning
4. Flemisch, Frank Ole (2017). The (uncanny and) unsafe valley of assistance and automation - description and safeguarding measures
5. Li, Shuo (2019). Evaluation of the effects of age-friendly human-machine interfaces on the driver's takeover performance in highly automated vehicles
6. Wessel, Ginn (2018). Learning from the Best - Naturalistic Arbitration for Cooperative Driving
7. Flemisch, F (2019). Joining the blunt and the pointy end of the spear: towards a common framework of joint action, human-machine cooperation, cooperative guidance and control, shared, traded and supervisory control
8. Johnson, Matthew (2017). Tomorrow's Human-Machine Design Tools: From Levels of Automation to Interdependencies
9. Biondi, Francesco (2019). Human-Vehicle Cooperation in Automated Driving: A Multidisciplinary Review and Appraisal
10. Marie-Pierre, Pacaux-Lemoine (2015). Towards vertical and horizontal extension of shared control concept

Fig. 9. Top 10 most citing articles to the largest cluster (#0).

Cluster #1 – Industry 4.0. For the second Largest-Cluster, cluster #1 containing 78 references that range a 13-year duration from 2008 to 2020. Both the duration and the start and end times indicate that this is a fairly active cluster. Its silhouette value is 0.951, which is slightly higher than the largest clusters #0, which means a better clustering effect. This cluster is dominated by representative technologies and terms such as mixed reality, augmented reality, IoT, and fog computing.

The development of cluster #1 has always been smooth, continuous, and stable. It can be seen on this timeline (See Fig. 10) that the frequency of literature citations is relatively average, except that there are two articles with citation frequency. An article by Michalos published in 2015 on the Human-Robot Collaboration in the assembly station [21]. According to different assembly process specifications, operators need to implement different controls. The design of the assembly station includes the assembly process, components, robotic equipment and variable station layout. And, this collaborative environment incorporates Real-Time monitoring of safety sensors, robot control safety functions, and augmented reality to ensure the safety and efficiency of the environment.

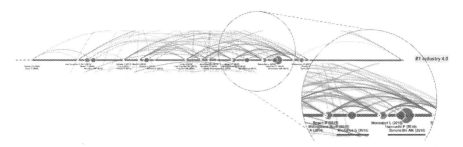

Fig. 10. Two key members of Cluster #1.

Another article is that Zanchettin proposed a kinematics control strategy for related practitioners in 2016 [22], which is used in a shared environment between humans and robots to enhance high safety and maintain the maximum productivity of robots. In order to meet different needs, according to the distance between human and robot, the speed of the robot is constrained under the minimum separation distance standard. Finally, in the open robot controller and the traditional closing scene, the Dual-Arm robot is tested and control strategy is discussed.

There are some other fields of research that are Co-cited frequently (See Fig. 11). The article by Woolley and Chabris [23] discovered evidence of collective intelligence through a study of 699 people, and the factors that affect collective intelligence can explain the performance of each group task. Among them, they proposed this "c factor" is related to the average social sensitivity of the group members, the equality in distribution of conversational Turn-Taking, and the proportion of females in the group. This discovery may make some late researchers pay more attention to the sociality of different people and gender differences in communication in team cooperation, since this may affect the degree of collaboration.

Freq	Burst	Degree	Centrality	Σ	Author	Year	Title	Source	Vol	Page	HalfLife	DOI	Cluster
13	11	0.01	1.00		Michalos G	2015		PROC CIRP	37	248	4	10.1016/j.procir.2015.0...	1
13	3	0.00	1.00		Zanchettin AM	2016		IEEE T AUTOM SCI ENG	13	882	3	10.1109/TASE.2015.24...	1
8	4	0.00	1.00		Tsarouchi P	2016		INT J COMPUT INTEG M	29	916	3	10.1080/0951192X.201...	1
7	5	0.00	1.00		Woolley AW	2010		SCIENCE	330	686	7	10.1126/science.11931...	1
6		0.00	1.00		Lasota Przemyslaw A	2014		2014 IEEE INTERNATIONAL CONFERE	0	339	6	10.1109/CoASE.2014.6...	1
5	4	0.00	1.00		Atton L	2010		COMPUT NETW	54	2787	8	10.1016/j.comnet.2010...	1
4	4	0.00	1.00		Zhang YF	2017		IEEE T IND INFORM	13	737	2	10.1109/TII.2016.26188...	1
4	10	0.00	1.00		Monostori L	2016		CIRP ANN-MANUF TECHN	65	621	2	10.1016/j.cirp.2016.06.0...	1
4	5	0.00	1.00		Tsarouchi P	2017		INT J COMPUT INTEG M	30	696	2	10.1080/0951192X.201...	1
4	3	0.00	1.00		Bonomi F	2012		P 1 ED MCC WORKSH MO	0	13	7	DOI 10.1145/2342509.2...	1

Fig. 11. Top 10 most Co-cited articles to the second cluster (#1).

Atzori's survey paper [24] on the Internet of Things (IoT) emphasizes the integration of multiple technologies and communication solutions, identification and tracking technologies, wired and wireless sensor and actuator networks, enhanced communication protocols (shared with the next generation Internet) and the distribution of smart objects intelligence is the most relevant factor in the development of the IoT. Any significant contribution to the development of the Internet of Things must be the result of collaborative activities carried out in different fields of knowledge (such as telecommunications, informatics, electronics and social sciences).

The articles on citing cluster members also provide us with Cutting-Edge information about the dynamics of this cluster #2. The top 10 citing articles ranked show more development directions, such as the digital twin in Human-Robot collaboration, occupational health and safety in the era of Industry 4.0, the future work scene of Human-Robot Collaboration, the Internet of Things for collective intelligence, and challenges for employee qualification in Human-Robot Collaboration (See Fig. 12).

1. **Malik, Ali Ahmad (2018).** Digital twins of human robot collaboration in a production setting
2. **Badri, Adel (2018).** Occupational health and safety in the industry 4.0 era: A cause for major concern?
3. **Petruck, Henning (2019).** Human-Robot Cooperation in Manual Assembly - Interaction Concepts for the Future Workplace
4. **Zedadra, Ouarda (2017).** Towards a Reference Architecture for Swarm Intelligence-Based Internet of Things
5. **Wang, Peng (2018).** Deep learning-based human motion recognition for predictive context-aware human-robot collaboration
6. **Daling, Lea M (2018).** Challenges and Requirements for Employee Qualification in the Context of Human-Robot-Collaboration
7. **Posada, Jorge (2018).** Graphics and Media Technologies for Operators in Industry 4.0
8. **Bakos, Levente (2019).** Human Factor Preparedness for Decentralized Crisis Management and Communication in Cyber-Physical Systems
9. **Lazaro, Olatz De Miguel (2019).** An Approach for adapting a Cobot Workstation to Human Operator within a Deep Learning Camera
10. **Wagy, Mark D (2015).** Combining Computational and Social Effort for Collaborative Problem Solving

Fig. 12. Top 10 most citing articles to the second cluster (#1).

Cluster #2 – Crowdsensing. The Third-Largest cluster(#2) contains 59 cited references. This cluster is active over 10 years from 2008 till 2017. There are two outstanding references from the timeline visualization of this cluster. One has a strong citation burstiness, and those two highly Co-cited (See Fig. 13).

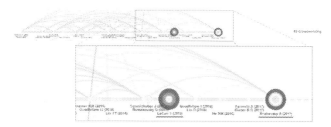

Fig. 13. Two citation burstiness of Cluster #2.

This highly Co-cited and strong burstiness article published LeCun Y in Nature is about breakthroughs in the field of deep learning [25]. Deep learning allows a computing model composed of multiple processing layers to learn data representations with multiple levels of abstraction. And by using a Back-Propagation algorithm, it indicates how the machine should change its internal parameters and discovers complex structures in large data sets. Deep convolutional networks bring breakthroughs in processing images, video, speech, and audio, while recursive networks inspire sequential data such as text and speech. The Second-Highest Co-cited reference in cluster #2 is a new method of convolutional neural networks. Krizhevsky [26] trained a deep convolutional neural network to train recognition images, which greatly reduced the test error rate and enhanced the GPU's computing speed. These technological breakthroughs inject a driving force into Human-Machine Cooperation and provide strong support for Multi-channel interaction.

Another highly Co-cited article published Quinn talks about the concept of human computation [27]. Human computation can bring many novel ideas, aiming to organize network users to do great things. This article classifies human computing systems to help identify similarities between different systems and reveal "holes" in existing work as an opportunity for new research.

As can be seen from the table cited in the top ten (See Fig. 14), the research field represented by cluster #2 is mainly about deep learning, convolutional neural networks, data set training, and other related knowledge. This means that a large number of research technologies and tools are being accumulated during this period, which is also an indispensable stage of development for Human-Machine Cooperation because smart machines (whether smart cars or robots) need to apply these new technologies to a wider range of Among the application fields. The rapid development of technology will greatly promote the progress of HMC research, and even change the transformation of the collaboration paradigm (this can be seen from the citation literature to see the direction of future transformation).

Freq	Burst	Degree	Centrality	Σ	Author	Year	Title	Source	Vol	Page	HalfLife	DOI	Cluster
17	5.27		0.00	1.01	LeCun Y	2015		NATURE	521	436	4	10.1038/nature14539	2
12		17	0.02	1.00	Krizhevsky A	2017		COMMUN ACM	60	84	4	10.1145/3065386	2
9		22	0.04	1.00	Quinn AJ	2011		29TH ANNUAL CHI CONFERENCE	0	1403	7		2
6		19	0.02	1.00	Lin TY	2014		LECT NOTES COMPUT SC	8693	740	4	10.1007/978-3-319-	2
5		9	0.01	1.00	Russakovsky O	2015		INT J COMPUT VISION	115	211	3	10.1007/s11263-01.	2
5		6	0.00	1.00	Schmidhuber J	2015		NEURAL NETWORKS	61	85	4	10.1016/j.neunet.20.	2
4		8	0.04	1.00	Wang FY	2010		IEEE INTELL SYST	25	85	8	10.1109/MIS.2010.1	2
4		8	0.01	1.00	Hassan H	2014		ARTIF INTELL REV	41	147	3	10.1007/s10462-91.	2
4		16	0.00	1.00	Nap J	2011		2011 IEEE INTERNATIONAL CONF	0	342	7	10.1109/ICSIPA.20.	2
4		8	0.00	1.00	Bhatkar J	2013		COMMUN ACM	56	116	7	10.1145/2380256.2.	2
4		4	0.00	1.00	Rogers Y	2011		INTERACTION DESIGN H	0	0	7		2

Fig. 14. Top 10 most Co-cited articles to the third cluster (#2).

The citing articles usually reflect the application field and future development of the cited references (See Fig. 15). Zou [28] introduced the robust WiFi-enabled device-free gesture recognition through unsupervised adversarial domain adaptation. Albini [29] identifies human hands from robot skin measurements. Wang [30] proposed to recognize human actions based on deep learning and predict the above mentioned related Human-Computer Collaboration. Zhong [31] pays attention to the analysis of the deep differences in face recognition with a similar appearance. The above article well reflects that intelligent agents based on technology and tools (such as deep learning, neural networks) can accurately recognize gestures, faces, motions, and even predict human behaviour, and establish trust and collaboration with humans.

1. **Zou, Han (2018).** Robust WiFi-enabled Device-free Gesture Recognition via Unsupervised Adversarial Domain Adaptation
2. **Albini, Alessandro (2017).** Human Hand Recognition from Robotic Skin Measurements in Human-Robot Physical Interactions
3. **Azevedo, Carlos R B (2017).** Vision for Human-Machine Mutual Understanding, Trust Establishment, and Collaboration
4. **Shirahama, Kimiaki (2016).** Towards large-scale multimedia retrieval enriched by knowledge about human interpretation
5. **Wang, Peng (2018).** Deep learning-based human motion recognition for predictive context-aware human-robot collaboration
6. **Tsvetkova, Milena (2015).** Understanding Human-Machine Networks: A Cross-Disciplinary Survey
7. **Zhong, Yaoyao (2018).** Deep Difference Analysis in Similar-looking Face recognition
8. **Guo, Bin (2015).** Mobile Crowd Sensing and Computing: The Review of an Emerging Human-Powered Sensing Paradigm
9. **Islam, Md Jahidul (2017).** Dynamic Reconfiguration of Mission Parameters in Underwater Human-Robot Collaboration
10. **Rupprecht, Christian (2018).** Guide Me: Interacting with Deep Networks

Fig. 15. Top 10 most Co-cited articles to the third cluster (#2).

4.4 Notable Specialties

Excessive attention to the Long-Term accumulation of highly Co-cited articles may ignore articles with short publication time but high value. Looking for some notable specialties in Human-Machine Cooperation can help to find potential papers, and thus find key breakthrough points that will trigger future research.

Betweenness Centrality. The betweenness centrality of a node in the citation network measures the importance of the position of the node in the network [9], which is a key node connecting one cluster to another completely independent cluster. Table 2 shows the top 10 structurally crucial references in the citation network. These nodes are mainly in clusters #0, #2, and #6, and each cluster is evenly distributed with 3 nodes. This also makes these three clusters more connected to other clusters. In our broadly defined field of Human-Machine Cooperation, these works can be regarded as crucial works that trigger exchanges between more research fields.

Table 2. Co-cited citations with the highest betweenness centrality.

Rank	Centrality	References	Cluster#
1	0.04	Quinn AJ, 2011, 29TH ANNUAL CHI CONFERENCE ON HUMAN FACTORS IN COMPUTING SYSTEMS, P1403	2
2	0.04	Wang FY, 2010, IEEE INTELL SYST, V25, P85	2
3	0.03	Abbink DA, 2012, COGN TECHNOL WORK, V14, P19	0
4	0.03	Flemisch F, 2012, COGN TECHNOL WORK, V14, V3	0
5	0.03	Mulder M, 2012, HUM FACTORS, V54, P786	0
6	0.03	Pacaux M P, 2011, IFAC P VOLUMES IFA 1, V18, P 6484	23
7	0.03	Lasota PA, 2015, HUM FACTORS, V57, P21	6
8	0.03	De Santis A, 2008, MECH MACH THEORY, V43, P253	6
9	0.03	Estelles-Arolas E, 2012, J INF SCI, V38, P189	2
10	0.03	Delton AW, 2011, P NATL ACAD SCI USA, V108, P13335	6

The first place is the survey of human computation published by Quinn [27] mentioned earlier in 2011. Quinn mentioned that many people working in the field of HCI tend to focus only on one human computing method, and in addition to new algorithms and designs, there is a more urgent problem to solve the problems related to ethics and labour standards. As designers, we should not only focus on the presentation of the design carrier but also consider the work adjustment arrangements and fair wages of workers who may face elimination due to the impact of technology. Future computing systems may also be more social in nature while maintaining the characteristics of performing computational work. Wang proposed that the enabling platform technology of CPSS (Cyber-Physical-Social Systems) will lead us into the era of intelligent enterprise and industry [32]. In complex space, CPSS technology can quickly respond and effectively collaborate and integrate. Physical space, cyberspace, physical word, mental work and artificial world form the CPSS system. But under the connected working environment and lifestyle supported by CPSS, social and personal safety will be an extremely important issue.

Citation Bursts. Table 3 lists the top 10 strong citation bursts. It is worth noting that there are 4 articles in cluster #10. Cluster #10 does not form a cluster because the modularity value is too small, which cannot be reflected in the landscape and timeliness graphs. But at the same time, due to its high burstiness, this kind of potential papers are likely to become the classic literature of the next cluster.

Table 3. References with the strongest citation bursts.

Citation bursts	References	Cluster#
8.01	Hoc JH, 2001, INT J HUM-COMPUT ST, V54, P509	10
5.27	LeCun Y, 2015, NATURE, V521, P436	2
5.19	Kruger J, 2009, CIRP ANN-MANUF TECHN, V58, P628	6
5.14	Hoc JM, 2000, ERGONOMICS, V43, P833	10
5.02	Castelfranchi C, 1998, ARTIF INTELL, V103, P153	10
4.78	Suchman Lucy, 1987, PLANS SITUATED ACTIO	24
4.34	Olson GM, 2000, HUM-COMPUT INTERACT, V15, P139	12
4.09	Hoc JM, 1998, INT J AVIAT PSYCHOL, V8, P1	10
3.9	Panchanathan K, 2004, NATURE, V432, P499	27
3.83	Parasuraman R, 2000, IEEE T SYST MAN CY A, V30, P286	41

Hoc's review [33] of cognitive collaboration has produced a great suddenness in the citation network. On the HCI research community, the recognized cognitive science knowledge system has achieved consistent results. However, under different frameworks and complex problems, it is difficult to develop new areas of Human-Machine collaboration. Under the dynamic situation of the time, the formation of small teams can cooperate on a cognition basis. Without neglecting the relevance of social methods and cooperation, it is very necessary to emphasize the collaboration of small groups to break through the cognitive dimension under dynamic circumstances.

Sigma. The Sigma metric measures both structural centrality and citation burstness of a cited reference. If a reference is strong in both measures, it will have a higher Sigma value than a reference that is only strong in one of the two measures. Table 4 lists the top 5 with the highest sigma value, which is also the only 5 (the sigma value of the rest article is 1). Interestingly, except for the third article from cluster #2, the rest exist in small clusters.

Table 4. References with the strongest citation bursts.

Sigma	Burst	Centrality	References	Cluster#
1.12	3.64	0.03	Pacaux M P, 2011, IFAC P VOLUMES IFA 1, V18, P 6484	23
1.06	5.19	0.01	Kruger J, 2009, CIRP ANN-MANUF TECHN, V58, P628	6
1.01	5.27	0	LeCun Y, 2015, NATURE, V521, P436	2
1.01	3.9	0	Panchanathan K, 2004, NATURE, V432, P499	27
1.01	3.81	0	Fehr E, 2002, NATURE, V415, P137	27

These articles have different focuses. Pacaux [34] proposed a method to define task sharing between operators and robots. Kruger [35] focused on investigating the form of collaboration and available technologies between people and machines on the assembly line. Panchanathan [36] showed that indirect reciprocity can stabilize cooperation. Ernst Fehr [37] believes that future research on the evolution of human cooperation should focus on explaining altruistic punishment.

5   Discussions and Conclusions

Through visual graph analysis, we review the development of Human-Machine Cooperation in the past few decades, which contains extremely rich content. In this Multi-interdisciplinary research, automated vehicle, robot, Internet of Things, deep learning, convolutional neural networks, these Automation-Related keywords are involved in. Shared control of human and automated vehicles has always been a topic of concern to practitioners. Compared to lose the perception and control of cars because of excessive dependence and trust, we are more inclined to have a relationship of guide and control. In a collaborative working environment, production efficiency and safety are what people and machines pursue through different forms and strategies of collaboration on the assembly line.

With the rapid development of various scientific technologies such as deep learning, convolutional neural networks, and data set training, the collaboration between humans and machines will become more convenient and diverse. In the same way that automation brings countless conveniences to human beings, we need to be vigilant, not only to be aware that excessive dependence may endanger our safety but also to consider the social issues that are replaced by machines. When people and machines collaborate in the future, while maintaining the purpose of performing tasks, they may also have social aspects of communication such as acceptance and trust by the public.

References

1. Hoc, J.-M.: From human–machine interaction to human–machine cooperation. Ergonomics **43**(7), 833–843 (2000)
2. Naujoks, F., Forster, Y., Wiedemann, K., Neukum, A.: A human-machine interface for cooperative highly automated driving. In: Stanton, N., Landry, S., Di Bucchianico, G., Vallicelli, A. (eds.) Advances in Human Aspects of Transportation. AISC, vol. 484, pp. 585–595. Springer, Cham (2017). https://doi.org/10.1007/978-3-319-41682-3_49
3. Biondi, F., Alvarez, I., Jeong, K.-A.: Human-vehicle cooperation in automated driving: a multidisciplinary review and appraisal. Int. J. Hum.-Comput. Interact. **35**(11), 932–946 (2019)
4. Kuhn, T.S.: The Structure of Scientific Revolutions. University of Chicago Press (1962)
5. Burt, R.S.: Structural holes and good ideas. Am. J. Sociol. **110**(2), 349–399 (2004)
6. Chen, C.: The centrality of pivotal points in the evolution of scientific networks. In: Amant, R.S., Riedl, J., Jameson, A. (eds.) IUI 2005, pp. 98–105. ACM (2005)
7. Kleinberg, J.: Bursty and hierarchical structure in streams. In: Proceedings of the 8th ACM SIGKDD International Conference on Knowledge Discovery and Data Mining. ACM Press (2002)
8. Chaomei, C.: Science mapping: a systematic review of the literature. J. Data Inf. Sci. **2**, 1–40 (2017)
9. Chen, C.: Predictive effects of structural variation on citation counts. J. Am. Soc. Inf. Sci. Technol. **63**(3), 431–449 (2012)
10. Navarro, J., Mars, F., Young, M.S.: Lateral control assistance in car driving: classification, review and future prospects. IET Intell. Transp. Syst. **5**(3), 207–220 (2011)
11. Flemisch, F.O., et al.: Towards cooperative guidance and control of highly automated vehicles: H-Mode and Conduct-by-Wire. Ergonomics **57**(3), 343–360 (2014)
12. Flemisch, F., et al.: Shared control is the sharp end of cooperation: Towards a common framework of joint action, shared control and human machine cooperation. IFAC-PapersOnLine **49**(19), 72–77 (2016)
13. Abbink, D.A., Mulder, M., Boer, E.R.: Haptic shared control: smoothly shifting control authority? Cogn. Technol. Work **14**(1), 19–28 (2012)
14. Mulder, M., Abbink, D.A., Boer, E.R.: Sharing control with haptics: seamless driver support from manual to automatic control. Hum. Factors **54**(5), 786–798 (2012)
15. Flemisch, F., et al.: Towards a dynamic balance between humans and automation: authority, ability, responsibility and control in shared and cooperative control situations. Cogn. Technol. Work **14**(1), 3–18 (2012)
16. Merat, N., et al.: Transition to manual: driver behaviour when resuming control from a highly automated vehicle. Transp. Res. Part F: Traffic Psychol. Behav. **27**, 274–282 (2014)
17. Itoh, M., Inagaki, T.: Design and evaluation of steering protection for avoiding collisions during a lane change. Ergonomics **57**(3), 361–373 (2014)
18. Mars, F., Deroo, M., Hoc, J.: Analysis of human-machine cooperation when driving with different degrees of haptic shared control. IEEE Trans. Haptics **7**(3), 324–333 (2014)
19. Blanco, M., et al.: Automated vehicles: take-over request and system prompt evaluation. In: Meyer, G., Beiker, S. (eds.) Road Vehicle Automation 3. LNM, pp. 111–119. Springer, Cham (2016). https://doi.org/10.1007/978-3-319-40503-2_9

20. Navarro, J.: Human–machine interaction theories and lane departure warnings. Theor. Issues Ergon. Sci. **18**(6), 519–547 (2017)
21. Michalos, G., et al.: Design considerations for safe human-robot collaborative workplaces. Procedia CIRP **37**, 248–253 (2015)
22. Zanchettin, A.M., et al.: Safety in human-robot collaborative manufacturing environments: metrics and control. IEEE Trans. Autom. Sci. Eng. **13**(2), 882–893 (2016)
23. Woolley, A.W., et al.: Evidence for a collective intelligence factor in the performance of human groups. Science **330**(6004), 686–688 (2010)
24. Atzori, L., Iera, A., Morabito, G.: The Internet of Things: a survey. Comput. Netw. **54**(15), 2787–2805 (2010)
25. LeCun, Y., Bengio, Y., Hinton, G.: Deep learning. Nature **521**(7553), 436–444 (2015)
26. Krizhevsky, A., Sutskever, I., Hinton, G.E.: ImageNet classification with deep convolutional neural networks. J. Commun. ACM **60**(6), 84–90 (2017)
27. Quinn, A.J., Bederson, B.B.: Human computation: a survey and taxonomy of a growing field. In: 29th Annual Chi Conference on Human Factors in Computing Systems, pp. 1403–1412 (2011)
28. Zou, H., et al.: Robust WiFi-enabled device-free gesture recognition via unsupervised adversarial domain adaptation, pp. 1–8 (2018)
29. Albini, A., Denei, S., Cannata, G.: Human hand recognition from robotic skin measurements in human-robot physical interactions, pp. 4348–4353 (2017)
30. Wang, P., et al.: Deep learning-based human motion recognition for predictive context-aware human-robot collaboration. CIRP Ann. **67**(1), 17–20 (2018)
31. Zhong, Y., Deng, W.: Deep difference analysis in similar-looking face recognition, pp. 3353–3358 (2018)
32. Wang, F.: The emergence of intelligent enterprises: from CPS to CPSS. IEEE Intell. Syst. **25**(4), 85–88 (2010)
33. Hoc, J.-M.: Towards a cognitive approach to human–machine cooperation in dynamic situations. Int. J. Hum.-Comput. Stud. **54**(4), 509–540 (2001)
34. Pacaux, M.P., et al.: Levels of automation and human-machine cooperation: application to human-robot interaction. IFAC Proc. Volumes **44**(1), 6484–6492 (2011)
35. Krüger, J., Lien, T.K., Verl, A.: Cooperation of human and machines in assembly lines. CIRP Ann. **58**(2), 628–646 (2009)
36. Panchanathan, K., Boyd, R.: Indirect reciprocity can stabilize cooperation without the second-order free rider problem. Nature **432**(7016), 499–502 (2004)
37. Fehr, E., Gächter, S.: Altruistic punishment in humans. Nature **415**(6868), 137–140 (2002)

Adoption of the HTA Technique in the Open Source Software Development Process

Rosa Llerena[1], Nancy Rodríguez[2]([⊠]), Lucrecia Llerena[2], John W. Castro[3], and Silvia T. Acuña[2]

[1] Ministerio de Educación, Quevedo, Ecuador
rosa.llerena@educacion.gob.ec
[2] Departamento de Ingeniería Informática, Universidad Autónoma de Madrid, Madrid, Spain
{nrodriguez,lllerena}@uteq.edu.ec, silvia.acunna@uam.es
[3] Departamento de Ingeniería Informática y Ciencias de la Computación,
Universidad de Atacama, Copiapó, Chile
john.castro@uda.cl

Abstract. The growth in the number of non-developer open source software (OSS) application users and the escalating use of these applications have led to the need and interest in developing usable OSS. OSS communities do not generally know how to apply usability techniques and are unclear about which techniques to use in each activity of the development process. The aim of our research is to adopt the HTA usability technique in the OpenOffice Writer OSS project and determine the feasibility of adapting the technique for application. To do this, we participated as volunteers in the project. We used the case study research method during technique application and participation in the community. As a result, we identified adverse conditions that were an obstacle to technique application and modified the technique to make it applicable to OSS projects. We can conclude from our experience that these changes were helpful for applying the technique, using web artifacts like forums and collaborative tools like Cacoo, although it was not easy to recruit OSS users to participate in usability technique application.

Keywords: Open source software · Usability techniques · Design · Hierarchical Task Analysis (HTA)

1 Introduction

OSS has spread so swiftly that it now rivals commercial software systems [1]. OSS communities do not as yet enact standard processes capable of ensuring that the software that they develop has the attributes of good software [2]. The inadequate definition of processes, activities, tasks and techniques within OSS development has led researchers from several areas to gravitate towards this field of research with the aim of correcting this situation. Usability is one of the key quality attributes in software development. In recent years, OSS has come to be an important part of computing.

However, several authors have acknowledged that the usability of OSS is poor [3–5]. In this respect, the empirical study conducted by Raza et al. [6] reports that 60% of

© Springer Nature Switzerland AG 2020
C. Stephanidis et al. (Eds.): HCII 2020, LNCS 12423, pp. 184–198, 2020.
https://doi.org/10.1007/978-3-030-60114-0_13

respondents (non-developer users) stated that poor usability is the main obstacle that OSS applications have to overcome if users are to migrate away from commercial software. On this ground, OSS projects must tackle the usability level and usability-related problems at length [5].

On one hand, the HCI field offers usability techniques whose key aim is to build usable software. However, they are applied as part of HCI methods and not within the OSS development process. On the other hand, the OSS development process focuses on source code and thus on the development of functionalities. The OSS development process has a number of features (like functionality-focused development) which prevent many of the HCI usability techniques from being adopted directly [7]. This community has now started to adopt some usability techniques. Most of the techniques taken on board by the community are for evaluating usability [7], whereas it has not adopted many techniques related to requirements analysis and design. Some techniques have been adapted ad hoc for adoption in OSS development projects [7]. Only a few research papers have reported the use of the HTA technique in OSS developments [8]. The HTA technique was applied in the Multiplex medical tool as described in Doesburg [8]. HTAs were used to decompose and compare various tasks related to the intravenous medication process. These HTAs were useful in comparing how various tasks are performed with both the current infusion system and the proposed control system. Participants were presented with five patient cases, designed with the help of an experienced ICU nurse (Intensive Care Unit). The cases were carefully created so that the decisions made by the participants do not influence the execution of the tasks. The tasks would be carried out both in the simulated environment and in Multiplex, to then contrast the results. Clicks, task time, errors and application response time were measured. The tests showed that users had difficulty understanding the buttons, which increased the probability of errors in the doses of intravenous therapies.

This paper addresses the research problem of how to adopt the HTA usability technique within the OSS development process, and particularly within a real OSS project called OpenOffice Writer. To do this, we previously identified which problems had to be solved in order to be able to apply the technique. Some authors claim that the main reasons for the generally poor usability of OSS developments are that OSS developers have tended to develop software for themselves [9] and that the development community is uninformed about who its users are [10]. HTA involves three linked stages: information gathering, diagramming, and analysis [11]. For the collection of information, existing information is reviewed (for example, operating manuals, procedures, etc.) to establish how things are done, what information is needed and whether or not the task is performed satisfactorily. To carry out the diagramming, hierarchical trees are used to facilitate the analysis of the tasks. The HTA technique was developed by Annette and Duncan [12]. HTA is the oldest and best-known task analysis technique, which is still valid, although there are new ways to apply the HTA technique [13, 14]. The main purpose of HTA is to understand how a system works and whether or not it achieves its objectives. This provides a functional analysis instead of a behavioral description. The difference between HTA and other task analysis techniques (e.g., GOMS and Object-Action Interface Model) is that in the other techniques a list of activities with cognitive aspects is made whereas in HTA the goals of the task are identified. On this ground, we have selected the HTA usability technique for adoption in the OpenOffice project.

This paper is organized as follows. Section 2 describes the research method followed to apply the usability technique. Section 3 describes the proposed solution. Section 4 discusses the results. Finally, Sect. 5 outlines the conclusions and future research.

2   Research Method

In order to validate our proposal for adopting the HTA technique in OSS development projects (particularly in OpenOffice Writer), we had to volunteer for this project. This is equivalent to being members of the OSS community of volunteers. We used a case study as the qualitative research method to validate our research [15]. We use a non-experimental design, since we do not randomly assign subjects or control the groups. From a case study, we learn about the experiences of applying usability techniques adapted to OSS projects. The case study is the best research method for carrying out this validation. On this ground, we followed the guidelines set out by Runeson et al. [15]. This research method is used when the phenomenon under study (in this case, the adoption of techniques with adaptations) is studied within its real-world context (in this case, OSS projects).

3   Proposed Solution

In this section, we briefly describe the HTA usability technique applied in an OSS Project. First, we specify the characteristics of the selected OSS project (OpenOffice Writer). Second, we describe the HTA technique as prescribed by HCI, followed by the details of the changes made to this technique for application to the OSS project. Finally, we report the results of applying the HTA technique.

3.1   Case Study Design

The case study is one of the most popular forms of qualitative empirical research. A case study investigates the phenomenon of interest in its real-world context. To be exact, the phenomenon of interest for this research is the adoption of the HTA technique with adaptations, whereas the real-world context is an OSS project. We will give a general description of the procedure enacted to perform the case study. Our case study is based on the research question: Is it possible to determine whether some adaptations of the HTA usability technique would enable its adoption in a real OSS project?

OpenOffice Writer is the selected OSS project in which the HTA technique is to be adopted. OpenOffice is currently one of the most popular OSS projects and a model of a successful OSS project. It is a large-scale, well-organized and structured OSS project, which also has a large user community.

3.2 Changes to the HTA Usability Technique

On the one hand, Annett [16] acknowledges that the HTA is based on copying how tasks are routinely performed, making it appropriate for task computerization projects (e.g., accounting records, product industrialization, etc.). On the other hand, Shepherd considers HTA as a strategy to examine tasks, focused on refining the performance criteria, concentrating on the skills of the members, understanding the contexts of the tasks and generating useful hypotheses to overcome performance problems [17]. Therefore, HTA is a very detailed study of a group of users that allows us to understand the current system and the information flows in it [18]. The HTA technique, belonging to the HCI Interaction Design activity, is an iterative process of identification and decomposition of tasks into sub-tasks, together with the precision of such decomposition [19]. This technique is very useful to structure the observed information about how the user organizes the tasks that usually carries out in his work. Therefore, the use of this technique can complement the Eduction and Requirements Analysis efforts when it comes to a system that aims to support the user in carrying out their common tasks. Also, this technique serves to model how users organize their activities and what means they use to carry them out [18].

Annett and Duncan [16] and other publications [13, 14, 19, 20] propose procedures to apply the HTA technique. Although these procedures are very similar to each other, for processes focused on user-centered development, a suitable approach is that of the work of Preece et al. [19]. For this reason, we have used the version of Preece et al. [19] as a reference, since it is the simplest among the authors studied to make the respective adaptations.

To adapt the HTA technique, it must first be formalized. Subsequently, modifications must be made to the formalized technique to be able to incorporate it to OSS development. It should be clarified that the formalization of the HTA technique is carried out in this work, since the proposed procedure is not explicitly defined by Preece et al. [19]. Below, the first five steps of the HTA technique by Preece et al. [19] are described and the unfavorable or inconvenient conditions that hinder their incorporation into OSS development are detailed.

The first step is the specification of the main work or task area, and it aims to recognize the main functions of the software tool to determine whether a failure may be occurring or not. Preece et al. [19] do not establish how to obtain the information to establish which are the main tasks. To overcome this unfavorable condition, we propose that this information be obtained by other means than those established by the HCI (for example, forums and surveys). The second step of this technique is to break down the main task into subtasks, each subtask corresponding to an action that needs to be performed in order to complete the task. Preece et al. [19] suggest breaking down each main task into four to eight subtasks specified in terms of objectives that cover the entire area of interest of the selected software project. Tasks should be written in such a way that they are easily recognized by the user. The output product obtained in this step is the document "list of tasks and subtasks". However, Preece et al. [19] do not specify the format of the document associated with this step. The third step corresponds to including the plans in the list of tasks and sub-tasks.

The plans describe under what conditions the users will perform the sub-tasks. Also, the plans control the order for the execution of the tasks. Preece et al. [19] do not specify the format of the document associated with this step.

The fourth step is known as drawing the subtasks, which consists of drawing the sub-tasks in an outline. Preece et al. [19] do not concisely suggest the type of schema to use to draw these sub-tasks. The output product obtained in this step is the hierarchical tree of tasks. This step does not explicitly identify the associated tasks for drawing these schematics, nor does it specify the format of this product associated with this step. The fifth step is to decide the level of detail that the decomposition of tasks requires and at what point to stop since in this step a consistent treatment of the situation is ensured. In this fifth step, Preece et al. [19] propose that the decomposition of tasks continues until the information flows were more easily represented from a much lower level of description to a higher level. In this step, it has been identified as a disadvantage that developers must come together to validate the level of detail defined in the decomposition of tasks obtained in the previous step. In other words, the developers must be physically together, a condition that cannot occur due to the characteristics of the OSS projects. Therefore, a modification to the technique must be made. To resolve this unfavorable condition, it is proposed to request feedback from the project developers via email.

Table 1 summarizes for each step of the technique the unfavorable conditions analyzed and the main adaptations proposed. There are mainly three adaptations: (i) Users participate online, (ii) it is necessary to obtain certain information to apply the technique by means other than those prescribed by the HCI and (iii) that the expert can be replaced by a developer or expert user of the OSS project. Particularly, in our case the expert was replaced by an HCI student under the supervision of two expert usability researchers. For this reason, there is no risk that the quality of the software will be negatively affected when applying the adaptation proposed for the HTA technique.

3.3   OpenOffice Writer Case Study Results

In this study, steps from the original HTA technique have been added to facilitate its application in OSS projects. Next, for each step in Table 2, the tasks carried out in the adaptation of the proposed HTA technique are detailed. By defining each task, new unfavorable conditions arise, and new adaptations are proposed to incorporate this technique into OSS projects.

To test the feasibility of our adaptation of the HTA technique, it was necessary to apply it in OpenOffice Writer. This tool is a cross-platform word processor that is part of the suite of applications of the Apache OpenOffice office suite. For the first task (Specifying the main work area or tasks), an analysis was made of the information obtained through means other than those established by the HCI (such as forums, emails and surveys). This obtained information refers to: (i) the problems reported in the OpenOffice Writer online forum, (ii) the problems reported by email and that are reported in the OpenOffice subscription lists and (iii) the results obtained in the survey applied for the Personas technique [21]. The Personas technique was applied in the first phase of the research to obtain the user profile of the OpenOffice Writer tool. In this step, we have specifically proceeded to extract and process the information from the following data sources: the "Personas" online survey,

Table 1. Summary of the identified adverse conditions and the proposed adaptations for the HTA technique.

Technique steps [19]	Adverse conditions	Proposed adaptations
1. Specify the area of work or main task	• It is necessary to obtain information (e.g., commonly recurring problems) to apply the technique in the way prescribed by HCI	• The information necessary to apply the technique is obtained through other means different to those established by HCI (e.g., through forums)
2. Break down tasks into subtasks 3. Include the plans to carry out the subtasks 4. Draw the subtasks	• The tasks associated to these steps are not explicitly identified	• The tasks associated to each step are detailed • The format for the output product is specified
5. Deciding the level of detail that the decomposition of the tasks requires 6. Deciding the level of depth and amplitude of the decomposition of tasks 7. Assigning numbering to tasks	• The face-to-face participation of the developers is necessary • The tasks associated to these steps are not explicitly identified	• Ask developers for feedback through email • The tasks associated to each step are detailed
8. Check the task analysis 9. Present the task analysis in written format	• The tasks associated to these steps are not explicitly identified • It is indispensable to employ a usability expert • The format of the document associated to these steps is not specified	• The tasks associated to each step are detailed • The expert can be a developer, an expert user of the OSS Project or an HCI student (under the supervision of a mentor) • The format for the output product is specified

the OpenOffice online forum, the Bugzilla repository, the emails received in Outlook from the subscription lists (users@openoffice.apache.org, dev@openoffice.apache.org, issues@openoffice.apache. org). Messages received from subscription lists were filtered by words that may be related to the OpenOffice Writer tool.

Regarding the online forum, its members' task is to support other users in their learning or solving specific problems with the OpenOffice Writer application. In addition, information was obtained on the specific page where errors are reported (bugs) of the OpenOffice tool called Bugzilla. Within Bugzilla, the Writer product and the messages with the User Interface (UI) component were examined, because this component is related to User Interface problems and most likely with usability issues related to user interaction with the application.

Table 2. Steps and tasks of the HTA technique adapted to apply it in an OSS project

Steps of the adapted HTA technique	Tasks
1. Specifying the main work area or tasks	• Define the main tasks to be analyzed • Specify names for the main tasks
2. Redrawing the hierarchical task tree	• Break down tasks into subtasks • List each task and subtask in decomposition
3. Drawing the subtasks	• Diagram the hierarchical tasks tree • Include plans that guide task development
4. Defining the level of detail for the decomposition of tasks	• Define the limit of the system description
5. Deciding the level of depth and amplitude	• Decide the stop condition for task decomposition • Decide depth and breadth level for decomposing tasks
6. Checking the task analysis	• Review task analysis
7. Requesting feedback for the task analysis	• Request feedback to improve task analysis
8. Selecting the users that are to participate in the application of the technique	• Act with the users who confirmed their participation in the research through their email contribution
9. Designing a format for data collection	• Design format for data recording
10. Executing the HTA of the defined tasks	• Executing the HTA of defined tasks with real users
11. Analyzing and interpreting the data obtained in the execution of tasks	• Analysis of the information provided by users in the development of tasks from the previous step
12. Redrawing the hierarchical task tree	• Perform the hierarchical tree diagram with the results obtained in the previous step by collaborative work • Include plans for the new hierarchical tree
13. Submit task analysis report	• Make the report with the pre-analysis and post-analysis of tasks • Present the report with pre-analysis and post-analysis of tasks

To extract the information from these two data sources (online forum and Bugzilla), we opted to use the Python tool. This tool is very easy to use and has a fast learning curve, which along with its versatility make it a high-quality language for data analysis. This programming language was selected to easily implement a source code using libraries that allow data mining. Once the information was extracted from these two data sources, the data analysis was carried out with the R tool to determine the patterns of problems or difficulties that users have with OpenOffice Writer. Table 3 shows some of the categories of problems identified in the online forum, emails and the Bugzilla website, as well as the difficulties registered in the online survey "Personas".

Table 3. Main problems reported in the forums, emails, Bugzilla and difficulties expressed in the "Personas" survey.

Category reported in	Forum	Emails	"Personas" survey	Bugzilla
Insert heading/footer	X			
Insertion of images	X		X	
Use of capital letters	X			
Use of tables	X	X	X	X
Use of the contextual menu to apply fonts	X			
Design formulas	X			

Based on this list of problems, we have defined five main tasks related to the purpose of our analysis and that are performed by users of the OpenOffice Writer tool. These tasks are to: (i) Write a document with capital letters, (ii) write a story that includes images, (iii) design a table with formulas, (iv) improve the design of a document, and (v) write a help manual.

For step two (breaking down the main task into subtasks), once the main tasks to be executed by OpenOffice Writer users have been defined, we break them down into subtasks considering them to have a minimum of six and a maximum of eight subtasks. As a result, we have the document "List of Tasks and Subtasks of task 1 Write a document with capital letter". For this step, it is proposed to use a conventional numerical system that emphasizes the hierarchy of tasks (for example: 1, 2, 3 for the first level, 1.1, 1.2, 1.3 for the second level, etc.).

Table 4 shows a fragment of the document that lists the tasks and subtasks in a numerical scheme specifying the type of Action (sequence, decision or iteration). Column 2 shows the type of action to be taken ((A)ction, (D)ecision, (I)teration).

For step three (drawing the subtasks), we draw the tasks and subtasks in the form of a tree diagram to have an overview of the tasks. The diagrams have been produced with the online tool CACOO 2.0, which provides a manipulable means for exploring information and increases cognitive resources, since it becomes a visual resource to expand human working memory. Each task is drawn with a box and the tasks that cannot be divided in turn are underlined (one line below the box). Figure 1 presents a fragment of the hierarchical tree designed with the collaborative tool CACOO 2.0 and is related to the main Task 1 (Writing a document with capital letters). The same was done for the rest of the tasks.

In the fourth step (defining the level of detail for the decomposition of tasks), the plans to control the sequence in which these subtasks are performed must be considered, and they show the conditions that indicate when the subtasks are applicable. The purpose of these plans is to exclude impossible scenarios and establish conditions for what can

Table 4. Fragment of the "Writing a document with capital letters" task

GOAL: To write a document in 2 columns, which includes capital letters and a page header	Type of action
1. Open the application OpenOffice Writer	A
2. Write the title of the document: "The core of the processor"	A
3. Apply two formats to the title: centered and bold	A
4. Type the following text into the document: Processor manufacturers are very clear; they want to create increasingly powerful PCs. To this end, taking advantage of improvements in the manufacturing process, they add the greater number of cores possible to the processor	A
5. Divide the document into two journalistic columns	A

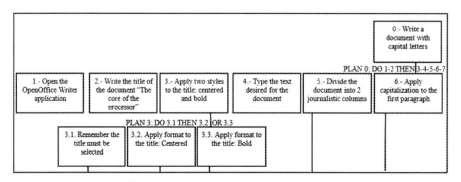

Fig. 1. Hierarchical tree of the "Writing a document with capital letters" task 1.

be prevented and what can happen. For example, in Task 1 (Writing a document with capital letters), PLAN 3: DO 3.1 THEN DECIDE BETWEEN 3.2 or 3.3, indicates that we must first run subtask 3.1 and then decide between running subtask 3.2 or subtask 3.3. Creating this detailed analysis of a main task in other simpler tasks has taken us a long time, in order to make each step explicit and making it less likely that the user will ignore any knowledge they require. At the same time, other opportunities have been identified to improve the user experience. For example, knowing that applying a capital letter style is a difficult option for a user to locate can influence the design and implementation of new functionality in the OpenOffice Writer tool. Developers should consider increasing the visibility of this option and making it easy for users to locate.

For the fifth step (deciding level of depth and amplitude), the detailed decomposition is performed according to the PxC rule that calculates the efficiency of continuing the analysis based on the probability of failure (P) x the cost of failure (C). In other words, the decomposition of the tasks that requires additional effort to analyze is only carried out when there are reasons to consider that the current performance is not acceptable. For example, in objective 7 (Apply capital letter) of Task 1 (Write a document with capital letters) (Table 3), we have considered this activity to be very important and difficult to execute (P = high and C = high), so all the additional effort of the analysis is concentrated here. In this case, developers have not adequately understood what tasks are essential and how the system should support users in performing them. Once we have defined the level of detail and the two dimensions (depth and breadth) we consult the developers via email if the decomposition of the tasks carried out in the previous step matches the conceptual and functional model that they expected to have on the application. Our hierarchical task analysis will allow any developer to quickly understand what their application does and how its capabilities translate into the system user experience.

In the sixth step (checking the task analysis), an HCI student under the tutelage of a mentor acts as an expert to perform the hierarchical task analysis check. Once the task analysis has been checked, it can serve as a system documentation, so developers can quickly understand how users interact with their software system. It is important to mention that the developers of the OpenOffice project are very aware that there is a need to look for new methods and practices of the HCI to improve the usability of this project. Therefore, hierarchical task analysis is an effective means of raising awareness among developers about reconsidering user engagement for software enhancement and being willing to listen to end users for that purpose.

Regarding the seventh step (requesting feedback for the task analysis), to reinforce the check of an initial version of the task analysis, feedback is requested from the project developers via email. An improved version of task analysis allows developers to explore various approaches to complete the same task or help optimize particular interactions between a user and a software system.

In the eighth step (selecting the users that are to participate in the application of the technique), the participation of representative users is necessary to discuss current or future tasks, but it is impossible to obtain a group of users that we can consider representative because they do not have enough time. Consequently, we dialogued with a group of volunteer users to collaborate with us in the application of the HTA technique. To do this, we made contact via email with some of the OpenOffice Writer users whom we knew were willing to participate in our research. Finally, we decided to invite an OpenOffice Writer user who was not involved in task decomposition to check the consistency of the task analysis.

In step nine (designing a format for data collection), once the diagrams of the tasks to be executed by the OpenOffice Writer user were produced, they were analyzed to determine possible human errors, especially those related to procedures or usability problems derived from the current design of the software product. This analysis is recorded in the document "Task Analysis Table". Table 5 contains the format of the document "Task Analysis Table" and is made up of four columns: the first column indicates the *action* performed by the user, followed by the *cause* and *effect* columns observed during the execution of the action and finally the *redesign* column where a possible task improvement is provided.

For the execution of step ten (executing the HTA of the defined tasks) the physical presence of users meeting with the evaluator or evaluators is necessary. This is impossible because the users of the OSS communities are spread out across the world. Therefore, a remote observing session is established to have an appropriate perspective with a guest user. It is important to mention that evaluators may need to contact users as many times

Table 5. Format of the document "Task Analysis Table"

TASK 1
USER NUM:
START TIME:
END TIME:
TASK DURATION:

ACTION	CAUSE	EFFECT	REDESIGN

as necessary to clarify all the questions that are necessary. However, because the work in the OSS community is done by volunteers in their spare time, it is difficult to apply several iterations to achieve greater precision in task analysis. In the execution of the HTA technique, it was agreed with the participant to carry out a remote observation on a specific day and time, all communication had to be done electronically, including explanations, supply of materials and data collection. Specifically, two tools were used: Skype, to be able to talk to the user and see their reactions, and TeamViewer, to visualize their interaction with the application by remotely accessing their screen view. Once the HTA was completed, an HCI student under the tutelage of a mentor acts as an expert to analyze and interpret the data obtained, which will finally allow the tasks to be redesigned and organized appropriately within the software system. Also, developers can be suggested to include new functions within the system and the user interface.

In step eleven (analyzing and interpreting the data obtained in the execution of tasks), the task analysis process is not only based on the registration of existing subtasks, but also provides possible improvements resulting from the introduction of new facilities for the development of a task. The implications of potential changes to these tasks should be re-recorded in the hierarchical task trees. Here the advantage of working with the CACOO platform is that it allows simultaneous collaborative work, that is, the same diagram can be edited at the same time by more than one person. This is related to step twelve (redrawing the hierarchical task tree). Therefore, the redesign of the hierarchical task trees was done jointly between the researchers and the developers of the OpenOffice Writer application. Finally, in step thirteen, to present the task analysis report, we designed a table that will document the details of the specific tasks, the details of the interactions between the user and the current system, as well as any problems related to these tasks. Table 6 presents a fragment of the document "HTA Report", which corresponds to the final product of the application of the HTA technique.

4   Discussion of Results

Communication with the OpenOffice community was troublesome because not all the users were willing to participate in the application of the usability technique. However, our experience of participating in large projects (e.g., LibreOffice Writer and OpenOffice Writer) has revealed that it is very difficult to recruit real end users to participate in the application of usability techniques in OSS projects generally [21, 22]. During the application of the HTA technique to the OpenOffice Writer project, the key problem

Table 6. Fragment of the document "HTA Report"

Higher-order task	Plan	Subtasks	Information flow through the interface	Information the user already knows	Pre-analysis notes	Post-analysis notes	Improvement in the user interface
Writing a document with capital letters	PLAN 0: DO 1-2, then 3-4-5-6-7-8	1. Open the OpenOffice Writer app	Start the OpenOffice Writer processor				
		2. Write the title "The core of the processor"	Type the title of the document				
		3. Apply formats to the title: centered and bold	Apply formats: centered and bold	Use of shortcuts			
		4. Type the text that will be contained in the document	Type text	The user removes centered and bold and applies bold without specifying it as an action			
		5. Dividing the document into 2 journalistic columns	Format>Columns>2	Use of shortcuts			
		6. Apply capital lettering to the first paragraph of the first column	Format>Paragraph>Initials>Show Initials		The user does not easily locate the "Capital Letters" option	The user, confused, reviews all the tabs of the "Paragraph" option to find the "Capital Letters" option	Directly show the Capital Letters option in the Format menu

was user availability, as many are volunteers and had very little spare time. This is preliminary research. In the HTA technique, the main adaptations made were three First, users participate online through web artifacts (forums). In the case of the HTA technique, the use of the forum allowed a reliable analysis of the tasks for developers to make decisions regarding improving the interface design. Second, the usability expert is replaced by a developer, expert user, or HCI student under the tutelage of a mentor. Particularly, in our case the expert was replaced by a team of junior experts supervised by a main expert. Third, it is necessary to obtain certain information to apply the technique in the manner prescribed by HCI. This information can be models or graphic representations of the tasks performed by users, becoming low-cost alternatives to achieve the same objectives that the HCI prescribes.

The HTA technique must be adapted and applied with the participation of users, for a better understanding of the tasks to be carried out and that is more understandable for the components of the team that are not accustomed to the notations typically of Software Engineering. Therefore, more cases studies are required to validate the proposed adaptations. Note that there are other usability techniques (for example, user profiles, heuristic evaluation) that might benefit from the proposed adaptations (for example, HCI students supervised by a mentor standing in for experts) to enhance technique adoption in the OSS development process.

5 Conclusions

The aim of this research was to evaluate the feasibility of adopting adapted HCI usability techniques in OSS projects. To be precise, we adapted the HTA technique for application in the OpenOffice Writer project. It was by no means easy to find users to volunteer to apply the HTA technique. As mentioned, users generally have very little time, and it was hard to get them to participate without an incentive. We identified three main adverse conditions that are barriers to the application of HTA in OSS development projects: (i) the need to have a usability expert to apply the technique, (ii) the unavailability of on-site users and (iii) the need to obtain certain information to apply the technique in the manner prescribed by HCI. In order to surmount these barriers, (i) a HCI student or group of HCI students supervised by a mentor substitutes the usability expert, (ii) OSS users participate remotely and (iii) the necessary information is obtained by means other than those established by the HCI (for example, in forums). We believe that it is necessary to educate users and OSS community members generally to raise awareness of the importance of application usability and publicize existing usability techniques in order to encourage participation. As future research, we intend to conduct further case studies to adapt and apply more usability techniques in OSS projects in order to validate the proposed adaptations and study new web artefacts that can be adapted to OSS communities to improve communication. This pilot study will be expanded by adapting and applying the HTA technique in the Libre OpenOffice project to confirm our findings.

Acknowledgements. Work funded by the Secretariat of Higher Education, Science, Technology and Innovation (SENESCYT) of the Government of Ecuador as part of an academic scholarship granted for postgraduate training, and Quevedo State Technical University through doctoral scholarships for university professors. Also, this research was funded by the FEDER/Spanish Ministry of Science and Innovation – Research State Agency: project MASSIVE, RTI2018-095255-B-I00, the R&D programme of Madrid (project FORTE, P2018/TCS-4314), and project PGC2018-097265-B-I00, also funded by: FEDER/Spanish Ministry of Science and Innovation – Research State Agency. Finally, this research received funding from the University of Atacama "DIUDA 22316" project.

References

1. Schryen, G., Kadura, R.: Open source vs. closed source software. In: 2009 ACM Symposium on Applied Computing, SAC 2009, pp. 2016–2023 (2009). https://doi.org/10.1145/1529282.1529731
2. Noll, J., Liu, W.-M.: Requirements elicitation in open source software development: a case study. In: 3rd International Workshop on Emerging Trends in Free/Libre/Open Source Software Research and Development, FLOSS 2010, pp. 35–40 (2010). https://doi.org/10.1145/1833272.1833279
3. Smith, S., Engen, D., Mankoski, A., Frishberg, N., Pedersen, N., Benson, C.: GNOME Usability Study Report. Technical Report, Sun Microsystems (2001)
4. Çetin, G., Gokturk, M.: A measurement based framework for assessment of usability-centricness of open source software projects. In: 4th International Conference on Signal Image Technology and Internet Based Systems, SITIS 2008, November 2008, pp. 585–592 (2008). https://doi.org/10.1109/sitis.2008.106
5. Raza, A., Capretz, L.F., Ahmed, F.: Users' perception of open source usability: an empirical study. Eng. Comput. 28(2), 109–121 (2012). https://doi.org/10.1007/s00366-011-0222-1
6. Raza, A., Capretz, L.F., Ahmed, F.: An empirical study of open source software usability: the industrial perspective. Int. J. Open Source Softw. Process. 3(1), 1–16 (2011). https://doi.org/10.4018/jossp.2011010101
7. Castro, J.W.: Incorporación de la Usabilidad en el Proceso de Desarrollo Open Source Software. Tesis Doctoral. Departamento de Ingeniería Informática. Escuela Politécnica Superior. Universidad Autónoma de Madrid (2014)
8. Doesburg, F.: Developing a System for Automated Control of Multiple Infusion Pumps, July 2012
9. Raza, A., Capretz, L.F., Ahmed, F.: An open source usability maturity model (OS-UMM). J. Comput. Hum. Behav. 28(4), 1109–1121 (2012)
10. Benson, C., Müller-Prove, M., Mzourek, J.: Professional usability in open source projects: GNOME, OpenOffice.org, NetBeans. In: CHI 2004, Extended Abstract on Human factors in Computing System, CHI EA 2004, April 2004, pp. 1083–1084 (2004). https://doi.org/10.1145/985921.985991
11. Granollers, T.: MPIu+a Una metodología que integra la Ingeniería del Software, la Interacción Persona Ordenador y la accesibilidad en el contexto de equipos de desarrollo mutidisciplinares. Tesis Doctoral. Departamento de Lenguajes y Sistemas Informáticos. Universidad de Lleida (2004)
12. Gray, M.J., Annett, J., Duncan, K.D., Stammers, R.B.: Task analysis. In: Department of Employment Training Information Paper 6. HMSO (1971)
13. Paternó, F.: Model-Based Design and Evaluation of Interactive Applications, Pisa, Italy (2000)
14. Stary, C., van der Veer, G.C.: Task analysis meets prototyping: seeking seamless UI-development. In: Extended Abstracts on Human Factors in Computing Systems, CHI 1999, pp. 104–105 (1999)

15. Runeson, P., Höst, M.: Guidelines for conducting and reporting case study research in software engineering. J. Empir. Softw. Eng. **14**(2), 131–164 (2009). https://doi.org/10.1007/s10664-008-9102-8
16. Annett, J., Duncan, K.D.: Task analysis and training design. Occup. Psychol. **41**, 211–221 (1967)
17. Shepherd, A.: HTA as a framework for task analysis. Ergonomics **41**(11), 1537–1552 (1998)
18. Ferré, X.: Marco de Integración de la Usabilidad en el Proceso de Desarrollo Software. Tesis Doctoral. Facultad de Informática. Universidad Politécnica de Madrid (2005)
19. Preece, J., Rogers, Y., Sharp, H., Benyon, D., Holland, S., Carey, T.: Human-Computer Interaction, 1st edn. Addison-Wesley Pub. Co. (1994)
20. Stanton, N.A.: Hierarchical task analysis: developments, applications, and extensions. Appl. Ergon. **37**(1), 55–79 (2006). https://doi.org/10.1016/j.apergo.2005.06.003
21. Llerena, L., Rodriguez, N., Castro, J.W., Acuña, S.T.: Adapting usability techniques for application in open source Software: a multiple case study. Inf. Softw. Technol. **107**, 48–64 (2019). https://doi.org/10.1016/j.infsof.2018.10.011
22. Llerena, L., Castro, J.W., Acuña, S.T.: A pilot empirical study of applying a usability technique in an open source software project. Inf. Softw. Technol. **106**, 122–125 (2019). https://doi.org/10.1016/j.infsof.2018.09.007

Exploring the Digital Native Assessment Scale as an Indicator for Building More Effective User Experiences

Lexy Martin[1]([⊠]), Steve Summerskill[1], Tracy Ross[1], Karl Proctor[2], and Arber Shabani[2]

[1] Loughborough University, Loughborough, UK
a.martin@lboro.ac.uk
[2] Jaguar Land Rover, Coventry, UK

Abstract. Building exceptional user experiences means designing for users of all digital skill level. An increased emphasis on personalization and, with it, adaptive interfaces exacerbates the necessity for digital inclusivity. However, how can designers ensure that they are meeting the needs of those with high and low skillsets? The research reported here employed semi-structured interviews to explore whether the Digital Native Assessment Scale (DNAS) can be used as a tool to classify users and act as a surrogate for predicting their digital profiles. Sixteen participants answered questions about their everyday technology behaviours, as well as their attitudes towards technology. Nine themes emerged through thematic analysis, however only one of these themes was associated with an even, dichotomous split between high scorers on the DNAS and low scorers on the DNAS. Therefore, the DNAS only clearly indicated digital behaviour in a limited number of issues and cannot be relied upon as a proxy for the participant characteristics to be supported in interface design.

Keywords: User experience design · Participant selection · Digital inclusivity

1 Introduction

Understanding users, and building empathy, is a main objective of exceptional user experience design, however this area, like the users themselves, is constantly evolving. Inclusivity, and catering to vastly different digital skillsets, is the driving force behind effective user experiences. This type of personalization is even more relevant with the increased prevalence of machine learning and AI. Different user groups have unique needs and demands that must be met to ensure a sufficiently pleasurable experience.

Two such user groups, digital native and digital immigrant, emerged from Mark Prensky's seminal 2001 paper, "Digital Natives, Digital Immigrants". The concept of 'digital natives,' meaning a person who was raised during the cyber age (Prensky 2001a), has sparked debate since it was first introduced. While its original ties to age have been largely refuted (Adams and Pente 2011; Akçayır et al. 2016; Bakla 2019; Bennett et al. 2008; Teo 2013), can the attributes Prensky identifies as the key characteristics of

© Springer Nature Switzerland AG 2020
C. Stephanidis et al. (Eds.): HCII 2020, LNCS 12423, pp. 199–210, 2020.
https://doi.org/10.1007/978-3-030-60114-0_14

'digital natives,' growing up with technology, comfort multitasking, reliance on graphics for communication and thriving on instant gratification, be tied to specific attitudes? Furthermore, can understanding these attitudes help designers better design for a wider range of technological skill levels?

The Digital Native Assessment Scale (DNAS) (Teo 2013) was developed as a means to identify whether or not an individual was a digital native. While predominantly used in the education sector, there is a potential for use within user centered design. Can the DNAS be used as a tool to identify different levels of digital skills?

This paper reports the parameters of effective user experience design, why they are needed, and how adaptive interfaces are the future of UX. Next, it looks at understanding digital natives and how the digital native assessment scale can be a possible means to evaluate digital skill level. Subsequently, the study methodology is presented. Results from the study are explained, then evaluated in relation to Digital Native Assessment Scale scores. The next section summarizes the findings and highlights the important conclusions. Finally, limitations are discussed, and future work ideas are presented.

2   Effective User Experiences

While user experience is present in all technology, there is a stark contrast between effective and ineffective experiences. In order to understand what would make an effective user experience, it is first necessary to understand what user experience is.

The term 'user experience,' or UX, was first introduced by Don Norman to describe the way an individual experiences reality around them (Norman 2016). This 'reality' can manifest as how someone interacts with a service, product or device (Norman and Nielsen n.d.). In 1991, Weiser proclaimed "...the most profound technologies are those that disappear" (Weiser 1999). This decree is still relevant today, an effective user experience is one that the user does not detect. The antithesis to this is the concept of 'dancing bear' software, where features are so good that users will overlook poor interaction design (Cooper 1999). However, despite whether a 'dancing bear' software has success, it could be exponentially improved with a good user experience (Cooper 1999). Ultimately for users, the interaction equates to the system, thus if they are required to exert past their normal effort threshold they will give up (Hartson and Pyla 2012). Larry Marine, a leader in UX, concisely explains this concept as "if the user can't use a feature, it effectively does not exist" (Marine in Hartson and Pyla 2012). Good user experience is dependent on users being able to access, and use, all features.

Designing for a wide variety of skillsets must be taken into account when designing user experiences. A feature for one user with vast digital expertise may provide an immensely different experience than for one with a limited amount of digital skill. Not only are some hindered by their overall skill, but users have different ability levels across applications and even across the same type of application (Fischer 2001). Thus, there are multiple avenues in which 'good' user experience has the potential to become obsolete. There have been a variety of avenues proposed to provide an inclusive user experience, with varying degrees of success. One avenue investigated, adaptation of user interfaces to fit with an individual's skill level, has proven to produce higher performance (Benyon 1993; Trumbly et al. 1993). The increased interest in Machine Learning and, with it, adaptive interfaces, demonstrates the need to develop experiences for multiple eventualities. Many view experts view "AI as the new UI," and thus, adaption as the most important way forward for improving user experience (Brownlee 2015; Kuang 2013)

2.1 UX, Adaptive Interfaces, and User Testing

With an adaptive system, it is necessary to design, and conduct user testing, for multiple eventualities. Adaptive user interface systems aim to automatically adjust the interface based on context or demands (Gemmell et al. 2002; Kubat et al. 1998). This is typically driven by user models and, more specifically, user modelling via stereotypes. Modelling via stereotypes is becoming more useful in the European Union due to adoption of the General Data Protection Regulation (GDPR), as this version can generate predictions based on a more limited amount of data (Rich 1989). These stereotypes can direct the user to experiences aimed at those with a high digital skillset or a low digital skillset. However, these two distinct experiences must be designed and tested to ensure that they achieve the desired interaction. It is paramount for designers to identify participants with the optimum skillset to adequately test these diverse experiences. This study will evaluate if the DNAS can serve as an effective measurement for participant recruitment.

3 Digital Natives

Rooted in the contrast of young and old or, more specifically, those born into a world with personal digital technology and those born into a world without, Prensky (2001a, b) presents the terms Digital Native and Digital Immigrant as the new way to describe individuals in the 21st century. Digital Natives are characterized as born on or after 1980, used to receiving information quickly, multi-taskers, graphics driven, thriving on instant gratification, and preferring games to 'serious' work (Prensky 2001a). Digital Immigrants, on the other hand, were born before the 1980's, turn to new technology second, learn "slowly, step-by-step, one thing at a time, individually, and above all seriously" (Prensky 2001a). Prensky's first paper focused on the repercussions of this divide on the educational community, as these Digital Natives learn differently to their Digital Immigrant teachers. The second paper (Prensky 2001b) explained how the brains of Digital Natives are different as they were socialized differently, surrounded by vast amounts of digital input, from a young age.

Despite the two initial papers (Prensky 2001a, b), and the subsequent additions and critiques (Kennedy et al. 2008; Stoerger 2009; Toledo 2007) it remains unclear what defines a Digital Native (Akçayır et al. 2016). It seems an "academic moral panic" arose with the introduction of the dichotomy, which presented those who resist the characterizations of Digital Native or Digital Immigrant as out of touch with reality (Bennett et al. 2008). Bennett et al's critique is of the language used in this "moral panic" which they say inhibits debate and gives creditably to unsupported claims.

3.1 Digital Native Assessment Scale (DNAS)

The Digital Native Assessment Scale (DNAS) was originally developed as a tool for teachers to understand how their students interacted with, and learned with, technology

(Teo 2013). It is a 21-item questionnaire that measures the degree to which an individual is a Digital Native by asking questions that are associated with Digital Natives. The DNAS uses a 7-point Likert scale that ranges from 'strongly disagree' to 'strongly agree.' The sum of the results of each of the scale's four factors, (1) growing up with technology, (2) comfortable with multitasking, (3) reliant on graphics for communication, and (4) thriving on instant gratifications and rewards, represents an individual's level of digital nativeness (Teo 2013). A higher score indicates that the individual is more digitally native. The scale was originally developed with 1018 students in Singapore and has been found to be "statistically valid and reliable" (Teo 2013). It has since been used in a variety of other Digital Native studies, albeit limited to the education sector (Akçayır et al. 2016; Huang et al. 2019; Teo 2016; Yong and Gates 2014).

Since its creation, the DNAS has served to inform Digital Native literature. However, while the scale is a means of determining if an individual is a Digital Native, it does not demonstrate how this score relates to other factors.

4   Methodology

This study comprised of semi-structured interviews with sixteen participants. The participants were drawn from a larger sample of 546 people who had completed an online survey. This survey enabled the DNAS score of each participant to be calculated and also indicated some of the behavioural and attitudinal factors that showed variability across the sample. The latter were used as a starting point for the development of the interview questions, to understand how high and low scorers vary in their technology behaviour.

4.1   Sampling Criteria

To be eligible for this study, participants needed to be:

1) Born between 1965–2001
2) A United Kingdom resident, as dictated by the UK immigration criteria

They also needed to take the Digital Natives Assessment Scale questionnaire, to enable their individual score to be generated

4.2   Recruitment Method

A purposive sample was recruited based on Digital Native Assessment Scores gathered in the previous online survey. Purposive sampling is used to achieve a sample that has specific characteristics that are important to a study's objectives (Palinkas et al. 2015). This type of sampling is often used in qualitative research, especially in selecting "information-rich cases" to best utilize limited resources (Palinkas et al. 2015; Patton 2002). It is necessary as the aim of the interviews is to understand and make sense of certain people's lived experiences, not to be a representation of all people (Gill 2005).

Figures 1, 2 and 3 show the rationale for the selection of participants. Figure 1 shows the range of scores based on the original DNAS scale (Teo 2013). Figure 2 shows the range of DNAS scores for the online survey sample from which the interview participants were drawn. The survey sample only included one participant with 'low' scores, the reason may have been tied to the fact that it was an online survey. As the sample for the interviews was drawn from this wider sample, a 'constructed low' of between 84 and 117 was used, along with a 'constructed high' of between 183 and 206. Eight 'high DNAS' participants were recruited along with eight 'low DNAS' participants.

DNAS SCALE (2013)

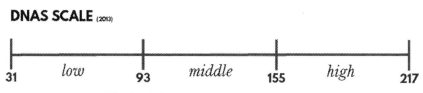

Fig. 1. Digital native assessment scale spread

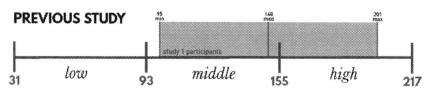

Fig. 2. Previous study

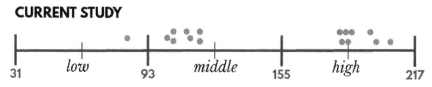

Fig. 3. Participants in current study

The Table below presents the different individuals that participated in this study, along with their DNAS scores, age, and self-reported gender (Table 1).

The interviews were conducted in Loughborough, Coventry, Glasgow and Derby. They were captured on a voice recorder, then fully transcribed by the researcher. All interviews fully complied with Loughborough University's ethics procedures.

Table 1. Participant table

Participant number	Age	DNAS score	Sex
P1	27	182	F
P2	31	117	F
P3	38	107	M
P4	42	107	F
P5	47	183	M
P6	42	117	F
P7	25	197	F
P8	25	187	F
P9	25	206	M
P10	24	114	M
P11	26	195	F
P12	50	184	M
P13	35	186	M
P14	28	84	F
P15	31	115	M
P16	36	105	M

4.3 Design of Semi-structured Interviews

To generate questions for interviews, it was important that the researcher investigate the background research fully. From here, it was necessary to develop a list of key topics that the questions were based upon. While some moderators can go into an interview scenario with only a list of themes, as these were semi-structured interviews, the researcher had a list of questions to provide a framework for the interview and guide it along. The questions developed to provide a framework were designed to stimulate information that is "factual', descriptive, thoughtful, emotional, or affectual" (Gill 2005). One of the main benefits of semi-structured interviews over structured interviews is the ability to adjust wording and order to best suit the participant (Bryman 2012). This deviation of question order can be done in semi-structured interviews for the purpose of exploring interesting areas and topics that might arise during the interview. While new questions may be aggregated in the moment, generally all the questions in the question list will be asked and in a similar wording (Bryman 2012).

The interviews comprised a core set of 24 open ended questions, with additional prompts and follow ups included on a case-by-case basis to facilitate clarification or expanding on answers. The topics covered by these questions were based on the results from the previous online survey. As these were semi-structured interviews, the number of questions posed varied depending on how the participant answered. Questions were added or adjusted based on the participant's response to previous questions.

4.4 Recording and Transcription

Recording and transcription serve as important steps in the understanding and analysis process. In order to fully immerse in the interview, audio recording is implemented as a key tool. This allows the researcher to focus on interactions rather than the pressure to put into writing every word of the conversation (Gill 2005). In addition to this, recording provides a more accurate record of the conversation, and the nuances, than relying on written notes (Gill 2005). However, the greatest benefit is the allowing the researcher to listen to the conversation over and identify ideas that might have been missed during the initial conversation (Gill 2005).

After each interview, the audio recording was transcribed by the primary researcher. The transcription process occurred as follows: audio was assessed for quality by listening to each recording and then was inputted into NVivo 12 (NVIVO 2020) transcribed, and timestamped (Welsh 2002). This system makes it easier to compare transcribed data with the original audio, maintaining the transcription's validity (Kvale and Brinkmann 2009). While transcription can take time, it allows for a re-familiarisation which can aid in data analysis (Crang and Cook 2012). NVivo 12 software was used as it can manage a large amount of different types of data, as well as serving as a powerful tool for analysis. Codes can easily be assigned and modified, if needed, to create more efficient analysis, as well as providing data visualizations for a clear overall understanding. Welsh (2002) elucidates that software such as NVivo "serves to facilitate an accurate and transparent data analysis process whilst also providing a quick and simple way of counting who said what and when, which in turn, provides a reliable, general picture of the data."

4.5 Data Analysis

Aided by NVivo, an in-depth thematic analysis was conducted on the responses from the interview. Thematic analysis is the method best suited to analyse semi-structured interviews. It is defined as: "A method for identifying, analyzing, and reporting patterns (themes) within data. It minimally organizes and describes your data set in (rich) detail. However, frequently it goes further than this, and interprets various aspects of the research topic" (Braun and Clarke 2006).

Themes are "specific patterns of meaning found in the data," and can contain manifest content or latent content (Joffe 2011). Manifest content refers to explicit mentions of an idea or phenomenon, whereas latent content provides implicit references (Joffe 2011).

The data analysis was carried out following the 'phases of thematic analysis' (Table 2) that were identified by Braun and Clark (2006).

These themes were then evaluated against the DNAS scores of the participants in each theme to understand how the digital behaviours and the scores related.

Table 2. Phases of thematic analysis (Braun and Clark 2006).

Phase		Description of the process
1	Familiarizing yourself with your data	Transcribing data if needed, reading and re-reading data, noting down initial ideas
2	Generate initial codes	Coding interesting features found in the data in a systematic way across the entire set of data, then collating data relevant to each code
3	Searching for themes	Assembling codes into potential themes, then gathering data relevant to each probable theme
4	Reviewing themes	Checking if the themes work in relation to the coded extracts and the entire set of data, then generating a thematic map of the analysis
5	Defining and naming themes	Ongoing analysis to refine the details of the themes, as well as the narrative the data tells, producing clear definitions and names for each theme
6	Producing report	The last opportunity for analysis. Selecting compelling examples, final analysis of selected examples, relating the analysis back to the research questions and wider literature, producing a scholarly report of the analysis

5 Results and Discussion

Using thematic analysis, 9 overarching themes relating to how individuals behave with technology were identified: (1) Attitudes, (2) Social Influence, (3) Tool, (4) Convenience, (5) Extension of Self, (6) Propinquity, (7) Awareness, (8) Connection, and (9) Consistency. The following sections explain each theme in turn, with a discussion of whether it showed a relationship with participants' score on the DNAS scale.

5.1 Attitudes

Certain attitudes, or emotions, are identified as most prevalent when discussing technological behaviours. Participants exhibit strong inclinations towards different actions in using smartphones and smart assistants. Confidence, trust, anxiety and curiosity portray different facets of users' feelings towards the devices that they own. However, this behaviour did not demonstrate a dichotomous relationship with DNAS score.

5.2 Society

Social norms dictate what is appropriate in society. These rules can vary among cultures, as well as between individual people. Rules around technology can be even more nuanced

(Tene and Polonetsky 2013). While individuals have their own set of rules for when it is appropriate to use their phones, the ambiguity of these rules is prevalent. Participant in this theme did not favor a behaviour based on their DNAS score.

5.3 Tool

A large number of participants see technology as a tool to use to achieve their goals, however the emotion attached to this tool differed. Some participants regarded their technology with no emotional attachment, that it is simply a vessel for information. However, these differences were not divided by DNAS score.

5.4 Convenience

In this theme, participants prioritized making things easier for themselves by optimizing their technology. Overall, the push for convenience was driven by three different mindsets: utilitarian with a lack of emotion, increasing speed of actions, or to bolster muscle memory. While the three mindsets may have slightly leaned towards one end of the DNAS scores, the relationship was not strong or direct.

5.5 Extension of Self

Technology is seen by some participants as an extension of the self, both physically and metaphorically. The notion that the phone has replaced the phonebook and the need to memorize phone numbers encapsulates this idea. Participants range from not caring at all to demonstrating heavily reliance on technology. Most of the individuals that make up this theme are in the high DNAS group, however there were a few on this theme from the low DNAS group.

5.6 Propinquity

Propinquity can be defined as the 'state of being close to something or someone' (OED 2020). In this instance, propinquity relates to how users interact with technology and those they are closest with, either by relation or by housing situation. Elements such as family, house rules, and sharing devices arise as avenues of interest. Attitudes and behaviours exhibited in Propinquity did not strongly indicate towards one end of the DNAS scale.

5.7 Awareness

While some participants do not reflect on their technology use, and how it could negatively affect them, others are very aware of the role technology plays in their lives. This understanding, and how it does or not affect behavior, is important to note as it relates to a person's aspirations and motivations. An even number of high and low were presented in this theme.

5.8 Connection

Participants articulate that the reality of constant connection is met with either strong positive or negative emotions. Technology can serve to keep individuals connected, especially when they are physically distanced. Participants who are partial to the connectivity benefits of technology, highlight the ease of staying in touch with those far away as a top benefit. The current minimum expectation is that connection is always available, thus frustration occurs when this threshold is not reached. Though many see connection as a benefit to their lives, there are some see the perpetual availability as too much pressure and prefer a more limited connectivity. This was the only theme with a clear, dichotomous split between behaviours. Participants with high scores on the DNAS favoured constant connectivity and those with low scores preferred constrained connection.

5.9 Consistency

Uniformity among the same type of device, such as smartphones, emerges as an important value for some participants. Users are particular about how their devices should be ordered and structured. Even when updating devices, participants expect their technology to stay consistent. These behaviours and expectations have no tie to either high or low DNAS scorers.

6 Conclusion

Results suggest that the DNAS is not a completely accurate indicator of any specific attitude or behavior, as most themes had a varied combination of high and low level DNAS participants. The only theme in which behaviors are split by DNAS group is Connection, with high scoring individuals highlighting constant connection as a priority and low scoring individuals seeing the same connection as a negative effect of technology.

This is important for practitioners to consider when designing for a variety of user groups, especially those with different levels of technological competence. While levels of connectivity may be more closely associated with the dichotomy of DNAS scores, the majority of attitudes and behaviours towards technology are not linked to a particular set of scores. This research demonstrates that DNAS score alone cannot be relied upon to define user groups for adaptive interfaces, thus it is not an effective tool for characterising participants in user experience design.

Future research could further explore the nine themes in order to understand how individuals vary according to the themes, whether clusters of themes can be used to create personas, and how this understanding can be used to improve user experience in system design.

Acknowledgements. The research reported in this paper was conducted as part of a PhD studentship at Loughborough University funded by Jaguar Land Rover.

References

Adams, C.A., Pente, P.: Teachers teaching in the new mediascape: digital immigrants or "natural born cyborgs"? E-Learn. Digit. Media **8**(3), 247–257 (2011). https://doi.org/10.2304/elea.2011. 8.3.247

Akçayır, M., Dündar, H., Akçayır, G.: What makes you a digital native? Is it enough to be born after 1980? Comput. Hum. Behav. **60**, 435–440 (2016). https://doi.org/10.1016/J.CHB.2016. 02.089

Bakla, A.: A study of digital nativeness and digital productivity: data from EFL and ESL contexts. Malays. Online J. Educ. Technol. **7**(1) (2019). https://doi.org/10.17220/mojet.2019.01.002

Bennett, S., Maton, K., Kervin, L.: The "digital natives" debate: a critical review of the evidence. Br. J. Edu. Technol. **39**(5), 775–786 (2008). https://doi.org/10.1111/j.1467-8535.2007.00742.x

Braun, V., Clarke, V.: Using thematic analysis in psychology. Qual. Res. Psychol. **3**, 77–101 (2006). https://doi.org/10.1191/1478088706qp063oa

Brownlee, J.: Apple Finally Learns AI is the New UI. Co. Design (2015). https://www.fastco mpany.com/3047199/apple-finally-learns-ai-is-the-new-ui

Bryman, A.: Social Research Methods Bryman. Oxford University Press (2012). https://doi.org/ 10.1017/CBO9781107415324.004

Buy NVivo Now | NVivo (2020). https://www.qsrinternational.com/nvivo/nvivo-products/nvivo-12-plus. Accessed 16 Feb 2020

Cooper, A.: The Inmates Are Running the Asylum: Why High Tech Products Drive Us Crazy and How to Restore the Sanity. The Inmates are Running the Asylum Why High Tech Products Drive us Crazy and How to Restore the Sanity (1999)

Crang, M., Cook, I.: Doing Ethnographies (2012). https://doi.org/10.4135/9781849208949

Gemmell, J., Bell, G., Lueder, R.: Adaptive interfaces for ubiquitous web access. Commun. ACM **45**(5), 34–38 (2002). https://dl.acm.org/doi/fullHtml/10.1145/506218.506240

Gill, V.: Tell me about . . . : using interviews as a research methodology. In: Methods in Human Geography Human Geography a Guide for Students Doing a Research Project (2005)

Hartson, R., Pyla, P.S.: The UX Book: Process and Guidelines for Ensuring a Quality User Experience. The UX Book: Process and Guidelines for Ensuring a Quality User Experience (2012). https://doi.org/10.1016/C2010-0-66326-7

Huang, F., Teo, T., He, J.: Digital nativity of university teachers in China: factor structure and measurement invariance of the Digital Native Assessment Scale (DNAS). Interact. Learn. Environ. 1–15 (2019). https://doi.org/10.1080/10494820.2019.1570278

Joffe, H.: Thematic analysis. In: Qualitative Research Methods in Mental Health and Psychotherapy: A Guide for Students and Practitioners (2011). https://doi.org/10.1002/9781119973249. ch15

Kennedy, G.E., Judd, T.S., Churchward, A., Gray, K., Krause, K.-L.: First year students' experiences with technology: are they really digital natives? Australas. J. Educ. Technol. **24**(1), 108–122 (2008). http://citeseerx.ist.psu.edu/viewdoc/download?doi=10.1.1.85.9526& rep=rep1&type=pdf

Kuang, C.: Why a New Golden Age for UI Design is Around the Corner (2013). https://www. wired.com/2013/08/design-and-the-digital-world/. Accessed 4 June 2020

Kubat, M., Holte, R.C., Matwin, S.: Machine learning for the detection of oil spills in satellite radar images. Mach. Learn. **30**(2–3), 195–215 (1998). https://doi.org/10.1023/A:100745222 3027

Kvale, S., Brinkmann, S.: Learning the craft of qualitative research interviewing. In: InterViews: Learning the Craft of Qualitative Research Interviewing (2009)

Norman, D.A.: Don Norman on the term "UX" (Video) (2016). https://www.nngroup.com/videos/ don-norman-term-ux/. Accessed 5 June 2020

Norman, D., Nielsen, J.: The Definition of User Experience (UX) (n.d.). https://www.nngroup. com/articles/definition-user-experience/. Accessed 5 June 2020

Palinkas, L.A., Horwitz, S.M., Green, C.A., Wisdom, J.P., Duan, N., Hoagwood, K.: Purposeful sampling for qualitative data collection and analysis in mixed method implementation research. Adm. Policy Ment. Health Ment. Serv. Res. **42**, 533–544 (2015). https://doi.org/10.1007/s10 488-013-0528-y

Patton, M.Q.: Qualitative research and evaluation methods. Qual. Inquiry (2002). https://doi.org/ 10.2307/330063

Prensky, M.: Digital natives, digital immigrants Part 1. Horizon **9**(5), 1–6 (2001a). https://doi.org/ 10.1108/10748120110424816

Prensky, M.: Digital natives, digital immigrants Part 2: Do they really think differently? Horizon **9**(6), 1–6 (2001b). https://doi.org/10.1108/10748120110424843

Propinquity | Definition of Propinquity by Oxford Dictionary on Lexico.com also meaning of Propinquity (n.d.). https://www.lexico.com/en/definition/propinquity. Accessed 5 June 2020

Stoerger, S.: The digital melting pot: bridging the digital native-immigrat divide. First Monday **14**(7), 1–9 (2009). http://firstmonday.org/htbin/cgiwrap/bin/ojs/index.php/fm/issue/view/292

Tene, O., Polonetsky, J.: A theory of creepy: technology, privacy and shifting social norms. Yale J. Law Technol. **16** (2013). https://heinonline.org/HOL/Page?handle=hein.journals/yjolt16&id= 59&div=&collection=

Teo, T.: An initial development and validation of a Digital Natives Assessment Scale (DNAS). Comput. Educ. **67**, 51–57 (2013). https://doi.org/10.1016/j.compedu.2013.02.012

Teo, T.: Do digital natives differ by computer self-efficacy and experience? An empirical study. Interact. Learn. Environ. **24**(7), 1725–1739 (2016). https://doi.org/10.1080/10494820.2015. 1041408

Toledo, C.A.: Digital culture: immigrants and tourists responding to the natives' drumbeat. Int. J. Teach. Learn. High. Educ. **19**(1), 84–92 (2007). http://www.isetl.org/ijtlhe/

Weiser, M.: The computer for the 21st century. ACM SIGMOBILE Mob. Comput. Commun. Rev. **3**(3), 3–11 (1999). https://doi.org/10.1145/329124.329126

Welsh, E.: Dealing with data: using NVivo in the qualitative data analysis process. Forum Qualitative Sozialforschung (2002). https://doi.org/10.17169/fqs-3.2.865

Yong, S.-T., Gates, P.: Born digital: are they really digital natives? Int. J. E-Educ. e-Bus. e-Manag. e-Learn. **4**(2), 2–5 (2014). https://doi.org/10.7763/ijeeee.2014.v4.311

The Aware User Experience Model, Its Method of Construction and Derived Heuristics

Jorge Maya$^{(\boxtimes)}$ (ID) and Natalia Ariza$^{(\boxtimes)}$

Universidad EAFIT, Medellín, Colombia
{jmayacas,narizav1}@eafit.edu.co

Abstract. Psychological experience possesses many different determinants of affective, cognitive, and behavioral order in complex interaction and mostly hidden to our consciousness. User experience models face this complexity by presenting a reduced set of variables and interactions. Most of these models have been created on a deductive but also largely intuitive basis. This poses three problems: First, the UX models' authors don't propose a systematic response to the question of "how to know what variables use into the UX model?" Second, most UX models overlook the components that arise to the user's consciousness. Third, even with this multitude of UX models, UX designers continue to rely heavily on intuition. Based on previous work, we propose the Aware UX Model, built systematically, and gathering empirical users' data. It focuses on the components, mostly thoughts, and feelings, that arise in the user's consciousness. The model provides their characterization and a rational account of its emergence in the UX. In addition, we propose a construction method for UX models based on our own process. We expose a case study to substantiate the Aware UX model and to contribute to its validation. Finally, we propose heuristics coupled to the Aware UX model components.

Keywords: UX · User consciousness · User modeling

1 Introduction

Psychological experience possesses many different determinants of affective, cognitive, and behavioral order. Their interaction is highly complex and mostly hidden to our consciousness: we manage to see just the tip of the iceberg. Most user experience models try to tackle that complexity by presenting a reduced set of variables and interactions; they simplify the user experience, UX, to decrease its complexity, turning it into a more manageable phenomenon. Most of these models have been created on a deductive but also largely intuitive basis. This poses three problems: First, the UX models' authors don't propose a systematic response to the question of "how to know what variables use into the model or, on the contrary, leave them out of it?". Second, even if UX happens in the user's consciousness, most UX models do not focus on identifying and characterizing what happens there. Ortiz-Nicolas (2014) shows that for 11 UX models, artifact, user, interaction and context are the main dimensions, and the so-called aggregates or properties, are subjective, conscious, emotional, interconnected, and dynamics. However,

© Springer Nature Switzerland AG 2020
C. Stephanidis et al. (Eds.): HCII 2020, LNCS 12423, pp. 211–233, 2020.
https://doi.org/10.1007/978-3-030-60114-0_15

none of the 11 UX models specify what probably happens in the user consciousness; this always appears difficult to specify and fragmented (Revonsuo 2009). In addition, every component has a different definition and role among the models (Ortiz-Nicolas 2014). This has led to uncertainty about the UX components that are important in UX design. Therefore, this poses a threat to the validity of those UX models too. Consequently, we want to propose a UX model that can specify what arises to the user's consciousness during the interaction: their inner thoughts, images, feelings of knowing, and so on, which have no clear location and extension in phenomenal space (Velmans 2009, p. 297) but are present in the consciousness, and are essential for UX design. Third, we believe that the large complexity of UX models, with so many components and properties, avoids their application to UX design, making them hardly actionable, and difficult to apply. Moreover, even with this multitude of UX models, UX designers continue to rely heavily on intuition (Tonetto and Tamminen 2015). This makes that many relevant aspects of the UX are missed, designers don't know how those aspects are related and don't know either their relative importance. We believe that the persistence of UX designers in relying mostly on their intuition is because UX models are not coupled to methods based on them. So, what type of UX design methods can be coupled to a specific UX model? In this paper, we try to contribute with answers to these three questions.

The paper is structured as follows: in the methods sections, we expose the methods used to answer each of the questions. In the results section, we expose the results of applying each method: for the first question, firstly, we reviewed the methods available to identify UX components, and secondly, we expose a method to systematically build UX models trying to avoid the biases from the researcher's intuition. For the second question, we propose the Aware UX Model resulting from the application of the aforementioned systematic method. Moreover, we present a case study to show how the Aware Model can explain the UX of a market successful product. For the third question, we propose a UX design method composed of heuristics extracted from different sources. The final section exposes the conclusions, limitations, and future work.

2   Methods

2.1   Question 1: How to Know What Variables Use into a UX Model or, on the Contrary, Leave Them Out of It?

We reviewed the methods available to identify UX variables. We expose a method to systematically build UX models trying to avoid bias from the researcher's intuition.

2.2   Question 2: Which Are the UX Components Important in UX Design?

We applied the aforementioned systematic method to propose a UX model. Moreover, we used the case study method to show how the UX model can explain the UX of a market successful product with a UX desired by users.

2.3   Question 3: What Type of UX Design Methods Can Be Coupled to a Specific UX Model?

We propose a UX method composed of heuristics extracted from different sources.

3   Results

3.1   Review of the Methods to Identify Affective and Cognitive Conscious Components

We have identified some approaches or methods to identify the human affective and cognitive components present in UX. We're just aware of the tip of the iceberg visible in consciousness. Consequently, we're not only interested in explicit, conscious, variables, but also in the unobserved, latent ones; all of them are causes or consequences of the user's observable behavior (Hoyle and Duvall 2004). Then, we review phenomenology, introspection, theory of mind, cognitive interviews (think-aloud protocols), self-report methods, and the Exploratory Factor Analysis (EFA) technique.

Phenomenology. Phenomenology is both a methodology and a philosophy to understand complex individuals' problems based on researching their intern and subjective experiences. It emerged as a philosophical movement concerning how to look at the world, providing insights to "understand certain phenomena" (Creswell 2007). Using it, we can get a deep comprehension of a phenomenon as experienced by several subjects (Creswell 2013). It provides an opportunity for systematic reflection on the lived experiences of people in certain circumstances. Its purpose is to "reduce individual experiences with a phenomenon to a description of the universal essence" (Creswell 2007). It has been used in organizational and consumer research but very few in product design. A phenomenon would be "an 'object' of human experience (van Manen cited by Creswell (2013), p. 163). These phenomena could be anything felt by the user while interacting with a product (Creswell 2013): try to find a song in the smartphone, experimenting anger because being unable to handle properly a drill, etc. Basically, the researcher collects data from people who have underwent the same experience and makes up a description from these multiple sources of the essence of the experience for all those persons. "This description consists of "what" they experienced and "how" they experienced it" (Creswell 2013). This method allows participants to express their experiences, which in turn, allow investigators to uncover the essence of the human experience (Creswell 2013).

What distinguishes phenomenology from other qualitative research is its emphasis on the subjective point of view (van Manen 1990). In addition, it provides the tools for discovering something meaningful and insightful, "through meditations, conversations, daydreams, inspirations, and other interpretive acts, we assign meaning to the phenomena of lived life" (van Manen 1990). However, one of the dilemmas of using a phenomenological method is whether it results in descriptive scientific research or in an interpretive personal inquiry. Can researchers avoid imposing their personal experiences and biases on the description or analysis of the experiences shared by the others? (Husserl 1982). Ajjawi and Higgs (2007) argue that it is impossible to achieve total objectivity because objectivity is situated in a reality constructed by subjective experiences.

Introspection. Introspection is a means by which we pay attention consciously to the mental conditions we are currently in (Rosenthal 2001). Introspection is different from our informal, transient, and fuzzy manner we are conscious of a lot of our mental states. Introspection encompasses the mental states being introspected and any mental representation of those mental states. Introspection collapsed as a psychological experimental method because of its lack of reliability: the results from distinct laboratories using it frequently disagree (Rosenthal 2001). Moreover, it has been shown that people invent their own introspective mental states to justify their behaviors as something acceptable or normal. However, many psychological experimental methods continue to rely on people's access to their actual mental states. All in all, introspection represents badly our mental states and misses to uncover a lot of concurrent mental states, both in usual and exceptional situations. It is probable that introspection only reveals a little part of the mental properties of the subject. As stated by Lashley's (1958, cited by Rosentahl) dictum "introspection never makes mental processes accessible, only their results". Nonetheless, it is fairly used among design practitioners because it is informal, flexible, and low-cost (Goodman-Deane et al. 2010). In conclusion, although introspection is easy to use, it is an unreliable method.

Theory of Mind (ToM). ToM is a branch of cognitive science regarding the comprehension of our minds and others' (Gopnik 2001). ToM is about our skill to attribute mental states (desires, beliefs, intentions, etc.) to others and understanding others' minds using our ordinary and intuitive comprehension of the mind (Gopnik 2001). ToM has been extensively researched in developmental psychology to understand when and how the different abilities of ToM arise and develop. The knowledge provided by ToM is theoretical, both for the mind of others and ours. ToM is related to folk psychology because it supports our comprehension of people's behavior in terms of desires, beliefs, expectations, intentions, etc. When we attribute a belief, we make a hypothesis of a mental state of the believer. The question is: do we have a method to understand our minds and others'? Some mechanisms of ToM have been researched, for instance, the ToM decoding (Lee et al. 2005). This is defined as the ability to use context information available such as tone of voice, body posture, and facial expressions, to identify and name precisely the others' mental state (Lee et al. 2005). However, we are talking about an innate ability deeply ingrained in our minds that would be hard to formalize as a method, in order to study the mental states of others. For instance, we're able to interpret which emotions someone is feeling by reading her facial gestures; notwithstanding, we're not able to do this on a systematic basis. For this matter, a method such as FACS, Facial Coding Action System, should be used (Ekman and Friesen 1978). There are two dilemmas of using an approach based on ToM to identify the UX components. First, it is easy to attribute false beliefs to other people if the researcher is not well trained since some mechanisms behind ToM acquisition are difficult to articulate to be easily tested at the neural level. ToM is a rather abstract construct that could take many forms at both the behavioral and neural levels (Mahy et al. 2014). Second, ToM's application mostly focuses on cognitive tasks rather than affective ones (Mahy et al. 2014).

Cognitive Interviews-Think Aloud Protocols. Cognitive interviews are a set of techniques for eliciting how a subject understands and responds to a diversity of situations, i.e., an interaction with a product. The most useful would be the think-aloud interviewing: the subject should say aloud what he is thinking while he is on a task (see "cognitive interview" by Knafl (2008)). In think-aloud protocols the verbal reports of the subject's own thinking processes are used as data. Think aloud protocol could be used insofar it was devised as a method to verbalize problem-solving activities, at every moment of that activity (Ericsson and Simon 1993). Since its creation by Newell and Simon in 1972 (Newell and Simon 1972), protocol analysis has been a central method in cognitive science. Two drawbacks of protocol analysis are, first, the method has been used mostly to study tasks where the cognitive elements are dominant, i.e., for sequences of thoughts: many tasks of problem-solving character, decision-making, judgment, expert tasks performance and learning (Ericsson and Simon 1993). And, second, it is not adapted to study affective phenomena.

Self-report Methods. Self-report is any method in which respondents relate their feelings, emotions, beliefs, etc., when they are asked to answer a question. Even if it is a very used method, its nature and lack of verifiability are a matter of debate (Robinson 2009). When considering the complexity of a self-report, at least concerning emotion self-reports, there are two types of components of distinct nature: dialecticism and granularity (Lindquist and Feldman-Barrett 2008). Basically, these two terms refer to people's ability to characterize their own experiences (Lindquist and Feldman-Barrett 2008). Dialecticism is the relationship between pleasant and unpleasant emotions as inversely related or as a dialectic experience (not seeing pleasurable and displeasurable experiences as opposed) feeling both pleasant and unpleasant emotions at the same time (Bagozzi et al. 1999). The other component, granularity, is the skill to verbally report the emotional experience precisely (Lindquist and Feldman-Barrett 2008). Emotional granular people use emotion qualifiers (i.e., angry, afraid, sad, joyful, etc.) to "represent discrete and qualitatively different experiences". The criticism of using self-reports is: one, self-reports rely on language which may not be equivalent to experience, sometimes experience is highly nuanced; two, we possess different skill levels to conceptualize or verbalize our experiences using language words. In this regard, a self-report would always be a flawed image of experience (Robinson 2009). Moreover, self-reports are problematic for cognitive scientists, on the one hand, because the conditions under which self-reports are to be trusted are unknown; and, on the other hand, the inferences from objective observations from states of consciousness are determined by the comprehension we have of the causal relations between the subjects' conscious states and what we observe on them (Natsoulas 2005).

Other Affective Information Assessment Methods. In this group, methods such as emotion-related vocal acoustics, specific affect coding system (SPAFF), affect rating dial, time sampling diary, facial image analysis such as FACS (Ekman and Friesen 1978), etc., should be used. Etc. These methods are highly specific focusing only on one affective phenomenon, look to obtain a global measurement of affect, or are highly complex and time-consuming. Consequently, they are not adapted to our needs.

Exploratory Factor Analysis (EFA). Even though latent variables cannot be measured by direct means, we can obtain information about them by measuring observed variables that represent them (Everitt and Howell 2005), in other words, we can measure them indirectly. Latent variables have the possibility of explaining a large number of behaviors using only a low number of constructs (Hoyle and Duvall 2004). Latent variables should be inferred, statistically, from data showing associations among observed variables, which presumably, are caused, to some extent, by one or more factors (Hoyle and Duvall 2004). Factor Analysis (FA) is a multivariable statistical analysis technique appropriate to analyze large numbers of variables and reduce them to a more manageable number or factors (Field 2009). Researchers in education, psychology, and cognate social fields have employed or evaluated their research with Factor Analytic procedures, including exploratory factor analysis (EFA) (Beavers et al. 2013). EFA describes associations among a very large number of observed variables or indicators, using a comparatively low number of factors (Hoyle and Duvall 2004). EFA works inductively because it allows, based on the observed variables data, to determine, *a posteriori*, the underlying factor model. None of the methods or approaches presented earlier to identify the UX elements seemed adapted to investigate our research problem. Consequently, we trust in EFA because of its long tradition to investigate many different and complex latent psychological phenomena, such as intelligence or personality (John and Srivastava 1999). EFA's main limitation is that the results should not be considered to provide a complete theory to a specific subject (John and Srivastava 1999). Nonetheless, a good application of FA provides a conceptual foundation that helps to examine theoretical issues and could be used as a base to develop further work (John and Srivastava 1999).

3.2   A Construction Method for UX Models

We propose a complete structured method to identify and characterize UX components using empirical data from users. This method uses a combination of techniques traditionally used in experimental psychology. The present research looks for identifying and classifying constitutive UX elements from an empirical study that integrates diverse latent variables behind the UX. Instead of a deductive process, based on existing theories on affective and cognitive phenomena to identify the UX elements, we propose a structured process of data gathering. The analysis is performed to finally identify, through EFA, the components that are crucial for an experience to occur, i.e., that arise in the user's consciousness, and, in this way, making them visible. The construction method has four stages responding to four objectives: first, identify the theoretical components of the UX by using thematic analysis; second, measure how those components are experienced by gathering user's data; third, reduce the number of components through EFA; fourth, construct the UX model. The three first parts provide the input or "bricks" to construct the UX model in the fourth part. Below, we expose the method.

First Part: Thematic Analysis. Use thematic analysis to identify systematically which the components of the UX are from a theoretical point of view. This technique is explained in Braun and Clarke (2006). It is very used to find patterns on a heterogeneous mass of qualitative text. It allows a structured process of coding and pattern recognition within the data avoiding researchers' biases. It provides themes and subthemes of variables present in the data, i.e., dimensions and groups and variables. These themes constitute the core for the construction of the further UX empirical study. One example of application in the context of UX modeling is in Ariza and Maya (2014a).

Second: Gathering Empirical User Data. Gather empirical evidence about how the different variables influence the final user experience. Construct a questionnaire transforming the theoretical variables into measurable ones; use Likert scales. Transform each variable into an empirical one, using the sub-themes to describe the variable in a more integral way. Improve the reliability and content validity of the instrument taking as reference questionnaires previously validated for other UX components. Design a protocol for the whole experiment. Select a product with features allowing to evaluate instrumental and non-instrumental aspects, according to your objectives. Have in mind that the product category will introduce a specificity in the people's responses to the whole experiment. Consider evaluating the UX in different stages corresponding to the prior expectations, the participants' immediate feelings, impressions and perceptions, the aftereffects, and the accumulative aspects. Before, during, after and long-after are common stages for this. Split the whole questionnaire into the questions corresponding to each stage. Propose a first draft of the questionnaire. Refine it by reviewing the definitions and questions to ensure a good relationship and clarity. Do a pilot test with some users. Design a sample according to EFA reliability requirements (usually in the hundreds of people). According to Field (2009) and Beavers et al. (2013), an EFA's good sample size is conditional upon the strength of the factors and variables, rather than a large sample size. These values must be validated while running the EFA. Apply the questionnaire to measure how those components are experienced by a representative group of users in real interaction with a product; to do so, choose, a free of disturbance, appropriate context. This will increase the ecological validity of the whole experiment. Allow the full manipulation and use of the product when needed. Use an online service to host the questionnaire and collect the data. One example of the application of these techniques for UX modeling is in Ariza and Maya (2014b).

Third: Apply EFA. Reduce the number of components to a manageable amount of factors by using EFA. EFA is a data reduction technique. It analyzes many correlations among observed variables reducing them to a more manageable number but retaining the essential (Field 2009). The main decisions for setting up the EFA are: (1) define which variables to include, (2) select a reliable sample, (3) determine the factor extraction method, and (4) define the model-fit considerations, rotation method, and reliability analyses. Choose a proper statistical package for EFA. Do the factorability test on the data. If the test is ok, validate the strength of the variables' relationships for the EFA study. Check the questionnaire's reliability by using Cronbach's alpha coefficient. Do a data optimization to check if the data is factorable. Choose the oblique rotation if, a-priori, the components are dependent, (i.e., they all belong to the UX). Finally, validate the factorial model through a Monte-Carlo simulation (Mooney 1997): this is a resampling technique that creates repeated samples from an original data sample while retaining the correlations. This allows to overcome the generalization problems of the EFA. Naming the factors in EFA is of paramount importance: look at the variable with the highest load on the factor and use it as a reference to label and describe the factor. Examine the other variables and see how they contribute to the full description of the component. This

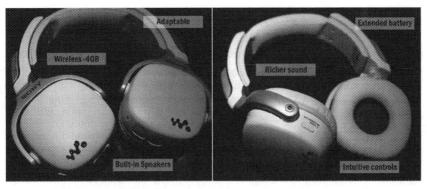

description should encompass the set of variables of the factor. The factors resulting from part three are the input, or "bricks" to construct the UX model sought. See one example of the application of EFA for UX modeling in Ariza and Maya (2014b).

Fourth: Construct the Model. Structure the factors to explain through a model how the UX arises for similar products and interactions. The construction of the UX model comprises several steps: (1) Rewrite the explanation of each factor to have a highly coherent explanation of what the factor is and how their variables are related. (2) Take the label alone of each factor to figure out how they are related and how is their temporal dynamics, i.e., the order of manifestation in the user's consciousness. (3) Propose a graphical scheme of this relation. (4) Check the meaningfulness of the whole model. (5) Check the explanatory capacity of the model by explaining the UX of three types of products: one of a similar category, with a very good UX; one of a similar category but with a failed UX; and one borderline case: a product with a UX where the model fails to explain some UX components. Apply the case study method for this. (6) Adjust the model following the pieces of evidence gathered through the three cases. (7) You will have a pre-model, which is the basis to make a backward process: starting from it, you have to devise an experiment to gather empirical data by operationalizing their variables as a questionnaire in a similar way as explained in part three of the method. (8) Apply Confirmatory Factor Analysis, CFA, to check if the factor model matches the relations posed by the pre-model. (9) If the match is correct, the pre-model reflects validly the user's UX. Otherwise, adjust the pre-model as necessary and repeat the CFA process.

3.3 The Aware UX Model

We propose the Aware UX model. It results from the application of the aforementioned systematic method until the case study step, which we use to begin its validation process. The model was constructed using the MP3 headphones of Fig. 1 as stimuli. In the case study, we explain the UX of a market successful product but of a different category (electric chainsaw) to the product used to construct our model.

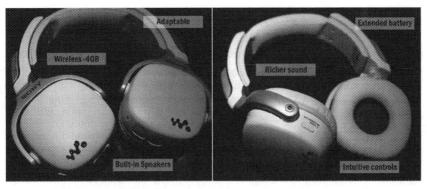

Fig. 1. Example of a product used in Ariza Maya (2014b): Sony WALKMAN® MP3 Player NWZ-WH303 headphones. Photo: Ariza.

The Aware UX Model Construction Process. In two previous publications we, first, identified UX variables and their dimensions for product design using thematic analysis applied to 13 UX models, 10 UX definitions, and 10 review papers (Ariza and Maya 2014a). Second, based on those dimensions-variables, we designed a study to get empirical user data (n = 200) while interacting with the MP3 headphones. Through an Exploratory Factor Analysis, we reduced the number of variables by identifying the factors behind them (126 variables to 32 factors) (Ariza and Maya 2014b). A further Montecarlo simulation (n = 1000) allowed us to confirm the quality of the factorial model. Based on that factor structure, we proposed the UX model below. The presentation of the Aware UX model is composed of two parts. First, in the components section, we explain each component of the model: we take each factor previously found and explained it as a coherent whole as a group of correlated variables. Each of these components are the different psychological constructs that would arise to the consciousness of the user during interaction. The Aware UX model explains three stages of the interaction. We only present here the components for the BEFORE Stage. For the DURING and AFTER stage see the Appendix. Secondly, in the model section, we fully describe the Aware UX model emphasizing the dynamics and causality relationships of the components.

A Detailed Explanation of the Components of the Aware UX Model for the BEFORE Stage

1. Attractiveness and Interest/Novelty of the product. In everyday language, attractiveness is the characteristic of an object of being "very pleasing in appearance", and "...causing interest" (Cambridge Dictionary Online 2019). Interest is aroused when the user needs to give selective attention to the product (APA 2015) because the product is significant. Significance can be threefold. The product must look attractive for the user: one way to arise the user's interest is to show him an attractive product. Interestingness is the quality of a product that arouses interest rather than aesthetic pleasure (APA 2015). Attractiveness can be obtained through multiple ways: combining the product's form supports (shape, colors, materials, textures,), through, manipulation of perceptual determinants (gestalt laws for instance) or cognitive determinants such as typicality, prototypicality, familiarity, etc. Once the product has arisen interest, the user's mood comes to the fore.

2. User's mood. Unlike emotions, the mood is an affective state "about nothing specific or about everything" (Fridja 2009a). The user's mood has cognitive effects. These are mood-congruent: encoding facilitation, recall, judgment biases, and attentional selectivity (Fridja 2009a). In other words, mood acts as a filter from a perceptual point of view. Certain pieces of information will be of relative interest depending on the user's mood. There are effects of mood on processing. Pleasant moods lead to "more superficial processing in precision tasks, and to more mental flexibility" while unpleasant moods favor deeper processing (Fridja 2009a, p. 258). The user's mood plays a paramount role because it can lead the user to abandon the exploration of the product, or, on the contrary, encourage the user to get more information from the product, i.e., to be more involved in the interaction. Depending on the user's mood, it leads to the product's specific concerns, component 3, or to 4, anticipation of buying and use.

3. Product's Specific concerns. "Concerns are the dispositional sources of emotions" (Fridja 2009b). Concerns are paramount for the interaction because they trigger emotions in the cognitive appraisal process (Demir et al. 2009). Emotions are the main component of the user experience. A concern is a specific state of the world that is important for the user. Many different types of concerns have been identified concerning the interaction with products: needs, goals, interests, etc. However, four types of concerns are central in the before phase of the user experience, from (3.1) to (3.5). (3.1) Interest in the Product's Functionality: ¿am I interested in this product's functionality? Functionality has been pointed out as the main need concerning a product (Jordan 2002). It is a gate for the interaction because if the user is not interested in the product's functionality, the interaction could be halted. (3.2) How valuable is the product? How curious I'll be? Economic concerns are omnipresent in our lives, especially with technological products that can be expensive. If the product is affordable for the user this judgment can lead him to be more curious about it and to try to gather more information that could lead him to the buying process. (3.3) Social approval: who uses the product. This concern is relatively important for every product, but if the product is to be used in public it becomes a very important one. This concern means that we want to know who uses the product to gain more information about affiliation processes such as belonging to the group of users of the product or being different from that group, even if oneself is the user of the product (Berghman and Hekkert 2017). (3.4) Product's professional look. This concern reflects the desire for the user of possessing a product with high performance, i.e., a robust product able to give a high-quality output for their main functions and at the same time able to withstand to small accidents and rough conditions during manipulation. This concern can be at the same time highly specific and highly general. Highly specific for technological products because they are delicate and prone to be easily damaged during rough manipulation. Highly general because it is a general human concern related to the duration of products and to our attachment to them. (3.5) Interest in the product's technology. This concern is highly specific to technological products specially if the product combines simultaneously different technologies in an innovative way. This interest should feed the anticipation of buying and use because it invites the user to judge different aspects of the product. This judgment made frequently based on partial information could lead the user to a buying process.

4. *Anticipation of buying and use.* Anticipation is a user's emotion involving an imaginative speculation process. This speculation concerns the future use and possession of the product. It is produced using information about the product or similar products saved in the user's brain. Anticipation can be pleasurable but at the same time a way to deal with the stress of facing the use of a new and not so easy to use product (Skynner and Cleese 1996).

The components for the DURING and AFTER Stage are explained in the Appendix.

The Three Stages of the Aware UX Model. For the BEFORE-UX and DURING-UX stages, we have a small number of factors (components) which allowed us to directly propose the model (Ariza and Maya 2014b). For the AFTER-UX stage, to have a more manageable group of components, we clustered again the factors obtained in two ways: using data from the EFA's correlation matrices and using the KJ method. Finally, the proposed model explains its components in terms of psychological constructs pertaining to the affect, cognition or behavior of the user. It explains some relationship among these components and some aspects of their dynamics while explaining what arises to the consciousness of the user. Even if the model pretends to be a generalization of the categories presented in the precedent section, the influence of the product's category (MP3 headphones) is clear. The numbers for each component are the same used in Ariza and Maya (2014b).

BEFORE Stage. For this stage, Fig. 2, (1) attractiveness and interest arise in the user's consciousness. The user is prompted to pay attention to the product because it offers some novel features to him. Even if the user is finally interested in the product his mood (2) modules his general affective tone: if good, all the downstream UX will tend to be felt positively or the contrary if the mood is negative. Then, the user's attention will address some typical concerns with the product (3), its functionality (3.1.) being, maybe, the most important. Other common concerns will pop up to the user's consciousness, not forcibly in this order: the value of the product (3.2), the social approval of the product (3.3.), if the product has a professional look because it conveys the idea of a sophisticated product (3.4.), and, finally, an interest in the product's technology (3.5). Probably, these concerns interact among them in an inextricable way. This stage finishes with an anticipation feeling to buy and use the product (4): the user imagine himself using and getting the benefits promised by the product.

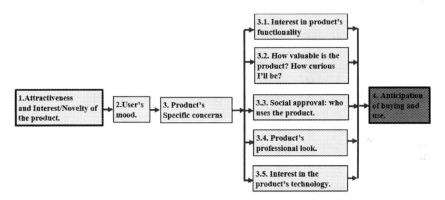

Fig. 2. The Before Stage UX model.

DURING Stage. In this stage, Fig. 3, the user should know how to use the product (1), he thinks or remembers how he has had previous experiences with similar products, (2), and remembers what the product does and how should be used (3). Components (2) and (3) make a loop where the user must figure out how to use the product to get all its functionalities. As he probably doesn't know how to use some functions, he tries the product's different controls and sees their effects; he iterates until he feels he's able to use the product at a minimum level. Due to its novel features, the product has different functions, (4), which the user could not know how to use, but in the end, he's satisfied with the principal function. Obtaining the main function is a fundamental support for the during stage; otherwise, if the user is not able to get it, he might abandon the interaction. If the user is in trouble trying to get the main function, he comes back to components (2) and (3) and the loop could be active again. When the product is working properly, the user would enter in a state of flow, (5), where no additional effort is required to get the benefits of the product and where the user enjoys the interaction, i.e., being connected to the product. When the user is in flow, components (2), (3) and (4) are no more of a concern during the UX. After the flow experience, in (6), the user is aware of how he can feel the aesthetic visual and tactile harmony of the product; he feels the product really comfortable on his hands. In conclusion, this stage is highly stimulating for the user: he felt the use of the product as very exciting and stimulating (7).

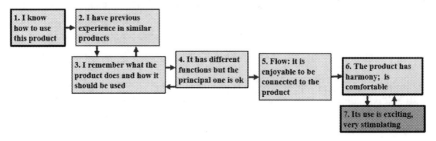

Fig. 3. The during stage of the UX model.

The AFTER Stage. This is the UX felt immediately after finishing the direct interaction. This stage can be very rich in components, as shown in Fig. 4, even if the user is no longer in contact with the product. This is the part of the Aware UX model that can give the most information about the other two UX stages. This stage begins with a global impression and general memory about the direct interaction that has just finished. This impression is a consequence of two groups of components. On the left side, there is a group of emotions made up of expectations that have been filled or not (3), if the user felt disconnected from the world using the product, (7), and if a recall or even nostalgia arose at the user's consciousness. On the right side, counterbalancing emotions, there is a large set of usability components. This demonstrates that a good usability is fundamental for the AFTER stage, even if there is no direct contact with the product. The set begins by the user asking himself if the product is easy to learn and understand, (2), which is a crucial component in this part because a negative answer will stop this usability cycle and would contribute to a very negative global impression. A clear entry point for the interaction is important, (10); this is made possible by clear marking functions. In turn, if the use of the product was possible, the user would ask himself how else he could use the product, (6), and how to use it in a context different to the original one, (9). To finish the usability group, there is a question about where the user can learn more about the product, (17). The comparison between the global use dimension and the global emotional group would lead the user to a reflection: he enjoyed using the product and he holds a position about it (13). This is important because it is a first evaluation of the UX that has just passed. If the enjoyment was present, the user would come into remembering details of the interaction, in the form of concerns: if the product's brand was ok, (11); if the performance of the product's technology was good (12); if the product's use matched its aesthetic appearance (14) and if the user looked good with the product in that context, (5), which makes the user think of other products with similar style (15), in a loop. After these personal concerns, leading to product evaluations, there would be a change in the user's perception of the product (16) in the form of an afterthought. If this change in perception is positive, the final component will be activated: the engagement with the product (1). This is important: engagement would be the final goal of a successful UX for designers.

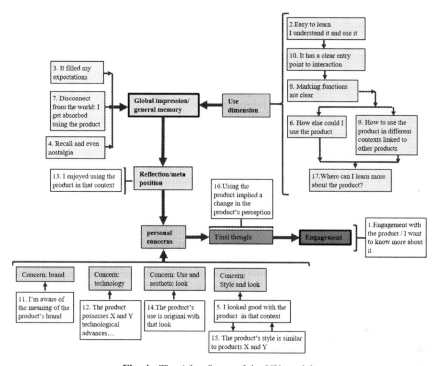

Fig. 4. The After Stage of the UX model.

Discussion. The Aware UX model is different from most models in the literature because is centered in the user and what arises to his consciousness. Even if the UX is felt as a whole, the model is highly analytical decomposing the UX in its many components. In this way, the model is explanatory. We do not hold that all these components arise in the user's consciousness during an interaction with a product similar to a headphone mp3; just some of them. However, they probably will be behind the UX as latent variables, influencing the contents of the user's consciousness. We use the model to make designers aware of the components by telling them that they exist, by explaining to them what they are and how they would influence the UX. We request designers to not forget the Aware model's components, because, even if latent, they are always there when designing for the UX.

A Case Study: The JawSaw Worx Electric Chainsaw
This case study concerns a market successful product: the JawSaw® electric chainsaw

from Workx®, Fig. 5. Chainsaws are intimidating for new users. The JawSaw has a safer chain saw to avoid accidents due to the exposed spinning chain. It was designed to be safer for the novice user. It can operate directly on the ground, so the user does not have to lift the logs off the ground and then bend down to cut them. It also has an extension handle for pruning high branches. It has 291 ratings with an average of 4.5 on Amazon.com (Amazon 2020), and an average of 4.6 for 478 ratings in Worx homepage (Worx 2020). The reviews of specialized sites were very good as well. For instance, the ChainsawJournal.com site said in its review that the "JawSaw was the best chainsaw alternative" (The Chainsaw Journal 2020). It won a Silver A' in the A' Design Awards in 2012 (A' Design Awards 2012). With this case study we want to substantiate the Aware UX model: to see if it possibly explains many different thoughts and feeling arising to the consciousness of a JawSaw's user, and to see if they could offer a coherent account of an UX. We did so by proposing supposedly user's self-taking, thoughts and feelings, belonging to each one of the stages and components of the UX Aware Model. The results of this case study should contribute to answer two questions: Do all these thoughts and feelings represent a whole UX experience? Are they important? We believe that designers have the answer to these two questions.

BEFORE stage (stimulus: the promotional videos of the product). 1. That product looks terrific in the video. Its shape is quite different, I've never seen one like that. 2. I'm in a very good mood for gardening this Spring. 3.1. That chainsaw cuts perfectly and it has many different safety features. 3.2. It's only U$110; it's worth the investment! 3.3. My neighbor will like it as well. 3.4. It looks so sturdy to endure very harsh conditions; it looks professional. 3.5. I don't know how it works. It seems they developed three patented systems for it. 4. I'm looking forward to buying it and use it.

DURING stage (stimulus: the real product in interaction). 1. Even if it looks different, I already know how to use this chainsaw. 2. I've used many chainsaws in my garden, some similar. 3. It cuts so well. I know how to cut the higher branches, it's a little bit tricky…I see it has security functions to avoid accidents. 5. What a pleasure to use this chainsaw! I really enjoyed doing all the gardening in one day. 6. The product looks so well. Its textures feel good; it's completely comfortable. 7. I found its use so stimulating; cutting logs on the ground for my first time was exciting, and without breaking my back!

AFTER stage (Stimulus is absent: the JawSaw is no longer present). 3. It's my first chainsaw to completely fill my expectations. 7. During the use I even felt disconnected from the world; it was absorbing to the point of doing all the Spring gardening in one day. 4. The use was terrific; I wonder when I would have the opportunity to use it again. 2. It was so easy to learn to use; I understood immediately all its functions. 10. The start button was the first thing to use. 8. The controls showed clearly what they were for. 6. If it's able to cut logs on the ground I wonder how else I could use it. 9. I might use it to cut branches over the roof if I use a proper ladder. 17. I wonder if there are more training videos on the internet. My global impression is that I bought a terrific product, I loved it! 13. I enjoyed its use all the time for my gardening. 11. That brand is very good and well evaluated on the Internet. 12. The security items are patented, and it has a new lubrication system. 14. Its shape was different which made its use different as well. 5. I think I looked good with the product on my hands. 15. Its style is similar to a high-end chainsaw's brand. 16. Oh my gosh: it made me change my mind about home chainsaws!

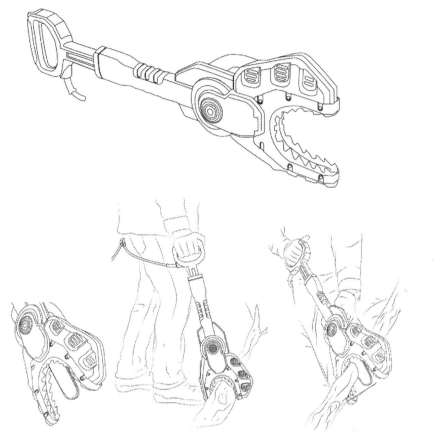

Fig. 5. Up, The Worx JawSaw electric chainsaw. Below, left, a close-up of the jaw system that keeps the blade and chain retracted until they're fully enclosed in the guard, avoiding accidents. Center, the JawSaw can cut logs on the ground. Right, it has an extensible pole. Illustrations: Angelica Rocha.

1. This chainsaw now has all my attention, It's really interesting. I want to use it over and over.

3.4   The Aware UX Heuristics Method

One criticism to UX models is that they are too broad and difficult to apply. Consequently, we propose a UX method composed of heuristics extracted from different sources. This is what a designer should do to design for UX. The features that are crucial for an UX to occur and the components that favor meaningful user engagement are difficult to grasp due to their different psychological nature. Therefore, instead of relying on highly structured methods for an already complex subject, those features would be easier to grasp through the deliberate application of simple design heuristics chosen from scientific, engineering and design literature. As an example, Table 1, we propose such heuristics for the DURING stage components. We propose two types of heuristics: the strategic heuristics, to be applied from the beginning and all through the UX design process, and component heuristics, to assist the design of the different UX design components of the Aware UX Model. The number in the beginning is the component of the DURING Stage. *Strategic Heuristic*: what the user wants during use is a lot of proper stimulation.

Table 1. Component Heuristics for the DURING Stage.

Component number	Heuristic
1, 2, 7	Use a mental model that clearly fits your product
1	Provide clear marking functions
1	Provide a clear entry point to the interaction
3	Use a proper color set for the user interface
3	Provide keys, pads and other control surfaces with a pleasant touch
3	Provide keys, pads and other control surfaces with a pleasant mechanical response and sound (clicks and other interaction sounds)
4	Make the product's functionality perfect
4	Provide delighter items in the product according to Kano model ("I didn't know I wanted it, but I like it")
5	Provide a flow experience while using the product (a smooth, pleasant and trouble-free interaction)
6	Provide a product's aesthetics high in unity
7	If the product's prototypical shape has been strongly changed provide clear clues to easily identify the product category

4 Conclusions, Limitations and Further Work

We believe that our work improves the theoretical and practical understanding of UX by increasing the designer's awareness of the UX, drawing her attention to many different UX's components that remain tacit and difficult to grasp and express, even for the designer's intuition. We identified and characterize the components of the UX with an information-technology product for listening to music, but, through the case study, we showed that the Aware UX model can explain the UX felt with products of other categories. When UX designers continue to rely heavily on intuition, many relevant aspects of the UX are missed, designers don't know how those aspects are related and don't know either their relative importance. We provide an easy to understand model that can be applied for different stages of interaction to always keep in mind that there are latent components of the UX that are worthwhile to think of. We provided a set of heuristics to do so. The granularity of all UX models is quite different among their different components (Forlizi and Ford 2000; Revonsuo 2009). We believe that this makes their application difficult. Consequently, we tried to propose a UX model with more regular granularity. We also hope that the factorial structure identified and used for the construction of the UX model would allow the refinement of future UX models and tools to improve UX design in design teaching and practice. One limitation of the Aware UX model is that it is built on EFA, so the results should not be considered to provide a complete theory to UX. We have to remember that what you put into an EFA is what you get out. As further work, we will advance on the validation of the Aware UX model by proposing more case studies and continuing to adjust the model all through the stages of the method proposed here. We will extract more heuristics for all the UX stages and evaluate the results of their application.

Acknowledgment. We would like to thank Universidad EAFIT for the grant awarded to the authors during 2014–2015 that made possible this research. We also thank Maria Angelica Rocha for the Chainsaw illustrations.

Appendix

The During-Stage Components of the Aware UX Model

1. I know how to use this product. This is a confirmatory belief of the user while using the product. The user arrives to get the services promised by the product's functionality without a problem. To do so, the user has evoked an appropriate mental model of the product. The mental models "are the conceptual models in people's minds that represent their understanding of how things work." (Norman, 2013, p. 26). This belief recognizes tacitly a correct usability with the product. Even if it seems a cognitive laden affirmation it could imply a positive or neutral affective state in the user.

2. I have previous experience with similar products. Experience is one stimulus that resulted in learning (APA, 2015). Being confronted with products with new and different functions and usability entails a significant cognitive-affective effort. According to the product appearance the user could take two paths. One, an exploratory path, where he undertakes a trial and error process to see if his manipulation works on the product. Two, he tries to recover appropriate mental models to use the product. Retrieval and memory resources must be assigned to this task. When a piece of retrieved information is good to solve the task at hand, mostly mental models of similar products, the mental content of "having experience" might come to our awareness. This goes hand in hand with part 3.

3. I remember what the product does and how it should be used. This confirmatory belief could be formed based on 2 and previous manipulation and direct knowledge of the product. It is a natural piece of thought in the flow of the experience because the user should strive to get the different functionalities the product has promised through advertising and other media. Especially during the first uses of the product, the user cannot be able to get all those different functions, so the next piece of thought, 4, comes up to experience.

4. It has different functions but the principal one is ok. This is the result of new products offering new architectures and integrating multiple technologies: even if the user explores it and try to get other functions, when he perceives that the product is offering him its main service, fluently, he stops exploring it. This is a necessary element to go into a good emotional state with the product, 5, leading finally to a state of flow.

5. Flow: it is not boring to be connected to the product. Flow is a state frequently present in the user experience. Flow is what makes an experience enjoyable (Csikszentmihalyi, 1997). Flow is present when a more or less difficult task is being faced effortlessly in a rather automatic way. The absence of negative emotions, such as boredom, and the presence of stimulating activity, 6, are paramount to flow. When there is flow the activities done with a product become autotelic, i.e., there is no reason to do the activity except because the user wants to feel the experience they make possible (Csikszentmihalyi, 1997).

6. The product has harmony; it is comfortable. Harmony refers in everyday language to a balance among all perceptual elements, i.e., to a product presenting a consistent whole. In empirical aesthetics harmony refers to a product presenting perceptual goodness, i.e. it has a good gestalt or Prägnanz (Palmer, Griscom, 2013). This factor is interesting because it is a sensory aesthetic factor, different from all the other factors in this stage (mostly of cognitive nature). This factor adds a layer of positive affect on the user experience. Comfort is the aesthetic sensation for the kinesthetic sense (proprioception). It refers to pleasurable sensations linked to the movements and body positions afforded by the product (Hekkert, & Leder, 2008).

7. Its use is exciting, very stimulating. The presence of a highly stimulating environment is, because of perceptual, 7, cognitive or affective reasons, essential for flow experience. By definition, flow is pleasurable (Csikszentmihalyi, 1997). Flow is a complex construct with at least nine elements contributing to it (Csikszentmihalyi, 1997). Being a complex construct, flow summarizes a good experience with a product by encompassing different feelings at the same time.

The After-Stage Components of the Aware UX Model

1. Engagement with the product. I want to know more about it. Engagement is a complex quality of user experience "characterized by attributes of challenge, positive affect, endurability, aesthetic and sensory appeal, attention, feedback, variety/novelty, interactivity, and perceived user control" (O'Brien, & Toms, 2008, p.938). This is the foremost element in the after phase: with no engagement, the interaction does not go further. Low levels of engagement lead to impoverished interaction. A user's high level of engagement with the product is an ideal objective. Engagement is a consequence of a global positive challenging experience that has turned out well for the product's user. Moreover, and because of the presence of variety and novelty in the experience, the user wants to gather more information about it, maybe to enrich his interaction through the availability of more elements and to gain control over the interaction itself.

2. Easy to learn. I understand it and use it. Learning is crucial in user experience: is a change in the user's behavior or capacities "brought about by experiences" (Reisberg, D., p. 460–461). Different forms of learning are caused in our interactions with products: associative learning and skill learning are common, especially to gain procedural knowledge (know how to perform some action with it). Skill learning should lead to automaticity for the skills involved during the interactions with the product, i.e., the skill is "run off as a single integrated action", (p.460) even though it was composed initially of many different actions. There is a learning curve reflecting how easy or difficult is to learn to use a product for the first time (Reisberg, 2001).

3. It filled my expectations. Expectations are generated from current and past experiences; these are a mental construct serving to narrow down the range of possible outcomes of an event (Geers, & Wellman, 2009). Expectations are beliefs about future occurrences. If an expectation is filled, our prediction of an outcome had a small error allowing us to give better responses to future contingencies, i.e. with more adaptive value (Geers, & Wellman, 2009).

4. Recall and even nostalgia (reminiscence). It is well known that recalling an experience can arouse emotions linked to that particular experience. Nostalgia, together with longing and poignancy, are a group of complex emotions characterized by "both hedonically positive and hedonically negative feelings" (Shaver, 2009, p. 243). It has no simple cognitive appraisal because the product is mentally portrayed as highly desirable but temporarily unattainable (Shaver, 2009).

5. I looked good with the product in that context. This is an aesthetic self-assessment (Palmer et al., 2019) of oneself on one's behalf. This evaluation is done by the individual but is referred to a context. "Looking…" has been identified as one indicator of aesthetic response. This shows how it depends on different elements contributing to the aesthetic response such as background colors, materials, illumination, etc.

6. How else could I use the product? This is imagination: it is a special "form of human thought characterized by the ability of the individual to reproduce images or concepts originally derived from the basic senses but now reflected in one's consciousness as memories, fantasies, or future plans" (Singer, 1999). The user can reshape these memories into rehearsals or planning future manipulations of the product. The product, being no longer in the user's sensory field, imagination is an economical method to explore and enrich the experience, all this happening in the user's stream of consciousness.

7. Disconnect from the world: I get absorbed using the product. This is one of the characteristics of the flow experience: distractions are kept out from consciousness, making the user focused on the here and now with the product (Csikszentmihalyi, 1997).

8. Marking functions are clear. They make visible the product's technical functions showing "how the product is to be handled or operated" (Bürdek, 2005, p. 312). Unclear marking functions make the user unable to get the service the product delivers through its technical functions.

9. How to use the product in different contexts linked to other products. This factor concerns how the user's mental model of the product (Norman, 2013, p. 26) shows the possibility of linking the product to other products in other contexts, i.e., connecting two different mental models. This factor is increasingly important due to trends in extending products into services by connecting them to the Internet.

10. It has a clear entry point to interaction. Having an appropriate mental model is not enough for the user to have a successful interaction: he must know where to begin the operation of the product. This is achieved by using good marking functions (Bürdek, 2005) providing hierarchy to the interaction, for instance, by applying a contrasting color to the product's start button.

11. Awareness of the product's brand meaning. There are four meanings delivered by the brand's identity (Kotler, 1999, p. 572): attributes (labels associated to the brand), benefits (customers buy benefits not attributes; they are functional and emotional), values (symbolized by the company, they attract customers who believe in them) and personality (similar to personality traits). Branding consists of developing this deep set of meanings. Cognitively, a brand is a concept that is recalled due to a prompt in the perceptual field of the user, for instance, the logotype of the brand or a certain brand's aesthetic style.

12. The product possesses X and Y technological advances. This is a comparison between the two product's concepts. A concept is composed of features that, in this case, are compared one to one to identify one as superior in a specific item. Product superiority is "the differentiation in characteristics found between similar products that leads to one product being perceived to be of higher value and/or quality to the customer" (Haverila, & Fehr, 2016, p.570). This superiority is vital for customer and user satisfaction (Haverila, & Fehr, 2016).

13. I enjoyed using the product in that context. Enjoyment is defined as "an emotional response to the experience of pleasure" (Sundarajan, L. 2009, p. 155). Enjoyment can be experienced at three levels: first, as acceptance wriggles that are movements that expand or increase the perception of the product (its sound, appearance, etc.). They serve to explore the different aspects of the stimulus in an effort to continue interaction; they can form an extensive repertoire (as in tasting wine (Fridja 2010)). Second, "enjoyment is a reportable pleasure derived from the awareness of pleasure" (Sundarajan, L., 2009). Third, enjoyment is like savoring: the user turns the event of use of the product over and over in his mind; this contributes to extend enjoyment beyond pleasure.

14. The product's use is original with that look. Consumers get bored with the typical appearance of their products, so an original and new product will get their attention (Veryzer, Hutchinson, 1998). However, originality in the use might produce an intense affective reaction because an incongruity of the use of the product with previous mental models of the product's usability can cause a higher arousal level. Consequently, solving this incongruity will be strongly experienced (c.f. Snelders, Hekkert, 1999).

15. The product's style is similar to products X and Y. Style conveys meanings and arises aesthetic, and emotional feelings in the user. Style is a way to make a product different or similar to competing products. Cognitively, presumably, comparing products' styles asks the user to compare meanings, aesthetic and emotional feelings. Style is important because it allows the user to belong to a group (the possessors of a product of certain brand) but, at the same time, allows the user to be different of other people who possess similar products but on other styles or brands (Berghman, & Hekkert, 2017).

16. Using the product implied a change in the product's perception. Using a new product implies new sensations for the user. Perception, by definition (Zimbardo et al., 2009), creates new interpretations of sensations, therefore, by using the product, a change in its perception is provoked.

17. Where can I learn more about the product? The question itself reveals the motivation to learn more about the product. The user wants to expand the possibilities of interaction with the product. This expansion is a consequence of a change in his pre-existing thoughts and behavior. Different ways of learning exist when interacting with a new product: by imitation, by trial and error and, through insight. (Strickland, 2001, p384-385).

References for the Appendix

1. Berghman, M. & Hekkert, P. (2017). Towards a unified model of aesthetic pleasure in design. *New Ideas in Psychology*, 47(136-144). Elsevier.
2. Bürdek, B. E. (2005). Design history, theory and practice of product design. Basel: Birkhäuser.
3. Csikszentmihalyi, M. (1997). *Flow and the Psychology of Discovery and Invention*. HarperPerennial, New York.
4. Fridja, N. (2010). On the Nature and Function of Pleasure. In: Kringelbach, M. L. & Berridge, K. C. *Pleasures of the Brain*. Edited Oxford University Press.
5. Geers, A.L., & Wellman, J.A. (2009). Expectation. In: Sander, D. & Scherer, K. (2009). *The Oxford Companion to Emotion and the Affective Sciences*. Oxford University Press.
6. Haverila, M. J. & Fehr, K. (2016). The impact of product superiority on customer satisfaction in project management. *International Journal of Project Management*, 34(4), 570–583. Elsevier.
7. Hekkert, P, & Leder, H. (2008). Product aesthetics. In Schifferstein, H.N.J., Hekkert, P. (Eds.), *Product experience* (pp. 259–285). Elsevier Science San Diego, CA.
8. Jordan, P. W. (2000). *Designing pleasurable products: An introduction to the new human factors*. CRC Press.
9. Kotler, Philip (1999). *Principles of marketing*. Pearson Education. 6th European edition
10. Norman, D. (2013). *The design of everyday things*: Revised and expanded edition. Basic books.
11. O'Brien, H. L. & Toms, E.G. (2008). What is user engagement? A conceptual framework for defining user engagement with technology. *Journal of the American Society for Information Science and Technology*, *59*(6), 938–955. Wiley Online Library.
12. Palmer, S. E. & Griscom, W. S. (2013). Accounting for taste: Individual differences in preference for harmony. *Psychonomic bulletin & review*, 20(3), 453–461. Springer
13. Palmer, S. E., Schloss, K. B. & Sammartino, J. (2013). Visual aesthetics and human preference. *Annual review of psychology*, 64, 77–107. Annual Reviews.
14. Reisberg, D. (2001). Learning in: Wilson, R. A. & Keil, F. C. (2001). The MIT Encyclopedia of the Cognitive Sciences (New Ed.). The MIT Press.
15. Shaver, P.R., 2009, Longing in: Sander, D. & Scherer, K. (2009). *The Oxford Companion to Emotion and the Affective Sciences*. Oxford University Press.
16. Singer, J. (1999). Imagination. In: Runco, M. A. & Pritzker, S. R. (1999). *Encyclopedia of creativity* (2 Vols.). Academic Press.
17. Snelders, D. & Hekkert, P. (1999). Association Measures as Predictors of Product Originality. *Advances in Consumer Research*, 26(1).
18. Strickland, B. (2001). Learning Theory. P384-385. In: *Gale Encyclopedia of Psychology*, 2nd Edition. Gale Group

19. Sundarajan, L., (2009). Enjoyment. In: Sander, D. & Scherer, K. (2009). *The Oxford Companion to Emotion and the Affective Sciences*. Oxford University Press.
20. Veryzer, J. R. W. & Hutchinson, J. W. (1998). The influence of unity and prototypicality on aesthetic responses to new product designs. *Journal of Consumer Research, 24*(4), 374–385. JSTOR.

References

A' Design Awards: JawSaw Silver A' (2012). https://competition.adesignaward.com/design.php?ID=23773

Ajjawi, R., Higgs J.: Learning clinical reasoning: a journey of professional socialisation. Adv. Health Sci. Educ. https://doi.org/10.1007/s10459-006-9032-4

Amazon: WORX WG307 JawSaw 5 Amp Electric Chainsaw (2020). https://www.amazon.com/WORX-WG307-JawSaw-Electric-Chainsaw/dp/B004SF8L9A?ref_=ast_sto_dp

APA: APA Dictionary of Psychology. American Psychological Association (2015)

Ariza, N., Maya, J.: Proposal to identify the essential elements to construct a user experience model with the product using the thematic analysis technique In DS 77: Proceedings of the DESIGN 2014, 13th International Design Conference, Dubrovnik, Croatia, pp. 11–22 (2014a). ISSN 1847-9073

Ariza, N., Maya, J.: Towards an empirical model of the UX: a factor Analysis study In: Proceedings of the 9th Design and Emotion Conference on the Colors of Care. Universidad de los Andes, Colombia, pp. 689–697 (2014b). ISBN 978-958-774-070-7

Attractiveness: Cambridge Dictionary Online (n.d.). https://dictionary.cambridge.org/es/diccionario/ingles/attractiveness

Bagozzi, R.P., Gopinath, M., Nyer, P.U.: The role of emotions in marketing. Acad. Mark. J. **27**(2), 184–206 (1999)

Beavers, A.S., Lounsbury, J.W., Richards, J.K., Huck, S.W., Skolits, G.J., Esquivel, S.L.: Practical considerations for using exploratory factor analysis in educational research. Pract. Assess. Res. Eval. **18**(6), 1–13 (2013)

Berghman, M., Hekkert, P.: Towards a unified model of aesthetic pleasure in design. New Ideas Psychol. **47**, 136–144 (2017). http://dx.doi.org/10.1016/j.newideapsych.2017.03.004

Braun, V., Clarke, V.: Using thematic analysis in psychology. Qual. Res. Psychol. **3**, 77–101 (2006)

Creswell, J.W.: Qualitative Inquiry and Research Design: Choosing Among Five Traditions, 2nd edn. Sage, Thousand Oaks (2007)

Creswell, J.W.: Qualitative Inquiry and Research Design: Choosing Among Five Approaches, 3rd edn. Sage, Thousand Oaks (2013)

Demir, E., Desmet, P., Hekkert, P.: Appraisal patterns of emotions in human-product interaction. Int. J. Des. **3**(2), 41–45 (2009)

Ekman, P., Friesen, W.: Facial Action Coding System: A Technique for the Measurement of Facial Movement. Consulting Psychologists Press, Palo Alto (1978)

Ericsson, K.A., Simon, H.A.: Protocol Analysis: Verbal Reports as Data. Bradford Books/MIT Press, Cambridge (1993)

Everitt, B., Howell, S., David, C.: Encyclopedia of Statistics in Behavioral Science. Wiley, New York (2005)

Field, A.: Discovering Statistics Using SPSS. Sage Publications (2009)

Forlizzi, J., Ford, S.: The building blocks of experience: an early framework for interaction designers. In: Proceedings of the 3rd Conference on Designing Interactive Systems: Processes, Practices, Methods, and Techniques, pp. 419–423 (2000)

Fridja, N.: Mood. In: Sander, D., Scherer, K. (eds.) The Oxford Companion to Emotion and the Affective Sciences. Oxford University Press, Oxford (2009a)

Fridja, N.: Concerns. In: Sander, D., Scherer, K. (eds.) The Oxford Companion to Emotion and the Affective Sciences. Oxford University Press, Oxford (2009b)

Goodman-Deane, J., Langdon, P., Clarkson, J.: Key influences on the user-centred design process. J. Eng. Des. 21(2–3), 345–373 (2010)

Gopnik, A.: Theory of mind. In: Wilson, R.A., Keil, F.C. (eds.) The MIT Encyclopedia of the Cognitive Sciences. MIT Press (2001)

Hoyle, R.H., Duvall, J.L.: Determining the number of factors in exploratory and confirmatory factor analysis. In: Kaplan, D. (ed.) Handbook of Quantitative Methodology for the Social Sciences. Sage, Thousand Oaks (2004)

Husserl, E.: Ideas Pertaining to a Pure Phenomenology and to a Phenomenological Philosophy. Trans. F. Kersten. The Hague: Nijhoff (1982)

John, O.P., Srivastava, S.: The big-five trait taxonomy: history, measurement, and theoretical perspectives. In: Pervin, L.A., John, O.P. (eds.) Handbook of Personality: Theory and Research, vol. 2, pp. 102–138. Guilford Press, New York (1999)

Jordan, P.W.: Designing Pleasurable Products: An Introduction to the New Human Factors. CRC Press (2002)

Knafl, K.: Cognitive Interview. In: Given, L. (ed.) The Sage Encyclopedia of Qualitative Research Methods. Sage, Los Angeles (2008)

Lee, K., Xu, F., Carlson, S.M., Moses, L.J., Sabbagh, M.A.: The development of executive functioning and theory of mind: a comparison of Chinese and US preschoolers. Psychol. Sci. 17(1), 74–81 (2005)

Lindquist, K.A., Feldman-Barrett, L.F.: Emotional complexity. In: Lewis, M., Haviland-Jones, J.M., Feldman-Barret, L.F. (eds.) Handbook of Emotions, 3rd edn. The Guilford Press (2008)

Mahy, C.E.V., Moses, L.J., Pfeifer, J.H.: How and where: Theory- of-mind in the brain. Dev. Cogn. Neurosci. 9, 68–81 (2014)

Mooney, C.Z.: Monte Carlo Simulation. Sage, Thousand Oaks (1997)

Natsoulas, T.: Stream of consciousness. In: Nadel, L. (ed.) Encylopedia of Cognitive Science. Wiley (2005)

Newell, A., Simon, H.A.: Human Problem Solving, vol. 104. Prentice-Hall Englewood Cliffs (1972)

Ortiz Nicolas, J.C.: Understanding and designing pleasant experiences with products. Ph.D. thesis, The Imperial College, London (2014)

Revonsuo, A.: Consciousness: the Science of Subjectivity. Psychology Press (2009)

Robinson, M.D.: Self-Report. In: Sander, D., Scherer, K. (eds.) The Oxford Companion to Emotion and the Affective Sciences. Oxford University Press, Oxford (2009)

Rosenthal, D.M.: Introspection and self-interpretation. Philos. Top. 28, 201–233 (2001)

Skynner, R., Cleese, J.: Life and How to Survive It. W. W. Norton & Company, London (1996)

The Chainsaw Journal: JawSaw was the best chainsaw alternative (2020). https://www.chainsawjournal.com/worx-jawsaw-review-the-safer-chainsaw/

Tonetto, L., Tamminen, P.: Understanding the role of intuition in decision-making when designing for experiences: contributions from cognitive psychology. Theor. Issues Ergon. Sci. 16(6), 631–642 (2015)

Velmans, M.: Understanding Consciousness. Routledge (2009)

van Manen, M.: Researching Lived Experience: Human Science for an Action Sensitive Pedagogy. Althouse Press, London (1990)

Worx: WORX WG307 JawSaw 5 Amp Electric Chainsaw (2020). https://www.worx.com/jawsaw-chainsaw-wg307.html

Is It Possible to Predict Human Perception of Video Quality? The Assessment of Sencogi Quality Metric

Maria Laura Mele[1,2](✉), Silvia Colabrese[1], Luca Calabria[1], and Christiaan Erik Rijnders[1]

[1] COGISEN Srl, Rome, Italy
{marialaura,silvia,luca,chris}@cogisen.com
[2] Department of Philosophy, Social and Human Sciences and Education, University of Perugia, Perugia, Italy

Abstract. Sencogi Quality Metric (SenQM) is a novel objective metric for video quality assessment. SenQM infers video quality scores from the spatio-temporal evolution of videos. The quality model behind SenQM is based on an algorithm developed by Cogisen for modelling dynamic phenomena generated by complex systems. In the field of video compression, Cogisen's algorithm uses machine learning to model human perception of video quality by extracting meaningful information directly from the video data domain and its frequency representation. The model has been trained over datasets of (i) x264 compressed videos as input data and (ii) the corresponding subjective Mean Opinion Scores as ground truth. This study introduces the model behind SenQM and how the proposed metric performs in subjective video quality prediction compared to the most used video quality assessment methods, i.e. PSNR, SSIM, and Netflix's VMAF. Results indicate a significantly higher prediction performance in terms of monotonicity, consistency, and accuracy than the compared metrics. SenQM quality scores show significantly higher variations for 352×288 resolution videos with equivalent levels of degradation, and outstands PSNR, SSIM, and VMAF in predicting subjective scores of increasing levels of compression without being affected by either the degradation level or the video content.

Keywords: Machine learning · Video quality assessment · Objective video quality

1 Introduction

Today, the effectiveness of video service providers is strictly related to how they meet the video quality expectations of their users. Subjective video quality plays an important role in affecting the user's quality of experience.

The Video Quality Assessment (VQA) methodology evaluates the quality of a video as perceived by an average human observer either by subjective or objective methods.

© Springer Nature Switzerland AG 2020
C. Stephanidis et al. (Eds.): HCII 2020, LNCS 12423, pp. 234–247, 2020.
https://doi.org/10.1007/978-3-030-60114-0_16

VQA is a key evaluation methodology for any digital video application that has a human-observer as its end-user [1].

Subjective VQA methods follow standard recommendations to directly involve human observers in assigning perceived quality scores to videos. This methodology is time-consuming and requires high costs. However, evaluating video quality directly with end users is still the most effective method to assess perceived quality [2].

Objective VQA methods have been proposed to predict video quality in a way that would be faster and less expensive than subjective VQA. The fidelity of an objective quality assessment metric is measured by standard robustness metrics which assess objective VQA methods compared to human video quality scores. VQA objective methods can be classified into four categories: handcrafted feature based, handcrafted feature plus learning based, feature learning based and end-to-end learning-based approaches [3].

Handcrafted feature-based methods include traditional methods for assessing image/video quality, which extracts and combines handcrafted features of frames (i.e., derived attributes that are relevant in video-frames) for quality prediction. Peak Signal to Noise Ratio (PSNR) and Structural Similarity index (SSIM) are the two most used state-of-the-art handcrafted feature-based metrics [3]. PSNR measures the mean squared error between a distorted video frame and its reference, pixel-by-pixel, returning a measure of distortion. SSIM computes the structural similarity between a distorted video and its reference. Compared to PSNR, SSIM specifically computes its index of similarity by weighting levels of luminance, contrast, and structure (i.e. how much pixel values change together with their neighbors) [4]. PSNR and SSIM are a universal validation standard for metrics comparison. In spite of their widespread use, PSNR and SSIM are not accurate enough to replicate the perceived quality in the Human Visual System (HVS) [5].

Developing VQA metrics that are consistent with the non-linear behavior of HVS [5] and adapting to different video contents is still a challenge in the video compression field [6]. As the understanding of human perception grows, incorporating brain-inspired features to VQA metrics can help for accurately predicting subjective quality of a video. Metrics that are based on machine learning algorithms, can find a more effective combination of features for visual quality prediction than only handcrafted feature-based methods.

One of the most used machine learning based algorithms is Video Multi-Method Assessment Fusion (VMAF) [7]. VMAF is a model that combines handcrafted features to a learning-based model. It uses a classifier to combine four metrics measuring visual information fidelity, loss of details, luminance, and noise. The model provides a Mean Opinion Score (MOS) for each video frame compared to a high-quality reference video, and returns an overall Differential Mean Opinion score (DMOS) normalized in the range 0–100, with higher values corresponding to higher quality scores, such as in MOS values. The main limit of VMAF is that the performance of the metric depends on the effectiveness of the extracted handcrafted features [3].

To overcome the weaknesses that handcrafted features have, machine learning can be directly applied to learn both the features and the model, either as subsequent steps (e.g. dictionary learning) or in an end-to-end fashion, where features and model for the VQA metric are learned jointly. The most successful end-to-end attempts reside in the deep learning framework [8–10]. However, the main challenge with deep learning is that training a model requires a considerable amount of labelled data, often not available in the context of VQA. Deep learning, though providing visual quality metrics that are often more accurate than any other machine learning attempt, raises the computational complexity. Metrics derived from deep learning have millions of parameters and their eventual embedding in a Rate-Distortion Optimization schema would make the encoding algorithm extremely complex [3]. In the literature, there are few VQA models not exploiting the deep learning framework, those proposed so far (e.g. [11–13] use higher level features that are still manually designed, thus their effectiveness greatly depends on the goodness of features design [3].

This work describes the assessment of a novel objective video quality metric called Sencogi Quality Metric (SenQM), an end-to-end approach that accounts for the spatio-temporal relevant components of videos, learned jointly with the model to train. The metric is based on machine learning training with the aim to estimate human perception of video quality by extracting features from specifically chosen spatio-temporal data. The non-linearity of the HVS is encoded in simple building-blocks within the model, different from those classically used in deep learning.

SenQM is an application derived from a new machine learning algorithm developed by Cogisen [14]. Cogisen's technique is flexible to accommodate several application to complex systems comprising dynamic phenomena that morph, such as video compression. Based on Cogisen's machine learning algorithm, the SenQM model works on selected portions of raw data from the input video. The model recombines selected pixels into meaningful sequences and transforms the linearized spatio-temporal domain onto relevant frequencies. Data in the transformed domain are combined into a model acting as video quality predictor. The training for the video quality metric consists of data selection and model parameters optimization, and it is driven by the fitting of subjective MOS values. The model, differently from VMAF and SSIM, is not highly dependent on the quality of the reference.

The study investigates the performance of SenQM as an objective video quality metric. The results show that SenQM performs significantly better than PSNR, SSIM, and VMAF in terms of prediction robustness, with higher variations of VQA scores for videos with equivalent levels of degradation, and without being affected by compression level and video content when predicting scores of increasing compression levels.

The paper is organized as follows. Section 2 describes in detail the model behind SenQM. Section 3 explains the methodology followed for the assessment of SenQM through the comparison with the main metrics used in the literature. Section 4 shows the results. Section 5 summarizes the findings.

2   Model

This section describes Cogisen's algorithm, used for developing the proposed SenQM quality metric, the dataset used for training, and how the training of SenQM has been conducted.

2.1 Sencogi Quality Metric

SenQM is obtained exploiting a new machine learning algorithm developed by Cogisen. Cogisen's algorithm is an original way of remapping data that does not exploit the deep learning framework. The algorithm maps raw data into a space where information is linearized and can be extracted with a high reduction in optimization parameters. The training algorithm is capable of extracting information directly from data frames and their temporal evolution [14].

The main steps of the method are summarized in Fig. 1 and can be called, in order of presentation: pixel selection, frequency selection and spectral combination. The output of the main steps is named feature (see F_i in Fig. 1). Features are obtained in parallel and their linear combination ($\sum_i F_i$) is used as video quality regressor. The number of features is a parameter related to the specific problem and its optimal value is decided as part of the training algorithm.

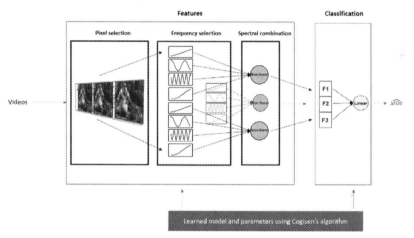

Fig. 1. Pipeline of Cogisen's algorithm. The main steps are underlined as separate boxes. We have: pixel selection, frequency selection and spectral combination. F_i stands for feature, while the final output, named $(\widehat{MOS})$, corresponds to the video quality predicted by the algorithm.

Pixel sequences and frequencies are selected jointly. While frequencies are scanned, a heuristic selects pixels from the video frames, reorders them, and evaluates their goodness after a transformation on the selected frequency. More formally, calling $x = \{x_1, \ldots, x_P\}$ a generic pixel sequence of length P, extracted from the video frames, its frequency transformation is named $y(\omega_k)$. Transformed data are combined in "zones". A zone is defined as the sum of Q power spectra, one for each of the pixel sequences selected from the input video, see Eq. 1:

$$Z = \sum_{i=1}^{Q} y_i(\omega_k)^2 \tag{1}$$

What we call feature is obtained combining two zones together, according to Eq. 2:

$$F = \frac{|Z_2 - Z_1|}{Z_1 + Z_2} \tag{2}$$

During the training, the model parameters, i.e. the frequencies involved, the subset of pixels, and the number of features, are selected by the optimization of a goodness function. Specifically, the SenQM model evaluated in Sect. 3 is obtained minimizing a Mean Square Error, where the error is defined as the Euclidean distance between the ground truth, i.e. the MOS of a video, and the model output $\widehat{MOS}$.

Qualitatively, the strength of Cogisen's approach lies in the fact that the algorithm is able to extract the full relevant information from the dataset without any loss in accuracy and generality. This is possible by selecting and recombining only a sparse subset of pixels both in the input domain and the frequency domain.

2.2 Video Quality Dataset

The SenQM model was trained over a dataset derived from sixteen videos at three pixel resolutions (426×224, 768×432, and 1920×1080) (Table 1).

The reference and compressed videos at 768×432 pixel resolution are taken from LIVE Public-Domain Subjective Video Quality Database[1], which provides distorted videos from reference using MPEG-2 compression, H.264 compression, simulated transmission of H.264 compressed bitstreams through error-prone IP networks and through error-prone wireless networks. The distortion strengths of the selected LIVE datasets videos were manually adjusted by the providers to guarantee a set of contours of equal visual quality for each distortion category [15].

The reference videos at 462×224 and 1920×1080 resolutions are taken from Netflix Video Quality Dataset[2]. Selected videos were compressed by the x264 encoder and at five Constant Rate Factors (CRF) values ($10, 21, 27, 33, 43$), in order to introduce a wide variability of video quality levels.

The datasets are paired with the related MOS, assigned in the range 0–100 by a cohort of observers. The MOS should reflect the human awareness of deliberate perception of video quality and acts as dataset ground truth. The Single-stimulus method with hidden reference [2] was used to obtain the MOS dataset. Five studies, with a mean of 30 participants each study, were used to compute the MOS. The Single-stimulus VQA method and the whole procedure of the subjective VQA test are explained in Sect. 3. More details about the datasets are summarized in Table 1.

---

[1] LIVE Public-Domain Subjective Video Quality Database: https://live.ece.utexas.edu/research/Quality/live_video.html, last accessed on 27 January 2020.

[2] Netflix Video Quality Dataset: https://github.com/Netflix/vmaf, last accessed on 27 January 2020.

Table 1. Details of the datasets used for training SenQM.

Video name	Resolution	Compression codecs and type	CRF			
Big buck bunny 1	426 × 224	h264	10	21 (×2)	27 (×2)	–
Crowd run						33
Tears of steel						–
Bouncing balls						–
Netflix ritual dance						–
Tractor	768 × 430	- Reference - h264 - mpeg2 - h264 compressed bitstreams through error-prone IP networks - h264 compressed bitstreams through error-prone wireless networks	–	–	–	–
Rush hour			–	–	–	–
Blue sky			–	–	–	–
Station			–	–	–	–
Pedestrian area			–	–	–	–
Big buck bunny 2	1920 × 1080	h264	–	–	–	33
Old town cross			–	–	–	33
Fox bird			21	27	33	–
Seeking						–
Tennis			–	–	33	43
Fox bird		VP9	–	27	–	–

2.3 Sencogi Quality Metric Training

The training was conducted on 63 videos (frame dimensions, 426 × 224, 768 × 430, 1920 × 1080) and their corresponding MOS values. Each video was separated into chunks of 12 frames each, sharing the same ground truth.

The SenQM was trained applying a decimation on the frame size, reduced to 352 × 288, and considering as search space, all the 12 frames for each chunk. The model finally selected as SenQM metric was made of one feature only, comprising 66 sequences, 33 for each zone. Short sequences were preferred, with a length between 23 and 78 pixels each.

3 Evaluation

The objective of the study is to evaluate the performance of SenQM in predicting subjective quality scores of videos different from those used for creating the SenQM model.

The Single-stimulus method with hidden reference [2] was used to obtain the subjective scores dataset for the assessment of SenQM.

The Single-stimulus method presents single videos to be assessed. The SS trials show both the videos under assessment and their corresponding reference sequence, which are presented without viewers being aware of it. The assessment trials are presented only once, in random order. The same content is not presented twice in succession. Some dummy sequences are shown at the beginning of the experiment to let observers practice the test. Each video is shown after a mid-grey adaptation field lasting 3 s. The video quality assessment scores are collected during display of a mid-grey post-exposure field.

An explicit viewing task was administered to human observers because specific tasks are better at controlling top-down influences than free viewing tasks, thus avoiding any intervening subjective factor [16]. A judgement task has been used as described in Sect. 3.2.

3.1 Material

Eight reference videos in the YUV 4:2:0 format, 25 frames per second, and CIF (352 × 288) resolution, were selected by the publicly available ETFOS CIF Video Quality (ECVQ) database[3] [17, 18]. The selected videos were compressed in the h.264 standard at three CRF levels (21, 27, 33). None of the videos used for modelling the metric was used to assess the ability of the model to generalize video quality scores.

3.2 Procedure

At the beginning of the subjective test, an example of a high-quality video is shown, then reference high quality videos and compressed videos are randomly presented to each participant per session. Viewers are asked to rate the perceived quality of each video by using a slider marked from 1 to 100. To help participants in their ratings, the scale was divided into 5 equal parts labelled with the adjectives "Bad", "Poor", "Fair", "Good", and "Excellent". The experimental task of judging the quality of 32 videos, 8 videos × 4 compression levels (reference, CRF 21, CRF 27, CRF 33) lasted about 15 min in order to prevent errors due to subjects' fatigue and loss of attention.

3.3 Assessment Metrics

Prediction, monotonicity, consistency, and accuracy define the robustness of a VQA metrics. In this study, the corresponding metrics recommended by the Telecommunication Standardization Sector (ITU) were used to assess the SenQM prediction model as described below [19].

Prediction monotonicity is the index of monotonic dependence on the level of degradation of a video. The index describes how much variation a VQA metric score has for different videos with equivalent levels of degradation. The prediction monotonicity of the objective metrics under assessment metric was measured by the Spearman Rank Order Correlation coefficient (SROC).

---

[3] Video Quality Group at Faculty of Electrical Engineering. URL: http://www.etfos.unios.hr/vqg/ Last access: 14 February 2020.

Prediction consistency measures how well a VQA metric is able to predict subjective scores without being affected by the degradation level of the video. The Pearson Linear Correlation Coefficient (PLCC), after applying a nonlinear regression with a logistic function [19] and the Outlier Ratio (OR) index were used in this study to assess prediction consistency. OR is defined as the percentage of the predicted numbers that falls outside 2 times the standard deviation of subjective MOS.

Prediction accuracy measures how well a VQA metric is able to predict subjective scores without being affected by the content of the video. In this study, prediction accuracy was measured by the Root Mean Square Error (RMSE).

4   Results

This section reports the results of the comparison between the scores computed by the proposed metric, SenQM, and the subjective video quality Mean Opinion Scores (MOS), obtained from the test with subjects. The performance of SenQM is also compared to the performance of the most used traditional metrics PSNR, SSIM, and Netflix's VMAF 1.3.14.

4.1   Subjects

An experimental test with twenty-one non-expert viewers (mean age = 36.8 years old, 50% male, 100% English speakers) was conducted through a crowdsourcing platform for psychological research called Prolific Academic[4]. All subjects declared normal or corrected-to-normal vision, normal contrast sensitivity, normal color vision, and no professional or extensive personal experience in dealing with video display systems or devices. Participants were rewarded for performing the test.

4.2   Subjective Video Quality Scores

Table 2 shows the MOS and the Difference Mean Opinion Scores (DMOS) assigned by each participant to each video (Table 2). DMOS were computed for each subject by subtracting the raw quality score assigned to the reference video to the score assigned to the distorted video. The internal consistency of the scale was validated by using Cronbach's alpha (alpha = 0.929) and Spearman Brown split-half index (rho = 0.848) (Cronbach's Alpha = 0.901 for the first half and alpha = 0.857 for the second half).

4.3   Performance Assessment of Sencogi Quality Metric

An analysis to see whether the metric is able to accurately predict human scores of perceived video quality and the comparison with other state-of-the-art VQA metrics was performed. Figures 2, 3 and 4 show the predicted scores for each VQA metric under assessment. Table 3 reports the results of the metrics used for assessing the robustness of each objective VQA metric.

---

[4] Prolific Academic. URL: www.prolific.co. Last access: 14 February 2020.

Table 2. Subjective video quality assessment scores. Higher MOS scores mean higher perceived video quality. For the DMOS scores, the higher the values, the worse the perceived video quality.

	CRF 21	CRF 27	CRF 33
MOS↑	58.345	54.673	43.679
DMOS↓	2.911	5.935	17.500

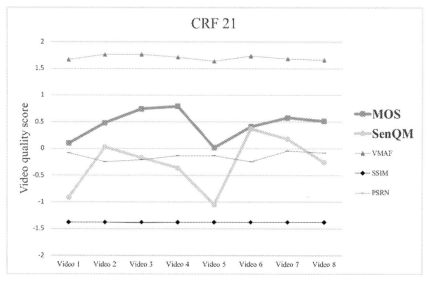

Fig. 2. Normalized video quality scores of each metric under assessment (PSNR, SSIM, VMAF, and SenQM) compared to the MOS assigned by the experimental subjects to videos at CRF 21.

Overall, SenQM obtained higher mean robustness scores compared to the other metrics (Table 3). The only exception is for the VMAF scores at CRF 21, which had a higher SRCC score than SenQM. SenQM returns lower RMSE compared to VMAF ($t = -5.602$, $p = 0.30$) and SSIM ($t = -37.758$, $p = 0.001$) (Table 3). Comparisons among the quality scores on all test videos (reference, CRF 21, CRF 27, CRF 33) returned no significant correlation between the SenQM scores and the scores calculated by the other objective measures (VMAF, $rho = 0.076$, $p > 0.05$; SSIM, $rho = 0.239$, $p > 0.05$; PSNR, $rho = -0.339$; $p > 0.05$).

A repeated measures ANOVA indicated significant differences in mean scores between SenQM and VMAF ($F_{(1,31)} = 198.512$, $p = 0.000$), SenQM and SSIM ($F_{(1,31)} = 138.811$, $p = 0.001$). No significant difference was found between the RMSE scores obtained by the SenQM scores and those obtained by the PSNR scores ($t = 1.323$, $p > 0.05$). Results on the OR analysis show that 75% of the values predicted by SenQM, 79% of the values predicted PSNR and 100% of VMAF and SSIM scores fall outside ± 2 of the SD (Table 3).

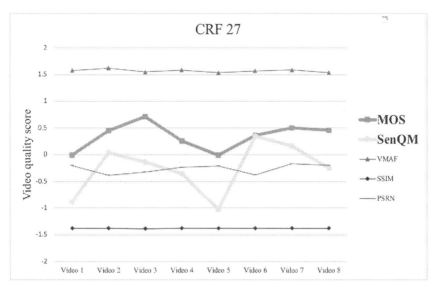

Fig. 3. Normalized video quality scores of PSNR, SSIM, VMAF, and SenQM compared to the MOS of videos at CRF 27.

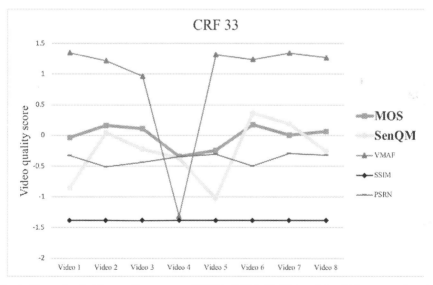

Fig. 4. Normalized video quality scores of PSNR, SSIM, VMAF, and SenQM compared to the MOS of videos at CRF 33. The x axis reports the name of each video used for the assessment.

Table 3. Statistical comparison between MOS and the objective scores computed by each metric under assessment. Low values of Spearman Rank Order Correlation (SRCC) and Pearson Linear Correlation (PLCC) mean high differences between the predicted score and the subjective MOS. High values of Root Mean Square Error (RMSE) and Outlier Ratio (OR) mean less ability to predict subjective scores with low error.

		SenQM	VMAF	SSIM	PSNR
SRCC↑	CRF 21	Rho = 0.286	Rho = 0.428	Rho = 0.071	Rho = 0.214
	CRF 27	Rho = 0.635	Rho = 0.143	Rho = 0.083	Rho = −0.381
	CRF 33	Rho = 0.786	Rho = −0.595	Rho = −0.147	Rho = −0.619
	Mean	**Rho = 0.569**	**Rho = 0.234**	**Rho = 0.232**	**Rho = 0.053**
PCC↑	CRF 21	r = 0.624	r = 0.615	r = 0.083	r = −0.155
	CRF 27	r = 0.769	r = 0.123	r = −0.124	r = 0.035
	CRF 33	r = 0.635	r = −0.341	r = −0.147	r = −0.643
	Mean	**r = 0.676**	**r = 0.285**	**r = 0.005**	**r = −0.125**
RMSE↓	CRF 21	25.487	39.581	57.942	20.813
	CRF 27	21.222	39.086	54.226	20.714
	CRF 33	13.586	39.944	43.826	13.183
	Mean	**20.098**	**39.444**	**51.998**	**18.237**
OR↓	CRF 21	0.875	1.000	1.000	0.750
	CRF 27	0.875	1.000	1.000	0.875
	CRF 33	0.500	1.000	1.000	0.750
	Mean	**0.750**	**1.000**	**1.000**	**0.792**

5   Discussion

The aim of this work was to verify whether SenQM is able to predict human perception of video quality with higher robustness levels compared to the most used VQA metrics. The results show that Cogisen's model of subjective video quality provides a method for predicting the subjective quality scores of videos that outperforms the most commonly used objective metrics.

Results on MOS and DMOS confirmed previous VQA studies [20–23] indicating that the higher the video quality degradation in terms of CRF, the lower the subjective quality scores. Similarly, all the VQA metrics under assessment reflect a decreasing trend in terms of quality scores (Figs. 2, 3 and 4).

SenQM scores to h264 videos, 352 × 288 pixel resolution, compressed at three compression CRF levels (21, 27, 33) obtained a significantly higher prediction performance in terms of monotonicity, consistency, and accuracy when compared to the traditional PSNR and SSIM metrics, and Netflix's VMAF. In particular, SenQM had significantly higher mean scores compared to the other metrics, thus indicating a higher variation of the SenQM mean scores for different videos with equivalent levels of degradation, especially for CRF 27 and CR 33 quality levels.

The proposed model is better than VMAF, SSIM and PSNR in predicting subjective scores of CRF 21, 27 and 33 compressed videos, without being affected by the degradation level and the content of the video. These results are likely because SenQM is driven by the fitting of MOS values assigned by humans to model subjective video quality in an end-to-end fashion. SenQM extracts meaningful information directly from the data frames and their temporal evolution, independently from the effectiveness of handcrafted features of video frames, such as for the other assessed metrics.

6 Conclusion

The study is the performance assessment of SenQM, a new metric for predicting the human awareness of deliberate perception of video quality that leads to a judgement process. The SenQM model is built on Cogisen's machine learning algorithm, which is able to recombine pixels into meaningful sequences and transform the linearized spatio-temporal domain onto relevant frequencies. SenQM model uses data in the transformed domain to predict subjective video quality. SenQM model has been trained over datasets of x264 compressed videos as input data and driven by subjective MOS values fitting. The scores computed by SenQM and the most used VQA metrics (PSNR, SSIM and VMAF) were compared with human MOS of video quality, derived from a judgment task on a selection of videos compressed with different codecs and at different CRF levels.

Findings show that SenQM is able to significantly predict subjective MOS of video quality without being dependent on the quality of the reference in its assessment process. The model outperforms the most commonly used video quality assessment metrics in the literature. In particular, SenQM performs significantly better with 352×288 resolution videos in terms of predicting robustness. The proposed metric showed greater variations for videos with equivalent levels of the degradation introduced by compression, without being influenced by the compression level or the video content when predicting scores of increasing levels of compression.

SenQM is trained on human quality scores and, differently from the most used metrics, it does not depend on the effectiveness of derived features of video frames because it extracts relevant information directly from the spatio-temporal domain. The machine learning algorithm behind SenQM does not demand for high amounts of labelled data, and provides a VQA metric that does not involve high computational costs.

Future works will focus on extending SenQM to different degradation levels, pixel resolutions, codecs, and viewing conditions (such as distance from screen, display size, or device) in order to generalize the model and provide an objective VQA metric that is consistent across wider ranges of variabilities.

References

1. Chikkerur, S., Sundaram, V., Reisslein, M., Karam, L.J.: Objective video quality assessment methods: a classification, review, and performance comparison (2011). http://dx.doi.org/10.1109/tbc.2011.2104671
2. International Telecommunication Union – ITU: Recommendation ITU-R BT.500-14 (10/2019). Methodologies for the subjective assessment of the quality of television images. BT Series. Broadcasting service (television), October 2019
3. Zhang, Y., Kwong, S., Wang, S.: Machine learning based video coding optimizations: a survey (2020). http://dx.doi.org/10.1016/j.ins.2019.07.096
4. Staelens, N., et al.: Assessing quality of experience of IPTV and video on demand services in real-life environments (2010). http://dx.doi.org/10.1109/tbc.2010.2067710
5. Wang, Z., Bovik, A.C., Sheikh, H.R., Simoncelli, E.P.: Image quality assessment: from error visibility to structural similarity (2004). http://dx.doi.org/10.1109/tip.2003.819861
6. Wang, Z., Bovik, A.C.: Modern image quality assessment (2006). http://dx.doi.org/10.2200/s00010ed1v01y200508ivm003
7. Li, Z., Aaron, A., Katsavounidis, I., Moorthy, A., Manohara, M.: Toward a practical perceptual video quality metric. Netflix Tech Blog. **6**, 2 (2016)
8. Bosse, S., Maniry, D., Muller, K.-R., Wiegand, T., Samek, W.: Deep neural networks for no-reference and full-reference image quality assessment (2018). http://dx.doi.org/10.1109/tip.2017.2760518
9. Kang, L., Ye, P., Li, Y., Doermann, D.: Convolutional neural networks for no-reference image quality assessment (2014). http://dx.doi.org/10.1109/cvpr.2014.224
10. Zhang, Y., Gao, X., He, L., Lu, W., He, R.: Objective video quality assessment combining transfer learning with CNN (2019). http://dx.doi.org/10.1109/tnnls.2018.2890310
11. Ye, P., Kumar, J., Kang, L., Doermann, D.: Unsupervised feature learning framework for no-reference image quality assessment (2012). http://dx.doi.org/10.1109/cvpr.2012.6247789
12. Shao, F., Li, K., Lin, W., Jiang, G., Yu, M., Dai, Q.: Full-reference quality assessment of stereoscopic images by learning binocular receptive field properties. IEEE Trans. Image Process. **24**, 2971–2983 (2015). https://doi.org/10.1109/TIP.2015.2436332
13. Zhang, Y., Zhang, H., Yu, M., Kwong, S., Ho, Y.-S.: Sparse representation based video quality assessment for synthesized 3D videos. IEEE Trans. Image Process. (2019). https://doi.org/10.1109/TIP.2019.2929433
14. Rijnders, C.E.: U.S. Patent Application No. 15/899,331 (2018)
15. Seshadrinathan, K., Soundararajan, R., Bovik, A.C., Cormack, L.K.: Study of subjective and objective quality assessment of video (2010). http://dx.doi.org/10.1109/tip.2010.2042111
16. Shen, J., Itti, L.: Top-down influences on visual attention during listening are modulated by observer sex. Vis. Res. **65**, 62–76 (2012). https://doi.org/10.1016/j.visres.2012.06.001
17. Rimac-Drlje, S., Vranješ, M., Žagar, D.: Foveated mean squared error—a novel video quality metric (2016). http://dx.doi.org/10.1007/s11042-009-0442-1
18. Vranješ, M., Rimac-Drlje, S., Grgić, K.: Review of objective video quality metrics and performance comparison using different databases. Sign. Process.-Image Commun. (2012). http://dx.doi.org/10.1016/j.image.2012.10.003
19. Corriveau, P., Webster, A.: The video quality experts group: evaluates objective methods of video image quality assessment (1998). http://dx.doi.org/10.5594/m00304
20. Mele, M.L., Millar, D., Rijnders, C.E.: The web-based subjective quality assessment of an adaptive image compression plug-in (2017). http://dx.doi.org/10.5220/0006226401330137
21. Mele, M.L., Millar, D., Rijnders, C.E.: Sencogi spatio-temporal saliency: a new metric for predicting subjective video quality on mobile devices. In: Kurosu, M. (ed.) HCI 2018. LNCS, vol. 10902, pp. 552–564. Springer, Cham (2018). https://doi.org/10.1007/978-3-319-91244-8_43

22. Mele, M.L., Millar, D., Rijnders, C.E.: Using spatio-temporal saliency to predict subjective video quality: a new high-speed objective assessment metric. In: Kurosu, M. (ed.) HCI 2017. LNCS, vol. 10271, pp. 353–368. Springer, Cham (2017). https://doi.org/10.1007/978-3-319-58071-5_27

23. Mele, M.L., Colabrese, S., Calabria, L., Millar, D., Rijnders, C.E.: The assessment of sencogi: a visual complexity model predicting visual fixations. In: Kurosu, M. (ed.) HCII 2019. LNCS, vol. 11567, pp. 332–347. Springer, Cham (2019). https://doi.org/10.1007/978-3-030-22643-5_26

Play to Improve: Gamifying Usability Evaluations in Virtual Reality

Abhijai Miglani[✉], Sairam Kidambi[✉], and Praveen Mareguddi[✉]

Philips Innovation Campus, Bengaluru, Karnataka, India
{abhijai.miglani,sairam.kidambi,praveen.mareguddi}@philips.com

Abstract. Objective: The research study focuses on evaluating how usability engineering related activities would look like in virtual reality from an exploratory point of view. Research questions for the study are: a) What quantitative impact does an environment have on the usability evaluation of software interface components? b) How is this impact different in virtual environment as compared to physical environment? c) What could be the best interaction design representation in virtual reality which could have a similar mental model for the users as having a mouse and keyboard in physical environment? d) What role does another user/a virtual mannequin and other elements/objects play on influencing the usability evaluation results in virtual reality?

Background: As per ISO 62366 and Food and drugs administration (FDA) guidelines, simulating usage environment when evaluating software components is crucial. However, with conventional lab environment usability testing sessions have no environment simulated in it.

The research focuses on how the transition path (moving from physical to virtual environment) would look like if a researcher wants to thoroughly evaluate a design concept in virtual reality.

Method: Participants ($N = 8$) participated in the experiment to evaluate 3 interaction design concepts in virtual reality (1) gaze timer: seeing the virtual monitor for 3 s to go to the next page in the workflow, (2) gaze click: seeing the virtual monitor and using controller to aim and go to the next page in the workflow, and (3) gaze gesture: seeing the virtual monitor and using controller to pick-drag-drop a page in the workflow stack to another location. The three interaction design concepts varied in physical workload, cognitive workload, familiarity, learning curve and readability. The experiment design was a within subject design.

Results: Participants preferred gaze click interaction design concept over gaze timer and gaze gesture concept.

Conclusion: Having a virtual environment added to a conventional lab/physical environment, transition could be possible. Replacement of controls like mouse and keyboard could be done by adding gaze click interaction.

Application: Results of the study could serve as providing design guidelines for simulation of software interfaces' usability evaluation in virtual reality.

Keywords: Virtual reality (VR) · Usability Engineering · Food and Drugs Administration (FDA) · Interaction design · Usage environment · Gamification

© Springer Nature Switzerland AG 2020
C. Stephanidis et al. (Eds.): HCII 2020, LNCS 12423, pp. 248–266, 2020.
https://doi.org/10.1007/978-3-030-60114-0_17

1   Introduction

The first Healthcare software components when manufactured follow ISO 62366 in the software development process they opt. As per ISO 62366, one of the major components to make the software products fail-safe from human error is to follow Usability Engineering or Human Factors Engineering. Usability Engineering requires the software manufactures to include multiple rounds of usability evaluation – formative and summative usability testing. This is also in accordance with the guidelines provided by Food and Drugs Administration (FDA). Moreover, these guidelines also suggest simulating usage environment when evaluating software components.

The type of environment or context – physical and social also effects the results of the components' usability evaluation as pointed by (Trivedi 2012). In this research, the researchers defined physical environment as refers to the environment in which user is tested and social environment as the environments having people involved. The laboratory evaluations do not simulate the context when usability testing is done with mobile phones, because laboratory settings lack the desired ecological validity. Similar claim also comes from (Park and Lim 1999) where they state that simulating the use settings is very hard, time consuming, expensive and lacks contextual factors. Field testing takes place in a more natural setting.

With respect to social context (Trivedi 2012) mentions people involved in usability evaluations can be the evaluators, the test monitors, the users, and other people who may not be directly involved with the evaluation, however, their presence can have a substantial effect on the results of usability evaluations.

(Tsiaousis and Giaglis 2008) examined the effects of environmental distractions on mobile website usability. They categorized the environmental distractions into auditory, visual and social. Results confirmed that environmental distractions have direct effect on mobile website usability.

Study by (Jacobsen et al. 1998) examines the evaluator effect in the usability tests. In their study four HCI research evaluators, all familiar with the theory and practice of usability analyzed four video tapes. The results indicate that only 20% of the 93 unique problems were detected by only a single evaluator. Severe problems were detected by more often by all four evaluators (41%) and less often by only one evaluator (22%), however, the evaluator effect remained substantial.

The product/prototype in the research study under focus offers an advantage over the conventional usability evaluation method by extending the method to include environment also as a component.

Similar work has been done by (Madathil and Greenstein 2011), where the researchers propose a synchronous remote usability testing, also using virtual environment for introducing environment in the traditional lab environment. The significance of this study is that the synchronous remote usability testing using virtual lab provides similar results as of the traditional lab method and in some respects it works better than the conventional approaches.

Interestingly, participants appeared to identify a slightly larger number of lower severity defects in the virtual lab environment than in the traditional lab and WebEx environments. The results of this study suggest that participants were productive and enjoyed the virtual lab condition, indicating the potential of a virtual world based approach as an alternative to the conventional approaches for synchronous usability testing.

Our research is novel in terms of the tools and the research methods opted. The research also has prime focus on evaluating the effect of virtual environment for usability evaluations (and less on remote usability testing). Also, due care was taken to address potential concerns that could arise due to acceptance of the prototype as a tool for usability evaluations. These concerns could arise because of user's familiarity and mental model with the tools used in the physical/lab environment for usability evaluations like mouse and keyboard for instance. Moreover, as part of exploration process, we are evaluating the contribution of different factors that would effect user's immersion in the environment and hence, acceptance of the prototype/tool.

As pointed out by (Rajanen and Rajanen 2017), for usability in gamification, there are some guidelines – define business objectives, delineate target behaviors, describe your behaviors, device activity loops, do not forget the fun and deploy the appropriate loops. The prototype designed to answer the research questions is a game (see section – prototype design) having components like instructions/demo given by a virtual mannequin, tasks being performed by the user, rewards obtained being the pleasure out of evaluation of design.

However, with the inclusion of environment and including all the components in virtual reality (that were part of physical environment), the accuracy of the results could change and could be different as when validated in physical environment.

The research focuses on how the transition path (moving from physical to virtual environment) would look like if a researcher wants to thoroughly evaluate a design concept in virtual reality. Results of the research study could serve as providing design guidelines for simulation of software interfaces' usability evaluation in virtual reality. These design guidelines if standardized by also including software as a medical device (SAMD) components, could help further in the FDA submissions.

Research questions for the study are: a) What quantitative impact does an environment have on the usability evaluation of software interface components? b) How is this impact different in virtual environment as compared to physical environment? c) What could be the best interaction design representation in virtual reality which could have a similar mental model for the users as having a mouse and keyboard in physical environment? d) What role does another user/a virtual mannequin and other elements/objects play on influencing the usability evaluation results in virtual reality?

For answering the research questions, two research hypotheses were framed. For the first research hypothesis, independent variable was chosen as environment realism and dependent variable was chosen as task success rate. Environment realism could be further segregated into components like social presence, objects in virtual reality, lighting – textures – materials and audiovisual cartography. Second hypothesis describes different constructs for the interaction modalities/prototype - independent variable and its behavior with respect to task success rate - dependent variable.

Figure 1 shows the first hypothesis - difference in task success rate for different environments with respect to environment realism.

Figure 2 shows the second hypothesis - difference in task success rate for different interaction modalities/prototypes with respect to modalities' properties.

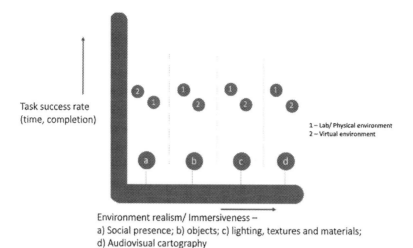

Task success rate
(time, completion)

1 – Lab/ Physical environment
2 – Virtual environment

Environment realism/ Immersiveness –
a) Social presence; b) objects; c) lighting, textures and materials;
d) Audiovisual cartography

Fig. 1. First hypothesis graph showing effect of environment realism on task success rate

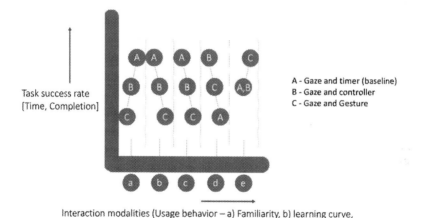

Task success rate
[Time, Completion]

A - Gaze and timer (baseline)
B - Gaze and controller
C - Gaze and Gesture

Interaction modalities (Usage behavior – a) Familiarity, b) learning curve,
c) Physical workload, d) Cognitive workload, and e) Readability)

Fig. 2. Second hypothesis graph showing effect of interaction design concepts' properties and task success rate

The research hypothesis was framed considering the unified technology acceptance model.

Environment realism variance is correlated to habit, effort expectancy, performance expectancy factor, social influence, hedonic motivation, age, gender, experience and facilitating conditions.

Interaction modality design intuitiveness is related to facilitating conditions and effort and performance expectancy, age, gender, experience, habit and hedonic motivation.

The independent variables are related to performance and effort expectancy and hence, user behavior (task success rate – dependent variable).

2 Method

2.1 Apparatus

A stock Oculus Rift was used with the two controllers. However, for the experiment, only right hand controller was used. The Oculus Rift also comes with two sensors for setting the space/boundary, which was also used.

The computer used for simulating the experiment was HP ZBook 15 G3 with 16 GB RAM and i7, 2.7 GHz.

In the experiment, Philips Ingenia 3.0 T MRi machine was simulated with appropriate noise coming from the machine.

2.2 Ethnography Studies

To study the environment that has to be simulated in virtual reality, a site visit was done where Philips Ingenia 3.0 T MR system is installed.

Philips Ingenia 3.0 T MR machine is a magnetic resonance machine by Royal Philips. The machine has a software user interface also to control the machine.

Position and movement of the objects in the room, movement of hospital staff, lighting and noise conditions were studied.

More importantly, tasks performed by the hospital staff were analyzed. In the room next to the room where MR system is installed, the technologist is responsible for initiating, capturing and analyzing patient's scans. The administrator is responsible for assisting the technologist with patient data entry and printing the scans.

2.3 Participatory Design Workshop

For ideation of the ethnographic research results, a participatory design workshop - Storyply was conducted. Storyply method was developed by (Atasoy and Martens n.d.). The method describes 9 steps to convert a research problem into design ideas. When ethnographic research results were presented to the participants in form of research problem, 3 design ideas came out, out of one was included in the prototype design. Participants suggested to have a demonstration of the usability session in virtual reality. This idea was included in the prototype design in form of stage-1 of the game - instructions. Please refer to section - prototype design for more details.

2.4 Prototype Design

Three set of prototypes were designed in virtual reality and each set was categorized as 3 stages for the participant to complete – introduction, performance and exit. The introduction and the exit was common across the 3 sets. Whereas, the performance stage varied based on the research hypothesis (interaction design in this case) to be evaluated. The prototype concepts were designed considering the heuristics suggested by (Sutcliffe and Gault 2004).

The three sets consisting of 3 stages each are shown as a storyboard in Fig. 3. As shown in the figure, based on the interaction design – gaze timer or gaze click or gaze gesture, the participants had to perform the task of undergoing through the workflow of MR Ingenia 3.0 software interface. The workflow of the application consists of pages - patient selection, exam routine selection, exam routine start, print area/layout mapping and end acquisition. Other than gaze timer and gaze click, in gaze gesture, the workflow pages were arranged as separate blocks (as a stack) on top of each other which the participant had to pick, drag and drop to another location. In gaze timer and gaze click, participants had to look at the pages (to initiate the workflow) and click using the right controller.

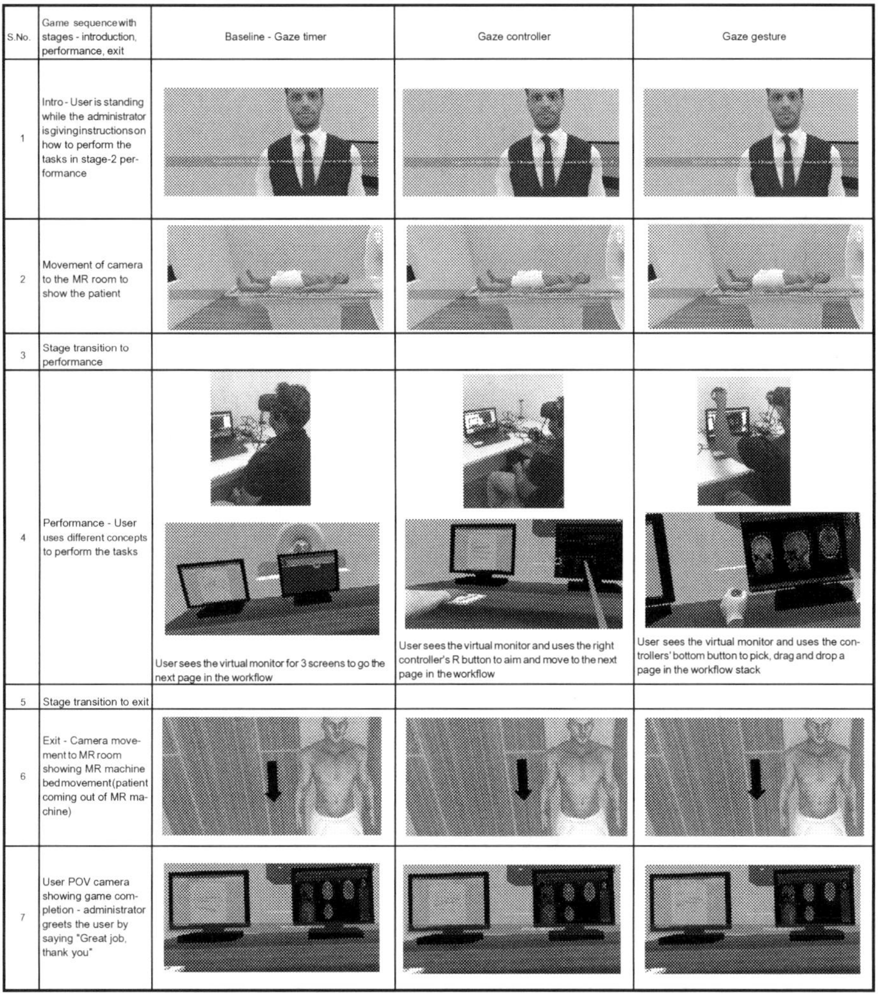

Fig. 3. Storyboard showing timeline for actions in Concept A: Gaze timer, Concept B: Gaze click and Concept C: Gaze gesture

For gaze timer, the gaze was denoted as a circular cursor/crosshair as shown in Fig. 3. For gaze click, the controller was used to aim at a point of any page followed by clicking on controller's 'A' button. The aiming was aided by showing a pink colored ray. In gaze gesture, virtual hands were present to aid picking of pages from the stack.

The interaction design concepts varied (refer to section - introduction) in terms of familiarity, learning curve, physical workload, cognitive workload and readability. For Concept – A: Gaze timer, familiarity and task success rate was hypothesized to be the highest followed by Concept B: Gaze click and Concept C: Gaze gesture. The hypothesis was based on the fact that more the familiarity, more would be the task success rate. As in Concept C, gestures were involved, it could come as something new to the participants. Whereas, in Concept A, participant just had to look at the virtual monitor to go to the next page in the workflow. Participants would be more familiar with the seeing task than the inclusion of gestures in the task. Learning curve for Concept C would be highest (with least task success rate) as participants would be least familiar with the gesture system.

With respect to Concept C, physical workload would be highest as it involves physical movements for picking-dragging-dropping the pages of a stack to another location. With physical workload highest for Concept C, task success rate would be least as it would take maximum time with respect to Concept A (just seeing would involve least physical workload) and Concept B.

With respect to cognitive workload, Concept A had the highest cognitive workload (with least success rate) followed by Concept C and B. For Concept A, participants would be looking at the virtual monitor for 3 s with 'proper focus' to go to the next page in the workflow. Concept B and C did not require participants to focus at the virtual monitor. However, concept C involved pick-drag-drop functionality which requires participants' attentional resources to complete the task.

In Concept-C pick-drag-drop functionality is provided, the participants can move a page of the workflow closer to have a better look at the content of the page (unlike in Concept A and B). Readability improves with having affordance of having the functionality to read the content of a page.

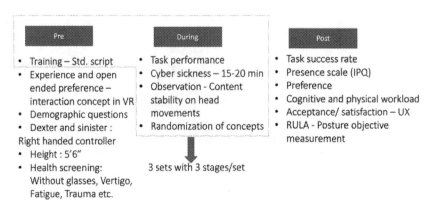

Fig. 4. Experiment design containing pre, during and post experiment sections

The prototype designed is modular in nature i.e. the same prototype could be used to evaluate any other system with the required adjustments in some components. There is a base component to the prototype which could be kept as common across any system evaluation.

Also, the 3 sets of game were designed keeping a time frame of 15–20 min into consideration. A game set having this time duration would ensure the participants do not feel cyber sick due to their continuous exposure to virtual reality.

As shown in the Fig. 3, the introduction stage had the assistant explaining the tasks to be performed by the participant in stage 2 - performance. As mentioned by (Junglas et al. 2007) trust in digital identities is crucial for immersion in virtual reality. To maintain the immersion levels, photorealistic mannequins were used with appropriate body joint movements and synchronization with the speech. Also spatial auditory noise was simulated to be coming from the MR room to enhance the immersion.

Furthermore, following the site visit done in ethnography studies stage, the usability room was designed in virtual reality taking the site visited as reference – with appropriate lighting, textures and materials applied on the objects in the room.

As pointed out in section – introduction, the virtual reality room was designed keeping the concept of gamification into consideration and designing different stages of the game accordingly. Each stage has a transition in between to make the movement between one stage to another a smooth one. With respect to the first and the third stage, some animations were designed including camera positions with its movements and subtitles on the footer.

2.5 Procedure

To evaluate the research hypothesis framed, a within experiment design was framed as shown in Fig. 4.

All participants had to fill a pre-experiment survey before they started participating in the experiment. The survey had questions related to participants' demographics (including height and if they wear eye glasses), experience with virtual reality technology, dexterity etc.

Due to the virtual mannequin of the assistant/administrator incorporated in the game and the eye point of the participant in virtual reality, it was crucial to ask the participants about their height. Also, the contrast of the overall prototype designed in virtual reality could have varied if the participants had eyeglasses. Hence, these parameters were covered as part of pre-experiment survey.

After filling the survey, the participants proceeded with wearing the Oculus Rift headgear. As mentioned before, the tasks to be performed by the participants were incorporated as a 'virtual speech script' in the game's introduction stage. The script also described how to go about performing the tasks using the three interaction modalities.

As mentioned above, the three interaction design concepts had variation in physical workload, cognitive workload, readability ease, familiarity/learnability. After the experiment was performed, the participants had to fill questionnaires pertaining to all these parameters/dependent variables. For workload, NASA – TLX was consulted and for acceptance/satisfaction – SUS scale was referred to.

Preference was also asked – which out of the 3 concepts would you prefer using?

Also, change in posture due to movements of head, elbow, hands, fingers and upper back portions of participants' body when experiencing the interaction design concepts was captured using rapid upper limb assessment (RULA) method.

Moreover, task completion rates were also captured.

Last but not the least, behavioral validity of the prototype having components like presence, realism etc. was captured using igroup presence questionnaire (IPQ).

3 Results

A convenience sample of 8 user interface/experience designers working at Philips Innovation Campus was taken. Out of the 8 participants, 5 participants wore glasses. It was critical to ask participants if they wear glasses as the virtual reality Oculus head-gear they had to wear did not allow glasses. Without the glasses, readability of the content could have been an issue.

Participants were also screened for health. All but one participant was found to be healthy as per the questionnaire designed. A participant had a history of migraines, had ear and balance problems and was claustrophobic.

Health screening questionnaire was essential to prevent participants feeling cyber sick. For the same reason, the content in virtual reality restrained to 15–20 min.

With respect to the demographics questionnaire, 7 out of 8 participants belonged to the age group 25–40 and one participant belonged to the age group 41–60. Gender wise, 5 participants were males and 3 were females.

All participants were working on different products and had no overlap in the work they were doing.

Participants were also asked to mention any other design idea (other than the design concepts) by which they would like to create a digital version of usability evaluations.

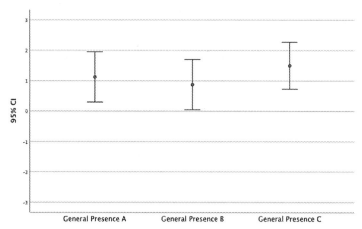

Fig. 5. General presence construct of IPQ scores for Concept A gaze timer, B gaze click and C gaze gesture

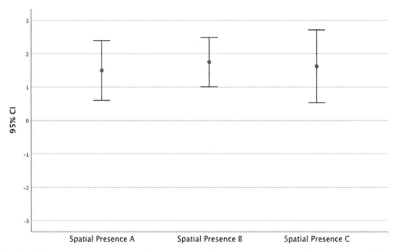

Fig. 6. Spatial presence construct of IPQ scores for Concept A gaze timer, B gaze click and C gaze gesture

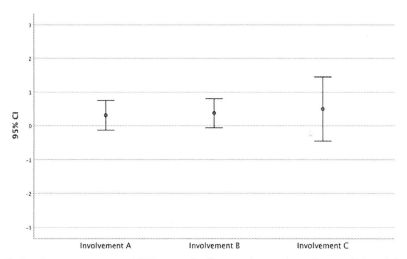

Fig. 7. Involvement construct of IPQ scores for Concept A gaze timer, B gaze click and C gaze gesture

Most of the participants had varied feedback varying from having voice feedback commands to having augmented reality based mobile application. Also, as per the participants, they considered having a digital version of usability evaluations as highly useful (75%) and neutral (25%).

Hands' dexterity was also asked from participants and majority were right-handed. One participant was ambidextrous. This question was essential to ask as participants had to use their right hand for controlling the right controller while evaluating concept B and C.

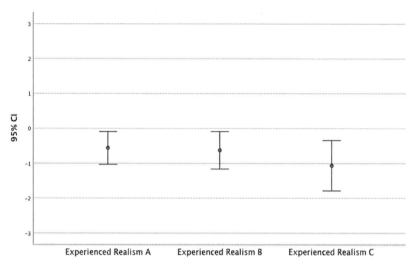

Fig. 8. Experienced realism construct of IPQ scores for Concept A gaze timer, B gaze click and C gaze gesture

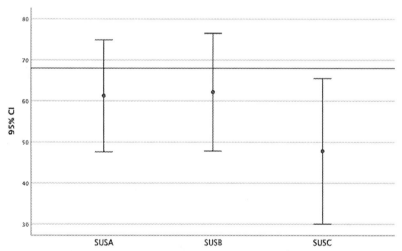

Fig. 9. System usability scale (SUS) scores with threshold value of 68 for Concept A gaze timer, B gaze click and C gaze gesture

Moreover, the most important need and most critical task if participants were playing a radiologist or a technologist was also asked. The tasks given as options were reading content, scrolling up/down or zooming in/out and using mouse to go to the next screen. Whereas the needs given as options were learnability of the application, readability of the content and comfortable workflow. Reading the content and comfortable workflow were the options majority of the participants marked as most important task and need respectively.

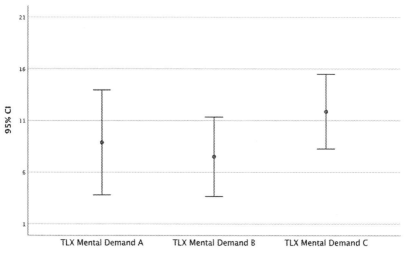

Fig. 10. Mental demand construct scores (Task load index – TLX) for Concept A gaze timer, B gaze click and C gaze gesture

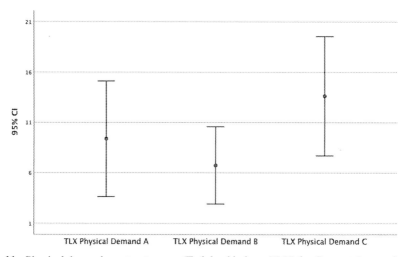

Fig. 11. Physical demand construct scores (Task load index – TLX) for Concept A gaze timer, B gaze click and C gaze gesture

First dependent variable being general presence, the order varied with different concepts as shown in Fig. 5. Concept C had the highest general presence followed by Concept A and B. Other than Concept A, normality tests (Shapiro wilk) showed the significance as more than 0.05. Hence, both ANOVA and Friedmann tests were conducted. Friedmann tests showed $x^2 = 2.381$, df $= 2$, p $= 0.304 > 0.05$. Furthermore, Mauchy's test of sphericity showed approx. x^2 value as 0.325 with p as 0.850. Hence, Huynh Feldt test was conducted to study effect of different concepts on general presence variable. It was

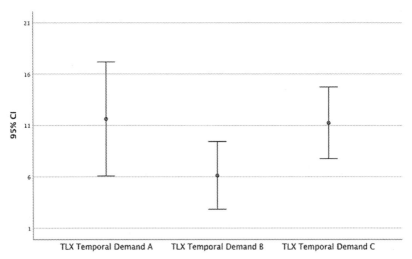

Fig. 12. Temporal demand construct scores (Task load index – TLX) for Concept A gaze timer, B gaze click and C gaze gesture

found out that F(2,14) – 1.727, p = 0.214 > 0.05 and quadratic trend was non-significant with F(1,7) – 2.054, P = 0.195 > 0.05.

Spatial presence being the second dependent variable has the order variation with different concepts shown in Fig. 6. Concept B had the highest spatial presence followed by Concept C and A. As per Shapiro-wilk test of normality, no concept had normally distributed data as significance for all concepts were more than 0.05. Hence, Friedmann test was done further. Friedmann tests showed the effect of different concepts on spatial presence as non-significant - x^2 = 0.471, df = 2, p = 0.79 > 0.05.

For involvement, the order variation with different concepts is as shown in Fig. 7. Concept C had the highest score followed by Concept B and A. Shapiro Wilk's test of normality did not show any significance for any concept and hence, Friedmann test was followed to test significance of effect of different concepts on Involvement scores. Friedmann test showed x^2 = 0.4, df = 2, p = 0.819 > 0.05.

Normality tests – Shapiro Wilk showed no significance for experience realism as per different concepts. Friedmann test was followed to test significance of effect of different concepts - x^2 = 2.471, df = 2, p = 0.291 > 0.05. The order for values of experienced realism as per different concepts was Concept A had the highest value followed by Concept B and C (Fig. 8).

For system usability, system usability score (SUS) was the highest for Concept B followed by Concept A and C. Normality tests – Shapiro Wilk showed significance for no concept and hence, Friedmann test were conducted to test effect of different concepts on system usability - x^2 = 1.742, df = 2, p = 0.419 > 0.05 (Fig. 9).

For task load index, Mental demand had the highest score for Concept C followed by Concept A and B. Normality tests – Shapiro Wilk showed significance for no concept and hence, Friedmann test were conducted to test effect of different concepts on Mental Demand - x^2 = 6.467, df = 2, p = 0.039 < 0.05 (significant) (Fig. 10).

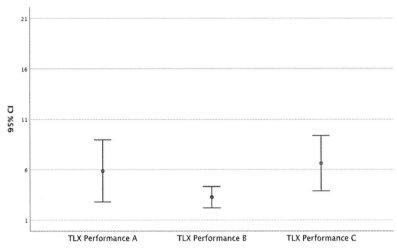

Fig. 13. Performance construct scores (Task load index – TLX) for Concept A gaze timer, B gaze click and C gaze gesture

On the other hand, Physical demand scored highest for Concept C followed by Concept A and B. Normality tests – Shapiro Wilk showed significance for no concept and hence, Friedmann test were conducted to test effect of different concepts on Physical demand - $x^2 = 6.870$, df $= 2$, p $= 0.032 < 0.05$ (significant) (Fig. 11).

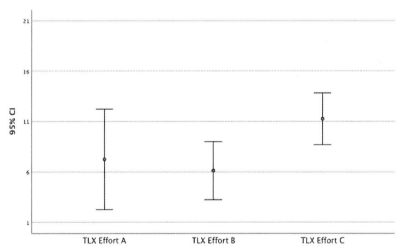

Fig. 14. Effort construct scores (Task load index – TLX) for Concept A gaze timer, B gaze click and C gaze gesture

Temporal demand construct had the highest score for Concept A followed by Concept C and B. Shapiro Wilk test for normality showed no significance for any concept and hence, Friedmann test was conducted to test effect of different concepts on Temporal Demand - $x^2 = 5.067$, df $= 2$, p $= 0.079 > 0.05$ (Fig. 12).

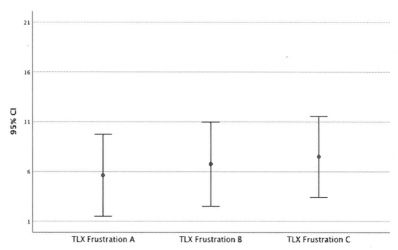

Fig. 15. Frustration construct scores (Task load index – TLX) for Concept A gaze timer, B gaze click and C gaze gesture

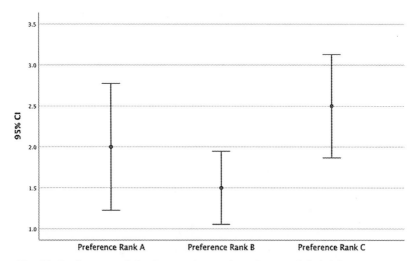

Fig. 16. Preference rank for Concept A gaze timer, B gaze click and C gaze gesture

Performance scored highest for Concept C followed by A and B. Shapiro wilk, the test for normality showed no significance for any concept. Friedmann tests concluded $x^2 = 3.267$, df $= 2$, p=0.195 > 0.05 (Fig. 13).

Effort scored highest for Concept C followed by A and B. Shapiro wilk showed no significance for normality of any of the concepts. Friedmann test scored $x^2 = 5.429$, df $= 2$, p $= 0.066 > 0.05$ (Fig. 14).

Frustration had highest score for Concept C followed by Concept B and A. Shapiro wilk showed significant normality for just Concept B. Friedmann test scored $x^2 = 1.786$, df = 2, p = 0.409 > 0.05. Whereas in ANOVA Mauchy's test for sphericity showed approx. x^2 value as 0.788 with p as 0.674. The effect of concepts on frustration was non-significant, Huynh Feldt scored $F(2,14) - 0.549$, p = 0.59 > 0.05. Linear trend of the frustration scores was also non-significant $F(1,7) - 1.305$, p = 0.291 > 0.05 (Fig. 15).

Rapid upper limb assessment (RULA) scores for concept B and C were measured and it came out to be 2 and 4–6 respectively showing actions needed for concept C. However, posture was acceptable for Concept B.

Most importantly, Preference scored rank 1 for Concept B, rank 2 for Concept A and rank 3 for Concept C. Normality test – Shapiro Wilk showed significance for all concepts. In ANOVA Mauchy's test of sphericity showed approx. x^2 value as 2.433 with p as 0.296. The effect of concepts on preference rank was non-significant, Huynh Feldt – $F(1.818, 12.727) - 2.333$, p = 0.140 > 0.05. The quadratic trend for different concepts' preference ranking was significant – $F(1,7) - 7$, P = 0.033 < 0.05 (Fig. 16).

For Concept A, qualitative feedback included comments about the timer – "timer was less, it should be more than what it is right now (3 s)", easiness – "The task was easy, no physical demand was required", control – "no control was sensed, I was not aware when I was controlling". A word cloud is shown in Fig. 17.

Fig. 17. Word cloud for comments and improvement suggestions received for Concept A gaze timer

Fig. 18. Word cloud for comments and improvement suggestions received for Concept B gaze click

Fig. 19. Word cloud for comments and improvement suggestions received for Concept C gaze gesture

For Concept B, feedback was positive – "I am able to control my actions, easy and smooth", "I am doing what I want to do" and "No focus required to complete the tasks" (Fig. 18).

For Concept C, feedback was mixed – "It takes effort to complete the tasks", "Readability is good", "Requires learning", "Tasks were not realistic with respect to physical model of screens in a monitor", "Experience was good as I can have more screens in front of me". Other improvement suggestions included having the functionality of grabbing the screens from a distance to avoid bending in the posture (Fig. 19).

4 Discussion

In this study, we used a prototype to simulate environment for the conventional usability lab environment. The prototype was designed to answer the research questions and were inclined towards the research hypothesis framed.

With respect to the first research question, as per (Trivedi 2012), physical and social environment can influence results in usability evaluation of a software component.

With respect to influence of different factors like visual, auditory and social on usability evaluation results, (Tsiaousis and Giaglis 2008) confirmed that environmental distractions have direct effect on direct impact on usability. Also, (Jacobsen et al. 1998) showed the impact of having another evaluator (social presence) on usability evaluation results.

For virtual environments, system usability scores (SUS) for the three interaction concepts designed namely, gaze timer, gaze click and gaze gesture had mean scores falling below the threshold value of 68. This shows that virtual environment does affect the usability when virtual environment interaction concepts are used (as compared to mouse or keyboard used in physical environment).

Moreover, positive correlations were found between gaze gesture concept and involvement construct (spearmann rho – 0.723, p-0.043) and experienced realism construct (spearmann rho – 0.704, p-0.051). Gaze gesture concept having lowest usability, had highest involvement and lowest experienced realism as compared to the other two interaction concepts.

For the third research question, participants preferred concept B: gaze click the most. Evidently, participants prefer to have control on the actions they are performing – similar to mouse and keyboard. Moreover, RULA scores also showed an acceptable posture for the concept. This is also in line with the usability scores (highest), mental demand scores (lowest), physical demand scores (lowest), temporal demand scores (lowest) and effort scores (lowest).

When making a transition from a physical environment or a conventional lab environment to having a virtual environment, gaze click concept can be used to control the workflow of pages. This guideline can be used further by other researchers working on usability engineering in virtual reality theme.

References

Trivedi, M.: Role of context in usability evaluations: a review. ACIJ (2012)
Park, K.S., Lim, C.H.: A structured methodology for comparative evaluation of user interface designs using usability criteria and measures. Int. J. Ind. Ergon. **23**, 379–389 (1999)

Tsiaousis, A.S., Giaglis, G.M.: Evaluating the effects of the environmental context-of-use on mobile website usability, pp. 314–322 (2008)

Jacobsen, N., Hertzum, M., John, B.: The evaluator effect in usability studies: problem detection and severity judgments. In: Human Factors and Ergonomics Society 42nd Annual Meeting, pp. 1336–1340 (1998)

Madathil, K.C., Greenstein, J.S.: Synchronous Remote Usability Testing - A New Approach Facilitated By Virtual Worlds. *CHI*. ACM, Vancouver (2011)

Rajanen, M., Rajanen, D.: GamiFIN, Pori, Finland (2017)

Atasoy, B., Martens, J.-B.: STORYPLY: designing for user experiences using storycraft. In: Markopoulos, P., Martens, J.-B., Malins, J., Coninx, K., Liapis, A. (eds.) Collaboration in Creative Design, pp. 181–210. Springer, Cham (2016). https://doi.org/10.1007/978-3-319-291 55-0_9

Junglas, I.A., Johnson, N.A., Steel, D.J., Abraham, D.C., Loughlin, P.M.: Identity formation, learning styles and trust in virtual worlds. DATA BASE Adv. Inf. Syst. **38**, 90–96 (2007)

Sutcliffe, A., Gault, B.: Heuristic evaluation of virtual reality applications. Int. Comput. **16**, 831–849 (2004)

Assessing the Human Factor of Cybersecurity: Can Surveys Tell the Truth?

Špela Orehek[1]([⊠]) [iD], Gregor Petrič[1] [iD], and Jan Šinigoj[2]

[1] Faculty of Social Sciences, University of Ljubljana, Ljubljana, Slovenia
{spela.orehek,gregor.petric}@fdv.uni-lj.si
[2] Plinovodi d.o.o., Ljubljana, Slovenia
jan.sinigoj@plinovodi.si

Abstract. Survey-based measuring plays an important role in exploring human behavior. In organizational context, self-reporting of behaviors, attitudes, norms etc. can often lead to people responding in line with expectations rather than reality. Particularly when answering sensitive questions, respondents can disguise the truth for various reasons. This is called a social desirability effect (SDE) and poses a key problem in the field of behavioral studies because it can significantly bias the findings of research. A number of methods to prevent or detect SDE exist. The aim of the paper is to test selected techniques for decreasing SDE in survey-based measuring of information security behavior and to propose an improved scale, minimally susceptible to SDE. We used a cross-sectional survey design with a split-ballot experiment across three companies of critical infrastructure in Slovenia (n = 414). Four groups of employees received versions of information security behavior scale with different combinations of negative, positive and forgiving item wording. No universal group and item type effect of forgiving and alternating item wording was found with testing of the Balanced Inventory of Desirable Responding (BIDR) scale. However, it turns out that the content of items matters because one of methods perform differently for different types of behavioral items. Moreover, the part of analysis showed that combination of forgiving and alternating item wording might be effective in minimizing SDE. Items with best properties were chosen to establish new information security behavior scale. The majority of items were chosen from groups with alternating item wording, especially the one combining positive and forgiving items.

Keywords: Information security behavior · Social desirability effect · Cybersecurity · Forgiving wording · Alternating item wording · Balanced Inventory of Desirable Responding (BIDR) scale

1 Introduction

In the last years a number of concepts were developed that address the human factor in information security, but it is clear that the most critical element is employee's behavior when using IT devices on workplace [36, 46]. Risky behavior increases the potential for various abuses and thus threatens the overall organizational security [7, 21].

© Springer Nature Switzerland AG 2020
C. Stephanidis et al. (Eds.): HCII 2020, LNCS 12423, pp. 267–281, 2020.
https://doi.org/10.1007/978-3-030-60114-0_18

It is thus very important to assess to what extent behaviors of employees are acting (in)securely. Currently different methods exist, from phishing simulations, to collecting data streams of employees' uses of IT devices as direct observation, and indirectly with surveys which enable more sophisticated statistical analyses. The latter remain especially important in attempts to provide socio-psychological explanation and predictions of user behaviors. While all methods have certain limitations, assessing behavior of employees via self-reporting can be problematic as respondents might provide answers in line with what is expected from them and not what is the reality. As employees are aware of the importance of information security, they may avoid providing honest answers regarding their activities. In social science research methodology this phenomenon is captured with the concept of social desirability effect (SDE), which can significantly bias the results of empirical study and hinders the validity and objectivity of research. This consequently leads to organizations making bad decisions [31]. Research offers a number of scales for survey-based measuring of information security behavior, but it is obvious that they are susceptible to social desirability bias [24]. Therefore, the aim of this paper is to present and test selected techniques to examine SDE in survey-based measuring of information security behavior and propose an improved scale considering the SDE. More specifically, we will examine to what extent forgiving and alternating item wording are prone to SDE in comparison with the negatively worded scale of information security behavior.

2 Theoretical Background

2.1 Information Security Behavior

Information security behavior is a key element to maintain the organizational information security [22]. The term is derived from organizational behavior, which signifies the patterns of employee' activities toward improving organizational performance and effectiveness [29, 37]. Therefore, information security behavior refers to employees' set of security activities and responses in critical moments that are manifested in the form of their behavioral patterns in their daily work [32, 39]. Some researchers define information security behavior as intention or actual compliance with information security policy [16, 21, 32, 47], which explicitly means following established rules regarding information security [16]. Information security behaviors are related to the interaction with organizational information and communication technologies (ICT) and are manifested through (a) device use (handling computers/mobiles), (b) internet use (opening e-mails and links/attachments, downloading software, Wi-Fi), (c) password management (handling and sharing passwords) and (d) dealing with organizational data [5, 13, 19, 40]. There are different versions of information security behavior. For example, risky behavior refers to behavior when employees intentionally disregard the information security policy even though they know it (the knowing–doing gap) [7], and insecure behavior that is mostly unintentional where employees subconsciously perform dubious security practices [13]. On the other hand, secure (compliant) behavior refers to expected and exemplary acting according the rules of information security. Within the theory of enlightened self-interest, the knowledge-attitude-behavior (KAB) model, which has been already studied in field of information security, substantiates that secure behavior is to some extent related to security knowledge [22, 33].

2.2 Social Desirability Effect

Social desirability reflects the tendency of people to deny socially undesirable traits and prefer to identify themselves with socially desirable traits that presents them in the best possible manner [9, 30]. Consequently, SDE is considered as a cognitive bias, resulting from the insincere responding to questions. Such answers may skew the findings of the study in terms of validity and reliability, especially in behavioral studies. From the view of information security behavior, most problematic are the individuals who (self)report more secure behaviors than they actually perform in their workplace. Therefore, this is a problem for researchers and organizational decision makers because they do not get insight into the true state of affairs regarding organizational information security. Main reasons for insincerity and socially desirable responses of employees are (a) a lack of self-confidence to disclose their true views, (b) intrusive (awkwardly asked) questions that encourage an individual's sense of embarrassment and discomfort with interfering with his privacy, (c) awareness or potential threat of disclosure to third parties in terms of anonymity and (d) a sense of satisfaction in a socially desirable response [11, 18, 45]. Threat to anonymity, in particular, might be most relevant in terms of organizational context, as employees have a sense that survey is intended primarily for their evaluation and the results can affect their career (in a negative or positive way). Another reason might be an employees' good feeling when giving a socially desirable response, as they often know what is the proper security behavior while acting differently.

In exploring human factor of information security, the possible bias of self-reporting was highlighted by Lebek et al. [24], while the issue of social desirability bias specifically has received only little (indirect) attention in this area [15]. Researchers used various techniques to reduce SDE, such as enabling anonymity, offering no incentive for participation and adjustments to the introductory text [16, 38], designing items with a fictional character scenario [27, 28] or hypothetical situations [17]. Furthermore, the predominant methods to detect SDE are inclusion of the Marlowe-Crowne social desirability scale in the survey questionnaire [48], testing the bias with the method of single unmeasured latent factor [15, 16] and analyzing the reliability of the over-claiming items [26]. Social science methodology offers numerous approaches to reduce the SDE using preventive or detective techniques. Preventive techniques seek to reduce the SDE prior to data collection, while detection techniques discover the SDE after it. In addition to above mentioned techniques, there are other useful (and suitable for online surveying) preventive methods like indirect questions, forgiving wording [23], negative formulation of questions [31] and others. In this paper we focus on three techniques for exploring SDE; preventive techniques of forgiving wording and alternating item wording and a detective method of Balanced Inventory of Desirable Responding (BIDR) scale. None of them have not been used in the field of information security.

2.3 Forgiving Wording and Alternating Item Wording

The forgiving wording technique refers to modifications of survey items by adding a prior (introductory) soothing sentence or a set of words with soothing function to a sensitive survey question or statement. The purpose of forgiving wording is to reduce the sense of intrusion and to explain the legitimacy of the question in the sense that each answer is correct or equally acceptable [10]. In this way, respondent is provided with socially acceptable reasons for his/her potentially unwanted social thinking or behavior [23, 45]. Consequently, this relieves the pressure of respondent on more sensitive topics and gives a hope for his/her response as honest as possible. Research on the use of such technique has shown that forgiving wording significantly contributes to the sincerity of answering on different sensitive topics [1, 2, 4]. Forgiving wording has a similar effect to the more often used technique of indirect questions because with both techniques we want to minimize the SDE using a prudent sets of words. They only differ in a way of presenting the questions; using forgiving wording we want to alleviate the critical situation with prior addressing, and with indirect questioning we use examples of hypothetical situations or characters and similarly do not put the respondent directly in an unpleasant position.

Alternating item wording is a common method to reduce acquiescent and extreme response bias. Acquiescent response bias reflects a tendency to select a positive response option without considering the question, while extreme response bias similarly reflects a tendency towards either lowest or highest response option. The alternation of positive and negative items encourages participants to consider the content of a question and thus provide a more meaningful response, thereby minimizing both biases [42]. We assume that more meaningful responses, elicited by alternating item wording should be less contaminated with SDE.

2.4   The BIDR Scale

The BIDR scale is commonly used measure of social desirability in surveys and it places a great deal of emphasis on exaggerated claims about an individual's positive cognitive attributes. Therefore, it is often treated as a measure of defense - people who achieve imaginary high self-esteem defend themselves against negative criticism by exposing inflated thinking stemming from their excessive self-evaluation [34]. In this way, they often express overconfident opinion in terms of rationality and sound judgement. The original scale consists of 40 statements on a 7-point Likert scale (where 1 means "*Not true*" and 7 means "*Very true*"). It was found out that short version of BIDR-16 demonstrates a high level of validity and reliability as well [14]. While the Marlowe-Crowne scale assumes one-dimensionality, the BIDR scale has two dimensions, self-deception enhancement (SE), which measures an individual's sincere but overly positive response, and impression management (IM), which measures the bias towards liking others [25]. However, the BIDR scale has not been used in the information security research so far but there are indications that it may perform well in this context as well [23].

3   Methodology

The data was collected in the context of master's degree [44] by means of a web survey that was prepared on platform 1KA. The design of our study combined a split-ballot experiment with a scale of information security behavior. It consists of 10 items on the 5-point Likert scale (where 1 means "*Definitely not true*" and 5 means "*Definitely true*"). Some items were adopted from one of previous studies [20], while others were formed by authors of this study. The experiment included one control group (insecure behavior scale) and three experimental groups with different versions of information security behavior scale, differentiated based on the two methods of preventing SDE. The effect of forgiving wording was examined in one experimental group and the effect of alternating item wording was examined in another group. The final experimental group combined the effects of both methods together. Additionally, the shortened version of the BIDR scale (6 items) was included in the last part of the questionnaire and was identical for all experimental groups. The empirical study was conducted in three companies of Slovenian critical infrastructure among 1320 employees. 448 questionnaires were returned with an overall response rate of 34%. Additionally, 34 units were deleted due to incompleteness (quick breakoff). The total sample size for the analysis is 414 employees. We used a pairwise deletion for treating the missing data. Table 1 presents basic sample characteristics.

Table 1. Basic sample characteristics.

	f / %
Returned questionnaires	448
Response rate	34 %
Gender	
Male	77.5 %
Female	22.5 %
Age	
Up to 29 years	3.8 %
30 to 49 years	61.0 %
50 years and more	35.2 %
Education	
High school or less	28.0 %
Undergraduate	64.0 %
Postgraduate	8.0 %

Table 2 presents the experimental design with detailed description of items and differences among groups. It also includes the example of one item per each group to illustrate different versions for different experimental groups.

In order to investigate the effect of forgiving and alternating item wording on susceptibility to SDE, we analyzed the item nonresponse, group means and distribution of information secure behavior items and their correlations with the BIDR scale. Firstly, in terms of item nonresponse, it was reported that more sensitive questions get more refusals [43]. Consequently, low item nonresponse rate using one of SDE prevention methods may indicate that these item versions are perceived as less threatening. Thus, they should be less prone to SDE. Secondly, reports of more common insecure behavior in a certain experimental group, indicated by a higher group mean and/or lower skewness

Table 2. Experimental design.

	Description	Example of item
Control group (n = 99)	All 10 items referring to insecure behavior (negatively worded items)	*I log into public (unsecured) Wi-Fi networks (e.g. at the airport, in bar), when I'm not at work.*
Experimental group – forgiving wording (n = 103)	All 10 items of insecure behavior with forgiving wording	*Because I need the internet to use my time off work productively, I log on to public (unsecured) Wi-Fi networks (e.g. at the airport, in bar).*
Experimental group – alternating item wording (n = 96)	Five items of insecure behavior and five reversed into secure behavior (positively worded items)	*I do not log into public (unsecured) Wi-Fi networks (e.g. at the airport, in bar), when I'm not at work.*
Experimental group – forgiving and alternating wording (n = 116)	Five items of insecure behavior (as in group 3) using forgiving wording and five reversed into secure behavior	*See example item from experimental group 2 and 3*

coefficients, might reflect more honest employees' responding. Thirdly, we calculated the scores of the BIDR scale. In scoring, each extreme answer (5 for SE and 4 or 5 for IM) yields one point (taking into account the alternating item wording). Higher scores are obtained by those respondents who give more socially desirable answers. The variable is an interval scale, ranging from 0 to 5. In this way we want to find out the sincerity of the respondents' answers and detect a size of SDE on employees' reporting about in(secure) behavior. Lastly, we also investigated the correlation between information secure behavior scale and employees' knowledge about information security, as theoretical framework of KAB model evidences the correlation between both variables [22]. Knowledge was measured as an index of four quiz questions, composing an interval scale, ranging from 0 to 4.

4 Results

We divided the results into four sections; the first part tests the effect of item wording on the overall insecure information behavior score, and the second part is intended to test the associations of items with the BIDR scale. The third part deals with correlations between behavioral items and knowledge. In the last section, we compose a new scale of information security behavior with minimized SDE out of best performing items, based on previous analyses.

4.1 Effect of Forgiving Wording and Alternating Item Wording

Table 3 presents some basic descriptive statistics (mean, skewness and kurtosis) of all behavioral items by experimental groups. We report all statistics (including five secure items in Group 3 and Group 4, marked with *) so that higher arithmetic means represent more insecure behavior.

Table 3. Descriptive statistics of information security behavior scale.

Items	Group 1			Group 2			Group 3			Group 4		
	M	Skew	Kurt	M	Skew	Kurt	M	Skew	Kurt	M	Skew	Kurt
Item 1	1.61	1.82	2.35	2.05	0.93	-0.71	2.16	0.73	-0.87	1.96	0.85	-0.18
Item 2	1.50	2.14	4.07	1.32	2.52	5.65	1.72	1.24	0.38	1.45	2.18	5.33
Item 3	2.24	0.48	-1.11	2.18	0.70	-0.90	2.04	1.05	0.46	2.09	1.10	0.40
Item 4	1.35	2.53	6.67	1.35	2.52	7.66	1.51	2.34	5.27	1.68	1.65	1.99
Item 5	2.07	0.88	-0.53	2.08	0.84	-0.63	2.61	0.21	-1.37	2.35	0.38	-0.96
Item 6	1.86	1.25	0.54	1.63	1.49	1.42	2.28	0.60	-0.91	1.62	1.38	1.59
Item 7	1.88	1.30	0.15	2.18	0.65	-1.23	2.08	0.96	-0.69	2.27	0.63	-0.91
Item 8	1.27	2.89	8.04	1.46	1.99	3.09	1.46	2.29	4.78	1.61	1.74	2.19
Item 9	2.29	0.69	-1.08	1.70	0.98	-0.09	1.57	2.03	4.26	1.63	1.77	3.27
Item 10	1.99	0.98	-0.27	1.77	1.17	-0.11	1.88	1.19	0.27	2.12	0.84	-0.53
Grand M	1.81	0.86	0.88	1.77	0.66	0.14	1.93	0.48	-0.22	2.13	0.34	0.12

Note: * reporting a negative wording item (recoded from the positive)

All items across the groups have right-skewed distributions, some of them are somewhat extreme (for items 4 and 8 in all groups). Three items from Group 2 (items 2, 7 and 8) have lower values of skewness than in Group 1 and similarly the majority of items from Group 3 have considerable lower skewness coefficients than those from Group 1. Grand (pooled) means of information security behavior items vary among groups ($M_1 = 1.81$, $SD_1 = 0.55$; $M_2 = 1.77$, $SD_2 = 0.55$; $M_3 = 1.93$, $SD_3 = 0.50$; $M_4 = 2.13$, $SD_4 = 0.39$). ANOVA showed significant differences between them (Welch's $F = 213.55$, $p < 0.001$), indicating that at least one group mean differs from another. Games-Howell and Tamhane's T2 post-hoc tests elaborated statistically significant mean differences between Group 4 and all others ($p < 0.001$ for Group 1 and 2; $p = 0.012$ for Group 3). Thus, the group with forgiving and alternating item wording shows a higher average compared to other groups. This might indicate it represents a truer state of employees' information security behavior. A more thorough analysis of group and item effect on SDE was done in 4.2.

The means of item nonresponse rates are 1.2% for Group 1, 3.9% for Group 2, 3.3% for Group 3 and 2.9% for Group 4. The lowest mean of nonresponse rate was obtained for Group 1 that (relatively) substantially differ from other three groups. Furthermore, item nonresponse rates vary across groups from 1.0% to 2.0% for Group 1, from 2.0% to 4.9% for Group 2, from 3.1% to 5.2% for Group 3 and from 2.6% to 5.2% for Group 4. The smallest variability of item nonresponse rate was also found in Group 1 (1.0%), while other groups have relatively higher variability (from 2.1% to 2.9%). We can conclude that items from Group 1 (negatively worded) obtained noticeable lower item nonresponse rates than from other three groups, indicating that forgiving wording did not decrease the nonresponse rate and therefore did not help reduce this aspect of SDE. It is important to note that experimental groups are approximately of same number of units so the findings are not dependent to this issue.

4.2   Item Correlations with the BIDR Scale

Our short version of the BIDR scale has a mean of 2.82 and is approximately normally distributed ($SD = 0.77$, skew $= -0.65$, kurt $= 1.29$). Confirmatory factor analysis of shortened BIDR scale with two factors showed a good fit after excluding one item ($\chi^2/df = 1.194$; GFI $= 0.995$; CFI $= 0.991$; RMSEA $= 0.023$; RMSR $= 0.021$). Cronbach's alpha coefficients for both factors are somewhat poor (0.459 for SE and 0.387 for IM) but it is common to find low values (e. g 0.50) on short scales with few items. For the reason of unattained restricted assumptions about Cronbach's alpha, it is more appropriate to report the mean inter-item correlation for the items. Briggs and Cheek [3] recommend an optimal range for the (mean) inter-item correlation between 0.2 and 0.4. In this case, all inter-item correlations on both factors are statistically significant. The mean inter-item correlation is 0.26 for the SE factor, and 0.24 for the IM factor. Composite reliability coefficient of the overall BIDR scale is 0.511 (below 0.60, but acceptable for the above reasons).

Table 4 presents Pearson's correlation coefficients of behavioral items with the BIDR scale across experimental groups. Absence of correlation between item and the BIDR scale indicates an item without SDE, while negative (or positive) correlation implies that item is problematic from perspective of SDE. Negative correlations mean that employees with more tendency for social desirability reported less insecure behavior on a certain item.

Each item of the information security behavior scale exists in either two or three versions, as shown in Table 4. First, we analyze items with three different versions (items 1, 3, 4, 9 and 10). There is no obvious item type effect. For example, positive wording yields the best result for item 1, but only in Group 4. For item 4, all but forgiving item wording performs well. Lastly, for item 9 both forgiving and positive wording (in Group 3) are acceptable. The next set of items (2, 5, 6, 7 and 8) consists of only two different versions of insecure behavior. As found before, no item type effect is apparent. For example, negative wordings of item 7 perform better than its forgiving version. Conversely, forgiving wording works better than negative wording for item 8.

We also found noticeable differences among items' overall performance. Item 3 has negative correlations in all four groups (-0.18 to -0.27) indicating that the item is prone to SDE in any case. On the other hand, all versions of items 5 and 6 seem to be acceptable (correlations from -0.01 to -0.13 and -0.10 to 0.16, respectively), indicating lower

Table 4. Correlations of behavioral items with the BIDR scale.

Items	Group 1		Group 2		Group 3		Group 4
Item 1	-0.303**	(f)	-0.203*	(s)	-0.229*	(s)	-0.067
Item 2	-0.125	(f)	-0.015		-0.121	(f)	-0.186*
Item 3	-0.187*	(f)	-0.211**	(s)	-0.193*	(s)	-0.266**
Item 4	-0.006	(f)	-0.322**	(s)	-0.035	(s)	-0.091
Item 5	-0.010	(f)	-0.125		-0.056	(f)	-0.022
Item 6	0.003	(f)	0.036		-0.096	(f)	0.156
Item 7	-0.128	(f)	-0.286**		0.117	(f)	-0.316**
Item 8	-0.203*	(f)	0.074		-0.171	(f)	-0.090
Item 9	-0.329**	(f)	-0.102	(s)	-0.016	(s)	-0.169*
Item 10	-0.110	(f)	-0.158	(s)	-0.277**	(s)	-0.088

Notes: * $0.05 < p < 0.1$; ** $p < 0.05$
(f) – insecure behavior (forgiving wording/item)
(s) – secure behavior (positive wording/item)
(no mark) – insecure behavior (negative wording/item)

tendency towards SDE. Some items, for example items 8 and 9 perform better when using one of selected preventive methods.

Lastly, we analyze if same versions of items perform differently in different groups. Small correlation differences (relative values from 0.004 to 0.099) of negatively worded items in Group 1 and Group 3 indicate no group effect on SDE. Comparison of items with forgiving wording in Group 2 and 4 does not show a clear trend. Items 2 and 6 perform better in Group 2, while item 5 performs better in Group 4. Items 7 and 8 are not equally prone to SDE, regardless of group (2 or 4). Similar findings apply to positively worded items (secure behavior). For example, positive wording in Group 4 works best for items 1 and 10 ($r = -0.07$ and $r = -0.09$ respectively). Interestingly, positive wording of both items gives a very different result in Group 3, where negative correlations ($r = -0.23$ and $r = -0.28$) imply a sensitivity to SDE. The situation is exactly opposite for item 9, where the same item version (secure behavior) performs better in Group 3.

To confirm previous findings, we performed two one-way ANOVAs with 40 items as data units, their correlations with the BIDR scale as the dependent variable and either item type or item group as factors. Results showed no significant main effect for either item type ($F = 0.31, p = 0.74$) or item group ($F = 0.31, p = 0.82$) on items' sensitivity to SDE. From this analysis no prominent experimental group which consists of only (or mostly) acceptable items was found.

4.3   Item Correlations with Information Security Knowledge

Index of knowledge has a mean of 1.35 ($SD = 1.65$, min $= 0$, max $= 4$) and is not normally distributed (skew $= -0.57$, kurt $= -1.43$). More than half of employees (56.8%) have low or no knowledge about information security. Concurrent criterion validity is used to test the existing scale with a criterion variable which should demonstrate the same underlying concept [8]. The concurrent criterion validity across experimental groups as four different scales of information security behavior was examined by the correlation with employees' knowledge about information security. In general, higher correlations implicate higher degree of validity[1]. Pearson correlation coefficients according to group averages are -0.15 for Group 1, -0.20 ($p = 0.051$) for Group 2, -0.26 ($p = 0.015$) for Group 3 and -0.28 ($p = 0.003$) for Group 4. In our case, negative correlation with items of information security behavior scale reflects that people with better knowledge of information security behave less insecurely. The highest and statistically significant correlation was found in Group 4 but it is still quite low to confirm the criterion validity. To provide a deeper insight of item correlations with knowledge, Table 5 presents Pearson's correlation coefficients across experimental groups per item.

Table 5. Correlations of behavioral items with knowledge.

Items	Group 1		Group 2		Group 3		Group 4
Item 1	-0.114	(f)	-0.236**	(s)	-0.209*	(s)	0.020
Item 2	0.052	(f)	-0.114		0.095	(f)	-0.050
Item 3	-0.113	(f)	-0.063	(s)	-0.147	(s)	-0.174*
Item 4	-0.159	(f)	-0.135	(s)	-0.178**	(s)	-0.006
Item 5	-0.021	(f)	-0.050		-0.114	(f)	-0.006
Item 6	0.015	(f)	-0.033		-0.131	(f)	-0.131
Item 7	-0.132	(f)	-0.176*		-0.260**	(f)	-0.201**
Item 8	-0.116	(f)	0.008		0.104	(f)	-0.217**
Item 9	-0.022	(f)	-0.085	(s)	0.102	(s)	-0.150
Item 10	-0.200*	(f)	-0.063	(s)	-0.261**	(s)	-0.165*

Notes: * $0.05 < p < 0.1$; ** $p < 0.05$
(f) – insecure behavior (forgiving wording/item)
(s) – secure behavior (positive wording/item)
(no mark) – insecure behavior (negative wording/item)

None of the correlations exceed the value of 0.3, although low negative correlations can be observed for each item in at least one group. In general, highest (but still low) correlations were found in Groups 3 and 4, where alternating items were used. Among them items 1, 4 and 10 perform better in Group 3, while items 3 and 9 perform better in Group 4. In case of forgiving wording only item 2 works better in Group 2, while items 6, 7, and 8 give best results in Group 4 as well. Although, two one-way ANOVAs with

---

[1] The methodological literature in the field of behavioral sciences suggests that criterion validity coefficient is expected to be up to 0.6 [12]. Although, according to some newest literature, the criterion validity is achieved if the coefficient is above 0.7 [35] or at least above 0.5 [41]. Anyway the majority max out at around 0.3 [6, 41].

40 items as data units did not show significant main effect for either item type ($F = 0.62$, $p = 0.54$) or item group ($F = 0.13$, $p = 0.95$) on items' relatedness to knowledge.

4.4 Establishing a New Scale

As found before, no group or item type effect about SDE were determined. Therefore, the content of items seems to be important. Based on combination of two selection criteria we propose a new scale that minimizes the SDE in measuring information security behavior. In the first step we selected the items according to smallest correlations between items and the BIDR scale. If there were no substantial differences among different versions of items, we considered higher item correlations with knowledge to form the most proper scale. Table 6 presents the chosen items according to experimental group and type of behavior.

Table 6. Information security behavior scale with minimized SDE.

	Content of item	Group (item type)
Item 1	Under no circumstances I do not give my password to my colleagues.	4 (s)
Item 2	If the e-mail contains an attachment, I open it regardless of its content because of my curiosity.	2 (f)
Item 3	-	-
Item 4	I do not enter my personal information (e.g. e-mail address, phone numbers, etc.) into unknown web pages.	3 (s)
Item 5	When I'm not at work, I log into public (unsecured) Wi-Fi networks (at airport, in a bar).	3
Item 6	I store sensitive data on a USB.	3
Item 7	Less than once a year I change my password to log in to my computer.	3
Item 8	Because of numerous and complex passwords I write them down on the sticky notes I have on my desk not to forget them.	4 (f)
Item 9	Before reading an e-mail, I check whether the subject and the sender are reasonable.	3 (s)
Item 10	When I leave the office, I log out of my computer.	4 (s)

Notes: * $0.05 < p < 0.1$; ** $p < 0.05$
(f) – insecure behavior (forgiving wording/item)
(s) – secure behavior (positive wording/item)
(no mark) – insecure behavior (negative wording/item)

It was found that item 3 behaves badly when detecting SDE so we didn't include it into the final scale. Of the remaining nine items, eight items were selected from experimental groups 3 or 4. It could indicate that alternating item wording has some effect in minimizing the SDE, since both experimental groups use a combination of positively and negatively worded items. The forgiving version of only items 2 and 8 were acceptable. This supports previous findings that forgiving wording solely is not effective in preventing SDE, but could be effective together with the method of alternating item wording.

5 Discussion and Limitations

This paper focuses on testing of SDE in survey-based measuring of (in)secure behavior. We employed two methods (forgiving and alternating item wording) to minimize the SDE. It turned out that using different wording methods separately did not have an effect on minimizing SDE. When testing with the BIDR scale, no group or item type effect was found. Nevertheless, some results point out that combination of forgiving and alternating item wording might reflect a truer state of employees' information security behavior. Furthermore, we aimed to draft a scale of information security behavior scale which is least prone to social desirability bias. The majority of items were chosen from groups with alternating item wording and a combination of alternating and forgiving item wording. As stated before, this might indicate that combining both methods to minimize SDE could prove effective and provides a starting point for further research with a slightly different experimental design. Due to the length of the overall questionnaire we were only able to include six items of the BIDR scale, resulting in a lower degree of reliability. Since the BIDR scale has not been used in the field of information security before, we only tested items based on an overall score. Besides, its two-dimensionality enables further analysis of correlations with the two factors of BIDR (SE and IM). Anyhow, this was a first attempt using these methods to deal with SDE in the studies of security behavior.

Acknowledgments. This work was supported by the Slovenian Research Agency within the "Young researchers" program [grant number P5-0168].

References

1. Belli, R.F., Moore, S.E., Van Hoewyk, J.: An experimental comparison of question forms used to reduce vote overreporting. Electoral. Stud. **25**(4), 751–759 (2006). https://doi.org/10.1016/j.electstud.2006.01.001
2. Bradburn, N.M., Sudman, S., Wansink, B.: Asking questions: the definitive guide to questionnaire design–for market research, political polls, and social and health questionnaires, 2nd edn. Wiley, San Francisco (2004)
3. Briggs, S.R., Cheek, J.M.: The role of factor analysis in the development and evaluation of personality scales. J. Pers. **54**(1), 106–148 (1986). https://doi.org/10.1111/j.1467-6494.1986.tb00391.x
4. Catania, J.A., Binson, D., Canchola, J., Pollack, L.M., Hauck, W., Coates, T.J.: Effects of interviewer gender, interviewer choice, and item wording on responses to questions concerning sexual behavior. Pub. Opin. Q. **60**(3), 345–375 (1996). https://doi.org/10.1086/297758

5. Chou, H.L., Chou, C.: An analysis of multiple factors relating to teachers' problematic information security behavior. Comput. Hum. Behav. **65**, 334–345 (2016). https://doi.org/10.1016/j.chb.2016.08.034
6. Cohen, J.: Statistical Power Analysis for the Behavioral Sciences, 2nd edn. Academic Press, New York (2013)
7. Cox, J.: Information systems user security: a structured model of the knowing–doing gap. Comput. Hum. Behav. **28**(5), 1849–1858 (2012). https://doi.org/10.1016/j.chb.2012.05.003
8. DePoy, E., Gitlin, L.N.: Introduction to Research: Understanding and Applying Multiple Strategies, 6th edn. Elsevier, St. Louis (2019)
9. Fisher, R.J.: Social desirability bias and the validity of indirect questioning. J. Consum. Res. **20**(2), 303–315 (1993). https://doi.org/10.1086/209351
10. Floyd, J., Fowler, Jr.: Improving Survey Questions: Design and Evaluation. SAGE, Thousand Oaks (2005)
11. Groves, R.M., Fowler Jr., F.J., Couper, M.P., Lepkowski, J.M., Singer, E., Tourangeau, R.: Survey Methodology, 2nd edn. Wiley, San Francisco (2009)
12. Guilford, J.P.: Fundamental Statistics in Psychology and Education, 5th edn. McGraw-Hill, New-York (1973)
13. Guo, K.H.: Security-related behavior in using information systems in the workplace: a review and synthesis. Comput. Secur. **32**, 242–251 (2013). https://doi.org/10.1016/j.cose.2012.10.003
14. Hart, C.M., Ritchie, T.D., Hepper, E.G., Gebauer, J.E.: The balanced inventory of desirable responding short form (BIDR-16). Sage Open **5**(4), 1–9 (2015). https://doi.org/10.1177/2158244015621113
15. Herath, T., Rao, H.R.: Encouraging information security behaviors in organizations: role of penalties, pressures and perceived effectiveness. Decis. Support Syst. **47**(2), 154–165 (2009). https://doi.org/10.1016/j.dss.2009.02.005
16. Hu, Q., Dinev, T., Hart, P., Cooke, D.: Managing employee compliance with information security policies: the critical role of top management and organizational culture. Decis. Sci. **43**(4), 615–660 (2012). https://doi.org/10.1111/j.1540-5915.2012.00361.x
17. Johnston, A.C., Warkentin, M., McBride, M., Carter, L.: Dispositional and situational factors: influences on information security policy violations. Eur. J. Inf. Syst. **25**(3), 231–251 (2016). https://doi.org/10.1057/ejis.2015.15
18. Kaminska, O., Foulsham, T.: Understanding sources of social desirability bias in different modes: evidence from eye-tracking. In: ISER Working Paper Series 2013-04, pp. 2–11. Institute for social and economic research, Essex (2013)
19. Karjalainen, M., Siponen, M., Sarker, S.: Toward a stage theory of the development of employees' information security behavior. Comput. Secur. **93**, 1–12 (2020). https://doi.org/10.1016/j.cose.2020.101782
20. Kaur, J., Mustafa, N.: Examining the effects of knowledge, attitude and behaviour on information security awareness: a case on SME. In: 3rd International Conference on Research and Innovation in Information Systems – 2013 (ICRIIS 2013), pp. 286–290. IEEE (2013). https://doi.org/10.1109/icriis.2013.6716723
21. Kim, S.S., Kim, Y.J.: The effect of compliance knowledge and compliance support systems on information security compliance behavior. J. Knowl. Manag. **21**(4), 986–1010 (2017). https://doi.org/10.1108/jkm-08-2016-0353
22. Kruger, H.A., Kearney, W.D.: A prototype for assessing information security awareness. Comput. Secur. **25**(4), 289–296 (2006). https://doi.org/10.1016/j.cose.2006.02.008
23. Kwak, D.H., Holtkamp, P., Kim, S.S.: Measuring and controlling social desirability bias: applications in information systems research. J. Assoc. Inf. Syst. **20**(4), 317–345 (2019). https://doi.org/10.17005/1.jais.00537

24. Lebek, B., Uffen, J., Neumann, M., Hohler, B., Breitner, M.H.: Information security awareness and behavior: a theory-based literature review. Manag. Res. Rev. **37**(12), 1049–1092 (2014). https://doi.org/10.1108/mrr-04-2013-0085
25. Leite, W.L., Beretvas, S.N.: Validation of scores on the marlowe-crowne social desirability scale and the balanced inventory of desirable responding. Educ. Psychol. Measur. **65**(1), 140–154 (2005). https://doi.org/10.1177/0013164404267285
26. McCormac, A., Calic, D., Butavicius, M., Parsons, K., Zwaans, T., Pattinson, M.: A reliable measure of information security awareness and the identification of bias in responses. Australas. J. Inf. Syst. **21**, 1–12 (2017). https://doi.org/10.3127/ajis.v21i0.1697
27. Menard, P., Warkentin, M., Lowry, P.B.: The impact of collectivism and psychological ownership on protection motivation: a cross-cultural examination. Comput. Secur. **75**, 147–166 (2018). https://doi.org/10.1016/j.cose.2018.01.020
28. Moody, G.D., Siponen, M., Pahnila, S.: Toward a unified model of information security policy compliance. MIS Q. **42**(1), 285–311 (2018). https://doi.org/10.25300/misq/2018/13853
29. Mullins, L.: Essentials of Organisational Behaviour, 2nd edn. Pearson Education, Harlow (2008)
30. Nederhof, A.J.: Methods of coping with social desirability bias: a review. Eur. J. Soc. Psychol. **15**(3), 263–280 (1985). https://doi.org/10.1002/ejsp.2420150303
31. Nuno, A., John, F.A.S.: How to ask sensitive questions in conservation: a review of specialized questioning techniques. Biol. Conserv. **189**, 5–15 (2015). https://doi.org/10.1016/j.biocon.2014.09.047
32. Padayachee, K.: Taxonomy of compliant information security behavior. Comput. Secur. **31**(5), 673–680 (2012). https://doi.org/10.1016/j.cose.2012.04.004
33. Parsons, K., McCormac, A., Butavicius, M., Pattinson, M., Jerram, C.: Determining employee awareness using the Human Aspects of Information Security Questionnaire (HAIS-Q). Comput. Secur. **42**, 165–176 (2014). https://doi.org/10.1016/j.cose.2013.12.003
34. Paulhus, D.L.: Measurement and control of response bias. In Robinson, J.P., Shaver, P.R., Wrightsman, L.S. (eds.) Measures of Personality and Social Psychological Attitudes, pp. 17–59. Academic Press, San Diego (1991). https://doi.org/10.1016/b978-0-12-590241-0.50006-x
35. Polit, D.E., Beck, C.T.: Essentials of Nursing Research, 6th edn. Lippincott Williams & Wilkins, Philadelphia (2006)
36. Rhodes-Ousley, M.: Information Security: the Complete Reference, 2nd edn. McGraw-Hill, New York (2013)
37. Robbins, S.P.: Organizational Behavior, 9th edn. Prentice-Hall International, Upper Saddle River (2001)
38. Rocha Flores, W., Ekstedt, M.: Shaping intention to resist social engineering through transformational leadership, information security culture and awareness. Comput. Secur. **59**, 26–44 (2016). https://doi.org/10.1016/j.cose.2016.01.004
39. Safa, N.S., Sookhak, M., Von Solms, R., Furnell, S., Ghani, N.A., Herawan, T.: Information security conscious care behaviour formation in organizations. Comput. Secur. **53**, 65–78 (2015). https://doi.org/10.1016/j.cose.2015.05.012
40. Safa, N.S., Von Solms, R., Furnell, S.: Information security policy compliance model in organizations. Comput. Secur. **56**, 70–82 (2016). https://doi.org/10.1016/j.cose.2015.10.006
41. Salkind, N.J.: Tests & Measurement for People Who (Think They) Hate Tests & Measurement, 3rd edn. SAGE, Los Angeles (2017)
42. Sauro, J., Lewis, J.R.: When designing usability questionnaires, does it hurt to be positive? In: Proceedings of the SIGCHI Conference on Human Factors in Computing Systems, pp. 2215–2224. Association for Computing Machinery, New York (2011)
43. Shoemaker, P.J., Eichholz, M., Skewes, E.A.: Item nonresponse: distinguishing between don't know and refuse. Int. J. Public Opin. Res. **14**(2), 193–201 (2002). https://doi.org/10.1093/ijpor/14.2.193

44. Šinigoj, J.: Informacijska varnostna kultura v izbranih energetskih družbah (in Slovene) (Information security culture in the selected energy companies). Master thesis, University of Ljubljana, Ljubljana (2020)
45. Tourangeau, R., Yan, T.: Sensitive questions in surveys. Psychol. Bull. **133**(5), 859–883 (2007). https://doi.org/10.1037/0033-2909.133.5.859
46. Tsohou, A., Karyda, M., Kokolakis, S.: Analyzing the role of cognitive and cultural biases in the internalization of information security policies: recommendations for information security awareness programs. Comput. Secur. **52**, 128–141 (2015). https://doi.org/10.1016/j.cose.2015.04.006
47. Vance, A., Siponen, M., Pahnila, S.: Motivating IS security compliance: insights from habit and protection motivation theory. Inf. Manag. **49**(3–4), 190–198 (2012). https://doi.org/10.1016/j.im.2012.04.002
48. Yazdanmehr, A., Wang, J.: Employees' information security policy compliance: a norm activation perspective. Decis. Support Syst. **92**, 36–46 (2016). https://doi.org/10.1016/j.dss.2016.09.009

Creating a Feedback Loop Between Persona Development and User Research Towards Better Technology Acceptance

Despoina Petsani[1]([✉]), Evdokimos Konstantinidis[1,5], Joanne Carroll[2], Richard Lombard-Vance[3], Louise Hopper[2], Maria Nikolaidou[1], Unai Diaz-Orueta[3], Wolgang Kniejski[4], and Panagiotis D. Bamidis[1]

[1] Medical Physics Laboratory, School of Medicine, Faculty of Health Sciences, Aristotle University of Thessaloniki, Thessaloniki, Greece
despoinapets@gmail.com, evdokimosk@gmail.com,
nikolaidou.med@gmail.com, bamidis@auth.gr
[2] School of Psychology, Faculty of Science and Health, Dublin City University, Dublin, Ireland
{joanne.carroll,louise.hopper}@dcu.ie
[3] Department of Psychology, Maynooth University, Maynooth, Ireland
{Richard.LombardVance,unai.diazorueta}@mu.ie
[4] INI-Novation GmbH, Muhtal, Germany
kniejski@ini-novation.com
[5] Nively Sas, Nice, France

Abstract. This work demonstrates the process of mapping real participants from the co-creation session in the user personas. The personas development that were used in co-creation sessions with older adults is presented. This paper provides also insights into how the ongoing user acceptance evaluation research has created a feedback loop into the development and enhancement of personas. The feedback collected improved the real users versus persona distribution while at the same time could provide early enough insights for the market research and drive the exploitation map.

Keywords: Co-creation · Personas · User acceptance evaluation · Technology · Older adults

1 Introduction

User-centered design (UCD) is vital for the design and implementation of technological and computer-based devices. Personas are a large part of UCD however there is limited research on describing the persona creation process in the health IT field [1]. A persona is typically a fictional representation of the target group (or market) of the technology or device, which can effectively communicate to developers the requirements, wants, needs and motivations of the group [7, 9]. Research from Holden and colleagues [5] maintains that while personas are used extensively in many fields, there is a dearth of persona use in the health sector where e-health or health technology is concerned.

© Springer Nature Switzerland AG 2020
C. Stephanidis et al. (Eds.): HCII 2020, LNCS 12423, pp. 282–298, 2020.
https://doi.org/10.1007/978-3-030-60114-0_19

When creating a persona, high level information will often be included such as names, gender, age, location (e.g., country/living status etc.), photos and personal attributes. More key information of interest to the developers will support the development of their technology or service. According to some research [12], personas can be used by developers to support qualitative research sessions with a group of individuals. They can often be a discussion point, providing a way for group members to examine the life of the persona in a way that is less personal making them more inclined to discuss issues. As a result, researchers can more clearly identify the motivations and requirements of the user group.

In addition, recent trends in eCare and eHealth markets are showing patients evolving into consumers as their share of health and care spending grows continuously [3]. This trend opens opportunities for innovative technologies to increase competition and drive further disruption into the market. Consequently, stakeholders will gain the means to be informed decision makers. This opens the ability to integrate feedback from different sources (persona) already in the development process and to consider stakeholders' interactions, values and unique selling propositions (USPs) in the design of business models and value-chains.

Personas can more than assist developers to construct and test their prototypes. The prototype will be developed with the persona in mind and during testing, participants can discuss how the persona may interact with the technology and their experiences of doing so. In 2019 research [6] considers how personas can also be used to make more effective decisions in the design of technology and services. From a HCI standpoint, the persona will influence developments from the earliest stages. Personas can also be used by organisations to demonstrate to target groups how technology or a service can be useful to themselves in their daily lives. Further, it can assist organisations in their marketing strategies. Research [8] was conducted to determine the specific benefits of personas on research based on the responses of experienced persona users. Their panel of experts identified several main benefits to persona use in research. These included re-focusing designers priorities on the user and their goals, prioritizing the requirements of the product/service and, ensuring designers do not design with their own requirements in mind. A lack of consistency was identified [5] in persona development and the lack of specific steps required for their development. However, personas can be developed using thematic analysis, affinity diagrams or even factor analysis of quantitative data. This view was supported [8] and further suggestions were made inferring that the development process is often incorrectly viewed as a singular procedure; something to be accepted or rejected, when in fact there are numerous methodologies which can be applied.

There are two major categories of personas, a proto-persona and a research persona [6]. Proto-personas are often developed as a precursor to work with participants. They involve the estimation of life details and are developed through indirect contact with the target group. They are based on assumptions and can often be influenced by stereotypes [8]. This assumed knowledge can enforce believability in a persona and ensures their 'story' is engaging [8]. While stereotypes can ease the cognitive load associated with the creation of personas [1], developers should be alert to the pitfalls associated with ethnicity and gender. While stereotypical personas may result in unintentional confirmation bias, they can also be used as an effective contradictory tool. Initially, the personas designed further validated the perspective of the frail older adult. However, the new personas better reflect a modern older adult perspective complete with varying abilities in digital literacy (a concept not previously included).

Further steps were recommended [6] when developing proto-persona and research personas. These include; creating a basic template, adding details, analyzing and merging personas, prioritizing important features and, design informed by qualitative data collection. The proto-persona will inform the development of the research persona. In this way, an enhanced persona is created which can lead to a 'gap analysis' to identify the breath of distance between the personas to provide developers with further insight in future persona development. However, some research [6, 9, 10, 13] has demonstrated serious faults with persona development. A time consuming process, the personas age rapidly and require regular updating and testing for validity. Often, personas are not used early in the design process and are less effective when design features have already been decided upon. Further faults were described in [9] including low representation rates when compared with big-data and the increased cost manual persona development incurs.

After completing this review, it is clear that the methodology described below is the best formulation to attain well developed personas based on the type of research being conducted. CAPTAIN is an iterative piece of design research with a small sample size and no real-time data capture abilities (at the time of writing). As such, initial proto-personas will be designed, followed by the creation of research personas. It is important to be able to validate the quality of the designed personas. Along with statistical demographics which will be discussed in the results section of this article, an evaluation of the personas based on the persona perception scale (PPS) [11] will be included. The scale distinguishes persona validity through the following dimensions, credibility, consistency, completeness, willingness, usefulness, empathy and similarity. Participants completed the PPS for both sets of personas (original and enhanced) and the results are discussed below. As a result, this paper is uniquely positioned to provide a review on the development of older adult personas in general, and specifically an account of the application of the PPS scale.

2   Methodology

2.1   The CAPTAIN System

The research presented in the current paper was conducted during the H2020 CAPTAIN project [4]. CAPTAIN aims to create an unobtrusive, virtual coach assistant that will support older adults in their everyday life at home. CAPTAIN provides support in four domains, cognitive and physical activity, nutrition and social participation using technologies for unobtrusive monitoring like 3D depth cameras for recognition of movements, speech recognition and generation as well as facial emotion recognition. The information is provided to the user through projection generation wherever and whenever needed leaving the home untouched when the system is not used.

Given the innovative nature of CAPTAIN, based on radically new ICT concepts an incremental, iterative delivery and empirical feedback approach was adopted that followed co-creation principles and methodologies was adopted. An active, trans-national and multidisciplinary community of stakeholders was engaged as the main source of requirements for the CAPTAIN system. This stakeholder's community has been meeting throughout the project's life cycle in order to assess the direction of the individual components of CAPTAIN during shorter development lifecycle, referred to as "Sprints".

In order to engage stakeholders early enough in the design process, the first version of user requirements produced for the system was based on literature and consortium expertise. User personas were created to gain a deeper understanding of the users and these were used to enhance the methodology and capture user expectations and anticipated behavior beyond demographics. CAPTAIN personas had a dual contribution, building understanding and empathy in the consortium and in end-user comprehension of the system's objectives.

2.2 First Matching Iteration

The first version of personas for the CAPTAIN system were created during face-to-face plenary project meeting. Five user personas were presented, that were based on the project's objectives and user groups, demographics and ethnographic details. Discussion was held on ideas that can offer some solutions to the problems, thoughts, fears and opinions of the personas previously created. The proposed template for the CAPTAIN proto-personas is shown below Fig. 1. The proposed solutions were gathered and consolidated in order to create a structured version of Personas. After that, one round of feedback from the stakeholder community took place, involving 2 older adults (1 healthy, 1 with mild cognitive impairment), 2 facilitators and 2 formal caregivers.

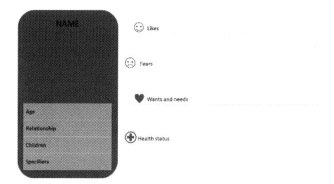

Fig. 1. CAPTAIN persona template

The resulting personas were used in participatory workshops in which older adults and other stakeholders were engaged, and the primary goal of which was to identify older adults' everyday life problems and needs. A larger group of participants (52 older adults, 29 healthcare professionals, 10 informal caregivers) were engaged during the first co-creation session in 5 European countries (Greece, Italy, Spain, Ireland and Cyprus) and provided feedback that was incorporated into the personas.

Following the creation of proto-personas and the enhancement of same from user feedback gathered, the intention was to investigate if the group of personas created can effectively represent the group of stakeholders that participated in the session. For each participant an enrolment booklet requesting mainly demographic information was collected. The existing personas also contained such information. The following table (Table 1) summarizes the demographics information that are available for each participant and the relative information from personas.

Table 1. CAPTAIN participant general demographics

	Information from participants	Information from personas
Age range	[60, 70)	[60, 70)
	[70, 80)	[70, 80)
	[80, ∞)	[80, ∞)
Living condition	Live alone at home	Live alone at home
	Live with a formal caregiver	Live with a formal caregiver
	Live with a partner at home	Live with a partner at home
	Live with an informal caregiver	
	Other	
Support needed	Instability	Physical exercise
	Insecurity with ADLs	Activities of Daily Living
	Nutritional style	Nutritional style
	Socialization/social participation	Social participation
	Frailty	Frailty
	Memory issues	Other
Physical impairments	None	None
	Leg motor impairment	Leg motor impairment
		Arm motor impairment
		Hemiplegia
		Tetraplegia
Sensory impairments	None	None
		Minor hearing impairment
		Minor visual impairment
		Major hearing impairment
		Major visual impairment

A matching procedure was defined in order to understand how many participants can be adequately represented by existing personas. For each category in the previous table, actual participant's information matching the persona's information receives 1 point towards the persona. For example, participant GR001 is in the same age range category, living condition and has the same physical impairments as the persona 'Carlo', but does not share the same needs (2 needs per persona) so achieves a score of 3/5. If the score was 0.6 or higher, the participant was considered as matched with the persona. If a participant was matched with more than one persona, the higher score was taken into account.

2.3 Persona Enhancement

Following the first analysis of proto-personas, it was obvious that there was important information missing from the personas. First and foremost, information about digital literacy, technology acceptance and perception are an important addition to the personas profile. The digital literacy score was based on the aggregated score from a questionnaire that was administered to the participants before their first interaction with the system. Digital literacy refers to the participants level of comfort using technology and participants scores were grouped as low, medium or high.

In order to create the new personas, a prioritization of information that will drive the persona enhancement was completed. The real participants are considered to be representative of the CAPTAIN target audience. Age and gender were considered as important demographic information. 'Living condition' is a factor that can influence a user's acceptance of the CAPTAIN system which is designed for in-home use. Low digital literacy may dissuade people from using a technology like CAPTAIN, which is why people with different digital literacy levels should be addressed, both in the personas and in the feedback Sprints. Lastly, the willingness to be supported and the impairments are considered the least significant factors that influence CAPTAIN system's acceptance. As a result, the priority of information was decided as:

1. Gender
2. Age
3. Living condition
4. Digital literacy
5. Willingness to be supported
6. Impairments (motor and sensory)

For each enhanced persona, the gender and age were decided first based on the gender and age distribution of the real participants. For the remaining information a similar approach was followed, always taking into account real participants' data. The information gathered for each persona were then analyzed in order to create a consistent story. Particular attention was paid to coherence and not to include multiple pieces of information that diverged from persona's scope and personality. Last but not least, the personas' photos were decided.

After the profiles of the new personas were created a new matching iteration was performed. Each new persona has a maximum score that can be achieved from a real participant as each has different types and numbers of support needed as well as deficiencies. A participant is considered matched to a persona only if the score percentage is higher than 60% and each participant is matched only with the persona having the highest percentage match.

3 Results

3.1 Persona Comparison

The enhanced persona creation was driven entirely by the participants' information. The gender and age distribution are presented in the following image (Fig. 2).

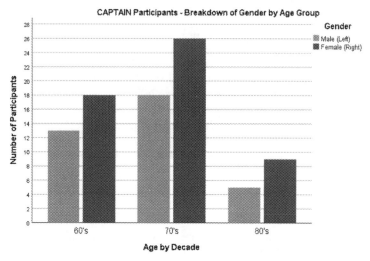

Fig. 2. CAPTAIN participants breakdown by gender and age

Based on that data three male and four female personas were created, two of the personas were in the first age range, three in the second and two in the third. In the previous version of personas there were three male and three female personas, four of which were in the second age range, one in the first and one in the last. Regarding the living condition, in the enhanced personas four are living with a partner at home, two are

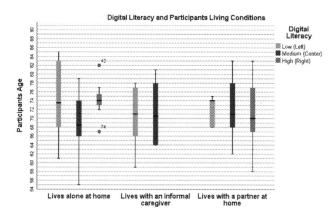

Fig. 3. Distribution of participants ages and digital literacy versus living conditions

living alone and one is living with an informal caregiver. In the previous version, there was no persona living with an informal or formal caregiver. The digital literacy group that the persona belongs to was decided taking into account both the living condition and the age range. For example, a persona that lives home alone and is in the higher age range will have low digital literacy (Fig. 3).

Below we present an original (Fig. 4) and the corresponding enhanced (Fig. 5) persona for comparison.

Carl

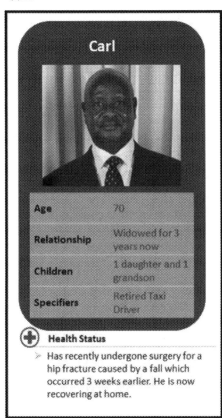

Likes:
- Going on road trips and driving his car
- Going to the park and playing with his grandson

Fears:
- Fears he might fall again, feels depressed because of some functional difficulties he encounters due to the surgery
- Loneliness because of his wife's death

Wants and Needs:
- He wants to stay in contact with his friends, he used to meet them 2 – 3 times a week in a local café but now he finds it difficult to do so
- Wants to communicate with his daughter but is afraid of burdening her

Further Information:
- Carlo had to take care of his wife during the last 3 years of her life. His daughter lives in the same city and in walking distance from his house.

Fig. 4. Original persona

Carl

Likes:
- Spending time with his grandchildren

Fears:
- Fears he will lose touch with his sons and grandchildren

Wants and Needs:
- Wants to communicate with his sons and grandchildren more often
- Wants to become more comfortable using technology to maintain contact.

Impairments:
- None

Age	67
Living Conditions	Lives with his partner at home
Children	Two Children
Specifiers	Retired taxi driver
Digital Literacy	Low
Willing to be supported	Social Participation & Nutrition

- **Further Information:**
  - Carl's children live far away and he would like to communicate with them more often. However, over the last few years his children have tried to promote the use of technology such as 'FaceTime', and 'Skyping'. Carl is uncomfortable with these methods and often feels foolish trying to interact this way. He is very happy that his children and grandchildren want to see him and show off their drawings etc. however, the computer and mobile phone are complicated to use. Carl would like a way to communicate with his family that is simple to control.

Fig. 5. Enhanced persona

An important difference between the two personas is that the digital literacy that was included in the enhanced persona completes the narrations and improves the consistency. Some information is removed, e.g., "…going on road trips and driving his car", as it does not add to the persona's narrative or personality and seems like surplus information.

3.2 Persona Mapping

The objective of this work is to define personas that can adequately represent the actual users of the designed system. For this reason, two mapping iterations were performed, for the original (Fig. 6) and the enhanced (Fig. 7) persona version., following the methods described in the Methodology section.

Number of participants matched with each original persona

Fig. 6. Distribution of real participants to original personas

Number of participants matched with each enhanced persona

Fig. 7. Distribution of real participants to enhanced personas

In the distribution of real participants across original personas, we notice that most participants are not matched with any persona and the user group is under represented. Though some participants may not be fully represented by the enhanced personas either, the distribution is wider.

3.3 Persona Perception Scale

Personas are a widely used technique in many technology-driven fields. However, until recently, there was no way to accurately assess the personas that were developed. The persona perception scale [11] was created to provide researchers with a way to test and validate the accuracy and credibility of development personas. The scale assesses personas based on a series of factors that are described in detail in their 2018 paper. The scale was assessed (Table 2) and high reliability scores were identified.

Upon analysis of the PPS, it was determined that there was no statistical difference between the original and enhanced personas. Inspection of the general descriptive

Table 2. The persona perception scale – factor reliability

Factor	Cronbach's Alpha
Credibility	0.90
Clarity	0.83
Completeness	0.93
Consistency	0.80
Empathy	0.94
Familiarity	0.90
Friendliness	0.91
Interpersonal attraction	0.84
Liking	0.89
Similarity	0.94
Usefulness & Willingness	0.93

statistics identified an interesting gender difference. PPS scores all improved for the male personas whereas, the female personas all got worse after being enhanced. The small sample size of our study may also have limited our ability to detect a significant difference (Fig. 8).

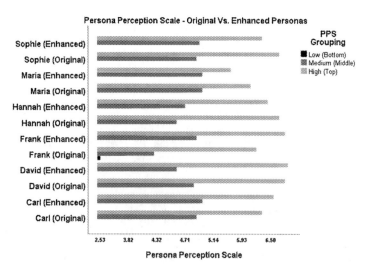

Fig. 8. Persona perception scale scores for original vs enhanced personas

4   Discussion

As a part of the agile methodology of the CAPTAIN system development, older adults were invited to discuss the wants, needs and requirements to create a system that would support them in the home. To assist these discussions, six personas were created. These personas included some personal information including; age, gender, marital status and some physical/sensory/cognitive impairments the persona may experience. These personas were supplemented by images (See Fig. 9 below) to help create a more realistic character.

Fig. 9. Original Persona Images

In the group sessions, only five personas were used due to time con-straints. Participants were asked to discuss the issues that may be experienced by these personas and what solutions may be offered to help these characters. Some participants would have preferred that the images used were a little younger, whereas others found the biographical information supplied to be an issue. Participants in Ireland found the personas to be unrealistic and at times, stereotypical. Participants suggested that the persona descriptions suggested that the personas were much 'older adults' than they represented themselves. Researchers also found some cultural differences across the personas which were a challenge. From a practical point of view, continental European health services appear to offer a substantial amount of support in the form of homecare assistance. However, in Ireland, participant's joked that individuals would be doing well to receive two hours of similar assistance. As a result, Irish participants did not feel the personas were realistic. Further, participants in Ireland had a more 'get-up-and-go' mentality, with very little patience for personas who were unable to manage their health or who spent undue time worrying about it. There was an expectation that everyone should just 'get on' with things, regardless of the issue. As such, this was a barrier to the Irish participants identifying with the personas in the way the researchers had hoped.

As populations age, and with over 149 million adults over the age of 65 expected to reside in the EU by 2050 [2] and more research is con-ducted with these population participants' concern about the stereotyping they felt was used in the creation of the personas is an issue of high importance. While some research [8] discusses stereotyping in persona creation, it focuses more on the gender misrepresentations rather than ageist views. Older adults are not satisfied with past views and many want others to accept that they are healthy and involved in their lives. The language and images used to create personas for adults over 65 is a vital area in the creation of realistic and relatable narratives. Terms like 'oldest old' to describe the older, older adults (85+) are used throughout the literature. However, even this term is being viewed negatively by participants.

After creating the new personas (see Fig. 10) based on the statistical demographics collected from 70+ older adults, they were offered to participants to evaluate based on the persona perception scale. The scale included items such as 'the persona seems like a real person' and 'I feel like I understand this persona'. These questions provided a complete view of participants' views of the personas. As such, this questionnaire was offered with the original personas along with the enhanced personas to provide researchers with information which could be directly compared. The results indicated that while there was no statistical significance between the original and enhanced personas, the male personas did receive more favorable results. This is interesting as only the male personas were improved upon, whereas the female persona scores got worse. Further study and discussion is required to determine whether there is a reason why participants found the female personas to be lacking. However, upon reflection, the researchers felt that simply asking participants to score a series of personas may not be enough for them to fully evaluate them. A simple group discussion before each personas is scored may have allowed participants to 'get-to-know' the persona first, before evaluating them.

Fig. 10. Enhanced persona images

4.1 Limitations

A further issue with the development of the personas was identified just after the initial data collection. There was confusion surrounding the term 'willingness to be supported'. Some of these issues arose due to language constraints and cognitive difficulties. Asking some older participants to imagine if 'they would be willing to be supported in the future if they developed a series of difficulties' was a challenging concept to understand and translate. After further discussion with participants another factor was identified which may have led to difficulty answering this item of the questionnaire. For younger older adults who were asked to report what areas they would be willing to be supported in, in the future, 'the future' was a further away concept than for the 'older', older adults. As a result, researchers thought it was possible that statistically, 'older' older adults who took part in the study would be less likely to agree to support in areas. However, there was no statistically significant difference between the two groups of older adults. Rather, with the exception of activities of daily living (ADL's), where more 'younger' older adults were willing to be supported, 'older' older adults were either as likely or more likely to be willing to be supported in the future. There is a possibility that older adults may be under-reporting their willingness to be supported in group discussion settings. By answering the question on willingness, the participants may be faced with exposing potential vulnerabilities or acknowledging concerns they have for the future. This may result in a form of dissonance which prevents the participant from thinking about the question fully. Using alternative methods might elicit responses of more detail and fidelity.

The presented personas and persona development methodology depends entirely on data from older adults. However, the CAPTAIN stakeholders' community and potential customers comprised a wider user group including healthcare professionals, informal and formal caregivers, and older adults' family members. Data from these groups can also be exploited to create more personas. This work focuses only on older adults as they are the primary user group of CAPTAIN technology.

4.2 Future Directions

Unlike the proto-personas and the research personas discussed above, data-driven personas incorporate a continuous stream digital data collected while the user engages with a service or piece of technology [9]. Data-driven persona development also addresses the issue associated with research personas. The time spent developing personas is decreased significantly and personas can be updated regularly [10]. However, this process cannot be completed without any human interaction. Due to the current limitations of technology (i.e., natural language processing), and issues such as the perception of personas including persona bias, human intervention is required.

There are several methodologies which can be used to direct data-driven persona development but these all require large quantities of quantitative data to be collected while the users are engaged with a service or piece of technology. Due to the small number of participants included in the research and the nature of data collected, it was not possible to use this methodology to inform persona development. However, as this process is being enhanced step-by-step (proto-persona, research personas) it is possible that when the CAPTAIN technology is available the real-time data that is collected could inform a round of data-driven persona development. As technology continues to advance, the amount of personal data which can be collected from technology is increasing. Effective data management, the regulatory environment (e.g. EU-GDPR and the ethical implications of data-driven persona development must be considered.

5   Conclusions

User-driven innovation is a key competitive factor for CAPTAIN; in this regard, one essential focus point for the definition of the value-generation chains and the service delivery models is not only the identification of stakeholders, but moreover their involvement to understand, at an early development stage, their expectations and the degree of acceptance of proposed systems. Persona development and research is valuable to empathize with the stakeholders and improve system acceptability. Furthermore, personas are valuable tools that can be used for customer validation and market analysis. Personas are potential customers that provide information to the marketing team on how to empathize with them and create targeted marketing plans.

The presented personas and persona development methodology depends completely on data from older adults. However, the CAPTAIN stakeholders' community and potential customers are comprised of a wider user group including healthcare professionals, informal and formal caregivers and older adults' family members. Data from these groups can also be exploited to create more personas. This work focuses only on older adults as they are the primary user group of CAPTAIN technology.

Appendix A

Persona Perception Scale

Persona Perception Scale - Salminen et al. 2018

Factor	Items
Consistency	The quotes of the persona match other information shown in the persona profile
	The picture of the persona matches other information shown in the persona profile
	The persona information seems consistent
	The persona's demographic information (age, gender, country) corresponds with other information shown in the persona profile
Completeness	The persona profile is detailed enought to make decisions about the customers it describes
	The persona profile seems complete
	The persona profile provides enough information to understand the people it describes
	The persona profile is not missing vital information
Willingness to Use	I would make use of this persona in my task of *[creating the YouTube video]
	I can imagine ways to make use of the persona information in my task of *[creating the YouTube video]
	This persona would improve my ability to make decisions about the customers it describes

(*continued*)

(*continued*)

Credibility	This persona seems like a real person
	I have met people like this persona
	The picture of the persona looks authentic
Clarity	The information about the persona is well presented
	The text in the persona profile is clear enough to read
	The information in the persona profile is easy to understand
Similarity	This persona feels similar to me
	The persona and I think alike
	The persona and I share similar interests
	I believe I would agree with this persona on most matters
Likability	I find this persona likable
	I could be friends with this persona
	This persona feels like someone I could spend time with
	This persona is interesting
Empathy	I feel like I understand this persona
	I feel strong ties to this persona
	I can imagine a day in the life of this persona

* [YouTube video] replaced with [designing the CAPTAIN technology]

References

1. Anvari, F., Tran, H.M.T., Richards, D., Hitchens, M.: Towards a method for creating personas with knowledge and cognitive process for user centered design of a learning application. In: 2019 IEEE/ACM 12th International Workshop on Cooperative and Human Aspects of Software Engineering (CHASE), pp. 123–130. IEEE, May 2019. https://doi.org/10.1109/chase.2019.00037
2. Eurostat: Ageing Europe: looking at the lives of older people in the EU (2019). https://ec.europa.eu/eurostat/documents/3217494/10166544/KS-02-19%E2%80%91681-EN-N.pdf/c701972f-6b4e-b432-57d2-91898ca94893
3. European Commission: Communication from the commission to the European parliament, the council, the European economic and social committee and the committee of the regions: eHealth action plan 2012–2020 - Innovative healthcare for the 21st century (2012). https://eur-lex.europa.eu/legal-content/EN/TXT/PDF/?uri=CELEX:52012DC0736&from=EN
4. Konstantinidis, E.I., et al.: A new approach for ageing at home: The CAPTAIN system. Stud. Health Technol. Inf. **264**, 1704–1705 (2019). https://doi.org/10.3233/shti1906
5. Holden, R.J., Kulanthaivel, A., Purkayastha, S., Goggins, K., Kripalani, S.: Know thy eHealth user: development of biopsychosocial personas from a study of older adults with heart failure. Int. J. Med. Inf. **108**, 158–167 (2017). https://doi.org/10.1016/j.ijmedinf.2017.10.006
6. Jain, P., Djamasbi, S., Wyatt, J.: Creating value with proto-research persona development. In: Nah, F.F.-H., Siau, K. (eds.) HCII 2019. LNCS, vol. 11589, pp. 72–82. Springer, Cham (2019). https://doi.org/10.1007/978-3-030-22338-0_6

7. Jung, S.G., Salminen, J., Kwak, H., An, J., Jansen, B.J.: Automatic persona generation (APG): a rationale and demonstrations. In: Proceedings of ACM SIGIR Conference on Human Information Interaction and Retrieval. 9CHIIR'18, New Brunswick, NJ, USA, 11–15 March 2018, 4 p. https://doi.org/10.1145/3176349.3176893
8. Marsden, N., Haag, M.: Stereotypes and politics: reflections on personas. In: Proceedings of the 2016 CHI Conference on Human Factors in Computing Systems, pp. 4017–4031, May 2016
9. Mijač, T., Jadrić, M., Ćukušić, M.: The potential and issues in data-driven development of web personas. In: 2018 41st International Convention on Information and Communication Technology, Electronics and Microelectronics (MIPRO), pp. 1237–1242. IEEE, May 2018
10. Salminen, J., Jung, S.G., Jansen, B.J.: The future of data-driven personas: a marriage of online analytics numbers and human attributes. In: 21st International Conference on Enterprise Information Systems, ICEIS 2019, pp. 596–603. SciTePress, January 2019. https://doi.org/10.5220/0007744706080615
11. Salminen, J., Kwak, H., Santos, J.M., Jung, S.G., An, J., Jansen, B.J.: Persona perception scale: developing and validating an instrument for human-like representations of data. In: Extended Abstracts of the 2018 CHI Conference on Human Factors in Computing Systems, pp. 1–6, April 2018. http://dx.doi.org/10.1145/3170427.3188461
12. Terlow, G., van't Veer, J.T.B., Kuipers, D.A., Metselaar, J.: Context analysis needs assessment and persona development: towards a digital game-like intervention for high functioning children with ASD to train social skills. Early Child Dev. Care 1–16 (2018). https://doi.org/10.1008/03004430.2018.1555826
13. Zhang, X., Brown, H.F., Shankar, A.: Data-driven personas: Constructing archetypal users with clickstreams and user telemetry. In: Proceedings of the 2016 CHI Conference on Human Factors in Computing Systems, pp. 5350–5359, May 2016. http://dx.doi.org/10.1145/2858036.2858523

Research on Kansei of Visual Literacy of Regional Cultural Experience in Product Shaping Design

Min Shi[✉]

Department of Product Design, School of Art and Design,
Fuzhou University of International Studies and Trade, Fuzhou, China
shimin@fzfu.edu.cn

Abstract. The purpose of the paper is to analyze and study the visual literacy of regional cultural experience in the product shaping design. First, the author collects the factors contributing to the formation of visual elements of the audience under the contexts of different regional cultures, learns about cultural differences under the influence of different cultural backgrounds and Kansei factors such as style and preference under regional culture and further clarifies the consumption demands of the audience in terms of style, preference and inclination under the cultural differences. Second, by studying the dynamic and interactive perception of factors such as cultural experience and analyzing the Kansei demand factors of visual literacy of customers under different cultural backgrounds in terms of their emotional experience in product shaping design, it will help us master these visual literacy factors of regional cultural experience in product shaping design and lay a theoretical foundation for design research. It will help designers grasp these design elements and infuse them into the creation of shaping, modeling and functions of the products, thus designing product shaping that meets the expectation of customers and enhancing the added value of product shaping.

Keywords: Product shaping · Design · Visual literacy · Kansei

1 Introduction

1.1 Research Background and Purpose

In our product shaping design, there are varied cultural differences such as regional characteristics, local conditions, folk customs, religion, art and values, which contribute to the Kansei demand of visual literacy in the corresponding product shaping design. The customers from different regions and cultural backgrounds vary in the establishment of visual literacy in the product shaping design (Zhiguo 2013). The visual literacy of regional cultural experience needs to be supported by knowledge and information of different disciplines. Therefore, it raises high requirements on cognition and understanding of visual literacy in product shaping, which facilitate the transformation of visual literacy information into visual performance of shaping. Therefore, on the basis of regional

© Springer Nature Switzerland AG 2020
C. Stephanidis et al. (Eds.): HCII 2020, LNCS 12423, pp. 299–306, 2020.
https://doi.org/10.1007/978-3-030-60114-0_20

cultural experience, the paper conducts a Kansei study on the visual literacy in product shaping design, analyzes and studies the Kansei factors contributing to visual literacy and its impacts, finds out the common demands of customers and provides references to development strategy for the conceptual design of product shaping.

1.2 Scope and Methodology

The author analyzes related literature and works, proposes methods for the concept of visual literacy in the course teaching of product shaping design and analyzes the cultural information consultation and visual system in product shaping design, thus improving the customers' understanding of visual literacy in product shaping.

Kansei engineering technology is mainly concerned with the following four directions (Canqun et al. 2006).

(1) To understand the feelings of customers in product shaping through the evaluation of human factors and psychology.
(2) To find out the design characteristics of product shaping from the feelings of customers.
(3) To establish a set of Kansei engineering for human factor technology.
(4) To correct the direction of product shaping design with the changes of society and the preference trend of the people.

2 Theoretical Support

Visual performance and its substance have always attracted attention from anthropologists and art scholars. The research is designed to reflect and analyze the regional traditions and material culture. The early focus of the academic circle is the development of the concept of art or traditional handicraft, which is mainly reflected in the diversified cultural landscapes and differences displayed by the connotation of regional culture and traditional culture and arts integrating music, ballads, dances, costumes and architectures, all of which show aesthetic effect in an artistic framework and form.

2.1 Concept of Visual Literacy

The argument of visual literacy is based on the high cognitive value of aesthetic effect (Qianwei 2002). From the perspective of visual symbol presentation, understanding the substance of regional culture and arts and analyzing the topics related with culture and aesthetics is the foundation of argument to interpret the regional culture and arts and development. Visual elements cover regional characteristics, local conditions, folk customs, religions, arts, etc., which are differences of visual elements that arise from inside out. Like the requirements and preference in architectures, it is an aesthetic habit supported by living environment, lifestyle and spiritual belief. Visual literacy is an ability that can be acquired, which can accurately explain visual information and create a message.

Visual literacy consists of three parts. First, visual thinking, which refers to the physical process of visual perception where thoughts, ideas and information are transformed into pictures, patterns or images that help convey related information. Second, visual communication. When pictures, patterns and other images are used to express ideas or conveyed to the audience, in order to achieve an effective visual communication, the audience should be able to construct a meaning out of the visual images they have seen. Third, visual learning, which refers to the learning process through pictures and media

2.2 Concept of Interdisciplinary Visual Literacy

The main components of visual literacy are design language, visual effects and forms. These components are produced in many ways and convey and explain different information in different communication environments. Therefore, visual literacy can be applied in almost all fields, the views and explanations of researchers from different disciplines and can be studied from the perspectives of different disciplines such as arts, biology, commercial demonstration, communication and engineering (Jin 2019). Visual literacy has attracted enough attention from the society. In the author's view, when we study communication and related issues, we need to consider language and visual information. That is the reason why consultation and design of different areas may play an important role in vision.

3 Kansei Analysis of Visual Literacy in Product Shaping

The main duty of a product shaping designer is to infuse form and content to product shaping and convey a meaningful symbol of the product itself. The Kansei cognition of visual literacy is very wide in the area of product shaping design. Therefore, very complex fields of knowledge are required. People from different regions show interest in visual literacy and different demands. A good utilization of visual literacy Kansei factors is necessary to product shaping design.

3.1 Influence of Human Factors and Mentality of Visual Literacy on Product Shaping

The visual literacy knowledge of products is very wide, which requires very complex fields of knowledge. Many people from different backgrounds show keen interest in visual literacy and shaping design. This occurs in different regions of the world. Product shaping design has its origin in different fields. Yet today it is a "receiving" discipline. Viewed from the process, the development of new application programs echoes with established disciplines. The experience, knowledge and skills acquired from visual literacy and product shaping design can be "infused" into many disciplines as a "catalyst" for the development of new product innovation language. New topics are conveyed to different audiences in specific fields. This might be the main trend of visual literacy and product shaping design in the future. All communication knowledge of these fields is necessary, particularly for the design of information. Visual literacy is utilized to propose a good design concept, which is a combination of the theory and the actual structure. For example, product shaping design requires theoretical knowledge and operating skills, which is intended to give a rational and effective response to theory and practice.

Meanwhile, visual literacy shows the influence and impetus of different cultural fields on design. In product shaping design, we should establish corresponding concepts based on related theories and knowledge acquisition and operating skills to describe the shapes. It indicates that the basic principle of product shaping design is to enable the audience to easily understand and access the complex data. In fact, visual literacy exists in all aspects of our daily life. Proper product shaping designs will appear in our life, so the information source of visual literacy itself will come up on its own.

3.2 Design Characteristics of Regional Product Shaping with Kansei Factors of Visual Literacy

With the changes of society, the data-based exploration ways of visual literacy keeps changing. The flexible uses of 5D technology, interactive technology and sound technology have been blended into all aspects of daily life in the form of digital information.

The origin and root of aesthetic literacy concerning product shaping design lie in the disciplines of language, arts and aesthetics, communication, behaviors and cognition, commerce and law, and to be more exact in construction and production. Among these wide fields, people have realized that visual information needs a clear, well-arranged and reliable introduction and explanation. It is difficult to define product shaping design, which is often replaced by other names. The author will describe product shaping design as follows.

To satisfy the information demands of intended receivers, product shaping design covers analysis, planning, demonstration and understanding of the content, language and form of information. Whatever medium is selected, well-designed information will satisfy the requirements of aesthetics, economy and consistency with ergonomic. Most product shaping designs contain the subjective factor of the designer. Under some situations, for example, those things with common values are expressed in a neutral way. In addition, some other yardsticks can test the effective shaping design. Repeated issues can be easily solved with such kind of measurement and evaluation. All these are issues that can define the new forms of product shaping design in the 21st century. The conveying form of information itself will become a meaningful signal (Fig. 1).

3.3 Kansei Design of Human Factor Technology in Visual Literacy of Products

Viewed from the perspective of vision, regional culture is abundant and diversified in traditional images. Therefore, by analyzing the texts of traditional images, we can interpret the connotation and value system of regional culture and arts. The interpreted images should be considered as a whole composed of symbolic elements, behind which there are associated meanings. Specific elements are extensively used or combined and arranged habitually, which may be the aesthetic judgement standard rooted in the cultural system (Yanzu 2003). When discussing regional culture and artistic images, we shall clarify that culture and its traditional social structure have a certain influence on the use of symbols. Under such an influence, the images that are applied repeatedly in

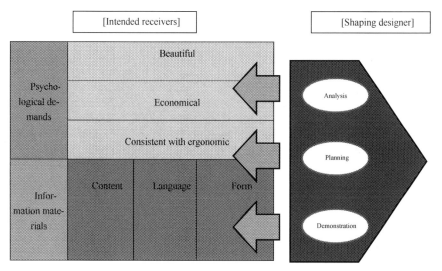

Fig. 1. Model of product shaping design (source of data: summarized in the research)

visual expression should be of a special significance, because in the process of cultural inheritance, it usually forms an aesthetic expression specific to the regional culture and becomes a common aesthetic standard to the population (Table 1).

Design does not remain unchanged. Similarly, product shaping keeps evolving, while new knowledge fields are developing. Such an expansion speed is usually based on excellent studies. Kansei factors of visual literacy have a great impact to product shaping design. Under many situations, Kansei factors of visual literacy are not just a presentation of visual effects in product shaping design, but more importantly a kind of communication and exchange between human and products.

4   Formation of Visual Literacy in Product Shaping

Visual literacy is a basic literacy of the public, which must be analyzed from the perspective of traditional culture and characteristics. Regional culture is closely connected with land and natural ecology and originates from traditional faith, lifestyle and common memory of a population. Therefore, the regional culture and handicraft reflect the conditions and characteristics of each population, family and community, and preserve the traits such as handicraft, nature, cultural perception and diversity. Such traits also continue to inherit and nourish the artistic creation of local culture. Different traits manifest the symbolism of corresponding regional culture (Table 2).

Basically regional culture represents the diversified decoration and beautification of costumes, accessories and articles for use, etc. Aesthetics exists in the demonstration of living contexts and ceremonial behaviors, which indicates the close connection between aesthetic judgement and emotions and cultural dignity. Whether cultural performance or visual form and elements, under the exhibition and exchange of artistic visual fields, the common experience, perception and awareness bring forth cultural aesthetics. The

Table 1. Glossary of terms to describe the culture (source of data: summarized in the research)

Japan	Taiwan	Korea	China
Texture	High tech	Innovative	Digital
Function	Fashionable	Thinness	Portable
Comfortable	Taste	Compact	Top-grade
Minimalist	Simplistic	Fashion	Delicate
Charming	Exquisite	Style	Pioneering
Handy	Durable	Colorful	Individualistic
Individualistic	New	Handy	Light
Cute	Popular	Particular	Popular
Light	Neat	Function	Eye-catching
Epochal	Particular	Smart	Extraordinary
Advanced	Individualistic	High tech	Intelligent
Creative	Compact	Curvaceous	Classical
Simple	Handy	Smooth	Boutique
Reassuring	Cute	Palmary	Reserved
Delicate	Classical	Shine	Luxurious
Exquisite	Thinness	Cute	Elegant
Gorgeous	Senior	Charming	Cute
Expressive	Young	Sport	Unusual
Senior	Business	Crazy	Dynamic
Straight	Leisure	Magic	Cool

aesthetics of product design is closely connected with the complex and prudent social structure and the derived national spirit, which is then expressed, received, exchanged and conveyed through various behaviors. Nowadays the ability to perceive and handle visual information has received more and more attention in life. The visual literacy level will naturally influence the delight and quality of people's life. It is a basic visual literacy and ability to discover and establish many intrinsic connections among things. People's aesthetic feelings are different from the sensory pleasure of animals, because it contains the elements of conception and imagination. Aesthetic is not an ordinary form, but a "significant form", because it has accumulated the natural form of social contents. Therefore, aesthetics exists in form, yet it is not form. Without form (natural form), there is no aesthetics. However, form (natural form) itself cannot guarantee aesthetics. Clive Bell argues that "aesthetics is a significant form". This famous argument emphasizes the aesthetic nature of pure forms (such as lines). However, his theory is stuck in circular reasoning. "Significant form" depends on whether it can arouse a special perceptual cognition. Defined and explained with the above theory of aesthetics accumulation, this is an outstanding theory on form (Chengli 2009). The visual literacy in product

Table 2. Cultural traits and symbolism of visual literacy of products

Type	Description
Shaping trait	Composed of or transformed from natural shapes or geometric shapes
	Symbolism: As the era evolves, the organic and geometric forms in the shaping are often endowed with new meanings
Color trait	The color using habit of a regional culture is implied in national character. If a people is enthusiastic, its products are often of bright and gorgeous colors. If a people is serious and precise, its products are often of conservative and pure colors
	Symbolism: Different cultures vary a lot. For example, yellow is noble and elegant, of a positive meaning in the East; while of a negative meaning in the West
Living behavior trait	Living behaviors develop into a unique culture with the passage of time. The image of behaviors and implements that are used will also become representatives of the culture
	Symbolism: The humankind's ceremonial behavior and the corresponding ceremony of products will contribute to different relationships among the human, objects and environment. Take the tea ceremony of Japan as an example. Other than tea drinking, it puts more emphasis on the emotional exchange among people

shaping in fact evolves from the realistic images. Its significance is accumulated in it and becomes "formal beauty". Thanks to its unique form of conception and imagination, it is different from the common emotions, affection and feelings, and becomes a specific "aesthetic taste". It contains a lot of conception and imagination elements, yet it cannot be interpreted clearly with reason, logic and concept. When it evolves and accumulates into sensory feelings, it naturally becomes a deep emotional response that cannot be described and expressed with concepts. Psychologists attempt to explain its mystery with the human's model of collective sub-consciousness. In fact, it is not mysterious. It exists in the form of accumulation and specific social contents and feelings. However, it is noteworthy that with the passage and change of time, the originally "significant form" has gradually lost the significant form and become regular and common formal beauty because of repeated imitation. As a result, this specific aesthetic feeling also gradually changes into a common sense of form. As such, such geometric ornamentation has become the earliest sample and specimen of various ornamental and formal aesthetics.

Product shaping design is a designing process of communicating with people and an inter-discipline of design and information construction. The design approach not only gives consideration to the establishment of information other than aesthetics in media, but also pays attention to the creation of new media form for conveying information to the intended receivers (Fei 2016). Product shaping design attempts to attract and stimulate people to respond to information for active changes, which might be the promotion of a brand, the change of sales or the fulfillment of other humanitarian purposes. This process involves thoughts of business strategy or the uses of approaches such as market research and creativity.

5 Conclusion

Through the above research, it indicates that visual literacy is very important in product shaping design and many other fields. Under many circumstances, the Kansei of regional visual literacy not only plays a certain role in the study of visual effect of product shaping. It is also a combination of information to be considered and studied when we study interaction with products.

The main duty of product designers is to endow contents with a form and convey the unique signal of the form itself so that it can become a symbolic sign. As long as there is a clear and confirmed target, it will be significant. Product shaping design is aimed to enable the audience to easily understand and access the complex data. In fact, such information exists in all aspects of our daily life. Properly designed product shaping will bring us an intimate perceptual cognition. The Kansei study of visual literacy requires a very wide scope of knowledge in terms of product shaping design. Under many situations and in many disciplines, it is necessary to apply visual literacy in product shaping design so that a good design and concept can be created and a rational and effective response can be made in theory and practice.

References

Shuyu, Z., Fan, W.: Cultivation of visual literacy and inheritance of national culture. Mod. Commun. **04**, 27–29 (2008)

Zhiguo, H.: Reflection on national and regional styles in environmental art design. Youth Litterateur (009), 173–173 (2013)

Canqun, H., Songqin, W., et al.: Approaches and exploration of Kansei engineering. Decoration **10**, 16 (2006)

Qianwei, Z.: Visual literacy education: a field urgent to be expanded. E-educ. Res. **03**, 6–10 (2002)

Rumei, O., Yonghai, Z.: Exploration and analysis of visual literacy education from the perspective of communication. Acad. J. Jiangsu Radio Telev. Univ. **23**(01), 19–22 (2012)

Jin, F.: Interdisciplinary content design of public art course in colleges based on visual literacy education. Acad. J. Chengdu Normal Univ. **35**(05), 31–36 (2019)

Changrui, B.: Visual literacy-necessary skills of the audience in the era of images. Mil. Correspondent **02**, 52–53 (2006)

Xiao, K.: Research on Restrictive Factors of Design from the Perspective of Inter-disciplines (2013)

Yanzu, L.: New concept of design: Kansei engineering. New Arts **04**, 20–25 (2003)

Chengli, Y.: Brief introduction to clive bell's thought on "significant form-reading of "arts" of clive bell. Res. Natl. Art **02**, 31–34 (2009)

A Journey of Aesthetics. Collection of Dialogues with Plato on Literature and Art (1959)

Fei, F.: Research on aesthetic psychology of the audience in visual communication design. Art Educ. Res. **06**, 83 (2016)

Shijian, L., Yunhe, P.: Research progress of Kansei image theory, technology and application in product design. J. Mech. Eng. **03**, 8–13 (2007)

Cassidy, M.F., Knowlton, J.Q.: Visual literacy: a failed metaphor? **31**(2), 67–90 (1983)

Burmark, L.: Visual Literacy: Learn To See, See To Learn (2002)

Research on Servicesecape Innovation Methods Based on Design Thinking

Ruiguang Tan[1](✉) and Jiayi Liu[2]

[1] School of Art Design and Media, East China University of Science and Technology,
M. BOX 286, No.130, Meilong Road, Xuhui District, Shanghai 200237, China
1981995@qq.com
[2] College of Fashion and Design, Donghua University, No.1882, West Yanan Rd,
Shanghai 200051, China
elynliu@foxmail.com

Abstract. Academic research on servicescape is mainly concentrated in the field of management, among which "connotation and dimension of servicescape" and "principle of servicescape" are the research focuses. The above studies are all based on actual cases. At present, there is a lack of research on servicescape innovation methods. Design thinking is an influential, efficient and widely used way of innovation. Design thinking can be widely expanded and integrated into all areas and levels of society. The focus of this paper is to combine design thinking with servicescape innovation, integrate the two frameworks, and explore a design method suitable for servicescape innovation. Firstly, the paper reviews the research results of servicescape and design thinking, and proposes the modification of servicescape dimensional model based on the innovation of servicescape. The research team proposed to use "Social Dimension", "Artificial Dimension", "Natural Dimension", "Time Dimension" as the four dimensions of servicescape innovation. Secondly, integrate the four dimensions of servicescape innovation with the process of design thinking, and explore the servicescape innovation model composed of "personage-site-time- event ". Finally, the research team applied the servicescape innovation method to the innovation of a design project. The results show that the servicescape innovation method based on design thinking can effectively innovate servicescape, the basic method is to cross combine the various dimensions of the servicescape to form the matters scenario of "personage-site-time-event". Such scenario organization will help designers to deeply understand the core matters faced by each project.

Keywords: Design thinking · Servicescape · Innovation method · User experience

1 Servicescape

Customers pay gradual attention on overall quality of commodities and service,and customer-experience-based mode has been dominate logic to market competition with

C. Stephanidis et al. (Eds.): HCII 2020, LNCS 12423, pp. 307–319, 2020.
https://doi.org/10.1007/978-3-030-60114-0_21

the development of service economy. As far as service enterprise is concerned, servicescape, which "will make possible main component to competition between services enterprises (Kotler, 1973)", is the significant component of commodity and service. The experiential service consumption such as theme shop, theme restaurant, theme parks, hotel, playground for children, rural complex and rehabilitation center, has already been consumption hotspots. Customers, who pay more attention on service environment of service enterprise, spend more time staying at sites, so service environment turns into the important component to make customer experience better.

Bitner [1] pointed out that "servicescape" was used to various environmental elements elaborately designed and conducted on sites, which has gradually been the general term when studying service environment. Bitner said that customers generally consume and experience in a tangible scape to analyze quality of service according to various tangible factors (here they are not visible ones but generally refers to all appreciable factors, such as odor, temperature). Servicescape may have effect on physiology, emotion, cognition of customers, and farther on their evaluation on quality of service as well as consuming intention. Bitner (1992).

Later, a collection of scholars did research about effect caused by environmental variables such as the external environment, effect and mechanics of servicescape, the interior(temperature, music, odor and color), layout and decoration, identification and decoration as well as servers in terms of effect and mechanism of servicescape, and they have obtained abundant research achievement, which provides dominant theoretical basis and practice guidance for servicescape management. However, we find that present research is bent on effect on physiology, emotion, cognition of customers caused by physics factors of servicescape after combing existed literatures. Related research on social element of servicescape has not got sufficient concern.

1.1 Dimension of Servicescape

Bitner (1992) divides servicescape into three dimensions, which are atmosphere elements, space layout and function, as well as identification, symbol and crafts, on the basis of which, "servicescape model" is creatively established to disclose the its function on user behaviors. Among them, "atmosphere elements" refer to music, temperature, lighting and odor; "space layout and function" refers to layout of facilities and furniture and their spatial relation; "identification, symbol and crafts" refer to pilot identifier and ornamental and so forth.

Interpersonal elements and social elements are involved in servicescape by Baker and so forth (1994) [2] who believes that servicescape ought to contain atmosphere elements, designing elements and social elements, among which, social elements refer to person-related elements, including other customers and servers.

By means of reviewing years of research, Turley and Milliman (2000) divide stimulation elements, one element of consumption environment, into external variables and general interior variable, layout and decoration variables, point-of-purchase and decoration variables, and human variables.

Rosenbaum (2009), however, takes attention restoration theory to disclose the essential effect of natural stimulation elements of servicescape on the field of public health, who classifies the natural elements into servicescape. On the basis of view raised by

Bitner (1992), servicescape model is expended by Rosenbaum and Massiah (2011) [3], including its physical dimension, social dimension, socially symbolic dimension and natural dimension, and among them, there is the same content both of physical and the servicescape, raised by Bitner (1992), which refers to those conductive, observable and measurable stimulation elements. The content of servicescape of servicescape model, mainly referring to servers, other customers, others' emotions and social density, has been extended by social dimension. Socially symbolic dimension refers to some identification, symbols and crafts which are of great symbolic significance to some groups. Its symbolic significance has different influence on individuals because of their various identities and status. Currently, researches on socially symbolic dimension focus on the point that servicescape has a special symbolic significance on some special consuming groups (such as certain nation, subcultural groups or marginalized social stratum),such as Jewish symbol (Rosenbaum, 2005). Researches on natural dimension are laid more on application of servicescape model into public health to arise a discussion on how to help customers recuperate, and disclose the essential effect of natural stimulation elements to public health. For example, some natural elements contribute to lighten customer's fatigue, such as boredom and depression.

Judging from development history of dimension classification of servicescape, its content has been constantly extended, which contains almost all elements present, not only tangible scape of sites. There are some difficulties and arguments on dimension classification, so classification standards are various. The main difficulty is that some elements are divided into "subjective and objective aggregation", such as atmosphere, symbol, which make sense on the basis of trace of people. Atmosphere dimension raised by Bitner refers to "music, temperature, lighting and odor". However, they are related to "space layout and function" as well as people. Atmosphere dimension is thus overall experience. Therefore, it is not suitable to make the atmosphere dimension an independent dimension. So does Baker dimension classification. When it comes to Turley and Milliman's, there are the same contents on "interior variables", "layout and design variables" and "point-of-purchase and decoration variables". Thus, dimension classification raised by Rosenbaum and Massiah is stricter relatively.

But there exist some matters if we make "socially symbolic dimension" independent, because symbolic significance both relies on external image and each independent individual. And individuals have different indexical meaning on the same image. Therefore, it is suggested to turn physical dimensions into artificial dimension, including symbolic subitem. Social dimension and natural dimension are as they were before. In addition, given that there exists a hidden important element for all scape, time, which is natural or artificial, but a new fictional definition which is related to user experience faithfully. So, it is necessary to add time dimension to be studied with other dimensions crosswise. According to specialties of specific items. The dimension contains first-degree subitem, second-degree subitem, even the third-degree subitem. (Table 1, servicescape dimension) such dimension classification applies not only to servicescape management, but also to servicescape creation. Basically, servicescape is about relationship between people and site. Natural dimension shall enlarge the application of scape, such as scape experience involving abundant natural elements such as "rural complex"," tourist destination", and "resort hotel". Therefore, the "site" contains "natural dimension" and "artificial dimension".

Table 1. Dimensions of servicescape

Dimensions	No	First-degree subitem	Second-degree subitem
Social dimensions	S1	Interested parties	List of interested parties
	S2	Interest appeal point	List of interest appeal point (behavior, psychology, economy) of interested parties
	S3	Benefits consistency	List of benefits consistencies of interested parties
	S4	Conflict interest	List of conflict interest of interested parties
Artificial dimensions	H1	Status of artificial environment	Buildings, Internal environment and external environment
	H2	Potential artificial environment	Potential materials, tech, facility, furniture, decoration, furnishings, lighting and colors, and so forth
Natural dimensions	N1	geographical environment	Natural landscape
	N2	Climatic environment	Airflow direction, illumination and temperature and so forth
Time dimensions	T1	Typical daily schedule	Workdays (daily routine), days of rest
	T2	Seasons	Spring, summer, autumn and winter
	T3	Special period	Festivals and so forth

With constantly thorough research on servicescape, scholars lead related knowledge of environmental psychology, cognitive psychology, managing organization behavior, and health professions into servicescape research. Transdisciplinary and multi-angle research makes the content of servicescape concept more and more abundant. Servicescape has been a transdisciplinary proposition focusing on relationship between people and site.

1.2   Organization Method of Customer-Experience-Based Servicescape

Early research pay attention on interaction of environment variables or effect of some environment variable for the sake of servicescape on the basis of cognitive psychology and environment psychology. Artificial elements such as music, lighting, temperature, odor, noise, color, layout and design, has prominent effect on psychological benefits such as customers' emotion, cognitive, service experience and satisfaction, behavior intention, and actual behavior. When studying these physical elements, scholars realized that some natural attributes or physical characteristics of those elements are closely and complexly connected with customers' emotion and cognitive, which includes volume, tone, rhythm and style of music; intensity of lighting; coordination degree between odor type or density and products or environment; color tone(cool color or warm color), lightness, saturation, high or low temperature, item location, spatial layout, internal decoration and furnishings in a shop. Recently, scholars concentrate on various distribution of artificial elements. For example, artificial elements shall match itself with target customers' preference, and different artificial elements ought to coordinate with each other at the same time to create harmonious scape atmosphere. For example, whether background music in shops are coordinated with sweet odor may prominently affect duration of stay as well as satisfaction of customers in the shops; the coordination between music style and its rhyme could obviously improve customers' evaluation on shops to promote their assessments and repurchase will. Subsequent researches emphasize the overall impression of customers on servicescape based on various element cognitive about servicescape. Various scape elements are regarded as an entirety by scholars, main effect and interaction effect caused by which to customers' emotion, cognitive, will and behaviors under the background of various service modes. As we look at some of those studies, on the one hand, all dimensions of servicescape have the prominent effect on customers' emotion; on the other hand, servicescape will also affect customers' cognitive and evaluation to service. Related research discloses the progressive psychological process of customers from cognitive (perceived service quality) to emotion (emotional reactivity) even to higher level emotion (perceived service value), which provides more thorough comprehension of relation between servicescape and customer behavior intention.

Servicescape is not only for the sake of satisfying functional consumer demand, but also for the sake of society demand and phycological demand, such as acquisition of self-identification, self-esteem, sense of belonging, social communication, social identity and social support. There are more scholars who have noticed socially symbolic elements transmitting certain social meaning. They found that symbolic elements shall arise customers' sense of belonging to make them feel welcomed by the site that is their "third space", and thus they repeatedly consume in the same shop, and set up long-run friendship with other customers or servers there. Researches on natural stimulation elements about customer—environmental behavior mainly focus on psychological area and medical area, with attention on natural effect on human health.

Research on mechanism of action of servicescape generally follows three theoretical pathways. The first one is based on the S-O-R(stimulation—organism–reaction), which believes servicescape, as external stimulation, applies to customers to cause them emotional reactivity, and eternally give rise to their advent behavior or avoidance behavior to service sites. Although S-O-R has the important significance on studying customers' environmental psychology, it is undeniable that emotion (perceptual elements) could merely provides partial explanation for relation between servicescape and customer behavior. Thus, some scholars such as Smith and Lazarus (1992) came up with another theoretical pathway—customer-based intermedium variables(customers' cognitive, image, perceived service quality, perceived service value on servicescape), which stresses that customers will take shape of cognitive and image to servicescape on the basis of various elements, and these shall affect their cognitive and evaluation, even their will and behaviors internally.

2   Design Thinking

2.1   Features of Design Thinking

At present, there exists no unified views about cognition of design thinking, because even there are some arguments on this term itself. From different perspectives, scholars come up with their own views. There is a common view that people oriented could build the future. People oriented is not people based, but involves lots of relevant shake holders, taking nature, artificiality, society and time as a system to creatively arrange, and thus achieve fresh value.

Design company, IDEO [4] defines design thinking as necessary rules available at technology and business strategy, transferable into customer value and market opportunity based on designers' perception and method. Therefore, design thinking shall be regarded as a new method and pathway to make innovation possible.

SIMON [5] defines design thinking as a process to search a better scheme with the existing conditions. In other words, we need to come up with a good idea or plan B that satisfy customers' need from the perspective of designer-styled thinking and method. He believes that design thinking involves three specific levels—cognitive, emotion express and interpersonal activity. So, what is different from traditional thinking (management, analysis) is that design thinking is a kind of design attitude and method on the basis of people based, a progress of generation, structure and realization of definition. This progress takes customers' need and behaviors into consideration as well as the possibilities on technology and commerce at the same time.

Method tackling problems by design thinking could also be used to handle management problem. The restraint regarded as implementation obstacles in traditional management thinking shall work as key element to promote design thinking progress. Because the essence of design thinking is abductive reasoning, not the simple deduction or induction in traditional management thinking. At the same time, design thinking has got its own analysis pattern, which is different from the traditional one. Such thinking lays importance on actual interactive effect among form, relation and behavior of human together with emotion. It is a kind of attitude with people-oriented features. Positive, contributive and experimental design thinking could analyze and tackle customer demands better, and find the requirements to satisfy those demands.

Design thinking stresses "customer value" ,"open thinking", and regard language as tools to promote group work to explore creative solutions. In addition, design thinking is divided into transdisciplinary area, which requires thorough consideration in the process of setting up multi-domain groups with various background as well as communication at different stages. In order to make the whole progress more effective, it is necessary to be different among designers. Coordination with multi-domain companies, between research department and factories, between factories and market is a must to extend innovative view to search for new opportunities.

There are two basic elements to successful design thinking.

First, keep an open mind without preconceived concepts or expectations;

Second, place the mind in a space of possibilities, allowing and embracing break-through ideas. In general, design thinking is a people-based with universal applicability, and interdisciplinary approach, a new way to discover solutions to problems and stimulate innovative thinking in a variety of ways.

2.2 Basic Approach of Design Thinking

Design thinking provides a way to stimulate customer demands and then generates a series of fast and simple problem-solving prototypes, and ultimately converges to innovative solutions finally. As a process of thinking, design thinking emphasizes the balance between image and abstraction, divergence and convergence, analysis and synthesis, logic and intuition. Design process is a high-level synthesis of image thinking and abstract thinking, which involves process of thinking such as association and intuition especially the intuition, which is difficult to be simulated by the computer, but which is often the necessity in the process of creative design. Design thinking is defined as an analytical and innovative process all the time that exposes customers to experiment, creation, domain model planning, feedback collection and redesign. From the perspective of customers, design thinking is an iterative process from the generation to test, even to implement actions about knowing more about customers, and about generating the idea. From the point of view of designers, they define (redefine) the matters or make them framework regularly in the process of design thinking by firstly applying the overall thinking mode, and then by sketching the prototype of possible ideas in the process of design. Collectively, the process of design thinking brings together different stakeholders to join in the discus, and quickly share or test their ideas, and then make a balance to arrive at actionable solutions.

When taking the economic and social elements into consideration.

In the actual operation of design thinking, researchers also provide certain strategies, patterns or processes on how to operate or implement it. CROSS [6] believes that there are three key strategic elements about design thinking in the matter of design theories:

1. The designer has extensive and systematic understanding of the matter, rather than just a fixed conditions matter;
2. The designer constructs the matter in a different or sometimes a personalized way;
3. The designer carries out the design on the basis of "first principles".

In BROWN's research, design thinking is divided into three stages:

1. Inspiration phase: collect opinions of related personnel l and search space for the expansion plan;
2. Conceptual phase: analyze actual customer demands to generate, develop and test a lot of concepts;

3. Implementation phase: record the process of program development, and apply the selected concepts, and then make improvements through monitoring, review and reporting. At the same time, BROWN believes that the process of design thinking is not a series of regular steps, but a system with overlap space, which are inspiration phase, conceptual phase and implementation phase. The three phases are called spaces rather than steps for they are not sequentially operated. The above three phases may be repeated more than once in a process to improve the original idea and explore new directions.

The D. school group at Stanford University has presented a five-stage process model of design thinking, which can be summarized as follows.

1. Empathy: At this stage, designers' cognition is expanded and enriched by talking with experts or conducting user surveys. On the basis of empathy, our understanding of customers' potential demands is expanded by means of experiencing the livelihood experienced by customers, by investigating mode of action between sites, action, customers and surroundings.
2. Definition: Transform user requirements obtained through empathy into deeper insights in order to describe "solutions to problems challenged by customers", which ultimately guides what changes can be taken to make the user experience better.
3. Concept generalization: At this stage, the ideas of all relevant people are collected. The basic principle makes no evaluation or restriction on generated ideas. the number of ideas and the co-operated ideas are emphasized at this stage Its main characteristics are creativity and imagination, which are embodied in the divergent thinking in order to explore wider solution space, including the numbers and differences of new concepts.
4. Prototyping: The expression of ideas in the mind is emphasized at this stage. A prototype can be anything substantial, such as a sketch, a wall covered with notes or an object. It is a method to express an idea at a high rate of speed. During the process of prototyping, a quick and flexible approach is needed to experiment with prototypes, and the earlier problems are identified, the better the process of design will be. Meanwhile, the process of prototyping can analyze whether a solution is too complex or too simple, whether a scope is too broad or too narrow so as to ensure rapid learning and the balance among different possibilities.
5. Testing: What is feasible and what is unfeasible will be found out at this stage and then make alteration repeatedly based on feedback. The purpose of testing is to refine and improve the solution. Place the solution in a real operational environment to connect the immature prototype with user's life by repeatedly testing to come up with a better solution with the help of advantages and disadvantages of parameters metric.

On the basis of d.school, the later researchers make supplement and improvement, for example "self-learning" stage, which requires learning and mastering the background in the field of innovation, design thinking and related knowledge to make the design thinking and its related contents generate a better understanding, is put before "empathy" stage by LUGMAYR. ARAUJO combines the "empathy" and "definition" stages into the "research" stage while RATCLIFFE has divided the "empathy" phase into two substages— "understanding" stage and "observation" stage in order to implement and operate design thinking.

3 Innovative Method of Servicescape Based on Design Thinking

Both design thinking and servicescape take user-experience-based thinking mode essentially. Design thinking provides the whole process for tackling matters, while servicescape provides a framework for thinking on matter analysis. The following is a case study of combining various stages of design thinking with the servicescape, which is proposed by D. School group.

3.1 Empathy Stage

At this stage, the designer conducts research on experts, users and sites. The dimensions of servicescape as well as their subitems provide a more comprehensive survey of objects and specific issues. In the process of research, users are often blind to their own demands. The value of design often lies in mining the potential demands of users, rather than simply following the instructions of users. Therefore, setting up a more comprehensive and open question library will be helpful for the in-depth research. The servicescape is composed of four dimensions. Variables of each dimension can be cross-combined with others to evolve the scene-based question library. The question scape consists of "personal - time - places – events". Dimensions may be of different importance in different items, so you can crossly combine them according to specific situations to find valuable question scape. The "Interested parties" subitem of the social dimension is to list as many stakeholders involved in each project as possible. The "Interest appeal points" is the basis for a full understanding of the concerns (or potential impact on stakeholders) of each stakeholder. "Interested parties" and "interest appeal points" are juxtaposed, and "Benefits consistency" and "conflict interests" are explored by means of ligature.

Example: In a residential community in Beijing, China, there was an architectural design studio with a small shop outside the studio. The shop housed a family of four. It was also an entrance to an underground air works inhabited by migrant workers. Due to the limited space here, there were often a lot of sundries piled up outside, mainly including beer boxes, cartons and so forth, and even their clothes were hung out there. (Fig. 1: the original condition of the design project), which has brought a negative impact on architectural design studios, which often required a good image. At this stage, the design group found the matter by means of listing "Interested parties" and "interest appeal points".

3.2 Definition Phase

The definition phase is the generalization and refinement of the above problem scenarios to clarify design issues, and provide initial ideas for problem solving. Stakeholders in this case include a family of four of the shop owners, design studio staff, basement residents, property management department, residents committee, community residents,

Fig. 1. Original situation of the project

studio visitors, etc. Through the investigation, it is found that the interest demands of all parties are different. Shop owners are more concerned about whether their business is good or not, and whether their life function will be affected. The design studio is more concerned about its brand image. In addition, due to the limited space, whether it is a shop or basement dwellers, design studio staff, residents of the community, hope that there are some places outside the shop can be carried out sitting, chatting and other rest functions, which is the interest of consistency. The conflicting interests are reflected in the destruction of public space by the living function of the canteen and the studio's demand for the brand image. If it can improve the external image of the shop and can be compatible with its living functions, it is also beneficial to its operation. Although this image confusion is caused by the canteen, the canteen has little incentive to change the environment. Therefore, if the environment is to be renovated, the main cost will be borne by the studio, and they do not want to invest too much on in this matter. Therefore, the demand of design can sum up as a simple question: how to create a beautiful and inexpensive space device that can accommodate leisure functions and life functions? (Fig. 2).

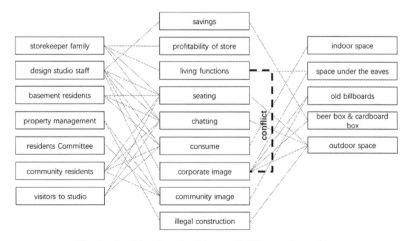

Fig. 2. Combination of subitems of different dimensions

3.3 Concept Generation

To solve the design matters, the team brainstormed what materials, structures and techniques could achieve the "beautiful and cheap" goal. "Extreme thinking" tools were introduced for analysis. "Extremely cheap" means that the materials used for construction are themselves free of charge for the entire life cycle of the project, and even do not incur transportation costs, installation costs, demolition costs, and transportation costs after demolition. Following this line of thinking, the design team first looked at whether there were materials that could be obtained from the site and that could be self-constructed to solve the construction matters. Finally, the beer box in the clutter came into view! If the structure is feasible, the beer box can be used for modular construction to build a "Functional Complex for Beer Box" : beer boxes can continue to be used to fill bottles, plant flowers and plants, set up chat seats, store items, and even set up some cultural interesting content. A little study on the structure of the beer box shows that this standardized box can be overlapped in both vertical and horizontal directions, but it needs to be reinforced in the structure to prevent the strong wind in Beijing autumn and winter and children from collapsing when climbing. In order to accommodate both leisure and living functions, the "beer box functional complex" is designed as a continuous "landscape wall", with holes in the orthogonal areas for people to sit and talk. The side of the "landscape wall" towards the design studio becomes a good image interface, while the side towards the canteen forms a storage space for the previously exposed sundries. As the beer crates are used as construction materials, the quantity of sundries is also reduced objectively.

3.4 Prototyping Stage

After the concept is generated, a picture of the solution becomes clear. Then the floor plan, elevation and perspective drawing are drawn according to the scale of the site using design software. (Fig. 3).

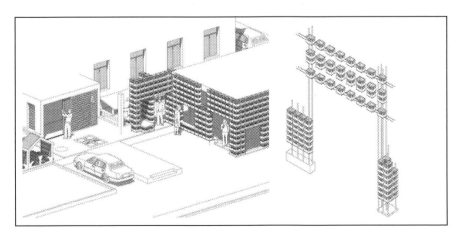

Fig. 3. Design prototype

To solve this spatial contradiction, a total of 320 beer crates were used, which were fixed vertically with PVC square pipes and fixed horizontally with steel bars. The structure was stable enough, but it was easy to dismantle. The dismantled beer crates can be used again without environmental waste. This solution is the result of innovation through the fusion of design thinking and servicescape. Although this is a small case, the dimensions of the servicescape involved are relatively simple. Still, this can be used as an innovative model for more complex projects.

3.5 Testing Phase

For ordinary products, the production and use of samples can be tested after the prototyping stage, but for environmental products, it is almost impossible to complete the pre-production testing. Therefore, post - use evaluation (POE) is the basic method in this field. The method of servicescape can also be combined with POE to study post usage evaluation. A special study on this topic will be carried out later. As far as the project is concerned, the major stakeholders are satisfied with the completion of the project. The design studio here solved the matters of the image of the external space, and the canteen solved the matters of insufficient space. For other stakeholders, improvements in the health and image of the community are also welcomed. (Fig. 4).

Fig. 4. Comparison before and after construction

4 Conclusions

The servicescape innovation method based on design thinking combines the two theoretical fields to seek innovative solutions to matters. The basic method is to cross combine the various dimensions of the servicescape to form the matters scene of "personage-site-time and event". Such scene organization will help designers to deeply understand the core matters faced by each project. For the first three stages of design thinking, "empathy", "definition" and "concept", the servicescape approach is conducive to the expansion of information and thinking. Combined with tools such as "divergent thinking" and "extreme thinking", servicescape innovation based on design thinking has more possibilities.

The case presented in this paper is a simple scenario, but such conflicts of interest are common in real life. Sometimes it is not necessarily the conflict of interests of different stakeholders, but the conflict of different interest demands of the same stakeholder (or the same group). More complex scenes are only composed of small and superimposed scenes such as a commercial complex or a resort hotel, hospital, etc. There are many different experience scenes, but these scenes can be hierarchically classified and modeled. The following research will select a composite scene to further explore the innovative method of servicescape based on design thinking.

References

1. Bitner, M.J.: Servicescapes: the impact of physical surroundings on customers and employees [J]. J. Mark. Des. Thinking **56**(2), 57–71 (1992)
2. Baker, J., et al.: The influence of store environment on qualityinferences and store imgage [J]. J. Acad. Mark. Sci. **22**(4), 328–339 (1994)
3. Rosenbaum, M.S., Massiah, C.: An expanded servicescape perspective [J]. J. Serv. Manag. **22**(4), 471–490 (2011)
4. Brown, T.: Design Thinking [M]. Harvard Business Review, Boston (2008)
5. Simon, H.: The Sciences of the Artificial [M], 3rd edn. MIT Press, Cambridge (1996)
6. Cross, N.: Design Thinking: Understanding How Designers Think and Work [M]. Berg Publishers, London (2011)

Cocreating Value with Customers: A Case Study of a Technology-Based Startup

Fang-Wu Tung[✉] and Shuo-De Lin

National Taiwan University of Science and Technology, Taipei, TW 10607, Taiwan
fwtung@ntust.edu.tw

Abstract. With developments related to the Internet and digital technology, consumers have shifted from passively receiving products to actively playing a role in new product development. This aim of this study was to elucidate how a technology-based startup cocreates value with customers to develop an Internet of things–based product and service. A single case study was conducted to identify a startup's cocreation motivations, cocreation forms, and engagement platforms throughout the entire new product development (NPD) process. Open-ended interviews with a set of cue cards were used for the research inquiry. The results show that customer cocreation occurs in all the stages of the NPD process, and the role of customers varied from ideation to the postlaunch stage. Customer cocreation assists startups in refining their offerings, generating content on a virtual platform, and establishing an active user community. We suggest that entrepreneurs consider customer cocreation as an open innovation method and search for viable cocreation opportunities to grow their business.

Keywords: Customer cocreation · Technology-based startup · New product development

1 Introduction

The boundary between consumers and producers is becoming blurred. Empowered by the Internet, consumers can participate in the new product development (NPD) process and serve as external resources for companies [1]. Companies are facing uncertainties related to this process in complicated and ever-changing markets. Therefore, companies have adopted various approaches to involve consumers in the NPD process to enhance their competitiveness. Several companies have embraced customer cocreation and pioneered the possibilities of cocreation with consumers through the Internet. Lego, for example, built the website "Lego Ideas," which invites consumers to submit their ideas. Such ideas are transformed into commercial products once the idea gains a certain level of support from others. The website "My Starbucks Idea" represents another approach to encouraging consumers to share their ideas and suggestions regarding the company's offerings, services, and even social responsibilities.

Compared with the aforementioned enterprises, startups have limited resources and R&D scales, which might hinder their innovation extent. Given that cocreation serves

© Springer Nature Switzerland AG 2020
C. Stephanidis et al. (Eds.): HCII 2020, LNCS 12423, pp. 320–330, 2020.
https://doi.org/10.1007/978-3-030-60114-0_22

as an external resource for implementing open innovation projects, value cocreation with customers could be a solution to compensate for startups' small size and the lack of internal research labs and structures. Value cocreation with customers enables startups to access customer knowledge and gain insights that can improve the chances of success from new product development [2]. Recently, many startups have set forth innovative ideas and solutions for the market. The number of technology startups has increased considerably. Many of these startups create Internet of things (IoT) products and services according to the IoT Startups Report & Database 2019 by IoT Analytics [3]. IoT technology has evolved in different industries; it has been involved, for example, in making health devices, vehicles, and home appliances "smart." Analysts estimate that IoT revenue worldwide will be $1.1 trillion by 2025 [4]. This provides considerably opportunities for startups and other companies to develop innovative products and services by leveraging existing and new technologies, leading to the formation of new business models. However, developing smart appliances with IoT technology poses a challenge for startups because the product concept is novel and requires entrepreneurs to devote effort to proving that the concept is feasible and desirable. With inputs from consumer cocreation, startups could optimize the use of limited resources and retrieve knowledge and usage patterns from customers to create and modify their offerings. This aim of this study was to understand how a startup develops an IoT product and its business through customer cocreation. To achieve the goal of this research, we adopted a case study methodology. In doing so, we contributed to the literature on customer cocreation in terms of entrepreneurship and the NPD process.

2   Literature Review

2.1   Ever-Changing Role of Consumers

With the evolution of the Internet, the role of customers has changed considerably. Previously, customers passively accepted products and services provided by enterprises, representing a unidirectional relationship between providers and recipients. However, currently, in the Web 2.0 context, bidirectional communication flows enable consumers to share their ideas and opinions with companies and others. Prahalad and Ramaswamy [5] discussed the new roles of customers and new possibilities for involving customers in the NPD process. Customers can actively play various roles in the NPD process as idea providers, makers, innovators, or brand advocates. Their inputs allow companies to discover consumer insights and needs that have not yet been met by the market [6]. This transformation suggests an unprecedented means for businesses to harness customers' ideas and knowledge.

Levine et al. [7] argued that markets are conversational and consumer roles in the production-consumption system have changed with the digital revolution, with consumers becoming prosumers. The term "prosumer" is a compound word made up of "producer" and "consumer." It was coined by Toffler in1980 [8] to describe consumers who produce goods and services for their own consumption. Digital technology empowers consumers with the time, ideas, and capital to become active consumers by becoming involved in various activities in the NPD process. In the proliferation of digital technology, the relationship between companies and users has changed to one with the potential for cooperative competition.

2.2 Cocreation

Chesbrough [9] advocated the concept of open innovation and stated that good ideas do not generated in internal departments; rather, they can also be produced by external actors. The need to collaborate with external partners has fostered the emergence of a new approach to generating innovations. Knowledge provides a competitive advantage because it fosters innovation [10, 11]. From a business perspective, cocreation with external actors can help businesses retrieve external knowledge to enhance their innovation and unlock new resources to create a competitive advantage [12]. Cocreation involves the actions of various entities or actors under the company's network, such as customers, suppliers, and distributors, to create value together [13]. The study focused on one stakeholder of companies: customers. Customer cocreation, as a form of open innovation, provides a crucial and promising direction for managers who wish to enhance their product quality, reduce risks, and increase market acceptance.

Hoyer et al. [14] proposed a conceptual framework of consumer cocreation in which cocreation can be valuable at all stages of the NPD process, including ideation, product development, commercialization, and postlaunch. Moreover, participation in the NPD process and cocreation with a company create an engaging experience for consumers [15]. This experience leads to an enhanced perception of the related brand and helps consumers develop a relationship with the company [16, 17].

Customers participate in several NPD activities, including product design, testing, and support [18]. To help firms identify cocreation opportunities, Frow et al. [19] proposed a structured framework for cocreation that incorporates multiple design dimensions and categories for revealing various cocreation opportunities. The framework outlines six dimensions: cocreation motivation, cocreation form, engaging actor, engagement platform, engagement level, and engagement duration. Each dimension contains specific categories. The cocreation design framework allows firms to discover viable cocreation alternatives through the formation of different morphotypes and by choosing suitable categories from relevant cocreation dimensions.

3   Methodology

A single case study was adopted, and a technology-based startup was selected as a case of successful consumer co-creation of an IoT product. The startup, Alchema, was selected because it represents a rare case of cocreation in the IoT product sector and among startups. Its first product was a smart homebrewing machine that empowers consumers to master making wine, mead, beer, and sake (Fig. 1). The brewing machine, featuring IoT-driven technology, has sensors that measure temperature, atmospheric pressure, alcohol level, and sweetness, and the data are sent to a cloud-based platform and analyzed through a tracking algorithm developed by Alchema. Additionally, the machine comes with an UV-C LED sanitizer for disinfecting the container and built-in weight sensors for automatically informing users of the quantity of ingredients added. The built-in scale and fermentation monitor track the progress from start to finish, instructing consumers about each step via the paired app. The mobile app, which is connected to machines and an IoT cloud service, guides users to finish the process, explore recipes, produce their own flavor, and monitor the progress of fermentation. The app contains hundreds of ready-to-use recipes created by Alchema and other users for brewing wine.

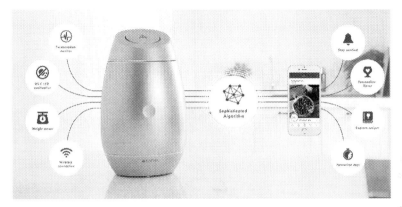

Fig. 1. The brewing machine, featuring IoT-driven technology, developed by Alchema [*1]

The aforementioned smart brewing machine and the app have not yet appeared in the market. Alchema conducted user research and engaged homebrewers and experts in cocreation activities to develop and verify the homebrewing flow through IoT technology. The device attracted the attention of the HAX hardware accelerator, which helped the company demonstrate a working prototype at Target and Brookstone. The founder of Alchema, Chang, was featured in the 2018 Forbes 30 Under 30 Asia List, which highlights 300 young entrepreneurs and innovators across 10 industries.

3.1 Data Collection and Analysis

A qualitative approach was adopted for data collection as the phenomenon under investigation is novel. Furthermore, the aim of the study was to understand how a startup conducts cocreation activities with customers to create a successful business using IoT products and services. Yin [20] proposed a combination of different sources of evidence for data collection. In the current study, interviews with the founder and secondary data, including nonparticipant observation of the website, documentation, and archival resources, were adopted. The primary data were collected through in-depth interviews. An artifact-based interview method was employed. On the basis of the cocreation design framework proposed by Frow et al., we developed a cocreation canvas and cards (Fig. 2). Cocreation cards contain various categories under the six cocreation dimensions: cocreation motivation, cocreation form, engaging actor, engagement platform, engagement level, and engagement duration. The interviewee, the Alchema founder, was asked to use the cards to illustrate how they cocreated with customers during the different stages of the NPD process. The interviewee was then given a semi-structured questionnaire covering (a) cocreation motivation, form, engagement platform, and engaging actor in each stage of the NPD process; outcomes of cocreation activities; the challenges involved; and questions about the overall results.

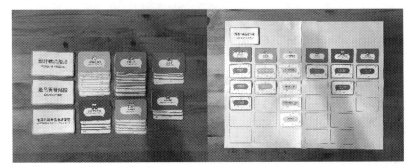

Fig. 2. Cocreation cards and canvas

The interviews, conducted face-to-face, were recorded, transcribed, and sent to the participants for their comments and approval. The secondary data covered media documentation, publicly available registers, and company social media, which ensured data triangulation through multiple sources of evidence. This data analysis involved defining the analysis content, analyzing the collected data, and discussing the implications. Regarding content analysis, we focused on understanding customers' cocreation throughout the NPD process, including ideation, development, commercialization, and postlaunch stages.

4   Results

4.1   Cocreation in the Ideation Stage

In the ideation stage, motives for cocreation activities were access to resources, hastening product development, creating competitive offerings, and enhancing customer experiences. The engagement platforms involved the use of working prototypes, physical spaces, and mobile applications. Alchema invited homebrewing aficionados and experts for cocreation. The cocreation included coevaluation, cotesting, and copromotion.

Cotesting. Alchema engaged participants in cotests on a series of working prototypes. The process was iterative, with *Alchema creating several initial working prototypes and modifying their functionalities based on testing and feedback.* The concept of a smart homebrewing machine embedded with sensors and connected to a mobile app is an innovative idea. Homebrewers could use the working prototype to produce wine and offer their usage experience and feedback to Alchema. The initial prototype had a pH sensor embedded in the top cap to maintain a certain pH level during fermentation. According to the testing feedback, Alchema modified the prototype by replacing the pH sensor with a UV-C light that keeps the pitcher sterilized and added sensors to monitor the temperature and air pressure during fermentation. The third version of the prototype had a weighing scale at the bottom of the machine because users must know the quantity of ingredients added. This version did make improved the results of homebrewing; however, Alchema observed that many participants placed the prototype in the living room, and sunlight affected fermentation. Therefore, they redesigned the prototype with a side door to prevent sunlight influencing fermentation. The product design involved iterative development based on a cyclic process of prototyping, testing, analyzing, and refining (Fig. 3). Moreover, the mobile application and algorithm were refined through the testing process. The participating consumers played the role of testers and thus assisted Alchema in creating an innovative homebrewing machine.

Fig. 3. Working prototypes were developed according to iterative cotesting activities (Courtesy of Alchema)

Coevaluation. In addition to cotests, Alchema involved homebrewers in online questionnaire surveys and interviews to evaluate insights gained and problems identified through cotests. The results of interviews and online questionnaires helped Alchema gain a better understanding of user requirements. Through cotests and coevaluations with homebrewers, Alchema gradually mastered product development and transformed the design concept into a market-ready product.

Copromotion. The series of cocreation activities, cotests, and coevaluations created a community of homebrewers at an early stage. The community mostly consisted of active homebrewers and early adopters. Many of them are influencers and willing to introduce the innovative homebrewing approach to others. This helps a startup with less resources form a homebrewing community and increase the new product's exposure through word of mouth.

4.2   Cocreation with Customers in the Product Development Stage

Alchema, as a startup, needed to raise fund to bring the product concept to manufacturing in the development stage. As crowdfunding can provide nascent entrepreneurs with access to capital, Alchema initiated a crowdfunding campaign through Kickstarter. The Alchema founder acknowledged that a crowdfunding campaign functions as a cocreation platform that attracts early adopters and active users to financially support the project and offer constructive feedback. The cocreation forms were colaunching, coevaluation, and copromotion.

Colaunching. To raise money to move to full production and market testing, Alchema initiated a crowdfunding campaign, which attracted 899 backers and raised US $344,231. Crowdfunding opened a new channel for accessing funds, and those backers financially supported the brewing machine and assisted Alchema in launching their business and initiating product manufacturing.

Coevaluation and Copromotion. Many backers not only sponsored the campaign project to facilitate its launch in the market but also helped promote the product through sharing the project with others During crowdfunding, Alchema received various questions, comments, and inputs from people who were interested in the novel method of homebrewing.

4.3   Cocreation with Customers in the Commercialization and Postlaunch Stage

In the commercialization and postlaunch stage, the cocreation forms become varied, including cooutsourcing, coevaluation, copromotion, coexperiencing, and cocreating meaning. The engagement platforms were homebrewing machine, the mobile application, social media, and events.

Cooutsourcing. Providing users with various recipes can enhance their experience of using the machine to develop diverse beverages. In addition to providing recipes developed by Alchema, the mobile app allows users to explore and share recipes. The recipe-sharing on the platform represents a type of user-generated content, contributing to the recipe database. Furthermore, Alchema analyzes user preferences according to their usage data and recommends recipes that may match their preferences. The platform and recommendation system effectively encourage users to experiment and share their recipes and insights. A community of recipe testers and editors has been built to enrich the recipe database.

Codeveloping. Alchema continuously develop new offerings to ensure the continued operation and growth of the firm. Involving customers in codevelopment activities at the postlaunch stage assists Alchema in improving their offerings and inspires them to develop new product lines. Customers may participate passively or actively in codevelopment activities in the postlaunch stage. Passive participation is that through the IoT system, which tracks the brewing progress of users using various recipe and ingredients. These data allow Alchema to understand user experiences and preferences, and they company can further improve related algorithms and develop new products or services to satisfy unmet requirements. Additionally, Alchema has hosted various events for which users and interested consumers are invited to drink homebrewed wine and share their experiences and insights of using the smart brewing machine. On the basis of the data gathered from user feedback, Alchema collaborated with other partners to develop new product lines such as ingredients to provide consumers with better homebrewing experiences.

Cocreating Meaning and Copromotion. Homebrewing is new in Taiwan, and it will take time to cultivate a related culture. Alchema users act as homebrewing advocates through sharing their homebrewing experiences with others and creating meaning together. Alchema maintains its user community on social media and regularly hosts gatherings to engage both current and potential customers, such as wine tasting events, homebrewing contests, and drinking meetups. The participation of their customers contributes to giving a meaning to homebrewing and as associating it with a particular lifestyle.

5   Discussion

5.1   Outcomes of Customer Cocreation for a Startup

Cocreation with customers is a strategy that involves collaborating with customers and harnessing their knowledge to achieve innovative product development. Customer knowledge serves as valuable resource for startups with a small budget. The present case study demonstrates how a technology startup created an innovative product (and service) and grew the business by conducting various co-creation activities with customers. The roles of customers in cocreation activities varied throughout the NPD process. During the ideation stage, homebrewers were invited to engage in cocreation activities as coevaluators and cotesters. Through *repeatedly testing* and validating product ideas with participants, Alchema obtained useful feedback to make decisions regarding the functionalities, user experience, and appearance of their homebrewing machines. The cocreation process allows a firm to develop a new product that meets customer needs, thereby increasing the possibility of success [21–23].

Moving to the product development stage, Alchema used crowdfunding to raise the funds needed to manufacture the product. The crowdfunding campaign became an effective cocreation platform, where backers could be involved in coevaluation, colaunching, and copromotion. Their participation enabled the firm to continuously optimize their products and services, access capital for manufacturing, gain exposure to increase brand awareness, and establish a customer base. Crowdfunding can be used as a channel for sourcing marketing intelligence in a rapid and cost-effective manner.

In the commercialization and postlaunch stages, Alchema has maintained a relationship with its customer community through social media and physical events. Alchema regularly organizes workshops, experience-sharing events, and homebrewing contests to attract users and people interested in homebrewing to participate in offline events. At the events, users, particularly power users, share experiences and knowledge of homebrewing by using the machine with other participants, thus crafting an experience with the smart machine. Moreover, the mobile application becomes a platform for users to share and create recipes, and the recipes shared by community members contribute to product content. The IoT system can be a platform for cocreation at the postlaunch stage. IoT-generated data can identify users' usage patterns and preferences; businesses leverage these to offer personalized items or services that enhance customer experiences. With the IoT system, Alchema collects data to optimize fermentation algorithms and user experiences.

5.2 Multiple Engagement Platforms

Effective cocreation requires an engagement platform that enables actors to share their resources and adapt their processes for use by others. The case study demonstrates that multiple platforms were adopted to engage customers in different forms of cocreation. The engagement platforms can involve multiple approaches to of engaging customers in the NPD process. Four main platforms were identified from the present study, namely working prototypes, an internet-based platform, offline events, and an IoT system. Working prototypes serve as an effective platform for engage homebrewing aficionados and experts in the cotesting activity at an early stage to obtain useful feedback and improve the product. As the smart homebrewing machine is a novel concept, collaborating with homebrewers is crucial to understanding usage patterns and verifying the concept's functionality and desirability. In addition to physical artifacts, the Internet-based platform involves the use of online surveys, social media, and crowdfunding websites, which provide entrepreneurs with an economical and efficient method of reaching potential customers and harnessing their opinions and knowledge. The advancement of Internet-based infrastructure offers firms with an unprecedent method of running a business and achieving innovation, such as by sharing, collaborating, and cocreating [24].

Although Internet-based platforms are beneficial, physical events are still essential as they allow a firm to have face-to-face interacts with current and potential customers. Events with a personal touch and engagement offer experiences that cannot be replicated online. Alchema regularly hosts meetup events to work on coexperience and cocreating meaning. The events help users build personal relationships with Alchema staff and share homebrewing experiences of using the smart machine. The founder of Alchema noted that their users, especially people in their 30 s, value real-life experiences and lifestyle. The gatherings allow Alchema and participants to cultivate a new meaning for homebrewing in modern life.

The homebrewing machine and service represents an unprecedent cocreation platform. IoT systems consist of sensors, and sensor-generated data provide useful contextual information, leading to improvements in the fermentation algorithm and a deeper understanding of customer usage and flavor profiles. The IoT system offers a novel opportunity for a company to collect data generated by users to synthesize multiple inputs and create new insights on optimizing products and services. In the IoT system, users contribute to data generation and obtain a positive user experience in return, leading to a new form of cocreation.

6 Conclusion

Open innovation strategies are often required for startups due to the lack of internal resources [25, 26]. Customers are valuable resources for companies, and the relationship between a company and its customers is not simply that of a one-off transaction. This case study demonstrates that successful cocreation with customers can occur, and customers can make further contributions at different stages of the NPD process. Customer cocreation can assist a startup in refining its offerings, increasing its access to capital and exposure, and establishing an active user community. The advancement of Internet-based infrastructure and technology enables companies to involve customers in the NPD process. Multiple engagement platforms and various cocreation forms were identified in the case study. The findings described herein provide entrepreneurs with a reference for discovering viable cocreation opportunities to grow their businesses.

Note
*1 Fig. 1 is retrieved from the official website of Alchema: https://www.alchema.com/pages/how_it_works.

Acknowledgement. This material is based upon work supported by the Ministry of Science and Technology of the Republic of China under grant MOST 108-2410-H-011-007-MY2.

References

1. Rayna, T., Striukova, L., Darlington, J.: Co-creation and user innovation: the role of online 3D printing platforms. J. Eng. Technol. Manag. **37**, 90–102 (2015)
2. Frishammar, J., Lichtenthaler, U., Rundquist, J.: Identifying technology commercialization opportunities: the importance of integrating product development knowledge. J. Prod. Innov. Manag. **29**(4), 573–589 (2012)
3. IoT Startups Report & Database (2019). https://iot-analytics.com/product/iot-startups-report-database-2019/
4. GSMA: New GSMA Study: Operators Must Look Beyond Connectivity to Increase Share of $1.1 Trillion IoT Revenue Opportunity (2018). https://www.gsma.com/newsroom/press-release/new-gsma-study-operators-must-look-beyond-connectivity-to-increase-share/
5. Prahalad, C.K., Ramaswamy, V.: Co-creating unique value with customers. Strategy Leadersh. **32**(3), 4–9 (2004)
6. Ernst, H., Hoyer, W.D., Krafft, M., Soll, J.H.: Consumer Idea Generation, working paper, WHU, Vallendar (2010)
7. Levine, R., Locke, C., Searls, D., Weinberger, D.: The Cluetrain Manifesto: The End of Business as Usual. Basic Books, New York (2001)
8. Toffler, A., & Alvin, T.: The Third Wave, vol. 484. Bantam Books, New York (1980)
9. Chesbrough, H.: Open Innovation: The New Imperative for Creating and Profiting, from Technology. Harvard Business School Press, Boston (2003)
10. Grant, R.: Toward a knowledge-based theory of the firm. Strateg. Manag. J. **17**, 109–122 (1996)
11. Nonaka, I., Kodama, M., Hirose, A., Kohlbacher, F.: Dynamic fractal organizations for promoting knowledge-based transformation-a new paradigm for organizational theory. Eur. Manag. J. **32**, 137–146 (2014)

12. Nambisan, S.: Designing virtual customer environments for new product development: toward a theory. Acad. Manag. Rev. **27**(3), 392–413 (2002)
13. Perks, H., Gruber, T., Edvardsson, B.: Co-creation in radical service innovation: a systematic analysis of microlevel processes. J. Prod. Innov. Manag. **29**(6), 935–951 (2012)
14. Hoyer, W.D., Chandy, R., Dorotic, M., Krafft, M., Singh, S.S.: Consumer cocreation in new product development. J. Serv. Res. **13**(3), 283–296 (2010)
15. Lee, S.M., Olson, D.L., Trimi, S.: Co-innovation: convergenomics, collaboration, and co-creation for organizational values. Manag. Decis. **50**(5), 817–831 (2012)
16. O'Cass, A., Ngo, L.V.: Examining the firm's value creation process: a managerial perspective of the firm's value offering strategy and performance. Brit. J. Manag. **22**, 646–671 (2011)
17. Nysveen, H., Pedersen, P.E., Skard, S.: Brand experiences in service organizations: exploring the individual effects of brand experience dimensions. J. Brand Manag. **20**, 404–423 (2012)
18. Nambisan, S., Baron, R.A.: Virtual customer environments: testing a model of voluntary participation in value co-creation activities. J. Prod. Innov. Manag. **26**, 388–406 (2009)
19. Frow, P., Nenonen, S., Payne, A., Storbacka, K.: Managing co-creation design: a strategic approach to innovation. Brit. J. Manag. **26**(3), 463–483 (2015)
20. Yin, R.K.: Case study Research and Applications: Design and Methods. Sage Publications, Thousand Oaks (2003)
21. Kristensson, P., Gustafsson, A., Archer, T.: Harnessing the creative potential among users. J. Prod. Innov. Manag. **21**(1), 4–14 (2004). The Value of Crowdsourcing. J. Prod. Innov. Manag. 2552012 **29**(2), 245–256
22. Magnusson, P., Matthing, R.J., Kristensson, P.: Managing user involvement in service innovation: experiments with innovating end-users. J. Serv. Res. **6**(2), 111–124 (2003)
23. Poetz, M.K., Schreier, M.: The value of crowdsourcing: can users really compete with professionals in generating new product ideas? J. Prod. Innov. Manag. **29**(2), 245–256 (2012)
24. Choi, N., Huang, K.-Y., Palmer, A., Horowitz, L.: Web 2.0 use and knowledge transfer: how social media technologies can lead to organizational innovation. Electron. J. Knowl. Manag. **12**(3), 174–184 (2014)
25. Henkel, J.: Selective revealing in open innovation processes: the case of embedded Linux. Res. Policy **35**, 953–969 (2006)
26. Van de Vrande, V., De Jong, J., Vanhaverbeke, W., De Rochemont, M.: Open innovation in SMEs: trends, motives and management challenges. Technovation 29, 423–437 (2009)

Strategies for Smart Service Prototypes - Implications for the Requirements Elicitation in the Early Development Stages

Tobias Wienken$^{(\boxtimes)}$ and Heidi Krömker

Ilmenau University of Technology, Ilmenau, Germany
`tobias.wienken@tu-ilmenau.de`

Abstract. The purpose of this paper is to investigate how can prototypes contribute to the requirements elicitation for smart services in the early development stages. Smart services are delivered to or via intelligent objects and are characterized by context awareness, connectivity, and data-driven value creation. Smart services and prototyping are emerging topics in requirements elicitation and pose challenges to existing approaches. This article creates a fundamental understanding for the requirements elicitation by characterizing smart services in a layer model that illustrates the structure, processes, and interaction of the networked components. Based on this, the strategies outline ways how prototypes for smart services can be composed in a result-oriented way and applied in requirements elicitation. The models are based on the results of a comprehensive literature review and demonstrate their relevance using case studies from the mobility sector.

Keywords: Requirements elicitation · Smart service · Prototyping · Early development stages · Mobility

1 Introduction

Technology has the potential to make users smart and overcome the limited capacities of the human mind [1]. To exploit the potential, it is important to understand how we can elicit user requirements and design solutions, to move from smart technologies to smart services that add value to users [2, 3]. In recent research on radical innovation, development of prototypes holds a considerable role [4, 5]. In tangible, fast learning cycles, the prototypes can be used to investigate newly emerging user behaviour and preferences and finally convert them into requirements.

Thus, the main objective of this article is to investigate how can prototypes contribute to the requirements elicitation for smart services in the early development stages. Based on the fundamental clarification of the concept of smart services, the theoretical section of the article examines the relevance of existing prototype approaches for applying to smart services. The lack of understanding of prototypes in the field of smart services is what motivates the attempt to define strategies for smart service prototypes. The strategy for prototypes defines the systematic design of the prototype components. The

© Springer Nature Switzerland AG 2020
C. Stephanidis et al. (Eds.): HCII 2020, LNCS 12423, pp. 331–351, 2020.
https://doi.org/10.1007/978-3-030-60114-0_23

goal is to systematically influence the way participants perceive and interact with the prototype to achieve the desired prototyping aims. Due to the high complexity of smart services, a comprehensive understanding of the nature of smart services is indispensably for the requirements elicitation. By discussing existing models for smart services, the layer model for smart services is established. This model aims to create a common ground, necessary for the understanding and prototyping of smart services in the early development phases. The findings are based on an extensive literature review and a multi-case study. Using case studies from public transport, a structured investigation will be carried out to determine to what extent strategies for prototypes can be applied to the field of smart services.

2 Background – a Literature Review

2.1 How Smart Services Are Understood in Current Research

Smart services go beyond the traditional understanding of services. The term "smart" is thereby assigned a variety of capabilities or requirements, from connected [6] to context-aware [7], data-based [8], intelligent [3] and even ubiquitous [9]. A comparison of the origins of the definitions reveals that each discipline has its understanding of smart services and sets its focus (see Table 1).

According to the theories of **service science**, the composition of a system of people, processes, technologies, physical evidence, and other resources is a prerequisite for smart services and thus essential for the creation of value [15]. In addition to the system thinking, the effects of smartness on value creation are investigated to better understand the nature of smart services and their evolution [7]. In contrast, **service engineering** explores new technologies and methodologies to improve the scalability [16]. This requires an intensive analysis of the networking of products and services and their technical implementation using integrated platforms [17]. Emphasis is placed on how services are combined on the integrated platforms. The individual service components are no longer orchestrated in a supplier- but rather in a customer-oriented manner [18]. According to Spohrer [16], **service management** deals with the question, how to invest to improve service systems. The focus lies on the investigation of the capabilities of smart services to optimize the value to customers and the cost efficiency for the providers simultaneously.

The comprehensive view into the disciplines helps to understand the diversity of the different approaches. A common capability emphasized by most approaches is the use of data. Based on this observation, services can be described as data-based, where the use of data plays a central role in the creation of value. In the first definition of smart services given by Allmendinger and Lombreglia [6], they also describe the basic prerequisite for data-driven value creation: "To provide them, you must build intelligence - that is, awareness and connectivity - into the products themselves".

Table 1. Comparison of smart service definitions from different disciplines

Author	Definition
Allmendinger and Lombreglia [6] 2005 Service Management	Smart services go beyond the kinds of upkeep and upgrades you may be bundling with your products, both in their value to customers and in their cost efficiency to you. To provide them, you must build intelligence - that is, awareness and connectivity - into the products themselves. And you must be prepared to act on what the products then reveal about their use
Wünderlich et al. [3] 2015 Service Management	A smart service – that is delivered to or, via an intelligent object, that is able to sense its own condition and its surroundings and thus allows for real-time data collection, continuous communication and interactive feedback [6]. The intelligent object of a smart service may be associated with an individual customer (e.g. health monitoring), a group of customers (e.g. family home monitoring) or a firm (e.g. monitoring of industrial equipment). Managers can use the information gathered through intelligent objects to improve their service offerings and let customers benefit from customized service features
Kagermann [8] 2015 Service Engineering	The Smart Service World is centred around the users who employ services in their respective roles as consumers, employees, citizens, patients and tourists. As far as the customer is concerned, smart services mean that they can expect to obtain the right combination of products and services to meet the needs of their current situation, anytime, anywhere. Smart service providers therefore require an in-depth understanding of their users' preferences and needs. This calls for them to intelligently correlate huge volumes of data (smart data) and monetise the results (smart services). To do this, they require data-driven business models. In order to develop these business models, providers need to understand the user's eco system and situational context. This understanding is based on data and its analysis. All the actors in a network collect data

(*continued*)

Table 1. (*continued*)

Author	Definition
Lim et al. [7] 2019 Service Science	Smart service systems are service systems in which value co-creation between customers, providers, and other stakeholders are automated or facilitated based on a connected network, data collection (sensing), context-aware computation, and wireless communications. These systems enable customers to accomplish their tasks efficiently and effectively. Using data from people and things (e.g., specific objects, processes, and resources) is the key in smart service systems to manage and improve the value co-creation and system operations
Carrubbo et al. [10] 2015 Service Science	Smart service systems can be understood as service systems that are specifically designed for the prudent management of their assets and goals while being capable of self-reconfiguration to ensure that they continue to have the capacity to satisfy all the relevant participants over time. They are principally (but not only) based upon ICT as enabler of reconfiguration and intelligent behavior in time with the aim of creating a basis for systematic service innovation [11] in complex environments [12, 13]. Smart service systems are based upon interactions, ties and experiences among the actors. Of course, among these actors, customers play a key role, since they demand a personalized product/service, high-speed reactions, and high levels of service quality; despite customer relevance, indirectly affecting every participating actor, smart service systems have to deal to every other actor's behavior, who's expectations, needs and actions directly affect system's development and future configurations
Spohrer and Demirkan [14] 2015 Service Science	Smart service systems are ones that continuously improve (e.g., productivity, quality, compliance, sustainability, etc.) and co-evolve with all sectors (e.g., government, healthcare, education, finance, retail and hospitality, communication, energy, utilities, transportation, etc.). […] Because of analytics and cognitive systems, smart service systems adapt to a constantly changing environment to benefit customers and providers. Using big data analytics, service providers try to compete for customers by (1) improving existing offerings to customers, (2) innovating new types of offerings, (3) evolving their portfolio of offerings and making better recommendations to customers, (4) changing their relationships to suppliers and others in the ecosystem in ways their customers perceive as more sustainable, fair, or responsible

However, the question is still open what exactly makes services smart? The comparison of the disciplines shows that there exists a lack of a common understanding. To approach a common understanding, a perspective from the user-centred design is used. Following Norman [19], designers who create modern, complex systems are studying the functionality, handling and interaction between humans and technology. Applying Norman's approach to smart services, the following questions need to be clarified for a comprehensive understanding:

- Structure of smart services – What elements and resources are required to provide the functionality?
- Functionality of smart services – What visible and non-visible functionalities are provided by a smart service for the user?
- Characteristics of smart services – What characteristics influence the handling and interaction between user and smart service?

2.2 Role of Prototypes in Requirements Elicitation

Creative thinking in the requirements engineering field is crucial to create new visions and discover requirements for future information systems [20, 21], such as smart services. A starting point for fostering creative thinking in requirements elicitation is the integration of creativity techniques [22]. Jensen et al. [23] consider that the use of prototyping techniques has significant potential to support the elicitation of requirements, especially when it comes to identifying uncertainties and unpredictability. In doing so, the prototype acts as a representative model or simulation of the final system [24]. A prototype can be interpreted as an approximation of the product or service along one or more dimensions of interest [25]. In addition to increasing creativity, prototypes pursue three main aims across disciplines. They allow early evaluation of design ideas, help designers to think through and solve design problems, and support communication within multidisciplinary design teams [26].

In contrast to general prototyping research, the investigation of the role of prototypes in requirements elicitation is still in its early stages. In prototyping research exist different streams that study prototyping and its effectiveness. Previous research has focused mainly on the following areas: Purpose of prototyping, prototyping process, anatomy of prototypes, involvement of users, and domain-specific application.

Above all, Houde and Hill [27] should be mentioned with their study on the purpose of the prototyping. They deal with the question which aspects of a product or service can be manifested by prototypes. They argue that by focusing on the purpose of prototyping, better decisions can be made for the structure of a prototype and its design. Houde and Hill [27] introduce three fundamental questions: "What role will the artefact play in a user's life? How should it look and feel? How should it be implemented?"

Numerous works are dedicated to the **prototyping process**. In addition to the process itself, the dominant topic is the approaches of rapid prototyping. Holtzblatt and Beyer [28] mention, for example, that the primary requirement of the prototyping process is ease and speed of building. Further research work addresses the simultaneous use of several prototypes. According to Dow et al. [29], parallel prototyping leads to better design results, more divergence, and increased self-efficacy. Furthermore, the **design of**

the prototypes is also being researched. For example, Lim et al. [30] create with the anatomy of prototypes a fundamental and systematic understanding of the structure and design of prototypes. On this basis, it is investigated which correlations exist between the prototype shape and the results of the prototyping. Several examples show how the levels of functionality influence the outcome of a prototypical interaction [cf. 5, 31, 32]. The aim is to show and measure the possibilities and limits of a design idea most simply and efficiently. Besides the prototypes themselves, other work focuses on the **participatory design approach** in prototyping. At the centre of this research is the use of prototypes with the active involvement of users to discover and create new solutions [cf. 33]. Finally, **applied prototyping research** is also worth mentioning. In this field, new techniques, such as hybrid prototyping, are investigated in particular. Hybrid approaches combine physical prototypes and digital models in virtual reality [34]. Complementing this, the transfer and application of prototyping approaches to other disciplines, such as service prototyping, is being studied [35, 36].

The present article focuses on the study of the prototype composition and more detailed on the design of prototypes for the requirements elicitation of smart services.

2.3   The Composition of Prototypes and the Existing Design Approaches

Discussions concerning the design of prototypes are mostly influenced by the approaches of **horizontal and vertical prototyping** as well as by the debate on fidelity. The motivation behind prototyping is to reduce the complexity of the implementation by eliminating parts of the entire system [37]. Horizontal prototypes reduce the level of functionality and therefore represent the user interface in its breadth. In contrast, vertical prototypes reduce the number of functions and implement the selected features in-depth. Nielsen's concept is complemented by scenario prototypes [37]. To meet the requirements of rapid prototyping, the number of features and the depth of the functional implementation is reduced. As a result, a minimum of the system will be implemented in one scenario, resulting in cost and speed benefits.

Another ongoing controversy is how exactly a prototype should represent the final product in form and function. This debate relates to the **fidelity of prototypes** and discusses whether prototypes must be complete, realistic or reusable to be effective [38]. In designing the prototype, the question of costs is always part of the equation. For this reason, the use of low-fidelity prototyping techniques has been emphasized, especially in the early stages of development [38]. Although the fidelity approach is helpful for orientation in prototyping, several research results show that the simple distinction between low and high fidelity prototypes can be problematic [39, 40]. The concept leads to the fact that several aspects of the prototypes are considered in their entirety [40]. Mostly it is not obvious whether the low fidelity refers to the degree of functionality, interactivity or other aspects, for example. McCurdy el al. [40] demonstrate the effectiveness of a mixed fidelity approach by combining low and high fidelity on different dimensions of the prototype. Lim et al. [39] also show that besides fidelity, other factors such as the material of the prototypes and the test settings affect the results.

The debate on these approaches is focused on the discussion of methods instead of further analyzing the underlying **composition of prototypes**. According to Lim et al. [30], a lack exists in the fundamental understanding of the prototypes themselves. They describe research in prototyping as a constant attempt to find out what to do with prototypes without understanding what they actually are [30]. This discourse stresses the distinction between prototypes and prototyping. A prototype is a representative model or simulation of the final system [24]. Consequently, this is an approximation of the product along one or more dimensions of interest [25]. Prototyping, on the other hand, is the process of developing such an approximation [25] and describes the activity of making and utilizing prototypes [30].

McCurdy [40] confirms this view and calls it an oversimplification of the prototypes. The existing approaches to characterize prototypes are too crude to ensure that prototyping resources can be used efficiently and that the prototype provides the desired output. Instead, authors from the discipline of human-computer interaction advocate designing prototypes along various orthogonal dimensions [40–42].

From the different approaches, five core **dimensions** could be extracted **for the characterization of the prototype composition**: Breadth of functionality, depth of functionality, level of interactivity, level of visual refinement, and level of data model. Besides the discipline of human-computer interaction, authors try to develop dimensions that are valid beyond disciplinary boundaries. Lim et al. [30] with the "anatomy of prototypes" can be named as representative of these classification efforts. The proposed anatomy of prototypes includes filter dimensions and manifestation dimensions. In analogy to the approaches from human-computer interaction, the filter dimensions consist of appearance, data, functionality, interactivity, and spatial structure. With these dimensions, the designer can focus on certain areas within the design space and exclude other areas that should not be investigated. Also, the cross-disciplinary classification approaches broaden the focus and consider the manifested form of the prototypes [30, 43]. Lim et al. [30] recommend in detail the consideration of material, resolution, and scope as further dimensions (Table 2).

In the scientific discussion, however, the question remains open to what extent the discussed dimensions can be transferred to smart service prototypes. Moreover, previous research focuses on the anatomy of the prototypes and how the anatomy changes when the dimensions are consciously influenced. However, the anatomy itself does not instruct engineers and designers how to design prototypes [30]. This research gap will be investigated with the strategies for prototypes in the present article.

3   Research Design and Methods

The design of the study is structured in three steps to take into account the different facets of the research work. The first two steps are characterized by theoretical studies. In the beginning, a comprehensive research review describes and evaluates the status quo of research on smart services and prototyping. The authors combine a systematic literature search in relevant scientific databases with a search using the snowball method. In a second step, the different theories and approaches are combined in new theoretical models: The layer model for smart services, the two-part prototyping diamond, and the strategy for prototypes. Based on the findings of the theoretical work, the third step is the analysis of a multi-case study. Based on three cases from the public transport sector, a structured investigation is carried out to determine the extent to which the identified

Table 2. Dimensions for prototype design in different disciplines

Author	Dimensions of prototype	
Arnowitz et al. [41] 2007 Human-computer interaction	Interaction design and navigation model Visual design Editorial content Brand expression System performance/behaviour	
McCurdy et al. [40] 2006 Human-computer interaction	Level of visual refinement Depth of functionality Breadth of functionality Level of interactivity Depth of data model	
Virzi et al. [42] 1996 Human-computer interaction	Breadth of features Degree of functionality Similarity of interaction Aesthetic refinement	
Blomkvist and Holmlid [35] 2011 Service design	Fidelity Representation	
Lim et al. [30] 2008 Transdisciplinary	**Filtering dimension:** Appearance Data Functionality Interactivity Spatial structure	**Manifestation dimension:** Material Resolution Scope
Extner et al. [43] 2015 Transdisciplinary	Form study Material study Proof of concept Proof of principle Proof of process Proof of function	

prototype strategies can be applied to the field of smart services. The evaluation of the case studies is based on secondary data collected by the authors in the context of three research projects.

4   Results

4.1   Understanding of Existing Smart Service Models and Implications for Prototyping of Smart Services

Service offerings are enabled by complex service systems [cf. 18]. Maglio et al. [15] define these systems as configurations of people, processes, technologies, physical evidence and other resources that enable value co-creation. For providing smart services, connectivity is a fundamental requirement [6]. Connectivity describes "the ability of a computer, program, device, or system to connect with one or more others" [44]. The existence of connectivity in smart services thus indicates that their underlying composition is characterized by systems structures. In addition to technological systems, e.g. for the communication of mobility data, socio-technical systems also arise out of the interdependence of stakeholders, such as in public transport between bus companies, car-sharing providers and passengers. Therefore Lim et al. [7] understand smart services as a system "in which value co-creation between customers, providers, and other stakeholders are automated or facilitated based on a connected network, data collection (sensing), context-aware computation, and wireless communications". In an idealized way, a smart service system consists of a triangular relationship between customers, providers, and things [7]. As representatives of the discipline of **service science**, Lim et al. [7] describe the structure of smart services from the perspective of value creation.

Service engineering, on the other hand, understands smart services as integrated platforms that enable data acquisition, data storage, data analysis and the design of smart services [17]. The focus here is on the resources required for the provision of services. To structure the smart service platforms, Bullinger et al. [17] divides them into three levels (networked physical level, software-defined level and service level) and thus provides a basic framework for service production. Across the different levels, smart service offerings can be composed by services, digital services, and intelligent products [cf. 17, 45].

All models listed are abstractions and simplifications of reality and therefore show only partial aspects [46]. Each of the previous approaches illustrates the structure and complex interrelationships of smart services from an isolated perspective. Lim and Maglio [7] emphasize value co-creation with their model. Bullinger et al. [17] focus on service production with a focus on the required resources and their feasibility. It is therefore important that a model is adequately meaningful for the situation and problem in prototyping. For a model in prototyping, value, look and feel, and implementation are particularly valuable perspectives [27, 36]. These enable engineers and designers to determine and analyse the object of investigation for prototyping.

Layer Model for Smart Services. The basic structure of smart services can be described as a layer model. In this representation, all components and functionalities required for the provision of a smart service are vertically orchestrated. The structure thus comprises five related layers: Smart space, smart product, smart data, smart service [cf. 8] and, smart interface. Horizontally, the sequential character of the service becomes apparent. Smart service is not a point interaction of components and functions, but rather generates its value in use [cf. 47], usually along the user journey. This phenomenon is indicated by the process, which is composed of individual activities of the user.

Perspective implementation—From a technological point of view, the realization of a smart service requires a complex structure of different resources. Using the layer model, the interplay between the components and functionalities of a smart service can be made transparent and provide valuable insights for the implementation. For example, in public transport smart service is used to inform passengers in real-time about changed departure times and available seats in the vehicles [cf. 48]. Buses and trains themselves act as smart products. Via sensors and microprocessors in the vehicles, the required information is transmitted to the control center system. The basic prerequisite for this communication is usually digital radio. It forms an intelligent environment (smart space) in which digitally connectable objects and devices, such as the on-board computers of the vehicles, can be networked. Coupled with smart space as the technical infrastructure, the networked information provider (smart products) form the prerequisite for the smart data layer. In this layer, the extracted data is collected, bundled and evaluated. Finally, at the service platform level, the data is combined and extended to smart services using context-specific algorithms and finally provided to users via the smart interface. For passengers, this means that they can use the passenger information system to request a forecast for departure times and seat occupancy directly from the control system and thus assess whether they will take their bus as planned or look for a more suitable alternative.

Perspective Value Creation—The value of smart services is created by the direct interaction between the user, the provider and the smart products. The central element here is the data, which is collected in the various layers, refined and provided to the user in the form of services. By analysing the different actors, components and functionalities along the data transformation process, the direct and indirect contribution to the value of a service can be identified. Using the value creation perspective in the model, it is thus possible to understand how the smart value chain is shaped by the data transformation. Continuing the example of public transport, it becomes apparent that the simple information about a free seat from the networked vehicle increases in value if this data is combined with the personal trip route of the passenger and is updated continuously.

Perspective Interaction—The difference between the layer model of smart service and other models is the interaction perspective. This perspective emphasizes the sequential nature of smart services and shows that user perception and feedback depend on the interaction with the provider and technology. Services are dynamic processes consisting of user and provider activities that extend over a certain period [49]. Shostack [50] distinguishes between activities visible to the user that directly influence the process and invisible activities in the background that indirectly affect the service (line of visibility). In the so-called backstage area, a distinction can be made between the physical infrastructure (line of infrastructure), which is the technological prerequisite for networking, and the software level. Both layers differ in their characteristics. The latter can, for example, use cloud computing to provide its activities largely independent of location.

4.2 Classification of the Strategy for Prototypes

The strategy for prototypes defines the systematic composition of a prototype. The goal is to systematically influence the way in which test persons perceive and interact with the prototype to achieve the desired prototyping aims.

To show the strategy and its significance, the strategy should be integrated into the concept of prototyping. For this purpose, the two-part prototyping diamond is introduced. The model structures the decision processes that engineers and designers have to face during the prototyping stage.

With the **aim** in mind, the fundamental question is raised: Why is a prototype created and what shall be achieved. It is common practice to use prototypes for the exploration, evaluation, and communication of future solutions [cf. 25, 27, 36, 51]. In the next step, the initial situation for prototyping is further specified by the **object of investigation**. For each prototyping iteration, it should be defined which aspect of the solution is being investigated. Houde and Hill [27] distinguish three main objects of investigation: "Role" investigates how the new solution creates value for users, "look and feel" explores the appearance and usability of the solution, and "implementation" looks at the feasibility of the solution. In addition, they introduce the "integration" as an additional object of investigation. The "integration" combines all three perspectives. Investigating how the various aspects work together in a prototype is also a relevant object of investigation for smart services. With the prototype and process, it now follows two elements in the model, which both influence the test persons and thus affect the output of the prototyping. In prototyping, designers are faced with the challenge of finding the simplest manifestation of the object of investigation without distorting the understanding of the whole [30].

The **composition of prototype** is always varied along different dimensions. The authors' field studies have shown that the dimensions representation, scope and functionality, interactivity, appearance as well as data model are particularly valuable for the design of smart service prototypes. Overall, the quality of the prototyping is evaluated by the achieved output. The prototype serves quasi as a means to an end, to collect the desired findings with the test persons. This is where the prototype strategy comes in. The strategy designs the composition of prototypes according to a systematic procedure. The goal is to design the interplay of the individual dimensions in such a way that certain perceptions and responses are triggered in the test persons. Similar to the prototype, all efforts in the **process** are focused on the output to be achieved. The process includes all questions concerning the prototyping sequence and defines the methodological framework. For example, it is defined which method is used for data collection, whether several prototypes are tested in parallel and how many iteration loops are performed.

All decisions concerning the process must also take into account their effects on the **probands**. Because their feedback is the primary motivation for prototyping. Traditionally, this role is taken by the future target group. But for the prototyping purpose communication, for example, when the prototype is presented to the management and decision-makers, then these stakeholders take on the role of the proband. Even the designer himself can test the prototype. In this case, the designer himself is the test person for the prototype. In addition to the selection of test persons, the questions of how many test persons participate in the test and to what extent the approaches of participatory design should be applied in prototyping must also be clarified.

The endpoint of the model represents the **output**. The findings are extracted from the aggregated perceptions and responses of the probands. The overall quality of the prototyping is revealed by reflecting the findings with the aims defined at the beginning. This reflection thus closes the circle and can lead to research questions for the new prototyping iteration.

4.3   Strategies for Smart Service Prototypes

The quality of a prototype is defined by the information and insights gained with its help. In accordance with this maxim, the prototype strategy is faced with the challenge of designing the prototype in such a way that a maximum of new and correct insights can be collected. For the sector of smart services three relevant strategies for prototypes in other design disciplines could be identified: Functional prototypes, experience prototypes and contextual prototypes (Fig. 3).

Each strategy has its own focus and thus influences how the prototype is perceived by the probands. The focus of a prototype is derived from its composition. For smart services, the composition consists of six different dimensions, along which a prototype can be characterized (see Table 3). A prototype can be designed and implemented for each of these six dimensions with low or high fidelity, depending on the findings the engineers or designers intend to gather as output. In the strategy, the dimensions are consciously selected to provoke responses from the probands with regard to the object of investigation. Despite the emphasis on one dimension, the test persons do not perceive the individual dimensions in isolation, but the probands are influenced by the interplay of all involved dimensions [cf. 38].

Crucial for the selection of a strategy is the assessment of the test persons. In line with Nielsen's findings in usability engineering [37], knowledge about the participants and their individual differences can also improve the outcome of a study in the requirements elicitation for smart services. To make a decision, engineers and designers have to ask themselves which strategy will produce the highest quality output from the test persons. In addition to the respondents, the prototyping diamond indicates two further dependencies for the selection of the strategy (see Fig. 2). The object of investigation should always be included in the strategy considerations, as well as the process.

Functional Prototypes Traditionally, the functionality of a prototype increases during the design stages with the understanding of the product [25]. However, innovation research in product design that aims to create radical innovations emphasizes the value of different functional prototypes already in the early stages of development [cf. 5]. Jensen et al. [23] as representatives from product design have developed the prototrials approach for this purpose. Prototrials cover high-functional prototypes used in the concept development phases for requirements elicitation, but with low fidelity compared with the final product [23]. Exactly this approach is used in the strategy of functional prototypes. According to the name, the dimension functionality is very prominent. Considering the layer model of smart services (see Fig. 1), it becomes clear that the layers below the line of visibility are the subject of these prototypes. Besides the software-based functionality in the smart service layer, the dynamic interdependencies and data transformation are also relevant for a functional investigation. This leads to the fact that elements from the layers smart data and smart product are also represented in functional prototypes. Engineers and designers must, therefore, decide which level of fidelity is sufficient for the dimension data in the prototype. Furthermore, the question also arises to what extent a representation of the smart products or a visualization of the data flows is relevant for explaining the functional relationships.

In research work for public transport, the orientation and navigation within subway stations were investigated from the passengers' point of view. One of the aims was to develop a tool that identifies the right wagon for the passenger according to individual needs when entering the subway [52]. In the first step, a prototype was developed to test its feasibility. The object of investigation was the data transmission and processing in real-time as well as whether the identification of a wagon is possible with the beacon technology. The researchers tested the prototype with 15 probands with the aim of

Table 3. Dimensions for the prototype composition of smart services

Dimension	Definition
Representation	The representation indicates how prototypes are presented, what they actually look like and how they are materialized [cf. 35]. Due to its immateriality, the representation in services design focuses on the service encounter to make the intangible parts of service tangible [49]. In smart services, the interaction takes place in the layer smart interface (see Fig. 1), but it can also be relevant to show the physical infrastructure and its relation to the software in the representation of the prototype
Scope	The scope defines the range of what is covered and manifested within the prototypes [30]. For smart services, this decision is challenged primarily by the service process and the context awareness of the services. Along the service process, it must be defined which touchpoint and which context of use should be considered in the prototype
Functionality	The functionality dimension contains the functions that can be simulated by the prototypes. Focusing on this dimension, engineers and designers determine to what level of detail is any one feature or sequence represented [40]
Interactivity	Interactivity defines how interactive elements are captured in the prototypes and communicated to the users [40]. The focus is on the way test persons can interact with the system, e.g. through feedback, input behaviour, operating behaviour and output behaviour [30]
Appearance	Appearance can occur in a variety of forms, especially in smart services. Above all, it is the visual refinement that shapes the appearance. For example, digital artefacts are represented on the low end of the fidelity scale with hand-drawn sketches and in contrast, the high end includes pixel-accurate screen designs. Apart from the visual appearance, the auditory and haptic aspects can also be relevant for the service interface, as well as the spatial context in which the interface appears
Data model	The dimension defines to what extent the data in the prototypes represent the actual domain data. The data model is relevant for two segments in the case of smart services. On the one hand, it must be decided to what extent real data must be presented to the test persons in the smart interface. On the other hand, it must be defined to what extent real data are relevant for the simulation of data acquisition, transmission and processing in the layers below the line of visibility for the findings of the prototyping

eliciting new requirements for further development. The prototype focused on the data exchange between beacon and a rudimentary information display on the smartphone. In addition to the functionality, the data had a high level of fidelity. For the test, real data was exchanged in real-time between the subway wagons and the smartphone. By integrating the wagon and the smartphone into the test, the probands were able to understand the dynamic interrelationships of the smart service. Compared to the final application, the dimensions of interactivity and appearance were hardly pronounced.

LAYER MODEL OF SMART SERVICES
Structure and Functionality

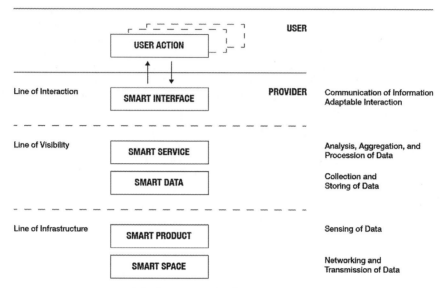

Fig. 1. Layer model for smart services

THE TWO-PART PROTOTYPING DIAMOND
Model

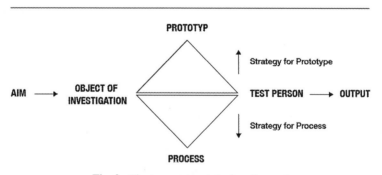

Fig. 2. The two-part prototyping diamond

The emphasis on the functional dimension leads the test persons to a structure-oriented view of the prototypes. In this way, the probands observe the functional elements of a system and their relationships, whereby the dynamic mechanisms and processes are of particular interest [cf. 46]. The focus is on how the functions are used to generate value for the user. Due to the concentration on the functional aspects, these prototypes have a significant demonstration character and only a low potential for immersion and involvement for the proband during the prototyping session.

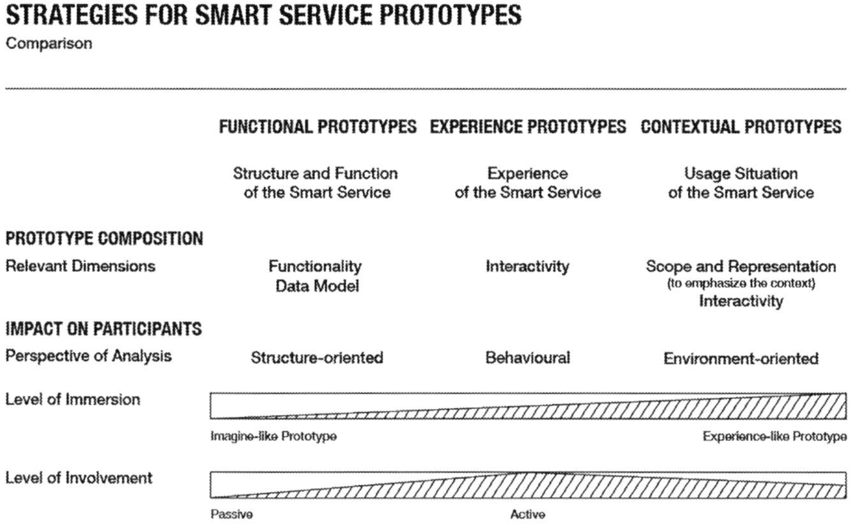

STRATEGIES FOR SMART SERVICE PROTOTYPES
Comparison

	FUNCTIONAL PROTOTYPES	EXPERIENCE PROTOTYPES	CONTEXTUAL PROTOTYPES
	Structure and Function of the Smart Service	Experience of the Smart Service	Usage Situation of the Smart Service
PROTOTYPE COMPOSITION			
Relevant Dimensions	Functionality Data Model	Interactivity	Scope and Representation (to emphasize the context) Interactivity
IMPACT ON PARTICIPANTS			
Perspective of Analysis	Structure-oriented	Behavioural	Environment-oriented
Level of Immersion	Imagine-like Prototype		Experience-like Prototype
Level of Involvement	Passive	Active	

Fig. 3. Strategies for prototypes of smart services

Experience Prototypes. By the term "experience erototype" Buchenau and Suri [53] mean to emphasize "the experiential aspect of whatever representations are needed to successfully (re)live or convey an experience with a product, space or system". The objective of the experience prototypes is the discovery of the probands' user experience. Based on the perceptions and responses of a test person resulting from the use of the system [cf. 54], new insights are generated for service development. The interaction of the test persons with the system is used as the central stimulus for the emergence of the user experience. Considering the experience prototypes in the layer model (see Fig. 1), it becomes clear that these prototypes concentrate on the smart interface layer. Experience prototypes can be described using the technique wizard of oz. While a test person interacts with a system that feels real, an engineer or designer simulates the system in the background [cf. 55]. The goal is to create a high degree of interactivity while maintaining low functionality in the prototype at the same time. The focus is on the dialogue between user and provider, which is made tangible through user inputs and system feedback. In service prototyping, there are special requirements due to the characteristics of the services. Stickdorn [49] therefore stresses that intangible services should be visualised in terms of physical artefacts. In general, the immaterial character of smart services is further reinforced. The reason for this is that interaction in smart service is characterized by automation and implicit interactions, which are fostered by adaptivity and context awareness. As a result, users perceive only a fraction of the activities of smart service. The majority of the activities are carried out in the backstage that is not visible to the user (see Fig. 1). For this reason, experience prototypes face the challenge to make the interaction tangible for the proband using the dimension representation. Another challenge for experience prototypes is the sequential nature of smart services. Stickdorn [49] recommends that the service should be visualised as a sequence of interrelated activities. For the prototype, this means that within the dimension scope all touchpoints along the user journey should be checked for relevance to the prototype. The focus on interaction promotes the behavioural analysis of the prototypes. The probands are primarily concerned with system behaviour and the generation of value creation during use, rather than focusing on internal, functional relationships. Furthermore, the interactive character of the experience prototypes promotes active participation [53] and the immersion of the probands in the test scenario.

Figure 4 shows a lego serious play prototype, which was carried out in combination with the technique service walkthrough. The aim of this experience prototype was to discover new requirements in the early phases of the research project within the first study with six test persons. The project explored the networking of local public transport and car-sharing with electric vehicles in a digital mobility platform [56]. Concretely, the process, as well as the interaction at the charging station and in the vehicles, was investigated. The basic structure for the session was defined using the service walkthrough method. Along the user journey, the test persons visited selected touchpoints, which became tangible artefacts for the test persons in the form of lego objects. At the individual touchpoints, interactions with the digital platform were simulated using paper prototypes to capture the mobility experience of the travel chain [cf. 57].

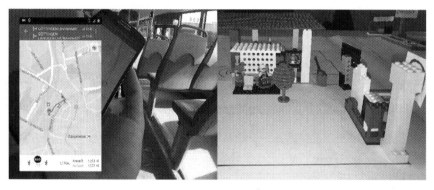

Fig. 4. Examples of contextual prototype (left) and experience prototype (right)

Contextual Prototypes. "Context […] characterize the situation of an entity. An entity is a person, place, or object that is considered relevant to the interaction between a user and an application" [58]. Contextual prototypes thus emphasize the situation in which the system is applied. At the same time, they take the context of use as a stimulus for the test persons in the prototyping session. Beaudouin-Lafon and Mackay [26] use the term "scenario prototypes" in this context and stress that prototypes are used in a more realistic scenario to simulate the system under real conditions. Hutchinson et al. [58] went one step further with their technology probes approach. Technology probes are simple, flexible, adaptable technologies that combine the social science goal of collecting information about the use and the users of the technology in a real-world setting [59]. Contextual prototypes use the realistic representation of the usage situation as a stimulus for the participants in the prototyping session. Consequently, when constructing the prototype, the usage context within the scope dimension must be considered in addition to the interaction at the touchpoint. Bittner [60] speaks in this context of servicescapes and mentions the possible factors influencing the user experience: Ambient conditions, spatial layout and functionality, signs, symbols, and artefacts as well as service typology, and environmental dimensions.

Due to the context awareness of smart services, contextual prototypes play a double role and contribute to the clarification of two questions. First, they provide information on how the context can hinder or improve the usage and experience of smart services. In this case, the focus of the prototypes lies on interactivity in combination with the representation to enable realistic interactions. Secondly, contextual prototypes offer the potential to understand how collected data from the usage context can contribute to the value generation of smart services. In doing so, no high fidelity in the dimensions data and functionality is required, but rather the logic of the system behaviour in the usage situation must be simulated. Both points lead to the fact that the participants analyse the prototypes from an environment-oriented perspective. The test persons perceive the external factors from the usage situation and their influence on the prototypes. Due to the real-world setting, a high level of immersion is generated among the probands during the prototyping session.

Figure 4 shows an example of a contextual prototype from a mobility research project. The project explored the agenda planning as a new mobility planning approach [cf. 48]. In this study with 25 test persons, it was examined how, for example, changed opening hours of shops and the current seat occupation of vehicles can be integrated into a digital planning application. The aim was to identify new requirements in the early development phases. The prototype included a rudimentary digital smartphone application that could be used in the local bus and train network. When composing the prototype, the focus was on interactivity and the usage context. It was important that all participants could perform their tasks independently in real-life usage situations.

5   Discussion—Contribution to Requirements Elicitation for Smart Services

The strategies for prototypes define the composition of prototypes and thus systematically influence how a prototype is perceived by the test persons. They constitute the missing link between the dimensions of a prototype and the targeted output. Based on the presentation of the strategies and the case studies carried out, the authors see two major contributions to requirements elicitation in the early development phases.

First, the strategies provide a critical thinking approach. The strategies can be used to better predict in advance of the requirements elicitation how a prototype will affect the test persons and which results can be achieved as output. The engineers and designers can thus better understand which features are important for prototyping in requirements elicitation. Furthermore, the strategy is the consequent continuation of the economic principle: "The best prototype is one that, in the simplest and the most efficient way, makes the possibilities and limitations of a design idea visible and measurable" [30]. By means of the output-oriented analysis, it is possible to assess in advance to what extent the effort for prototyping is cost-effective. Secondly, the strategies provide a guideline for the creation of prototypes in requirements elicitation. Following the example of a pattern language [cf. 61], the strategies provide engineers and designers a kind of pattern for the composition of the different prototype dimensions. On the other hand, in conjunction with the layer model of smart services, the strategies show which dimensions are relevant for the investigation of the different layers.

As a limitation, it must be noted that the strategies are a mindset for the composition of prototypes for smart services. The strategies do not contain concrete recommendations for the efficient use of prototype resources in economic terms. This requires controlled and detailed studies to prove the effect of single dimensions on the output of prototyping [cf. 32, 39, 62]. Furthermore, the three strategies for smart service prototypes are only a selection. Although the various strategies have proven themselves in practice, they have their origins in other design disciplines. The question remains unanswered whether new strategies are better suited for requirements elicitation in the early development phases. With novel approaches, the complex structure of smart services could be addressed more precisely. One possible approach would be to focus on data-driven value creation, for example.

6 Conclusion

In this article the question is investigated, how can prototypes contribute to the requirements elicitation for smart services in the early development stages. An elementary prerequisite for the use of prototypes in requirements elicitation is the comprehensive understanding of smart services. The present article reveals through extensive literature research that the understanding of smart services varies from discipline to discipline and that the existing models address only rudimentary prototyping issues. To overcome this shortcoming, the authors introduce the layer model of smart services and build the foundation for the investigation of smart service prototypes. The review of the existing approaches for the systematic design of prototypes shows that the relationship between the composition of a prototype and the output has been insufficiently investigated so far but is becoming increasingly relevant for smart services. The layer model demonstrates that five layers with different functionalities are required for the provision of smart services and that a conscious focus must, therefore, take place every time a prototype is created. The lack of discussion motivated the authors to define the strategies for the composition of prototypes and to work out the approach for the requirements elicitation of smart services. The strategies systematically guide the composition of prototypes in order to influence how a prototype is perceived by the test persons. They thus form the missing link between the dimensions of a prototype and the targeted output. For smart services, the authors identify three relevant strategies in related design disciplines: Functional prototypes, experience prototypes and contextual prototypes. The relevance of the defined strategies is reviewed and illustrated by case studies from the mobility sector.

References

1. Norman, D.: Things That Make Us Smart: Defending Human Attributes in the Age of The Machine. Diversion Books (2014)

2. Norman, D.: The Design of Future Things. Basic Books (2009)
3. Wünderlich, N.V., et al.: Futurizing smart service: implications for service researchers and managers. J. Serv. Mark. **29**, 6 (2015)
4. Haines-Gadd, M., et al.: Cut the crap; design brief to pre-production in eight weeks: rapid development of an urban emergency low-tech toilet for Oxfam. Des. Stud. **40**, 246–268 (2015)
5. Leifer, L.J., Steinert, M.: Dancing with ambiguity: causality behavior, design thinking, and triple-loop-learning. Inf. Knowl. Syst. Manag. **10**(1–4), 151–173 (2011)
6. Allmendinger, G., Lombreglia, R.: Four strategies for the age of smart services. Harv. Bus. Rev. **83**(10), 131 (2005)
7. Lim, C., Maglio, P.P.: Clarifying the concept of smart service system. In: Maglio, P.P., Kieliszewski, C.A., Spohrer, J.C., Lyons, K., Patrício, L., Sawatani, Y. (eds.) Handbook of Service Science, Volume II. SSRISE, pp. 349–376. Springer, Cham (2019). https://doi.org/10.1007/978-3-319-98512-1_16
8. Kagermann, H., et al.: Smart service welt: Umsetzungsempfehlungen für das Zukunftsprojekt Internetbasierte Dienste für die Wirtschaft. acatech, Berlin (2014)
9. Bruhn, M., Hadwich, K.: Dienstleistungen 4.0 – Erscheinungsformen, Transformationsprozesse und Managementimplikationen. Dienstleistungen 4.0, pp. 1–39. Springer, Wiesbaden (2017). https://doi.org/10.1007/978-3-658-17552-8_1
10. Carrubbo, L., Bruni, R., Cavacece, Y., Moretta Tartaglione, A.: Service system platforms to improve value co-creation: insights for translational medicine 2015, Service Dominant Logic, Network and Systems Theory and Service Science: Integrating three Perspectives for a New Service Agenda (2015)
11. IfM and IBM: Succeeding through service innovation: a discussion paper. In: Cambridge Service Science, Management and Engineering Symposium. University of Cambridge Institute for Manufacturing, Cambridge (2007)
12. Basole, R.C., Rouse, W.B.: Complexity of service value networks: conceptualization and empirical investigation. IBM Syst. J. **47**(1), 53–70 (2008)
13. Demirkan, H., Kauffman, R.J., Vayghan, J.A., Fill, H.G., Karagiannis, D., Maglio, P.P.: Service-oriented technology and management: perspectives on research and practice for the coming decade. Electron. Commer. Res. Appl. **7**(4), 356–376 (2008)
14. Spohrer, J.C., Demirkan, H.: Introduction to the smart service systems: analytics, cognition, and innovation minitrack. In: 2015 48th Hawaii International Conference on System Sciences, pp. 1442–1442. IEEE, January 2015
15. Maglio, P.P., Vargo, S.L., Caswell, N., Spohrer, J.: The service system is the basic abstraction of service science. Inf. Syst. e-bus. Manag. **7**(4), 395–406 (2009)
16. Spohrer, J., Maglio, P.P., Bailey, J., Gruhl, D.: Steps toward a science of service systems. Computer **40**(1), 71–77 (2007)
17. Bullinger, H.-J., Ganz, W., Neuhüttler, J.: Smart Services – Chancen und Herausforderungen digitalisierter Dienstleistungssysteme für Unternehmen. Dienstleistungen 4.0, pp. 97–120. Springer, Wiesbaden (2017). https://doi.org/10.1007/978-3-658-17550-4_4
18. Winter, A., et al.: Manifest-Kundeninduzierte Orchestrierung komplexer Dienstleistungen. Informatik-Spektrum **35**(6), 399–408 (2012)
19. Norman, D.: The Design of Everyday Things: Revised and Expanded Edition. Basic Books (2013)
20. Robertson, J.: Requirements analysts must also be inventors. IEEE Softw. **22**(1), 48 (2005)
21. Hoffmann, O., Cropley, D., Cropley, A., Nguyen, L., Swatman, P.: Creativity, requirements and perspectives. Australas. J. Inf. Syst. **13**(1) (2005)
22. Nguyen, L., Shanks, G.: A framework for understanding creativity in requirements engineering. Inf. Softw. Technol. **51**(3), 655–662 (2009)
23. Jensen, M.B., Elverum, C.W., Steinert, M.: Eliciting unknown unknowns with prototypes: introducing prototrials and prototrial-driven cultures. Des. Stud. **49**, 1–31 (2017)

24. Warfel, T.Z.: Prototyping: a Practitioner's Guide. Rosenfeld Media (2009)
25. Eppinger, S., Ulrich, K.: Product Design and Development. McGraw-Hill Higher Education (2015)
26. Beaudouin-Lafon, M., Mackay, W.E.: Prototyping tools and techniques. In: Human-Computer Interaction, pp. 137–160. CRC Press (2009)
27. Houde, S., Hill, C.: What do prototypes prototype?. In: Handbook of Human-Computer Interaction, pp. 367–381, North-Holland (1997)
28. Holtzblatt, K., Beyer, H.: Contextual design: evolved. Synth. Lect. Hum.-Cent. Inform. 7(4), 1–91 (2014)
29. Dow, S.P., Glassco, A., Kass, J., Schwarz, M., Schwartz, D.L., Klemmer, S.R.: Parallel prototyping leads to better design results, more divergence, and increased self-efficacy. ACM Trans. Comput.-Hum. Interact. (TOCHI) 17(4), 1–24 (2010)
30. Lim, Y.K., Stolterman, E., Tenenberg, J.: The anatomy of prototypes: prototypes as filters, prototypes as manifestations of design ideas. ACM Trans. Comput.-Hum. Interact. (TOCHI) 15(2), 1–27 (2008)
31. Blackler, A.: Applications of high and low fidelity prototypes in researching intuitive interaction (2009)
32. Hare, J., Gill, S., Loudon, G., Lewis, A.: The effect of physicality on low fidelity interactive prototyping for design practice. In: Kotzé, P., Marsden, G., Lindgaard, G., Wesson, J., Winckler, M. (eds.) INTERACT 2013. LNCS, vol. 8117, pp. 495–510. Springer, Heidelberg (2013). https://doi.org/10.1007/978-3-642-40483-2_36
33. Sanders, E.B.N.: From user-centered to participatory design approaches. In: Design and the Social Sciences, pp. 18–25. CRC Press (2002)
34. Exner, K., Sternitzke, A., Kind, S., Beckmann-Dobrev, B.: Hybrid prototyping. In: Gengnagel, C., Nagy, E., Stark, R. (eds.) Rethink! Prototyping, pp. 89–127. Springer, Cham (2016). https://doi.org/10.1007/978-3-319-24439-6_8
35. Blomkvist, J., Holmlid, S.: Existing prototyping perspectives: considerations for service design. NorDes, vol. 4 (2011)
36. Stickdorn, M., Hormess, M. E., Lawrence, A., Schneider, J.: This is Service Design Doing: Applying Service Design Thinking in the Real World. O'Reilly Media Inc. (2018)
37. Nielsen, J.: Usability Engineering. Morgan Kaufmann (1994)
38. Rudd, J., Stern, K., Isensee, S.: Low vs. high-fidelity prototyping debate. Interactions 3(1), 76–85 (1996)
39. Lim, Y.K., Pangam, A., Periyasami, S., Aneja, S.: Comparative analysis of high-and low-fidelity prototypes for more valid usability evaluations of mobile devices. In: Proceedings of the 4th Nordic Conference on Human-Computer Interaction: Changing Roles, pp. 291–300, October 2006
40. McCurdy, M., Connors, C., Pyrzak, G., Kanefsky, B., Vera, A.: Breaking the fidelity barrier: an examination of our current characterization of prototypes and an example of a mixed-fidelity success. In: Proceedings of the SIGCHI Conference on Human Factors in Computing Systems, pp. 1233–1242, April 2006
41. Arnowitz, J., Arent, M., Berger, N.: Effective prototyping for software makers. Elsevier (2010)
42. Virzi, R.A., Sokolov, J.L., Karis, D.: Usability problem identification using both low-and high-fidelity prototypes. In: Proceedings of the SIGCHI Conference on Human Factors in Computing Systems, pp. 236–243, April 1996
43. Exner, K., Lindow, K., Stark, R., Ängeslevä, J., Bähr, B., Nagy, E.: A transdisciplinary perspective on prototyping. In: 2015 IEEE International Conference on Engineering, Technology and Innovation/International Technology Management Conference (ICE/ITMC), pp. 1–8. IEEE, June 2015
44. Cambridge University Press. https://dictionary.cambridge.org/de/worterbuch/englisch/connectivity. Accessed 24 Feb 2020

45. Neuhuettler, J., Ganz, W., Liu, J.: An integrated approach for measuring and managing quality of smart senior care services. In: Ahram, T., Karwowski, W. (eds.) Advances in The Human Side of Service Engineering, vol. 494, pp. 309–318. Springer, Cham (2017). https://doi.org/10.1007/978-3-319-41947-3_29

46. Haberfellner, R., de Weck, O., Fricke, E., Vössner, S.: Systems Engineering–Grundlagen und Anwendung. 12. Auflage, Orell Füssli, Zürich (2012). 978-3280040683

47. Grönroos, C., Voima, P.: Critical service logic: making sense of value creation and co-creation. J. Acad. Mark. Sci. **41**(2), 133–150 (2013)

48. Wienken, T., Schoppe, C., Krömker, H.: Auf dem Weg zur Agendaplanung– Weiterentwicklung der Fahrplanauskunft zum Service-System für Mobilität. Nahverkehr, **35**(9) (2017)

49. Stickdorn, M., Schneider, J., Andrews, K., Lawrence, A.: This is Service Design Thinking: Basics, Tools, Cases, vol. 1. Wiley, Hoboken, NJ (2011)

50. Shostack, G.L.: Designing services that deliver. Harv. Bus. Rev. **62**, 133–139 (1984)

51. Voss, C., Zomerdijk, L.: Innovation in experiential services: an empirical view. AIM Research (2007)

52. Krömker, H., Schöne, C., Wienken, T., Steinert, T.: DiMo-FuH - Digitale Mobilität - Fahrzeug und Haltestelle - Schlussbericht. Technische Universität Ilmenau, Ilmenau (2018)

53. Buchenau, M., Suri, J.F.: Experience prototyping. In: Proceedings of the 3rd Conference on Designing Interactive Systems: Processes, Practices, Methods, and Techniques, pp. 424–433, August 2000

54. International Standards Organization: Ergonomics of Human-System Interaction—Part 210: Human Centred Design for Interactive Systems (2010). ISO 9241-210

55. Kelley, J.F.: An iterative design methodology for user-friendly natural language office information applications. ACM Trans. Inf. Syst. (TOIS) **2**(1), 26–41 (1984)

56. Schmermbeck, S., et al.: Mobil im ländlichen Raum dank innovativer Dienstleistungen. Dienstleistungen als Erfolgsfaktor für Elektromobilität, pp. 128–139. Fraunhofer Verlag, Stuttgart (2017)

57. Wienken, T., Krömker, H.: Experience maps for mobility. In: Kurosu, M. (ed.) HCI 2018. LNCS, vol. 10902, pp. 615–627. Springer, Cham (2018). https://doi.org/10.1007/978-3-319-91244-8_47

58. Abowd, G.D., Dey, A.K., Brown, P.J., Davies, N., Smith, M., Steggles, P.: Towards a better understanding of context and context-awareness. In: Gellersen, H.-W. (ed.) HUC 1999. LNCS, vol. 1707, pp. 304–307. Springer, Heidelberg (1999). https://doi.org/10.1007/3-540-48157-5_29

59. Hutchinson, H., et al.: Technology probes: inspiring design for and with families. In: Proceedings of the SIGCHI Conference on Human Factors in Computing Systems, pp. 17–24 (2003)

60. Bitner, M.J.: Servicescapes: the impact of physical surroundings on customers and employees. J. Mark. **56**(2), 57–71 (1992)

61. Alexander, C.: A Pattern Language: Towns, Buildings. Construction. Oxford University Press, Oxford (1977)

62. Sefelin, R., Tscheligi, M., Giller, V.: Paper prototyping-what is it good for? A comparison of paper-and computer-based low-fidelity prototyping. In: CHI 2003 Extended Abstracts on Human Factors in Computing Systems, pp. 778–779, April 2003

An Integrated Framework of Product Kansei Decision-Making Based on Hesitant Linguistic Fuzzy Term Sets

Yan-pu Yang[1]([✉]), Jun-wen Shi[2,3], and Gang-feng Wang[1]

[1] School of Construction Machinery, Chang'an University, Xi'an 710064, China
yangyanpu@chd.edu.cn, 420803947@qq.com
[2] Xi'an Zhongqing Packaging Machinery Co. Ltd., Xi'an 710086, China
270867535@qq.com
[3] Light Industrial Xi'an Mechanic Design Research Institute Co. Ltd., Xi'an 710086, China

Abstract. Kansei adjectives have the advantage of close to consumers' perception of a product. But consumers may show hesitation and opinion discrepancy while expressing their preferences through comparative Kansei adjectives. To address this, this article investigates hesitant linguistic expression and its application in product Kansei decision-making. An integrated framework is firstly presented based on hesitant fuzzy linguistic term sets (HFLTSs), which involves a consensus model for assessing consistency of consumers' preferences, particle swarm optimization (PSO) method for adjusting Kansei opinions when agreement fails, and the technique for order preference by similarity to an ideal solution (TOPSIS) for yielding ranked product solutions. An example of charging piles design was used to illustrate the necessity of considering consumers' hesitation in Kansei decision-making. With the proposed method, the consensus level of consumers' preferences is enhanced from 0.8339 to 0.9052, and the overall satisfaction degree is also improved. Furthermore, the results of Kansei decision-making through optimizing Kansei preferences are significantly different from that without optimization. This improvement demonstrates that hesitance and consensus change will influence design decision-making and they should be considered in product Kansei decision-making. The given example shows the validity and suitability of the proposed approach.

Keywords: Kansei engineering · Product Kansei decision-making · Hesitant fuzzy linguistic term sets · Consensus reaching · Particle swarm optimization

1 Introduction

In today's rapid growing and competitive market, consumer-centered approach has attracted increasing attentions of many companies as a vital strategy for product development. It can help enterprises to enhance their market competitiveness and save time and costs during product development. The core of consumer-centered approach is to have a better understanding of consumers' requirements, which includes two aspects:

© Springer Nature Switzerland AG 2020
C. Stephanidis et al. (Eds.): HCII 2020, LNCS 12423, pp. 352–366, 2020.
https://doi.org/10.1007/978-3-030-60114-0_24

physiological and psychological. The former mainly involves functional attributes of products while the latter refers to subjective needs and feelings [1]. It is widely believed that similar products will have equivalent function, and it may be difficult for consumers to differentiate products only by their function [2, 3]. Moreover, good quality products are not enough for a company to survive in the increasing competitive market [4]. In this regard, satisfying consumers' needs not only depends on the reliability and physical quality of products, but also the affective aspects evoked by various product design elements [5]. One of the influential factors is attractive product appearance, which can affect consumers' intuitive perception and first impression, generate affective resonance, and lure them into making purchase decisions. The unique emotional value related to beauty or aesthetics of a product is also used to attract the attention of potential consumers [6].

To study the affective influence on consumers, Kansei Engineering (KE) has been proposed and used to link emotions to product properties [7, 8]. Covering the meanings of sensibility, impression and emotion, Kansei means all the senses of an individual's subjective impression and recognition from a certain artifact, environment, or situation, as described by Nagamachi [9]. KE methodology aims to integrate consumers' psychology and translate them into appropriate product design elements [10]. It has been proven that this technique is capable of testing the different feeling and shows their relation with characteristics of real production requirements by associating with consumers' physiological and psychological feelings [11]. For decades, KE has been developed as a consumer-oriented technique and connected to the industrial world to create numerous successful products and innovations [12].

An important KE type is KE modeling for assessing consumers' feeling of Kansei words [7]. It mainly involves attribute classification, preference modeling, and priority analysis [13]. When performing these operations, a common practice taken by many researchers is to convert users' Kansei preferences to numerical values for quantifying qualitative perception. However, it may result in loss of information because consumers tend to prefer Kansei adjectives or words to express their preferences rather than numerical values [14, 15]. Another common practice is that users' preferences are depicted by discrete concrete numbers or fuzzy numbers. Nevertheless, this may not accurately reflect the true intentions of users due to respondent bias when users are unable or unwilling to provide accurate answers. The third issue for Kansei assessment is hesitance in making preference, which reflects consumers' uncertainty about comparative linguistic terms. For example, a consumer's perception may be irresolute and swing between "very comfortable" and "comfortable", but the exact description cannot be given and the final perception may be "no worse than comfortable". In this situation, both "comfortable" and "very comfortable" should be used for preference representation. The three issues mentioned above are the key to elevating the quality of design decision-making and affect consensus reaching of group opinions.

In general, Kansei preference data is better to be treated as semantic variables than SD method [16], and using fuzzy linguistic term sets to deal with consumers' Kansei preference as continuous variables is more in line with their perception. Besides, hesitance and opinion discrepancy often happen when consumers make a choice. However, these problems have got little attention in product Kansei decision-making process.

Aiming at these issues of product Kansei decision-making, this paper presents an integrated framework based on hesitant fuzzy linguistic term sets (HFLTSs), which involves a consensus model for assessing consistency of consumers' preferences, particle swarm optimization (PSO) method for adjusting Kansei opinions when agreement fails, and the technique for order preference by similarity to an ideal solution (TOPSIS) for yielding ranked product solutions. Accordingly, the remainder of the paper is organized as follows: Sect. 2 introduces preliminaries of the proposed method, including linguistic variables and HFLTSs. In Sect. 3, an integrated framework is proposed. Then, a numerical example is provided to illustrate the detailed implementation of the proposed method in Sect. 4. Finally, Sect. 5 makes the concluding remarks and contribution of this paper.

2   Preliminaries

2.1   Linguistic Variables

The essential part of fuzzy linguistic approach are fuzzy sets as they provide a means of modeling vagueness underlying most natural linguistic terms [17, 18]. For Kansei decision-making problems, adjectives of emotional connotations can be regarded as a fuzzy set U defined by its membership function $\mu : U \rightarrow [0, 1]$, where U is a nonempty set [19]. With fuzzy sets, fuzzy linguistic approach can be founded based on linguistic variables introduced by Zadeh [20–22], which takes words or sentences to model the linguistic information. A linguistic variable is formally defined as follows.

Definition 1 [20].   A   linguistic   variable   is   characterized   by   a quintuple $(L, T(L), U, S, M)$ in which L is the name of the variable; $T(L)$ denotes the term set of L, i.e., the set of names of linguistic values of L, with each value being a fuzzy variable that is denoted generically by X and ranging across a universe of discourse U, which is associated with the base variable u; S is a syntactic rule (which usually takes the form of a grammar) for the generation of the names of values of L; and M is a semantic rule for associating its meaning with each L, $M(X)$, which is a fuzzy subset of U. With triangular fuzzy numbers, the composition of a quintuple of Kansei adjective "comfortable" is illustrated in Fig. 1.

Using ordered linguistic term sets, Xu [23] defined a set of linguistic terms as $S = \{s_\alpha | \alpha \in \{-\tau, \cdots, 0, \cdots, \tau\}\}$ with 0 as the symmetric center and odd number of linguistic terms. Let $\tau = 3$ then we can get a Likert-7 scale which is often used in measuring consumers' Kansei preferences, shown as follows:

$S = \{s_{-3}$: not at all, s_{-2}: low, s_{-1}: slightly, s_0: neutral, s_1: moderately, s_2: very, s_3: extremely$\}$.

With ordered finite subset of consecutive linguistic terms, it is obvious that $s_\alpha \leq s_\beta \Leftrightarrow \alpha \leq \beta$. If a negation operator exists, then we can have $\text{Neg}(s_\alpha) = s_{-\alpha}$.

In order to preserve all given information, Xu [24] further extended the discrete linguistic term set S to the continuous linguistic term set $\overline{S} = \{s_\alpha | \alpha \in [-t, t]\}$, where t is a sufficiently large positive integer. In general, the linguistic terms $s_\alpha (s_\alpha \in S)$ are given by decision makers while the extended linguistic terms $\bar{s}_\alpha (\bar{s}_\alpha \in \overline{S})$ only appear in operations.

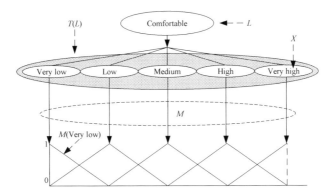

Fig. 1. A quintuple of the Kansei adjective "comfortable"

Let $\mu, \mu_1, \mu_2 > 0$, $s_\alpha, s_\beta \in \bar{S}$. The basic operation rules of linguistic variables are as follows [25].

(1) $s_\alpha \oplus s_\beta = s_{\alpha+\beta}$;
(2) $\mu s_\alpha = s_{\mu\alpha}$;
(3) $(\mu_1 + \mu_2)s_\alpha = \mu_1 s_\alpha \oplus \mu_2 s_\beta$;
(4) $\mu(s_\alpha \oplus s_\beta) = \mu s_\alpha \oplus \mu s_\beta$.

2.2 HFLTSs

For product Kansei decision-making, consumers' preferences may sway or hesitate between two or more options. In such situation, singleton linguistic term may be not suitable to represent their judgment. To denote the hesitancy over several linguistic terms, HFLTSs are employed to represent and aggregate consumers' Kansei preferences.

Definition 2 [26]. Let S be a linguistic term set, $S = \{s_\alpha | \alpha \in \{-\tau, \cdots, 0, \cdots, \tau\}\}$. An HFLTS, H_S, is an ordered finite subset of the consecutive linguistic terms of S.

Using the example from the previous section, we can get two different HFLTSs as:

$$H_S^1 = \{s_{-1} : \text{slightly}, s_0 : \text{neutral}\},$$
$$H_S^2 = \{s_1 : \text{moderately}, s_2 : \text{very}, s_3 : \text{extremely}\}.$$

The basic operations and computations that will be performed on the HFLTS in this paper are as follows.

(1) The upper bound H_{S+} and lower bound H_{S-}:

$$H_{S+} = \max\{s_i | s_i \in H_S\}, \quad H_{S-} = \min\{s_i | s_i \in H_S\}.$$

(2) The envelope $\text{env}(H_S)$ of the HFLTS:

$$\text{env}(H_S) = [H_S^-, H_S^+].$$

In order to operate correctly when comparing two HFLTSs, Zhu and Xu [27] proposed a method to add linguistic terms in a HFLTS:

$$\bar{H}_S = \xi H_{S+} \oplus (1 - \xi) H_{S-} \tag{1}$$

where $\xi (\xi \in [0, 1])$ is an optimized parameter. $\xi = 1$ and $\xi = 0$ correspond with the optimism and pessimism rules, respectively. Without loss of generality, we set $\xi = 0.5$ in this paper.

3   An Integrated Framework for Kansei Decision-Making

On account of the function of HFLTSs for aggregating consumers' Kansei preferences, an integrated framework of product Kansei decision-making is proposed, including a consensus model, PSO and TOPSIS. The flow chart of the proposed framework is shown in Fig. 2.

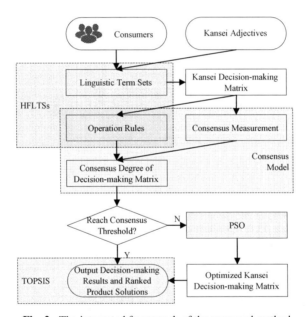

Fig. 2. The integrated framework of the proposed method

In the framework with HFLTSs employed, a consensus model is built to gauge their consistency, as is expected that the final decision should be reached based on a wide enough agreement. When disagreement fails to meet an acceptable consensus degree, PSO will be adopted to adjust the Kansei opinions and finally the ranked product solutions will be output with TOPSIS. The following expounds the details of the framework.

3.1   Consensus Model

Let $D = \{d_1, d_2, \cdots, d_q\}$ $(q \geq 2)$ be a set of consumers who are invited to participate in product Kansei decision-making about a set of product design alternatives $X = \{x_1, x_2, \cdots, x_n\}$ $(n \geq 2)$. Assume that the set of Kansei indicators is $C = \{c_1, c_2, \cdots, c_m\}$ $(m \geq 2)$. A linguistic term set, $S = \{s_\alpha | \alpha \in \{-\tau, \cdots, 0, \cdots, \tau\}\}$, is used to collect consumers' preference information. Then we have the decision matrix of HFLTS:

$$A^{(k)} = [H_{ij}^{(k)}]_{n \times m} \tag{2}$$

where $k = 1, 2, \cdots, q$; $H_{ij}^{(k)}$ represents the judgment of product alternative x_i given by consumer d_k in terms of Kansei indicator c_j.

In product Kansei decision-making process, the opinions of consumers will be aggregated when they reach a certain level of agreement or consensus to assure a high reliability of decision-making result. In order to evaluate the consistency of decision matrix, similarity function is an effective tool, which is usually used to build mathematical consistency model by measuring the proximity of consumers' preferences [28].

For a Kansei indicator, suppose that $H_S^1 = \{s_{\delta_l^1} | s_{\delta_l^1} \in S\}$ and $H_S^2 = \{s_{\delta_l^2} | s_{\delta_l^2} \in S\}$ are two HFLTSs given by two consumers, and $l(H_S^k)(k = 1, 2)$ represents the number of elements in H_S^k. Then the Euclidean distance between H_S^1 and H_S^2 can be defined as [29]:

$$D(H_S^1, H_S^2) = \left(\frac{1}{L} \sum_{l=1}^{L} \left(\frac{|\delta_l^1 - \delta_l^2|}{2\tau + 1} \right)^2 \right)^{1/2} \tag{3}$$

where $L = l(H_S^1) = l(H_S^2)$ (otherwise, the shorter one should be extended by adding the linguistic terms given as Eq. (1)).

Let $w_j(j = 1, 2, \cdots, m)$ represent the weight of Kansei criteria. The distance between two product Kansei decision matrices $A^{(k)} = [H_{ij}^{(k)}]_{n \times m}$ and $A^{(l)} = [H_{ij}^{(l)}]_{n \times m}$ can be described as:

$$d(A^{(k)}, A^{(l)}) = \frac{1}{n} \sum_{i=1}^{n} \sum_{j=1}^{m} w_j d(H_{ij}^{(k)}, H_{ij}^{(l)}) \tag{4}$$

Accordingly, the consensus degree between $A^{(k)}$ and $A^{(l)}$ can be computed as:

$$CON(A^{(k)}, A^{(l)}) = 1 - d(A^{(k)}, A^{(l)}) \tag{5}$$

Then the consensus level of all consumers whose judgements are represented in the set $(A^{(1)}, A^{(2)}, \cdots, A^{(q)})$ can be obtained as follows:

$$CONS = \frac{1}{q(q-1)} \sum_{\substack{k=1 \\ k \neq l}}^{q} \sum_{l=1}^{q} CON(A^{(k)}, A^{(l)}) \tag{6}$$

3.2 PSO for Consensus Reaching by Adjusting Consumers' Preferences

Agreement of the majority of consumers is essential for design decision-making. However, it is likely not to reach a consensus easily due to cognitive discrepancy. Comparing to ask consumers to change their opinions, it is more effective to employ intelligent algorithms to search for satisfactory solutions of consumers' opinions that meet a consensus threshold instead of finding the optimal value. With the advantage of ease of implementation, high degree of stability and fast convergence to acceptable solutions [30–32], PSO is suitable for consensus optimization. As a population based self-adaptive, stochastic optimization technique [33], all population members in PSO survive from the beginning of a trial until the end rather than are selected and evolve in evolutionary algorithms. Due to that particle interactions result in iterative improvement of the quality of problem solutions over time with few or no assumptions about the problem being optimized and can search very large spaces of candidate solutions [34], the PSO techniques are taken to seek consensus with adjustment of consumers' preferences. Each candidate solution in PSO, called a particle, flies in the N-dimensional search space according to a speed. Suppose that there are M particles in the swarm, and then particle p_j has a position $p_j = (p_{1j}^T, p_{2j}^T, \cdots, p_{mj}^T)^T$ and a velocity $v = (v_{1j}, v_{2j}, \cdots, v_{mj})$, where $p_{1j}^T, p_{2j}^T, \cdots, p_{mj}^T$ represents the automatically adjusted preferences of consumers. The velocity decides the flying distance and direction, and Eq. (6) is used as target optimization function. Thus, the velocity and location updating of a particle can be calculated as follows:

$$\begin{cases} v_{\alpha\beta}(t+1) = \omega v_{\alpha\beta}(t) + c_1 r_{1\beta}(t)(pbest_{\alpha\beta}(t) - x_{\alpha\beta}(t)) + c_2 r_{2\beta}(t)(gbest_\beta - x_{\alpha\beta}(t)) \\ x_{\alpha\beta}(t+1) = x_{\alpha\beta}(t) + v_{\alpha\beta}(t+1) \end{cases}$$

(7)

where t is the iteration number; $v_{\alpha\beta}(t)$, $x_{\alpha\beta}(t)$ represent the velocity and position of particle α in the β dimension, respectively; $pbest_{\alpha\beta}(t)$ is the current best position of particle α; $gbest_\beta$ shows the best fit that any particle of the swarm has ever achieved; $r_{1\beta}(t)$ and $r_{2\beta}(t)$ are two random numbers ranging from 0 and 1; c_1 and c_2 are two positive constants, denoting the cognitive and social components respectively; ω is the inertia of the particle which is employed to improve the convergence of the swarm. Linearly Decreasing Inertia Weight (LDW) is often used to enhance the global exploration ability for searching in a larger space by increasing the value of ω when the evolution speed of the swarm is fast, and maintain the particles searching in a small space to find the optimal solution more quickly by decreasing the value of ω if the evolution speed of particles slows down. ω can be calculated as follows [35]:

$$\omega = \omega_{max} - \frac{\omega_{max} - \omega_{min}}{t\_max} \times t$$

(8)

where t_max is the maximal iteration generations of PSO; ω_{max} and ω_{min} represent the maximum and minimum of ω respectively. Generally, ω linearly decreases from 0.9 to 0.4.

3.3 TOPSIS

When consumers' preferences come to an agreement, the TOPSIS [36] method will be employed to determine the orders of product alternatives. The basic principle of TOPSIS is to calculate the distance between each HFLTS and the hesitant fuzzy linguistic positive ideal solution, and the distance between each HFLTS and the hesitant fuzzy linguistic negative ideal solution, respectively. The closer to the positive ideal solution and the farther from the negative ideal solution, the better the alternative.

Kansei adjectives utilized to describe consumers' perceptions reflect their expectations about a product. They are benefit-type criteria. Hence, for each HFLTS in $A^{(k)} = [H_{ij}^{(k)}]_{n \times m}$, utilizing the upper bound H_{S+} and lower bound H_{S-}, the hesitant fuzzy linguistic positive ideal solution A_+ and the hesitant fuzzy linguistic negative ideal solution A_- can be defined as follows:

$$\begin{cases} A_+ = \{H_S^{1+}, H_S^{2+}, \cdots, H_S^{m+}\} \\ A_- = \{H_S^{1-}, H_S^{2-}, \cdots, H_S^{m-}\} \end{cases} \tag{9}$$

where $H_S^{j+} (j = 1, 2 \cdots, m) = \max\limits_{\substack{i=1,2,\cdots,n \\ k=1,2,\cdots,q}} \{s_{\delta_l} | s_{\delta_l} \in H_{ij}^{(k)}\}$, $H_S^{j-} (j = 1, 2 \cdots, m) = \min\limits_{\substack{i=1,2,\cdots,n \\ k=1,2,\cdots,q}} \{s_{\delta_l} | s_{\delta_l} \in H_{ij}^{(k)}\}$.

For ranking the product design schemes according to the idea of TOPSIS, the distance between each HFLTS and the positive ideal solution A_+ (denoted by $d(A_j^{(i)}, A_+)$), and the distance between each HFLTS and the negative ideal solution A_- (denoted by $d(A_j^{(i)}, A_-)$) are computed using Eq. (4) respectively. Then the Kansei satisfaction degree of a product design alternative can be defined as:

$$\eta(x_i) = \frac{1}{q} \sum_{j=1}^{q} \frac{(1 - \theta)d(A_j^{(i)}, A_-)}{\theta d(A_j^{(i)}, A_+) + (1 - \theta)d(A_j^{(i)}, A_-)} \tag{10}$$

where the parameter θ denotes the risk preferences of the decision maker: $\theta > 0.5$ means that the decision maker is pessimists; while $\theta < 0.5$ means the opposite. Without loss of generality, we choose $\theta = 0.5$.

4 Case Study

A case study of charging piles design for electric vehicles was used to determine the proposed method's ability for reaching consensus in product Kansei decision-making process. To collect consumers' Kansei needs effectively, various charging piles were involved in this research, covering current production and concept design. 43 Kansei adjectives about product samples were collected from websites, literatures, product manuals, magazines, experts, industrial designers, experienced users and dissertations. Adjectives with antonyms were paired up and others were endowed with right antonyms, and based on this we used an NDSM-GA based approach which was discussed in our previous research [37] to cluster consumers' Kansei needs into several categories and clarify primary adjectives. Finally, we obtained 4 Kansei adjectives to evaluate consumers' response about product design alternatives, shown as follows: (1) technological; (2) dynamic; (3) modern; (4) futuristic. 3 industrial designers were asked one each to

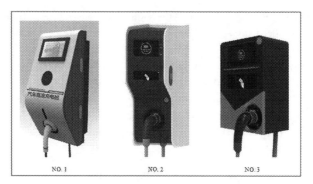

Fig. 3. Charging piles design solutions

give a design solution according to consumers' Kansei needs and the requirement of the principal, who requested the product to be processed by sheet metal (seen in Fig. 3).

Through questioning the designers, the styling features of 3 product solutions were articulated to consumers. 5 consumers who intended to buy or use charging piles were randomly selected and invited to give their preferences about the alternatives according to the Kansei indices, which were represented through linguistic terms of $S = \{s_{-3}$: not at all, s_{-2}: low, s_{-1}: slightly, s_0: neutral, s_1: moderately, s_2: very, s_3: extremely$\}$.

The Kansei decision-making matrices are shown below:

$$A^{(1)} = \begin{bmatrix} \{s_2, s_3\} & \{s_2, s_3\} & \{s_3\} & \{s_1, s_2\} \\ \{s_1\} & \{s_2, s_3\} & \{s_1, s_2\} & \{s_2\} \\ \{s_1, s_2\} & \{s_0\} & \{s_2\} & \{s_1\} \end{bmatrix};$$

$$A^{(2)} = \begin{bmatrix} \{s_2\} & \{s_3\} & \{s_2, s_3\} & \{s_2\} \\ \{s_1, s_2\} & \{s_1, s_2\} & \{s_1\} & \{s_0, s_1, s_2\} \\ \{s_2\} & \{s_0, s_1\} & \{s_{-2}\} & \{s_1\} \end{bmatrix};$$

$$A^{(3)} = \begin{bmatrix} \{s_0\} & \{s_1\} & \{s_{-1}, s_0\} & \{s_1, s_2\} \\ \{s_1, s_2\} & \{s_1, s_2\} & \{s_1\} & \{s_0, s_1\} \\ \{s_0, s_1, s_2\} & \{s_0, s_1\} & \{s_1, s_2\} & \{s_1, s_2\} \end{bmatrix};$$

$$A^{(4)} = \begin{bmatrix} \{s_1, s_2\} & \{s_{-1}, s_0\} & \{s_2, s_3\} & \{s_1\} \\ \{s_2\} & \{s_1, s_2\} & \{s_0, s_1, s_2\} & \{s_1\} \\ \{s_1, s_2\} & \{s_{-1}\} & \{s_2\} & \{s_0\} \end{bmatrix};$$

$$A^{(5)} = \begin{bmatrix} \{s_{-2}\} & \{s_0, s_1\} & \{s_2\} & \{s_{-1}, s_0\} \\ \{s_1, s_2\} & \{s_0\} & \{s_1, s_2\} & \{s_0, s_1\} \\ \{s_1, s_2\} & \{s_0\} & \{s_{-1}, s_0\} & \{s_1, s_2\} \end{bmatrix}.$$

The 4 Kansei indices were given equal weight by investigating consumers' opinions. Using Eq. (1)–Eq. (6), the consensus matrix can be obtained as:

$$CON = \begin{bmatrix} 1 & 0.86363 & 83287 & 0.86980 & 0.79250 \\ 0.86363 & 1 & 0.83630 & 0.82562 & 0.80895 \\ 0.83287 & 0.83630 & 1 & 0.84212 & 0.84917 \\ 0.86980 & 0.82562 & 0.84212 & 1 & 0.81783 \\ 0.79250 & 0.80895 & 0.84917 & 0.81783 & 1 \end{bmatrix}$$

The consensus threshold value was set as 0.9, and the overall consensus of consumers was 0.8339, which did not reach the specific threshold and the Kansei decision-making matrices should be adjusted using PSO.

Generally, particle swarm size ranges from 10 to 50 depending on different applications and problems [30], and here its value was set as 10. c_1 and c_2 belong to the range of [0, 4], and $c_1 = c_2 = 2$ may be preferable. t_max was set to 500. By asking consumers' advice, the adjustment space of consumers' preferences was set to [−0.5, 0.5]. Yet the adjusted value should fall in the range of −3 and 3. There were 120 parameters that would be adjusted and searched in the bound. The adjustment rules are as follows: (1) if there is only one element in an HFLTS, it will be extended to three equal elements; (2) if there are two or three elements, the lower bound and the upper bound will be extended by −0.5 and 0.5 respectively, and the intermediate elements are calculated according to Eq. (1).

After 100 operations by using PSO, the optimal consensus value distribution was obtained, shown in Fig. 4. Figure 5 shows the convergence process of the algorithm and Fig. 6 depicts the mean deviation change in one of the operations. It can be seen that the optimal consensus value was found in each generation and mean deviation between the optimal matrix and the original matrix did not outnumber 0.07.

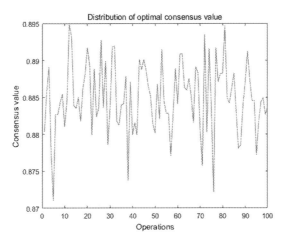

Fig. 4. Distribution of optimal consensus value in 100 operations

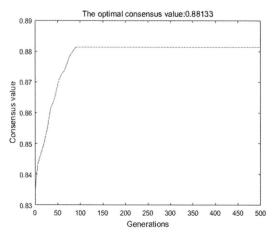

Fig. 5. The change curve of optimal consensus value

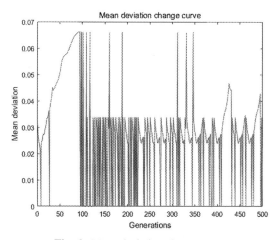

Fig. 6. Mean deviation change curve

However, the optimization results failed to meet the expected requirement of consensus threshold. In terms of the mean deviation and consumers' suggestion, the adjustment space was extended to $[-0.6, 0.6]$ and the consensus value was recalculated, shown in Fig. 7. The results show that the optimal consensus degree reached the threshold requirement in operations of 4, 12, 20, 28, 31, 41, 43, 46, 52, 60, 66, 68, 72, 76, 79, 83 and 86. The maximum appears in the 43th operation which equals to 0.9052. The distribution of mean deviation shown in Fig. 8 demonstrates that the overall deviation between the optimal matrix and the original matrix does not exceed 0.032.

The adjusted Kansei decision-making matrices are listed as follows:

$$A_t^{(1)} = \begin{bmatrix} \{s_{1.4}, s_{1.9}, s_{2.4}\} & \{s_{1.4}, s_{1.9}, s_{2.4}\} & \{s_{2.4}, s_{2.4}, s_{2.4}\} & \{s_{1.6}, s_{1.6}, s_{1.6}\} \\ \{s_{1.6}, s_{1.6}, s_{1.6}\} & \{s_{1.4}, s_{1.9}, s_{2.4}\} & \{s_{1.6}, s_{1.6}, s_{1.6}\} & \{s_{1.4}, s_{1.4}, s_{1.4}\} \\ \{s_{1.393513}, s_{1.3967565}, s_{1.4}\} & \{s_{0.128705}, s_{0.128705}, s_{0.128705}\} & \{s_{1.4}, s_{1.4}, s_{1.4}\} & \{s_{1.3984}, s_{1.3984}, s_{1.3984}\} \end{bmatrix}$$

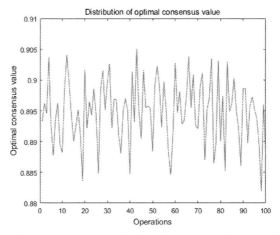

Fig. 7. Distribution of optimal consensus value in 100 operations after extending the adjustment space

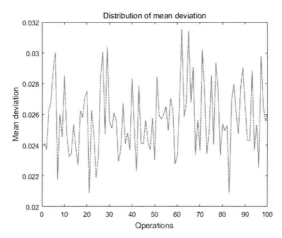

Fig. 8. Distribution of mean deviation in 100 operations after extending the adjustment space

$$A_t^{(2)} = \begin{bmatrix} \{s_{1.4}, s_{1.4}, s_{1.4}\} & \{s_{2.4}, s_{2.4}, s_{2.4}\} & \{s_{2.400927}, s_{2.400927}, s_{2.400927}\} & \{s_{1.4}, s_{1.4}, s_{1.4}\} \\ \{s_{1.6}, s_{1.6}, s_{1.6}\} & \{s_{0.609128}, s_{1.2445585}, s_{1.879989}\} & \{s_{1.6}, s_{1.6}, s_{1.6}\} & \{s_{0.6}, s_1, s_{1.4}\} \\ \{s_{1.4}, s_{1.4}, s_{1.4}\} & \{s_{-0.01036}, s_{0.19482}, s_{0.4}\} & \{s_{-1.4}, s_{-1.4}, s_{-1.4}\} & \{s_{1.398742}, s_{1.398742}, s_{1.398742}\} \end{bmatrix}$$

$$A_t^{(3)} = \begin{bmatrix} \{s_{0.6}, s_{0.6}, s_{0.6}\} & \{s_{1.6}, s_{1.6}, s_{1.6}\} & \{s_{-0.4}, s_{0.1}, s_{0.6}\} & \{s_{1.6}, s_{1.6}, s_{1.6}\} \\ \{s_{1.6}, s_{1.6}, s_{1.6}\} & \{s_{0.605709}, s_{1.2481525}, s_{1.890596}\} & \{s_{1.6}, s_{1.6}, s_{1.6}\} & \{s_{0.6}, s_{0.99972}, s_{1.39944}\} \\ \{s_{0.6}, s_1, s_{1.4}\} & \{s_{-0.01046}, s_{0.19477}, s_{0.4}\} & \{s_{1.253859}, s_{1.3269295}, s_{1.4}\} & \{s_{1.393535}, s_{1.3967675}, s_{1.4}\} \end{bmatrix}$$

$$A_t^{(4)} = \begin{bmatrix} \{s_{1.6}, s_{1.6}, s_{1.6}\} & \{s_{-0.4}, s_{0.1}, s_{0.6}\} & \{s_{2.398064}, s_{2.399032}, s_{2.4}\} & \{s_{1.6}, s_{1.6}, s_{1.6}\} \\ \{s_{1.4}, s_{1.4}, s_{1.4}\} & \{s_{0.4}, s_{1.1455025}, s_{1.891005}\} & \{s_{0.6}, s_{1.193672}, s_{1.787344}\} & \{s_{1.119032}, s_{1.119032}, s_{1.119032}\} \\ \{s_{1.390762}, s_{1.395381}, s_{1.4}\} & \{s_{-0.4}, s_{-0.4}, s_{-0.4}\} & \{s_{1.4}, s_{1.4}, s_{1.4}\} & \{s_{0.6}, s_{0.6}, s_{0.6}\} \end{bmatrix}$$

$$A_t^{(5)} = \begin{bmatrix} \{s_{-1.4}, s_{-1.4}, s_{-1.4}\} & \{s_{0.6}, s_{1.1}, s_{1.6}\} & \{s_{2.6}, s_{2.6}, s_{2.6}\} & \{s_{-0.4}, s_{0.1}, s_{0.6}\} \\ \{s_{1.6}, s_{1.6}, s_{1.6}\} & \{s_{0.6}, s_{0.6}, s_{0.6}\} & \{s_{1.6}, s_{1.6}, s_{1.6}\} & \{s_{0.6}, s_{0.998952}, s_{1.397904}\} \\ \{s_{1.390743}, s_{1.3953715}, s_{1.4}\} & \{s_{0.129997}, s_{0.129997}, s_{0.129997}\} & \{s_{-0.4}, s_{-0.125955}, s_{0.274045}\} & \{s_{1.6}, s_{1.6}, s_{1.6}\} \end{bmatrix}$$

After getting the adjusted matrices of consumers' Kansei decision-making about charging piles design solutions, Eq. (9) and (10) will be used to determine their ranking orders. The positive ideal solution A_+ and the negative ideal solution A_- of adjustment matrices are as follows:

$$\begin{cases} A_+ = [\{s_{2.4}\}, \{s_{2.4}\}, \{s_{2.6}\}, \{s_{1.6}\}] \\ A_- = [\{s_{-1.4}\}, \{s_{-0.4}\}, \{s_{-1.4}\}, \{s_{-0.4}\}] \end{cases}$$

Table 1 shows the satisfaction degrees of each product solution. In contrast, the satisfaction degrees calculated with the original matrix are also included in the table. Data from Table 1 displays that the ranking order of charging piles design solutions according to adjustment of consumers' preferences is $NO.1 \succ NO.2 \succ NO.3$, which is significantly different from that without optimization ($NO.2 \succ NO.1 \succ NO.3$). With the consensus level lifted from 0.8339 to 0.9052, the overall satisfaction degrees of consumers have also been improved. The satisfaction degrees of scheme 1 and 2 are promoted, while that of scheme 3 is slightly reduced.

Table 1. Comparison of satisfaction degrees

Charging piles design solutions	Satisfaction degrees of adjusted HFLTSs	Satisfaction degrees of original HFLTSs
1	0.71764	0.64303
2	0.70790	0.67383
3	0.53812	0.55172

5 Conclusion

As continuous linguistic variables are more in line with consumers' perception than concrete values or discrete Kansei adjectives, and hesitance and opinion difference exist extensively in Kansei decision-making process, it is conducive to employ HFLTSs to analyze consumers' preferences with the characteristics of uncertainty, imprecision and subjective vagueness. By studying the theories and operation rules of linguistic variables and HFLTSs, a consensus model is constructed to analyze the consistency of consumers' Kansei preferences. When disagreement fails to meet an acceptable consensus degree, PSO is deployed to adjust consumers' opinions aiming at lifting consensus level. With adjusted Kansei preferences, the final decision-making results are determined by HFLTSs-based TOPSIS. The case study of charging piles design for electric vehicles is taken as an example to verify the proposed method's ability in product Kansei decision-making process. Results show that with the consensus level lifted from 0.8339 to 0.9052, the overall satisfaction degrees of consumers have also been improved.

However, it should be noted that hesitance will affect preference consistency. The normalization of HFLTSs to ensure that the HFLTSs have the same number of linguistic terms mainly relies on the subjectivity of decision makers, but the determination of risk preference is an intractable task, which may distort the original preferences and will be further studied. Future research will focus on the development of Kansei decision-making software for dealing with consumers' perceptual opinions, and hesitance of online consumers' Kansei preference with big data technology.

Acknowledgements. This research is supported by National Natural Science Foundation of China (Grant No. 51805043), the Fundamental Research Funds for the Central Universities, CHD (Grant No. 300102259202), the China Postdoctoral Science Foundation (Grant No. 2019M663604), and Shaanxi innovation capability support project of China (Grant No. 2020PT-014). We are grateful of their support. We would also like to thank the anonymous reviewers for their invaluable comments and suggestions.

References

1. Petiot, J.-F., Yannou, B.: Measuring consumer perceptions for a better comprehension, specification and assessment of product semantics. Int. J. Ind. Ergon. 33(6), 507–525 (2004)
2. Jiao, J., Zhang, Y., Helander, M.: A Kansei mining system for affective design. Expert Syst. Appl. 30(4), 658–673 (2006)
3. Yan, H.B., et al.: Kansei evaluation based on prioritized multi-attribute fuzzy target-oriented decision analysis. Inf. Sci. 178(21), 4080–4093 (2008)
4. Nagamachi, M., Lokman, A.M.: Innovation of Kansei Engineering. CRC Press, Taylor & Francis Group, Florida (2011)
5. Djatna, T.K., Wenny, D.K.: A system analysis and design for packaging design of powder shaped fresheners based on kansei engineering. Procedia Manuf. 4, 115–123 (2015)
6. Tama, I.P., Azlia, W., Hardiningtyas, D.: Development of customer oriented product design using Kansei engineering and Kano model: case study of ceramic souvenir. Procedia Manuf. 4, 328–335 (2015)
7. Nagamachi, M.: Kansei engineering: a new ergonomic consumer oriented technology for product development. Int. J. Ind. Ergon. 15(1), 3–11 (1995)
8. Nagamachi, M.: Kansei engineering as a powerful consumer oriented technology for product development. Appl. Ergon. 33(3), 289–294 (2002)
9. Nagamachi, M.: Kansei engineering and kansei evaluation. In: International Encyclopedia of Ergonomics and Human Factors, 2nd edn. 3 Volume Set. CRC Press (2010)
10. Nagamachi, M.: Kansei engineering: a powerful ergonomic technology for product development. In: Helander, M.G., Khalid, H.M., Tham, M.P. (eds.) Proceedings of the International Conference on Affective Human Factors Design, pp. 9–14. ASEAN Academic Press, London (2001)
11. Huang, Y.X., Chen, C.H., Khoo, L.P.: Kansei clustering for emotional design using a combined design structure matrix. Int. J. Ind. Ergon. 42(5), 416–427 (2012)
12. Lévy, P.: Beyond kansei engineering: the emancipation of kansei design. Int. J. Des. 7(2), 83–94 (2013)
13. Chou, J.-R.: A Kansei evaluation approach based on the technique of computing with words. Adv. Eng. Inform. 30(1), 1–15 (2016)
14. Herrera, F., Martinez, L.: An approach for combining linguistic and numerical information based on the 2-tuple fuzzy linguistic representation model in decision-making. Int. J. Uncertainty Fuzziness Knowl.-Based Syst. 8(5), 539–562 (2000)

15. Chuu, S.-J.: Interactive group decision-making using a fuzzy linguistic approach for evaluating the flexibility in a supply chain. Eur. J. Oper. Res. **213**(1), 279–289 (2011)
16. Chou, J.-R.: Applying fuzzy linguistic preferences to Kansei evaluation. In: Proceedings of the 5th International Conference on Kansei Engineering and Emotion Research, KEER 2014, vol. 100, pp. 339–349, Linköping, June 2014
17. Zadeh, L.A.: Fuzzy logic = computing with words. IEEE Trans. Fuzzy Syst. **4**(2), 103–111 (1996)
18. Lawry, J.: A methodology for computing with words. Int. J. Approx. Reason. **28**(2–3), 51–89 (2001)
19. Zadeh, L.A.: Fuzzy sets. Inf. Control **8**(3), 338–353 (1965)
20. Zadeh, L.A.: The concept of a linguistic variable and its applications to approximate reasoning-part I. Inf. Sci. **8**, 199–249 (1975) (2012)
21. Zadeh, L.A.: The concept of a linguistic variable and its applications to approximate reasoning-part II. Inf. Sci. **8**, 301–357 (1975)
22. Zadeh, L.A.: The concept of a linguistic variable and its applications to approximate reasoning-part III. Inf. Sci. **9**, 43–80 (1975)
23. Xu, Z.S.: Linguistic Decision Making: Theory and Methods. Science Press, Beijing (2012)
24. Xu, Z.S.: Deviation measures of linguistic preference relations in group decision making. Omega **33**(3), 249–254 (2005)
25. Xu, Z.S.: Uncertain Multiple Attribute Decision Making: Methods and Applications. Tsinghua University Press, Beijing (2004)
26. Rodriguez, R.M., Martinez, L., Herrera, F.: Hesitant fuzzy linguistic term sets for decision making. In: Wang, Y., Li, T. (eds.) Foundations of Intelligent Systems, Advances in Intelligent and Soft Computing, vol. 122, pp. 287–295. Springer, Heidelberg (2011). https://doi.org/10.1007/978-3-642-25664-6_34
27. Zhu, B., Xu, Z.S.: Consistency measures for hesitant fuzzy linguistic preference relations. IEEE Trans. Fuzzy Syst. **22**(1), 35–45 (2014)
28. Chiclanala, F., et al.: A statistical comparative study of different similarity measures of consensus in group decision making. Inf. Sci. **221**, 110–123 (2013)
29. Liao, H.C., Xu, Z.S., Zeng, X.J.: Distance and similarity measures for hesitant fuzzy linguistic term sets and their application in multi-criteria decision making. Inf. Sci. **271**(3), 125–142 (2014)
30. Eberhart, R., Kennedy, J.: A new optimizer using particle swarm theory. In: International Symposium on Micro Machine and Human Science, pp. 39–43. IEEE Press, Nagoya, October 1995
31. Kennedy, J.: Particle swarm optimization. In: Sammut, C., Webb, G.I. (eds.) Encyclopedia of Machine Learning. Springer, Boston (2011). https://doi.org/10.1007/978-0-387-30164-8
32. Jiang, H.M., et al.: A multi-objective PSO approach of mining association rules for affective design based on online customer reviews. J. Eng. Des. **29**(7), 381–403 (2018)
33. Jain, N.K., Nangia, U., Jain, J.: A review of particle swarm optimization. J. Inst. Eng. (India): Ser. B **99**(4), 407–411 (2018). https://doi.org/10.1007/s40031-018-0323-y
34. Kennedy, J.E., Russell, C.: Swarm Intelligence. Academic Press. San Diego (2001)
35. Shi, Y.H., Eberhart, R.C.: Parameter selection in particle swarm optimization. In: Porto, V.W., Saravanan, N., Waagen, D., Eiben, A.E. (eds.) Evolutionary Programming VII. EP 1998. LNCS, vol. 1447, pp. 591–600. Springer, Heidelberg (1998). https://doi.org/10.1007/BFb0040810
36. Hwang, C.L., Yoon, K.P.: Multiple Attribute Decision Making: Methods and Applications. Springer, New York (1981)
37. Yang, Y.P., et al.: Consumers' Kansei needs clustering method for product emotional design based on numerical design structure matrix and genetic algorithms. Comput. Intell. Neurosci. **2016**, 1–11 (2016)

Positioning Participant Engagement in Participatory Design

Ziheng Zhang[✉] and Francesco Zurlo

Politecnico di Milano, Via Giuseppe Candiani 72, 20158 Milan, MI, Italy
ziheng.zhang.polimi@gmail.com

Abstract. The approach of Participatory Design (PD) is the direct involvement of people as participants in the process of shaping design artifacts. Thus the facilitation of participant engagement is a priority for designers and researchers within this field. However, there are few reviews of how PD research interprets and employs the concept of engagement. In this paper, we shall first briefly introduce the related concepts. Then provides a systematic literature review of engagement on 81 PD related (PD, co-design, co-creation, etc.) publications, concerning its diverse perspectives, engaged participants, interpretations, and facilitation. We provide the attributes of participant engagement to further define this concept, as well as a guideline for the strategy of facilitating it. In the end, gaps within the literature have been pointed out as the challenges and opportunities for further work.

Keywords: Participant engagement · Participatory design · Co-design · Design process

1 Introduction

Participatory design (PD) emerged in the early 1970s in Scandinavian, motivation to involve people in the policy-making to empowering the end-users for catalyzing democratic engagement [1]. Over the years of development, it derived various forms and concepts include co-design, co-creation, etc. As a distinct set of the design approach, it has been applied extensively in various fields including the design of products, interactions, services and thought [2], mainly intended to facilitate user engagement and target a specific group of users, for example, disabled children, elderly people, hospital patients, etc. The designers invite them or other stakeholders to participate in certain phases of the design process [3, 4]. In practice, organizing effective participation is one of the cornerstones of PD [5], it largely depends on the engagement of participants. However, it is a concept that continues to pose challenges for researchers and designers. How to interpret engagement in the context of PD? What is the relation between participation and engagement? What contributes to and supports participant engagement?

1.1 From Participation to Engagement

Participation is a defining trait of PD and related activities [1]. summarize five fundamental perspectives of participation has interpreted and manifested from the central

© Springer Nature Switzerland AG 2020
C. Stephanidis et al. (Eds.): HCII 2020, LNCS 12423, pp. 367–379, 2020.
https://doi.org/10.1007/978-3-030-60114-0_25

literature of PD research (See Table 1). Although it remains a central concern for PD researchers, the implication of it is rarely defined and polyvocal [3]. In spite of a large amount of research as well as a rich diversity of practices address participation in their central concern, due to the complexity and the blurred boundary, designers are still facing an army of challenges related to facilitating participation in the design process. With this in mind, engagement as a smaller scope of concept turns out to be used to describe the positive state of experience of participants in PD with high frequency.

Table 1. Fundamental perspectives of participation.

Perspectives	Description
Politics	People who are affected by a decision should have right to influence it
Users	People play critical roles in design by being experts in their own lives
Methods	Methods are means for users to gain influence in design processes
Context	The use situation is the fundamental starting point for the design process
Product (out-comes)	The goal of participation is to design alternatives, improving quality of life

A difference can be distinguished between "participation" and "engagement". "Participation" tends to emphasize a perspective of methodology and outcome of the PD process [1]. While "engagement" more to underline participant's autonomy, needs, motivations. Promising the potential contribution to design activities by facilitating positive, interesting and immersive experiences [6].

On the other hand, several authors arguing that design activities include PD is a social process where involves communication, negotiation and entering compromises [7–9]. They claim that designing the design process itself is of equal importance as designing the final artifact. Many scholars shared this view in the later research, and also stresses that participant engagement is a crucial indicator of organizing effective participation. It should be concerned and designed in the design process [5].

1.2 Related Concepts

For the motivation of design engagement, it is most frequently interpreted as a dynamic state [10]. Several definitions were cited in different situations, the most singled out one is from Sidner et al.: "By engagement, we mean the process by which two (or more) participants establish, maintain and end their perceived connection. This process includes initial contact, negotiating a collaboration, checking that other is still taking part in the interaction, evaluating whether to stay involved and deciding when to end the connection" [11].

O'Brien and Toms frame engagement as a favorable experience with detailed attributes: "Engagement is a quality of user experiences that are characterized by challenge, aesthetic and sensory appeal, feedback, novelty, interactivity, perceived control and time, awareness, motivation, interest, and affect [10]." Douglas and Hargadon bridge it to the theories of gaming, immersion, and flow, they state engagement with a distinct hedonic perspective: "The pleasures of immersion stem from our being completely absorbed within the ebb and flow of a familiar narrative schema. The pleasures of engagement tend to come from our ability to recognize a work's overturning or conjoining conflicting schemes from a perspective outside the text, our perspective removed from any single schema [6]." Similarly, Laurel connected engagement to an emotional joy state: "Engagement refers to the emotional state of mind the user must attain to enjoy the representation, that is, a willing suspension of disbelief [12]."

The concept of engagement has been employed to understand user experience (McCarthy and Wright 2004), facilitating learning motivation [13], investigate online interaction [14, 15], guide autonomous systems [16], understand video game model, and evaluate technologies for wellbeing, civil services, social networks, etc. [17–19]. Definitions can be different by context due to the diverse purpose and motivation, Doherty explained a feasible way to further defining this versatile concept is to reduce its scope by applying an appropriate prefix [20]. For instance, user engagement as a concept, linked individuals' experience with the designed system, is become a universal goal in the design of products, interactions and services [20]. We shared this concept by using participant refers to the user when the context shifted into PD.

However, comparing to "users", participants in PD are experience hybrid states, engagement that "take place neither in the users' domain, nor in the technology developers' domain, but in an in-between region that shares attributes of both spaces" [21]. This unique position leads to more conflicted and hidden interpretations. Difficulties persist in adopting the concept in PD research and practice.

2 Review Methods

2.1 Search Criteria

Concern the questions

1. How to interpret and understand the concept of engagement in the process of PD.
2. How to facilitate participant engagement in PD related activities.

This paper presents a systematic review from multiple sourced literature, include the ACM indexed publication of PDC (participatory design conference), CHI (Conference on Human Factors in Computing Systems), journal of Codesign, CoCreation, etc. Across the disciplines and fields of design, HCI, computer science, psychology, Sociology and so on.

The review material was searched and collected from the July of 2019. A initial search gathered 440 results included the keywords "participatory design" or "co-design" in title, and the keyword "engagement" in either title or abstract. The first round minimal exclusion has been carried out based on the criteria of

1. If the material is dissertation format.
2. It is book format or chapters of book.
3. It did not focus on engagement of human been.

Finally, after a round of full-text review, this method resulted in 81 samples. Those were ruled out during the second screening if

1. It did not address descriptions, cases or experiments of PD related activities.
2. It only concern user engagement as a outcome of design.
3. It addresses the term of engagement with certain prefixes.
4. There is a limited discuss on the design process in the paper.

2.2 Coding

Samples have been coding during the analyze process according to several aspects.

1. General coding: recording each paper's date, title, authors, department of authors and the publisher.
2. Content coding: recording the goal and the conclusion of the paper, as well as methods, focused field, cases and experiments.
3. Engagement coding: recording the definitions, descriptions and theories mentioned toward engagement, as well as recording the participatory methods in design process for facilitate engagement.

The coding scheme (see Fig. 1) leading to a detailed analysis of the current engagement research in the context of PD, explained in the next section.

Good to See You Again: Engaging Users in Design	Tuuli Mattelmäki	2011	DPPI	School of art and design	Detail of user-driven innovation processes in an industrial context.
	Design probes kit(14 students):1.Timeline of the daily thoughts and activities of the participants. 2. Questions 3. Stories telling.(self-expression) 4. drawing exercise.				Codesign workshop(5 students): 1. present finding 2. present demo 3.based on 1,2. use PLEX card to create playful interactions. 4. present second demo and play Kapteeni game
Engaging users in the early phases of the design process	ya Ozcelik ITU	2011	DPPI		ous user engagement method. improve user engagement in the early stages of the des
	Challenges in Engaging Users in the Design Process: 1 Company culture plays an important role in the motivation of companies for engaging users in their design process. 2 The role of the designer				
Empowering Children through Design and Making: towards	Netta Iivari	2018	PDC18	INTERACT Research Unit	Engaging children in design and making activities
	PD(38 children) divided into groups of 4-5 children and supposed to ideate, design, and implement one game spot. The children had a possibility to use many playful tools in their game spots including robots, Legos, and MakeyMakey. Activities : 1. Introductory meeting. 2. survey on interests and expertise. 3. two design session 4.				1. The maker movement seems to encourage children to take a strong role in shaping technology development. 2. Playing the game is the most enjoyable part of the project. 3.
Increasing Engagement in Workshops: Designing a Toolkit	K.J. Schelle	2015	tional Conference	User System Interaction Program	Enhance engagement in creative workshops
	The use of the templates toolkit and games arguably has an impact on engagement, none of them is directly targeted at participant engagement. Trotto and Hummels is only actively design tools for creating engagement.				Problem-clusters related to engagement 1. Managing expectations. Problems of taking user's point of view; participants having wrong expectations. 2. Keeping the energy high. Relates to participants getting distracted or tired and tasks being too complex. 3. Breaking the ice. Relates to the facilitator having trouble to break the ice between participants and participants underestimating their own creativity. 4. Creating right attitude by showing value. Relates to participants not seeing the added value of
Critical Participatory Design: Reflections on Engagement and	n Goldkind Vikra	2018	PDC18	Computing and Society	th a community-based organization towards developing a technology supporting their h
	Purpose of PD remains primarily for: probing the participants and encouraging engagement, priming the participants for immersion in the design process, gaining an understanding of the users' current experiences and context, and generating ideas and concepts				
The Library of Engagements	Emily Crompton	2018	tional Conference	School of Architecture	Participatory Design tool for engaging citizens in the production of space, urban and arc
	The Library of Engagements is a highly personalised method of sharing the knowledge of participatory design.				
ParScipatory Design of DIY Digital AssisSve Technology in	Foad Hamidi	2018	AfriCHI18		mmunity-building activities to investigate the possibilities and challenges of maker appr
					Overall, the majority of students in both schools showed signs of engagement and excitement in using the system.
Subversive Participatory Design: Re?ections on a case study	Michela Cozza	2016	PDC16	Business, Society and Engineering	Engaging older people as co-designers of several wearable and in-house technologies.
					Useing bodystorming method to engaging older people
you what I want": Engaging indivi	Melissa Dawe	2007	CHI2007	Computer Science	Engage with individual with significant cognitive disable
					This research uncovered how technology probes can connect emotionally with individuals with cognitive disabilities, enabling them to engage more deeply with the technology and the design process. For example, in early
Empowerment Through Design: Engaging Alternative High School	Aneisha DuMon	2012	IDC2012	f Instructional Technology and Lea	Engage struggling students in sophisticated learning through design projects.
	Youth are engage successfully in the design process with tangible technology.				Students fix a series of pre-programmed bugs in a prototype tangible digital pet. After, students designed, developed and crafted their own tangible digital pets. Students were encouraged to use and modify code from the prototype pet.

Fig. 1. The coding scheme (portion).

3   Unfold Participant Engagement

Designers in decades face the unique and messy challenge related to facilitating participation in PD process [1]. The term engagement then becomes a priority use to describe the state of participants when they are motivated in a PD process. However, although practitioners continuously design for participant engagement, there is a surprising lack of detailed defines of this concept: most of the publications that adopt engagement without a definition. Facing this challenge, we turn to first investigate what approaches and methods are applying for engaging participants in PD (See Table 2). Then analyze the different perspectives of the engagement and the attributes of the engaged participants. (The approaches and methods mentioned are sometimes overlapping, one PD case may applying multiple methods.)

Table 2. The approaches and methods for engaging participant.

Approaches and methods for engagement	Mentions
Game and play	18
Board/card games, gamification, game/toy pieces, playful challenges, roll-play, etc.	
Tangible prototyping	17
Prototyping with/by participants, prototype/product presenting, mapping, drawing, etc.	
Telling and talking	13
Stories telling, brainstorming, interviewing, playing video, inspiration card, etc.	
Create atmosphere	10
Trust-building, creating friendly/freedom/relaxing atmosphere, design fictions, etc.	
Physical actions	9
Bodystorming, physical space design, acting, etc.	
Others3	3
Offering money/gifts, free lunch, etc.	

3.1   Perspectives of Engagement

As the value of, an identity transformation between end-users/stakeholders and designers is the priority result of participant engagement. Therefore, we put forward an analysis of how these approaches and methods facilitate this transform with three perspectives: emotional, cognitive and behavioral [22–24].

Emotional. Laurel suggests that engagement should primarily be understood as emotions [12]. An emotional perspective may lead to a more subjectively interpretation of engagement. People could have diverse outcomes of experience like identification, belonging, encompassing, attitudes, disappointment or desperation evoked by different emotions such as interest, boredom, stress, sadness, etc. These emotions are the key indicators of the assessment of engagement. Schelle et al. emphasize the need for consideration of several problems related to PD engagement. For an emotional concern, the problem of keeping the vitality, prevent participants from getting distracted or tired and tasks being too complex. As well as the ice-breaking between participants and facilitators/participants also efforts to avoid the facilitation of negative emotions such as embarrassing, nervousness and suspicion [25]. Gennari et al. adopted the control-value theory to link children's engagement, emotion, and performance in a PD experiment [26]. In a game and play based activity, the research found that by the evidence of the activity triggered positive emotions more than negative emotions (the intensity of enjoyment and relaxation is higher than anxiety and boredom), on average, the PD activity engaged the children successfully. Like Churchill positions engagement as a state between boredom and stress [27], the employ of flow theory in PD process design is another significant example of this perspective [28]. Flow theory declared an immersive and enjoyable emotional state evoked by the design of balanced challenge, authorization of control and immediate feedback [29]. Approaches based on a game metaphor could encourage multiple flow symptoms often employed as emotional indicators of engagement. Contrary, an unbalanced challenge is most likely to reduce the participant's engagement. A sense of nervousness caused by too challenging tasks can be considered as a sign of disengagement [26]. Approaches for creating atmosphere also have a significant impact on facilitating positive emotions. Multiple authors emphasize that the key to engagement is to build trust and create a friendly and relaxing atmosphere [30, 31].

Cognitive. Cognitive engagement is valued the most in PD activities for educational purposes. Conscious components like effort [24], awareness [31], and attention [32] are all considered as secondary objectives in numerous PD cases. Moreover, compared with the emotional and behavioral perspective, cognitive components can potentially shape a long-term engagement, which is an exclusive goal in this situation. In general, there is also a widespread concern in PD related to the cognitive factors: Problems of expectation management, how to taking users' points of view and letting participants recognize appropriate expectations [25]. Review shows that the approaches of tangible prototyping made the major contributions to the cognitive aspect, for example creating the right attitude and showing value through a tangible prototype [33]. Participation in the tangible making instead of design an intangible concept can make participants recognize their importance and being critical enough. This focus of engagement also provides a feasibility to quantify measure the engagement in PD. Fredricks et al. developed a cognitive engagement scale to evaluate and measure engagement based on an individual's voluntary efforts to understand and master challenging tasks [34]. However, so far, it seems there are few similar measure methods adopted in PD related research.

Behavioral. The perspective of behavior emphasizes the actions of participants especially physical actions, which occupy a large proportion of methods in the actual design stage (different from the stage of ice-breaking, background telling, feedback, etc.). PD cases are more or less report effectively adoptions of action-based methods. For instance, tangible making and playful action. Research shows the maker movement could encourage participants to play a strong role in shaping technology design [35]. participants especially teens and children are express on multiple occasions that playing the game (generalized game-like activities in ice-breaking, ideation process, evaluating prototype, etc.) is the most enjoyable part of the project [25, 36]. Similarly, body storming as a more physically action (compare to brainstorming) are adopting increasingly in PD projects [37]. behavioral components of engagement promising more objective analysis. Observation methods have been used toward behavioral matters [26].

3.2 Engaged Participants

To understand different engaged participants always require the consideration of their age, gender, profession, motivation, expectation, predispositions, and also their role in PD. For example, Harrington et al. organized community-based PD research among low-income, African-American, older adults in Chicago. The traditional PD tools have been using to facilitate the ideation process (materials include markers, colored pencils, sketching paper). The participants however put forward that the materials provided were "infantilizing and belittling". Researchers believe that due to multiple reasons related to the history and participants' characteristics, classic materials and activities might lead to an implication of their participation and contribution were not being taken seriously [38]. Despite the diverse participants features lead to numerous interpretation of engaged participants, there is still a consistency based on the objective of each PD projects. As followed, we present an analysis of three types of engaged participants with considering their role played in PD primarily.

Interested. In the most common situations, engaged participants can be interpreted primarily as being interested. Review shows that PD studies link game metaphor the most to engagement [39]. Game and play based methods are proved can facilitate positive emotions which could potentially immerse participants in the PD activities. Nicholas et al. describe the "uninterested and unengaged participants" as the people who have less concern or experience on the design objective, who potentially hold negative views [31]. As an example, teens are likely to consider that doing taxes is less favorable and boring. This predisposition may let them being "design excluded" when issuing a design project toward tax-related policies [31]. As expected, research shows that action-based activities especially playful design facilitate most engagement of these teens.

Empowered. From a historical perspective, the emphasis of democratic empowerment is a distinguishing set of traditional participatory design rooted in the Scandinavian approach of cooperative design. The famous UTOPIA project was set to democratic empowering workers by engaging them to co-design to improve their work situation [40]. Today PD activities are not necessarily to facilitating democratic empowerment, but the empowerment of awareness, willingness, and ability of design persist.

Sanders et al. present a framework of the Tools and Techniques using for organizing PD activities. They further explain the purposes of tools and techniques include: encouraging engagement by probing participants and priming them aim to immerse them in the domain of interest, understand their current experience, and generate ideas or concepts for the future [36]. Thinyane et al. shared this view as the purpose of common PD activities [41]. The interpretation of engagement here still remains the focus of interest, and also an emphasis on empowering participants. The engaged participants are empowering to control the design project and gain feedback from it. The design ability, willingness, awareness are also empowered aim to let them making self-expression, which is seen as one of the core insights that designers can be gain within participants. Hansen and Iversen carried out a project "LiTiRUM" to develop an augmented school installation and new social technology application that aims to support informal learning in public schools. They emphasized that the students as participants were involved and endorsed as experts instead of invited as pupils. Researchers gave the student enough recognition and control, in return, they were taking the design project seriously and been encouraged to participate [42]. There is a large number of cases reflect that in certain PD project, end-users are involved as experts of "been themselves". High school students participate in PD as experts of been teenagers, elders as experts in their everyday lives of being old [30, 37, 43, 44].

Aroused. Across the PD literature, researchers also link the engagement with not only the PD process but also an outcome of it. Most commonly, adopting the PD method to promote user engagement of the final artifact. However, despite the extended scope, the engaged participants still played the same role as been "experts of their everyday lives". Designers gain insight from the participation expect for the designed outcome can promote greater engagement towards the broader range of end-user who may share some characteristics with their participants in the PD process. However, the review shows that there is an increase in the PD project's effort to build long-term engagement with participants. Especially when the PD object related to civic/public engagement and educational purposes. Schofield organized a participatory interaction design project "Time Telescope" in an art gallery, aims to engage teenagers with the heritage of their local area. The design objective is to strengthen the gallery's links to its younger audiences. During a year-long project, the teenagers have participated in every stage of the design, from brainstorming to rapid prototyping. By the end of this project, participants showed a strong interest and a sense of belonging towards local heritage even began to volunteer to continue research [45]. Similar to exteriorly engaging students in PD for doing tax [31], but the real goal is towards civic responsibilities education. In these cases, the engagement of participants tends to emphasize a state of arousal, may lead to the absorption of knowledge, change of mindsets, attitude, reception of negotiation, compromises, and a possibility to remain a long-term engagement [25, 42, 46].

3.3   Attributes of Participant Engagement

Participant engagement is a versatile concept. Interpretations can be distinct and conflicting due to numerous different goals, focus, participants, methods, etc. Through the investigation of each perspective of engagement and the engaged participants, consistency can be summarized. As a result, we present a description of the attributes of participant engagement and link it with the approaches which could potentially contribute to it (see Fig. 2).

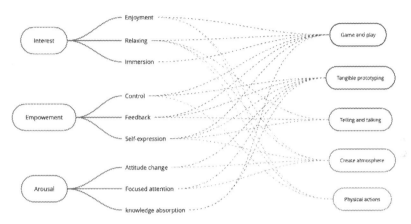

Fig. 2. Attributes of participants engagement and the connection with engagement approaches.

Participant engagement shall first generalized interpret as a sense of *interest*. Due to a surprising consistency of hedonic inclination, shared with numerous definitions and interpretations out the scope of PD, a sense of interest can be considered as fundamental of engagement. Ideally, a sense of interest may lead participants to certain positive emotions includes *enjoyment* and *relaxing*, finally immerse them in the PD process even possibly enter a state of flow. However, participants who have hybrid experience (in-between user and designer) [21] are expected to not only hedonic engaged but also in need of *empowerment* to contribute to the design projects. Empowerment can be reflected in two perspectives. 1. Through PD tools, techniques, systems and/or facilitators' assistance, non-designers can empower more capability and willingness to make *self-express*, thereby contribute more to design projects. 2. Based on the principle of "people should have the right to participate in the design of politics if they are potentially influenced by it [1]". Link to democratic empowerment, amplify the end-users' voices by giving them *control* and *feedback* in the design process. Engagement in certain PD also reflects an educational purpose. Participants are expected to be aroused towards certain *attitudes*, mindsets, *attention, knowledge*, etc.

4   Discussion

Motivated by the potential of the versatile implications of engagement, numerous suggestions, intimations, and hidden interpretations have addressed without consensus in

PD research. We consider one primary reason for this situation is too flexible language. The result of this review to some extent could facilitate more clearly articulating towards this concept. Further, analyze and adopting this concept still requests an awareness of the limitations and contributions of each perspective. A diverse methodology should be embracing in the future work.

4.1 Gaps Within the Literature

There are several gaps been found through the review. Due to the complexity of design activities and the blurred understanding of engagement, few studies conducted a measurement of engagement in PD research. In contrast, the conception of engagement is very often tied to measurement in other fields. There are many approaches to measurement in HCI and gaming studies including questionnaires, interviews, measures of outcomes, and digital behavior logging [21]. Is it possible to adopt similar approaches to measure engagement in the context of the PD process?

From a practice perspective. A game metaphor is widely used for engagement. But regard that Patricio's suggestion of gamification "engagement should go hand in hand with coordination.... Although actors may be engaged in the process because it is playful and more relaxed, coordination is necessary to maintain the focus on the project goals [47]". As well as the finding of higher degrees engagement does not always imply improved learning, wellbeing, or experience [48, 49]. It is crucial to understand which symptoms of engagement can promote focus participation in the PD process, and which are invalid or even obstacles. This requires a detailed understanding of how the game metaphor triggers motivation toward PD activities.

5   Conclusion

The paper position participant engagement at a central concern of PD related research, presents a detailed mapping of the landscape of PD related research regarding the concept of participant engagement. By the evidence scattered in the literature and the analysis of multiple perspectives, the review provides a result of engagement attributes. We have examined the motivations and results of approaches and methods applied for engaging participants, linking to the engagement attributes, we present a potentially guideline of the strategy of engaging participants in practice. At last, we point out the gaps in the literature and identify them as challenges and opportunities for future work.

References

1. Halskov, K., Hansen, N.B.: The diversity of participatory design research practice at PDC 2002–2012. Int. J. Hum.-Comput. Stud. **74**, 81–92 (2015)
2. Buchanan, R.: Design research and the new learning. Des. Issues **17**(4), 3–23 (2001)
3. Bratteteig, T., Wagner, I.: Unpacking the notion of participation in participatory design. Comput. Support. Coop. Work (CSCW) **25**(6), 425–475 (2016). https://doi.org/10.1007/s10606-016-9259-4

4. Andersen, L.B., Danholt, P., Halskov, K., Hansen, N.B., Lauritsen, P.: Participation as a matter of concern in participatory design. CoDesign **11**(3–4), 250–261 (2015)
5. Brandt, E.: Designing exploratory design games: a framework for participation in participatory design?. In: Proceedings of the Ninth Conference on Participatory Design: Expanding Boundaries in Design, vol. 1, pp. 57–66, August 2006
6. Douglas, Y., Hargadon, A.: The pleasure principle: immersion, engagement, flow. In: Proceedings of the Eleventh ACM on Hypertext and Hypermedia, pp. 153–160, May 2000
7. Bucciarelli, L.L., Bucciarelli, L.L.: Designing Engineers. MIT press, Cambridge (1994)
8. Habraken, N.J., Gross, M.D.: Concept design games: a report submitted to the national science foundation engineering directorate, design metholodogy program. Department of Architecture, Massachusetts Institute of Technology (1987)
9. Horgen, T., Joroff, M.L., Porter, W.L., Schon, D.A.: Excellence by Design: Transforming Workplace and Work Practice. Wiley, Hoboken (1999)
10. O'Brien, H.L., Toms, E.G.: What is user engagement? A conceptual framework for defining user engagement with technology. J. Am. Soc. Inf. Sci. Technol. **59**(6), 938–955 (2008)
11. Sidner, C.L., Kidd, C.D., Lee, C., Lesh, N.: Where to look: a study of human-robot engagement. In: Proceedings of the 9th International Conference on Intelligent User Interfaces, pp. 78–84, January 2004
12. Laurel, B.: Computers as Theatre. Addison-Wesley, NewYork (1991)
13. Fredricks, J.A., McColskey, W.: The measurement of student engagement: a comparative analysis of various methods and student self-report instruments. In: Christenson, S., Reschly, A., Wylie, C. (eds.) Handbook of Research on Student Engagement, pp. 763–782. Springer, Boston, MA (2012). https://doi.org/10.1007/978-1-4614-2018-7_37
14. Lehmann, J., Lalmas, M., Yom-Tov, E., Dupret, G.: Models of user engagement. In: Masthoff, J., Mobasher, B., Desmarais, M.C., Nkambou, R. (eds.) UMAP 2012. LNCS, vol. 7379, pp. 164–175. Springer, Heidelberg (2012). https://doi.org/10.1007/978-3-642-31454-4_14
15. Thomas, L.N., et al.: Exploring the role of visualization and engagement in computer science education. ACMSIGCSE Bull. **35**(2), 131 (2002)
16. Bohus, D., Horvitz, E.: Models for multiparty engagement in open-world dialog. In: Proceedings of the SIGDIAL 2009 Conference: The 10th Annual Meeting of the Special Interest Group on Discourse and Dialogue, pp. 225–234. Association for Computational Linguistics, September 2009
17. Jungx S., Lee, S.: Developing a model for continuous user engagement in social media. In: Proceedings of the 10th International Conference on Ubiquitous Information Management and Communication, vol. 19. ACM, September 2016
18. Kim, B.J., Kleinschmit, S.W.: A logistic multilevel model for civic engagement and community group impact in the digital age. In: Proceedings of the 6th International Conference on Theory and Practice of Electronic Governance, pp. 34–37, October 2012
19. Linnemeier, M., Lin, Y-Y., Laput, G., Vijjapurapu, R.: StoryCubes: connecting elders in independent living through storytelling. In: Proceedings of the 2012 ACM Annual Conference Extended Abstracts on Human Factors in Computing Systems Extended Abstracts (CHIEA 2012), vol. 1321. ACM Press (2012)
20. Doherty, K., Doherty, G.: Engagement in HCI: conception, theory and measurement. ACM Comput. Surv. (CSUR) **51**(5), 1–39 (2018)
21. Muller, M.J.: Participatory design: the third space in HCI. In: The Human-Computer Interaction Handbook, pp. 1087–1108. CRC press (2007)
22. Zyngier, D.: (Re) conceptualising student engagement: doing education not doing time. Teach. Teach. Educ. **24**(7), 1765–1776 (2008)
23. Bouta, H., Retalis, S.: Enhancing primary school children collaborative learning experiences in maths via a 3D virtual environment. Educ. Inf. Technol. **18**(4), 571–596 (2013)

24. Islas Sedano, C., Leendertz, V., Vinni, M., Sutinen, E., Ellis, S.: Hypercontextualized learning games: fantasy, motivation, and engagement in reality. Simul. Gam. **44**(6), 821–845 (2013)
25. Schelle, K.J., Gubenko, E., Kreymer, R., Gomez Naranjo, C., Tetteroo, D., Soute, I.A.C.: Increasing engagement in workshops: designing a toolkit using lean design thinking. In: ACM International Conference Proceeding Series, 29–30 June (2015). https://doi.org/10.1145/281 4464.2814481
26. Gennari, R., et al.: Children's emotions and quality of products in participatory game design. Int. J. Hum Comput Stud. **101**(January), 45–61 (2017). https://doi.org/10.1016/j.ijhcs.2017. 01.006
27. Churchill, E.F.: Enticing engagement. Interactions **17**(3), 82 (2010)
28. Long, D., McKlin, T., Weisling, A., Martin, W., Guthrie, H., Magerko, B.: Trajectories of physical engagement and expression in a co-creative museum installation. In: C and C 2019 - Proceedings of the 2019 Creativity and Cognition, pp. 246–257 (2019). https://doi.org/10. 1145/3325480.3325505
29. Mirvis, P.H., Csikszentmihalyi, M.: Flow: the psychology of optimal experience. Acad. Manag. Rev. **16**(3), 636 (1991). https://doi.org/10.2307/258925
30. Lindsay, S., Jackson, D., Schofield, G., Olivier, P.: Engaging older people using participatory design. In: Proceedings of the Conference on Human Factors in Computing Systems, pp. 1199–1208 (2012). https://doi.org/10.1145/2207676.2208570
31. Nicholas, M., Hagen, P., Rahilly, K., Swainston, N.: Using participatory design methods to engage the uninterested. In: ACM International Conference Proceeding Series, vol. 2, pp. 121–124 (2012)
32. Trotto, A., Hummels, C.: Engage me, do!, p. 136 (2013). https://doi.org/10.1145/2513506. 2513521
33. Zurlo, F., Nunes, V.D.G.A.: Designing Pilot Projects as Boundary Objects: A Brazilian Case Study in the Promotion of Sustainable Design. Springer, Heidelberg (2015)
34. Fredricks, J.A., Blumenfeld, P.C., Paris, A.H.: School engagement: potential of the concept, state of the evidence. Rev. Educ. Res. **74**(1), 59–109 (2004)
35. Iivari, N., Kinnula, M.: Empowering children through design and making: towards protagonist role adoption. In: PDC 2018: Proceedings of the 15th Participatory Design Conference, vol. 1, pp. 1–10 (2018). https://doi.org/10.1145/3210586.3210600
36. Sanders, E.B.N., Brandt, E., Binder, T.: A framework for organizing the tools and techniques of participatory design. In: ACM International Conference Proceeding Series, pp. 195–198 (2010). https://doi.org/10.1145/1900441.1900476
37. Cozza, M., Tonolli, L., D'Andrea, V.: Subversive participatory design: reflections on a case study C3. In: ACM International Conference Proceeding Series, vol. 2, pp. 53–56 (2016). https://doi.org/10.1145/2948076.2948085
38. Harrington, C.N., Borgos-Rodriguez, K., Piper, A.M.: Engaging low-income African American older adults in health discussions through community-based design workshops, pp. 1–15 (2019). https://doi.org/10.1145/3290605.3300823
39. Vaajakallio, K., Mattelmäki, T.: Design games in codesign: as a tool, a mindset and a structure. CoDesign Int. J. CoCreation Des. Arts (2014). https://doi.org/10.1080/15710882.2014. 881886
40. Sundblad, Y.: UTOPIA: participatory design from Scandinavia to the world. In: Impagliazzo, J., Lundin, P., Wangler, B. (eds.) HiNC 2010. IAICT, vol. 350, pp. 176–186. Springer, Heidelberg (2011). https://doi.org/10.1007/978-3-642-23315-9_20
41. Thinyane, M., Bhat, K., Goldkind, L., Cannanure, V.K.: Critical participatory design: reflections on engagement and empowerment in a case of a community based organization Mamello. In: Proceedings of the 15th Participatory Design Conference on Full Papers - PDC 2018, vol. 1, pp. 1–10 (2018). https://doi.org/10.1145/3210586.3210601

42. Hansen, E.I.K., Iversen, O.S.: You are the real experts! - studying teenagers' motivation in participatory design. In: ACM International Conference Proceeding Series, pp. 328–331 (2013). https://doi.org/10.1145/2485760.2485826
43. Harrington, C.N., Erete, S., Piper, A.M.: Deconstructing community-based collaborative design: towards more equitable participatory design engagements. Proc. ACM Hum.-Comput. Interact. 3(CSCW) (2019). https://doi.org/10.1145/3359318
44. Randall, N., Sabanovic, S., Chang, W.: Engaging older adults with depression as co-designers of assistive in-home robots. In: ACM International Conference Proceeding Series, pp. 304–309 (2018). https://doi.org/10.1145/3240925.3240946
45. Schofield, G.: Time telescope: encouraging engagement with heritage through participatory design. In: Proceedings of the Conference on Designing Interactive Systems: Processes, Practices, Methods, and Techniques, DIS, pp. 117–120 (2014). https://doi.org/10.1145/2598510.2598517
46. Ozcelik, D., Quevedo-Fernandez, J., Thalen, J., Terken, J.: Engaging users in the early phases of the design process: attitudes, concerns and challenges from industrial practice. In: Proceedings of the DPPI 2011 - Designing Pleasurable Products and Interfaces (2011). https://doi.org/10.1145/2347504.2347519
47. Patrício, R., Zurlo, F.: Gamification approaches to the early stage of innovation, pp. 499–511, June 2018. https://doi.org/10.1111/caim.12284
48. Bickmore, T., Schulman, D., Yin, L.: Maintaining engagement in long-term interventions with relational agents. Appl. Artif. Intell. 24(6), 648–666 (2010)
49. Boyle, E.A., Connolly, T.M., Hainey, T., Boyle, J.M.: Engagement in digital entertainment games: a systematic review. Comput. Hum. Behav. 28(3), 771–780 (2012)

Design Case Studies

Increasing Awareness of Avalanche DANGER: Redesigning a Bulletin

Bojan Blažica[1]([⊠]), Franc Novak[1], Špela Poklukar[1], Peter Novak[1], and Vanja Blažica[2]

[1] Jožef Stefan Institute, Jamova 39, 1000 Ljubljana, Slovenia
{bojan.blazica,franc.novak,spela.poklukar,peter.novak}@ijs.si
[2] Slovenian Environment Agency, Vojkova 1b, 1000 Ljubljana, Slovenia
vanja.blazica@gov.si

Abstract. We present the redesign of the Slovenian avalanche bulletin, published regularly during the winter season to warn against avalanche danger and to provide specific information for advanced users. The former version included an estimation of danger on a scale from one to five with supporting text for the whole country, while the new one offers an additional graphical description, specified for several geographical regions. The paper highlights the importance of usability testing with users to understand how they think about avalanches (problem first vs location first), what information they use to decide etc. Among the key findings is the fact that the word "danger" should be emphasized in all aspects of communication of avalanche conditions, starting with the name of the bulletin.

Keywords: Usability testing · Avalanche danger · Warning systems

1 Introduction

Behind the idyllic scenery of snow-covered mountains lies a hidden threat of unstable mass that can unpredictably slide downhill.

Avalanches endanger local communities in the mountain villages, road and railway traffic and infrastructure, ski resorts and winter sports enthusiasts away from secured ski runs. More than 150 people are killed worldwide each year due to avalanches. The majority of fatalities occurs in the European Alps (about 100–40-year average (Techel et al. 2016)), followed by the USA Rockies (about 28 – 10-year average (Page et al. 1999)). The numbers have increased over the years and shifted from controlled terrain (settlements, transportation corridors) to uncontrolled terrain (Techel et al. 2016); all due to the popularity of winter sports. Climbers, backcountry skiers, out-of-bounds skiers, and more recently snowmobilers constitute the majority of the victims (Techel et al. 2016; Page et al. 1999). The numbers however show the benefit of avalanche prevention strategies: the number of deaths decreased among groups that benefit from avalanche control programs (Page et al. 1999).

Avalanche warning services (AWSs) issue regular avalanche bulletins to warn the endangered population and to inform the public about the current snow and avalanche

© Springer Nature Switzerland AG 2020
C. Stephanidis et al. (Eds.): HCII 2020, LNCS 12423, pp. 383–393, 2020.
https://doi.org/10.1007/978-3-030-60114-0_26

situation. The sources on which the forecasters base their warnings depend on characteristics of each AWS. Among these are automatic measurements and observations of weather and snowpack conditions, manual measurements by AWS team, terrain reports from other sources (mountain rescue service, winter sports enthusiasts etc.), results from numerical models (weather forecast and analysis, snowpack structure, avalanche simulation etc.) and, above all, the forecasters' expertise to combine their knowledge with the information provided. The created warning is disseminated through established channels for communication with users, mainly web pages and mobile applications. The bulletins are aimed at "all those who are exposed to potential avalanche danger in the mountains in winter, whether in a professional or recreational capacity, and those who are responsible for the safety of others"

To improve avalanche safety of the public, the local, regional and national AWSs in Europe formed the European Avalanche Warning Services (EAWS) in 1983. Since then, the AWSs jointly develop standards, exchange experiences and operational procedures and prepare graphical output guidance. Their 5-scale European avalanche danger scale (Fig. 1) is universally accepted in Europe as the most fundamental description of avalanche danger. The AWSs are renovating their bulletins in accordance with the guidelines, which helps users that transit from one region to another to comprehend the local bulletin easily and thus improves the efficiency of the warnings, a common goal of all the AWSs.

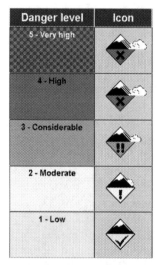

Fig. 1. Internationally recognized and used 5-point avalanche danger scale. Each level has an associated description of snowpack stability and avalanche triggering probability, see http://www. avalanches.org/eaws/en/main_layer.php?layer=basics&id=2.

To add to this common knowledge, the current case study presents the renovation process for the Slovenian avalanche bulletin and the lessons learned.

2   State of the Art

The structure of bulletins should, according to the EAWS, have the form of information pyramid with 6 levels, from most important to least important information: danger level, avalanche prone locations (aspects, elevation), avalanche problems, danger description, other information (snowpack, weather) and measured values (unchecked raw data). Because bulletins with well implemented use of graphics perform best in presenting critical information (Burkeljca 2013), as much content as possible should be presented in a graphical way. The icons for danger level and avalanche problems are already agreed upon and promoted by EAWS, the others will likely follow. The majority of AWSs have adapted the guidelines and put much information into internationally understandable graphical components of the bulletin. For example, the extensive renovation of the Swiss bulletin and accompanying processes is well documented, evaluated and presented in a series of articles (Ruesch et al. 2013; Winkler et al. 2013; Winkler et al. 2014]. The benefits of renovation, as stated by the Catalan AWS (Marti et al. 2010), are the possibility of avalanche forecasts database and improved dissemination options (e.g. pdf, xml). From the forecaster's point of view, the application allows to elaborate the bulletin in a friendly way while the hierarchical structure allows the user to reach more detailed information step by step (Marti et al. 2009). The findings from these renovations are very useful guidelines for other AWSs, of course for each in extent of their resources

3   Renovation Process

The **first step** of the redesign, performed by Slovenian Environment Agency, was an extensive study of other avalanche bulletins to find examples of good practice and of visualization options. In the **second step**, the extent of the information that would be presented in the new bulletin had to be decided. On the one hand, the bulletin needs to be as informative as possible while avoiding information overload and, on the other hand, we had to balance the resources needed to provide the data for the bulletin, e.g. data availability and human resources needed to process the data. Based on the agreed extent of information, several drafts of the new bulletin were prepared and tested with target groups. The **third step** was to design a new database and interface to support forecasters' new workflow. The **fourth step** was to achieve further improvements by asking stakeholders (mountain rescue service, mountain guides, alpine association etc.) for comments on the nearly-final version. After the final corrections, the new bulletin was issued along with explanatory material and a follow-up survey.

4   Methodology of User Testing

The aim of testing with user was to answer the following research questions: 1) which version of the bulletin is most effective for the users, 2) which information is most relevant for the users (danger level, problem description etc.), 3) how fast and successful are users when searching for relevant information, 4) how well is the placement of the information aligned with the cognitive processes of the users, 5) how well do the users understand the icons used, 6) for each version of the bulletin, which are the tasks most quickly and effectively completed by the users, 7) which are the most emphasized pros and cons of each version of the bulletin, 8) how does the interactivity of the bulletin fulfill users' expectations?

4.1 Avalanche Bulletin User Profiles

Avalanche bulletin users are people who visit mountains in snow conditions. Based on their motivation to visit mountains and frequency, we can divide them in two groups: Group A: users who have to go to the mountains (mountain rescue workers, lodge managers, ski slopes workers, mountain unit of the army, plow drivers) and Group B: Users going to the mountains for "sport" (alpinists, tourers, hikers, snowmobile drivers). Users have different levels of knowledge, but we assume all are aware of the existence of threats, the avalanche bulletin and the five-level danger scale.

4.2 Study Outline

The study was exploratory in nature and collected qualitative data. The design of the study was within-subjects (all participants performed all tasks, with the order of the tasks different to counter the effect of accommodation to icons when evaluating different versions). The timeframe of each session was around 55 min (2 min introduction, 2 min mountaineering habits survey, 30 min moderated tasks using think-aloud, and 10 min after-test interview).

Evaluation of Different Versions of the Bulletin. The most important goal of the test was to evaluate three different versions of the bulletin. Versions vary by the amount of information on the bulletin:

- Version 1 (Fig. 2 left): Danger level across all regions and a more detailed description of the danger also across all regions
- Version 2 (Fig. 2 right, Fig. 3 left): Danger level across all regions, while a single more detailed description for the whole of Slovenia with only one major problem exposed
  Version 3 (Fig. 3 right): One danger for all regions and a detailed description for the whole of Slovenia, but for two main problems (sometimes it can be only one).

The main difference between the bulletins is in the detailed description of the danger (for Slovenia or individually by regions) and the main problem (one or two for Slovenia or individually by region). In this regard, it was necessary to establish: 1) do users (especially Group B) decide in advance where to go or they choose the region based on the situation, 2) are users interested in general information about hazards wherever they are going or only in detailed information about the particular region of interest, 3) are users aware of the different types of problems at all, and 4) if users are aware of the various types of problems, how important are they to them?

Order and Naming of Icons on the Bulletin. Regarding the icons, which explain in detail the danger associated with the avalanche, the questions were whether they are

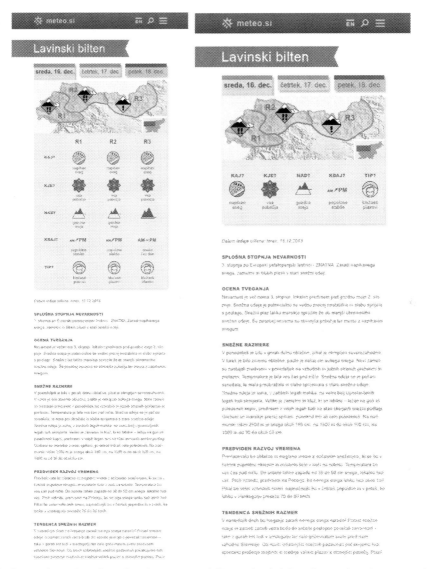

Fig. 2. Version 1 describes all regions at once (left), version 2.1 describes each region separately placing location first (right).

understandable to the users and which ones are the most important to them. The icons used represented the aspect of slopes with higher danger for avalanches (Fig. 7 top), the altitude above or under which the danger is more pronounced (Fig. 7 middle), the time of pronounced danger over the course of the day due to temperature increase over the day (Fig. 7 bottom), the main cause for the avalanche (Fig. 4), the type of avalanche expected (Fig. 5) and the tendency of avalanche danger in the course of the next 3 days (Fig. 6).

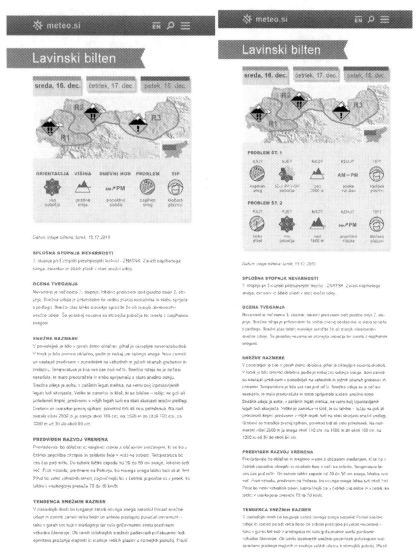

Fig. 3. Version 2.2 describes each region separately placing problem first (left), version 3 describes each region separately while emphasizing two problems for each region if two problems occur in nature (right).

The question of understanding icons is crucial for proper communication of the danger level, while the importance of the icons is related to the mental processes of the users. For example:

– "In Julian Alps, cornices formed. Due to this, the danger increases above 1700 m and on northern slopes. The danger increases during the day. Slab avalanches may occur." or

Fig. 4. Typical avalanche problems (from left to right): persistent weak layers, new snow, wind-drifted snow, wet snow, gliding snow, stable snowpack

Fig. 5. Types of avalanches (from left to right): glide-snow avalanches, loose-snow avalanches, wet-snow avalanches, slab avalanches, cornice fall.

Fig. 6. The tendency of avalanche conditions over the next days (Wednesday, Thursday, and Friday).

Fig. 7. Top: Representation of slope aspect with pronounced danger (darker color indicates higher risk); Middle: representation of altitudes with pronounced danger (darker color indicates higher risk). Attitude is also communicated explicitly with a number below the icon; Bottom: Representation of the time in day with pronounced danger if this is the case due to changes in temperatures during the day.

– "In Julian Alps the danger increases above 1700 m and on northern slopes. The danger increases during the day. The danger is caused by cornices and by slab avalanches."

To test the user's understanding of the icons, we showed them to the users without a description and asked to identify what the icon is about. After that, we showed the descriptions as well and asked if s/he thinks the icons and descriptions match.

Information About the Textual Part of the Bulletin. The textual part of the bulleting is the one that gives the forecaster space to express situations that are too complicated to fit in slots defined by the graphical aspect of the bulletin. Here, we wanted to know what the users' preferences in terms graphics vs. text are, which parts of the text (as usually produced by the Slovenian Environment Agency) is relevant to the users and which not, is the textual part too short or too lengthy and whether there is some information missing and how this differs across user groups.

General Questions. Finally, we tested two basic assumptions: 1) are the users are fully aware that with snow there is always danger of avalanches and 2) the users are familiar with the 5-level avalanche danger scale.

Testing Protocol. Testing took place in our lab on two consecutive days. 9 participants came in on scheduled times; besides the moderator and observer, a recorder taking notes was present. Testing was filmed after written consent from the participants. Testing resulted in 9 h of footage. After analysis, videos were deleted. The participants completed the following three tasks with paper prototypes of the bulletin:

– **Task #1:** You are headed for ski touring on Grintovec mountain. To be sure, you check the avalanche bulletin for the next days and based on what you see, you decide whether you will actually go or not. Describe the snow conditions for each day, your decision about going or not and the reasons for your decision in as much detail as possible.
– **Task #2:** On Tuesday your boss surprises you with news that you can be missed at work for one day in the current week. You are happy and plan to spend this day in the mountains. You immediately go online to check the avalanche bulletin and, based on given information, you decide on which day and where exactly will you go. Please explain your decision and the reasons for it in as much detail as possible.
– **Task #3:** On Thursday, December 17th (2015), a friend calls you in the morning. He tells you he has just parked his car near the barracks on Pokljuka plateau and intends to go ski touring with his wife on Viševnik mountain. He forgot to check show conditions prior to departure and asks you to check the bulletin for him and describe it over the phone.

5   Results and Discussion

The new bulletin was positively accepted: All users complimented the design and content of the redesigned bulletin.

  The new bulletin should further accentuate the danger of avalanches: According to some users, the bulletin understated the danger associated with snow avalanches, which was also confirmed by testing with less experienced users - some of them were not aware that the bulletin was talking about danger at all but was interpreted only as a description of snow conditions. They were only aware that the situation was problematic, when presented the versions of the bulletin that explicitly used the word "problem" to describe the type of avalanche. Regarding the danger of avalanches, experienced users talked about 'acceptable' or 'unacceptable' level of risk and therefore suggested that the bulletin should be named, for example, the "Avalanche danger bulletin".

Knowledge and experience are an important factor in decision making: Advanced users decide whether to go in the mountains and where to go primarily on the basis of their own knowledge of avalanches, knowledge of micro-location and experience. They are mainly interested in weather forecasts and weather and snowpack conditions in the past days. The degree of danger is only an indicative information for them, while for less experienced users, the degree of danger is the main decision factor.

Problem first, aspect second: Concerning the importance of the problem for the user, we encountered two different mental models, which largely depend on the user's experience. More experienced users first think about the problem, and only then about the location, aspect and altitude, while less experienced users think in reverse - location, aspect and attitude first, problem second. We believe this is caused by the lack of a deeper understanding of avalanches and awareness of the danger involved.

Given the expressed desire of users that the bulletin emphasizes the danger more clearly, the layout of the icon with the problem in the first place appears reasonable. Such an arrangement considers, inter-alia, the educational aspect of the bulletin, since it informs the users of the importance of the problem itself.

The type of avalanche and the problem are related and should appear next to each other: Due to the association of information on the problem and the type of avalanches, more experienced users suggested that these two icons be placed together.

General meteorological forecast: All users used weather data directly or indirectly in their decision making. Most users also explicitly expressed the desire for a weather forecast.

The desire for additional information in graphic form: the temperature, wind direction and intensity, the increment of the snow cover and the height of the snow cover at different altitudes: The most frequent response to the question "Do you miss any key information in the bulletin?" was "specific weather information, preferably in graphic form" and with the history of the last few days. This helps create a picture of the developments in time.

Missing legend and explanation of the avalanche danger scale: Since the vast majority of users, including the most experienced, do not know the icons of the avalanche danger scale by heart, they expressed the desire that the full scale should always be clearly displayed on the bulletin.

The textual part of the bulletin is especially important for advanced users: In the case of advanced users (guides and rescuers), we noticed that they based their decisions primarily on the basis of text and detailed information in it. Some of them had entirely skipped the graphic display at the top.

Users expect the text to change in days, not just the graphic display: Most users expected that the text was adapted to each day, as users of the text did not perceive it as a general description of snow conditions on the day the bulletin was issued (in Slovenia the bulletin is not issued every day).

Users would choose Version1: After performing the tasks, we asked what version users would choose. Version 2 was the most intuitive, but Version 1 was chosen as it contains more information.

Version 3, which emphasizes two problems, creates confusion: The two-problem version was generally poorly understood. It was not clear to most users why it had two problems. They wondered which region the icons relate to and which problem is more important. After presenting the main idea of Version 3 to users, they appreciated the larger amount of information, but decided it was too complex.

The tendency is not evident from the graphic display: At first glance, only two users found out that the snow conditions worsened. Most of them answered negatively when asked "Do you think the tendency of snow conditions is evident from the graphic part of the bulletin?" Following explanation that this is evident from the colors of the tabs, they appreciated the solution as sensible and imaginative.

The icons combined with labels are sufficiently clear: We showed the users the icons for avalanche type and avalanche problem without labels. Given the complexity of the problem presented by icons, the degree of recognition among experienced users is satisfactory. If using labels, all icons were completely clear to all users.

The initial theoretical work done before designing the first prototypes payed of as all were considered satisfactory and a huge improvement over the old version. Reviewing available bulletins and literature as well as current procedures needed to issue bulletins allows everybody involved in the redesign to better grasp the problem. This was essential especially because the problem is very specific and characterized by a gap between how it is seen by those who are familiar with it (forecasters who issue bulletins, expert mountaineers) and those not (less experienced mountaineers, designers or other outside experts who might be working on the redesign). This initial step helps getting everybody on the same page and allows those issuing the bulletin to get an understanding of what are the areas of avalanches and avalanche warnings that are obvious only to them and not others. On the other hand, external experts working on the redesign get an initial understanding of the problem, how it can be solved and, most importantly, what are the limitations when issuing bulletins (e.g. resources available to update in real time or on a daily basis).

The usability testing then lead to the following actionable items and improvements to the bulletin: 1) version V1 is used, 2) the title of the bulletin is corrected to "Bilten plazovnega tveganja" (eng. Avalanche risk bulletin), 3) above the textual part, the title "Snow conditions on the day [date of issue of the bulletin]" is added 4) at the date of the issue of the bulletin, the anticipated date of issuing the new bulletin and the link to the archive of the bulletins is added, 5) for the naming of icons, the terms "problem", "avalanche type", "aspect", should be used, 6) the icon for the avalanche problem is placed first, the avalanche type icon is second, 7) a general weather forecast is added to the bulletin, 8) the legend of icons is added, especially for the five-level danger scale, 9) in line with the educational purpose of the bulletin, a link to a general description of possible problems related to snow conditions, a description of the various types of avalanches and information related to their occurrence should be added.

6 Conclusion

The presented case study offers insight in an avalanche bulletin redesigned process and highlights the importance of testing bulletins with users. We would advise all AWSs to perform such tests to better understand how their users think and what they expect. In our case, user testing helped us sort out graphical and layout details, but also showed us the importance of textual information to expert users and, most importantly, revealed the fact that the word danger should be over-emphasized to achieve the desired warning effect of the bulletin.

Acknowledgements. We thank all the volunteers involved in the study. The authors acknowledge the financial support from the Slovenian Research Agency (research core funding No. P2-0098).

References

Burkeljca, J.: Shifting audience and the visual language of avalanche risk communication. In: Proceedings of the International Snow Science Workshop, ISSW 2013, pp. 415–422 (2013)

Martí, G., et al.: A new iconographic avalanche bulletin for the Catalan Pyrenees: a beginning for a future avalanche forecasting database. In: Proceedings of the International Snow Science Workshop, ISSW 2009, pp. 361–365, Davos (2009)

Page, C.E., et al.: Avalanche deaths in the United States: a 45-year analysis. Wilderness Environ. Med. **10**(3), 146–151 (1999)

Ruesch, M., Egloff, A., Gerber, M., Weiss, G., Winkler, K.: The software behind the interactive display of the Swiss avalanche bulletin. In: Proceedings of the International Snow Science Workshop, ISSW 2013, pp. 406–412, ANENA, IRSTEA, Météo, Grenoble (2013)

Techel, F., et al.: Avalanche fatalities in the European Alps: long-term trends and statistics. Geograph. Helv. **71**(2), 147–159 (2016)

Winkler, K., et al.: Swiss avalanche bulletin: automated translation with a catalogue of phrases. In: Proceedings of the International Snow Science Workshop, ISSW 2013, pp. 437–441, Grenoble (2013)

Winkler, K., Kuhn, T., Volk, M.: Evaluating the fully automatic multi-language translation of the swiss avalanche bulletin. In: Davis, B., Kaljurand, K., Kuhn, T. (eds.) CNL 2014. LNCS (LNAI), vol. 8625, pp. 44–54. Springer, Cham (2014). https://doi.org/10.1007/978-3-319-102 23-8_5

Explore an Evolution of Physical Education Based on Virtual Reality Lab for Traditional Ethnic Minorities' Sports

Wenmei Dong[1](✉) and Jingyan Yu[2]

[1] Physical Education Department, Minzu University of China, Beijing, China
dongwenm@163.com
[2] University of Rochester, Rochester, NY, USA
yujingyana@163.com

Abstract. Purpose: Ten-year Plan for the Development of Education Informatization (2010–2020) was issued in China, which had its unique impact on improving the quality of education, promoting the evolution of educational concept, and cultivating the innovative talents with international competitiveness. This paper was to explore why and how we could establish virtual reality for traditional ethnic minorities' sports, and aimed to teach traditional ethnic minorities culture, achieve visualization and retention with virtual reality and cloud computing technologies.

Methods: We choose archery, firecrackers, and curling to construct 3D models of sports field, participants, costumes, and facilities of the three sports. Students putting on VR/AR gargles to immerse in and interact with virtual scenes.

Results: 1. The construction of traditional ethnic minorities' sports virtual reality is aiming to meet the need of P.E. development, apply the computer simulation technology, and realize the digitization, visualization, and operationalization of P.E. discipline. 2. The laboratory is consists of three sections: computer room, exploration zone, and observation zone. The processes of the lab were modeling 3D scene, constructing traditional ethnic minorities' sports, interacting with virtual scenes, and evaluating the previous interaction.

Conclusions: By the help of cloud computing and VR technology, MUC is aiming to protect and inherit the culture of traditional ethnic minorities' sports, realize the visualization and operationalization of traditional ethnic minorities' sports, and enhance students' understanding of those sports and the culture of traditional ethnic minorities' sports.

Keywords: Traditional ethnic minorities' sports · Virtual reality · Physical education

1 Introduction

The Virtual Lab has been rapidly developed around the world since it was first proposed by Professor William Wolf of the University of Virginia in 1989. At present, many universities in the United States, the United Kingdom, Canada, Australia, Spain, New

© Springer Nature Switzerland AG 2020
C. Stephanidis et al. (Eds.): HCII 2020, LNCS 12423, pp. 394–401, 2020.
https://doi.org/10.1007/978-3-030-60114-0_27

Zealand, and India have established virtual reality laboratories and are committed to building a virtual simulation experimental network platform covering the whole country. With the continuous development of the information industry, the informationization of education has received great attention from China. According to the Ten-year Plan for the Development of Education Informatization (2010–2020), education informatization has its unique impact on improving the quality of education, promoting the evolution of educational concept, and cultivating the innovative talents with international competitiveness, etc. It is also a momentum for the process of education modernization in China (Zhai 2014). In the public document Notice on the Construction of National Virtual Simulation Experimental Teaching Center, the ministry of education points out that 'virtual reality experimental teaching is an important part of information construction of higher education and of experimental teaching center construction, it is also the in-depth combination of information technology and discipline construction.' Now that Minzu University of China (MUC) is supporting the establishment of virtual reality experimental teaching center, it is a great opportunity for MUC to improve its education quality and train more innovative talents. Meanwhile, virtual reality is known for its scenario construction, the ultimate goal of physical education (P.E.) is to improve students' emotional, cognitive, and physical ability. As a result, virtual reality (VR) technology can help physical education to 'build up scenarios' in order to expand the depth and range of teaching materials, and to extend the teaching time and space. To fulfill MUC's goal of executing the 'Double First Class University Plan' and to meet the need of the development of Faculty of Physical Education, traditional ethnic minorities' sports VR laboratories are required to be built.

2   Virtual Reality Lab Overview

2.1   The Meaning of Virtual Reality Lab

Based on virtual reality, human-computer interaction, multimedia, database and network technologies, etc., the virtual simulation laboratory is used to build highly simulated virtual experimental environments and experimental scenarios. Under the conditions of virtual experiments, students can independently carry out virtual experiments, select experimental subjects, change control factors, observe different experimental results and conduct diagnosis analysis of the results, and write experimental reports to meet the requirements of the syllabus. The development of virtual reality experiments cannot be separated from the development of virtual reality resources. Virtual reality resources refer to various explicit or hidden conditions and elements that can be used. They generally include four parts: simulation model, simulation data, simulation software, and simulation platform. They involve all available infrastructure and software equipment.

2.2   Features of Virtual Reality Lab

High Simulation and Intelligence. In the virtual experiment scenario, all the equipment provided by the virtual reality laboratory has high simulation and intelligent setting functions. Students can conduct simulation experiments, operate autonomously, and observe experimental phenomena just like the actual experimental environment.

Intuitive and Open. Virtual simulation experiments can visually display some abstract concepts through animation, making up for the lack of traditional experimental teaching. Moreover, virtual simulation experiments can strengthen students' understanding of abstract concepts, promote the improvement of teaching effects, and be able to break time and space constraints. Users can log in to the interface to enter the virtual experiment platform at any time.

Security and Immunity. Some of the traditional experiments with toxic side effects or high risks are difficult to carry out. Virtual simulation experiments can overcome adverse factors and carry out simulation experiments to deepen students' understanding of knowledge. In addition, the virtual simulation experiment can avoid the situation that the experiment cannot be carried out on time due to factors such as instrument failure and poor contact, and has certain anti-interference performance.

Economy. The virtual simulation laboratory can effectively avoid problems such as aging, damage, and depreciation of the instrument, and can meet the requirements of repeated use by users. Therefore, it can save teaching expenses and reduce experimental costs.

3   The Construction of Virtual Reality Lab of Traditional Ethnic Minorities' Sports Conforms to MUC's Requirement

Among all the universities of nationalities in China, MUC is the only one that participates in the construction of 'Double Frist Class University Plan (Class A)'. It represents MUC's leading position in fulfilling national strategies, promoting national unity, serving ethnic minorities, accelerating economic and social development in regions inhabited by ethnic minority groups, and constructing the consciousness of Chinese national community (Zhang 2018). At present, the main tasks for MUC are to make solid progress in the construction of first-class disciplines to have its own characteristics and to improve social visibility. The development of P.E. is lagging behind other disciplines, so it needs to seize the opportunity and become a first-class discipline. Meanwhile, the development of P.E. can help MUC to form its own characteristics and improve its social visibility.

Among the world's top 100 universities, almost 50% of them are located in the U.S. Why would more and more Chinese parents send their children to the U.S. regardless of the huge cost? Are they simply following suit or is there a gap between China and the U.S. in education? In terms of scientific research achievements, student training, and student services, China might be able to keep up with the universities in the U.S., but their long history of physical education has far exceeded that in China. According to the mission statement of Stanford University, 'from its founding in 1891, Stanford University's leaders have believed that physical activity is valuable for its own sake and that vigorous exercise is complementary to the educational purposes of the university.' On the webpage of Brown University, it says, 'The athletic program plays an essential role in teaching students to conduct themselves with honesty and integrity, make sacrifices, strive for excellence, persevere through adversity, and compete with dignity and pride while developing a commitment to teamwork and service to the community. (Yang 2011)'

A student from University of South California remarks, 'for students from USC, nothing can be more important than watching a match!' Students from University of Florida have reached a consensus that, 'Life is movement! College life cannot be full without football matches!' In conclusion, P.E. can help universities to reach their educational objectives and cultivate fully-developed talents.

The development of P.E. in MUC has a comparatively short history, so it is essential to sort out the discipline's characteristics for its future progression. Each year, the discipline of P.E. is responsible for thousands of students, and it always faces the challenges as follows: the lack of spaces and facilities, bad weathers, the lack of teachers, the small selection of courses due to safety concerns, students' lack of enthusiasm for P.E. classes, etc. The construction of virtual reality experimental teaching center for P.E. will expand the depth and breadth of learning. Students can enhance their cognition and understanding for sports, and build up motivations of learning through man-machine interaction. Thus, they can also establish the life-time habit of exercising their bodies. Traditional ethnic minorities' sports, on the one hand, can help improve people's health, on the other hand, is the heritage of traditional ethnic culture. As a result, it has the function of carrying on ethnic culture and enhancing the consciousness of Chinese nation. In conclusion, the establishment of VR laboratory of traditional ethnic minorities' sports conforms to MUC's requirement of becoming a 'Double First Class' university.

4   The Characteristics of the Traditional Ethnic Minorities' Sports VR Laboratory

Based on the concept of 'Double First Class University Plan', the construction of traditional ethnic minorities' sports VR laboratory is aiming to meet the need of P.E. development, apply the computer simulation technology, and realize the digitization, visualization, and operationalization of P.E. discipline. The characteristics of the laboratory are as follows:

4.1   Discipline Characteristics

As is required by the 'Outline of Physical Education Instruction for Undergraduates' issued by Ministry of Education, MUC has set up courses for public P.E., among them, 'Traditional Ethnic Minorities' Sports' is one of the optional courses. However, due to the lack of teachers, the limitation of facilities, and the replacement by western sports, traditional ethnic minorities' sports are gradually forgotten. As a result, even though MUC has offered the course, there are only a few traditional sports for option, and only a few classes are taken.

The disciplinary background of MUC has laid a solid foundation for the Faculty of Physical Education to choose traditional ethnic minorities' sports as the teaching content. In order to enhance the competitiveness and to raise the profile of the Faculty of Physical Education, MUC has to focus on developing the discipline of traditional ethnic minorities' sports, so as to build characteristics for the Faculty of Physical Education. To solve the problems faced by the course of traditional ethnic minorities' sports, including the lack of teachers, the limitation of facilities and spaces, the endangerment of some sports, and the high level of risks of some other sports, MUC is planning to build VR laboratories to teach students about traditional ethnic minorities' sports culture and national solidarity.

4.2 VR and Cloud Computing Technologies

VR technology uses computer to generate 3-dimensional realistic images and uses graphic technology to generate sounds, touch, vision and other sensations that simulate a user's physical presence in a virtual environment. By implementing the VR technology, Faculty of Physical Education can realize the visualization, enablement, and operationalization of traditional ethnic minorities' sports. This is because, students would only enhance their understanding of and cultivate their interests on traditional ethnic minorities' sports when they experience them sensually. Moreover, the simulation of costumes, rules, and scenarios can enhance the education in ethnic minorities' traditional culture and the mutual-understandings among ethnic groups. Thus, it improves national unity.

With the help of the advanced cloud computing technology, students can download the application on their phone before taking classes, so that they can watch videos, read articles about traditional ethnic minorities' sports, and get prepared for their future study.

4.3 Digitalization and Permanent Preservation

Traditional ethnic minorities' sports are originated from people's daily life, so they have distinctive national characteristics and a broad mass base. It is not only an essential part of China's physical culture, but it is also a significant part of China's traditional culture. According to the statistics, there are over 900 types of traditional ethnic minorities' sports. In the quadrennial National Traditional Games of Ethnic Minorities, there are 17 different sports including fire cracker ball, pearl ball, wooden ball, shuttlecock, dragon boat, single-bamboo drifting, swing, crossbow, spinning top, and Tibetan tug of war. The courses opened in MUC including fire cracker ball, stilt race, spinning top and so on. The options are limited, but each of the course has its own characteristics.

By the help of cloud computing and VR technology, firstly, the depth and breadth of traditional ethnic minorities' sports education can be expanded in a way that it enables the dangerous but popular sports, like horse-riding and archery, can be learned in the VR classrooms. Secondly, through VR technology, students can be introduced to the costumes, culture, and game rules that could not be presented in traditional classrooms. These show that VR laboratories of traditional ethnic minorities' sports can realize the digitalization of traditional ethnic minorities' sports: it does not only promote the development of P.E., but it also protects and inherits the culture of traditional ethnic minorities' sports, so that the culture can be used and kept in a long-term basis.

4.4 High Level of Visibility and Operationally

In the laboratory room, a computer is set up to generate various scenarios of traditional ethnic minorities' sports, so as to realize the visualization of the learning projects and help students to understand. In the experience area, students can wear VR/AR glasses to interact with the virtual scene and experience the learning process of skills. There is a large screen projection in the laboratory's observation area, for students to watch virtual games.

5 Experiment Script

5.1 Purposes

- Expand the depth and range of teaching materials, and extend the teaching time and space of the teaching content of traditional ethnic minorities' sports.
- Protect and inherit the culture of traditional ethnic minorities' sports with the technology of cloud computing and VR.
- Realize the visualization and operationalization of traditional ethnic minorities' sports, enhance students' understanding of the sports and of the culture behind the sports, and motivate students to participate in the sports.

5.2 Principles

VR technology can help traditional ethnic minorities' sports to 'build scenarios', expand the depth and range of teaching materials, and extend the teaching time and space.

Traditional ethnic minorities' sports is the heritage of fine traditional culture of different ethnic groups. However, due to the limitation of space, faculty, facility, rule, and security concern, some of the most popular sports cannot be introduced into the classrooms. With the help of VR technology, faculty of physical education can provide students a much more abundant amount of information, from the origin of the sports to their costumes, and further to the match scenarios. Besides, students can have both the visual and the sensual experience of the sports.

5.3 Overview and Processes

Overview of the Laboratory. The laboratory consists of three sections: the computer room, exploration zone and observation zone. In the computer room, there are computers that can generate scenarios for different traditional ethnic minorities' sports. In the initial period of laboratory construction, the room requires 5 high-performance computers, servers, and graphic cards. It can provide service for 20 students at the same time. In the exploration zone, students can put on VR/AR gargles and interact with virtual scenes. In the initial period of laboratory construction, the sports being chosen, archery, fire cracker ball, and curling, are the sports that are widely practiced in ethnic minority areas. These sports have a certain level of complexity and are popular among students. In the observation zone, there are giant screen projection for students to watch virtual matches.

Processes. *3D scene modeling: In the initial period of construction, the three sports chosen are archery, fire cracker ball, and curling.* The main task is to construct 3D models of sports field, participants, costumes, and facilities of the three sports.

Constructing traditional ethnic minorities' sports: to organize, set rules and do behavioral modeling for the three sports mentioned above.

Students putting on VR/AR gargles to immerse in and interact with virtual scenes, so that they can obtain virtual experience of participating in the sports.

Evaluating the previous interaction.

5.4   Progress of Lab Construction

The "National Traditional Sports Virtual Simulation Experiment Project" was approved for the Beijing Virtual Simulation Experiment Teaching Project in 2019, and was also recommended by Beijing as a national project. This project has been registered in the national virtual simulation experimental teaching project sharing platform. Through 3D modeling, animation, speech recognition, human-computer interaction and other technologies, the project not only created "scenes of tall horses, pearl balls, gyro and other projects" in the "virtual environment" but also restored the historical origins, skills of these three projects, tactical rules and the process of the game. The picture is as follows:

6   Sustainable Development

6.1   Professional Team

The research team formed by the faculty of physical education can be ranked as the top in China, as MUC has a number of researchers (including Professors and PhDs) who are experienced in the area of traditional ethnic minorities' sports. The experts and researchers from the team are the guarantees of establishing characteristics for the discipline. Meanwhile, MUC will cooperate with Universities that also have courses related to traditional ethnic minorities' sports, including Yunnan Minzu University and Jishou University from Hunan Province, to build VR laboratories together.

Among the laboratory construction team, there are a professor who has been working on the research and development of virtual reality technology for many years with his company team. Professional technicians are guaranteed of constructing laboratories.

6.2   Laboratory Site

The laboratory consists of three sections: computer room, exploration zone, and observation zone. There might be some obstacles in the initial period of construction, but the project can start in a smaller-scale and the site of laboratory can be expanded when the new campus of MUC is built.

6.3   Funding

With the financial support of MUC for building the VR laboratories, faculty of physical education can have the opportunity to build VR labs, and it is possible to establish their discipline characteristics through building traditional ethnic minorities' sports VR laboratories. At the same time, this project has gotten its approval from the Beijing Key Laboratory, and will get sustainable funding from that.

6.4 Sustainable Development

The construction of traditional ethnic minorities' sports VR laboratories is a sustainable task. The education of traditional ethnic minorities' sports culture is essential for all MUC students, and this physical education resource can be shared by other universities. Over 600 traditional ethnic minorities' sports are the treasures of Chinese traditional culture. It is a long-term and sustainable task to digitalize and visualize those sports, and keep them in permanent preservation.

7 Conclusion

Virtual reality experimental teaching is not only an important part of information construction of higher education and of experimental teaching center construction, but it is also the in-depth combination of information technology and discipline construction. By the help of cloud computing and VR technology, MUC is aiming to protect and inherit the culture of traditional ethnic minorities' sports, realize the visualization and operationalization of traditional ethnic minorities' sports, and enhance students' understanding of those sports and the culture of traditional ethnic minorities' sports. By all counts, this project has a wide-spread prospect.

References

Wang, H.: Thoughts on the construction of comprehensive virtual simulation experimental teaching center in application-oriented local colleges. Jiangsu Sci. Technol. Inf. **5**, 75–79 (2019)

Ceng, W., Yang, Y.: Research on innovation and entrepreneurship based on virtual reality technology. Res. Curric. Teach. **10**, 12–13 (2016)

Yang, Z.: Core American Universities' concepts of sports. Sports Cult. Guide **4**(4), 104–106 (2011)

Zhai, Z.: Take the development of MOOC as an opportunity to promote the deep integration of information technology and higher education. China High. Educ. Res. **6**, 1–4 (2014)

Zhang, J.: Strengthening the Consciousness of Maintaining National Unity, Developing Higher Education of Ethnic Minorities. Guangming Daily, vol. 12, p. 14 (2018)

Liu, Q., Yang, S.: Constructing a virtual simulation laboratory to promote the cultivation of innovative talents in agriculture. Equip. Manag. Maint. **5**, 5–6 (2019)

Gong, M., Li, G.: Thoughts and suggestions on creating a basic medical virtual simulation laboratory. China Educ. Technol. Equip. **4**, 59–60 (2016)

Wang, W., Jin, H.: Status and development of virtual simulation experiment teaching in foreign universities. Res. Explor. Lab. **34**(5), 214–219 (2015)

Office of the Working Group on the Outline of the National Medium- and Long-term Education Reform and Development Plan. The Outline of the National Medium- and Long-term Education Reform and Development Plan (2010–2020) (2010)

Liang, C.: Analysis on the path of specialty construction based on the construction of virtual simulation laboratory. Sci. Technol. Innov. **13**, 145–146 (2017)

Information Design to Save Lives: Visualizing Data in the Design of Overdose Kits

Gillian Harvey[1]([⊠]) and Katherine Bubric[2]

[1] University of Alberta, Edmonton, AB, Canada
gharvey@ualberta.ca
[2] Alberta Health Services, Calgary, AB, Canada

Abstract. This paper visualizes and discusses the data collected in an iterative design project to improve the design of instructions for how to use naloxone kits. In addition to a discussion about participant demographics, it presents the usability testing data and will use several data visualizations to illustrate the information that could be found, information that was used correctly and accurately, and overall performance level achieved. This paper will also present the observations that were made in the testing and comment on how the variations in design affected the comprehension of the instructions. It will visually explain and discuss the data collected in the design and comment on the importance of data collection and visualization in an interdisciplinary health design project. The project has proven the need for an evidence-based, human centred design approach to the redesign of any kind of procedural instruction that is to be read and understood in an emergency situation.

Keywords: Data visualization · Healthcare · Design thinking · Usability testing

1 Introduction

The broad accessibility of data and digital tools has dramatically increased the quantity of information directed toward policy makers and the general public. By some estimates, the average person is inundated with the information equivalent of 147 newspapers daily [7]. Because infographics leverage the brain's most dominant capacity—visual processing—they can be a faster and more effective way of communicating information than text alone. As Noel, Joy and Dyck [6] acknowledge, healthcare is one of the areas where data visualization is most useful. Quality Improvement (QI) projects are familiar for those in healthcare as projects that aim to improve processes or services for patients, but the way that the data collected from these initiatives is used is still not well understood.

A different sort of data visualization is noticeable in the public health field with the use of infographics to inform the public of everything from outbreaks of listeria in the United States to the global health worker shortage [1]. Information visualization is also becoming a more accepted way of showing research studies in healthcare as well, however there is little known about how to do it effectively. Given the enormity of data used in healthcare, it may be surprising to designers that user-centered design is not firmly entrenched in this field. In order to use data to drive action, data must be meaningful to people [5].

© Springer Nature Switzerland AG 2020
C. Stephanidis et al. (Eds.): HCII 2020, LNCS 12423, pp. 402–414, 2020.
https://doi.org/10.1007/978-3-030-60114-0_28

2   Context

In December 2018, a group of designers and design researchers undertook the evaluation and redesign of the Community Based Naloxone Kit (CBNK) instructions for Alberta Health Services (AHS) in Alberta, Canada. The province of Alberta, Canada, in the last 3 years has seen some frightening statistics: in 2016, more people died from opioid overdoses than from motor vehicle crashes [2].

Naloxone kits are used to help people – specifically individuals who are not medically trained – inject an antidote (naloxone) into someone who is experiencing opioid poisoning. This could happen in an emergency situation, after emergency personnel has been called, but before they have time to respond. Often it is a bystander, and not a medical professional, that intervenes in these situations. For example, a friend or a family member may find themselves in the presence of someone who has overdosed from opioid poisoning. Sometimes the person that intervenes has had experience dealing with injections, and sometimes they have not. While we usually hear about the overdoses that are due to the use of recreational/street drugs, it is important to realize that anyone has the potential to be a victim of an opioid overdose. Studies have found that most overdoses occur in the presence of another person; this provides an opportunity for someone to intervene [2]. The Community Based Naloxone Kit instructional sheet was designed by medical professionals in response to an opioid epidemic in Alberta, but had not been formally evaluated prior to implementation.

The Alberta Health Services (AHS) Harm Reduction team develops programs and initiatives aimed to reduce risks and harm associated with the use of psychoactive substances, which includes overseeing the province's naloxone kits. The team identified an opportunity to improve the design of the naloxone kit instructions, as they were thought to be too clinical, as opposed to being designed for a more novice audience. An initial analysis of the naloxone kit instructions by our research team found several shortcomings (Fig. 1) including:

- Insufficient and unclear labelling of contents in the kit. A photo of the kit contents show overlapping medical equipment and contents are not labelled.
- The hierarchy and importance of the information was not clear. Subtitles within the kit did not allow people to understand the sequence of the procedure and did not provide detail on how to use the contents of the kit.
- Critical information was hard to find. It was not clear that calling 911 before starting rescue breathing is essential.
- Lack of information on how to inject naloxone, dispose of the needle, and care for the patient.
- Use of medical jargon. Words were written from a medical perspective rather than in layman's terms.
- Overuse of acronyms and unintuitive icons.
- Inadequate sequencing of the procedure.
- A disconnect between the images and the text.
- A folding layout was used that did not consider the context of use.

The challenges identified with the current instructions are significant when the task and context of use are considered. Naloxone kits are intended to be used to save the life

Fig. 1. Original naloxone kit challenges and opportunities for improvement

of someone who has overdosed, which is an inherently stressful task, and even more so for individuals that have no experience with needles or giving injections. Because of the clear patient safety risks associated with an inability to quickly and accurately follow the instructions in the naloxone kits, a quality improvement project was initiated to improve the design of the instructions of the kits. "Quality improvement (QI) in healthcare refers to the varied initiatives across healthcare organizations that aim to improve health outcomes for patients" [6]. Often the context for QI initiatives is inpatient populations, however, in this case the focus was on opioid users, who are a vulnerable, high risk, marginalized population. QI projects can focus on a range of issues and outcomes, and there is no standardization in terms of how data is collected or analyzed. Often these projects use quantitative comparisons to measure the effectiveness of an intervention, however a clear measure of success is not always available. Consequently, sometimes QI projects are more subjective in nature. In the naloxone kit study, it was not possible to use a single measure to determine the effectiveness of each new iteration of the instructions (i.e. it was not possible, or ethical, to implement each new design of the instructions and compare how many overdoses were successfully prevented). Rather, a number of individual data points were collected including background demographics as well as errors and completion rates during scenario-based usability testing. There was a clear need for a structured framework to make sense of the wide range of data collected in order to apply the results to future iterations and ultimately produce a final, usable design. In addition, in this, as well as other, quality improvement initiatives, there is a need to be able to present the collected data in a clear and compelling manner to the stakeholder team who are ultimately responsible for deciding whether to implement the outcome of the improvement initiative or not. This research study was approved by the Research Ethics Board of the University of Alberta, Edmonton, Alberta, Canada.

3   Description of Methods

3.1   Literature Review

A literature review was done to understand and gather scientific evidence with regard to the design of the documents. A number of relevant themes were identified in the literature:

Plain Language and Word Order. Use plain language and short, concise phrases clarify content. As, Wright, who has often written about the benefit of graphic communication over written communication suggests, it is helpful to have "the order of mention match the order of action" [9]. For example, in an instructional sequence such as "Call 911, then proceed to rescue breathing" is much more effective than the sentence, "Before rescue breathing, call 911".

Layout and Typography. Use short sentences with few words and bullets wherever possible to aid comprehension. Waller, in his writing about type, emphasizes this point by adding that typography "adds the diagrammatic quality that can make such a structure accessible to the browsing or less committed reader" [8]. Using this logic, the large numbers, and short subheadings should make the steps in the procedure salient and easier to read, providing a "typographic roadmap" [8]. The typographic roadmap in these instructions are emphasized by the steps that are in the same place down the left-hand side of the insert and the headings which, when read alone without the detailed instructions, will allow the reader to understand the procedure.

Pictorial Simplification. Images should provide visual information to the reader. This is different than in other publications where they are used to provide pleasure or visual stimulation. Goldsmith says that "semantic unity requires recognition of the image, and representation adequate for this purpose relies not on slavish imitation of an object, but on the clarity of distinguishing features which give relevant information" [3].

3.2 Usability Testing

An iterative approach to designing and testing the naloxone kit instructions was used. A total of 40 participants participated in three rounds of usability testing, with each round testing a new version (i.e. prototype) of the instructions. Participants included individuals who had used opioids and those who had not. The sample also included a mix of individuals who had used a naloxone kit and those who had not. A description of the sample of participants can be found in Table 1.

Table 1. Participant demographics

	PROTOTYPE I		PROTOTYPE II		PROTOTYPE III	
	Yes	No	Yes	No	Yes	No
currently use opioids	10	20	0	4	2	4
previously used opioids	17	13	0	4	4	2
has witnessed an overdose	18	11	0	4	3	2
has administered naloxone	8	21	0	4	1	4
has experience with needles	13	16	2	4	3	2

Each prototype was designed with consultation from a Human Factors Specialist as well as members of the local Harm Reduction team from AHS. Through consultation with medical experts, the design team was able to define performance specifications. These performance specifications are goals of the instructions that isolate information that needs to be tested with users.

Participants needed to be able to do three types of tasks with the instructions (Fig. 2).

BASIC TASKS	IDENTIFICATION TASKS	USAGE TASK
Provide a summary of the steps involved	Define an overdose	Know how to respond to an overdose
Know how to care for a casualty	Know when to call 911	Know how to inject naloxone
Know that naloxone is safe to use if a person has not overdosed		Know what to do if first naloxone dose does not work

Fig. 2. Types of tasks involved in successful completion of naloxone administration

Each usability testing session involved a participant completing a simulated scenario in which they used the naloxone kit instructions to administer naloxone to someone who had collapsed. The simulated scenario involved a CPR mannequin on a table and a facilitator who re-enacted an emergency situation. Rather than injecting into the mannequin, participants were instructed to inject the naloxone into a training device that is designed to be punctured, and to indicate on a diagram which body part they would have injected in. As the participants completed the scenario, they were asked to verbalize what they were thinking and doing, including anything that is confusing or frustrating. Throughout the scenario, an observer recorded whether the participant successfully completed each key step in the naloxone administration process (i.e., whether the performance specifications were achieved), any errors that occurred, and any challenges that were observed or verbalized. At the end of the session, a debrief session occurred with predetermined open-ended questions. The goal of the debrief was to understand if the participants understood key information contained in the instructions, how they used the instructions, if there was anything they did not understand, and any improvement opportunities. Following each round of usability testing, the data was compiled, and recurring challenges and errors were identified. A design solution was identified for each key challenge, which was translated into the next prototype.

4   Results

All results provided show the combined data from the three rounds of usability testing.

4.1   Overall Performance

Figure 3 illustrates participant performance on each step of the naloxone administration task. This data was used to identify areas to focus on during each round of redesign. For example, the task of calling 911 was missed during 44% of the simulated scenarios, so this information was made more salient in the final version of the instructions. In step 3, most participants (91%) Attempted rescue breaths, but only 58% of participants performed them correctly, meaning that this needed to be clarified in the instructions. In addition, participants only re-evaluated the person correctly 69% of the time. When it came to injecting naloxone, 94% of participants were able to do this, but only 78% were able to do this in the correct location on the body. This led to design changes that drew attention to the injection location in the instructions.

4.2   Role of experience

Experience as an opioid user – especially experience with injections – played an important role in evaluating the participants' performance. The two groups were:

- Experienced: participants who had previous experience using opioids.
- Inexperienced: participants who did NOT have previous experience using opioids.

Performance of experienced and inexperienced participants differed for each step of the naloxone administration process (Fig. 4). Participants who did not have previous experience using opioids performed better than those with opioid experience on a number of measures including: checking response with sternal rub (75% vs. 65%), knowing rescue breaths were required (100% vs. 65%) and performing them correctly (71% vs. 41%), calling 911 (100% vs. 32%), and injecting in the correct location (86% vs. 73%).

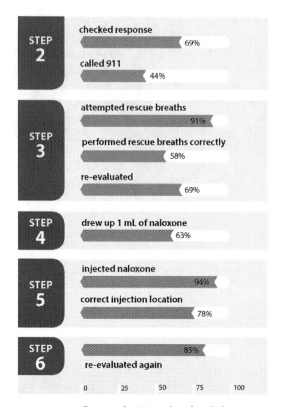

Percentage of participants who performed task

Fig. 3. Frequency of correct completion of each step in the procedure for administering naloxone using the new instructions.

Conversely, the experienced group performed better than the inexperienced group on successfully drawing up naloxone (68% vs. 50%), knowing the needle would retract after the injection (67% vs. 0%), and knowing that administering naloxone to someone who had not actually overdosed would not cause harm (32% vs. 14%). Despite the differences in performance on individual tasks, the average percent completion was similar between the two groups: 73% in the inexperienced group versus 71% in the experienced group.

Separating the results by user group allowed the design team to understand additional nuances about the data that led to targeted improvements to the instructions. For example, it was mentioned that the step of calling 911 was only performed by 44% of the participants, but when this was broken down further, it was revealed that this step was only missed by participants with opioid experience. This indicates that the problem may not be related to the saliency of this instruction, but a result of other variables such as the notion that opioid users may feel reluctant to call 911 in fear of a negative experience. Understanding this allowed the design team to consider including language informing users of the kits that dialing 911 would not result in any repercussions.

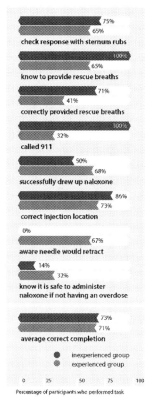

Fig. 4. Percentage of experienced and inexperienced participants that correctly completed each step

4.3   Additional Detail on Errors

Figures 5 and 6 are data visualizations that expand on the errors described in Figs. 3 and 4. Figure 5 displays information about the relationship between effectively drawing up naloxone and injection locations. Although 94% of participants were ultimately able to inject naloxone, only 67% were able to draw up the naloxone from the vial correctly. Visualizing the specific challenges related to drawing up naloxone allowed the design team to isolate and clarify shortcomings in the instructions. For example, in order to draw up naloxone the vial must be inverted. This is a critical step that would not be known by many users of the naloxone kits, so must be salient in the instructions, but was not clear in the early designs. In addition, there is a small, plastic cap on the top of the vial that participants must see and remove in order to insert the syringe into the vial. Again, this must be clear in the instructions. This level of data was required in order to determine how to address some of the high-level errors identified, e.g. not able to successfully draw up naloxone.

Ensuring that naloxone is injected in the correct location is also critical, as naloxone travels through the bloodstream much more quickly with an intramuscular injection. 78% of participants injected into the correct location, meaning that 12% of participants

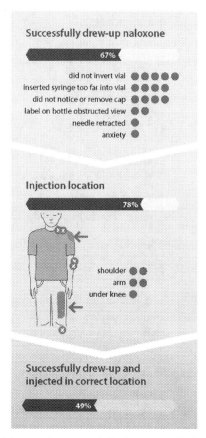

Fig. 5. Percentage of participants who successfully drew-up and injected naloxone using the new instructions with common errors from participants who did not perform the steps correctly

injected into other locations such as the shoulder, arm, or under the knee; locations that would not be effective in an emergency. This led the design team to further clarify and emphasize the image of the intramuscular injection site in the instructions with a drawing and additional highlight using colour.

Figure 6 displays information about the safety of administering naloxone. A bystander may come across someone they think has overdosed, but it may not be clear that they have. In these cases, it is safe to inject naloxone and there will be no adverse effects if the person had not actually overdosed. Only 39% of participants knew that it was safe to inject naloxone in someone who is not having an overdose. The majority responded that nothing happens after it is injected, however, some indicated that they thought that patients may become angry, they may have a potential allergic response, would make them "high" again, or it might result in withdrawal.

In contrast to the 39% of participants who said that naloxone was safe, 58% of participants indicated that they did not know the effects of naloxone, or whether or not it was safe to inject. Interestingly, 2% indicated that it was unsafe. It is important that

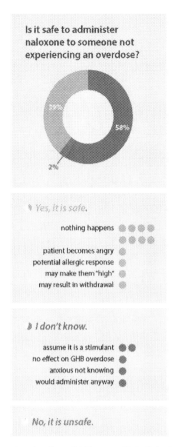

Fig. 6. Percentage of participants who thought it was safe to inject naloxone in someone who had not actually overdosed

the people who are using naloxone kits feel safe and empowered to do so. Information related to consequences of injecting naloxone was not included in earlier iterations of the instructions but was added based on these results. Being able to clearly understand the misconceptions held by participants provided the researchers with specific content to include in the instructions.

5   Discussion

The data that was collected indicates that there needs to be general information provided to experienced and inexperienced users about what naloxone is, as there are a number of existing misconceptions. As demonstrated in Fig. 6, while people can inject naloxone, they often cannot tell you why it is important to do so, or what will happen as a result. In addition, people may feel reluctant to administer naloxone to someone if they are not clear on the consequences of doing so, whether the person has actually overdosed or not. This speaks to a need for a general, consistent education program where messaging about naloxone, its use, and effects is communicated clearly to audiences both experienced and inexperienced with opioids.

5.1 Following Directions vs. Using Previous Experience

This study showed that people with and without opioid experience may benefit from different components of the instructions. Participants who did not have previous experience with opioids performed better than those with opioid experience on a number of technical steps including checking response with sternal rub, providing rescue breaths, calling 911, injecting in the correct location. It is suspected that this performance is due to the fact that due to the lack of experience with opioids and naloxone kits these participants relied more heavily on the instructions provided in the kits, which is what was observed to be the case during the evaluation. Conversely, participants who had used opioids performed better on tasks related to the use of the needle itself, such as drawing up the naloxone and expecting the needle to retract. Often, people who use drugs are familiar with naloxone kits, and are used to having to act in an emergency situation. Experienced users generally know that naloxone kits save lives, however, they may be less likely to follow all the steps or get all the technical details correct, such as completing a sternal rub, providing rescue breaths correctly, and injecting the naloxone into the correct location. This is why the graphic presentation of the information is critical. For example, it is important that instructions in naloxone kits isolate the spot where a muscular injection should be and it should be easy to read and understand, without complexity in an emergency. Overall, experienced participants were less likely to rely on the instructions, which further highlighted the need to make them short, clear, and pictorial.

5.2 Considerations for Other Languages

People learn through pictures and words together, but consideration needs to be given to people whose first language is not English. Going forward, there needs to be consideration into the design for people who use English as a Second Language. Participants noted: "Get rid of the words, just keep the pictures."; "Make it more efficient and better for people who are ESL"; and "Translation may be required for foreigners. It's pretty much good. Pictures are good". Notably, they scored higher when they checked for a response to the casualty than native English speakers (Fig. 7).

5.3 Training

It was discovered that participants who had previous training on the use of naloxone kits were successfully, at 100% accuracy, able to check for rescue breaths, evaluate whether the person is breathing, prepare naloxone, inject naloxone, and locate the correct injection location. Those who had training were able to recall that the needle retracted and that they should re-evaluate after injection. In contrast, the participants who had had no training on how to use the kits were able to inject correctly in the correct location, likely due to their use of the instructions, but most of themdid not know that the needle retracted. However, when they used the new instructions, they were all able to know that the needle would retract and successfully re-evaluated the person after the injection.

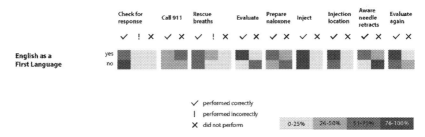

Fig. 7. Percentage of participants that were able to perform the procedure correctly, incorrectly or did not perform whose first language was not English

5.4 Stress Leading to Inaccuracy

Of all of the steps to be performed in the procedure, participants started off well but erred in later steps thus failing to complete the procedure accurately. Completing a procedure in a simulated stress situation may impair function and cognition in short term memory. In this study, participants were able to follow a sequence of steps but were often unable to follow through on the entire sequence. For example, 91% of participants attempted rescue breaths, but only 58% performed rescue breaths correctly. Similarly, 94% of participants were able to inject naloxone, but the percentages fell as soon as participants were asked to locate where the needle is inserted 67% percent of participants were able to draw up naloxone.

6   Conclusion

In this study, the data visualizations were crucial in making the large data set meaningful and translating the findings into design changes. For example, initial findings and trends that were observed such as that participants did not often call 911 were clarified through subsequent visualizations that broke the data down by participant group. Had this not occurred, the design change would have been to make the instruction to call 911 larger and more salient, rather than focusing on the reasons why an opioid user may feel reluctant to call 911 for help. In addition, using graphics to illustrate the variety of specific challenges experienced by participants trying to inject naloxone was a quick and obvious way to identify design improvements but also communicate the challenges to the rest of the design team. This enhanced the efficiency of the iterative design process and allowed the entire team to quickly get on the same page and understand key themes in the data.

The results of this study underscore the need for data visualization in QI projects. In QI, just as in data visualization, there is no one-size-fits-all solution. It must be recognized that for each type of data set, optimum data solutions require different data visualizations. Just as in healthcare, practitioners diagnose a problem and then come up with a solution that best suits the diagnosis. Information design is similar and many parallels can be drawn between these two disciplines proving the need for more willingness to acknowledge each other's working processes. As Jones suggests, "These two fields are similar in many ways. Both are performed as an expert-informed skilled practice that is learned by doing. And both are informed by observation and feedback, by evidence of their beneficial effects. Both disciplines are motivated by a deep desire to help people manage and improve their lives, individually and culturally. Modern medicine is guided by scientific inquiry much more than design, but then designers and engineers in healthcare often have scientific backgrounds. In medicine, evidence of outcome is gathered by measures of health and mortality, controlled experiments, and validated in peer-reviewed research. For clinical practice and organizational change, however, validation is often based on the proof of adoption in practice. Design interventions in healthcare are often assessed by the analysis of empirical evidence, but in few cases would experimental validation be appropriate for service or interaction design. Different evaluation methods are valid in their contexts, a proposition that may not yet be acceptable across healthcare fields" [5].

Data must be visually compelling and well-designed, enabling frontline staff to work effectively and save lives. In this study, we demonstrated that gathering data from a QI study and then displaying it graphically could demonstrate opportunities for improvement in a set of instructions. The instructions, as a result, went through another round of iteration and design and were eventually included in first aid kits in Alberta. Well-designed healthcare information will resonate and affect change in the healthcare system. In any QI project, designers and their colleagues must consider their audience and the context of use for the designs for in order to be able to make significant change possible.

References

1. Brigham, T.J.: Feast for the eyes: an introduction to data visualization. Med. Ref. Serv. Q. **35**(2), 215–223 (2016)
2. Freeman, L.K., et al.: Alberta's provincial take-home naloxone program: a multi-sectoral and multi-jurisdictional response to overdose. Can. J. Publ. Health = Revue Canadienne De Sante Publique **108**(4), e398–e402 (2017)
3. Goldsmith, E.: Comprehensibility of illustration: an analytical model. Inf. Des. J. **1**, 204–213 (1980)
4. Government of Alberta: Opioid-related deaths in Alberta in 2017: review of medical examiner data (2019). https://open.alberta.ca/publications/9781460143421. Accessed Sep 2019
5. Jones, P.H.: Design for Care: Innovating Healthcare Experience. Rosenfeld Media, Brooklyn (2013)
6. Noël, G., Joy, J., Dyck, C.: Improving the quality of healthcare data through information design. Inf. Des. J. **23**(1), 104–122 (2017). https://doi.org/10.1075/idj.23.1.11noe
7. Otten, J.J., Cheng, K., Drewnowski. A.: Infographics and public policy: using data visualization to convey complex information. Health Aff. (Millwood) **34**(11), 1901–1907 (2015). https://doi.org/10.1377/hlthaff.2015.0642
8. Waller, R.: Using typography to structure arguments: a critical analysis of some examples' to be published. In: Jonassen, D.H. (ed.) The Technology of Text: Principles for Structuring, Designing and Displaying Text, vol. 2. Educational Technology Publications, Englewood Cliffs (1983)
9. Wright, P.: Printed instructions: can research make a difference? In: Zwaga, H., Boersema, T., Hoonhout, H. (eds.) Visual Information for Everyday Use: Design and Research Perspectives, pp. 45–56. Taylor and Francis, London (1999)

Policy Making Analysis and Practitioner User Experience

Dimitris Koryzis[1], Fotios Fitsilis[1], Dimitris Spiliotopoulos[2]([✉]) [ID],
Theocharis Theocharopoulos[3], Dionisis Margaris[4] [ID], and Costas Vassilakis[2] [ID]

[1] Hellenic Parliament, Athens, Greece
{dkoryzis,fitsilisf}@parliament.gr
[2] Department of Informatics and Telecommunications, University of the Peloponnese,
Tripoli, Greece
{dspiliot,costas}@uop.gr
[3] Department of Cultural Technology and Communication, University of the Aegean,
Lesvos, Greece
theocharopoulos@aegean.gr
[4] Department of Informatics and Telecommunications, University of Athens, Athens, Greece
margaris@di.uoa.gr

Abstract. This article presents the work on social media analysis-driven policy-making platforms that are powered by classic social media analysis technologies, such as policy modelling, linguistic analysis, opinion mining, sentiment analysis and information visualization. The approach examines the user design perspective towards user experience in policymaking for all the innovative modules used. The technology behind such complex task is presented while the resulting platform is appraised on the potential for real world application. The findings drive the development and the requirements for the summative usability assessment tests. We also report on the level the practitioners adopted the policy formulation tools.

Keywords: Policy making · Social network analysis · Opinion mining · Content analysis · Natural language interfaces · User experience

1 Introduction

The increasing computational power and the adoption of modern software frameworks have driven the development of more and more impressive user-friendly interface designs for different users' requirements [1]. Successful approaches formulate the suitable design, functionalities and satisfying user experience for their target users as main stakeholders [2]. It is evident that identifying correctly the stakeholders needs, even analysing and visualizing various sources of big data on any level (quantitative, qualitative, semantic, etc.), is a prerequisite. Identifying the end-users and what they really need from an interface, module or application can make the difference between success and failure of the design, especially in complex environment like the policy making stages [3].

The article examines a set of Information Communication Technology (ICT) tools in the policy making process especially in parliamentary policy cycle. These tools use

© Springer Nature Switzerland AG 2020
C. Stephanidis et al. (Eds.): HCII 2020, LNCS 12423, pp. 415–431, 2020.
https://doi.org/10.1007/978-3-030-60114-0_29

crowdsourcing, data analysis, brand monitoring, content analysis and opinion mining to visualise critical insights to assist the decision makers. The decision makers utilise the integrated policy making analytics tools to gain a clear and fast overview of the citizens' arguments, sentiments, opinions and trend analyses in the policy making arena.

The relevant market for software products, offers several tools for policy formulation and validation, but it is relatively new and limited when it comes to dedicated analysis for policy making. On the other hand, the market for data collection, sentiment analysis, opinion mining, argument extraction, linguistic analysis for web content is already quite developed and highly competitive as there are solutions from a variety of organisations already in market [4–6].

One may find several applications for potential customers like political institutions, mass media organisations, individual politicians and policy makers based on the social media analysis. But these tend to ignore the user experience of these stakeholders and the accuracy of the data provided. It must be noted that it is rather difficult to create, promote and distribute an integrated tool suite for policy making as a package. During the last 10 years, a lot of individual stand-alone modules were advertised and sold individually, especially in the more competitive market of big data, artificial intelligence and content analysis. That is why in this work the end users or the major stakeholders evaluate the tools for policy making before the general public.

This work presents results from multiple usability assessment tests, as well as contributes towards best practices in user-driven design. The proposed methods are implemented and validated by users/participants in formal evaluation. The findings and UX facilitator meta-evaluation provide insights that can lead to optimization towards the number of participants, selection of evaluators and problem severity identification via specific views from domain experts as they have been utilised in this work.

2   Related Work

An array of new ideas, research projects, platforms, techniques and products are emerging through the massive use of the social web into the policy-making process, based mainly on social media analysis. The empowerment of citizens, businesses and other organizations is a strategic priority realised through the use of new technological tools facilitating digital interaction between administrations and citizens/businesses for high-quality public services. Such empowerment would aim at giving citizens access to better services, designed around their needs and in collaboration with them, while, at the same time, allowing their effective involvement in the policy-making process [7].

The basic framework concept and the actions derived from this strategic priority are incorporated in the following words: Listen, Analyse, Receive, Act (Fig. 1).

Listening and Monitoring what people say, then *Analysing* with ICT tools the conversations and get the main stakeholder opinions in order to *Receive* all responses and data properly displayed for an effective use and finally *Act* based on this information.

In this way, citizens could be directly involved in the policy making stages of the Policy Cycle (Agenda Setting, Policy Formulation, Policy Adoption, Policy Implementation, Policy Evaluation) using simple ICT tools with social networks and user-friendly capabilities offered by Web 3.0 tools and channels. Recent research introduced

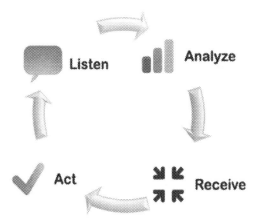

Fig. 1. Policy makers concept framework.

approaches that exploit the identification of "reputation models" [8] with advanced linguistic analysis of social web texts, emphasising on policy implementation and evaluation [9, 10].

Additionally, organisations like Parliaments and mainly NGOs, Civil Society Organisations or Governmental Institutions in several European Countries have developed a series of non-sustainable tools, online platforms for public consultation, crowdsourcing, citizens' engagement and e-participation in the law making process [11].

Although there is not a clear methodology, roadmap or pathway from user design to user experience covering all the stages of policy making. overall, based on the results of several research projects, it seems that there is a need for user-friendly integrated ICT tools that allows policy makers to have, among others [12]:

- an interpretation of citizens' discussions, for or against a policy agenda (Agenda Setting Stage and Evaluation Stage),
- a stable feedback loop between the vast amount of crowd opinion on the web and the agenda of the decision-maker, for a given policy during the Policy Formulation Stage,
- a clear and complete plan on the understanding of how the citizens' opinion, arguments and needs can (or should) affect the policy-making agenda during the Policy Formulation Stage,
- a novel and valuable resource of ideas and opinions for the Policy Formulation Stage,
- a complete set of tools for the discovery, aggregation, analysis and visualization of arguments, expressed in the web in support or against a given policy, during the discussion in the Policy Adoption Stage and during the Policy Implementation Stage,
- a continuous usability testing bringing closer digital transformation and the digital society, as a continuous horizontal process,
- a full integration of multimedia archives (video, image, text) with customized services addressed to citizens' needs,
- transparent, with access to interconnectivity, open prototypes, open source tools, open data and open architecture,
- evidence-based accountable results in the Policy Evaluation Stage, and

• an integrated platform or a tool suite with a modular, open architecture, naturally lending itself to future improvements on each of its modules (and the techniques each one applies).

Meanwhile, the past decade, research in policymaking, tried to elaborated proto-type web-based tools having as main purpose to provide the decision-makers, users and stakeholders with a semi or fully automated solution for data acquisition, argument extraction, opinion mining, sentiment analysis, argument summarization and visualization that works in a collaborative form in the policy-making regime [13]. Primary, it was foreseen to create an integrated Tool Suite that successfully integrates all selective modules that perform the aforementioned tasks under a simple work environment making it easy for the users to switch between these modules. The following figure indicates the perception of the policy lifecycle that is rather compatible with the five Policy Stages described before [14], having four Policy Stages –as the Policy Implementation is not

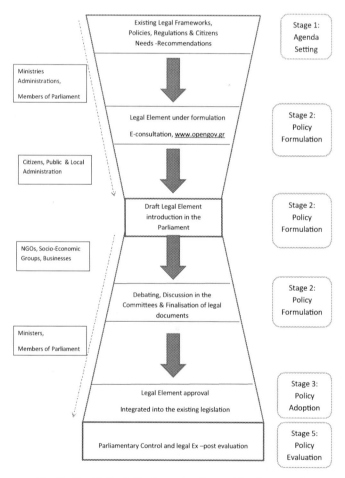

Fig. 2. The Hellenic Parliament policy making framework.

part of the Parliamentary Work– incorporated in the following scheme of the policy cycle that has been used in the use case of the Hellenic Parliament (Fig. 2).

3 Innovative ICT Approaches in Policymaking

The main two constraining factors that hinder the generation of a trusted relationship between citizens (and especially young people) and decision makers are (a) existing ICT approaches that focus on tools/modules/components for isolated stages of the decision-making cycle, making it impossible for decision makers to adopt a unified and coherent solution that covers their needs and satisfies engagement requirements for more than one decision-making cycle, and (b) the undisputed fact that public opinions and outputs are not considered sufficiently by decision makers, because of the lack of practical and technical opportunities, as well as knowledge, on how to embed them into the formal decision-making mechanisms.

In essence, there was a need for an open source, trusted cloud-based service-delivery prototype that will:

1. Link the different steps of the public decision-making process with existing tools and services used by parliamentary institutions.
2. Support decision makers to choose the right blend of tools and services through a guided template that will evaluate a-priori the impact of their generated actions (in terms of engagement) based on open service cataloguing.
3. Deliver case-specific and customised service mashups to public authorities in a smart and integrated manner to allow for instant deployment and operation without the need for intense ICT investments.

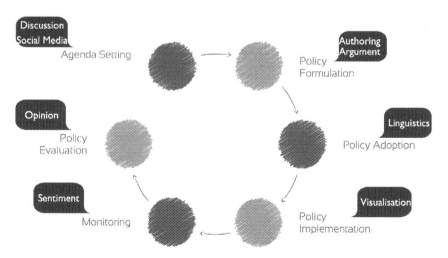

Fig. 3. ICT tools in the policy making cycle.

4. Cater for the innovation growth of software developers by offering the option for promoting their services through an open innovation platform where various tools, services and components may be included and promoted (Fig. 3).

Having at hands these policy-making stages, the users/stakeholders and their needs, the question that arises is which ICT tools, modules or innovative approaches could be used in a parliamentary environment.

The development and application of the mentioned policymaking tools has the additional advantage of fitting nicely into the greater European interoperability Framework, as provided through the ongoing ISA2 programme [15]. More specifically, the greater objectives of legal Interoperability, i.e. to enable smooth implementation of European public policies through better legislation, can be essentially supported by appropriate configuration of the policymaking tools. Furthermore, digital support of evidence-based decision and policymaking is difficult to be imagined without appropriate, structured data formats and xml-based web-standards, exactly as proposed in the tested solution. For this reason, the proposed Integrated ICT approach should be a sustainable open platform that integrates tools for policy making.

To summarize, it is more than evident that the users need a customised integrated web-based accessible policymaking analytics approach that successfully integrates all policymaking tools under a single work environment making it easy for users to switch between tasks and applications, while allowing them to complete all steps of the policy-making cycle. The following paragraphs refer to the tools that have been found to be of use for end-to-end policymaking.

3.1 Policy Model Authoring Environment

The Policy Model Authoring Environment is the environment for authoring the models with respect to policy domains and the policies themselves. This tool allows for the visual representation of the policy argumentation models. It facilitates the needs of non-ICT skilled end-users to assist policy makers in policy formulation on a conceptual level and deliver a machine-readable representation of the respective models. The authoring tool enables the domain experts that support policy makers with creating and maintaining policy models. It supports authoring of the policy models for all domains, it deploys all the computational tools necessary and it brings together the arguments about the introduced policies.

User interface visualization aids users to create advanced and complex models with minimal cognitive load. It could be an integral part of the system, seamlessly allowing the authorship of policy models, also being fully compatible with all modern web browsers [16]. This solution is highly portable, only requiring the use of the web interface. It can be easily accessed by policy makers, assistants, researchers and other end-users, using simple user accounts. Other potential users like NGOs, market researchers and business analysts could make use of it as well.

3.2   Open Data Acquisition and Analysis

Open data has generated a great deal of excitement around the world for its potential to empower citizens, change how government works, and improve the delivery of public services. Analytics powered by open data can help uncover citizens' preferences, reveal problems, anomalies and variations in public administrations' performance [17]. This module can communicate with and draw data from a variety of text sources, based on ad hoc needs. The sources can be websites, RSS feeds, search engine results, such as Google or Yahoo, and social media, such as Twitter and Facebook.

It provides a unique point of entry for the gathering of data from a variety of sources, minimizing the effort for configuration. The module can be critical for a variety of domains, such as reputation management, news updates and policy making. All these domains of application require a constant stream of information from multiple text sources to enable acting and reacting efficiently. The module is built as a web service, which enables integration in any system setting that uses web services [18–20], practically all contemporary applications.

The module is usable by and useful for any company that exploits online text. For example: news agencies, reputation management service providers, online analytics providers and decision-support system designers. It must be noted that there are several companies that focus on a specific data provider, Twitter, for instance, or provide analytics services, such as SumAll, BigPanda, Looker and AWS Data Pipeline. However, to the best of the authors' knowledge, there is no unified, broad solution for textual data gathering from all the aforementioned sources.

3.3   Linguistic Analysis

This module analyses and pre-processes textual information that collected from a variety of sources to transform free text into a set of structured data, usable by business analytics or text analytics modules. It provides a unified set of well-established tools that can be used to pre-process and structure free text for follow-up use by business intelligence tools. The cleaning up of data can reflect significant effort. Its lack, on the other hand, can lead to erroneous or nonsensical business analysis results. The Linguistic Analysis module, also built as a web service, covers a variety of aspects from character encoding considerations to tokenization and sentence splitting in the pre-processing of free text, so as to provide a common, established tool, useable in a data analytics pipeline [21].

3.4   Argument Extraction

The Argument Extraction module can discover and extract arguments from free text (including texts from social media, blogs, news sites, etc.) [22]. Thus, it can help gain intuition and understanding to support a claim, be it a proposed policy or a generic subject of conversation. The module is the only known software detecting and extracting arguments in many languages, such as English, Greek and German. It can provide precious information regarding a policy or a product, empowering business intelligence with the logic of every internet user. The module can detect tendencies and stances related to specific subjects, so that a policy maker can act and react in a timely, efficient manner, taking into account the public (or target-group) arguments on a subject, such as a policy or a product. This is also built as a web service [23, 24].

3.5 Opinion Mining and Sentiment Analysis

This module, offered as a web service, can assign sentiment values (positive, negative, neutral) to multi-lingual text and especially to arguments. Thus, it can provide at-a-glance information about the public (or target-group) reaction to an issue, an event or a policy. It provides a unified solution for sentiment analysis across different languages (e.g. English, Greek, and German). The module can be critical for a variety of domains, such as reputation management, news updates and policy making. All these domains of application analyse the public sentiment from text data, to enable acting and reacting efficiently [25].

3.6 Visualisation

The visualization modules provide intuitive access to the data crawled and analysed by external text analysis techniques, similar to the works presented in [26, 27]. It is realized as a web application and can therefore be accessed via a browser [28]. The visual interface supports the exploration of statistical features within thematic categories identified in the underlying content. Besides the quantity of information present for the respective categories, the extracted sentiment scores (from positive to negative) are depicted. Moreover, the content of the respective documents can be accessed via most frequent terms. Both the analysis of the evolution of thematic categories over time and of demographic information about the authors of the screened documents are supported (Fig. 4).

The visual interface enables the view on the underlying data structures from different perspectives. The techniques used constitute the front-end of a document processing pipeline. The techniques have been chosen and designed in order to allow for a comprehensive view on the evolving topics and sentiments of the discussion. In addition, the user may pursue its interests from different perspectives. In effect, through application of design principles from information visualization, "questions to the data" may be asked.

The visual interface enables users to analyse the evolution of topics with respect to sentiments, keywords and quantitative information. It supports the user to extract emerging trends in predefined categories and to compare different audiences with respect to their underlying opinions. The user gains a detailed insight about the supporters or opponents of a given opinion.

The visual interface can be used as Graphical User Interface to access any data reflecting the described structure. These again are analysed and stored in a database. The main stakeholders to be addressed with this solution are policy makers. However, the visual interface offers a generic view on textual content that is categorized and analysed with keyword extraction and sentiment analysis techniques. Therefore, it can also be considered for application in the domains of journalism or marketing, with respect to brand monitoring.

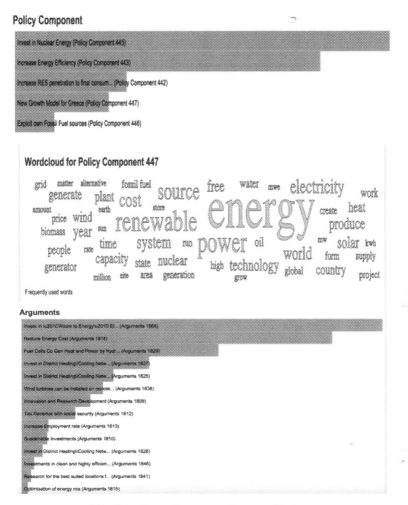

Fig. 4. Policy and argumentation visualisation.

3.7 Public Dialogue

This module provides public dialogue capabilities, including discussions, comments, forums, feedback services, deliberation and structured argumentation systems. It ensures seamless integration with major social media networks, similar to the works presented in [29, 30], allowing citizens to use popular and familiar discussion services and, thus, to increase the visibility and outreach. The module is using graph visualization technologies and can be easily accessed, among others, by policy makers, aids and researchers using simple user accounts. The Public Dialogue module would also be fully compatible with all modern web browsers, which can again be accessed by other modules and users [31, 32].

3.8   E-Participation Services

The right to petition constitutes one of the basic rights all citizens enjoy, characterized by such essential traits as extension, compulsion, popularity as well as participation [33], and actually entails the capability of the former to freely, either alone or as part of a group. The Petition Tool is accessible in external locations allowing users to create petitions easily and at any time, mostly for free, through user-friendly interfaces. It aspires to leverage e-petitioning to provide an additional channel for connecting citizens, communities and other groups of people, especially the young generation, with decision makers, and thereby inducing action, political or not, with regard to issues that are of interest to a great mass of people [34].

Another facet of democratic participation and engagement in the decision-making process is manifested through voting. The voting Tool combines the best of breed features of current online polling approaches (e.g. user-friendliness, simplicity, ubiquitous engagement, prevention of fraud etc.) to provide appropriate voting tools that will allow on one side decision makers to obtain tangible evidence on what citizens think and on the other will enable citizens to voice their opinion and actively drive developments on various social levels.

3.9   Social Media Campaign

This Module monitor how social media activity might be a useful capability, especially from a policy perspective, both for detecting new or emergent issues, as well as for getting a better situation awareness of how citizens react to a particular issue or person (e.g. MP, Policy, discussion). The focus will be put upon improving public authorities' ability to actually listen & communicate directly through social media with the population/citizens, especially youth and take into consideration their discussions in all Social Networks for a certain Policy domain [35]. By defining the scope, concept and needs of each user, i.e. of each public authority, it will propose the services and tools that suit each user's needs best [36]. Thus, this integration of innovative services and tools in one platform or tool suite, enhances aspiration to make the most out of social media, by gleaning data and actually listening to what targeted audiences, especially young people, have to say about a certain issue, as well as by analysing the gathered data, in a similar way that a recommender system works [30, 37, 38].

4   Evaluation

Before the assessment of the users' acceptance, the authors evaluated the use of these modules as innovative ICT approaches in policymaking. The main research question is their suitability in the different stages of policymaking. Table 1 presents the Policy Making Stages, the main users involved and their needs versus the main ICT modules that satisfy them.

The mentioned suite can be used and marketed as an integrate tool to assist evidence-based policymaking. The next table presents a SWOT-like analysis of the tool's strengths, weaknesses, opportunities and threats concerning its positioning within the future software market. The SWOT analysis was based on the evaluation results, the users' needs,

Table 1. Using the appropriate ICT components for all policy making stages.

Policy making stages	Users	Needs	Target analysis
Agenda setting	Government, MPs	Discussions	Dialogue, opinion, sentiment, argument, open data, E-participation, social media
Policy formulation	Citizens	Crowdsourcing, opinion, feedback	Authoring, visualisation, E-participation, social media
Policy adoption	MPs	Aggregation	Linguistics
Policy implementation	Government	Transparent, user friendly	Visualisation
Policy evaluation	MPs, Citizens, government	Effects, accountability	Dialogue, opinion, sentiment, argument, open data, E-participation

the analysis of the ICT environment and the components related to digital strategy of the Strategic plan 2018–2021 of the Hellenic Parliament [39] (Table 2).

Table 2. Evidence-based policymaking SWOT analysis.

Strengths	Weakness
Satisfactory interaction with users	GDPR ethical issues
Empowers citizens' participation	No accuracy of arguments
User friendly	NLP processing difficulties
Integration of different features	Time consuming
Opportunities	**Threats**
Emerging markets	Niche market
Growing societies	Similar software business products
Web 3.0 research opportunities	Advanced ICT technologies

Despite the above-mentioned difficulties, the tool Suite can benefit from the fact that it is a unique product that aims to address specific audiences, including policy makers, advisors, governmental officials, NGO's, academics, communication specialists, researchers and media institutions.

5   Validation in Parliamentary Settings

Complex applications require intuitive design and respective usability testing that can provide feedback to accommodate the proposed design. The specific problem of "too much data from many interaction modules" is tackled through collective problem severity identification by involving a mixed-initiative (as opposed to top-down or bottom-up) appropriateness selection of usability testing assessments and rules for adaptation. This approach contributes to the mitigation of the "observer effect", which is one of the most pronounced problems in the design and testing of complex applications.

5.1   Use Case Scenario

Using the Evaluation Results, Hellenic Parliament Users participated in a study to validate a policy domain (in our case, Energy) with the aforementioned tools following the steps indicated in Fig. 5.

Fig. 5. Use case scenario deployment in the Hellenic Parliament.

Table 3. Use case scenario in the Hellenic Parliament.

Use case description	User	Relation to the policy stages
Create the ENERGY domain model	Domain author	Agenda Setting/policy formulation
Add terms on the domain	Domain author	Agenda setting/policy formulation
Load the domain	Domain author to policy scientific assistant	Agenda setting/policy formulation
Create the model for the "green energy" policy and "renewable energy" policy	Policy maker & policy scientific assistant	Policy formulation
Add policy components for the relevant policy	Policy maker/scientific assistant	Policy formulation
Load the domain model	Scientific assistant	Policy formulation/policy argumentation
Load existing policies on renewable energy	Scientific assistant	Policy formulation/policy argumentation
Get sentiment for the domain entities	Policy maker, policy advisor	Policy formulation/policy debating
Filter sentiment for the domain entities	Policy maker, policy advisor	Policy formulation/policy debating
Predict sentiment for the domain entities	Policy maker	Policy formulation/policy evaluation
Add new arguments for the policy component of the RES policy model as a key component in optimizing the policy model	Policy analyst/scientific associate to policy makers & standing committee	Policy argumentation
Upload new policy structure	Policy makers	Policy evaluation
Browse argumentation polarity	Policy makers & standing committee members	Policy evaluation
Filter argumentation polarity for the selected policy model	Policy makers & plenum	Policy evaluation
Predict the evolution of polarity for the arguments in the selected policy model	Policy makers & plenum	Policy evaluation

Table 3 lists the tasks, the target users that engage in the tasks and the respective policy formulation stages.

5.2 Results

Two rounds of evaluation have been conducted with 22 participants in total. MPs, governmental officials, scientific advisors, policy domain experts, researchers, administrators and policy consultants were part of the evaluation design, which included three phases. The goal was to evaluate the load of information presented in real time to the user in order to achieve completeness and informativeness in real time. The authors also evaluated the analysis modules and the integrated tool for policymaking before the general public. Furthermore, the participants were asked to fill in an online form after the end of all sessions (a typical procedure, performed in many research works [40, 41]). Each session was adapted to the feedback from the preceding one.

After presentation of the modules, the participants were debriefed on the interaction experience and system feedback, mainly on the visualization module and the authoring tool. Furthermore, an online questionnaire survey was compiled, and focus group discussions were organized to collect feedback and opinions, to better identify the necessary features of the proposed approach. The focus groups involved 4 Members of the Parliament, 3 politics-oriented advisors, 2 policy experts, 5 parliamentary officers, 4 policy analysts as scientific advisors, 2 Political Parties representatives, 2 interaction and content designers.

The main outcomes of these sessions were the following:

- The suite could use public consultation results from selective websites (e.g. Open-Gov.gr) directly and feedback from the legislative process (Stage 2 Policy Formulation)
- Missing transparency of the suite background process, such as which modules presented each set of results, accuracy, demographics and web sources reliability,
- Modules are more appropriate in post-legislative scrutiny [42] assisting the parliamentary control function (Stage 5 Policy Evaluation),
- Tool Suite and modules sustainability is an issue that the authors need to take care of based on the results of the SWOT evaluation.

However, the use of innovative ICT tools poses significant challenges to parliaments, many of which do not seem to be technology-affine [43].

The perception of individual participants was more or less positive, in a Likert scale of 1–5 they have provided the following validation results:

- Usability score: 3.59;
- Suitability to Policy Making score: 3.52;
- Technological readiness score: 3.19.

As a result, the users/stakeholders have acquired some knowledge of standard analyses and the social media analytics, but most have not yet been able to use them in a

highly successful manner or yet to incorporate them efficiently into their working procedures. These facts are also certified by recent research, as the aforementioned innovative
approaches failed so far to widely involve important stakeholders, both on the policy
and the society side, in the overall process [13]. Moreover, it is at hand that there are still
many unsolved challenges regarding the use of ICT in policymaking. Such challenges
do not allow policy makers to provide sustainable and inclusive decisions and citizens to
engage in policy-making stages [44]. However, the use of state-of-the-art intuitive integrated tools such as the ones that have been demonstrated in this article has the potential
to advance digital transformation of the policy cycle.

6   Conclusion and Future Work

This work reports on the need to fine-tune accurate analysis to efficient approaches to
for collaborative policy formulation. The integrated tools included nine modules, the
results of which had technical complexity requiring extensive user training sessions and
several iterations of design prototyping, in order to ensure usability. The results of the
investigated tool adaptation in the four Policy Cycle Stages, particularly during the Policy
Formulation Stage where a lot of users/stakeholders are typically involved, appear to
be rather limited. On the other hand, the market for crowdsourcing, consultation, data
collection, sentiment analysis and argument extraction for Web 3.0 content is already
quite developed and highly competitive.

Future work includes the use of the proposed methodology with recommender systems and especially incorporation in social related recommendation applications [45,
46] and combination with collaborative filtering techniques [47–50] in order to have
flexibility on the users' perspective, their preferences and to capture inherent subtle
characteristics.

References

1. Capano, G., Pavan, E.: Designing anticipatory policies through the use of ICTs. Policy Soc.
   38, 96–117 (2019). https://doi.org/10.1080/14494035.2018.1511194
2. Spiliotopoulos, D., Dalianis, A., Koryzis, D.: Need driven prototype design for a policy
   modeling authoring interface. In: Marcus, A. (ed.) DUXU 2014. LNCS, vol. 8518, pp. 481–
   487. Springer, Cham (2014). https://doi.org/10.1007/978-3-319-07626-3_45
3. Knecht, T., Weatherford, M.S.: Public opinion and foreign policy: the stages of presidential
   decision making. Int. Stud. Q. **50**, 705–727 (2006). https://doi.org/10.1111/j.1468-2478.2006.
   00421.x
4. Jasti, S., Mahalakshmi, T.S.: A review on sentiment analysis of opinion mining. In: Mallick,
   P.K., Balas, V.E., Bhoi, A.K., Zobaa, A.F. (eds.) Cognitive Informatics and Soft Computing.
   AISC, vol. 768, pp. 603–612. Springer, Singapore (2019). https://doi.org/10.1007/978-981-
   13-0617-4_58
5. Murray, G., Hoque, E., Carenini, G.: Opinion summarization and visualization. In: Sentiment
   Analysis in Social Networks, pp. 171–187. Elsevier (2017). https://doi.org/10.1016/B978-0-
   12-804412-4.00011-5
6. Liu, B.: Sentiment Analysis and Opinion Mining. Synth. Lect. Hum. Lang. Technol. **5**, 1–167
   (2012). https://doi.org/10.2200/S00416ED1V01Y201204HLT016

7. Hardina, D.: Strategies for citizen participation and empowerment in non-profit community-based organizations. Community Dev. **37**, 4–17 (2006). https://doi.org/10.1080/155753306 09490192
8. Braga, D.D.S., Niemann, M., Hellingrath, B., Neto, F.B.D.L.: Survey on computational trust and reputation models. ACM Comput. Surv. **51**, 1–40 (2019). https://doi.org/10.1145/323 6008
9. Tambouris, E., et al.: eParticipation in Europe. In: E-Government Success around the World: Cases, Empirical Studies, and Practical Recommendations, pp. 341–357 (2013). https://doi.org/10.4018/978-1-4666-4173-0.ch017
10. Alexopoulos, C., Lachana, Z., Androutsopoulou, A., Diamantopoulou, V., Charalabidis, Y., Loutsaris, M.A.: How machine learning is changing e-government. In: Proceedings of the 12th International Conference on Theory and Practice of Electronic Governance - ICEGOV2019, pp. 354–363. ACM Press, New York (2019). https://doi.org/10.1145/3326365.3326412
11. Rowledge, L.R.: CrowdRising: Building a Sustainable World through Mass Collaboration. Routledge, Abingdon (2019). https://doi.org/10.4324/9780429285905
12. Schefbeck, G., Spiliotopoulos, D., Risse, T.: The recent challenge in web archiving: archiving the social web. In: Proceedings of the International Council on Archives Congress, pp. 1–5 (2012)
13. Fitsilis, F., Koryzis, D., Svolopoulos, V., Spiliotopoulos, D.: Implementing digital parliament innovative concepts for citizens and policy makers. In: Nah, F.F.-H., Tan, C.-H. (eds.) HCIBGO 2017. LNCS, vol. 10293, pp. 154–170. Springer, Cham (2017). https://doi.org/10.1007/978-3-319-58481-2_13
14. Howlett, M., Cashore, B.: Conceptualizing public policy. In: Engeli, I., Allison, C.R. (eds.) Comparative Policy Studies. RMS, pp. 17–33. Palgrave Macmillan UK, London (2014). https://doi.org/10.1057/9781137314154_2
15. Sartor, G.: Legislative information and the web. In: Legislative XML for the Semantic Web, pp. 11–20. Springer, Dordrecht (2011). https://doi.org/10.1007/978-94-007-1887-6_2
16. Kouroupetroglou, G., Spiliotopoulos, D.: Usability methodologies for real-life voice user interfaces. Int. J. Inf. Technol. Web. Eng. **4**, 78–94 (2009). https://doi.org/10.4018/jitwe.200 9100105
17. Hossain, M.A., Dwivedi, Y.K., Rana, N.P.: State-of-the-art in open data research: Insights from existing literature and a research agenda. J. Organ. Comput. Electron. Commer. **26**, 14–40 (2016). https://doi.org/10.1080/10919392.2015.1124007
18. Margaris, D., Georgiadis, P., Vassilakis, C.: On replacement service selection in WS-BPEL scenario adaptation. In: Proceedings - 2015 IEEE 8th International Conference on Service-Oriented Computing and Applications, SOCA 2015, pp. 10–17 (2015). https://doi.org/10.1109/SOCA.2015.11
19. Margaris, D., Vassilakis, C., Georgiadis, P.: Improving QoS delivered by WS-BPEL scenario adaptation through service execution parallelization. In: Proceedings of the 31st Annual ACM Symposium on Applied Computing, pp. 1590–1596. Association for Computing Machinery, New York (2016). https://doi.org/10.1145/2851613.2851805
20. Margaris, D., Georgiadis, P., Vassilakis, C.: A collaborative filtering algorithm with clustering for personalized web service selection in business processes. In: 2015 IEEE 9th International Conference on Research Challenges in Information Science (RCIS), pp. 169–180 (2015). https://doi.org/10.1109/RCIS.2015.7128877
21. Spiliotopoulos, D., Xydas, G., Kouroupetroglou, G.: diction based prosody modeling in table-to-speech synthesis. In: Matoušek, V., Mautner, P., Pavelka, T. (eds.) TSD 2005. LNCS (LNAI), vol. 3658, pp. 294–301. Springer, Heidelberg (2005). https://doi.org/10.1007/115 51874_38
22. Risse, T., et al.: The ARCOMEM architecture for social- and semantic-driven web archiving. Future Internet **6**, 688–716 (2014). https://doi.org/10.3390/fi6040688

23. Margaris, D., Vassilakis, C., Georgiadis, P.: An integrated framework for adapting WS-BPEL scenario execution using QoS and collaborative filtering techniques. Sci. Comput. Program. **98**, 707–734 (2015). https://doi.org/10.1016/j.scico.2014.10.007

24. Margaris, D., Georgiadis, P., Vassilakis, C.: Adapting WS-BPEL scenario execution using collaborative filtering techniques. In: Proceedings - International Conference on Research Challenges in Information Science, pp. 174–184 (2013). https://doi.org/10.1109/RCIS.2013.6577691

25. Kauffmann, E., Peral, J., Gil, D., Ferrández, A., Sellers, R., Mora, H.: Managing marketing decision-making with sentiment analysis: an evaluation of the main product features using text data mining. Sustainability **11**, 4235 (2019). https://doi.org/10.3390/su11154235

26. Margaris, D., Vassilakis, C., Spiliotopoulos, D.: What makes a review a reliable rating in recommender systems? Inf. Process. Manage. **57**, 102304 (2020). https://doi.org/10.1016/j.ipm.2020.102304

27. Margaris, D., Vassilakis, C., Spiliotopoulos, D.: Handling uncertainty in social media textual information for improving venue recommendation formulation quality in social networks. Soc. Netw. Anal. Mining **9**(1), 1–19 (2019). https://doi.org/10.1007/s13278-019-0610-x

28. Pino, A., Kouroupetroglou, G., Kacorri, H., Sarantidou, A., Spiliotopoulos, D.: An open source/freeware assistive technology software inventory. In: Miesenberger, K., Klaus, J., Zagler, W., Karshmer, A. (eds.) ICCHP 2010. LNCS, vol. 6179, pp. 178–185. Springer, Heidelberg (2010). https://doi.org/10.1007/978-3-642-14097-6_29

29. Margaris, D., Vassilakis, C.: Exploiting Internet of Things information to enhance venues' recommendation accuracy. Serv. Oriented Comput. Appl. **11**(4), 393–409 (2017). https://doi.org/10.1007/s11761-017-0216-y

30. Margaris, D., Spiliotopoulos, D., Vassilakis, C.: Social relations versus near neighbours: reliable recommenders in limited information social network collaborative filtering for online advertising. In: Proceedings of the 2019 IEEE/ACM International Conference on Advances in Social Networks Analysis and Mining (ASONAM 2019), pp. 1160–1167. ACM, Vancouver (2019). https://doi.org/10.1145/3341161.3345620

31. Xydas, G., Spiliotopoulos, D., Kouroupetroglou, G.: Modeling improved prosody generation from high-level linguistically annotated corpora. IEICE Trans. Inf. Syst. **E88-D**, 510–518 (2005). https://doi.org/10.1093/ietisy/e88-d.3.510

32. Spiliotopoulos, D., Stavropoulou, P., Kouroupetroglou, G.: Acoustic rendering of data tables using earcons and prosody for document accessibility. In: Stephanidis, C. (ed.) UAHCI 2009. LNCS, vol. 5616, pp. 587–596. Springer, Heidelberg (2009). https://doi.org/10.1007/978-3-642-02713-0_62

33. Mallan, K.: Gateways to digital participation. In: Digital Participation through Social Living Labs, pp. 333–349. Elsevier (2018). https://doi.org/10.1016/B978-0-08-102059-3.00018-6

34. Demidova, E., et al.: Analysing and enriching focused semantic web archives for parliament applications. Future Internet **6**, 433–456 (2014). https://doi.org/10.3390/fi6030433

35. Androutsopoulos, I., Spiliotopoulos, D., Stamatakis, K., Dimitromanolaki, A., Karkaletsis, V., Spyropoulos, C.D.: Symbolic authoring for multilingual natural language generation. In: Vlahavas, I.P., Spyropoulos, C.D. (eds.) SETN 2002. LNCS (LNAI), vol. 2308, pp. 131–142. Springer, Heidelberg (2002). https://doi.org/10.1007/3-540-46014-4_13

36. Antonakaki, D., Spiliotopoulos, D., Samaras, C.V., Ioannidis, S., Fragopoulou, P.: Investigating the complete corpus of referendum and elections tweets. In: Proceedings of the 2016 IEEE/ACM International Conference on Advances in Social Networks Analysis and Mining, ASONAM 2016, pp. 100–105 (2016). https://doi.org/10.1109/ASONAM.2016.7752220

37. Margaris, D., Vassilakis, C., Georgiadis, P.: Knowledge-based leisure time recommendations in social networks. In: Alor-Hernández, G., Valencia-García, R. (eds.) Current Trends on Knowledge-Based Systems. ISRL, vol. 120, pp. 23–48. Springer, Cham (2017). https://doi.org/10.1007/978-3-319-51905-0_2

38. Margaris, D., Vassilakis, C., Georgiadis, P.: Recommendation information diffusion in social networks considering user influence and semantics. Soc. Netw. Anal. Mining **6**(1), 1–22 (2016). https://doi.org/10.1007/s13278-016-0416-z

39. Eckardt, M.: The Impact of ICT on policies, politics, and polities an evolutionary economics approach to information and communication technologies (ICT). SSRN Electron. J. **20** (2012). https://doi.org/10.2139/ssrn.2445839

40. Margaris, D., Vassilakis, C.: Exploiting rating abstention intervals for addressing concept drift in social network recommender systems. Informatics. **5**, 21 (2018). https://doi.org/10.3390/informatics5020021

41. Aivazoglou, M., et al.: A fine-grained social network recommender system. Soc. Netw. Anal. Mining **10**(1), 1–18 (2019). https://doi.org/10.1007/s13278-019-0621-7

42. Norton, P.: Post-legislative scrutiny in the UK Parliament: adding value. J. Legis. Stud. **25**, 340–357 (2019). https://doi.org/10.1080/13572334.2019.1633778

43. Griffith, J., Leston-Bandeira, C.: How are parliaments using new media to engage with citizens? J. Legis. Stud. **18**, 496–513 (2012). https://doi.org/10.1080/13572334.2012.706058

44. Makri, E., Spiliotopoulos, D., Vassilakis, C., Margaris, D.: Human behaviour in multimodal interaction: main effects of civic action and interpersonal and problem-solving skills. J. Ambient Intell. Hum. Comput. **1**, 1–16 (2020). https://doi.org/10.1007/s12652-020-01846-x

45. Margaris, D., Vassilakis, C., Georgiadis, P.: Query personalization using social network information and collaborative filtering techniques. Future Gener. Comput. Syst. **78**, 440–450 (2018). https://doi.org/10.1016/j.future.2017.03.015

46. Margaris, D., Kobusinska, A., Spiliotopoulos, D., Vassilakis, C.: An adaptive social network-aware collaborative filtering algorithm for improved rating prediction accuracy. IEEE Access. **8**, 68301–68310 (2020). https://doi.org/10.1109/ACCESS.2020.2981567

47. Margaris, D., Vassilakis, C.: Improving collaborative filtering's rating prediction quality in dense datasets, by pruning old ratings. In: Proceedings - IEEE Symposium on Computers and Communications, pp. 1168–1174 (2017). https://doi.org/10.1109/ISCC.2017.8024683

48. Margaris, D., Vassilakis, C.: Improving collaborative filtering's rating prediction accuracy by considering users' rating variability. In: Proceedings of the 2018 IEEE 16th International Conference on Dependable, Autonomic and Secure Computing, 16th International Conference on Pervasive Intelligence and Computing, 4th Intl Conf on Big Data Intelligence and Computing and Cyber Science and Technology Congress, pp. 1022–1027 (2018). https://doi.org/10.1109/DASC/PiCom/DataCom/CyberSciTec.2018.00145

49. Margaris, D., Vasilopoulos, D., Vassilakis, C., Spiliotopoulos, D.: Improving collaborative filtering's rating prediction accuracy by introducing the common item rating past criterion. In: 10th International Conference on Information, Intelligence, Systems and Applications, IISA 2019, pp. 1022–1027 (2019). https://doi.org/10.1109/IISA.2019.8900758

50. Margaris, D., Vassilakis, C.: Improving collaborative filtering's rating prediction quality by considering shifts in rating practices. In: 2017 IEEE 19th Conference on Business Informatics (CBI), pp. 158–166 (2017). https://doi.org/10.1109/CBI.2017.24

Research on the Smartable Design Paths of Modern Museum — A Case Study on Jingzhou Museum

YaoHan Luo[✉]

WuHan University of Technology, Wuhan, People's Republic of China
511574206@qq.com

Abstract. With the rise of the wave of personalized consumption, the emergence of emerging technologies can often push the arts and tourism industry to break through the traditional bottleneck, thus creating a new tourism experience. Emerging technologies and applications including Cloud Computing, 5G, AI (Artificial Intelligence) and Big Data are changing the existing pattern of the cultural and tourism industry. Information technology is opening a new chapter in the development of the cultural and travel industry. The 2019 Government Work Report points out that China's development of new momentum has grown rapidly over the past year. New kinetic energy is profoundly changing the way of production and shaping China's new advantages in development. The government keeps encouraging the application of information technology to enhance the protection of cultural relics and the inheritance of intangible cultural heritage.

Keywords: Modern museums · Smartable design path · IP · Cultural and creative product design · Digital upgrade · AI

1 Typical Features of Modern Museums

Modern museums can be traced back to two ancient origins, one is the "muse" as the prototype of the pursuit of knowledge and education, and the other is the "rare treasure chest" as the symbol of the display and collection of objects. Nowadays, the forms and functions of the museum are expanding and enriching. However, traditional physical museums are constrained by time and space, unable to let the audience visit whenever they want and wherever they are. In addition, the static display form of traditional museums gives only a one-dimensional experience. This kind of spatial presentation and narrative form only allows the audience to passively accept knowledge, lacking new technologies to achieve more interactions between the audience and the museums.

Modern museums have two characteristics: national and epochal. Nationality refers to the integration and collision of different languages, religions, morals, thinking habits, aesthetic concepts, social conditions, and local customs in a certain region and a certain nation, forming its characteristics that are different from other regions. The epochal nature of the museum, that is, the manifestation of people's technology, culture, aesthetic

C. Stephanidis et al. (Eds.): HCII 2020, LNCS 12423, pp. 432–440, 2020.
https://doi.org/10.1007/978-3-030-60114-0_30

consciousness and value orientation on exhibits in a certain period and era, reflects the cultural features and aesthetic characteristics of that era. The museum is a treasure house of local human geography and cultural connotation, the carrier of the protection and dissemination of the achievements of human civilization, and an important symbol of the continuous progress of social civilization. For a long time, traditional museums have formed a decentralized management model, resulting in poor communication of information and difficulties in sharing resources. It urgently calls for the support of new technologies to complete the intelligent transformation, thus breaking the restrictions of the physical wall to better spread the culture of Jingzhou.

2 Analysis of the Current Situation of Jingzhou Museum

Jingzhou's history and culture are rich and diverse and have a long history. Jingzhou has been an upper class since ancient times. During the Six Dynasties, it became a political, economic, and military center at the time. Therefore, it has always been said that "Jingzhou is a place where soldiers must fight". In the late Eastern Han Dynasty, Jingzhou was carefully created by Liu Biao to avoid the war and attracted a large number of bachelors to avoid chaos, solemnly become the late Han Dynasty national academic center. Among them, Jingzhou School is a key school of ideological academic transformation. The influence of Jingzhou school is multi-faceted, including academic, political, ritual system and art, resulting in more academic works. In ancient China, Jingzhou was the political, economic and military center of the Six Dynasties. Now, Jingzhou Museum is the most important display platform for Jingzhou history and culture.

For a long time, traditional museums have formed a decentralized management model, resulting in poor communication of information and difficulties in sharing resources. The outdated and extensive operation management model lacks the overall planning of one-stop services of visitor management, resource management, service management, safety management, and traffic management. It has been unable to cover the increasingly diversified and personalized scenes, leading to museum visitor experience not good enough. In terms of hardware facilities, the traditional static display form of the Jingzhou Museum has not been able to meet the viewing needs of tourists conveniently and efficiently, and the phenomenon of queuing, congestion, and insufficient commentary by tour guides during the visit will also affect visitors' perception of history and culture. On the other hand, the traditional museum, for the sake of cultural relics protection, often has a limited amount of cultural relics displayed, thus restricting the function of the museum's social education and cultural communication. Among the supporting facilities, the Jingzhou Museum lacks a resting place. When tourists need to rest, they have to sit on the bench next to the flower bed in the museum or near the entrance of the museum; There are fewer restaurants around Jingzhou Museum and lack of local specialty snacks, and parking spaces are relatively scarce during the peak holiday period; Lack of dedicated transportation and transportation guidance systems connected to the attractions. Traffic accessibility, parking convenience, resting places, and catering services need to be improved; In terms of interactive product display, the application of information exhibits based on artificial intelligence and virtual reality in Jingzhou Museum is not widespread enough. Due to the limitation of space and time, visitors cannot observe ancient cultural relics in close range, for a long time, and immersively. In terms of online operation, Jingzhou Museum's relatively single mode of communication has limited the viewing effect, and the degree of informatization is obviously lagging behind. The Jingzhou museum is a typical example, with the problems of the obsolete exhibition form, insufficient integration of online and offline activities, lack of delicacy management and propaganda strategy, low tourist satisfaction, etc. It urgently calls for the support of new technologies to complete the intelligent transformation, thus breaking the restrictions of the physical wall to better spread the Jingzhou culture.

3   The Smartable Design Path of Jingzhou Museum

As a high-quality historical and cultural resource carrier in a specific area, modern museums urgently need to be equipped with engines of new technologies to move towards the future "smart city vision". In response to the opinion of the State Administration of Cultural Relics on "The Internet and the Construction of Chinese Civilization", Jingzhou Museum should rely on the Internet, based on traditional Chinese culture and spiritual civilization, and continuously promote Jingchu cultural heritage and innovation through intelligent design ideas and applied practices.

3.1   Creative Product Design Based on IP of Jingzhou Museum

In today's "Internet Plus" environment, IP (Intellectual Property) as the core of the cultural production becomes one of the new trends in the new era. There are four types of IP, including story IP, image IP, product IP and cultural IP. The specific story is called the story IP; a concrete cultural relic or historical figure is the image IP; story IP or image IP generates a series of product IP; by extracting historical and cultural elements from the above three types of IP and evolving them into souvenirs with the symbol of cultural, it comes the cultural IP. Ways to develop new media communication resources with cultural heritage as the theme, mainly including digital creative product forms, such as online news, short videos, H5, panoramas, applets, APPs, online videos, e-books, 3D, micro movies, VR, Online games, anime, MV, etc. Based on the IP creative design of Jingzhou Museum, it will promote the creation of a widely influential local cultural symbols and promote the unity of cultural value and industrial value.

For example, the Jingzhou Museum can achieve "digitalization of traditional culture" by developing IP-themed silk mobile applications. On the client, Jingzhou Museum can vividly display the full picture of silk fabrics in the museum through LBS technology, and provide visitors with online exhibits overview, route planning, location search, cultural relics explanation, catering, accommodation, customer service consulting and other services. At the scenic spot, Jingzhou Museum can establish analysis of tourist characteristic behavior data, master big data of user portraits, and then tap the deep value of big data to help provide services and construction of Jingzhou Museum. IP-based Jingzhou cultural and creative product design not only combines digital creativity with traditional culture, but also provides the feasibility of achieving a complete and high-quality offline supply chain: creative interaction, design research and development, packaging proofing, product production, mini-program e-commerce, Logistics and other links throughout the industry chain. Jingzhou Museum can develop a creative interactive mobile application, in which visitors can DIY their own "customized swords of the king" online, and order to purchase the physical swords with one-click. The extension of the cultural industry chain turns content IP into one of the selling points to attract tourists and stimulate consumption, so that the commercial profits of museums come from different revenue channels in every part of the industrial chain (Fig. 1).

Fig. 1. IP-based cultural and creative products

3.2 Digital Upgrade of the Museum's Resources

As a new form of service, "Internet Plus" holds the idea of integrating the online operation mode with the offline experience service. It requires that the interactions of the intelligent terminals should be more suitable to museum's resources. In the context of "Internet Plus", the digital upgrade of the Jingzhou Museum is imperative. For online, digital work requires scientific methods to process and store documents in electronic format, and to be able to efficiently insert, delete, modify, retrieve, provide access interfaces and protect information resources. As to offline, smart end devices such as mobile phones, iPads and ticketing devices are increasingly used in museums, such as the Crystal Bridge Museum of Art in the United States, where iPads are installed as digital tags on the left side of artwork, and visitors can view artist biographies, artists' works, and a voting question about their work. The upgrade of the collection's resources and smart terminals not only makes it easier for visitors to learn more about the exhibits at the Jingzhou Museum on their mobile devices, but also gives visitors a refreshing viewing experience.

Jingzhou Museum can try to use classic features such as The Sword of GouJian, Taoist Ancient Architecture Groups and Triple Courtyard Architecture Art to develop some games, movies and so on, including the online and offline ones. The digital upgrade of the Jingzhou Museum will not only effectively develop the collection resources, but also vigorously promote the integrated development of the Jingzhou Museum business and the cultural industry. The digital form of Jingzhou Museum will essentially realize the content of sharing and dissemination.

3.3   Intelligent Operation and Maintenance of Background Management System

The background management system of modern museums supervises the background operation of infrastructure networks and other critical equipment, which is a strong guarantee for the efficient operation of digital museums. Jingzhou Museum may formulate a standardized digital backstage management system, in order to facilitate the allocation, storage and management of the museum's digital resources.

Take the Cleveland Museum of Art as an example. The museum has used DAM (Digital Asset Management System) for several years. During these years, it has added three integrated systems: main system, collection online and ArtLens. The management system (CMS) is integrated as an externally-oriented interactive application for dynamic use. Specifically, the main system of the digital asset management system (that is, the internal system) stores all artwork photos, editable photos, and images to be filtered for archival purposes for library staff. The digital asset management system is connected to the collection management system. It mainly provides: (1) the digital asset management system supports collections online and provides additional content such as electronic publications and course programs for the website; (2) the collection management system is the collection in the exhibition area. The wall and the ArtLens mobile app provide artwork descriptions and images, which can not only do a lot of supporting work for a large number of multimedia and themed tours, but also provide more than 1,000 video materials. The main source of metadata for all visual art works on the Cleveland Museum of Art collection walls and on the ArtLens mobile app is the ArtLens catalog. It is composed of about 100 tables, which can provide 40 customized views and more than 20 storage methods, enabling it to provide the latest dynamic collection catalog data for the collection wall. The success of the Cleveland Museum of Art's back-end system provided valuable experience for the Jingzhou Museum to build an excellent back-end system.

3.4   The Construction of Digital Cloud Exhibition Platform

In 2018, the National Cultural Relics Bureau commissioned the Cultural Relics News Agency to build an "Online Museum Exhibition" cloud platform, which reflects the future direction of the transformation of modern museums. And there are more than 100 exhibitions on the line, including the Palace Museum, Nanjing Museum, Shanghai Museum, Shan Xi History Museum, Qin Emperor's Mausoleum Museum, China National Museum, Digital Wuhan Museum, The Digital Museum of The Traditional Village in Southeast Fujian, etc. (Fig. 2).

Digital cloud exhibitions in modern museums include physical exhibitions and virtual exhibitions. Applications in physical exhibitions in major museums include augmented

Fig. 2. Digital cloud exhibition platform of the Palace Museum

reality technology, giant screen projection technology, and holographic projection technology. Applications in virtual exhibitions include phantom imaging technology, virtual reality technology. For example, in the future digital cloud exhibition process, the Jingzhou Museum can use phantom imaging technology to tell the public the stories behind artifacts such as jade, lacquer, and silk. Based on the combination of "real-world modeling" and "phantom" optical imaging, the captured images (people, objects) are projected into the main model landscape in the set box, and then an innovative spatial narrative interpretation method is formed. It is characterized by a combination of real-world environments, creating a magical atmosphere and cool three-dimensional effects that allow visitors to have an immersive experience without wearing 3D glasses.

It should be emphasized that in the construction of the Jingzhou Museum cloud exhibition platform, the integration of traditional spatial display and narrative form with digital media technology will become an important point of modern museum research. The multi-dimensional and multi-sensory experiences provided by the museum can make the audience understand cultural relics through perception rather than simply browsing the exhibits and reading the introduction, which also gives the audience the right to think dialectically and objectively. It makes the audience possible to switch roles from viewer to participant, collector, commenter, and finally creator.

3.5 The Intelligent Application of AI

After the era of personal computer, network and mobile, the whole society has entered into the era of Artificial Intelligence. Some AI technologies such as intelligent robots, smart ticketing, smart navigation, smart recommendations and virtual experiences can be applied to modern museums. Artificial intelligence has reached or surpassed the human level in many aspects such as visual image recognition, speech recognition, and text processing, and it has also begun to emerge in the visual arts and program design, which is amazing.

1. Intelligent robot. In recent years, the state has introduced policies to continuously promote the application of service robots in venues. For example, in the National "13th Five-Year Plan" for cultural heritage protection and public cultural science

and technology innovation, it is mentioned that the use of artificial intelligence technology and human-computer interaction technology, the development of natural language dialogue can be achieved service robots, reduce the intensity of personnel work, improve service quality. Now China's major museums also have "you catch up with me" competition to try to introduce robots, for example, cheetah mobile robot "Panther small secret" figure has been all over Shanxi Geological Museum, Zhejiang Deqing Geographic Information Technology Museum, Jiangxi Jingdezhen China Ceramic Museum, Shandong Art Museum. "small robot" which based on Baidu AI technology were used in Hunan Province Museum landing pilot, become the front desk smart small assistant. Smart robots will gradually develop into "new employees" of museums.

2. Smart Ticketing. Jingzhou Museum's smart ticketing system can be used by electronic tickets. Visitors can make reservations through this system, purchase, and the museum's daily visitor numbers will be more scientifically planned. The information can be connected to the Internet and can be obtained remotely. Jingzhou Museum can also be equipped with handheld mobile terminal equipment or vertical electronic access control, to achieve automatic identification of tickets.

3. Wisdom guide. Jingzhou Museum's intelligent navigation system can provide users who are visiting the site with accurate navigation and cultural relics based on the user's location. Through graphics, audio, video and other ways to provide users with a set of display, interaction, explanation, entertainment in one of the integrated navigation and navigation services. When the user is not on site, it can also remotely pass through the system for virtual tour, and support to watch and listen to the explanation (Fig. 3).

4. Smart recommendation. Based on artificial intelligence, Jingzhou Museum's own data and OTA data collision, you can pull some of the data away, visitors can be restored to a three-dimensional image. On the one hand, one-on-one marketing actions can be achieved, such as Jingzhou local food recommendations, souvenirs or creative products recommended, and then stimulate tourist demand for tourism. On the other hand, under the decision-making of artificial intelligence and the service of intelligent terminals, it can provide visitors with personalized tour route recommendations, cultural relics recommendations that may be of interest, cultural activities, etc.

5. Virtual experience. On the one hand, Jingzhou Museum can interact with the user through VR, AR, MR as the representative of the three-dimensional panoramic technology, so as to obtain the immersive experience and greatly enrich the user's sensory experience. Based on multimedia and VR technology, the interaction of static two-dimensional interface has developed into the interaction of multi-dimensional information, so that users can enjoy a visual feast from the art of cultural relics in a virtual environment, and can carry out high-quality visibleimmersive virtual interaction experience, which not only narrow the distance between Jingzhou Museum and the viewer, It is also convenient to display Jingzhou Museum and cultural relics in all aspects. On the other hand, in the rapid development of artificial intelligence, the use of robots or artificial intelligence can customize their own story lines, so that visitors can according to their own preferences for interactive viewing, and everyone

Fig. 3. XiaoDu AI Robot

comes to different exhibition halls with their own unique and exclusive emotional experience (Fig. 4).

Fig. 4. Lost in Play2

4 Summary

With the development of the technology, traditional museums like Jingzhou Museum will be transformed into a innovation-driven, cultural inherited and scientific museum. In order to better spread the history and culture of China, the modern museums should rethink the exhibition methods, derivative design and cultural industry. Through the application of AI technology, modern museums can expand the cultural connotation, and upgrade the traditional museums' authoritative, educational, and indoctrinating styles into participatory, immersive, and heuristic styles. Thus to reach the realm" Beyond The Form, Get The Hub", that is, beyond the appearance to get the essence of history, culture, aesthetic and philosophy.

References

1. Quan, W.: Research on museum audience experience. Master's thesis of Central Academy of Fine Arts, 01 May 2019
2. Yang, D.: Museums: the future of traditions. Fine Arts News (2019)
3. Industrial Internet Smart Cultural Travel Research Report. Tencent Cultural and Creative Industry Research Institute
4. Feng, Y., Zhong, S.: Research on the development of museum cultural tourism from the perspective of global tourism—a survey based on tourist satisfaction. J. Northwest Uni. Natl. (03) (2018)
5. Yang, H.: Research on Digitalization of Intangible Cultural Heritage. Social Science Literature Press (2014)
6. Julie, D.: Technology and Digital Initiatives—Museums' Innovation. Shanghai Science and Technology Education Press (2017)
7. Gu, X.: Historical Review and Development Status of Artificial Intelligence. Nat. Mag. (3) (2016)

Multisensory HCI Design with Smell and Taste for Environmental Health Communication

Paula Neves$^{(\boxtimes)}$ (ID) and António Câmara (ID)

Faculty of Science and Technology, New University of Lisbon (FCT-UNL),
2829-516 Caparica, Portugal
pc.neves@campus.fct.unl.pt

Abstract. In the field of Multisensory Human-Computer Interaction (HCI) Design, integration of chemical senses has been increasingly explored. Nevertheless, smell and taste senses are still underrepresented in HCI. This underrepresentation limits Environmental Health Communication, which should incorporate those senses. The exploratory study presented in this paper describes Multisensory HCI design process with the chemical senses as mediators of environmental health communication. To do so we formulated design hypothesis and divided our research design process into two phases: the chemical sense experience for cross-sensory analogies research and the digital media experience for meaning and communication research. Thereby, we describe the conceptualization, design and evaluation of our design project *Earthsensum*. Our approach accomplished symbolic displaying of smell and taste and led us to a new multi-sensorial interaction system using Mobile Virtual Reality (MVR) and Mobile Augmented Reality (MAR). The results of our findings confirmed our design hypothesis, and showed that the purposed interaction system lead not only to a better understanding of smell and taste perception, as well as of environmental challenges. We discuss our results in the context of the HCI design strategies for chemical senses inclusion.

Keywords: Multisensory HCI design · Sustainable HCI · Chemical senses · Environmental health communication · Mobile virtual reality · Mobile augmented reality

1 Introduction

Based on the recognition that human health and well-being are intimately linked to the environment, raising environmental literacy within communities and citizens is crucial to foster pro-environmental behavior [1]. By definition, environmental health is the science and practice of preventing human injury and illness, promoting well-being by identifying and controlling environmental sources and hazards agents [2]. These comprise all the physical, chemical, and biological factors external to a person, and all the related factors impacting behavior [3]. Present environmental problems, such as global warming, reflect human activities impact since the Industrial Revolution [4]. Recent report trends are pointing towards progressive global socio-economic pressure [5] and population health risks [6–8]. These trends were announced already by pioneering studies of 20th century

© Springer Nature Switzerland AG 2020
C. Stephanidis et al. (Eds.): HCII 2020, LNCS 12423, pp. 441–463, 2020.
https://doi.org/10.1007/978-3-030-60114-0_31

[9] alerting that the quest of unlimited economic growth would lead to system collapse, due to the earth's limited resources. Meanwhile, the 21st-century evolving environmental hazards have led to new policy efforts [10], such as transition to low-carbon economy and sustainable food systems [11]. These lines of actions fall within the scope of the latest environmental health strategies recommended by the World Health Organization (WHO) [12]. These includes the commitment to sustainable patterns of consumption and production, as well as it tackles the misuse of natural resources and the large-scale generation of waste. WHO argues that if these strategies could be implemented on time, more economic and health risks could be reduced. Accordingly, we assume, that the more people know how to interpret their environment, the more they will act in accordance with these transition strategies.

Our goal is to test these environmental health communication design strategies benefit from multisensory interaction systems which include chemical sense experiences. Our approach relies on the fact that human organism can be reached by environmental exposure vectors through air, food, soil and water conditions [13]. This implies that through breathing and ingestion, environmental pollutants enter imperceptibly into the human body triggering health issues [13–15]. To evidence these events, the chemical senses are the most relevant. They comprise the senses of smell (olfaction), taste (gustation) and trigeminal stimulation which rely on signal transduction by the human brain. The olfactory bulb is stimulated via orthonasal and via retronasal route. By "sniffing" air through the nostrils (orthonasal) or by swallowing reaching the back of the throat (retronasal), neural signals are sent to key areas of the brain involved in speech, emotions, memories and reward [16]. Taste involves sensations that arise from the stimulation of the tongue's taste buds, which comprise sweet, sour, salty, bitter and umami [17]. When smell is fused through the retronasal route with taste information, it generates flavor perceptions [18]. Trigeminal stimulation also contributes to flavor experiences, as involved biting and chewing actions process temperature, spiciness, body and touch information in the mouth and tongue [19]. Hence, chemical sense perception results from these intertwined senses, leading to interpretation and communication.

We state that smell and taste lead to multi-sensorial experiences which convey multi-layered information about environmental events [20]. However, to the best of our knowledge, these senses are usually absent when those events are represented in digital systems. Geographic Information Systems (GIS) enabled multidimensional environmental systems [21] to evolve since the event of the World Wide Web (WWW) [22]. As broadband and technological advances provided web mapping and location-based services, which enabled the public to interact with geographic data. Platforms and services have evolved to collect, monitor, predict and interpret environmental data through governmental and public sources [23, 24]. Nevertheless, the chemical sense dimension is absent from these representations. Despite reporting tools are improving related to environmental smell experiences [25, 26] there is no correlation with taste. Overall, there is a lack of design solutions which embraces the inherent representative dimensions [27] of this correlation.

In this paper, we describe our exploratory study, which aims to demonstrate how chemical senses allow representing environmental problems within digital forms and how Multisensory HCI Design can be used for non-scientific audiences to communicate environmental health. We wanted to know if by providing tools to acknowledge and communicate smell and taste experiences, people could make sense of environmental events and make more informed choices. Our Multisensory HCI design project *Earthsensum,* offered environmental smell and taste experiences about real geolocations to participants of the study. These experiences were represented digitally using Mobile Virtual Reality (MVR) and Mobile Augmented Reality (MAR) prototypes. The project comprised two main design phases. The first phase provided smell and taste experiences without contextual clues. The second provided the contextualization using digital media. Finally, we describe the qualitative and quantitative results from the participant's evaluation of these experiences.

2   Related Work

This research is rooted in Multisensory HCI framework pursuing chemical sense inclusion in digital systems [28]. Ongoing efforts tackle digitalization of smell and taste [29, 30] for delivery, transmission or substitution of senses. Within this context, stimulation occurs via chemical exposure (LOLLio [31]; InStink [32]; oPhone [33]), electrical or thermal stimulation (Digital Lollipop [34]; Vocktail [35]) as also acoustic levitation (TastyFloats [36]). Regarding sensory interpretation, cross-modal correspondences research [37, 38] has shown how sensory modalities interaction (e.g. sound, colour) influence smell and taste perception [19]. Application of these studies in Multisensory HCI are projects that explore sensory substitution, such as how senses can be altered by its appearance or scent (MetaCookie [39]; Straw-user Interface [40]). However, attempts of digital representation of those senses as communication systems, have shown limited success [32, 41] mainly due to inter-subject perception and interpretation variances. Despite overall experiments proved technological feasibility, its dissemination depends on relevant consumer centred application developments [42]. This work refers also to Sustainable HCI, a research field that studies how technology is applied to increase environmental awareness by giving users information about the environmental impact of their actions, and hopefully motivating pro-environmental behavior [43]. Within this context, inspiring HCI projects include *Smell Pittsburgh,* a collaborative system that enables community members to report and track air pollution. Public online available data reports comprise air quality metrics, self-reported health symptoms and personal stories with images. These reports are sent directly to the local health department and visualized on a map along with air quality data from monitoring stations [44]. *SmellyMaps* is an interactive map that captures urban "smellscapes" from social media data (i.e., tags on Flickr pictures or tweets) of some cities. It lets sort city's streets by emissions, nature, food, waste and animal smell with 258 smell triggers classified in ten categories. Specific categories (e.g. industry, transport, cleaning) correlate with governmental air quality indicators. Additionally, it also provides basic emotional dimensions correspondences. *ActNow.Bot* is an interactive and responsive chatbot harnessing Artificial Intelligence (AI) to engage people to take climate action. Conceived as a social media campaign, it recommends and tracks daily actions to reduce human carbon footprint. By registering and sharing these actions, it aims to inspire these behaviors collectively [45]. From the Sensory Arts and Design field [46] we highlight *Climate Pod,* an art installation made up of five geodesic domes, emulating polluted environments in cities globally. Within each dome, the air quality of five global cities is recreated. It starts with breathing clear smelling air of Tautra (Norway) and then continuing through to the cities of London (United Kingdom), New Delhi (India), Beijing (China) and São Paulo (Brazil). It aims to raise awareness about air pollution and health in different regions of the world [47] by providing the public with the near to real situation of breathing in distant places. *Ghost Food Project* is an art installation which explores cross-modal research. It includes a customized food truck, trained performers, synthetic scents and a lab-made olfactory device which is worn on the face and positions a pod with a scented displayer under the wearer's nose. Three taste experiences are offered based on scent-food pairings that simulate the taste experiences of foods threatened with extinction due to the impact of climate change. Sensory substitution of the perceived scent combines a facsimile food with a custom-designed synthetic smell. When ordering a taste experience from the menu, the visitor expects to get something, which is combined with the simulation via the olfactory device [48]. The ultimate goal is to raise questions about safe food systems and climate change. Whereas, *Talking Noses* is an art installation which aims to translate the urban "smellscape" of Mexico City in olfactory terms. Using headspace technology, key smells of neighbourhoods were decoded and recreated in a scratch and sniff map of the city. These smell displays are accompanied by looping video footage of Mexico City residents close up sniffing noses. Only words are heard in the video, describing smells with words. In this manner, the artwork translates the invisible olfactory narrative of the city in terms of its identity and also of its surroundings, such as air pollution [49].

Summing up, the background research helped us to reflect on HCI which include the chemical senses. From our perspective, a transdisciplinary approach of science, engineering, design and art [50] could benefit utmost environmental health communication strategies.

3 *Earthsensum* Multisensory HCI Design Process

Based on the recognition that human health and well-being are intimately linked to the state of the environment, raising environmental knowledge capital within communities and citizens is crucial to pursue mitigation and adaption of new environmental conditions. Our design study rationale is based on the statement that chemical senses, elements and places are in a continuous relationship with the environment. As the world is compound by atoms and molecules, humans and environment exchange these through breathing and ingestion. Breath and food are then vehicles which transfer into human blood cells not only oxygen and nutrients, as also air, water and soil conditions of the environment. Targeting the non-scientific public, we presume that the communication of this intertwined environmental-human health relationship could lead to enhanced environmental literacy and foster behaviour change.

Our exploratory study aims two answer research questions: (i) How can chemical sense experiences communicate environmental health information on digital systems?

(ii) How is the Design of such Multisensory HCI System? Targeting non-scientific audiences, we wanted to explore how chemical senses could represent environmental problems within digital forms and how these can be applied to communicate environmental health. We wanted to inquire if by providing tools to acknowledge and communicate smell and taste experiences, people could make sense about their chemical sense experiences, environmental events and behaviour change. To answer these questions, we applied research through design methodology within HCI research [51], based on hypothesis formulation [52]. We build our Multisensory HCI Design process considering synesthetic design methodology [53] for *Earthsensum* prototype ideation. Its guidelines provide design process strategies to encompass sensory modal connections. They include aligning cross-sensory analogies with congruent iconic, symbolic and semantic attributes. The process implies first a first step "selecting those strategies which enable connecting modalities with respect to the intended product" [53, p. 16], followed by a second step in which these strategies are fused into the product conceptualization. Therefore, this design process builds up along two main design phases - first, a cross-sensory analogy and symbolic construction layer, followed by a meaning and communication construction layer. *Earthsensum's* first design phase offered environmental smell and taste experiences about real geolocations without contextual clues. It comprises exploring cross-modal association data for digital representation research purposes. The second provides the contextualization of the experience for meaning-building. Strategically, we opted for Mobile Virtual Reality (MVR) and Mobile Augmented Reality (MAR) technology, as they provide technical features which support our design intent. This phase comprises prototype development for proof-of-concept validation which we describe in this section.

Design Hypotheses. To proof our design concept baseline's comprehensibility and feasibility, we formulated two design hypotheses for prototype development.

Design Hypothesis 1. An educational tool exploring immersive technology provides virtual tours to environmental hazard locations related to smell or taste experiences. Its mission is to transfer the user into remote places where environmental problems happen. By having tasted or smelled an ingredient, to which its related remote location the user is transferred, we assume it is possible to establish an association between a geographic location and the chemical senses. This cognitive association is then complemented with additional meaning layers. These are delivered by multimedia contents, addressing topics such as condition influences, human life impact and prevention.

Design Hypothesis 2. Building an annotation tool of smell and taste experiences enables to articulate cognitively an otherwise volatile perception. By providing a symbolic representation system, these personal chemical sense experiences can be communicated and shared with wide audiences. In this line, augmented reality technology allows to index smell and taste representation by geographic coordinates and link these to geo-context driven information. Thereby, the platform has the ability not only to provide chemical sense annotation facilities but also deliver local related environmental health information. Hence, the content design addresses multi-purpose objectives: information, education and behavior change.

Considering both design hypothesis, we believe that Multisensory HCI Design framework enables successfully to communicate environmental health with the chemical senses, fostering environmental awareness and behavior change. Positive evaluation results of its conceptual design and impact on environmental awareness, would prove if where right.

Participants. In total, 16 participants (Females = 2) between the ages 17 and 64 years (M = 18.5 years, SD = 13.46) volunteered to take part in the study. They were recruited on an opportunity-sampling basis. The education level of participants ranged from undergraduate (n = 11), bachelor (n = 3) and doctoral degree (n = 2). Reported expertise area comprised "Technology and Informatics" (n = 13), "Augmented Reality" (n = 1), "Chemistry" (n = 1), and "Research and Development" (n = 1). Participants agreed about the outline and procedure of the complete test setting. We asked permission to audio and video recording, as also taking photos. All volunteers read and signed an informed consent before participating, not receiving any compensation. The experiment was conducted at Tech Start Up company "Aromni" equipped Showroom, located on the University Campus of FCT NOVA - (Faculty of Science and Technology - New University of Lisbon). Our study adopted a within-group design. We assigned eight participants for the smell experience group and eight participants for the taste experience group. Each experiment was carried on separate time schedules.

3.1   Design Phase 1: Chemical Sense Experience

In this section of our study, we explore cross-sensory analogies and symbolic construction layer of our Multisensory HCI design process. It encompasses defining an "environmental chemical senses correspondence chart", selecting and producing stimuli samples and providing association attribution options.

Stimuli Selection. We circumscribed emergent environmental themes about environmental health [54], world trade [55] and pro-environmental strategies, [56, 57]. For each topic, we selected its representative smell or taste. Next, we defined an "environmental chemical sense correspondences chart" organized by stimuli; molecule highlight, location, geo coordinates, sample source and call for action themes (Table 1). This categorization provided basic guidelines for content development throughout *Earthsensum's* conceptualization process.

Stimuli Production and Presentation. Our ammonia sample was produced by diluting 3 ml household ammonia in 300 ml of water. The hydrogen sulfide sample by leaving one fresh egg yolk in an unclosed recipient for seven days on open air. Whereas dimethyl sulfide sample resulted from soaking dry wakame algae in 300 ml seawater for seven days. These samples were presented in the form of three jars and were manually delivered. Each jar was also wrapped in tape paper to avoid visual cues of its content. This procedure is based on previous studies in the fields of experimental psychology such as Velasco et al. [58]. Taste sample production of chlorophyll resulted from cooking fresh spinach leaves with steam vapour. Soybean experience consisted of cooked white rice seasoned with Shoyu Soy Sauce by Clearspings. For clove's eugenol experience we seasoned cooked

Table 1. Chemical Sense correspondences chart for sample and content development.

Sample	Stimuli	Molecule highlight	Location	GPS	Sample Source	Call for action themes
Smell A	Solid waste	Ammonia	Waste treatment Station, Portugal	38.744959, −9.326482	Household Ammonia	Waste prevention and recycling
Smell B	Cellulose	Hydrogen Sulfide	Pulp industry, Portugal	40.053199, −8.865728	Rotten Eggs	Paper waste reduction
Smell C	Sea	Dimethyl Sulfide	Seacoast, Portugal	38.804254, −9.484806	Seaweed	Plastic waste reduction; Sustainable fish and seafood consumption
Taste A	Spinach	Chlorophyll	Tehran, Iran	35.664816, 51.359608	Spinach Leaves	Car use reduction; Plastic waste reduction
Taste B	Soybean	Water	Beijing, China	39.907256, 116.375481	Soy Sauce	Discarded electronics reduction; Meat consumption reduction
Taste C	Clove	Eugenol	Dhaka, Bangladesh	23.811389, 90.421289	Biryani Spice	Clothing waste reduction

white rice with Bombay Biryani Mix by Shan. These food samples were served on ceramic spoons as "amuse-bouche", inspired on previous cross-modal study by Spence et al. [58].

Procedure and Methods. After participants aforementioned agreement protocol and explanation of the proceedings, they were guided to the test setup. Smell and Taste experiments were performed at different times with different participants. Concerning the smell experience, jars with smell samples were displayed on a table. Participants were instructed to hold each jar 20 cm away from their nose while sniffing. We suggested the smelling order by increasing arousal properties (from low to high). Whereas for the taste experience, ceramic spoons were displayed on a table with food samples. We recommended participants taking small bites suggesting taste order by arousal intensity (from low to high). After completion, we asked participants to translate their perceptions by associating semantic, haptic, graphic and affective attributes.

(Step1) Semantic Associations. Olfactory and gustatory language is predominantly shaped by cultural factors and vocabulary [59–61]. Hence, we wanted to study participants skill and preferences to describe chemical sense experiences. To this end, we applied two methods: (1) choosing words from a predefined list and (2) description with own vocabulary. For the first method, we compiled a list of smell and taste descriptors organized by source, category and affect (Table 2), based on different sources of classification systems [62–64]. Immediately after stimuli experience, participants were asked to choose any words from the list which best matched their stimuli perception for quantitative analyses. The second method was performed at the conclusion of this section of the study. We asked participants to recall what they perceived and express it their own words, for qualitative analyses. At this stage, we also inquired about method description preference.

Table 2. List of Semantic descriptors for smell and taste experiences.

	Smell descriptors	Taste descriptors
Source	animals, cleaning, coffee, complex, construction, emissions, food/beverage, humans, industrial, nature, non-food, smoke, subway, synthetic fragrance, tobacco, waste	dairy products, fruits, leaves, legume, meat, poultry, root, seafood, seeds, spice, whole grain
Category	acid, ammonia/ruinous, bakery, burnt, chemical, cold, decayed, fish, flower, fruit, garlic, grass, musky, sour, spices, sweaty, sweet, warm, wood	bitter, bland, crunchy, dry, greasy, moist, piping hot, rich, salty, savory, scrumptious, sour, spicy, sugary, sweet, tasty
Affect	agreeable, aromatic, bad, characteristic, delicate, delicious, delightful, disgusting, distinct, evil, exquisite, faint, fresh, grateful, heavy nasty, nauseous, offensive, peculiar, penetrating, pleasant, powerful, pungent, rich, sickening, strange, strong, suffocating, unpleasant	amazing, appealing, appetizing, delectable, delicious, delightful, disgusting, divine, enjoyable, enticing, excellent, exquisite, extraordinary, fantastic, finger, heavenly, licking, lip smacking, luscious, marvelous, mouth-watering, palatable, pleasant, pleasing, satisfying, scrumptious, strange, superb, tantalizing, tasty, terrific, unpleasant, wonderful, yummy

(Step2) Haptic associations. In general, our surroundings are perceived by colours, patterns and structures engaging all sensorial modalities. Within this context, we looked into Gestalt psychology research [65] for non-verbal communication processes. Considering our project scope, we wanted to study how volumetric shapes and textures represent chemical senses experiences [66]. We selected three shape options of round, point edged and angular objects (tennis ball, trigger ball, cube) and three texture options of rough, regular and soft (sandpaper, denim, velvet). Shape objects and textures were displayed on a tray in random order. Participants were instructed to choose one shape and one texture option for each *stimuli* experience for quantitative analyses (Fig. 1).

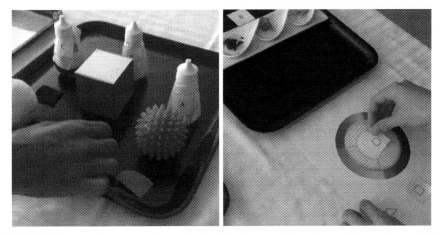

Fig. 1. Left image shows participant selecting haptic associations for smell experience. Right image shows graphic associations process of taste experience.

(Step3) Graphic components associations. Form and colour enable symbolic construction of meanings [67]. Hence, we wanted to study what graphic forms, textures and colours would represent smell and taste perceptions. We provided basic geometric shapes based on their symbology [66, 68] (triangle, square, circle), colour palettes based on Plutchik's wheel of emotions [69] and graphic texture representations (zigzag, diagonals, waves, circle) based on visual communication formulations [70] for quantitative analyses. Participants selected these components by handling a paper interface prototype that we build for this purpose [71] (see Fig. 1).

(Step4) Affective associations. Sensorial experiences are mediated by emotional responses. In this line, we measured psychometric variables with Bradley's Self-Assessment Manikin (SAM) scale [72]. We asked participants to fill out online Self-Assessment questionnaire answering questions about Pleasantness - "Did you like the smell/taste? (1 = "Strongly Disagree"; 5 = "Strongly Agree")"; Valence - "How does this smell/taste make you feel? (1 = "Sad"; 5 = "Happy")" and Arousal - "What impact has this smell/taste on you? (1 = "Calm"; 5 = "Excited")".

Results.   In this section we summarize the main findings from Design phase 1, following the four main association dimensions.

(Results Step 1) Semantic Association. The first method applies quantitative analysis focused on the word association task. Figure 2 presents the most frequently selected words for each chemical sense experience. Figure 3 provides a summary of these words. The size of the words depends on their frequency of use, with larger words being more frequent than smaller words. Words like "strong", "chemical" and "powerful" were more often selected when describing the ammonia smell experience. Whereas the most words associated with hydrogen sulphide were "burnt", "decayed", "fish", "fruit", "sour" and "sickening", among others. Finally, "grass", "food", "nature", "wood", "agreeable" and "aromatic" were dimethyl sulphide's word choices. Regarding the taste experience,

spinach most associated words were "enjoyable", "leaves ", "legume" and "moist". The soy experience comprised "seafood", "seeds" and "spice". At last, the clove experience most frequent word choices were "spice", "moist" and "piping hot".

The second method applies qualitative analysis to determine participants personal translation strategies of these experiences. Two main themes emerged: functional and creative. The functional theme contains essential descriptive word choices. The creative theme refers to the use of metaphors. We present herein representative quotes for each smell and taste experiences. Ammonia: "Burning" (P3); "Disgusting, urge to escape, a terror movie" (P5). Hydrogen sulphide: "Industrial" (P2); "A day of autumn" (P4). Dimethyl sulphide: "Strange" (P8); "It is a soft and characteristic smell" (P7). Spinach: "Unpleasant" (P13); "Feels like a connection with pure nature" (P14). Soy: "Neutral" (P15); "Rice fields, rivers and birds" (P16). Clove: "Spicy and horrible" (P11); "Above the real world, sublime" (P16). Out of total 16 participants, the preferred description method is from a predefined list (56,25%). Pointed reasons are convenience and speed. Selecting words from a list helps to overcome lack of vocabulary and it is perceived as a faster method than using personal vocabulary.

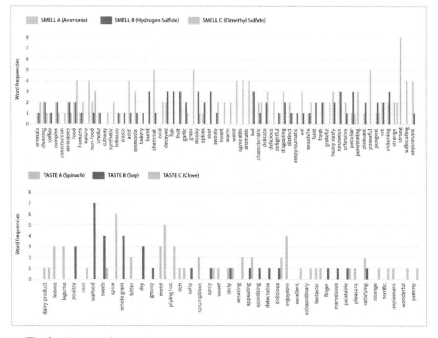

Fig. 2. The most frequently selected words smell (upper row) and taste (lower row).

(Results Step 2) Haptic Association. Quantitative results of volumetric shape and texture options revealed a collective sensorial profile. Ammonia was perceived as a point shape object (6P) with a rough texture (6P); Hydrogen sulfide an angular object (6P) with a hard texture (6P); Dimethyl sulfide a round object (5P) with a soft texture (8P). Regarding taste association, Spinach was represented by a round object (5P) and regular texture

(5P); Soy an angular object (4P) and soft texture (4P); Clove as a point edged object (7P) and rough texture (7P) (see Table 3 for data distribution, Fig. 3 for results overview).
(Results Step 3) Graphic Components Association. Quantitative analysis revealed that graphic representation options enabled individual abstract communication of smell and taste experiences. Data collections disclosed a collective formal representation of these.

Table 3. Haptic association attribution of smell and taste experiences evaluated by 8 participants (100%) of each group.

Variables		Smell A (Ammonia)	Smell B (Hydrogen Sulfide)	Smell C (Dimethyl Sulfide)	Taste A (Spinach)	Taste B (Soy)	Taste C (Clove)
		%	%	%	%	%	%
Shape	Cube	12,5%	75%	12,5%	37,5%	50%	12,5%
	Tennis Ball	12,5%	12,5%	62,5%	62,5%	25%	0
	Trigger Ball	75%	12,5%	25%	0	25%	87,5%
Texture	Denim	25%	75%	0	62,5%	37,5%	0
	Sandpaper	75%	25%	0	0	12,5%	87,5%
	Velvet	0	0	100%	37,5%	50%	12,5%

Table 4. Graphic association attribution of smell and taste experiences evaluated by 8 participants (100%) for each group

Variables		Smell A (Ammonia)	Smell B (Hydrogen Sulfide)	Smell C (Dimethyl Sulfide)	Taste A (Spinach)	Taste B (Soy)	Taste C (Clove)
		%	%	%	%	%	%
Color	Purple	50%	37,5%	0	5%	25%	25%
	Orange	25%	25%	0	0	12,5%	75%
	Green	12,5%	25%	37,5%	62,5%	12,5%	0
	Blue	12,5%	12,5%	62,5%	12,5%	50%	0
Texture	Zigzag	62,5%	25%	0	0	12,5%	75%
	Wave	12,5%	62,5%	12,5%	12,5%	37,5%	12,5%
	Diagonal	12,5%	12,5%	37,5%	87,5%	0	0
	Circles	12,5%	0	50%	0	50%	0
Shape	Square	12,5%	87,5%	0	25%	62,5%	12,5%
	Triangle	75%	0	25%	37,5%	12,5%	50%
	Circle	12,5%	12,5%	75%	37,5%	25%	37,5%

Ammonia was purple (4P), zigzag texture (5P), triangle shape (6P). Hydrogen sulfide was purple (3P), wave texture (5P), square shape (7P). Dimethyl sulfide was blue (5P), circle texture (4P), circle shape (6P). Spinach was green (5P), diagonal texture (7P), triangle shape (3P) and circle shape (3P). Soy was blue (4P), circle texture 4P), square shape (5P). Clove was orange (6P), zigzag texture by (6P), triangle shape (4P) (see Table 4 for data distribution, Fig. 3 for results overview).

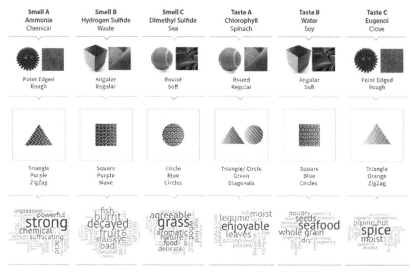

Fig. 3. Overview of haptic (first row), graphic (second row) and semantic associations (third row) results for smell and taste experiences.

(Results step 4) Affective Associations. We performed quantitative analyses pleasantness, valence and arousal response. Data revealed that Ammonia was "strongly unpleasant" (6P), evoked feelings of "unsatisfied" (4P), and had an "excited" (3P) arousal effect on participants. Hydrogen sulfide was "unpleasant" (6P), evoked feelings of "unsatisfied" (5P) and arousal effect was "dull" (5P). Whereas, Dimethyl sulfide was rated as "neutral" either for pleasantness (5P), valence (4P) and arousal (6P) dimension. Spinach was "pleasant" (5P), its valence "neutral" (4P), with a "calm" (5P) impact. Soy was perceived as "neutral" for pleasantness (5P), valence (4P) and arousal (5P) dimensions. Clove instead was ranked as "pleasant" (5P), evoking "happy" feelings (4P) with arousal dimension of "excited" (3P) and "dull" (3P) (see Fig. 4).

Summary of Design Phase 1. In this section of our study, we explored cross-sensory analogies and symbolic construction possibilities of semantic, haptic, graphic and affective association with smell and taste experiences. Association features allowed individuals to describe smell and taste perceptions. Additionally, data collection sets enable collective profiling of these experiences. Adaptation of these association features on interface modules enables symbolic displaying of chemical sense experiences. This first

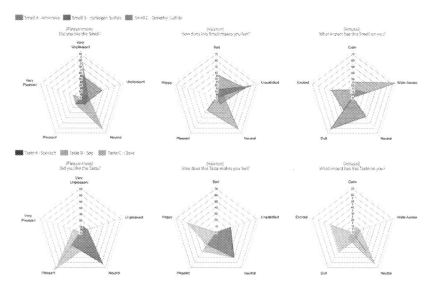

Fig. 4. Results of participants affective evaluation of smell and taste experiences for pleasantness, valence and arousal dimensions.

design phase provided smell and taste experiences without contextual clues. The second design phase provides the contextualization of these experiences using digital media.

3.2 Design Phase 2: Digital Media Experience

In this section of the study, we explore the meaning and communication construction layer of our Multisensory HCI design process. We present the conceptualization, design and implementation of digital media experiences, following our design hypothesis formulations. The main objective our study was to explore if by providing tools to acknowledge and interact with smell and taste experiences, people could make sense about their chemical senses, environmental events and pro-environmental behaviour. To this end we developed a Mobile Virtual Reality (MVR) App and a Mobile Augmented Reality (MAR) App.

Mobile Virtual Reality App. Based on the aforementioned design hypothesis 1 formulation, we developed the *Earthsensum's* MVR App for prototype evaluation.

Specifications. Entering the main scene, users are guided to take time to *"Breath"* on the virtual location as also to *"Smell your Environment"* or *"Taste your Environment"*. Following, the main menu options are displayed. These include "molecular signature", "context story" and "call for action". The contents provide information about molecules, location, economic activity, cultural tradition, as also associated environmental impacts and courses of action to mitigate them.

Design Development. For the purpose of our design hypothesis evaluation, we decided to implement a basic demo prototype. Requirements comprised interaction with User

Fig. 5. MVR prototype implementation process with Unity 3d. Left image present the starting scene suggesting the user to "breath" local air of Dhaka, Bangladesh. Right image shoes "Molecules" section option featuring 3d eugenol molecule composition on Dhaka location.

Interface (UI) components and moving through the scenes. Our design process covered user flow analyses, information architecture diagram, storyboard for content flow planning and asset production. We produced all graphic assets and motion design. For imaginary we took 360° photos with Samsung Gear 360 Camera, otherwise we used "Street View Download 360" online tool [73]. For background audio we used online service providers [74, 75], whereas locution audio was recorded with Voice Memo App for iPhone. Finally, digital 3D model libraries [76] supplied featured Molecule compositions.

Interaction Design and Implementation. We decided on eye-gaze based interaction as input method for a natural sense of navigation with a standalone Head Mount Displays (HDM). We followed common VR methodology design recommendations for Human Ergonomics [77]. Interaction zones for content placement where defined by its range of motion attributes. Main menu options were placed on the main content zone for easiness, whereas section options were placed on the peripherical zone to stimulate content exploration through head movement. Graphic elements, motion graphic and 3d Models were placed along depth axis of 1 m to 10 m, to guarantee comfortable depth and content separation effects. Next, [78] we tested navigation and content flow with Low-Fi wireframing. Final demo prototype was implemented with Unity3D [79] and exported as a standalone app (see Fig. 5).

Mobile Virtual Reality App Evaluation

Apparatus and Test Procedure. We used mobile device Samsung Galaxy S8 coupled with Samsung Gear VR, a standalone Head Mounted Display (HMD). At start of session, participants were given a spoken introduction and written task scenarios to complete:

- Smell Experience Task - *"You pass by a location. A distinguished smell has an impact on you. You want to know more about this smell"*.
- Taste Experience Task - *"You pass by a street food market. You have tasted a certain ingredient. You want to know more about this ingredient"*.

We explained the navigation settings and demonstrated them on an external screen and handed out the HMD. Next, participants tested the VR experience while seated in a revolving chair as recommended for experiments involving 360-degree contents [80].

Evaluation Method. We applied the walkthrough method [81] for the prototype evaluation. We took notes about verbal and non-verbal clues while keeping an eye on what the participant was looking at and how they interacted. Additionally, we recorded navigation flow and body movements. At conclusion, we inquired about the system and content experience. To this end, we adapted Witmer's questionnaire [82] for navigation and presence evaluation, besides inquiring about emotional engagement and content exploration. At last, we asked participants about the usefulness and environmental awareness impact. Answers were registered through self-report questionnaires with Likert evaluation scale (5-point).

Evaluation Results. All 16 participants executed movements and navigation actions with success. Navigation targets were recognized "easily" - smell group: 75% (6P); taste group: 100% (8P). Presence perception of having a sensation of being in the real place was "somehow" for 50% (4P) of each group. The average number of total participants enjoyed the scenes and contents were rated as comprehensible. 75% (6P) of each group confirmed that a clear message was provided. Near all rated the content experience as useful - smell group: 75% (6P); taste group: 87,5% (7P). Out of total 16 participants 75% (12P) would recommend the VR App as an education tool. Regarding environmental behaviour impact, the average of both groups agreed that content experience improved their awareness about the environment - 68,75% (11P), made them think about their behaviour towards the environment - 75% (12P) and inspired them positively to take action towards their environment - 87,50% (14P).

Mobile Augmented Virtual Reality App. In line with the aforementioned design hypothesis 2 formulation, we developed the *Earthsensum* MAR App for prototype evaluation.

Specifications. Interaction modules providing formal, hedonic and semantic associations options enable chemical sense annotation. These allow to build a personal visual symbol in accordance with user's geolocation. Signing up to the *Earthsensum* community allows the user to consult his area for previous "geolabeled" experiences and decide to "join" or to "place" a symbol. To join a symbol means that a predominant sensory experience is prevailing in the area. To "place" a new symbol represents a new experience. Finally, the user is able to consult, connect and share this data with the community (Fig. 6). Additional information is provided through main content sections of "Molecules" and "Take Action". The "Molecules" section enables to access of molecule information and air quality indicators pulled by official data sources in real-time [83–85]. Its most accentuated indicator determines what molecular information is displayed. By contrast, the taste experience is labelled by its ingredients. Databases identify the most common molecule presence for an ingredient (e.g. Spinach – Chlorophyll) and provide information about the main export country [55]. This process enables to approach air quality indexes of the remote location to which the ingredient is related. Finally, the main section "Take Action" provides further contextualized information about social-economic and behaviour change information. Users are able to suggest their own pro-environmental actions to *Earthsensum's* community.

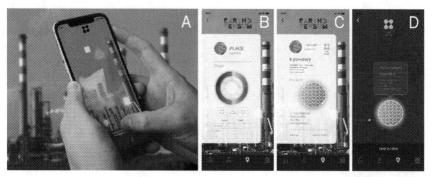

Fig. 6. MAR prototype concept (a). Example of wireframe development of association options (b), symbolic representation summary (c) and map view of icon placement (d).

Design Development. For the purpose of our design hypothesis evaluation, we implemented a basic interactive prototype based on graphic images. We also build a paper prototype to study interaction functionality with graphic association components. Our design process covered visual design development as also functional specification and content analyses.

Interaction Design and Implementation. Common design recommendations for Augmented Reality [86] guided our design process. To avoid information overload, we decided symbols display blending with the physical world should be placed facing the same direction. Symbol information would be also displayed on map visualization mode. Main and second level menus display lists of related options following User Usability Principles [87]. For navigation fluidity, we applied navigation drawers for association components (Fig. 6). After defining the information architecture, Low-Fi wireframing [88], allowed us to test navigation and content flow. Next, we build our Hi-Fi prototype with web-based online tool [89] for heuristic evaluation [90].

Mobile Augmented Virtual Reality App Evaluation

Evaluation Apparatus and Test Procedure. We used a MacBook Pro Desktop for heuristic evaluation through walkthrough methodology. At start of the session, we introduced product concept and its underlying technology with visual and spoken information. Next, we presented three task scenarios to complete:

- Task 1 - *"You perceive a certain smell/taste in your environment. You want to label and share this experience on your location".*
- Task 2 - *"You want to find out more about this kind of smell/taste".*
- Task 3 - *"You would like to have a more participative attitude towards your environment. You want to know how to take action".*

Evaluation Method. We applied the first click testing method [91] and took notes of participants interaction behaviour. At the test conclusion we conducted a qualitative and quantitative study. We provided self-report questionnaires with Likert evaluation scale (5-point) and conducted semi-structured Interviews. We asked about system experience (navigation) and content experience (relevancy, satisfaction, usefulness). At last, we asked participants about environmental awareness impact.

Evaluation Results. Total of 16 participants, all recognized navigation targets easily. Relevancy evaluation of the experience design was high, as near all participants declared that their smell and taste awareness increased - smell group: 87,5% (7P); taste group: 100% (8P). Participants confirmed that the system enabled them to express chemical sense experiences - smell group: 75% (6P); taste group: 100% (8P). All participants enjoyed the content experience. They rated it as useful - smell group: 87,5% (7P); taste group: 100% (8P), and recommend it as an education tool - smell group: 100% (8P); taste group: 87,5% (7P). Finally, 87,5% (14P) confirmed that the chemical sense annotation system increased their environmental awareness.

Summary of Design Phase 2. In this section of our study, we explored the meaning and communication construction layer of our Multisensory HCI design process. Using digital media, we provided the contextualization of smell and taste experiences. We conceptualized and developed two design hypotheses for prototype evaluation: (i) MVR experience for educational purposes addressing remote environmental events and (ii) MAR experience consisting of enhancing a smell and taste annotation system with local environmental information. Evaluation of these design concepts was positively rated in terms of system, user and content experience. Furthermore, results revealed awareness increment about chemical senses and environmental challenges, after the prototype experience. Regarding our goal to know if by providing tools to acknowledge and communicate smell and taste experiences, people could make sense of environmental events and make informed choices, our results are encouraging.

4   Discussion

Two key factors influenced our experience design: the natural environmental setting and the situational context. We evoked the natural setting by presenting smells and tastes derived from the real world. Technology mediated the situational context by communicating the environmental setting. As environmental events are bounded to time and space of occurrences, MVR experience brought closer remote events, whereas the MAR experience evidenced local events. Our study design implied from the start participants engaged with smell and taste experiences, followed by the experiences with prototypes. The experiment sequence assumed that participants had to engage with their chemical sense perceptions before elaborating about their environmental meaning correspondence. We observed how participants showed surprise and curiosity while they progressed along the experiment path. As attribution choices were mandatory, they ended up discovering new perspectives about their sensorial experiences. When they engaged with the prototypes, participants were already imprinted with their previous chemical sense experience and thereby more available to construct meaning through the digital content experience. This strategy may have contributed to the overall positive results. Haverkamp stresses that "intuitive strategies based on cross-modal analogy, association and symbolism are suitable for creating a design that provides connections between the senses, which directly appear appropriate and easy to interpret" [53, p. 139] Nevertheless, to avoid misinterpretation it is prerequisite "that associative and symbolic contents are known to the user" [53, p. 139]. This cognitive association congruency has to be consistent along the design process, taking into account contextual factors. Regarding our design concepts, even if smell and chemical perceptions and associations did not rely on universal assumptions, participants of the study were able to uncover their connotations and message. In fact, we found that both digital media experiences increased their chemical sense and environmental awareness. Overall, the conceptual approach of linking smell and taste to environmental events was understood and highly supported as an innovative concept for environmental health communication. Our study results revealed that linking chemical senses with environmental health benefits environmental health communication strategies.

Verbeek states that interaction design is "designing relations between humans and the world, and, ultimately designing the character of the way in which we live our lives" [92, p. 31]. If we pretend to attain a more sustainable future, we have to design these desirable actions. Addressing chemical sense education first, to unfold its application possibilities could benefit Multisensory HCI design. By this means the foundations would be placed upon which its framework could expand.

Limitations. The main limitations of our testing were related to the early stage of the prototypes. Participants had high immersive expectations while testing our basic prototype demos, but they could not observe digital object blending with the physical world. This fact did not interfere with their prototype conceptual evaluation. However, it might influence scores like presence and satisfaction.

5   Conclusion and Future Work

In this paper, we provided a description and reflection about the design and evaluation of *Earthsensum*, a Multisensory HCI design project with smell and taste to inform the design of future interactive technologies in the context of environmental health communication. We wanted to know if providing exploration and annotation tools that capture smell and taste experiences, can be an enabler for individuals to make informed health choices. Our approach was based on the recognition that human health and well-being are intimately linked to the state of the environment and raising environmental knowledge capital within communities and citizens is crucial to foster pro-environmental behaviour.

This work explored the link between chemical senses and environmental problems, reflecting on the fact that human organism can be reached by environmental exposure vectors through air, food, soil and water conditions. We suggest that the chemical senses are fundamental to put in evidence these events. Trough breathing and ingestion, environmental pollutants enter imperceptibly into the human body triggering health issues. We formulated design hypothesis which addressed the design of (i) MVR experience for education on remote environmental events and (ii) MAR experience which combines annotation features of smell and taste with local environmental information. We believed that these design experiences would result in higher literacy about smell and taste perception and its connection with environmental health. Results of our study validated positively our conceptual approach and hypothesis assumptions. This work makes specific contributions. First, it provides guidelines on how to design with chemical senses for digital systems. Secondly, it adds new perspectives on environmental health communication strategies with Mobile Virtual Reality and Mobile Augmented Reality technologies, contributing to the role of HCI in the challenges of sustainability.

Future developments intend to develop the conceptual approach with more technical refined prototypes. We aim to explore further our chemical sense annotation system in terms of association possibilities and interaction modules for mixed and immersive media platforms. We also aim to test these systems on real locations where smell and taste experiences occur, instead of lab indoor environment. Our ultimate goal is to develop further our environmental health communication strategy with chemical senses, centred on behaviour change.

Acknowledgements. This Work is funded by Foundation for Science and Technology – grant FCT (SFRH/BD/52545/2014).

References

1. Finn, S., O'Fallon, L.: The emergence of environmental health literacy-from its roots to its future potential. Environ. Health Perspect. **125**(4), 495–501 (2017)
2. The National Environmental Health Association: Definitions of Environmental Health: National Environmental Health Association: NEHA. https://www.neha.org/about-neha/definitions-environmental-health. Accessed 02 Dec 2018
3. WHO: World Health Organization, Environmental health. https://www.who.int/phe/health_topics/en/. Accessed 20 Jan 2020
4. Crutzen, P.J.: The "Anthropocene". In: Ehlers, E., Krafft, T. (eds.) Earth System Science in the Anthropocene, pp. 13–18. Springer, Heidelberg (2006). https://doi.org/10.1007/3-540-26590-2_3
5. World Economic Forum: The global risks report 2020 (2020)
6. IPCC - SR15: Global warming of 1.5°C. Intergovernmental panel on climate change (2018). https://www.ipcc.ch/report/sr15/. Accessed 02 Dec 2018
7. World Health Organization: WHO: First WHO Global Conference on Air Pollution and Health, 30 October–1 November 2018. World Health Organization (2018)
8. Neira, M., Prüss-Üstün, A., Wolf, J., Corvalàn, C., Bos, R.: Preventing Disease Through Healthy Environments: A Global Assessment of the Burden of Disease from Environmental Risks, p. 147. World Health Organization (2016)
9. Meadows, D., Randers, J., Meadows, D.: Limits to Growth: The 30-Year Update. Earthscan Publications, London (2005)
10. United Nations Framework Convention: The Paris Agreement: UNFCCC (2018). https://unfccc.int/process-and-meetings/the-paris-agreement/the-paris-agreement. Accessed 28 Nov2018
11. European Environment Agency (EEA): The European Environment - State and Outlook 2020. Knowledge for Transition to a Sustainable Europe. Publications Office of the European Union, Luxembourg (2019)

460   P. Neves and A. Câmara

12. Executive Board: Health, environment and climate change: draft WHO global strategy on health, environment and climate change: the transformation needed to improve lives and well-being sustainably through healthy environments: report by the Director-General. World Health Organization (2018)
13. Landrigan, P.J., et al.: Health consequences of environmental exposures: changing global patterns of exposure and disease. Ann. Glob. Health **82**(1), 10–19 (2016)
14. World Health Organization: COP24 special report: health & climate change (2018)
15. Schiffman, S.S., Nagle, H.T.: Effect of environmental pollutants on taste and smell. Otolaryngol. Head Neck Surg. **106**(6), 693–700 (1992)
16. Lundström, J.N., Boesveldt, S., Albrecht, J.: Central processing of the chemical senses: an overview. ACS Chem. Neurosci. **2**(1), 5–16 (2011)
17. Delwiche, J.: Are there 'basic' tastes? Trends Food Sci. Technol. **7**(12), 411–415 (1996)
18. Auvray, M., Spence, C.: The multisensory perception of flavor. Conscious. Cogn. **17**(3), 1016–1031 (2008)
19. Spence, C.: Multisensory flavor perception. Cell **161**(1), 24–35 (2015)
20. World Health Organization: WHO: Public Health, Environmental and Social Determinants of Health. WHO (2019). https://www.who.int/phe/en/. Accessed 08 Oct 2019
21. Câmara, A.S.: Environmental Systems: A Multidimensional Approach. Oxford University Press, Oxford (2002)
22. Berners-Lee, T.: The original proposal of the WWW, HTMLized. CERN. https://www.w3.org/History/1989/proposal.html. Accessed 30 Jan 2020
23. NASA: Visualize Data: Earthdata. https://earthdata.nasa.gov/earth-observation-data/visualize-data. Accessed 24 Oct 2019
24. Keeling, C.D.: The keeling curve: a daily record of atmospheric carbon dioxide from Scripps Institution of Oceanography at UC San Diego. https://scripps.ucsd.edu/programs/keelingcurve/. Accessed 28 Nov 2018
25. Hsu, Y.-C., Cross, J., Dille, P., Nourbakhsh, I., Leiter, L., Grode, R.: Visualization tool for environmental sensing and public health data. In: Proceedings of the 19th International ACM SIGACCESS Conference on Computers and Accessibility - DIS 2018, pp. 99–104 (2018)
26. AirVisual: Air quality monitor and information you can trust. https://www.airvisual.com/. Accessed 30 Jan 2020
27. Henshaw, V., McLean, K., Medway, D., Perkins, C., Warnaby, G.: Designing with Smell: Practices, Techniques and Challenges, 1st edn. Routledge, New York (2017)
28. Obrist, M.: Mastering the senses in HCI: towards multisensory interfaces. In: Proceedings of CHI 2017, Cagliari, Italy, September 2017 (2017)
29. Obrist, M., Tuch, A.N., Hornbaek, K.: Opportunities for odor. In: Proceedings of the 32nd Annual ACM Conference on Human Factors in Computing Systems - CHI 2014, pp. 2843–2852 (2014)
30. Obrist, M., Comber, R., Subramanian, S., Piqueras-Fiszman, B., Velasco, C., Spence, C.: Temporal, affective, and embodied characteristics of taste experiences: a framework for design. In: Proceedings of the 32nd Annual ACM Conference on Human Factors in Computing Systems - CHI 2014, pp. 2853–2862 (2014)
31. Murer, M., Aslan, I., Tscheligi, M.: LOLLio - exploring taste as playful modality. In: TEI 2013 - Proceedings of the 7th International Conference on Tangible, Embedded and Embodied Interaction, pp. 299–302 (2013)
32. Kaye, J.N.: Symbolic olfactory display. Massachusetts Institute of Technology (2001)
33. This New App Wants to Be the iTunes of Smells: WIRED. https://www.wired.com/2015/04/ophone-onotes-itune-of-smell/. Accessed 06 Jan 2020
34. Ranasinghe, N., Do, E.Y.-L.: Digital lollipop: studying electrical stimulation on the human tongue to simulate taste sensations. ACM Trans. Multimed. Comput. Commun. Appl. **13**(1), 5:1–5:22 (2016)

35. Ranasinghe, N., Nguyen, T.N.T., Liangkun, Y., Lin, L.-Y., Tolley, D., Do, E.Y.-L.: Vocktail. In: Proceedings of the 2017 ACM on Multimedia Conference - MM 2017, pp. 1139–1147 (2017)

36. Vi, C.T., et al.: TastyFloats: a contactless food delivery system. In: Proceedings of the 2017 ACM International Conference on Interactive Surfaces and Spaces, ISS 2017, pp. 161–170 (2017)

37. Spence, C.: Crossmodal correspondences: a tutorial review. Atten. Percept. Psychophys. **73**(4), 971–995 (2011). https://doi.org/10.3758/s13414-010-0073-7

38. Parise, C.V.: Crossmodal correspondences: standing issues and experimental guidelines. Multisensory Res. **29**(1–3), 7–28 (2016)

39. Narumi, T.: Multi-sensorial virtual reality and augmented human food interaction. In: Proceedings of the 1st Workshop on Multi-Sensorial Approaches to Human-Food Interaction - MHFI 2016, pp. 1–6 (2016)

40. Hashimoto, Y., et al.: Straw-like user interface. In: Proceedings of the 2006 ACM SIGCHI International Conference on Advances in Computer Entertainment Technology - ACE 2006, p. 50 (2006)

41. Dmitrenko, D., Maggioni, E., Vi, C.T., Obrist, M.: What did i sniff? Mapping scents onto driving-related messages. In: 9th ACM International Conference on Automotive User Interfaces and Interactive Vehicular Applications (AutomotiveUI 2017), pp. 154–163 (2017)

42. Spence, C., Obrist, M., Velasco, C., Ranasinghe, N.: Digitizing the chemical senses: possibilities & pitfalls. Int. J. Hum Comput Stud. **107**, 62–74 (2017)

43. DiSalvo, C., Sengers, P., Brynjarsdóttir, H.: Mapping the landscape of sustainable HCI. In: 2010 Proceedings of the Conference on Human Factors in Computing Systems, vol. 3, pp. 1975–1984 (2010)

44. Hsu, Y.-C., et al.: Smell pittsburgh, pp. 65–79, January 2019

45. United Nations Climate Change Summit. Actnow.Bot - take climate action (2018)

46. Heywood, I.: Sensory Arts and Design, 1st edn. Bloomsbury Academic (2017)

47. Pinsky, M.: Pollution pods (2018). http://www.michaelpinsky.com/project/pollution-pods/. Accessed 06 Dec 2018

48. GhostFood: Miriam songster. https://songster.net/projects/ghostfood/. Accessed 29 Jan 2020

49. Talking nose. http://www.ediblegeography.com/talking-nose/. Accessed 29 Jan 2020

50. Oxman, N.: Age of entanglement. J. Des. Sci. (2016). MIT Media Lab, MIT Press. https://doi.org/10.21428/7e0583ad, https://jods.mitpress.mit.edu/pub/ageofentanglement. Accessed 23 Nov 2018

51. Zimmerman, J., Forlizzi, J., Evenson, S.: Research through design as a method for interaction design research in HCI. In: Proceedings of the SIGCHI Conference on Human Factors in Computing Systems - CHI 2007, pp. 493–502 (2007)

52. Bang, A., Krogh, P., Ludvigsen, M., Markussen, T.: The role of hypothesis in constructive design research. In: Proceedings of the Art of Research Conference IV (2012)

53. Haverkamp, M.: Synesthetic Design: Handbook for a Multi-Sensory Approach. Birkhäuser Verlag, Basel (2012)

54. IQAir AirVisual: World most polluted cities in 2018 - PM2.5 ranking (2019). https://www.airvisual.com/world-most-polluted-cities. Accessed 08 Oct 2019

55. Simoes, A.: OEC: the observatory of economic complexity. https://oec.world/en/. Accessed 07 Oct 2019

56. Club of Rome: the club of Rome climate emergency plan (2019). https://www.clubofrome.org/project/the-club-of-rome-climate-emergency-plan/. Accessed 08 Oct 2019

57. Akenji, L., Lettenmeier, M., Koide, R., Toivio, V., Aryanie, A.: 1.5 degree lifestyles. Aalto University (2019)

58. Spence, C., et al.: On tasty colours and colourful tastes? Assessing, explaining, and utilizing crossmodal correspondences between colours and basic tastes. Flavour **4**(1), 23 (2015)

59. Rouby, C.: Olfaction, Taste, and Cognition. Cambridge University Press, Cambridge (2002)
60. Kaeppler, K., Mueller, F.: Odor classification: a review of factors influencing perception-based odor arrangements. Chem. Senses **38**(3), 189–209 (2013)
61. McLean, K.: Comparative smell vocabularies (2016). https://sensorymaps.com/portfolio/comparative-smell-vocabularies/
62. Quercia, D., Aiello, L.M., Schifanella, R.: The emotional and chromatic layers of urban smells, May 2016
63. Suffet, I.H., Rosenfeld, P.: The anatomy of odour wheels for odours of drinking water, wastewater, compost and the urban environment. Water Sci. Technol. **55**(5), 335–344 (2007)
64. World Food and Wine: Describing taste and flavor. https://world-food-and-wine.com/describing-food. Accessed 23 July 2019
65. Köhler, W.: Gestalt Psychology. Liveright, Oxford (1929)
66. Larson, C.L., Aronoff, J., Steuer, E.L.: Simple geometric shapes are implicitly associated with affective value. Motiv. Emot. **36**(3), 404–413 (2012). https://doi.org/10.1007/s11031-011-9249-2
67. Atkin, A.: Peirce's Theory of Signs, Summer 201. Metaphysics Research Lab, Stanford University (2013)
68. Munari, B.: Bruno Munari: Circle, Square, Triangle, 1st edn. Princeton Architectural Press, New York (2015)
69. Plutchik, R.: The nature of emotions: human emotions have deep evolutionary roots, a fact that may explain their complexity and provide tools for clinical practice. Am. Sci. **89**, 344–350 (2001)
70. Arnheim, R.: Art and Visual Perception: A Psychology of the Creative Eye, 2nd edn. University of California Press, Berkerley (2004)
71. Buxton, B.: Sketching User Experiences - Getting the Design Right and the Right Design. Morgan Kaufmann Publishers (2007)
72. Bradley, M.M., Lang, P.J.: Measuring emotion: the self-assessment manikin and the semantic differential. J. Behav. Ther. Exp. Psychiatry **25**(1), 49–59 (1994)
73. Orlita, T.: Online viewer for street view. https://mapio.app/CGiD1-c4hdAno5GjKVxnTg. Accessed 10 Aug 2019
74. SoundSnap: Soundsnap sound library. https://www.soundsnap.com/. Accessed 10 Aug 2019
75. SoundBible: Free sound clips. SoundBible.com. http://soundbible.com/. Accessed 10 Aug 2019
76. TurboSquid: 3D models for professionals. TurboSquid. https://www.turbosquid.com/. Accessed 10 Aug 2019
77. Jerald, J.: The VR Book: Human-Centered Design for Virtual Reality. Association for Computing Machinery and Morgan & Claypool (2015)
78. GoPro: GoPro official website - capture + share your world - GoPro VR player 2.0. https://gopro.com/en/us/news/gopro-vr-player-2-now-available. Accessed 09 Aug 2019
79. Unity3D. https://unity3d.com/unity
80. Van den Broeck, M., Kawsar, F., Schöning, J.: It's all around you. In: Proceedings of the 2017 ACM on Multimedia Conference - MM 2017, pp. 762–768 (2017)
81. Sutcliffe, A.G., Kaur, K.D.: Evaluating the usability of virtual reality user interfaces. Behav. Inf. Technol. **19**(6), 415–426 (2000)
82. Witmer, B.G., Singer, M.J.: Measuring presence in virtual environments: a presence questionnaire. Presence Teleoperators Virtual Environ. **7**(3), 225–240 (1998)
83. European Environment Agency (EEA): European air quality index. European Environment Agency. https://www.eea.europa.eu/themes/air/air-quality-index/index. Accessed 04 Oct 2019
84. Yale University: Environmental performance index (2019). https://epi.envirocenter.yale.edu/. Accessed 04 Oct 2019

85. World's air pollution: Real-time air quality index. https://waqi.info/. Accessed 04 Oct 2019
86. Dünser, A., Grasset, R., Seichter, H., Billinghurst, M.: Applying HCI principles to AR systems design. In: Mixed Reality User Interfaces: Specification, Authoring, Adaptation (MRUI 2007: 2nd International Workshop at the IEEE Virtual Reality 2007 Conference), pp. 37–42 (2007)
87. Shneiderman, B.: The eight golden rules of interface design. University of Maryland. https://www.cs.umd.edu/~ben/goldenrules.html. Accessed 13 Aug 2019
88. Balsamiq. https://balsamiq.com. Accessed 21 July 2019
89. Figma. https://www.figma.com/. Accessed 21 July 2019
90. Nielson, J.: 10 usability heuristics for user interface design. Nielson Norman Group (1994). https://www.nngroup.com/articles/ten-usability-heuristics/. Accessed 13 Aug 2019
91. Nielson, J.: Usability testing for mobile. Nielson Norman Group (2014). https://www.nngroup.com/articles/mobile-usability-testing/. Accessed 13 Aug 2019
92. Verbeek, P.P.: Cover story: beyond interaction: a short introduction to mediation theory. Interactions **22**(3), 26–31 (2015)

Designing Palpable Data Representations

Jessica J. Rajko[✉]

Wayne State University, Detroit, MI 48202, USA
jessicarajko@wayne.edu

Abstract. This paper discusses a multisensory approach to data representation with a specific focus on haptic media. In this, I provide a philosophical and methodological overview of my design process informed by the following themes and topics: 1) the haptic subject; 2) touch as political; 3) co-formed knowledge; and 4) arts-based research methods. The overview is further contextualized by a thorough analysis of collaborative work *Vibrant Lives*, a 4-year project that includes a suite of unique, custom-designed, vibrotactile interfaces that give audiences a real-time experience of their own personal data output. I continue my analysis by sharing observations from a series of workshops I conducted with haptified archive data. In conclusion, I reflect on issues of user ethics, agency, and control when designing touch-based experiences of data in a multisensory installation setting.

Keywords: Haptics · Data representation · Ethical design · Arts-based design

1 Introduction

Multisensory data representation is a complex and complicated endeavor, in part because of our extensive use of data *visualization.* Given the use of visual media in data creation and collection, the dominance of data visualization may come as no surprise. This form of data representation is pervasive to the point that imagining data outside of a predominantly visual context to many may be an interesting artistic exploration in *aesthetics,* rather than a deep inquiry into the politics of information and interface. However, new research into the possibilities of data sonification (auditory data representation) [1] and more recently data haptification (tactile data representation) [2] have seen a dramatic increase in the last two decades. Furthermore, efforts to sonify and haptify data thoughtfully weave aesthetic exploration into transdisciplinary research approaches that investigate important questions of what it means to understand, witness, and be in relation with data. Questions such as: How are we creating stories about our world through the use of data? What stories are best told in a multisensory context? How can multisensory data representations impact users' data understanding and experience? The goal here is not to argue for a reworking of sensorial priority, nor is it to claim that tactile or auditory representations must be researched in isolation from vision to 'catch up' with visualization research. The aim is instead to consider how we might begin to understand our other senses' role in building data representations that allow us to interface with data's affective and cultural contexts. Given that we experience our world through all our senses, I am more interested in creating work that thoughtfully includes touch and sound within a multisensory framework. To do this I employ collaborative practices within an arts-based research approach to better understand how we work with touch and sound as compositional tools. Furthermore, I encourage approaches that build frameworks for understanding touch and sound without reducing them to a set of standards or best practices.

In this paper I will discuss my philosophy and approach to designing multisensory data representations and interfaces with a specific focus on haptic media. This discussion extends my research in embodied practices for interaction design [3] and non-taxonomic methods for designing touch [4]. The broader philosophical discussion articulated throughout this paper will be augmented with design examples from my work *Vibrant Lives*, a collaboratively designed haptic/sonic infrastructure that gives people a real time sense of how much data they output from their personal mobile devices [5]. Methods cultivated in *Vibrant Lives* extend into my current research designing multisensory data representations of archival data with a focus on haptic aesthetics. In this paper, I discuss novel methods for representing large, complex datasets in multisensory formats that are both immersive and legible.

2 Transdisciplinary Approaches to Sensory Research

Comprehending the complex web of haptics research requires a broad understanding of the practices, trends, politics, and ethical dilemmas manifested by engaging haptics as an area of study, particularly within user experience. This is in no small part because we are in a time where how we create haptic media determines the processes and protocols we will effectively use to define the field. In my work, I address problems with designing haptic interfaces that reinforce sensory isolation, efficiency, utilitarianism, knowledge acquisition, and bodily control. Whether or not these are the explicit design intentions, it's worth articulating that such priorities are embedded in the cultural and methodological fabric of many contemporary user design processes, particularly those with empirical roots and aspirations toward adoption by industry. As such, the following section discusses tensions between scientific sensory research methods and haptic design. Furthermore, I highlight a growing body of haptics research that extends beyond empirical design methods into the areas of media studies, digital music, dance and movement practices, philosophy, and sociology to name a few. The purpose here is to highlight some key issues and topics that inform my own work in multisensory data representation design, including the following: 1) the haptic subject; 2) touch as political; 3) co-formed knowledge; and 4) arts-based research methods.

2.1 The Haptic Subject

The transformation of touch into a conscious target of empirical study and computational mediation lead to the emergence of what Parisi calls the *haptic subject*.

> This haptic subject embodies the self-conscious efforts of scientists, engineers, and marketers made to transform touch, as they sought to give tactility a new utility

in a political economy of sensations vital to a society with a growing dependency on the circulation of information through sensing bodies [6, p. 4].

The haptic subject is marked by a need to control, reproduce, and commodify touch as a concept or even *object* that can live outside of the subjective lens of any one person, community, culture, or society. To do this, researchers aspire to transform touch into an acultural commodity that can be controlled by scientific methods and tools. Efforts to simplify or standardize touch are pursued so that findings may be shared and reproduced; however, such efforts also pressure users to normalize their touch experience to that which can be defined within the scientific parameters bound to the haptic subject. Furthermore, as Classen points out, attempts by science to define touch speaks more to the culture of science than to any possible standard features of touch. [7, p. 4] Research working toward the haptic subject is often articulated as a necessary response to participating in contemporary society as it relates to validation, valuation, and access to monies and resources. Returning again to Parisi, he discusses the technologizing of touch as including the following interrelated developments:

> [...] the institutionalized and formalized knowledge production networks that rose up around touch, the new intellectual and financial resources funneled into the study of touch, the training and regimentation of tactility demanded by the new machines, and the motivations – explicit and implicit – of the various researchers who set themselves to work at the immense challenge of bringing touch under the control of scientific and technical apparatuses [6, p. 10].

The collective scientific hopes for a haptic subject speaks to a yearning for touch research to be validated within the constructs of empirical epistemology, which has very specific assumptions about how knowledge and information should be organized and handled as a utility largely decoupled from personal, subjective, cultural, and communal readings of touch experience.

2.2 Touch as Political

The decoupling of touch from its connection to lived experience is what Erin Manning describes as a process of normalization in which bodies become "stabilized within national imaginaries in preordained categories". [8, p. xv] Politics are often affiliated with the workings of governments, but the term "politics" can also be used to describe decision-making and enforced organizational control over a group of members. Considering touch within a dialogue of politics, Manning points to the inherent political nature of engaging and mediating touch as a static, finite object or thing. In this, the haptic subject props up the politically organized, collective consciousness of science–prioritizing that which can be rendered visible, logical, quantifiable, and categorizable. Conversely, that which eludes, evades, or escapes the bounds of the haptic subject is rendered unnecessary, invaluable, irrelevant, and even problematic. This not only includes physiological experiences of touch, but subjective and cultural understandings of touch that do not fit within the empirical framework and related political imaginary of the haptic subject. Normalizing here is also considered a form of policing, not only of our sense of touch, but of what bodies are, can be, and should do. How we choose to ask users to physically engage with an interface expresses our own beliefs about how bodies should act and behave.

Further complicating the politics of mediated touch is how haptic technologies are appropriated across fields and design practices. Haptic technologies such as tactile transducers and force feedback devices are often adopted by designers working outside the device's originally intended application. Teoma Naccarato and John MacCallum discuss the ethical dilemmas posed when appropriating technologies in their work with biomedical sensors [9]. Their paper investigates the "ethical and aesthetic implications of the appropriation of biomedical sensors in artistic practice" and discusses the pitfalls of appropriating any form of technology from one field for use in another [p. 1]. Their work highlights the importance of acknowledging that the transition of a technology outside its intended domain is not only an appropriation of technologies and their functional uses, but also an appropriation of cultural practices specific to the original discipline in which it was used. This cultural appropriation happens whether we recognize it or not, and can result in a wide array of consequences, some of which deeply impact user experience. Here, they suggest adopting a *critical appropriation*:

> Critical appropriation involves the process of intentionally and explicitly deconstructing the ontology of technologies in order to rebuild them with and through a value system shared by all participants in the collaboration [p. 6].

Building new interface designs means that we are not only responsible for our own design intentions, but we must also be aware of how we are introducing the design goals of those who made the technologies we use. While Naccarato and MacCallum do not explicitly talk about the haptic subject, they observe a similar socio-political transition in how biosensors are being used within the design process that reinforce a need to control and police the bodies observed. In their observations, the results can be deeply impactful for those whose bodies do not conform to normalized interaction settings, as is seen in this example from their paper:

> As Tom improvised with the particular movement patterns and qualities available in his body, the software had trouble tracking his gestures, and as such, kept losing him. The choreographer repeatedly asked Tom to "just stand still", so that the tracking system could calibrate his skeleton. It was not possible for Tom to "just stand still". Jokingly, but perhaps also with a hint of frustration, the choreographer said to Tom "you broke my system". Because Tom's particular movements did not conform to the expectations of the software (as preset by the human designers), his body was literally invisible to the tracking system. Despite the choreographer's desire to market his motion-tracking system for people with disabilities, he created a program that was very limited in its capacity to process—never mind embrace—bodily differences [p. 5].

2.3 Co-formed Knowledge

Knowledge is co-formed in the relationship between those in the exchange. One does not inform the other. One is not static while the other transforms. Both transform and become new. Returning to Manning, she writes, "I accept this paradox and offer *Politics of Touch* not as a reading of what touch is, but as an exploration of what might happen if we are willing to direct our thinking toward movement, toward a relational stance that makes it impossible to pin down knowledge but asks us instead to invent". [8, p. xvi] What does it mean to design a user experience from this perspective? For me, it means the following: 1) creating experiences that acknowledge the mutually transformative act of exchanging touch and its vast impact on a shared experience between users and interface; 2) designing tactile interfaces as an invitation to co-create meaning; and 3) engaging the design process as an act of facilitation rather than as a series of commands. It is impossible to fully control, impact, manipulate, or know the outcome of a mediated touch experience. In explicitly naming its impossibility, I recognize I am not stating something novel. Rather, I name the futility of controlling touch to emphasize that to design with the intention of inciting control is not only futile, but potentially an act of violence.

Susan Kozel highlights the potential for violence in her thoughtful reflection on performing in Paul Sermon's installation work, *Telematic Dreaming* [10]. In this installation performance, two separate rooms with beds were projected upon each other using livestream camera feeds. Kozel performed on one bed and audiences were invited to interact with her on the other bed so that each body was projected onto the other space. [p. 439] While the interactions between Kozel and audience members were digital, she describes the physical responses she had to various forms of digital touch including pain when being virtually punched, sexual intimacy when digitally caressed, and the threat of violence when virtually accosted with a knife. Kozel's work demonstrates a very clear co-formed techno-mediated exchange between herself and other. Similarly, I suggest that touch experiences between users and digital interfaces can elicit similar visceral, physical responses.

2.4   Arts-Based Research Methods

Artists and artistic methods have been longtime contributors to design methodology. More specifically, somatics and first-person, arts-based research methods are widely engaged within cognitive science and human computer interaction to augment the rise in embodiment research within these fields [11]. Contributing to this, artists have engaged haptics within various contexts. Musician Lauren Hayes designs haptic interfaces that explore haptic/acoustic relationships that extend beyond a simple reinforcement of touch as an extension of sound [12, 13]. Her work is informed by musicians such as Eric Gunther and Sile O'Modhrain [14], and Kaffe Mathews and Lynn Pook [15] who similarly explore haptic aesthetics in relation to sound and music. Within dance and somatic practices Susan Kozel [16] and Thecla Schiphorst [17] explore first-person design approaches to haptic media in performative wearable technology design. When creating her work *soft(n)* Schiphorst explored a "somaesthetics of touch" to investigate a *poetic* approach to touch design supported by somatic practices and first-person arts-based research approaches in designing mediated touch experiences.

A poetics of interaction supports a somaesthetics framework because it acknowledges that meaning is simultaneously constructed on multiple levels: conceptual, experiential, material, and computational (or technological). Meaning derives from our experience and the imaginative interplay between our self and our environment [18, p. 2432].

Arts-based approaches to design, particularly those informed by self-study, first-person methods, and somatic practices by their very nature resist the *haptic subject.* By integrating personal experience into the design process, subjective human experience becomes entangled with the resulting design. This work is not without structure or repeatable methods, rather it focuses on methods for facilitating shared exploration and reflection through the use of workshops, open questions, dialogue, and iterative refinement. For example, when creating *whisper[s]* Schiphorst held a series of workshops that focused on various sensory experiences such as hearing one's own body or making physical contact with another participant [19]. The purpose here, "was to explore how people pay attention to their own body states and share those states with others in a space [19, p. 226]." Users were asked to improvise and interact with various props and objects and then respond to open-ended questions such as, "What did it feel like?" [19, p. 227] Similarly, Loke and Khut engaged workshop participants in activities specifically informed by the somatic practice Feldenkrais and used this work to create design workshops in which people somatically explored interactive systems [20]. Building from these somatically-informed, arts-based design methods, my own work engages in various models of facilitated exploration, reflection, and discussion – all of which influences the resulting design choices.

2.5 Moving Toward Multisensory Data Representation

I envision my work as an ongoing effort to refine a process of design inquiry, rather formalize a specific haptic infrastructure. The results of which are not standardized systems, but a stronger protocol for designing faciliatory touch experiences between users and data. In my design process, I consider many aspects of touch, not only including the vibrotactile actuators themselves, but also the material, shape, and texture of the interface and the user's physical action of approaching the interface. My interest in bringing touch into the domain of data representation is twofold. Firstly, I am interested in haptic aesthetics that are not explicitly concerned with replicating real-world touch experiences, which is a common feature of contemporary haptic design [21]. Secondly, I wish to explore the potential for haptic data representations that make the cultural contexts, stories, and people embedded within the data more intimate, palpable, and emotionally resonant to users. This second point amplifies the import of engaging haptics outside of the *haptic subject* and recognizing the power of touch politics. In my case, I see the intimate, personal, cultural, and political resonances of touch as an asset to my work, rather than a hinderance.

3 Vibrant Lives

My research began with a 4-year exploration of haptic data through the project *Vibrant Lives,* which includes a suite of unique, custom-designed, vibrotactile interfaces that give audiences a real-time experience of their own personal data output [5]. The project was constructed through a series of intimate workshops and unique performance installations, conducted with my core collaborators Jaqueline Wernimont and Eileen Standley. User interfaces include wearable devices, hanging tapestries, and large sculptures that engage audiences in personal data output (see Fig. 1).

Over the course of four years, *Vibrant Lives* evolved into multiple, unique installations that offer various bodily, spatial, auditory, material, and social relationships between people, interface, and data. Across all iterations, we used a software/hardware system specifically designed for the project that reinterprets people's mobile phone data output as auditory and vibrotactile feedback. Simply described, as users produce more data through their mobile phone activities the sound volume and vibrotactile sensation increases. Conversely, when their activities produce let data output, the sound and sensation decrease. The custom system includes vibrotactile actuators, a sound-producing smartphone app, and custom server software. Together, our haptic infrastructure allows people to feel and hear their data output in real time. (see Fig. 2) A detailed description of the technical infrastructure is discussed in a previous publication [5]. Throughout the design of *Vibrant Lives*, I conducted several individual and collaborative workshops exploring haptic aesthetics and data representation, including workshops at the following events and locations:

- ACM Tangible, Embedded and Embodied Interaction Conference, March 2019.
- Dance Program at Davidson College, February 2018.
- Alliance of Women in Media Arts and Technology Conference, February 2018.
- ART Lab at University of New Mexico, November 2017.
- Synthesis Center at Arizona State University, November 2016.
- Signal/Noise: FemTechNet Conference on Feminist Pedagogy, Technology, & Transdisciplinarity, April 2016.

The haptic workshops served as an open forum for user exploration, discussion, and participant documentation and observation.

3.1 Initial User Study

Conceptually grounding *Vibrant Lives* was a question of how to give users a very real sense of the massive amounts of data their mobile devices output in a given moment. Also embedded within our line of inquiry was a critical investigation of how and why companies and governments find user data acquisition to be a useful and necessary activity. Given the gravity of a discussion about personal data acquisition, we knew we were asking people to move into a space of possible discomfort and unease. Our first user study included guided discussions about the initial interface design [5]. Once users connected to our wireless network and opened the custom mobile phone app, I asked them to set aside their phones as I led them through a series of verbal prompts meant to heighten their sensory and spatial awareness using proprioceptive, kinesthetic, and cutaneous cues [22]. After I completed verbal prompts, users returned to their phones, ran the app in the background, and experienced the feeling of data output via the portable/wearable tactile transducer. The app ran in the background as they conducted various mobile phone activities. During and after user exploration, I asked the following questions:

- As you navigate, what do you notice?
- What stands out to you?
- What do you feel (from the device) and how does that make you feel?
- What thoughts come to mind?
- How does this inform you/make you feel about your own data output?
- How does this experience inform you/make you feel about your mobile phone?
- What does this make you want to do (if anything)?
- What part of this experience was the most impactful for you?
- What will you take away from this experience?

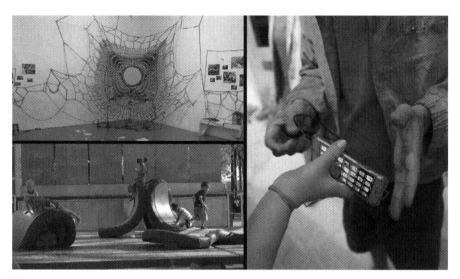

Fig. 1. The images represent the various interfaces created for *Vibrant Lives*. The top-left image shows the hanging crocheted tapestry, the bottom-left image is of three wood/fabric sculptures, and the right image is of the portable/wearable tactile transducer users connected to their mobile phone.

User responses were permeated with sadness, frustration, confusion, surprise, and curiosity as to who is gathering their data, how, and why. A full overview of the study is

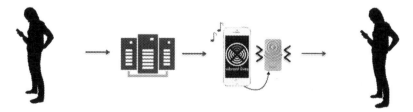

Fig. 2. This image shows the system used for all iterations of *Vibrant Lives*. Users connect to our custom server via our wireless network. Their data output is then captured and sent back to their mobile device using our mobile phone application. The mobile phone application creates a data sonification, which is transformed into vibrotactile stimulation using the tactile transducer.

available in an earlier publication [5]; however, I highlight this work because it greatly impacted how we moved forward with our various installation designs. We thought deeply about what it meant to foster environments of curiosity and compassion rather than spaces that reinforced the themes of surveillance and governmental monitoring so easily elicited by the project. This is where visual elements became critical. We integrated bright colors, playful, improvisatory dance performances, and surprising use of other tangible media such as torn paper, dust, and household objects to reinforce our conceptual themes without reinforcing the negative and oppressive undertones of the tactile infrastructure. The visual elements that augmented our haptic infrastructure were devised during movement workshops involving various contributors that flowed in and out of the project.

During the first movement workshop we brought in a group of dancers to engage with cyber security experts and digital humanists. We discussed packet sniffing and packet capture software uses, devised various physical gestures and choreographies, and composed touch-based exercises that elicited the characteristics and behaviors of various data acquisition protocols. This process created a suite of rich, mutually understood physical, tactile, and visual metaphors we then used to anchor the performative and visual elements. This process helped us create interactions that avoided some of the common sociocultural affiliations with vibrotactile interfaces, such as relaxation or erotic pleasure. To see video of the performative elements of the work, visit the online video documentation [23].We also learned the importance of including performers whose job was to "host the space" by verbally and nonverbally inviting users to touch and physically interact with the haptic data infrastructures. This helped users drop into the experience and consciously focus on their own touch experience with the haptified data.

3.2   Sculptures and Shared Data Experiences

The first public exhibition of *Vibrant Lives* invited users to feel their personal data output by holding or wearing a tactile transducer while navigating a multi-room installation. The exhibition was in conjunction with a dance concert at Arizona State University, and the *Vibrant Lives* audience was mostly comprised of concertgoers. During the exhibition, we noticed that while users were able to navigate the installation together, the solitary nature of the wearable/portable haptic interface kept people from interacting. (see Fig. 1). This created a quiet space in which individual people were absorbed in their own experience. We would see and hear people talk to each other at times, but only on occasion or with prompting. Also, several users shared their discomfort with having the mobile phone app on their phone when exiting the exhibition. All audience members were assured that the *Vibrant Lives* project was not saving any of the data captured through the custom server, but our assurances did not assuage the visceral experience of feeling one's own data output. The act of having to download and use the mobile app on a personal device was its own act of political touch. We learned from the first installation that this performative gesture of touch was incredibly powerful, prompting users to uninstall the app quickly after navigating the installation. We decided to make the mobile app a unique feature of the first installation. In later iterations, the project's software/hardware infrastructure stayed relatively the same; however, we transitioned from engaging individual data to working with the collective data output of every device connected to our custom sever.

The group data vibrated larger objects that could be touched by multiple people. This includes a series of large sculptures and tapestries that allow for a shared experience of data output. The transition from individual to collective data haptification meant users did not need to download the mobile phone app, only connect to our server network. Logistically, removing the additional mobile phone app step made it easier for users to move in and out of the installation experience.

Vibrant Lives: Data Play. The second iteration of *Vibrant Lives* included a suite of three wood sculptures upon which we attached large bass shakers called ButtKickers. (see Fig. 3) We worked with artist Bobby Zokaites to design and construct the sculptures, which were exhibited at large, family-friendly festivals and outdoor events. The sculptural nature of *Vibrant Lives: Data Play* allowed for multiple users to sit, stand, and lie on the same structure. This collective experience meant people could co-witness haptic data output and more easily dialogue about their shared experience. We often saw families sit together and collaborate to discover different methods for interacting with the installation. The soft, curvy design of the sculptures also invited a playful interaction that offered many possibilities of physical contact with various bodily surfaces. We intentionally created shapes that leveraged a cultural familiarity with benches, ottomans, and chairs without offering obvious, flat surfaces. The precarity of this design choice hinted at the possibility of sitting but invited other possibilities, which many users explored. Some of the activities we saw were rolling, sliding, lying down, and climbing.

Fig. 3. The left images show the ButtKickers attached inside the sculptures. The right images show users collectively and individually engaging with the completed interfaces.

Additionally, our reference to a socially familiar object meant that people would often happen upon the haptics themselves, sitting down and then expressing surprise when they felt sculptures vibrate. Many users expressed subtle joy in discovering the dynamic haptic feature of the sculptures, which prompted them to seek out information about the sculptures' intent. We always kept an installation host on hand to answer questions, but users would most often find each other and willingly share their knowledge about how the installation worked. The opportunity for self-discovery and collective knowledge sharing across users were strong attributes of *Vibrant Lives: Data Play*; however, the sculptures also quickly became jungle gyms for family audiences – particularly when the installation saw large waves of people. In these moments, the busy activity of the space decreased the likelihood that people would spend time with the haptic data.

From our conversations with users, we learned that people were fascinated by the conversation of data output and surprised by the haptic representation of personal data. Users most often expressed a sense of excitement, enthusiasm, and play. Overall, the affective response to *Vibrant Lives: Data Play* was much more positive and joyful than the first installation. User response was fostered by the ease in which they happened upon a collective experience of the data, which allowed for users to maintain a sense of agency in their own experience and discovery process. The affective user response is also due to the event environment. Users were often with other family and friends enjoying an outdoor festival. This was a very different environment than the initial installation, which was an indoor exhibition connected to a contemporary modern dance concert. Finally, users were able to come and go from the installation without downloading the mobile app, which avoided some of the concerned response we received from earlier users.

Vibrant Lives: The Living Net. Our final iteration was *Vibrant Lives: The Living Net*, which involved a vertically hung crocheted tapestry visually designed to look like a generic data visualization. (see Fig. 4). Tactile transducers were crocheted into the nylon cord, which transmitted vibration across the tapestry. Our goal with the installation was to create a piece that could grow and evolve over the duration of an exhibition. During exhibitions, I continued to crochet the net across various objects and surfaces in the space, increasing its size and reach. (see Fig. 4). This performative element served two purposes. First, it enlivened the haptic interface by giving it sense of growth and spread, which reinforced previous user observations about the pervasive, creeping nature of their own data. Second, it allowed me to be nearby as the installation host without idly standing and waiting for people to ask questions. Users appeared to be comfortable with my presence, even though the installation was mostly preformed in quiet gallery-like spaces. In our first performance of *Vibrant Lives: The Living Net*, I invited dance performers to improvise and transform the space by moving and reshaping objects. This prompted users to also rearrange and transform the space. In later iterations, we invited users to leave personal objects behind and annotate their contribution on a tag. We would crochet the objects into the net, essentially leaving visual traces of those who touched the installation. (see Fig. 4).

The flat, two-dimensional nature of the net combined with the personal objects meant people most often assumed the piece was meant to be a visual sculpture until invited to touch or lean upon it. These moments of host invitation resulted in many rich discussions, but also impacted the sense of personal agency to create one's own touch experience. Users often referred to me as the host for the "correct" way to experience the work, ultimately predefining the interaction. This was something we were seeking to avoid in our design process. To help users discover the haptic elements, we used

Fig. 4. The top-left image shows the net after being crocheted across the room during live performance. The bottom-left image shows the tactile transducer crocheted into the net. The right images show users' personal objects crocheted into the net.

speakers to amplify the data sonification that drove the tactile transducers. The sound was very effective in inviting users to touch the tapestry for much longer than when it was not present. I also noticed that the reinforced sound amplified the haptic experience. When the sound would increase, users would perform visceral responses through facial expressions of surprise, a deep inhalation, and/or a slight postural receding from the installation. Conversely, as sound volume decreased, users would soften in their stance, at times leaning toward the installation.

3.3 Haptifying Data Archives

The initial work with *Vibrant Lives* provided many rich, multilayered experiences from which to consider haptic design. As described in Sect. 2, data haptification is a relatively new concept. Since people are generally accustomed to looking at data, there is a nuance to providing enough context so that people can settle into a haptic data experience without providing so much information that people don't feel the need to touch data to feel satisfied with their own understanding of how it works. We found that if a haptic data experience was over explained, either by an installation host or accompanying signage, people were less likely to physically engage with the work. Also, what initial information we provide and how we provide it drastically impacts user experiences. Fortunately, in the case of *Vibrant Lives* the relationship between personal data and haptic sensation was tightly coupled to users' physical interactions with their own mobile devices. Meaning, when people engage with their mobile devices and simultaneously feel vibration, there is a very clear pairing of the user's physical gesture and the haptic output. It is worth noting here that sculpture installations still required users to use connect their mobile device to our network to generate data output. While the haptified data was a sum of all mobile data moving through our custom server, users were often still able to feel their individual spikes in activity. We learned about the power of this implicit gesture/haptic pairing when we began working with archival datasets.

In the case of archival data, the data is still about people and human activity, but it is not directly connected to user activity. The separation of data from the physical gesture of a user adds another layer of complexity and requires a more thorough investigation of how we contextualize the haptic/data relationship through a multisensory experience.

3.4 Haptic Archive Workshops

I have conducted a few small experiments with archival datasets along with my collaborators Jaqueline Wernimont and Eileen Standley. We used various sonified archival datasets to resonate tactile transducers connected to unique materials and objects. (see Table 1). None of the installations were visually encoded with explicit details about the dataset parameters used to create haptic feedback. As such, users typically needed a thorough verbal overview of the dataset parameters before they could drop into the haptic experience. In this, we were compelled to verbally describe how the data was rendered over time, much like describing a graph. Once users had an understanding of the data, they could experience it in haptic form. However, for several users, the simple verbal description of the data itself was enough to satisfy their curiosity. As a result, some users would spend little time with the haptic data before moving onto the next installation. This was particularly true for installations in which the structure, texture, and gesture toward the haptified object did not elicit any strong metaphors for how the data should be understood.

Table 1. Dataset/object pairings.

Title	Dataset	Haptified object
The Sandbox	Global Warming data	plastic bin with play sand
The Balls	Eugenic Rubicon data	white beachballs
The Braid	Iraq War Body Count data	hand braided cotton rope
The Skirt	Vibrant Lives real-time data	women's hoop skirt

The most compelling objects were the white beachballs and the sandbox. The white, inflated beachballs resonated with data from the Eugenic Rubicon project, which represents the over 20,000 voluntary and forced sterilization recommendation records from the state of California from 1920–1960 [24]. Most workshop participants chose to hold the balls near their chest or abdomen with their hands or arms so that data was felt across the upper torso and limbs. The use of a large circular object conjured many metaphors and images across users. Given the size and shape of the ball, it fostered connections to fertility, pregnancy, and the loss of the ability to bear children by those forcibly sterilized. For some, this experience was quite powerful and helped them connect to the data; however, for others our form of data representation was considered too intimate, exploitative, and even a misrepresentation of the data itself. Some participants also found the use of beachballs inappropriate because they were objects of play. In these cases, users were not able to decouple their experience from the cultural connotations of what a beachball is and is used for. The Eugenic Rubicon installation led to many deep discussions about who the data is for, who should have access to it, and how to appropriately represent data.

The small sandbox represented global warming data, which sonified and haptified global warming trends over time. Participants would rest or dig their hands into the sand to feel the data. The use of sand was a very clear metaphor for global warming, inciting images of deserts and dry land. Some users would almost caress the sand or find themselves shaping it in ways pleasing to them. One person said they felt it necessary to take care of the sand as they felt the data. Like the ball installation, users found the sandbox compelling because the installation's physical materials intuitively connected to the data itself.

The initial workshop explorations helped us understand what to consider when haptifying archival data within a multisensory installation. The first is the importance of intentionally pairing the physical elements of the installation with the data itself. In this, we learned not only to consider size, shape, structure, and texture of the physical installation elements, but also: 1) user's personal and cultural familiarity with the objects and materials, 2) likely user gestures for entering into, exiting, and sustaining touch, and 3) discrete visual and aural information for contextualizing the dataset parameters. These considerations and how I use them are highly contingent upon the user group and larger environment in which the data representation is situated.

4 Discussion

The design of tactile data representations surfaces many questions that are not only specific to touch but elicit deeper questions about how we are using data as a form of storytelling. Offering data as touch heightens awareness of the people and human infrastructures present enmeshed with the data. In the case of *Vibrant Lives*, users became more attuned to the unnamed people who were collecting their data, often asking questions such as, "Who wants my data and why?" During our first installation, one participant said she already knew her data was being collected by companies, but in touching her data, she felt far more implicated by her decision *not* to change her behavior or do something about it. This points to the *livingness* of the data installation as it takes on qualities of movement. Haptic data evokes the materialist theories of Jane Bennett, who inspired our initial conceptual work on *Vibrant Lives*. In this, our work amplifies the ways in which non-living things like our devices and data are themselves "quasi-agential" forces that shape lived experience [25]. In all iterations of my work, users were not so much focused on discrete data points or static renderings of the data, as one might see in a static data visualization, rather users focused on the overall changes in haptic sensation over time, noting major spikes and drops in sensation. These major shifts would become places for inquiry and discussion, mostly of what the data represented and why such representations were meaningful to various stakeholders producing, using, and consuming the data.

4.1 Ethical Data Representation

Initially, my research goal was to understand the ethical implication of using haptic aesthetics in data representation. This is a key area of my research and something I continue to engage throughout my work. However, moving my work toward data archives surfaces many questions related to data representation. The first is, how are we treating the people embedded within the data, and do we have the right to work with the data at all? Working within *Vibrant Lives*, the data we used throughout our preliminary research was inherently our own. I began to make intimate relationships with the information. When a colleague would share their data with me, it was conducted with great generosity as a gesture of self-offering. We were able to cultivate a mutually respected ethos of care between the data creator, researcher, and research process because we were all physically in the same room. However, working with archival data means engaging with people who are not in the room and thus, do not have the ability to decide if and how the data should be used. In these cases, how do we make a mutual contract of care between those within the data, the designers, and the users? How do we create ethical processes for publicly representing data when the people represented cannot participate in the ethical debate? I don't think these questions are important just because I am working with touch, or because I continue to work with highly political and emotionally charged datasets, but the importance of these questions is more *palpable* because I am working with haptics. I feel the implications differently, and I am ever-ruminating on the ethical implications of data representation as a form of storytelling and narrativizing information. Discussions such as this would have perhaps been merely an intellectual exercise rather than a serious consideration prior to beginning my haptic research. Now, I am deeply considering ethical questions of access and use before moving forward with future archival datasets.

5   Conclusion

In this paper, I discuss my philosophy and approach to designing multisensory data representations and interfaces with a specific focus on haptic media. This includes designing for both real-time data and data archives. I discuss the importance of resisting the haptic subject and thus separating users from their personal and cultural understandings of touch. I also articulate why I consider touch design as an inherently political act in which knowledge is co-formed. The results of my design work suggest that the physical materials imbued with haptic data impact how users interpret the data itself. When designing physical infrastructures for data haptification, I suggest considering not only size, shape, structure, and texture of the physical installation elements, but also: 1) user's personal and cultural familiarity with the objects and materials, 2) likely user gestures for entering into, exiting and sustaining touch, and 3) discrete visual and aural information to help contextualize the dataset parameters.

Throughout my work, my goal is to create multisensory experiences that thoughtfully generate dialogue between the information inscribed within the data and the users themselves. The process of entangling users with various data attributes imbues data representations with palpable, culturally specific elements that speak to the broader histories and social contexts of the data. I do not wish to eradicate data visualization from the design process, but to balance its impact on the user experience by deprioritizing vision as the primary means of consciously consuming and analyzing data. I do this as an embodied mediation between people and data, examining what it means to care for and create affective spaces for large datasets that are often about people but leave little trace of human experience within their representations.

References

1. Hermann, T., Ritter, H.: Listen to your data: model-based sonification for data analysis. Adv. Intell. Comput. Multimedia Syst. (1999)
2. Paneels, S., Roberts, J.: Review of designs for haptic data visualization. IEEE Trans. Haptics **3**(2), 119–137 (2009)
3. Rajko, J.: A call to action: embodied thinking and human-computer interaction design. The Routledge Companion to Medind Digital Humanities, pp. 195–203. Routledge, London, UK (2018)
4. Hayes, L., Rajko, J.: Towards an aesthetics of touch. In: Proceedings of the 4th International Conference on Movement Computing. ACM (2017)
5. Rajko, J., et al.: Touching data through personal devices: engaging somatic practice and haptic design in felt experiences of personal data. In: Proceedings of the 3rd International Symposium on Movement and Computing. ACM (2016)
6. Parisi, D.: Archaeologies of Touch: Interfacing with Haptics from Electricity to Computing. U of Minnesota Press, Minneapolis, MN (2018)
7. Classen, C.: The Book of Touch. Berg Publishers, Oxford, UK (2005)
8. Manning, E.: Politics of Touch: Sense, Movement, Sovereignty. U of Minnesota Press, Minneapolis, MN (2007)
9. Naccarato, T., MacCallum, J.: Critical appropriations of biosensors in artistic practice. In: Proceedings of the 4th International Conference on Movement Computing. ACM (2017)
10. Kozel, S.: Spacemaking: experiences of a virtual body. The Book of Touch, pp. 439–446. Berg Publishers, Oxford, UK (2005)
11. Dourish, P.: Where the Action is: The Foundations of Embodied Interaction. MIT press, Cambridge, MA (2004)
12. Hayes, L.: Skin music (2012): an audio-haptic composition for ears and body. In: Proceedings of the 2015 ACM SIGCHI Conference on Creativity and Cognition, pp. 359–360. ACM (2015)
13. Hayes, L.: Vibrotactile feedback-assisted performance. In: Proceedings of New Interfaces for Musical Expression, pp. 72–75. NIME (2011)
14. Gunther, E., O.Modhrain, S.: Cutaneous grooves: composing for the sense of touch. J. New Music Res. **32**(4), 369–381 (2003)
15. Morita, S.: Sonic art for intersensory listening experience. In: Proceedings of the Electroacoustic Music Studies Network Conference, Electroacoustic Music Beyond Performance, pp. 1–11 (2014)
16. Susan, K.: Closer: Performance, Technologies, Phenomenology. MIT press, Cambridge, MA (2007)
17. Schiphorst, T., Andersen, K.: Between bodies: using experience modeling to create gestural protocols for physiological data transfer, 1–8 (2004)

18. Schiphorst, T.: soft (n) toward a somaesthetics of touch. In: CHI'09 Extended Abstracts on Human Factors in Computing Systems, pp. 2427–2438 (2009)
19. Schiphorst, T.: Body matters: the palpability of invisible computing. Leonardo **42**(3), 225–230 (2009)
20. Loke, L., et al.: Re-sensitising the body: interactive art and the Feldenkrais method. Int. J. Arts Technol. **6**(4), 339–356 (2013)
21. Salisbury, K., Mandayam, S.: Phantom-based haptic interaction with virtual objects. IEEE Comput. Graph. Appl. **17**(5), 6–10 (1997)
22. Bainbridge Cohen, B.: Sensing, Feeling and Action: The Experiential Anatomy of Body-Mind Centering. Contact Editions, Northampton, MA (1993)
23. Rajko, J.: Vibrant Lives Performance Installation (2015). https://vimeo.com/143582781
24. Wernimont, J., Minn, A.: Eugenic Rubicon (2017). https://scalar.usc.edu/works/eugenic-rubicon-/index
25. Bennett, J.: Vibrant Matter: A Political Ecology of Things. Duke University Press, Durham, NC (2010)

Personal Air Pollution Monitoring Technologies: User Practices and Preferences

Nina Sakhnini[1] , Ja Eun Yu[1] , Rachael M. Jones[2] ,
and Debaleena Chattopadhyay[1(✉)]

[1] University of Illinois at Chicago, Chicago, USA
debchatt@uic.edu
[2] The University of Utah, Salt Lake City, UT, USA

Abstract. Long-term exposure to air pollution can cause adverse health effects. Many efforts are underway to develop affordable, portable, and accurate technologies to help people monitor air pollution regularly. Although personal, wearable air pollution monitoring technologies are popular among some technology enthusiasts and citizen scientists, we know little about air pollution monitoring practices and preferences of lay individuals. We conducted a sequential explanatory mixed-methods study ($n = 321$) to understand people's current air pollution monitoring practices and their requirements for personal air pollution monitoring technologies. Although concerned about the adverse effects of air pollution (94%), less than 10% reported checking the levels of air pollution at least once a week. Respondents were more likely to carry a monitoring device as a bag accessory (74%) or wear it on their wrist (42%), than around their shoes, waist, or neck. If monitoring were available, however, it was unclear how much that would manifest behavior changes in individuals. We discuss how our findings can inform future technology design.

Keywords: Air pollution monitoring · Wearable · User survey · Ubiquitous computing · User requirements · Design

1 Introduction

Long-term exposure to air pollution is a well-established risk factor for several chronic diseases [1–3]. The World Health Organization attributes about 7 million premature deaths globally to air pollution [4]. Most recently, an increase of $1\mu g/m^3$ in $PM_{2.5}$ exposure was reported to be associated with an 8% increase in the COVID-19 (coronavirus disease) death rate [5]. Air pollution exposure accumulates over time, as individuals repeatedly come in contact with air pollutants, such as Carbon Monoxide (CO), Nitrogen Dioxide (NO_2), Ozone (O_3), or Particulate Matter (PM).

Traditionally, air pollution exposure is assessed retrospectively, at the population level, using kriging or land-use regression modeling based on highly sophisticated monitoring networks that collect data over time [6, 7]. In recent years, many low-cost air quality sensors have emerged. While there are some limitations to their performance,

© Springer Nature Switzerland AG 2020
C. Stephanidis et al. (Eds.): HCII 2020, LNCS 12423, pp. 481–498, 2020.
https://doi.org/10.1007/978-3-030-60114-0_33

including sensitivity to relative humidity and aerosol composition [8–10], the latest generation of sensors have been found to have good long-term performance [9] and reasonable accuracy and precision with calibration [11, 12]. These sensing advances have inspired many ubiquitous computing solutions to better understand the air pollution landscape of urban areas—via mobile measurement stations [13–15] or participatory urban sensing [16, 17].

The advances in low-cost air quality sensors have also made personal air pollution monitoring feasible, i.e., directly monitoring one's own exposure to air pollution over time. While the traditional air quality sensors (found in governmental monitoring stations) are large, expensive (>$20,000), stationary, and needs routine maintenance, the latest sensors are small (~5 cm), mobile, low-cost ($50–$500), and do not require domain expertise to use when paired with appropriate data processing algorithms. Systems utilizing these low-cost air quality sensors can now (reasonably) accurately measure different air pollutants—from volatile organic compounds, like CO and O_3, to particulate matters, like PM_{10} and $PM_{2.5}$ [17–20].

Nevertheless, the design and development of personal air pollution monitoring systems have just begun. Although portable and stationary indoor air quality monitoring devices have garnered some popularity among mainstream consumers [21], wearable environmental monitoring systems [22] still largely cater to citizen science and scientific research [17, 20, 23, 24]. Only a few, introduced most recently, target the general public [25, 26]; the extent of their acceptance, challenges, or use, however, remains unexplored.

Although prior research has repeatedly demonstrated the technological feasibility of affordable and accurate personal air pollution monitoring wearables [18, 19, 27], we know little about how people currently monitor air pollution around them or their preferences in personal air pollution monitoring technologies. To address this gap in the human-computer interaction (HCI) literature, we conducted a mixed-methods study to understand people's current air pollution monitoring practices and elicit their requirements for personal air pollution monitoring technologies. Drawing on empirical data, this paper contributes user requirements and design tradeoffs for personal air pollution monitoring technologies.

2 Methods

We adopted a sequential explanatory mixed-methods design to examine air pollution monitoring practices and preferences [28]. A mixed-methods design combines quantitative and qualitative methods to complement each other and allow for a more robust analysis than using only either one of the methods. A sequential explanatory mixed-methods design includes two distinct phases: collecting and analyzing quantitative data followed by collecting and analyzing qualitative data. The quantitative phase informs the research questions of the qualitative phase. In turn, the qualitative data provides refinement and explanation of the statistical results in the quantitative data.

In our study, a set of qualitative interviews with technology probes ($n = 7$) followed an online survey ($n = 314$). Next, we discuss the quantitative results from the survey in Sect. 3 and the qualitative interviews in Sect. 4.

3   User Survey

3.1   Method

We designed an online survey with twenty-seven multiple-choice questions (Appendix A) to elicit (1) air pollution monitoring practices, (2) preferences about monitoring air pollution exposure, (3) sociodemographic characteristics, and (4) environmental attitudes. The survey was open for responses between April and November 2019. The target population was adults living and/or working in a metropolitan area. Recruitment occurred via advertisements on social media outlets, university mailing lists, and distributed by local community organizations. One participant was randomly selected to receive a $50 gift card. This study was reviewed and approved by the university's institutional review board (IRB).

3.2   Results

Demographics. A total of 314 respondents completed the survey. Respondents were 53.8% male and 43.3% female. Most of the respondents were between 18 to 44 years old (88.8%), Caucasian (44.1%), and employed (63.7%). Nearly half of the respondents' annual household income was less than $50,000 (46.6%), and only a quarter reported to be in a technical industry (25%). Respondents were largely from the greater Chicago area in the midwestern United States. Detailed demographics are shown in Table 1.

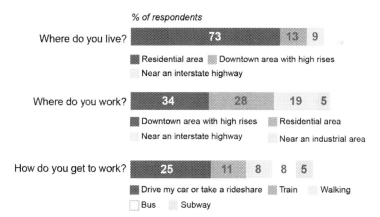

Fig. 1. Most of the respondents lived in a residential area (73%) and worked in a downtown area with high rises or a residential area (62%).

Table 1. Participant Sociodemographics.

Participant characteristics ($n = 314$)	Descriptive statistics
Gender, n (%)	
Male	169 (53.8)
Female	136 (43.3)
Other	9 (2.9)
Age, n (%)	
18–24	164 (52.2)
25–44	115 (36.6)
45–64	24 (7.6)
65 or older	11 (3.5)
Ethnicity, n (%)	
Caucasian	137 (44.1)
African American	24 (7.7)
Hispanic or Latino	52 (16.6)
Education Level, n (%)	
Less than 4-year college	127 (40.5)
4-year college or more	187 (59.5)
Annual household income, n (%)	
Less than $50,000	132 (46.6)
$50,000–$100,000	84 (29.7)
More than $100,000	67 (23.7)
Employed, n (%)	200 (63.7)
Primary industry, n (%)	
Scientific or Technical Services	29 (10.2)
Software	42 (14.8)
Computers and Electronics Manufacturing	17 (6)

Most respondents lived in a residential area (73%), worked in a downtown or residential area (62%), and went to work by car (Fig. 1). Most respondents considered environmental pollution as an important global problem and expressed concern about the adverse health effects of chronic exposure to air pollution (Fig. 2).

Pollution Monitoring Practices. Although concerned about air pollution and its adverse effects (Fig. 2), less than 10% of the respondents reported checking the levels of air pollution at least once a week. A majority of the respondents (60%) never checked air pollution levels (Fig. 3).

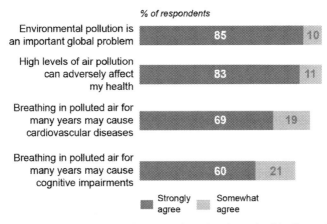

Fig. 2. A majority of respondents showed concern about the adverse health effects of air pollution. (5-Point Likert Scale)

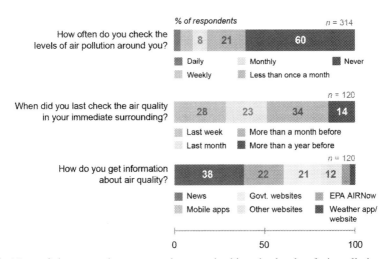

Fig. 3. Most of the respondents reported never checking the levels of air pollution around them. Among those who did, the top three sources of information were news, mobile apps, and government websites.

Among respondents who did check the air quality around them, diverse sources of information were used, including: the news (38%), mobile apps (22%), government websites (21%), or other websites (12%). Only nine (2.9%) respondents (either college students or people with an annual income of $100,000 or more) reported using any air quality monitoring devices. Those devices varied widely, from custom-made sensor boards to off-the-shelf products, like AirBeam[1], Dyson Pure Cool[2], Foobot[3] and, Awair[4]. Two respondents reported using air purifiers as air quality monitors, although such devices do not directly offer air quality data to users. One person referred to his body as an air pollution monitoring device.

Most respondents were aware of how to minimize exposure to air pollution when air quality was poor, such as: to use a dust mask (74.5%), minimize time outdoors (69.4%), or close the windows of a room (78%). Respondents, however, rarely took all those steps (Fig. 4).

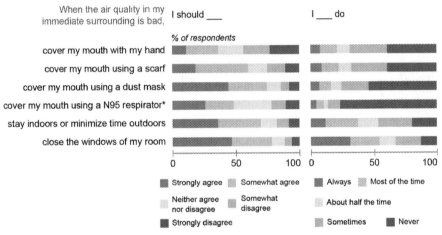

Fig. 4. Most respondents were aware of how to minimize exposure to air pollution, but few always took those steps. (*survey conducted before the 2019–20 coronavirus pandemic)

Pollution Monitoring Preferences. Majorities of respondents wanted to know how much air pollution they breathe in, both over the long-term (e.g., over the last year, 84%) and short-term (e.g., during last evening's commute, 84%). While 82% of respondents were willing to have a portable air quality monitoring device at home, 59% were willing to wear one. Most respondents (76%) valued portability in an air quality monitoring device (Fig. 5). When suggested that a personal device may more accurately measure their exposure to air pollution than estimates across neighborhoods from fixed monitoring sites, respondents were more likely to carry a device as a bag accessory (74%) or wear a device on their wrist (42%), than a device on or near their shoes, waist, or neck (Fig. 6).

Summary. In a convenience sample of 314 people living/working in a midwestern US metropolitan area, who were concerned about the adverse effects of air pollution, we

---

[1] https://www.habitatmap.org/airbeam.

[2] https://www.dyson.com/purifiers/dyson-pure-cool-overview.html.

[3] https://foobot.io/.

[4] https://getawair.com/.

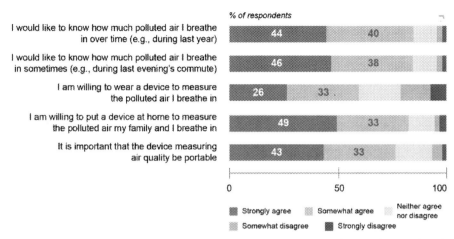

Fig. 5. The majority of respondents (84%) wanted to know how much air pollution they breathe in with time and were more willing to have a portable air quality monitoring device at home (82%) than to wear a device (59%).

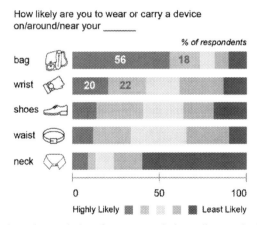

Fig. 6. The top two form-factor choices for a personal air quality monitoring device were bag accessory and wristwear.

found a considerable preference for monitoring personal pollution exposure (Fig. 5). However, most respondents reported that they currently do not check or measure air pollution levels around them (Fig. 3). Nevertheless, more people wanted to have a portable at-home air quality monitoring device than a wearable (Fig. 5).

Greater Chicago has relatively low air pollution than many other parts of the world, which may have been why many respondents in this study reported never checking air pollution levels. The infrequent use of air pollution monitors may be due, in part, to the relatively high cost of consumer-grade air quality monitoring devices ($200+), and/or their recent availability in the marketplace.

With respect to the design of personal air quality monitoring devices, respondents preferred to clip it on a bag or wear it on the wrist (Fig. 6). Note that the age of our survey respondents was skewed toward the young (Table 1); thus, all our results may not extend to an older population. Furthermore, the levels of education and income do not appropriately reflect the full gamut of socioeconomic statuses (SES); air pollution monitoring practices and preferences of people with low SES or less formal education might be different from our survey findings.

While the survey results indicated a general preference toward personal air pollution monitoring, the data could not clarify 1) why people might not want to monitor air pollution, 2) why they preferred a keychain or wrist-wear-like form factor, and 3) how would they use the monitoring data (given that most people rarely take actions to reduce their air pollution exposures). To find out, we designed an in-depth qualitative study with a technology probe.

4 Technology Probe Study

4.1 The Technology Probe

Technology probes are commonly used in HCI to collect information about the use and users of a technology. In this approach, users explore a fully functional technology prototype to think about how and whether the technology can support their needs and desires [29]. As a technology probe, we designed a personal air pollution monitoring tool using off-the-shelf air quality monitoring sensors (Fig. 7).

Fig. 7. Using a low-cost, off-the-shelf air quality sensor (a), we developed a technology probe for our interviews—a keychain device (b) with a companion smartphone application (c).

The probe used a $30 off-the-shelf particle concentration sensor, Plantower PMS7003 (48 mm × 32 mm × 12 mm). The PMS7003 operates using the principle of light scattering to measure the number concentration of airborne particles with aerodynamic diameters <2.5 µm ($PM_{2.5}$) in real-time. The sensor was mounted on a third-generation single-board computer, Raspberry Pi 3b+(85 mm × 56 mm × 17 mm), which included a 1.4 GHz 64-bit quad-core processor, a Bluetooth module, Wi-Fi, 1 GB

RAM, and 16 GB storage. The Pi was powered with a 1000 mAh rechargeable LiPo battery at 3.7 V (30 mm × 40 mm × 7 mm). The device weighed about 100 gms.

Python scripts read data from the PMS7003, wrote data to a local or cloud database, and sent data to a companion smartphone application. When the device could connect to a wireless network, the sensor readings were logged to the cloud database (Amazon Web Services); otherwise, sensor readings were logged onto the smartphone via Bluetooth and sent to the cloud by the app when an internet connection became available. An Android application visualized the airborne particle concentrations so that users could monitor their current exposure to $PM_{2.5}$ (Fig. 7c) and logged geolocation using the smartphone's global positioning system (GPS) receiver.

4.2 Method

In this phase, we targeted people who resided near an industrial area and/or belonged to a vulnerable group (e.g., older adults, people with cardiovascular or respiratory conditions). We chose this group as they could get a more immediate advantage from personal air pollution monitoring technologies as well as have specific system requirements that might not have emerged from the survey. Participants were recruited via social media posts and partnerships with local community organizations. Participants were not affiliated with the authors' institution.

Participants explored the technology probe, asked questions about it to the researchers, and then discussed whether they would use similar technology, why or why not, and how. The study session lasted for about 30 to 40 min. The study was approved by the institutional IRB and participants were compensated with a $10 gift card for their time. Sessions were audio-recorded and iteratively analyzed for themes via memoing and group discussions (Fig. 8).

Fig. 8. A study participant exploring the technology probe during the study.

4.3 Results

We interviewed seven individuals residing in the greater Chicago area. Their demographics are shown in Table 2. All participants reported strong concerns about the adverse health effects of air pollution. The first and last authors open coded the data to uncover themes. Initial themes included how people see or smell air pollution around them, health concerns due to bad air quality, behaviors around bad air quality, advocacy, and interest in monitoring air pollution exposure. After further reflection and analysis via memoing and axial coding, the following five themes emerged[5].

Table 2. Participant Sociodemographics

Participant	Age	Gender	Characteristic(s)
1	35	Male	Lives in/near a heavy industrial area
2	72	Female	Older adult, cardiovascular condition
3	27	Female	Chronic respiratory condition, lives near a heavy industrial area
4	55	Female	Chronic respiratory disease
5	70	Male	Older adult
6	69	Female	Older adult
7	47	Male	Chronic respiratory condition

Smaller, Lighter, Modular. Participants wanted a system they could use both on-the-go and at home:

> *I'd think just with you. And then if you've it on your home, you could just mount it, if it needs to be charged, and that's your home system —P1*

> *I think it should be… especially for people like me…I have sinus problems and dust triggers sinus I think it will be very beneficial for people to use everywhere…in and out…with asthma and sinus infection —P7*

After exploring the technology probe, people wanted a smaller and lighter version ("*consolidated, compressed…size, maybe half of this*", "*an option of a watch is a good one*", "*like a television remote control*", "*it's too bulky*"), something modular enough to wear, carry, or stow at home:

> *You can use a bigger one at home because you are putting it in one place [...] and then much more portable when you are out —P5*

> *Or almost similar to the air fresheners they have in the car and as you are driving wherever you go … in the same context…because then you could just bring it home —P1*

---

[5] Negative or less than enthusiastic comments about personal air pollution monitoring are emphasized in red.

To Monitor or Not to Monitor. Monitoring attitudes differed across participants. Some wanted to know the air quality in their immediate surroundings to take actions, while others expressed apathy, anxiety, and almost a comfort in not knowing.

Well I guess I'd avoid if it was indicating that it was high levels ... I'd try to avoid it [the place] —P2

It's good to know if the air around us is polluted with some of these [...] that could cause cancer at the long run right. So we get ahead of that [...] if we can detect it early enough then we can save the younger generation

—P7

Would I like to [monitor air quality]? Well ... the problem is if you monitor it what can you do about it. [...] To me it's almost better not to know. —P6

If we went from red green yellow [...] will it give a person a sense of panic to a certain degree [...] I will be panicked..I will be like I gotta get out of here. I mean it's good but like do I really wanna panic all the time about seeing something..uhm..I don't know. —P3

Access to Longitudinal Data. People wanted easy access to their long-time exposure data—to understand triggers to their chronic health conditions, inform others, and be aware of their neighborhood air quality.

Yeah, I think year long would be good. Just because I'd like to know if the pollutions are actually irritating me more and when ... are they really correlating to when I get sick because it's the cold or they're correlating because there is something in the air. —P3

[...] it could tell you the quality of the air per where you were in the day. So now you have a better idea ok the air was terrible [...] you could look at where was I, what was I doing while I was there, and then you could even send that back to those people and say hey can you do something about your air quality there —P1

I might consider at some point where can I move to where there is less pollution. If I can compare like living here in the city to maybe [...] depending on how it affected me personally like noticing that my health was being affected where can I live that there's less of this —P4

Ambivalence toward Lifestyle Changes. If personal pollution monitoring were available, how much people would change their behaviors to reduce air pollution exposure was fraught with ambivalence. Some were optimistic about actions they could/would take, while others were realistic about the lack of actionable steps outside home.

I will analyze it and see how safe to live in that area and if it is not safe either we do something about it and if it's not in our power we move —P7

how can I better it like presenting this stuff to your bosses and you coworkers to say this is how bad the air is here, what can we do to clean it —P1

If it's indoors [...] I can maybe install a filtration or air cleaning system. I don't know what I can really do about it [pollution] as far as what's outside unless we start wearing those [...] protective masks or walk around in those hazmat suits —P4

There's not much really that you can do other than promote like carpool or walking —P3

Advocacy Goals. An interest in using the data to advocate for environmental changes at a community or state level emerged.

well if your neighbors all had something similar you could petition to your alderman to do something about the air quality or if there's a city bureau. I mean if you have data that's why you go up there [town hall, local government] you don't use opinions—P6

4.4 Summary

The interview data elaborated our survey findings. The limited options in controlling personal exposure to air pollution appeared to demotivate the use of any personal air pollution monitoring tool. The qualitative data also elaborated the form factor requirements of a personal air pollution monitoring tool beyond a particular accessory type. Different ways of using exposure data emerged, such as to correlate with sick days, to decide which neighborhood to live in, or to share it with community leaders to facilitate changes beyond one's personal control. Next, we discuss the user requirements that emerged from the mixed-methods study and identify the associated design tradeoffs.

5 Discussion

Study results indicate that among people who are concerned about the adverse effects of air pollution, there is a high preference for monitoring personal pollution exposures over time (84%, Fig. 5). However, despite that, and the current pollution monitoring technologies available at no additional cost, such as government websites[6] or smartphone apps, most people never check the levels of air pollution around them (60%, Fig. 3). One could reasonably argue that this might be because those widely available air pollution monitoring technologies are rarely *personal*; they offer air pollution estimates at the county or neighborhood level. For instance, there are four $PM_{2.5}$ governmental monitoring stations in greater Chicago, and most operate on a 1-in-6 or 1-in-4-day sensing schedule [30]. Nevertheless, other factors emerged from our study that has important implications for the future uptake and use of personal air pollution monitoring technologies.

---

[6] https://www.airnow.gov/.

5.1 Design Issues

Our study revealed a set of preferences for a personal air pollution monitoring device, such as high mobility, lightness, and easy access to longitudinal data. From what we know technologically about how current personal air pollution monitoring works [22], user requirements did not always align with the optimal operating conditions. User preferences for form factors may have been biased by the ubiquitous computing devices in wide use today, like smartphones and smartwatches. Table 3 lists the user requirements that emerged from our study, some design solution examples, and design tradeoffs associated with those solutions. In describing the design requirements for personal air pollution monitoring systems, we do not anchor to a particular technology or sensor; rather, we acknowledge the current technological limitations in the personal air pollution monitoring field [22].

5.2 Socioeconomic Issues

Very few people (2.9%) reported owning/using an air pollution monitoring device. Furthermore, higher levels of education and income correlated with the ownership of a personal air pollution monitoring technology. This was expected given the current innovation stage of personal pollution monitoring technologies. As sensing technology advances, these systems are expected to get affordable and widely available.

Nevertheless, the qualitative data indicated that people perceive air pollution as a public health issue, not a personal issue. Thus, participants expected air pollution monitoring devices to be made freely available by the city or state as a utility, not something they would want to buy personally. This view was expressed by three older participants (P4, 55; P5, 70; P6; 69) in our interviews. Older adults, however, are more vulnerable to air pollution and could get a more immediate advantage from personal air pollution monitoring. Note that participants self-selected for our study, which already indicated an interest in the technology. We observed that the willingness to pay (WTP) widely varied by age. Future controlled studies with larger sample sizes are needed to confirm this trend. Nevertheless, it is worth noting that personal air pollution monitoring can be most beneficial to older adults and people with low SES.

5.3 Sociotechnical Issues

Our interviews revealed that even if an affordable and accurate air pollution monitoring device is available, some people may not want to use it regularly because of *the lack of tangible steps* available to an individual to reduce personal air pollution exposure. This finding unveils an interesting dichotomy. If enough people are monitoring and trying to reduce their personal air pollution exposure, apart from individual lifestyle changes, their awareness and advocacy can bring about big societal changes. Unfortunately, the prospect of only a long-term reward may not be enough for general technology adoption and use. Future personal monitoring systems must think about how to present tangible steps to users to not only monitor their air pollution exposure but significantly reduce it over time and thus, get personal health benefits. For example, predicting to a runner how running at a different time of the day or taking a different route may result in x% less PM

Table 3. User Requirements for Personal Air Pollution Monitoring Systems.

User requirement	Design solution (for example)	Associated design tradeoff(s)
A small, light, carriable system	A wearable wrist-worn monitor using low-cost sensor components	• Accuracy may be unreliable at certain concentrations of air pollutants • A smaller battery implies repeated charging • Human skin emissions may interfere with air pollutant readings
Good accuracy	A correction model to calibrate the sensor performance	• Additional environmental sensors may be needed to achieve good calibration; thus, making the system bulkier and/or larger • Multiple calibrations may be needed to address sensor aging effects, seasonal changes, or any prior calibration errors
Easy access to daily, weekly, monthly, and yearly average air pollution exposure data	Offer a companion app/website with daily, weekly, monthly, and yearly average air pollution exposure and levels for adverse health effects	• Long-term air pollution exposure affects health outcomes differently for different demographics, but that research is still in its early stages and not yet fully standardized • Data may generate anxiety and helplessness among users without the means to take any steps to reduce pollution exposure
Tangible actions to reduce air pollution exposure	Use time and location (GPS) information to identify pollution hotspots	• Asking users to always have their GPS on will have privacy issues • Logging users' location information to aggregate long-term pollution exposure data will make them vulnerable to security breaches

exposure in the next month compared with the last. In sum, this is a hard sociotechnical problem that remains to be addressed.

5.4 Study Limitations

Our study is not without limitations. The survey used a convenience sample, which may have impacted the results. Greater Chicago does not have pollution levels comparable to some of the most polluted areas globally. People residing in those areas may have different perceptions and practices toward air pollution monitoring, not only because of the levels of pollution but also due to sociocultural factors. Future studies focusing on vulnerable populations may elicit additional user requirements that we missed due to our participant demographics.

6 Conclusion

In this paper, we presented empirical data on people's air pollution monitoring practices and preferences. Results indicate a preference for air pollution monitoring devices that can be used both outside and inside home. Whether people would adopt and heavily use personal air pollution monitoring devices will depend on how monitoring devices offer tangible steps for them to reduce pollution exposures. At present, few people monitor the levels of air pollution around them, and way fewer own or use an air pollution monitoring device. But the increasing affordability of these systems, as technology advances, may increase adoption in the future. Nevertheless, the sociotechnical issue of short-term vs. long-term reward may hinder a wider uptake and use of personal air pollution monitoring technologies.

Acknowledgments. We thank all our participants for their time and the City Tech Collaborative, Environmental Law and Policy Center, and Chicago Hyde Park Village for their assistance in study recruitment.

Appendix A: Survey Questions

Q1. How often do you check the levels of air pollution (i.e., air quality) around you?
   Never Less than once a month Monthly Weekly Daily
Q2. When did you last check the air quality in your immediate surrounding? (e.g., measured using a device or visited a government website, such as https://airnow.gov)
   Never More than a year before More than a month before Last month Last week
Q3. How do you get information about air quality? (Choose all that apply.)
   News Government website Other websites EPA AIRNow mobile app Other mobile apps Other I don't
Q4. Do you use any air quality monitoring devices?
   Yes No
Q5. Do you own/use any of the following air quality monitoring devices? (Choose all that apply.)
   Dylos Airbeam Foobot Dyson Pure Cool Xiaomi Mi Air Purifier Pro Awair uHoo PurpleAir Healthy Home Coach by Netatmo AirVisual Pro Blueair Aware Other I don't own any device.

Q6. The air quality in your immediate surrounding is bad. Now consider the following statements.

I should cover my mouth with my hand.

Strongly disagree   Somewhat disagree   Neither agree nor disagree   Somewhat agree   Strongly agree

I should cover my mouth using a scarf.

I should cover my mouth using a dust mask.

I should cover my mouth using a N95 respirator.

I should stay indoors or minimize time outdoors.

I should close the windows of my room.

Q7. The air quality in your immediate surrounding is bad. How often do you?

Cover your mouth with your hand.

Strongly disagree   Somewhat disagree   Neither agree nor disagree   Somewhat agree   Strongly agree

Cover your mouth using a scarf.

Cover your mouth using a dust mask.

Cover your mouth using a N95 respirator.

Stay indoors or minimize time outdoors.

Close the windows of your room.

Q8. Research has shown that pollution levels measured with a personal device are little different and more personal than estimated across neighborhoods from fixed monitoring sites. Please state how much you agree or disagree with the following statements.

I would like to know how much polluted air I breathe in over time (e.g., during last year).

Strongly disagree   Somewhat disagree   Neither agree nor disagree   Somewhat agree   Strongly agree

I would like to know how much polluted air I breathe in sometimes (e.g., during last evening's commute).

I am willing to wear a device to measure the polluted air I breathe in.

I am willing to put a device at home to measure the polluted air my family and I breathe in.

It is important that the device measuring air quality around me be portable.

Q9. You are offered a device that can measure your daily exposure to air pollution. The device needs to be worn outside, over your topmost layer of clothing, to accurately measure the air quality around you. How likely are you to wear or carry a device like this? Please rank in the order of your preference. (Rank 1 means highly likely, rank 5 means least likely. Images show some examples.)

– on or near your bag

– around or near your waist

– around or near your neck

– on or near your shoes

Q10. Please state how much you agree or disagree with the following statements:

Environmental pollution is an important global problem.

Strongly disagree   Somewhat disagree   Neither agree nor disagree   Somewhat agree   Strongly agree

High levels of air pollution can adversely affect my health and my family's health. Breathing in polluted air for many years may cause cardiovascular diseases. Breathing in polluted air for many years may cause cognitive impairments. Demographics

References

1. Rajagopalan, S., Al-Kindi, S., Brook, R.: Air pollution and cardiovascular disease. J. Am. Coll. Cardiol. **72**(17), 2054–2070 (2018)
2. Johannson, K., Balmes, J., Collard, H.: Air pollution exposure: a novel environmental risk factor for interstitial lung disease? Chest **147**(4), 1161–1167 (2015)
3. Tzivian, L., et al.: Long-term air pollution and traffic noise exposures and mild cognitive impairment in older adults: a cross-sectional analysis of the heinz nixdorf recall study. Environ. Health Perspect. **124**(9), 1361–1368 (2016)
4. World Health Organization (WHO) Air pollution. https://www.who.int/health-topics/air-pollution#tab=tab_1. Accessed 15 Jun 2020
5. Wu, X., Nethery, R.C., Sabath, B.M., Braun, D., Dominici, F.: Exposure to air pollution and COVID-19 mortality in the United States. medRxiv (2020)
6. Özkaynak, H., Baxter, L., Dionisio, K., Burke, J.: Air pollution exposure prediction approaches used in air pollution epidemiology studies. J. Expo. Sci. Environ. Epidemiol. **23**(6), 566–572 (2013)
7. Kloog, I., Koutrakis, P., Coull, B.A., Lee, H.J., Schwartz, J.: Assessing temporally and spatially resolved PM2.5 exposures for epidemiological studies using satellite aerosol optical depth measurements. Atmos. Environ. **45**(35), 6267–6275 (2011)
8. Levy Zamora, M., Xiong, F., Gentner, D., Kerkez, B., Kohrman-Glaser, J., Koehler, K.: Field and laboratory evaluations of the low-cost plantower particulate matter sensor. Environ. Sci. Technol. **53**(2), 838–849 (2019)
9. Liu, X., et al.: Low-cost sensors as an alternative for long-term air quality monitoring. Environ. Res. **185**, 109438 (2020)
10. Kelly, K.E., et al.: Ambient and laboratory evaluation of a low-cost particulate matter sensor. Environ. Pollut. **221**, 491–500 (2017)
11. Zusman, M., et al.: Calibration of low-cost particulate matter sensors: model development for a multi-city epidemiological study. Environ. Int. **134**, 105329 (2020)
12. Morawska, L., et al.: Applications of low-cost sensing technologies for air quality monitoring and exposure assessment: How far have they gone? Environ. Int. **116**, 286–299 (2018)
13. Lin, Y., Dong, W., Chen, Y.: Calibrating low-cost sensors by a two-phase learning approach for urban air quality measurement. Proc. ACM Interact. Mobile Wearable Ubiquit. Technol. **2**(1), 1–18 (2018)
14. Kim, Y., Eberle, J., Hanninen, R., Un, E.C., Aberer, K.: Mobile observatory: an exploratory study of mobile air quality monitoring application. In: Proceedings of the 2013 ACM Conference on Pervasive and Ubiquitous Computing Adjunct Publication - UbiComp 2013 Adjunct, pp. 733–736 (2013)
15. Chattopadhyay, D., Toward a bayesian approach for self-tracking personal pollution exposures. In: Proceedings of the 2018 ACM International Joint Conference and 2018 International Symposium on Pervasive and Ubiquitous Computing and Wearable Computers - UbiComp 2018, pp. 1166–1171 (2018)
16. Budde, M., El Masri, R., Riedel, T., Beigl, M.: Enabling low-cost particulate matter measurement for participatory sensing scenarios. In: Proceedings of the 12th International Conference on Mobile and Ubiquitous Multimedia - MUM 2013, pp. 1–10 (2013)

17. Nikzad, N., et al.: CitiSense: improving geospatial environmental assessment of air quality using a wireless personal exposure monitoring system. In: Proceedings of the Conference on Wireless Health - WH 2012, pp. 1–8 (2012)
18. Maag, B., Zhou, Z., Thiele, L.: W-air: enabling personal air pollution monitoring on wearables. Proc. ACM Interact. Mobile Wearable Ubiquit. Technol. **2**, 1–25 (2018)
19. Sakhnini, N., Yu, J.E., Chattopadhyay, D.: myCityMeter: helping older adults manage the environmental risk factors for cognitive impairment. In: Proceedings of the 2018 ACM International Joint Conference and 2018 International Symposium on Pervasive and Ubiquitous Computing and Wearable Computers - UbiComp 2018, pp. 235–238 (2018)
20. Piedrahita, R., et al.: The next generation of low-cost personal air quality sensors for quantitative exposure monitoring. Atmos. Meas. Tech. **7**, 3325–3336 (2014)
21. Kim, S., Li, M.: Awareness, understanding, and action: a conceptual framework of user experiences and expectations about indoor air quality visualizations. In: Proceedings of the 2020 CHI Conference on Human Factors in Computing Systems, pp. 1–12 (2020)
22. Al Mamun, M.A., Yuce, M.R.: Sensors and systems for wearable environmental monitoring toward iot-enabled applications: a review. IEEE Sensors J. **19**(18), 7771–7788 (2019)
23. AirBeam is a low-cost, palm-sized air quality instrument, https://www.habitatmap.org/airbeam/. Accessed 15 Jun 2020
24. MicroPEM™ Sensor for Measuring Exposure to Air Pollution. https://www.rti.org/impact/micropemsensor-measuring-exposure-air-pollution. Accessed 15 Jun 2020
25. Plume Flow2. https://plumelabs.com/en/flow-2/store/. Accessed 15 Jun 2020
26. Oz Robotics: Air Pollution Monitor that helps you breathe cleaner, healthier air. https://ozrobotics.com/shop/atmotube-portable-air-pollution-monitor/. Accessed 15 Jun 2020
27. Tian, R., Dierk, C., Myers, C., Paulos, E.: MyPart: personal, portable, accurate, airborne particle counting. In: Proceedings of the 2016 CHI Conference on Human Factors in Computing Systems, pp. 1338–1348 (2016)
28. Creswell, J.W., Clark, V.L.P.: Designing and Conducting Mixed Methods Research. Sage publications (2017)
29. Hutchinson, H., et al.: Technology probes: inspiring design for and with families. In: Proceedings of the Conference on Human Factors in Computing Systems - CHI 2003, pp. 17–24 (2003)
30. Illinois PM2.5 Daily Averages - Illinois EPA Bureau of Air. http://www.epa.state.il.us/air/pm25/index.html. Accessed 04 May 2020

On Designing a Slot Sharing E-Platform for Liner Shipping Services

Xiaoning Shi[1]([⊠]) [iD], Lin Ma[2] [iD], and Stefan Voß[1] [iD]

[1] University of Hamburg, Von-Melle-Park 5, Hamburg, Germany
{xiaoning.shi,stefan.voss}@uni-hamburg.de
[2] Dalian University of Foreign Languages, South Lvshun Road W6, Dalian, China
malin@dlufl.edu.cn
http://www.bwl.uni-hamburg.de/iwi.html, http://www.dlufl.edu.cn/en/

Abstract. Slot sharing phenomena are often observed in the liner shipping industry. When some liner shipping companies are providing container transportation service, they offer slots on board of their possessory vessels to their competitors in a cooperative manner. The liner shipping companies are amplifying their physical transport network coverage jointly and shortening service time accordingly. Such physical transport service is implemented nowadays after associated shippers book the service via online portals, i.e., E-platforms. The physical network and its related layout of the physical transport network has been changing dramatically during the past five years. The behavior of combining service links in the network and its related design of the E-platform could be interesting to practitioners as well as researchers. The booking business existing in the liner shipping alliances is similar to the booking system in the airline industry. However, the containers are not as selective as a human passenger when she/he is booking seats. Therefore, the potential design of the E-platform of the slot sharing business is different in its own way. By considering the similarities and differences, in this paper we propose some ideas regarding the design of the slot-sharing E-platform.

Keywords: Slot sharing · Liner shipping · E-platform · Design · Smart shipping · Complex networks

1 Background

Disparities in wealth distribution, turbulence of real economies as well as instability of the location advantages could cause global supply chain vulnerability and maritime shipping disruptions [3]. As a result, by providing transport service for containerized goods, e.g., relatively high valued trade, the liner shipping business sees great dynamics especially in the past five years [1,35]. Before 2014, small-to-medium-size liner shipping carriers were mostly engaged in setting up

Supported by National Science Foundation of China with Project No. 11602137.

C. Stephanidis et al. (Eds.): HCII 2020, LNCS 12423, pp. 499–513, 2020.
https://doi.org/10.1007/978-3-030-60114-0_34

cooperative container shipping networks to compete against the largest liner shipping companies, as found by research in [5].

However, as the horizon in front of the world trade is keeping fluctuation, individual liner shipping companies have to keep organizing their fleet management and slot agreements based on demand forecasting, collaborative trends [2] on one hand, and even the largest liner shipping companies started to join slot sharing agreements which is different from what [5] has previously found. On the other hand, these liner shipping companies deploy mega ships to cater for the long hauls [24] and to negotiate better tariffs at ports and push for volume discounts [17]. Consequently, some links between involved ports might have imbalanced trade volumes. Therefore, idle slots onboard occur. Based on that, some liner shipping companies become slot providers and some others become slot charterers, or some liner companies play both roles simultaneously, i.e., slot sharing [34,35]. Nevertheless, liner shipping companies have to deal with the problem of assigning container slots onboard to the right customer (including both end customers and slot charterers) at the right price to maximize their revenue [42].

This paper is devoted towards enhancing insights into slot sharing E-platforms. After some literature review we discuss mechanisms (Sect. 3) as well as modeling aspects (Sect. 4). Finally, we conclude with some managerial implications.

2   Literature Review on Slot Sharing E-Platform

E-platforms could facilitate the data flow and the information quality of slot sharing agreements in the liner shipping business, due to the fact that E-platforms are actually implementations of theoretical communication frameworks between various actors [9]. However, the impacts and performances of the E-platforms can only be positive if all actors involved have the willingness of using these E-platforms. Aforementioned actors include slot providers and slot charterers. Based on the willingness and capabilities of implementing the idea of E-platforms, a review on categories and designs of slot sharing E-platforms in the liner shipping industry is performed in detail in this section.

2.1   Categories of Slot Sharing E-Platforms

Several in-operation E-platforms of the liner shipping business are investigated and categories are groomed based on E-platforms of slot providers and pure 3rd party service integrators and pure 4th party engines. Characteristics of the abovementioned E-platforms are identified, and deigns are discussed, respectively.

- E-platform initiated by slot providers
  An example in this category can be found in a liner shipping company associated platform [13], which is a slot provider and charterer simultaneously.

- E-platform initiated by 3rd party service integrators
  An example in this category can be found in a third party freight forwarder associated platform [26,32], which is not a slot provider.
- E-platform functions as pure 4th party engine
  Such an E-platform can be regarded as an online marketplace where slot-related service is provided by multiple third parties with transactions processed by the marketplace operator [16]. By far, such 4th party engine enabling a slot sharing E-platform has not been widely accepted by practitioners though there are some pilot projects.

2.2 Design of Slot Sharing E-Platforms

Besides the fact that physical transport networks are often investigated, some vital research problems in the information networks and systems are often addressed, too. They need to be reflected and improved in the E-platform design. The design might result in differences of performance of computational processes and simulation, for instance, when it comes to the 'recommendations' provided by the slot providers to their customers. In this context, the interpretation of complex slot-sharing networks and forecasting techniques on link related behavior would be of relevance. Other than that, there exists flocking behavior from the capacity provider side along certain links in the liner shipping network, which is defined as overcapacity in business reality, i.e., too many idle slots, along some regional routes or international trade lanes. Therefore, abovementioned free capacities are to be shared among the consortium or strategic alliance [22]. However, from time to time there also exist slot sharing agreements with some parties who are not within the same consortium or alliance [18,36]. Both former and later business scenarios imply that the design of a slot-sharing E-platform in such context can consider slots as inventory where an operational policy is designed for an integrated inventory system with controllable lead time and buyers' space limitation [40].

The E-platform then would help to balance between the slot rates (slot price) collected and the actually implemented slot costs paid in the physical transport network, and do not recommend such slots to its customers. Therefore, timeline of structuring internally and recommending externally to the outside customers are both vital, and need to be reflected in the E-platform via different levels of authorities. When it comes to the question of slot allocation, pricing and revenue management, many existing literatures investigated feasible revenue management models and mechanism designs [15,28,37]. Some literature investigates feasible inventory routing models with a focus on the routing perspective [31,38]. Some literature on coordination with a focus on inventory policies [23,41], and its consignment agreement representing the storage-holding costs could also be replicated in slot agreement containing slot pricing tactic.

Furthermore, although slot and empty container are two different terminologies in real-world business, there are some similarities when overcapacity is investigated and congestion is caused in some nodes of transport networks. Idle slots onboard can be regarded as one kind of overcapacity and empty containers can be regarded as another kind of overcapacity. An example of an empty container exchange E-platform can be found in Germany [8]. There are also differences between idle slots and empty containers. Idle slots have the feature of perishable products such as, e.g., 'newspaper' and 'flower' in classic operations research problems, due to the fact that these obtained but unused slots of a slot charterer become 'out-of-date newspaper' and 'withered flowers' once the associated ships depart the ports. Empty containers could bear relatively longer time windows without so tight restriction. Therefore, pricing strategies [7] could also advance the research of slot agreement. When designing inventory and pricing policies for perishable products, return policy plays a role [11,21] and back-order discounts have been investigated [39] However, regarding slot agreements there is yet neither return policy nor back-order discount considered in practice, which could also be an aspect to advance designing of the slot-sharing E-platform.

Regarding the feature of perishable products, slots onboard of container ships and seats in aircrafts share similarity. For controlling seat inventory of aircrafts, airlines develop fare class 'buckets' and 'last-minute discount' so to manage the overall yield [4]. A theoretical discussion on swap allowance in terms of sensitivity analysis on slot purchase prices has been conducted in [30]. However, in practice there is no such pricing buckets and discount strategy so far offered by liner shipping companies, which could also be an angle to advance designing of the slot-sharing E-platform.

Based on above discussion, it is obvious that deploying slot-sharing agreements involves the decision on numbers of slots to be either shared or purchased, as well as the decision on price. The numbers of slots under consideration should take into account some demand forecast, i.e., mostly a deterministic approach for slot-sharing on a yearly basis, and mostly a stochastic approach for slot-chartering (purchasing) on a spot basis. When designing a slot-sharing E-platform, priorities could also be distributed with different degrees to yearly-based agreements and spot contracts. Such priority policies have been reflected in the existing literature [12]. Especially the prices of slots would need to consider a dynamic pricing scheme with stochastic demand over finite horizons [19], and an empirical analysis is conducted to test the influences of changing slot price for sale [30].

One step further, once we take into account the flocking behavior of deploying slots in advance, i.e., overcapacity by taking into account demand forecast, then the distribution of slots via E-platforms can embed features of complex networks. Complex networks can further be optimized by either decentralized or centralized control mechanism [33]. Decentralized mechanism would work, to some extent, as motivation to related stakeholders with information asymmetry [14]. Similar to centralized and decentralized mechanisms, to better discuss fair risk sharing between the parties involved in agreements, an overview and classification of coordination contracts is conducted from both viewpoints of cooperative games and non-cooperative games [20].

From the perspective of progressive evolution of the liner shipping business game, new levels of organization evolve when the competing units on the lower level begin to cooperate. Accordingly, in the liner shipping industry, cooperation at the level of regional slot agreement may lead to cooperation at the level of strategic alliances later on [27].

From the perspective of compatibility of slot-sharing agreement parties, trade imbalance in some legs of the liner shipping networks would need to be considered so that load factors of each leg could be leveraged [29]. On designing the slot-sharing E-platform, it is not compulsory to satisfy the exact amount of demand. In contrast, partial satisfaction of demand is allowed [25], which is reflected as non-static load factors of container ships.

From the perspective of cooperation structure, the 'small-world' network could interpret the high connectivity between nodes (or in other words, low remoteness among the nodes) [6]. Other than that, hierarchical structure of the complex liner shipping networks is also observed on a global level [10]. In the liner shipping business setting, these properties shed light on slot related agreements, e.g., the connections among ports can in fact create clusters of small specialized ports that function as satellites and feeder ports around a hub port. Then purchasing slots to reach feeder ports that are not called by its own ships, makes it possible for the liner shipping company to build a more sophisticated service network and to attract its final customers.

3 Mechanisms Designed for a Slot Sharing E-Platform

In this section, we define a slot as the specific space on board a container ship to be occupied by a container. Service retailing in the liner shipping business has created an unprecedented market place for the slot owner (potential provider of slots) and the slot charterer (buyer of slots and competitor of the slot owner simultaneously) to cooperate on distributing as well as offering their slots as service to final consumers, i.e., shippers in the liner shipping market. Recently these business structures have entailed the continued creation of innovative forms of contracting arrangement between liner shipping business partners, i.e., slot owners and slot charterers, for managing their commercial relationship. Such innovative forms include slot sharing E-platforms. In this section, we do not distinguish the commercial relationships including slot sharing and slot chartering in detail. Slot chartering agreements are also included in a slot sharing E-platform, because eventually a 'slot' is the target to be either shared with or without monetary payment. To simplify and generalize, a slot sharing E-platform is dealing with contracts (agreements) between partners who buy and sell a defined allocation of slots on a 'used or unused' basis at an agreed price and for a minimum defined period of time or selected legs of physical transport networks.

Based on the practices of the slot sharing related business, understanding the effectiveness and efficiency of these contracting arrangements has in turn become a major interest of practitioners as well as academic researchers. The economic impact of coordinating E-platforms is of importance; however, their design is often inadequate in real-world commercial operations. Therefore, there is a need to investigate this mechanism design problem thoroughly in the liner shipping business, including pricing schemes and structures of E-platform participants.

3.1 Pricing Schemes

The following pricing schemes can be distinguished:

- Capacity-based pricing means that the price of using a slot depends on the capacity constraints given by the liner carriers. An apparent example is the soaring freight rate retained to an upcoming peak season, i.e., when supply falls short of demands. Despite the carriers being competitors all the time, they might build a temporary pricing partnership so that each of these carriers can obtain a freight rate increment simultaneously.
- Time-based pricing means the price of using a slot depends on the Total Travel Time (TTT) of this specific voyage. When a service ordered by a shipper cannot be performed by one single voyage, one or more transshipments occur. Generally speaking, the more transshipments are involved, the longer the TTT can be expected. However, the liner carrier might offer some priority to certain carriages so that even if transshipment is involved, these carriages can still enjoy quite efficient connections, which results in shorter TTT. Obviously, such time-saving service as fast-lane or quick-connection, no matter how to name it, costs more to the shipper.
- Service-based pricing means the price of using a slot depends on the service quality offered by the carrier. For instance, in case a reefer container is to be carried, the price of providing carriage of such cargo is expected to be relatively high.

The above mentioned pricing scheme is set between the seller (provider) of the slots and the buyer (charterer) of the slots. The seller can be the owner of a container ship and/or operator of container ships. The buyer of the slots, in most cases, can be a shipper and/or consignee. However, taking into account the cooperation among liners, the buyer of slots can also be a liner who rents slots, i.e., buys service from her business partner based on designed slot charter agreements.

Among these three pricing schemes, the capacity-based pricing more likely happens during highly congested seasons or specific capacity-restricted geographical regions. Some of the objectives of adopting a slot agreement mechanism are to have a best possible interplay between covering as much of a service network as possible and deploying the smallest capacity (or handling volume) as possible, and obtain maximal expected profits. Therefore, the pricing scheme also plays a vital role as one aspect of general principles of slot agreements.

3.2 Structuring Agreements

In this subsection, the E-platform participants' agreements and actions are structured as follows. A seller of slots can choose the retail price based on the pricing schemes in the previous subsection as well as listing quantity for selling his loaded slot at the slot charterer online marketplace, and the slot owner collects a fee from the slot charterer based on the slot charter agreement only when a slot related service is sold. The slot owner calculates the fee to charge based on a predetermined percentage of the list price of a loaded slot.

Towards gaining managerial insights on this issue, we consider building a slot related agreement consisting of one slot owner and one slot charterer. The slot owner incurs a constant unit cost to offer a slot with unlimited shipping capacity, and the slot charterer incurs a constant unit cost for chartering and later selling the slot to the liner shipping market. As a start of this line of research, we assume that market demand for the liner shipping service during a selling season is uncertain and depends on the freight rate offered.

Prior to the selling season, the slot owner announces a revenue share, as the percentage of the list price for the slot (e.g., 55% in the slot owner's case), that he wants to charge the slot charterer for each slot sold. In response to this revenue share, the slot owner chooses the list price for chartering out a slot. Based on this list price and the predetermined revenue share, the slot charterer then decides the final freight rate for selling the slot to the market and a corresponding slot charter order quantity. This final freight rate chosen by the slot charterer is the actual price that the shipper will pay for using the slots, and it does not have to be equal to the list price set up by the slot owner. The calculation of the slot charterer's fee payable to the slot owner on each unit sold, however, is always based on the list price.

We assume that demand information, about the service price-sensitivity and its nature of uncertainty, is common knowledge to both participants of the slot related agreement. All decisions, i.e., the revenue share, the list price, the final freight rate and the slot order quantity, have to be made before the start of each selling season (i.e., every year or every half year to match existing business reality). In addition, for simplicity, we assume that there is no salvage value or disposal cost for any unsold slot at the end of voyages, and there is no shortage penalty beyond the loss of profit margin for any unmet demand.

We model the above decision-making procedures as a 3-stage Stackelberg (leader-follower) game. At the first stage, the slot charterer, acting as the Stackelberg-leader, offers the Slot owner a take-it-or-leave-it contract, specifying the percentage allocation of the revenue between these two parties. At the second stage, the slot owner, acting as the follower, chooses the list price, which is actually the unit cost of this specific slot charterer of using the slot. At the third stage, the slot charterer determines the freight rate per unit as well as the slot charter order quantity.

3.3 Decision Making Procedures

In this subsection, we will characterize the solutions of non-cooperative behaviors under the two kinds of agreements in Subsect. 4.1 and Subsect. 4.2, respectively. In order to provide a brief framework on these two kinds of agreements, i.e., the General Slot Agreement and the Modified Slot Agreement, players and their decisions are listed in Table 1.

Table 1. General and modified slot agreements

Participants	General slot agreement	Modified slot agreement
Slot owner provides	- list price	- list price - quantity of slots to sell to the slot charterer
Slot charterer decides	- quantity of slots to buy - selling price of the slots to the market - stocking factor	- selling price of the slots to the market

4   Model

4.1   Assumption Based on Collective Decision

Consider a liner shipping service where a slot owner provides slots and sells slots through a slot charterer to the market. The slot owner, i.e., the carrier, produces the service at a constant unit cost of c_s, and the slot charterer incurs a unit cost of c_R for handling and re-selling the service via the E-platform to the market.

Define $c = c_s + c_R$ as the total unit cost, and $\alpha = \frac{c_R}{c}$ as the share of the collective cost that is incurred by the slot charterer (or by the slot agreement-based business). Market demand for the service, denoted by D, is price-dependent as well as uncertain. We use the following multiplicative function form to model demand:

$$D(p) = y(p) \cdot \epsilon \tag{1}$$

p is the freight rate offered to the final customer, i.e., shipper; $y(p)$ is a deterministic and decreasing function of p, and ϵ is a scaling factor, representing the randomness of demand. Let $\epsilon \in [A, B]$.

Assume $y(p)$ takes the following form:

$$y(p) = ae^{-bp} \tag{2}$$

with $a, b > 0$.

Before the implementation of the slot charter agreement, the slot owner provides Q units of slots and delivers them to the slot charterer who consequently tries to sell them to the liner shipping market at selling price (i.e., a freight rate) p. The slot charterer and the slot owner operate according to a slot charter agreement that specifies who makes which decisions and how payments are transferred between the participants. We will consider and compare two different contractual arrangements, to be labeled as the General Slot Agreement and the Modified Slot Agreement, respectively.

When operating the slot charter business under the General Slot Agreement, the slot charterer and the slot owner negotiate sequentially in three stages, which can be shown as follows.

- Negotiation Stage 1: the slot charterer sets up a payment schedule which states that for each unit of the product he sells to the market, he pays $(1-r)$ % of a list price p_L to the slot owner.
- Negotiation Stage 2: the slot owner chooses the list price p_L to determine the final payment he will get back from the slot charterer for each slot sold.
- Negotiation Stage 3: the slot charterer decides the quantity Q for the slot owner to deliver and the final freight rate p of selling the slot to the liner shipping market.

Then, in order to derive a solution to such agreement, a backward-induction procedure is applied for analyzing these stages.

For the rest of this section we derive the optimal solution for a cooperative behavior, which will serve as a benchmark for comparing the performance of the Slot Charter Agreements. In the case of a slot charter business based on cooperative behaviors from both parties, the slot charter agreement between the slot seller (i.e., slot owner) and the slot buyer (i.e., slot charterer), the decision is to simultaneously choose the selling price p and the quantity Q with the objective to maximize the expected collective revenue which can be written as:

$$\Pi_c(p,Q) = pE\{min(D,Q)\} - cQ = pE\{min(y(p)\epsilon, Q)\} - cQ \qquad (3)$$

We define $z = \frac{Q}{y(p)}$ and call it the stocking factor of unused idle slots, which to some extent reflects the service level of the slot owner. Then, due to the one-to-one correspondence between (p,z) and (p,Q), for maximizing $\Pi_c(p,Q)$, choosing (p,Q) is equivalent to choosing (p,z). Furthermore, based on the demand function form (1) that for given (p,Q), the stocking factor is computed as:

$$P_s\{D(p) \le Q\} = P_s\{\epsilon \le \frac{Q}{y(p)} = z\} \qquad (4)$$

For a given distribution of ϵ, each z value corresponds to a unique stocking factor, and thus choosing a value for z is equivalent to setting up a service level for the slot owner. Substituting $Q = y(p)z$ into the formula, the objective function can be rephrased as:

$$\Pi_c(p,z) = y(p)\{pE[min(\epsilon,z)] - cz\} = y(p)\{p[z - \int_A^Z (z-x)f(x)\mathrm{d}x] - cz\}, \quad (5)$$

$$\text{where } \Lambda z = \int_A^Z (z-x)f(x)\mathrm{d}x. \qquad (6)$$

To find the optimal solution, denoted as (p_c^*, z_c^*), which maximizes $\pi_c(p,z)$, we first find the optimal price $p_c^*(z)$ for any given z, and then maximize $\pi_c(p_c^*(z), z)$ with respect to z to find the optimal z_c^*.

For any given $z \in [A,B]$, the unique optimal freight rate $p_c^*(z)$ is given by:

$$p_c^*(z) = \frac{cz}{z - \int_A^Z (z-x)f(x)\mathrm{d}x} + \frac{1}{b} \qquad (7)$$

Moreover, if the probability distribution function $f(\cdot)$ satisfies the property of increasing failure rate (IFR), the optimal z_c^* that maximizes $\Pi_c(p_c^*(z), z)$ is uniquely determined by:

$$\frac{cz}{z - \int_A^Z (z - x)f(x)\mathrm{d}x} + \frac{1}{b} = \frac{c}{1 - F(z_c^*)} \tag{8}$$

Then,

$$\Pi_c^* = ae^{-b\{\frac{cz_c^*}{z_c^* - \int_A^Z (z-x)f(x)\mathrm{d}x} + \frac{1}{b}\}}\frac{z_c^* - \int_A^Z (z-x)f(x)\mathrm{d}x}{b}$$

$$= ae^{-b\{\frac{cz_c^*}{z_c^* - \Lambda(z_c^*)} + \frac{1}{b}\}}\frac{z_c^* - \Lambda(z_c^*)}{b} \tag{9}$$

At Stage 3 of the decision procedure, for a given revenue share r, allocated by the slot charterer at the Stage 1, and a given list price p_L, chosen by the slot owner at Stage 2, the slot charterer's problem is to simultaneously choose the selling price p and the order quantity Q to maximize her own expected profit which can be calculated as:

$$\Pi_{d,R}(p, Q \mid r, p_L) = [p - (1 - r)p_L]E\{min(D, Q)\} - c_R Q. \tag{10}$$

As before, the stocking factor is $z = \frac{Q}{y(p)}$. Then, for the slot charterer, choosing (p, Q) is equivalent to choosing (p, z). Hence, the above profit function can be rewritten as:

$$\Pi_{d,R}(p, z \mid r, p_L) = y(p)\{[p - (1 - r)p_L][z - \Lambda(z)] - c\alpha z\} \tag{11}$$

Although the selling price p via the E-platform to the market is decided by the slot charterer, it should be close to or almost the same as the slot owner's offer to the same market in case the slot owner would like to sell directly these slots to the market (shippers). Note that in the liner shipping market, a slot owner and a slot charterer can be liner shipping carriers at the same time, which means that, generally speaking, they simultaneously are competitors besides the fact that slots are chartered from one player to the other on some specific voyage, i.e., some legs of the liner shipping service networks.

4.2   Performance of the Designed Model

Backward-induction is applied in this subsection so that stages of decision making procedures are analyzed. The decision making procedure 1 is applied during Stage 3. In other words, the decision making procedures follow a reversed sequence of the negotiation stages. Decision making procedures are listed as follows:

- Decision making procedure 1: The slot charterer decides the selling price
- Decision making procedure 2: The slot owner decides the list price
- Decision making procedure 3: The slot charterer decides the revenue share

Slot Charterer Decides the Selling Price. In order to find the optimal solution, denoted by (p_d^*, z_d^*), for maximizing the output of the profit function $\Pi_{d,R}(p, z|r, p_L)$, the optimal selling price $p_d^*(z)$ for any given z needs to be derived. Then the optimal z_d^* that maximizes $\Pi_{d,R}(p, z|r, p_L)$ with respect to z is to be determined. The results are summarized as follows.

For any given $z \in [A, B]$, list price $p_L > 0$, and revenue share $r \in (0, 1)$, the unique optimal selling price $p_d^*(z)$ is given by:

$$p_d^*(z) = (1-r)p_L + \frac{c\alpha z}{z - \Lambda(z)} + \frac{1}{b} \tag{12}$$

In addition, if the demand distribution satisfies the property of IFR, the optimal z_d^* that maximizes $\Pi_{d,R}(p_d^*(z), z|r, p_L)$ is uniquely determined by:

$$\frac{c\alpha z_d^*}{z_d^* - \Lambda(z_d^*)} + \frac{1}{b} = \frac{c\alpha}{1 - F\{z_d^*\}} \tag{13}$$

The IFR, i.e., $h(x) = f(x)/(1 - F(x))$ being increasing in x is a relatively weak condition satisfied by most commonly applied probability distributions like normal, uniform, and exponential distribution, etc., Eq. (13) implies that under this condition about the demand distribution, the optimal stocking factor z_d^* is in fact independent of the list price p_L and revenue share r. Rather it is uniquely determined by the demand distribution and other system parameters. Furthermore, Eqs. (12) and (13) indicate that the slot charterer's optimal selling price p_d^* consists of two main parts, i.e., the amount paid to the slot owner, namely, $(1 - r)p_L$, and for each unit sold plus a constant revenue margin for herself, namely, $c\alpha z/(z - \Lambda(z)) + 1/b$.

Note that the slot owner provides the slot charterer a list price according to z. Later on in the following analysis, we will further discuss whether z and the list price really affects the expected revenue.

Slot Owner Decides the List Price. At this stage of the decision making procedure, namely stage 2, knowing that the slot charterer chooses according to (12) and (13) at stage 3, the slot owner aims to set the list price p_L to maximize his own expected profit, for any given revenue r proposed by the slot charterer at Stage 1. The slot owner's profit function, denoted by $\Pi_{d,s}(p_L|r)$, is expressed as:

$$\Pi_{d,s}(p_L|r) = (1-r)p_L E\{min(D, Q_d)\} - c_s Q_d \tag{14}$$

After integrating $D = y(p_d)\epsilon$ and $Q_d = y(p_d)z_d$ into (14), the following equation can be obtained:

$$\Pi_{d,s}(p_L|r) = y(p_d)\{(1-r)p_L\{z_d - \Lambda(z_d)\} - c(1-\alpha)z_d\} \tag{15}$$

Since $y(p_d) = ae^{-bp_d}$ and (p_d^*, z_d^*) are determined in (12) and (13) during Stage 3, (15) can further be rephrased as:

$$\Pi_{d,s}(p_L|r) = ae^{-b\{(1-r)p_L + \frac{(c\alpha z_d^*)}{(z_d^* - \Lambda(z_d^*))} + \frac{1}{b}\}}\{(1-r)p_L\{z_d^* - \Lambda(z_d^*)\} - c(1-\alpha)z_d^*\} \tag{16}$$

For any given revenue share $r \in (0,1)$, the slot owner's unique optimal list price $p_L^*(r)$ is given by:

$$p_L^*(r) = 1/(1-r)\left\{\frac{cz_d^*(1-\alpha)}{z_d^* - \Lambda(z_d^*)} + \frac{1}{b}\right\} \tag{17}$$

From (17) we can see that the optimal list price p_L^* is increasing in slot charterer's revenue share r. Since the optimal z_d^* does not depend on the revenue share r, (17) further implies that the amount earned by the slot owner on each unit sold, namely, $(1-r)p_L^*$, is a constant. For instance, if the slot charterer raises her share r of the revenue, the slot owner would accordingly increase the optimal list price p_L^* to ensure the amount that he gets from each sold unit is not affected, which is very realistic in the liner shipping business. This is as expected, since from the slot owner's point of view, given that all money transfers are based on the units sold, what matters to himself is how much he earns on each unit sold. This also indicates that the slot charterer does not create any real bargain power by moving first, as a leader of this game, to set up the revenue share scheme, as what can be seen based on Stage 1 of this section of the analyses. Incorporating (17) into (12), we then have:

$$p_d^*(z_d^*) = (cz_d^*)/(z_d^* - \Lambda(z_d^*)) + 2/b \tag{18}$$

Therefore, the slot charterer's bargain power might superficially been reflected as revenue share. However, the slot charterer's optimal selling price does not really depend on that revenue share allocation r. This is a vital finding of this research as food for thought for the slot charterer, which is beyond the slot charterer's first instinct over the slot agreement related business.

5   Implications to the Slot Agreement Business Stakeholders

In this paper, we have investigated slot sharing E-platform mechanisms and modeling for liner shipping services. Finally, some implications to stakeholders, i.e., E-platform designers, slot owners (providers) and slot charterers (buyers) are provided.

- Roles of slot owners (providers), slot charterers (buyers) and customers need to be clearly defined in the design of the E-platforms. By so doing, all kinds of participants obtain feelings of ownership of the slot agreement E-platform and it might increase the overall number of participants involved.
- Timeliness of making decisions internally and externally makes sense for the overall performances of the E-platforms. An E-platform could pop-up options via user interfaces either to slot owners (providers) or to slot charterers (buyers) step by step according to the designed decision procedures, respectively.
- Centralized or decentralized structure of the E-platforms affect their outcome, therefore, the design needs to take into account business scenarios in various contexts, which could be further investigated in future research.

References

1. Alphaliner (2017). https://www.alphaliner.com/
2. Alphaliner: Top 100 liner carriers (2020). https://alphaliner.axsmarine.com/PublicTop100/
3. Bell, M.G., Liu, X., Angeloudis, P., Fonzone, A., Hosseinloo, S.H.: A frequency-based maritime container assignment model. Transp. Res. Part B Methodol. **45**(8), 1152–1161 (2011). https://doi.org/10.1016/j.trb.2011.04.002
4. Belobaba, P.P.: Airline yield management an overview of seat inventory control. Transp. Sci. **21**(2), 63–73 (1987). https://doi.org/10.1287/trsc.21.2.63
5. Caschili, S., Medda, F., Parola, F., Ferrari, C.: An analysis of shipping agreements: the cooperative container network. Netw. Spat. Econ. **14**(3–4), 357–377 (2014). https://doi.org/10.1007/s11067-014-9230-1
6. Caschili, S., Medda, F.R.: A review of the maritime container shipping industry as a complex adaptive system. Interdisc. Descr. Complex Syst. **10**(1), 1–15 (2012). https://doi.org/10.7906/indecs.10.1.1
7. Chen, X., Pang, Z., Pan, L.: Coordinating inventory control and pricing strategies for perishable products. Oper. Res. **62**, 284–300 (2014). https://doi.org/10.1287/opre.2014.1261
8. DAKOSY: DAKOSY launches myboxplace.de-the digital exchange platform for empty containers (2018). www.hafen-hamburg.de/en/news/dakosy-launches-myboxplace-de-the-digital-exchange-platform-for-empty-containers---35922
9. Di Febbraro, A., Sacco, N., Saeednia, M.: An agent-based framework for cooperative planning of intermodal freight transport chains. Transp. Res. Part C Emerg. Technol. **64**, 72–85 (2016). https://doi.org/10.1016/j.trc.2015.12.014
10. Ducruet, C., Notteboom, T.: The worldwide maritime network of container shipping: spatial structure and regional dynamics. Glob. Netw. **12**(3), 395–423 (2012). https://doi.org/10.1111/j.1471-0374.2011.00355.x
11. Emmons, H., Gilbert, S.M.: Note: The role of returns policies in pricing and inventory decisions for catalogue goods. Manag. Sci. **44**(2), 276–283 (1998). https://doi.org/10.1287/mnsc.44.2.276
12. Erdelyi, A., Topaloglu, H.: Computing protection level policies for dynamic capacity allocation problems by using stochastic approximation methods. IIE Trans. **41**(6), 498–510 (2009). https://doi.org/10.1080/07408170802706543
13. Eshippinggateway: Eshippinggateway platform functions-2019 (2019). https://www.eshippinggateway.com/win2door-lcl/enquiry-price.html?isConciseModel=true
14. Fang, X., Ru, J., Wang, Y.: Optimal procurement design of an assembly supply chain with information asymmetry. Prod. Oper. Manag. **23**(12), 2075–2088 (2014). https://doi.org/10.1111/poms.12199
15. Feng, C.M., Chow, I.C., Chang, C.H.: An optimal slot allocation in intra Asia service for liner shipping. In: Proceedings of the Eastern Asia Society for Transportation Studies, vol. 6 (The 7th International Conference of Eastern Asia Society for Transportation Studies 2007), p. 386, 11 p (2007). https://doi.org/10.11175/eastpro.2007.0.386.0
16. FreightHub: Online freight marketplaces vs. freight forwarders-2017 (2017). https://freighthub.com/en/blog/online-freight-marketplaces-vs-freight-forwarders/
17. FreightHub: Shipping alliances-what do they do and what does it mean-2017 (2017). https://freighthub.com/en/blog/shipping-alliances-mean/

18. FreightWaves: HMM forms space-sharing agreement with Maersk-2016 (2016). https://www.freightwaves.com/news/hmm-forms-space-sharing-agreement-with-maersk-msc

19. Gallego, G., Van Ryzin, G.: Optimal dynamic pricing of inventories with stochastic demand over finite horizons. Manag. Sci. **40**(8), 999–1020 (1994). https://doi.org/10.1287/mnsc.40.8.999

20. Govindan, K., Popiuc, M.N.: Overview and classification of coordination contracts within forward and reverse supply chains. University of Southern Denmark, Discussion Papers on Business and Economics, No. 7 (2011)

21. Granot, D., Yin, S.: On the effectiveness of returns policies in the price-dependent newsvendor model. Naval Res. Logist. (NRL) **52**(8), 765–779 (2005). https://doi.org/10.1002/nav.20114

22. Guericke, S.: Liner shipping network design: decision support and optimization methods for competitive networks. Ph.D. thesis, Fakultät Wirtschaftswissenschaften, Universität Paderborn (2014)

23. Gümüş, M., Jewkes, E.M., Bookbinder, J.H.: Impact of consignment inventory and vendor-managed inventory for a two-party supply chain. Int. J. Prod. Econ. **113**(2), 502–517 (2008). https://doi.org/10.1016/j.ijpe.2007.10.019

24. Hsu, C.I., Hsieh, Y.P.: Routing, ship size, and sailing frequency decision-making for a maritime hub-and-spoke container network. Math. Comput. Model. **45**(7–8), 899–916 (2007). https://doi.org/10.1016/j.mcm.2006.08.012

25. Kjeldsen, K.H.: Routing and scheduling in liner shipping. University of Aarhus, Department of Economics (2012)

26. Kuehne+Nagel: Kuehne+Nagel is expanding its digital seafreight platform sea explorer into a smart gateway-2018 (2018). https://newsroom.kuehne-nagel.com/kuehne-nagel-is-expanding-its-digital-seafreight-platform-sea-explorer-into-an-smart-gateway-for-all-liner-services-in-container-shipping/

27. Lam, J.S.L., Yap, W.Y.: Dynamics of liner shipping network and port connectivity in supply chain systems: analysis on East Asia. J. Transport Geogr. **19**(6), 1272–1281 (2011). https://doi.org/10.1016/j.jtrangeo.2011.06.007

28. Liu, D., Yang, H.L.: Optimal slot control model of container sea-rail intermodal transport based on revenue management. Procedia-Soc. Behav. Sci. **96**, 1250–1259 (2013). https://doi.org/10.1016/j.sbspro.2013.08.142

29. Liu, X.: Port choice: a frequency-based container assignment model. Ph.D. thesis, Department of Civil and Environmental Engineering, Imperial College London (2012). https://core.ac.uk/download/pdf/9833237.pdf

30. Lu, H.A., Chen, S.L., Lai, P.: Slot exchange and purchase planning of short sea services for liner carriers. J. Mar. Sci. Technol. **18**(5), 709–718 (2010). https://doi.org/10.6119/JMST.201010_18(5).0011

31. Papageorgiou, D.J., Cheon, M.S., Nemhauser, G., Sokol, J.: Approximate dynamic programming for a class of long-horizon maritime inventory routing problems. Transp. Sci. **49**(4), 870–885 (2015). https://doi.org/10.1287/trsc.2014.0542

32. Safety4sea: New digital seafreight platform launches to help container shipping-2018 (2018). https://safety4sea.com/new-digital-seafreight-platform-launched-to-help-container-shipping/

33. Schmidt, K.: Cooperative Work and Coordinative Practices: Contributions to the Conceptual Foundations of Computer-Supported Cooperative Work (CSCW). Springer, London (2011). https://doi.org/10.1007/978-1-84800-068-1

34. Shi, X., Meersman, H., Voß, S.: The win-win game in slot-chartering agreement among the liner competitors and collaborators. In: Proceedings of the IAME 2008

Conference Sustainability in International Shipping, Port and Logistics Industries and the China Factor, pp. D2/T2/S2-3, 1–26. IAME, Dalian (2008)

35. ShipHub: Alliances in container shipping (2020). https://www.shiphub.co/alliances-in-container-shipping/

36. Supply Chain Dive: ZIM will join 2M alliance on Asia-US East coast trade-2018 (2018). https://www.supplychaindive.com/news/ZIM-slot-sharing-2M-Maersk-MSC/528178/

37. Ting, S.C., Tzeng, G.H.: An optimal containership slot allocation for liner shipping revenue management. Marit. Policy Manag. **31**(3), 199–211 (2004). https://doi.org/10.1080/0308883032000209553

38. Wang, S.: Formulating cargo inventory costs for liner shipping network design. Marit. Policy Manag. **44**(1), 62–80 (2017). https://doi.org/10.1080/03088839.2016.1245879

39. Wu, J.W., Lee, W.C., Lei, C.L.: Optimal inventory policy involving ordering cost reduction, back-order discounts, and variable lead time demand by minimax criterion. Math. Prob. Eng. 2009 (2009). Article ID: 928932. https://doi.org/10.1155/2009/928932

40. Yi, H., Sarker, B.R.: An operational policy for an integrated inventory system under consignment stock policy with controllable lead time and buyers' space limitation. Comput. Oper. Res. **40**(11), 2632–2645 (2013). https://doi.org/10.1016/j.cor.2013.05.001

41. Zahran, S.K., Jaber, M.Y., Zanoni, S.: Comparing different coordination scenarios in a three-level supply chain system. Int. J. Prod. Res. **55**(14), 4068–4088 (2017). https://doi.org/10.1080/00207543.2016.1249431

42. Zurheide, S., Fischer, K.: A revenue management slot allocation model with prioritization for the liner shipping industry. In: Hu, B., Morasch, K., Pickl, S., Siegle, M. (eds.) Operations Research Proceedings 2010. ORP, pp. 143–148. Springer, Heidelberg (2011). https://doi.org/10.1007/978-3-642-20009-0_23

Smart City Through Design: Preparation of a New Wayfinding System in Prague

Petr Štěpánek[✉]

Faculty of Multimedia Communication, Tomas Bata
University in Zlín, Univerzitní 2431, 760 01 Zlín, Czech Republic
`petr.stepanek@thesign.cz`

Abstract. The City of Prague decided to prepare and implement a new wayfinding system for public transportation. The analytical part of the project is being prepared for the second year and will culminate with a call for participation in the international graphic competition. The project outputs are the result of interdisciplinary research and idea disputes of many experts and stakeholders.

The cross-sectional paradigm of the project is to increase the economic, social and environmental sustainability of the city through its more attractive and accessible public transport. Project preparation demonstrated the need for greater interaction between different disciplines and the need to confront their professional dogmas.

Although the methodological, creative and technological framework of the wayfinding system is described more than enough, there are countless specific problems that hinder their innovation.

A separate topic is the elaboration of substantive and formal parameters of the competition, taking into account the specificities of the project and the necessary legislative framework of public procurement.

Keywords: Design competition · Prague · Public transport · Smart city · Wayfinding system

1 Introduction and Purpose

1.1 Wayfinding System

Wayfinding refers to information (today graphic, architectural, electronic, and virtual) systems that guide people through the physical environment (indoor and outdoor) and improve their understanding of the place. It´s a very interdisciplinary field that goes beyond the limits of graphic design. A good wayfinding system is increasingly important in the environment of cities (including railway stations, airports, hospitals and other large complexes).

Complex systems for wayfinding often combine maps, colors, symbols and other units of communications. When designing wayfinding systems, the crucial application is the paradigm of the semantic concept of design. These systems integrate interactive interfaces, smart phone applications and other digital technologies.

© Springer Nature Switzerland AG 2020
C. Stephanidis et al. (Eds.): HCII 2020, LNCS 12423, pp. 514–526, 2020.
https://doi.org/10.1007/978-3-030-60114-0_35

The approach to wayfinding systems is changing. It can be said that they are constantly improving, responding to more specific needs and challenges, their content is also reflecting the global character of traveling public.

1.2 Smart City Concept

The Smart City is a concept of an environmentally, economically, and socially sustainable city. It mainly includes *technological* (mobility, energy, buildings, environmental infrastructure, digital technologies, etc.) and *social* (participation, community, housing) components, which are characterized by a high level of innovation (use of best available technologies), extensive data use, and sophisticated management. Many smart city projects concern sustainable mobility and the use of data in transport. Optimization of driving, walking or parking, use of public transport and other data applications are becoming part of navigation systems.

One of the paradigms of the Smart City concept is also the attractiveness of public transport, the restriction of individual car transport and the motivation to walk and use public space. The Smart City is also the most harmonized way of managing cities and regions using the highest achievable level of knowledge, and the sustainable development of cities and regions is a key objective and determinant.

In practice, two types of smart city projects are generally realized:

- Long-term, interdisciplinary projects at the level of the whole city or an integral part (urban district).
- Sector related project, i.e. mobility, renewable energy sources, housing.
- Individual, rather autonomous, but highly innovative (infrastructure, social, environmental) projects based on BAT, the impact of which meets the concept and objectives of Smart City (and compatible with the public interest).

Smart City projects usually have a public character and are implemented mainly at the level of towns, partially regions (self-governing territorial units) or through state (state-controlled) organizations, so municipalities are therefore a key partner. The Smart City concept is (unfortunately) also often just a marketing label and a business channel.

The upgrade of the Prague wayfinding system is directly related to the Prague concept of the smart city titled Smart Prague 2030. A significant part of its projects concerns transport and information related to it. Information on the functioning of public transport cannot be dealt with autonomously. It is important to interact with other information determining the movement in the city, the use of data and sensors.

1.3 Prague Public Transport

Prague Public Transport (the exact name of the system is Prague Integrated Transit) is an integrated transport system, including metro, trams, railways, trolleybuses, city and suburban bus lines, cable car, several river ferries and a network of P+R (Park and Ride) car parks. It covers the territory of the capital city of Prague and a large part of the Central Bohemian Region.

Several organizations participate in the provision of public transport: ROPID (coordinator of Prague integrated transport), the Prague transport company, private carriers, railways, transport companies of the cities of the Central Bohemian region, taxis etc.

2 Historical Aspects

First thoughts on the underground railway in Prague date back to the period before WWII, but the project was introduced in the 1960s. The Prague metro is one of the key construction projects of the so-called normalization period (socialist regime in Czechoslovakia after 1969) and its showcase. Therefore, the best available resources were concentrated on its implementation. Although its model was the Moscow metro and the USSR participated in the construction, the aesthetic language of the metro reflected the style of post-war modernity.

The level of graphic design used in post-war Czechoslovakia was ambivalent. On one hand, we adore theater and film posters and some books of the time, on the other hand, the denial of the market economy has actually degraded the level of corporate identity, packaging design, advertising and most print media. A large qualitative barrier was also the technological deficit of reproductive technologies. The profession of graphic designer was exclusive, tied to membership in a trade union and conditioned by loyalty to the regime. At the same time, however, there was a tradition of pre-war design, of which the most prominent figure was probably Ladislav Sutnar[1].

The design of the wayfinding system in the Prague metro was designed by two important graphic designers: Jiří Rathouský and Rostislav Vaněk. At the time of its inception, there was an orientation system that was competitive with the level of design in the world. Their design is an integral part of the aesthetic face of the metro, whose architecture was also shaped by the authors of ceramic tiles, sculptures, reliefs, furniture, etc. From today's point of view, the wayfinding system is perceived as iconic.

A special font was designed for the stations, the whole system uses pictograms harmonized with the typography.

The orientation in the metro also includes architectural elements in the stations and their colors. This ambitious project was to include an orientation system for other transportation means (tram, bus), but it was never implemented. The navigation of surface transport was reduced to the bare minimum, ascetic, gray, unaesthetic – like all public space and life of the time.

The last thirty years have brought visual smog advertising to the subway and also the need to renovate stations. The interventions of architects and traffic engineers into the wayfinding system were often fatal and nonconceptual. In the metro, various variants of logotypes, pictograms, and color scales multiplied. Not all authors of the new stations understood the paradigm of metro navigation. The current situation is still functional, but it is far from comparable with the level of similar metropolises (and not at all with innovated wayfinding systems, e.g. in London).

Nevertheless, the design of the Prague metro is perceived as a cult matter (Pavelková 2013). There are several reasons: it is undoubtedly a well-functioning transport system,

[1] Ladislav Sutnar (1897–1976) was Czech-American graphic designer, a pioneer of information design and information architecture.

tourists also perceive it positively (EY 2019), and the interest in brutalist and technical architecture of the post-war period (1960s to 1980s) has revived in recent years. With growing awareness of the quality of design and the importance of public space, a debate also began about the need to deal with the problem of navigation, not only in the metro, but in the whole Prague public transport system as well as in the cityscape itself.

Although sentiment towards the current system can be expected (as one of the few quality graphic design projects from the times of normalization), the professional public prefers a radical and complex change and solution, including underground transport. The main reasons are the fragmentation of this subsystem as a consequence of desynchronized reconstructions of metro stations.

3   Wayfinding System Requirements

3.1   Strategical Project Goals

The project reflects the requirements of the Strategic Plan of Prague, Smart City Prague concept and the Plan for Sustainable Mobility of Prague (and the metropolitan area). The project set the following requirements for a new system of orientation and navigation in public transport and public space:

- Wayfinding will be an important part of the overall presentation of the city and its branding.
- It will address all types of mobility (public, pedestrian, bicycle and individual motor transport) with an emphasis on the preference for sustainable types of mobility and the promotion of multimodality.

  The following strategic goals were defined for the project implementation:

- Raise public awareness with an emphasis on mobility services.
- Increase the comprehensibility of information.
- Increase the share of sustainable types of mobility.
- Increase the quality of public spaces.
- Increase the cultural identification of residents with the city.
- Increase the efficiency of administration and maintenance of the information and orientation (navigation) system.
- Unify the design and increase the quality of providing the information and orientation system while respecting the visual style of the city of Prague.

3.2   Environmental, Social and Economic Aspects

Wayfinding systems are similarly quite standardized in their visible (graphic) and basic form. There are several reasons: globalized adopting of the best case studies, international standards for accessibility for the disabled, technological globalization and unification of traditional inactive interfaces. Nevertheless, the quality of design that affects public space varies from country to country and city to city.

3.3 Public Interest

From the beginning, the paradigm of fulfilling the public interest through this project was emphasized. Any project is better promoted through the argument that it fulfills already adopted strategies, policies and action plans. The emphasis on such a fact confirms that it fulfills the codified public interest. For decision makers from different sectors, it is difficult to accept the cost of (not necessary) redesign. The analysis therefore emphasized the positive impacts of the project on solving environmental and social problems and its positive externalities.

The following aspects were emphasized:

- Promoting the environmental, economic and social sustainability of a city directly dependent on attractive, socially non-stigmatized, accessible and easy-to-use public transport.
- The need to develop the competitiveness of the city and the adjacent region, which is limited, among other things, by the quality of public space and includes the intention to support the creative industries in the metropolis and build the concept of Smart city.
- Building and protection of cultural heritage (of which the wayfinding system is a part).
- The need to improve the quality of the physical public space and the motivation for its use.
- Maintaining a sufficient degree of social cohesion also dependent on quality public transport.
- Ensuring the permeability and accessibility of physical public space, as well as maintaining the accessibility and permeability of the city for the disabled.
- Ensuring the maximum possible information intelligibility for the inhabitants of the city and its visitors.
- The intention to support a sustainable tourism industry in the metropolitan area.
- The intention to support the brand of the capital, whose reputation is directly affected by the quality of public transport and of which the new wayfinding system should become a visible part.
- Meeting the objectives of the political representation program statement[2].

3.4 Accessibility Issues

From the beginning, the issue of inclusion of the wayfinding system for the disabled (in terms of sight, hearing, or movement) and for users who cannot use electronic devices for any reason was addressed. It turned out that the standards of the Czech Republic are stricter than the EU standards. Devices for visually impaired users work (from a design point of view) independently and sufficiently.

The mandatory condition for participation in a design competition is compliance with all the necessary standards, thus a methodology reflecting this issue is required.

---

[2] This is a formal but key argument for the political enforcement of the project.

4 Interdisciplinary Approach and Confrontation of Professional and Sectoral Paradigms

4.1 Project Management

Contracting authority of the project of innovation of the unified information system (wayfinding system) was ROPID – Regional Organizer of Prague Integrated Transport. This organization, managed by the capital city of Prague, harmonizes transport in Prague and in the metropolitan area around Prague, a significant part of the self-governing Central Bohemian Region, from which 140,000 inhabitants commute daily to Prague.

The analytical part of the project was implemented by the consulting company Ernst & Young and the consulting company CEDOP (Center for Efficient Transport). The team also included representatives of the Institute of Planning and Development of Prague, the Prague Transport Company and later also representatives of the city management.

The output of the project for the preparation of a new wayfinding system for Prague public transport is six implementation studies. The new wayfinding system will emerge from the author's competition. The implementation of the navigation system will be divided between the institutions managed by the capital city of Prague and coordinated by ROPID. The project is currently awaiting the approval from the political representation.

The planned budget of the project is approximately EUR 150 million.

4.2 Conflict of Professional Approaches

Participation in the public contract for project preparation was conditioned by strict requirements for formal qualification and real competence of members of the expert team. This condition reflected the high degree of interdisciplinarity of the project and a similar approach was reflected in the preparation of the author's design competition. The team included an architect and designer, traffic engineers, economists and project managers. In a wider team of experts from the organizations that the project was to affect, then also lawyers, vehicle technicians and others.

It turned out that participation of different professions is necessary to balance and harmonize the various expert, often fundamental, approaches that needed to be corrected. Several fundamental and conflicting approaches can be described as follows:

- Fetishism of (changeable) norms, binding (not always relevant) to the legislative framework and bureaucratic caution typical especially of corporate lawyers. The flexibility of the project management of a large corporation (transport company) is limited (legal framework of public tenders, powerful unions etc.).
- Aesthetic relentlessness of architects and professions associated with the protection of culture heritage. The project had to overcome the distrust of fans of existing navigation design and at the same time explain the need for some technological interventions in public space. It was also necessary to set a realistic approach to the existence of advertising in the public transport premises.

- One-dimensional perception of public space by transport engineers, who tend to reduce the city to transport infrastructure and mobility only as a matter of logistical efficiency. It was also very challenging to enforce the emotional, psychological and aesthetic aspects of mobility in the city[3].

A typical example of the conflict of different approaches was the question of the intensity of the deployment of navigation elements in the city. Fundamentalists from the transport sector were confronted with the fact of various (medieval, modernist) urban structures of the city or the agenda of cultural heritage protection. Architects had to accept that the design of a wayfinding system is not just an agenda of creative disciplines.

4.3 Participation and Project Communication

The participatory dimension of the project was absolutely crucial. For this reason, a PR agency also joined the implementation consortium. The communication of the project proved to be a key determinant of its success. Participation and communication had to solve the following problems, barriers and risks:

- Ensuring the support of municipal political representation. The implementation of the project is ensured by organizations that are established or managed by the capital city of Prague. In case of disagreement of the capital's management, the project will not be executed. Currently (May 2020) the project is awaiting approval. Politicians were concerned about how the public would accept such an expensive redesign, because only some of its constituents are aware of the need of change. The change in the approach of part of the new political representation with a different value framework was positive (one of the politicians is a top graphic designer).
- Trust in professionals. There is a (gradually disappearing) distrust of public tenders among graphic designers. There are many cases where the impartiality of a jury or its competence can be questioned. Many contracts were won by low level suppliers due to the very low bid price (or non-transparent or incompetent procurement management). Different generational attitudes are represented by two organizations: the Union of Graphic Design and the Association of Applied Graphics.
- Internal resistance to change. Especially within the Prague transport company, the atmosphere was not conducive to changes that are not considered important and involve large costs. Some employees also have a strong affection for the original design.
- The topic of the wayfinding system is sensitive for experts who deal with this issue (no one wants to be left out). Communication with stakeholders was also a guarantee of their loyal or at least neutral attitude towards the project.
- The results of quantitative research (EY 2019) have shown that the public and tourists are satisfied with the current state of the information system. It is very difficult

---

[3] We can say that e.g. architects are more aware of the cultural and social dimension of the use of public space including public transport. City dwellers choose less logistically efficient, but subjectively more pleasant (more stimulating, safer, etc.) ways to achieve their goals (Gehl 2010).

to inspire the public to change the information infrastructure, when benefits of the upgrade are perceived only by experts[4].

Therefore, the project also included extensive individual interviews with stakeholders (including graphic designers, publicists and theorists, local politicians and other opinion makers). At the same time, institutional negotiations took place with representatives of non-governmental organizations representing disabled citizens, with experts for the protection of cultural heritage, and organizations associating graphic design.

There were three large multimedia streaming presentations in cooperation with the Prague Institute of Planning and Development, two workshops with graphic artists and representatives of art schools, a public opinion poll and ongoing presentations of the project in the media.

5   Key Parameters of the Proposed Wayfinding System

5.1   General Paradigm

From the confrontation of various expert approaches, the analysis of examples of good practice from abroad, interviewing public transport users, and taking into account other activities of the city (redesign of furniture, smart city concepts), the requirements for a new wayfinding system were distilled.

It turned out that the public interest associated with the implementation of this project is identical to the public interest, which fulfills the smart city concept. General support for smart cities can also be a crucial factor in promoting and funding a project[5].

In general and in accordance with the strategic plan, the Prague wayfinding system innovation project must positively contribute to the environmental, social and economic sustainability of the city and region, to the physical and social permeability of the city, support smart city approach (data use, climate protection) and sustainable forms of mobility.

5.2   Quality Requirements

The specific requirements for the new wayfinding system were formulated in areas as follows:

- **Complexity.** The wayfinding system must support all types of mobility as well as all system statutes, situations and planned and extraordinary traffic events.

---

[4] Exaggerated emphasis on participation can also have a negative effect. For example, the Vienna Public Transport company included an unsuccessful (too naturalistic) pictogram of a sports hall in its wayfinding system. Its form was selected in a survey.

[5] The project was brought to the attention of the planned investment platform for Smart cities in the Czech Republic, which should use the financial instruments of the European Investment Bank.

- **Accessibility.** The information must be provided in such a way that it depends as little as possible on the user's knowledge of the territory, language skills, information literacy, physical and sensory abilities or ownership of electronic devices[6].
- **Openness and multimodality.** The system must be open to future changes in the transport system[7].
- **Ubiquity.** The system must ensure the information security of the passenger at all times (where he is, what his options are, what will follow)[8]. The system must support passengers' decision-making at all times (even at the cost of more frequent repetition of information) and provide information in various forms.
- **Safety.** The wayfinding system must not conflict with safety rules and promote the safe behavior of all transport participants.
- **Validity and flexibility.** The system must be ready to update information quickly.
- **Connectivity.** The system must interconnect other information and navigation systems (railways, airports) and support their use[9].

Traffic information should respect the following principles:

- **The principle of mass.** The form of communication is determined by the number of recipients.
- **Speed of information.** Reduced but fast information is passed on to people on the move. In other cases, the maximum amount of structured information is preferred.
- **The rule of entropy.** Standard conditions require less information than emergencies. Extraordinary events should be covered by multiple information channels.
- **User friendliness.** In addition to accessibility standards (readability, comprehensibility), a client approach based on maximum user friendliness must also be taken into account. The passenger is not the enemy.
- **Intuitiveness and semantic logic.** The same type of information is presented by the same means and using the same graphic attributes in all media.
- **Hierarchisation of information.** Prediction of decision-making processes must be reflected in the form and quantity of information provided.
- **Continuity of objectives.** Once set, the goal must not be neglected.
- **Specification of minimum and confirmatory information.**
- **Same place for wayfinding system.** Navigation information must be maximally concentrated in one place. Concentration of navigation information in one (intuitively searchable) place facilitates their search and increases the subjective comfort of passenger transport.

---

[6] Many public transport users are dependent on their smartphones. It turned out that people move differently on familiar routes and differently in an unknown neighborhood, subway station, etc. Navigation uncertainty often motivates them to use a car (EY 2019).

[7] Such a change may be new modes of transport, shared means of transport, new types of urban infrastructures, requirements for the resilience of the city, changes (extension of lines, etc.).

[8] This requirement applied to walking in the city was the subject of disputes with architects. Architects do not want to prioritize navigation over design. It is a conflict of professional paradigms and priorities.

[9] This can be achieved, for example, by unifying the signage, duplicating, combining or substituting the labeling of public transport elements.

- **Association of basic and supplementary information**. Presentation of information in various forms (color, pictogram, number, text, possibly also architectural elements, sound, etc.).

All of this shows how important it is to confront the knowledge bases of different fields. Relatively well and extensively codified rules for wayfinding systems are not applied in the design of interactive interfaces. It is governed by other paradigms, often technologically or professionally conditioned.

The socio-demographic aspect also has a great influence. Different generations (and different social groups) receive information in different ways and have different preferences. This aspect must also be taken into account, for example, in order to maintain the social cohesion and social permeability of public transport and public space.

5.3 Design as a Tool of Smartification

The concept of smart cities in Prague is based on the Strategic Plan of the City of Prague, the very concept of smart city is then codified in several European and Czech methodologies[10].

In the Czech Republic, SC projects are methodologically based on documents prepared in the university and research sectors for the needs of the public sector (government, cities) and NGOs. Methodological trends associated with SC projects are as follows:

- Links to Industry 4.0 and Company 4.0.
- Greater accent on social projects, regional cohesion and social innovation, which reflect demographic challenges in the near future.
- Higher participation (public, stakeholders) rate.

As part of the Prague Strategic Plan and the Smart cities concept, the preparation of a new wayfinding system fulfills several specific objectives, including objectives that are part of EU cohesion policy:

- A smarter Europe supporting innovative and smart economic transformations.
- A greener Europe with low CO_2 emissions.
- A more interconnected Europe that increases mobility and makes ICT accessible.
- Social Europe.
- Europe closer to the citizens and promoting the sustainable and integrated development of all regions through local initiatives.

---

[10] Czech SC approach is based on two upgraded documents: Smart Cities methodology (Ministry of regional development): Methodology for the preparation and implementation of the Smart Cities concept at the level of cities, municipalities and regions (2019) and Project outputs SMART Czechia, prepared on the premises of the Union of Towns and Municipalities of the Czech Republic (2020). In addition, there are partial sectoral methodologies, especially for the area of environment protection, urban and spatial planning, housing, Industry 4.0 and mobility.

Meeting these objectives increases the chance of at least partial use of ESIF 2021–2027 or EIB financial instruments. The redesign of the wayfinding system also fulfills five priorities for the Czech Republic:

- Low carbon economy and environmental responsibility.
- Development of knowledge economy.
- Educated and cohesive society.
- Availability and mobility[11].
- Sustainable development of the territory[12].

If an attractive wayfinding system is implemented for the Prague metropolitan area, more positive impacts compatible with the goals of the smart city concept can be expected. Prague suffers from suburbanization (urban sprawl), which generates too much individual car traffic. Part of this traffic load is transferable to public transport, provided that it will be (especially emotionally, functionally) an attractive alternative. The intention to build an attractive city brand is also related to the redesign of its communication attributes. Higher physical and consequently social permeability is the key to cohesion. Attractive public space is a tool for reducing car traffic. More similar effects of improving the wayfinding system on quality of life, cohesion and sustainability can be found.

6 Design Competition

6.1 Design Competition Goals

The design competition is the key part of the project. The result of the design competition is the design of graphic attributes and the related use design of a unified information style of Prague integrated transport system, as well as the public spaces in the capital. That is, a functional and comprehensive orientation and information system for all types of mobility.

The ambition of the new wafinding system must be a top quality proposal, ranking among the best projects in the world, reflection of new (smart) technologies and the paradigm of sustainable mobility. The general public (unlike the professional) will not evaluate the current design very critically and the new wayfinding system will be critically compared with the original one. Although the analysis can greatly refine the assignment of the project, the quality of the result depends on the ability to interpret the requirements into the subtle nuances of the graphic language.

The aim of the competition is mainly:

---

[11] Specific objectives: Development and improvement of transport infrastructure, development and improvement of transport integration, introduction of new technologies for organization of transport and reduction of traffic load, efficient use of multimodal freight transport, increase of use and availability of alternative drives in transport.

[12] Protection, development and support of cultural heritage, improvement of public spaces, sustainable tourism, quality of public space, development of non-motorized transport.

- Selection of a qualified supplier of wayfinding system design with proven competence and capacity to design it in its entirety and capable of long-term contractual cooperation.
- Obtaining a quality proposal that is competitive in the international context, which will enable its further development and implementation in the next decades,
- Providing functional documents for the subsequent implementation of the project,
- Effective progress and fulfillment of the overall objectives of the project.

6.2 Competition Parameters

The parameters of the competition were mainly influenced by the public status of the contracting authority, positive and negative experiences from similar competitions, participatory activities and the attitude of stakeholders and, above all, the goals to be achieved.

The competition parameters are designed[13] as follows:

- International competition.
- Anonymity of applicants and proposals.
- Requirement for the level of qualification of the research team.
- Two-phase competition.
- Public tender based on relevant Czech legal framework.

International benchmarking will be applied to the outputs. Graphic design is a completely internationalized sector of the creative industry, in the field of design of so-called wayfinding systems determined by universal global standards.

The international character of the competition will be reflected in the composition of the jury. Inviting foreign candidates can have a positive effect on its competitive nature and level of innovation, ensure a reflection of current discourse and trends in the field and eliminate the effects of the jurors' subjective perception of reputation and competence of candidates.

With regard to the interdisciplinary nature of the project, it is also required to meet the qualifications of the supplier team. The supplier must be able not only to prepare a tender proposal, but also to develop it into a comprehensive system. The team must understand the methodological framework of wayfinding systems, links to the smart cities agenda, understand the psychological, technological and social aspects of mobility.

The anonymity of candidates and proposals should enforce the independence of the competition. At the same time, it is conditioned by the chosen legislative framework[14].

The applicant's qualification requirements reflect the interdisciplinary character and importance of the project, the financial ambitiousness of its implementation, the need for the holistic approach and to the knowledge of the professional discourse, the project's impact on public space and last but not least the expected scope of proposals.

Each candidate must demonstrate that he has the following qualified experts:

---

[13] But not yet announced (delayed due to the COVID-19 as well as political reasons).

[14] Two options were discussed: a competitive dialogue and finally a selected design competition, followed by a dialogue with a maximum of three selected teams.

- Graphic designer with history of experience in wayfinding systems.
- Methodologist with demonstrable knowledge of standards, technical and legal aspects of wayfinding systems.
- Typographer with demonstrable experience in the design of author's fonts.
- UX designer.
- Architect or designer/ sculptor with experience in spatial realizations,
- Sociologist, psychologist.

The requirements for the composition of the jury are that it be internationally, generationally, institutionally and regionally diversified. Only experts can vote on the proposals in the jury. The participation of independent non-voting opponents and representatives of the contracting authority is limited.

7 Conclusion

The preparation of a project for the new Prague wayfinding system is an example of the interdisciplinary nature of design. The conflict of interests of different stakeholders and the confrontation of many expert approaches underlined the importance of design management. At the same time, it uncovered what the design can provide to the current environmental, social and technological challenges, including those, associated with the concept of smart cities.

The information system should be designed to support the natural movement of the city, to remove mental barriers in understanding of the city and to support the spatial memory of the inhabitants. It should also serve as a means of navigation between individual types of public transport, especially their interconnectivity. Last but not least, it should lead the people to prefer sustainable modes of transportation, in particular walking, cycling and public transit.

The new Prague wayfinding system for public transport and public space has the ambition to become not only a functional navigation system for the city, but also one of the pillars of its city image and a mirror of the value system of its inhabitants.

References

EY, CEDOP: Implementation study. Integrated information system. Analytical part A3–A4 (2019)

Gehl, J.: Cities for People (2010)

GEOtest: URBIS – Smart Cities Investment Platform – CZ. Assignment report (2020)

Ministry of Regional Development of the CR, Czech Technical University in Prague: Methodology for preparation and implementation of the Smart Cities concept at the level of cities, municipalities and regions (2019)

Pavelková, M.: Jiří Rathouský – Grafický design pražského metra. Palacky University, Olomouc (2013)

Prague Institute of planning and Development: Strategic plan of Prague (2015)

Stepanek, P. (EY): Implementation study. Graphic design competition. Implementation part R2 (2019)

Mystery Shopping in Public Transport: The Case of Bus Station Design

Stefan Voß[1]($\boxtimes$)(ID), Gonzalo Mejia[2](ID), and Alexander Voß[1]

[1] Institute of Information Systems, University of Hamburg,
Von-Melle-Park 5, 20146 Hamburg, Germany
stefan.voss@uni-hamburg.de, alexander.voss@hamburg.de
[2] Universidad de La Sabena, Bogota, Colombia
gonzalo.mejia@unisabana.edu.co

Abstract. In times of extended awareness regarding climate change and emission control, the use of public mass transit comes into the forefront of discussions regarding mobility of people especially in metropolitan areas. This includes multiple modes such as subway, light rail, bus and many others. In this paper we survey the state-of-the-art regarding bus station design and extend earlier approaches by combining mystery shopping as a marketing-oriented method with appropriate modeling (using Business Process Modeling Notation, BPMN) and concepts from virtual reality. Moreover, we reflect on possible disturbances and bus station design.

Keywords: Public transport · Bus station design · BPMN · Virtual reality · Mystery shopping · Disturbance · Covid19

1 Introduction

Whenever we use public transport, we are supposed to reach a target place, leaving some origin and arriving at some destination. We have a purpose and possibly walking is too much, a bicycle not available (or the hill is too steep) and the car may be difficult to park. So, we use public transport. This could be subway, bus, many others. And we have a given system that provides us what we want. Does it? Very often it works, but there is also hesitation in many places around the world. For instance, in the United States we often hear that public transport is for poor people, those who cannot afford a big car. This is prejudice, though, but unfortunately not always untrue.

Whenever we want to use public transport, we need information; for instance, which means of transportation is available at what time, how much do we need to pay and how to access transport? We expect that clever people have done some proper investigation and that everything works. This would be an ideal world. Then, however, we meet disturbances, problems and alike (for a recent survey see [14]). This could be a small delay and it could be a major pandemic like Covid19 with a lockdown. It could be a high-probability low-impact event or a very low-probability very high-impact event. No matter, the question remains

C. Stephanidis et al. (Eds.): HCII 2020, LNCS 12423, pp. 527–542, 2020.
https://doi.org/10.1007/978-3-030-60114-0_36

on how could we make the public transport system better (or, better, those who are responsible for running the system)?

An interesting observation is that many people including the general public are discussing about the quality of public transport, even if it might only be handwaving. But then nothing changes. May be the users should pay attention. May be the users could even provide some input on how to improve the public transport system. May be, we are not properly trained in marketing but that might even be an advantage. We are not bound to use predefined, sometimes useless (sorry), knowledge from academia. May be, we just need to be careful in observing. In that sense we could all be so-called mystery shoppers in public transport.

Extending earlier work [17,18], this research focuses on modeling and analyzing bus stations within public transit. As an example, consider a Bus Rapid Transit (BRT) station. BRT refers to a "bus-based rapid transit system that can achieve high capacity, speed, and service quality at relatively low cost by combining segregated bus lanes that are typically median aligned with off-board fare collection, level boarding, bus priority at intersections, and other quality-of-service elements (such as information technology and strong branding)" [22]. The components of BRT include: vehicles, stops, stations, terminals, and corridors. A wide variety of rights-of-way, pre-board fare collection, use of modern information and communication technologies (ICT), all-day service, and brand identity can be aligned with a BRT system. To be specific, consider the TransMilenio system, as it is found in Bogota, Colombia (see Fig. 1).

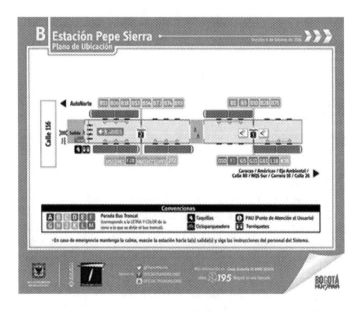

Fig. 1. Typical layout of a TransMilenio station, from [37]

Classical concepts like BPMN for modeling or also living labs [33] may help to advance the knowledge about bus stations as major access points for public transport. Nevertheless, when it comes to improving the mobility needs of todays' populations in metropolises and mega-cities, new avenues of research need to be undertaken. That is, beyond classical modeling approaches, one may use a virtual reality environment as well as the concept of mystery shopping to gain new insights into the design of bus stations. *Virtual reality* (VR) deals with the computer-generated emulation of real-world environments or the creation of fictional environments [34]. Users can immerse themselves in three-dimensional digital environments and simulations through the use of devices such as head-mounted displays. *Augmented reality* (AR) is concerned with enhancing the perception of a real-world environment with virtual effects or additional information as opposed to the entirely virtual environment created by VR [5]. That is, a user's perception of the surroundings is extended through information that would not be visible in reality by use of digital devices such as digitally-enabled glasses or displays.

Mystery shopping (MS) is a concept mostly used in marketing when it comes to measure quality of service (QoS), or compliance with regulation, or to gather specific information about products and services [41]. With the combined use of these technologies, i.e. VR and MS, new insights may be gained at the interface of people using public transport systems and the system itself, especially allowing the consideration of different user groups that may want to use public transport, as there are, among others, elderly, handicapped, young children or pregnant women. A major takeaway from our research is that classical questionnaire-based research as it is commonly found in recent literature (see, e.g., some contributions on https://link.springer.com/journal/volumesAndIssues/12469) is too short-sighted when it comes to advancing and influencing the managerial insights of policy makers within public transport. AR, VR and MS in combination are able to change this.

The exposition of the subsequent sections first elaborates on various aspects regarding bus station design and provides a related survey. Then, Sect. 3 is devoted to MS and its use in public transport. This is moderately interleaved with our intention to combine this topic with modern ICT. Section 4 concludes and summarizes some future research needs.

2   Bus Station Design

Bus stations are access points to public transport systems (and, as the name says, especially bus systems). They can be just simple sign posts for a single stop of a single line and they can be versatile transfer centers where many bus lines or even different means of transport meet and allow for transfer. Various aspects need to be considered when designing a bus station as there are, foremost, functionality requirements and safety. Moreover, it may need to be subjectively pleasing, fulfill information management requirements as well as other types of aspects.[1]

2.1 Functionality

The initial functionality requirement refers to a station being an access point to public transportation. Whatever one sees gives a first indication. And certainly the (*mystery shopping*) views in Fig. 2 are not necessarily typical ones.

Various measures are related to the functionality of bus stations including size, location, capacity, time of use and alike. Moreover, beyond functionality various other factors may be considered. As we started with a BRT system in the previous section, let us focus on BRT. The BRT Standard is an evaluation tool for world-class bus BRT based on international best practices. It is also meant to be a tool to exemplify a unified view on BRT systems. The somewhat initial 2014 Standard reinforces the basic BRT elements and provides some modifications to earlier drafts. The latest version dates back to 2016 [22].

For the case of Stockholm (Sweden), [2] undertake a study regarding the capacity of bus terminals. While the study does not clarify to full extent why a specific Swedish way is needed (as claimed), the study is interesting in its own right, taking into account various indicators to provide insights into the capacity of those terminals. In the same spirit, but more comprehensively, [39] also consider capacities. A microscopic simulation study is performed to analyze

Fig. 2. Sign posts; traveling through the world as a public transport mystery shopper (Source: own figures; Lisbon, Portugal, on the left, Brisbane, Australia, on the right and Melbourne, Australia, as the inset)

---

[1] Our survey is supposed to be narrative rather than a so-called structured one as in the latter case important aspects would be lost.

capacity. In the first of two stages, a mathematical model is presented for bus-side capacity with bus to bus interference and in the second, a model is used to estimate the relationship between average queue and degree of saturation. Results are conducted for various dwell times. A comparison between different BRT systems is provided in [19].

Especially for larger stations the question arises whether traffic flows resulting from transfer needs have to be directed in an appropriate way to avoid clashing or colliding of different flows with implied delays; see, e.g., related thinking based on [18] and Fig. 1. The functionality and design are also considerably affected by the size and location of a station. A location may be (to some extent) small, positioned at the curbside (with its relative location towards, say, the beginning, middle or end of a street segment). Beyond this, type, position and size may also be influenced by the street-side circumstances like the types of traffic flow considered in the streets where a station is built. An example of a related model based on ideas from cellular automata is given in [8]; other references include [16].

A survey has been conducted by [13]. The authors used existing transit agency manuals to gain state-of-the-practice information on bus stations. More-over, transit agencies have been investigated and questioned. The results of [12] can be used to aid in the selection of a preferred bus stop design for a given location and traffic volume. Their analysis is divided into two separate stud-ies: curbside versus bus bay/open bus bay, and queue jumper versus no queue jumper.

While being a silent observer, not to say a MS, we may see or encounter deficiencies [17]. If everything follows some predefined rules, everything would be nice. But this seems not the case. According to various authors including [38] one can distinguish different time periods associated with a bus stop. Assuming the perspective of a bus and also assuming a single berth, these periods can be specified as follows: Queuing time is the time spent by a bus in a queue prior to entering the bus stop, if at all (see also Fig. 7 below). Clearance time is the minimum [theoretical] time between the departure of one bus and the arrival of a subsequent bus in the bus berth. Dead time is the time that elapses in opening and closing of doors plus the time associated with extending ramps/lifts/other equipment to facilitate alighting and boarding of disabled persons, if any. Pas-senger service time is the time elapsed while passenger exchange takes place. Internal delay is the time spent by a bus waiting to leave the bus berth after it is ready to leave, but cannot actually leave as it is obstructed by other bus(es) in the bus stop area. External delay is the time spent by a bus waiting to leave the bus berth after it is ready to leave, but cannot actually leave as it is obstructed by other traffic outside the bus stop area. Having stated this, a case study in a British context can be found in [1].

In [23] we see the description of a model that includes not only a set of elements to determine the safety level of a public transport company but also a set of indicators and criteria to evaluate these elements by a team of auditors Regarding safety we also see the development of low-floor vehicles and related bus stations for improving the accessibility of urban buses to mobility-restricted people. In [10] we see some research and development project for the public transit system in Grenoble (France) that attempts to reduce the gaps at bus stations. Investigations regarding operating conditions of accessibility equipment on the buses (kneeling, access ramp) as well as driver capability to dock at the bus station are described with the result of an improved bus station design.

Bus stations are also social areas. An interesting study may be to observe passengers while using a bus station. This relates to accessing, deboarding and eggressing as well as waiting. Depending on various design criteria of a station this may be varying considerably. Different postures of waiting passengers can be observed such as sitting or upright standing and leaning against a wall, depending on different bus station designs. Culture may require queuing or people are just walking around. In [42] the authors investigate different standing postures providing an ergonomic perspective towards bus station design. While the implications from this study are still limited, they open up an area that deserves consideration regarding the comfort of passengers in different ways. As a next step one needs to differentiate passengers due to their specific needs, e.g., when mobility-restricted people are concerned. For instance, in [44] indicators are described measuring to some extent the quality of a station in this respect (considering aspects such as being barrier-free, incorporating height differences and alike).

Different user groups may require different design aspects based on their specific needs. These groups can be related to elderly, handicapped, small children, pregnant women etc. Specific examples considering related requirements include, e.g., [27], who provide a first investigation of the case of a kindergarten-based safety requirement.

Functionality requirements also include safety. Then the question arises, whether unexpected disturbances are included, too; see, e.g., Sect. 2.4 to think about corona-based design. Finally, we mention the issue of service systems being required to be subjectively pleasing (and eventually causing happiness [11]).

2.2   The Arts Component

Bus stations may reflect cultural aspects of a city and can be used not only regarding their functionality but reflect also other measures that might reflect more arts-based functionality or touristic aspects, but this may need further investigation. In [26] the idea of building a harmonic bus station in light of the surroundings and the culture of the place to be reflected is considered.

Researchers from the Offenbach University of Design (Germany) are concerned with the question of the role of design in promoting multimodal mobility behavior. Mobility design, focusing not necessarily on vehicles but on the design of infrastructure like bus stations and processes like accessing a station, have been an integral part of studies and research. Examples of some projects that they are developing use new visualization methods such as AR and VR. Examples include the service points of German railways as well as a related bus station design operationalized in South Korea [20]. The possible design of a mobility hub as a new extended project is shown in Fig. 3.

Fig. 3. Mobility hub from [20]

2.3   Information and Communication Technology

Over time passenger information and modern ICT of the related times had been incorporated into the interplay of customers with the public transport system and especially with their access to the system; older ideas and systems as envisaged years ago [9] have now been incorporated into station design as a natural endeavour [28].

The use of various techniques can be *simulated* in various ways. Living labs, as an example, can be seen as a real simulation environment that can be enhanced by various other technologies; see, e.g., Fig. 4, [33]. Extending this towards new designs is realized on a continuous basis; see, e.g., the examples in Fig. 8 below. Marrying this with AR allows for extended visualization and information provision; see, e.g., Fig. 5.

2.4   Miscellaneous

Beyond the issues raised above, several additional aspects may be considered. This may be, e.g., the question of how to get energy to and at the bus station if needed (see an example for a case study in [3]) or the recent case of modified thinking related to social distancing as indicated below.

The recent pandemic has influenced all areas of life. For instance, in times of a lockdown the operations of public transport (including bus, rail, ferry and taxi) have been suspended or at least been reduced considerably in many places; cf. Fig. 6. Stations were temporarily closed or not served. For instance, in Wuhan as a starting point of the Covid19 pandemic, the municipal government expropriated, among others, bus stations to build shelter hospitals rather than using

Fig. 4. Living lab bus station from [33]

them for public transport purposes [45]. Obviously, following the requirements of a pandemia like in the case of Covid19 requires quite a few drastic changes in public transport. For instance, if social distancing is followed in an appropriate way, then systems that are already beyond their limits might need even more capacity and infrastructure. Handwaving says that not only countries like India require a multitude of buses to allow commuters to effectively perform social distancing.[2] Bus stations require different forms of queuing. Complying with social distancing already applies during access implying rethinking of station design. Similarly, bus station maintenance requires different and more intensive thinking in the same spirit.[3] The question of social distancing may also ask whether this can be enforced by the station design. Regarding the above-mentioned concerns of enabling efficient transfer becomes even more important if social distancing can be enforced through a clever assignment of buses to berths allowing for appropriate (separated or non-overlapping) transfer paths.

3   Mystery Shopping

As indicated above, *mystery shopping* is a marketing research-based method intended to measure QoS, gather specific information about a market, com-

---

[2] See, e.g., https://www.intelligenttransport.com/transport-news/100881/india-req uires-24-times-more-buses-to-allow-commuters-to-social-distance-effectively/, last access June 19, 2020.

[3] See, e.g., https://www.transit.dot.gov/regulations-and-programs/safety/fta-covid-19-resource-tool, last access June 19, 2020.

Fig. 5. Augmented reality adoption in bus usage

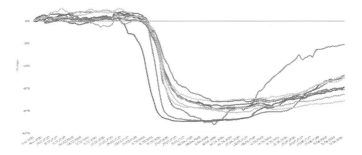

Fig. 6. Decline of bus patronage worldwide; https://moovitapp.com/insights/en/ Moovit_Insights_Public_Transit_Index-countries, last access June 19, 2020.

petitors, or even economies. Mystery shoppers are intended to mirror common consumer behavior and to investigate the habits of customers, sellers and service providers. It is also a tool allowing to measure compliance with regulations etc. General considerations include [29,41].

The history of MS goes way back into the 1940s. The focus was on manufacturing and retail with the financial sector coming next. Specific observers or people were trained to act as normal customers realizing or simulating real sales and customer situations.

MS as a tool in the service industries has been explored especially in [41]. Other sources include [24]. While known and applied in practice, MS in public transport has not yet been fully explored in academic literature and only few papers are available including [7,15,35,40]. Those are building the base of our elaboration below. Finally, with mystery shopping in mind we return towards bus station design.

Another option to undertake mystery shopping is to some extent known under the name of *field studies*.

3.1 Questionnaire-Based Studies in Public Transport

Customer satisfaction surveys are part of important research. For instance, once performing customer surveys, public transport companies or authorities gain insights into the areas where possible improvements are needed. Our criticism, though, is that recently quite a few of these studies have been published or submitted for publication without bringing any additional value. That is, while this methodology is important for public transport companies and regulating bodies, their one-dimensional application in academia is often lacking good reasoning. Older questionnaire-based papers with that type of reasoning for existence include [13,21,31].

What we should gain are factors influencing QoS and also hints on how to use scarce financial resources. While it seems interesting to see whether, just to name a few examples, station cleanliness and on-time arrival of buses are important in one place or another based on some, say, 384 interviewees being users of a public transport system, the resulting numbers might not really tell us on how to use scarce financial resources to improve the system and they also lack to explain anything about non-users of the system if they are not considered. In that sense we claim that other types of methodology should be appended (as indicated below) while public transport companies still undertake these studies. They should also be published, but rather as company-oriented quality reports than academic papers.

Again, a major concern relates to those who are involved into customer satisfaction surveys, i.e., is it just customers or also non-customers (those who might be interested or even need to be motivated to switch to public transport). Moreover, detailed information regarding access points and places where questionnaires were handed out are often missing (like enhancements by additional information about the station design etc. considering using a single signpost versus major transfer stations).

3.2 Examples for Mystery Shopping Applications in Public Transport

To exemplify, we refer to four cases as they are London (UK) [40], Thessaloniki (Greece) [15], Moscow (Russia) [35] and Hamburg (Germany)[4].

Copying from [29], one may ask upfront about how to set up a MS application. Among several steps one should start with the scope of the MS assessment (e.g., which attributes are to be tested). Next, the way on how to conduct the study should be defined. This may include benchmarking, a way to find out about the strengths and weaknesses of something or an ongoing effort to continuously measure and improve an offered service. Then comes the simulation of an actual

---

[4] Quality reports from HVV are available including mystery shopping hints; see, e.g., https://www.hvv.de/resource/blob/29930/3e91642bcb98d022ed75fadcf71f4f8a/ qualitaetsbericht-2018-data.pdf for 2018 and https://www.hvv.de/resource/blob/ 22478/5b50e752c34a9924c40dcb6fe8863879/qualitaetsbericht-2017-data.pdf   for 2017; access on June 19, 2020.

customer experience. Beyond that, quite a few additional mostly self-explanatory aspects need to be considered touching base regarding the way MS results are reported, how employees are informed about the implementation of MS etc.

An interesting question relates to who is going to set up the mystery shoppers. For instance, in case of several transit companies working together in a transport association (say the Hamburger Verkehrsverbund (HVV) in case of Hamburg, Germany), should it be the single bus company or the association. In case of Hamburg, the above mentioned reports are provided by the association and the MS program is set up to allow for year-round check-ups. The different modes of transportation within the HVV have different sets of quotas. That is, all buses and half of all bus stops are visited at least once a year. There are three groups of indicators for buses and ferries and their corresponding attributes:

– Stop sign/mast: stop-symbol, name line, tariff line, route line, color of mast
– Passenger information (related to the bus station): schedules, tariff information, possibly network plan
– The stations themselves are also monitored, but the responsibility for them lies often not with the HVV member, but other parties, which poses another issue.

For London the well-documented study of [40] focuses more on London Underground rather than the bus system, but they provide useful reasoning why MS should be superimposed on customer satisfaction results. Especially the allocation of funds regarding different attributes requires detailed business cases defining the scope of the study. MS teams of two were deployed four times a year on strictly specified routes. On their journey they collected measurements of 26 train-specific and 116 station-specific attributes using a paper questionnaire.

Also the Moscow study of [35] focused more on metro than other means of transportation, though, testing a comprehensive number of vehicles overall. Different from Hamburg and London this was a one-shot endeavour in summer 2014. Moreover, the extent of the study was to some extent focused (cleanliness, wifi quality etc.). The Thessaloniki case [15] is interesting in its own right as the related authority had no prior experience on MS so that a pilot study is reported providing insights on how to set up such an endeavour.

3.3   Mystery Shopping and Bus Station Design

While the previous sections revealed the possible use of MS in public transport it has not really been used in literature for bus station design. Modeling attempts like the one in [18] may be extended but have not used the concept of MS. Narrative papers could also be seen as educated MS attempts on how to design bus stations, like in [25,46], but the real attempt is still missing.

As a first attempt, we utilize the visualization tools of some simulation to design an *ideal* bus station; see, e.g., Fig. 7 for a first step in that direction. This may overcome some of the deficiencies encountered in various places in the world as very briefly sketched in [17]. That is, if a way can be found to let bus drivers behave appropriately and train them in a sustainable way, that might help a lot. Moreover, issues as those related to ICT adoption in bus station design as indicated in Fig. 8 may be encountered, too, especially if they can be married with those attempts performed related to the living lab concept of [33]. VR would allow to let MS with different background to not only use the system but also to envisage possible design changes in a simulated environment. While this does not compensate for the real experience, it still allows for upfront measures to incorporate meaning and comprehension of mobility restricted people, minors or pregnant women, just to mention some groups of interest. For the hybridization of BPMN and VR, tools are available; see, e.g., [32]. That is, regarding bus station design MS may provide a lot of food for thought.

Fig. 7. Simulation of a bus station

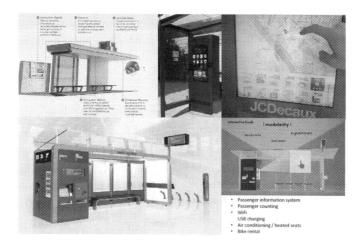

Fig. 8. ICT adoption in bus station design

4   Conclusions

In this paper we have looked at bus station design based on selected literatures. Implicitly an information management approach and incorporating a marketing-based mystery shopping idea as well as modern ICT (including augmented reality and virtual reality) gave us a slightly different edge over existing references. In passing, we have seen quite a few issues that are worth being explored further. In that sense we can see the value of this paper as one providing food for thought and initializing further research. Let us distinguish between some food for thought and some explicit future research directions.

The upcoming idea of autonomous vehicles allows to conceptualize quite a few ideas of innovative public transport systems, including private rapid transit (PRT) and mobility-as-a-service (MaaS) [43]. During the 1990s, PRT was mainly envisaged for automated people movers in airports, but more recently, individualized solutions seem to become more and more possible. While these systems are built and/or simulated, their possible station design needs to be considered, too. The interesting issues relate to differently-sized vehicles that need to be accommodated in an appropriate way, like car-sized electric vehicles running on a separated (say, underground road) network; see, e.g., [30,36]. In [4,6] the authors suggest layouts and operations strategies for transfer stations between PRT and heavy rail.

Moreover, we claim that public transport companies need more research on mystery shopping married with augmented and virtual reality-based simulation rather than academic questionnaire-based studies. This methodology should be applied inhouse by public transport companies, though. While this methodology seems well understood, especially if they consider the sharing of scarce resources (which many of them do not do), ideas on mystery shopping still seems to be underrepresented and need more evidence.

Acknowledgement. We appreciate the fruitful discussion with our former bachelor student Marc Rebal as well as the support from Leonard Heilig regarding Figs. 8 and 5 and Figen Guenyar regarding Fig. 7.

References

1. Adhvaryu, B.: Design of bus station: a case study in Brighton. Traffic Eng. Control **47**(5), 182–187 (2006)
2. Al-Mudhaffar, A., Nissan, A., Bang, K.L.: Bus stop and bus terminal capacity. Transp. Res. Procedia **14**, 1762–1771 (2016). https://doi.org/10.1016/j.trpro.2016.05.142
3. Alikhanova, A., Kakimzhan, A., Mukhanov, A., Rojas-Solórzano, L.: Design of a bus shelter based on green energy technologies for extreme weather conditions in Nur-Sultan, Kazakhstan. Sustain. Energy Technol. Assess. **36**, paper #100544 (2019). https://doi.org/10.1016/j.seta.2019.100544
4. Andréasson, I.J.: Personal rapid transit as feeder-distributor to rail. Transp. Res. Rec. **2275**, 88–93 (2012). https://doi.org/10.3141/2275-10

5. Barsom, E.Z., Graafland, M., Schijven, M.P.: Systematic review on the effectiveness of augmented reality applications in medical training. Surg. Endosc. **30**(10), 4174–4183 (2016). https://doi.org/10.1007/s00464-016-4800-6
6. Chen, C., Wu, X., Chen, A., Liu, H., Xiang, S.: Research on PRT station design using unmanned vehicles based on Petri net. In: 3rd International Conference on Electronic Information Technology and Computer Engineering (EITCE), pp. 210–213. IEEE (2019). https://doi.org/10.1109/EITCE47263.2019.9094984
7. Collard, D.: Les enquêtes "client mystère": une technique de contrôle des comportements. Politiques et Management Public **30**(4), 519–535 (2013). https://doi.org/10.3166/pmp.30.519-535
8. Cui, C., Quan, J.: Bus stop setting problem based on cellular automaton traffic model. Artif. Life Robot. **24**(2), 135–139 (2018). https://doi.org/10.1007/s10015-018-0470-x
9. Daduna, J.R., Voß, S.: Efficient technologies for passenger information systems in public mass transit. In: Pirkul, H., Shaw, M. (eds.) Proceedings of the First INFORMS Conference on Information Systems and Technology, pp. 386–391. INFORMS, Washington (1996)
10. Dejeammes, M., et al.: Bus stop design and automated guidance for low-floor buses: evaluation of prototypes with investigation of human factors. Transp. Res. Rec. **1666**, 85–91 (1999). https://doi.org/10.3141/1666-10
11. Duarte, A., Garcia, C., Giannarakis, G., Limão, S., Polydoropoulou, A., Litinas, N.: New approaches in transportation planning: happiness and transport economics. Netnomics **11**, 5–32 (2010). https://doi.org/10.1007/s11066-009-9037-2
12. Fitzpatrick, K., Nowlin, R.: Effects of bus stop design on suburban arterial operations. Transp. Res. Rec. **1571**, 31–41 (1997). https://doi.org/10.3141/1571-05
13. Fitzpatrick, K., Perkinson, D., Hall, K.: Findings from a survey on bus stop design. J. Public Transp. **1**(3), 17–27 (1997). https://doi.org/10.5038/2375-0901.1.3.2
14. Ge, L., Voß, S., Xie, L.: Robustness and disturbances in public transport. Technical report, Institute of Information Systems (IWI), University of Hamburg (2020)
15. Georgiadis, G., Xenidis, Y., Toskas, I., Papaioannou, P.: A performance measurement system for public transport services in Thessaloniki, Greece. In: Transport Research Arena (TRA) 5th Conference: Transport Solutions from Research to Deployment, Paris (2014)
16. Gjersø K.: Granåsen case study: how can location and design of a bus stop influence the use of public transport? (2017). http://hdl.handle.net/11250/2453841, Master thesis, NTNU, Department of Civil and Environmental Engineering
17. Gonzalez-Lopez, F., Mejia, G., Voß, A., Voß, S.: Bus station design. Institute of Information Systems, University of Hamburg (2018). https://www.bwl.uni-hamburg.de/iwi/forschung/busstationdesign.pdf, Research poster, Accessed 11 Oct 2019
18. Gonzalez-Lopez, F., Mejia, G., Voß, S.: Bus rapid transit station CP-net modelling for multi-objective performance evaluation: passenger overcrowding, driving safety, and bus congestion. In: IT/AI for Manufacturing (IT), Proceedings of the 24th International Conference on Production Research. IFPR, Posnan, Poland, p. 5 (2017)
19. Guarda, P., Velásquez, J.M., Tun, T.H., Chen, X., Zhong, G.: Comparing Chinese and non-Chinese bus rapid transit systems: Evidence from evaluating global systems on the basis of bus rapid transit design indicators. Transp. Res. Rec. **2647**, 118–126 (2017). https://doi.org/10.3141/2647-14
20. HfG - University of Art and Design: Unit design, bus stop city of Paju (2008/09). https://www.unit-design.de/de/projekte/paj-busstop.php. Accessed 11 Oct 2019

21. Hutchinson, T.: The customer experience when using public transport: a review. Proc. Inst. Civil Eng. - Municipal Eng. **162**(3), 149–157 (2009). https://doi.org/10.1680/muen.2009.162.3.149

22. ITDP: The BRT Standard 2016 Edition (2016). www.itdp.org, Institute for Transportation and Development Policy. Accessed 11 Oct 2019

23. Izquierdo, F., Sesemann, Y., Alonso, J.: Safety management evaluation in bus and coach companies. Transp. Rev. **29**(6), 665–684 (2009). https://doi.org/10.1080/01441640902750106

24. Jacob, S., Schiffino, N., Biard, B.: The mystery shopper: a tool to measure public service delivery? Int. Rev. Adm. Sci. **84**(1), 164–184 (2018). https://doi.org/10.1177/0020852315618018

25. Kim, Y.C.: A study of bus station design considering pedestrian environment based on main road bus stations in Gwangju, a metropolitan city in Korea. Des. Res. **6**(6), 123–128 (2011)

26. Li, J.: The analysis of design thinking of harmonious bus station. Appl. Mech. Mater. **357–360**, 345–348 (2013). https://doi.org/10.4028/www.scientific.net/amm.357-360.345

27. Liu, Z., Ng, W.K.: Based on usability experience-enhanced potential community transportation design study in China: a case of Kindergarten bus stop design. In: Marcus, A., Wang, W. (eds.) HCII 2019. LNCS, vol. 11585, pp. 85–100. Springer, Cham (2019). https://doi.org/10.1007/978-3-030-23538-3_7

28. Lu, L., Baotian, D.: Design of mobile electronic bus station board based on BPEL. In: Sixth International Conference on Intelligent Human-Machine Systems and Cybernetics, vol. 2, pp. 75–78 (2014). https://doi.org/10.1109/IHMSC.2014.121

29. Lubin, P.: What's the mystery? ABA Bank Mark. **33**(7), 28–33 (2001)

30. Mueller, K., Sgouridis, S.P.: Simulation-based analysis of personal rapid transit systems: service and energy performance assessment of the Masdar City PRT case. J. Adv. Transp. **45**(4), 252–270 (2011). https://doi.org/10.1002/atr.158

31. de Oña, J., de Oña, R.: Quality of service in public transport based on customer satisfaction surveys: a review and assessment of methodological approaches. Transp. Sci. **49**, 605–622 (2015). https://doi.org/10.1287/trsc.2014.0544

32. Oberhauser, R., Pogolski, C., Matic, A.: VR-BPMN: visualizing BPMN models in virtual reality. In: Shishkov, B. (ed.) BMSD 2018. LNBIP, vol. 319, pp. 83–97. Springer, Cham (2018). https://doi.org/10.1007/978-3-319-94214-8_6

33. Schrenk, M., et al.: Bus Stop 3.0 - Bushaltestelle der Zukunft. In: REAL CORP 2010 Proceedings, pp. 1019–1025 (2010)

34. Sherman, W., Craig, A.: Understanding Virtual Reality: Interface, Application, and Design, 2nd edn. Morgan Kaufmann, Cambridge (2019)

35. Sidorchuk, R., Efimova, D., Lopatinskaya, I., Kaderova, V.: Parametric approach to the assessment of service quality attributes of municipal passenger transport in Moscow. Mod. Appl. Sci. **9**(4), 303–311 (2015). https://doi.org/10.5539/mas.v9n4p303

36. Sohn, K.: An investigation into the station capacities for personal rapid transit systems. Proc. Inst. Mech. Eng. Part F: J. Rail Rapid Transit **226**(5), 457–468 (2012). https://doi.org/10.1177/0954409711433737

37. TransMilenio S.A.: Plano de estaciones y portales de TransMilenio, TransMilenio, Bogota (2014)

38. Tyler, N.: Accessibility and the Bus System: Transforming the World, 2 edn. ICE Publishing, London (2016). https://doi.org/10.1680/aabs2ed.59818

39. Widanapathiranage, R., Bunker, J.M., Bhaskar, A.: Modelling the BRT station capacity and queuing for all stopping busway operation. Public Transp. **7**(1), 21–38 (2014). https://doi.org/10.1007/s12469-014-0095-y
40. Wilson, A., Gutmann, J.: Public transport: the role of mystery shopping in investment decisions. Market Res. Soc. J. **40**(4), 1–9 (1998). https://doi.org/10.1177/147078539804000401
41. Wilson, A.M.: Mystery shopping: using deception to measure service performance. Psychol. Market. **18**(7), 721–734 (2001). https://doi.org/10.1002/mar.1027
42. Wong, S.F., Chen, Q.: Posture analysis in ergonomic study for bus station design. In: IEEE International Conference on Industrial Engineering and Engineering Management (IEEM), pp. 701–705 (2015). https://doi.org/10.1109/IEEM.2015.7385738
43. Wong, Y.Z., Hensher, D.A., Mulley, C.: Mobility as a service (MaaS): charting a future context. Transp. Res. Part A: Policy Pract. **131**, 5–19 (2020). https://doi.org/10.1016/j.tra.2019.09.030
44. Yangsheng, J., Yanru, C., Liang, Y.: Study on the evaluation indexes system of barrier-free public transportation system quality. In: International Conference on Optoelectronics and Image Processing, vol. 2, pp. 460–464 (2010). https://doi.org/10.1109/ICOIP.2010.152
45. Yu, X., Li, N.: How did Chinese government implement unconventional measures against COVID-19 pneumonia. Risk Manag. Healthcare Policy **13**, 491–499 (2020). https://doi.org/10.2147/RMHP.S251351
46. Zhang, W., Zhang, N.: Several problems of city bus station design - take Qingdao city bus station as an example. Archit. Cult. **160**(7), 138–139 (2017)

Preliminary Design of an 'Autonomous Medical Response Agent' Interface Prototype for Long-Duration Spaceflight

Melodie Yashar[1]([✉]), Jessica Marquez[2], Jayant Menon[3,4], and Isabel Torron[1]

[1] San Jose State Research Foundation, M/S 262-4, Moffett Field, CA 94035, USA
melodie.yashar@nasa.gov
[2] NASA Ames Research Center, M/S 262-2, Moffett Field, CA 94035, USA
[3] Nahlia Inc., 95 1st Street, Los Altos, CA 94022, USA
[4] Department of Neurosurgery, Stanford University, Stanford, CA, USA

Abstract. An autonomous medical response agent (AMRA) is envisioned to help astronauts address medical complaints, develop a differential diagnosis, and guide self-treatment until a healthy state is restored. AMRA develops a process of personalized diagnosis and treatment through a Bayesian predictive control system that recommends therapeutic control actions to crewmembers (Menon 2020). The Human Computer Interaction (HCI) lab from NASA Ames Research Center's (ARC) Human Systems Integration Division has collaborated with Nahlia Inc. in order to develop a human-centered design for AMRA. Funded by the Translational Research Institute for Space Health (TRISH), this design introduces an interactive user-interface prototype that guides astronauts through self-diagnosis, treatment, and rehabilitation while communicating with remote specialists in ground support (most notably a patient's flight surgeon). The interface prototype, AMRA Aggregate Information Display (AMRA AID), is an integrated information system for comprehensive autonomous medical guidance of in-flight medical conditions experienced by crewmembers. This paper describes the interaction design process contributing to the user interface design and workflow of a crewmember using AMRA AID, developed through user research, iterative prototyping, and usability testing.

Keywords: User experience · Autonomous medical response · Space medicine · Space health · Intelligent agent · Medicine for extreme environments · Wilderness · Environmental medicine

1 Introduction

1.1 Project Objectives

Future long duration exploration missions (LDEM) operations will require an astronaut crew to self-monitor health more autonomously than current spaceflight missions and pose new risks to the management of crew health compared to current International Space Station (ISS) operations. Unlike ISS operations, Private Medical Conferences

© Springer Nature Switzerland AG 2020
C. Stephanidis et al. (Eds.): HCII 2020, LNCS 12423, pp. 543–562, 2020.
https://doi.org/10.1007/978-3-030-60114-0_37

(PMCs) will not be possible with flight surgeons and seeking definitive medical care on Earth could take days, weeks or even months. Major challenges for astronauts in future LDEMs will be that crewmembers are not expected to be medical professionals, may be under high workload and stress, are facing physiological challenges caused by spaceflight, and will have limited, delayed voice communications with medical support from Earth.

For LDEMs, an autonomous medical response agent (AMRA) is envisioned to help astronauts address medical complaints, develop a differential diagnosis, and guide self-treatment until a healthy state is restored. An intelligent, on-board medical system requires an interface that enables an astronaut and a caretaker to work with AMRA in reviewing, diagnosing, and treating a chief medical complaint. AMRA's algorithms monitor the crew's normative or healthy state, provide a means for developing a differential diagnosis, and identify a protocol for diagnostic and treatment response to a medical incident. AMRA's interface must therefore communicate and synchronize with human health monitoring from ground support so that feedback, interventions and treatments may be communicated appropriately. Despite the fact that communication between the crew and ground will be challenging due to time delays and bandwidth limitations, flight surgeons on the ground will still need an effective means to monitor astronaut health for LDEMs (Love and Reagan 2013).

An autonomous medical response agent must consider decision-making support systems for self-diagnosis of medical complaints in times when feedback or guidance from ground support is not immediately available, and must consider recommendations of appropriate treatment protocols which integrate with pre-existing databases of medical manuals for spaceflight and otherwise. As such, our team set out to design, validate, and assess a prototype interface that: 1) provides an optimal work flow of actionable recommendations for self-care of the crew while 2) building trust between Mission Control Center (MCC) flight surgeons and astronauts on LDEMs with limited bandwidth for communications.

The final project prototype introduced an enhanced workflow and treatment guidance for two medical scenarios (headache and shortness of breath) for a non-specialist user base with various levels of medical training. The interaction design process considered speech (conversational user interface) elements and on-screen interactions to be developed in future iterations of the project, and determined communication design and functional requirements relevant to self-care versus caring for another astronaut. The AMRA AID prototype was tested for usability with an international space medical community.

1.2 Impact for Earth and Space

Numerous analogous domains identified within our research, particularly medical care in extreme environments such as military hospitals, submarine missions, disaster response, or scientific expeditions (i.e. Antarctica), will benefit from the development of AMRA corresponding between crew and a remote support team (mission control), as they demonstrate parallels to the experience of crewmembers in LDEMs.

Our project subscribes to the Medical System Concept of Operations developed by NASA's Human Research Program's Exploration Medical Capabilities Element

(ExMC), which considers transit operations only (not surface, extravehicular activity, or launch/landing operations) (Urbina et al. 2016). We are assuming a Mars design reference mission transit phase with a crew of 4 or 5 individuals, where return to Earth will take months. Unlike the International Space Station (ISS), there is no evacuation capability and there is no potential for definitive medical care in transit. Because there will be limited real-time telemedical consultations for information guidance, no regular resupply (hence limited pharmaceutical resources), and a high level of risk, technologies for autonomous care throughout diagnosis, treatment, and rehabilitation must be advanced (Urbina et al. 2016).

2 Problem Space

Future LDEM operations will require an astronaut crew to self-monitor health more autonomously than current spaceflight missions, and pose new risks to the management of crew health as compared to current ISS operations. To date, human spaceflight missions have operated with near-instantaneous two-way communication with Earth. As crews venture beyond low-earth orbit, the time delay of communications will increase. For example, the one-way light travel time from Earth to Mars can range from 4 to 22 min. In contrast, this communication delay was about 1.25 s for the Apollo astronauts on the moon missions. Unlike current ISS operations, real-time Private Medical Conferences (PMCs) will not be possible with flight surgeons and seeking definitive medical care on Earth could take days, weeks or even months. Individual crew training and experience will vary in future LDEMs and the crew may or may not have specialized medical expertise or training relevant to unplanned or emergency medical procedures arising in a mission.

Currently, medical treatment on board the ISS relies not only on extensive emergency medical manual protocols but on the availability of mission control to provide real-time help and guidance. ISS and exploration-class missions require radically different capabilities from an on-board medical system; and while AMRA AID comes to demonstrate a number of hypothetical 'chains of command' between the autonomous

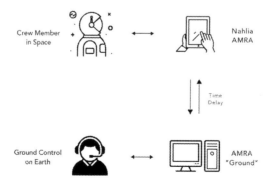

Fig. 1. Representation of communications between the crewmember in space, AMRA's onboard medical system, AMRA's projected ground based medical system on Earth, as well as ground control.

medical response technology, the crew, and mission control, new protocols relevant to communication will need to be identified and validated (see Fig. 1).

2.1 Scoping

For the purposes of this project, our scope was to demonstrate diagnosis, treatment, and management of patient care in addition to demonstrating the requirement (from a human systems integration perspective) that the front-facing user interface for the medical system integrate mission-critical information from flight sub-systems such as vehicle information and crew schedule. While a technology platform such as AMRA may potentially provide and integrate resources for in-flight training and task execution support, our focus was restricted to demonstrating that the medical system synthesize and aggregate pertinent updates relevant to crew decision-making over the course of an unplanned medical incident. Our scope was also restricted to demonstrating user interactions between a patient-crewmember, crew medical officer (CMO) or caregiver, and AMRA over the course of two unplanned medical scenarios: headache and shortness of breath.

2.2 Assumptions

The following are assumptions relevant to the scope, process, and research of this project:

State-of-the-art in Medical Response. Our research indicated that medical response hardware, medical response protocols, and computational processes relevant to diagnosis and treatment for future LDEMs are still in early development. Furthermore, the consistency with which ground support will be able to receive updates from the in-flight medical system for reliable vitals monitoring remains inconclusive. The capability and protocols for high-bandwidth communications with crew (audio and video) rather than simply text communications over the course of a mission must be examined in greater detail (Krihak et al. 2019). For these reasons, we tailored our approach to being as technology- and system- agnostic as possible for long-duration spaceflight.

Level of Care. NASA-STD-3001 has designated basic medical Level of Care capabilities. The NASA Human Research Program's Exploration Medical Capabilities Element (ExMC) has expanded these standards and applied them to 5 design reference mission architectures ranging from <8 day missions in LEO to 210+ day lunar or planetary missions. Assumptions relevant to Mars Exploration Mission Medical System ConOps include that: both crewmembers and caregivers have varying medical skill sets and the Medical System will complement the Caregiver's skillset, and furthermore the Medical System has varying levels of support and the Caregiver can utilize the system as much or as little as needed (Mindock et al. 2017). Therefore, within Level of Care V, the physician-caretaker is considered self-sufficient, relies on ground support for consultation and advice, and may choose whether to follow the recommendations of a medical support technology. For this reason and others, our project prototype supports a range of autonomy from ground. Maintaining ground awareness despite the capability to interface with AMRA remained an integral concept for promoting trust between ground and crew.

Crew Makeup. The stakeholders relevant to the two high-impact medical response scenarios are: an astronaut onboard a future LDEM with some emergency response training but limited expertise in medicine, a CMO who will likely be a trained physician on-board, and a flight surgeon monitoring and responding to crew medical incidents from ground control and reporting mission-critical incidents to the flight director. While our project initiated with an assumption that medical support and guidance should be provided as universally as possible to crewmembers with little to no medical expertise, our research indicated that we must assume individuals on exploration class missions will have had sufficient medical training to stabilize a patient-crewmember in an emergency, as an example.

3 Process and Methodology

As part of domain-specific user research, a literature review was conducted of NASA guidelines and standards (e.g. NASA STD-3001; NASA 2007), current medical training protocols (NASA JSC-48522-E4 and Ball and Evans Jr. 2001), as well as previous medical incidents in spaceflight including how they were managed (Clement 2014). For analogous domain research, we reviewed the current state of the art for medical care in extreme environments (e.g. Antarctica). We reviewed examples of emergency medical care such as in telemedicine and synthesized lessons learned from these analogous domains. In collaboration with Nahlia Inc., we hosted multiple collaborative review sessions with Nahlia Inc. stakeholders to coordinate and synthesize ongoing research.

Next we identified and methodically outlined sequence flows for headache and shortness of breath user scenarios within a mission context. In our project, a headache scenario was chosen to represent a chronic illness. Shortness of breath was chosen as an acute emergency condition. These two scenarios were chosen to demonstrate AMRA's capability to guide astronauts through both complex short term and long-term self-treatment. The design prototyping process consisted of: establishing an overall information architecture for the interface, paper prototyping & wireframing for the user interface, establishing essential interactions and core features of a minimum viable product (MVP), and establishing additional features or interactions to be considered in future stages of the project. Astronauts, physicians, flight surgeons as well as non-experts were identified for user testing. Multiple rounds of usability testing were conducted using both heuristic evaluation as well as think-aloud evaluation methods (Nielsen 1993, 2000) with practitioners of space medicine as well as HCI. Our goal in user testing was to iteratively verify that the features and interactions of the interface provided: intuitive recommendations requiring minimal training, improved efficiency, improved usability, and improved satisfaction over the course of self-treatment in a medical response scenario.

3.1 Headache Scenario

The headache scenario represents a chronic condition and demonstrates integration of diagnostic exams within the interface and the integration of a follow up procedure. In the scenario, the patient experiences a mild headache, prompting AMRA to ask four diagnostic questions to arrive at a preliminary evaluation of whether the patient's condition is extreme or not. AMRA validates that the headache is 'not extreme' and prescribes Tylenol to the patient. AMRA identifies where in the vehicle the Tylenol may be found, updates vehicle inventory, and autonomously schedules a follow up with the patient. Our project focused on integration of the medical response technology within the context of a mission to demonstrate needed integrations between the medical system and other vehicle systems.

3.2   Headache Follow Up

The headache follow up scenario demonstrates additional development significant to defining the requirements for data integration of the on-board medical system with vehicle and other mission-critical information. In this portion of the scenario, an hour passes since the patient had last taken Tylenol for a mild headache. The patient reports back to AMRA that the headache has worsened, and simultaneously high CO_2 levels are reported within two areas of the vehicle. AMRA then prompts all crewmembers to report on any potential symptoms. AMRA then recommends a neurological exam be administered by the CMO. By prompting the involvement of the CMO, the headache follow up demonstrates a potential communication workflow where collaboration with multiple crew members may be required. Once confirmed, AMRA provides reference material for the neurological exam and sends a summary report of the incident and exam results to ground once the exam is completed.

3.3   Shortness of Breath Scenario

The shortness of breath scenario represents an emergency condition necessitating collaboration from the CMO (the caregiver) and demonstrates a potential communication workflow with limited pre-established protocols. We decided to focus on an emergency pneumothorax condition to demonstrate how AMRA might recommend a routine ultrasound procedure to the crew. The extent to which the autonomous medical response technology might interfere or interact with the crew in an emergency condition remains questionable. We demonstrated how AMRA may play a supporting role to the CMO within the emergency scenario. AMRA recommends an ultrasound procedure be scheduled as a follow up to the incident, however mission critical tasks prevent the ultrasound from being scheduled that day. AMRA communicates the schedule conflict directly to mission control, demonstrating needed integration of the medical system with vehicle and mission communications.

3.4   Prototype Development and Static States

The user scenarios determined the interactions and functional requirements necessary for AMRA's capability as an on-board medical response assistant. The user scenarios were diagrammed as sequence flows and were instrumental to derive key portions of information communication and integration. The scenarios were selected and developed to examine collaboration between the patient, crew medical officer, and AMRA while keeping the flight surgeon in-the-loop. Requirements for an MVP for the interface prototype are summarized below. Most significantly, the features, interactions, design and integration requirements specified here may equally be applied to the design of autonomous medical decision support technologies in multiple analogous domains identified within our research—such as in (terrestrial) remote medical response, disaster response, or scientific expeditions:

Communication Design Requirements:

- Straightforward, conversational interactions with the medical system requiring little-to-no training to engage all aspects of diagnosis, treatment, and rehabilitation.
- Leveraging the potential of natural-language processing to establish an intelligent conversational user interface for seamless data input and hands-free interaction with the medical system.
- Individual communication channel provided between the patient, medical response agent, and ground support.
- Individual communication channel between the patient, caregiver (if relevant), the medical response agent, and ground.
- Individual communication channel for all crewmembers, the medical response agent, and ground support.
- Ability for the flight surgeon (or remote support) to offer feedback or input relevant to a recommendation from the medical response agent.

Medical System Integration Requirements:

- Integration with vitals monitoring as well as prior medical history for crewmembers.
- Integration with medical system protocols for treatment, diagnostic tests, and rehabilitation.
- Integration with reference and training materials.
- Integration with crew schedule for scheduling medical procedures but also for general purposes of developing symptomatology.
- Integration with vehicle and environmental monitoring of pressure, oxygen levels, CO_2 levels, etc.

The sequence flows identified hypothetical communication orders between the patient, caretaker, AMRA, and ground input for seamless diagnostic evaluation and treatment to occur while considering the ramifications of a 20-min communications delay. Within the project's final prototype, one such communication order was identified and demonstrated.

The sequence flows were then used to derive 'static states,' or non-interactive screen representations of a hypothetical user flow, for AMRA's user interface. The static states capture key interactions, changes, and updates within the interface representative of key moments the user will likely confront when interacting with the prototype. The static states show how mission-critical information could be interrelated to the medical system without assuming a causal relationship. The static states were used to develop key interaction features within the preliminary, low-fidelity prototype of the interface. Over the course of our design process, four prototype iterations were created, beginning with low fidelity prototyping and culminating in a high fidelity, multi-screen interactive prototype compiled within the InVision platform. With each iteration, key research findings and evaluations were synthesized and ranked to inform changes and revisions in subsequent iterations.

4   AMRA AID Prototype

AMRA AID is an integrated information display system for comprehensive autonomous medical guidance, diagnosis, and treatment of in-flight medical conditions experienced by crewmembers. AMRA AID refrains from relying on input from ground or mission control for self-treatment of medical issues—though ground awareness and communication with ground is maintained as a means of ensuring trust between mission control and crew. AMRA AID demonstrates how the crew's on-board medical system might integrate with information from vehicle monitoring and crew schedule without assuming causal relationships. The 4 screens within AMRA AID include: AMRA Log, Crew Medical System, Vehicle & Environmental Manager, and Crew Schedule; these screens are intended to be viewed simultaneously by users. AMRA AID's comprehensive view enables efficient information access for both crew and ground support, reducing cognitive burden in the event of an unplanned or emergency medical incident and enabling informed analytical decisions to be made based on both crew and vehicle health (see Fig. 2).

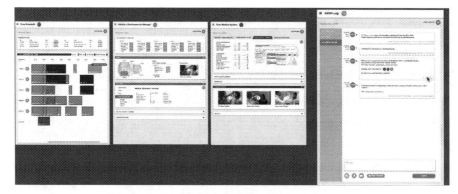

Fig. 2. Screenshot of the AMRA AID user interface

4.1   AMRA Log

AMRA Log functions as the communications interface for crew to report a medical incident, ask AMRA questions relevant to crew health, respond to AMRA's diagnostic questions following a chief complaint, and for AMRA to provide references to procedures, manuals, or other informational resources. AMRA Log guides crewmembers through diagnostic questions relevant to a chief medical complaint and makes recommendations to the crew relevant to diagnosis and treatment.

We assume that reliable voice-to-text capabilities will enable AMRA to function as a conversational user interface, enabling crewmembers to interact with AMRA hands-free should that be required in patient caretaking or in responding to unplanned medical incidents. As mentioned previously, we are assuming a time delay of 20 min for any message to reach Earth, and likewise for any message from Earth to reach the crew. To promote trust and confidence between crew and ground support, flight surgeons and ground support retrieve time-stamped information through AMRA Log in order to: acknowledge protocols have been followed successfully, offer additional guidance to a patient following a recommendation or diagnosis made by AMRA, or provide general medical input or feedback should it be needed. AMRA Log develops features supporting asynchronous communication as demonstrated within Playbook's Mission Log, a multimedia chat software interface provided within Playbook, an execution web-application for mission operations (Marquez et al. 2019).

4.2 Integration Functionality

AMRA Log communicates the integration of crew schedule and vehicle information with the health status of each crew member in a manner that would be most informative, efficient and productive for both the crew and the flight surgeon. Both planned and unplanned medical incidents will demand situation-awareness of information such as crew schedule, the health state of fellow crew members, and vehicle performance. Three supplemental screens are provided to convey and integrate information crucial for both medical support and the mission overall. The Crew Medical System features an individual crewmember's health records, diagnostic test results, vital signs information, as well as training and reference material. The Vehicle & Environmental Manager (V&EM) monitors environmental conditions and tracks inventory aboard the vehicle. Finally Crew Schedule features information on the mission as well as scheduling.

Comprehensive and inclusive access to data from mission operations, communications, and vehicle/environmental information will be critical to integrate with the onboard medical system from a human systems integration perspective. The in-mission medical system should therefore be viewed as a component of the overall integrated vehicle system, and when appropriate, medical data and information should be shared with other vehicle system components, and vice versa (Mindock et al. 2017). To best align with the assumptions developed for the ExMC medical scenarios, we considered all medical resources (e.g. equipment, medication, software) to be a subset of the medical system and represented these resources within the AMRA AID interface accordingly. Additionally, we assumed the medical system will use the vehicle system for communications to ground. Lastly, we assumed the vehicle system would monitor the environment. These assumptions are consistent with and parallel the medical scenarios developed by NASA and ExMC to date.

4.3 Prototype Development and Demo

The visual and interactive elements of the AMRA AID user interface (UI) were determined based on functional requirements and validated within the static states. These states were expanded and developed into two demo scenarios described below. Each demo scenario presents a potential user interaction with the AMRA AID prototype in order to highlight key features, interactions, and information integration requirements relevant to AMRA as an in-flight medical system. A demo was created for both user scenarios researched within the project—headache and shortness of breath.

The Headache scenario demonstrates the patient's chief complaint, AMRA's initial diagnostic questions, AMRA's evaluation that the headache is not extreme, recommendation for Tylenol as well as reference to location and inventory of Tylenol aboard the vehicle, and autonomous scheduling of a follow-up. Within the Headache follow up demo, AMRA initiates a communication thread between the crew medical officer (CMO), the patient, and the flight surgeon in order to conduct a neurological exam on the patient, whose headache has now worsened. Information pertinent to a neurological exam is provided within the Crew Medical System, V&EM, and the procedure is updated in the Crew Schedule. Within the shortness of breath scenario demo, AMRA recommends an ultrasound as a follow up to an emergency pneumothorax procedure. A mission critical activity prevents the ultrasound from being scheduled for the patient and crew medical officer (also the caretaker). AMRA initiates communication to the flight director via the V&EM informing of the issue.

5   Usability Testing

Four iterations of AMRA AID were designed and tested. The following represents the version iterations of AMRA AID as well as user subjects involved within testing and evaluation of those iterations:

Table 1. Version iterations of AMRA AID prototype and testing relevant to each iteration.

Prototype version	Usability testing	Test subjects
V.1	Heuristic Evaluation & Think-aloud	Subject matter experts at Johnson Space Center and in remote video-conferencing which included: 3 NASA scientists affiliated with ExMC, 3 emergency medicine specialists, 2 current and 2 former NASA flight surgeons, 1 current and 1 former NASA astronaut
V.2	Think-aloud	Internal AMRA AID team within the Human Computer Interaction Group
V.3	Think-aloud	1 Subject matter expert in remote & emergency medicine, also a former NASA flight surgeon
V.4	Heuristic Evaluation & Think-aloud	8 Members of the NASA-ARC Human Systems Integration Division (Code TH) in the Human Computer Interaction Group

5.1   HCI Evaluation Methods

We conducted heuristic evaluation on the interface iterations as a usability engineering method for finding and addressing usability problems (Neilson 1993, 2000). In this process, the interface was examined and its compliance with Jakob Nielsen's usability heuristics was evaluated (Nielson 2000). Nielson's research has identified that utilizing five evaluators is generally recommended, as this number has been demonstrated to be most effective in discovering approximately 75% of all usability issues, with diminishing returns found with the participation of additional evaluators.

Think-aloud testing is another usability engineering method championed by Jakob Nielsen and is a direct observation method of user testing that asks users to report on their cognitive process as the demo occurs in real-time (Nielsen 1993). Users are asked to share thoughts with each interaction in the demo as a means of identifying what information the user pays attention to, how the user brings prior knowledge to bear, and what the predominant usability issues may be based on the user's reasoning. Think-aloud testing was instrumental in determining users' expectations while interacting with AMRA AID and in identifying what aspects of the multi-screen interface the user found confusing.

Versions 1–3 of the prototype were tested with subject matter experts as well as non-experts in space and emergency medicine (see Table 1). Version 4 of the prototype was tested with a target audience of Human-Computer Interaction (HCI) practitioners from NASA-ARC Human Systems Integration Division who had experience identifying usability issues with the interfaces and user experiences. None of the participants considered themselves to be medical specialists or have any medical or emergency response training. Users did not have prior knowledge of protocols referenced within the scenarios. A goal of testing with the Ames HCI group was to reveal friction points of the multi-screen AMRA AID experience and illustrate confusing experiences relevant to information integration over the course of the two medical incidents. Factors used to test the prototype's usability included: 1) the capacity for AMRA AID to integrate mission critical information required for situation awareness as medical decision support recommendations are offered, 2) intelligibility and clarity in communication design of recommendations provided, as well as 3) visual appeal and clarity of the interface to the user.

5.2   Usability Testing: Sessions and Evaluation Tasks

Usability testing sessions evaluating the V.4 AMRA AID prototype lasted approximately 1 h per participant and consisted of the subject using the AMRA AID graphical user interface followed by an interview to evaluate the software, tools, and capabilities demonstrated in the AMRA system. In user testing the prototype, subjects viewed all four screens of AMRA AID simultaneously yet were only asked to interact with AMRA Log. The interface guided the user through a "medical incident" scenario and the user was prompted to input "symptoms" to the interface, which then guided users through treatment options, follow-up procedures, or information on possible diagnoses. In Scenario 1 users were asked to respond to AMRA in the first-person as the patient. Users were given a description of headache symptoms and were instructed to report these symptoms to AMRA and respond to its recommendations and suggested workflow. For Scenario 2, users were informed of a series of events taking place over the course of an emergency needle thoracostomy (needle procedure) performed by the Crew Medical Officer (CMO), on a patient-crewmember with tension pneumothorax. Once the patient is stable and the needle decompression procedure is complete, the CMO reports the incident to AMRA, and a series of interactions between the CMO, patient, and AMRA were then demonstrated in the interface.

5.3 Usability Testing Findings

Usability issues were categorized as either: a usability catastrophe, a major severity, or a minor severity. The severity of a usability problem is a combination of the frequency with which the problem occurs, the impact of the problem (whether it might be easy or difficult for the users to overcome), and the persistence of the problem. In this context, a usability catastrophe is classified as a problem imperative to fix before the release of a product, a major usability problem is important to fix and thus should be given high priority, a minor usability problem should be given low priority, and cosmetic problems need not be fixed unless extra time is available on a project (Nielsen 1994). Nielsen elaborates that using the mean of a set of severity ratings from just three evaluators is satisfactory for practical purposes. For this reason, results (below) are discussed as either being demonstrated by all users, a majority of users, or few users (less than 50%).

The key usability findings from testing the V.4 AMRA AID prototype are as follows:

a. In regard to the capacity for AMRA AID to integrate mission critical information required for situation awareness as medical decision support recommendations are offered—a majority of users understood the general premise of AMRA AID as an information integration tool as well as assistant in integrating multiple pieces of mission critical information. A majority of users identified the information displayed within the secondary screens had some relevancy (though not necessarily a causal relationship) with the scenario development. For example, all users identified that the "All Crew" notice to report individually on symptoms was a result of changing (potentially problematic) vehicle conditions. A majority of users identified that the inventory and location of Tylenol was being identified within the V&EM. A majority of users identified that AMRA found an appropriate opening in schedule as the highest likelihood for autonomously scheduling a follow up procedure because of constraints.
b. In regard to intelligibility and clarity in communication design of recommendations provided—all users understood AMRA's conversational mode of issuing diagnostic prompts, recommendations for treatment, and updates relevant to information being sent from ground or to ground.
c. In regard to visual appeal and clarity of the interface to the user—a majority of users found great benefit in being able to see all four screens of AMRA AID at once. A majority of users felt the color scheme between the different screens assisted the legibility and separation of information. All users understood the relationship between the icons representing AMRA Log, V&EM, Crew Schedule, and Crew Medical with their corresponding screens with ease.

Significant usability issues introduced through testing also included the following:

- Usability catastrophe: A majority of users did not notice an update within the 'All crew' message thread, and thus were unclear the 'All crew' message thread must be clicked on to proceed in the demo. This issue prevented users from advancing within the demo. Within a mission context, an information gap caused by an inability to adequately alert 'All crew' of a message could potentially have catastrophic consequences.
- Major Severity:

  - Some users were unclear how the "Acknowledge" or "Confirm" buttons embedded within a message might differ from natural-language (spoken) interactions.
  - A majority of users felt that profile icons (currently with initials) are difficult to tell apart. This issue obstructs the intelligibility of the interface and if improved may result in improved usability.
  - Few users failed to understand the significance of 'Caregiver Mode' or why this would be necessary within the emergency (Shortness of breath) scenario.
  - Few users felt the Summary Report sent to the flight surgeon should also be referenced in the patient's medical and health record.
  - Some users were unclear as to the meaning of "Diagnostic Calculations" or why this was being provided as a hyperlink.

Consequently, key recommendations relevant to the AMRA AID graphical user interface within the current demo include to: differentiate message threads and updates conversations more substantially, differentiate graphical user icons more substantially (especially from AMRA), and provide updates relevant to individual screens in separate messages, so the user can better identify which screens are updating relevant to individual tasks.

6 Research Findings

Based on the two elaborated LDEM medical scenarios—headache and shortness of breath—the research demonstrated the need for additional data relevant to information integration, confidentially, and communications to enable trust. The following represent the core research findings and takeaways. Numerous possibilities for advancement of present research are likewise introduced. These findings may reasonably be applied to the design of autonomous medical response agent technologies within analogous domains in remote and emergency medicine.

6.1 Integration Requirement

Our research validated that integration of mission-critical information and vehicle data with autonomous medical decision support technologies is critical from a human systems integration perspective. The onboard medical system should provide comprehensive health management relevant to prevention, diagnosis, treatment, and long-term management of crew health. The onboard medical system should also: minimize crew burden while using the system, share a common user interface with the overall vehicle system to minimize crew training and cognitive burdens, reduce operations complexity, and lower mission medical risk (Mindock et al. 2017).

The expectation for crew to collect and input data to the medical system over the course of an unplanned medical incident, consolidate that data, and then send to ground will likely add unnecessary workload and stress to the crew and inhibit situation awareness. Despite the fact that future design reference missions empower and enable physician-caretakers to operate with full autonomy from ground, we must ensure capabilities for flight surgeons to remain updated and be provided with sufficient just-in-time information so that they may offer guidance in the event of a medical emergency. Automated data capturing of unplanned incidents by the autonomous medical response agent (or its equivalent) would be of significant benefit to the crew, particularly if this information could be parsed from the on-board medical system and sent to be synchronized with the ground medical system automatically and in a routine manner. Ensuring that the medical system does not add additional workload to the crew in the event of an emergency will be critical, and relying on crew for time-dependent input of information may prove unreliable.

6.2 Crew Autonomy

Technologies for medical decision support are critical to augment and enable crew autonomy—but the degree of autonomy will depend on the communication time delay and the training of the crew. The assumed or implied agency of an autonomous medical system such as AMRA within an emergency scenario where a physician-crewmember cares for a patient-crewmember is particularly under-examined. ExMC rightly specifies the caretaker as a physician, and not just a CMO. The mission physician-astronaut serves as director of care during real-time medical events and thus acts as the primary source for in-mission medical decision making. Therefore, autonomous care models for exploration require flight surgeons and other medical support staff on the ground to take on a consultant role and their input may be considered secondarily (Mindock et al. 2017).

All the same, an emergent scenario introduced by our research poses the question of what happens when the mission physician-astronaut becomes ill and needs care? We assume that in future LDEMs, to best empower and augment the autonomy of the crew in circumstances of unplanned, remote medical care, medical decision support technologies must be provided. The onboard medical system should provide enhanced resources to complement both the physician-astronaut and other crew members' knowledge base in the form of onboard medical references and decision support systems (Mindock et al. 2017). The crew, regardless of their level of expertise, will need enough information and instruction to respond to both time-critical incidents and as well as chronic conditions independently and without specialist support.

6.3 Crew Confidentiality

Designing for or assuming crew confidentiality (such as in protecting the privacy of personal health information) in future LDEMs requires further research and investigation.

We found there is insufficient data indicating how crew confidentiality would differ substantially from ISS medical operations, and additional research is necessary to identify how the role of the mission physician-astronaut will replace or impact the role of the flight surgeon in mission control today. Crewmembers (not just physicians or CMOs) may need access to another crewmember's health information in the event of a medical emergency. In such circumstances a CMO may also be a patient. The flight surgeon is generally the go-between between the crew, those handling vehicle information, and the flight director. In rethinking the role of flight surgeons in autonomous crew operations, it is important to consider that the commander may not be aware of medical conditions that have operational consequences.

6.4   Communications Protocols

Emergency (pre-approved) protocols (such as in medical manuals) will still be extremely critical when time is of the essence. Today aboard ISS, the crew is instructed to go through the Medical Manual checklist and then call a flight surgeon for next steps. The establishment of communications protocols for self-care of an unplanned incident between the patient, on-board medical system, and ground versus directed care through both planned and unplanned incidents with a patient, caretaker, on-board medical system, and ground is a significant area of research with unique requirements still demanding consideration. Guidance must be provided on when and in what circumstances decision support technologies should replace the need for directed communication with the flight surgeon and ground. There is an implicit understanding that the role of the flight surgeon will change, and the crew will need to be empowered to have more decision-making capabilities.

ISS currently relies heavily on real-time communication for guidance and recommendations. Real-time video and audio communications with ground through Private Medical Conferences are integral aspects of crew medical treatment and care. A flight surgeon or physician can distinguish key differences in tone of voice, behavior, physical appearance, etc. through real-time video, which proves integral to quickly formulating diagnoses. In future LDEMs, there may be times in which video, audio, or text communications be regulated due to bandwidth limitations. Which modes of communication that would be most appropriate for distinct medical tasks and levels of risk is an area of research requiring additional investigation. Additional research is needed to determine the limitations, types, and frequency of high-fidelity communications (audio and video) over the course of routine medical check-ins for chronic conditions or for unplanned emergencies (Krihak et al. 2019).

6.5   Ground Awareness and Trust

Crew to ground synchronization of medical records (such as the EMR) and documentation of unplanned incidents will prove challenging and represent an unprecedented paradigm shift from ISS. Regardless of whether an acute or chronic condition is being diagnosed or treated, information must be sent to flight surgeons on the ground in order to remain 'in-the-loop'. The on-board medical system will maintain ground awareness of crew health as flight communication constraints permit (Mindock et al. 2017). Even though the synchronization of in-mission and ground medical data systems depends on a variety of factors such as telemetry bandwidth, distance from earth, priority of data, and more, ground support must continue to be informed on the state of the crew to assess impacts to the mission and provide support as needed. (Mindock et al. 2017).

While we did not measure trust specifically, and while the flight surgeon interface was not demonstrated in the final prototype, the following hypotheses can be drawn to support trust between ground support and crew. Mirrored, delayed data presentation for situational awareness may augment trust within medical emergencies or when time is of the essence. In the event of an emergency, critical information to be provided to the flight surgeon such as vital signs information and responses from advanced cardiac life support algorithms would ideally be packaged and sent to the flight surgeon for an immediate response without requiring the crew collect and integrate information. In such circumstances, a simple, one-sentence update may be more valuable than a data-dump in treating a chronic condition or an unplanned medical incident when time is of the essence. These updates may reasonably be provided by an autonomous medical support technology. The frequency of such updates (given bandwidth capabilities, for example) and their content requires further consideration.

7   Conclusion

In conclusion, AMRA AID proposes a multi-screen dashboard which frames the in-mission medical system as a component of the overall integrated vehicle system, and demonstrates how we might ensure crew autonomy, increase the crew's medical capabilities, and decrease cognitive burden within a front-end user interface. AMRA AID refrains from relying on input from ground or mission control for self-treatment of medical issues—though ground awareness and communication with ground is maintained as a means of ensuring trust between mission control and crew. This project arrives at critical findings regarding usability needs, communication requirements, and integrated information requirements for a future technology interface aimed to increase confidence between ground support and LDEM crewmembers.

Acknowledgments. We would like to thank the NASA flight surgeons, astronauts, and subject matter experts affiliated with NASA ExMC who consulted on this project as well as all usability test subjects at NASA Johnson Space Center and Ames Research Center who participated in studies relevant to the grant. This work has been supported by the Translational Research Institute through NASA Cooperative Agreement NNX16AO69A.

Appendix

(See Figs. 3, 4 and 5).

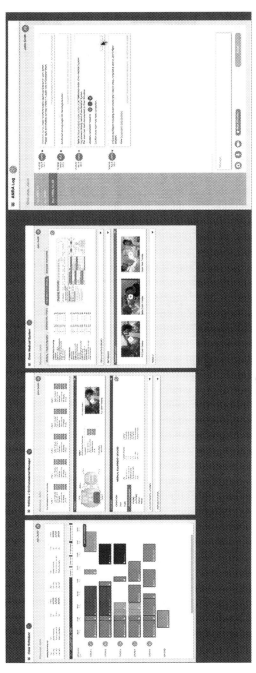

Fig. 3. Screenshot of AMRA AID user interface.

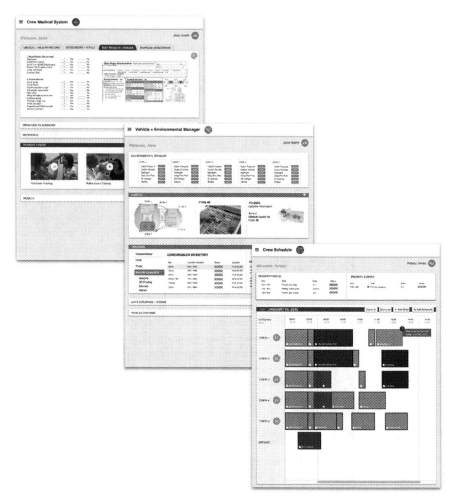

Fig. 4. Screenshot of supplementary screens.

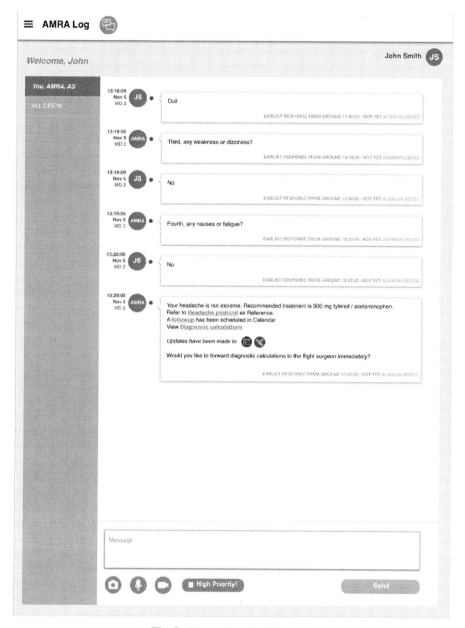

Fig. 5. Screenshot of AMRA Log.

References

Antonsen, E., et al.: Evidence report: risk of adverse health outcomes and decrements in performance due to in-flight medical conditions. Human Research Program Exploration Medical Capabilities Element, JSC-CN-39542 (2017)

Ball, J.R., Evans Jr, C.H. (eds.): Safe Passage: Astronaut Care for Exploration Missions. Institute of Medicine (US) Committee on Creating a Vision for Space Medicine During Travel Beyond Earth Orbit. National Academies Press US, Washington (DC) (2001)

Blue, R., Nussbaum, D., Antonsen, E.: Development of an Accepted Medical Condition List for Exploration Medical Scoping Capability. NASA/TM-2019-220299 (2019)

Clément, G.: Fundamentals of Space Medicine. Operational Space Medicine, December 2010

Krihak, M., et al.: Communication Bandwidth Considerations for Exploration Medical Care during Space Missions. NASA/TM-2019-220335

Love, S.G., Reagan, M.L.: Delayed voice communication. Acta Astronaut. **91**, 89–95 (2013)

Marquez, J.J., et al.: Enabling communication between astronauts and ground teams for space exploration missions. IEEE Aerospace (2019)

Menon, J.: Autonomous medical repose agent prototype. In: NASA HRP Investigators Workshop (2020)

Mindock, J., et al.: Exploration Medical Capability ConOps and Systems Engineering: Technical Interchange Meeting Summary. JSC-CN-39099 (2017)

Nielsen, J.: Usability Engineering. Academic Press, Cambridge (1993)

Nielsen, J.: Why You Only Need to Test with 5 Users. Nielsen Norman Group, 19 March 2000. https://www.nngroup.com/articles/why-you-only-need-to-test-with-5-users/

Nielsen, J.: Severity Ratings for Usability Problems. Nielsen Norman Group, 1 November 1994. https://www.nngroup.com/articles/how-to-rate-the-severity-of-usability-problems/

NASA JSC-48512-E1: International Space Station Complex Operations Emergency Procedures All Expedition Flights, Mission Operations Directorate Operations Division (2000)

NASA JSC-48522-E4: International Space Station Integrated Medical Group (IMG) Medical Checklist. ISS - All Expeditions (2001)

NASA-STD-3001: NASA Space Flight Human-System Standard (2014)

Urbina, M., Rubin, D., Hailey, M., Reyes, D., Antonsen, E.: Medical system concept of operations for mars exploration missions. In: NASA HRP Investigators Workshop (2016)

The Kansei Images of Blister Packaging Through Tactile Perception

Shang-Ru Yu and Hsi-Jen Chen[✉]

Department of Industrial Design, National Cheng Kung University, No. 1, University Road,
East District, Tainan 701, Taiwan
eatcandys1213@gmail.com, hsijen_chen@mail.ncku.edu.tw

Abstract. With the growing importance of User Experience (UX), Kansei design become the key elements of competitive advantages between products, and consumer demand gradually changes from functional to psychological. As the first medium contacted between consumers' senses in the process of consumption, previous researches on Kansei engineering have paid more attention to the image of products and materials.

Blister packaging is common in the marketspace, and its physical factors and texture changes are rarely discussed. Thus, the purpose of this study is to investigate the correlation between perceived meanings and the hardness of blister package in order to explore the image of blister package through Kansei engineering and establish the relation between geometric form, hardness and the image.

The results showed the importance of package hardness on consumer psychology, indicating that the high hardness package provided the sense of luxury and delicate. It is also found that the hardness of tactile is similar with the Fechner law. Meanwhile, geometric perceptions affect sense of touch. Our results contribute to the HCI community by delivering knowledge about the packaging design of interaction.

Keywords: User Experience · Packaging · Kansei engineering · Tactile · Visual

1 Introduction

Previous review has revealed that User Experience (UX) is an important factor in influencing consumers in an environment of market commodity diversity. In order to satisfy the consumer experience, information can be collected through the human senses, which contain the sensations of the stimuli received by the human five senses [1]. Using the information derived from the five senses to create a more attractive design is currently an object that the Kansei engineering is committed to exploring. Kansei engineering is a consumer-oriented technology approach designed to develop new products, and its consumer-centric thinking design model, which translates consumer perceptions and images into new product design elements. With the improvement of product performance and technology, perceptual design become the key to competitive advantage between products [2]. Nowadays, Kansei engineering is widely applied in products, perceptual

© Springer Nature Switzerland AG 2020
C. Stephanidis et al. (Eds.): HCII 2020, LNCS 12423, pp. 563–575, 2020.
https://doi.org/10.1007/978-3-030-60114-0_38

design can affect consumers' behavioral motivation, enhance customer evaluation and even brand impressions [3].

On the other hand, Kansei research in the past were mostly focused on products, materials and vision [4], and less on packaging, an important medium between products and consumers. Packaging has basic functions such as cladding, protecting products, and experiencing product content [5]. With the evolution of consumption habits, there are strong competitiveness between products and the emotional design in the packaging become one of the factors to increase product value and drive consumers' purchasing behavior [6], which has also become a vital part of marketing, packaging can influence consumer perception of product features and their consumption value, which affects purchasing motivation and brand impression [7].

In order to meet people's psychological preferences, recent years have explored how to improve the emotional design of products and confirmed the importance of consumers' emotional needs [8]. But previous studies have focused less on plastic packaging and its physical properties. In the process of consumption, the interaction between consumers and packaging affects the target behavioral motivation through the senses [9]. Thus, this paper conducted a questionnaire, semi-structured interviews and tactile experiment, to investigate consumers' perception about blister packaging.

2   Literature Review

2.1   Blister Packaging

Blister package (see Fig. 1) is made by vacuum forming (see Fig. 2), which is a thermo-forming method. The manufacturing principle is to heat the thermoplastic material until it is softened and then to stretch and mechanically compress the plastic material to the mold [10].

Fig. 1. Blister packaging

Vacuum forming can be used to produce a wide range of products, such as product packaging, modelmaking, carrying trays and etc. [11]. Because of its low cost, high reuse rate, fast production speed, vacuum forming has become a widely used plastic processing method. The process can be divided into the following three stages:

1. The heating stage: the machine first places the plastic sheet, and then uses the heating device to soften the material.
2. The molding stage: when the plastic sheet is heated to the softening point, the plastic sheet will be pressed onto the mold by vacuum and then form.
3. The release phase: after forming, wait for the plastic to cool down and then it can be separated from the mold.

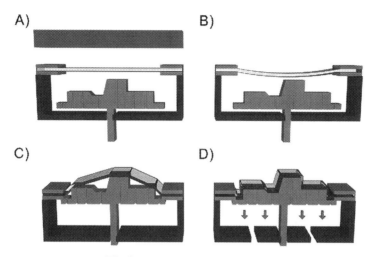

Fig. 2. Process of vacuum forming

2.2 Sensations and Perceptions

The sensation of human organs can usually be divided into five sensory systems, which are vision, touch, smell, taste and hearing. Each system is interconnected and interdependent [12]. It is a continuous process between sensations, the basis of perception, and perceptions. Sensation is a psychological response triggered by the physiological sensations of the body's senses receiving from the external environment. Meanwhile, perception is the psychological function of the sensory message that is processed by the brain.

Visual. Visual is the most developed system in human. Visual can receive messages, such as the shape, size, color, proximity and etc. At least 80% of the messages in life are obtained through vision [13]. When the human body interacts with any object, vision is often the first sensory re-impact of receiving messages [14]. Vision can also provide the most information in the shortest possible time, so visual cognition, before other sensory messages are involved, is the primary factor to influence individual actions such as making decisions and evaluating judgments [15].

Tactile. Tactile is also known as sense of pressure which is caused by skin irritation. Tactile is the first sense of human connection to the outside world, but the message of complex cognitive mechanisms are less explored [16]. In the process of consumption, when experiencing products and touching the surface, tactile is the most important source of perception [17]. The various sensory stimuli and messages presented by the commodity, which in turn affect personal cognition, are among the factors that contribute to the motivation of consumption, especially when the human body comes into contact with the object, and the information generated by the senses of touch is irreplaceable by other senses, such as temperature, hardness and texture [18].

Scholars Elder and Krishna [19] point out that using visual to describe a product would visualize mental simulation, and tactile can increase confidence in the product. Thus, if the sense of touch can be involved in the process of consumption, it not only increases consumers product experience, but also increases the purchasing intention [20]. In addition, Peck and Shu [21] indicated that the emotional connections between objects and human beings occur immediately while touching products.

2.3 Kansei and Kansei Engineering

Kansei. The word sensibility means the psychological feeling and image of events or objects, or the expected psychological feeling of something. Sensibility can be divided into three parts: the sensibility process (emotion analyzing system of brain), sensibility medium (how human body feels) and sensibility outcome (the result of sensation analysis). The sens outcome is the comprehensive sensory delicate of the meaning, viewpoint and value of the environment created by humanity in the process of perceptuality [22].

Kansei Engineering. Kansei Engineering is to provide market information and design applications for products [23]. Kansei engineering is a technique that translates people's sensibility and impressions into physical design elements. The purpose of Kansei engineering is primarily to translate the sensory perception and demand of consumers on the product into design [24].

3 Method

In this article, we conducted a questionnaire, semi-structured interviews and tactile experiment, to investigate the perception of blister packaging among consumers. Prior researches on Kansei engineering were reviewed to have a comprehensive understanding of perception. Through the tactile senses can distinguish the surface characteristics and feelings of the object, the way of touch will also be related to the shape of the object, different object shapes will induce the toucher different touch movements, so there are different aspects of the surface texture of the object, and human through the hands to perform touch action on the object to evaluate.

In an experiment, scholars Lederman and Klatzky observed the behavior patterns of subjects when touching objects, and the results showed that most people used typical actions, called tactile exploration, to organize a total of six haptic ways of exploring. For example, when the subject wants to feel the hardness, they will apply force to press the material, and if they want to feel the overall shape, they will be covered objects with his hand [25].

We referred to the studies form Lederman and Klatzky [25]. During the experiments, we asked the subjects to feel the geometry and hardness of the sample by pressing and covering the sample with touch (see Fig. 3). The sample size is based on the average size of adult palms in Taiwan [26].

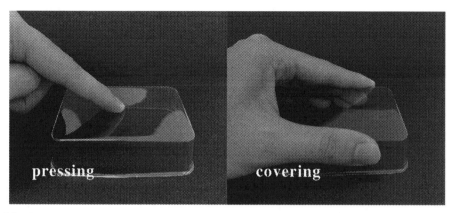

Fig. 3. Two ways to touch the samples. Pressing to feel the hardness, covering to feel the geometry

3.1 Kansei Vocabulary and Questionnaire Design

Kansei Vocabulary. Through literature review, we collected about 200 Kansei vocabularies, and invited six industrial designers to conduct focus group method. The selected vocabulary will be used in the questionnaire design. The vocabulary selection steps are explained below:

1. First, explain the research purpose to six industrial designers, provide the 200 Kansei vocabularies collected previously as a reference, and then ask them to screen the vocabulary for blister packaging images.
2. Use the KJ Method to group and rename the screened vocabulary.
3. Finally, six groups of Kansei vocabulary were selected. In order for the vocabulary in the questionnaire to comprehensively cover the product experience dimension, we confirmed that all Kansei vocabularies fit the five categories of sensory perception, "object/measurable", "evaluative/aesthetics", "social status and positions", "emotion" and "interface delicate", etc. [27].

Questionnaire Design. In order to avoid the confusion caused by too many choices for a single question, and reduce the accuracy of the evaluation, the five- and seven-point semantic difference method can more accurately, and the results are more significant [28]. Therefore, this experimental questionnaire uses five-point Semantic Differential Method (SD Method).

3.2 Product Form and Hardness

Product Form. Scholar Lauer and Pentak [29] pointed out that most figurative objects are composed of several geometric shapes. After simplification, these shapes can be distinguished into basic geometric components. The decomposed geometric elements help researchers to study on pure forms to obtain people's psychological feelings about geometric forms [29].

Therefore, we collected about 100 samples of Blister Packaging on the market, and then analyzed them through a focus group of six industrial designers to restore the basic geometric form. Finally, we used card sorting method to classify the two main shapes, arc and square.

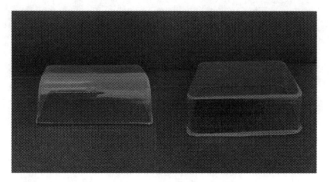

Fig. 4. The sample of experiments (arc and square).

Hardness. The hardness of the blister pack is controlled by the thickness of the plastic sheet. After discussing with three experts who have more than five years of experience in blister packaging production, in order to obtain the consumer's perceptual image of different hardness, the most commonly used plastic sheet thickness in the industry was selected as the sample material, allowing the subject to perceive the change in hardness. Plastic thickness: 0.4 mm~0.8 mm, a total of five thicknesses.

3.3 Tactile Experiment

The tactile experiments were conducted in a one-to-one manner, and the subjects evaluated the blister packaging by haptic. In the experiment, the samples will be placed in a dark box to prevent the subject from visually associating past experience and thus affecting the experimental results. The subject touches the sample in a prescribed manner (see Fig. 4). Score the Kansei vocabulary on the questionnaire and accept interviews. The experimental content includes two shapes, five hardness, and six groups of Kansei vocabulary.

The subjects were all educated in design for four years. The subjects who were educated in design are more sensitive to material texture changes and can clearly express and understand the meaning of Kansei vocabulary.

We eventually gathered 15 valid data from aged 20 to 25. Next step, we used SPSS software to analyze our data based on the scores from each item in our questionnaire.

4   Results

First, we performed reliability analysis (Table 1) on two questionnaires to ensure the accuracy of the questionnaires.

Table 1. The reliability between two questionnaires.

Questionnaires	Cronbach's alpha
Arc questionnaire	.895
Square questionnaire	.886

We then analyze the questionnaire scores of the square and arc shapes. In order to know the image scores of the two shapes in each hardness, the SPSS software was used for ANOVA analysis. Therefore, we served the number of groups of hardness as the independent variables, and the seven groups of Kansei vocabularies as the dependent variables for comparing the differences between the groups.

4.1   Cheap/Luxury

There is significant association between cheap, luxury and thickness ($p < .01$). In the shape of square, there are differences between thickness 0.4 mm and thickness 0.7 mm, 0.8 mm and 0.9 mm. There are differences among thickness 0.6 mm, 0.8 mm and 0.9 mm, however, there is no difference between thickness 0.6 mm and 0.7 mm. On the other hand, there is no difference between the thicker samples such as 0.8 mm and 0.9 mm, but each of them is different from others.

When it comes to arc, there is no difference between thickness 0.7 mm and 0.8 mm, but the thickness 0.9 mm is different to the lower thickness (see Fig. 5).

4.2 Traditional/Modern

Traditional and modern are found to be related to thickness ($p < .01$). A square of thickness 0.4 mm and 0.6 mm only have significant differences with the higher thickness 0.8 mm and 0.9 mm, and there is no significant differences in the thickness 0.7 mm. In the shape of arc, the results are similar to the results of square (see Fig. 6).

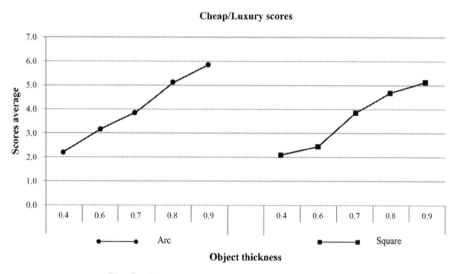

Fig. 5. Cheap/luxury meaning scores of prototypes.

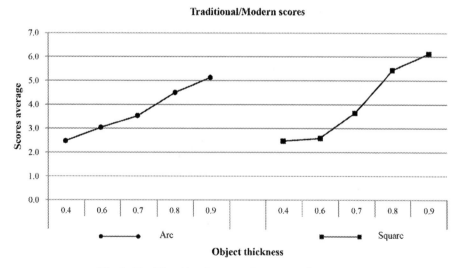

Fig. 6. Traditional/modern meaning scores of prototypes.

4.3 Simple/Delicate

There is significant association between simple, delicate and thickness ($p < .01$). The significant differences of square shape are only found among thickness 0.4 mm, 0.6 mm and 0.9 mm. As the arc shape, there are significant differences between 0.4 mm, 0.6 mm, 0.7 mm and 0.9 mm (see Fig. 7).

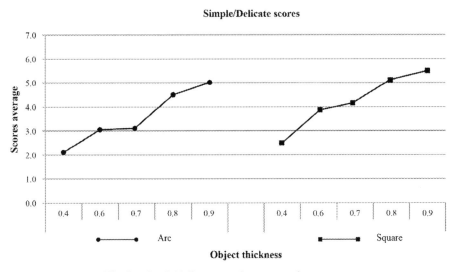

Fig. 7. Simple/delicate meaning scores of prototypes.

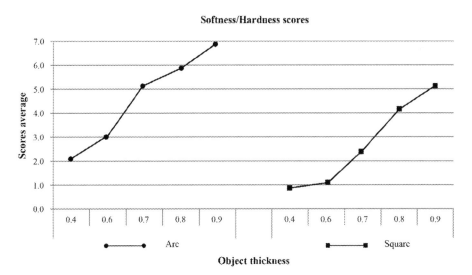

Fig. 8. Softness/hardness meaning scores of prototypes.

4.4 Softness/Hardness

Softness and hardness are found to be significant (p < .01). In the case of square shape package, the thickness 0.4 mm and 0.6 mm are significant different from all the other thickness, so does the thickness 0.6 mm. Therefore, above the thickness 0.7 mm there are significant different from the lower thickness such as 0.4 mm and 0.6 mm.

When it comes to square, there are no difference between the thickness 0.4 mm and 0.6 mm, and above the thickness 0.8 mm there are significant different from the lower thickness such as 0.4 mm and 0.6 mm (see Fig. 8).

4.5 Nature/Geometry

Nature and geometry are found to be significant (p < .01). In the shape of square, there are differences between 0.4 mm, 0.6 mm and 0.9 mm. And the results of lower thickness 0.4 mm and 0.6 mm of square package are similar with the square package (see Fig. 9).

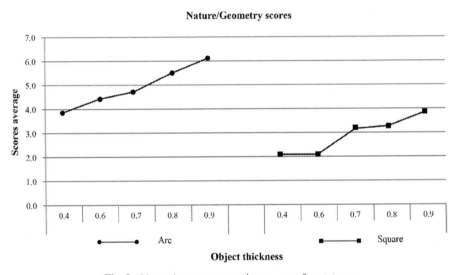

Fig. 9. Nature/geometry meaning scores of prototypes

4.6 Fancy/Practical

There is significant association between fancy, practical and thickness (p < .01). The significant differences of square shape are only found among thickness 0.4 mm, 0.6 mm, 0.8 mm and 0.9 mm. As the arc shape, the results are similar with the results of square (see Fig. 10).

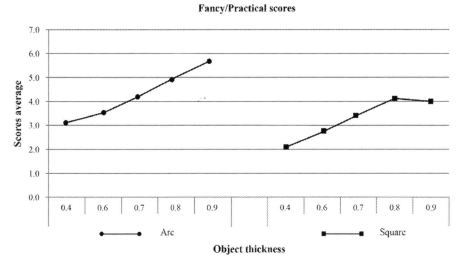

Fig. 10. Fancy/practical meaning scores of prototypes

5 Discussion

On square packaging, the sense of luxury is easy to detect after the thickness reaches 0.8 mm, while the arc packaging is detected at 0.9 mm. When the thickness is higher, the square and curved packaging samples are considered to be more modern, especially when the thickness of the arc packaging reached more than 0.8 mm, is the most obvious. Similarly, the higher the thickness, the higher the sense of touch is delicate to the packaging of both shapes.

Participants also find the blister packaging with higher thickness to be more hardness than those with lower thickness blister packaging, when square packaging reaches 0.7 mm in thickness and arc packaging reaches 0.8 mm in thickness, the sense of higher hardness is the most obvious. Blister packaging that are at the extreme hardness with 0.4 mm and 0.9 mm thickness received higher meaning scores, and the blister packaging close to extremes (0.6 mm and 0.8 mm thickness) received meaning scores similar to extremes.

Similarly, packaging with lower thickness are found to be fancy whereas packaging with higher thickness are found to be more practical. As for the effect of thickness on geometric and nature Kansei vocabulary, it is more affected by the shape of the package itself, but the increase in hardness will still increase the tactile perception of geometry.

Results suggest that overall Kansei vocabularies presents a positive relationship to thickness. Regardless of blister packaging shape, when the thickness become higher, they are all considered as more luxury. Through interviews, the participants also indicated that through the sense of touch, the feeling of blister packaging can be easily sensed, and the feeling will vary with the change in hardness. Through the results, it was found that after the hardness of the square blister packaging reached 0.7 mm and arc packaging reached 0.8 mm, the other evaluations of the package also increased. Depending on the hardness change, the shape of the package will also affect the tactile feeling. According to the data, it can be found that the arc shape is considered to be fancy, nature and softness, but delicate and modern than square.

However, the research still needs to be improved, increasing the number of participants and different groups of participants, so that the research can be more effectively. In the future, the research can be directed to the research of cognitive behavior impact on the operation interface of plastic materials.

6   Conclusion

The current study investigated the influence of physical qualities of packaging, particularly hardness, on perceived meanings. The results suggest that a minor change in thickness might lead to a greater impact on perceived meanings, when the packaging have lower or higher hardness, subjects' perception of Kansei vocabularies will be more obvious, whereas their perception are fuzzier when the hardness of blister packaging is in the middle of the range.

In this study, we classified the Kansei vocabularies of blister packaging, and finally, six groups of Kansei vocabularies which can be used to operate perceptual elements in the design of blister packaging. Moreover, we have collected the common blister packaging styles in the market and classified them into two geometric forms, square and arc, and analyzed consumers' image towards the geometry of packaging. This paper discovered the importance of the hardness change of blister packaging on consumer psychology, similar to the Fechner law, the packaging after reaching a certain hardness affected the feeling of the tested and improved the evaluation.

In conclusion, the past research of Kansei engineering has mainly focused on products and visual applications. However, with the increasing importance of user experience, the role of packaging in the consumer experience process is worthy of discussion. The research results are based on preliminary research on blister packaging and the findings of the study contribute to HCI Community by delivering knowledge about packaging design of interaction. The results can provide suggestions for packaging interaction related on the design of hardness and geometry, and as the basis for subsequent research on the interface of plastic materials.

References

1. Choi, K., Jun, C.J.A.E.: A systematic approach to the Kansei factors of tactile sense regarding the surface roughness. Appl. Ergonomics **38**(1), 53–63 (2007)
2. Barlow, J., Maul, D.: Emotional Value: Creating Strong Bonds with Your Customers. Berrett-Koehler Publishers, San Francisco (2000)
3. Streicher, M.C., Estes, Z.: Multisensory interaction in product choice: grasping a product affects choice of other seen products. J. Consum. Psychol. **26**(4), 558–565 (2016)
4. Ryu, T., Park, J.: Will product packaging density affect pre-purchase recognition? Food **8**(8), 352 (2019)
5. Stewart, B.: Packaging Design Strategy. Pira International, Leatherhead (1994)
6. Mackenzie, D.: Green Design: Design for the Environment. Books Nippan, London (1997)
7. Krishna, A., Cian, L., Aydinoglu, N.Z.: Sensory aspects of package design, (in English). J. Retail. Article **93**(1), 43–54 (2017)

8. Van Egmond, R.: The experience of product sounds. In: Product Experience, pp. 69–89. Elsevier (2008)
9. Littel, S., Orth, U.R.: Effects of package visuals and haptics on brand evaluations. Eur. J. Mark. **47**(1/2), 198–217 (2013)
10. Yamaoka, J., Kakehi, Y.: DrawForming: an interactive fabrication method for vacuum forming. In: Proceedings of the TEI 2016: Tenth International Conference on Tangible, Embedded, and Embodied Interaction, pp. 615–620. ACM, (2016)
11. Hussain, B.I., Safiulla, M.: Comparative study of cooling systems for vacuum forming tool. Mater. Today Proc. **5**(1), 30–36 (2018)
12. Schultz, L.M., Petersik, J.T.: Visual-haptic relations in a two-dimensional size-matching task. Percept. Motor Skills **78**(2), 395–402 (1994)
13. Berger, A.A.: Seeing is believing: an introduction to visual communication. ERIC (1989)
14. Ludden, G.D., Schifferstein, H.N., Hekkert, P.: Visual tactual incongruities in products as sources of surprise. Empirical Stud. Arts **27**(1), 61–87 (2009)
15. Schifferstein, H.N., Desmet, P.M.: The effects of sensory impairments on product experience and personal well-being. Ergonomics **50**(12), 2026–2048 (2007)
16. Prytherch, D., McLundie, M.: So what is haptics anyway? Res. Issues Art Design Media **2**, 29 (2002)
17. Schifferstein, H.N.: The perceived importance of sensory modalities in product usage: a study of self-reports. Acta Psychol. **121**(1), 41–64 (2006)
18. Grohmann, B., Spangenberg, E.R., Sprott, D.E.: The influence of tactile input on the evaluation of retail product offerings. J. Retail. **83**(2), 237–245 (2007)
19. Elder, R.S., Krishna, A.: The "Visual Depiction Effect" in advertising: facilitating embodied mental simulation through product orientation. J. Consum. Res. Article **38**(6), 988–1003 (2012). (in English)
20. Peck, J., Childers, T.L.: To have and to hold: The influence of haptic information on product judgments. J. Mark. **67**(2), 35–48 (2003)
21. Peck, J., Shu, S.B.: The effect of mere touch on perceived ownership. J. Consum. Res. Article **36**(3), 434–447 (2009). (in English)
22. Lévy, P., Nakamori, S., Yamanaka, T.: Explaining kansei design studies. In: Design and Emotion Conference 2008 (2008)
23. Roy, R., Goatman, M., Khangura, K.: User-centric design and Kansei Engineering. CIRP J. Manuf. Sci. Technol. **1**(3), 172–178 (2009)
24. Ogawa, T., Nagai, Y., Ikeda, M.: An ontological approach to designers' idea explanation style: towards supporting the sharing of kansei-ideas in textile design. Adv. Eng. Inform. **23**(2), 157–164 (2009)
25. Lederman, S.J., Klatzky, R.L.: Hand movements - a window into haptic object recognition. Cogn. Psychol. Article **19**(3), 342–368 (1987). (in English)
26. Wu, S.W., Wu, S.F., Liang, H.W., Wu, Z.T., Huang, S.: Measuring factors affecting grip strength in a Taiwan Chinese population and a comparison with consolidated norms. Appl. Ergonomics **40**(4), 811–815 (2009). (in English)
27. Krippendorff, K.: The Semantic Turn: A New Foundation for Design. CRC Press, Cambridge (2005)
28. Dawes, J.: Do data characteristics change according to the number of scale points used? An experiment using 5-point, 7-point and 10-point scales. Int. J. Market Res. **50**(1), 61–104 (2008)
29. Lauer, D.A., Pentak, S.: Design Basics. Cengage Learning, Boston (2011)

User Experience Case Studies

A Study on User Preference: Influencing App Selection Decision with Privacy Indicator

Sven Bock[1][✉] and Nurul Momen[2]

[1] Technische Universität Berlin, Berlin, Germany
`sven.bock@mms.tu-berlin.de`
[2] Karlstad University, Karlstad, Sweden
`nurul.momen@kau.se`

Abstract. This paper investigates how the use of privacy indicators in app stores can influence user behavior, and if the added information can improve consumer transparency. After a pre-study on the design and symbology, a visual privacy indicator was implemented and evaluated in an app market prototype. A total of 82 participants were asked to select a number of task-specific apps. By varying the degrees of participatory background information, we show that impact of a privacy indicator on app selection behavior has statistical significance and such privacy preserving behavior can be invoked by mere presence of the indicator.

Keywords: Privacy · Transparency · Indicator design · Decision making · Mobile interface · User study

1 Introduction

The telephone with a wire has transformed into smartphone over the last couple of decades and became a charismatic tool with an ability to keep human beings captivated for a considerable amount of their life-time. Users remain of the opinion that the services offered would be free of charge while their personal data is being monetized by Big Data. Though users pay with personal data, the price is invisible for them. Certainly, there is much to gain from such data analysis, but the notion to brush privacy risks under the carpet poses new challenges ahead. Users face hindrances to be aware of and to take preventive measures because of poor means to observe and to assess the consequences of data disclosure. Though users can solve numerous daily-life problems through finding a convenient app from online stores, their decisions to grant access to personal data could result to privacy implications [3,17,45]. Thus, informed decision making about privacy by an ordinary user is hard to come by.

Today's app market offers popularity-based ranking which is entirely dependent on crowd-sourced user opinion. Convenience, ease of use, rich features and functionality are the established criteria for rating an app [20]. The excessive

© Springer Nature Switzerland AG 2020
C. Stephanidis et al. (Eds.): HCII 2020, LNCS 12423, pp. 579–599, 2020.
https://doi.org/10.1007/978-3-030-60114-0_39

data harvesting nature of apps hardly features in the rating procedure [19]. As this negative attribute is rather kept hidden from the interface, apps' privacy invasive behavior mostly does not play an important part in a users' decision making process while selecting an app. This paper addresses this shortcoming and seeks for introducing a privacy indicator within app selection scenarios. We chose the Android app market for our study due to the open source nature of the platform and implementation feasibility.

In order to address the aforementioned issue, we hypothesize that providing privacy-indicating cues in the app-store, could help the user in making informed decisions. The main research objective of this study is to analyze the impact of such *ex-ante*[1] cues [37] on the decision making process of users and to address the following questions: *(a)* Is the privacy indicator able to lead to a better judgment regarding the apps' trustworthiness and to provide the ease of selection? *(b)* Is there a significant difference in privacy-preserving decision making behavior while selecting an app for a certain task? and *(c)* Is the indicator an adequate tool to illustrate the intrusiveness of apps in terms of privacy?

This paper presents our design, implementation and evaluation processes of a privacy indicator for the app-store. Our contributions are: *(i)* Through an online study and an empirical study that included 82 participants, we show that the impact of privacy indicators on app selection behavior has statistical significance. *(ii)* By varying the degrees of participatory background information and introduction, we show that the mere presence of the indicator caused participants to select more privacy-friendly apps for six out of eight app categories. *(iii)* For Messaging and Video-call categories, the indicator had limited or no impact. We suspect this is because of background preferences for very popular apps, suggesting that privacy concern decreases with respect to app popularity.

The rest of this article is organized as following: Sect. 2 provides a brief overview of prior research works conducted within this area. Section 3 describes how we designed indicators, conducted the online study and selected an indicator that is easy to perceive. Section 4 documents how the empirical study was performed along with the results collected from it. Section 5 elaborates interpretations, evaluation, limitations of the findings and our future research plans. We draw a conclusion of this paper in Sect. 6.

2   Background

There are numerous prior research works on the security and privacy aspects of Android apps. This section outlines the related work on apps' security and privacy issues, efforts to aid the user to protect privacy and users' decision dilemma. Studies were also conducted to report on users' awareness and concerns regarding privacy, identifying privacy leaks, the usability challenges of privacy controls. Hence, many solutions were introduced to aid users in managing privacy. We briefly discuss the relevant background to formulate the problem and hypothesis.

---

[1] Before the event (data disclosure) takes place.

2.1 App Behavior and Privacy Friendliness

The Android operating system relies on a permission-based access control model that is placed to guard user data and sensors [13]. Depending on type of permissions, approval from the user is required during the first use of the app for granting access to resources [12]. As the platforms offer binary choices (accept/decline), it is difficult to perceive consequence for granting access and assess the risk, if not impossible. Moreover, information is hardly available about the usage of user data once access has been granted. So, a white-card privilege to the available system resource is given to the app that leaves access decisions about sensitive personal data to arbitrary programs and services. This is a problem for the data subject who suffers the lack of appropriate information to make decisions regarding privacy preferences. Several prior works pointed out this problem that mostly put emphasis on apps' data access potential, frequency, consequences and privacy implications [16,19,21,32,34,36].

We intend to consider the outcome of app behavior analysis as the input to our indicator ranking mechanism. For example, [19,35] judge app behavior based on four parameters: data access potential (permission requirement), frequency of resource usage (runtime access), regulatory (GDPR—General Data Protection Regulation [9]) compliance according to corresponding privacy policy and user review analysis. Before including a comprehensive privacy score generating mechanism into our research, the prime goal is to find out whether a privacy cue can make a difference in user decisions within this evolved context or not. However, indicator ranking mechanism remains out of scope for this article.

2.2 Addressing Decision Dilemma

Though a decent amount of research effort has been invested to study app behavior, the app market is mostly inclined with ratings that are harvested from crowd-sourced user feedback. So, apps' data access potential is not easy to unearth and the user usually struggles to deal with individual privacy while deciding upon installing mobile apps [1,5,26]. There exists an array of prior works that shed light on users' remorse and struggle with understanding privacy risks associated with apps [39,41,43,46] and offer solutions to aid the user [2,33,42].

Rajivan and Camp used visual cues to support the user in decision making before giving consent to requested permissions [38]. Kraus et al. used a permission scale to communicate potential risks to the user [27]. Gu et al. concluded that a high level of malaise is perceived by users when an app requires accesses to rights (perceived permission sensitivity) [18]. This raises users' privacy concerns while downloading apps. In contrast, the apps' popularity reduces these concerns and the effect of justifying access rights on privacy concerns is heavily dependent on previous bad experiences that the user has faced regarding privacy with mobile devices.

Kelley et al. found that certain contextual notices, such as privacy symbols, can be effectively used to influence the subsequent use of privacy [25]. In [26], Kelley et al. performed another study which contained 20-participant lab study and a 366-participant online experiment. In this study, participants were presented with a short display about privacy facts that included a brief description about potential consequences. However, all these privacy cues from [25–27,38] are addressing secondary user interface—app details to communicate privacy risks. It is possible to see the privacy cue after selecting an app which implies to decisions being made without cues' influence. Once the user has selected an app and become aware of the warning from privacy cue, it is cumbersome to go back to the app selection; although the user is aware of the aggressiveness of the app. Therefore, these studies are not supporting decision making comparison in primary interface—app store and they require more cognitive effort besides technical knowledge, e.g. permission.

Moreover, these studies were conducted in a different context compared to ours because, Androids' access control model had gone through several changes and before evolving into the current one; most notable changes were the run-time permissions in 2016 [14] and restrictions on app-behavior in 2018 [11]. So, the user does not see permission requirements prior to installation because their consent is required during run-time. Thus, it can be deduced that privacy hardly plays any part in decision-making process of the user while choosing an app for installation. These significant context changes require pursuing exploration with renewed challenges.

2.3   Considering Privacy in Decision-Making

Understandably, users hardly pay attention to data disclosure and/or to permission requirements prior to app installation [4,40]. However, users are more concerned about their privacy when they realize that their decisions have put them at risk of data leakage through third-party apps [15,23,44]. Also, revealing apps' data access and sharing practice can upset the user [43] and thus, they seek for remedy [46]. So, we can infer that privacy-facts (that inherit complexity) under-perform against app-ratings (that come with simplicity) while users decide upon app installation.

Two significant research efforts can be noticed from prior works: (a) to develop a comprehensive mechanism to determine apps' privacy-friendliness and (b) to communicate privacy risks to the user through an easily perceivable illustration. We see the potential to fill the gap between them through this work. To address the challenge against overcoming complexity issues and support informed decision making in ex-ante scenarios, we put priority on designing easy-to-perceive indicators. To keep the effort of users' as low as possible when selecting an app, the indicator should bring a high degree of intuitiveness. Hence, we first elaborate on the design process of privacy indicators and then, evaluate them based on their cognitive appeal.

Fig. 1. An instance of the app-store demo with arrow-scale meter, one of the five indicators, for online survey.

3 Pre-study: Indicator Selection

Here, we elaborate on the design process of five different variants of the privacy indicator. Then we describe how an online survey was run to choose an indicator that is easy to perceive, to understand and has the potential to cause awareness. The outperforming indicator was then implemented in a simulated app market for conducting a user study that is going to be discussed later. Our approach to design a privacy indicator and results from an online study to choose an outperforming indicator are detailed in this section.

3.1 Finding an Appealing Indicator

In the design phase, we addressed one question—*How can we construct an easily perceivable indicator with potential to yield spontaneous awareness?* For a comparative analysis, five indicator instances were chosen to demonstrate different levels of privacy risks associated with apps which are shown in Table 1. Our indicator design process is elaborated in this section.

Designing Indicators. In [24], Kelley et al. presented privacy labels with detailed privacy facts, similar to nutrition facts on labels of food produce. We argue that complex and multi-dimensional information could compel the user to ignore. So, a goal was set to design a unidirectional information based and cognitively easy to perceive indicator. In this design process, color is considered as a critical attribute for accurate identification, while other attributes such as size, brightness, and shape can vary without affecting identification [7]. In [8], Cimbalo et al. conducted a study of children and students in terms of emotionally-colored images and color choices. Green is always attributed to happy and therefore positive emotions, while red is more likely associated sad and negative emotions.

In [6], Benbasat et al. conducted a study that classified information as more understandable and better in terms of decision-making when it was presented in multiple colors compared to monochrome. Thus, for our design, we adopted subdivision of the indicator into five different color sections from dark-green to light-green, yellow, and orange to red. The indicator should require little cognitive effort to understand it, so that the information provided can be better taken into account in decision-making. The visual cues, in this case, the color-coded symbols of the privacy indicator, contribute to informed decisions as previously demonstrated by Hibbard and Peters in [22].

Table 1. Statistical description of survey on different privacy indicators. Respondents (N = 168) could rate the indicators between 1–10. *Label bar* stood out among the rest, based on calculated average and standard deviation (SD).

Indicator	Appearance	N	Min	Max	Average	SD
Arrow-scale bar		168	1	10	6.64	2.66
Label bar		168	1	10	8.25	2.28
Arrow-scale meter		168	1	10	7.80	2.45
Smiles		168	1	10	7.64	2.50
Bubbles		168	1	10	7.02	2.68

Having decided on a color-coded indicator, the next task was to find the right shape for it. An extensive literature research unfortunately did not yield any further information about an optimized indicator shape. Due to this reason, a focus group (participated by several researchers from two research groups) discussion yielded indicators that can also be found in everyday life and that are already familiar to the users: *(a)* Arrow-scale bar from the thermometer, *(b)* Label bar from the product test, *(c)* Arrow-scale meter from the speedometer, *(d)* Smiles from the evaluation of customer satisfaction in retail, and *(e)* Bubbles from a traffic light. Both *a* and *c* show range of the scale and point towards the indicating instance. On the other hand, *d* and *e* visualizes the indicating instance. Only *b* shows the instances with written descriptions.

Furthermore, we decided on a five-point scale, because of the cognitive limitation of humans to process information. In [31], Miller states that a human being can keep 7 ± 2 units of information (chunks) in the short-term memory. This ability is genetic with individual exceptions and cannot be increased by training. We took the lower limit of chunks that can be stored in short-term memory, so that the majority of end-users can use the indicator with low cognitive effort. In addition, we opted for an odd-numbered scale so that apps can be labeled as *moderate* besides *secure* or *insecure*.

Online Survey. To verify which design is the most appropriate one, an online survey was conducted. The participants were presented with app store demo as shown in Fig. 1, but with five variants of indicator as shown in Table 1. They were asked to rate each scale from 1 to 10 according to following attributes:

Discriminability: Are the colors discriminable?
Ambiguity: Is the indicator/graphic unambiguously/clearly understandable?
Readability: How well readable is the information that is presented by the indicator/graph?
Comprehension: Do you understand the information which is illustrated by the indicator/graphic?
Color (Appeal): Is the intensity of the color of the indicator/graphic appropriate?
Size (Appeal): Is the size of the indicator/graphic appropriate?

Their rating scores were recorded to determine visual and cognitive appeal of the indicators. The survey was active from the end of August, 2018 until the end of December, 2018. During this time, a total of 55 individuals participated in the survey. Unfortunately, only 28 individuals completed the questionnaire with all five indicators. So, only the completed results are taken into account. The survey consisted of 28 people, who gave ratings in the six categories, and in the end, it resulted in 168 ratings per indicator.

Fig. 2. Demography of participants in lab study.

3.2 Pre-study Results

The descriptive evaluation in Table 1 shows the following mean values, Standard Deviation (SD), in descending order for a span of one to ten: *Label bar* M = 8.25 (2.28), *Arrow scale bar* M = 7.80 (2.50), *Smiles* M = 7.64 (2.51), *Bubbles* M = 7.02 (2.68) and *Arrow-scale Bar* M = 6.64 (2.66). The data sets of the responses of each scale were then tested for normal distribution using the Kolmogorov-Smirnov test [29]. The outcome was significant for all scales ($p < .000$), so that a normal distribution can not be assumed. Then a non-parametric Friedman test [10] was used and it resulted in a significant difference ($x^2 = 54.35, p < .000$). In addition, we compared the individual groups of pairs with the help of the Wilcoxon test and found significant differences in all pairs with p = .000 apart from the pair Arrow Scale Bar and Bubbles with p = .188.

Based on the analysis of ratings from respondents, a favoritism for the *Label Bar* could be recognized. The Friedman test showed a significant difference between the scores of each scale, so a decision regarding implementation was made in favor of the *Label Bar*. Justifications for the assessments were not included in the study. However, there is reason to believe that the *Label Bar* can be interpreted with less cognitive effort than the other indicators and therefore, has received better rating. It can also be considered as achromatopsia-friendly.

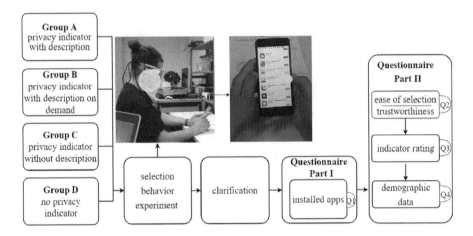

Fig. 3. An overview of the lab study procedure.

4 Lab-Study: User Preference

This section elaborates the lab-study to illustrate user preference towards privacy indicator on app store. First, we discuss the study's work-flow and the corresponding parameters that we measured. Second, We describe the results, highlighting on the app selection behavior of participants. We also reflect on the statistical significance of our findings and feedback from participants regarding the privacy-indicator-embedded app store.

4.1 Empirical Study Procedure

To evaluate the outcome of the pre-study, we implemented the *Label bar* in an app-market prototype. As shown in Fig. 3, the *Label bar* was placed right next to the app logo, so that the user could view and compare the list of apps along with their data access potential and make a decision on the primary interface without needing to explore details of every app. We then invited people to participate in a semi-structured lab study. Our goal was to determine users' app selection behavior during given scenarios. They were asked to perform selection tasks and then interviewed to explain their actions.

Table 2. Statistical significance of participants' app selection behavior: Highest and lowest mean values amongst the four groups per category are colored in green and red, respectively.

Groups		Messenger	Video-call	Weather	E-mail	Music	Fitness	Games	News
A: indicator with detailed description & explanation	Mean	3.10	1.24	1.00	1.19	4.05	4.71	4.38	4.86
	N	21	21	21	21	21	21	21	21
	St. dev.	0.94	0.54	1.00	0.94	0.22	0.64	1.07	0.65
B: indicator with description & explanation on-demand	Mean	3.00	3.90	3.65	3.30	3.5	4.74	4.76	60
	N	20	20	20	20	20	20	20	20
	St. dev	1.03	0.64	0.99	1.30	0.51	0.81	0.66	1.05
C: indicator without description or explanation	Mean	2.57	4.09	3.33	3.48	4.00	4.33	4.29	3.86
	N	21	21	21	21	21	21	21	21
	St. dev.	1.12	0.83	1.32	1.36	0.95	1.20	1.15	1.56
D: app store without any indicator	Mean	2.95	3.80	2.65	3.00	3.90	3.30	2.95	3.10
	N	20	20	20	20	20	20	20	20
	St. dev.	0.68	0.89	0.93	0.65	0.72	1.59	1.10	1.52

Ethical Consideration. Our study was approved by the Ethics Committee with appropriate authority. In compliance with the prescribed policies, the most important precautions to minimize the risk for human participants are considered. An appropriate ratio of the investigations' benefit and subjects' risk was established in the investigation. Further, it is assured that participants take part voluntarily and all regulations for the protection of privacy are adhered, too. As a result of the review by the Ethics Committee, the tests in the framework of this research project have been deemed as ethically unobjectionable by the committee unanimously.

Recruitment of Participants and Demography. Advertisement of our study was circulated through online platforms which included blogs, social media, etc. as well as offline means that included posters hanging on notice boards of several institutions located within reachable proximity. Due to the fact that participants need to be physically present in the lab, most of them are recruited from our geographically convenient location. Nonetheless, majority of the participants have a background that is diverse due to the cosmopolitan nature of a big city. Each subject has been compensated €10 for participating in the study. If the study lasted longer than one hour, the subject was compensated with an additional €2.50 per 15 min elapsed.

A total of 82 German-speaking individuals participated in the lab study who were aged between 18 and 68. Among them, 43 were male and 38 were female; one person identified thyself as neither male nor female. Their educational background varied from middle school to higher academic degrees: 6 went through middle school level, 28 had high school diploma, 7 had vocational training and 41 possessed higher academic degree from universities. Figure 2 illustrates the demography based on age, sex, highest educational qualification obtained and technology affinity (time spent on mobile phone per day).

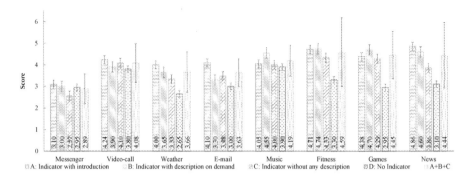

Fig. 4. Comparison of participants' app selection behavior. Distribution of participants: Group A—participants received introduction and explanation about indicator, Group B—explanation was provided to subjects on demand, by clicking on the privacy indicator, Group C—app-store interface is presented with privacy indicator, but without any explanation, and Group D—app-store interface is presented with no privacy indicator (control group).

Distribution of Participants. This empirical study was constructed with a 4×1 between-subjects design. The subjects were randomly assigned, considering a mix of age, sex, occupation, academic and geographical backgrounds, to one of the following four groups with different experimental conditions, based on the different availability of information in the app market. Thus, the subjects from one group only went through one of the four experimental conditions:

- Group A: An app-store interface is presented with privacy indicator, along with a detailed description as an introduction.
- Group B: An app-store interface is presented with privacy indicator, along with a detailed description on demand, by clicking on the privacy indicator.
- Group C: An app-store interface is presented with privacy indicator, but without any detailed description.
- Group D: An app-store interface is presented with no privacy indicator. This group represents the control group of this experiment.

Our aim was to find out if the participants were paying attention to the privacy indicators, to analyze the decisions they make and to combine them with a questionnaire.

Scenarios and App-Categories. The app-store demo consisted of eight categories and they were associated with mock up scenarios. Each category had ten apps and their ratings were removed due to possibility of interference in decision-making. All the participants had to go through each of the scenarios. The scenarios and app-categories are described below:

1. Messenger: Imagine you want to schedule a dinner with a friend. Write her a short message.

2. Video calling: Imagine you are on a trip and want to talk to a friend. Start a video call with her.
3. Weather: Imagine you are packing your suitcase for a trip and want to look at the weather forecast to pack the right things.
4. E-mail: Imagine you want to invite a friend to a concert. Write her an e-mail.
5. Music: Imagine you want to hear a song from the current charts on your smartphone.
6. Fitness: Imagine that you want to track your physical activities. Set up a fitness app for it.
7. Games: Imagine you are about to board on a long flight. For entertainment, you want to download the game Sudoku, which you can play on your smartphone.
8. News: Imagine you want to know the latest news. Open a news app.

Workflow of an Experimental-Session in Lab. Participants are left unaware of the purpose of the study. They decided to join the study under the pretext to rate the usability of an app-store. Upon appointment confirmation, they are randomly assigned to group A, B, C, and D. Figure 3 shows the lab environment. To accelerate the study for each and every app, an account was already created, if needed. Upon completion of all tasks, they were interviewed and had to complete a questionnaire to examine acceptance, trustworthiness, and usability. To identify the interference in decision making, they were asked if the apps used in the experiment were already installed in their private devices. The steps of the lab-session are listed below in a chronological order:

1. The participant comes in the laboratory.
2. An elaborate description is provided to them in both written and oral form in order to explain the purpose of experiment (this step varies based on group).
3. The participant gets the form to declare freely given consent regarding processing of data collected during the experiment.
4. The procedure of the experiment is told and being demonstrated to them.
5. An eye-tracker-mounted glass is worn by them.
6. The device (a mobile phone - Nokia 5) is handed over to them.
7. The eye tracker glass has to be calibrated before commencing the first task.
8. The first scenario is read aloud orally.
9. The participant is presented with the app store on mobile interface.
10. They choose an app according to the scenario presented to them and carry on completing the tasks.
11. They are asked to repeat from the step 8 for rest of the scenarios (if they are confused, spontaneous explanation and/or assistance is provided against queries, depending on which group they belong to.)
12. They participate in a semi-structured interview using recorded video to provide feedback reflecting on his/her own app selection decisions.

Table 3. Responses from participants about ease of app selection and apps' trustworthiness. Highest mean values among the four groups per category are colored in green.

Category	Statement	Group A			Group B			Group C			Group D		
		Mean	N	SD	Mean	N	SD	Mean	N	SD	Mean	N	SD
Messenger	Apps was easy to choose	6.24	21	1.04	6.35	20	0.93	5.86	21	1.24		20	0.76
	App seemed trustworthy	4.43	21	1.75		20	1.45	4.62	21	1.12	3.70	20	1.81
Video-call	Apps was easy to choose	6.11	19	1.20	5.90	20	0.91		21	0.87	6	19	1.20
	App seemed trustworthy	5.00	21	2.1		20	1.68	5	21	1.34	3.95	20	1.73
Weather	Apps was easy to choose	5.86	21	1.56		20	1.01	5.14	21	1.15	5.75	20	1.71
	App seemed trustworthy	5.48	21	1.83		20	0.97	5.05	21	0.92	5	19	1.80
E-mail	Apps was easy to choose		20	1.41	5.25	20	1.65	4.67	21	1.28	5.11	19	1.56
	App seemed trustworthy		20	1.27	5.3	20	1.42	4.4	20	1.39	4.37	19	1.42
Music	Apps was easy to choose		20	0.72	6.05	20	1.43	6.05	21	1.24	6.47	19	1.12
	App seemed trustworthy		20	1.57	5.45	20	1.05	5.29	21	1.06	5.47	19	1.26
Fitness	Apps was easy to choose		18	1.32	4.95	19	1.35	4.19	21	1.66	4.29	17	1.11
	App seemed trustworthy		17	1.83	5.21	19	1.27	4.48	21	1.33	3.82	17	1.74
Games	Apps was easy to choose		20	1.40	5.3	20	1.63	4.52	21	1.25	5	18	1.37
	App seemed trustworthy		20	1.46	5.4	20	1.23	4.71	21	1.01	4.53	17	2.15
News	Apps was easy to choose	5.71	21	1.52		20	0.73	5.14	21	1.15	5.52	19	1.58
	App seemed trustworthy	5.62	21	1.28		20	0.91	4.90	21	0.83	5	19	1.63

4.2   Empirical Results: Users' App Selection Behavior

We assumed that implementing a privacy indicator in an app-store would result in a more appropriate selection of apps in terms of privacy. To compare the selection behavior with respect to the indicator illustrated beside the app, we assigned each app selection step a rating (ranging from 1 to 5; considering 1 as very critical and 5 as very safe). The mean values in Table 2, also highlighted in Fig. 4, show a tendency of a higher value for the groups (A, B, and C) with indicator compared to the group (D) without indicator. This primarily confirms the assumption that the subjects who had illustrated an indicator selected an app that was classified as less critical.

Comparative Analysis. To check whether the results in Table 2 and in Fig. 4 differ significantly, a Kolmogorov-Smirnoff test [29] was performed on normal distribution. The test showed that all data sets deviated significantly from a normal distribution, so that the non-parametric Kruskal Wallis test [28] for more than two independent samples was performed. A significant difference regarding the selection behavior among all four groups resulted in the following app categories:

1. Weather $(x^2 = 14.591, p < .002)$,
2. E-Mail $(x^2 = 12.309, p < .006)$,
3. Music $(x^2 = 17.572, p < .001)$,
4. Fitness $(x^2 = 15.716, p < .001)$,
5. Games $(x^2 = 25.720, p < .000)$ and
6. News $(x^2 = 20.062, p < .000)$.

No significant difference could be determined for the outcomes of the Messenger and Weather app categories. Subsequently, the first three groups were combined into one group to perform a Mann-Whitney U test [30], which examines two distributions for significant differences. The test showed significant differences in the same categories that were considered significant in the Kruskal Wallis test [28]:

1. Weather ($U = 319.500, z = -3.342, p < .001$)
2. E-Mail ($U = 396.500, z = 2.627, p < .009$),
3. Music ($U = 477.000, z = -2.031, p < .042$),
4. Fitness ($U = 332.000, z = -3.778, p < .000$),
5. Games ($U = 212.000, z = -4.951, p < .000$) and
6. News ($U = 336.000, z = -3.776, p < .000$)

In addition, the individual groups were examined for significant differences with each other using the Mann-Whitney-U test [30]. Additionally, Bonferroni-correction was carried out to counteract the problem of multiple comparisons. The corrected p-Value now equals .0062. While comparing groups A and B only significant difference can be found in the app category, Music ($U = 104.500; z = -3.491; p < .000$).

When comparing group A and C, no significant difference was found. When comparing the groups A and D, significance was observed in the following categories:

1. Weather ($U = 73.000, z = -3.678, p < .000$),
2. E-Mail ($U = 79.500, z = -3.791, p < .000$),
3. Fitness ($U = 106.000, z = -3.093, p < .002$),
4. Games ($U = 76.000, z = -3.728, p < .000$) and
5. News ($U = 84.000, z = -3.917, p < .000$).

Notably, they are the same app categories found significant in the Kruskal Wallis test [28], which compares every group with each other. Furthermore, no significant difference was found in the comparison of group B and C, for the Music category. When comparing group B and D, significant differences were found in the following categories:

1. Weather ($U = 97.000, z = -2.889, p < .004$),
2. Music ($U = 95.500, z = -3.464, p < .001$),
3. Fitness ($U = 93.000, z = -3.186, p < .001$),
4. Games ($U = 48.000, z = -4.460, p < .000$) and
5. News ($U = 95.500, z = -3.213, p < .001$).

The last comparison between group C and D showed a significant difference in the Games category: $U = 88.000, z = -3.437, p < .001$.

Table 4. Evaluation of indicators by participants: highest and lowest mean values among the three groups (with indicator) per category are colored in green and red, respectively.

Statement	Group A			Group B			Group C			Total		
	Mean	N	SD	Mean	N	SD	Mean	N	SD	Mean	N	SD
The indicator is trustworthy	5.57	21	1.32	5.50	20	1	4.95	20	1.32	5.38	61	1.24
The usability of the indicator is good	6.10	21	0.89	5.95	19	0.91	5.90	20	0.91	5.98	60	0.89
The indicator is easy to understand	6.33	21	0.91	6.1	20	0.85	6.05	21	0.87	6.2	62	0.87
The indicator is intuitive	5.48	21	1.63	5.80	20	1.32	5.67	21	1.07	5.65	62	1.34
The indicator is valid	5.43	21	1.33	5.39	18	1.09	4.57	21	1.25	5.12	60	1.28
The indicator is reliable	5.43	21	1.25	5.26	19	1.24	4.86	21	1.32	5.18	61	1.27
The indicator had an impact on my choice	5.68	21	1.56	5.2	20	1.57	4.90	21	1.81	5.32	62	1.68
The indicator is confusing	2.10	21	1.14	2.20	20	1.58	2.19	21	1.08	2.16	62	1.26
The information provided is not sufficient	3.05	21	1.69	3.1	20	1.37	1.62	21	1.86	3.6	62	1.79
The indicator increases the sense of privacy protection	5.86	21	1.32	5.90	20	1.17	5.57	21	1.69	5.77	62	1.40
I want privacy indicator in my own app market	5.80	20	1.61	5.65	20	1.60	5.62	21	1.69	5.69	61	1.61
The privacy indicator is unnecessarily complex	2.10	21	1.3	2.45	20	1.82	2.10	21	1.55	2.21	62	1.55
With possibility to enable/disable, I would enable it	5.71	21	1.26	5.9	20	1.55	5.62	21	1.88	5.92	62	1.58
The indicator increases trustworthiness of apps	6.24	21	0.94	6.1	20	1.33	5.76	21	1.34	6.03	62	1.21

Ease of App Selection and Apps' Trustworthiness.

Considering the results shown in Table 3, the ease of app selection and trustworthiness of the app (on a scale of 1 = strongly agree, to 7 = strongly disagree), the highest averages, with the exception of ease of selection in Messenger category, are all to be found in Group A, B, and C. Thus, it could be assumed that with the exception of the Messenger category, the indicator has led the participants to find it easier to choose an appropriate app to accomplish the task and rated the app as more trustworthy than the participants without indicator. To test this assumption, a Kruskal Wallis test [28] was performed due to the absence of a normal distribution shown by the Kolmogorov-Smirnov test [29]. This resulted into findings with significant differences in terms of trustworthiness of the app in the following categories:

1. Video-call ($x^2 = 8.463, p < .037$),
2. Weather ($x^2 = 9.854, p < .020$),
3. E-mail ($x^2 = 12.129, p < .007$),
4. Fitness ($x^2 = 9.152, p < .027$) and
5. News ($x^2 = 8.723, p < .033$).

For the ease of app selection, significant difference in the averages could be found for Weather ($x^2 = 9,854, p < .020$) and Fitness ($x^2 = 12,892, p < .005$) category.

In addition, we compared the individual groups of pairs with the help of the Mann-Whitney-U Test and were not able to find a significant difference comparing all pairs in Group A and B after carrying out a Bonferroni-correction. While having a closer look comparing all pairs of Group A with Group C a significant difference could be found following pairs:

- E-mail: $U = 103.500, p < .004$ for ease of selection and $U = 99.500, p < .005$ for trustworthiness.

– Fitness: $U = 123.000, p < .004$ for ease of selection.

Comparing Group A with Group D:

– E-Mail: $U = 94.500, p < .006$ for trustworthiness.
– Fitness: $U = 79.000, p < .001$ for ease of selection.

Comparing Group B with Group C:

– Weather: $U = 104.500, p < .004$ for ease of selection and $U = 95.000, p < .002$ for trustworthiness.
– News: $U = 99.500, p < .002$ for trustworthiness.

No significant difference can be found while comparing Group B and Group C with Group D.

Indicator Evaluation by Participants. Table 4 presents a summarized result of participants' indicator evaluation ratings. It is noticeable that on a scale of $1 =$ strongly agree, to $7 =$ strongly disagree, overall a positive rating was given to positive statements (trustworthiness, usability, understanding, intuitiveness, validity, reliability, impact, feeling of protection, demand, willingness to use, apps' trustworthiness). Overall, the negative statements (ambiguity, lack of information, complexity) were disagreed by the majority.

In order to archive the subjective opinion of the testee, we did not define in detail how to interpret the given terms. Comparing the groups with each other, a tendency for better rating in group A can be found. Group C gave the worst scores, while group B's evaluations are mostly found between group A and C. The means and standard deviations can be seen in Table 4.

Subsequently, the different means were tested for normal distribution using the Kolmogorov-Smirnov test ($p < 0.002$) [29]. This precluded a normal distribution for all value pairs. Furthermore, the non-parametric Kruskal Wallis test was applied [28], which, however, could only show a significant difference for the lack of information ($x^2 = 10, p < .010$).

5   Discussion

In this section, we discuss the interpretation of results collected and analyzed. From Fig. 4, a comparative user awareness can be observed in the app selection behavior for all the given scenarios. From the analysis of collected data, a general observation can be made: *privacy concern decreases with app-popularity.* Participants deliberately ignored the indicators due to apps' popularity attribute. In Fig. 4, this observation is prominent in Messenger and Video-call category due to frequent selection of Whatsapp and Skype. However, skeptic and cautious app selection behavior, by choosing safer options often if more privacy details provided, can be observed in case of Weather, Fitness and News apps. Our theory behind causing this phenomenon is that the large amount of press and media releases highlighting negative aspects of apps' personal data collection have raised awareness. Weather apps' location data gathering, Fitness apps' data collection resulting in revelation of army bases' map, and 'fake-news' becoming buzzword about misinformation, may have led to more privacy-aware app selection.

5.1   Assisting the User in App Selection

At first glance on Table 3, it can be seen that, with an exception of the Messenger category, the mean values for ease of app selection were highest in the groups (A, B, and C) with indicator. When evaluating the trustworthiness of the app, it was possible to find the highest mean values in these groups. The results also indicate that (for the category Video-call, Weather, E-mail, Fitness, and News) users having indicator assisted interface were significantly more adequate at evaluating the trustworthiness of the app than users who did not have the indicator available. Here, the results could again be explained by the popularity of the app. Using the example of Skype, a popular app in combination with a secure indicator leads to a higher rating in the trustworthiness, as an app without indicator. A popular app with an insecure indicator, within a category like the messenger app WhatsApp, leads to a lower trustworthiness rating because the app is chosen for its popularity despite the unsafe classification by the indicator, but the subject is aware of the insecurity of the app and thus indicates a lower trustworthiness.

If the app is not known and the indicator categorizes it as safe, then the trustworthiness of the app is considered high. An unpopular app with an insecure classification by the indicator is usually not selected and thus has no influence on the rating. A popular app without an indicator is heavily dependent on its reputation, which is evident from the collected data. A similar pattern can be seen in the case of ease of selection. There, only Weather and Fitness categories had a significantly higher mean. There was no favored app in these two categories, which led to a significantly higher ease of selection for the participants with an indicator.

5.2   Influencing App Choice?

Comparing the privacy-preserving app selection scores in Table 2, the highest means of the scores belong to Group A (Messenger, Video-call, Weather, and E-Mail) and to Group B (Music, Fitness, Games, and News). It should be noted that the lowest scores are always to be found in group D (without indicator), with an exception in the Messenger category. The Kruskal Wallis Test revealed significant differences in all app categories except Messenger and Video-call. Thus, the indicator had a significant impact on the selection behavior, leading to a selection of less invasive apps in Weather, Email, Music, Fitness, Games, and News categories. The lack of significance in comparison of Messenger and Video-call can be explained by the nullifying parameter—popularity of the app. The interviews point that most subjects chose an app they already knew. Also, the first part of the questionnaire denotes that most of the selected apps for the task were already known to the users, or are currently used by them. Furthermore, the results show that 63% of the participants chose WhatsApp and the remaining 37% were split between the other apps. Similar results can be found in the Video-call category: Skype was chosen by 74% and Viber by 17% of the participants. The remaining 9% were divided between the other apps. The reason for the lack of significant differences could be seen if we compare the values with those of the Weather category, which are clearly distributed more homogeneously. Thus, it could be concluded that with increasing popularity of the app, the influence of the indicator decreases (Wetter-Online $= 24\%$, Wetter.com $= 26\%$, Wetter.de $= 22\%$, More-cast $= 20\%$, Weatherzone $= 2\%$, Bayer Agrar Wetter $= 2\%$, Yr $= 1\%$).

Furthermore, the importance of description can be seen by comparing the group D with each of the individual groups: A, B and C. While in group A significant differences can be found in 6 categories and in group B in 5 categories, between C and D only 2 app categories (Fitness and Games) can be found, whose mean values differ significantly. However, it should be noted that all averages of group A to C, except for the category Messenger, are higher than the averages of group D.

5.3   Privacy Indicator: Good or Bad?

The tendency of Group-A to rate the positive statements high could be related to the fact that the they received a detailed explanation of the indicator. Thus Group-A paid more attention to the indicator and had background knowledge of the functionalities. This would also explain the significant difference over the statements for the lack of information. Group C, with the highest score on information poverty, did not get an explanation about the indicator and did not have the possibility to view a description of the indicator. Nevertheless, the indicator was rated consistently positive.

5.4   Limitations and Future Work

Here, we would like to discuss the limitations of our contributions and claims which are intended to be addressed in future. This work is exploratory and it should be noted that the interpretation of null results in statistical tests also has limitation—a lack of detected statistical significance does not imply an absence of effect.

During the empirical study, we noticed that some apps were generally considered as safe by several participants, but marked as unsafe in our implemented app-store demo, e.g. Telegram due to vendors' advertisement on end to end encryption. This partly confused the participants and perhaps had an impact on their decisions. So, there exists a probable error margin, because sometimes the app was selected despite facing the poor classification. Mostly this behavior is justified by the reputation and the private use of the app. We intend to counteract this limitation in near future by constructing a realistic indicator from app-behavior analysis data.

Another limitation was that the participants used glasses to operate the mobile phone. As a result, the eye movements in the video was recorded with poor quality. An attempt was made to counteract by asking the subject during the interview to describe more precisely on which characteristics was focused upon. However, we decided to limit the scope of this paper by excluding qualitative analysis of their opinion and we intend to do it in future work.

In further exploratory analysis, the exact time that the subject spent paying attention to the indicator can be determined using the eye tracking videos. In addition, the time needed by the subjects to select an adequate app to perform the task could be compared.

This study did not recruit any individuals that were minors (aged below 18). Consequently, a large user base for Games, Social, Messaging and Lifestyle category remained out of consideration. Also limited app selection options were offered to the participants, which could hinder in showcasing actual user behavior. Our future research plan also includes conducting studies with unknown apps to avoid popularity bias and with app ratings to determine comparative impact of the privacy indicator.

6 Conclusion

In this paper, we investigate the potential to introduce a simple privacy indicator within the ecosystem of smartphone apps. Our investigation includes designing and evaluating five variants of privacy indicators. Then we elaborate on the evaluation process of outperforming indicators and present results of a user study consisting of 82 participants which was focused on documenting their app selection behavior. The major findings from the collected data and statistical analysis of this study are: *(i)* A unilateral and simple privacy indicator is able to lead to a better judgment regarding the apps' trustworthiness and to provide ease of selection; *(ii)* Adequacy in privacy-preserving decision making by subjects having indicator-illustrated interface, compared to the control group, can be observed; and *(iii)* According to the collected feedback from the participants, adequacy of the indicator as a transparency and privacy enhancing tool can be confirmed.

In addition, the result denotes that the indicator is generally perceived as positive and helpful. Feedback from participants point out that the indicator is able to initiate cautious thoughts and has a privacy-preserving influence on the selection behavior. However, it is also evident that app popularity can cause bias in decision making which can be inferred to the obvious factor—the marketplace facilitates a user to choose apps based on popularity only. Though privacy indicator poses requirement of a brief introduction for proper interpretation, it has the potential to bring greater use in avoiding privacy implications from apps' growing ability to collect, process and transmit data about the surroundings of the user.

References

1. Acquisti, A.: Nudging privacy: the behavioral economics of personal information. IEEE Secur. Priv. **7**(6), 82–85 (2009)
2. Acquisti, A., et al.: Nudges for privacy and security: understanding and assisting users' choices online. ACM Comput. Surv. **50**(3), 44:1–44:41 (2017). https://doi.org/10.1145/3054926. http://doi.acm.org/10.1145/3054926
3. Acquisti, A., Brandimarte, L., Loewenstein, G.: Privacy and human behavior in the age of information. Science **347**(6221), 509–514 (2015)
4. Alohaly, M., Takabi, H.: Better privacy indicators: a new approach to quantification of privacy policies. In: Twelfth Symposium on Usable Privacy and Security ({SOUPS} 2016) (2016)
5. Balebako, R., Jung, J., Lu, W., Cranor, L.F., Nguyen, C.: Little brothers watching you: raising awareness of data leaks on smartphones. In: Proceedings of the Ninth Symposium on Usable Privacy and Security, p. 12. ACM (2013)
6. Benbasat, I., Dexter, A.S., Todd, P.: An experimental program investigating color-enhanced and graphical information presentation: an integration of the findings. Commun. ACM **29**(11), 1094–1105 (1986)
7. Christ, R.E.: Review and analysis of color coding research for visual displays. Hum. Factors **17**(6), 542–570 (1975)
8. Cimbalo, R.S., Beck, K.L., Sendziak, D.S.: Emotionally toned pictures and color selection for children and college students. J. Genet. Psychol. **133**(2), 303–304 (1978)
9. European Commission: Regulation (EU) 2016/679 of the European Parliament and of the Council of 27 April 2016 on the protection of natural persons with regard to the processing of personal data and on the free movement of such data (General Data Protection Regulation). Off J Eur Union p. L119 (2016)
10. Conover, W.J., Iman, R.L.: Rank transformations as a bridge between parametric and nonparametric statistics. Am. Stat. **35**(3), 124–129 (1981)
11. Android Developers Documentation: Android 9.0 changes. https://developer.android.com/about/versions/pie/android-9.0-changes-all (2019). Accessed 12 Sept 2019
12. Android Developers Documentation: Dangerous permissions (2019). Accessed 12 Sept 2019
13. Android Developers Documentation: Permissions overview. https://www.developer.android.com/guide/topics/permissions/overview (2019). Accessed 12 Sept 2019
14. Android Developers Documentation: Runtime permissions. https://developer.android.com/distribute/best-practices/develop/runtime-permissions (2019). Accessed 12 Sept 2019
15. Felt, A.P., Ha, E., Egelman, S., Haney, A., Chin, E., Wagner, D.: Android permissions: Uuser attention, comprehension, and behavior. In: Proceedings of the Eighth Symposium on Usable Privacy and Security, p. 3. ACM (2012)
16. Fritsch, L., Momen, N.: Derived partial identities generated from app permissions. In: Open Identity Summit (OID) 2017. Gesellschaft für Informatik (2017)
17. Gross, R., Acquisti, A.: Information revelation and privacy in online social networks. In: Proceedings of the 2005 ACM Workshop on Privacy in the Electronic Society, pp. 71–80. ACM (2005)
18. Gu, J., Xu, Y.C., Xu, H., Zhang, C., Ling, H.: Privacy concerns for mobile app download: an elaboration likelihood model perspective. Decis. Support Syst. **94**, 19–28 (2017)

19. Hatamian, M., Momen, N., Fritsch, L., Rannenberg, K.: A multilateral privacy impact analysis method for android apps. In: Naldi, M., Italiano, G.F., Rannenberg, K., Medina, M., Bourka, A. (eds.) APF 2019. LNCS, vol. 11498, pp. 87–106. Springer, Cham (2019). https://doi.org/10.1007/978-3-030-21752-5_7

20. Hatamian, M., Serna, J., Rannenberg, K.: Revealing the unrevealed: mining smartphone users privacy perception on app markets. Comput. Secur. (2019). https://doi.org/10.1016/j.cose.2019.02.010. http://www.sciencedirect.com/science/article/pii/S0167404818313051

21. Hatamian, M., Serna, J., Rannenberg, K., Igler, B.: FAIR: fuzzy alarming index rule for privacy analysis in smartphone apps. In: Lopez, J., Fischer-Hübner, S., Lambrinoudakis, C. (eds.) TrustBus 2017. LNCS, vol. 10442, pp. 3–18. Springer, Cham (2017). https://doi.org/10.1007/978-3-319-64483-7_1

22. Hibbard, J.H., Peters, E.: Supporting informed consumer health care decisions: data presentation approaches that facilitate the use of information in choice. Annu. Rev. Public Health **24**(1), 413–433 (2003)

23. Jung, J., Han, S., Wetherall, D.: Short paper: enhancing mobile application permissions with runtime feedback and constraints. In: Proceedings of the Second ACM Workshop on Security and Privacy in Smartphones and Mobile Devices, pp. 45–50. ACM (2012)

24. Kelley, P.G., Bresee, J., Cranor, L.F., Reeder, R.W.: A "nutrition label" for privacy. In: Proceedings of the 5th Symposium on Usable Privacy and Security SOUPS 2009, pp. 4:1–4:12. ACM, New York (2009). https://doi.org/10.1145/1572532.1572538. http://doi.acm.org/10.1145/1572532.1572538

25. Kelley, P.G., Consolvo, S., Cranor, L.F., Jung, J., Sadeh, N., Wetherall, D.: A conundrum of permissions: installing applications on an android smartphone. In: Blyth, J., Dietrich, S., Camp, L.J. (eds.) FC 2012. LNCS, vol. 7398, pp. 68–79. Springer, Heidelberg (2012). https://doi.org/10.1007/978-3-642-34638-5_6

26. Kelley, P.G., Cranor, L.F., Sadeh, N.: Privacy as part of the app decision-making process. In: Proceedings of the SIGCHI Conference on Human Factors in Computing Systems, pp. 3393–3402. ACM (2013)

27. Kraus, L., Wechsung, I., Möller, S.: Using statistical information to communicate android permission risks to users. In: 2014 Workshop on Socio-Technical Aspects in Security and Trust, pp. 48–55. IEEE (2014)

28. Kruskal, W.H., Wallis, W.A.: Use of ranks in one-criterion variance analysis. J. Am. Stat. Assoc. **47**(260), 583–621 (1952)

29. Lilliefors, H.W.: On the kolmogorov-smirnov test for normality with mean and variance unknown. J. Am. Stat. Assoc. **62**(318), 399–402 (1967)

30. McKnight, P.E., Najab, J.: Mann-whitney u test. In: The Corsini Encyclopedia of Psychology, p. 1 (2010)

31. Miller, G.A.: The magical number seven, plus or minus two: some limits on our capacity for processing information. Psychol. Rev. **63**(2), 81 (1956)

32. Momen, N.: Towards measuring apps' privacy-friendliness. Ph.D. thesis, Karlstads Universitet (2018)

33. Momen, N., Bock, S., Fritsch, L.: Accept-maybe-decline: introducing partial consent for the permission-based access control model of android. In: Proceedings of the 25th ACM Symposium on Access Control Models and Technologies, pp. 71–80 (2020)

34. Momen, N., Fritsch, L.: App-generated digital identities extracted through android permission-based data access-a survey of app privacy. In: SICHERHEIT 2020 (2020)

35. Momen, N., Hatamian, M., Fritsch, L.: Did app privacy improve after the GDPR? IEEE Secur. Priv. **17**(6), 10–20 (2019)
36. Momen, N., Pulls, T., Fritsch, L., Lindskog, S.: How much privilege does an app need? Investigating resource usage of android apps. In: The Fifteenth International Conference on Privacy, Security and Trust-PST 2017, 28–30 August 2017, Calgary, Alberta, Canada. IEEE (2017)
37. Murmann, P., Fischer-Hübner, S.: Tools for achieving usable ex post transparency: a survey. IEEE Access **5**, 22965–22991 (2017)
38. Rajivan, P., Camp, J.: Influence of privacy attitude and privacy cue framing on android app choices. In: Twelfth Symposium on Usable Privacy and Security (SOUPS 2016). USENIX Association, Denver, CO, June 2016. https://www.usenix.org/conference/soups2016/workshop-program/wpi/presentation/rajivan
39. Ramokapane, K.M., Mazeli, A.C., Rashid, A.: Skip, skip, skip, accept!!!: A study on the usability of smartphone manufacturer provided default features and user privacy. Proceedings on Privacy Enhancing Technologies **2019**(2), 209–227 (2019)
40. Rosen, S., Qian, Z., Mao, Z.M.: Appprofiler: a flexible method of exposing privacy-related behavior in android applications to end users. In: Proceedings of the Third ACM Conference on Data and Application Security and Privacy, pp. 221–232. ACM (2013)
41. Schneegass, S., Poguntke, R., Machulla, T.: Understanding the impact of information representation on willingness to share information. In: Proceedings of the 2019 CHI Conference on Human Factors in Computing Systems CHI 2019, pp. 523:1–523:6. ACM, New York (2019). https://doi.org/10.1145/3290605.3300753. http://doi.acm.org/10.1145/3290605.3300753
42. Shih, F., Liccardi, I., Weitzner, D.: Privacy tipping points in smartphones privacy preferences. In: Proceedings of the 33rd Annual ACM Conference on Human Factors in Computing Systems CHI 2015, pp. 807–816. ACM, New York (2015). https://doi.org/10.1145/2702123.2702404. http://doi.acm.org/10.1145/2702123.2702404
43. Shklovski, I., Mainwaring, S.D., Skúladóttir, H.H., Borgthorsson, H.: Leakiness and creepiness in app space: perceptions of privacy and mobile app use. In: Proceedings of the 32nd Annual ACM Conference on Human Factors in Computing Systems, pp. 2347–2356. ACM (2014)
44. Thompson, C., Johnson, M., Egelman, S., Wagner, D., King, J.: When it's better to ask forgiveness than get permission: attribution mechanisms for smartphone resources. In: Proceedings of the Ninth Symposium on Usable Privacy and Security, p. 1. ACM (2013)
45. Watson, J., Lipford, H.R., Besmer, A.: Mapping user preference to privacy default settings. ACM Trans. Comput.-Hum. Interact. (TOCHI) **22**(6), 32 (2015)
46. Wijesekera, P., Baokar, A., Hosseini, A., Egelman, S., Wagner, D., Beznosov, K.: Android permissions remystified: a field study on contextual integrity. In: 24th {USENIX} Security Symposium ({USENIX} Security 15), pp. 499–514 (2015)

User Experience of Alexa, Siri and Google Assistant When Controlling Music – Comparison of Four Questionnaires

Birgit Brüggemeier[1]([envelope]) [iD], Michael Breiter[1] [iD], Miriam Kurz[1,2], and Johanna Schiwy[1]

[1] Fraunhofer Institute for Integrated Circuits IIS,
Am Wolfsmantel 33, 91058 Erlangen, Germany
{birgit.brueggemeier,michael.breiter}@iis.fraunhofer.de
[2] Institute for Psychology, Friedrich-Alexander University,
Nägelsbachstr. 49b, 91052 Erlangen, Germany

Abstract. We evaluate user experience (UX) when users play and control music with three smart speakers: Amazon's Alexa Echo, Google Home and Apple's Siri on a HomePod. For measuring UX we use four established UX metrics (AttrakDiff, SASSI, SUISQ-R, SUS). We investigated the sensitivity of these four questionnaires in two ways: firstly, we compared the UX reported for each of the speakers, secondly, we compared the UX of completing easy single tasks and more difficult multi-turn tasks with these speakers. We find that the investigated questionnaires are sufficiently sensitive to show significant differences in UX for these easy and difficult tasks. In addition, we find some significant UX differences between the tested speakers. Specifically, all tested questionnaires, except the SUS, show a significant difference in UX between Siri and Alexa, with Siri being perceived as more user friendly for controlling music. We discuss implications of our work for researchers and practitioners.

Keywords: User experience · Voice User Interfaces · Measuring · SUS · SASSI · SUISQ · AttrakDiff · Validity

1 Introduction

Speech assistance is a growing market with a 25% yearly growth predicted in the next three years [1]. Speech assistants can be integrated in different devices, like smartphones, personal computers and smart speakers, which are dedicated

This work has been supported by the SPEAKER project (01MK20011A), funded by the German Federal Ministry for Economic Affairs and Energy. The co-author Johanna Schiwy contributed significantly to this study while she was an employee of Fraunhofer IIS in 2019. The author currently has no affiliation.

speakers that can be controlled by voice commands. In our work we focus on smart speakers. Within six years approximately 53 Million Americans bought a smart speaker, which is a market development comparable to the rapid spread of smart phones [2]. This market trend is not confined to the North American market, but is present throughout the world, in Europe, as well as Asia, Africa and Latin America [3–6], showing that smart speakers are of broad public interest.

The consumer speech assistance market in the English speaking world, as well as in Europe, is dominated by three manufacturers and assistants: Amazon with Alexa, Google with Google Assistant and Apple with Siri [5,7]. These three assistants cover more than 88% of the market in the US [7]. Intuitively, these three assistants are named as the most commonly known Voice User Interfaces (VUIs) [8] and featured as smart speakers in numerous product reviews [9–11]. We will refer to speech assistants and smart speakers interchangeably in our paper, that is when we mention Siri, we refer to Siri on HomePod, which is the smart speaker we used in our study. The same is true for Alexa and Echo Dot, as well as Google Assistant and Google Home. A number of product reviews compare the three devices and highlight how these devices may differ [9–11], which can be used by prospective customers to make purchasing decisions. However, a comprehensive analysis and comparison of these devices seems challenging [12]. Siri, Google Assistant and Alexa can be used for a wide range of applications, including playing music, answering questions, reading news, controlling smart devices, telling jokes and more [13]. Moreover, there are infinite ways of addressing the assistants, considering variability of language, accents and tone. What is more, the devices differ in how they look, feel, and sound and these differences may affect how users experience interactions with them. Product reviews make up a rich source of information for customers as well as for Human-Computer-Interaction researchers and practitioners. A downside of this rich information is the lack of quantification. Qualitative information as presented in reviews can be supplemented by quantitative estimations of user experience (UX) and usability.

User experience is a construct first introduced by Don Norman in the 1990s [14]. Norman introduced UX because he found usability, which is a prevalent concept in Human-Computer Interaction (HCI), too narrow to capture all aspects that Norman considered relevant for creating satisfying interactions with computers [14]. Hence, usability may be considered a part of UX. UX is arguably broader than usability and may not be fully covered by it. Notably, there are multiple conceptualizations of UX [15] and conversational interactions with machines may introduce additional factors to UX that may not be part of current UX theories [16], like perceptions of the system as a dialogue partner [17,18].

One of the most commonly used questionnaires for assessing usability is the System Usability Scale (SUS) [19]. SUS is one of the four questionnaires we use in our study to assess interactions with smart speakers. In addition to SUS we use the questionnaires *Subjective Assessment of Speech System Interfaces (SASSI)*, *Speech User Interface Service Quality questionnaire – Reduced Version (SUISQ-R)* and AttrakDiff, which are used for assessing aspects of UX in interactions with speech devices [16,20]. No gold standard exists for measuring UX with speech assistants and each of the named questionnaires has drawbacks that are discussed in detail by Kocaballi et al. [16] and Lewis [20].

Brüggemeier et al. studied UX of interactions with Alexa when users were asked to perform single tasks [21], which are commands that can be accomplished in one turn [22]. For example, a user asks "Play songs by Queen" and the speech assistant starts playing songs by the band Queen. In our present study, we compare UX scores reported for both single tasks and multi-turn tasks [22], that is tasks that are not accomplished within one turn, but require multiple turns and encompass more than one goal, like in this example:

[*User*]: "Play songs by Queen."
[*System starts to play 'Don't stop me now'.*]
[*User*]: "When was this song first released?"
[*System*]: "The song 'Don't stop me now' by Queen was first released in 1978."

Multi-turn tasks require more capabilities from a system than single tasks in order to be successfully completed. For example the user question "When was this song first published?" requires a speech assistant to parse "this song" and deduce that it refers to "Don't stop me now" by the band Queen. Single tasks do not require such deduction to be successfully completed. Thus, multi-turn tasks are arguably more difficult to complete than single tasks. In this study, we investigate whether UX scores of the four investigated questionnaires reflect task difficulty. If task difficulty affected UX of smart speakers, it should be reflected in scores, and we would expect single tasks to score higher in UX than multi-turn tasks.

In our work, we investigate UX scores of the three smart speakers Alexa's Echo Dot, Apple's HomePod, and Google Home. Smart speakers of Apple, Google, and Amazon are compared in the media a lot. However, there is little scientific work published on comparisons between these three smart speakers [12,23]. Media reports suggest that the audio playback quality of Apple's HomePod is superior to Google Home and Alexa's Echo [9–11]. A superior audio playback quality may affect the UX in our experiments, in which we ask participants to play music. Controlling music is one of the most frequent applications of speech assistants [8,24]. If audio playback quality or other factors affect UX of speech assistants, this should be reflected by scores of the UX questionnaires we study.

Speech assistant and task type may interact, which would result in some speech assistants gaining high UX scores for one task type but not the other, while other assistants would reach high scores for both task types. The online publication TechRadar concludes on the intelligence of speech assistants "Interacting with Google Assistant has the most natural feel. It understands your commands better than Alexa. (...) HomePod's Siri is the least intelligent of the three." [9]. If true, Siri may gain high UX scores at simple, single tasks and lower scores at more difficult multi-turn tasks, while Google might reach similarly high scores for both task types.

Our research questions for this study are:

1. Do UX ratings differ between single turn and multi-turn interactions?
2. Do UX ratings differ in interactions with Siri, Google Assistant and Alexa respectively?
3. Do UX ratings display an interaction between speech assistant and task type?

We expect that single tasks have a higher UX than multi-turn tasks. If the evaluated questionnaires fail to show such differences, this would challenge their validity as UX metrics for smart speakers. We have no a priori expectations on UX of different smart speakers. Reviews and research suggests that smart speakers do differ and that differences are complex [9–12,23]. If questionnaires can distinguish UX of smart speakers, this indicates that they may be useful for applied research. Moreover, we have no a priori expectations regarding interactions between task type and smart speakers. If some metrics show interactions and others do not, this would suggest that questionnaires differ in what they measure, and this could motivate future research.

2 Methods

To address our research questions we invited 51 participants to interact with Amazon's Alexa, Google Assistant, and Apple's Siri. All participants used all three speech assistants. After interacting with them, participants were asked to fill out four questionnaires (AttrakDiff, SASSI, SUISQ-R, SUS).

2.1 Participants

We recruited participants within our institute and externally. Internal participants were recruited through mailing lists. External participants were recruited through notice boards and social media channels. The only requirements for participating in our study was a good command of (spoken) English (self reported) and being over 18 years of age.

In total 51 participants took part in the study. Three participants were excluded from the analysis. We excluded a male and a female participant because of technical problems with the speech assistants. Another male participant was excluded because he did not show any variation in his responses. The participant selected the same value for all items within each questionnaire, which was either always the maximum value or always the minimum value, depending on the questionnaire. This response pattern is unusual for filling our questionnaires [25]. We ran all analysis with and without the outlier and found that the overall results did not change. Thus, we included 48 participants in the analysis we present here. 22 were female (46%) and 26 male (54%). Age ranged between 20 and 53 years, mean age was 26.63 years ($SD = 6.87$). 24 participants were employees at our institute, eight were students. Two participants were native English speakers. The majority of participants had little or no experience with speech assistants. Thirteen had never used an assistant before, 23 used them less than once per month in the past year, four less than once per week, three once per week, two used speech assistants several times per week, and three used them daily.

2.2   Questionnaires

We included four questionnaires that are discussed in two recent works on metrics for UX in interactions with conversational systems [16,20]: AttrakDiff, SASSI, SUISQ-R, SUS. These articles did not address smart speakers, however. Note, that we focus on assessing conversational quality, and this is why we did not include Mean Opinion Scale (MOS), which assesses quality of synthetically generated speech [16,20]. For a detailed description of the evaluated questionnaires see [21].

2.3   Study Design

The experiment was conducted in an office room with low ambient noise between 9 am and 6 pm on work days. Participants were first briefly introduced to the three speech assistants by the experimenter. We explained that the aim of the present study was to evaluate UX-questionnaires and that they would therefore interact with the assistants and rate their experience afterwards. After the informed consent procedure, which included a privacy statement according to GDPR, participants filled out a short online questionnaire asking for demographic variables (age, gender) and prior experience with speech assistants.

Subsequently, the experimenter explained the general procedure of the experiment and introduced them to the tasks they would perform. Participants were divided into two groups, one was given *single tasks*, the other *multi-turn tasks* [22]. Single tasks can be completed in one turn. A turn can be described as a single exchange between user and assistant. Half of the participants ($n = 24$) were assigned to single tasks, the other half to multi-turn tasks. Participants in the single task group were given four tasks in total, each consisting of a request for playing music. Participants were instructed to request (1) a song, (2) an artist, (3) a playlist, and (4) a genre, in this order. Participants in the multi-turn tasks group were presented with three multi-turn tasks. The first was concerned with keeping up to date with popular music. Participants were instructed to ask the assistant to play popular music and then get additional information about the song being played (e.g. the song's and the artist's name). The second multi-turn task consisted of creating a playlist for a specific mood. Participants first had to create a playlist and name it according to the mood they chose. Participants could freely choose the mood but several examples were given (happy, melancholic, hungover). Subsequently, they had to request a song matching this mood and add it to the playlist. Note that this task could not be completed with any of the assistants. It was included because we assumed that it would be frustrating for participants, resulting in a less positive user experience. We expected that the resulting difference in UX would be large enough to be detected by a valid UX-questionnaire. For the third task, participants were asked to get music recommendations. They were instructed to request their favourite song and then ask the assistant for similar songs. The order in which the tasks were presented corresponded to the one described above and it was the same for all participants. Each participant interacted with all three assistants while trying to accomplish the respective tasks. The order in which the assistants were used was fully randomized. Participants were informed that they were free to retry a task as often as they liked. Furthermore, they were instructed to stop playback after a few seconds.

The duration of the experiment for participants in the single task group was on average approximately 45 min. Participants in the multi-turn task group took on average a bit longer with approximately 60 min. Institute policy does not permit to reimburse internal participants monetarily. Thus we offered internal participants sweets as appreciation for their time. External participants were reimbursed for their time with sweets and a monetary compensation of 12€ per hour, students additionally received credit points for their courses. The course was not run by any of the authors, nor were any of the student participants supervised by the authors.

The way tasks are presented to users can bias how users complete a task. In interaction with conversational systems users speak with the system, formulating requests in natural language. If the task description includes example phrases, like "Try saying 'I want to listen to classical music' participants may be biased to produce "I want to listen to classical music" rather than alternatives like "Play some songs featuring violins". Such biased commands are less likely to reflect variability in natural interactions with speech assistants. Wang et al. [26] investigated different methods of presenting tasks and measured how much each method biased speech production. They found that a list-based approach biases speech production the least. Thus we presented tasks with a list-based approach, in order not to bias how participants phrase requests. Tasks were presented in written form as abstract goals, e.g.

Goal: *Play an artist.*
Artist: *Play someone, who was popular in your childhood.*

In addition, we presented participants with a written explanation of the experimental procedure and a brief instruction on how to use the smart speakers. After giving participants an oral explanation, letting them read through the written explanations, and asking if they had any questions, the experimenter left the room.

After participants completed these tasks, they filled out the four questionnaires mentioned in Sect. 2.2 on a computer. The order in which the questionnaires were presented was fully randomized. Participants were instructed to answer the questionnaires intuitively and without much deliberation. In addition, we told participants that they could terminate taking part in our study at any point during the experiment, without experiencing any disadvantages.

Speech Assistants. For interacting with Amazon's Alexa, an *Amazon Echo Dot* (3rd gen., firmware version 2584226436) was used. It was set to American English. For Google Assistant, a *Google Home* smart speaker was used (1st gen., firmware version 1.42.171861), set to American English. Interaction with Apple's Siri took place via a *HomePod* (1st gen., firmware version iOS 12.4) which was set to British English. Playback via *Spotify Premium* was enabled and set as the default for playing music on the Echo Dot and Google Home. On the HomePod Apple Music was used for playback.

2.4 Data Analysis

Preprocessing. Scales for negatively-phrased items were inverted before calculating questionnaire scores. For the AttrakDiff, the SASSI, and the SUISQ-R the scores for the subscales are the average of the scores of all corresponding items, so that the score for each subscale ranges between 1–7 points. A higher score indicates a better UX. The SUS score was calculated following the scoring procedure described by Brooke [27], and the total score is in a range of 0–100 points. A higher score indicates a better usability. We did not find a published procedure for calculating a global score across subscales for AttrakDiff and SASSI (similar to [20]). In order to facilitate the comparison of the different questionnaires, the average of the subscale-scores was used as a total score for these. Consequently, the resulting total score ranges between 1–7 points and a higher score indicates a better UX. We appreciate the multi-dimensionality of UX and our choice of creating global measures does not presume unidimensionality. In fact, creating global measures, despite multi-dimensionality is common practice in differential psychology (e.g. intelligence tests [28]) and usability research (e.g. SUS [27]) and can be explained with a hierarchical model, that assumes a global measure, e.g. UX, to be made up of multiple factors. Two participants did not provide information regarding their age. In our implementation of Linear Mixed Effect Analysis, missing values at individual level were not accepted. Thus we set the age for the missing values to the mean age of the remaining 46 participants. We tested if extreme values for the two missing data points (e.g. 99 years) would affect the results of our analysis, and they did not. Hence, our procedure likely does not distort true age effects.

Statistical Analysis. For the statistical analysis we chose a multilevel modeling approach to account for dependencies in repeated measures [29]. In our work, we repeatedly asked participants to report UX of different speech assistants using different questionnaires. Note, that intraclass coefficient (ICC) can be used as a criterion to decide whether it is appropriate to conduct multilevel analysis. For our data ICC assesses how much of the overall variance can be attributed to differences between individuals rather than to factors like task type or speech assistant. If the ICC is high, and thus a lot of overall variance is due to differences between participants, it is useful to employ multilevel modelling, as it allows to further investigate individual differences in a statistically sound way. As a rule of thumb, multilevel modeling is required if the ICC is higher than 0.05 [30]. Multilevel modeling can be regarded as a generalization of linear regression and is also known as hierarchical linear modeling or linear mixed-effect modeling. The interpretation of such models is similar to multiple regression [29]. For an in-depth treatment of the subject see for example [29] or [31]. For the present analyses, intercepts were allowed to vary, which assumes that participants may vary in their baseline rating of UX as measured by questionnaires.

A separate model was fitted for each questionnaire. Model structure was similar across models and included the following predictors as fixed effects: (1) Assistant, with three levels relating to Alexa, Google Assistant and Siri, (2) task type, with two levels representing multi-turn and single tasks, (3) interaction between assistant and task type, (4) gender, with the two levels female and male, (5) prior use, with the two levels not used before and used before, and (6) age. The categorical predictors 'assistant', 'gender', and 'task type' were effect-coded. When asking participants for their gender, we allowed them to choose one of three options: *female*, *male*, and *other*. None of the participants chose *other*, thus we analysed two levels for gender. For prior use we analysed the two levels *never used* and *used before*. Models only differ in their dependent variable, which is the total score of the respective questionnaire. Questionnaire scores were treated as interval scales.

For significance testing of fixed effects, we used F-tests in combination with the Kenward-Roger approximation [32]. Correction for multiple comparisons were applied if post-hoc tests were used. For testing random parameters, we performed likelihood-ratio tests. The intercepts were the only random parameters. We compared a model with varying intercepts with a model in which the intercepts were fixed (i.e. the same) for all participants. To assess violation of the underlying assumptions of mixed-effect models, level one and level two residual plots were visually inspected. For level one residuals there was no indication of a violation of normality or homoscedasticity for any of the four questionnaires. This was true for level two residuals also. Similarly, there was no evidence for level two residuals to be not normally distributed and not centered around zero.

3   Results

Our analysis shows similar patterns of results across questionnaires. We find significant main effects for assistant and task type (see Table 1) which means that both factors affect UX. Ratings for single tasks are consistently higher than for multi-turn tasks, which suggests that single tasks have a better UX than multi-turn tasks. Interestingly, participants rated HomePod to have a higher usability and UX than Echo Dot and Google Home.

There is no significant interaction between task type and assistant, which indicates that rankings of assistants are consistent across task type. Neither age, gender, nor prior use show significant effects on ratings. Detailed statistics can be found in Table 1.

3.1   AttrakDiff

For the AttrakDiff the ICC is .274, which suggests that multilevel modelling should be conducted to account for dependencies in the data. Analysis of fixed effects with multilevel modelling shows significant main effects for assistant

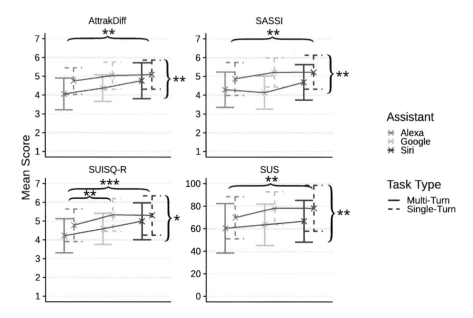

Fig. 1. Total questionnaire scores split by task type and assistant for the four questionnaires (raw values). Exes (X) represent mean values, error bars standard deviations, brackets significant differences of the multi-level analyses; $^*p < .05.^{**}p < .01.$ $^{***}p < .001.$

$(F(2, 92) = 7.27, p = .001)$ and task type $(F(1, 43) = 9.63, p = .003)$. The interaction between assistant and task type is not significant $(F(2, 92) = 1.08, p = .343)$. Post-hoc tests show that UX for the single-tasks condition was rated higher compared to the multi-tasks condition $(t(43) = 2.97, p = .005,$ see also Fig. 1). Furthermore, they reveal that UX for Siri was rated significantly higher compared to Alexa $(t(92) = 3.80, p < .001)$, while ratings for Siri and Google Assistant did not differ significantly $(t(92) = 1.62, p = .243)$. The difference between Google Assistant and Alexa is also not significant $(t(92) = 3.18, p = .080)$. None of the covariates we measured (age, gender, prior use) exhibits a significant influence on the total questionnaire score (see Table 1).

Conditional R^2 and marginal R^2 provide an estimate for the amount of explained variance, since classical R^2 cannot be computed for multilevel models. Conditional R^2 is an estimate of the amount of variance explained by the full model, marginal R^2 for the amount explained by the fixed factors only [33–35]. For the model fitted for the AttrakDiff marginal R^2 was .185, conditional R^2 was .408.

3.2 SASSI

The ICC for SASSI is .423. The effect pattern of SASSI is similar to AttrakDiff. We find significant main effects of assistant $(F(2, 92) = 4.20, p = .018)$ and

Table 1. Results of the linear mixed effect analyses: Type III tests of the fixed effects of the total UX-questionnaire scores

	Sum Sq	Mean Sq	Num. df	Den. df	F	p
AttrakDiff						
Assistant	6.73	3.36	2.00	92.00	7.27	.001**
Task Type	4.08	4.08	1.00	43.00	8.83	.005**
Assistant x Task Type	1.00	0.50	2.00	92.00	1.08	.343
Age	0.13	0.13	1.00	43.00	0.28	.598
Gender	0.39	0.39	1.00	43.00	0.84	.365
Prior Use	0.32	0.32	1.00	43.00	0.70	.408
SASSI						
Assistant	3.70	1.85	2.00	92.00	4.20	.018*
Task Type	5.25	5.25	1.00	43.00	11.93	.001**
Assistant x Task Type	2.21	1.11	2.00	92.00	2.51	.086
Age	0.12	0.12	1.00	43.00	0.27	.605
Gender	0.02	0.02	1.00	43.00	0.04	.839
Prior Use	1.60	1.60	1.00	43.00	3.64	.063
SUISQ-R						
Assistant	10.86	5.43	2.00	92.00	11.47	<.001***
Task Type	2.76	2.76	1.00	43.00	5.83	.020*
Assistant x Task Type	1.14	0.57	2.00	92.00	1.20	.306
Age	0.03	0.03	1.00	43.00	0.07	.795
Gender	0.02	0.02	1.00	43.00	0.04	.836
Prior Use	0.17	0.17	1.00	43.00	0.36	.551
SUS						
Assistant	1443.84	721.92	2.00	92.00	3.82	.026*
Task Type	1477.78	1477.78	1.00	43.00	7.82	.008**
Assistant x Task Type	178.21	89.11	2.00	92.00	0.47	.626
Gender	5.79	5.79	1.00	43.00	0.03	.862
Age	5.20	5.20	1.00	43.00	0.03	.869
Prior Use	738.77	738.77	1.00	43.00	3.91	.055

Note. $*p < .05.$ $**p < .01.$ $***p < .001.$

task type ($F(1, 43) = 14.367, p < .001$) while the interaction is not significant ($F(2, 92) = 2.51, p = .086$). Again, ratings for the single-tasks condition are significantly higher compared to the multi-tasks condition, as indicated by post-hoc tests ($t(43) = 3.45, p = .001$). Scores for Siri are significantly higher compared to Alexa ($t(92) = 3.79, p < .001$). The difference between Siri and Google Assistant is not significant ($t(92) = 2.01, p = .096$), as is the difference between Google Assistant and Alexa ($t(92) = 0.68, p = .774$). Neither age, gender or prior use demonstrate significant main effects (see Table 1). Marginal R^2 was .217, conditional R^2 was .559.

3.3 SUISQ-R

The ICC for SUISQ-R is .462. Results for SUISQ-R again mirror previous results. Assistant $(F(2, 92) = 11.47, p < .001)$ and task type $(F(1, 43) = 6.87, p < .012)$ show significant main effects and their interaction is not significant $(F(2, 92) = 1.20, p = .306)$. Post-hoc tests reveal that scores for the single-tasks condition are significantly higher compared to the multi-tasks condition $(t(43) = 2.42, p = .020)$. Furthermore they show that Siri achieves significantly higher scores compared to Alexa $(t(92) = 4.65, p < .001)$, while ratings for Siri and Google Assistant do not differ significantly $(t(92) = 1.34, p = .380)$. In contrast to the other questionnaires, scores for Google Assistant are also significantly higher than those of Alexa, $(t(92) = 3.32, p = .004)$. Again, age, gender and prior use do not exhibit main effects (see Table 1). Marginal R^2 is .155, conditional R^2 is .543.

3.4 SUS

The ICC for SUS is .457. Results for SUS are in line with those of the other questionnaires. We find significant main effects for assistant $(F(2, 92) = 3.82, p = .026)$ and task type $(F(1, 43) = 7.82, p = .008)$, but not for their interaction $(F(2, 92) = 0.47, p = .626)$. For the SUS, post-hoc tests show again higher ratings for the single-tasks condition compared to the multi-tasks condition $(t(43) = 2.80, p = .008)$. Ratings for Siri are significantly higher compared to Alexa $(t(92) = 2.62, p = .028)$, but not higher than those of Google Assistant $(t(92) = 0.54, p = .853)$. The difference between Alexa and Google Assistant is not significant $(t(92) = 2.08, p = .010)$. None of the covariates (age, gender and prior use) shows a significant main effect (see Table 1). Marginal R^2 was .164, conditional R^2 was .546.

3.5 Evaluation of Model Choice

We have chosen a multilevel approach because we expected dependencies in our data due to the repeated measures design. That the ICC values of all questionnaires are considerably higher than the threshold of .05 [30] indicates that this is indeed the case. To test whether the variation in participants baseline UX is significant, we compare the multi-level approach here with the more widely-used linear regression approach. For the comparison we use multiple criteria that are commonly used to compare models, namely AIC, BIC and likelihood-ratio tests [29]. Note that the only difference between the multi-level and the linear models is that the former allow random variation of intercepts of participants' ratings and the latter do not. In our data, intercepts of participants' ratings are equivalent to their average UX ratings. By allowing average ratings to vary, we assume that participants differ in their baseline ratings of UX. Allowing for random intercepts leads to a significantly better model fit for all four questionnaires, indicated by both the likelihood ratio test and the information criteria (see Table 2 in the appendix) for details. This implies that there is substantial variation in participants baseline ratings of UX.

4   Discussion

In our study, consistent patterns emerge across the evaluated questionnaires. This suggests valid differences in UX between task types and smart speakers. We measured UX for goal-oriented tasks (playing music) and usability may be a primary factor influencing user ratings for those tasks [36], which may explain why we see similar patters across UX metrics. All evaluated questionnaires differentiate UX of single and multi-turn tasks as well as of smart speakers, which indicates that they can be used to measure differences in UX of interactions with smart speakers.

4.1   UX Metrics for Smart Speakers

As UX differences are measured consistently, which of the four evaluated questionnaires should one pick, when wanting to measure UX with smart speakers? This question is important both for practitioners and researchers working in companies or institutes who may use UX as key performance measure of smart speakers. One can argue that, as all of the evaluated questionnaires measure similar differences and constructs [21], it does not matter which questionnaire is used. However, Lewis [20], Kocaballi et al. [16] and Brüggemeier et al. [21] note that each of the questionnaires has drawbacks like lack of norms, reliability and validity tests [20], incomplete measurement of UX [16] and differences in face validity and length [21]. Kocaballi et al. [16] suggest to combine multiple questionnaires so that some drawbacks can be compensated for. However, there may be situations in which using only one questionnaire may be preferable, for example when we do not learn more from using more than one questionnaire [21], or when repetitive exposure to questionnaires can be tiring to users [21], or when there are time restraints. For such situations we suggest to use SUISQ-R to measure UX in interactions with smart speakers. In our set-up, differences in UX were consistently measured across questionnaires, including SUISQ-R. SUISQ-R (14 items) is shorter than SASSI (34 items) and AttrakDiff (28 items). Moreover, SUISQ-R has a higher face validity than AttrakDiff and SUS for interactions with smart speakers [21].

Future work can evaluate other questionnaires with smart speakers. For example UEQ+ [37] could be assessed. UEQ+ is modular and has 16 scales that can be added or omitted to fit product and use context. Scales include factors of UX like stimulation, which comprises fun, and fun has been reported to be insufficiently covered by other metrics [16]. Moreover, UEQ+-scales like 'Trust' may be of interest for speech interfaces also, given privacy and trust scandals

[38]. Furthermore, research into designing questionnaires specifically for smart speakers is indicated.

4.2 Multi-turn Tasks vs Single Tasks

We find that single interactions unanimously score higher in UX than multi-turn interactions. This demonstrates that the number of tasks (one vs. more than one) might affect UX of smart speakers. This is not surprising, as multi-turn interactions constitute challenges for conversational systems [22]. In our study we asked participants in the multi-turn task condition to tackle two or three tasks that were related to each other. We found marked reductions in UX compared to single tasks. An example for a multi-turn task scenario is someone playing music and then asking for information about the music (e.g. when it was first released).

One of the three multi-turn tasks we presented (creating playlists) was not supported by any of the smart speakers. The experience of not being able to solve this task may have negatively affected UX scores for multi-turn tasks. Hence, the differences we find between single and multi-turn tasks may be due to the fact that one of the three multi-turn tasks could not be completed. Future research should investigate the effect of task success on UX in interactions with smart speakers. In addition, it would be interesting to investigate if there is a correlation between UX and the number of tasks in interactions with smart speakers. If the number of connected tasks increases, does the UX in interactions with smart speakers decrease?

4.3 UX Differences in Smart Speakers

Our data suggest that for music control UX of Apple's HomePod exceeds UX of Amazon's Alexa. Moreover, scores for Siri were consistently higher compared to Google Home, however, differences were not or only marginally significant. This finding is true for both single and multi-turn tasks. This indicates that participants in our study had a superior user experience when interacting with Siri than with the other two assistants. Apple's HomePod is praised in product reviews for its sound quality when playing music [10,11,39], which may be a reason why we find higher UX scores for HomePod than other speakers. However, most participants stopped music playback after a few seconds. If playback quality explained the ranking of speech assistants, brief periods of playback must have been sufficient to cause differences in UX. Another possible explanation is that Siri's language setting was British English, while the other two assistants were set to American English. It could be that participants preferred interacting with British over American speech assistants. Also, speaker accent influences lexical choices of users, which may affect the overall interaction and user experience [18]. Moreover, the conversational quality of Siri might be superior to the other assistants. This however, is in contrast with reviews suggesting that "Interacting with Google Assistant has the most natural feel. It understands your commands better than Alexa. (...) HomePod's Siri is the least intelligent of the three"

[9]. Such reviews are in agreement with findings by Berdasco et al. [12] which suggest that correctness and naturalness of Alexa and Google Assistant are rated as superior to Siri. Another potential explanation for the result that users in our study report Siri to have the best UX is brand expectations [23]. Indeed, Thomas Brill [23] demonstrates that user expectations are a strong predictor of user satisfaction and he argues that users want their expectations to be fulfilled, which may bias their evaluation of speech assistants. Further, Brill suggests that expectations are based on the company brand [23]. Thus companies like Apple may profit from positive brand expectations.

Users in our study knew what product they were interacting with, as we introduced them to the three smart speakers by mentioning their names and the companies that produce them before participants started the experiment. We did not further comment on the products. Hence we measured UX confounded with brand and these scores may differ if users would not be able to identify product brands. This could be achieved for example by letting users interact with smart speakers behind a visual cover. However, even if users do not see speakers, they still hear them and voices of Alexa, Siri and Google Assistant might be recognized by participants. Hence a blind assessment of smart speakers may not be sufficient to exclude brand effects. Researchers would have to implement Alexa, Siri and Google Assistant such that they use the same voice. In addition, users would have to be able to activate each assistant with the same wake word, for example "Computer" instead of "Alexa", to prevent users recognizing assistants based on their names. Moreover, speaker hardware and appearance may affect UX and our participants were able to see the speakers. If the three speech assistants were implemented to run on three similar speakers, effects of hardware and appearance would be controlled. Thus future studies could anonymize smart speakers, to test only their conversational abilities.

4.4 Limitations

We present a purely quantitative approach here, which misses important aspects of user experience, which are captured by qualitative approaches. For example product reviewers comment on prize, setting-up process, compatibility with other devices, number of skills and other aspects [10,11,39] that are not covered in our experiment. We believe that qualitative and quantitative information on user experience (UX) and usability are complementary. Future research could include qualitative methods like interviews, thinking out loud, diary studies, or behavioral analysis from video as they may shed light on questions such as why Apple's Siri rates higher in UX than the other two assistants.

Participants in our study filled out four questionnaires after completing each interaction with each speech assistant. This means UX was measured repeatedly and this may be problematic, as participants may get tired or annoyed, when they fill out questionnaires repeatedly. We controlled for potential effects of fatigue or mood on responses by randomizing the presentation of questionnaires. Each of the questionnaires had the same probability to be filled out as first, second, third or last. In addition, we randomized the order of interactions with smart speakers, so that each smart speaker was equally likely to be used as first, second or last speaker. Still, the fact that we see similar patterns in UX scores across questionnaires may be due to our repeated measure approach. Hence, future work may evaluate UX questionnaires with independent user groups.

The multi-turn condition was designed so that one of the tasks was impossible to complete. However, we did not include details on whether participants managed to complete the other tasks, even in the single-task condition. It would be good to know whether there were differences, for example, between participants who could complete all the other tasks apart from the impossible one, and participants who could not complete some of the other tasks, perhaps because the smart speaker did not understand the command. Also, perhaps some people could complete all the tasks at the first attempt, while others took more than one attempt. These are all differences that likely influence the perceived UX.

Participants in our study were mostly non-native English speakers. Only two out of the 48 included participants were natives. In our recruiting we asked people to register only if they had a good command of spoken English, however it is still possible that testing mostly non-natives affects UX with speech assistants [40]. Thus future research should evaluate UX questionnaires with native and non-native speakers.

We computed global scores for all questionnaires to facilitate comparison. However, not all questionnaires are designed for global scores. For example, SASSI is not designed to be used as a global measure. Computing a global score for SASSI may have distorted results for that questionnaire.

5   Conclusion

We quantify UX with commercial smart speakers and find consistent differences between task types and speakers. To the best of our knowledge, we are the first to describe these UX patterns for smart speakers. Other use contexts, tasks and metrics may show different patterns in UX of virtual assistants. We believe that the HCI community will profit from a data repository of UX scores for interactions with speech assistants. Such data may help to identify factors that are relevant for UX in interaction with VUI. Some of the factors that are commonly mentioned in reviews of smart speakers, like sound quality, compatibility with Smart Home devices, and difficulty of set-up [9–11] are not covered in any of the questionnaires we analyzed. The definition and assessment of UX with speech assistants may have to be extended to cover attributes that are identified as relevant by qualitative reviews. Our data suggest that UX differs across task types and smart speakers and that we should keep track of scores for different set-ups as such data are necessary for creating meaningful norms that act as basis for evaluation [20]. Norms facilitate meaningful evaluations and comparisons and so far none of the evaluated metrics have norms for interactions with speech assistants [20]. It will be challenging to create comprehensive norms for interactions with speech assistants, as they are complex and datasets from different laboratories and experiments have limited comparability. Despite these challenges, data repositories with UX scores of interactions with speech assistants are a step towards answering a question that is relevant for both researchers and practitioners: "What is good-enough user experience?".

Appendix

Table 2. Results of the linear mixed effects analysis for the Random Effects.

Model	df	AIC	BIC	logLik	Deviance	χ^2	$df(\chi^2)$	p
AttrakDiff								
No RE[a]	10	352.61	382.31	−166.30	332.61			
With RE	11	346.56	379.23	−162.28	324.56	8.05	1	.005**
SASSI								
No RE	10	380.90	410.59	−180.45	360.90			
With RE	11	360.69	393.35	−169.34	338.69	22.21	1	<.001***
SUISQ-R								
No RE	10	398.03	427.73	−189.02	378.03			
With RE	11	374.84	407.51	−176.42	352.84	25.19	1	<.001***
SUS								
No RE	10	1259.22	1288.92	−619.61	1239.22			
With RE	11	1236.60	1269.27	−607.30	1214.60	24.62	1	<.001***

Note. [a]RE = Random Effects; $^*p < .05$. $^{**}p < .01$. $^{***}p < .001$.

References

1. Kinsella, B.: Juniper estimates 3.25 billion voice assistants are in use today, Google has about 30% of them (2019). https://voicebot.ai/2019/02/14/juniper-estimates-3-25-billion-voice-assistants-are-in-use-today-google-has-about-30-of-them/
2. Gibbs, S.: How smart speakers stole the show from smartphones. The Guardian, January 2018. https://www.theguardian.com/technology/2018/jan/06/how-smart-speakers-stole-the-show-from-smartphones
3. Statista: Market shares of smart speakers in the United Kingdom (UK) Q1 2018 (2018). https://www.statista.com/statistics/953755/smart-speaker-market-shares-uk/
4. Statista: Vernetzte Lautsprecher mit Sprachassistenten in Deutschland 2017—global consumer survey. Technical report ID 810003 (2017)
5. GlobalData: Informationen zu Smart Speakern und Voice-Technology aus lizensierter Datenbank, July 2019. https://www.globaldata.com/

6. IMARC: Intelligent virtual assistant market: global industry trends, share, size, growth, opportunity and forecast 2019–2024. Technical report 4775648, IMARC (2019)
7. voicebot.ai: Voice assistant consumer adoption report. Technical report, voicebot.ai, November 2019
8. Splendid Research: Digitale Sprachassistenten. Technical report, Splendid Research, Hamburg (2019)
9. Porter, J., Pino, N., Leger, H.: Amazon echo vs apple homepod vs google home: the battle of the smart speakers (2019). https://www.techradar.com/news/amazon-echo-vs-homepod-vs-google-home-the-battle-of-the-smart-speakers
10. Van Camp, J.: The 8 best smart speakers with alexa and google assistant (2019). https://www.wired.com/story/best-smart-speakers/
11. Gebhart, A., Price, M.: The best smart speakers for 2019 (2019). https://www.cnet.com/news/best-smart-speakers-for-2019-amazon-echo-dot-google-nest-mini-assistant-alexa/
12. Berdasco, A., López, G., Díaz-Oreiro, I., Quesada, L., Guerrero, L.A.: User experience comparison of intelligent personal assistants: Alexa, Google assistant, siri and cortana. In: Bravo, J., González, I. (eds.) Proceedings of the 13th International Conference on Ubiquitous Computing and Ambient Intelligence - UCAm I 2019. MDPI Proceedings, vol. 31, pp. 51–58. MDPI (2019). https://doi.org/10.3390/proceedings2019031051
13. NPR, Edison Research.: The smart audio report 2019. Technical report, NPR and Edison Research (2019)
14. Hellweger, S., Wang, X.: What is user experience really: towards a UX conceptual framework (2015). arXiv:1503.01850
15. Law, E., Roto, V., Vermeeren, A.P., Kort, J., Hassenzahl, M.: Towards a shared definition of user experience. In: CHI 2008 Extended Abstracts on Human Factors in Computing Systems, pp. 2395–2398. Association for Computing Machinery, New York (2008). https://doi.org/10.1145/1358628.1358693
16. Kocaballi, A.B., Laranjo, L., Coiera, E.: Measuring user experience in conversational interfaces: a comparison of six questionnaires. In: Proceedings of the 32nd British Computer Society Human Computer Interaction Conference - HCI 2018, pp. 1–12 (2018). https://doi.org/10.14236/ewic/HCI2018.21
17. Branigan, H., Pickering, M., Pearson, J., McLean, J.: Linguistic alignment between people and computers. J. Pragmat. 42, 2355–2368 (2010). https://doi.org/10.1016/j.pragma.2009.12.012
18. Cowan, B.R., et al.: What's in an accent? In: Proceedings of the 1st International Conference on Conversational User Interfaces - CUI 2019 (2019). https://doi.org/10.1145/3342775.3342786
19. Lewis, J.R., Sauro, J.: Can I leave this one out? The effect of dropping an item from the SUS. J. Usability Stud. 13(1), 38–46 (2017)
20. Lewis, J.R.: Standardized questionnaires for voice interaction design. Voice Interact. Des. 1(1), 1–16 (2016)
21. Brüggemeier, B., Breiter, M., Kurz, M., Schiwy, J.: User experience of alexa when controlling music–comparison of face and construct validity of four questionnaires. In: Proceedings of the 2nd International Conference on Conversational User Interfaces CUI 2020, July 2020. (in Press)

22. Kiseleva, J., Williams, K., Hassan Awadallah, A., Crook, A.C., Zitouni, I., Anastasakos, T.: Predicting user satisfaction with intelligent assistants. In: Proceedings of the 39th International ACM SIGIR Conference on Research and Development in Information Retrieval - SIGIR 2016, pp. 45–54 (2016). https://doi.org/10.1145/2911451.2911521

23. Brill, T.M., Munoz, L., Miller, R.J.: Siri, Alexa, and other digital assistants: a study of customer satisfaction with artificial intelligence applications. J. Market. Manag. 35(15–16), 1401–1436 (2019). https://doi.org/10.1080/0267257X.2019.1687571

24. voicebot.ai: Voice assistant consumer adoption report. Technical report, voicebot.ai, November 2018

25. Menold, N., Bogner, K.: Design of rating scales in questionnaires (version 2.0). GESIS - Leibniz Institute for the Social Sciences, Mannheim, Germany (2016). https://doi.org/10.15465/gesis-sg_en_015

26. Wang, W.Y., Bohus, D., Kamar, E., Horvitz, E.: Crowdsourcing the acquisition of natural language corpora: methods and observations. In: Proceedings of 2012 IEEE Workshop on Spoken Language Technology, SLT 2012, pp. 73–78 (2012). https://doi.org/10.1109/SLT.2012.6424200

27. Brooke, J.: SUS - a quick and dirty usability scale. Usability Eval. Ind. 189(194), 4–7 (1996)

28. Schneider, W.J., Newman, D.A.: Intelligence is multidimensional: theoretical review and implications of specific cognitive abilities. Hum. Resour. Manag. Rev. 25(1), 12–27 (2015). https://doi.org/10.1016/j.hrmr.2014.09.004

29. Hox, J.J.: Multilevel Analysis: Techniques and Applications. Quantitative Methodology Series, 2nd edn. Routledge and Taylor & Francis, New York (2010)

30. Hedges, L.V., Hedberg, E.C.: Intraclass correlation values for planning group-randomized trials in education. Educ. Eval. Policy Anal. 29(1), 60–87 (2007). https://doi.org/10.3102/0162373707299706

31. Gelman, A., Hill, J.: Data Analysis Using Regression and Multilevel/Hierarchical Models. Analytical Methods for Social Research. Cambridge University Press, Cambridge (2007). https://doi.org/10.1017/CBO9780511790942

32. Kenward, M.G., Roger, J.H.: Small sample inference for fixed effects from restricted maximum likelihood. Biometrics 53, 983–997 (1997)

33. Johnson, P.C.: Extension of Nakagawa & Schielzeth's $R^{2}\textsc{glmm}$ to random slopes models. Methods Ecol. Evol. 5(9), 944–946 (2014). https://doi.org/10.1111/2041-210X.12225

34. Nakagawa, S., Schielzeth, H.: A general and simple method for obtaining R^2 from generalized linear mixed-effects models. Methods Ecol. Evol. 4(2), 133–142 (2013). https://doi.org/10.1111/j.2041-210x.2012.00261.x. http://doi.wiley.com/10.1111/j.2041-210x.2012.00261.x

35. Nakagawa, S., Johnson, P.C.D., Schielzeth, H.: The coefficient of determination R^2 and intra-class correlation coefficient from generalized linear mixed-effects models revisited and expanded. J. R. Soc. Interface 14(134), 1–11 (2017). https://doi.org/10.1098/rsif.2017.0213

36. Hassenzahl, M., Ullrich, D.: To do or not to do: differences in User Experience and retrospective judgments depending on the presence or absence of instrumental goals. Interact. Comput. 19, 429–437 (2007). https://doi.org/10.1016/j.intcom.2007.05.001

37. Schrepp, M., Thomaschewski, J.: Handbook for the modular extension of the User Experience Questionnaire (2019)

38. Lynskey, D.: Alexa, are you invading my privacy? - the dark side of our voice assistants. The Guardian, October 2019. https://www.theguardian.com/technology/2019/oct/09/alexa-are-you-invading-my-privacy-the-dark-side-of-our-voice-assistants

39. Caddy, B., Pino, N., Leger, H.: The best smart speakers: 2019 which one should you buy? (2019). https://www.techradar.com/news/best-smart-speakers

40. Pyae, A., Scifleet, P.: Investigating differences between native English and non-native English speakers in interacting with a voice user interface: a case of google home. In: Proceedings of the 30th Australian Conference on Computer-Human Interaction OzCHI 2018, pp. 548–553. Association for Computing Machinery, New York (2018). https://doi.org/10.1145/3292147.3292236

A Study on the Cross-Screen User Experience of Watching Live Streaming News

Liang Yuan Che$^{(\boxtimes)}$ and Chien-Hsiung Chen

National Taiwan University of Science and Technology, Taipei, Taiwan
a3n7156@gmail.com

Abstract. With the wide spread of smart handheld device and the rapid development of Internet technology, the opportunity for global population to use live broadcast technology across screens has been increasing. Traditional ways of watching TV news via cable or air broadcasting are no longer the primary media receiving channel for users. In fact, in the modern era, many media corporates also provide instant and fast news to the public by using different communication channels on different devices. By adopting the behavior of cross-screen live streaming news watching, the authors hope to explore innovative interaction styles with users and, at the same time, increase their cross-screen user experience. The purpose of this study is to explore the users' task performance regarding information search while conducting cross-screen interactions. The experiment was a two-factor mixed factorial design, i.e. 2 (viewing style) × 2 (graphic/text focus). A total of four prototypes were created for the experiment. Twelve participants were invited to take part in the experiment by convenient sampling method. The participants were asked to conduct five tasks. Among them, two of the participants' task performance were collected for further statistical analysis. After the tasks were conducted, each participant was required to answer the questionnaire of System Usability Scale (SUS), NASA Task Load Index (NASA-TLX), and subjective preference. A semi-structured interview was also conducted after the participant completed the experimental tasks.

The generated results of this study revealed that: (1) The viewing style tended to be different according to users' use scenarios. Their degrees of interests were related to the information contents. (2) The recommended information visualization is to adopt graphic first with text as supportive information. That is, when the user could not understand the meaning of the graphics, they can confirm by reading the texts or click on the relevant icon for more information. (3) In task 1, most participants preferred to interact with the device in the horizontal style with texts first and graphics as supportive design. This is because the toolbar is placed on the right side of the screen for better click-on position. (4) In task 5, most participants preferred interact with the device in the vertical style with graphics first and texts as supportive design. This is because the page was placed in the lower right corner of the screen after zooming out and it was displayed as an icon.

Keywords: Cross screen · Live streaming news · User experience · Graphic · Text · Vertical · Horizontal

© Springer Nature Switzerland AG 2020
C. Stephanidis et al. (Eds.): HCII 2020, LNCS 12423, pp. 619–634, 2020.
https://doi.org/10.1007/978-3-030-60114-0_41

1 Introduction

Television is a popular form of entertainment in modern families. With the spread of the Internet and the rise of the concept of smart homeownership, more and more TV sets have been installed, and more users are receiving reply via the Internet's cross-screen. It can receive instant news messages through various channels, such as streaming video, sharing on the forum, etc. The authors have also discovered this phenomenon and have shown an extension of the second screen through handheld devices (i.e. mobile phones or tablet PCs) so that viewers can directly discuss their interactions with the content of the TV program.

Even though hand-held devices are well developed, many users are accustomed to watching the news on the TV and getting instant messages through the Internet. Because users enjoy watching TV during the same period, they visit the web pages related to the topic or share their own interesting topics with friends to join the discussion. This interaction has also encouraged the number of people watching the news live through the Internet and across the screen. As a result of this interactive mode, TV production units are gradually planned to increase audience dependence on the program. For example, viewers are encouraged to call live programs and send comments to share their views on the topic. Finally, through the use of the TV as the first screen and the handheld device as the second screen, the film consumer obtains more relevant information and interacts with the TV program to demonstrate that personal opinions have become the mainstream multi-media interaction mode.

This study aims to explore the effect of viewing patterns and graphical interface design on users' experience and performance during cross-screen viewing of news live broadcast. Neem and Dozier [6] pointed out that the cost of cross-screen viewing can be divided into two types (i.e. the passive cross-screen viewing and the active cross-screen viewing) [11], and active cross-screen viewing such as information search, social media discussion, etc. Excluding users' social burden (i.e., social affordances), the effect is that users will be immersed in a multi-screen viewing experience to view the audio and video channels. The internal product is more viscous and is more willing to raise the level of discussion in the community media. How to improve user interaction and enhance user interaction is an important topic for human-machine interaction.

This study also tries to explore the interaction between the interface design and the user during the live broadcast of news on the cross-screen viewing line. The main intention is to understand the user's use of the interface, the burden of the work and the subjective preference in watching the news. The information function provided by the handheld device is of great importance to the viewer in a cross-screen viewing attitude. The above topics are still yet to be clarified and will be investigated and discussed in this study.

2 Background

Cross-screen viewing was first used for related research on PDAs which requires people to performing tasks while watching TV. With the expansion of the Internet service area and the popularity of handheld devices, users are still used to using home television as the main medium for receiving information. At the same time, they are using mobile phones to further search for relevant information or share discussions. Shin [10] suggested that "social" (e.g., interaction) is the main reason for the transition from a single screen to a cross-screen [12]. The production unit also found that when the film and video consumers are keen to meet their needs, the interaction between the screen and the screen gives them control over the consumption of the medium. Once consumers get a sense of satisfaction and joy from this interaction, they will become more dependent on the event's purpose.

Pavlik [9] argued that the second screen not only conveys the content of the TV program but also provides added value for the enjoyment of the experience [10]. The synergy between the main screen and the second screen can enhance the overall enjoyment of the audience. The interactive effect can be achieved through the two types of screens, which will make the user more immersed in the program. Kari and Savolainen [5] pointed out the context created by television and the second screen is important for understanding the content of the program [7]. Without the context, it is not very meaningful to use the information in different ways. The application of the second fluorescent screen has been widely used in a variety of programming situations, creating opportunities for the industry to advertise in a wide range of advertisements, as well as allowing users to become more immersed in the event's content. As a result, it has become very important in the design of cross-platforms. Levin (2014) proposed the 3C model. It contains consistency (consistent), Continuous design (Continuous), complementary design (Complementary). Consistency design is the same experience that has been reproduced to all the devices, such as internal flow, structure and main functions so that the participants can enjoy the whole experience independently on any device. Persistent design is transmitted from one setup to another, regardless of whether the same activity (or shifting to different contexts) moves towards the same goal. Finally, the inter complementary scheme is to create a new experience by pretending to help each other (i.e., using the relevant information function) by integrating two types of installation (cooperation, control) (e.g. cross-screen "cooperation" to produce a common visual experience, and "controlling" to use hand-held devices as a remote control.

Visual search on a handheld device when viewing across screens is very relevant to the user's viewing mode. Visual search is the process of finding a target in a certain scene. Yang et al. [13] mentioned that the Islamic scholar Alhazen once divided the visual process into aspectus and inuitio obtutus. That is, the entire scene can be seen at first glance, and then carefully observed [6]. To the processing of individual perception messages. If the viewing scene is between 2–30°, people can observe by moving the eyes. If the viewing target exceeds the above angle, you need to move your head to see all the details. Visual search is a time-consuming process, and the process depends on people's interest and expectations about the scene. There are also many related types of research on viewing modes and the visual search efficiency of text. For example, Ojanpää, Näsänen, and Kojo [8] proposed that there is significant evidence for the overall speed of horizontal scanning and vertical scanning [9]. Deng, Kahn, Unnava, and Lee [4] also mentioned that because the eyes of a person are horizontal and match the direction of eye movement required to process the horizontal direction, the horizontal comparison the vertical display is smoother and faster in information processing [5]. However, whether such differences apply to handheld devices for cross-screen viewing remains to be clarified. The follow-up of this study will also focus on the preliminary interviews for visual scanning and search efficiency of handheld devices under cross-screen viewing.

Because cross-screen viewing is an activity that switches between attention categories, participants watch the audiovisual program through the first screen, while operating the second screen (e.g., a hand-held device) to perform advanced functional operations. How participants can successfully find the required function depends on the design of the menu. In previous research, Benbasat and Todd (1993) discussed the menu text and email ratio and visual search performance of the email system earlier [1]. In the experiment, icons and text were used as experimental samples. In this study, there is no significant difference between icons and text. In Theil and Hwang's [12] experiment, the elderly were invited to make corresponding gestures in the air according to the experimental samples they saw [3]. The study divided the experimental samples into text, static graphics, and dynamic graphics. Finally, it was found that pictures can produce the correct corresponding gestures as quickly as possible. From the above studies, it can be found that under different operating situations, interfaces, menus, and even the interface graphic ratio will affect the user's visual search performance. How to understand people's viewing habits and visual search preferences in the context of cross-screen viewing is also the focus of this study.

Imagine the process in which a user operates a task in front of two screens and switches attention. How to make people and machines work more smoothly through interface design is the core task of user interface design. Designers can refer to Norman [7]'s "Seven Principles of User-centered Design" [8] and Shneiderman [11]'s "Law of Eight User Interface Designs" [13] passed this category, through these design principles will effectively enhance the user's operational experience. Once the user has better experience or experience than any other product, he or she is more inclined to repeat the product and develop a feeling of trust.

Cross-screen viewing is generally possible through various display devices. However, there are still a number of applications for cross-screen viewing. Apart from the low availability of the system interface and the technical problems such as breakage, users still hope to be able to transfer or connect the system through enhanced visual experience. This study tries to explore the impact of interface design in different viewing modes on the effectiveness of information search in cross-screen viewing. Finally, the user's preferences in the various operational tasks are understood from the usability scales, the workload scales, and the subjective preference scales. The following is a brief introduction to the quantity scale used in this experiment:

2.1 System Usability Scale, SUS

SUS is a well-known experimental scale for usability testing (see Table 1). Since its creation by John Brooke (1986) [2], it has been widely used in the rapid test of testing product system interface and website pages. SUS contains a total of ten questions, each of which gives five options (1 strongly disagree, 5 strongly agree). According to about 500 studies in the past, the average SUS score is 68 points. It is generally considered that a system score higher than 68 points is easy to use, and a system score lower than 68 is not easy to use.

Table 1. System usability scale

1. I think that I would like to use this system frequently
2. I found the system unnecessarily complex
3. I thought the system was easy to use
4. I think that I would need the support of a technical person to be able to use this system
5. I found the various functions in this system were well integrated
6. I thought there was too much inconsistency in this system
7. I would imagine that most people would learn to use this system very quickly
8. I found the system very cumbersome to use
9. I felt very confident using the system
10. I needed to learn a lot of things before I could get going with this system

John Brooke [2]

2.2 The NASA Task Load Index, NASA-TLX

NASA-TLX is a widely used perceived workload assessment tool (see Table 2). The rating scale developed by Human Performance Group at NASA's Ames Research Center has more than 4,400 research applications in various fields so far. NASA-TLX contains a total of six subjective subscales, with seven options given to each question (1 is extremely low and 7 is extremely high). Each scale participant has a description, and participants can score on the content of the experiment.

Table 2. NASA-TLX (The NASA Task Load Index)

	Subjective subscales	Description
1	Mental Demand	How much mental and perceptual activity was required? Was the task easy or demanding, simple or complex?
2	Physical Demand	How much physical activity was required? Was the task easy or demanding, slack or strenuous?
3	Temporal Demand	How much time pressure did you feel due to the pace at which the tasks or task elements occurred? Was the pace slow or rapid?
4	Effort	How hard did you have to work (mentally and physically) to accomplish your level of performance?
5	Frustration Level	How irritated, stressed, and annoyed versus content, relaxed, and complacent did you feel during the task?
6	Overall Performance	How successful were you in performing the task? How satisfied were you with your performance?
7	Overall Task Load	Overall Task Load score

3   Method

This study is intended to understand the interactive research on information search efficiency between interface design and viewing mode when viewing across screens (see Fig. 1). Generally, in the interface design of a handheld device, the graphic ratio will affect the efficiency of the user's reading information. When viewing video and audio media on a handheld device, under different viewing modes, its graphic ratio may also affect the user's operating efficiency due to different situations. In other words, how to use a handheld device as a second screen to view audiovisual media, the interface graphic ratio is a very important issue.

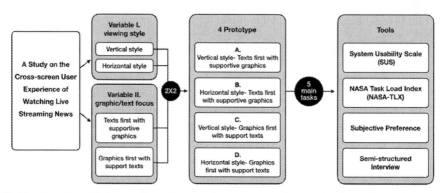

Fig. 1. Experimental design. Note: The experiment is a two-factor mixed experiment design. A total of four prototypes are generated. Each participant will be assigned two different prototypes to perform five main tasks. After each prototype is completed, three scales will need to be filled out.

This study established a series of cross-screen news broadcast scenes and introduced the inter-screen viewing scenarios and follow-up experiments to the participants before the experiment began. Four different handheld device interfaces were created by Proto-io, a Prototype Production Tool, and the iPhone 6S was used as the first screen and the second screen viewing device to provide the participants with simulation and experimental operation.

The design prototype was created through an analogue application and the participants would operate five tasks in the experimental flow. The experiment was a two-factor mixed factorial design, i.e. 2 (viewing style) × 2 (graphic/text focus). A total of four prototypes were created for the experiment. The prototype interface framework contains five pages: the home page, the search page, the live streaming page, the chat room page, and the narrowing of the live streaming page. The page design for both viewing style is shown in Fig. 2 and Fig. 3.

Prototype Interface framework	Vertical style		Horizontal style	
	Texts first with supporti-ve graphics	Graphics first with supportive texts	Texts first with supporti-ve graphics	Graphics first with supportive texts
首頁 Home page	24:76:0	80:20:0	16:72:12	72:18:10
搜尋 Search page	1:46:53	36:24:40	0:49:51	64:29:7
播放頁 Live streaming page	11:59:30	50:20:30	8:30:62	38:0:62
聊天頁 Chat room page	1:69:30	18:52:30	0:20:80	20:0:80
縮小模式 Narrowing of the live streaming page	24:76:0	68:29:3	16:75:9	79:14:7

(Graphic: Texts: Background color)

Fig. 2. Interface design of the experimental prototype. (Note: This study planned the prototype interface according to the grid-scale and experimental design variables. The page design, text, and background color ratios areas above.)

Based on the user interface design, the prototype is combined with live news and simulates the live news (see Fig. 3 below for details) and invites the participants to perform task operations according to the experimental process (see the Experimental procedure below). The main task operation purpose in this study is to sort out the operation process and apply the 3C model of cross-device experience mentioned in the Levin (2014) literature. Reference task 1 refers to the "consistency" method and task 5 refers to "continuity" Approach, and in the final results discussion section focus on the relationship between these two tasks.

Before the experiment officially starts, the experiment introduction and prototype group assignment will be conducted, so that the participants can understand the experimental simulation scene, understand the interaction method and the subsequent method. Because the experimental design is distributed using a two-factor mixed experimental design, each participant will be assigned two different prototype interfaces for segmented operations.

After the start of the formal experiment, the participants will follow the main tasks in steps. During the operation, the researchers will record the operation seconds as reference performance data. After completing the first-stage prototype operation, the participants will fill in the System Usability Scale (SUS), NASA-Task Load Index (NASA-TLX), and subjective preference scale in order, and then proceed to the second-stage prototype operation. After the two-stage prototype operation is completed, a semi-structured interview will be conducted to help the participant recall the prototype characteristics and operation process and to understand the participants' problems and difficulties during the operation through the interview. Participant population data will also be collected before the end of the experiment. We hope to explore the problems of interface interaction through rigorous process design and further propose solutions to improve it.

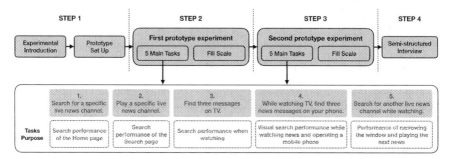

Fig. 3. Experimental procedure. Note: The experimental process will be divided into four steps. At the beginning of the experiment, researchers will explain the main purpose of this study and how it will be performed. Steps two and three will perform five main tasks based on the assigned prototype and fill out the scale. After completion, the researcher will lead the participant to process review and semi-structured interview record.

In this study, the purposeful sampling method was used to invite twelve participants to participate in a cross-screen viewing online news live research, to obtain user needs and improve solutions through experimental design and data collection.

4   Results

In this experiment, a total of twelve participants watched live online news across screens and performed five main tasks, such as finding a specific online live news channel, reducing the screen and playing the next news. Each participant will operate a total of two experimental prototypes, two System Usability Scale (SUS), NASA-Task Load Index (NASA-TLX), and subjective preference scale in two stages to collect subjective feelings of the user's operational interactions. The research results are summarized.

The participants found that there were no significant differences in the use of SUS in the two variables among the four experimental prototypes (P = 0.6 > 0.05). In the experimental sample, the prototype of the straight text master figure auxiliary (M = 64) prototype is less than 68 points, which is insufficient. The MEAN value in descending order is: Vertical style with graphics first with supportive texts (M = 71.5) = Horizontal style with graphics first with supportive texts (M = 71.5) > Horizontal style with texts first with supportive graphics (M = 70.0) > Vertical style with texts first with supportive graphics (*M = 64.0) (see Table 3).

Table 3. Two-way ANOVA Table of SUS

Sources	SS	df	MS	F	P
Viewing style	18.00	1.00	18.00	0.16	0.73
Graphic/text focus	40.50	1.00	40.50	0.88	0.45
Viewing style X graphic/text focus	18.00	1.00	18.00	0.39	0.60

*P < .05

From the Two-way ANOVA Table (see Table 4). of NASA-TLX in "Mental Demand", it was found that the participants considered there was no significant difference between two viewing styles (P = 0.65 > 0.05) and two visual scales (P = 0.50 > 0.05). And also no significant interaction between two variables (P = 0.35 > 0.05). Observe MEAN value from high to low: Horizontal style with graphics first with supportive texts (M = 3.5) > Vertical style with texts first with supportive graphics (M = 2.8) > Vertical style with graphics first with supportive texts (M = 2.7) > Horizontal style with texts first with supportive graphics (M = 2.5).

In "Physical Demand", participants feel no significant difference between two viewing styles (P = 0.63 > 0.05) and in two visual scales (P = 0.41 > 0.05). Also no significant difference between the interactions of the two variables (P = 0.07 > 0.05), which its MEAN value in descending order is: Horizontal style with graphics first with supportive texts (M = 3.0) = Vertical style with texts first with supportive graphics (M = 3.0) > Vertical style with graphics first with supportive texts (M = 2.5) > Horizontal style with texts first with supportive graphics (M = 1.8).

Results in "Temporal Demand", participants considered there was no significant difference between two viewing styles (P = 0.21 > 0.05), but have a significant difference in two visual scales (*P = 0.01 < 0.05) and also in the two variables interactions (*P = 0.01 < 0.05). "Temporal Demand" MEAN value from high to low: Horizontal style with graphics first with supportive texts (M = 5.3) > Vertical style with graphics first with supportive texts (M = 2.4) > Vertical style with texts first with supportive graphics (M = 2.2) > Horizontal style with texts first with supportive graphics (M = 1.3).

With "Effort" result shown that participants concluded that there was no significant difference between the two viewing styles (P = 0.39 > 0.05) and that there was no significant difference between the two visual scales (P = 0.32 > 0.05) and also no significant difference between the interaction of the two variables (P = 0.84 > 0.05). Which MEAN value in descending order is: Horizontal style with texts first with supportive graphics (M = 3.8) > Vertical style with texts first with supportive graphics (M = 3.5) > Horizontal style with graphics first with supportive texts (M = 3.0) > Vertical style with graphics first with supportive texts (M = 2.3).

The participants in the "Frustration Level" concluded that there was no significant difference between the two viewing styles (P = 0.72 > 0.05) and that there was no

Table 4. Two-way ANOVA Table of NASA-TLX

	Sources	SS	df	MS	F	P
1. Mental Demand	Viewing style	0.30	1.00	0.30	0.22	0.65
	Graphic/text focus	0.83	1.00	0.83	0.50	0.50
	Viewing style X graphic/text focus	1.63	1.00	1.63	0.97	0.35
2. Physical Demand	Viewing style	0.67	1.00	0.67	0.25	0.63
	Graphic/text focus	0.67	1.00	0.67	0.74	0.41
	Viewing style X graphic/text focus	3.94	1.00	3.94	4.35	0.07
3. Temporal Demand	Viewing style	4.00	1.00	4.00	2.01	0.21
	Graphic/text focus	16.54	1.00	16.54	18.38	*0.01
	Viewing style X graphic/text focus	13.54	1.00	13.54	15.04	*0.01
4. Effort	Viewing style	1.41	1.00	1.41	0.82	0.39
	Graphic/text focus	5.21	1.00	5.21	1.13	0.32
	Viewing style X graphic/text focus	0.21	1.00	0.21	0.05	0.84
5. Frustration Level	Viewing style	0.20	1.00	0.20	0.14	0.72
	Graphic/text focus	0.20	1.00	0.20	0.33	0.58
	Viewing style X graphic/text focus	5.00	1.00	5.00	8.33	*0.02
6. Overall Performance	Viewing style	1.34	1.00	1.34	2.30	0.17
	Graphic/text focus	1.60	1.00	1.60	0.98	0.36
	Viewing style X graphic/text focus	1.60	1.00	1.60	0.98	0.36
7. Overall Task Load	Viewing style	0.53	1.00	0.53	0.29	0.60
	Graphic/text focus	4.80	1.00	4.80	12.80	*0.01
	Viewing style X graphic/text focus	4.80	1.00	4.80	12.80	*0.01

*P < .05

significant difference between the two visual scales (P = 0.58 > 0.05). And there was a significant difference between the interaction of the two variables (*P = 0.02 < 0.05). The MEAN value from high to low: Vertical style with texts first with supportive graphics (M = 2.8) > Horizontal style with graphics first with supportive texts (M = 2.4) > Horizontal style with texts first with supportive graphics (M = 1.6) = Vertical style with graphics first with supportive texts (M = 1.6).

In "Overall Performance", participants considered that there was no significant difference between two viewing styles (P = 0.17 > 0.05), and there was no significant difference between the two visual scales (P = 0.36 > 0.05). There was also no significant difference between the variable interactions (P = 0.36 > 0.05). The overall MEAN value in descending order is: Horizontal style with texts first with supportive graphics (M = 5.4) > Vertical style with texts first with supportive graphics (M = 4.3) = Vertical style with graphics first with supportive texts (M = 4.3) > Horizontal style with graphics first with supportive texts (M = 4.2).

Finally, the participants in "Overall Task Load" think that there was no significant difference between the two viewing styles (P = 0.60 > 0.05) and that there was a significant difference between the two visual scales (*P = 0.01 < 0.05) and there was also a significant difference between the interaction of the two variables (*P = 0.01 < 0.05). The MEAN value from high to low: Horizontal style with graphics first with supportive texts (M = 3.5) > Vertical style with texts first with supportive graphics (M = 2.8) = Vertical style with graphics first with supportive texts (M = 2.8) > Horizontal style with texts first with supportive graphics (M = 1.5).

From the "Subjective Preference" analysis of Two-way ANOVA Table (see Table 5), it shows that the participants concluded that there was no significant difference between the two viewing styles (P = 0.86 > 0.05) and no significant difference between the two visual scales (P = 0.17 > 0.05) and also no significant difference between the interaction of the two variables (P = 0.17 > 0.05). With MEAN value in descending order is Horizontal style with texts first with supportive graphics (M = 5.5) > Vertical style with texts first with supportive graphics (M = 5.0) = Vertical style with graphics first with supportive texts (M = 5.0) > Horizontal style with graphics first with supportive texts (M = 4.3).

Table 5. Two-way ANOVA Table of subjective preferences

Sources	SS	df	MS	F	P
Viewing style	0.04	1.00	0.04	0.03	0.86
graphic/text focus	2.04	1.00	2.04	2.17	0.17
Viewing style X graphic/text focus	2.04	1.00	2.04	2.17	0.17

*P < .05

From the Two-way ANOVA Table of the Information search performance in Task 1 (see Table 6), it was found that the participants considered there was no significant difference between two viewing styles (P = 0.25 > 0.05) and two visual scales (P = 0.81 > 0.05). And also no significant interaction between two variables (P = 0.81 > 0.05). Observe MEAN value from high to low: Vertical style with texts first with supportive graphics (M = 5.75) = Vertical style with graphics first with supportive texts (M = 5.75) > Horizontal style with texts first with supportive graphics (M = 5.00) > Horizontal style with graphics first with supportive texts (M = 4.25).

In the Information search performance in Task 5, it was found that the participants considered there was a significant difference between two viewing styles (*P = 0.04 < 0.05). But no significant difference between two visual scales (P = 0.17 > 0.05), also no significant interaction between two variables (P = 0.39 > 0.05). Observe MEAN value

Table 6. Two-way ANOVA Table of the Information search performance

	Sources	SS	df	MS	F	P
Task 1	Viewing style	5.06	1.00	5.06	1.61	0.25
	graphic/text focus	0.56	1.00	0.56	0.06	0.81
	Viewing style X graphic/text focus	0.56	1.00	0.56	0.06	0.81
Task 5	Viewing style	108.48	1.00	108.48	2.52	*0.04
	graphic/text focus	39.05	1.00	39.05	0.91	0.17
	Viewing style X graphic/text focus	315.08	10.00			0.39

*P < .05

from high to low: Horizontal style with texts first with supportive graphics (M = 21.67) > Horizontal style with graphics first with supportive texts (M = 12.67) > Vertical style with texts first with supportive graphics (M = 11.5) > Vertical style with graphics first with supportive texts (M = 9.25).

5 Discussions

During this study, users were required to perform five tasks in the two designated prototypes, fill in the scoring scale after each operation, and conduct semi-structured interviews as the reference basis for interpreting the data after the completion of all experiments.

From this study by SUS, it seems that in the two viewing styles, the graphics first with supportive texts average score of is 71.5 (higher than the SUS standard score which is 68 points), followed by the texts first with supportive graphics in the horizontal style. Finally comes to the usability score assisted by the texts first with supportive graphics in the vertical style was the lowest. It is estimated that in some interviews with the participants, graphics first with supportive texts assisted in the two viewing styles, the video page operation experience will be richer, and it is easier to immerse in the context of cross-screen viewing. The horizontal style with texts first with supportive graphics is more usable than vertical style with texts first with supportive graphics. Which can be estimated by participants that the layout assisted by the vertical style is more difficult to search the text information, and also feel more crowded in vertical style with texts first with supportive graphics.

Comparing the NASA-TLX results with the participant's interview response found out that the results of "Mental Demand" may be compared with the participants looking for information in a horizontal style. The main text of the picture is because the screen size and channel picture are horizontal. The amount of information is small, and the operation of sliding up and down affects the load on psychological perception. When looking for information in a straight view, the leading figure of the author, because of the large amount of information, caused a sizable psychological perception load on the text reading.

The result of the "Physical Demand" was to estimate that the participants had more information about the text during direct viewing and therefore more action was required to be. The cross-sectional aspect of the participant was that the participant's action during the cross-section was more burdened by the fact that the participant was unable to determine when the required information would appear.

The result of "Temporal Demand" was to estimate that the information on the graphics first with supportive texts was relatively trivial and the information was more likely to cause visual disturbances under vertical observation. And when the picture was more significant, so the time burden was higher than the other. During horizontal viewing, participants were limited by the layout of the graphics first with supportive texts. They were not sure when the task information would appear. As a result, the temporal Demand of the horizontal style was much higher.

However, the results of the "Effort" may be more focused and energy-consuming in texts first with supportive graphics when referring to the data search tasks conducted by the participants, regardless of the format (straight/crosswise) of the participant.

The "Frustration Level" results estimated that when participants in vertical viewing with texts first with supportive graphics, they might have more details of the information presented by the Master Diagram, and that it would take time for them to take a closer look. Thus, the participants felt that it was not easy to find the information. In horizontal viewing, when picture take a lot of space, because of the rolling up and down relationship, it is not easy for participants to find the information they need.

The result of "Performance and Satisfaction" was to infer that when the participants referred to vertical viewing with texts first with supportive graphics, the visual search was more demanding and adverse. Therefore, the participants generally expressed a low degree of Self-satisfaction and a low level of Self-evaluation. In horizontal viewing, the participants find out that texts first with supportive graphics can see more information with a glance, and compare to graphics first with supportive texts, texts first with supportive graphics shows relatively more and required less time to look for it. As compared with the fact that the participant was able to see more frequently, the results were satisfactory.

Last, "Overall Task Load", the respondents noted that in vertical viewing it both waste of some attention between two visual scales. In horizontal style, graphics first with supportive texts will be more crowded and limit by layout the information will be cut down. So participants prefer in horizontal viewing with texts first with supportive graphics which can catch the resource at a glance.

The results of the participant's subjective preference interview can be inferred that the participants' subjective preference in vertical viewing is neutral, and there is no particular preference difference in the proportion of text. In the horizontal viewing, the participants preferred the texts first with supportive graphics. Although it was more strenuous under visual searching, they could see the information they needed at a glance. However, it is estimated that the channel picture contains a small amount of text and graphic, that will cause visual disturbances, congestion, and participants were also more likely to overlook important information.

As the second screen is operated as a function to assist the progression of the first screen (TV), the usability of interface will be explored first. The results show that the usability of the graphics first with supportive texts will be higher in both two viewing style. Obviously, the participants still preferred to see the video on the inter-screen viewing. This would allow the audience to blend in with the video. The second reason for this is that the horizontal viewing of the participant is in line with the direction of the eye, and the visual perception is more comfortable. Last, the tools bar for horizontal viewing are concentrated on the left side of the screen and are similar to the gestures used in people's operations.

The task performance part is mainly to segment the cross-screen viewing presentation method. Under task one (consistency), the vertical viewing requires more time to operate, and the horizontal viewing form requires less time. In the horizontal viewing mode, the graphics first with supportive texts can complete the task-one operation more quickly. From the interview, it can be found that when user in the task 1 is synchronized with the second screen, the handheld device is in the horizontal mode like the TV, and the specific viewing experience is more consistent. And the toolbar is easier to find and click when viewing in horizontal style. However, some participants mentioned that in the horizontal viewing with graphics first with supportive texts, the graphic is usually large relatively, that the viewing range of the participant will be limited by the screen size, which may cause the participant to produce more high sense of temporal demand, workload, and led visual screening mechanism larger.

Task 5 in vertical viewing is more straight forward than horizontal viewing. In horizontal style, both visual scales require more time for the participants to operate, meaning that the participants are more effective under vertical viewing. In the direct viewing mode, the Master Literary Supplement can perform task 5 operation more quickly. The conclusion of the interview was to find that the participants generally believed that, the vertical style as a result of the page design, it would be easier to think of the direct film as an interactive area during the interview with a sliding motion to reduce the size of the picture and to look for more individual channels. Contrast horizontal style, since the screenplay is full, it is not easy to think of direct manipulation, and the reduced number of channels is relatively small. It is estimated that the performance of the two viewing modes is different from that of the above.

6   Conclusions and Future Work

Cross-screen viewing is an interactive design based on the application of the TV media base extended to handheld devices. Cross-screen viewing is an interactive design based on the application of the TV media base extended to handheld devices. As this type of interaction has arisen and the number of users has increased, the demand for instant access to information and transmission has rapidly growing. Understanding user needs through relevant contexts, improving user operational processes and experience, and, finally, understanding user preferences is a topic that is eagerly explored in all areas. This study was mainly conducted through contextual and prototype design of cross-screen, followed by investigation of participants' operating habits in different viewing modes, final interface use, and subjective preference. Based on the pilot experiment, conduct two variables (Viewing style, Graphic/text focus) of the experiment was set up. Finally, based on the respondents' questionnaire and the feedback from interviews, the following future design references and suggestions were put forward:

First, the use of context and the level of importance of video content can affect viewing style: Using mobile device as the second screen, vertical viewing mode is more suitable for auxiliary TV (as the first screen) to perform continuously activities other than watching movies. (e.g. interactive chatting, etc.).

Graphics first with supportive texts: Tool bar are not recommended for full image presentation. It is recommended that the user be given a second confirmation when they are not sure whether they understand the graphic correctly.

Last, this experiment revealed that Task 1 (Home Page) The horizontal view with the graphics first with supportive texts is better. The main reason for this is because of the left-hand side of the tool line, which is assumed to be consistent with the direction of the user's eyes and the way we hold it. Task 5 (Narrowing of the live streaming page) has a better performance in vertical style, and may be due to its direction design (comparing to horizontal, full-screen viewing) that can guide users through the movement of sliding gestures.

This study found that the design of the interface affected the viewing style of the handheld device according to the viewing situation, or even the level of interest of the users. Due to the size of the mobile phone, the viewing format will also affect the placement of the functional columns. It is recommended that media productions of cross-screen should consider the platform features that are expected to be broadcast so that their channels become more prominent among competitors. In the end, this study also suggests that future researchers can extend more sophisticated design plans for different program content, context, and interactive content.

References

1. Benbasat, I., Todd, P.: An experimental investigation of interface design alternatives: icon vs. text and direct manipulation vs. menus. Int. J. Man-Mach. Stud. **38**(3), 369–402 (1993)
2. Brooke, J.: System Usability Scale (SUS): a quick-and-dirty method of system evaluation user information. Digital equipment co ltd. 1-7 (1986)
3. Chen, C.H., Chen, S.C.: Effects of 2D wedge design as a wayfinding facilitator in a 3D virtual environment. J. Soc. Inf. Disp. **23**(1), 27–35 (2015)
4. Deng, X., Kahn, B.E., Unnava, H.R., Lee, H.: A "wide" variety: effects of horizontal versus vertical display on assortment processing, perceived variety, and choice. J. Mark. Res. **53**(5), 682–698 (2016)
5. Kari, J., Savolainenb, R.: Relationships between information seeking and context: a qualitative study of Internet searching and the goals of personal development. Library Inf. Sci. Res. **29**(1), 47–69 (2007)
6. Neem, R.C., Dozier, D.M.: Second screen effects: linking multiscreen media use to television engagement and incidental learning. Convergence **23**(2), 214–226 (2017)
7. Norman, D.A.: The Psychology of Everyday Things. Basic Books, New York (2013)
8. Ojanpää, H., Näsänen, R., Kojo, I.: Eye movements in the visual search of word lists. Vis. Res. **42**(12), 1499–1512 (2002)
9. Pavlik, J.V.: Digital Technology and the Future of Broadcasting: Global Perspectives. Routledge, Abingdon (2015)
10. Shin, D.-H.: Defining sociability and social presence in Social TV. Comput. Hum. Behav. **29**(3), 939–947 (2013)
11. Shneiderman, B., Plaisant, C.: Designing the User Interface: Strategies for Effective Human-Computer Interaction. Pearson Education India, New Delhi (2009)

12. Theil, C.A., Hwang, F.: Text or image? Investigating the effects of instruction type on mid-air gesture making with novice older adults. Paper presented at the Proceedings of the 10th Nordic Conference on Human-Computer Interaction (2018)
13. Yang, G.-Z., Dempere-Marco, L., Hu, X.-P., Rowe, A.: Visual search: psychophysical models and practical applications. Image Vis. Comput. **20**(4), 291–305 (2002). https://doi.org/10.1016/S0262-8856(02)00022-7

How Contextual Data Influences User Experience with Scholarly Recommender Systems: An Empirical Framework

Zohreh Dehghani Champiri[1]([✉]), Brian Fisher[1], Loo Chu Kiong[2], and Mahmoud Danaee[2]

[1] School of Interactive Arts and Technology, Simon Fraser University Vancouver, Vancouver, Canada
{z.champiri,bfisher}@sfu.ca
[2] Department of Artificial Intelligence, Faculty of Computer Science and Information Technology, Department of Social and Preventive Medicine, Faculty of Medicine, University of Malaya, Kuala Lumpur, Malaysia
{ckloo.um,mdanaee}@um.edu.my

Abstract. Since the advent of Recommender Systems (RSs), many papers have been published with the majority focusing on creating more accurate algorithms. The more accurate the algorithm is, the better the recommendation is predicted to be for users. Recently, RSs researchers pointed out that the embedding of the recommendation methods in the User Experience (UX) dramatically affects the recommender systems' value to users. This paper proposes a framework to explore how contexts influence UX with Scholarly recommender systems and identifies relevant contexts to be incorporated in the UX. We first review existing models and theories of UX that are most applicable to RSs and identify gaps in existing work. The framework clarifies how contexts can influence UX with SRSs and enriches our conceptual understanding of how contextual information influences UX of scholarly recommender systems. It can serve as a foundation for further theoretical and empirical investigation. An experiment evaluating the user experience is performed using the quantitative method of Partial Least Squares (PLS) Regression and Structural Equation Modeling (SEM) to examine the developed conceptual framework.

Keywords: Scholarly Recommender System · Research paper recommender system · User Experience · Contextual data · Context- aware · User-centric evaluation · Human-computer interaction · User testing · Imperial framework

1 Introduction and Problem Statement

Since the advent of Scholarly Recommender Systems (SRS), more than 200 papers on the topic have been published [1, 2]. Most of this aim to create more effective algorithms that will generate better recommendations for users. Recently, RSs researchers pointed out that the embedding of the recommendations methods in the User Experience (UX)

© Springer Nature Switzerland AG 2020
C. Stephanidis et al. (Eds.): HCII 2020, LNCS 12423, pp. 635–661, 2020.
https://doi.org/10.1007/978-3-030-60114-0_42

dramatically affects the effectiveness of scholarly RSs [3–5]. Because UX is inherently a subjective metric, however, it is extremely difficult to measure without explicitly asking a user how good a recommendation is [6, 7]. UX can be seen as an umbrella term used to stimulate (motivate) research in Human Computer Interaction(HCI) to focus on aspects which are beyond usability and its task-oriented instrumental values [8]. UX proposes that researchers examine the qualitative experience of interacting with a product [9], e.g., a mobile phone [10, 11]. The current ISO (ISO 9241-110:2010 (clause 2.15)) definition on UX focuses on a "person's perception and the responses resulting from the use or anticipated use of a product, system, or service". Kraft [12] described UX as any feelings (positive or negative) that the user experiences while using a product, device, or system. He emphasized that the UX is not about creating the newest and cutting-edge technologies, UX is about creating a product that invokes good feelings in the user. It is indeed the key battleground for all kinds of product in the consumer business market [13]. As it is defined, UX is affected by the nature of human perception and the preconceptions of the individual. Researchers state that factors such as personal and situational characteristics, which are mostly considered as contextual information, affect the user experience [6, 14]. In this paper the authors proposed to improve classical recommender methods by modelling contextual information. This contextual information plays an important role in the recommendation because it can represent the status of people, places, objects, and devices in the environment. It is often assumed that more personalization results in higher levels of UX. In other words, the best UX begins with personalization. This perspective motivates RS researchers to work to deliver the highest possible level of personalization in an attempt to provide the best user experience [7, 15]. While it has been claimed that incorporating contextual information is an effective approach to enhance personalization and consequently user experience with RSs, it is not easy to decide which contextual information must be incorporated into scholarly RSs. Nor is it clear how contextual information influences UX of SRSs. So far, SRS studies have given little attention to user experience with SRSs [11]. To understand and improve the user experience of recommender systems, it is necessary to conduct studies that consider the entire process of how the user experience comes about. Our framework describes how contextual information influences the UX which provides a deeper understanding of how user, environment and system contexts influence the user experience and behaviour through perceived system aspects. It allows for a better understanding of why and how certain aspects of the system result in a better UX and others do not, which helps future user-centric research and development of SRSs. To understand and improve the user experience of recommender systems, it is necessary to conduct studies that consider the entire process of how the user experience comes about. Therefore, this research aims to develop a conceptual framework that describes how contextual information influences the UX, providing a deeper understanding of how user, environment and system contexts influence the user experience and behaviour through perceived system aspects. It will allow for a better understanding of why and how certain aspects of the system result in a better UX and others do not, which supports future user-centric research and development of SRSs. An experiment is performed using the quantitative method of Partial Least Squares (PLS) Regression and Structural Equation Modeling (SEM) to examine the developed conceptual framework.

2 Conceptual Framework Development

For conceptual construction of the framework, five steps are performed as shown in Fig. 1.

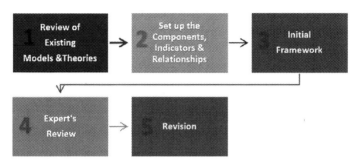

Fig. 1. Conceptual formulation of the framework

2.1 Review of Existing Theories and Models

The main goal of the proposed framework is to present a set of structurally relevant contexts influencing UX of SRSs which can be embedded into both back-end (algorithms) and front- end (user interface) of SRS development in order to enhance the UX. Researchers indicated that UX is a subjective phenomenon. However, its impacts might be reflected by the users' observable behaviors [6]. Since the 1980s, several models and theories have including normative & attitudinal models, UX models, and UX models for RSs been developed to illuminate the interactive experience of using digital technologies [16]. Once researchers discovered that usability does not account for subjective emotions, UX emerged to explain the personal experience when a user is interacting with a product or a system and led to a shift from designing for users to designing with users [17]. This shift mostly brought concepts such as fun [18], pleasure [19], aesthetics [20] and hedonic qualities [8] to our understanding of UX. Some of the models have considered UX as a cognitive process that can be modelled and used to measure or evaluate changes in perception and judgement over time. "Sander's Experience Model" [17, 21] postulates that experience is an intersection of memories of the past, current experience, and future dreams that is felt individually. Sander believes that UX can be involved in the process of design once we have access to people's experiences (past, present and potential) [21]. Over time, the three levels of design theory are also considered as part of cognitive process of UX. This theory was proposed by Don Norman [22], who is most well-known for his advocacy of user-centric design. He discussed that there are three different levels of experience and that these experiences can be triggered by three different levels of design including visceral, behavioral, and reflective. The visceral reaction, immediate and often beyond our control, is the one precipitated by the initial sensory scan of the experience. The limitation and advantage of the relevant existing models have been discussed in Table 1 which also are utilized as a basis for establishment of proposed framework in this study. The key limitation of existing models is that they have not discussed how contextual data affect the UX. This is actually a paradigm shift in RSs research field since researchers in the past have been trying to develop more accurate algorithms but not specifically to enhance user experience [4, 6]. Another key limitation of existing models is that they have neglected in looking into long-term user experiences. UX should not only be something valuable after interacting with an object, but also before and during the interaction. While it is relevant to evaluate short-term experiences, given dynamic changes of user goals and needs related to contextual factors, it is also important to know how (and why) experiences evolve over time.

Besides, in the models that have been proposed specifically for RSs, users' perceptions or beliefs have not been elaborated completely. For example; Pu and Chen's framework [23] relies on a user-centric approach to RS evaluation and links user's perception of quality to the user's beliefs. While user's beliefs are antecedents of their attitudes which are themselves antecedents of behavioral intentions (inspired by TRA), only four indicators of "control", "ease of use", "usefulness" and "transparency" have been considered. We contend that users' perceptions, as perceived by the users, are more than the indicators mentioned in the past models. This framework brought a new approach to user's perception of recommendation quality that becomes the hallmark of this approach compared to the existing frameworks. However, the framework does not explain which factors influence user's perceptions. Perceptions such as visual aesthetics, personalization, and fun that are also very important in user-centric evaluations have long been ignored by the existing models. Bart P. Knijnenburg et al.'s [6] in their Framework disputed that for analyzing the UX of SRs, the accuracy of recommendations is insufficient. Consideration of other aspects also is essential. They advocated an evaluation framework that examines the influence of subjective system aspects such as recommendation and interaction into objective user behaviors such as purchase and personal use. They found that the subjective aspects such as perception of quality, usability and appeal have strong correlation with users' behaviors. In addition, their experiments showed that "why" and "how" subjective system aspects contribute to the user experience of RSs. However, they have not elaborated the subjective system aspects and the relationships with situational characteristics and personal characteristics. Finally, among the existing models and theories, only five models are related to the recommenders and among those three the HRI Model [24, 25] was also examined for the domain of research paper recommenders. The focus of this model is not the impact contexts have on the UX. This is a prominent limitation of this model.

2.2 Set up Components, Indicators and Relationships

Based on our assessment of the limitation of existing models, particularly in the field of RSs, the main components of the framework have been developed.

Derivation of Components. As shown in Table 2, the framework in this research has four main components: context, perception, attitude, feeling and appraisal. They incorporate advantages of current models while compensating for their limitations.

Contexts are taken as a starting point because in most current models contextual factors such as users' background, characteristics, goals, task are the starting point of

Table 1. Advantage and limitation of existing studies

Model/theory	Advantage	Limitation	Reference
TRA, TAM, UTAUT Theories	-Discuss understanding of person's behavior intention -Discuss attitude towards using a technology -Discuss the factors influence acceptance and Use of Technology	-Not discuss the impact of contexts -Not discuss UX -Not discuss UX of RSs -Not examine the results empirically	[26–28]
Sander's Experience Model	-Discuss UX -Discuss explicit, tacit knowledge and, observed experience influencing UX		
Cognitive Process of UX	-Discuss UX -Discuss visceral, behavioral, and reflective	-Not examine the results empirically	[22]
Components of User (CUE) Experience Model	-Discuss UX -Discuss context -Discuss instrumental, non-instrumental and the emotional reactions	-Not discuss the impact of the whole contexts -Not discuss UX of RSs -Not discuss long term impact of UX	[17, 21]
Hartmann et al.'s Model	-Discuss the user interface quality assessment Discuss users' background, goals, and task have an impact on the system assessment as well as decision-making criteria (usability, aesthetics)	-Not examine the results empirically	[29]
Hassenzahl UX Model	-Discuss UX -Discuss pragmatic quality and hedonic quality	-Not discuss the impact of contexts -Not discuss UX of RSs -Not discuss long term impact of UX -Not discuss how contexts influence UX	[8, 29]
Ozok et al.'s	-Discuss RS usability -Discuss the impacts of specific system aspects		[30]

(continued)

Table 1. (*continued*)

Model/theory	Advantage	Limitation	Reference
Zins and Bauernfield's Model	-Discuss traveling RSs -Discuss how user's satisfaction is influenced by trust, flow, and browsing behaviour		[31]
HRI Model	-Discuss UX of SRSs and users' needs -Discuss users' seeking behaviors		[24, 25]
Xiao and Benbasat Framework	-Discuss the business and marketing-oriented research on RSs -Characteristics of RSs influencing users' trust and satisfaction -Discuss personal and situational characteristics		[32]
Pu & Chen's Framework	-Discuss RS evaluation from a user centric viewpoint -Results were examined empirically	-Not discuss the impact of contexts -Not discuss long term impact of UX	[23]
Bart P. Knijnenburg et al.'s Framework	-Discuss UX of RSs -Results were examined empirically	-Not elaborated the subjective system aspects Not elaborated the relationships with situational characteristics and personal characteristics - Not discuss long term impact of UX	[6]

Table 2. Derivation of the components and relationships

Component	Reference	Relationships	Reference
Context	[6, 24, 25, 33]	Context → Perception	[6, 23, 29, 33]
Perception	[6, 23, 33]	Perception → Feeling	[8, 23, 33]
Feeling	[8, 23, 29, 33]	Feeling → Appraisal	[8, 33]
Appraisal	[8, 33]	–	

frameworks for understanding users' perceptions [6, 23, 29, 33]. A few studies in RSs have proposed that incorporating contexts into recommending process can enhance UX [34–36]. Therefore, our research devotes considerable attention to conceptualization user, system and environment contexts and investigation of their impact on the users' perceptions and UX of SRS. Second, based on the [6] and CEU models, contexts affect users' perceptions. Pu and Chen's [23] framework conceptualizes that the user's perception of quality is initiated by recommendation diversity, novelty, accuracy, interaction adequacy, interface adequacy, information sufficiency and transparency. However, Pu and Chen [23] did not discuss context influencing UX. Our research bears much similarity to Pu and Chen's framework, but takes a step back to explore how these quality perceptions originate and a step beyond examine other contextual information. Furthermore, as mentioned before, a key shortcoming of current models is that they have considered only a few perceptions such as "control", "ease of use", "usefulness" and "transparency", while in the literature perception of fun, personalization and visual aesthetics are additional factors. Hassenzahl's UX model emphases consideration of visual aesthetics, a factor that has been ignored in most current models particularly in RSs models. This research takes these perceptions into consideration and aims to evaluate them in a UX study. Third, the TRA, TAM, UTAUT theories have demonstrated that the person's behavioral intention is influenced by attitudinal and normative factors. Based on the aforementioned theories, we differentiate between attitudes and behavioral intention that are created by attitudes in this framework for SRSs. Forth, CUE model, perceptions and attitudes influence emotional reactions or feelings; hence, in the initial proposed framework, feeling is presented after attitudes [19, 37]. Users might feel pleasure during the experience of interaction with the RS. For example, when user revives a good and unexpected recommendation that can meet his/her information need, he/she might feel pleasure. Hassenzahl emphasizes pleasure moments and design for happiness, which embraces both features of a product; functionality and aesthetics [37]. Like Hassenzahl's model, pleasure and trust are considered in this framework. Fifth, according to the TAM, UTAUT, CUE models, people' behaviors and reactions are a product of emotional responses. This is called appraisal in the CUE model. Knijnenburg et al. [6] also revealed that what users' feel about the system impact on the subjective system aspects such as user satisfaction in this way the appraisal component is derived to end up the flow of the proposed framework. Finally, a major shortcoming of existing UX research in the field of RSs is that UX happens over a longer interval and this long-term aspect of UX is largely ignored in the existing models. This framework is also inspired by Norman and Sander's theories whereas the influence of long-term variable is conceptualized as a moderator variable on of users' feeling and appraisal.

Derivation of the Indicators. Each component consists of a few determinants or indicators taken from the literature of RSs. In the following, the derivation components' indicators have been described. Also, each indicator is discussed accordingly. Table 3 shows an overview of the whole indicators. The indicators mostly have been identified using a Systematic Literature Review (SLR) conducted by [11].

As mentioned earlier, the contexts are taken as a starting point for the UX. Considering Dey's definition of context as any information that can be used to characterized the situation of an entity [119], the results of a systematic review by Champiri et al. [11]

Table 3. Derivation of the indicators

Component	Indicators	Ref.	Component	Indicators	Ref.
User Situation (Context)	*Profile*	[11]	Paper Quality (Context)	*Accuracy*	[5, 38]
	Task	[39–45]		*Novelty*	[5, 25, 38, 46, 47]
	Pre-Knowledge	[48–50]		*Popularity*	[5, 51]
	Scholarly network	[52, 53]		*Diversity*	[51, 54, 55]
	Search logs	[43, 56–60]	Interaction Design Adequacy (Context)	*Preference elicitation*	[24, 61, 62]
	Learning style	[63]		*Preference refinement*	[58, 62, 64–66]
	Mood	[59, 67]		*Explanation*	[62, 68–71]
	Personality trait	[5, 72–75]		*Privacy consideration*	[76–81]
	Search Status	[22]	Interface Design Adequacy (Context)	*Visualization*	[82–84]
Environment Situation	*Time*	[85–89]		*Gamification*	[90–92]
	Location	[85–89]		*Consistency*	[93, 94]
				Info. sufficiency	[2, 30, 95]
				Display	[6, 96–99]
				Visualization	[82–84]
Interaction	*Fun*	[94, 100]	Feeling & Attitude	*Trust*	[101–104]
	Transparency	[23, 64, 83]		*Pleasure*	[37]
	Personalization	[105–107]		*Surprise*	[108]
	Usefulness	[30, 111–114]	Appraisal	*Usage*	[28]
	Visual authentic	[27] [62]		*Overall satisfaction*	[23, 115–118]
	Dominance	[4, 84]		*Expectation*	[118]

has revealed that contextual information applied in SRSs has been categorized into three classes: user situation, environment and system contexts. These three categories and their indicators are listed in Table 3. In addition, in this study interaction and interface contexts are considered as system contextual data. Furthermore, most studies have considered accuracy as the main part of resource context or quality while accuracy partially constitutes UX of SRSs and researchers have recommended to apply other features such as diversity, novelty and popularity to make a better list of recommendation and improve UX of RSs [120–122].

Initial Framework. After considering the limitations of existing models particularly in the field of RSs and setting up the component, indicators, relationships, a framework draft has been developed as shown in Fig. 2 that includes component, indicators, and relationships. This framework can inform design and development of new SRSs in which

UX has been centralized. The initial conceptual framework is also validated through the expert review technique explained in the next section.

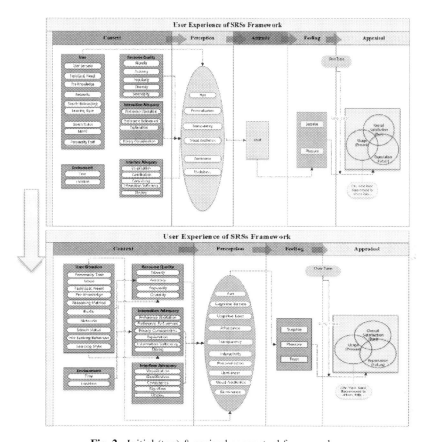

Fig. 2. Initial (top) & revised conceptual framework

Expert Review. The aim of this expert review is designed to validate the proposed conceptual framework, its components, indicators, and relationships and to examine the utility of the terminologies, the logical relevancy of component indicators for each component as well as the relationships. We also examine the usability & readability of the framework to demonstrate how contexts can influence UX of SRSs. The interviews were conducted online, and the experts had knowledge of RSs, SRSs, and HCI. The majority of the experts agreed that the most selected terminologies were sufficiently clear. They recommended that two terminologies "Info Seeking Behavior" and "Overall Feeling" should be replaced with "Search history (logs)" and "feeling". All experts agreed that two components, "Attitude" and "Feeling", should be merged into a single component. Consequently, "trust", "pleasure" and "surprise" were moved into the "overall feeling" component. In analysis of logic relevancy of indicators four experts recommended that "Information Sufficiency" be moved under the "IxD" component because it refers to a piece of information about the recommendations that users would like to see once recommendations are presented to them. It was recommended that this be categorized under the "IxD". According to the reviewers' recommendations the indicator of "Serendipity" should be removed because the indicator of "Novelty" is more appropriate to explain the paper quality. The experts also recommended a few indicators be added into the components which do not trace back to the literature of RSs shown in Table 4. The experts pointed out that there are interrelationships between the contexts that should be added to the initial framework such as the impact of user context on the interaction interface adequacy and paper quality. There may be additional relationships between some of the indicators, for example, signifier might influence affordance, however such relationships

Table 4. New indicators recommended by reviewers

Component	New indicator	Description/justification
User Context	*Reasoning methods*	Each person applies the exiting knowledge for making judgements, predictions, and explanations or drawing conclusions which are reasoning methods including deductive, inductive, and abductive
IxD Adequacy	*Dialog*	Dialog design is to yield closure to prevent users to think much or guess what to do or what is the next action. The dialogue make the system fool-proof as possible using messaging box, flags, and icons
UiD Adequacy	*Signifier*	Signifiers are communication signs/signals that tell users what this object for and help users to understand what to do and where to do it, what is happening and what is the alternative
Perception	*Interactivity*	It is about building systems and platforms that allows interaction between product/service and its users. It aims to build meaningful relationships between people and the product/services they use
	Affordance	If users perceive affordance, it means that the UI design's clues or identifiers are visually clear enough to guide users what to do. Some of the studies in the field of RS have used term of "Ease of Use" which is defined as "the degree to which a person believes that using a certain system would be free of effort"
	Cognitive barrier	If something temporary put a stop to users' actions required to complete in order to gain their goal, it called cognitive barrier. The less the user perceives cognitive barriers, the more they have a better experience
	Cognitiveload	It is about the amount of the required memory being used by the working memory of the user to achieve his goal. The less cognitive load is the more the pleasure is

are not examined in this research to avoid increasing framework complexity. The usability and readability of the framework, and. the ease of framework understanding were acceptable by the experts.

Revised Conceptual Framework. Before the empirical examination, the framework was reviewed by five experts in the field. After applying the comments and recommendation of the experts, the framework was revised as depicted in Fig. 2. It is important to mention that the time (context) can characterize different situations. For example, it might represent the time a user spends to receive recommendations which influence UX, in this case time is considered as a systemic context not environmental context [123]. Moreover, there are other factors such as accessibility of recommendations. For examples, in most systems, recommendations are free, however some SRSs such as Mendeley provides paper recommendations only as a premium service [123] which is unappealing for many users. Also, the impact of the accessibility of recommendations was excluded from this research. As indicated earlier, this is assumed that the perceptions mediate the impact of contexts on users' feelings. In this framework, context influences user's perceptions and there are interrelationships between the contexts.

3   Empirical Examination and Results

In this section, it is examined that if the proposed conceptual framework is empirically valid. To do so, we use the quantitative method of PLS-SEM. This method is a predictive technique [124] and useful for exploratory research objectives [125] where theory is less developed [126] and for studying phenomena that are relatively new [127]. In addition, it helps to estimate relationship models with latent variables which are mostly subjective and not directly measurable. Also, a few pre- processing assumptions such as large sample size and normality have been avoided in this method [128, 129]. This method also can be considered as one of the useful methods for data or dimension reduction to reduce the complexity and ambiguity in the system [130] which helps SRSs researches which context or indicator is more important. As illustrated in Fig. 3, five multi-stage processes have been applied. A summary of the stages is discussed in the following.

3.1   Identification of Hypotheses

The hypotheses examine the impacts of contexts on users' perception (H_1-H_{11}), perception on users' feelings (H_{12}), feeling on users' appraisal (H_{12}) and finally the impact of long- term variable on the users' appraisal (H_{14}).

3.2   Model Specification (Inner and Outer Models)

Based on the PLS-SEM method guidelines [128], the second step is modulation or model specification made of two sub-models of structural model (inner model) and measurement model (outer model) (Fig. 4). The structural model displays the relationships (paths) between the constructs or latent variables. The measurement models display the relationships between the latent variables and indicators (measurable variables) [131].

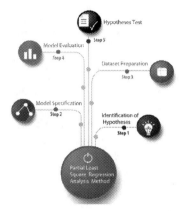

Fig. 3. Empirical examination procedures

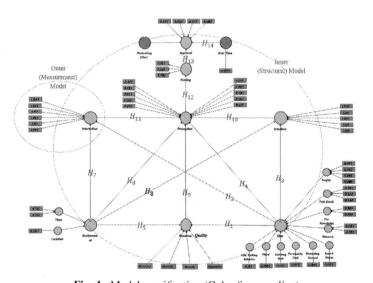

Fig. 4. Model specification (Color figure online)

As Fig. 4 depicts, user, resource, environment, interface, and interaction contexts along with the perception, feeling and appraisal compose the latent constructs that build up the structural or inner model (Grey circles and relationships between them). Each of constructs along with its indicators (Green rectangular) establishes measurement or outer model (Grey circle and green rectangular). The pink circles show the impact of moderator variable of "over time" on the relationships between "feeling" and "appraisal" variables. The hypothesized relationships also have been shown.

3.3 Dataset Preparation

Before evaluating the validity of proposed model and examining the research hypotheses, the preparation of the adequate dataset is required. A few activities discussed in the following sections have been performed to prepare the dataset.

Measurement of Latent Variables: Questionnaire. Generally, for meaning the conceptual variable (latent variable), there are two methods. One is to use existing measurement scales from the literature if there are and the other is to create new measures. To decide the best scale for each of our latent variables, a thorough literature review of existing measurement scales was conducted. The past studies of Pu and Chen [62] and Knijnenburg et al. [6] provided extensive questionnaires to test several concepts related to UX of RSs. The scales which are like this research are utilized. However, because the scales are for a scholarly RS domain and UX is highly contingent upon the purpose of the system [6], the necessary wording modifications were made to the original scales to suit them to the measurement needs of this study without affecting the original conceptual bases of such scales. In addition, past studies mostly do not include latent variables of contexts therefore in this study, these scales were developed. In this research, most of the second ordered constructs such as learning style, reasoning method are measured by single scales. The reason of measuring them by a single scale because of preventing too many questions which make participants to quit the survey however for all the single scales, the question is clarified by presenting a few examples or specification. For validity and consistency examination of the measuring tool (questionnaire), through a panel of experts, Pre-test (face validity and Content validity (Q-Sorting)) and Pilot-test (Test-retest) have been performed for measuring the reliability, respectively. Pre-test examine the validity of the test instrument or measuring tool.

After pre-test, the validity of indicators empirically was examined and, a few scales were developed that need to be validated. Two validities have been performed; 1. Face validity [132] that can be examined by the expert interviews and 2. Content validity by using user card sorting exercises (also called Q-Sorting) [133, 134]. The results of face validity showed that all indicators found to be relevant and valid. Some indicators or statements, however, needed some language improvements. Such improvements were made, and all indicators were taken to the next stage of the scale development process. The Q- sorting was used to double-check the validity of the initial conceptual classification of the pre- prepared statements using participants' feedback and to discover any wording or language issues that made a misunderstanding for participants.

The aim of the Pilot-test is to examine the consistency of the test instrument. The test-retest reliability was performed by running the questionnaire twice over a period of two weeks by the 15 scholarly participants including PhD, Master Students, post-doc researcher and lecturers who already accepted to participate two times. Correlation coefficient (Spearman's rho) was applied and tested the reliability of all indicators. Table 5 summarizes the results of Spearman's rho test.

According to the results all correlation coefficients were above 0.7 which indicates that all indicators can be reliable and there is no confusing or correlated item. After examining the validity and consistency of the indicators, a web application was developed which enables the scholarly participants (PhD, Master Students, post-doc

Table 5. Correlation between test and re-test survey for all indicators

Indicator	r	Indicator	r	Indicator	r	Indicator	r
Q-AC1	0.783	U-SS1	0.938	U-PR1	0.950	I-CO1	0.919
Q-AC2	0.811	U-MO1	0.890	U-PR2	0.883	I-VI1	0.955
Q-PO1	0.826	U-PT1	0.944	U-PR3	0.930	I-GA1	0.902
Q-PO2	0.793	U-RM1	0.985	U-PR4	0.725	I-SI1	0.954
Q-PO3	0.813	U-LS1	0.970	U-PK1	0.822	I-DI1	0.950
Q-PO4	0.883	U-IS1	0.951	U-PK2	0.902	P-CB1	0.906
Q-NO1	0.843	E-TI1	0.977	U-TA1	0.865	P-AF1	0.922
Q-NO2	0.874	E-TI2	0.980	U-TA2	0.888	P-CL1	0.909
Q-NO3	0.871	E-LO1	0.700	U-TA3	0.964	P-PR1	0.943
Q-NO4	0.726	I-PE1	0.712	P-FU1	0.895	F-PL1	0.862
Q-DI1	0.870	I-PR1	0.777	P-IN1	0.853	F-TR1	0.859
Q-DI2	0.926	I-EX1	0.948	P-US1	0.896	A-SA1	0.867
Q-DI3	0.911	I-IS1	0.912	P-VI1	0.849	A-EX1	0.897
U-NE1	0.841	I-PI1	0.909	P-TR1	0.884	A-US1	0.983
U-NE2	0.879	I-DA1	0.938	P-DO1	0.854	A-US2	0.986

researcher and lecturers) to express their feedbacks in 5-point Likert scale ranging from 1 (strongly disagree) to 5 (strongly agree). The bachelor students in this examination were excluded because it was assumed that under-graduate students are not seriously involved in research and scholarly tasks such as finding appropriate papers. The Questionnaire went live for 6 months and a total of 177 useful responses were received and the dataset was prepared to be used in Smart-PLS tool.

3.4 Model Evaluation

The model evaluation consists of two experiments of 1) The assessment of the measurement (outer) model, 2) The assessment of the (inner) structural model. According to [128], the outer model is examined by two metrics of Variance Inflation Factor (VIF) and Outer Weights (OWs) for formative constructs. The results of the VIF for the constructs after running the PLS algorithm, were all lower than 10 which indicates the absence of multicollinearity in the indicators. The Outer Weights (OWs) are checked to examine the significance and relevance of indicators using bootstrapping of 3000 sample data. The OWs should be different from zero (p-value < 0.05; T-values > 1.96). However, if the OWs is different from zero but p-value $\geq$ 0.05, in such cases, as suggested by [128, 130, 135], the Outer Loadings(OLs) should be checked for the particular indicators to see if they pass a minimum threshold of 0.5 (OL > 0.5). If they pass, the indicators should be retained in the analysis otherwise the item is retained but it is interpreted as absolutely important and not as relatively important. If the item is not significant neither the OW nor OL, the researcher should decide whether to retain or remove the indicator by examining its theoretical relevance and potential content overlap with other indicators of the same construct [130]. Table 6 shows the results of significance relevance of indicators by representing of OWs and OLs which meet the above-mentioned thresholds (Significant level: 95%). A high indicator weight suggests that the indicator is making a significant contribution to the formative latent variable.

Two metrics were applied to assess the structural model including Coefficient of determination (R^2) and Effect size (f^2) [130]. The R^2 of the dependent variables indicate that the variance of UX of SRSs is explained substantially only by the effect of user context (Fig. 5).

R2 explains how much of the variability of a factor (latent or dependent variable) can be influenced by its relationship to another factor (independent variable). Overall, R2 values of 0.75, 0.50, or 0.25 for dependent variables are viewed as substantial, moderate, or weak [13].

Table 6. Significance & relevance assessment of indicators

Indicator	P (OW)	P- (OL)	Indicator	P (OW)	P (OL)	Indicator	P (OW)	P (OL)
E.TI2	0.033	0.001	x.EX1	0.005	0.001	P.VI1	0.001	0.186
I.DI1	0.008	0.001	P.AF1	0.031	0.485	P.IN1	0.016	0.027
I.CO1	0.014	0.001	P.FU1	0.038	0.000	F.SU1	0.001	0.001
I.VI1	0.001	0.001	X.DA1	0.029	0.000	F.PL1	0.005	0.001
I.GA1	0.011	0.001	P.CB1	0.009	0.458	F.TR1	0.002	0.001
I.SI1	0.021	0.001	P.CL1	0.035	0.000	A.EX1	0.029	0.071
X.PE1	0.031	0.001	P.TR1	0.012	0.000	A.SA1	0.031	0.065
X.PR1	0.002	0.000	P.DO1	0.057	0.000	A.US1	0.002	0.055
X.PI1	0.003	0.001	P.PR1	0.045	0.000	A.US2	0.002	0.005
X.IS1	0.014	0.000	P.US1	0.001	0.000			

Effect size (f^2) is an important tool in reporting and interpreting the impact of a construct on another one. The values of 0.35, 0.15, and 0.02 signify respectively large, medium, and small effects. f^2 values of less than 0.02 indicate that there is no effect. Based on the f^2 values, the smallest effects are between the environment context and other constructs which means that environment changes such as location, time might not be influence on the interaction adequacy, interface adequacy and user's perception however the environment changes may impact on resource quality which includes novelty, accuracy, diversity and popularity of a paper in this research. For example, the academic time can impact on the recommended paper. Also, there is a small correlation between the overtime construct (moderating variable) and appraisal. As mentioned before, f^2 does not necessarily mean that the change in one variable is the cause of the change in the values of the other variable. The following constructs have obtained the large effect

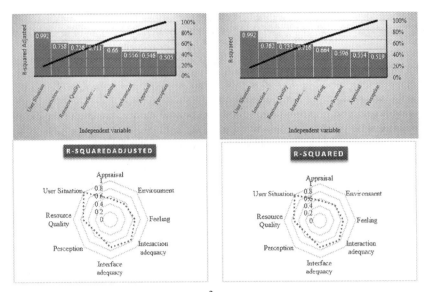

Fig. 5. R2s and adjusted R^2s of the independent variables

and the correlations between the user's context and resource quality is the largest effect.

Largest f^2 = [(ρ (U, Q), 0.376), (ρ (U, I),0.351), (ρ (U, X),0.356), (ρ (Q, P), 0.375),(ρ (P,F), 0.354)), (ρ (P,F,A), 0.371)), (ρ (F, A), 0.374)]

3.5 Hypothesis Testing (β Test)

To examine the hypothesized relationships between the constructs, the path coefficients (β) are assessed which have standardized values of linear regression weights between -1 and $+1$ [130]. Estimated path coefficients close to $+1$ represent strong positive relationships (and vice versa for negative values) that are almost always statistically significant (p-value < 0.05; T-values > 1.96) [130]. The closer the estimated coefficients are to 0, the weaker the relationships are (normal data distribution). In other words, very low values close to 0 are usually none-significant. The data are normal, and Fig. 6 shows a sample of normal data distribution for contexts.

The obtained path coefficients (p-value < 0.05; T-values > 1.96) examined the relationships between the constructs. Among the hypothesized relationships, all relationships were found statistically significant other than the relationship of the Moderating Effect (over time) $\rightarrow$ Appraisal (p-value = 0.201) which is discussed in the next section (Table 7). The results also revealed that the strongest relationships are between the constructs listed below.

$User_{context}$ → Resource $_{quality}$ 0.790
$User_{context}$ → IxD $_{adequacy}$ 0.788
$User_{context}$ → UiD $_{adequacy}$ 0.786
Resource $_{Quality}$ →Perception   0.760

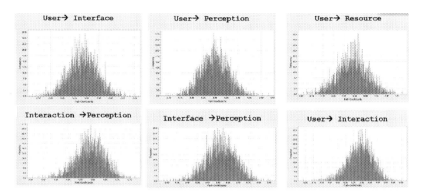

Fig. 6. Normal distribution samples

Table 7. Significance & relevance assessment of indicators

Constructs	P-value	+→	Hypo. Testing	Constructs	P-value	+→	Hypo. testing
$E \rightarrow X$	0.000	Weak	Supported	$O \rightarrow A$	**0.201**	–	**N-Supported**
$E \rightarrow I$	0.000	Weak	Supported	$P \rightarrow F$	0.000	Strong	Supported
$E \rightarrow P$	0.022	Weak	Supported	$U \rightarrow X$	0.000	Strong	Supported
$E \rightarrow Q$	0.037	Moderate	Supported	$U \rightarrow I$	0.000	Strong	Supported
$F \rightarrow A$	0.000	Moderate	Supported	$U \rightarrow P$	0.354	Moderate	Supported
$X \rightarrow P$	0.002	Moderate	Supported	$U \rightarrow Q$	0.000	Strong	Supported
$I \rightarrow P$	0.005	Moderate	Supported	$Q \rightarrow P$	0.003	Strong	Supported

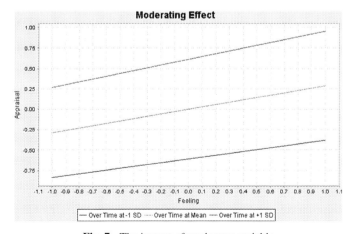

Fig. 7. The impact of moderator variable

As mentioned above, the results of path coefficients showed that the moderating effect indicator (over time) does not surpass the minimum threshold of p-value (p-value overtime $= 0.201$) which means that there is not statistically significant relationship between this construct and overall appraisal (Fig. 7).

As discussed earlier, researchers have emphasized that the UX is not built one night. The users' appraisal of SRSs might be changed over the time and it is not stable. Therefore, from the conceptual viewpoint, there must be a relationship between these two constructs. However, the empirical results revealed no relationship. One main reason might be that the ratings collected in this research, were provided by the users not while experiencing the paper recommendations but by imagining the situation and providing judgments. Hence, the impact of "over time" construct has not been assessed significant.

4   Discussion: Advantages of the Proposed Framework

In this section, the advantages of the proposed framework are discussed and at the end a few recommendations for the future studies is proposed.

4.1   Decipher of Context and UX in SRSs Research Using Empirical Method

UX is becoming the key competitive factor in more and more industries [13]. Users demand products that are not only easy to use but also joyful and fun to use. UX is affected by contexts, and is subjective, which can cause difficulties for researchers [6, 11]. The lack of understanding of the subjective concepts not only leads to more complexity in the system but also causes the system failure from the end user's perspective. Our framework bridges the user's contexts with the system contexts and provides finer insights into both back-end (recommending feature algorithms) and front-end (User Interface) of RSs development from a UX design perspective.

4.2   Insights on User Interface and Interaction Design Adequacy in SRSs

It is worth mentioning that no matter how accurate the algorithms are, if the UI and interaction design are poorly designed and evaluated, this will degrade the interaction between the user and system in a way that users might find the system intrusive, annoying or distracting, and perceive it as a factor that negatively affects their experience [30]. Based on the results, display (I. DI1, 0.396), consistency (I. CO1, 0.387) and gamification (I.GA1, 0.374) have the highest weights among the UiD's indicators. And for the IxD construct, the preference elicitation, refinement, and privacy consideration have received the highest weights in contribution to the IxD the formative latent variable. $IxD_{weight}= [(X.PE1, 0.526), (X.PR1, 0.529), (X.PI1, 0.553), (X.IS1, 0.460), (X.DA1, 0.132), (X.EX1, 0.298).$

4.3   Detection of the Most Relevant Contexts

Due to the issues of the impact of irrelevant contexts, it is necessary to estimate and analyze the impact of contextual information on UX before actually collecting and exploiting it in the recommending process [136]. Figure 8 shows the relevant contexts.

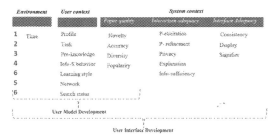

Fig. 8. The most relevant contexts

The R2s of the dependent variables indicated that the variance of UX of SRSs is explained substantially only by the effect of User $_{context}$ variable. In addition, based on the outputs of Outer Weights (OWs), among the indicators of one construct, the indicator which have more weight is relevant for the construction of the formative index demonstrates a sufficient level of validity. Among the user context construct, respectively profile (PR_Mean, 0.901), task (TA_Mean, 0.685), learning style (LS_Mean, 0.664), pre-knowledge (PK_Mean, 0.561) and, information seeking behavior have obtained the highest weights which confirm that they have a significant contribution to the formation of user contexts for a SRS. U$_{weight}$= [(PR_Mean, 0.901), (TA_Mean, 0.685), (LS_Mean, 0.664), (PK_Mean, 0.561), (IS, 0.460)]. Also, between time (TI_Mean, 0.430) and location (E.LO1, 0.052) for the environment context, time is more relevant for the construction of the formative the environment context and demonstrates a sufficient level of validity. Although the weight of location is low but the value of 0.52 still surpasses the threshold. Therefore, it is not removed. Additionally, the results of f^2 test showed that the following constructs have obtained the large effect and among them, the correlations between the user's context and resource quality is the largest effect. Largest effects = [(ρ (U, Q), 0.376), (ρ (U, I),0.351), (ρ (U, X),0.356), (ρ (Q, P), 0.375),(ρ (P,F), 0.354)), (ρ (P,F,A), 0.371)), (ρ (F, A), 0.374)]

4.4 Insights on Appropriate Paper Recommending List

Paper quality or appropriate paper refers to the attributes that each paper must be matched with a specific scholar. Researchers argued that apart from the accuracy, other qualities such as diversity, novelty and popularity of the recommended papers are also important for the users [137–139]. This framework emphasis on developing algorithms that can generate a list of appropriate papers. Among the paper quality context constructs, novelty (NO_Mean, 0.574) and diversity (DI_Mean, 0.563) have more weights. Q$_{weight}$= [(AC_Mean, 0.388), (DI_Mean, 0.563), (NO_Mean, 0.574), (PO_Mean, 0.336)].

4.5 The Importance of Affordance, Fun, Cognitive Barriers & Surprise in SRSs

Among the perception indicators, the highest weight respectively belongs to affordance (P.AF1, 0.398), fun (P.FU1, 0.385) and, cognitive barrier (P.CB1, 0.361 can be considered for the SRSs development. Surprise refers to the feeling of receiving useful and unexpected recommendation [108, 109]. Recommending the novel papers might make feeling of surprise for the users [110]. The surprise feeling is considered as an indicator to measure the impact of overall feeling which should be provided in SRSs development.

5 Recommendation for the Future

Development of this framework continues existing lines of research that aim to better understand the UX of SRSs and does not stop here. Here is some recommendation for the future studies.

- Exploit contextual information in recommending: Among the identified contextual information, this research has not incorporated contexts such as users' reasoning method, mood, academic social network as well as personality traits. Therefore, future studies are encouraged to consider the above-mentioned contexts in developing systems for recommending papers.
- Extension of the proposed framework: The framework proposed in this research is a specialised framework as it allows SRSs designers and researchers to target contexts associated with users' experience while they are working with the SRSs. The details of the framework components can further be enriched so that it can be utilised and evaluated for various domains. The details may include investigation of all the users' perceptions related to the identified contexts. For example, how contexts can be influential in providing fun for the users of SRSs.
- Identification of users' needs in long term: Meeting of the user's information need is the main contribution of a good scholarly recommender. Users have different information needs due to different knowledge, preferences, goals, and contexts. In this research, the user model aimed to diagnose the users' information needs, however, the problem is that the identification of users' information is not an easy task and needs better understanding of the users' information needs not only when they are working with the system but also before and after that. Therefore, it requires monitoring the users' needs in a long term in order to provide good service and recommend adequate items.

References

1. Beel, J., et al.: Research paper recommender system evaluation: a quantitative literature survey. In: Proceedings of the International Workshop on Reproducibility and Replication in Recommender Systems Evaluation. ACM (2013)
2. Beel, J., et al.: Paper recommender systems: a literature survey. Int. J. Digit. Libraries 17(4), 305–338 (2016)

3. McNee, S.M., Riedl, J., Konstan, J.A.: Being accurate is not enough: how accuracy metrics have hurt recommender systems. In: CHI 2006 Extended Abstracts on Human Factors in Computing Systems. ACM (2006)

4. Konstan, J.A., Riedl, J.: Recommender systems: from algorithms to user experience. User Model. User-Adapt. Interact. **22**(1), 101–123 (2012)

5. Nguyen, T.: Enhancing user experience with recommender systems beyond prediction accuracies. Ph.D Dissertation, The University of Minnesota (2016)

6. Knijnenburg, B.P., et al.: Explaining the user experience of recommender systems. User Model. User-Adapt. Interact. **22**(4–5), 441–504 (2012)

7. Champiri, Z.D., et al.: User experience and recommender systems. In: 2019 2nd International Conference on Computing, Mathematics and Engineering Technologies (iCoMET). IEEE (2019)

8. Hassenzahl, M., Tractinsky, N.: User experience-a research agenda. Behav. Inf. Technol. **25**(2), 91–97 (2006)

9. McCarthy, J., Wright, P.: Technology as experience. Interactions **11**(5), 42–43 (2004)

10. Law, E.L.-C., et al.: Understanding, scoping and defining user experience: a survey approach. In: Proceedings of the SIGCHI Conference on Human Factors in Computing Systems. ACM (2009)

11. Champiri, Z.D., Shahamiri, S.R., Salim, S.S.B.: A systematic review of scholar context-aware recommender systems. Expert Syst. Appl. **42**(3), 1743–1758 (2015)

12. Kraft, C.: User Experience Innovation: User Centered Design that Works. Apress, New York (2012)

13. Bernhaupt, R.: Evaluating User Experience in Games: Concepts and Methods, p. 277. Springer, London (2010). https://doi.org/10.1007/978-1-84882-963-3

14. Dehghani Champiri, Z., Asemi, A., Siti Salwah Binti, S.: Meta-analysis of evaluation methods and metrics used in context-aware scholarly recommender systems. Knowl. Inf. Syst. **61**(2), 1147–1178 (2019). https://doi.org/10.1007/s10115-018-1324-5

15. Champiri, Z., Salim, S.S., Shahamiri, S.R.: The role of context for recommendations in digital libraries. Int. J. Soc. Sci. Humanity **5**(11), 948–954 (2015)

16. Hart, J.: Investigating user experience and user engagement for design (2015)

17. Visser, F.S., et al.: Contextmapping: experiences from practice. CoDesign **1**(2), 119–149 (2005)

18. Monk, A., et al.: Funology: designing enjoyment. In: CHI 2002 Extended Abstracts on Human Factors in Computing Systems. ACM (2002)

19. Green, W.S., Jordan, P.W.: Pleasure with Products: Beyond Usability. CRC Press, Boca Raton (2003)

20. Tractinsky, N., Katz, A.S., Ikar, D.: What is beautiful is usable. Interact. Comput. **13**(2), 127–145 (2000)

21. Sanders, E.B.-N., From user-centered to participatory design approaches. In: Design and the Social Sciences: Making Connections, vol. 1, no. 8 (2002)

22. Norman, D.: The Design of Everyday Things, Revised and expanded edition edn. Basic Books, New York (2013)

23. Pu, P., Chen, L., Hu, R.: A user-centric evaluation framework for recommender systems. In: Proceedings of the Fifth ACM Conference on Recommender Systems. ACM (2011)

24. Mcnee, S.M.: Meeting user information needs in recommender systems. Proquest (2006)

25. McNee, S.M., Riedl, J., Konstan, J.A.: Making recommendations better: an analytic model for human-recommender interaction. In: CHI 2006 Extended Abstracts on Human Factors in Computing Systems. ACM (2006)

26. Fishbein, M., Ajzen, L.: Belief, Attitude, Intention and Behavior: An Introduction to Theory and Research, pp. 181–202. Addison-Wesley, Reading (1975)

27. Davis, F.D., Bagozzi, R.P., Warshaw, P.R.: User acceptance of computer technology: a comparison of two theoretical models. Manag. Sci. **35**(8), 982–1003 (1989)
28. Venkatesh, V., et al.: User acceptance of information technology: toward a unified view. MIS Q. **27**, 425–478 (2003)
29. Hartmann, J., Sutcliffe, A., Angeli, A.D.: Towards a theory of user judgment of aesthetics and user interface quality. ACM Trans. Comput.-Hum. Interact. (TOCHI) **15**(4), 15 (2008)
30. Ozok, A.A., Fan, Q., Norcio, A.F.: Design guidelines for effective recommender system interfaces based on a usability criteria conceptual model: results from a college student population. Behav. Inf. Technol. **29**(1), 57–83 (2010)
31. Bauernfeind, U., Zins, A.H.: The perception of exploratory browsing and trust with recommender websites. Inf. Technol. Tour. **8**(2), 121–136 (2005)
32. Xiao, B., Benbasat, I.: E-commerce product recommendation agents: use, characteristics, and impact. MIS Q. **31**(1), 137–209 (2007)
33. Thüring, M., Mahlke, S.: Usability, aesthetics and emotions in human–technology interaction. Int. J. Psychol. **42**(4), 253–264 (2007)
34. Adomavicius, G., Tuzhilin, A.: Context-aware recommender systems. In: Ricci, F., Rokach, L., Shapira, B., Kantor, P.B. (eds.) Recommender Systems Handbook, pp. 217–253. Springer, Boston, MA (2011). https://doi.org/10.1007/978-0-387-85820-3_7
35. Panniello, U., Gorgoglione, M.: Context-aware recommender systems: a comparison of three approaches. In: DART@ AI* IA (2011)
36. Baltrunas, L., et al.: Context relevance assessment and exploitation in mobile recommender systems. Pers. Ubiquitous Comput. **16**(5), 507–526 (2012)
37. Hassenzahl, M., et al.: Designing moments of meaning and pleasure. Exp. Des. Happiness Int. J. Des. **7**(3), 21–31 (2013)
38. Felfernig, A., Burke, R., Pu, P.: Preface to the special issue on user interfaces for recommender systems. User Model. User-Adapted Interact. **22**(4), 313–316 (2012)
39. Kuo, J.-J., Zhang, Y.-J.: A library recommender system using interest change over time and matrix clustering. In: Chen, H.-H., Chowdhury, G. (eds.) ICADL 2012. LNCS, vol. 7634, pp. 259–268. Springer, Heidelberg (2012). https://doi.org/10.1007/978-3-642-34752-8_32
40. McNee, S.M., Kapoor, N., Konstan, J.A.: Don't look stupid: avoiding pitfalls when recommending research papers. In: Proceedings of the 2006 20th Anniversary Conference on Computer Supported Cooperative Work. ACM (2006)
41. Marko A., Rodriguez, D.W.A., Shinavier, J., Ebersole, G.: A recommender system to support the scholarly communication process. CoRR abs/0905.1594 (2009)
42. Konstan, J.A., et al.: Techlens: Exploring the use of recommenders to support users of digital libraries. In: CNI Fall Task Force Meeting Project Briefing. Coalition for Networked Information, Phoenix, AZ (2005)
43. Dehghani, Z., et al.: A multi-layer contextual model for recommender systems in digital libraries. In: Aslib Proceedings, vol. 63, no. 6, pp. 555–569 (2011)
44. Patton, R., Potok, T., Worley, B.: Discovery & refinement of scientific information via a recommender system. In: The Second International Conference on Advanced Communications and Computation INFOCOMP 2012 (2012)
45. Rodriguez, M.A., et al.: A recommender system to support the scholarly communication process. arXiv preprint arXiv:0905.1594 (2009)
46. Rana, C.: New dimensions of temporal serendipity and temporal novelty in recommender system. Adv. Appl. Sci. Res. **4**(1), 151–157 (2013)
47. Adamopoulos, P., Tuzhilin, A.: On unexpectedness in recommender systems: or how to better expect the unexpected. ACM Trans. Intell. Syst. Technol. (TIST) **5**(4), 54 (2015)
48. Strangman, N., Hall, T.: Background knowledge. National Center on Assessing the General Curriculum, Wakefield, MA, vol. 26, p. 2005 (2004). Accessed Sept 2004

49. Amini, B., et al.: Incorporating scholar's background knowledge into recommender system for digital libraries. In: 2011 5th Malaysian Conference in Software Engineering (MySEC). IEEE (2011)
50. McNee, S.M., et al.: On the recommending of citations for research papers. In: Proceedings of the 2002 ACM Conference on Computer Supported Cooperative Work. ACM (2002)
51. Jannach, D., Lerche, L., Gedikli, F., Bonnin, G.: What recommenders recommend – an analysis of accuracy, popularity, and sales diversity effects. In: Carberry, S., Weibelzahl, S., Micarelli, A., Semeraro, G. (eds.) UMAP 2013. LNCS, vol. 7899, pp. 25–37. Springer, Heidelberg (2013). https://doi.org/10.1007/978-3-642-38844-6_3
52. Serrano-Guerrero, J., et al.: A Google wave-based fuzzy recommender system to disseminate information in University Digital Libraries 2.0. Inf. Sci. **181**(9), 1503–1516 (2011)
53. Yang, W.-S., Lin, Y.-R.: A task-focused literature recommender system for digital libraries. Online Inf. Rev. **37**(4), 581–601 (2013)
54. Tsai, C.-H.: An interactive and interpretable interface for diversity in recommender systems. In: Proceedings of the 22nd International Conference on Intelligent User Interfaces Companion, pp. 225–228. ACM, Limassol and Cyprus (2017)
55. Adomavicius, G., Kwon, Y.: Maximizing aggregate recommendation diversity: a graph-theoretic approach. In: Proceedings of the 1st International Workshop on Novelty and Diversity in Recommender Systems (DiveRS 2011) (2011)
56. Hwang, S.-Y.H., Hsiung, W.C., Yang, W.S.: A prototype WWW literature recommendation system for digital libraries. Online Inf. Rev. **27**(3), 169–182 (2003)
57. Tsuji, K., et al.: Use of library loan records for book recommendation. In: 2012 IIAI International Conference on Advanced Applied Informatics (IIAIAAI). IEEE (2012)
58. Middleton, S.E., Shadbolt, N.R., De Roure, D.C.: Ontological user profiling in recommender systems. ACM Trans. Inf. Syst. (TOIS) **22**(1), 54–88 (2004)
59. Jung, S., et al.: SERF: integrating human recommendations with search. In Proceedings of the Thirteenth ACM International Conference on Information and Knowledge Management ACM (2004)
60. Yoshikane, F., Itsumura, H.: Book recommendation based on library loan records and bibliographic information. Procedia-Soc. Behav. Sci. **147**, 478–486 (2013)
61. Pommeranz, A., et al.: Designing interfaces for explicit preference elicitation: a user-centered investigation of preference representation and elicitation process. User Model. User-Adapted Interact. **22**(4–5), 357–397 (2012)
62. Pu, P., Chen, L., Hu, R.: Evaluating recommender systems from the user's perspective: survey of the state of the art. User Model. User-Adapted Interact. **22**(4–5), 317–355 (2012)
63. Dunn, R., Beaudry, J.S., Klavas, A.: Survey of research on learning styles. California J. Sci. Educ. **2**(2), 75–98 (2002)
64. Swearingen, K., Sinha, R.: Interaction design for recommender systems. In: Designing Interactive Systems (2002)
65. Kelly, D., Fu, X.: Elicitation of term relevance feedback: an investigation of term source and context. In: Proceedings of the 29th Annual International ACM SIGIR Conference on Research and Development in Information Retrieval. ACM (2006)
66. Beel, J., et al.: Research paper recommender system evaluation, pp. 15–22 (2013)
67. Herlocker, J., Jung, S., Webster, J.G.: Collaborative filtering for digital libraries (2012)
68. Felfernig, A., Burke, R.: Constraint-based recommender systems: technologies and research issues. In: Proceedings of the 10th International Conference on Electronic Commerce. ACM (2008)
69. Herlocker, J.L., et al.: Evaluating collaborative filtering recommender systems. ACM Trans. Inf. Syst. (TOIS) **22**(1), 5–53 (2004)
70. Sinha, R., Swearingen, K.: The role of transparency in recommender systems. In: CHI 2002 Extended Abstracts on Human Factors in Computing Systems. ACM (2002)

71. Beel, J., Langer, S., Nürnberger, A., Genzmehr, M.: The impact of demographics (age and gender) and other user-characteristics on evaluating recommender systems. In: Aalberg, T., Papatheodorou, C., Dobreva, M., Tsakonas, G., Farrugia, C.J. (eds.) TPDL 2013. LNCS, vol. 8092, pp. 396–400. Springer, Heidelberg (2013). https://doi.org/10.1007/978-3-642-40501-3_45

72. Gosling, S.D., Rentfrow, P.J., Swann, W.B.: A very brief measure of the big-five personality domains. J. Res. Pers. **37**(6), 504–528 (2003)

73. McCrae, R.R., Costa, P.T.: Validation of the five-factor model of personality across instruments and observers. J. Pers. Soc. Psychol. **52**(1), 81 (1987)

74. Kraaykamp, G., Van Eijck, K.: Personality, media preferences, and cultural participation. Pers. Individ. Differ. **38**(7), 1675–1688 (2005)

75. Rentfrow, P.J., Gosling, S.D.: The do re mi's of everyday life: the structure and personality correlates of music preferences. J. Pers. Soc. Psychol. **84**(6), 1236 (2003)

76. Resnick, P., Varian, H.R.: Recommender systems. Commun. ACM **40**(3), 56–58 (1997)

77. Ackerman, M.S., Mainwaring, S.D.: Privacy issues and human-computer interaction. Computer **27**(5), 19–26 (2005)

78. Knijnenburg, B.P., Willemsen, M.C.: The effect of preference elicitation methods on the user experience of a recommender system. In: CHI 2010 Extended Abstracts on Human Factors in Computing Systems. ACM (2010)

79. Tinschert, J., et al.: Fracture Resistance of Lithium Disilicate–, Alumina-, and Zirconia-based three-unit fixed partial dentures: a laboratory study. Int. J. Prosthodontics **14**(3), 231–238 (2001)

80. Bollen, J., Van de Sompel, H.: An architecture for the aggregation and analysis of scholarly usage data. In: Proceedings of the 6th ACM/IEEE-CS Joint Conference on Digital Libraries. ACM (2006)

81. Geyer-Schulz, A., Neumann, A., Thede, A.: An architecture for behavior-based library recommender systems. Inf. Technol. Libraries **22**(4), 165–174 (2003)

82. Hiesel, P., et al.: A user interface concept for context-aware recommender systems. Mensch und Computer 2016-Tagungsband (2016)

83. Murphy-Hill, E., Murphy, G.C.: Recommendation delivery. In: Robillard, M.P., Maalej, W., Walker, R.J., Zimmermann, T. (eds.) Recommendation Systems in Software Engineering, pp. 223–242. Springer, Heidelberg (2014). https://doi.org/10.1007/978-3-642-45135-5_9

84. di Sciascio, C.: Advanced user interfaces and hybrid recommendations for exploratory search. In: Proceedings of the 22nd International Conference on Intelligent User Interfaces Companion. ACM (2017)

85. Luo, J., et al.: A context-aware personalized resource recommendation for pervasive learning. Cluster Comput. **13**(2), 213–239 (2010)

86. Chen, C.M., Yang, Y.C.: An intelligent mobile location-aware book recommendation system with map-based guidance that enhances problem-based learning in libraries. In: Zeng, Z., Wang, J. (eds.) Advances in Neural Network Research and Applications. LNEE, vol. 67, pp. 853–860. Springer, Heidelberg (2010). https://doi.org/10.1007/978-3-642-12990-2_99

87. Biancalana, C., et al.: An approach to social recommendation for context-aware mobile services. ACM Trans. Intell. Syst. Technol. **4**(1), 1–31 (2013)

88. Gómez, S., et al.: Context-aware adaptive and personalized mobile learning delivery supported by UoLmP. J. King Saud Univ. – Comput. Inf. Sci. **26**(1), 47–61 (2014)

89. Li, Q.C., Dong, Z.-H., Li, T.: Research of information recommendation system based on reading behaviour. In: Proceedings of the Seventh International Conference on Machine Learning and Cybernetics, Kunming (2008)

90. Feil, S., et al.: Using gamification to tackle the cold-start problem in recommender systems. In: Proceedings of the 19th ACM Conference on Computer Supported Cooperative Work and Social Computing Companion. ACM (2016)

91. de Ziesemer, C.A., Müller, L., Silveira, M.S.: Just rate it! gamification as part of recommendation. In: Kurosu, M. (ed.) HCI 2014. LNCS, vol. 8512, pp. 786–796. Springer, Cham (2014). https://doi.org/10.1007/978-3-319-07227-2_75
92. Hussain, J., Khan, W.A., Afzal, M., Hussain, M., Kang, B.H., Lee, S.: Adaptive user interface and user experience based authoring tool for recommendation systems. In: Hervás, R., Lee, S., Nugent, C., Bravo, J. (eds.) UCAmI 2014. LNCS, vol. 8867, pp. 136–142. Springer, Cham (2014). https://doi.org/10.1007/978-3-319-13102-3_24
93. Nielsen, J.: 10 usability heuristics for user interface design. Nielsen Norman Group, Fremont [Consult. 20 maio 2014]. Disponível na Internet (1995)
94. Shneiderman, B.: Designing for fun: how can we design user interfaces to be more fun? Interactions 11(5), 48–50 (2004)
95. Farooq, U., et al.: Design and evaluation of awareness mechanisms in CiteSeer. Inf. Process. Manag. 44(2), 596–612 (2008)
96. Garrett, J.J.: Elements of User Experience, The User-Centered Design for the Web and Beyond. Pearson Education, London (2010)
97. Swearingen, K., Sinha, R.: Beyond algorithms: an HCI perspective on recommender systems. In: ACM SIGIR 2001 Workshop on Recommender Systems (2001)
98. Rim, R., Amin, M.M., Adel, M.: Bayesian networks for user modeling: predicting the user's preferences. In: 2013 13th International Conference on Hybrid Intelligent Systems (HIS). IEEE (2013)
99. Chen, L., Tsoi, H.K.: Users' decision behavior in recommender interfaces: impact of layout design. In: RecSys 2011 Workshop on Human Decision Making in Recommender Systems (2011)
100. Malone, T.W.: What makes things fun to learn? A study of intrinsically motivating computer games. Pipeline 6(2), 50 (1981)
101. Viriyakattiyaporn, P., Murphy, G.C.: Challenges in the user interface design of an IDE tool recommender. In: Proceedings of the 2009 ICSE Workshop on Cooperative and Human Aspects on Software Engineering. IEEE Computer Society (2009)
102. Montaner Rigall, M.: Collaborative recommender agents based on case-based reasoning and trust. Universitat de Girona (2003)
103. Panniello, U., Gorgoglione, M., Tuzhilin, A.: In CARSWe trust: how context-aware recommendations affect customers' trust and other business performance measures of recommender systems (2015)
104. Lim, B.Y.: Improving understanding and trust with intelligibility in context-aware applications. Oregon State University (2012)
105. Neves, A.R.M., Carvalho, Á.M.G., Ralha, C.G.: Agent-based architecture for context-aware and personalized event recommendation. Expert Syst. Appl. 41(2), 563–573 (2014)
106. Luo, J., et al.: A context-aware personalized resource recommendation for pervasive learning. Cluster Comput. 13(2), 213–239 (2009)
107. Joonseok Lee, K.L., Kim, J.G.: Personalized academic research paper recommendation system. arXiv preprint arXiv:1304.5457 (2013)
108. Kaminskas, M., Bridge, D.: Measuring surprise in recommender systems/serendipity. In: Proceedings of the Workshop on Recommender Systems Evaluation: Dimensions and Design (Workshop Programme of the 8th ACM Conference on Recommender Systems) (2014)
109. Reisenzein, R.: The subjective experience of surprise. In: The Message Within: The Role of Subjective Experience in Social Cognition and Behavior, pp. 262–279 (2000)
110. Kaminskas, M., Bridge, D.: Measuring surprise in recommender systems. In: Proceedings of the Workshop on Recommender Systems Evaluation: Dimensions and Design (Workshop Programme of the 8th ACM Conference on Recommender Systems) (2014)
111. Cyr, D., Head, M., Ivanov, A.: Design aesthetics leading to m-loyalty in mobile commerce. Inf. Manag. 43(8), 950–963 (2006)

112. Deaton, M.: The elements of user experience: user-centered design for the Web. Interactions **10**(5), 49–51 (2003)
113. Hekkert, P.: Design aesthetics: principles of pleasure in design. Psychol. Sci. **48**(2), 157 (2006)
114. Karvonen, K.: The beauty of simplicity. In: Proceedings on the 2000 Conference on Universal Usability. ACM (2000)
115. Anderson, J.C., Narus, J.A.: A model of distributor firm and manufacturer firm working partnerships. J. Market. **54**, 42–58 (1990)
116. Storbacka, K., Strandvik, T., Grönroos, C.: Managing customer relationships for profit: the dynamics of relationship quality. Int. J. Serv. Ind. Manag. **5**(5), 21–38 (1994)
117. Seddon, P., Kiew, M.-Y.: A partial test and development of DeLone and McLean's model of IS success. Australas. J. Inf. Syst. **4**(1) (1996)
118. Keiningham, T.L., Perkins-Munn, T., Evans, H.: The impact of customer satisfaction on share-of-wallet in a business-to-business environment. J. Serv. Res. **6**(1), 37–50 (2003)
119. Dey, A.K.: Understanding and using context. Pers. Ubiquitous Comput. **5**(1), 4–7 (2001)
120. McCay-Peet, L., Toms, E.: Measuring the dimensions of serendipity in digital environments. Inf. Res.: Int. Electron. J. **16**(n3), 6 (2011)
121. Kotkov, D., Veijalainen, J., Wang, S.: Challenges of serendipity in recommender systems. In: WEBIST 2016: Proceedings of the 12th International Conference on Web Information Systems and Technologies, vol. 2. SCITEPRESS (2016). ISBN 978-989-758-186-1
122. Kotkov, D., Wang, S., Veijalainen, J.: A survey of serendipity in recommender systems. Knowl.-Based Syst. **111**, 180–192 (2016)
123. Beel, J., Langer, S.: A comparison of offline evaluations, online evaluations, and user studies in the context of research paper recommender systems (2014, Under Review, Pre-print). http://www.docear.org/publications
124. Pratley, A., van Voorthuysen, E., Chan, R.: A step-by-step approach for modelling complex systems with Partial Least Squares. Proc. Inst. Mech. Eng. Part B: J. Eng. Manuf. **229**, 847–859 (2014)
125. Hulland, J.: Use of partial least squares (PLS) in strategic management research: a review of four recent studies. Strateg. Manag. J. **20**(2), 195–204 (1999)
126. Henseler, J., et al.: Common beliefs and reality about PLS comments on Rönkkö and Evermann. Org. Res. Methods **17**, 182–209 (2014)
127. Sharma, P.N., Kim, K.H.: Model selection in information systems research using partial least squares based structural equation modeling (2012)
128. Hair Jr., J.F., et al.: Partial least squares structural equation modeling (PLS-SEM) an emerging tool in business research. Eur. Bus. Rev. **26**(2), 106–121 (2014)
129. Urbach, N., Ahlemann, F.: Structural equation modeling in information systems research using partial least squares. J. Inf. Technol. Theory Appl. **11**(2), 5–40 (2010)
130. Hair, J.F., Ringle, C.M., Sarstedt, M.: The use of partial least squares (PLS) to address marketing management topics. J. Market. Theory Pract. **19**(2), 135–138 (2011)
131. Vinzi, V., et al.: Handbook of Partial Least Squares. Springer, Heidelberg (2010). https://doi.org/10.1007/978-3-540-32827-8
132. Lewis, B.R., Templeton, G.F., Byrd, T.A.: A methodology for construct development in MIS research. Eur. J. Inf. Syst. **14**(4), 388–400 (2005)
133. Moore, G.C., Benbasat, I.: Development of an instrument to measure the perceptions of adopting an information technology innovation. Inf. Syst. Res. **2**(3), 192–222 (1991)
134. Stephenson, W.: The Study of Behavior. Q-Technique and its Methodology. Chicago University Press, Chicago (1953)
135. Hair, J.F., Ringle, C.M., Sarstedt, M.: Editorial-partial least squares structural equation modeling: rigorous applications, better results and higher acceptance. Long Range Plann. **46**(1–2), 1–12 (2013)

136. Rubens, N., Kaplan, D., Sugiyama, M.: Active learning in recommender systems. In: Ricci, F., Rokach, L., Shapira, B., Kantor, P.B. (eds.) Recommender Systems Handbook, pp. 735–767. Springer, Boston (2011). https://doi.org/10.1007/978-0-387-85820-3_23
137. Hurley, N.J.: Robustness of recommender systems. In: Proceedings of the Fifth ACM Conference on Recommender Systems. ACM (2011)
138. Sridharan, S.: Introducing serendipity in recommender systems through collaborative methods (2014)
139. Adamopoulos, P., Tuzhilin, A.: On unexpectedness in recommender systems: or how to expect the unexpected. In: Workshop on Novelty and Diversity in Recommender Systems (DiveRS 2011), at the 5th ACM International Conference on Recommender Systems (RecSys' 11). ACM, Chicago (2011)

rScholar: An Interactive Contextual User Interface to Enhance UX of Scholarly Recommender Systems

Zohreh Dehghani Champiri[1](✉), Brian Fisher[1](✉), and Luanne Freund[2](✉)

[1] School of Interactive Arts and Technology, Simon Fraser University, Vancouver, Canada
{z.champiri,bfisher}@sfu.ca
[2] School of Information, University of British Columbia, Vancouver, Canada
luanne.freund@ubc.ca

Abstract. Scholarly recommender systems attempt to reduce the number of research resources or papers presented to scholars and predict the utility of resources for their scholarly tasks. Industry practitioners and academic researchers agree that the interface of a recommender system may have as profound an effect on users' experience as the recommender's algorithmic performance. Despite this, little attention has been given to User Interface and Interaction Design of scholarly recommender systems. Scholarly recommender systems rarely use contextual data, such as personal and situational characteristics, that can dramatically affect the user experience (UX) and effectiveness of SRSs. This research presents rScholar, a scholarly recommender system interface that utilizes User Interface and Interaction Design adequacy indicators as well as the user contextual data to enhance the user experience. The evaluation of rScholar is performed by user studies and expert review of feedback by users and by comparison to the UI of the recommendation display of Google Scholar.

Keywords: Scholarly recommender systems · Research paper recommender systems · User experience · User interface · User experience · Context-Aware · Contextual data · Human-Computer interaction

1 Introduction

Scholarly recommender systems (SRSs) attempt to reduce the number of research resources or papers on a topic and predict the utility of new resources that can assist scholars with their scholarly tasks [1, 2]. Development of RSs can be divided into two parts: the back-end that decides what to recommend, and the front-end that delivers the recommendation [3]. Both industry practitioners and academic researchers argue that the interface of a RS may have as profound an effect on users' experience with the recommender as can the recommender's algorithmic performance [4]. According to the RecSys09 keynote by Francisco Martin, up to 50% of the value of recommenders comes from a well-designed interface [5]. However, there is little attention given to User Interface (UiD) and Interaction Design (IxD) of SRSs. This might derive from the fact

C. Stephanidis et al. (Eds.): HCII 2020, LNCS 12423, pp. 662–686, 2020.
https://doi.org/10.1007/978-3-030-60114-0_43

that they have been mostly implemented as a backend component of digital libraries, reference management tools, and bibliographic databases [6]. Despite this, RSs are considered to be one of the critical components of e-commerce websites such as Amazon and e-Bay [7]. In addition, SRSs have not been developed with an eye to using contextual data such as personal and situational characteristics, but rather have been heavily topic and content focused. Such characteristics can dramatically affect the user experience (UX) and effectiveness of SRSs [8]. This paper presents rScholar (recommendations for Scholars) that considers UiD and IxD adequacy indicators as well as user contextual data in order to enhance the UX. The evaluation of rScholar is carried out through user studies and in comparison, with the recommendation UI of Google Scholar.

1.1 Why Do UiD and IxD Matter?

Some researchers have suggested that, regardless of the accuracy of recommendation algorithms, a poor UiD and IxD can degrade the interaction between the users and a system such that users find the system intrusive, annoying or distracting, thereby negatively affecting their experience [9]. For example, the recommendation algorithm might perform well and retrieve an appropriate set of novel and accurate recommendations for a target user. If the delivery of those recommendations is not well designed [5], users may be confused and unable to find the connections between their needs and the recommendation set, reducing system acceptance [8–10]. Contextual information is also critical for the application of probabilistic User Models [10] which can establish a link between user actions, contexts and system events and synchronise the interaction in a way that users experience positive feelings when they interact with the system [11, 12]. Effective UiD and IxD indicators might also be used to help users visually understand the logic behind the recommendations (algorithm functionality) and the usefulness of these recommendations. Design of the interface and selection of items to be presented to users for rating can reduce the "new user problem" in RSs [13]. Therefore, the quality of UiD and IxD can have a critical and decisive effect on users' perceptions and experiences of SRSs.

2 The UI Development Process

Figure 1 depicts the five steps of the rScholar design process, which are inspired by the design principles introduced by Saffer [14]. These principles emphasize IxD adequacy by improving the interactions between or among humans and UI affordances. The steps of the design process for rScholar are described in the sections to follow.

2.1 User Research

In the User research phase, UiD and IxD guidelines are reviewed to identify use requirements. While general webpage design guidelines can be applied to RSs, it should be noted that the RS is a component of the page that is strongly related to the item (e.g. the paper) that is delivered to the user rather than other content of the Web page. The impact of recommender UIs on user behavior has been discussed in various studies and have

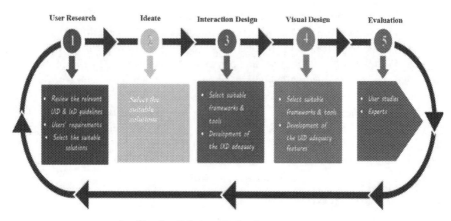

Fig. 1. rScholar: UI development steps

resulted in a few design guidelines and rules. The applicability of these guidelines to specific RS components have rarely been tested empirically [15, 16]. Ozok et al. [9] and Pu and Chen (2011) provide an in-depth analysis of common design pitfalls when developing UIs for preference elicitation, preference revision, page layout and explanation. Felfernig et al. (2006) analyze the impact of different recommender UI functionalities such as explanations, product comparison pages, and repair actions on factors such as perceived increase of domain knowledge, increase of usability and trust. In another study, Felfernig et al. [9] analyze different preference elicitation interfaces through three user studies. The results are four design guidelines for preference elicitation interfaces: (1) users willing to spend more effort in preference elicitation should be able to do so; (2) affective feedback interfaces (e.g., in terms of so-called affect buttons) should be considered as a means of detailed preference feedback; (3) interfaces should be designed to support exploration, where the consequences of preference shifts are easily visible; and (4) preference elicitation processes should rely on initial system preference suggestions, rather than starting from scratch.. Table 1 presents an overview of features identified in the design rules and guidelines reported in several RSs studies.

Some detailed user studies of contextual data were conducted as part of this stage and reported in [27, 28]. The most relevant contextual data were identified as research interest, research interests, learning style, task, and pre-knowledge. Also, Pu and Chen's framework conceptualizes that the user's perception of recommendation quality is initiated by recommendation diversity, novelty, accuracy [29]. Moreover, other researchers argued that apart from the accuracy, other qualities such as diversity, novelty and popularity of the recommended papers are also important for the users [30–32]. In regard to UiD and IxD design, the results of the studies conducted by [10, 15, 16] have revealed that the major UiD indicators are display, consistency, and signifier and the IxD indicators are pre-elicitation, pre- refinement, privacy, explanation, and information-sufficiency. Therefore the main UI requirements are to find efficient mechanisms to 1) obtain user's data (user context) 2) to obtain the environment's data (environment context) 3) to display four paper recommendation displays of diverse, novel and popular and accurate papers 4) meet the UiD adequacy (system context) 5) meet IxD adequacy (system context).

Table 1. Design rules and guidelines for the RSs

Study Title	Feature											
	PE	PR	IS	SC	DN	EX	RL	RD	PC	PL	NA	*Ref*
Beyond algorithms: An HCI perspective on recommender systems				✓						✓	✓	[17, 18]
Evaluating recommender systems from the user's perspective: survey of the state of the art	✓	✓	✓		✓	✓	✓	✓		✓		[19]
Design guidelines for effective recommender system interfaces based on a usability criteria conceptual model: results from a college student population			✓	✓	✓	✓	✓	✓		✓	✓	[9]
Advanced user interfaces & hybrid recommendations for exploratory search						✓					✓	[20]
Adaptive user interface and user experience based authoring tool for recommendation systems	✓											[21]
The effect of preference elicitation methods on the user experience of a recommender system				✓		✓		✓	✓			[22]
Interaction design for recommender systems	✓	✓	✓			✓				✓	✓	[18]
Interfaces for eliciting new user preferences in recommender systems					✓	✓						[23]
Is seeing believing? how recommender system interfaces affect users' opinions	✓							✓				[24]
Recommendation delivery	✓									✓	✓	[3]
Recommender systems: from algorithms to user experience		✓					✓			✓	✓	[25]
User interface patterns in recommendation-empowered content intensive multimedia applications				✓		✓				✓	✓	[26]

(*continued*)

Table 1. (*continued*)

Study Title	Feature											
	PE	PR	IS	SC	DN	EX	RL	RD	PC	PL	NA	*Ref*

Preference Elicitation = PE; Preference Refinement = PR; Information Sufficiently = IS;
Size & Composition of recommendation sets = SC; Dialog & Natural Language = DN;
Explanation = EX; Recommendation Label = RL; Recommendation Display = RD; Privacy
Consideration = PC; Signifier = SI; Page Layout = PL; Navigation = NA

2.2 UI Ideate

Considering the above requirements, user profile-based design not only makes rScholar
serve as a scholarly search engine and a recommender but also as a scholarly personal
web page which allows the scholars to share their scholarly profile and upload their
CVs. This follows findings from a major review of SRs [19], guideline #9, to emphasize
specific goals of users to motivate them to contribute. Table 2 presents the final eighteen
selected design elements applied in order to meet these requirements.

2.3 rScholar Interaction and Visual Design Development

In this section we describe how interaction and visual design was conducted to meet
the requirements in the previous section. Once the user logs in (Fig. 2), a home page
(Fig. 3) that has been designed based on the user profile and personalised for each user
is presented. In this page, the user is able to submit their academic information such
as name, major, contact number etc. as well as social media accounts and upload their
photo (Oval 1: Fig. 3). The user is able to submit their research interests and areas
of expertise, with a maximum of 10 allowed inputs per user [33]. The sliders can be
applied to rate the degree of his/her knowledge from a range of 0 to 100% (Oval 2:
Fig. 3). The user can input profile information such as learning style, task, and current
academic semester (Oval 3: Fig. 3). Navigation through different pages (discussed later)
in enabled via the menu bar, including homepage, profile, privacy setting and about
rScholar and the page layout (list and pie) can be changed through the menu bar (Oval 5:

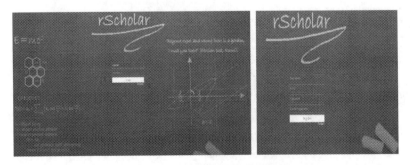

Fig. 2. rScholar - Home page

Fig. 3. rScholar - Home page

Fig. 3). The user is able to search in the datasets and the results of their search are shown (Oval 6: Fig. 3/Fig. 5 and Oval 7, 8 and 9: Fig. 3) together with recommendation label, recommendation presentation (in four categories: novel, diverse, accurate and popular papers) and gamification, respectively, which are discussed in the next section in detail.

Figure 4 shows the dropdown lists, which present options for learning style, task, and academic term. These pieces of contextual information can be later utilized to make better recommendations for users. This approach to employing task specification for contextual search draws inspiration from earlier work on enterprise search [34].

Figure 5 shows the results of users' searches. The user can view the abstract of the paper and save the papers to a personal library (Oval 1: Fig. 5). This library is a self-created library by the userThere are a few icons as Oval 2 presents. The user can remove a paper that is not relevant, send the paper to someone else, see the full text, and cite the paper. These options can also be considered as the options for preference elicitation and refinement, which are discussed in Sect. 2.4.

Table 2. Design element selection

Requirements/ Features		Influential in Perception										Selected Design Element(s)																	
		AF	FU	CB	CL	TR	IN	PR	US	AV	DO	1	2	3	4	5	6	7	8	9	10	11	12	13	14	15	16	17	18
UI & Ix adequacy Features	PE	✓	✓	✓	✓						✓	✓	✓			✓		✓	✓		✓	✓	✓	✓		✓			
	PR	✓	✓	✓	✓						✓	✓	✓			✓		✓	✓		✓	✓	✓	✓		✓			
	IS			✓	✓				✓		✓	✓	✓	✓		✓	✓	✓			✓	✓		✓		✓		✓	
	EX/RL			✓	✓	✓						✓	✓	✓	✓			✓			✓					✓		✓	
Obtain users / environment data	PC	✓						✓		✓	✓	✓	✓	✓		✓	✓	✓	✓	✓	✓	✓		✓	✓	✓	✓	✓	✓
	RD	✓	✓					✓	✓	✓	✓	✓	✓	✓	✓	✓	✓	✓	✓	✓					✓				
	SC			✓	✓				✓	✓										✓									
	SI	✓									✓			✓						✓					✓				
	CO	✓		✓	✓						✓		✓	✓	✓		✓	✓				✓							✓
	PR						✓	✓	✓							✓	✓	✓			✓								
	TA						✓	✓	✓								✓	✓											
	PK						✓	✓	✓								✓	✓											
	LS						✓	✓	✓								✓												
	IS			✓			✓	✓	✓								✓												
	TI						✓	✓	✓		✓						✓	✓				✓							✓
Bayesian Model outputs	NO	✓		✓	✓		✓	✓	✓			✓	✓			✓		✓	✓		✓	✓	✓	✓	✓	✓	✓	✓	
	DI	✓					✓	✓	✓			✓	✓			✓		✓	✓		✓	✓	✓	✓	✓	✓	✓	✓	✓
	PO						✓	✓	✓			✓	✓						✓			✓	✓	✓	✓	✓	✓	✓	✓
	AC						✓	✓	✓			✓	✓					✓				✓		✓		✓	✓	✓	✓

Design Solution: User Persona

Features: Preference Elicitation= PE, Preference Refinement= PR, Information Sufficiently= IS, Explanation= EX, Recommendation Label= RL, Privacy Consideration= PC, Size & Composition of recommendation sets=SC; Recommendation Display= RD; Signifier = SI, Consistency= CO

User/ Environment contexts: Profile = PR; Task= TA, Pre-knowledge= PK, Learning style= LS, Info-seeking behavior= IS, Tune= TI;

Paper context: Novelty= NO; Diversity= DI; Popularity= PO, Accuracy= AC

Perception: Affordance =AF, Fun= FU, Cognitive barrier= CB; Cognitive Load= CL, Transparency=TR, Interactivity=IN, Personalization=PR, Usefulness=US; Visual authentic=VA Dominance= DO

Design Elements: Sliders =1; Icons =2; Dropdown lists =3; List boxes = 4; Buttons = 5; Dropdown Button= 6; Toggles (Switches)= 7; Text fields= 8; Search Field= 9; Pagination= 10; Tags= 11; Notifications= 12; Tool Tips = 13; Message Boxes =14; Modal Window (pop-up) =15; Accordion =16; Menu Bar= 17; Tabs= 18

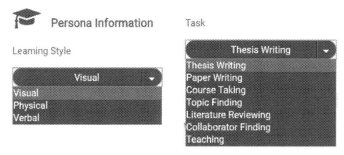

Fig. 4. Available options for learning style & task (dropdown lists)

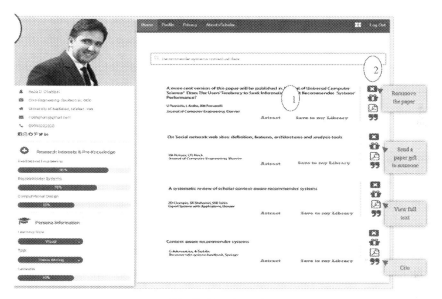

Fig. 5. Search results

Figure 6 depicts two different layouts of pie and list design and shows how rScholar displays recommendations. Based on recent studies, paper quality or appropriate paper refers to attributes of each paper that can be matched to a specific scholar. Researchers emphasized that that apart from the accuracy, other qualities such as diversity, novelty and popularity of the recommended papers are also important for the users [10, 35]. Therefore, the recommendations are displayed to in four categories (Oval 1: Fig. 6).

As Fig. 7 shows, in the profile menu, the user is able to input information about him/herself and edit the data. The user can manage his/her recommendation delivery time interval by choosing three options of daily, weekly, and monthly (Oval: Fig. 7). In addition, the user can set if s/he is willing to get mail notifications or not (Oval 2: Fig. 7).

If the user is a faculty member and has students to supervise, s/he might input the students' research interests or topics so that s/he may receive some recommendations related to students' research interests (Oval 3: Fig. 6). The user's CV can also be uploaded

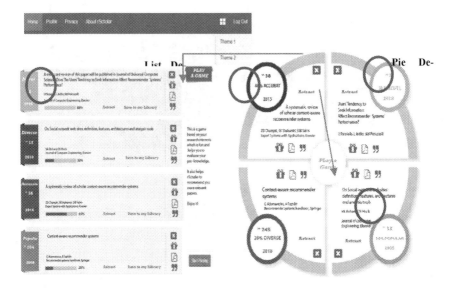

Fig. 6. Page layout options

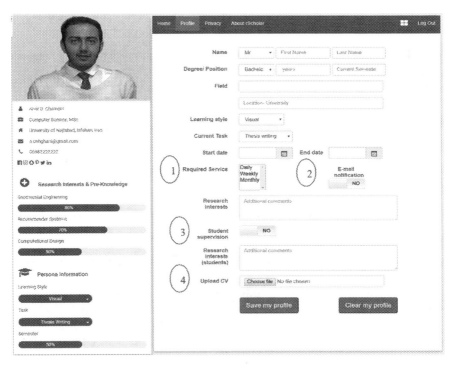

Fig. 7. Page layout options

by using the last option in the profile page (Oval 4: Fig. 6). As mentioned earlier, one of the advantages of the proposed UI is that rScholar can serve as a personal web page/profile for the scholars.

All the fields in the homepage are editable through two ways on the homepage and profile menu as shown in Fig. 7. Guideline #9 in [19] emphasizes setting goals for users to motivate them to contribute. The scholarly personal web page/profile also helps users identify themselves with their scholarly communities, motivating them to contribute more. Beenen et al. [36] discovered that most users are "social loafers" rather than contributors and they may work harder when their effort is important to the group's performance and when their contributions to the group can be identified. As mentioned before, the aim of the rScholar is to develop an efficient mechanism to obtain user's data (user context) and environmental data (environment context) and is also an efficient mechanism to show a list of appropriate papers. In the following sections, we discuss how an efficient mechanism is applied to meet UiD and IxD quality requirements for rScholar.

2.4 Meeting IxD Quality Requirements

In the following, it is discussed how the features influencing the IxD quality based on the design guidelines (Table 1 and 2) have been designed in rScholar.

Preference Elicitation & Refinement. The preference elicitation method is the way in which the RS discovers what the user likes and/or dislikes [29, 37]. In rScholar, there are a few methods for discovering the users' preferences implicitly and explicitly. In the explicit mode, users are asked to rate items or specify preferences on features of the products, such as user profile, item rating and filtering and Questionnaire. In implicit mode, the system makes estimates of the users' preferences by observing users' browsing, searching, selecting, purchasing, and rating behaviors. Feature-based preference elicitation has previously been applied to high-risk and high-involvement products, such as cars, computers, houses, cameras, items for which users rarely have experience, making it difficult to obtain their ratings. It is it is feasible, however, to ask them to identify criteria on specific features [38]. Figure 7 shows the implicit and explicit preference elicitation applied in the design of rScholar. Based on the interface design guidelines for preference elicitation indicated in [39], the profile/interest selection serves as an low effort starting point for eliciting default preferences that can be adapted subsequently by the users.

Guideline #11 in Pu et al.'s research (2011) indicates that refinement facilities, such as critiquing helps the system increase recommendation accuracy and the users' sense of control. Table 3 illustrates the preference refinement methods used in rScholar. In other words, users take these actions towards the recommended papers to refine their preferences.

This preference elicitation is designed to establish a more accurate user model for finding the users' information needs. According to [18, 40], this aspect is highly correlated to the users' trust in the system. Games are also an implicit method for obtaining users' preferences; however, this has not considered in this research. Amazon employs a

Table 3. Preference elicitation/refinement methods

Method	rScholar
Deleting/removing	(Oval 1: Fig. 7)
Viewing the full text	(Oval 1: Fig. 7)
Saving to the library	(Oval 2: Fig. 7)
Viewing the full text	(Oval 2: Fig. 7)
Citing	(Oval 1: Fig. 7)
Sending as a gift to a friend	(Oval 1: Fig. 7)
Changing the rate of paper	(Oval 2: Fig. 7)
Updating the user profile	(Fig. 7)

simple preference refinement method. It asks users to rate some specific items under the box that says, "Improve Your Recommendation". This facility may convince users that their work leads to more accurate recommendations and encourage them to put forth more effort.

Recommendation Label. The recommendation label identifies the area on the screen where the recommended items are displayed. "Recommendation for you" (by Amazon), "Movies you'll like" (by Netflix), or simply "Suggestion" (by YouTube) are samples of recommendation labels [3]. In rScholar, the statement: "'[User's name], rScholar thinks that you may enjoy these papers" is applied as the recommendation label (Fig. 8).

Explanation. In addition to labels, recent recommenders employ explanatory techniques to help users understand the recommender's logic and to increase transparency of the user interaction [3]. This is one of the IxD indicators that plays a highly important role in the success of the recommenders [9, 15].

As shown in Fig. 8, rScholar papers are recommended to the user in four categories of novel, accurate, popular and, diverse. The recommendations in these four categories can be generated by considering the users' situation and preferences. Accuracy represents the papers that are most likely similar to a user profile/search keyword. These papers are chosen to be similar to the users' preferences and past ratings [15, 41]. Novel papers are those that users have not yet rated or used. Also, it could be an unknown item that the user has never encountered [15, 41, 42]. Popular items are those that are widely recognized in a community. For example, a paper that has a high citation count in a field might be considered as a popular item [43]. Recently diversity has been the a focus of a few studies in RSs and Information Retrieval (IR) to improve user satisfaction [43–45]. It refers to recommendations that are not exactly similar to the users' interests or preference but yet may be relevant [45]. To date, many researchers have demonstrated that providing good explanations for recommendations could help inspire users' trust and satisfaction, increase users' involvement and educate users on the internal logic of the system [18, 25, 40, 46]. Table 4 summarizes the explanation type and methods for recommendations stated in various studies.

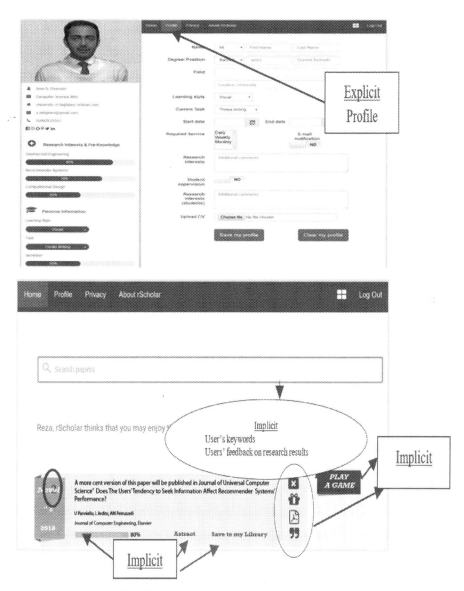

Fig. 8. Implicit & explicit preference elicitation

It should be noted that rScholar recommendations are based on more than one criterion. Describing the rationale for the recommendations is not as straightforward as simply flagging similar research interests. Textual descriptions may be used to clarify the situation [3]. This is something we are considering for future enhancement.

Information Sufficiency. Information sufficiency refers to the content of the recommendation and specification that should be sufficient for users to confidently make their decisions while saving time and effort [9]. In rScholar, as Fig. 9 depicts, paper title,

Table 4. Methods for the recommendation explanation

Type	Method/Technique	References
Textual	Comments, feedback, chat box, social texture	[47, 48]
Graph	Statistical presentations, images, graphs, Star ratings	[18, 25, 40, 46, 49, 50]
Cascaded	Displays only the category of information sources	[51]
Labelling	"Customers who bought/viewed this item also bought/viewed:"	[52]
Tabular	Tables	[9, 29]

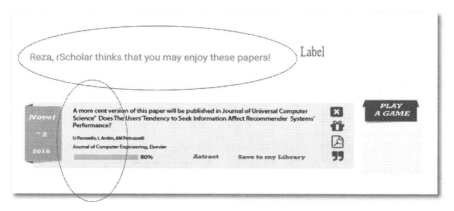

Fig. 9. Recommendation labelling

paper author(s), abstract, full text (if accessible), citations, journal publication date, and publisher are presented to the users and the detailed information such as abstract are provided by additional link. Based on the study of [9], participants mostly want short and concise information.

Privacy Consideration. Figure 10 shows that users are asked to give permission to the rScholar to access their social media information and search logs while apprising them that their information is kept confidential and only is used for making more personalized recommendations for them.

This method protects users' information appropriately and might help users trust the system; however, according to [53], it is still far from dealing with the privacy issues in RSs. Privacy is a critical issue for RSs, regardless of whether the adopted user modeling method is explicit or implicit [54, 55]. To know users well enough to make effective recommendations, a recommender must acquire sufficient information (e.g., demographic information, preference information, personality information etc.) about the users. The privacy concern becomes more important when the required information is more personal, and the users want to keep it confidential. Finding the optimal balance

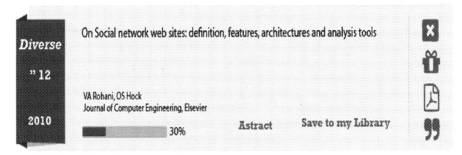

Fig. 10. Information sufficiency in rScholar

between privacy protection and personalization remains a challenging task [56]. There is a general assumption that people are sensitive to privacy issues. However, a mismatch exists between people's privacy preferences and their actual behavior. The results suggest that people overlook privacy concerns once they are highly involved in the system [57]. In addition, when users decide whether to provide personal information or not, they would like to know who is able to access the information and its specific purpose [58].

2.5 Meeting UiD Quality Requirements

Based on the results of an empirical study conducted by [10]; recommendation display, consistency and, signifier are major contributors to the recommendation perceptions. In online RSs, interface issues such as page layout and navigation are the most important factors relating to the overall ease of use and perceived usefulness of RSs [9, 18].

Recommendation Display. Page layout, color, icons, number of recommendations, recommendation notification, recommendation time, and navigation design patterns all can address the recommendation display.

Page Layout. Guideline #14 in [19] places special importance on attractive layout design and effective labeling in order to enhance users' perceived accuracy, and explains how the systems compute the recommendations (recommendation explanation: IxD quality indicators). Doing so can increase users' perception of the system's effectiveness, their overall satisfaction of the system, their readiness to accept the recommended items, and their trust in the system. In one of the earlier studies examining the HCI aspects of such systems, Swearingen et al. [18] found that some of the interface issues including graphics and color are not strongly correlated to the ease of use and perceived usefulness of RSs. In the survey conducted by [9], participants overwhelmingly (85.5%) preferred to see RSs as part of the regular web page content. Chen (2011) has indicated that most of current RSs follow the list structure, where recommended items are sited one after another. The grid layout, a two-dimensional display with multiple rows and columns, has also been applied in one movie recommender sites to display the items. As the third alternative design, pie layout has been rarely used in RSs. However, it has been proven as an effective menu design for accelerating users' selection process and has significantly enhanced the users' decision confidence, enjoyability, perceived recommender competence, and usage intention via user evaluation [59]. Therefore, as mentioned before and shown in Fig. 6, two-page layouts, list, and pie, have been designed in this research. The effectiveness of page layouts for SRSs is evaluated and discussed in the next section.

Number of Recommendation (Size). The number of recommendations, which is also called set composition or recommendation set size, is another concern of RSs researchers [9, 16]. Studies indicate that while showing one item is too few, showing more than five items increases users' choice difficulty. Hence, it seems that an appropriate recommendation number is three [9]. In this research, we have four recommendations because the recommendations are based on four paper categories of novel, accurate, popular, and diverse. Another implication of prior research is that different kinds of items should be mixed and balanced to make up the final set.

Recommendation Presentation. Presentation is also a crucial factor in persuading users to accept the recommended items; therefore, each RS must carefully employ strategies that are sensitive to users' information needs as well as the business goals of the RS. To create an adequate recommendation set in this research, a set of four paper recommendations consisting of novel, popular, accurate and diverse is offered (Fig. 6).

Recommendation Delivery Time & Method. There are two ways of delivering recommendations: reactive (manual), in which the recommendations are sent to users when they ask for them; and proactive initiation (automatic), in which the recommendations are sent at prescheduled times [3]. Several user interface techniques have been proposed to help balance the need for timely recommendations with the need to avoid distracting users. These inform the user that a recommendation is available without forcing the user to acknowledge it immediately. It seems that providing both methods and a combination of them is preferable by users. In another perspective, Ho and Tam [60] indicate that in the early stage of the decision process, users are more likely to accept and review the recommendations; therefore, it is better to present some recommendations to them at that time. In rScholar, users receive recommendations at the time they explicitly ask for them at a set time or after searching and interacting with the system. rScholar has two methods of recommendation delivery in three-time intervals of daily, weekly, and monthly including recommendations that are delivered via email notification and those presented in the rScholar homepage. The user can set his/her preferable method. If the email method is set, the recommendations are sent to the users' mail inbox at a set time (Fig. 11). The user is also able to view more detailed information about the recommendations. The deactivation (unsubscribe) of receiving recommendations is provided by the link at the bottom of email notification (Fig. 12).

Consistency. Consistency is using familiar icons, colors, menu hierarchy, call-to-actions, and user flows when designing similar situations and sequence of actions. It helps users to perceive the system as easy to use and stable [61, 62]. Past studies have not discussed the relationships between consistency and UX of SRSs however this factor in rScholar was considered using simple icons and design in a way that users do not perceive cognitive barriers and load.

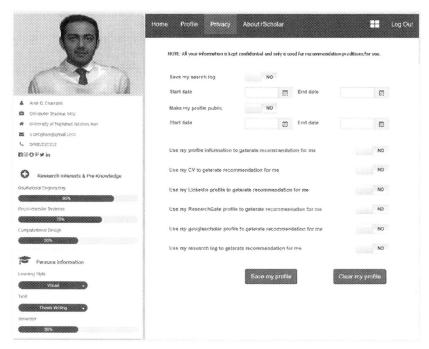

Fig. 11. Privacy consideration in rScholar

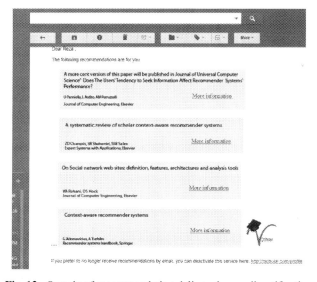

Fig. 12. Sample of recommendation delivery by email notification

Signifier. Signifiers are communication signs or signals that tell users what an object is for. Signifiers help users understand what to do and where to do it, what is happening and what are the alternatives. They convey possible actions to the individual [63]. The signifier should be clear for the user who wants to use the product, so it is easy to understand. In rScholar clear text labels, tooltips, simple and easy to understand icons help users to understand affordances.

2.6 Evaluation and Results

UX evaluation of RSs has only started recently and is still in its infancy. Knijnenburg et al. [16] and Pu and Hu [19] have proposed frameworks and guidelines for the evaluation of RSs from a user- centric perspective. For the rScholar evaluation, survey questionnaires (UI and Ix aspects) of the above-mentioned studies have served as the inspiration for design of a questionnaire. Expert evaluation and user studies have been performed to evaluate the UI.

Expert Evaluation. Expert evaluation has been accepted as a significant way to improve the quality of a developed software and as a complement for testing other products [64]. Thus, this study adopted this approach for the evaluation of rScholar. The objectives were to gather feedback on the rScholar and to compare it with the UI of Google Scholar. The experts were selected based on their UX/UI professional backgrounds. The invitations, along with the details of the validation study were sent to 15 experts within the field. Nine experts agreed to participate. Both the rScholar and the questionnaire were accessible through www.rscholar.com and first, the experts were asked to work with Google scholar for five minutes without providing any information or guidance to how to use it. Then, the experts were asked to use the rScholar and rate the features indicated in questionnaire in a 5- Likert scale for both Google scholar and rScholar separately. Before examining the UiD and IxD differences of rScholar and Google scholar from the experts' viewpoints, Normality test were performed and parametric T-tests (sig. < 0.05) and non-paramedic Mann- Whitney (MW) tests (sig. > 0.05) were applied for comparison of rScholar and Google scholar's features. Based on the results of MW and T tests shown in Table 5, there are no statistically significant differences (sig. $= .622 > .05$) between UiD and IxD features in rScholar and Google scholar, however, by means comparing (r_CS $=$ $4.00 < g\_CS = 4.27$; r_RD $= 4.22 > g\_RD = 3.77$).

Experts rated Google scholar's consistency higher than that of rScholar and rated rScholar recommendation display higher that that of Google scholar. The reason for rating consistency higher for Google scholar might be the familiarity of experts with Google products and their design. Among the other examined UiD and IxD features, there is significant difference (sig. $< .05$) in PE, PR, EX features between rScholar and Google scholar. The means comparison reveals that experts have rated rScholar higher for the features of Preference Elicitation (PE) (r_PE $= 4.22 > g\_PE = 3.22$), Preference Refinement (PR) (r_PR $= 4.38 > g\_PR = 2.38$), as well as Explanation of recommendation (EX) (r_EX $= 4.44 > g\_EX = 1.77$) than Google scholar.

rScholar: User Study Evaluation. The objective of this end user evaluation is to examine the UiD and IxD features influencing UX two times in a three-month interval. The user studies took place in two intervals with individuals who agreed to participate in

Table 5. UiD & IxD differences in rScholar & Google scholar (MW& T-test)

MW: *Decision Null Hypo.		Sig.	Feature	Mean
PE	✗	.006	r-PE	4.22
			g-PE	3.22
PR	✗	.000	r-PR	4.38
			g-PR	2.38
PC	✗	.000	r-PC	4.61
			g-PC	3.27
EX	✗	.000	r-EX	4.44
			g-EX	1.77
IS	✓	1.00	r-IS	4.00
			g-IS	4.00
SI	✓	.190	r-SI	3.94
			g-SI	4.22

T-test	Feature	N	Sig.	Mean	Std. Deviation	Std. Error Mean
CS	r_CS	9	.622	4.0000	.66144	.22048
	g_CS	9		4.2778	.44096	.14699
RD	r_RD	9	.622	4.2222	.23810	.07937
	g_RD	9		3.7778	.23810	.07937

r→ rScholar; g→Googlescholar; PE→Preference Elicitation; PR→ Preference Refinement; PC→Privacy Consideration.; EX→Explanation; IS→ Information Sufficiently; SI→Signifier; CS→Consistency RD→Recommendation Display

the evaluation phase. Four groups of Master, PhD students, Post-doc researchers, and Faculty members participated in this research. Each group consisted of five participants for a total of twenty participants. Bachelor students were excluded because of our focus on research expertise and knowledge of scholarly tasks. As in our expert evaluation, both the rScholar and the questionnaire were accessible through www.rscholar.com. First, the participants were asked to work with rScholar for five minutes without any information or guidance on how to use it. Then, they were asked to provide their ratings on the features indicated in the questionnaire on a 5-point Likert scale. The rest of the evaluation is similar to our expert's evaluation. To measure the changes resulting from the experimental environment, pretest-posttest designs were used to compare the changes in different groups and times. High changes in pre-test and post-test scores indicate low reliability [65]. To examine the reliability and consistency of users' scores, the data was collected in two times with three months' time interval. The first data collection is a pretest and the second is a post-test (after three months). After performing the Normality test (Sig. $= .00 < 0.05$)., the Wilcoxon signed ranks test is used to determine if the time (three months) as an intervention has a significant effect on the users' scores on UiD and IxD features as well as on users' overall evaluation. As the results in Table 6 reveal, the median of differences between Pre-test and Post-test equals zero (0) for all features which indicates that there is no significant difference between the scores of participants. In other words, there is no change in scores from the first time to the second time after three months, therefore, it can be discerned that the users' rates are reliable.

Table 6. Related samples test results-scale data (Wilcoxon signed ranks)

Decision Null Hypo.	Sig.	Decision Null Hypo.	Sig.	Decision Null Hypo.	Sig.	Decision Null Hypo.	Sig.
re_ Post_PE	.180	Pre_ Post_PC	.060	Pre_Post_CS	.581	Pre_ Post_RD	.216
Pre_Post_PR	.157	Pre_ Post_EX	.396	Pre_Post_SI	.083	Pre_Post_IS	.157

* Retain null hypothesis (✓): The median of differences between Pre-test and Post-test equals zero (0)
* Rejected null hypothesis (✗): The median of differences between Pre-test and Post-test does not equal zero (0)

By using the Friedman Two- way Analysis of Variance (ANOVA) and Kendall's Coefficient of Concordance tests it revealed that there is not statistically significant differences between the different groups of users' ratings and the distribution in different groups (Master, PhD student, Post-doc researcher, and Faculty member) are the same (Sig. = .00 < 0.05). Figure 11 depicts, the mean users' rates on rScholar UiD and IxD features vs Google scholar as well as users' overall perception on rScholar and Google scholar in term of dominance, fun, cognitive load, and cognitive barrier. Like the experts' evaluation, rScholar consistency obtained the lowest rate and participants have perceived more dominance when interacting with Google scholar. However, users have rated rScholar higher on sufficient information and recommendation explanations, privacy considerations and preference elicitation and refinements methods than Google scholar (Fig. 13).

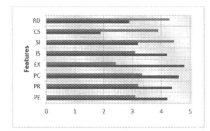 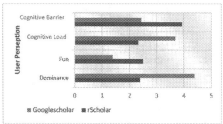

Fig. 13. Users' Evaluation Results

3 Discussion and Recommendation

The rScholar design and evaluation were based on the most powerful indicators of UiD and IxD quality including preference elicitation, preference refinement, privacy consideration, explanation, and info-sufficiency for IxD adequacy, and UiD quality measures such as display, consistency, and signifier. It is obvious that users' satisfaction and experience are also associated with usefulness and quality of recommendations, but in this study, rScholar does not generate recommendations for the users, which is a shortcoming of the study. To prevent biased results, the users were asked to evaluate rScholar with the assumption that they are receiving relevant and appropriate recommendations.

A comprehensive research examination of UX of RSs must consider both the back-end that decides what to recommend, and the front-end that delivers the recommendation [3]. However, there are more than 200 research studies on SRS mostly focused on back-end (accuracy of algorithms) [66] and there has been given little attention to UI design for RSs and particularly SRSs. rScholar is one of the first serious attempts in the field of UI design for the SRSs. Therefore, this research does not end here and encourages further studies on UI and IxD design for RSs and SRSs. Some of the possible areas are discussed in the following section.

3.1 Consistency

As the evaluation results showed, both experts and users gave the lowest rates to rScholar consistency. Consistency suggest that users perceive the system as easy to use and stable which leads to less cognitive load while using the system [67]. It also helps with user control; however, it is not an easy task to design consistent interfaces for these complex recommendations.

3.2 Trade-off Between User Contribution and Data Acquisition

Making this trade-off is not always easy since, first, the users perceive rating-time costs which means they perceive benefits as those that outweigh the costs they pay [41]. Second, users are often more satisfied when they are given control over how the recommender functions on their behalf, even when that control increases the effort that is required of them, and even when the resulting recommendations are objectively less accurate. Therefore, a recommender should provide a balance between the control/dominance which users desire and an effective recommendation service [25]. McNee et al. [23] compared three interface strategies for eliciting movie ratings by 192 users and found that a higher level of user control over the interaction gives rise to a more accurate preference UM/algorithm. The experiment also revealed that although the user-controlled group spent more time, they did not perceive any additional effort. Besides, design of adaptive RSs, which tailors the user interaction effort to his/her individual characteristics and motivates users to expend this effort might be a good solution and ultimately help to create a pleasant experience for the users.

3.3 Users' Control and Dominance

User control or dominance of SRSs is about letting users decide what to do and to control their preferences, which motivates them to rate more indicators in the future [20, 25]. The privacy and recommendation delivery time/method in rScholar helps users to feel dominance, however since the users do not receive real recommendations, their perceptions might be invalid. This aspect needs more investigation.

3.4 Visualization

Visualization has shown significant impact on the UX of SRSs [10], but they have received less attention in the rScholar design since data visualization for SRSs requires separate extensive investigations in both design solutions and data analysis. Recently, a few studies have utilized visualization techniques specially to denote the user's current context such as time, location and weather along [68] and also multidimensional visualization to promote the diversity of recommended items through an interpretable and interactive interface [44]. Like the dashboard on a car, RS dashboards typically integrate recommendations of different types from different sources allowing the user to glance at recommendations frequently and with low commitment [3]. Besides, visualization techniques are used in RSs to support transparency, acceptance, and controllability of the recommendation process. PeerChooser and SmallWorlds are good examples of visual interactive recommenders that show relationships between users and recommended items [3].

3.5   Fun and Gamification

Although it seems that SRSs are not required to be fun for the scholars interacting with them, gamification has a significant effect on users' experiences with SRSs and perceived fun [10]. Gamification could be one of the preference elicitation methods. In rScholar, we included a game icon that we designed, and feedback showed that around 54% of users like to have fun while they are looking for an appropriate paper. However, it is still debatable as some of the users also indicated that they need to find the paper instantly and in a straightforward way. Hence, providing fun in RSs needs more investigation and is highlighted here to offer insights for SRSs in the future studies.

3.6   Dialog and Interactive Chatbots

Chatbots or conversational agents are able to support interactions with the users. The aim of dialogue design is to yield closure and to reduce cognitive load. An effective dialogue makes the system as reliable as possible by, for example using messaging box, flags, and icons [62]. Moreover, the medium that presents the recommendations also influences the user's satisfaction of RS [69]. According to Global Web Index statistics, it is said that 75% of internet users are adopting one or more messaging platforms. And with new advancements coming every year like AI, NLP and Machine Learning which makes the bot more intelligent. In rScholar chatbots were not considered but some part of contextual data (profile information) such as users' task, research interests, and pre-knowledge could be obtained through interactive chat with the users.

References

1. Champiri, Z.D., Shahamiri, S.R., Salim, S.S.B.: A systematic review of scholar context-aware recommender systems. Expert Syst. Appl. **42**(3), 1743–1758 (2015)
2. Dehghani Champiri, Z., Asemi, A., Siti Salwah Binti, S.: Meta-analysis of evaluation methods and metrics used in context-aware scholarly recommender systems. Knowl. Inf. Syst. **61**(2), 1147–1178 (2019). https://doi.org/10.1007/s10115-018-1324-5
3. Murphy-Hill, E., Murphy, Gail C.: Recommendation delivery. In: Robillard, Martin P., Maalej, W., Walker, R.J., Zimmermann, T. (eds.) Recommendation Systems in Software Engineering, pp. 223–242. Springer, Heidelberg (2014). https://doi.org/10.1007/978-3-642-45135-5_9

4. Nguyen, T.T., et al.: Rating support interfaces to improve user experience and recommender accuracy. In: Proceedings of the 7th ACM Conference on Recommender Systems, pp. 149–156. ACM, Hong Kong (2013)
5. Ge, M., Delgado-Battenfeld, C., Jannach, D.: User-perceived recommendation quality-factoring in the user interface (2010)
6. Abdrabo, W., Wörndl, W.: DiRec: a distributed user interface video recommender. In: IntRS@ RecSys (2016)
7. Calero Valdez, A., Ziefle, M., Verbert, K.: HCI for recommender systems: the past, the present and the future. In: Proceedings of the 10th ACM Conference on Recommender Systems. ACM (2016)
8. Champiri, Z.D., et al.: User experience and recommender systems. In: 2019 2nd International Conference on Computing, Mathematics and Engineering Technologies (iCoMET). IEEE (2019)
9. Ozok, A.A., Fan, Q., Norcio, A.F.: Design guidelines for effective recommender system interfaces based on a usability criteria conceptual model: results from a college student population. Behav. Inf. Technol. 29(1), 57–83 (2010)
10. Champiri, Z.D.: A contextual bayesian user experience model for scholarly recommender systems. Doctoral dissertation, University of Malaya (2019)
11. Xiao, B., Benbasat, I.: E-commerce product recommendation agents: use, characteristics, and impact. MIS Q. 31(1), 137–209 (2007)
12. Mcnee, S.M.: Meeting user information needs in recommender systems. Proquest (2006)
13. McNee, S.M., Riedl, J., Konstan, J.A.: Being accurate is not enough: how accuracy metrics have hurt recommender systems. In: CHI'06 Extended Abstracts on Human Factors in Computing Systems. ACM (2006)
14. Saffer, D.: Designing for Interaction: Creating Innovative Applications and Devices. New Riders, Indianapolis (2010)
15. Felfernig, A., Burke, R., Pu, P.: Preface to the special issue on user interfaces for recommender systems. User Model. User-Adapt. Interact. 22(4), 313–316 (2012). https://doi.org/10.1007/s11257-012-9120-5
16. Knijnenburg, B.P., et al.: Explaining the user experience of recommender systems. User Model. User-Adapt. Interact. 22(4–5), 441–504 (2012). https://doi.org/10.1007/s11257-011-9118-4
17. Swearingen, K., Sinha, R.: Beyond algorithms: an HCI perspective on recommender systems. In: ACM SIGIR 2001 Workshop on Recommender Systems (2001)
18. Swearingen, K., Sinha, R.: Interaction design for recommender systems. In: Designing Interactive Systems (2002)
19. Pu, P., Chen, L., Hu, R.: Evaluating recommender systems from the user's perspective: survey of the state of the art. User Model. User-Adapt. Interact. 22(4), 317–355 (2012). https://doi.org/10.1007/s11257-011-9115-7
20. di Sciascio, C.: Advanced user interfaces and hybrid recommendations for exploratory search. In: Proceedings of the 22nd International Conference on Intelligent User Interfaces Companion. ACM (2017)
21. Hussain, J., Khan, W.A., Afzal, M., Hussain, M., Kang, B.H., Lee, S.: Adaptive user interface and user experience based authoring tool for recommendation systems. In: Hervás, R., Lee, S., Nugent, C., Bravo, J. (eds.) UCAmI 2014. LNCS, vol. 8867, pp. 136–142. Springer, Cham (2014). https://doi.org/10.1007/978-3-319-13102-3_24
22. Knijnenburg, B.P., Willemsen, M.C.: The effect of preference elicitation methods on the user experience of a recommender system. In: CHI'10 Extended Abstracts on Human Factors in Computing Systems. ACM (2010)
23. McNee, S., et al.: Interfaces for eliciting new user preferences in recommender systems. In: User Modeling 2003, p. 148 (2003)

24. Cosley, D., et al.: Is seeing believing?: how recommender system interfaces affect users' opinions. In: Proceedings of the SIGCHI Conference on Human Factors in Computing Systems, pp. 585–592. ACM, Ft. Lauderdalep (2003)
25. Konstan, J.A., Riedl, J.: Recommender systems: from algorithms to user experience. User Model. User-Adap. Inter. **22**(1), 101–123 (2012). https://doi.org/10.1007/s11257-011-9112-x
26. Cremonesi, P., Elahi, M., Garzotto, F.: User interface patterns in recommendation-empowered content intensive multimedia applications. Multimed. Tools Appl. **76**(4), 5275–5309 (2016). https://doi.org/10.1007/s11042-016-3946-5
27. Dehghani Champiri, Z., et al.: A multi-layer contextual model for recommender systems in digital libraries. In: Aslib Proceedings. Emerald Group Publishing Limited (2011)
28. Champiri, Z.D., Salim, S.S.B., Shahamiri, S.R.: The role of context for recommendations in digital libraries. Int. J. Soc. Sci. Human. **5**(11), 948 (2015)
29. Pu, P., Chen, L., Hu, R.: A user-centric evaluation framework for recommender systems. In: Proceedings of the Fifth ACM Conference on Recommender Systems. ACM (2011)
30. Hurley, N.J.: Robustness of Recommender Systems. In: Proceedings of the Fifth ACM Conference on Recommender Systems. ACM (2011)
31. Sridharan, S.: Introducing serendipity in recommender systems through collaborative methods (2014)
32. Adamopoulos, P., Tuzhilin, A.: On unexpectedness in recommender systems: Or how to expect the unexpected. In: Workshop on Novelty and Diversity in Recommender Systems (DiveRS 2011), at the 5th ACM International Conference on Recommender Systems (RecSys 2011). ACM, Illinois (2011)
33. Freund, L., et al.: Exposing and exploring academic expertise with virtu (2010)
34. Yeung, P.C., Freund, L., Clarke, C.L.: X-site: a workplace search tool for software engineers. In: Proceedings of the 30th Annual International ACM SIGIR Conference on Research and Development in Information Retrieval (2007)
35. Hurley, N.J.: Towards diverse recommendation. In: Workshop on Novelty and Diversity in Recommender Systems (DiveRS 2011). Citeseer (2011)
36. Beenen, G., et al.: Using social psychology to motivate contributions to online communities. In: Proceedings of the 2004 ACM Conference on Computer Supported Cooperative Work (2004)
37. Pu, P., Chen, L., Hu, R.: Evaluating recommender systems from the user's perspective: survey of the state of the art. User Model. User-Adap. Inter. **22**(4–5), 317–355 (2012). https://doi.org/10.1007/s11257-011-9115-7
38. Herlocker, J.L., et al.: Evaluating collaborative filtering recommender systems. ACM Trans. Inf. Syst. (TOIS) **22**(1), 5–53 (2004)
39. Pommeranz, A., et al.: Designing interfaces for explicit preference elicitation: a user-centered investigation of preference representation and elicitation process. User Model. User-Adap. Interact. **22**(4–5), 357–397 (2012). https://doi.org/10.1007/s11257-011-9116-6
40. Sinha, R., Swearingen, K.: The role of transparency in recommender systems. In: CHI 2002 Extended Abstracts on Human Factors in Computing Systems. ACM (2002)
41. Nguyen, T.: Enhancing user experience with recommender systems beyond prediction accuracies. Ph.D. Dissertation. The University of Minnesota (2016)
42. Rana, C.: New dimensions of temporal serendipity and temporal novelty in recommender system. Adv. Appl. Sci. Res. **4**(1), 151–157 (2013)
43. Jannach, D., Lerche, L., Gedikli, F., Bonnin, G.: What recommenders recommend – an analysis of accuracy, popularity, and sales diversity effects. In: Carberry, S., Weibelzahl, S., Micarelli, A., Semeraro, G. (eds.) UMAP 2013. LNCS, vol. 7899, pp. 25–37. Springer, Heidelberg (2013). https://doi.org/10.1007/978-3-642-38844-6_3

44. Tsai, C.-H.: An interactive and interpretable interface for diversity in recommender systems. In: Proceedings of the 22nd International Conference on Intelligent User Interfaces Companion, pp. 225–228. ACM, Limassol (2017)

45. Adomavicius, G., Kwon, Y.: Maximizing aggregate recommendation diversity: a graph-theoretic approach. In: Proceedings of the 1st International Workshop on Novelty and Diversity in Recommender Systems (DiveRS 2011). Citeseer (2011)

46. Tintarev, N., Masthoff, J.: A survey of explanations in recommender systems. In: 2007 IEEE 23rd International Conference on Data Engineering Workshop. IEEE (2007)

47. Kim, J.K., Kim, H.K., Cho, Y.H.: A user-oriented contents recommendation system in peer-to-peer architecture. Expert Syst. Appl. **34**(1), 300–312 (2008)

48. Cosley, D., et al.: Is seeing believing? How recommender system interfaces affect users' opinions. In: Proceedings of the SIGCHI Conference on Human Factors in Computing Systems (2003)

49. Konstan, J.A.: Introduction to recommender systems: algorithms and evaluation. ACM Trans. Inf. Syst. (TOIS) **22**(1), 1–4 (2004)

50. Konstan, J.A., et al.: Techlens: exploring the use of recommenders to support users of digital libraries. In: CNI Fall Task Force Meeting Project Briefing. Coalition for Networked Information, Phoenix, AZ (2005)

51. Pu, P., Chen, L.: Trust-inspiring explanation interfaces for recommender systems. Knowl.-Based Syst. **20**(6), 542–556 (2007)

52. Vig, J., Sen, S., Riedl, J.: Tagsplanations: explaining recommendations using tags. In: Proceedings of the 14th International Conference on Intelligent User Interfaces (2009)

53. Lam, S.K.T., Frankowski, D., Riedl, J.: Do you trust your recommendations? An exploration of security and privacy issues in recommender systems. In: Müller, G. (ed.) ETRICS 2006. LNCS, vol. 3995, pp. 14–29. Springer, Heidelberg (2006). https://doi.org/10.1007/117661 55_2

54. Resnick, P., Varian, H.R.: Recommender systems. Commun. ACM **40**(3), 56–58 (1997)

55. Konstan, J.A., Riedl, J.: Recommender systems: from algorithms to user experience. User Model. User-Adap. Interact. **22**(1–2), 101–123 (2012). https://doi.org/10.1007/s11257-011-9112-x

56. Knijnenburg, B.P., Berkovsky, S.: Privacy for recommender systems: tutorial abstract. In: Proceedings of the Eleventh ACM Conference on Recommender Systems. ACM (2017)

57. Ramakrishnan, N., et al.: Privacy risks in recommender systems. IEEE Internet Comput. **6**, 54–62 (2001)

58. Kobsa, A., Schreck, J.: Privacy through pseudonymity in user-adaptive systems. ACM Trans. Internet Technol. (TOIT) **3**(2), 149–183 (2003)

59. Chen, L., Tsoi, H.K.: Users' decision behavior in recommender interfaces: Impact of layout design. In: RecSys 2011 Workshop on Human Decision Making in Recommender Systems (2011)

60. Tam, K.Y., Ho, S.Y.: Web personalization as a persuasion strategy: an elaboration likelihood model perspective. Inf. Syst. Res. **16**(3), 271–291 (2005)

61. Nielsen, J.: 10 usability heuristics for user interface design. Fremont: Nielsen Norman Group. [Consult. 20 maio 2014]. Disponível na Internet (1995)

62. Shneiderman, B.: Designing for fun: how can we design user interfaces to be more fun? Interactions **11**(5), 48–50 (2004)

63. Norman, D.: The Design of Everyday Things: Revised and, Expanded edn. Basic Books, New York (2013)

64. Wiegers, K.E.: Peer Reviews in Software: A Practical Guide. Addison-Wesley, Boston (2002)

65. Dimitrov, D.M., Rumrill Jr., P.D.: Pretest-posttest designs and measurement of change. Work **20**(2), 159–165 (2003)

66. Beel, J., Breitinger, C., Langer, S., Lommatzsch, A., Gipp, B.: Towards reproducibility in recommender-systems research. User Model. User-Adap. Interact. **26**(1), 69–101 (2016). https://doi.org/10.1007/s11257-016-9174-x
67. Shneiderman, B., Plaisant, C.: Designing the user interface: strategies for effective human-computer interaction. Pearson Education India, Delhi (2010)
68. Hiesel, P., et al.: A user interface concept for context-aware recommender systems. Mensch und Computer 2016-Tagungsband (2016)
69. Beel, J., et al.: A comparative analysis of offline and online evaluations and discussion of research paper recommender system evaluation. In: Proceedings of the International Workshop on Reproducibility and Replication in Recommender Systems Evaluation. ACM (2013)

An Observation on the Behavior of Smartphone Addicts at Taipei Mass Rapid Transportation Station

Miao Huang$^{(\boxtimes)}$ and Chien-Hsiung Chen

National Taiwan University of Science and Technology, Taipei, Taiwan
huangmia11@gmail.com

Abstract. The purpose of this study is to explore the impact of smartphone addiction on users in public settings. The experiment was conducted using non-participant observation to observe the smartphone addicts in the metro station. The study investigated: (1) The attendances of the smartphone addicts at different time periods of the day in the MRT station. (2) A study on the behavior of smartphone addicts in MRT, such as the entry route, stay time, etc. The experiment took three days of the week, i.e., the weekdays day on Mondays and Wednesdays, and the weekends on Saturdays. The time for each observation period is 15 min, divided into four time periods: 10:00 am, 13:00, 17:00, and 20:00. The generated results revealed that: (1) Smartphone addicts have higher attendance rates on weekdays than on weekends. (2) The direction indicator of the gate was ignored by some of the smartphone addicts. (3) We propose the design improvement of the direction indicator and suggest an interactive space at MRT station.

Keywords: Non-participation observation · Smartphone addicts · MRT station · Indicator design

1 Introduction

In modern society, more and more people rely on using mobile devices. The user who over-uses mobile devices is called "smartphone addicts." In many countries, there have been tragic incidents in which smartphone users focus on mobile screens on the roads and encounter traffic accidents. Founded in current research on the adverse consequences of overusing technology, "mobile phone overuse" has been proposed as a subset of forms of "digital addiction", or "digital dependence", reflecting increasing trends of compulsive behavior amongst users of technological devices. Researchers have variously termed these behaviors "smartphone addiction". Grant et al. (2010) believed that smartphone addiction can be classified as a behavioral addiction, such as Internet addiction. Behavioral and chemical addictions have seven core symptoms in common, that is, salience, tolerance, mood modification, conflict, withdrawal, problems, and relapse.

The Chartered Society of Physiotherapy has issued a report stating that smart mobile devices, such as smartphones and tablets having unwittingly prolonged users' working hours and exploited their health. The Association surveyed 2010 white-collar workers

© Springer Nature Switzerland AG 2020
C. Stephanidis et al. (Eds.): HCII 2020, LNCS 12423, pp. 687–695, 2020.
https://doi.org/10.1007/978-3-030-60114-0_44

in the UK and found that more than two-thirds of those surveyed had to continue working outside working hours due to the popularity of smartphones and other devices, on average two hours more than the legal working hours. The Association warns that smart mobile devices are turning users into "screen slaves." The Association also pointed out that, whether it is work or leisure, people usually do not pay attention to maintaining a reasonable posture when using handheld smart devices, thus causing a greater risk of health problems. Abo-Jedi (2008) also pointed out that smartphone addiction can affect physical and mental health. The negative physiological health effects of excessive smartphone use include the neurological disorders, the weakened immune system, some problems with the eardrum, the pain in wrists, neck, and joints and so on (Cha and Seo 2018). Psychologically, smartphone addiction can cause poor social support and higher levels of loneliness (Nie and Erbring 2000).

On the other hand, urbanization and demands for mobility have spurred the development of mass rapid transit infrastructure in industrializing Asia (Townsend and Zacharias 2010). Thus, it is necessary to examine how transit systems better applied locally. The tracks and stations of the Metro Rapid System in Taipei include underground, ground, and elevated sections. Passengers must enter or leave a Metro Rapid Transit (MRT) station either through stairs, escalators, or elevators. In 2000, the accident rate for escalator riding was about 0.815 accidents per million passenger trips through Taipei MRT heavy capacity stations. The results from the analysis indicated that the majority of the escalator riding accidents were caused by passengers' carrying out other tasks (Chi, Chang and Tsou 2006). Besides, there are safety hazards. Some people walk, bike, or even drive without forgetting to check their phones, which can be dangerous and may lead to injuries or even death in an emergency. This is not only not responsible for their own, but also for the passers-by around irresponsible, because of the use of smartphone caused by the accident of the news is often reported in the newspaper.

In many countries, smartphone users have focused on their phones on the road, resulting in tragic accidents, some of which have resulted in death. South Korea, a country where smartphones and mobile Internet are the most popular in the world, has launched a special traffic warning signal to warn smartphone users not to focus on their mobile screens in an accident-prone area, foreign media reported. The government of Seoul, South Korea, has even launched an experimental scheme to design several warning signs for smartphone users, in conjunction with traffic authorities. The warning signs will be set up in five accident-prone areas of Seoul to remind passersby not to focus on their mobile phone screens and cause serious accidents (Fig. 1).

While mobile smart devices bring convenience, they also virtually increase work pressure and even cause more physical and psychological risks. Therefore, the problems and needs of smartphone addicts need to be addressed. This article develops and explores the impact of excessive use of smart mobile devices in the public MRT station.

2 Purpose

The study investigates the effects of the phenomenon that smartphone addiction in a public environment pertinent to users. The experiment was conducted using a non-participant observation technique to observe the smartphone addicts at Taipei Mass Rapid Transportation (MRT) Station. The purpose of this study includes that:

Fig. 1. The warning signal of the smartphone addicts in Seoul

- Explore the attendance of the smartphone addicts at different times of the day in the MRT station
- Observe the behavior of smartphone addicts in the MRT regarding the entering route, stay area, etc.
- Propose the design improvement of the MRT station for smartphone addicts by adopting the universal design concept for the MRT station to benefit everyone.

3 Methods

This study uses a non-participant observation technique to explore the behavior of mobile phone addicts in the Taipei MRT station.

The experiment site was at Gate 2 of the Gongguan Station in Taipei City. Gongguan Station is located on the southwest side of the National Taiwan University campus. Exits 1 and 2 are at the southern end of the station, exits 3 and 4 are at the northern end of the station. The observation area was from the entrance of exit 2 to the gate (Fig. 2).

The experiment took three days of the week to perform, the weekdays were on Mondays and Wednesdays, and the weekends were on Saturdays. The observation time for each period was 15 min, divided into four-time periods: 10:00 am, 13:00, 17:00, and 20:00. The experimental data were collected regarding the number of smartphone addicts entering the station and the number of smartphone addicts staying in the public space. The judgment of the smartphone addicts: (1) looking down at the screen while walking. (2) The people who staying and watching the screen for more than five minutes.

(1)   (2)   (3)

Fig. 2. The observation area of exit 2 of Gongguan Station (1) Gate 2 of the Gongguan Station, (2) Perspective of observation, (3) Escalator entrance

4   Observation Results

4.1   The Entering Route

The process of taking the metro from exit 2 to the platform is roughly four steps: entering the station, going downstairs, to the gate, and swiping the card. The plan of exit 2 of the Gongguan station is shown in Fig. 3. There were 4 steps at the entrance. After entering, people need to turn right and go downstairs. There are three connecting up and down passages, of which the descending escalator is in the middle and the stairs are on the right. There are seven gates, two on the far left are entrances, four are exits, and one is barrier-free.

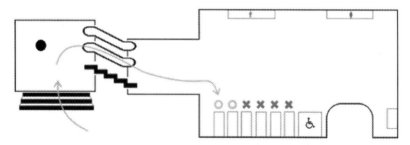

Fig. 3. The entering route of smartphone addicts

The observation results indicated that the route taken by smartphone addicts was showed in Fig. 3. Black dots indicate the location of the entering route observation. After entering, smartphone addicts would prefer to go to the escalator instead of the stairs, the observation result is consistent with the research of Chi et al. (2006) who suggested that the Escalators seem to be the favorite choice by people. Then they would turn right to the speed gate and choose the nearest door to swipe the card.

4.2 Usage Behavior of Smartphone Addicts

Almost everyone standing in the public space outside the gate is looking at their smartphones, they are usually waiting for someone. Figure 4 showed the location of smartphone addicts outside the gate. The black dots indicate the location of the observer, the star symbol indicates that smartphone addicts often like to stand close to the wall near the toilets and the vending machine. The bottom right corner of the map shows the temporary charger for the subway station, and smartphone addicts stay here longer than in other spaces.

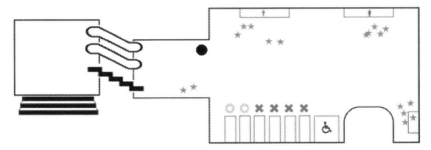

Fig. 4. Standing areas of smartphone addicts

In addition, observations found that this phenomenon is most common around 1:30 and 5:30 pm, with more weekends than weekdays. It may be inferred that because the number of commuters and students who take the MRT on weekends is less than on weekdays, the purpose of traveling has changed from for the work or school, and the travelers have also changed. In reality, an increase in social time will increase the waiting and staying time of smartphone addicts at MRT stations. Figure 5 shows the real situation of usage behavior of smartphone addicts who stay outside the gates for a long time.

Fig. 5. The usage behavior of the smartphone addicts in MRT station.

4.3 Numbers of the Smartphone Addicts

Table 1 illustrated that the total number of entering people on Monday was 174, of which 43 were smartphone addicts. The probability is about 24.7%. The total number of entering people on Wednesday was 211, of which 54 were smartphone addicts. The probability is about 25.6%. On Saturday the number was 276, of which 48 were smartphone addicts with a probability of 17.4%. The result indicated that smartphone addicts had higher attendance rates on weekdays than on weekends.

Table 1. The number of smartphone addicts entering the station at different times

		10:00–10:15	13:00–13:15	17:00–17:15	20:00–20:15	All day total
MON.	Total entering	27	44	72	31	174
	Smartphone addicts	5	16	17	5	43
WED.	Total entering	31	54	91	35	211
	Smartphone addicts	3	22	19	10	54
SAT.	Total entering	51	67	87	62	276
	smartphone addicts	7	11	14	16	48

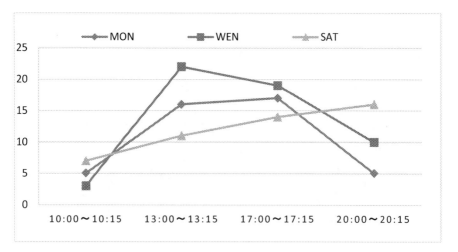

Fig. 6. The number of smartphone addicts at each period

Figure 6 showed that on Mondays and Wednesdays, smartphone addicts showed up more frequently at noon, and then gradually decreased. On Saturday, the number of smartphone addicts showed up increased, and the highest time was at 8:00 pm.

5   Discussion and Suggestion

The observation of this study found that the majority of the smartphone addicts are traveling alone and their ages are around 18 to 30. The usage behavior at the MRT station is mainly to watch smartphones while walking, standing at charging stations, and watching smartphones while waiting. Among the smartphone addicts who walked and looked at the phone, two people nearly tripped on the steps and one went to the escalator running in the opposite direction. The behavior of looking down at the phone while walking may increase the occurrence of escalator accidents, this is consistent with the research of Chi, Chang and Tsou (2006).

Moreover, the longest stay area for smartphone addicts on MRT stations is the charging station. The mobile devices used include smartphones, tablets, and laptops. Observations show that they usually stay at the charging station for more than 20 min, and they just lean on the table of the charging station instead of charging. Smartphone addicts using charging stations for long periods may reduce resource utilization.

Based on the above observational results, this study makes suggestions from two aspects. The first is to reduce the possibility of smartphone addicts encountering accidents at MRT stations. The second is to reduce the time that smartphone addicts use their smartphones at MRT stations.

There is a height difference between the topography of the MRT station. Smartphone addicts are prone to accidents while walking because they are too obsessed with phones. Therefore, it is recommended to add a warning landmark at the MRT station to remind smartphone addicts to pay attention to the current position. Figure 7 showed the design of warning landmarks. The left is the step warning landmark at the entrance outside the MRT station, which is consistent with the width of the steps. On the right is the escalator direction warning landmark, which is marked with a triangle to guide the direction of the escalator and avoid riding in the opposite direction. Landmarks are all in red which is more visible and targeted. It can also reduce the possibility of injury caused by looking down at the phone.

In addition to the design of warning landmarks, the in and out indicator of the gates also can be improved. The visible range of the existing gate direction indication is limited and can only be seen when approaching to swipe the card. We suggest adding an indicator light above the gates shown in Fig. 8. Thus, people can be seen from a distance to avoid congestion.

The second is to reduce the time that smartphone addicts use their smartphones at MRT stations. We suggest that the size of the desktop of the charging station can be appropriately reduced, so users cannot comfortably occupy for a long time. It can only be open to those who really need charging. Moreover, we suggest that a public reading area, such as a mobile library, can be set up at the MRT station in the future so that smartphone addicts can read without having to wait for time to watch the smartphone.

(1)   (2)

Fig. 7. Design improvement of the warning landmarks (1) The step warning landmark (2) The escalator direction warning landmark

Fig. 8. Design improvement of the direction indicator of the gate

6   Conclusion

Through this non-participant observation, the generated results indicate:

1. Smartphone addicts have higher attendance rates on weekdays than on weekends.
2. Some smartphone addicts ignore the gate's direction indicator causing them to collide with the opposite crowd.
3. We propose the design improvement of the direction indicator and suggest setting up an interactive space at the MRT station.

This study used a non-participative observation technique to understand some of the habits of smartphone addicts and conducted a design study with the Taipei MRT station as an example. The primary result of the study is to understand the usage habits of smartphone addicts and solve some problems in the design of the MRT station direction indicators.

Of course, this study has limitations. Nowadays, the phenomenon of smartphone addiction is highly concerned. This study only concerns with the travel problems of smartphone addicts. They may also have special usage habits at other times. In the future research, we may pay more attention to the interaction between smartphone addicts and phones, such as preferred application types, frequency of checking phones, etc., in order to reduce the chance of becoming a smart phone addict.

References

Abo-Jedi, A.: Cellphone addiction and its relation to self-closure in a sample of Jordanian university and Amman private university students. Jordan. J. Educ. Sci. **4**, 137–150 (2008)

Ahn, H., Wijaya, M.E., Esmero, B.C.: A systemic smartphone usage pattern analysis: focusing on smartphone addiction issue. Int. J. Multimedia Ubiquit. Eng. **9**, 9–14 (2014)

Cha, S.S., Seo, B.K.: Smartphone use and smartphone addiction in middle school students in Korea: prevalence, social networking service, and game use. Health Psychol. Open **5**(1), 2055102918755046 (2018)

Chi, C.F., Chang, T.C., Tsou, C.L.: In-depth investigation of escalator riding accidents in heavy capacity MRT stations. Accid. Anal. Prev. **38**(4), 662–670 (2006)

Grant, J., Potenza, M., Weinstein, A., et al.: Introduction to behavioral addictions. Am. J. Drug Alcohol Abuse **36**, 233–241 (2010)

Nie, N.H., Erbring, L.: Debating the societal effects of the Internet: connecting with the world. Public Perspect. **11**, 42–43 (2000)

Sun, L., Lee, D.H., Erath, A., Huang, X.: Using smart card data to extract passenger's spatio-temporal density and train's trajectory of MRT system. In: Proceedings of the ACM SIGKDD International Workshop on Urban Computing, pp. 142–148. ACM, August 2012

Townsend, C., Zacharias, J.: Built environment and pedestrian behavior at rail rapid transit stations in Bangkok. Transportation **37**(2), 317–330 (2010)

Yeo, S.K., He, Y.: Commuter characteristics in mass rapid transit stations in Singapore. Fire Saf. J. **44**(2), 183–191 (2009)

Subjective Usability and Will of Use on mHealth Application for Postpartum Emotional Disorder - A Case of We'll

Ding-Hau Huang[1]([✉]), Shih-Chen Lai[2], Liang-Ming Lo[3], Tai-He Hong[3], and Wen-Ko Chiou[4]

[1] Institute of Creative Design and Management, National Taipei University of Business, Taoyuan City, Taiwan
hauhuang@ntub.edu.tw
[2] Department of Industrial Design, Ming Chi University of Technology, Taoyuan City, Taiwan
down_120@hotmail.com
[3] Department of Obstetrics and Gynecology, Chang Gung Memorial Hospital, Taipei City, Taiwan
{lmlo,thh20}@cgmh.org.tw
[4] Department of Industrial Design, Chang Gung University, Taoyuan City, Taiwan
wkchiu@mail.cgu.edu.tw

Abstract. Patients having serious postpartum emotional disorder could have the intention of committing suicide or be in the danger of harming the new-born baby. Some researchers have developed a postpartum emotional disorder assistance mobile application, We'll, with social support as its core structure. Emotional support for the patients suffering postpartum emotional disorder can be enhanced through the interactive function of making wishes to further ease their depression problems. The study aimed to understand the subjective usability and willingness of use for the target users of We'll APP and discuss the actual needs of the users to further propose the optimized plans and suggestions for the mobile application. In this study, 15 subjects, satisfied the criteria of being a Taiwanese puerpera around 20 to 40 years old with child-birth experience, were recruited. The subjects are required to operate the We'll APP and perform 12 predetermined tasks for the evaluation of system usability scale (SUS). The willingness of use, satisfaction and other suggestions to the APP can be understood from semi-structured interview. The overall average score of SUS is 79.5, which is higher than the previous study. Hence, it is known that the usability of We'll APP satisfied the standards. We proposed and suggested the following plans to make subsequent optimization and revision based on the feedback of the subjects during the interview: (1) Create personal pregnancy experience database for users. (2) Set up prompt reminder function. (3) Create mothers' forum. (4) Enhance online real-time professional medical care consultation.

Keywords: Postpartum emotional disorder · Postpartum depression · Mobile health management · Mobile APP · Usability

© Springer Nature Switzerland AG 2020
C. Stephanidis et al. (Eds.): HCII 2020, LNCS 12423, pp. 696–709, 2020.
https://doi.org/10.1007/978-3-030-60114-0_45

1 Introduction

The probability of women suffering from depression is around two times of the probability of men [1, 2], and in addition, pregnant women and puerpera are one of the groups that has a high probability of suffering from depression. This is because most women can easily have emotion reaction aroused from huge hormone changes during their menstrual cycle, pregnancy and menopause. Hence, women suffering postpartum emotional disorder during pregnancy are quite common where they have common symptoms, such as postpartum blues (or baby blues) and postpartum depression (PPD). Around 40% to 80% puerpera had experienced unstable emotion and temporal postpartum blues [3]. However, most symptoms that puerpera suffered can be improved within a short amount of time with appropriate social support (including husband, family members, friends) and sufficient assistance. Postpartum depression could occur if the depression symptoms, such as being down in the dumps, has been prolonged for at least two weeks. The prevalence rate of postpartum depression is around 10% to 15% [4–7].

The combination of e-mental health (EMH) and social support is an important link to effectively improve and reduce the risk of puerpera suffering postpartum depression [7]. Currently, EMH services have become a trend in non-medicine therapy applications as the technology advances rapidly. Professional functions and effective information can be provided to the users through social media network to improve mental health issues. The form of EMH has gradually transformed to mobile health (mHealth) service with the prevalence in smart phones and tablet devices. In the mental health field, there were studies describing some relevant advantages of pregnant women and puerpera using EMH. For instance, women can use these APPs anonymously, so they are more likely to share some sensitive information related to their mental health [8, 9]. Moreover, smart phones exist everywhere in our daily life so the entry barrier for EMH APP is low. Women can use the EMH APP at their own appropriate time, which enhanced the flexibility of usage [8, 9]. From the society point-of-view, EMH applications can increase the possibility of postpartum depression discovery and therapy as well as reducing the costs to the maximum since the time in contact with a physician was reduced. Moreover, due to diagnosis, the chances of being cured can be increased rapidly. [8]. With all these advantages, more people have devoted in the development and test on EMH applications for postpartum depression in recent years. These methods result in active effects [8, 11, 12] with users having high acceptability and feasibility [9, 10, 13].

Previous studies [14] developed emotion assistance APP, We'll, based on social support theory. Such system takes on the concept of enhancing the social support and self-efficacy of puerpera users [15] as its core and provided a self-screening function by the Edinburgh postnatal depression scale (EPDS) [16], hoping that puerpera can ease and prevent postpartum blues and depression problems with the assistance of We'll APP. The postpartum emotion assistance system consists of management devices for data collection and organization, user data module, self-inspection module, medical information module, interactive game module, social media module and data storage module. Emotion after delivery can be expressed and self-controlled through the mental psychological inspection and suggestions from self-inspection module, the professional suggestions from medical information module, positive expectations from interactive game module and the online interaction with multiusers experiencing same emotions by the social media platform.

To extend the research results of We'll usability test [17], we applied qualitative research method on the revised version of We'll APP in this study. The current willingness of use and satisfaction of the system can be understood from the interview and objective usability analysis after puerpera actually operated the We'll APP. In addition, improvement plans and suggestions can be proposed based on the interface operation and function problems of the system from the users. We hope that the actual needs of puerpera from the EMH app can be understood and the willingness of use can be enhanced from our research results.

2 Literature Review

2.1 Current Status and Development of Mobile Health and E-Mental Health for Depression a Subsection Sample

Depression is currently one of the most common mental illnesses. Relevant symptoms of the patients include mental and work disabilities as well as unbalanced life, which could have a further impact on social economy and result in a huge burden. Hence, depression is ranked as the fourth in the global burden of disease [18] and is the most urgent illness to be eased due to its impact. Regarding therapy for depression, cognitive behavior therapy (CBT) and behavioral activation therapy (BA) have been recognized as the first-line treatment [19] in recent years. Both methods are the most common mental therapy channels currently. The difference between the two is explained in the following: cognitive behavior therapy is a treatment process with assistance provided by the proccessional psychotherapist in order to guide them into positive thinking; with the required professional training and treatment cost are relatively higher. Behavioral activation therapy, on the other hand, can be provided by mental health personnel with less training, making treatment costs and professional training costs relatively lower; this method has become a new treatment option to patients with tight budget. In the aforementioned two psychological treatments, patients are required to meet with their therapist regularly. However, the population suffering from depression has increased by day [20]. Hence, some research proposed network model for the provision of mental treatment services [21–23]. That is, patients suffering from depression can get treatment through the mobile application on their smart phones or mobile devices, providing an option thinking outside the box of traditional limited psychological consultation model and achieving the popularity of screening and treatment services.

Huguet et al. [19] organized 117 applications related to depression in their research. Based on their classification on the type of services provided by the applications for patients suffering depression, they pointed out that the most widely used types were education, screening and diagnosis; state induction was ranked next; and the most uncommon application type was tracking and social support (refer to Table 1). Chan et al. [24] also pointed out in their research that there are many mobile applications to assist the patients suffering depression on the market with mental health service functions including self-monitoring, self-management, diagnosis and treatment. Currently, there is no limitations on the creation of applications which can be downloaded and used from public open platform. Passing the application procedure is the only requirement to make to the shelf. The applications do not require strict verification on reliability and validity. The study suggested that mobile applications providing mental health services should conduct strict evaluation to verify its effects and clinical usability based on their functions so that reliable mental health services with evidence can be provided to the users through mobile devices.

Table 1. Organization of the application type related to depression

APP type	Quantity (%)
Tracking	10(8.55)
CBT/BA treatment	12(10.26)
State induction	18(15.38)
Diagnosis and screening	30(25.64)
Education	32(27.35)
Social support	3(2.56)
Others	28(23.93)
Total number of APPs	177(100)

(Organized from [19])

Dol et al. [7] discovered in their recent literature review that there is sufficient evidence showing that mHealth intervention can improve social support during postpartum period. In addition, comparing with those without intervention, it has been discovered that mHealth intervention can reduce postpartum depression. Baumel et al. [25] also show in their research that it is feasible and acceptable for women with postpartum depression to use 7Cups digital platform as mHealth intervention measures and there are also actual effects clinically. For women suffering postpartum depression, 7Cups digital platform can provide them adjunct treatment and self-support tools, including the following: the ability to connect with people from the community (24/7 emotional support will be provided by trained volunteers); personalized growth path function (providing an orderly route for the treatment activities or information, including appreciation practice, psychological education, tools for practice, evaluation and feedback under the principle of accepting and committing to treatment); and audio-based mindfulness exercises.

2.2   Research Related to the Evaluation on the Willingness of Using MHealth APP

Smart phones are the most widely used technology, and thus, all kinds of APP have been developed vigorously in respond to all kinds of needs and fields. Among them, the applications related to medical type have grown 25% each year [26], including adjunct management on chronic disease, self-diagnosis, general physical and mental health and fitness, etc. [27]. Most of the research on the APPs focused on the interaction between the users and the human-machine interface and verified only whether the application design matched the theory [28–30]. The impact, intention of use and needs of the APP users are poorly understood. Currently, there are lots of health-related mobile applications, however, users do not continue to use them or completely unwilling to use them after using short amount of time in the beginning, or users even do not know the existence of these kinds of applications. If discussed from the user point-of-view, then users' past experiences, use habits, use awareness and needs can be used as the evaluation principle to accurately analyze the willingness of use from the users.

Some researchers discussed the design and content elements of health-related applications by qualitative research and pointed out the important factors affecting the use of health-related applications through inductive topic analysis (refer to Table 2) [31]. In order to understand why the users are willing to use or unwilling to use, Peng et al. [31] understood the APP use situation and preference of the use subjects and explained their experiences and needs through focus group interview; in addition, they analyzed the true willingness of use through the interview content. They can even optimize the APP by the needs of the users and the reason of unwillingness to use so that the users will be willing to continue using or their willingness of use in the future can be enhanced.

Table 2. Factors impeding and driving the use of health applications

Factors impeding the use of health applications		Factors driving the use of health applications
The obstacles of starting to use health applications	The obstacles of continuing to use health applications	
Low awareness of health apps	Lack of time (and effort)	Motivators
Lack of need for health apps	Lack of motivation and discipline	Information and personalized guidance
Lack of app literacy		Tracking for awareness and progress
Cost		Credibility
		Goal setting
		Reminders
		Sharing personal information

(Organized from [31])

Recent retrospective research also pointed out that many studies applied the user-centered design process and some novel methods to enhance user-engagement during the development of mental health applications. Applying user point-of-view for designing mental health applications can greatly improve the usability and satisfaction of these kinds of applications [32].

2.3   Usability Analysis on mHealth APP

Usability is the criteria for the success of health and health care mobile applications and is the key factor for whether the users adopted these applications. Thus, Liew et al. [33] discussed the usability indicators jointly cared by mHealth developers and users in their research where satisfaction, learnability and error rate are the usability issues cared by the two groups jointly. Satisfaction refers to interface familiar and comfort, contributes to health objectives, address specific needs; learnability is integrated with habit/daily life; and error rate is for the control of providing accurate information. Moreover, Zapata et al. [34] investigated 22 studies related to mHealth applications through systematic literature overview and organized the indicators in the usability evaluation, including attraction, learnability, operability and understandability, shown in Table 3.

Table 3. Usability evaluated characteristic of mHealth app

Characteristics	Description
Attractiveness	a. The colour black is often found to be repulsive b. The colour of components should contrast with the background c. Adults are not interested in gaming applications, unlike teens
Learnability	a. Training is important to reduce the time needed by users to learn how to use the app b. A monotonous user interface causes poor learnability c. A tutorial at the start of the app is desired by users to guide them d. Users learn how to use a touchscreen after a few tries
Operability	a. It takes a young adult a 1/4 of the time required by an older. adult to complete a task b. Free text inputs should be avoided c. Dropdown menus with prewritten options improve efficiency d. Difficulty in scrolling despite the existence of visual hints e. Difficulty in performing swipe gestures f. Difficulty in holding the tablet and interacting at the same time g. There is no interaction between time and self-rated smartphone. Confidence
Understandability	a. Texts should be easily understood to avoid confusing terms or actions b. Need for bigger font sizes, even on the keyboard c. Buttons need to look like real buttons d. Too much information or commands on a single screen should. be avoided e. Tendency to press icons but not the text associated with it f. Difficulty in managing navigation levels, relying on the back. button as a safe option

(Organized from [34])

3 Method

3.1 Research Design

The research aimed to discuss the willingness of puerpera using We'll APP and propose optimized plan for the system from the qualitative feedback from the subjects as the as references for subsequent enhancement on willingness of use. The experiment procedure was conducted as follows: (1) Recruit the subjects; (2) Explain research and experiment test; (3) Test by scenario tasks; (4) Evaluate by usability scale; (5) Conduct semi-structure interview after the test. Before the test started, the research content was explained to the subjects, including the test procedure and purpose, the basic operation of the APP interface and the introduction on scenario tasks. First, the subjects were familiarized themselves with operating the experiment device (ASUS ZenPad 8.0 tablet device). After making the introductory explanations, the subjects were guided to operate the We'll APP to conduct the predetermined tasks for the experiment. There were 12 items in the scenario tasks, covering all the functions provided by the application. After completing the test, the usability evaluation was conducted, including basic survey questionnaire to record the basic information of the subjects and system usability scale (SUS) to evaluate the usability of We'll APP. In the end, semi-structure interview was conducted based on the feeling of subjects operating the system. The use experience and willingness of use for We'll from the subjects were collected during the interview process. The interview time for each subject was 25 to 40 min. Video and audio recording were conducted during the interview. After the interview, the recordings will be organized as transcript for analysis. During the data analysis process, the transcript will be cross compared repetitively to clarified the subjective differences between the subjects and the research. Optimized plans were proposed after organizing.

3.2 Subjects

In this study, 15 subjects were recruited to participate in the experiment. The recruitment criteria were the following: (1) Women with pregnancy experience and have a child (or children); (2) Aged between 18 to 45 years old who have pregnancy plans or does not exclude child birth opportunity; (3) Had over 4 years of experiences using smart phones and have the habit of using tablet devices in their daily life. The following conditions in the subjects were excluded: (1) Aged over 45; (2) Experienced pregnancy period before but had no experiences in child birth; (3) Foreign puerpera or those who cannot read Chinese characters were being excluded since current version of the system and the scale were both in Chinese.

3.3 In-Depth Interview Procedure

Before the interview, we explained to the subjects about the purpose of the interview and the interview outline in detail again and asked the subjects to devote themselves during the interview. The estimated time for the interview was 25 to 40 min. The interview procedure and time were flexibly adjusted according to the personal situation of the different subjects. The design of the interview procedure is shown in. The interview location is the same as the usability test (mainly the puerpera health education classroom in the Obstetrics and Gynecology; however, we also satisfied the convenience of the subjects to conduct the interview at their home, the reception room of apartment, coffee shop, etc.). The application devices used during the interview were the built-in recording software in smart phone, paper and pen. Hardware was used to record all the content during the interview. The interviewer also recorded the emotion of the subjects and some notes with paper and pen at the same time in order to assist in the subsequent analysis on the words and sentences in the interview. After all interviews were completed, the interviewer transformed the content in the recording audio to transcript according to the time order and repetitively listen to the interview content and label the key sentences. The research procedure and relevant tools were confirmed and approved by IRB committee of Chang Gung Hospital (Table 4).

Table 4. Design of interview procedure

Interview order	Required time	Interview outline	Content design
1	Around 5 min	Interview introduction	Introduce the interview outline to the subjects, explain the interview procedure and ask for their permission for audio recording
2	Around 10 min	Past experiences	Ask the subjects about their use experiences on relevant APP in the past, their use situation of Edinburgh Postnatal Depression Scale and the problems required most assistance and the person that they asked for help most often during pregnancy
3	Around 10 min	We'll usability	Know whether the users are satisfied with the interface and function of We'll
4	Around 10 min	User needs	Understand whether We'll satisfied user needs and discuss the actual user needs

3.4 In-Depth Interview Outline

Interview outline can be divided into three aspects: (1) past experiences, (2) usability, (3) actual user needs. The details of the interview questions are shown in Table 5.

Table 5. Interview content outline

Outline type	Question no.	Content
Past experiences	1	Do you have past experiences using puerpera assistance APP?
	2	Have you heard of Edinburgh Postnatal Depression Scale?
	3	Have you filled out Edinburgh Postnatal Depression Scale before?
	4	Please describe the emotion changes during pregnancy
	5	Who is the one that mostly accompanied and supported you during pregnancy?
	6	What is the matter that required most support during pregnancy?
We'll usability	7	Please describe your feeling for We'll system before/during/after the test
	8	What is the biggest challenge among the executed tasks?
	9	Which of the executed tasks made the most impression on you?
	10	How do you feel about the current We'll interface?
	11	Is there any current function in We'll that helped you?
	12	Please list the current advantages and disadvantages of We'll (each two)?
User needs	13	Does the We'll interface match your expectation?
	14	Which of the function in We'll matched your needs?
	15	Which current function do you think existed but not required?
	16	Which function do you think is required but not yet provided?
	17	Are you willing to download and use We'll during pregnancy in the future? Why?
	18	Are you willing to introduce your family and friends to use We'll? Why?
	19	We would like to hear your suggestions for We'll

4   Result and Discussion

4.1   Analysis on Subjects

In this study, 15 subjects were recruited and interviewed during the period from August 22, 2019 to December 22, 2019. Subjects included 75% primipara and 25% with child-birth experiences (that is, having at least one child). There were 70% of the subjects used adjunct APP during their pregnancy. All the subjects had over 4 years of experiences using smart phones.

4.2 System Usability Analysis Results

The overall average score of the system usability scale (SUS) from the 15 subjects is 79.5, which is greater than the average score of SUS, 68. It can be seen from this that the satisfaction of We'll matched the standards. The average score from the Android version used in the early-stage research was 70.5 [17]. The SUS score enhanced obviously after revision and optimization, representing that the satisfaction of the current version was approved and recognized by users.

4.3 Interview Results

Analysis and coding on the transcript were conducted based on the interview content of the subjects. Coding was done based on the research purpose and can be divided into two topics: (I) willingness of use in the future; and (II) actual user needs. Coding was conducted two times based on the aforementioned topics and organized into Table 6.

Table 6. Code

Topic	Code
Willingness of use in the Future	Ease of use in terms of interface and operation
	Function usefulness
	Use satisfaction
Actual user needs	Past experiences
	Need awareness
	Family and friend support
	Professional support

Willingness to Use in the Future. In the aspect of ease of use in terms of interface and operation, we discovered the following: most users thought the interface icons in We'll are cure and have soft color matching and affinity, etc. through the interview and observation; they said that the interface design matched user visual perception and can arouse willingness of use. In the previous version, the function of interface icons was not obvious and there are some errors in the navigation. However, the problems were reduced after revision. We can determine that the ease of use in terms of We'll interface is enhanced after revision.

In the aspect of function usefulness, We'll provides users with functions in three different aspects: (1) Real-time inspection: Edinburgh Postnatal Depression Scale was provided; (2) Formal support: Professional health education knowledge for puerpera was provided; (3) Non-formal support: Wishing well function was provided; social support is enhanced by making wishes and interacting with family and friends. This function obtained positive feedback and recognition from users.

In the aspect of user satisfaction, significant increase in the score of system usability scale proved that user satisfaction increased after the interface and usability were being optimized; and in addition, users also proposed during the interview that the ductility (such as the reasons for the same puerpera reuse We'll when having the second child or the third child, including the past record and database of first-child pregnancy or other kinds of inducement) of We'll, other than ease of use and usability, will be the key element for their willingness of use in the future.

Actual Needs of the Users. In the aspect of users' past experiences, we discovered that postpartum depression was very common in the current society. Women with child-birth experiences will reference their own pregnancy experience in the past while women with first pregnancy will reference the prompt information from their family and friends, the elders or the internet. They required a reliable and effective information channel for the symptoms of postpartum depression and how to ease the symptoms.

In the aspect of need awareness, postpartum blues or depression can mainly be blamed by the significant changes of female hormone affecting their emotion. Those suffered from postpartum can hardly determine whether they required assistance regarding their own physical and mental status.

In the aspect of family and friend support, family members, spouse, friends and colleagues are the social support network of the puerpera (and non-formal supporting source). If emotional, practical, evaluation support can be given at appropriate time during the postpartum blues and temporal depression, then the mental discomfort can be improved effectively. Some subjects said that if mothers' forum or social community was created on We'll, then it can also become an effective supporting method.

Professional support refers to the support required from formal medical personnel or relevant specialists to provide professional knowledge for new-born baby care and relevant assistance methods to ease postpartum emotional disorder problems. In the aspect of professional support, how and where can they obtained professional assistance in-time was also a need proposed by the subjects.

4.4 Discussion

In the aspect of willingness of use in the future, we categorized the interview with the subjects into ease of use in terms of interface and operation, function usefulness and satisfaction for discussion. Among them, the information and the score of system usability scale obtained during the interview can verify that the navigation errors and ease of use have been improved in the revised interface and operation from the early-stage research [17] and the Edinburgh Postnatal Depression Scale function and social support structure provided in We'll obtained positive feedback and recognition from the subjects. The results were consistent with other recent relevant studies [7]. We can know from this that the willingness of use for We'll from the subjects is positive and can be extended. As mentioned by the subjects that We'll aimed for easing postpartum depression in its development, hence there are specific use group for the APP. To maintain the willingness of use, it is required to maintain the personal database or We'll use social community so that the willingness of use can be extended effectively during long term and more target users will have the willingness to use. Regarding this, 7cup platform model [25] can be referenced, where they systematically built a non-formal support system.

In the aspect of user actual needs, we divided the interview process of the subjects into past experiences, need awareness, family and friend support and professional support for discussion. We learned from the interview that women with first pregnancy were often perplexed and had no sense of security towards childbirth. They probably required We'll intervention as the tools for easing their emotion or assistance. In addition, the scope of the social support function can be further expanded. For example, creating mothers' experience forum for those with childbirth experiences to help and connect with those having their first childbirth and share their experiences and offer actual support. Then with the current evaluation screening, professional information and family and friend interaction in We'll, the actual needs for the puerpera can be satisfied comprehensively.

5 Conclusion

In this study, we analyzed the willingness of use for We'll from the interview with the subjects and discuss whether the current functions in We'll matched their needs. We incorporated the actual needs of the subjects as references for subsequent optimization in the function of We'll so that We'll can be optimized towards the direction of matching closely and satisfying target users.

According to the aforementioned results and discussion, we suggested the following for subsequent optimization:

(1) Create personal pregnancy experience database for users so that they can review or compare the history as records and references for the time after delivery or during future pregnancy; also, their willingness of use can be enhanced.

(2) Set up prompt reminder function so that the puerpera users and their family and friends (family members, spouse or friends) can use the We'll account to link the reminder function; reminder will be given to the linked account after their usage status (making wishes, complete the scoring and evaluation on emotion inspection) is completed.

(3) Create mothers' forum so that the puerpera can build a peer-supporting network by sharing their own process and experience.

(4) Enhance online real-time professional medical care consultation so that the users can promptly get professional knowledge and caring methods through We'll network.

References

1. Burt, V.K., Stein, K.: Epidemiology of depression throughout the female life cycle. J. Clin. Psychiatr. **63**, 9–15 (2002)
2. Kessler, R.C.: Epidemiology of women and depression. J. Affect. Disord. **74**(1), 5–13 (2003)
3. Evins, G.G., Theofrastous, J.P.: Postpartum depression: a review of postpartum screening. Prim. Care Update Ob/Gyns **4**(6), 241–246 (1997)
4. Cox, J.L., Murray, D., Chapman, G.: A controlled study of the onset, duration and prevalence of postnatal depression. Br. J. Psychiatr. **163**(1), 27–31 (1993)

5. Gavin, N.I., Gaynes, B.N., Lohr, K.N., Meltzer-Brody, S., Gartlehner, G., Swinson, T.: Perinatal depression: a systematic review of prevalence and incidence. Obstet. Gynecol. **106**(5–1), 1071–1083 (2005)

6. Darcy, J.M., Grzywacz, J.G., Stephens, R.L., Leng, I., Clinch, C.R., Arcury, T.A.: Maternal depressive symptomatology: 16-month follow-up of infant and maternal health-related quality of life. J. Am. Board Family Med. **24**(3), 249–257 (2011)

7. Dol, J., Richardson, B., Murphy, G.T., Aston, M., McMillan, D., Campbell-Yeo, M.: Impact of mobile health interventions during the perinatal period on maternal psychosocial outcomes: a systematic review. JBI Evid. Synth. **18**(1), 30–55 (2020)

8. O'Mahen, H.A., et al.: Internet-based behavioral activation—treatment for postnatal depression (netmums): a randomized controlled trial. J. Affect. Disord. **150**(3), 814–822 (2013)

9. Danaher, B.G., et al.: Web-based intervention for postpartum depression: Formative research and design of the mommoodbooster program. JMIR Res. Protocols **1**(2), e18 (2012)

10. Haga, S.M., Drozd, F., Brendryen, H., Slinning, K.: Mamma mia: a feasibility study of a web-based intervention to reduce the risk of postpartum depression and enhance subjective well-being. JMIR Res. Protocols **2**(2), e29 (2013)

11. Barrera, A.Z., Wickham, R., Muñoz, R.F.: Online prevention of postpartum depression for spanish- and english-speaking pregnant women: a pilot randomized controlled trial. Internet Interv. **2**(3), 257–265 (2015)

12. Maloni, J.A., Przeworski, A., Damato, E.G.: Web recruitment and internet use and preferences reported by women with postpartum depression after pregnancy complications. Arch. Psychiatr. Nurs. **27**(2), 90–95 (2013)

13. Osma, J., Barrera, A.Z., Ramphos, E.: Are pregnant and postpartum women interested in health-related apps? Implications for the prevention of perinatal depression. Cyberpsychol. Behav. Soc. Netw. **19**(6), 412–415 (2016)

14. Chiou, W.-K., Kao, C.-Y., Lo, L.-M., Huang, D.-H., Wang, M.-H., Chen, B.-H.: Feasibility of utilizing e-mental health with mobile app interface for social support enhancement: a conceptional solution for postpartum depression in Taiwan. In: Marcus, A., Wang, W. (eds.) DUXU 2017. LNCS, vol. 10289, pp. 198–207. Springer, Cham (2017). https://doi.org/10.1007/978-3-319-58637-3_15

15. Shaw, L.H., Gant, L.M.: In defense of the Internet: the relationship between internet communication and depression, loneliness, self-esteem, and perceived social support. J. Obstet. Gynaecol. Canada **41**(10) (2004)

16. Shen, N., et al.: Finding a depression app: a review and content analysis of the depression app marketplace. JMIR mHealth uHealth **3**(1), e16 (2015)

17. Chiou, W.-K., Lai, S.-C., Huang, D.-H.: Usability testing of a mobile application for alleviating postpartum emotional disorders: a case of we'll. In: Duffy, Vincent G. (ed.) HCII 2019. LNCS, vol. 11582, pp. 23–40. Springer, Cham (2019). https://doi.org/10.1007/978-3-030-22219-2_2

18. World Health Organization: The global burden of disease: 2004 update (2008, 2011)

19. Huguet, A., et al.: A systematic review of cognitive behavioral therapy and behavioral activation apps for depression. PLoS ONE **11**(5), e0154248 (2016)

20. Kessler, R.C., Chiu, W.T., Demler, O., Walters, E.E.: Prevalence, severity, and comorbidity of 12-month DSM-IV disorders in the National Comorbidity Survey Replication. Arch. Gen. Psychiatr. **62**(6), 617–627 (2005)

21. van't Hof, E., Cuijpers, P., Stein, D.J.: Self-help and Internet-guided interventions in depression and anxiety disorders: a systematic review of meta-analyses. CNS Spectr. **14**(S3), 34–40 (2009)

22. Ly, K.H., et al.: Behavioural activation versus mindfulness-based guided self-help treatment administered through a smartphone application: a randomised controlled trial. BMJ Open **4**(1), e003440 (2014)

23. Moss, K., Scogin, F., Di Napoli, E., Presnell, A.: A self-help behavioral activation treatment for geriatric depressive symptoms. Aging Mental Health **16**(5), 625–635 (2012)

24. Chan, S., Torous, J., Hinton, L., Yellowlees, P.: Towards a framework for evaluating mobile mental health apps. Telemed. e-Health **21**(12), 1038–1041 (2015)

25. Baumel, A., Tinkelman, A., Mathur, N., Kane, J.M.: Digital peer-support platform (7Cups) as an adjunct treatment for women with postpartum depression: feasibility, acceptability, and preliminary efficacy study. JMIR mHealth uHealth **6**(2), e38 (2018)

26. Becker, S., Miron-Shatz, T., Schumacher, N., Krocza, J., Diamantidis, C., Albrecht, U.V.: mHealth 2.0: experiences, possibilities, and perspectives. JMIR mHealth uHealth **2**(2), e24 (2014)

27. Boulos, M.N.K., Brewer, A.C., Karimkhani, C., Buller, D.B., Dellavalle, R.P.: Mobile medical and health apps: state of the art, concerns, regulatory control and certification. Online J. Public health Inform. **5**(3), 229 (2014)

28. Direito, A., Dale, L.P., Shields, E., Dobson, R., Whittaker, R., Maddison, R.: Do physical activity and dietary smartphone applications incorporate evidence-based behaviour change techniques? BMC Public Health **14**(1), 646 (2014). https://doi.org/10.1186/1471-2458-14-646

29. Middelweerd, A., Mollee, J.S., van der Wal, C.N., Brug, J., Te-Velde, S.J.: Apps to promote physical activity among adults: a review and content analysis. Int. J. Behav. Nutr. Phys. Act. **11**(1), 97 (2014). https://doi.org/10.1186/s12966-014-0097-9

30. Zahry, N.R., Cheng, Y., Peng, W.: Content analysis of diet-related mobile apps: a self-regulation perspective. Health Commun. **31**(10), 1301–1310 (2016)

31. Peng, W., Kanthawala, S., Yuan, S., Hussain, S.A.: A qualitative study of user perceptions of mobile health apps. BMC Public Health **16**(1), 1158 (2016)

32. Mehrotra, S., Tripathi, R.: Recent developments in the use of smartphone interventions for mental health. Curr. Opin. Psychiatr. **31**(5), 379–388 (2018)

33. Liew, M.S., Zhang, J., See, J., Ong, Y.L.: Usability challenges for health and wellness mobile apps: mixed-methods study among mHealth experts and consumers. JMIR mHealth uHealth **7**(1), e12160 (2019)

34. Zapata, B.C., Fernández-Alemán, J.L., Idri, A., Toval, A.: Empirical studies on usability of mHealth apps: a systematic literature review. J. Med. Syst. **39**(2), 1 (2015). https://doi.org/10.1007/s10916-014-0182-2

Understanding User Engagement in Information and Communications Technology for Development: An Exploratory Study

Tochukwu Ikwunne(✉) ⬡, Lucy Hederman ⬡, and P. J. Wall ⬡

ADAPT Centre, Trinity College Dublin, Dublin, Ireland
{ikwunnet,hederman,pj.wall}@tcd.ie

Abstract. User engagement is often associated with successful information systems implementation, with this being particularly true in developing countries in the Global South. However, the term remains poorly understood with many seemingly conflicting definitions and the term "user engagement" has come to mean a variety of things in the literature. Also, it is unclear at what stage(s) of the design, development, implementation and use phase(s) that user engagement should apply to. This research examines the meaning of user engagement with the objective of bringing some level of clarity to suit the information communication technology for development (ICT4D) context. To this end, we propose an expanded definition of the term user engagement. The research also suggests what stages of the design, development, implementation and use phase of the technology this expanded definition of user engagement most usefully applies to by drawing lessons on user engagement in a variety of mobile health projects from the Global South. Qualitative methods of data analysis were used in collecting data which show that user engagement as applied to a specific phase of each of the projects was essential for the ongoing success of each project.

Keywords: User engagement · Global South · ICT for development · ICT4D · Mobile-health applications · Mobile health · mHealth

1 Introduction

It is widely accepted that implementation of any technology-based project for development in the Global South (ICT4D) is difficult [1] and usually has a high failure rate [2]. There have been many technical [3, 4] and socio-technical [5] reasons put forward to explain this including lack of user engagement in the process. This would seem to be obvious but is problematic for a variety of reasons. Firstly, user engagement has diverse meaning and its actual form and strategies for effective user engagement are poorly defined and understood [6] with many seemingly conflicting definitions, with the term meaning a variety of different things in the literature. In addition, other similar terms such as user participation [7] have appeared to confuse the situation even further. Secondly, it is unclear at what stage(s) of the design, development, implementation and use phase(s) that user engagement should apply. This research thus perceived a gap. Based

C. Stephanidis et al. (Eds.): HCII 2020, LNCS 12423, pp. 710–721, 2020.
https://doi.org/10.1007/978-3-030-60114-0_46

on this gap we propose the research question "how can an improved understanding of the concept of user engagement be achieved in the design, development, implementation and use of mHealth projects in Global South countries?". The objective of this study is to provide an extended definition of user engagement and to apply this to a variety of ICT4D and mHealth projects in African and India. We do this in an attempt to show how our extended notion of user engagement elicits a better understanding of user engagement in the ICT4D context. A further objective is to show whether user engagement may have impacted the success or otherwise of each ICT4D project. In addition, this work attempts to bring some level of clarity to the situation by firstly reviewing the various meanings and interpretations of user engagement from the literature, and secondly by proposing a definition of user engagement that is appropriate to ICT4D. Finally, the work attempts to extend existing definitions of user engagement to better suit the ICT4D context. We also suggest what stages of the design, development, implementation and use phase of the technology this expanded definition of user engagement most usefully applies to. This work is supported by providing a qualitative analysis of data collected primarily by semi-structured interview from 5 mobile health (mHealth) projects in Africa and India which show that user engagement (as defined by our extended definition) as applied to a specific phase of each of the projects was essential for the ongoing success of each project. The paper concludes by suggesting that a clear, expanded and widely accepted definition of user engagement is essential in both ICT4D and mHealth, and also that some level of clarity is needed on when and how users can be engaged in such projects.

2   Literature Review

2.1   Meaning of User Engagement

User engagement within the broad field of information systems (IS), and more recently its important sub-discipline of ICT4D, has been widely discussed since the 1960's [6]. This is an important discussion as the research suggests that higher levels of user engagement lead to a higher chance of system success [7]. This is particularly important in the ICT4D field given the estimated 80% failure rate of technology implementations in such environments [8]. Any discussion of user engagement must start with a definition of the term as this has been poorly defined in the literature [6]. User engagement usually refers to the engagement of users in the design, development, implementation and use of technology, but many other varying definitions have also been provided. O'Brien and Toms [9] propose that user engagement as a category of user experience characterized by attributes of challenge, positive affect, endurability, aesthetic and sensory appeal, attention, feedback, variety/novelty, inter-activity, and perceived user control. Furthermore, O'Brien [10] viewed user engagement as a quality of user experience characterized by the depth of an actor's investment when interacting with a digital system.

Many aspects of user engagement have been written about including development of models for measuring and validating the factors required for successful user engagement in IS development [11]. A variety of models have also been suggested to measure this including the User Engagement Scale [12]. In addition, methodological issues around user engagement are widely discussed in the literature including by Bhatt et al. [1] who consider issues in putting together methodology that create what they call active user engagement which is designed to overcome various socio-cultural barriers such as language and culture.

This paper relies on the definition of user engagement as provided by Kappelman and McLean [13] as *"the total set of user relationships towards IS and their development, implementation, and use"*. We rely on this definition for a number of important reasons. Firstly, this is one of the earliest and more widely accepted definitions of the term. Secondly, the definition distinguishes between engagement in the design, development, implementation and the use phases of the technology. Thirdly, it identifies behaviors and attitudes (i.e. the component dimensions) of system users in each stage of the technology development, implementation and use process. According to Kappleman and McLean [13] a user can be engaged in the development process or in the use of the product, but it is not possible for a single user to be engaged in only one of the component dimensions (i.e. behavior and attitude). Finally, the definition allows for the various ways in which users can be engaged in the processes of information technology development, implementation and use.

2.2 Various Interpretations of User Engagement and the Need for an Extended Definition

As already mentioned, a number of definitions of user engagement already exist and these are now discussed in brief. We suggest a wider discussion about user engagement in ICT4D (a subsection of Information System Development ISD) needs to occur, and that this should be based around the work already done in the field of ICT4D and the broader ISD field. This is because of the ambiguous terminology associated with the roles of system users in the process(es) of IS development, implementation and use [13]. Furthermore, ICT4D is the practice of utilizing technology to assist poor and marginalized people in developing communities, hence, the role of users in IS development and implementation has received a great deal of research focus. However, the value of such roles is mixed because social, cultural, political and environmental factors of the users are not captured as regards the various ways users can be engaged in the processes of IS development, implementation and use, especially in the Global South. This is not to say that the previous definitions of user engagement are "not correct" to a certain extent, but that the field is evolving as the subject of study becomes more clearly understood. The prior definitions played a valuable role in helping to focus on this need for clarity and hence the quest for an extended definition.

We start this discussion by looking at the existing work on user engagement in ICT4D where the notion of successful user engagement is closely tied to the success of any ICT4D project [14–16]. The Department for International Development in the UK (DFID) regards engagement as individuals moving from simply accessing or consuming the content and services offered by an online platform to becoming more involved in the platform, recommending or promoting it and actively co-creating the content [17]. Engagement has also been viewed as the state of mind that must be attained in order to enjoy a representation of an action so that we may experience computer worlds directly, without mediation or distraction [18]. This view aligns with the concept of "direct engagement" that focusses on the interaction between human and machine, by which users' cognitive intentions can be realized through the physical manipulation of the interface [19]. Another view is provided by Attfield [20] who perceived engagement as the quality of user experience that emphasizes the positive aspects of interaction, in particular the phenomena associated with being captivated by technology. Additionally, Attfield [20] defined user engagement as the emotional, cognitive and behavioral connection that exists, at any point in time and possibly over time between a user and a resource. Other conceptions of user engagement have sought to shift focus from the individual user's perspective to the designer's perspective. One example of this is Jacques [21] who examined the ability of the system or application to catch and captivate user interest, while Quesenbery [22] looked at methods of drawing people in and encouraging interaction. Additionally, Saariluoma [23] had interest in motivating and enhancing the user experience with the use of the application, while O'Brien and Toms [12] defined engagement based on their synthesis of aesthetic, flow, play, and information interaction theories, as well as on previous work in the application areas of video games, online shopping, web searching, and educational software [21, 24]. Other definitions have been linked with user experience, specifically McCarthy and Wright's [25] spatio-temporal, compositional, emotional, and sensual "Threads of Experience", with many studies considering user engagement beyond user experience qualities. One example of this is Lukoff [26] who defined user engagement in connection with self-actualization and fulfilment. In addition, Lalmas [27] highlighted a broad definition of user engagement, identifying emotional, cognitive, and behavioral experience of a user with a technological resource that exists at any point in time and over time.

It is important to agree a shared understanding of the specific meaning of user engagement as the various interpretations have led to much misunderstanding [13] and it is not clear how useful these interpretations have been to practicing designers [28]. A clear and widely accepted definition of the term is also important in order to allow theorisation and a deeper understanding of how users actually "engage" with technologies, with this being of particular importance in developing country contexts. Furthermore, user engagement is a success factor in IS development, implementation and use [11].

However as already mentioned, and as in the IS literature, user engagement remains poorly defined in the ICT4D body of work [29, 30] which results in an inability of the concept to be clearly communicated amongst practicing designers [28]. While this work is valuable, we suggest that existing definitions of user engagement need to be extended for the ICT4D context. Thus, we propose an extended definition of user engagement and this is discussed in the next section.

3   Extending the Definition of User Engagement for ICT4D

As previously mentioned, we suggest that it necessary to extend the existing definition of user engagement as given by Kappelman and McLean [13] to include some elements of end user experiences in the different stages of the IS. Thus, we propose an extended definition of user engagement as follows: *"the total set of user relationships towards IS in their development and use stages, where this set of user relationships is dictated by users experience of interacting with the different stages of the system"*. This extended definition of user engagement takes into account how users relate with the IS in each stage of the development or use, in order to improve the efficiency and effectiveness of the IS's users. Also, it involves more than working with the users. It requires working with local ecosystem partners and to build their trust in and support for the use of the solution. We adopted three user experiences dimensions; cultural, psychological and social as described by Robert and Larouche [31] to describe user engagement in the development process and product of ICT4D or in the broader ISD domain. The user experience encompasses the attitude, behavior and cultural identity of users in the process and the product of ISD. Hence, user engagement is used here to refer to the combinations of user attitudinal, behavioral and cultural associations with the developmental process and product of ICT4D or a broader ISD. Figure 1 shows a diagrammatic representation of our proposed extension of the definition of the user engagement.

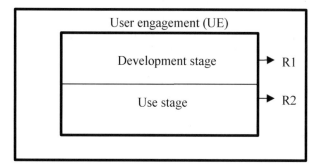

Fig. 1. Our extended definition of user engagement definition represented diagrammatically where R1 & R2 represent sets of relationships

User engagement is important in ICT4D because users are making decisions about what technologies to invest their time and effort into based on how those technologies make them feel [32]. It is not only whether an application is efficient, effective, or satisfying, but how well it is able to engage users and provide them with an experience [33, 34]. This is particularly relevant to users of ICT4D-related technologies and applications as these technologies and apps need to be both functional and engaging [34].

As already mentioned, successful user engagement can result in increased success when implementing and using technology in the Global South [9], but there are a number of difficulties with existing notions of user engagement in ICT4D. It bears critical significance, not just for informing the design and implementation of the interface, but also for creating improved and advanced interfaces that can adapt to users [35]. Taking healthcare as an example, user engaged technology-enabled applications can result in improved health outcomes [36]. Bush [37] examined the impact of user engagement on mHealth technology and pregnancy outcomes and found that strong user engagement in the use of the app resulted in significant performance by community health workers (CHWs) [38]. Furthermore, Torous [39] linked successful user engagement with higher levels of engagement with mental health apps. This aligns with the view of Kim [40] that the study of users' engagement from the use of mobile technologies can provide insights to further explain their success and continuous engagement behavior in the use of the technologies. It is believed that the ability to engage and sustain engagement in digital environments can result in positive outcomes not only for mHealth projects but for citizen inquiry and participation, web search, e-learning, and so on [41].

All of this implies that user engagement is paramount and key to ICT4D and mHealth success. This is why we are proposing an expanded definition that takes three user experiences dimensions; cultural, psychological and social into account in the development, implementation and use of the system.

4   Methodology: Data Collection, and Data Analysis

In this section we apply our extended definition of user engagement to five case studies of mHealth in India and Africa in order to provide clarity on the extent and nature of our expanded notion of user engagement in each case. The rationale for choosing these five cases studies of mHealth projects was because of the need to engage users which is among the key issues raised in e-government systems implementations and use [42–45] in different countries in the Global South. Each of the mHealth projects were partnered with government organisations and other stakeholders to ensure shared knowledge about the various mHealth projects and extended opportunities for learning and development through ICT. We also discuss briefly how user engagement has influenced the outcome and success of each case.

Qualitative research methodology was used in this research. Data collection consisted of 5 semi-structured interviews that lasted for 60 min each with key people in 5 separate mHealth projects. We focused on user engagement in the various stages of the development and use of the mHealth systems. Interviewees were identified based on their involvement in the development and use of the mHealth systems, and the interviewee had detailed knowledge of the development and use stages of the technology in each case. Each person also had in-depth knowledge of the manner and extent of the level of user engagement in each case. Each of the mHealth systems had various levels of success, with none of the 5 cases being seen as having totally failed.

All interviews were transcribed, and thematic coding and analysis were carried out using NVivo. The thematic analysis looked across all the data collected from the interviews to identify common issues that occurred around user engagement and identified the main themes that summarized all the views from the experts that were interviewed. Thereafter, a coding scheme was generated and proceeded iteratively, with constant comparisons being made between codes to identifying recurring themes. Codes that had similar elements were merged to form categories and the codes were clustered around each major theme. We arrived at three themes as follows: (1) user engagement in the development stage, (2) user engagement in the use of the product, and (3) user experience dimensions with interactive products. This method was chosen to understand expert's perspectives and experiences in working with users in the developmental process and product of ICT4D in order to provide answers to the research question. These were formed to support the reason for our proposed definition of user engagement which are to show what stage(s) of the design, development, implementation and use phase of the technology that our definition of user engagement most usefully applies to and to include some elements of user experiences.

For ethical and confidentiality reasons each case was assigned a case number from 1 to 5. Also, the experts interviewed are assigned with E1-E5, with these designations being associated with each case (i.e. E1 is the interviewee associated with Case 1, E2 is the interviewee associated with Case 2, and so on for Cases 2–5). The cases are as follows:

- Case 1: Gender based violence and child protection in Malawi - this project uses a mobile app to record child protection and gender-based violence data. The targeted users of the app were CHWs.
- Case 2: Diabetes control in India - this project is focused on the development, implementation and use of an app to test diabetes in remote areas of India. The targeted users of the apps are ASHAs (Indian CHWs).
- Case 3: HIV & TB in Africa - this project consists of an mHealth initiative that was conducted in four countries; South Africa, Mozambique, Zimbabwe, and Malawi. The project was based on clinicians using an app to collect data on routine viral load of each patient. The data was recorded, and the result was then sent to patients in the form of an SMS.
- Case 4: Handover report in India - this is an mHealth project based on a handover report system. The project was conducted in India, and the users of the handover report system were nurses. The technology was designed for handing over reports about patients within hospitals at the end of the nurses shifts.
- Case 5: Pregnancy care in India - this is an mHealth project based in India. It uses a mobile app to provide education and counselling to pregnant women on how to take care of themselves and babies when they are delivered.

5   Findings and Discussions

As previously stated, user engagement is used here to refer to the combinations of user attitudinal, behavioral and cultural associations with the developmental process and product of ICT4D or a broader ISD. The three user experience dimensions (psychological, social and cultural) were used to show users' attitudes, how the importance of users' relationships with other stakeholders can impact in the development, implementation and use of the technology, and how the user experience can contribute to defining user's cultural identity. In order to give a clear view of our extended definition, we organized our findings around three key themes from our proposed extended definition: (1) user engagement in the development stage (2) user engagement in the use of the product (3) user experience dimensions with interactive products. These themes are explained in greater detail below.

5.1   User Engagement in the Development Stage

The first theme involves examining how users were engaged during the development stages of the project and what made the projects succeed or not. Each of the mHealth projects were partnered with government organisations, research or academic institutions, NGO or not-for profit organisations, private organisations and the wider community to ensure shared knowledge about the various mHealth projects and extended opportunities for learning and development through ICT. According to E5 in Case 5 *"end users were very involved in designing the app. Tested with 10 ASHA's[1], focus groups, observation, etc. There was lots of feedback from ASHA's for over 1 year, and they got a lot of quality feedback".* In the same vein in Case 3, *"end users in Zimbabwe and Malawi were involved in focus groups and they provided information whether SMS with cryptic message would be available for them".*

Another important point was that users of the app could record messages that were provided to pregnant women with their local dialects during the development stages of the app. E5 stated that *"The entire app was translated to Hindi. Local health workers have recorded the messages in local dialect. Images were adapted to suit local contexts. The local health workers recorded their voice in the local language on the app in Hindi and the local dialect."* The conscious intent of engaging users at the development stage of the project created personal experience for the users which resulted in improving users' confidence. E5 stated that *"The voice on the phone is the ASHAs, but they sometimes tell the patient that the voice is from a doctor in Delhi. The whole thing has improved both the ASHAs confidence in themselves, and other people's confidence in the ASHAs."* This supports the reason we extended the definition we relied on, to include users' experience dimensions. The project was implemented successfully because of the feedback sessions provided by the ASHAs. E5 stated that *"There was a significant amount of feedback in the first year during the app development and there was newborn component every month and Prenatal app was good enough. When project becomes very big, reinstall a new version. 285 ASHAs involved in 285 villages provided feedback."*

This applies to our extended definition of user engagement because it clearly shows users relationships towards the development stage of the app by providing their local language and images in the app to engage users.

5.2   User Engagement in the Use of the Product

Next, we asked the interviewees their thoughts on how users were engaged in the use of each of the mHealth products. We are examining our expanded definition of user engagement in the context of the use of each of the mHealth products. In Case 5, it was explained that the pregnant women preferred listening to the voice from a male doctor or ASHA based in Delhi as opposed to other doctors or ASHA that are based locally. The male doctor voice engaged the pregnant women and they always gather around to share information (E5).

In Case 3, patients were engaged in always checking for their viral loads. According to E3, *"all information about patients' viral load was encrypted and patients logged in with a unique id".* E2 believed the cause of users' engagement with the app was because users received SMS that were encrypted.

In Case 2, the AV tool brought out conversations about diabetes which engaged people. E2 believed that what caused this engagement was because of the local dialects used in the AV tool. This facilitated engagement in conversations among the patients and created personal and emotional experiences for the patients. One major outcome

---

[1] An ASHA is an accredited social health activist or CHW usually based in India. The ASHA programme was initiated by the Indian Ministry of Health and Family Welfare may years ago.

highlighted by E2 was that the AV tool caused the patients to discuss subjects that were traditionally taboo, the stigma of diabetes, the genetic component and the implications this might have for marriage prospects for them and their daughters. This reflects on the important point that users engaging in the product creates experiences for the users.

5.3   User Experience Dimensions with Interactive mHealth Applications

We discussed three user experience dimensions to explain how mHealth apps were used and users' experiences. Every product creates an experience for its users, and that experience can either be the result of planning and conscious intent or the unplanned consequence of the product designer's choices [46]. According to E1 in Case 1, *"The project is run by community volunteers as well as community child protection workers and community development workers. The Government employs the health workers to record the data on mobile phones. The data includes age, gender, incident, how incident was resolved, etc."* These community workers understand the language, culture, and needs of the users and that made easier communication with the users.

Robert and Larouche [31] explained psychological dimension of user experience as when respondent talks of the emotions generated by the interaction with the product, of the impact of the product on his/her attitudes, opinions, motivations, identity, satisfaction. S/he discusses the underlying values of the product in relation with his/her own emotions. In the mHealth project, the experts discussed emotions generated by the interaction with the product, of the impact of the product on users' attitudes, opinions, motivations, identity, satisfaction. In relation to Case 4, E1 stated that *"An issue was getting the nurses to understand that there is no extra work involved, you are only pressing a number of buttons, there is no extra work."* This was because the nurses felt that they were doing an extra work by working with the app.

Robert and Larouche [31] explained social dimension of user experience as the respondent talks of the importance of others (e.g., parents, friends, work colleagues, etc.) and his/her relations with them when s/he uses the product. S/he talks of the impact of different representatives of enterprises on his/her relationship with the product (e.g., customer service). This dimension arises in the case studies as the experts talked about the importance of users' relations with their friends, relations when using the product. In Case 5, E5 stated that, *"Family members of literate ASHA's were trained. They could help ASHAs to use the phone and the app."* The trained ASHA's family members were literate, and they assisted in the challenge of bringing low literate ASHA's to level of literate users. This resulted in successful implementation of the project and assisted in providing education and counselling to pregnant women on how to take care of themselves and babies after giving birth.

6   Summary and Conclusions

User engagement in ICT4D and more broadly ISD is important because of the link between higher levels of user engagement and a better chance of system success. It is, therefore, important to provide a clear and extended definition of user engagement. We did this and applied our new extended definition to five cases of mHealth projects in the

Global South. The objective of this study is to show how our extended notion of user engagement may have impacted the success or otherwise of each case. The reason for the extended definition is to capture and include the experiences created by users from the design, implementation and in the use of the technology.

Also, this work brought some level of clarity to this situation by firstly reviewing the various meanings and interpretations of user engagement from the literature, and secondly by proposing a definition of user engagement that is appropriate to ICT4D. Finally, the work extended existing definitions of user engagement to better suit the ICT4D context. We also suggested what stages of the design, development, implementation and use phase of the technology this expanded definition of user engagement most usefully applies to.

We demonstrated how users were engaged in the cases of the mHealth projects and explained how our extended version of user engagement impacted each project. This is important because it clearly showed how engaging the use of the technology created experience for the users.

This is a complex context for research and design which presents many opportunities for future work. It should be emphasized that this is a call to action for other researchers to work on this because little attention has been paid to integrate measures of user engagement within a design, and implementation process of mHealth apps. We plan future interactions to include more focus groups and interviews from developers, design exports, local partners and end-users in order to measure and evaluate user engagement in line with our expanded definition of that term.

Acknowledgement. This publication has emanated from research supported in part by a grant from Science Foundation Ireland under grant number 18/CRT/6222.

References

1. Bhatt, P., Ahmad, A.J., Roomi, M.A.: Social innovation with open source software: User engagement and development challenges in India. Technovation **52**, 28–39 (2016)
2. Heeks, R.: Information systems and developing countries: failure, success, and local improvisations. Info. Soc. **18**(2), 101–112 (2002)
3. Baccarini, D., Salm, G., Love, P.E.: Management of risks in information technology projects. Ind. Manag. Data Syst. **104**(4), 286–295 (2004)
4. Nawi, H.S.A., Rahman, A.A., Ibrahim, O.: Government's ICT project failure factors: a revisit. In: 2011 International Conference on Research and Innovation in Information Systems, pp. 1–6. IEEE (2011)
5. Dada, D.: The failure of E-government in developing countries: a literature review. Electron. J. Inf. Syst. Dev. Ctries. **26**(1), 1–10 (2006)
6. Chan, C.M., Pan, S.L.: User engagement in e-government systems implementation: a comparative case study of two Singaporean e-government initiatives. J. Strateg. Inf. Syst. **17**(2), 124–139 (2008)
7. Maail, A.G.: User participation and the success of development of ICT4D project: a critical review. In: Proceedings of the 4th Annual Workshop. ICT In Global Development. Pre-ICIS Meeting (2011)
8. Heeks, R.: ICT4D 2.0: the next phase of applying ICT for international development. Computer **41**(6), 26–33 (2008)

9. O'Brien, H.L., Toms, E.G.: What is user engagement? A conceptual framework for defining user engagement with technology. J. Am. Soc. Inform. Sci. Technol. **59**(6), 938–955 (2008)

10. O'Brien, H.: Theoretical perspectives on user engagement. In: O'Brien, H., Cairns, P. (eds.) Why Engagement Matters, pp. 1–26. Springer, Cham (2016). https://doi.org/10.1007/978-3-319-27446-1_1

11. Abusamhadana, G.A., Elias, N.F., Mukhtar, M., Asma'mokhtar, U.: User engagement model in information systems development. J. Theoret. Appl. Inf. Technol. **97**(11), 2908–2930 (2019)

12. O'Brien, H.L., Toms, E.G.: Examining the generalizability of the User Engagement Scale (UES) in exploratory search. Inf. Process. Manag. **49**(5), 1092–1107 (2013)

13. Kappelman, L.A., McLean, E.R.: User engagement in the development, implementation, and use of information technologies. In: HICSS, no. 4, pp. 512–521 (1994)

14. Bailur, S.: Using stakeholder theory to analyze telecenter projects. Inf. Technol. Int. Dev. **3**(3), 61 (2006)

15. Puri, S.K., Sahay, S.: Role of ICTs in participatory development: an Indian experience. Inf. Technol. Dev. **13**(2), 133–160 (2007)

16. Hunton, J.E., Beeler, J.D.: Effects of user participation in systems development: a longitudinal field experiment. Mis Q. **21**(4), 359–388 (1997)

17. Harris, R.W.: How ICT4D research fails the poor. Inf. Technol. Dev. **22**(1), 177–192 (2016)

18. Laurel, B.: Computers as Theatre Reading. Addison-Wesley Publishing Company, Mas (1991)

19. Hutchins, E.L., Hollan, J.D., Norman, D.A.: Direct manipulation interfaces. Human-Comput. Interact. **1**(4), 311–338 (1985)

20. Attfield, S., Kazai, G., Lalmas, M., Piwowarski, B.: Towards a science of user engagement (position paper). In: WSDM Workshop on User Modelling for Web Applications, pp. 9–12 (2011)

21. Jacques, R.D.: The nature of engagement and its role in hypermedia evaluation and design. Doctoral dissertation, South Bank University (1996)

22. Quesenbery, W.: Dimensions of usability. In: Albers, M., Mazur, B. (eds.) Content and Complexity: Information Design in Technical Communications, pp. 81–102. Lawrence Erlbaum, Mahwah (2003)

23. Saariluoma, P.: Explanatory frameworks for interaction design. In: Pirhonen, A., Saariluoma, P., Isomäki, H., Roast, C. (eds.) Future Interaction Design, pp. 67–83. Springer, London (2005). https://doi.org/10.1007/1-84628-089-3_5

24. Webster, J., Ho, H.: Audience engagement in multimedia presentations. ACM SIGMIS Database: DATABASE Adv. Inf. Syst. **28**(2), 63–77 (1997)

25. Wright, P., McCarthy, J.: Technology as Experience. MIT Press, Cambridge (2004)

26. Lukoff, K., Yu, C., Kientz, J., Hiniker, A.: What makes smartphone use meaningful or meaningless? Proc. ACM Interact. Mobile Wearable Ubiquitous Technol. **2**(1), 1–26 (2018)

27. Lalmas, M., O'Brien, H., Yom-Tov, E.: Measuring user engagement. Synth. Lect. Inf. Concepts Retrieval Serv. **6**(4), 1–132 (2014)

28. Doherty, K., Doherty, G.: Engagement in HCI: conception, theory and measurement. ACM Comput. Surv. (CSUR) **51**(5), 1–39 (2018)

29. Cavaye, A.L.: User participation in system development revisited. Inf. Manag. **28**(5), 311–323 (1995)

30. Markus, M.L., Mao, J.Y.: Participation in development and implementation-updating an old, tired concept for today's IS contexts. J. Assoc. Inf. Syst. **5**(11), 14 (2004)

31. Robert, J.M., Larouche, A.: The dimensions of user experience with interactive systems. In: IADIS International Conference Interfaces and Human Computer Interaction 2012 (part of MCCSIS 2012), pp. 89–96 (2012)

32. O'Brien, H.L., Toms, E.G.: The development and evaluation of a survey to measure user engagement. J. Am. Soc. Inform. Sci. Technol. **61**(1), 50–69 (2010)

33. Bannon, L.J.: A human-centred perspective on interaction design. In: Pirhonen, A., Saariluoma, P., Isomäki, H., Roast, C. (eds.) Future Interaction Design, pp. 31–51. Springer, London (2005). https://doi.org/10.1007/1-84628-089-3_3

34. Overbeeke, K., Djajadiningrat, T., Hummels, C., Wensveen, S., Prens, J.: Let's make things engaging. In: Blythe, M.A., Overbeeke, K., Monk, A.F., Wright, P.C. (eds.) Funology. Human-Computer Interaction Series, vol. 3, pp. 7–17. Springer, Dordrecht (2003)

35. Goethe, O., Salehzadeh Niksirat, K., Hirskyj-Douglas, I., Sun, H., Law, E.L.-C., Ren, X.: From UX to engagement: connecting theory and practice, addressing ethics and diversity. In: Antona, M., Stephanidis, C. (eds.) HCII 2019. LNCS, vol. 11572, pp. 91–99. Springer, Cham (2019). https://doi.org/10.1007/978-3-030-23560-4_7

36. Sama, P.R., Eapen, Z.J., Weinfurt, K.P., Shah, B.R., Schulman, K.A.: An evaluation of mobile health application tools. JMIR mHealth uHealth 2(2), e19 (2014)

37. Bush, J., Barlow, D.E., Echols, J., Wilkerson, J., Bellevin, K.: Impact of a mobile health application on user engagement and pregnancy outcomes among Wyoming Medicaid members. Telemed. e-Health 23(11), 891–898 (2017)

38. Doherty, K., et al.: Engagement with mental health screening on mobile devices: results from an antenatal feasibility study. In: Proceedings of the 2019 CHI Conference on Human Factors in Computing Systems, pp. 1–15 (2019)

39. Torous, J., Nicholas, J., Larsen, M.E., Firth, J., Christensen, H.: Clinical review of user engagement with mental health smartphone apps: evidence, theory and improvements. EVID.-BASED MENTAL Health 21(3), 116–119 (2018)

40. Kim, Y.H., Kim, D.J., Wachter, K.: A study of mobile user engagement (MoEN): engagement motivations, perceived value, satisfaction, and continued engagement intention. Decis. Support Syst. 56, 361–370 (2013)

41. O'Brien, H.L., Cairns, P., Hall, M.: A practical approach to measuring user engagement with the refined user engagement scale (UES) and new UES short form. Int. J. Hum. Comput. Stud. 112, 28–39 (2018)

42. Carter, L., Bélanger, F.: The utilization of e-government services: citizen trust, innovation and acceptance factors. Inf. Syst. J. 15(1), 5–25 (2005)

43. Evans, D., Yen, D.C.: E-Government: evolving relationship of citizens and government, domestic, and international development. Gov. Inf. Q. 23(2), 207–235 (2006)

44. Tan, C.W., Pan, S.L.: Managing e-transformation in the public sector: an e-government study of the Inland Revenue Authority of Singapore (IRAS). Eur. J. Inf. Syst. 12(4), 269–281 (2003)

45. Tan, C.-W., Pan, S.L., Lim, E.T.K.: Managing stakeholder interests in e-government implementation: lessons learned from a Singapore e-government project. J. Glob. Inf. Syst. 13(1), 31–53 (2005)

46. Garrett, J.J.: Customer loyalty and the elements of user experience. Des. Manag. Rev. 17(1), 35–39 (2006)

The Impact of Advertisements on User Attention During Permission Authorization

Yousra Javed[1]([✉]), Elham Al Qahtani[2], and Mohamed Shehab[2]

[1] National University of Sciences and Technology, Islamabad, Pakistan
yousra.javed@seecs.edu.pk
[2] University of North Carolina, Charlotte, USA
{ealqahta,mshehab}@uncc.edu

Abstract. Advertisements are an integral part of websites and play an important role in generating revenue. Many websites also present users with permission authorization windows. For instance, Facebook's third-party application authorization window is displayed when playing a game on various gaming websites. Although researchers have investigated the impact of advertisements on user frustration and their ability to process content, the extent to which advertisements distract the users during permission authorization has not been explored. This paper investigates the impact of advertisement's presence and its content type on user's attention during permission authorization. We conducted a between-subjects experiment on the mockup of a popular gaming website that contained banner advertisements. The control group was presented with no advertisements above the permission authorization dialog. Whereas, the treatment group was presented with static or animated advertisements. Eye-gaze tracking was performed while participants interacted with the applications. We observed that the presence of animated advertisements that contain sound significantly distracted participants away from the permission authorization window. Our findings suggest that increasing the number of distraction elements (e.g., animation and sound) increases the likelihood of users ignoring text on important windows such as permission authorization windows. Moreover, the use of shopping and politics related advertisements, can attract more attention compared to food and sports related advertisements.

Keywords: Advertisements · Eye-gaze tracking · Permission authorization windows · Distractions · User attention

1 Introduction

Advertisements are an integral part of websites and applications. Companies around the world spend billions of dollars to advertise their brand name to consumers due to their impact on consumers' buying behavior [7].

There are various forms of advertisements. One of the most common and well-known form of advertising is the use of banner advertisements [12] which show up above or below the content. Banner advertisements can either be animated, animated with sound, or static [2,11,13]. A second form of advertisement is video advertisement which is shown when the content is loading a new screen, or through incentive-based

© Springer Nature Switzerland AG 2020
C. Stephanidis et al. (Eds.): HCII 2020, LNCS 12423, pp. 722–739, 2020.
https://doi.org/10.1007/978-3-030-60114-0_47

advertising, where the user gets either an in-game reward or Facebook credits (i.e., money) for watching the advertisement. In addition, there are product placement advertisements, which are injected in the content in some way for example, a McDonald's product placed in a farm inside the game FarmVille. Zynga, a provider of popular games such as Farmville on Facebook displays these forms of advertisements in the games it provides on Facebook (see Fig. 1) [6].

(a) Banner advertisements above Facebook Zynga game   (b) Product placement advertisement in Facebook Zynga game   (c) Advertisements in a third-party Android game

Fig. 1. Advertisements inside third-party applications

Several researchers have investigated the impact of advertisements on user frustration and their ability to process website/application content or to perform certain tasks. For example, salient web ads disrupt users' reading due to their closeness to the text area [13,15]. Similarly, animated ads increase user frustration and mental demand of visual search tasks [2]. Although the impact of advertisements on user attention has been studied before, the context of security/privacy has not been investigated. One usecase is Facebook's third-party application authorization window, which shows requested permissions to the user, and is displayed on various gaming websites upon starting/installing a game. To the best of our knowledge, our work is the first one to use eye-gaze tracking to study the impact of advertisements while making such authorization decisions. Our goal is to understand whether the existing claims regarding advertisements hold for the security/privacy context. More specifically, in this paper, we investigate the following research questions:

RQ1: Does the introduction of advertisements above the permission authorization dialogs cause the users to pay less attention towards permissions?
RQ2: Does the type of advertisements (e.g., static, or animated) have an effect on the user's visual attention?
RQ3: Does the content type of an advertisement (e.g., shopping or food) play a role in a user's attention towards permissions?

We conducted a between-subjects experiment on 120 participants who installed game applications on a mockup gaming website. During this process, eye-tracking was used to log participants' eye-movements. The participants' attention on authorization dialogs in the absence of advertisements was compared with that in the presence of three types of banner advertisements. Treatment group participants were exposed to four advertisement content types. The impact of advertisement content-type on attention was also evaluated. Our results show that the presence of advertisements can further distract users away from the permissions text on the authorization window. The distraction level for the animated ads with sound is the highest compared to the animated ads without sound, which have the second highest level of distraction, and the static ads, which have the third highest level of distraction from permission text. Additionally, shopping and politics related advertisements, attract more attention compared to food and sports related advertisements.

The remainder of this paper is organized as follows. Section 2 presents the literature related to our work. Section 3 explains our study design. Section 4 presents the results of our study. Section 5 provides a discussion of our results. Finally, we conclude our work in Sect. 6 and discuss future directions.

2   Related Work

This section presents the literature most relevant to our work, which includes the effect of advertisements on user frustration and content processing, and dialog readability and risk signal communication.

2.1   Effect of Advertisements on User Frustration and Content Processing

Simola et al. [15] conducted three eye-tracking experiments on web pages to assess whether ads were ignored or if they attract user attention and affect their reading performance. The authors found that salient web ads (onset) attract users' visual attention and disrupt their reading due to ads' closeness to the text area.

Pasqualotti et al. [13] studied the impact of advertisement's distance from the text and its animation on two tasks, namely, word search and reading. Using eye-gaze fixations, they showed that advertisements close to the text cause cognitive processing difficulties. However, the impact of static vs animated ads varies according to the cognitive task. Burke et al. [2] studied the impact of animated banner ads on visual search task. After performing the task, participants were interviewed. Participants reported greater workload and stated that animated ads increased their frustration and mental demand of the search task.

Henderson et al. [11] conducted a study on 50 freshman women. The participants were asked to study in the presence music playing in the background. Their results showed that popular music served as a distraction and affected participants' efficiency on the vocabulary and paragraph sections of the reading test.

Wojdynski et al. [16] used eye-tracking to study users' ability to process news websites' content in the presence of relevant and irrelevant ads. They observed that readers paid more attention to the news story content when it was presented alongside relevant ads.

2.2   Dialog Readability and Risk Signal Communication

Harbach et al. [8] explored the use of readability measures on the descriptive text of warning messages to estimate how understandable a warning is for the user. The linguistic properties of warning message texts also has an effect on its perceived difficulty

[9]. Keeping headlines simple, using as few technical words as possible and creating short sentences without complicated grammatical constructions makes warning messages more pleasant for the user.

Egelman et al. [3] proposed design changes to the Facebook Connect dialog by presenting the actual information requested by the public profile permission. They observed that the changes were noticed, but because users had such low expectations for privacy, the additional information did not dissuade them. Passive eye-tracking was used to analyze the readability of this dialog design compared to others by observing the frequency and duration of a user's eye-gaze fixations over the dialog content [5]. The results showed that, although the participants who were shown information verbatim took longer to read the dialog, it did not affect their decision to authenticate using Facebook Connect.

Several researchers have made efforts to improve the risk communication for authorization dialogs. Harbach et al. [10] proposed a modified permission dialog for Android applications to improve security risk communication to the end-user. They display a personal information example along with each permission to help the user understand the risk associated with a permission's authorization. Their study showed a significant difference in the behavior of participants who were presented with the modified dialog design compared to the ones who were presented with the default design. The participants who were shown information examples for each permission spent more time on the dialog and appeared to be more aware of the security and privacy risks.

Sarma et al. [14] proposed a mechanism for creating effective risk signals for Android applications that 1) are easy to understand by both the users and the developers, 2) are presented by a small percentage of applications, and 3) are triggered by malicious applications. They use the permissions that an application requests, the category of the application, and the permissions requested by other applications in the same category to better inform users whether the risks of installing an application are commensurate with its expected benefits.

Social navigation is defined as the use of social information to aid a user's decision. Besmer et al. [1] explored the use of social navigation cues (i.e., the percentage of users who have allowed/denied a particular permission) to help users make better permission authorization decisions when installing Facebook applications. They found that social cues have minimal effect on users' Facebook privacy settings. Hence, only a small subset of users who take the time to customize their settings may be influenced by strong negative social cues.

3   Study Design

To answer our research questions, we designed a between-subjects study comprised of four groups:

1. **Control Group** - Participants in this group were not shown any advertisements. The advertisement area displayed the game application logo (see Fig. 2(a)).
2. **Static Ads Group** - The participants in this group were shown advertisements displaying a static image (see Fig. 2(b)).

3. **Animated Ads Group** - The participants in this group were shown advertisements as images in Graphics Interchange Format (gif).
4. **Animated Ads with Sound Group** - The participants in this group were shown advertisements as images in Graphics Interchange Format (gif) along with a background sound related to the ad.

All treatment groups were exposed to four types of advertisement content, namely, shopping, food, politics and sports.

3.1 Hypotheses

We formulated the following hypotheses based on our research questions:

H1: The participants who are presented with advertisements will pay less attention to the permission text as compared to the control group participants

H2: The participants who are presented with animated advertisements will pay less attention to the permission text as compared to those presented with static advertisements and the control group

H3: The participants who are presented with advertisements will be distracted by certain advertisement content types more than the others

3.2 Mockup Gaming Website

We developed a mockup of a popular gaming website that hosted four popular Facebook applications, namely Candy Crush, FarmVille, Angry Birds, and Criminal Case (Fig. 2(a)). Upon clicking a specific game's icon, the Facebook permission authorization window is displayed along with four advertisements related to one of the four content types above it. For example, four shopping related ads were displayed upon clicking the Angry Birds game icon (see Fig. 2(b)). Each content type was assigned to each game application as follows. Shopping-related ads were assigned to the Angry Birds game, food-related ads were assigned to the Candy Crush game, sports-related ads were assigned to the Criminal Case game, and politics-related ads were assigned to the FarmVille game.

3.3 Study Session

The study was approved by the IRB Protocol#13-0330. We recruited our participants from the university through email announcements and flyers. Our participants were older than 18 years and had an active Facebook account. Each participant spent an average of 30 min on the tasks and received a $5 gift card in return for their participation.

In order to avoid bias, we did not inform the participants about the existence of advertisements in the experiment or that we were studying the effect of advertisements on their attention. Participants were informed that *"the purpose of this research study is to utilize eye-gaze tracking to understand how users interact with applications. Participants in the study will use a set of third-party applications and their eye-gaze will be tracked in the background"*. Each participant first followed a 12-point eye-tracking calibration procedure on the eye-tracking device. The participant's calibration evaluation

(a) Website displaying applications used in the experiment

(b) Advertisements displayed above the application authorization dialog upon clicking on an application

Fig. 2. Mockup of the gaming website Zynga used in our experiment

was checked (See Fig. 3(b)). If a participant received excellent or good results, they had a high gaze accuracy. If they received poor results, they had to re-calibrate until they achieved good results. After completing the calibration process, the participants logged into their Facebook account and were presented with a mockup website containing four game applications. The participants were instructed to explore the website and play the games in any order. Clicking on a game application's icon popped up the Facebook permission authorization window.

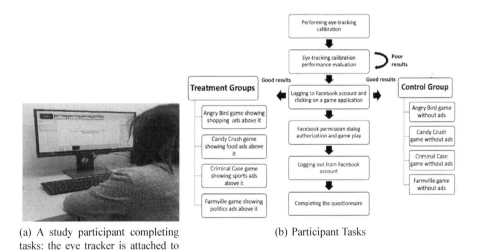

(a) A study participant completing tasks: the eye tracker is attached to the monitor

(b) Participant Tasks

Fig. 3. Study design

Participants who were assigned to the treatment groups were shown different types of advertisements above the permission authorization window. At the end of the experiment, participants logged out from their Facebook accounts and completed a questionnaire (See Appendix). Participants were asked whether they noticed any advertisements, were they distracted by these advertisements, and which advertisements distracted them the most. Figure 3(b) shows the participant tasks.

We used the iMotions[1] eye-tracker to collect participants' eye-gaze movements. The participants were not informed about the purpose of eye-tracking to avoid any biased results.

3.4 Evaluation Metrics

We defined Areas of Interests (AOIs) around the dialog's permission text, application logo, and advertisements to analyze eye-gaze data in a specific region on screen as shown in Fig. 4. The following metrics were calculated from the eye-tracking data to measure participant attention on authorization dialogs in the presence of advertisements:

- The proportion of eye-gaze fixations on an area of interest
- The proportion of revisits to an area of interest
- The proportion of total time spent on an area of interest (based on the total duration of eye-gaze fixations)

Fig. 4. AOIs are highlighted in red color (Color figure online)

3.5 Data Analysis

We utilized the Area of Interest (AOI) metrics generated by the eye tracking software for our analysis. These metrics include eye-gaze fixation counts, number of revisits, and the percentage of the total time spent in an AOI.

---

[1] https://imotions.com.

We analyzed our data using the Statistical Package for the Social Sciences (SPSS) [4]. Using tests of normality, normal Q-Q plots, and histograms we found that our data was not normally distributed. Therefore, we transformed the skewed continuous variables (measuring proportions) to be normally distributed using log transformation [4]. We conducted the Kruskal-Wallis test (non-parametric version of one-way ANOVA test) on non-normally distributed ordinal data of four groups. We conducted the one-way ANOVA test on the proportions of eye-gaze fixations, revisits, and time spent on advertisements/permission text among the four groups. Lastly, we conducted the mixed ANOVA test to compare each advertisement content-type e.g., food, shopping, politics, and sports. The post-hoc test was used to perform pairwise comparisons.

In addition, heatmaps were used to present the visual distribution of participant's attention by using different colors to represent various concentration levels.

4 Results

4.1 Demographics

We recruited our participants from the university. Therefore, a majority of them were students. The total number of participants in our experiment were 120 (30 per group). 57.5% of the participants were female, and 42.5% were male. The Chi-Square test showed no significant differences between the number of participants with respect to gender ($\chi^2(3) = 2.83$, p = .42). 61.7% of the participants were between the ages 20–29. The Kruskal-Wallis test showed no significant differences between the number of participants in each of the four age groups (H(3) = 5.81, p = .12). Therefore, our sample contained an equal number of participants from each gender and age group.

4.2 Effect of Ad Presence on Attention Towards Permission Text

We hypothesized that the participants who were presented with advertisements would pay less attention to the permission text area compared to the control group participants.

To test this hypothesis, we measured participants' visual attention on advertisement AOIs and the authorization dialog's permission text AOI for each of the four groups using a number of metrics. Our first metric is the proportion of eye-gaze fixations on permission text AOI calculated as:

$$\text{Proportion of eye-gaze fixations on permission text} = \frac{\text{No. of fixations on permission text}}{\text{No. of fixations on permission text} + \text{No. of fixations on ads/app logo}}$$

In order to conduct a one-way ANOVA test on the dependent variable *proportion of eye-gaze fixations on permission text*, we first performed log transformation on the variable to normalize values between 0 and 1. The test showed a significant difference between the proportion of eye-gaze fixations on permission text of the four groups (F(3,120) = 3.91, p = .011, with a medium effect size $\eta_p^2 = .09$). The Tukey post-hoc comparison test showed significant differences between the proportion of eye-gaze fixations for Animated-Ads-Sound and Control groups (p = .021), Animated-Ads and Control groups (p = .045), and between Static-Ads and Control groups (p = .031). Table 1 shows the means, standard deviations, and confidence intervals for each group regarding the proportion of eye-gaze fixations on permission text.

Table 1. Descriptive statistics for the proportion of eye-gaze fixations on permission text

Group	M	SD	95%CI
Animated-Ads-Sound	.24	.16	(.18, .29)
Animated-Ads	.25	.16	(.19, .31)
Static-Ads	.25	.19	(.17, .32)
Control	.38	.23	(.29, .47)

To further analyze the impact of advertisement presence on participants' attention towards permission text, we calculated the proportion of time spent on permission text in milliseconds as:

$$\text{Proportion of time spent on permission text} = \frac{\text{Time spent on permission text}}{\text{Time spent on ads/app logo} + \text{Time spent on permission text}}$$

A one-way ANOVA test was conducted on the dependent variable *proportion of time spent on permission text* after performing log transformation on the variable. We found a significant difference between the proportion of time spent on permission text among the four groups ($F(3,120) = 4.63$, $p = .004$, with a large effect size ($\eta_p^2) = .11$). The Tukey post-hoc comparison tests showed significant differences between the Animated-Ads-Sound and Control groups with $p = .006$, and between Static-Ads and Control groups with $p = .017$. However, we found no significant difference between the Animated-Ads group and Control groups at $p = .06$. The means (milliseconds), standard deviations, and confidence intervals for each group are shown in Table 2.

Table 2. Descriptive statistics including the mean (M), standard deviation (SD) and 95% Confidence Intervals (CI) for the proportion of time spent on permission text

Group	M	SD	95% CI
Animated-Ads-Sound	.21	.14	(.15, .26)
Animated-Ads	.25	.16	(.19, .31)
Static-Ads	.22	.19	(.15, .29)
Control	.37	.19	(.28, .46)

Based on these results, we can conclude that our first hypothesis is supported. We found that the proportion of eye-gaze fixations and time spent on the authorization dialog's permission text was higher for the control group, which was not shown any ads. In other words, participants in the control group were less distracted from the permission text since they spent relatively more time and had relatively more eye-gaze fixations on the permission text area compared to the treatment groups. The visual attention towards the permission text was lower for the Animated-Ads-Sound, Static-Ads, and Animated-Ads groups who were distracted due the presence of ads.

To further validate the results regarding participant attention towards permission text, we considered participants' responses to post-task questionnaire. The participants were asked if any of the presented applications requested permissions to their information during installation (responses were "Yes", "No", or "I do not know"). 90% of the participants from Animated-Ads-Sound, Animated-Ads and Control groups, and 80% from the Static-Ads group replied "Yes". Participants were also asked if they read the text in the installation window (responses were "Ignore it", "I tried to read a little", or "I read every word"). We did not find a significant difference among the groups at $p = 0.78$ regarding reading the permission text. As shown in Table 3, most participants stated that they read a part of the permission text in the authorization window.

Table 3. Percentage of participants who read the permission text in the authorization window

Response for reading text	Animated-Ads-Sound	Animated-Ads	Static-Ads	Control
"I Ignored it"	40%	23.3%	36.7%	33.3%
"I tried to read a little"	53.3%	73.3%	53.3%	60%
"I read every word"	6.7%	3.3%	10%	6.7%

A majority of the participants stated that these applications asked for their personal information in the authorization window. However, percentages in Table 3 showed that most participants ignored the permission text. This correlates with the eye-tracking results proving that participants paid less attention to the text during the permission authorization due to the presence of different type of advertisements. Based on these results, 40% of the participants ignored reading the permission text from the Animated-Ads-Sound group and 60% from the Control group read a part of the permission text in the authorization window.

4.3   Effect of Ad Type on Attention Towards Permission Text

Our second hypothesis was that the participants who were presented with animated advertisements would pay less attention to the permission text compared to the participants presented with static or no advertisements. Therefore, we investigated participants' revisits to the advertisement areas in the presence of each advertisement type (static, animated, animated with sound). The number of revisits to the advertisement area was calculated as:

$$\text{Proportion of revisits to advertisement/app logo area} = \frac{\text{No. of revisits to ads/app logo area}}{\text{No. of revisits to permission text} + \text{No. of revisits to ads/app logo area}}$$

We conducted a one-way ANOVA test on the proportion of revisits to the advertisement areas. We found a significant difference among the four groups ($F(3,120) = 5.76$, $p = .001$, with a medium effect size ($\eta_p^2 = .13$). The Tukey post-hoc comparison test showed significant differences with higher revisits for the Animated-Ads-Sound group compared to the other groups: Static-Ads ($p = .002$) and Control ($p = .003$). We did not find a significant difference between the Animated-Ads and Animated-Ads-Sound group ($p = .16$) due to the high revisits to the animated ads in both groups. The means, standard deviations, and confidence intervals for each group are shown in Table 4.

Table 4. Descriptive statistics for the proportion of revisits to advertisement areas

Group	M	SD	95% CI
Animated-Ads-Sound	.65	.29	(.54, .76)
Animated-Ads	.46	.34	(.33, .59)
Static-Ads	.31	.38	(.17, .45)
Control	.31	43	(.16, .48)

To further interpret the results visually, we utilized heatmaps to analyze participant attention areas using colors on the advertisement areas, application logos and permission text. The red color represents the highest participant attention, whereas the green color represents the lowest attention. We have presented the heatmaps of visual attention distribution on the FarmVille game as an example (Fig. 5) for the Animated-Ads-Sound and Control groups. Figure 5(a) shows how participants' attention was distributed on politics-related ads for the Animated-Ads-Sound group during the authorization process. We can see the green color is distributed on the advertisement areas above the authorization window, specifically the last part of the ad. Regarding Fig. 5(b) for the Control group, participants concentrated more on the Facebook authorization dialog than the area that included game application logos above the authorization dialog. Table 5 shows the average eye-gaze fixations on the advertisement areas in the treatment groups and the application logos in the Control group. The average eye-gaze fixations for all game applications were higher on the advertisement areas compared to the Control group.

Table 5. Average eye-gaze fixations on ads and application logos above the authorization window

Game application	Animated-Ads-Sound	Animated-Ads	Static-Ads	Control
Angry Birds	4.6	2	1.2	1.1
Candy Crush	6.1	1.4	2	0.8
Criminal Case	5.5	2.8	1.5	1
FarmVille	5.2	1	1.6	0.9

(a) Heatmap of FarmVille for Animated-Ads-Sound   (b) Heatmap of FarmVille for Control

Fig. 5. Heatmap of visual attention distribution on FarmVille game application for Animated-Ads-Sound and Control groups

We also analyzed participants' responses to the survey question: *"Did you notice any advertisements above the application's permission authorization dialog?"*. Participants responded with either "Yes", "No", or "I don't know". 83.3% of participants from the Animated-Ads-Sound, 73.3% from the Static-Ads, and 70% from the Animated-Ads responded "Yes", meaning that they noticed the existence of ads above the authorization dialog. 56.7% of the Control group participants answered either "No" or "I don't know". The Kruskal-Wallis test showed a significant difference between the responses of the four groups at p<.001 (H(3)=17.8 with a small effect size, $\eta^2 = 0.1$). The Bonferroni post-hoc comparison test was performed to see the differences between each pair (see Table 6). Significant differences were found between Control and Animated-Ads-Sound groups at p = .009, Control and Animated-Ads groups at p = .020, and Control and Static-Ads groups at p = .009.

Table 6. Post-hoc comparison test for whether participants noticed advertisements above the authorization dialog

Group comparison (Mean ranks)	Adj.Sig.
Control (41.9) vs. Animated-Ads-Sound (70.9)	p = .001
Control (41.9) vs. Animated-Ads (63.7)	p = .020
Control (41.9) vs. Static-Ads (65.5)	p = .009

The results indicated that the number of participants who revisited the advertisement areas for the Animated-Ads-Sound and Animated-Ads groups was higher compared to the other groups. In contrast, both Control and Static-Ads groups had the lowest number of revisits due to static ads and the fixed position of the game application logo above the authorization window, respectively. Also, a majority of the participants (83.3%) from the Animated-Ads-Sound group, noticed the presence of ads above the authorization dialog because of changing images with a musical sound, which attracted their visual attention and led them to revisit these ads several times compared to the other groups.

Y. Javed et al.

4.4 Effect of Ad Content-Type on Participant Attention

Our third hypothesis focuses on the effect of advertisement content-type on participant attention towards the permission text. We hypothesized that the participants who were presented with advertisements would be distracted by a certain advertisement content type, namely, shopping, food, politics, and sports, more than the others.

To test this hypothesis, we calculated the proportion of eye-gaze fixation counts on an advertisement content-type as:

$$\text{Proportion of eye-gaze fixations on an ad content-type} =$$
$$\frac{\text{No. of fixations on ad content-type}}{\text{No. of fixations on permission text} + \text{No. of fixations on ad content-type}}$$

We conducted a mixed ANOVA test to compare the proportion of eye-gaze fixations on each ad content-type among the treatment groups. The Mauchly's test of sphericity for equality of variances and all other assumptions were met ($\chi^2(5) = 2.8$, $p = .72$). The test showed a significant main effect of eye-gaze fixations on each advertisement content-type among the treatment groups ($F(3, 261) = 10.2$, $p < .001$, with a medium effect size ($\eta_p^2) = .10$). The Bonferroni post-hoc tests showed that there were significant differences at $p < .001$ between sports-related ads and shopping-related ads, between food-related ads and shopping-related ads, and between politics-related ads and shopping-related ads. The means, standard deviations, and confidence intervals among treatment groups for this test are presented in Table 7.

Table 7. Descriptive statistics for proportion of eye-gaze fixations on advertisement content-types

Ad Content Type	M	SD	95%CI
Shopping	.47	.39	(.39, .55)
Politics	.26	.34	(.19, .33)
Food	.25	.30	(.19, .32)
Sports	.23	.33	(.16, .30)

To further interpret the visual attention on each content-types' AOIs for the treatment groups, the average eye-gaze fixation counts are presented in Table 8. Overall, the average eye-gaze fixation counts on all ad content-types were higher for the Animated-Ads-Sound group as compared to the Animated-Ads and Static-Ads groups.

We also analyzed participants' responses to the survey question: *"Which advertisement content-types distracted you the most?"* Participants selected one or more from shopping, politics, food, and sports. This question was asked from both the treatment groups and the control group. 33.3% of Animated-Ads-Sound group participants selected all four ad content types, whereas only 13.3% of Animated-Ads group, and 13.3% of Static-Ads group participants selected all four ad content types. 80% of participants from the Control group chose "I don't remember".

Table 8. Average eye-gaze fixation counts on each advertisement content-type

Content-type (content position)	Animated-Ads-Sound	Animated-Ads	Static-Ads
Shopping (1)	1.3	0.9	0.8
Shopping (2)	1.4	0.7	0.2
Shopping (3)	1.1	0.2	0.1
Shopping (4)	0.7	0.2	0.1
Food (1)	1	0.2	0.3
Food (2)	3.2	1	1.2
Food (3)	1.1	0.2	0.3
Food (4)	0.8	0.1	0.1
Sport (1)	0.6	0.4	0.8
Sport (2)	2.1	0.9	0.3
Sport (3)	2.2	1.3	0.4
Sport (4)	0.6	0.2	0.1
Politics (1)	0.8	0	0.2
Politics (2)	0.8	0.1	0.6
Politics (3)	1.4	0.3	0.4
Politics (4)	2.2	0.5	0.3

Table 9. Post-hoc comparisons regarding which advertisement content types distracted participants the most

Group comparison (Mean ranks)	Adj.Sig.
Control (39.5) vs. Animated-Ads-Sound (67.7)	p = .005
Control (39.5) vs. Animated-Ads (67.7)	p = .005
Control (39.5) vs. Static-Ads (67.1)	p = .007

We performed the Kruskal-Wallis test on participant responses, which showed significant differences at p = .001 (H(3) = 16.9 with a small effect size, $\eta^2 = 0.1$). The Bonferroni post-hoc comparison test (see Table 9) shows significant differences between Control and Animated-Ads-Sound groups at p = .005, Control and Animated-Ads groups at p = .005, and Control and Static-Ads groups at p = .007.

Based on these results, the third hypothesis is supported. We found that shopping-related ads and politics-related ads attracted participant attention the most. Based on analyzing participants' responses regarding the most distracting content-type, we found that a higher percentage (33.3%) of participants from the Animated-Ads-Sound group identified all four advertisement content types, namely, shopping, food, sports, and politics as equally distracting.

5 Discussion

Our study illustrated the differences in attention towards the authorization dialog's permission text for three types of ads. Similar to Simola et al. [15], we found that ads attract users' visual attention and disrupt their reading due to ads' closeness to the text area.

While investigating the presence of different ads during permission authorization, we found that participants who were presented with animated ads that contained a background sound related to ads were distracted from reading the permission text more as compared to the other groups. Adding sound to the animated ads appeared to be an effective factor of distraction, confirming the results of Henderson et al. [11] and Burke et al. [2]. Animated ads without sound and static ads emerged as the second level of distraction. Based on the results of the first hypothesis, we found that the proportion of eye-gaze fixations and time spent towards the permission text was higher for the control group, who was not shown any ads. This shows that participants in the control group were not distracted noticeably during permission authorization due to the fixed game logos and the absence of ads.

Also, in support of the second hypothesis, we investigated what type of advertisements attracted participants' attention the most (static ads, animated ads, animated ads with sound) by measuring the proportion of participants' revisits to the advertisement areas. We found that the Animated-Ads-Sound and Animated-Ads group participants revisited advertisement areas several times compared to the Static-Ads and control groups due to the moving elements in the animated ads which attracted participants' visual attention. In addition, 83.3% of the participants from the Animated-Ads-Sound group noticed the presence of ads above the authorization dialog. On the other hand, both Static-Ads and Control groups had fewer revisits due to the static images in the ads of different content types (food, shopping, sports, political ads), and the fixed position of all game applications' logos above the authorization dialog in the Control group.

Furthermore, when we analyzed participants' response to the question: "Were you distracted by these advertisements?", we found that 40% of participants from Animated-Ads-Sound and Animated-Ads, and 37.5% from the Static-Ads group responded "Yes". For the Control group, 80% of participants responded "No" or "I do not remember". Participants who responded "No" were asked "why were you not distracted by these advertisements?". Examples of treatment group participants' responses are as follows: "I'm so used to seeing these types of advertisements", "I ignored these ads", "because I was trying to concentrate on the music", and "Over time, I have learned to ignore advertisements while playing a game or conducting some other activity". The Control group participants commented, "I didn't notice any ad" and "Focused on game". We can see that most participants from the treatment groups thought that these ads did not distract them; even though the eye-tracking data showed that they were distracted. In contrast, most participants from the Control group stated that ads did not divert their visual attention at all because they could not see any ads.

Overall, the data in our study was based on eye-tracking information-based metrics, and participants' responses to the questionnaire. The evaluation using eye-tracking information-based metrics (eye-gaze fixations, revisits, and time spent during fixation) showed that the presence of different ad types distracted participants' visual attention towards the permission text. As a result, the distraction level for the Animated-Ads-Sound group was the highest compared to the Animated-Ads, which had the second highest level of distraction, and the Static-Ads, which had the lowest level of distraction from the permission text. Due to the absence of ads in the Control group, participants had the lowest level of distraction from the permission text during the dialog authorization process. The second evaluation was based on the participants' responses, and the results showed that a higher percentage of participants from the Animated-Ads-Sound group noticed the presence of ads above the authorization dialog and identified all four content-types (politics, shopping, sports, and food) as distracting compared to the other groups.

6   Limitations and Future Work

Our study is not without limitations. We faced the following issues during our experiment. Firstly, we conducted our study in the usability lab at our campus; so our sample was recruited from the university, which may limit the generalizability of our results.

Secondly, we only focused on one advertisement location (above the authorization dialog) and did not study the effect of an advertisement's location on user attention. In other words, would the user be more distracted if the same advertisement is above the dialog vs on the left, right, or bottom.

Thirdly, most participants did not know what the third-party applications are. Therefore, we had to explain what these different games are and that the games can be played in any order. This explanation could have lead the participants to be biased towards playing the games and might have affected their actual behavior of accepting or rejecting the permissions. For this reason, we were unable to study the impact of advertisements on user decision on authorization dialogs. A future study is needed to address this limitation.

Lastly, we did not randomize the order of displaying advertisement content type (food, politics, sports, shopping) on the game applications. Therefore, a specific game always displayed advertisements of a particular content type. This could have biased the results regarding participant attention towards specific advertisement content types.

Our future work will investigate different factors, such as advertisement location, advertisement content type randomization, and using a demographically diverse sample from different communities outside the university. We will also study the impact of advertisements on user decisions (allow/deny) on permission authorization dialogs.

7   Conclusion

In this paper, we investigated the impact of advertisements on user attention during permission authorization. We conducted a between-subjects experiment on 120 participants and studied three types of advertisements (static, animated, and animated with sound). We used eye-tracking data-based metrics (proportion of eye-gaze fixation counts on permission text, proportion of revisits to ads, and proportion of time spent on permission text during fixation) and participants' responses to the questionnaire in our analysis. Our results show that the presence of advertisements can significantly distract users away from the permission authorization window. Moreover, the use of shopping and politics related advertisements, can attract more attention compared to food and sports related advertisements. The distraction level for animated ads with sound is the highest compared to that for animated ads, and static ads suggesting that increasing the number of distraction elements (e.g., animation and sound) increases the likelihood of users ignoring text on important windows such as permission authorization windows.

A   Survey Questions

1. You were presented with four applications in this study. Which applications did you enjoy using?
2. Did any of the these applications request permissions to your information during installation?
3. Did you notice any advertisements above an application's installation window?
4. If you answered yes to the previous question, what type of advertisements were displayed above the application installation window?
5. Were you distracted by these advertisements? If you answered "No" to this question, why were you not distracted by these advertisements?
6. Which advertisement content type distracted you the most?
7. On most of the installation windows you saw, did you intentionally read the text in the installation window?
8. What is your gender?
9. What is your age?

References

1. Besmer, A., Watson, J., Lipford, H.R.: The impact of social navigation on privacy policy configuration. In: SOUPS (2010)
2. Burke, M., Hornof, A.J.: The effect of animated banner advertisements on a visual search task. Technical report. Oregon University Eugene Department of Computer and Information Science (2001)
3. Egelman, S.: My profile is my password, verify me!: the privacy/convenience tradeoff of facebook connect. In: Proceedings of the SIGCHI Conference on Human Factors in Computing Systems, pp. 2369–2378. ACM (2013)
4. Field, A.: Discovering Statistics Using IBM SPSS Statistics. Sage, Los Angeles (2013)
5. Furman, S., Theofanos, M.: Preserving privacy – more than reading a message. In: Stephanidis, C., Antona, M. (eds.) UAHCI 2014. LNCS, vol. 8516, pp. 14–25. Springer, Cham (2014). https://doi.org/10.1007/978-3-319-07509-9_2
6. Gobry, P.E.: How Zynga makes money (2011). http://www.businessinsider.com/zynga-revenue-analysis-2011-9
7. Haider, T., Shakib, S.: A study on the influences of advertisement on consumer buying behavior. Bus. Stud. J. 9(1), 1–13 (2018)
8. Harbach, M., Fahl, S., Muders, T., Smith, M.: Towards measuring warning readability. In: Proceedings of the 2012 ACM Conference on Computer and Communications Security, CCS 2012, pp. 989–991. ACM, New York (2012). https://doi.org/10.1145/2382196.2382301

9. Harbach, M., Fahl, S., Yakovleva, P., Smith, M.: Sorry, i don't get it: an analysis of warning message texts. In: Adams, A.A., Brenner, M., Smith, M. (eds.) FC 2013. LNCS, vol. 7862, pp. 94–111. Springer, Heidelberg (2013). https://doi.org/10.1007/978-3-642-41320-9_7
10. Harbach, M., Hettig, M., Weber, S., Smith, M.: Using personal examples to improve risk communication for security & #38; privacy decisions. In: Proceedings of the 32nd Annual ACM Conference on Human Factors in Computing Systems, CHI 2014, pp. 2647–2656. ACM, New York (2014). https://doi.org/10.1145/2556288.2556978
11. Henderson, M.T., Crews, A., Barlow, J.: A study of the effect of music distraction on reading efficiency. J. Appl. Psychol. **29**(4), 313 (1945)
12. Marketing, A.: 7 types of online advertising (2018). https://www.antevenio.com/usa/7-types-of-online-advertising/
13. Pasqualotti, L., Baccino, T.: Online advertisement: how are visual strategies affected by the distance and the animation of banners? Front. Psychol. **5**, 211 (2014)
14. Sarma, B.P., Li, N., Gates, C., Potharaju, R., Nita-Rotaru, C., Molloy, I.: Android permissions: a perspective combining risks and benefits. In: Proceedings of the 17th ACM Symposium on Access Control Models and Technologies, SACMAT 2012, pp. 13–22. ACM, New York (2012). https://doi.org/10.1145/2295136.2295141
15. Simola, J., Kuisma, J., Öörni, A., Uusitalo, L., Hyönä, J.: The impact of salient advertisements on reading and attention on web pages. J. Exp. Psychol.: Appl. **17**(2), 174 (2011)
16. Wojdynski, B., Bang, H.: Distraction effects of contextual advertising on online news processing: an eye-tracking study. Behav. Inf. Technol. **35**, 654–664 (2016). https://doi.org/10.1080/0144929X.2016.1177115

User Experience in Kiosk Application for Traceability of Fishery Products

José Oliveira[1]([⊠]), Pedro Miguel Faria[1][iD],
and António Miguel Rosado da Cruz[1,2][iD]

[1] Escola Superior de Tecnologia e Gestão, Instituto Politécnico de Viana do Castelo,
Viana do Castelo, Portugal
`j.o.oliveira@ipvc.pt`, {`pfaria,miguel.cruz`}`@estg.ipvc.pt`
[2] Centro ALGORITMI, Escola de Engenharia, Universidade do Minho,
Guimarães, Portugal

Abstract. Nowadays it is very important to understand the origins of most products because there is an increased product quality challenge and awareness from the customers about environmental and social aspects. Food traceability information must reach customers where they need to choose which products to buy. One of the best ways to provide this traceability information for the customers is to add kiosks on the points of sale of those products. This paper describes the development of Fish products traceability kiosk user interface and experience, in the scope of ValorMar R&D project, that will allow all kiosk devices in a supermarket, shop or other type of point of sale, to consult an online RESTfull API about the traceability of fish product lots. At the end of this development stage, a System Usability Scale questionnaire has been deployed to test the usability of this kiosk application, which was well accepted by the majority of the participants.

Keywords: Interactive application · Usability · User experience · System usability scale · Kiosk application

1 Introduction

Food traceability is an increasing demand, driven by increased product quality challenges and customers' awareness about social and environmental aspects, related, for instance, with working conditions of the fishermen and other workers in the supply chain, the care taken in maintaining the species in question or the respect for the public health and the environment when using certain fishing methods.

Food traceability allows to trace back and recall product lots from the market, in case of threats to the public health. It also checks all actions carried out along the supply chain, from harvesting, capture or production until the sale to the final costumer. This transparency needs to reach the customer in an easy way. One of the ways this transparency can be delivered to the customer is through

© Springer Nature Switzerland AG 2020
C. Stephanidis et al. (Eds.): HCII 2020, LNCS 12423, pp. 740–751, 2020.
https://doi.org/10.1007/978-3-030-60114-0_48

a kiosk application that allows customers to anonymously consult and search for traceability information about the products or product lots available on the supermarket where they are acquiring their goods.

Fish and fisheries products travel a long way from the sea, where fish species are captured, or aquaculture farms, until the final customer. It is important to trace back fish, fishery products or any other food product, both to inform the consumer or to be able to recall fish lots in case of threats to the public health [5]. Therefore, it was decided to develop an application for a kiosk, supported on mobile application development technology (e.g. for smartphones and tablets).

The ValorMar R&D project is developing a traceability platform of fish and fishery products, originating both from fisheries and aquaculture [3,4]. The traceability information must be entered, in the platform, by all the supply chain operators.

The Polytechnic Institute of Viana do Castelo is also in charge of creating two different applications that will use the traceability platform developed. One of the applications is targeted for regular users and it is almost finished for both Android an iOS operating systems. This application allows the user to check information about a products lot such as the origin, quality, when was it registered the first time. This information is later used to create a graph and a map containing all information about the product. The second application under development is a kiosk application that runs inside fishery products stores and allows the clients to see available lots as well as information of the fish species that they select. For example, after selecting tuna, the kiosk shows a product details page with all the lots available of that species, with different price ranges and information such as nutrition data, possible recipes, an oriented graph and a map containing all the traceability information.

This paper is organized as follows: In Sect. 2 we explain the Traceability in the ValorMar Project; Sect. 3 explains the development of the kiosk application with information about hardware and available technologies; The forth section is about the kiosk application itself, containing the architecture and the screens flow, page by page; Sect. 5 is about the User Interface, information displayed and the importance of that information; Sect. 6 is about the System Usability Scale questionnaire developed and deployed to multiple participants to evaluate the application as it is; And, finally, Sect. 7 presents our conclusions.

2   Traceability in the ValorMar R&D Project

Fisheries supply chain starts at the sea, where fish species are captured, or at aquaculture farms. Fresh fish is then typically sold at fishery auction traders, and then continues its way through the value chain (e.g. logistics, industry) until the final customer. Sometimes, while still at sea, the fish is transformed, in industrial fishing vessels, into, for example, frozen or salted fish products. These fish products also make their way through the value chain until the final customer. The ValorMar R&D project has been developing a traceability platform of fish products, originating both from fisheries and aquaculture [3,4]. The traceability information must be inserted, in the developed platform, by all the involved stakeholders, that is by all the supply chain operators.

The traceability of fish or fishery products, like other food products, is very important, both to inform the consumer about the path of the fish through the value chain and to be able to recall fish lots in case of threats to the public health [5].

3   Architecture of a Kiosk Application

Kiosk usage is different than using a laptop, desktop or mobile devices. Gestures, sensors and location data may be used on consoles and computers but they play a specially important role in applications on mobile devices. Being targeted for a tablet device, this kiosk application has some of the requirements and limitations of mobile applications.

According to [10], an application on a mobile device has technical requirements that are not usually found on other applications, which includes the integration with the device hardware and security, performance, reliability and, of course, storage limitations. Some of the requirements are:

- Handling sensors
- Native and hybrid applications. Mobile devices usually include applications that use services over the Internet with the web browser that affects data and displays on the device.
- Hardware and Software. Most devices execute code that is custom-built for the properties of the device.
- Security. Mobile platforms are open which allows the installation of new malware applications that can compromise the regular operation of the device.
- User Interfaces (UI) must be built according to specific guidelines due to the display dimensions.
- The complexity of testing. Mobile web applications have the same issues of web apps but with additional concerns such as the transmission through gateways and the telephone network.
- The power consumption.

Smaller displays or different styles of interaction also have impact on interaction design for kiosk applications which has a strong influence on application development. Kiosk applications often have to be redesigned to highlight the most used functions and to make most effective use of the display. The user interface for kiosk applications is based on widgets, touch, physical motion and keyboards rather than the WIMP (Windows, Icons, Menus, Pointer) interface style of apple iOS and Microsoft Windows. Another aspect that may influence the application design might be the sensor usage or any other device feature activation.

Usually, kiosk applications include their user interface libraries and also guidelines which is why many applications share a common aspect. The platform standards are of the interest of the developer specially the on touch-screen devices where users are expecting a set of gestures which is different on every platform.

Kiosk applications may be written in different languages according to the target operating system (OS) of the device [8]. For developers, this is quite problematic because each OS uses its own API for accessing sensors or to create the aspect of the application. Cross-platform mobile development tools can possibly solve this issue. Using this tools, a developer can use the same code for multiple OS without writing application code in different languages. From [8], cross-platform mobile development tools have benefits such as:

- Lower skills required because the application is built using the same technology
- Reduction of coding because the source code is the same for every OS
- Development time and long term maintenance costs reduced
- Reduction of APIs knowledge because it is not needed to know the API for each OS, but only the provided by the tool
- Easier compared to native applications

The goal of these tools is to allow expanding the application offering, and sale, on more markets to increase the gain.

The authors in [8] suggest that, when selecting the tool for cross-platform development, some requirements must be gathered first such as the OS that we are targeting, the license of the tool, programming languages accepted and the APIs provided with the aim to get an idea of hardware parts accessible in the OS and how to access them.

On this paper we describe a kiosk application built with *Apache Cordova* which is an open-source cross-platform development framework that allows standard web technologies such as HTML5, CSS3, and JavaScript for cross-platform web and mobile development. Applications operate within wrappers targeted to each platform, and rely on standards-compliant API bindings to access each device's capabilities such as sensors, data, network status and more.

For the kiosk application project we have selected *Apache Cordova* essentially because of the ease to generate oriented graphs, one of the main outputs with traceability information to the user (refer to Sect. 5). Other alternative tools required much more effort or the libraries were paid. *Cordova* enables the use of SigmaJS, a JavaScript library dedicated to drawing graphs that makes it easy to publish them to web and mobile applications. *Cordova* also offers the possibility to extend the tool by using custom made plugins.

Essentially *Cordova* is a "wrapper" that allows enclosure of applications written in known web languages into mobile native applications. *Cordova* applications can be considered hybrid as they may yield mobile and web apps. These applications are neither native nor web apps.

4   ValorMar Kiosk Application

The developed kiosk application allows customers to view the available fish products' information, such as the traceability of the product lot, nutritional table, as well as recipes requiring the product. Thus, a user interface has been created, towards the idea that most of its users are not IT or food experts, and require a minimal and clean interface to navigate the application's features. I was supported by a Javascript library called Vuejs (https://vuejs.org).

The kiosk also enables in-store administrators to make changes, such as adding products (from the central traceability platform) and editing and removing products on the internal database maintained by the application. After saving the changes, the kiosk application will send a package to the kiosk applications on the same local network, containing new instructions of what to do on the local database, synchronizing all kiosks' databases. Note that each kiosk application has its own embedded lightweight database using SQLite. After making the changes the administrator can simply log out and use the application as a regular customer.

Figure 1 shows an illustration of how the system is currently working considering all clients as both client and server devices.

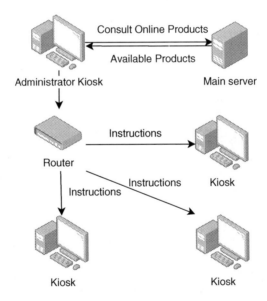

Fig. 1. Administrator consults online catalog and adds products available locally while the application sends the new data to the connected kiosks

Every device communicates with each other using a router as middleware. This router must accept broadcast in order for the devices to keep communicating with every new device that may connect or be connected to the network.

The application installed on each device adds a small local database that gets updated with the packages that a tablet neighbor sends. These updates are deployed every time an authenticated user changes the local database of the device that it is using. After applying the changes the system proceeds to update the connected databases which on this case are the remaining tablet neighbors working as a client for this server device.

The databases on this system are not synchronizing, instead the device where the changes were made has to communicate a new instruction such as add, edit, remove, build a JSON package with the product information and previous instruction and then send it to the tablet neighbors connected on the network.

To have permission to make changes to the system, the user has to be authenticated using an administrator account. The administrator has to consult an online catalog of available products and select every product that is also available on that current store. While adding products the kiosk application will send a new update to every other kiosk connected to update their databases as well (Fig. 1).

The application also has to import product information from the traceability application database using a RESTfull API. To do this, it is required to use specific authentication that will generate an access Token that will be used on every request to authenticate the application and obtain the information required. Such information will later be added to the product detail page inside the application. With this product information comes the traceability which will allow us to generate a graph with SigmaJS (found in http://sigmajs.org/) and a map using OpenLayers (found in https://openlayers.org/) with the graphical information. Check [7] for more details about this application network architecture.

5   Customers User Interface

Subsequently, it was necessary to develop a user interface for customers, to be made available on the kiosk. It was decided to design and develop an interface having in mind that its usability would promote a good user experience for the customer when consulting information about fish products available for sale. The screens structure is represented in Fig. 2. The main screen of this kiosk application was built considering three different categories for marine products available on every store. There are Fresh, Frozen and Canned products as seen in Fig. 3. These three boxes on the main screen are used as a filter to the products that belong to one of these categories. After the customer has chosen one of the categories, the kiosk application opens the next screen on which the products available on the store will be filtered according to the category selected.

The kiosk application accesses its offline database with all the products, previously added by an administrator, and dynamically creates new boxes for every product item. As more products are added by an administrator to one of the kiosk applications on the store, more products will appear on every individual kiosk application, since they are all synchronizing instructions.

Figure 3 shows an image of the main screen of the kiosk application. This application has been designed to run on multiple android tablet devices and allow these devices, running the application, to seamlessly communicate with each other. The kiosk application has a login feature that allows an administrator to login and make changes to the database, on any of the connected devices. At

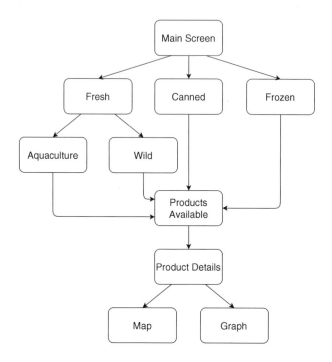

Fig. 2. Kiosk application page flow

Fig. 3. Kiosk user interface entry screen

any moment, an administrator can authenticate with his/her account on the application and gain permissions to make changes about the available products inside the store.

The boxes used to represent the available products contain the name of the product, e.g. tuna, or codfish, the image of the product and the price. If the product has a discount, the application calculates the amount of discount according to the old price and a new price for the product. These values were also added on the item box for the products that have a discount. The customer can select one of these products by touching the correspondent box of the product. After selecting a product, the kiosk application will jump to a new screen (Product Details) on which the user may see all the information gathered about this product. This information is obtained through the access to an external API also developed during the Valormar R&D project.

The Product Details page has all the information about the product selected by the customer. On the beginning of the product details page, the customer can verify all the lots available for a specific product and a table containing information such as the scientific species name, the price, how it was obtained (e.g. Aquaculture, nets, etc.) and the date when it was created. The price of one lot can be different from the other lots, which is why every lot has its own price parameter. With this information, the customer has access to all the available lots and every other information associated to them, such as the events with temperature, quality, origin, and dates for every single lot. This page also includes a more generalized content about the product itself, not just the lot that it belongs to. As the customer scrolls down the page, he finds more important information about the product, which includes some of the possible recipes using the specific product, the beneficial effects for human health and a nutritional table. To complement all this information available to the user, the application also creates an interactive map and a supply chain events' oriented graph, providing information about products traceability, according to the lot selected before and identified on the top of the page (Fig. 4).

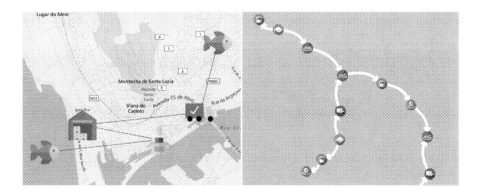

Fig. 4. OpenLayers map and SigmaJS graph on product page

As indicated, both the map and the graph are interactive, meaning that the customer can play around with both to get a better view of the information associated to the fish product. In the case of the graph, for example, if the customer presses one of the events, the kiosk application opens a small window on the top of it, with some information additional information, such as the temperature, the event name, the date, and some other information. The map was created using the OpenLayers technology (https://openlayers.org) and the graph using the SigmaJS (http://sigmajs.org/). Both widgets are still being under development, in order to improve the experience of the customer when interacting with them, and to obtain more information about the lot traceability.

6   Kiosk Usability Test and Results

In order to test the usability of the application it was decided to use the System Usability Scale (SUS) method. This method consists in a questionnaire having ten questions, each one evaluated from strongly disagree to totally agree, using a Likert scale with five points, according to [1,6]. There are five positive statements and five negative statements. All the questions can be seen on Table 1. The general measure of the perceived usability is obtained by calculating the sum of the 10 questions rating. The value obtained is used to verify the global usability of the application, indicated by the users. The range of a SUS questionnaire goes from 0 to 100 and the product has potential only if the final score is above 68 [9]. Additional research has been made to map adjectives such as "worst imaginable", "poor" and "excellent" to range the scores for additional insight [2]. The SUS Score can be measured in a few different grades[1]. Below 51 it's considered to be awful, from 51 to 67 it's poor, 68 means the application is ok, between 68 and 80.3 is good and above this last value can be considered excellent. This kiosk passed the usability test with a score of 81, meaning that it is more than acceptable.

Table 1. Questions used on the questionnaire

1	I think that I would like to use this system frequently
2	I found the system unnecessarily complex
3	I thought the system was easy to use
4	I think that I would need the support of a technical person to be able to use this system
5	I found the various functions in this system were well integrated
6	I thought there was too much inconsistency in this system
7	I would imagine that most people would learn to use this system very quickly
8	I found the system very cumbersome to use
9	I felt very confident using the system
10	I needed to learn a lot of things before I could get going with this system

[1] https://www.usabilitest.com/system-usability-scale.

After a week in which the questionnaire was available, 35 responses were obtained, from 21 women and 14 man, between 18 and 54 years old. The average results can be seen in Fig. 5. From the results it is possible to verify that most male participants indicated to have a reduced difficulty using the application, while female participants are more convinced to use the application, despite the increased difficulty using the kiosk. Female participants agreed that the application should be less complex but also that is very easy to learn how to use the kiosk.

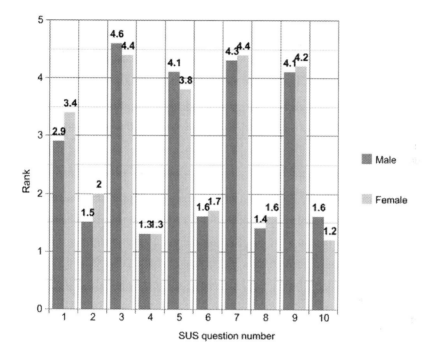

Fig. 5. Average results grouped by gender of participant.

Additionally, few suggestions from the participants were also collected and some were considered to be added to the application. The top bar with the back button and the logo of the application should follow the user while it scrolls down the page of the product, otherwise the user will have to scroll the entire page up again to use the back button. Other user asked for sections on the product page, instead of only having one big page with all the content. The idea was to add sections so that the user could select the section of interest such as traceability or recipes for that product. Other users prefer the map over the graph, which can be confusing for some users, and ask for lot details on the map itself rather than the graph.

Most of the problems identified by the users were already under developers knowledge and are already being considered for resolution.

Overall, the application has been well accepted by most users and some of the users that might disagree with the application purpose might be convinced after a few updates to the applications user interface and flow and might feel tempted to use it in the future.

Another question was also added during this SUS questionnaire but not taken into account for the final score of 81. The participants were asked if the application features were enough and adequate. 91% of the users considered that to be true.

7   Conclusions

The presented kiosk application has been developed under the premise that not every system user is an expert in technology or in food quality. The kiosk network requires only that all the kiosk devices (Android Tablets) connect to the same network and then, using ZeroConf technology they will connect to each other and communicate every single instruction without the administrator having to insert it manually on each device or having another device in the middle running as a server. The only requirement for this network to work is that the router on which the kiosk devices will connect is configured to allow broadcast, so that they can emit the packages to all other kiosk device neighbors. The network implemented on this application was already discussed on [7].

The user interface of this application has been built towards this same principle, allowing users to check products detailed information, without too much effort. With only three finger clicks on the screen the user will be able to find the products origin, quality, temperatures as well as their traceability information.

An important objective to achieve with the work here described was to do an usability study, concerning the kiosk customer user interface. Thus, it was decided to use a SUS questionnaire to gather useful information about the user perspective on using the kiosk.

Despite having a more finished and robust template of the user interface and experience to work on, the kiosk application will continue to be improved. According to the results of the SUS questionnaire (See Sect. 6), the application was well accepted and some suggestions indicated by the participants are already taking in consideration. As it stands, this kiosk application is looking quite attractive for most participants.

For future work, the user interface of the kiosk application developed and the flow will be updated as well as some technical features that were discussed in [7] and a new SUS questionnaire might be developed and deployed to test a final version of this product.

Acknowledgments. This contribution has been developed in the context of Project "ValorMar – Valorização integral dos recursos marinhos: potencial, inovação tecnológica e novas aplicações (reference POCI-01-0247-FEDER-024517) funded by FEDER (Fundo Europeu de Desenvolvimento Regional) through Operational Programme for Competitiveness and Internationalization (POCI).

References

1. Bangor, A., Kortum, P., Miller, J.: Determining what individual SUS scores mean: adding an adjective rating scale. J. Usability Stud. **4**, 114–123 (2009)
2. Brooke, J.: SUS: a retrospective. J. Usability Stud. **8**(2), 29–40 (2013)
3. da Cruz, A.M., et al.: On the design of a platform for traceability in the fishery and aquaculture value chain. In: 14th Iberian Conference on Information Systems and Technologies (CISTI 2019) (2019). https://ieeexplore.ieee.org/document/8760891
4. Cruz, E.F., Cruz, A.M., Gomes, R.: Analysis of a traceability and quality monitoring platform for the fishery and aquaculture value chain. In: 14th Iberian Conference on Information Systems and Technologies (CISTI 2019) (2019). https://ieeexplore.ieee.org/document/8760755
5. Cruz, E.F., da Cruz, A.M.R.: A food value chain integrated business process and domain models for product traceability and quality monitoring. In: 21st International Conference on Enterprise Information Systems (ICEIS). INSTICC, Heraklion, April 2019
6. Devy, N.P.I.R., Wibirama, S., Santosa, P.I.: Evaluating user experience of English learning interface using user experience questionnaire and system usability scale. In: 2017 1st International Conference on Informatics and Computational Sciences (ICICoS), pp. 101–106 (2017)
7. Oliveira, J., da Cruz, A.M.R., Faria, P.M.: Zeroconf network retail kiosk for fish products traceability. In: 15th Iberian Conference on Information Systems and Technologies (CISTI), Sevilla, Spain (2020)
8. Palmieri, M., Singh, I., Cicchetti, A.: Comparison of cross-platform mobile development tools. In: 2012 16th International Conference on Intelligence in Next Generation Networks, ICIN 2012, pp. 179–186 (2012). https://doi.org/10.1109/ICIN.2012.6376023
9. Sharfina, Z., Santoso, H.B.: An Indonesian adaptation of the system usability scale (SUS). In: 2016 International Conference on Advanced Computer Science and Information Systems (ICACSIS), pp. 145–148 (2016)
10. Wasserman, A.I.: Software engineering issues for mobile application development. In: Proceedings of the FSE/SDP Workshop on Future of Software Engineering Research, FoSER 2010, p. 397–400. Association for Computing Machinery, New York (2010). https://doi.org/10.1145/1882362.1882443

Authentication of Choice on Mobile Devices: A Preliminary Investigation

Akintunde Jeremiah Oluwafemi$^{(\boxtimes)}$ and Jinjuan Heidi Feng$^{(\boxtimes)}$

Towson University, Towson, USA
{aoluwafemi,jfeng}@towson.edu

Abstract. Authentication is a security measure designed to allow authorized users to use the system securely with minimum interference on the usability of the system. Although numerous user studies had examined various authentication methods such as traditional alphanumeric password, graphical password, and biometrics, very limited research investigated users' performance and preference when they were allowed to choose the authentication method(s) of their choice for a specific application. This study was conducted as an initial attempt to fill in that gap. We developed a mobile application called the 'Event manager' that offers calendar and file management functions. Regarding the authentication, the 'Event manager' app provides users the freedom to choose their preferred authentication method(s) among five commonly adopted authentication mechanisms. We conducted an empirical user study with a 'within-group' design to investigate users' initial interaction with three different types of authentication processes: alphanumeric passwords, one-factor authentication of choice, and two-factor authentication of choice. 75 participants completed the study. The result of the study will help understand users' general perception regarding the 'authentication of choice' approach as well as their preferred authentication method or combination of methods in the context of mobile devices.

Keywords: Access control · Authentication of choice · Usability · Security

1 Introduction

Access control is one of the most important measures to ensure the security of a system. Access control is used to prevent unauthorized access to a system and involves three key steps; identification, authentication, and authorization. Identification is the process of providing identity to the system, which can be a claim or a set of claims about the user. Authentication is the process of verifying the identity of the user, device, or other entity in a system before granting the entity access to the system (O'Gorman 2003). Authorization is the process of granting permissions or privileges to the authenticated entity (Clarke 2010). This study focuses on the authentication process in the context of mobile devices.

The main goal of authentication is to ensure that users can perform their primary tasks securely on a system with minimal impact of the authentication method on the

© Springer Nature Switzerland AG 2020
C. Stephanidis et al. (Eds.): HCII 2020, LNCS 12423, pp. 752–761, 2020.
https://doi.org/10.1007/978-3-030-60114-0_49

completion of their primary tasks (Beautement et al. 2010). Previous research confirmed the tradeoff between the security and usability of authentication mechanisms. Typical measures that improve the security of the authentication mechanism (e.g., increasing the length of passwords, requiring a frequent change of passwords, reduction in false acceptance rate, etc.) usually negatively affect the usability of the system (Yee 2002). To make a system usable and secure, system developers need to go beyond the traditional human-centered design techniques and adopt design techniques that allow users to make decisions (Cranor et al. 2014). Ben Schneiderman's golden rules of interface design also state that system should allow users to make decisions to increase the usability of that system. Although numerous user studies had examined various authentication methods such as traditional alphanumeric password, graphical password, and biometrics, very limited research investigated users' performance and preference when they are allowed to choose the authentication method(s) of their choice for a specific application. We conducted an online empirical study to provide a preliminary understanding of the 'authentication of choice' approach in the context of mobile devices. The focus of this study is to investigate users' initial interaction and perception when they have the freedom to select authentication methods of their choice.

2   Related Work

2.1   Authentication Methods

There are various authentication methods that can generally be grouped into four categories based on the factor used for authentication:

Knowledge-based authentication is based on what the user must know to verify his identity to the information system. This is done in the form of challenge and response, in which the user responds to the challenge with something he knows (Katsini et al. 2016). Examples include numeric password, also referred to as personal identification number (PIN), alphanumeric password, or graphical password. Knowledge-based authentication methods are the most widely adopted form of authentication because they are relatively easy to implement and have lower operating cost (Lampson 2004). However, the major limitation of this type of authentication is the memorability requirement in that users have to commit information to memory and recollect the information during authentication. This memorability problem does affect the usability and security of the knowledge-based authentication methods (Katsina 2016). Users find it difficult to remember password or PIN and many end up writing down their passwords or choosing simple passwords that can lead to compromise of the system security.

Inherent factors authentication, also known as biometrics, uses the physiological or behavioral traits of the user for authentication. Examples of the inherent factors include fingerprint, iris, retina, voice, face, signature, typing patterns, physical movement, etc. Biometric authentication is relatively more usable and secure compared to knowledge-based authentication that involves committing information to memory (Cohen et al. 2011). One of the challenges of the biometric authentication approach is that once the factor is compromised, the compromise will be permanent. If hackers can find matching fingerprints for a user, there is no way that the user can change his fingerprint like in the case of knowledge-based or possession-based authentication (Cohen et al. 2011).

Another issue with inherent factor authentication is that the user's environment can affect the functioning of the authentication method (Stephanidis et al. 2013). For instance, a health worker in the emergency room wearing gloves and mask would not be able to use fingerprint or face recognition for authentication until they remove their protecting gear.

The Possession-Based Authentication relies on what users have or possess for authentication. Examples of possession include smart card, common access card, token, etc. This authentication approach is relatively more acceptable to users compared to other authentication factors, but it is more difficult to manage, and the device can get lost, stole or shared (Habtamu 2006).

Location-based Authentication involves using the geographical location of the user or device to authenticate and validate access to the information system. A common implementation of this approach is when banks deny customer transaction on their debit or credit card in an unauthorized location until the customer calls the bank to provide additional validation. This authentication approach can provide an additional level of security for the system by preventing access from unauthorized areas, but it is not easy to implement and has to be combined with another authentication approach to identify a specific user (Sailer et al. 2004).

2.2   Multifactor Authentication Method

Multifactor authentication is the combination of two or more authentication methods to authenticate a user (i.e., smart card (possession-based authentication) and PIN (knowledge-based authentication)). Multifactor authentication was introduced because of the insufficient level of security provided by single-factor authentication especially for sensitive systems (Konoth et al. 2017). This approach provides a higher level of security especially for government and military systems as well as other critical services (Banyal 2013) but does affect the usability of those systems (De Cristofaro et al. 2013).

2.3   Authentication on Mobile Devices

There has been a rapid increase in the use of mobile phones in the past decade. It was reported in 2016 that almost two-thirds of the world's population has a mobile phone (Kemp 2017). Mobile devices have improved the quality of life by providing a variety of services anytime and anywhere. However, the mobility and portability of mobile devices pose significant threat to privacy and security of the information stored on the device (Marcin et al. 2013). User authentication is one of the security measures to counter the threat to security and privacy of the information on mobile devices. The most popular authentication approach on mobile devices is knowledge-based authentication methods such as PIN, password, and pattern or graphical passwords. More recently, fingerprint authentication and facial authentication have been widely adopted as well (Teh 2019). Knowledge-based authentication in mobile devices is vulnerable to threats such as smudge attack, which detects the oily smudges left behind by user's finger when operating the mobile device (Aviv et al. 2010). Shoulder surfing and brute force attack are other major threats to knowledge-based authentication on mobile devices (Zakaria et al. 2011). Poor lighting may affect face authentication. Fingerprint authentication can fail if the user's hand is dirty, dry, or injured (Park et al. 2011).

2.4 Authentication of Choice

There is no single authentication mechanism that can accommodate the needs of all users (Renaud 2004). It is difficult to design a universally accessible authentication method for users without knowing their abilities and disabilities (Fairweather et al. 2002). People have different preferences for authentication methods based on their cognitive skills or physical abilities (Belk et al. 2013). Systems are usually designed with one authentication method out of a variety of authentication methods that are currently in use. To enhance the security of the system, some systems may be designed to require two-factor authentication that requires higher workload from the user (Jain et al. 2011; Gutmann et al. 2005). In either one-factor of two-factor authentication, providing the freedom of choice in selecting the authentication method(s) preferred by each individual user may help improve the usability of the system. To date, there is very limited empirical research in the authentication of choice approach. The online study reported in this paper was conducted as an initial attempt to fill in the gap.

3 Methods

The goal of this online study is to examine users' initial interaction and perception of different authentication methods when using the freedom of choice process. The study adopted a within-group design with three conditions for authentication:

- Alphanumeric username and password
- One-factor authentication of choice: In this condition, the participant chose one authentication method out of five options (alphanumeric passwords, pin, fingerprint authentication, facial authentication, and One Time Password (OTP))
- Two-factor authentication of choice: In this condition, the participant chose two authentication methods out of the five options listed above.

3.1 Participants

75 participants completed the study. Participants didn't receive any financial or other types of incentives for taking part in the study. The age of participants varies, with 47 participants in the age range of 18–30 years, 18 in the range of 31–40 years, 8 in the range of 41–50 years and 2 above 50. Out of the 75 participants, 43 claimed they were male while 32 claimed to be female. 71 of the participants were professionals working in various fields such as business, education, science, engineering and IT, and healthcare. Three participants were students. One participant didn't identify his/her career.

3.2 Event Manager Application

An Android-based mobile device application called 'Event manager' was developed to provide a realistic setting for this study. The 'Event Manager' supports five authentication methods and provides a calendar for managing daily schedule. The calendar setting was chosen because it was provided on almost all mobile phones and its' security and privacy related expectation was representative of many tasks conducted on mobile devices on a daily basis. The five authentication methods supported are commonly adopted on mobile devices:

- Alphanumeric username and password
- Personal Identification Number (PIN)
- Fingerprint authentication
- Facial authentication
- One-Time-Password (OTP)

The design of the application followed general usability guidelines and underwent several rounds of refinement according to user feedback. The home page and the registration page of the application are demonstrated in Fig. 1 below. Users can create three types of account on the application using the same email:

Type 1 (T1): alphanumeric username and password,
Type 2 (T2): One-factor authentication of choice with five options
Type 3 (T3): Two-factor authentication of choice with five options

 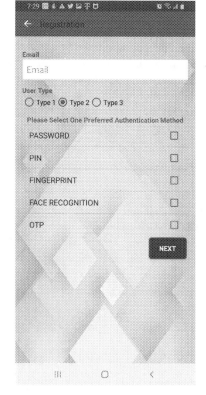

(a) Home page   (b) Registration page

Fig. 1. a. Home page b. Registration page

3.3 Procedure

The study was conducted online. Instructions for the study environment and procedure were sent out to participants via email. After providing consent to take part in the study, participants first downloaded the 'Event Manager' app from Google Play and installed it on their Android phones. Then each participant created and logged into an account under all three conditions. After they logged into an account, they added or revised an event on the calendar. The order of the three conditions was counterbalanced among the participants to control the learning effect. After the participant completed the tasks under all 3 conditions, they answered a questionnaire via a Google form and rated their preference for each of the three authentication processes. A demographic questionnaire was completed at the very end of the study. The authentication methods chose during the one-factor and two-factor authentication of choice processes were automatically logged by the system.

4 Results

We counted the number of participants who chose each authentication method when using the one-factor or two-factor authentication of choice processes. Table 1 illustrates the number of participants who chose each method under each of the 2 processes.

Table 1. The number of participants who chose each specific authentication method under the one-factor and two-factor authentication of choice conditions.

Authentication method	Type 2	Type 3	Type 2%	Type 3%
Password	1	13	1.3%	17.3%
Pin	35	68	46.7%	90.7%
Fingerprint	11	34	14.7%	45.3%
Facial authentication	28	35	37.3%	46.7%
OTP	0	0	0	0
Total	75	150	100	200

The number of participants who chose each specific authentication method under the one-factor and two-factor authentication of choice conditions. Note that in the two-factor authentication of choice condition, each participant chose 2 methods for the account. Therefore, the total number of participants choosing all methods is 150 and the total percentage of participants is 200%.

As illustrated in Table 1, the PIN is the most frequently chosen method in both the one-factor (46.7%) and the two-factor (90.7) authentication of choice conditions. In the one-factor condition, the 2nd most frequently chosen method was the 'facial authentication' method, which was almost doubled that of the 'Fingerprint' method. In the two-factor authentication condition, there was a tie between the 'facial authentication' method and the 'fingerprint' method, each counting towards 46.7% and 45.3% of the participants, respectively. Only one participant chose the traditional password method in the one-factor condition, while 13 participants chose this method in the two-factor condition. Figure 2 illustrates the percentage of participants who chose each authentication method under the two authentication of choice conditions.

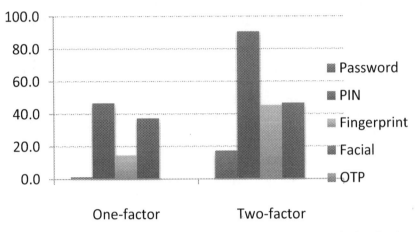

Fig. 2. The percentage of participants who chose each authentication method under the two authentication of choice conditions.

Table 2. Number and percentage of participants who ranked each of the three conditions as their first, second, and third choice.

Rank	Alphanumeric password number (%)	One-factor authentication of choice number (%)	Two-factor authentication of choice number (%)	Total
Top	3 (4%)	63 (84%)	9 (12%)	75
2nd	33 (44%)	12 (16%)	30 (40%)	75
3rd	39 (52%)	0 (0)	36 (48%)	75
Total	75	75	75	

The participants were asked to rank their preference towards the three test conditions. Table 2 illustrates how the participants ranked each test condition. Regarding the top choice, 84% of the participants chose the one factor authentication of choice condition, 12% chose the two-factor authentication of choice condition, only 4% chose the alphanumeric password condition. As to the second choice, 44% chose the alphanumeric condition, 40% chose the two-factor authentication of choice condition and 16% chose the one-factor condition. Regarding the least preferred condition, 52% chose the alphanumeric condition and 48% chose the two-factor authentication of choice condition. A Chi-squared test suggests that there is a significant difference in the participants' ranking between the 3 conditions ($X^2(4) = 135.36$, $p < 0.001$). Participants overwhelmingly prefer the one-factor authentication of choice condition over the other two conditions (Fig. 3).

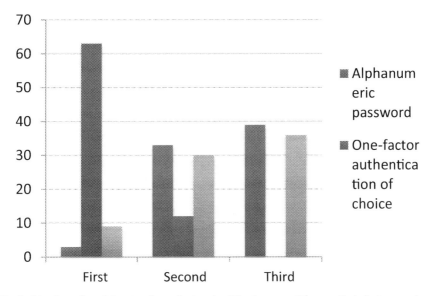

Fig. 3. Number of participants who ranked each of the three conditions as their first, second, and third choice.

5 Discussions and Conclusion

The results suggest that, when given the freedom to choose the authentication method(s) for their mobile devices, most participants prefer PIN, followed by facial authentication and fingerprint authentication. OTP is the least preferred method under both authentication of choice conditions. Participants overwhelmingly preferred the one-factor authentication of choice condition over the other two conditions. Participants' preference towards the one-factor authentication of choice condition over the alphanumeric password condition implies that participants like the freedom of selecting authentication method for their mobile phones. The reason that participants prefer the one-factor authentication of choice over the two-factor condition might be due to the increased workload required by the two-factor authentication.

The study suggests there is potential to adopt the authentication of choice approach on mobile devices to improve user satisfaction, However, the results should be interpreted with caution due to several limitations. First, the study only involved Android users. Second, the authentication methods supported were either knowledge-based or biometrics. Possession-based and location-based authentication were not examined. Third, because the participants logged into each account only once during the study, the results only apply to the very initial interaction with the authentication processes. Future studies are planned to evaluate the authentication of choice approach involving more diversified authentication methods, on more platforms, and through a longer period of time.

Acknowledgements. We would like to thank Edward Miklewski for his assistance in data collection. We also want to thank all the participants.

References

Aviv, A.J., Gibson, K., Mossop, E., Blaze, M., Smith, J.M.: Smudge attacks on smartphone touch screens. In: Proceedings of the 4th USENIX Conference on Offensive Technologies, pp 1–7. USENIX Association, Berkeley (2010). http://dl.acm.org/citation.cfm?id=1925004.1925009

Banyal, R.K., Jain, P., Jain, V.K.: Multi-factor authentication framework for cloud computing. In: Proceedings of the Fifth International Conference on Computational Intelligence, Modelling and Simulation (CIMSim), Seoul, Korea, 24–25 September 2013, pp. 105–110 (2013)

Beautement, A., Sasse, M.A., Wonham, M.: The compliance budget: managing security behavior in organizations. In: Proceedings of the Workshop on New Security Paradigms, pp. 47–58 (2010). https://doi.org/10.1145/1595676.1595684

Belk, M., Fidas, C., Germanakos, P., Samaras, G.: Security for diversity: studying the effects of verbal and imagery processes on user authentication mechanisms. In: Kotzé, P., Marsden, G., Lindgaard, G., Wesson, J., Winckler, M. (eds.) INTERACT 2013. LNCS, vol. 8119, pp. 442–459. Springer, Heidelberg (2013). https://doi.org/10.1007/978-3-642-40477-1_27

Clarke, R.: Sufficiently Rich Model of (id)Entity, Authentication and Authorization (2010). http://www.rogerclarke.com/ID/IdModel1002.html#MAc

Cohen, S., Ben-Asher, N., Meyer, J.: Towards information technology security for universal access. In: Stephanidis, C. (ed.) UAHCI 2011. LNCS, vol. 6765, pp. 443–451. Springer, Heidelberg (2011). https://doi.org/10.1007/978-3-642-21672-5_48

Cranor, L.F., Buchler, N.: Better together: usability and security go hand in hand. In: IEEE Security & Privacy, vol. 12, no. 6, pp. 89–93 (2014). https://doi.org/10.1109/msp.2014.109

De Cristofaro, E., Du, H., Freudiger, J., Norcie, G.: A comparative usability study of two-factor authentication. arXiv preprint arXiv:1309.5344 (2013)

Fairweather, P., Hanson, V., Detweiler, S., Schwerdtfeger, R.: From assistive technology to a web accessibility service. In: Proceedings of the 5th International ACM Conference on Assistive Technologies (ASSETS). pp. 4–8. ACM (2002)

Gutmann, P., Grigg, I.: Security usability. IEEE Secur. Priv. 3(4), 56–58 (2005)

Habtamu, A.: Different Ways to Authenticate Users with the Pros and Cons of each Method, Norsk Regnesentral, Norwegian (2006)

Jain, A., Ross, A., Nandakumar, K.: Introduction to Biometrics. Springer, Boston (2011). https://doi.org/10.1007/978-0-387-77326-1

Katsini, C., Belk, M., Fidas, C., Avouris, N., Samaras, G.: Security and usability in knowledge-based user authentication: a review (2016). https://doi.org/10.1145/3003733.3003764

Kemp, S.: Digital in 2017: global overview. We are social (2017). https://wearesocial.com/specialreports/digital-in-2017-global-overview

Konoth, R.K., van der Veen, V., Bos, H.: How anywhere computing just killed your phone-based two-factor authentication. In: Grosasklags, J., Preneel, B. (eds.) FC 2016. LNCS, vol. 9603, pp. 405–421. Springer, Heidelberg (2017). https://doi.org/10.1007/978-3-662-54970-4_24

Lampson, B.W.: Computer security in the real world. IEEE Comput. 37(6), 37–46 (2004)

Marcin, R., Khalid, S., Mariusz, R., Marek, T., Marcin, A.: User authentication for mobile devices. In: 12th International Conference on Information Systems and Industrial Management (CISIM), Krakow, Poland, September 2013, pp. 47–58 (2013)

O'Gorman, L.: Comparing passwords, tokens, and biometrics for user authentication. Proc. IEEE 91(2003), 2021–2040 (2003)

Park, Y.H., et al.: A multimodal biometric recognition of touched fingerprint and finger-vein. In: 2011 International Conference on Multimedia and Signal Processing, vol. 1, pp. 247–250 (2011)

Renaud, K.: Quantification of authentication mechanisms - a usability perspective. J. Web Eng. 3(2), 95–123 (2004)

Sailer, R., Zhang, X., Jaeger, T., Van Doorn, L.: Design and implementation of a TCG based integrity measurement architecture. In: Proceedings of the 13th Conference on USENIX Security Symposium, SSYM 2004, vol. 13, p. 16. USENIX Association, Berkeley (2004)

Mayron, L.M., Hausawi, Y., Bahr, G.S.: Secure, usable biometric authentication systems. In: Stephanidis, C., Antona, M. (eds.) UAHCI 2013. LNCS, vol. 8009, pp. 195–204. Springer, Heidelberg (2013). https://doi.org/10.1007/978-3-642-39188-0_21

Teh, P.S., Zhang, N., Tan, S.: Strengthen user authentication on mobile devices by using user's touch dynamics pattern. J Ambient Intell. Human Comput. (2019). https://doi.org/10.1007/s12 652-019-01654-y

Yee, K.-P.: User interaction design for secure systems. In: Deng, R., Bao, F., Zhou, J., Qing, S. (eds.) ICICS 2002. LNCS, vol. 2513, pp. 278–290. Springer, Heidelberg (2002). https://doi. org/10.1007/3-540-36159-6_24

Zakaria, N.H., Grifths, D., Brostof, S., Yan, J.: Shoulder surfing defense for recall-based graphical passwords. In: Proceedings of the Seventh Symposium on Usable Privacy and Security, pp. 6:1– 6:12. ACM, New York (2011). https://doi.org/10.1145/2078827.2078835

Measuring Users' Psychophysiological Experience in Non-linear Omnichannel Environment

Ariane Roy[1]([✉]), Sylvain Sénécal[1], Pierre-Majorique Léger[1], Bertrand Demolin[1], Émilie Bigras[2], and Julie Gagne[2]

[1] HEC Montréal, 3000 Chemin de la Côte-Sainte-Catherine, Montréal, QC H3T 2A7, Canada
{ariane.roy,sylvain.senecal,pierre-majorique.leger,
bertrand.demolin}@hec.ca
[2] Vidéotron, 612 rue Saint-Jacques, Montréal, QC H3C 1C8, Canada
{emilie.bigras,julie.gagne}@videotron.com

Abstract. As the use of technological products in complex user journeys has increased, both the physical and digital worlds need to be considered in measuring the customer's experience. Hence, measuring the customer experience requires to embody multiple sets of non-linear interactions. The uniqueness of the user's physical experience and the ecological validity issues have to be taken into account in a physical context of interactions. Various methods already exist to measure customer journeys, but they rely mostly on self-reported and retrospective measures, like questionnaires, interviews, or focus groups. The objective of this research is to mirror the actual complexity of the omnichannel customer interactions by mobilizing quantitative and qualitative data with implicit measures. In this article, we propose a methodology for collecting and analyzing insightful psychophysiological data in non-linear physical interactions. We build upon an illustrative case study where 24 participants had to install new cable equipment. Implicit psychophysiological measures and explicit qualitative assessment were used to obtain a rich perspective on the user's emotional and cognitive experience. Through psychophysiological variables and self-reported metrics, this article serves as a comprehensive methodological approach for experts to have a precise overview of the emotional journey of consumers.

Keywords: User experience (UX) · Evaluation methodology ·
Psychophysiological measures · Psychophysiological pain points · User journey

1 Introduction

As the use of technological products in the complex user journeys has increased, both the physical and digital worlds need to be considered in measuring the customer's experience. Enabled by technology, users expect to interact with companies interchangeably across channels (Carroll and Guzmán 2013). Consequently, consumers' path can be more or less direct, but the use of different channels within the same journey favor non-linearity. Their journey can encompass multiple and much less predictable exits, even as

C. Stephanidis et al. (Eds.): HCII 2020, LNCS 12423, pp. 762–779, 2020.
https://doi.org/10.1007/978-3-030-60114-0_50

consumers can circle back to previous choices and steps until their final purchase (Carroll and Guzmán 2013). Hence, measuring customer experience requires to embody multiple sets of non-linear interactions. In a physical context of interactions, the uniqueness of the user's experience and the ecological validity issues have to be taken into account. Various methods already exist to measure customer journeys, but those methods rely mostly on retrospective measures, like questionnaires, interviews, or focus groups. For example, Customer Experience Modelling has been used in the service sector to gain an accurate picture of the whole customer journey, by exploring touchpoints sequence with customer-centric soft goals (Verma et al. 2012). Indeed, user journeys have been observed more frequently in qualitative and retrospective assessments.

The field of user experience (UX) research is defined by the *International Organization for Standardization (ISO)* as the set of user perceptions and responses resulting from the use or anticipation of the use of a system, a product, or a service (ISO 2018). User experience encompasses all consumer-firm touchpoints and interactions encountered within the user journey. Generally, to measure this experience, user testing has been mostly associated with online interactions. Indeed, UX professionals create tasks to replicate real interactions that are logically organized and monitor the user in this artificially rational process (Nielsen 2012). In the assessment of this experience, most UX research focuses on explicit and self-reported and retrospective measurement tools, such as questionnaires. However, prior research also shows that there is an important discrepancy between what users feel during the experience and how they recall it afterward (Cockburn et al. 2017; Eich and Schooler 2000).

In order to mirror the actual complexity of the omnichannel customer interactions, a quantitative analysis must be combined with qualitative, judgment driven evaluations (Rawson et al. 2013). As such, implicit psychological measures are favorable to overcome the potential self-reported biases (Léger et al. 2014). Indeed, cognition and affect are psychological constructs that have been proved to influence customer behavior and customer experience (Bagozzi et al. 1999; Frow and Payne 2007; Tynan and McKechnie 2009). Recent research also showed the effectiveness of implicit psychological pain points in insights during peak emotional responses in a user's experience (Giroux-Huppé et al. 2019). Implicit pain points are defined here as a moment, in reaction to an event during the interaction, during which the user experiences an automatic physiological activation characterized by a high level of emotional arousal and negative emotional valence (Giroux-Huppé et al. 2019). But to use psychological measures and tools, ecological validity is necessary and easier to ensure in an online experience, where the user does not have to move or to manipulate an object. In omnichannel shopping, however, as more frequent business-consumer interactions with technology take place within a physical context, challenges arise in measuring the emotional and cognitive user experience.

In this article, we propose a methodology to collect and analyze insightful psychophysiological data in a non-linear physical interaction. We will use the case study of a telecommunication provider's equipment set up using implicit psychophysiological measures and explicit qualitative assessment. The task consisted of completing the un-installation and installation of technological equipment for cable and television services, with the sole support of the instruction manual to replicate as close as possible the real-life context. We aim to measure the cognitive and emotional experience of a user in their interaction sequence from uninstalling existing equipment to installing a new technological experience, using novel types of equipment in the telecommunication industry.

2 Description of the Proposed Methodology

The proposed methodology aims to overcome the different challenges raised by measuring user experience in physical interactions. Physiological measures, such as electrocardiography (ECG), respiration rate, skin-based measures (EDA), and psychological measures (EEG) allow a deeper understanding of the emotional and cognitive experience of a user without interfering with the interaction (Dufresne et al. 2010). Moreover, the use of non-intrusive psychophysiological measures provides the opportunity to assess multiple aspects of an experience that cannot be accurately reported by the users at a precise moment in time. Many of those measures are related to the user experience field, such as emotional valence, arousal, and cognitive load (de Guinea et al. 2009). However, the main disadvantage when using physiological tools is that their use requires great execution precision and minimum external noise, which are complicated to overcome in the case of physical interactions with technology.

3 Illustrative Case

3.1 Experimental Procedure

The objective of this case study is to demonstrate the feasibility of the proposed methodology. The context of this illustrative case is an auto-installation of a new entertainment platform using novel types of technological equipment. In order to acquire valid data, it is important to replicate the setting of real-life usage. In a laboratory setting, the participant completed the tasks in a room arranged to resemble as close as possible the living room environment of the installation. The laboratory setting allowed for a mirror room for researchers to observe and follow the experiment closely.

We anticipated an average of two and a half hours for each participant, including tool installation. It is important to be mindful of the length of the experiment to minimize the exhaustion of the participant. Indeed, participants' fatigue caused by the context of an experiment can skew the data and lead to biased conclusions. Thus, it is crucial to pretest the protocol of the experiment to ensure the quality of the data recorded but also that the tools used, and the tasks' steps order run fluently and consistently from one participant to another. For running experiences in physical contexts, we suggest pretesting the protocol with at least three participants, as improvements from the first one to the last will make this more complex experiment easier to run when collecting the real data. Then, once the protocol has proved to run smoothly, each experiment should be closely observed by researchers. Detailed notetaking on any predetermined events of interest or on participants' actions should be recorded.

In the end, our final sample consisted of 24 participants (10 women, 14 men). All participants provided signed consent. Participants recruited from research panels each received money as compensation. This experiment was approved by the research committee of our institution.

3.2   Experimental Tasks

The study was divided into five sub-tasks to successfully complete the installation, as shown in the instruction booklet support given to participants. In general, determining sub-tasks allows for more control over the potential non-linearity factor of any physical interaction. Indeed, dividing the ideal path to success into smaller steps will help to maintain the same user journey language throughout participants, and also facilitates the elaboration of a user's path to completion. Finally, sub-tasks can also be used as event markers during or after the test, to dissect the overall task into several pieces. In our case, participants performed all five sub-tasks with the support of an instruction booklet:

- *Unboxing*: This task is the first step of the experiment and the first contact the customer has with the new product. Participants needed to take the equipment out of the delivery box.
- *Uninstalling*: This task is crucial to the process flow for a successful installation. Since the equipment already in place can be unique to each user, participants needed to follow the instructions carefully in order to take out the right cables and equipment.
- *Installation*: This task includes the installation of the two different pieces of equipment (Gateway and Terminal) needed to assess the experience fully.
- *Remote control configurations*: To finalize the installation, the participant has to activate the smart remote control equipped with a voice command. A pairing of the remote control and the TV is the last step to fully complete the installation.

The proper order of those tasks was as stated above in the instruction booklet. However, the participants were free to complete the auto-installation as they would at home. To keep the results as close as possible to reality, only a general verbal explanation of the test was given to participants (Fig. 1).

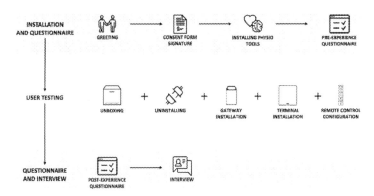

Fig. 1. The figure above provides an overview of the experimental procedure.

Before the experiment, all events of interest identified with the help of the experimental procedure were coded into the behavioral and analysis software used, in our case we opted for Observer XT (Noldus, Wageningen, Netherlands). An event can be defined as an action or situation of interest expected to happen or that has happened during the interaction measured. Those events are the results of variations in constructs such as emotional valence, arousal, and cognitive load. The value of analyzing events resides in the interpretation of concrete observations of the emotional and cognitive experience within a certain time frame in the overall interaction. For example, in a relatively linear website interaction, one can predict, prior to the test, that in order to complete a purchase (the final objective), the user will have to create an account first. Hence, the account creation step will be considered as an event and can be interpreted as a moment of interest in the evaluation of the emotional and cognitive user experience. The early identification of those events—i.e., defining tasks or subtasks—lightens the post-processing of the data and facilitates the understanding of the context. Hence, those events should be aligned with the objectives of the research. It is highly possible that some of the defined events will require modifications or adjustments post-experience, but at least this pre-experience preparation gives a general guideline as to what should be closely observed and noted. We use those events to average values of psychophysiological data in between each of them. During the experiment, the execution of those events can be done by pressing on the existing marker pre-coded when the participant reaches this event. However, when the interaction measured is exposed to non-linear steps in the journey, a manual codification of those events of interest can be done posterior to avoid errors.

3.3 Instruments and Apparatus

A total of five cameras were placed around the experiment room to record movements from different angles. Those cameras not only facilitate the observation of the participant's reactions at every step of the experience but also allow us to review all the actions that could be reported in synchronization with the other tools. Indeed, recordings grant a posteriori identification of the specific moments in time coupled with varying levels of arousal and cognitive load. Hence, the cameras ensure a safe recall option of all the micro-actions performed by the participants to complete the notes taken via an observation grid during the experiment. If needed, this gives researchers a more accurate view of the participant's actions even during the analysis phase.

While determining cameras' placement, it is crucial to choose adequately room locations where a sync markers' light would be visible to the researcher, to ensure the cameras are working properly throughout the experience. Indeed, the use of a sync light issued by all five cameras secures that all cameras start recording seamlessly and that they function in sync during the whole experiment. In fact, the cameras should be synchronized using a sync box to facilitate the analysis. We followed Léger et al. (2014) guidelines for synchronization. The automatic data stream will allow additional precision when placing markers in Noldus Observer XT (Wageningen, Netherlands) during the analysis phase.

Finally, the cameras were placed in strategic places to cover all the room's angles to the maximum extent (see Fig. 2):

- One camera on the ceiling over the unboxing table (initial place of the box)
- One camera on the ceiling, on the top of the coaxial wire (to see if fixated correctly)

- One camera on the wall to see the side of the television (to see the connection—the disconnection of wires)
- One camera below the TV furniture (to see from the TV the participants during the remote-control configuration)
- One camera on the wall in front of the TV (to see what was displayed).

Fig. 2. One view of the laboratory room where cameras' placement is highlighted.

Depending on the objects of interest to observe, the Go-Pro camera can simply be strapped around the participant's chest, since the EEG helmet prevents the support of any other devices on the participant's head. Indeed, the use of a Go-Pro camera (San Mateo, United States) is optional but allows for more precise visuals on participants' manipulations. The Go-Pro camera (San Mateo, United States) can act as a zoom on an event of interest that can be too subtle for long-range camera recording.

4   Research Variables

4.1   State Factors

This illustrative case focuses on three physiological state factors: emotional arousal, valence, and cognitive load. Users' emotions are considered an important factor in their experience since the emotional evaluation of that experience allows them to compare possibilities (Russell 2003) and substantiate future behavior (Hassenzahl 2013).

Valence. Emotional valence can be defined as "the value associated with a stimulus as expressed on a continuum from pleasant to unpleasant or from attractive to aversive" according to the APA Dictionary of Psychology (Online APA Dictionary of Psychology, 2020). Emotions are of interest since they are an omnipresent part of consumers' decision-making and behavior (Schiffman et al. 2010). Measuring the emotional experience of a user allows for the identification of unwanted negative emotional states.

Arousal. Arousal refers to the user's emotional state indicating physiological activity (Deng and Poole 2010; Russell 2003). A measure of a user's arousal will allow to nuance its affective state, since different level combinations of valence and arousal lead to diverse states, for example, a positive valence with high arousal (happy) will be different than a positive valence with low arousal (pleasant).

Cognitive Load. Cognitive load refers to the mental effort required to carry out certain tasks (Fredricks et al. 2004). In this experiment, participants are to achieve goals, such as the installation. Fredericks et al. (2004) showed that cognitive and metacognitive strategies are crucial to achieving the aforementioned goals. Namely, metacognitive strategies refer to the setting and planning of goals when performing a task. Hence, cognitive load can influence how the user will employ the best strategies to install new electronic devices.

4.2 Attitudinal Factors

Attitudinal factors can be examined in relation to variations in emotional experiences. For example, Maunier et al. (2018) explored the level effect of valence, arousal, and cognitive load on the impact of success rates during a task. Attitudinal factors can be used as discriminant elements that can explain variation in a user's emotional journey. This illustrative case focuses on two attitudinal factors that could be of interest in measuring the emotional and cognitive experience of a user: self-efficacy and task success.

Self-efficacy. Perceived self-efficacy is concerned with people's beliefs in their capabilities to produce given outcomes (Bandura 1997). Indeed, self-efficacy plays a key role in the likeliness of task accomplishment. Previous research suggests that individuals with a high level of self-efficacy think they possess the capacity to succeed in specific tasks (Walker et al. 2006). Consequently, individuals who believe they are self-efficient at completing a task will in fact generate the necessary efforts to succeed (Bandura 1993).

By using a measurement scale to assess self-efficacy, the performance results of the study can be separated into groups based on the high and low levels to examine significant differences between groups, if any. Given the usefulness of a theoretical construct, it is relevant to find previously established constructs and measurement scales, appropriate for the research objectives. Indeed, using additional self-reported behavioral measures will nuance the physiological data collected. Especially within studies involving a spatial context, attitudinal measures can help understanding and explaining the sequence of actions undertaken by the participant. Moreover, researchers suggest that combining complementary methods of assessment offers a deeper understanding of user experience, while adding implicit measurement, such as physiological tools, allows for a more rigorous measure of the participant's emotional journey (Bigras et al. 2018). Self-reporting measures of emotions, like the Self-Assessment Manikin (Bradley and Lang 1994), can also be administered to be able to see the personal differences across participants.

Success Variable. To evaluate the success of each user's path, which could be different from one another, we developed thresholds of success for each identified task. Installation task success was measured using sub-tasks success thresholds (such as the completion of the task, the appropriate installation of the wire connections, the firmness of the cable fastening, etc.). Thus, overall success was achieved when the participant completed the installation with few or no mistakes.

5   Measurement

5.1   Psychophysiological Measures

In order to accurately measure users' reactions and behaviors, it is crucial to choose measurement tools that are adequate for a moving subject. Aligned with the objectives of the experiment, psychophysiological measures were used to capture participants' emotional valence, arousal, and cognitive load (Riedl and Léger 2016).

A precise measure of arousal is needed to assess a quantitative activation level of emotion, from not aroused to excited. For this study, arousal was measured using the electrodermal activity with the Acqknowledge software (Biopac, Goleta, USA) as pictured in the figure below. Sensors (BIOPAC, Goleta, USA) were applied in the palm of the non-dominant hand of participants to measure skin conductance during the experience (Fig. 3).

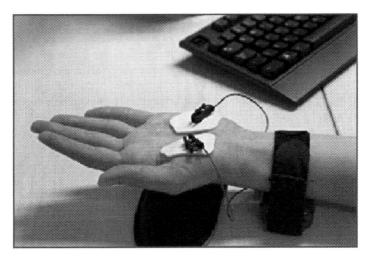

Fig. 3. A measure of electro-dermal activity using the Acqknowledge software (Biopac, Goleta, USA), with sensors in the palm of the hand.

Valence is typically measured through facial expressions (Ekman 1993), as micro-movement on the user's face can be detected using a video webcam. However, the constant movement of participants does not allow for precise facial detection, hence valence and cognitive load needed to be measured with tools that can easily move with the participant. As such, a wireless EEG cap (Brainvision, Morrisville, NC) was used, which allows to detect "inner" emotions and cognitive load. The mobile EEG cap contains 32 Ag-AgCl electrodes and an amplifier (Brainvision, Morrisville, NC), and was used to measure variations in brainwave activity in the θ (4–8 Hz), α (8–12 Hz) and β (12–30 Hz) bands, isolated by a bank of filters. Previous research has also used EEG signals to detect emotions (Maunier et al. 2018; Chanel et al. 2007; Brown et al. 2011) and to collect cognitive load data (Teplan 2002; Anderson et al. 2011; Park et al. 2014; Maunier et al. 2018).

5.2 Psychophysiological Pain Points

Among the different models of emotion classification, Russel (1979) proposed the use of a two-dimensional Arousal-Valence model, where pleasure-displeasure and level of arousal are sufficient to represent a wide range of emotional states (Russel 1979). As such, the implicit pain point identification method used in this article allows arousal, cognitive load, and valence data to be triangulated into specific points in time that we can identify as implicit psychophysiological pain points (PPPs) (see Fig. 4). An implicit psychophysiological pain point can be defined as a precise moment in time, when the user both feels a high level of emotional arousal and negative emotional valence, compared with his baseline state (Giroux-Huppé et al. 2019). However, PPPs are easier to diagnose in an online interaction context since recordings of the interaction are clearer to interpret via a 2D screen recording. In fact, identification of precise points in a user's journey using mouse movement is more straightforward than with physical actions performed by moving subjects.

Consequently, the objective of PPPs in this experiment would relate to portray users' emotional frictions throughout the tasks of the physical experience to avoid relying solely on emotional memory recall (Cockburn et al. 2017; Eich and Schooler 2000), as shown in Fig. 4. The main actionable insight of PPPs analysis is the possibility to rectify and optimize the experience to promote users' autonomy during any interaction. Frustrations along the user journey can serve as optimization's starting points in the physical interaction stage with a new technology, where the quality of the first experience can be a crucial determinant of future usage and adoption. Indeed, an unpleasant first experience can have negative consequences for the user's experience and perceptions of the brand (Brakus et al. 2009). Therefore, PPPs can be used as a preventive tool to ensure satisfaction and future usage.

5.3 Psychometric Measures

Perceived self-efficacy was measured via questionnaire before and after the experiment, to evaluate any discrepancies that can be linked to the effects of the tasks performed. A 6-item measure was used to assess the perceived self-efficacy construct (Sherer et al. 1982).

6 Analysis

Once the data collection is completed, the extraction of the data is necessary to proceed to the analysis phase. Depending on the software used to collect the data, this step will be

Measuring the physiological experience - Individual journeys and pain points

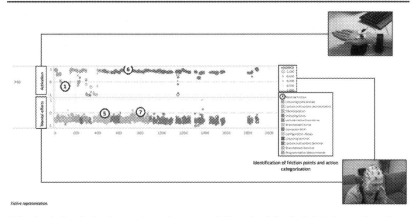

Fig. 4. A detailed schema shows how to mobilize physiological data into pain points.

different; see the software provider's specific instructions to ensure optimal extraction. Once all the recordings and the psychophysiological data are exported into separate files under the participants' number (e.g., P01), the first step consists of viewing the video recordings in a behavioral coding and analysis software (e.g., Noldus Observer XT) in order to place the proper markers, which correspond to the event of interests previously established. To avoid multiple rounds of review, it is essential to examine the notes taken during each experiment to see if any new events should be added to the existing list entered before the beginning of the experiment. If this is the case, new event markers should be added to Noldus Observer before the viewing process.

Then, once all the markers are in place in each participant's recording file, it is easier to code each of them with the different views offered by the five angles of the cameras. The markers always need to have a "start" and an "end," in order for the analysis to be performed accurately. Precision is key in this process since coding errors in the timeline could lead to false results and interpretation. It is also crucial that every marker is properly coded into each participant's file (if the case may be) before extracting the data for further analysis. Indeed, all events of interest, including the tasks, coded into the software will allow for an interpretation of the physiological data in time. The next step in the analysis process is to transform the physiological data to allow their use in the interpretation of the participants' emotional and cognitive experiences.

6.1 EEG-Based Valence and Cognitive Load

In order to extract the valence and cognitive load of the raw data files, cleaning of the files is needed. We used the NeuroRT software (Mensia, Rennes) to analyze the EEG data. The acquisition rate was 500 Hz. The following steps were performed: Decrease the acquisition rate up to 256 Hz, filters 1–50 Hz, cleaning the ocular artifacts with the help of source separation, re-referencing to the mean reference, and artifact detection by calculating the Riemannian distance between the covariance matrix and the real-time mean. Then, we apply a MATLAB transformation to clean the data using ASR. It is important to verify after the cleaning that no critical channel was lost. After a cleanse of the raw files, we export the clean data into NeuroRT Studio to pass it into a pre-existing general EEG pipeline. Cognitive load was calculated as a ratio using (power) $\beta/(\alpha + \theta)$ from F3, F4, O1, O2 on the international 10–20 system, following procedure from Pope (1995). Valence, collected by EEG technology, will be detected as follows: "Valence: positive, happy emotions result in a higher frontal coherence in alpha, and higher right parietal beta power, compared to negative emotion" (Bos 2006). Once the process stops, a ".csv" file should be ready to import into the next step, a triangulation software.

6.2   Identifying Pain Points

Once each physiological data file is properly transformed and the recordings are properly set with the relevant markers to speed up the visualization and interpretation steps, we have to prepare the necessary data files to allow for a triangulation of the separated data files into a valuable and understandable output. We previously developed a methodology to be able to easily find the implicit frustrations in a user journey (Giroux-Huppé et al. 2019). We will use the same method here to be able to identify more accurately the difficulties faced by users in physical interaction.

To facilitate PPPs triangulation and identification, CubeHX software was used (Courtemanche et al. 2019; Patent US10,368,741 B2 2019), which is cloud-based lab management and analytics software for triangulated human-centered research (Léger et al. 2019). This software used to triangulate all the data accumulated during the experiment generates outputs of UX attentional, emotional, and cognitive heat maps, and can also export to statistical packages from one or multiple projects (e.g., cross-project analyses, compatibility with third-party visualization software, i.e. Tableau software) (Léger et al. 2019).

Concretely, calculations of pain points are performed using a specific threshold, built on previous research, with the statistical software SAS 9.4. In this context, to be qualified as a pain point, the data point needed to be both in the ninetieth percentiles of EDA (i.e., high arousal) and in the tenth percentile of valence (i.e., large negative valence) (Giroux-Huppé et al. 2019). Once a list of all the PPPs experienced throughout the experiment's relevant time frame is generated, the researcher has to manually identify and interpret the users' actions during the window of time when the pain point occurs. To ensure a precise interpretation, unique micro-moments pain points can be regrouped into pain points moments if they are consecutive seconds apart. Using the same software for video recordings' viewing (Noldus Observer XT), one must put himself in the shoes of the participant by reviewing, using the different angles of the multiple cameras, the moments when each of friction points are experienced (± 10 s before and after the precise time listed to gain context). Having the same researcher interpreting all the pain points moments will limit labeling errors. To compensate for the researcher's potential bias, another researcher can then perform the same exercise separately and a combination of the two labeling lists can allow for more reliable classification. Whenever there is a discrepancy of interpretation, a third researcher should do the same exercise, as to serve as a decisive interpretation. Once the micro-moment regrouped into pain points moments and interpreted, they can be classified and arranged into similar categories across participants, as to improve the actionable insights from a high-level overview instead of per individual participant. Precise interpretation is central to benefit from decoding the root of the frustrations, and the regrouped categories of pain points are an easy and understandable way to present the problems to the rest of the research team and to high-level management.

7   Results from the Illustrative Case

7.1   Visualization of Users' Emotional Journey

Once all the psychophysiological data is treated, we may be able to build user experience journey maps and identify the different pain points in a more visual way. In addition to the interpretation of each moment of frustration, another mobilization of users' intense frustration is the visualization of PPPs across the tasks in the form of journey maps (see Fig. 5). Timeline visualization of PPPs allows the researchers to gain a deeper understanding of the participants' emotional journey. Using Tableau software (California, USA), individuals' journey maps coded with the sub-tasks simplify the recognition of the most problematic tasks or subtasks but also the most critical implicit pain points in time (see figure below).

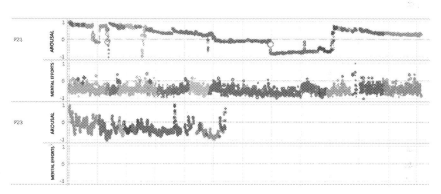

Fig. 5. Visualization of the psychophysiological user journey by task with clear pain points moments identification (red dots). (Color figure online)

As Fig. 6 below shows, the colored circles on the following cards illustrate all the different psychophysiological points in time through tasks undertaken by participants. Second, the user's moments of frustration are illustrated by the red colored points. The size of the circles represents, from the smallest, a lower intensity PPP to the largest, most intense PPP. Finally, the scale on the y-axis represents the user's activation and cognitive effort from the lowest to the highest. The x-axis represents the timeline of each task performed per participant. The most intense or most frequent moments of frustration can then be visually prompted by a legend similar to Fig. 6. This way, one quick look at the journey map can reveal the unique emotional journey of each participant, as well as how the moments of frustration unfold through the task completion.

This visualization of an emotional journey has multiple advantages granted by its comparison elements. First, it is easy to compare users' journeys with each other for the

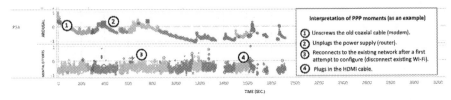

Fig. 6. Visualization of an individual psychophysiological user journey by task with pain points interpretation. (Color figure online)

same task (see Fig. 7), thus being able to tell a real story for each identified user. Common difficulties can be identified and classified with users' same frustrations, therefore emphasizing the need for a change in the experience process. Second, users' journeys can be compared with competitors,' in order to benchmark the emotional experience across different approaches or paths of a similar product or service. Within the same test, participants can be asked to perform a similar task with two different products or websites, then the intra-subject data can be used to assess opportunities originated by the comparison of a competitor's experience. Third, the users' journeys can also grant an overview of the sub-tasks' effects on a user's emotions. Certain sub-tasks can create more accumulation of frustrations than others, hinting at the source of problematic instances instead of re-evaluating the whole journey process. Finally, the visualization of the users' physical journeys can serve as a common tool to evaluate user experience across all touchpoints. Ultimately, the emotional and behavioral journey of users can be compared equally across each channel, no matter their nature.

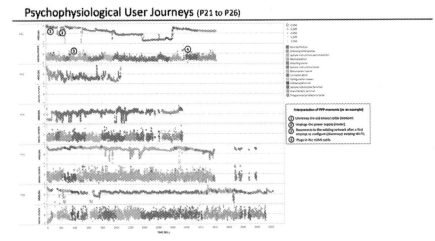

Fig. 7. An example of the complete visualization of the psychophysiological user journey for different participants.

7.2   Complementarity of Quantitative and Qualitative Data

The use of physiological data and retrospective measures allow a more complete under-standing of the users' experience with the technology. Self-reported measures are an interesting addition to physiological measures because they allow us to see if there are any differences between groups of different attributes. For this study, self-efficacy was used in the elaboration of two different groups, low and high self-efficacy, to test for any significant differences in overall success rates between the two groups. As portrayed in Table 1, no statistically significant difference was found between the high and low self-efficacy groups. However, results lean towards an overall higher success rate for the low self-efficacy group.

Table 1. The difference in success rates between high and low self-efficacy groups.

Groups	Average success rate (%)	Wilcoxon sum rank test two-tail p-value
Low self-efficacy	69%	0.675 (NS)
High self-efficacy	55%	

Furthermore, as self-efficacy was measured before and after the experiment, it can be useful to uncover any significant differences. As shown in Table 2, participants signif-icantly felt more confident about their own capacities after they accomplished the task. Such findings could imply that the task has some empowerment implications and could encourage users to do it again.

Table 2. The difference in average self-efficacy before and after the task

Individuals	Average score (scale 1 to 7)	Wilcoxon sum rank test two-tail p-value
Self-efficacy pre-experience	4.5	0.0011*
Self-efficacy post-experience	5	

* $p < .05$

Moreover, the success variable was used as an overall presentation of the journey flow undertaken by all the participants. This variable can support the identification of problems in the subtasks by comparing success rates across the journey. This refining of the overall task is useful for constructing a step-by-step success map. Compared with the emotional journey, similarities between the two journeys are raised to strengthen the insights uncovered.

All in all, each additional retrospective measure included in the study must have relevant insight potential, even if the hypothesis is not sustained after the analysis. The combination of psychophysiological, behavioral, and psychometric measures provides, beyond insights about task successes, a complete picture of emotional and cognitive influences and impacts on the user experience.

8   Discussion and Conclusion

The simultaneous use of physical technology (e.g., mobile phones) and online resources (e.g., websites) in various day-to-day activities call for a closer exploration of each user interaction with a brand. As user experience is a consolidation of all consumers' touchpoints throughout its journey, tangible interactions with technology are to be of interest. As the omnichannel approach suggests, a unified experience has to be maintained across all touchpoints (Verhoef et al. 2015). Despite the need for consistency across channels, there was still no established methodology, to our knowledge, to measure and compare user experience across both on—and offline interactions. Indeed, frequent switches between offline and online touchpoints result in higher complexity of user journeys. The combination of interactions can almost be unique to each consumer, with various exit points in their journey as they want to compare other options, retrieve more information, and then as they circle back to previous choices (Carroll and Guzmán 2013).

This article presented a methodology better suited to measure users' experience in the omnichannel environment. Through psychophysiological variables and self-reported metrics, this article serves as a comprehensive methodological approach for experts to have a precise overview of the emotional journey of consumers. Overall, we succeeded in demonstrating the interest of this methodological approach through an illustrative case study. This methodology can help businesses evaluate with precision in-store experiences as well as face-to-face interactions. Consequently, our case study demonstrated that the measure of user experience has to include a fair assessment of emotional and behavioral influences, impacts, or consequences across all touchpoints, regardless of the online-offline element. Despite the cost of resources to run an experiment with moving subjects, the methodology presented shows the potential for faster and more accurate identification of dissatisfaction and intense frustrations, which is a tremendous competitive advantage for companies.

Although the usefulness of the proposed methodology is clear, it is still the first exploration into the preservation of ecological validation in a physical interaction study. A few recommendations are stated for replication intention or future research. First, we recommend pretesting the whole experiment until the protocol runs seamlessly and the quality of physiological data recorded is high. By doing so, we make sure the synchronization of the data is adequate, and the noise is reduced to the minimum. Since the methodology proposed requires the mobilization of EEG data, we suggest having individuals with cognitive science expertise or previous experience with EEG technology within the team. This will facilitate the execution of the tests but also ensure the quality of the data during the data collection and analysis. Also, it is important to consider that although it is a systematic approach, there is still a human factor embedded in the analysis process, in order to identify and interpret psychophysiological data. Hence, it is critical to be mindful of potential interpretation biases. We suggest relying on consistency throughout the analysis by ensuring that the same researcher performs all analysis interpretation first (event coding, pain points analysis), and then repeating the process with another researcher to compare interpretation results. In addition, it is recommended to keep the analysis period short in order to avoid bias or memory loss that can happen when there are long periods of inactivity.

As businesses tend to be competitive on all channels, modern consumer behavior urges companies to approach commerce in an omnichannel way. The user experience does not end when the purchase is completed on the website and is rather an ongoing process of interactions with the physical product or service, before and after. It is usually difficult to measure the interaction with ecological validity in a non-linear physical experience because of the noise created by the subject's movements. This article proposed a complex yet simple methodology that allows for researchers to grasp the users' experience using a combination of psychophysiological metrics and qualitative data, despite barriers such as movements, bias, and noise. The proposed methodology allows companies to optimize and cultivate a relationship with the user throughout the channels, identify opportunities within the interactions, and correct service failures even outside the Internet world. As usability testing prevents missteps that could be fatal to the user-business relationship, it is of equal importance to consider the physical interactions with the technology, pre-and post-purchase. Indeed, all interactions, no matter their nature, can have an impact on users' future usage and satisfaction. This new approach consolidates user-centric data, as well as a multi-method evaluation of user experience to be applied in each step of a consumer journey, from their search of information to their unboxing at home. Not to mention that conducting valuable user testing, even in physical contexts, can assure a constant experience quality in an increasingly omnichannel world, without compromising the ecological validity of the experiments.

References

Anderson, E.W., Potter, K.C., Matzen, L.E., Shepherd, J.F., Preston, G.A., Silva, C.T.: A user study of visualization effectiveness using EEG and cognitive load. Paper presented at the Computer Graphics Forum (2011)

Bagozzi, R.P., Gopinath, M., Nyer, P.U.: The role of emotions in marketing. J. Acad. Mark. Sci. 27(2), 184–206 (1999)

Bandura, A.: Perceived self-efficacy in cognitive development and functioning. Educ. Psychol. 28(2), 117–148 (1993)

Bandura, A.: Self-Efficacy: The Exercise of Control. Worth Publishers, New York (1997)

Bigras, E., et al.: In AI we trust: characteristics influencing assortment planners' perceptions of AI based recommendation agents. In: Nah, F.F.-H., Xiao, B.S. (eds.) HCIBGO 2018. LNCS, vol. 10923, pp. 3–16. Springer, Cham (2018). https://doi.org/10.1007/978-3-319-91716-0_1

Bos, D.O.: EEG-based emotion recognition. The Influence of Visual and Auditory Stimuli 56(3), 1–17 (2006)

Bradley, M.M., Lang, P.J.: Measuring emotion: the self-assessment manikin and the semantic differential. J. Behav. Ther. Exp. Psychiatry 25(1), 49–59 (1994)

Brakus, J.J., Schmitt, B.H., Zarantonello, L.: Brand experience: what is it? How is it measured? Does it affect loyalty? J. Mark. 73(3), 52–68 (2009)

Brown, L., Grundlehner, B., Penders, J.: Towards wireless emotional valence detection from EEG. Paper presented at the 2011 Annual International Conference of the IEEE Engineering in Medicine and Biology Society (2011)

Carroll, D., Guzmán, I.: The new omni-channel approach to serving customers. Accenture.com (2013)

Chanel, G., Ansari-Asl, K., Pun, T.: Valence-arousal evaluation using physiological signals in an emotion recall paradigm. Paper presented at the 2007 IEEE International Conference on Systems, Man and Cybernetics (2007)

Cockburn, A., Quinn, P., Gutwin, C.: The effects of interaction sequencing on user experience and preference. Int. J. Hum.-Comput. Stud. **108**, 89–104 (2017)

Courtemanche, F., et al.: U. S. patent (2019)

De Guinea, A.O., Markus, M.L.: Why break the habit of a lifetime? Rethinking the roles of intention, habit, and emotion in continuing information technology use. MIS Q. **33**(3), 433–444 (2009)

Deng, L., Poole, M.S.: Affect in web interfaces: a study of the impacts of web page visual complexity and order. MIS Q. **34**(4), 711–730 (2010)

Dufresne, A., Courtemanche, F., Tep, S.P., Senecal, S.: Physiological measures, eye tracking and task analysis to track user reactions in user generated content. Paper presented at the 7th International Conference on Methods and Techniques in Behavioural Research (Measuring Behaviour, 2010) (2010)

Eich, E., Schooler, J.: Cognition/emotion interactions. In: Eich, E., Kihlstrom, J.F., Bower, G.H., Forgas, J.P., Niedenthal, P.M. (eds.) Cognition and Emotion, pp. 3–29. Oxford University Press, New York (2000)

Ekman, P.: Facial expression and emotion. Am. Psychol. **48**(4), 384 (1993)

Fredricks, J.A., Blumenfeld, P.C., Paris, A.H.: School engagement: potential of the concept, state of the evidence. Rev. Educ. Res. **74**(1), 59–109 (2004)

Frow, P., Payne, A.: Towards the "perfect" customer experience. J. Brand Manag. **15**(2), 89–101 (2007). https://doi.org/10.1057/palgrave.bm.2550120

Giroux-Huppé, C., Sénécal, S., Fredette, M., Chen, S.L., Demolin, B., Léger, P.-M.: Identifying psychophysiological pain points in the online user journey: the case of online grocery. In: Marcus, A., Wang, W. (eds.) HCII 2019. LNCS, vol. 11586, pp. 459–473. Springer, Cham (2019). https://doi.org/10.1007/978-3-030-23535-2_34

Hassenzahl, M.: User experience and experience design. In: The Encyclopedia of Human-Computer Interaction, 2nd edn. (2013)

Léger, P.-M., Courtemanche, F., Fredette, M., Sénécal, S.: A cloud-based lab management and analytics software for triangulated human-centered research. In: Davis, F.D., Riedl, R., vom Brocke, J., Léger, P.-M., Randolph, A.B. (eds.) Information Systems and Neuroscience. LNISO, vol. 29, pp. 93–99. Springer, Cham (2019). https://doi.org/10.1007/978-3-030-01087-4_11

Léger, P.-M., Sénecal, S., Courtemanche, F., Ortiz de Guinea, A., Titah, R., Fredette, M., Labonte-LeMoyne, É.: Precision is in the eye of the beholder: application of eye fixation-related potentials to information systems research. J. Assoc. Inf. Syst. **15**(10), 3 (2014)

Maunier, B., et al.: Keep calm and read the instructions: factors for successful user equipment setup. In: Nah, F.F.-H., Xiao, B.S. (eds.) HCIBGO 2018. LNCS, vol. 10923, pp. 372–381. Springer, Cham (2018). https://doi.org/10.1007/978-3-319-91716-0_29

Nielsen, J.: Usability 101: introduction to usability (2012). https://www.nngroup.com/articles/usability-101-introduction-to-usability/

Park, W., Kwon, G.H., Kim, D.-H., Kim, Y.-H., Kim, S.-P., Kim, L.: Assessment of cognitive engagement in stroke patients from single-trial EEG during motor rehabilitation. IEEE Trans. Neural Syst. Rehabil. Eng. **23**(3), 351–362 (2014)

Pope, A.T., Bogart, E.H., Bartolome, D.S.: Biocybernetic system evaluates indices of operator engagement in automated task. Biol. Psychol. **40**(1–2), 187–195 (1995)

Rawson, A., Duncan, E., Jones, C.: The truth about customer experience. Harv. Bus. Rev. **91**(9), 90–98 (2013)

Riedl, R., Léger, P.-M.: Fundamentals of NeuroIS: Studies in Neuroscience. Psychology and Behavioral Economics. Springer, Heidelberg (2016). https://doi.org/10.1007/978-3-662-450 91-8

Russell, J.A.: Affective space is bipolar. J. Pers. Soc. Psychol. **37**(3), 345 (1979)

Russell, J.A.: Core affect and the psychological construction of emotion. Psychol. Rev. **110**(1), 145 (2003)

Schiffman, L.G., Kanuk, L.L., Wisenblit, J.: Consumer Behavior. Pearson Prentice Hall, London (2010)

Sherer, M., Maddux, J.E., Mercandante, B., Prentice-Dunn, S., Jacobs, B., Rogers, R.W.: The self-efficacy scale: construction and validation. Psychol. Rep. **51**(2), 663–671 (1982)

ISO 9241-11:2018(en): ergonomics of human-system interaction—part 11: usability: definitions and concepts. Switzerland, Geneva (2018)

Teplan, M.: Fundamentals of EEG measurement. Measur. Sci. Rev. **2**(2), 1–11 (2002)

Tynan, C., McKechnie, S.: Experience marketing: a review and reassessment. J. Mark. Manag. **25**(5–6), 501–517 (2009)

Verhoef, P.C., Kannan, P.K., Inman, J.J.: From multi-channel retailing to omni-channel retailing: introduction to the special issue on multi-channel retailing. J. Retail. **91**(2), 174–181 (2015)

Verma, R., et al.: Customer experience modeling: from customer experience to service design. J. Serv. Manag. **23**(3), 362–376 (2012)

Walker, C.O., Greene, B.A., Mansell, R.A.: Identification with academics, intrinsic/extrinsic motivation, and self-efficacy as predictors of cognitive engagement. Learn. Individ. Differ. **16**(1), 1–12 (2006)

The Effect of Experience on Learnability and Usability of a Neuroimaging Platform

Thomas Ruel[1]([✉]), Pierre-Majorique Léger[2], Gregory Lodygensky[3], David Luck[3], Yang Ding[3], Bertrand Demolin[2], and Sylvain Sénécal[2]

[1] Polytechnique Montréal, Montréal, Canada
thomas.ruel@polymtl.ca
[2] HEC Montréal, Montréal, Canada
{pierre-majorique.leger,bertrand.demolin,sylvain.senecal}@hec.ca
[3] CHU Sainte-Justine, Montréal, Canada
glodygen@gmail.com, david.luck.prof@gmail.com, it@cnbp.ca

1 Introduction

As the diagnostic power of medical imaging technologies continues to develop, its utilization in healthcare research has proliferated (Sandoval et al. 2018). Consummate with such proliferation has been the aggregation of a large amount of high-quality research medical imaging data across research centres. Henceforth, there is a rising need for an accessible, intuitive, and approachable web interface to organize, visualize, and share the large repertoire of medical imaging data effectively and easily (Sandoval et al. 2018). Since these platforms are complex and aimed at a trained medical or research scientific personnel, efforts to ensure usability are often not the main concern.

However, acceptance or turndown of new medical systems depend largely on their degree of usability (Kushniruk et al. 1997). Medical application developers must cope with the added challenge of designing systems that provide complex functionalities while remaining easy to learn and use. Additionally, since many adverse events in medicine are the result of poor interface design rather than human error, unresolved usability issues can represent serious safety concerns (Fairbanks et al. 2004), thus making usability testing a crucial part of development for such applications. Rigorous usability testing has been proved to be effective at reducing common and consequential health care systems errors, like the generation of duplicate medical records (Khunlertkit et al. 2017).

With the rapidly changing interface types in medical applications, there is a need for methodology, tools and techniques in practice to integrate Human Factors and Usability (HF/U) elements in design (Nagarajan et al. 2019). The tests are centered around cognitive tasks analysis, which consist of characterizing the decision-making skills of subjects, as they are asked to perform activities requiring the processing of complex information (Kushniruk et al. 1997). Data collection often includes self reporting methods, like questionnaires or interviews. Also, since self-reports tend to rely heavily on the subjects' memory to identify issues, studies also suggest the use of video analysis to identify more performance deficiencies and their contributory factors (Mackenzie et al. 1996).

One of the main hurdles of conducting usability tests with medical applications is to recruit valid participants. Recruiting test subjects is challenging in all fields, but getting access to the medical experts and to convince them to participate in a usability test has often shown to be particularly tricky. Thus, we frequently need to rely on participants with less expertise and experience to validate the usability of applications. In this paper, we are investigating the past medical experience of participants in medical usability testing. If there would be no or little differences between novices and experts, this would help facilitate user testing in medical domains with subjects that are more easily accessible.

To answer this research question, we have conducted a study to investigate the effect of medical experience on various usability metrics during a usability test on a new neuroimaging application. As a case study, we also try to uncover major usability issues of said application. The interface studied is a deployed instance of Longitudinal Online Research and Imaging System (LORIS) v19 (Das et al. 2012) for the Canadian Neonatal Brain Platform (CNBP). The Loris system has extensively developed over the past decades and has become a prominent choice among the neuroimaging specialists community for organizing and managing data across the world. For CNBP to be truly successful, aspects of the LORIS system require continuous user validation and feedback during its customization and improvement over the upcoming decades.

2 Materials and Methods

2.1 Experimental Design and Participants

We conducted a correlational study where all participants were asked to accomplish the same tasks in LORIS. The tasks were based on procedures a medical researcher would need to perform in the software. The study was approved by the Research Ethics Board of HEC Montréal before data collection. Upon completion of the experiment, participants were given a 50 CAN$ compensation.

2.2 Sample

The participant sample consisted of 16 professionals in the field of medical imaging at the CHU Sainte-Justine, a large children's hospital in Canada. Participants had no prior experience with the LORIS interface, but had varying expertise accomplishing similar tasks using other online software interfaces. Participants occupation mostly included imaging technicians and developers. The sample was composed of 9 women and 7 men, and the average age was 26.

2.3 Experimental Tasks and Stimuli

Participants were asked to complete six different tasks of varying difficulty and specificity. All the tasks were on a deployed instance of LORIS v19 for the CNBP. The tasks were designed to cover the principal functions of the interface as well as some crucial key functions. The tasks were:

1. View a specific MRI scan
2. Report a patient's information as incomplete
3. Report a patient's scan as a failure
4. Trigger an image analysis routine on a specific scan
5. Download a patient's scan
6. Download a patient's information

For illustration purposes, Fig. 1 shows the correct paths for task 3 (report a patient's scan as a failure). All tasks start at the homepage (top center). For task 3, the participants need to access a patient's imaging data through the candidate tab (left path) or the imaging path (right path). They then need to find the scan and report it as a failure by opening the drop-down bar in the "QC status" section and selecting fail. For the task to be complete, the participant then needs to save their changes.

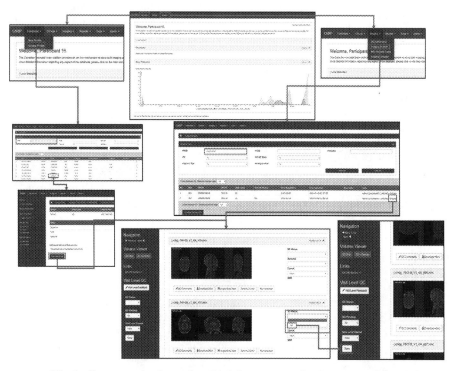

Fig. 1. Correct navigation paths of task 3; report a patient's scan as a failure

2.4 Experimental Setup

Participants were isolated in a small room with a computer, mouse and keyboard. The moderator was installed in another room, also with a computer, and had control over the subject's computer with Teamviewer (Göppingen, Germany). Communication between the moderator and the subject was assured with microphones and speakers. More detailed instructions on the tasks were available to the participants on a tablet.

2.5 Operationalization of the Research Variables

Performance. Subject's performance was assessed by their ability to finish the task (failure, partial success or success) and by measuring the time necessary to accomplish the task. If unable to complete the task by 7 min, the participants were stopped, and the task was considered a failure. The timer was stopped when the participants announced they were done with the task, not necessarily when the task was successfully completed.

Experience. Since the participants' experience potentially varied heavily depending on the nature of the task, experience was measured for each task. Experience was assessed through a questionnaire with two measures: Years of experience (no experience, 0–1 year, 1–2 years, 2–3 years, 3–4, 5+ years) and frequency (never, everyday, a few times a week, a few times a month, a few times a year). The participants were asked to refer to the times they do the same task with another interface or software. Since the questionnaires consisted of multiple-choice questions, experience distribution was discrete.

Usability and Learnability. A self perceived measure of usability was obtained with a System Usability Scale (SUS) (Brooke 1996). This scale has been validated as a reliable tool to ordinally compare two or more systems (Peres et al. 2013). It consists of a 10-item questionnaire with five response options for respondents; from Strongly agree to Strongly disagree. It then attributes a score relating usability. In this study, this score was interpreted as relative usability (between tasks and between participants), rather than absolute usability. A more qualitative measure of usability was obtained with questions on the platform in general, like their likelihood of using this software if available. Other open-ended questions, like their ideas for improving the software or general comments, were used to confirm conclusions drawn from other measures.

Since this interface is aimed at professionals who will most likely use it for an extended duration, learnability is an essential part of the usability of the system. The definition of learnability used in this study differentiates initial learnability from extended learnability. The former refers to "allowing users to reach a reasonable level of usage proficiency within a short amount of time", while the later refers to the "ease at which new users can begin effective interaction and achieve maximal performance" (Grossman et al. 2009). Since the study only consists of 6 tasks and that the participants will not be exposed to the interface for an extended duration, only the initial learnability of the system will be evaluated. Additionally, since the order of the tasks was randomized, some data processing is needed in order to obtain the evolution of performance through the experiment.

2.6 Experimental Protocol

The experiment started with the participant filling out a consent form. Then, a short video tutorial of 2 min was presented, in which the very main navigational components of the interface were introduced. No measures were taken during viewing. The participants then proceeded to accomplish their first task. The task number depended on a randomized order. Immediately after the task, participants were asked to fill out a questionnaire (SUS and expertise assessment). In this fashion, the participants completed the 5 other tasks, followed by the same questionnaire. The final questionnaire also included open-ended questions on the platform in general.

2.7 Data Processing

To measure correlation between experience and other variables of interest, participants have been divided into groups for each task; low experience, medium experience and high experience. The cut off points for each experience group were chosen to maximize between-group variance. Correlation with success, time and SUS score were calculated with a wilcoxon rank sum test.

To uncover usability issues, SUS score, time and success rate were calculated by task. Higher time and lower success rate do not necessarily equate to usability issues and could just mean the task was harder. Thus, conclusions were made considering both performance and SUS score. Screen recordings were also analysed to determine participants' navigation paths for every task. Divergences from correct paths were noted. Reproductible divergence locations could be the result of usability issues.

Initial learnability was assessed by calculating performance by order of task. Correlation between experience and learnability was also explored by splitting the participants into groups, for every order of task; no experience and at least some experience. The learning curves of each group were plotted, and a wilcoxon rank sum test was performed for each order of task.

3 Results

Following our wilcoxon rank sum test, we found no statistical correlation between experience and performance for any of the tasks. Table 1 shows the p-values of each hypothesis of correlation between experience and the three measures (SUS, time and success), for every task. We can see the only hypothesis we can accept with a degree of confidence of 95% is the correlation of SUS and experience for task 1 (p-value = 0,0507). We can conclude that the participants who have more than 1 year of experience seem to give a higher SUS score, for task 1; View a specific MRI scan.

To obtain learning curves, the results were then arranged by the order the task was made in the experiment. Participants were classified into two groups; No experience and at least some experience. Figure 2 shows how the performances of the two groups evolve in the experiment. With no surprises, performances do get better for the two groups as the experiment progresses. Between the first and last task, mean success rates have improved by 48% for the low experience group (from 0,60 to 0,89) and by 71% for the high experience group (from 0,5 to 0,86). Time has decreased by 58,2% for the low experience group (from 275 s to 115 s) and by 57,1% for the high experience group (from 216 s to 94 s).

Table 1. Results of wilcoxon rank sum test for experience by task

Task	Variable	Statistic	Z	p-value
1	Success	46	−1,1619	0,375
	Time	61	1,0304	0,3132
	SUS	33	−1,908	0,0507
2	Success	61	0,1316	1
	Time	61,5	0,1594	0,8574
	SUS	51	−0,8493	0,3898
3	Success	46	0,4225	1
	Time	50	0,7942	0,4224
	SUS	51	0,9076	0,3617
4	Success	49,5	−1,3382	0,2615
	Time	52	−0,7415	0,4521
	SUS	69	0,9534	0,3366
5	Success	57	1,0394	0,5
	Time	49	−0,1628	0,8538
	SUS	43,5	−0,7615	0,4436
6	Success	50	−0,0674	1
	Time	53	0,1633	0,8493
	SUS	52,5	0,1088	0,9071

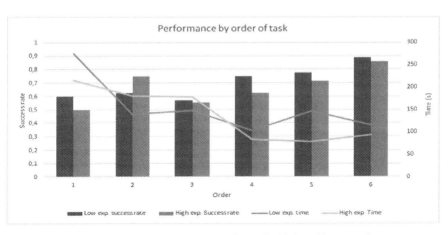

Fig. 2. Evolution of performance in the experiment for high and low experience groups

The same Wilcoxon rank sum test was made on these results. The tests yielded no statistical difference between the groups for SUS, time or success. Table 2 shows the p-values associated with each hypothesis.

Table 2. Results of wilcoxon rank sum test for experience by order

Order	Variable	Statistic	Z	p-value
1	Success	56	0,5669	0,6329
	Time	49	−0,1639	0,8521
	SUS	54,5	0,3261	0,7315
2	Success	64	−0,5427	1
	Time	66	−0,1575	0,8785
	SUS	69,5	0,106	0,8981
3	Success	68	0,9836	0,3575
	Time	60	0	0,9799
	SUS	50,5	−0,9011	0,3637
4	Success	56	−1,5014	0,2821
	Time	72	0,3676	0,7209
	SUS	58,5	−0,9494	0,3374
5	Success	57,5	−0,2113	1
	Time	47	−1,2711	0,2003
	SUS	70,5	1,1155	0,2615
6	Success	58,5	−0,0922	1
	Time	63	0,3185	0,7571
	SUS	68,5	0,9031	0,3648

The SUS results by task were plotted to reveal tasks with usability issues (see Fig. 3). Presence of these issues were then confirmed with the analysis of navigation paths, and their contributory factors were identified. From their lower scores, we can see task 2 and 3 seem to present lower usability than the other tasks (70 and 71,7). These tasks were "Report a patient's information as incomplete" and "Report a patient's scan as a failure". They both asked the participant to deal with the quality control (QC) interface of the platform. The difference was that task 2 was for the patient, and that task 3 was for a specific scan. According to overall comments collected in the final questionnaire, most participants were confused when dealing with QC tasks, mainly because differences between patient-specific and scan-specific QC review weren't clear enough.

Navigation paths for task 2 and 3 go in line with the lower SUS scores and the comments collected from the questionnaire. For task 2, of the 11 participants that managed to complete the task by leaving a patient-specific QC comment, 6 of them first tried to

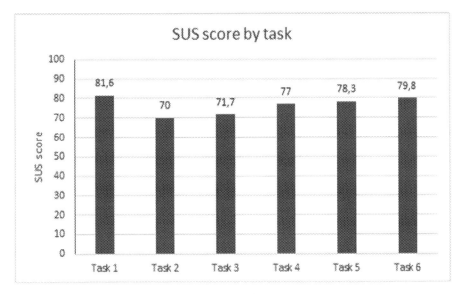

Fig. 3. SUS score for all tasks

leave a scan-specific QC comment instead. For task 3, of the 14 participants that managed to mark a specific scan as a failure, 3 of them first tried to leave a patient-specific QC comment and 4 of them first tried to leave a scan-specific QC comment. Another big usability issue of task 3 is revealed by the fact that most of the participants did not complete the task fully. Of the 14 people that marked the scan as a failure, only 5 of them saved their modification and completed the task. However, since participants were not told whether they completed the task successfully or not, this issue did not affect their perceived performance or the perceived usability of the platform.

The analysis of the navigation paths for tasks 1, 4, 5 and 6 did not present the same reproducibility in the locations of divergence from correct paths. The causes behind divergences seemed rather random, and these observations are supported by the higher SUS scores and by the absence of comments pointing out specific usability issues for these tasks.

4 Discussion

Our statistical analysis yielded no correlation between experience and the usability metrics in our study. Novices and experts do not differ in terms of performance or usability appreciation. These findings could mean that high levels of medical experience are not a necessary selection criterion for participants in order to obtain a valid assessment of the usability of a medical platform. This would make recruitment much easier, since novices are usually easier to recruit because of their higher numbers and availability.

This research has been conducted with a single application using a post hoc categorization of experts and novices. We recommend that future studies use a more differentiated separation of the participants in their experimental design and ensure a wider range of expertise. Studies across different softwares and participant samples are required in order to generalize the use of novices as proxies for experts in the medical field. If those results are replicated, this would reduce the effort needed to test medical applications, and usability testing could occur more often and sooner in the development process. Future research should consider measuring the visual attention of medical professionals to establish more precisely, via eye tracking, the role of expertise in using medical platforms (e.g. Boutin et al. 2019). Using a rich user experience methodology (Alvarez et al. 2019), a more precise understanding of experts' cognitive (e.g. Léger et al. 2014a, b) and emotional state (e.g. Léger et al. 2014a, b) would allow UX professionals to better assess what makes some applications easier to use and learn.

References

Alvarez, J., Brieugne, D., Léger, P.-M., Sénécal, S., Frédette, M.: Towards agility and speed in enriched UX evaluation projects. In: Human-Computer Interaction. IntechOpen (2019)

Boutin, K.-D., Léger, P.-M., Davis, C.J., Hevner, A.R., Labonté-LeMoyne, É.: Attentional characteristics of anomaly detection in conceptual modeling. In: Davis, F.D., Riedl, R., vom Brocke, J., Léger, P.-M., Randolph, A.B. (eds.) Information Systems and Neuroscience. LNISO, vol. 29, pp. 57–63. Springer, Cham (2019). https://doi.org/10.1007/978-3-030-01087-4_7

Das, S., Zijdenbos, A.P., Vins, D., Harlap, J., Evans, A.C.: LORIS: a web-based data management system for multi-center studies. Front. Neuroinformatics **5**, 37 (2012)

Fairbanks, R.J., Caplan, S.: Poor interface design and lack of usability testing facilitate medical error. Joint Comm. J. Qual. Saf. **30**(10), 579–584 (2004)

Brooke, J.: SUS—a quick and dirty usability scale. In: Jordan, P.W., Thomas, B., Weerdmeester, B.A., McClelland, A.L. (eds.) Usability Evaluation in Industry. Taylor and Francis, London (1996)

Khunlertkit, A., Dorissaint, L., Chen, A., Paine, L., Pronovost, P.J.: Reducing and sustaining duplicate medical record creation by usability testing and system redesign. J. Patient Saf. (2017)

Kushniruk, A.W., Patel, V.L., Cimino, J.J.: Usability testing in medical informatics: cognitive approaches to evaluation of information systems and user interfaces. In: Proceedings of the AMIA Annual Fall Symposium, p. 218. American Medical Informatics Association (1997)

Léger, P.-M., Riedl, R., vom Brocke, J.: Emotions and ERP information sourcing: the moderating role of expertiseInd. Manag. Data Syst. **114**(3), 456–471 (2014a)

Léger, P.M., et al.: Precision is in the eye of the beholder: application of eye fixation-related potentials to information systems research. Association for Information Systems, October 2014 (2014b)

Mackenzie, C.F., Jefferies, N.J., Hunter, W.A., Bernhard, W.N., Xiao, Y.: Comparison of self-reporting of deficiencies in airway management with video analyses of actual performance. Hum. Factors **38**(4), 623–635 (1996). LOTAS Group. Level One Trauma Anesthesia Simulation

Nagarajan, K., Silva, A.: Tailor-made design guidelines for human factors and usability for medical device application: a proposed methodology. In: Proceedings of the Design Society: International Conference on Engineering Design, vol. 1, no. 1, pp. 995–1004. Cambridge University Press, July 2019

Peres, S.C., Pham, T., Phillips, R.: Validation of the system usability scale (SUS): SUS in the wild. In: Proceedings of the Human Factors and Ergonomics Society Annual Meeting, vol. 57, no. 1, pp. 192–196 (2013)

Sandoval, G.A., Brown, A.D., Wodchis, W.P., Anderson, G.M.: Adoption of high technology medical imaging and hospital quality and efficiency: towards a conceptual framework. Int. J. Health Plann. Manag. **33**(3), e843–e860 (2018)

Grossman, T., Fitzmaurice, G., Attar, R.: A survey of software learnability: metrics, methodologies and guidelines. In: CHI 2009 Conference Proceedings: ACM SIGCHI Conference on Human Factors in Computing Systems, pp. 649–658 (2009)

Multiuser Human-Computer Interaction Settings: Preliminary Evidence of Online Shopping Platform Use by Couples

Armel Quentin Tchanou[(⊠)], Pierre-Majorique Léger, Sylvain Senecal,
Laurie Carmichael, Constantinos K. Coursaris, and Marc Fredette

HEC Montréal, Montréal, QC H3T 2A7, Canada
{armel-quentin.tchanou,pierre-majorique.leger,sylvain.senecal,
laurie.charmichael,constantinos.coursaris,marc.fredette}@hec.ca

Abstract. The phenomenon of multiple users interacting together with a single shared system interface to perform a task (i.e., a multiuser human-computer interaction) is under-investigated in the Human-Computer Interaction (HCI) literature, yet it shows promising avenues for research. For example, little is known about cross-level influences driving collaborative use of a shared system interface, and the literature lacks knowledge about collective adaptation of users to triggers in this setting. The present work contributes to contemporary research on multiuser HCI with system interfaces. As an initial effort, it focusses on the joint use of online shopping platforms by couples. A survey is conducted with 390 respondents in the USA about couples' habits regarding joint online shopping. Results suggest that joint online shopping is overwhelmingly common among couples and that they engage in such activity in a wide variety of ergonomic layouts. Our findings constitute preliminary evidence and intrinsically call for more researchers' interest in investigating emotional, cognitive and behavioral dynamics taking place when multiple users jointly use system interfaces. Such research endeavors may ultimately inform and optimize multiuser system designs and corresponding products and services.

Keywords: Multiuser human-computer interaction · Shared system interface · Collaborative use · Joint online shopping · Couples' online shopping · Joint system use

1 Introduction

The phenomenon of study addressed in this paper is that of multiple users interacting together with a single shared system interface to perform a task. This perspective is important for several reasons. Although most computer systems are designed for use by a single user, they are frequently used in multiuser settings. Examples include individual shopping systems such as e-commerce platforms (e.g., [1–3]). To illustrate further, a recent study revealed that 53% of online purchases by households are operated by two or more users shopping online together [4]. Hence, it is common that individuals use

© Springer Nature Switzerland AG 2020
C. Stephanidis et al. (Eds.): HCII 2020, LNCS 12423, pp. 790–811, 2020.
https://doi.org/10.1007/978-3-030-60114-0_52

information technologies collaboratively with other users by interacting with a single system interface [5].

Despite its importance, this perspective of multiuser interaction with a shared system interface is scant within the human-computer interaction (HCI) literature. Introducing this perspective may contribute to addressing several limitations in extant literature. First, the HCI literature on collaborative system use has been examined mostly through studies focused on group-level use of systems made to be used by groups of users separately, such as with group support systems (e.g., [6]) and collaborative systems (e.g., [7]). Very few studies on group-level system use focus on collaborative task processing jointly performed through a shared system interface. Second, past research has essentially conceptualized system use at a single level of analysis (e.g., individual level or group level), without explicitly addressing cross-level associations, that is, possible influences from or to other lower or higher levels of analysis [8]. Third, the literature on user adaptations during interactions with a system addresses the question of patterns of user coping with triggers (e.g., [9]); however, this literature only considers single-user system use. Hence, little is known about how multiple users, both collectively and individually, adapt to triggers while they jointly interact with a system.

The objective of the present paper is to contribute to contemporary research on multiuser interaction with system interfaces. As an initial study, this research focuses on the collaborative use of online shopping platforms by couples. Two research questions are investigated: (1) to what extent do couples jointly use online shopping platforms; (2) in what settings do couples shop together using online platforms?

To answer these questions, an online survey was conducted on couples' habits of joint online shopping. Based on a sample of 390 responses, detailed results are presented on a variety of perspectives showing the extent to which, as well as settings in which, couples jointly use online shopping platforms. Findings suggest that couples spend a significant amount of time jointly navigating the Internet, with 43.95% of couples spending more than 3 h/week in this activity. Findings also suggest that couples shop together in different ways. During this activity, they use a wide variety of ergonomic layouts and are significantly more physically collocated, though may sometimes be separated. Analyses revealed that during joint online shopping couples most frequently use two separate smartphones, followed by comparable frequencies of using either the same computer or two separate computers. In terms of screen layout, during joint online shopping, couples mostly use the same website window when they use the same screen, whereas they use different windows when they use separate screens. Regarding the location of this joint activity, couples engage in it mostly from home, and specifically either in the living room or the bedroom, and tend to do so physically separated (i.e., remotely) from each other, with men maintaining control of the mouse significantly more than women. Finally, couples engage in joint online shopping mostly on websites related to travel and tourism, computers and electronics, and classified ads.

The remainder of this paper is structured as follows: the study's methodology is presented first, followed by the results, and ending with a discussion of emergent implications.

2   Methodology

To answer the above-mentioned research questions, a survey in the U.S.A. was conducted regarding couples' habits of joint online shopping (note: participants were asked to report on their habits under normal times/conditions). Participants were randomly recruited from a general online population through Amazon Mechanical Turk (MTurk), a crowd sourcing online platform having a United States user base of approximately 85,000 "Turkers" [10]. Participants were required to be in a relationship, without taking into account their marital status or whether they lived with their partner. The survey had to be completed by a single respondent. Finally, the study was approved by the ethics committee of the authors' institution, and each participant provided informed consent.

A total of 490 respondents participated to the study. Excluded from the analysis were responses from participants, who: (i) reported not being in a relationship, (ii) failed one of the attention check questions on MTurk, (iii) completed the survey multiple times, or (iv) completed the survey in an extremely fast pace that would not allow for meaningful processing of the questions and answer options (i.e., 3 s per question, on average). After this meticulous review and cleansing of the questionnaire data collected, the final dataset comprised 390 usable responses.

In addition to demographic information, participants reported on various aspects of their joint online shopping habits, including the extent to which: they buy certain categories of products together; shop together in different types of locations; use different device setups; use different types of screen layouts, in terms of device screen(s) (i.e., same or separate) and website window(s) (i.e., same or different); and each partner controls the mouse during joint shopping. The product categories chosen based on existing product categories that were investigated in the literature in the context of online shopping by couples [1], which were refined and extended following working sessions with two marketing experts. The added product categories are Real Estate, Clothing and Fashion, Leisure Activities, And Cars. The questionnaire was administered through the Qualtrics.com platform. Table 1 presents the participants' demographics.

Several visualizations of various aspects of the collected data and analyses were produced. Significance tests on differences observed were performed using linear regression with random intercept, at $\alpha = 0.05$ significance level and using two-tailed p-value adjusted for multiple testing using the Holm-Bonferroni method. The analyses were performed using the SAS statistical software.

3   Results

Results are presented in Fig. 1, 2, 3, 4, 5, 6, 7, 8, 9, 10, 11, 12, 13, 14, 15 and 16. Differences observed in bar charts are generally statistically significant. The statistics related to the pairwise comparisons are presented in Appendix A.

Regarding which device setup – smartphone, tablet, or computer, and whether single or multiple devices were used – couples used when they jointly shop online, Fig. 1 shows that couples use two separate smartphones significantly more than using the same smartphone; in fact, the former is the most frequently used of all device setups. Regarding the use of computers, couples reported using the same computer more frequently than separate computers but not to a statistically significant different level. Finally, the least used device setups by couples during joint online shopping were the use of the same smartphone, the same tablet, and two separate tablets. In terms of response data distribution, Fig. 2 shows that the same trend as in Fig. 1 was observed, except for the two most used setups. A total of 93.59% of couples appear to jointly shop together at least occasionally using the same computer, while 92.05% use two smartphone occasionally, 86.67% use two separate computers, 82.56% use the same smartphone, 68.97% use the same tablet, and 61.28% use two separate tablets. Figure 3 shows relative frequencies per device setup, suggesting higher frequencies for the use of two smartphones or the same computer.

Table 1. Participants' demographics

Demographics variables		Frequency (n = 390)	Percentage
Participant's gender	Male	218	55.90%
	Female	170	43.59%
	Other	2	0.51%
Partner's gender	Male	174	44.62%
	Female	215	55.13%
	Other	1	0.26%
Participant's age	18–25 years	41	10.51%
	26–35 years	197	50.51%
	36–45 years	87	22.31%
	46–55 years	43	11.03%
	Greater than 55	22	5.64%
Participant's education level	High school	61	15.64%
	College	69	17.69%
	Undergrad	104	26.67%
	Graduate	115	29.49%
	Post-graduate	41	10.51%
Household income	Less than $30,000	29	7.44%
	$30,000–$49,999	73	18.72%
	$50,000–$69,999	102	26.15%
	$70,000–$89,999	86	22.05%
	$90,000 or more	100	25.64%

Concerning which screen layouts couples use when they jointly shop online, Fig. 4 shows that when they use the same screen, they mostly use the same website window. Also, using the same window within the same screen appears to be the most used of all four screen layout options. On the other hand, when couples use separate screens to jointly shop online, they tend to use multiple windows as opposed to using the same window. The next most used layout is the use of multiple website windows within separate screens. The least popular setups reported were the use of the same shared window within separate screens and finally the use of different website windows within the same screen. The same trend was observed with the data distribution as shown in Fig. 5. A total of 93.33% of couples appear to at least occasionally use the same website window when they use the same screen for joint online shopping, while 71.03% use different websites windows. Finally, 87.69% use different website windows when they use separate screens, while 78.72% use a same shared website window. Figure 6 shows relative frequencies per screen layout, suggesting higher frequencies for the use of a shared window when using the same screen and the use of different windows when using separate screens.

Regarding the physical location from where couples shop online together, as shown in Fig. 7, results show that couples do so mostly being physically collocated, specifically in their living room, followed by their bedroom. The third most common location to jointly shop online is to be physically remote from each other and in different rooms. This setting was not statistically significantly different from joint shopping in the kitchen, in separate rooms at home, and at the same location out of the home. Lastly, joint shopping in the yard or in the garage were also reported albeit at the lowest frequencies.

Regarding what categories of products are shopped for online by couples (or in other words, the categories of online shopping platforms accessed), as depicted in Fig. 8, Travel and Tourism appears to be most shopped for online. The Cars category follows, with no significant difference with Art and Shows, Groceries, and Real Estate. Leisure Activities

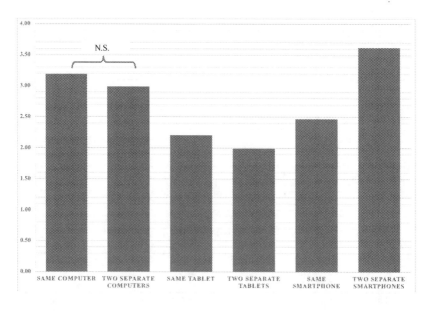

N.S. = Non-Significant

Fig. 1. Extent to which couples use each device setup during joint online shopping

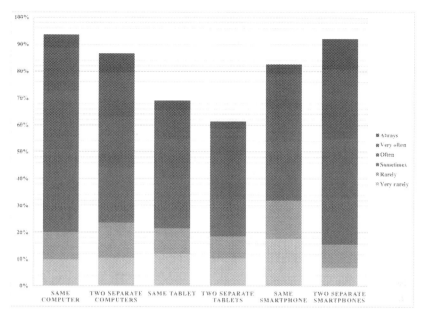

Fig. 2. Frequencies of device setup use during couples' joint online shopping

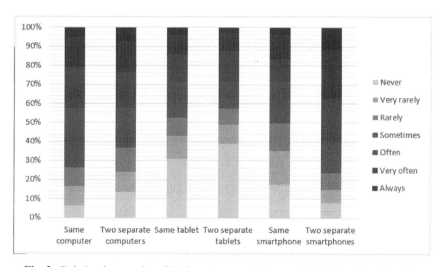

Fig. 3. Relative frequencies of device setup use during couples' joint online shopping

and Clothing and Fashion. The Cars category is followed by the Furnitures and Appliances category, which shows no statistically significant difference with Classified Ads, Leisure Activities, and Clothing and Fashion. The Furnitures and Appliances category is followed by the Computers and Electronics category, with no statistically significant difference with Leisure Activities. The Computers and Electronics category is followed

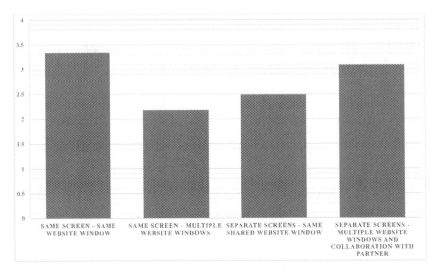

Fig. 4. Extent to which couples use each screen layout during joint online shopping

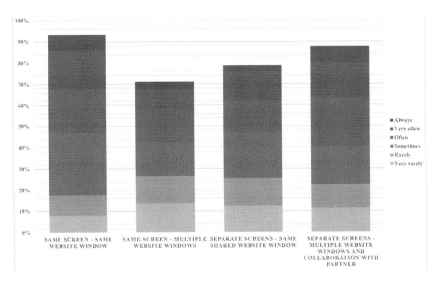

Fig. 5. Frequencies of screen layout use during couples' joint online shopping

by Art and Shows, with no statistically significant difference with the Paper Magazine category.

Also answered was the question as to what extent each partner by gender keeps control of the mouse during the couple's joint online shopping. As shown in Fig. 9, men reported to keep control of the mouse during the activity to a significantly greater extent than women do.

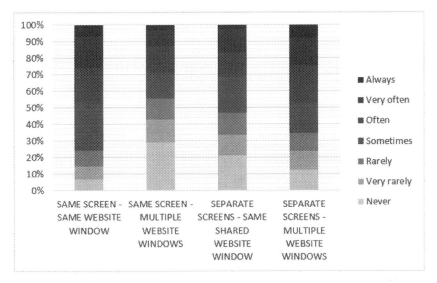

Fig. 6. Relative frequencies of screen layout use during couples' joint online shopping

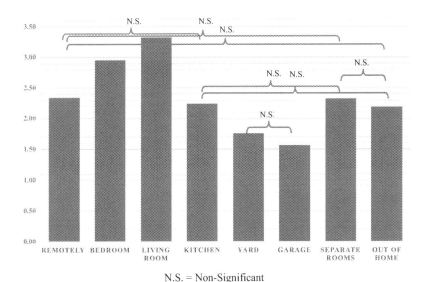

N.S. = Non-Significant

Fig. 7. Extent to which couples jointly shop online by location

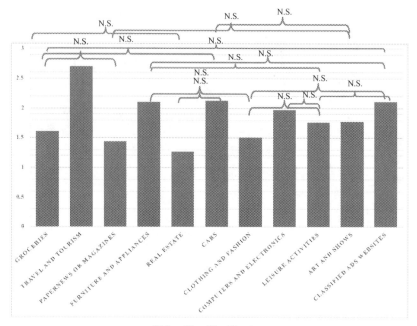

N.S. = Non-Significant

Fig. 8. Extent to which couples jointly shop online by product category

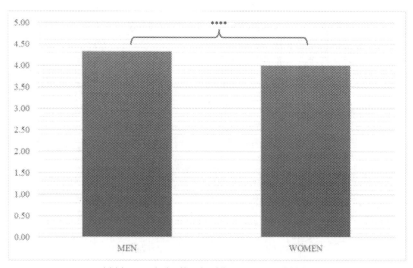

**** = statistically significant at α = .0001

Fig. 9. Extent to which partners keep control of the mouse, by gender

The remaining results are provided against more than one dimension. Figure 10 presents a heatmap representing the extent to which couples were reported to jointly shop online for each product category. This information is reported by the extent to which they use each device to conduct the activity. The heatmap suggests that couples which jointly shop the most for Art and Show are those who always use the same tablet to do so. On the other hand, couples who jointly shop the most for Cars are those which always use the same smartphone to do so, followed by those who always use the same tablet. The result for Cars also applies for the Classified Ads, Clothing and Fashion, Computers and Electronics, Furnitures and Appliances, Groceries, and Paper and News categories. Moreover, it appears that couples which shop the most for Leisure Activities

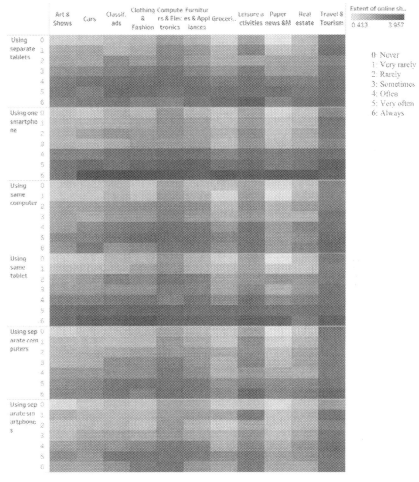

Vertical axis: Extent to which couples jointly shop online using each device setup.
Horizontal axis: Product categories.

Fig. 10. Extent of joint shopping per product category and by device setup

are those which very often use either separate tablets, the same tablet, or the same smartphone to jointly shop online. Those couples which jointly shop online most often for Real Estate are those which always use the same smartphone to shop online. Finally, those couples which shop most often for Travel and Tourism are those which either most often use the same smartphone or always use the same tablet.

The next view is provided in Fig. 11, which shows the extent to which couples jointly shop online for the different product categories, reported according to the extent to which they jointly shop online in various location settings. It appears that the Art and Shows category is mostly shopped for jointly when the couple tends to do joint shopping very often in separate rooms at or when they are collocated out of home. As for Cars, couples who jointly shop online for this category are those who tend to do joint shopping very often in the yard or out of home at the same location. Moreover, couples jointly shopping very often in the garage are those mostly shopping for Clothing and Fashion. As for Computers and Electronics, couples who jointly shop for this category are those who tend to do joint shopping very often in the yard or in the kitchen or in the garage at home. As for Furnitures and Appliance, couples who jointly shop for this category tend to engage in joint shopping very often in the garage, in the kitchen, or at the same location out of their home. As for Groceries, they are mostly jointly shopped by couples which tend to shop together very often in the yard or in the garage. Leisure Activities are most shopped for by couples which shop together online very often remotely from each other or collocated in the garage or in the kitchen. Paper and News are most shopped for by couples which shop together online very often in the garage or in the same location out of home, or in separate rooms at home. Couples mostly shopping for Real Estate together are those which tend to shop together online very often in the yard. Finally, couples mostly shopping together for Travel and Tourism are those which tend to shop together online very often in the yard.

The following graphs, Fig. 12, 13, 14, 15 and 16 depict the extent to which couples were reported to jointly shop online using either two smartphones or the same computer, i.e. the two device setups that were reported to be the most used. Results are shown against the "Travel and Tourism" product category, which was reported to be the most frequently jointly shopped for online.

As Fig. 12 shows, couples which use separate smartphones for joint online shopping within the Travel and Tourism product category the most are those reported to very rarely do so being physically. As Fig. 13 shows, couples also use two smartphones the most for either collocated or physically separated joint online shopping of the same product category.

As depicted in Fig. 14, couples jointly shopping using the same computer to the greatest extent to shop for Travel and Tourism are those which shop for that product category very often but rarely do so being collocated. Moreover, Fig. 15 shows that couples jointly shopping using the same computer to the greatest extent to shop for Travel and Tourism are those which sometimes shop for that product category but very rarely jointly shop online at the same location from each other.

Regarding the use of two separate computers, Fig. 16 shows that the couples jointly shopping using separate computers to the greatest extent to shop for Travel and Tourism are those which sometimes shop for that product category and very often jointly shop at remote locations from each other.

4   Discussions and Conclusion

4.1   Findings

The present paper presented detailed results on several perspectives showing the extent to which as well as settings in which couples jointly use online shopping platforms. It was observed that couples spend a significant amount of time jointly navigating on the internet, with 44.62% of couples spending 3 h/week, 28.21% spending more than 6 h/week, and 11.79% spending more than 10 h/week in this activity. These observations

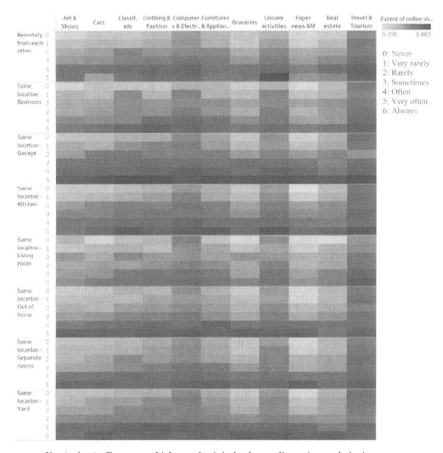

Vertical axis: Extent to which couples jointly shop online using each device setup.
Horizontal axis: Product categories.

Fig. 11. Extent of joint shopping per product category and by location

suggest that an important proportion of couples consistently jointly use web applications, websites, or other web-based software, including online shopping platforms.

Results also suggest that couples shop together in different ways, using a variety of device setups. More couples were reported to jointly shop online using two smartphones separately (93.59%), using the same computer (92.05%) or using two separate computers (86.67%). However, aggregated data revealed that couples shop together online to the greatest extent using two separate smartphones, the same computer, or two separate computers, respectively.

Just as with device setup, couples use different ergonomic layouts to shop together online. The highest proportion of couples were reported to use same website window when using the same screen (93.33%), multiple website windows when using separate screens (87.69%), and same shared window within separate screens (78.72%), respectively. Besides, this same trend was observed with regard to the extent to which couples use each device layout. Hence, it was observed that couples jointly shop online more usually using the same shared window within the same screen.

Regarding the location relative to each other when shopping together online, results suggest that couples engage in the activity in a variety of location settings. They do so mostly at the same location from each other, and they mostly do so at home in the living room and in the bedroom. However, couples were generally reported to shop online together occasionally remotely from each other.

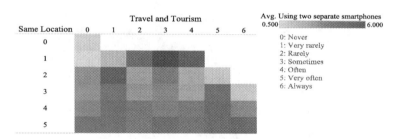

Vertical axis: Extent to which couples jointly shop online at the same location from each other.
Horizontal axis: Extent to which couples jointly shop online for travel and tourism.

Fig. 12. Extent of collocated joint shopping, using two separate smartphones, and by location, for Travel and Tourism

Regarding the types of online platforms (i.e., product categories) jointly used by couples, results revealed that they shop online in a greater proportion for Travel and Tourism, Furniture and Appliances, and Cars.

Finally, results reveal a statistically significant difference in behavior between men and women during couples' joint online shopping: men tend to keep control of the mouse and keyboard more than women.

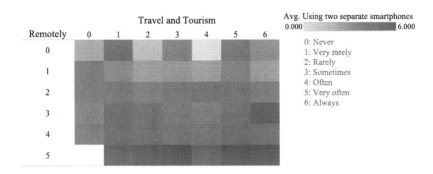

Vertical axis: Extent to which couples jointly shop online at the same location from each other.
Horizontal axis: Extent to which couples jointly shop online for travel and tourism.

Fig. 13. Extent of physically remote joint shopping, using two separate smartphones, and by location, for Travel and Tourism.

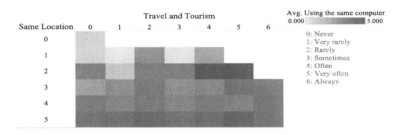

Vertical axis: Extent to which couples jointly shop online at the same location from each other.
Horizontal axis: Extent to which couples jointly shop online for travel and tourism.

Fig. 14. Extent of collocated joint shopping by couples, using the same computer, and by location for Travel and Tourism

4.2 Implications and Conclusion

This paper aimed at contributing to contemporary research in the area of multiple users interacting together with a single shared system interface to perform a task. Based on a survey of 390 participants, preliminary results in the context of online shopping platforms offer support for this paper's premise in that that the phenomenon warrants deeper exploration. The study results provide straightforward answers to the research questions. Overall, it was observed that most couples jointly use online platforms to accomplish the shopping task together. Moreover, they do so in a wide variety of settings, generally to a significant (frequent) extent. These settings include variety of device setups, ergonomic layouts, physical locations relative to each other, and product categories. The main limitation of this study is that the questionnaire considers the different settings independently from one another. Future research could examine direct links, such as the extent of joint use of systems relative to specific combinations of settings.

804   A. Q. Tchanou et al.

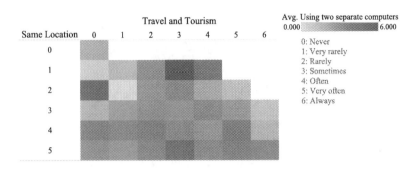

Vertical axis: Extent to which couples jointly shop online at the same location from each other.
Horizontal axis: Extent to which couples jointly shop online for travel and tourism.

Fig. 15. Extent of collocated joint shopping, using two separate computers, and by location, for Travel and Tourism

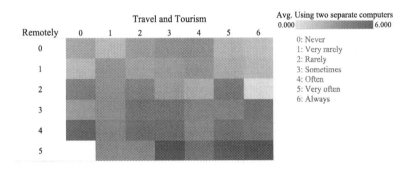

Vertical axis: Extent to which couples jointly shop online remotely from each other.
Horizontal axis: Extent to which couples jointly shop online for travel and tourism.

Fig. 16. Extent of physically remote joint shopping, using two separate computers, and by location, for Travel and Tourism

This study's findings in the context of online shopping platforms pose a call for more research in multiuser human-computer interaction, which is currently lacking within the HCI literature. Hence, several avenues for research can be considered. First, research could propose theoretical frameworks, which may subsequently facilitate the development of research models to be tested. Such frameworks could associate relevant higher-order constructs into logical layers. Second, as with past HCI literature (e.g., [9]), mechanisms of joint use of shared interfaces can be investigated in terms of emotions, cognitions, and behaviors of groups of users. For instance, a working paper proposes a new index for measuring gaze convergence of a user dyad during their joint use of a system interface, and it demonstrates that gaze convergence of a user dyad jointly interacting with a system interface is negatively associated with dyad cognitive load and positively associated with dyad performance [11]. Third, antecedents and consequences of these mechanisms can be examined. As an illustration, this study revealed that couples using a shared system interface during joint shopping, men tend to control the mouse to a significantly greater extent. Research could examine how the structure of a group of users jointly interacting with an interface shapes the emotional, cognitive, and behavioral dynamics during the task. Figuring out configurations through which groups of users perform optimally during the joint use of system interface may contribute to better system design, ultimately enabling collaborative innovation in organizations. Finally, research could investigate cross-level influences between individual and collective levels during multiuser system use, as per past recommendations about multilevel theorizing (e.g., [5, 8, 12, 13]).

Finally, this study also puts forth a call for practitioners to take into account whenever possible relevant multiuser interactions in various contexts. To illustrate, system designers should develop user scenarios involving multiple users for systems that are often jointly used by multiple users. An example emerging from this study is the design of online shopping platforms for travel and tourism. Likewise, marketers should consider possible influences from other users jointly using such online shopping platforms.

Appendix A: Pairwise Comparisons of Bar Charts' Levels

Dependent variable	Level 1	Level 2	t value	Adjusted p-value
Type of products	Clothing and Fashion	Furniture and Appliances	0.07	1
Type of products	Clothing and Fashion	Groceries	5.79	<.0001
Type of products	Clothing and Fashion	Travel and Tourism	−6.80	<.0001
Type of products	Clothing and Fashion	Classified Ads Websites	0.65	1
Type of products	Clothing and Fashion	Art and Shows	5.04	<.0001
Type of products	Clothing and Fashion	Cars	3.88	0.00
Type of products	Clothing and Fashion	Computers and Electronics	−3.15	0.03
Type of products	Clothing and Fashion	Leisure Activities	−1.43	1
Type of products	Clothing and Fashion	Paper News and Magazines	7.75	<.0001
Type of products	Clothing and Fashion	Real Estate	4.01	0.00
Type of products	Furniture and Appliances	Groceries	5.72	<.0001

(*continued*)

(continued)

Dependent variable	Level 1	Level 2	t value	Adjusted p-value
Type of products	Furniture and Appliances	Travel and Tourism	−6.87	<.0001
Type of products	Furniture and Appliances	Classified Ads Websites	0.58	1
Type of products	Furniture and Appliances	Art and Shows	4.97	<.0001
Type of products	Furniture and Appliances	Cars	3.81	0.00
Type of products	Furniture and Appliances	Computers and Electronics	−3.23	0.02
Type of products	Furniture and Appliances	Leisure Activities	−1.50	1
Type of products	Furniture and Appliances	Paper News and Magazines	7.67	<.0001
Type of products	Furniture and Appliances	Real Estate	3.93	0.00
Type of products	Groceries	Travel and Tourism	−12.59	<.0001
Type of products	Groceries	Classified Ads Websites	−5.14	<.0001
Type of products	Groceries	Art and Shows	−0.75	1
Type of products	Groceries	Cars	−1.91	0.67
Type of products	Groceries	Computers and Electronics	−8.94	<.0001
Type of products	Groceries	Leisure Activities	−7.22	<.0001
Type of products	Groceries	Paper News and Magazines	1.96	0.66
Type of products	Groceries	Real Estate	−1.78	0.82
Type of products	Travel and Tourism	Classified Ads Websites	7.45	<.0001
Type of products	Travel and Tourism	Art and Shows	11.84	<.0001
Type of products	Travel and Tourism	Cars	10.68	<.0001
Type of products	Travel and Tourism	Computers and Electronics	3.65	0.01
Type of products	Travel and Tourism	Leisure Activities	5.37	<.0001
Type of products	Travel and Tourism	Paper News and Magazines	14.55	<.0001
Type of products	Travel and Tourism	Real Estate	10.81	<.0001

(continued)

(*continued*)

Dependent variable	Level 1	Level 2	t value	Adjusted p-value
Type of products	Classified Ads Websites	Art and Shows	4.39	0.00
Type of products	Classified Ads Websites	Cars	3.23	0.02
Type of products	Classified Ads Websites	Computers and Electronics	−3.80	0.00
Type of products	Classified Ads Websites	Leisure Activities	−2.08	0.52
Type of products	Classified Ads Websites	Paper News and Magazines	7.09	<.0001
Type of products	Classified Ads Websites	Real Estate	3.36	0.02
Type of products	Art and Shows	Cars	−1.16	1
Type of products	Art and Shows	Computers and Electronics	−8.19	<.0001
Type of products	Art and Shows	Leisure Activities	−6.47	<.0001
Type of products	Art and Shows	Paper News and Magazines	2.70	0.10
Type of products	Art and Shows	Real Estate	−1.03	1
Type of products	Cars	Computers and Electronics	−7.03	<.0001
Type of products	Cars	Leisure Activities	−5.31	<.0001
Type of products	Cars	Paper News and Magazines	3.87	0.00
Type of products	Cars	Real Estate	0.13	1
Type of products	Computers and Electronics	Leisure Activities	1.72	0.85
Type of products	Computers and Electronics	Paper News and Magazines	10.90	<.0001
Type of products	Computers and Electronics	Real Estate	7.16	<.0001
Type of products	Leisure Activities	Paper News and Magazines	9.18	<.0001
Type of products	Leisure Activities	Real Estate	5.44	<.0001
Type of products	Paper News and Magazines	Real Estate	−3.74	0.00
Device	Using one computer	Using two separate computers	1.82	0.11
Device	Using one computer	Using one tablet	9.02	<.0001

(*continued*)

(*continued*)

Dependent variable	Level 1	Level 2	t value	Adjusted p-value
Device	Using one computer	Using two separate tablets	10.96	<.0001
Device	Using one computer	Using one smartphone	6.59	<.0001
Device	Using one computer	Using two separate smartphones	−3.85	0.00
Device	Using two separate computers	Using one tablet	7.20	<.0001
Device	Using two separate computers	Using two separate tablets	9.13	<.0001
Device	Using two separate computers	Using one smartphone	4.77	<.0001
Device	Using two separate computers	Using two separate smartphones	−5.68	<.0001
Device	Using one tablet	Using two separate tablets	1.94	0.11
Device	Using one tablet	Using one smartphone	−2.43	0.05
Device	Using one tablet	Using two separate smartphones	−12.87	<.0001
Device	Using two separate tablets	Using one smartphone	−4.37	<.0001
Device	Using two separate tablets	Using two separate smartphones	−14.81	<.0001
Device	Using one smartphone	Using two separate smartphones	−10.44	<.0001
Location	Remotely from each other	Same location - Bedroom	−7.30	<.0001
Location	Remotely from each other	Same location - Living room	−11.70	<.0001
Location	Remotely from each other	Same location - Kitchen	1.22	0.89
Location	Remotely from each other	Same location - Yard	6.97	<.0001
Location	Remotely from each other	Same location - Garage	9.29	<.0001
Location	Remotely from each other	Same location - Separate rooms	0.21	1
Location	Remotely from each other	Same location - Out of home	1.83	0.40

(*continued*)

(*continued*)

Dependent variable	Level 1	Level 2	t value	Adjusted p-value
Location	Same location - Bedroom	Same location - Living room	−4.40	<.0001
Location	Same location - Bedroom	Same location - Kitchen	8.53	<.0001
Location	Same location - Bedroom	Same location - Yard	14.27	<.0001
Location	Same location - Bedroom	Same location - Garage	16.59	<.0001
Location	Same location - Bedroom	Same location - Separate rooms	7.52	<.0001
Location	Same location - Bedroom	Same location - Out of home	9.14	<.0001
Location	Same location - Living room	Same location - Kitchen	12.93	<.0001
Location	Same location - Living room	Same location - Yard	18.67	<.0001
Location	Same location - Living room	Same location - Garage	20.99	<.0001
Location	Same location - Living room	Same location - Separate rooms	11.92	<.0001
Location	Same location - Living room	Same location - Out of home	13.54	<.0001
Location	Same location - Kitchen	Same location - Yard	5.75	<.0001
Location	Same location - Kitchen	Same location - Garage	8.07	<.0001
Location	Same location - Kitchen	Same location - Separate rooms	−1.01	0.94
Location	Same location - Kitchen	Same location - Out of home	0.61	1
Location	Same location - Yard	Same location - Garage	2.32	0.14
Location	Same location - Yard	Same location - Separate rooms	−6.75	<.0001
Location	Same location - Yard	Same location - Out of home	−5.13	<.0001
Location	Same location - Garage	Same location - Separate rooms	−9.08	<.0001
Location	Same location - Garage	Same location - Out of home	−7.46	<.0001

(*continued*)

(*continued*)

Dependent variable	Level 1	Level 2	t value	Adjusted p-value
Location	Same location - Separate rooms	Same location - Out of home	1.62	0.53
Screen layout	Same screen - Same website window	Same screen - Multiple website windows open	10.85	<.0001
Screen layout	Same screen - Same website window	Separate screens - Same shared website window	7.95	<.0001
Screen layout	Same screen - Same window	Separate screens - Multiple website window	2.37	0.02
Screen layout	Same screen - Multiple website windows open	Separate screens - Same shared website window	−2.90	0.01
Screen layout	Same screen - Multiple website windows open	Separate screens - Multiple website windows	−8.48	<.0001
Screen layout	Separate screens - Same shared website window	Separate screens - Multiple website windows	−5.58	<.0001
Mouse usage	Men	Women	4.86	<.0001

References

1. Berrada, M.A.: Trois essais sur l'influence relative et les stratégies de résolution de conflit lors d'une prise de décision d'achat en ligne en couple. Dissertation/thesis. H.E.C. Montréal (2011). c2011 U6 - ctx_ver = Z39.88-2004&ctx_enc = info%3Aofi%2Fenc%3AUTF-8&rfr_id = info%3Asid%2Fsummon.serialssolutions.com&rft_val_fmt = info%3Aofi%2Ffmt%3Akev%3Amtx%3Abook&rft.genre = dissertation&rft.title = Trois + essais + sur + l%27influence + relative + et + les + strat%C3%A9gies + de + r%C3%A9solution + de + conflit + lors + d%27une + prise + de + d%C3%A9cision + d%27achat + en + ligne + en + couple&rft.DBID = T5A&rft.au = Mekki + Berrada%2C + Abdelouahab&rft.externalDocID = 303785&paramdict = en-US U7 - Dissertation
2. Yue, Y., Ma, X., Jiang, Z.: Share your view: impact of co-navigation support and status composition in collaborative online shopping, pp. 3299–3308
3. Zhu, L., Benbasat, I., Jiang, Z.: Investigating the role of presence in collaborative online shopping. In: AMCIS 2006 Proceedings, vol. 358 (2006)
4. al., B.e.: Ecommerce in Canada 2018. eMarketer, New York (2018)
5. Burton-Jones, A., Gallivan, M.J.: Toward a deeper understanding of system usage in organizations: a multilevel perspective. MIS Q. **31**, 657–679 (2007)
6. Dennis, A.R., Wixom, B.H., Vandenberg, R.J.: Understanding fit and appropriation effects in group support systems via meta-analysis. MIS Q. **25**, 167–193 (2001)

7. Doll, W.J., Deng, X.: The collaborative use of information technology: end-user participation and systems success. Inf. Resour. Manag. J. (IRMJ) **14**, 6–16 (2001)

8. Markus, M.L., Rowe, F.: Is IT changing the world? Conceptions of causality for information systems theorizing. MIS Q. **42**, 1255–1280 (2018)

9. de Guinea, A.O., Webster, J.: An investigation of information systems use patterns: technological events as triggers, the effect of time, and consequences for performance. MIS Q. **37**, 1165–1188 (2013)

10. Robinson, J., Rosenzweig, C., Moss, A.J., Litman, L.: Tapped out or barely tapped? Recommendations for how to harness the vast and largely unused potential of the mechanical turk participant pool. PLoS ONE **14**, e0226394 (2019)

11. Tchanou, A.Q., Léger, P.-M., Boasen, J., Senecal, S., Taher, J.A., Fredette, M.: Collaborative use of a shared system interface: the role of user gaze – gaze convergence index based on synchronous dual-eyetracking. Appl. Sci. **10**(13), 4508 (2020)

12. Zhang, M., Gable, G.G.: A systematic framework for multilevel theorizing in information systems research. Inf. Syst. Res. **28**, 203–224 (2017)

13. Burton-Jones, A., Straub Jr., D.W.: Reconceptualizing system usage: an approach and empirical test. Inf. Syst. Res. **17**, 228–246 (2006)

Author Index

Printed in the United States
By Bookmasters